SOCIOLOGY

Second Edition

SOCIOLOGY

Second Edition

GENERAL EDITOR
ROBERT HAGEDORN

Holt, Rinehart and Winston of Canada, Limited Toronto

Canadian Cataloguing in Publication Data
Main entry under title:
Sociology
ISBN 0-03-921636-5
1. Sociology-Addresses, essays, lectures.
Includes bibliographies.
I. Hagedorn, Robert, 1925–
HM51-S63   1983   301   C83-098012-1

Acquisitions Editor: Anthony Luengo
Managing Editor: Dennis Bockus
Copy Editor: James Wills
Design: Jim Ireland
Cover Design: Maher & Murtagh Inc.

Printed in the United States of America

1 2 3 4 5 87 86 85 84 83

PREFACE

This book presents in clear and simple prose an overview of the discipline of sociology using the best Canadian data available. Its goals include describing how sociologists view the social world, how they discover what that world is, and what we currently know about that world.

There are two major problems in accomplishing these goals. The first is that sociology, like other physical and social sciences, is faced with growing specialization. As the amount of information in each of the areas of sociology increases, it becomes impossible to know everything about all of them. Increasingly, there is specialization even within a single area – formal organizations, the family, and political sociology, for example. This means that no one person is an expert in "sociology." Some idea of the diversity can be seen in the fact that over forty different courses are listed in guides to graduate departments of sociology. Along with these courses and sections there has been a tremendous increase in the number of journals related to subareas.

A simple solution to the problem of specialization is to use specialists to write the various chapters. This is the approach taken here. A question arises as to why such a solution is rarely used in writing introductory sociology textbooks. The answer lies in the problem of presenting writing that is always clear, interesting, and consistent in style. The solution to this problem was twofold. First, all authors were asked to use three perspectives, which helped to tie the chapters together. Second, each chapter was carefully edited for style, clarity, and interest. Whether we have achieved our goals will be determined by you.

Consistent with these goals are the book's organization and features. The text's seventeen chapters are divided into six sections. The sections represent very general but distinct sociological categories that unite the individual chapters. The chapters present an overview of the major sociological areas. Many of these areas (for example, deviance and the family) are upper division and graduate courses. In this sense, each chapter is an introduction to an area of specialization in sociology.

Features of the book are designed to make learning and remembering easier. These include cross-references between chapters to integrate important ideas and information, the use of pictures to reinforce the written text, boldface type to identify important terms, and boxed readings to illustrate major points. At the end of each chapter is a summary of the major points, a glossary that simplifies looking up definitions, and an annotated list of further readings.

The instructor's manual contains test banks of objective questions contructed by the authors, as well as study questions, research projects, and, in many cases, suggestions of films to supplement the text.

I would like to express a special thanks to the teachers and students who constructively criticized the first edition. Due to them, two new chapters have been added, and all chapters have been simplified and shortened. We encourage teachers and students to let us know how this edition could be improved.

Victoria
February 1983   ROBERT HAGEDORN

COAUTHORS

Reginald W. Bibby
University of Lethbridge

James Curtis
University of Waterloo

Leo Driedger
University of Manitoba

Ellen Gee
Simon Fraser University

A.R. Gillis
Erindale College, University of Toronto

J. Paul Grayson
Atkinson College, York University

L.M. Grayson
Legislative Research Service, Queen's Park, Ontario

John Hagan
University of Toronto

Robert Hagedorn
University of Victoria

R. Alan Hedley
University of Victoria

Kathryn M. Kopinak
King's College, University of Western Ontario

Ronald D. Lambert
University of Waterloo

Jos. L. Lennards
Glendon College, York University

Marlene Mackie
University of Calgary

Victor W. Marshall
University of Toronto

Emily M. Nett
University of Manitoba

R. Ogmundson
University of Victoria

Carolyn J. Rosenthal
University of Toronto

Terrence H. White
University of Alberta

CONTENTS

DETAILED CONTENTS

I
THE FIELD OF SOCIOLOGY

The first chapter, or section, of this book provides an overview of what is generally called theory. Chapter 1, *What Is Sociology?*, examines the nature of sociology and pays particular attention to current perspectives in sociology, and their historical development. The theoretical perspectives of sociology are the lenses through which sociologists see. The answers you get depend on the questions you ask, and the questions you ask depend on the perspective you use. Perspectives determine what you look at and how you see it. Perspectives, therefore, define sociology.

Is a group of people a collection of individuals, or does it have properties of its own? Is society stable, or changing? Do we share basic values, or are we essentially in conflict? The answers to these questions define sociological perspectives, which in turn determine what you will measure, what you will look for, which then determines what you find and answers you get.

In sociology there are three major perspectives: conflict, structural functionalism, and symbolic interaction. These are discussed in the first chapter, and are used throughout the book.

CHAPTER
1
WHAT IS SOCIOLOGY?

CHAPTER 1
WHAT IS SOCIOLOGY?

ROBERT HAGEDORN

THREE EARLY VIEWPOINTS
Emile Durkheim, 1858-1917
Max Weber, 1864-1920
Karl Marx, 1818-1883

CURRENT PERSPECTIVES
Macrosociology
Microsociology
An Overview

SOCIOLOGY AND SCIENCE
The Naturalist Position

TABLE 1-1. EMPLOYMENT OF SOCIOLOGY BACHELOR GRADUATES BY COUNTRY.

Vocational Categories	Jobholders in		
	United States	Canada	Total
Educational/Academic	19%	42%	37%
Business and Commerce	22	21	21
Social Services	31	15	19
Research, Data Processing, Communications	5	6	6
Professions, Professional Assistance	8	5	5
Government	5	4	4
Other	10	7	7
Total	100%	100%	98%[1]
Number of Jobholders	(610)	(2366)	(2976)

SOURCE: Hedley, Alan R., and Susan M. Adams. "The job market for bachelor degree holders," *The American Sociologist*, Volume 17, #3, 1982.
NOTE: [1]The difference between column sums and 100 is due to rounding error.

Right now you are probably asking yourself: What am I getting into? What is this book about? What is sociology?

To many people, sociology is the most exciting subject on earth, a fresh, lively, coherent, and valuable way of understanding people and the world in which we live. For some people, sociology is so compelling that they invest their entire professional careers in learning it, teaching it, and doing it. As Table 1-1 shows, people trained in sociology work in a wide variety of jobs where their knowledge and research influence many decisions that affect our everyday lives.

Sociology is a young science, only about a hundred years old. Like all youngsters, sociology ripples with energy, with promise, with insights, and with the sure sense that what it is doing is important.

Sociology is important because it deals with the stuff of everyday life, but in a new way. What we tend to see as almost boringly familiar, such as the smallest details of human interaction and the largest events of the evening news, take on new meaning and make more sense in light of the basic sociological insight that our behavior is affected by social forces beyond our control. Not only do we, as individuals, influence society; society also influences us.

This may surprise you. In this country, individuals are important. So is individual effort. People work hard to get what they want – money, power, a better life for their children, a university education, a flashy car, a house of their own. But most of this individual effort takes place in social groups – in businesses, in classrooms, in organizations. These social groups affect our behavior and can significantly determine how successful we are in achieving our goals. Look around at the students in your class. Most of them had to work hard all through school for good grades. Some have probably worked at a part-time job to help meet expenses. But hard work is only part of the story. Look around again. Are there more women or men? How many native Canadians are in the class? Are these students rich or poor? In fact, the best indicator of who goes to university is not the individual's ability, but his or her parents' occupation. Social forces influence us and our lives in profound ways, many of which are not at all obvious.

For some of you this may seem trivial. Of course, society influences us. In many ways the essential insight of sociology, and many of its discoveries, seem deceptively like common sense. Common sense tells you that the more severely you punish people, the less likely they are to repeat the forbidden act. Common sense tells you that reading pornography increases the likelihood of sex crimes. Common sense tells you that capital punishment will reduce crime. Common sense tells you that happy workers are productive workers. Common sense tells you that these statements are obvious. What is not so obvious is that each of these statements is false. Far from being trivial, sociological insight, with its emphasis on groups and social interaction, increases human knowledge, extends our awareness of ourselves as human beings, and can expand our power over our own destinies.

Each of the chapters that follow will add to your awareness of the social forces that affect your destiny.

In them you will encounter a broad panorama of important social issues – power and the political process, the quality of education, life in the city, the growth of large organizations, crime, discrimination, poverty and wealth, class conflict, to name only a few. More important, you will see how these issues influence your life. Consider the following questions:

1. Do I have any values?
2. How does a person become a criminal?
3. Can an individual have feminine qualities and masculine qualities at the same time?
4. Why don't more women study math and science?
5. What is the difference between a dirty old man and a sexy senior citizen?
6. When I am too old to work, will society be able to support me?
7. If I work hard, will I get ahead?
8. If I marry, what are the chances my partner and I will be happy?
9. Why do people join religious cults?
10. How did Joe Clark beat Pierre Trudeau in 1979?
11. Will I get a good job when I graduate?
12. How long can I expect to live and what will probably kill me?
13. What motivates people to work hard?
14. What would it take to get me out on a picket line?

The answers to some of the questions may surprise you. Sociology can give you important insights into the forces that shape you and your world.

Most sociologists agree on the importance of their work and the basic sociological insight that groups shape behavior. But many disagree among themselves as to precisely what they should study and how they should study it. This is not unusual. Most of the social sciences contain within themselves similar disagreements and debates. It might be convincingly argued that the social sciences get the spark for many of their most important discoveries and ideas directly from the interaction of conflicting factions within the disciplines. Fortunately for a new student of sociology, most of the internal disagreements divide the discipline, more or less, into three basic perspectives.

Before we begin to discuss these three perspectives, and the three early theorists whose work underlies these perspectives, we need a definition of **sociology**. The usual textbook solution is to give a short definition, with a cautionary note that it is not really sufficient. Here are some examples: sociology is "the scientific study of man's social life" (Horton and Hunt, 1972); sociology is "the scientific study of human relationships and their consequences" (Caplow, 1971); sociology is "the scientific study of human society and social behavior" (Robertson, 1977).

Our definition is that sociology is the description and explanation of social behavior, social structures, and social interaction in terms of these social structures, and/or in terms of people's perceptions of the social environment. This definition is longer and more complex than those cited above. But we believe it to be more complete and accurate. In the balance of this chapter, you will study the three basic sociological perspectives around which this book is organized, the three early theorists whose ideas underlie these perspectives, and some examples of how the different perspectives contribute to the sociological fund of knowledge. Then we will return to our definition of sociology. At that time it should make more sense to you, and give you a more complete and accurate idea of what sociology is all about.

THREE EARLY VIEWPOINTS

Each of the three theorists to be discussed – Durkheim, Weber, and Marx – is seen by different people as the most important sociologist. Such assessments indicate that these men were seminal thinkers, profound, original, and influential. They also wrote a great deal, and they changed over time. Sometimes their later work was inconsistent with their own earlier views. But they have strongly influenced what sociology is today. It is no exaggeration to say that very little has been added to their basic perspectives. What follows is a description of how these theorists viewed the sociological world, with emphasis on how their viewpoints have affected current sociology. As you read, remember that we are less concerned with the "rightness" or the "wrongness" of one viewpoint or another, than with

the established usefulness of all three in shedding light on the social world around us.

Emile Durkheim, 1858-1917 _STRUCTURE FUNCTIONALISM_

Durkheim's main concern was to make sociology a separate and unique science. His solution was to define sociology as the scientific study of **social facts**, of things that are external to, but constraining upon, the individual.

Born in France to middle-class Jewish parents, Emile Durkheim spent most of his life as an academic and is considered by many to be the father of modern scientific sociology as well as the originator of the functionalist school or position in that field (it had other forerunners in anthropology). He is probably best known for _Suicide_ (1897), which is a model of empirical research and statistical/probabilistic reasoning. Durkheim's other major works include his doctoral dissertation _On the Division of Labor in Society_ (1893), _The Rules of Sociological Method_ (1895), and _The Elementary Forms of the Religious Life_ (1912). One of Durkheim's major goals in life was to establish sociology as a scientific discipline in his country. While he did not succeed during his lifetime (though he held the first professorship in sociology ever to be established in France), his influence on modern Canadian sociology is extensive.

Sociology: What We Study. Most of you would agree with the following statements: Canadians wear clothes in public; rich people are different from poor people; priests behave differently from football players; and large classes are different from small classes. If your reasons or explanations for these statements are: because it is the custom or the law to wear clothes in public; or income, occupation, and class size make a difference; you are talking about social facts. For Durkheim, the key characteristics of social facts are that they are *external* to individuals and *coercive* upon them.

These external and coercive facts are seen as a separate and distinct variety of phenomena, "and it is to them the term 'social' is to be applied." Because they represent a new order of phenomena that is distinctly social, Durkheim argued bluntly that they could not be explained psychologically: "Consequently, every time that a social phenomenon is directly explained by a psychological phenomenon, we may be sure that the explanation is false" (Durkheim, 1964c, originally published in 1895).

Durkheim's classic analysis of suicide is a good example of his view of sociology. He had observed that certain rates of suicide were stable over time and across countries. He found that rates for married persons were lower than rates for divorced persons, and that Catholics had lower rates of suicide than Protestants. (See Chapter 17 for a discussion of Durkheim's method of measurement.) He argued that since the rates were stable, that is, since Protestants everywhere and at different times committed more suicides than Catholics, you could not explain the rates by the motivations of individual Protestants and Catholics. Durkheim insisted that you must look to social facts for the explanation of suicide rates. Specifically, you must look to the degree of integration of the groups into society. What explained these rates was the social fact of integration. Both married people and Catholics were more integrated into society than divorced people or Protestants. Durkheim's study of suicide was a bold attempt to look at a problem that had been seen as u..iquely psychological and to treat it instead as uniquely sociological.

Durkheim's crucial suggestion was that **social structure** – that is, social facts external to the individual – can offer an explanation for social behavior and other facts. He isolated what he saw as unique to sociology, a science which studies social facts independently of individuals. Society is not only more than the sum of its parts, it is coercive or constraining on the parts.

One example of a social fact would be the position of Prime Minister in Canada. It exists independently of a specific individual. In a real sense, it is out there external to any individual. Further, it is coercive or constraining upon any individual elected to the position. Whoever is Prime Minister is greatly affected by this social fact. Another example of a social fact would be the prestige of a particular department in a university. Certain departments are ranked high in prestige, something which is an important social fact affecting future employment.

As with all three men we shall discuss, it is not the correctness of the particular explanation that is crucial, but rather the general approach and the possibilities it suggests. What is important in Durkheim's case, and therefore worth repeating, is the suggestion that social structure, or social facts, can offer an explanation for social behavior and other social facts.

Durkheim's approach is evident in a contemporary study by Blau and Schoenherr (1971), who comment:

The formal structure of organizations exhibits regularities of its own. Although organizations are made up of people, of course, and what happens to them is the result of decisions of human beings, regularities are observable in their structure that seem to be independent of the personalities and psychological dispositions of individual members. . . . In short . . . organizations are not people.

Sociology: How We Study It. Durkheim believed that social facts could be studied and explained in the same way we study the physical and biological world – that is, scientifically. For Durkheim, the explanation of social facts involved establishing their causes and the functions they fulfill. Durkheim wanted both *causal* explanations and *functional* explanations. An example that he gives is, "The social reaction that we call 'punishment' is due to [caused by] the intensity of the collective sentiments which the crime offends; but, from another angle, it has the useful function of maintaining these sentiments at the same degree of intensity, for they would soon diminish if offenses against them were not punished" (Durkheim, 1964c, originally published 1895). This quote suggests that, for Durkheim, the more intense the collective feelings about a certain crime the more severe the punishment. This is a fairly obvious statement of cause and effect. But he also notes that punishment serves the purpose of maintaining this feeling within the group. This is the function of punishment.

It is clear, throughout Durkheim's works, that he wanted to establish sociology as a distinct subject that could not be explained by other disciplines, especially psychology, and as a science, because social facts could be explained scientifically. Furthermore, Durkheim believed that science could determine what is best, or the ends which we should seek. He asked: Why strive for knowledge of society if this knowledge cannot serve us in life? Durkheim's theorizing led him to the view that science could determine ends as well as means. In other words, science can determine what society should be (the ends), as well as the means of achieving those ends. As we will see, Durkheim's question of why strive for knowledge of society is still being asked. But most of those who accept sociology as a science reject Durkheim's solution, that science can determine ends.

Max Weber, 1864-1920 *SYMBOLIC INTERACTION*

It is hard to believe that Weber and Durkheim did not know each other's work. However, there is no indication that Weber, a German, was in communication with his French colleague or that they regarded each other as important figures in the development of sociology. This lack of awareness may have been due to the fundamental differences between their approaches. These differences can be seen by contrasting Durkheim's definition of sociology with Weber's.

Sociology: What We Study. Weber (1964) defined sociology as, "a science which attempts the interpretive understanding of social action in order thereby to arrive at a causal explanation of its course and effects." "Action" refers to all human behavior to which an actor attaches subjective meaning. For example, a traveler was at a museum in Spain and wanted to find a particular painting that he thought was in another building. He asked the guard for directions, and the guard put his arm out, palm down, and moved his hand up and down. The traveler took this to mean "Go away from me," and toward the other building. But as he proceeded to the other building, the guard moved his hand up and down more violently. When he got to the door, he saw that the building was completely dark. He looked back at the guard, who kept his hand wildly moving up and down. Then he remembered that in Spain this motion meant, not "Go away," but "Come forward." The guard and the traveler had different subjective meanings of the symbols being used for communication. The only way to understand this social action would be to know what these subjective meanings were. As Weber (1964) noted:

Action is social in so far as, by virtue of the subjective meaning attached to it by the individual (or individuals), it takes account of the behavior of others and is thereby oriented in its course.

A **social action** occurs between two individuals when each person takes into account the actions of the other. For Weber, sociology was concerned with the subjective meanings by which people are guided in their social conduct. The purpose of sociology for him, then, was to achieve an objective understanding of how people evaluate, use, create, and destroy their social relationships.

In this view, the individual is the basic unit of analysis. For Weber, sociologists studying a nation should concern themselves with the subjective meaning the nation has for its members, because it is in terms of what the nation means to its members that it is a reality. Contrast this with Durkheim's view that a nation is a reality in and of itself (a social fact), which therefore cannot be explained by its parts, that is, by the subjective meanings of individuals.

Weber believed that the individual is the sole carrier of meaningful conduct, because only the individual

Though he suffered from ill health most of his life, the German academic Max Weber exercised a profound influence over European and North American sociology as a consequence of the work he accomplished during productive periods. Often said to have been engaged in a lifelong dialogue with Marx, Weber directed the thrust of many of his major works to the criticism or elaboration of what he regarded as simplistic elements in Marxian thought. He is probably best known for his classic *The Protestant Ethic and the Spirit of Capitalism* (translated in 1930). But the thesis of this book – the influence of ideology on social structure – is also carried forward in *Ancient Judaism* (translated in 1952), *The Religion of China* (translated in 1951), and *The Religion of India* (translated in 1958). His major work, still incompletely translated into English, is *Wirtschaft und Gesellschaft* (Economy and Society, 1922).

can attach subjective meaning or motives to behavior. The social scientist can impute motives to individuals and thereby go beyond merely predicting human behavior to understanding it. This kind of understanding is not part of the physical sciences, where the subjective states of the things investigated are irrelevant. It is important to note at this point that both Durkheim and Weber were defining sociology by stating what is unique to the field of sociology, and therefore what separates it from other social sciences. Their definitions are diametrically opposed. This opposition is important, because it is still with us.

Sociology: How We Study It. Two of Weber's major statements concerning science have had a great impact on contemporary sociology. One concerns the notion of science as **value free**, or ethically neutral. The second concerns a method for studying social action which he called **Verstehen** (in German, literally "understanding").

You will recall that for Weber sociology had the advantage of access to subjective aspects of behavior, the meanings and motives of the individual. Weber would grant that people can be partly understood by external manifestations, social facts, or structures. For these phenomena, the methods of natural science were applicable for establishing general laws. Structure is inadequate for a full understanding of people, however, because it ignores what is unique to humans. Unlike atoms and molecules, humans think, feel, pursue goals, and have motives.

In Weber's view, general laws explaining human behavior were possible but inadequate. Just as we can observe natural objects like plants, stars, and chickens, we can also observe from the outside how people behave, and explain the regularities in their behavior by abstract causal laws. But with humans we can do more than with natural objects. We can impute motives by interpreting actions and words. We can get at the subjective meanings that actors attach to their own behavior and the behavior of others. But how do we study motives?

In order to get at what is unique to humans, we need a different approach. This new approach for Weber was Verstehen, or the interpretive understanding of social behavior. Weber suggested that this type of understanding could be achieved in two ways. The first was to reproduce in ourselves the purposive reasoning of the actor. For example, if we see a woman walking with a book under her arm, we might conclude that she is going to read, or that she is returning the book to the library. The second and more important way of understanding, however, was empathy. Sociologists should put themselves in the place of the actor and understand things as the actor sees them. For example, a sociologist today who wanted to study the use of marijuana could begin by determining who smokes, how often different people smoke, and the age and social class differences of smokers to see if there are any trends or empirical generalizations. But this is inadequate. Our sociologist must also find out what smoking grass means to the people who use it, what motivates them to try it, and what prompts them to continue with it. To do this the sociologist might "associate" with marijuana users, talk to them, observe them, and imaginatively try to experience their situation as they experience it. Only then would the researcher have access to what is uniquely sociological. Weber stated that this approach was scientific.

According to Weber, science by its very nature abhors value judgments. He believed that social scientists can gather information that is not affected by their values. An atheist, for example, can gather accurate data on religious beliefs. He also believed that scientific data and theories, in and of themselves, contain nothing that tells the scientist what *should* be done. There is nothing in the theory of relativity that tells the scientist that it is bad to drop atomic bombs. Good and bad, right and wrong, are beyond science.

To Weber, the physician's only job is to cure the patient. The physician, as a physician, has no right to say whether life is worth living or not. We can ask science, What shall we do? But we will get no answer, for on questions of value, science is mute.

Karl Marx, 1818–1883 CONFLICT THEORY

Durkheim and Weber were both directly concerned with creating a separate, distinct field of sociology and consequently took great pains to define what sociology

Born and educated in Germany, Marx went to England after the failure of the socialist revolution of 1848 and spent the remainder of his life there, much of it pursuing his studies in the British Museum. He collaborated with Friedrich Engels in writing *The Communist Manifesto* in 1848. The writing of his major work, *Das Kapital* (Capital), stretched over the years 1867 to 1894; Engels edited and completed the last two volumes after Marx's death. With V. I. Lenin, Marx is generally considered the father of modern communism.

is. Because of this, most of their contributions are directly related to that discipline. Karl Marx is different.

Sociology: What We Study.
Karl Marx stands alone among the writers we have considered, because of his impact on the world. A man of his stature, who wrote many books, articles, and speeches, who changed over time, who was a scientist and a revolutionary, becomes all things to all people. He called himself a philosopher, but some members of every social science claim him as one of their own.

One of the main difficulties in clearly summarizing Marx is that he wanted not only a science of society, he also wanted to change society. Therefore, his theory of society is also a revolutionary program. It is mainly since the 1960s that sociologists have openly paid their debt to Marx. For a long time, particularly in North America, his work was largely ignored or avoided for political reasons, and for these same reasons some members of every social science disclaim him, sometimes bitterly. But no one ignores him.

Essentially, Marx argued, everything that happens in society is caused by economic relationships. Society is divided into two basic economic classes, each having interests that are fundamentally antagonistic. The class that owns the wealth is the *bourgeoisie*, and the class that produces it is the *proletariat*, or working class. The masses of workers are exploited by a small privileged elite that manages to control most of the wealth without actually producing it themselves. Society, therefore, consists of classes of people with unequal power. The inequality of power is due to the differences in their relationships to the means of production, such as land, factories, and so on. The antagonism between these classes is **class conflict**. Periodically, the exploited class revolts and in turn becomes the exploiting class. As Marx put it, "The history of all hitherto existing society is the history of the class struggle" (Feuer, 1959). Marx saw revolution as necessary for social change, since the haves will not voluntarily give up their power. In capitalist societies the haves are the bourgeoisie, the people who own the land and the factories, and therefore the people who employ laborers in exchange for wages. The have-nots are the prole-tarians or working class who, because they do not own the means of production, are forced to sell their labor in order to survive. In this evolutionary stage, the working class revolts against the bourgeoisie and socializes the means of production. In other words, through the revolution the workers become the owners of the means of production. Since classes are based on ownership of the means of production, and after the revolution the workers own the means, the result theoretically is a classless society.

Marx also saw the economic system as a major force in determining other elements which make up the *superstructure* of society. Examples of such elements are law, politics, religion, art, and philosophy. The elements of the superstructure also are to be understood in their relationship to the means of production. However, once developed, the elements can play an independent role and can affect each other. For example, Marx referred to religion as "the opium of the people," because religion urged workers to forego rewards in this life and strive to build up rewards in an afterlife. Religion, therefore, justifies the current economic system (Bottomore, 1964).

Marxist concepts that have influenced present-day sociology include:

1. viewing society as constantly changing and change as inevitable; this is in contrast to those sociologists who stress the stability of society
2. the importance of economic structures as they determine other structures in society, and as they determine an individual's economic standing, life-chances, values, and behavior
3. stress on the interrelations among parts of the superstructure, so that any one part, to be understood, must be seen in relation to the others, especially economic institutions.

Furthermore, as an analyst of the class content of historical movements, Marx is unique. He must be seen as one of the major contributors to the study of revolutions. It is remarkable that so few sociologists have concerned themselves with the study of revolutions, given their importance both throughout history and today. (See Chapter 16 for some tentative explanations of this apparent disinterest.) In more general terms, Marx has contributed to our understanding of the roles of conflict and power as major elements of society.

Sociology: How We Study It. Both Durkheim and Weber were directly concerned with defining sociology and describing why sociology could be or was a science. These were not Marx's concerns. Nevertheless, some of his views on science are important in understanding the current state of sociology.

Marx considered himself a scientist and attempted to construct a historical science distinguishable from philosophy. He believed that his theories were based on scientific fact, not just opinion, and that his conclusions were derived from the empirical study of history and society. He also tried to construct a theory of social structure and social change. However, Marx's view of science was pragmatic in that he felt scientists should apply their knowledge in the service of humanity. In this aspect of his thought he was directly opposed to Weber, for whom science was value free.

A second important difference between Marx and the other two theorists was that Marx believed science to be historically specific. In this sense, there are no general laws of social change, other than that change will occur. Each problem must be looked at within a historical context. This historical specificity is well illustrated in Marx's reply to one critic who wrote: "According to Marx's philosophical system, Russia, like every other nation, would be obliged to pass through a stage of capitalist development." Marx answered: "Thus we see that events of a striking similarity, but occurring in different historical contexts, produced quite different results" (Bottomore, 1964). Marx's empirical generalizations were always applied to historically specific conditions. For Marx, then, social relations and ideas were grounded in historical periods and were therefore transitory. All historical periods had class struggles, but these struggles differed according to the historical period, and the type of people who participated in class struggles changed over time.

Of these two Marxist views, the first (that scientists should use their knowledge to improve the life of humankind) has had the greatest impact. For certain modern sociologists, however, the second (the idea that sociological analysis must be historically specific) has also been important.

In sum, Marx, Durkheim, and Weber each saw himself as a scientist and believed that a science of society, human behavior, and history was possible. They meant very different things, however, by the term "science." The major questions they posed were: Can general laws of social behavior be established? Can the general methods of natural science be used to study social behavior and social structure; if they can, are they sufficient? Can and should scientists use their knowledge for the betterment of humanity? Is science value free? These questions are still with us, and sociologists are still divided in their answers.

CURRENT PERSPECTIVES

Theoretical perspectives are more than attempts to define the subject of sociology. In a sense, a perspective is a pair of glasses for viewing a part of the world. The world is not just there, but is seen and interpreted through the perspective used. A high rate of suicide, for example, can be seen as the result of rainy weather or a chemical imbalance, a product of capitalist society, the result of a lack of integration of the individual into society, or the result of large numbers of people defining their situation as hopeless. Each perspective, by stating what sociology is, is also suggesting what questions to ask. Therein lies the usefulness of these perspectives, alone and in combination.

What part of the world you look at and what questions you ask about that part of the world are therefore largely determined by the perspective you use. The **sociological perspectives** discussed so far suggest that certain parts of the world are more important than others. All sociologists would agree that human behavior is shaped by social groups. But what behavior is shaped, how it is shaped, and what groups are crucial in the shaping process are viewed very differently, depending on the sociologist's perspective.

The various specific disagreements aside, there is general agreement that the views of Durkheim, Weber, and Marx form the basis of current perspectives in sociology. Structural functionalism is traced to Durkheim, conflict theory to Marx, and symbolic interaction to Weber. In the following sections we examine these current perspectives and classify them as macrosociology or microsociology. A macro-perspective studies the large scale structures and processes of society. A micro-perspective studies the small scale structures and processes of society.

Macrosociology

Generally, **macrosociology** refers to a set of factors, characteristics, dimensions, or variables that exist in society independently of individuals and that are believed to constrain them to behave and think in particular ways. It is assumed that individuals experiencing the same structure will behave in the same way and that certain parts of the structure affect other parts.

This approach is not unique to sociology. Structural statements are used often by people in their everyday lives. Young people who contend that no one over thirty should be trusted are assuming that regardless of individual characteristics (such as personality or conviction) there is something about passing this age that constrains people to behave in a certain way. In fact, a structural argument may be used to support this lack of trust. By age thirty, most people are well integrated into society. They are out of school and have been working in an occupation for a few years. Most are married, are in or are supporting a family and have accumulated some material goods. In short, they are closely tied to established society and have something to lose by criticizing it or changing it. They are, moreover, entrenched in a web of relationships that further constrains them to behave in respectable and predictable ways.

Another illustration of a structural statement is found in the question, "What do you do?" The question asks for one's occupation, and the person asking it is imputing to occupation a dominant influence on life-style. When we find out a person's occupation, we adjust our behavior accordingly. We are not likely to tell "dirty" jokes to a priest, and we may feel uneasy in the presence of a powerful figure like the Queen or the Prime Minister.

Actually, macrosociology may be used in two rather distinct ways that can be stated as basic sociological assumptions. The first assumption is that *a specific structure of society determines its other structural characteristics*. For example, Marx was using a structural approach when he suggested that capitalist countries are likely to experience one economic crisis after another. These countries, he argued, are characterized by the profit motive, and workers receive only a subsistence wage. Profits are plowed back into the corporation and production increases rapidly. But workers, he argued, are not paid enough to buy the products. This situation leads to an economic crisis like financial depression.

The second assumption is that *social structures constrain individual behavior*. People from cities, for example, behave differently from those in rural areas; and individuals in certain positions, like physicians or lawyers, are likely to wield greater personal power than postal carriers or streetcar conductors. Occupation, the last example, is often used by sociologists as an important determinant of behavior, and in its extreme form may be summed up in such statements as, "the office makes the person" and "bank presidents are conservative." Both structural-functionalism and conflict theory are kinds of macrosociology.

Structural Functionalism. Structural functionalism is one of the three main contemporary perspectives. It stresses:

1. that a society cannot survive unless its members share at least some common perceptions, attitudes, and values
2. that each part of the society makes a contribution to the whole
3. that the various parts of society are integrated with each other, each part supporting the other parts as well as the whole
4. that these forces keep societies relatively stable

Structural functionalism is directly related to the work of Durkheim, and the concept of social system is central to it.

Think of your body as a system. The system has certain needs or requirements to maintain its existence (for example, a certain temperature range). When the system is maintaining a proper temperature it is in a state of equilibrium, or balance. When your body gets too hot, the equilibrium is threatened, and the system adjusts or adapts by perspiring, returning it to a state of equilibrium. Perspiring is functional in that it helps the body adjust. In this example, the concept of system is *integral*. In structural functionalism, the social system is likewise integral.

The **social system** can be defined by four characteristics: boundaries, interdependence of parts, needs or requirements, and equilibrium.

A system must have boundaries. This means you can identify what parts are in the system and what parts are outside of it. An example would be your university. What it owns, the buildings, and the people who are members are parts of the university system. Non-members are not part of the system.

The parts of the university system are interrelated or interdependent. What happens to one part in the system affects the other parts. If student membership declines, all parts of the system (number of faculty, number of programs, standards, the budget) are affected.

The university system has needs or requirements if it is to survive (for example: no students, no university). The university also needs funds for its programs and salaries for its teachers and other personnel. And the university must have some control over its members to see that they perform at an acceptable level.

When, at a particular time, the university has adequate funds, adequate numbers of students, faculty and staff, it is in a state of **equilibrium**. If this equilibrium is threatened (if, for example, the number of students increases very rapidly), then the university system will be obliged to adapt itself to a new set of circumstances. It is in the use of equilibrium that social systems differ from human systems. In the case of the human body, the only change that takes place is a return to the original state. In our example, 37 degrees Celsius is the equilibrium state. If the body is hot, perspiring will cool it to 37 degrees. Social systems, however, change over time. The university grows. As

it grows, a balance or equilibrium – more money, more faculty, more students – is maintained. To describe this condition the structural-functionalist uses the term **dynamic equilibrium.**

It is the concept of social system that makes this analysis structural. What makes it a functionalist analysis is the interpretation of the parts in terms of the system. The parts of a system can be functional, dysfunctional, or nonfunctional. Usually, a functional analysis of structures stresses the functional aspects of a part for the system. A part is **functional** if it helps meet the needs of the system, if it helps contribute to the adjustment of the system. A part of the system that is harmful to the rest of the system is **dysfunctional**. A part that is irrelevant to the system is nonfunctional. Gans (1972), for example, in his functional analysis of poverty, concluded that poverty persists when it is functional for the rich and dysfunctional for the poor and that it will persist as long as the elimination of poverty would create dysfunctions for the rich. In the same way, job discrimination against women is dysfunctional for women, but functional for men, and nonfunctional for the retired.

In a functional analysis the system is seen as being in a state of equilibrium, or balance, when the needs of the system are being met and the parts are interdependent. But the social systems that structural-functionalism analyzes are made up of individuals. For the system to be integrated and stable the assumption is usually made that the individuals making up the system are committed to the general values of the system. In other words, the structural functionalist assumes that societies have value systems that are shared by their members. If most of the people in a society did not agree on the values of that society, the society would fall apart. In the structural functionalist perspective, consensus on the major values, such as laws, is seen as a requirement of a social system.

Thus, the structural functionalist perspective stresses the order and stability in society. Institutions like the family, education, and religion are analyzed according to how they help meet the needs of society, the role they play in maintaining society's stability. Education, for example, teaches the basic values and skills necessary in an industrial society and fits people into

Harvard sociologist Talcott Parsons was a prominent modern structural functionalist whose work stressed equilibrium.

the appropriate societal positions. As you will see in Chapter 14, the educational system accomplishes this latter function by sorting people out on the basis of their achievements and their ability.

In this way individuals are matched with various positions or jobs, and society gets the doctors, lawyers, teachers, machinists, and engineers that it needs. Not everyone can be a doctor, and the educational system identifies those who can and want to, as well as those who can't and don't have the desire. The general view is, therefore, that modern education serves positive functions for society. The maintenance of social order is one outcome of education. Other social institutions and their functions would include the economic system, which operates to produce and distribute necessary goods; the family, which performs the functions of early socialization, sexual regulation and satisfaction, and the rearing of children; and the political system, which organizes and legitimates power.

The Conflict Perspective.

The **conflict perspective** is macrosociological because it assumes that social structure affects human behavior. But where structural functionalism emphasizes integration, shared values, and social stability, the conflict perspective stresses conflict, power differences, and social change. While conflict theorists do not necessarily follow the class conflict assumptions of Marx, they do follow his general orientation.

The basic elements (adapted from Dahrendorf, 1959) in the conflict perspective are:

1. societies are always changing
2. conflict and *dissensus* (lack of general agreement) are always present in society
3. there are elements or parts of every society that contribute to change
4. coercion is always present in society; that is, in every society some people have more power than others

In this perspective, society is seen as ever changing, as a precarious balance of power groups trying to maintain or improve their positions. Structural functionalists tend to view institutions and groups as integrated and complementary. Conflict theorists, by contrast, suggest that such groups usually work at cross purposes, the goals of one group frequently at odds with the goals of another. Conflict is seen as pervasive, as each group attempts to improve or maintain its position. These continuous power struggles between groups result in a constantly changing society. What stability there is occurs during (usually brief) periods in which there is domination by one group or a balance of power between groups.

Another characteristic of the conflict perspective is that it tends to view values, ideas, and morality as rationalizations for existing power groups. The basic causes for change are thus not to be found in the values of individuals but in the structure of society. By the same token, power is not seen as due to individual characteristics, but due to position in society. The Prime Minister, for example, has power because of the nature of the office, not because of any individual characteristics. Or persons are seen as having power because they control resources, such as money or the

Modern conflict theorist Ralf Dahrendorf, director, London School of Economics, in his office near the Strand, 1974.

means of production. This view also stresses that social facts are part of society and are external to and constraining upon the individual.

A conflict theorist studying education would likely view modern mass education in the following manner. First, it teaches the values and skills of the dominant groups in society in the hope that their values will be accepted and that they themselves will not be challenged. Second, it selects individuals so that the power structure of society will be maintained. As we pointed out at the beginning of this chapter, the best predictor of who goes to university is not the individual's ability but the parents' occupation, suggesting that to a certain extent higher education functions to perpetuate status structure. The conflict theory of education is discussed in more depth in Chapter 14.

In summary, both conflict theorists and structural-functionalists are oriented toward the study of social structures and institutions. Structural-functionalists see society as basically static and orderly, its integrated parts contributing to its stability, and shared values creating cohesion. In contrast, the conflict perspective views society as constantly changing. The parts of society are viewed as contributing to this change, and the role of power in maintaining order is stressed. Dissension and conflict, rather than agreement and order, are taken to be the natural state of society.

Microsociology

Many microsociologists will grant that social facts exist, but they will also insist that social facts are relevant only to the extent that people attach meaning and significance to them.

Suppose you are walking down a garden path, you turn a corner and suddenly see a large snake. You may say, "Hey, that snake will be a great addition to my dance act," or "Wow, here comes dinner," or, "Poor snake, it might get hurt on this path." The point is that we can agree that this is a snake, a fact, but our responses to it depend on the meaning we attach to it. A snake may mean good luck or bad, may be beautiful or ugly, may cause joy or fear.

The basic assumption of **microsociology** is that the explanations of social life and social structures are to be found at the individual level and/or in social interaction.

Symbolic Interaction. The dominant microsociological approach is **symbolic interaction**, which looks primarily at the subjective states of the actor, both as a result of social learning and as these subjective states affect the actor's environment. Symbolic interaction is the third of the three main contemporary sociological perspectives. Everyday statements that typify symbolic interaction are: "I know how she feels, because I have gone through it;" "I understand his depression, because I too have worked on an assembly line;" and "I once lost my job, so I can understand the feelings of those who are forced to retire." That you can know how other people feel in different situations is implicit in such statements as, "People are on relief, because they are too lazy to work;" "Anyone can succeed who really tries;" "A good teacher cares about the students;" "You're only as old as you feel;" and "He is a good salesman, because he is aggressive." (Contrast this last statement with "He is aggressive, because he is a salesman," which is a structural argument implying that there is something about being a salesman that makes people aggressive.) These examples express the theme that subjective states of individuals are basic for understanding their acts.

A large percentage of sociological research on delinquency, attitudes, company morale, job satisfaction, and social values stems from Weber's notion of social action. (Remember the story of the tourist in Spain.) The following interpretation of symbolic interaction is based on the writings of Herbert Blumer (1962), which are directly related to Weber's social action theory.

Symbolic interaction focuses on people. To the symbolic interactionist social facts are not things that control, coerce, or constrain people; they are little more than the framework for the real subject of sociology. The symbolic interactionist is not inclined to treat society as a set of real structures distinct from people.

Humans are feeling, thinking beings who attach meaning to the situations they are in and behave in accordance with that interpretation. In this perspective, people are considered to be far more creators of society than passive recipients of society's norms and values. Not only are they capable of learning the norms and values of their society, but they also discover, invent, and initiate new norms and values. They create, interpret, plan, and control their values, their environment. People not only react, but act. Blumer (1962) writes:

The term symbolic interaction refers to, of course, the peculiar and distinctive character of interaction as it takes place between human beings. The peculiarity consists in the fact that human beings interpret or "define" each other's actions instead of merely reacting to each other's actions. Their response is not made directly to the actions of one another but instead is based on the meaning which they attach to such actions. Thus, human interaction is mediated by the use of symbols, by interpretation, or by ascertaining the meaning of one another's actions.

The similarity between Blumer and Weber should be apparent. Both stress the subjective meanings of individuals as the fundamental subject of sociology. A basic difference, however, is the symbolic interactionist's emphasis on symbols, that is, on signs, gestures and – most importantly – language.

A **symbol** is something that stands for something else. A word, for instance, can stand for a thing. Language, gestures, and flags are symbols. The meanings of symbols are arbitrarily determined by the people who create them. For the symbolic interactionist, it is the use of words, or language, that makes human beings unique among all other forms of life. It is our capacity to represent symbolically ourselves, each other, ideas, and objects, that makes us human. To a great degree, humans are free from instincts and must rely on symbols to adapt and survive. Human social organization, therefore, is created, maintained, and changed largely due to our capacity to create symbols.

Because humans can agree on the meanings of symbols and share these meanings, they can effectively communicate. Furthermore, because meanings of symbols are learned, they are necessarily social and are learned through interaction. We communicate and interact by interpreting the symbols that others convey. In this process of interaction, humans learn to anticipate each other's responses and to adjust to each other. This ability to anticipate the reponses of others, or to imagine the viewpoint of others, Mead (1934) calls **role taking**, or "taking the role of the other." Role taking for symbolic interactionists is the basic process by which interaction occurs; we take into account the attitudes, feelings, and subjective intentions of others. In a sense, we can see ourselves from the outside – that is, from the viewpoint of another. Role taking is the process by which we develop self-awareness and a concept of ourselves. This process is examined at length in chapter 3, *Socialization*.

If the symbolic interactionists are correct, the self-awareness of individuals, whether they see themselves as popular or unpopular, good or bad, bright or dull, depends on their perception of how others think about and treat them. Symbolic interactionists believe also that people are generally correct in their judgment of how they are perceived and treated by others. This development of the self through the process of role taking is a central concept of the interactionist perspective and shows how our very humanness and distinctiveness as individuals are the result of interaction in society. Closely related to this capacity for self-development is the assumption that we are capable of examining and finding symbolic solutions to future problems – are capable, that is, of planning.

Consider W.I. Thomas' (1928) notion of the "definition of the situation." He claimed that if people "define the situation as real, it is real in its consequences." This again stresses the notion of people as active; it is not the structure that determines their behavior but their definition of that structure. Through interpreting and defining the situation, an individual is making and remaking the environment. This emphasis on the meanings that the situation and interaction have for the individuals involved has led the symbolic interactionists to focus on social behavior in everyday life, to try to understand how people create and define the situations they experience. For example, street gangs, communes, and work groups have been studied using this perspective.

George Herbert Mead introduced the concept of symbolic interaction, showing how people interact through symbols, especially language.

To summarize the symbolic interactionist perspective: humans create, use, and communicate with symbols. Through the process of interaction we develop that which is uniquely human: a self and the ability to think.

To illustrate these various sociological perspectives, we can ask ourselves how each might be used in studying the students in a classroom. A structural functionalist, focusing on what is common to classrooms, might analyze the functions of tests. A conflict theorist could look at the effects of the power differences between teacher and students. A symbolic interactionist might want to determine how the individual students interpret the class, or the effect of the teacher on the development of their self-images.

Ethnomethodology. A fairly new microsociological approach which has much in common with symbolic interaction is called ethnomethodology. **Ethnomethodology** is primarily concerned with understanding how people carry out the ordinary, routine activities of their everyday lives by means of language and meaning, and the way in which people construct, interpret, and use rules or norms of conduct.

According to the first point, ethnomethodologists emphasize the direct study of everyday life activities. These activities include interactions and communications – the way people discuss, argue, flirt, teach, leer, question, and order their world into a comprehensible form. Rather than investigating the "products" or "reflections" of activities such as occupational prestige, formal level of education, or degree of isolation, the stress is on directly observing the individual activities involved in prestige, education, or isolation. A person may use a different kind of grammar or initiate new interactions with others, for example, which may be reflected in occupational prestige.

The second point is the emphasis on understanding the language and meanings of the people under consideration. In this regard, ethnomethodology is somewhat similar to the orientations of social action and symbolic interaction, which also stress language and communication between individuals. The everyday activities of life, like arguing and questioning, can be viewed as having a grammar or form. The task of the ethnomethodologist is to establish the appropriate categories and rules of such grammar or form. To do so, you need to understand the subtle meanings of language and how people use language in their everyday lives. Ethnomethodologists look unfavorably on the use of questionnaires and interviews, because they believe the subtleties of language are not well enough understood for the formulation of useful questions. For them, consequently, the only valid technique is some form of participant observation, which requires being a member of a group so that the observer can understand what is going on. In this sense, the orientation is somewhat similar to the method of Weber's Verstehen.

Social rules, or **norms**, and the way people use them – the third point – play a prominent part in ethnomethodological investigations. Briefly stated, norms are standards that specify how people should behave. (See Chapter 2 for a more detailed definition.)

To the ethnomethodologist, norms are considered to be general and abstract. They must be interpreted by the individual in an ad hoc manner applied to specific situations. For example, a No Smoking sign in an auditorium really does not apply to the specific situation where, as part of his role, an actor smokes a cigarette. The general norm of no smoking must be interpreted for the specific situation. How norms are interpreted and used by people is a major aspect for ethnomethodological investigation.

Exchange Theory. Another and distinctive microsociological approach is **exchange theory** as developed by George Homans (1961). In this view, the proper area of study for sociology is the overt (observable) patterns of behavior occurring in interpersonal relations. The emphasis is on what individuals and human groups do in behaving with and toward one another, rather than on their subjective states or motivations. Exchange theory focuses on establishing the patterns of behavior of interacting individuals. Homans uses a model for explaining social interaction which is based on certain psychological and economic considerations. The major proposition of exchange theory is that every human interaction is an exchange of goods and services. Marriage is one such relationship. An exchange theorist would analyze the goods and services, such as money and affection, that each partner receives. Interaction does not persist unless there is a profit to both parties. Two individuals will interact as long as the interaction is perceived as beneficial to both.

For exchange theorists, behavior is determined by the previous give and take of rewards and the cost of the interaction. For a relationship to continue people must feel that what they are receiving is equal to what they are giving.

An Overview

These, then, are the major sociological perspectives. Which is right? A better question is: Which of them has been useful in helping us come to an understanding of society? And the answer to that is all of them. They are all based on different assumptions. But so far each has provided a useful way of viewing part of the social world.

Early in the chapter we defined sociology as the description and explanation of social behavior, social structures, and social interaction in terms of these

Historian and economist Harold Innis significantly influenced Canadian sociology with his analyses of socioeconomic and urban conditions. Innis headed the Department of Political Economy at the University of Toronto, and sociology was placed under his direction. His contribution has been recognized in the naming of Innis College, part of the University of Toronto.

social structures, and/or in terms of people's perceptions of the social environment. This definition is built around the three theoretical perspectives we have just examined. It contains elements of structural functionalism, conflict theory, and symbolic interaction.

Having considered the what and how of sociology (what it is and how we study it) from various points of view, we will now consider a question toward which our discussion has been tending all along: the question of sociology *and* science.

SOCIOLOGY AND SCIENCE

According to Aristotelian physics, the motion of material objects was governed by motives and goals. Earthly matter sought the center of the earth as its natural goal. And because heavenly bodies were al-

leged to be composed of a "quintessence," they were supposed to move only in circular orbits at a uniform speed. These theories led to conclusions that conflicted with observations of falling bodies and the motions of planets.

Slowly, through careful observation, more direct knowledge was gathered about the physical world, first about the stars and much later about human anatomy. Astronomy and physiology became *empirical*, that is, based on observation. "Prove it" became "Show me." As an example, through controlled experiments in which physicists observed balls rolling down planes and objects falling under different conditions, it was suggested that a feather will fall as fast as a rock in a vacuum. Physicists did not actually observe this because they could not then effect the necessary near-perfect vacuum. But using this assumption they could account, for instance, for the rate at which objects do fall under stated conditions, as well as why we do not fly off the earth. Much later, using the theory of gravity, they would predict where a rocket to the moon would land and be correct to within one foot.

But the social world in Aristotle's time gave rise to pretty much the same sorts of questions as we ask today. Why are some people warlike? Why are some rich and others poor? Why are we civilized and they are barbarians? Why do some people go crazy? Why do some men have many wives and some only one? The answers to these questions, like the answers to questions about the earth's surface, the sun, the functioning of the body, and madness, were based on authority, tradition, revelation, or intuition. All are ways of knowing. It was Auguste Comte who, in the early 1800s, first suggested that sociology should use the scientific method as its way of knowing.

The Naturalist Position

The naturalist view of science holds that scientific method can be applied to study social behavior, and that through the use of the scientific method causal and law-like statements can be established in sociology. This **naturalist view** is accepted by some members of the three sociological perspectives: structural-functionalism, conflict theory, and symbolic interaction.

In the naturalist view, **science** is basically a method for collecting and explaining facts. The primary goal of this method for sociology is to discover patterns of social behavior and to explain these patterns by developing laws. A fact or relationship is explained if it can be subsumed under a **scientific law**. Scientific laws contain predictive statements that certain effects will occur given specified conditions. Scientific laws, then, are statements of relations between two or more **variables**. These relations have been supported or proved repeatedly by **objective** test. That we can walk on earth is explained by the law of gravity. If some of us go flying off the face of the earth, this law would have to be modified. Thus the law, in order to be a law, must predict correctly. If it does not, if there are negative cases that do not conform to it, the law must be revised.

In order to make such predictive statements and establish laws, the assumption is made that there is order in the physical and social universes. It is assumed that systematic relations exist that can be observed and formulated into laws. The task for sociologists is to find the order in social phenomena and express it using the scientific method.

Characteristics of Science.

The goal of the scientific method is to construct scientific laws. But how do we reach this goal? According to the naturalist position, we reach it in three ways:

1. by verifiability
2. by unbiased observation
3. by unbiased interpretation

Verifiability means that an observation can be confirmed by independent observers. If we walk out of a movie and you say the heroine had red hair and I say she did not, we have two independent observations that contradict each other. Who is right? We ask 20 friends and 19 say she had red hair and one says no. But on further questioning we determine that the one who said no is color blind and therefore not a competent observer. Then we agree that you are right. Your observation is verified, because several other observers made the same observation, and we can say it is a fact that the heroine had red hair. We say something is a

What is love? Sexual attraction, companionship, a physical sensation, or a spiritual communication? For social researchers, defining what they observe and how they measure it is essential.

fact when several qualified observers, after careful observation, achieve the same results.

It should be clear that, for science, the final arbiter of knowledge is *observation*. Consequently, science can answer only questions on phenomena that can be directly or indirectly observed. It is important to recognize that observation can be indirect. In many instances, concepts are formed from things which we may not observe at the time, molecules and atoms for example. However, these are employed in science theoretically so that there is an observable outcome. If atoms behave as we theoretically think they do, then when we split them, the bomb should go off. If it does, we say it is useful to accept the existence of atoms as fact. If the observable outcome predicted from our theory does not occur, then we conclude it is not useful.

It follows from this that while science has proven to be a powerful way of viewing the world, it is restricted to those problems that deal with the observable world. In turn, it should be apparent that some very important problems and concerns cannot be resolved by the scientific method: Thou shalt not kill; We should obey the law; What is beauty?; Is there a God? These are questions and statements that are not empirical. In other words, they cannot be resolved by observation. We may use logic, tradition, authority, common sense, revelation, faith, or intuition to answer these questions, but we cannot answer them by observation. We cannot answer them by science. In restricting science to the realm of the observable, scientists are limited to studying facts. The bomb goes off, crime rates increase, a higher proportion of women were in the labor force in 1980 than in 1960. Such statements are factual; they can be verified by observation. Factual statements are distinguished from statements or questions of preference or values. *Should* the bomb go off? A high crime rate is *bad*. Is it *good* that more women are working?

Science cannot help us answer such questions. Most Canadians, for example, want capital punishment for certain crimes. Sociologists cannot, as scientists, state that capital punishment is right or wrong. They can say that there is no clear relationship between capital punishment and a reduction in the crime rate. They can also state that a poll (Gallup 1981) showed that as many as 74 percent of the Canadians sampled favored the return of capital punishment for certain crimes Sociologists can study scientifically what people *do* want, but there is nothing in this method that enables them to tell individuals what they *should* want.

Science, then, is concerned with questions that have observable answers. The color of the heroine's hair can be observed. The color of a unicorn's hair or a witch's hair is not at this time observable and is thus outside the scope of science. It should be noted that the frequently mentioned conflicts between religion and science can occur only over questions of fact, that is questions that pertain to the world of observation. In this perspective, science is objective or unbiased, meaning that it is assumed that observations can be made that are unaffected by beliefs, values, or preferences.

It follows from the idea that science is based on verifiable knowledge that if the observations are biased, if we see what we want to see, rather than what

is, there can be no science. Unbiased observation, the second way we reach our goal of constructing laws, assumes that the researchers' values can be controlled adequately in doing social research. For example, if you are a democratic socialist and I am a conservative, is it possible for us to conduct a survey poll such that our political biases do not affect our results? Can an anti-abortionist conduct an objective (value-free) study of abortion?

Sociologists who accept the naturalist position say yes, it is possible to control bias. They would also say that the amount of bias can be determined by other independent observers. If your poll has the N.D.P. winning and mine has the Progressive Conservatives winning, we do not know who is right. It might be that just by looking at how the polls were conducted we could determine who is most likely correct. However, if several other pollsters support your findings, then the evidence suggests either that I did a bad job of polling or that my biases affected my observation.

Besides the problem of unbiased observation, there is also the problem of unbiased interpretation, the third way we reach our goal. If, for example, you do a study on aggressiveness in salespeople as compared to several other occupations, how do you interpret this information? A sociologist with a social-action perspective, who sees motives as important, might argue that being a salesperson requires a certain amount of aggressive behavior, and aggressive people are attracted to this type of occupation. A sociologist with a structuralist orientation might suggest that salespeople become aggressive because the occupation causes the behavior and attitude, rather than the reverse. The problem is that most facts or relationships can be interpreted in more than one way. Consequently, our biases frequently affect our interpretations.

The naturalist offers a solution to this problem by requiring that the interpretation must be stated so it is capable of being tested. In other words, the interpretation becomes a *hypothesis*, a testable statement asserting a relationship between two or more variables. If the structuralist is right, then a study of people before they become salespeople and people who go into other occupations should show no difference in aggressiveness. If the study shows further that salespeople become

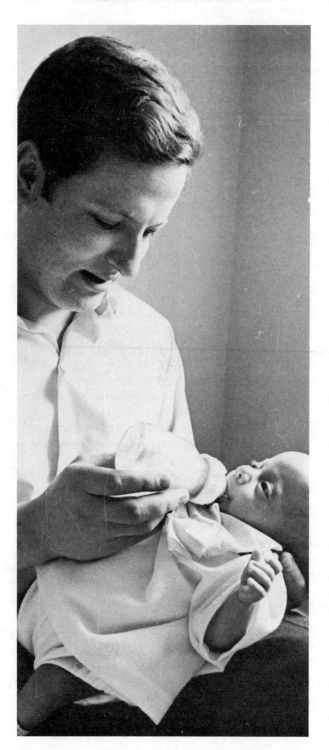

more aggressive over time, this would also support a structuralist interpretation. If a study has not been conducted, then either interpretation is plausible. In any case, what is required is that the interpretation be stated so that observations can determine the truth or falsity of the statement. Some interpretations are by definition not able to be tested. If I state that the plague was caused by God's wrath, there seems to be no way that I could test this to determine whether it is scientifically true or false.

A last example of the problems of interpreting facts is dreaming. The question of whether people dream is easily answered. We remember our dreams and can relate them. Other behavior, such as rapid eye movements during sleep, indicates that people dream. It has been found that every time we observe rapid eye movements and wake the subjects, they say that they were dreaming. However, do dogs dream? Most people say yes. But how do we know? We see the dog asleep, and we see the creature tremble and make noises and infer from this that the dog is dreaming. But we cannot ask the dog. We have no way of observing directly or indirectly whether a dog dreams. Consequently, other interpretations are possible, such as indigestion or some other physical cause. Because neither of these interpretations is testable scientifically, we do not know if dogs dream. At this point you say, "Science is a waste of time. I know dogs dream." But if you know, your knowledge is based on intuition, authority, or common sense – something other than science.

The ability to test whether one interpretation or another is correct is a way of controlling for bias in interpretations of observations. Another aid is the fact that science is public. There is nothing more sobering and conducive to careful analysis for sociologists than the knowledge that their colleagues will carefully read

This father has normal aspirations for his child's intelligence. Sir Cyril Burt claimed that children inherit intelligence. But in the late seventies Burt's findings were exposed as fraudulent. Some of his studies proved to be pure fiction.

and criticize what they say. When something is public, if it is wrong, sooner or later someone will point this out. It may take time, and the reasons for the delay are not always clear. One reason is that sometimes a given theory fits the biases of most people. In this case, there may be a gap before the error is identified, because most people want to believe it. Another possible explanation is that the scientist who made the statement is very powerful or has a great deal of prestige in the discipline.

An important example of what can happen in the social sciences is the case of the late Sir Cyril Burt, an internationally known and respected British psychologist whose studies of identical twins raised apart had been cited as the best evidence that intelligence is hereditary. Burt's publications span a period from 1912 to 1969, and he was knighted in 1946 for his service to British education.

Since Burt's death in 1971, however, his findings have been exposed as fraudulent. It seems that his twin studies were fabricated, he invented co-authors, and the other data he presented were fraudulently derived. As Gillie (1979) puts it: "Today there is little doubt that Sir Cyril Burt, apparent guardian of intellectual rigor, hero of educational conservatives, defender of a future to be given over to the genetically pure, was one of the most formidable confidence men British society has produced." The reasons he went unquestioned so long were probably that many liked what he was "proving," that he enjoyed considerable prestige, and that most scientists believe that other scientists simply do not make up data. His fame was dependent upon publication. But public record can be checked and rechecked, and if unsound will be exposed sooner or later.

To summarize this naturalist view, scientists can and must try to keep their values and preferences from affecting what they see and how they interpret what they see. Science is value free, but scientists are not. Therefore, by adhering to the rules of science scientists can reduce the effects of values, and by verification and retesting they can determine the extent to which values may have intruded upon their research. Chapter 17 provides more details about the scientific methods used by social researchers.

We have just considered some of the qualities of science that make it science and some of the qualities that sociology must have or acquire to be considered a science. Is sociology now, or can it be, a science? It all depends, as we have seen, on what you mean by "science." Opinions vary, sociologists differ.

These differences have existed for a long time and seem likely to continue. Like those associated with the other perspectives, these differences are not unique to sociology. Nor are they unhealthy. If you know what stance a given sociologist takes, you should be in a good position to evaluate what is being said and done. There is no one right way to view the world. It is probably true that most sociologists accept a naturalist position as a goal, while realizing that it is extremely difficult in social research to exclude personal values. At the same time, most sociologists are increasingly aware of ethical responsibilities toward the people they study and the results of their study. And in a book such as this, written by many people, it becomes necessary that the reader be aware of these diverse perspectives, since in various chapters you will encounter all of them.

This chapter has presented an overview of the discipline of sociology. Necessarily, much has been omitted and simplified, but the stress has been on the potential value and usefulness of diverse and multiple viewpoints, as opposed to the one right way of seeing society. The chapters to come will provide you with good illustrations of this valuable diversity.

SUMMARY

1. Durkheim and Weber defined sociology in diametrically opposed ways. For Durkheim, sociology was concerned with social facts which are external to individuals and which constrain their behavior. Explanations of social behavior and social facts must themselves be explained by other social facts. Weber, on the other hand, believed that what was uniquely sociological was our ability to understand the subjective states of individuals. The subject of sociology is the individual's subjective meanings, motives, or definitions of the situation.

2. Marx did not define sociology, but his influence has been direct and profound. For Marx, society is seen largely in terms of the relationships people have to the means of production and the class conflict that results. Change and conflict, in his view, are fundamental characteristics of society.

3. Three major current perspectives are derived from these three classical thinkers: structural functionalism is traced to Durkheim, conflict theory stems from Marx, symbolic interaction is clearly related to Weber.

4. Structural functionalism stresses order and stability in society. This perspective emphasizes that a society cannot survive unless its members share some common values, attitudes, and perceptions; that each part of the society contributes to the whole; that the various parts are integrated with each other; and that this interdependence keeps societies relatively stable.

5. The conflict perspective emphasizes that societies are always changing; that conflict and dissensus are always present in society; that parts of every society contribute to change; and that coercion is always present in society because some people have more power than others.

6. Symbolic interaction focuses on people and how they create, use, and communicate with symbols, especially language.

7. Naturalists argue that sociology is based on objective, verifiable data and the attitude that science can be value-free.

GLOSSARY

Class conflict. Antagonism between social classes, especially between the class that owns the means of production and the classes that do not.

Conflict perspective. A sociological view emphasizing that conflict, power, and change are permanent features of society.

Dynamic equilibrium. Parsons' term for the orderly change that constantly occurs among the interrelated parts of a social system.

Dysfunctional. Adjective applied to an element or part of a system that disrupts or is harmful to the system.

Equilibrium. In structural-functionalism, the overall balance that exists among the elements in a system.

Ethnomethodology. Sociological perspective concerned with the methods people use to carry out their everyday activities, language and meanings, and the implicit norms that govern behavior.

Exchange theory. Set of propositions that relates interaction of persons to the level of the satisfying outcomes they experience and that specifies the consequences of these outcomes.

Functional. Adjective applied to parts of a social system that contribute to the overall stability of the system.

Macrosociology. Study of large social units.

Microsociology. Study of small scale structures and processes of society.

Naturalist position. View that the scientific method, as in the physical sciences, can be used to study social phenomena. Facts are established by reliable and verifiable observation.

Norms. Standards of conduct. Statements of how people should and should not behave.

Objectivity. Ability to observe and interpret reality in such a way that subjective judgments and biases are eliminated.

Role taking. Process of imaginatively putting yourself in the role of another and seeing the world from that person's perspective.

Science. Systematic methods by which reliable, empirical knowledge is obtained. Also refers to the actual body of knowledge obtained by these methods. See also **Naturalist position.**

Scientific law. An hypothesis that has been repeatedly supported by empirical tests.

Social action. Human behavior that is subjectively meaningful to the persons involved.

Social facts. Durkheim's term to indicate things that are external to, and coercive or constraining upon, the individual.

Social structure. Factors that are persistent over time, are external to the individual, and are assumed to influence behavior and thought.

Social systems. Within the structural-functionalist perspective, a series of interrelated parts in a state of equilibrium with each part contributing to the maintenance of other parts.

Sociological perspective. Point of view about society and social behavior that provides an overall orientation for examining sociological problems.

Sociology. The description and explanation of social behavior, social structures, and social interaction in terms of these social structures, and/or in terms of people's perceptions of the social environment.

Structural functionalist perspective. View that society is a social system comprised of interrelated parts that contribute to the stability of the system.

Symbol. Anything that can stand for or represent something else, such as a word or gesture.

Symbolic interactionism. Sociological perspective that focuses on the micro order and emphasizes the interactions between people that take place through symbols, especially language.

Value-free sociology. The position, held by naturalists, that personal judgments and biases can and should be excluded from social observations and interpretations.

Variable. Measurable characteristic that takes on two or more values (such as age, gender, or violent behavior.)

Verifiability. Characteristic of a conclusion or factual statement by which it can be subjected to more than one observation or test.

Verstehen. Weber's term for the subjective interpretation of social behavior and intentions, usually based on empathy. In German, literally "understanding."

FURTHER READING

Churchill, Lindsey. "Ethnomethodology and measurement." *Social Forces*, 50: 182-91, 1971. A clear statement of the basic assumptions of this perspective.

Goffman, Erving. *The Presentation of the Self in Everyday Life.* New York: Doubleday/Anchor, 1959. A well written, unique approach to microsociology. Goffman follows a symbolic interactionist perspective but develops his own "dramaturgical" model of society.

Gouldner, Alvin W. "The sociologist as partisan: sociology and the welfare state." *American Sociologist*, 3: 103-17, 1963. One of the best statements on why science cannot be value free.

Hagedorn, Robert, and Sanford Labovitz. *Sociological Orientations.* New York: John Wiley, 1973. A slightly different view of the major perspectives on schools of sociological thought.

Merton, Robert K. *Social Theory and Social Structure.* Glencoe, Ill.: Free Press, 1968. A clear statement of what functionalism is and what it isn't. See especially pp. 19-84.

Mills, C. Wright. *The Sociological Imagination.* New York: Oxford University Press, 1967. A classic introduction to sociology from the conflict perspective.

Ritzer, George. *Sociology: Multiple Paradigm Science.* Boston: Allyn and Bacon, 1975. A more advanced discussion of theories in sociology, which is compatible with this chapter.

II
THE INDIVIDUAL IN SOCIETY

At birth we are color coded, blue or pink. We are tagged with names, usually according to gender. We are fed the types of food that society deems best. Sooner or later we are toilet trained, introduced to eating schedules, and taught the "proper" way to eat. We learn to be polite. We learn whom and what to love, and whom and what to fear. Thus we are born into, and adapt to, a social and (more or less) orderly world.

Our world is ordered by the beliefs, norms, and values of the group into which we are born. Every society has rules governing who is responsible for taking care of children, who is an eligible marriage partner, how to behave when our fathers die, what to eat and how often. Chapter 2, *Culture*, discusses the variations and uniformities in these rules and values.

Implied here is the notion that human beings are systematically taught how to behave, feel, and think. This process of learning to become a member of society continues throughout life. What we learn is part of our culture, how we learn it is called *socialization*, which is discussed in Chapter 3.

Chapter 4 talks about gender: how sex has been used to categorize people, what this means, what the consequences of gender roles are, and how they are changing.

Chapter 5 examines age and aging. All societies expect different behaviors from the young, mature, and old. As with gender roles, the expectations may vary greatly from society to society, but within each society the expectations are usually very clear. While people in different societies have different life expectancies, everyone gets older and nobody gets out alive.

Every society has deviants. These are people who are different – people who break the rules. Lawbreakers are deviants, but so are people who break unwritten rules. The question of what is deviant, the puzzle of who becomes a deviant, and the attempts of various sociological perspectives to explain deviance are the topics of Chapter 6.

CHAPTERS

CHAPTER 2
CULTURE

JAMES CURTIS
RONALD D. LAMBERT

In ordinary language, you may describe someone as cultured, meaning that he or she speaks a second language, is well versed in history and philosophy, and has an appreciation of literature and art. It is in this sense that universities are sometimes thought of as places where one goes to "get culture." There is also the related distinction between "high" and "low" cultures, with the implication that the former is superior to the latter.

Sociologists do not ordinarily use the concept of culture in this value-laden and invidious fashion. So far as sociologists are concerned, everybody possesses culture as a member of society. To be human is, in a very real sense, to be cultured. **Culture** refers to shared symbols and their meanings prevailing in any society or parts of society. These symbols and their meanings include ideas about facts, ideas about desirable goals, and ideas about how people should or should not act.

The operation and effects of culture can be witnessed in the most mundane situations. Imagine people waiting for a bus, for example. They stand close together but do not speak, apparently oblivious of each other's existence. As the bus approaches, a woman steps back to permit an obviously elderly person to board first. This act is just one indication that the people have, in fact, taken account of each other while waiting. Wherever this "taking into account" occurs we say that *social interaction* has happened. In stepping back, the woman has acknowledged the unwritten rule that we should defer to the elderly in such circumstances. By contrast, an apparently less generous person chooses to protect her position in the queue, adhering to the rule of "first come, first served." She has decided that this rule supersedes rules having to do with age. These rules – indeed all rules of behavior – are part of culture.

Social interaction is typically patterned and ordered because people share in a culture. Take automobile traffic on city streets, for example. Drivers know what to expect of other drivers, as well as of pedestrians, on the basis of commonly understood rules of the road. Drivers can make reasonably accurate predictions about others' behavior on the basis of what others *should* do. As drivers and pedestrians, we routinely stake our lives on the assumption that other people's behavior is governed by rules.

Something as simple as boarding a bus or driving a car, or as complex as sending a rocket to the moon, is possible because people can depend on others to behave in more or less predictable ways. Without this dependability, of course, society would be impossible. No wonder, then, that people have devised rules to insure that we act and interact in a predictable and acceptable manner. Because rules are so pervasive and fundamental to social life, a dominant theme in the sociological image of people is that they are rule-oriented. The task for the sociologist is to identify the origins, characteristics, and consequences of these rules, and of people's understandings of them.

Having people do what is expected is more fully assured when the individuals involved possess reciprocal, or shared, understandings, with each person knowledgeable about and motivated to abide by the same rules. All regularly occurring or repetitive social relationships involve shared understandings. Spouses respond to each other in more or less regular ways over time because of shared understandings. The same is true of the relationships between customers and sales clerks, between parent and child, between the police and criminals, between ministers and members of the congregation, and between people waiting in a queue. These shared understandings of how to behave are not always to our liking. We sometimes violate them, but when we do we often experience feelings of guilt and remorse, or we make efforts to keep violations secret. Each of these responses testifies to the power of these understandings over us, even when we oppose or violate them.

DEFINING CULTURE

Shared Symbols and Meanings

Culture, then, involves shared meanings. In other words, what is important is the ideational content of culture. In contrast, some social scientists, especially some anthropologists, emphasize the material side of culture. **Material culture** consists of all manner of material objects that people create and use, ranging from simple tools to advanced machinery, such as computers, to works of art. For anthropologists, it is often the case that the only remaining evidence of past cultures is contained in material artifacts.

Artifacts are an aspect of culture, but only one aspect. To describe culture fully requires drawing on the meanings attached to objects by their producers and users; that is, it requires looking at objects as symbols. Crossed sticks may mean firewood in one culture and Christ's crucifixion in another. Automobiles, part of our material culture, may be taken as a symbol of social standing, as a practical or impractical means of transportation, as a social problem in energy depletion, or as some combination of these three definitions, depending on the social group doing the defining. Material artifacts embody culture and communicate their meanings to those versed in the culture, but they do not in themselves constitute the whole of culture.

Let's consider symbols and meanings in more detail. As you saw in Chapter 1, a **symbol** is anything taken by people to stand for something else as a matter of convention. It may be any object, sound, word, gesture, or action useful for communicating with others. In other words, symbols achieve much of their significance because they are the means of communication. To talk about a society or a group within society is to talk about a community of interaction – that is, of communication – within which culture is affirmed and modified in varying degrees.

One such community of interaction is sociologists thought of as a professional group. It is the purpose of a textbook such as this, or of a course in sociology, to introduce the student to the culture of sociologists – that is, to the shared symbols that have meaning for sociologists.

Most of the symbols presented here, as you will see, are common to speakers in the larger society, although the meanings attached to them by sociologists are more circumscribed and precise. Other symbols are more or less peculiar to sociologists who have fashioned words to refer to specific meanings for which the existing language did not seem entirely adequate. To the unsympathetic outsider or to the novice, these words have the appearance of jargon. As the student becomes familiar with them and begins to share their meanings with sociologists, however, they will be seen as useful tools for communicating sociological ideas.

It should be emphasized that a symbol, while referring to something else, is not itself the thing that is symbolized. A flag bearing a maple leaf symbolizes the nation; but it is not the nation itself. The word "freedom" symbolizes a certain type of relationship between humans; it is not the relationship itself.

It follows, then, that the same object or concept may mean different things in different contexts. In one context a red light is a symbol for stopping traffic; in another it may stand for the availability of sexual services. In other words, when we respond to symbols, we react to the meaning commonly attached to them in particular situations.

The meanings assigned to symbols, at least originally, are often quite arbitrary. The expressions "pigs is pigs" and "a rose by any other name would smell as sweet" imply the arbitrary way in which we attach words to things. The difference between defining a distance, or the speed of a car, in miles versus kilometers is another example of this. It is historically arbitrary. Having agreed upon the definition of distance, however, we respond and think in these terms.

We have indicated that the symbols and meanings making up culture are shared. Some aspects of culture

---

Shared Meanings

The idea that culture is shared is basic to the concept. This is a distinction that sets culture apart from concepts dealing exclusively with individuals. Unfortunately, shared meanings are abstract; they can neither be weighed nor photographed.

Thomas Schelling, an economist, devised some interesting puzzles to illustrate the invisible existence of shared meanings. He wanted to show how important shared meanings are for communication and for interpersonal coordination. The first two problems illustrate tacit coordination without the benefit of communication in situations where people share common interests.

1. You are to meet somebody in (your home town or university). You have not been instructed where to meet; you have no prior understanding with the person on where to meet; and you cannot communicate with each other. You are simply told you will have to guess where to meet and that he is being told the same thing and that you will just have to make your guesses coincide.
2. Name "heads" or "tails." If you and your partner name the same, you both win a prize.

The next problem illustrates tacit bargaining, again without the benefit of communication, but this time people have divergent interests.

3. You and your two partners (or rivals) each have one of the letters A, B, and C. Each of you is to write these three letters, A, B, and C, in any order. If the order is the same on all three of your lists, you get prizes totaling $6, of which $3 goes to the one whose letter is first on all three lists, $2 to the one whose letter is second, and $1 to the person whose letter is third. If the letters are not identical on all three lists, none of you gets anything. Your letter is A (or B, or C); write here the three letters in the order you choose.

—; —; —;

The task that is common to all of these problems is that respondents must predict not only what other people might say, but they must also anticipate other people's predictions about their own answers. To be successful, you must predict my prediction of your answer. On what basis shall we make our predictions? The kind of answer that respondents look for, Schelling says, is one that has "some kind of prominence or conspicuousness. But it is a prominence that depends on time and place and who the people are." In other words, it will depend upon our beliefs about shared meanings in our culture.

Source:

Adapted from Schelling, Thomas C. *The Strategy of Conflict.* New York: Oxford University Press, 1963, ch. 3.

are shared by almost all members of a society. Examples from Canadian society include ideas about the monetary value of different coins and paper bills, the rules of traffic governing drivers and pedestrians, and the meaning of parents, police, teachers, and so on. No individual knows or has need of all the culture of a society, however. Some aspects of culture are shared by only a few people, such as the specialized knowledge of medicine, engineering, and law. The point is that culture is like an idea bank upon which all members of the society draw, though different groups of people may make use of different sections of the bank more than other groups. How much sharing takes place, by which groups and for what aspects of culture, is a research question of special interest to the sociologist. The economist Thomas Schelling was particularly interested in shared meanings, and the direction his work took is outlined in the boxed insert on page 31.

Loyalty to Culture

If culture is as important and as pervasive as our discussion has implied, then we should expect people to develop intense loyalties to it. We can see this in the loyalty many Canadians feel for the imperial system of weights and measures, and their hostility toward metrication. Culture is external to individuals, in the sense that they learn about it, but it is also internal, as it is made part of them and bestows meaning on their lives. So the loyalty of people to their culture is a very intensely personal matter.

Since we tend to have such an emotional investment in our own culture, we are often skeptical about the worth of ideas and practices in other groups and societies. Would it not be best for everybody if others' beliefs and values corresponded to our own? Would it not be best, for example, if French Canadians simply abandoned their language and adopted a more vital and progressive language – such as our own? This kind of loyalty to one's own culture and belittling of others is called **ethnocentrism**.

Ethnocentrism reveals itself in judgments about all kinds of beliefs and practices. We may wonder, for instance, how any culture would think that filed teeth are attractive, or how an "uncultured" group can hold

to the belief that country and western music is interesting and enjoyable. Until recently we questioned the "misguided" notion that acupuncture had significant medical benefits since our own doctors did not practice it. We can detect similar processes between townspeople and students in university communities, between members of the military and civilians, between young and old, between religious groups, between sociologists and psychologists, and so on. Ethnocentrism is involved, then, in our judgments of other cultures and of the ideas of other subcultures within our society. Some social scientists regard this very human tendency as the seed from which most intergroup prejudice grows (LeVine and Campbell, 1972).

William Sumner was one of the first social scientists to emphasize the pervasiveness of ethnocentric thinking. He argued that it seemed to be a universal phenomenon that people see the world in terms of us versus them, as we disapprove of the ways in which they see and do things.

Why do people think ethnocentrically? There are a number of reasons, including the previously mentioned preference for predictability. Confronting significantly different ideas about how to do things implicitly challenges the judgments inherent in one's own culture. It is easier simply to reject differences out-of-hand than systematically, and repeatedly, to embark on a major reevaluation of one's beliefs.

In addition, families, schools, churches, peer groups, and so on, do more than simply teach specific beliefs and values. The culture they transmit is linked to self-images in such a way that acting in culturally approved ways affirms people's self-worth. Acting in culturally disapproved ways, on the other hand, arouses feelings of shame and guilt. Much of what is transmitted is further justified by invidious comparisons with out-groups and their cultures. Consider, for example, how religious culture is transmitted in some groups in our society. Beliefs having to do with sin, damnation, and salvation may be taught as catechism and as sacred duty to young children well before they can exercise critical and independent judgment. Children learn to judge their own worth, as well as the worth of other groups outside the faith, in terms of these emotionally charged symbols.

The personal disorientation experienced when one is immersed in a foreign culture has been labelled culture shock. The experience is shocking in the sense that the things one has taken for granted are profoundly challenged. This happens, for example, when people travel to, or through, other cultures for the first time. It may even occur within our own society when moving from English to French Canada, from the farm to the large city, from high school to university. The point is less dramatically made when we interact with people from different cultures on our "home turf." These contacts may prove awkward, even if they do not produce shock. Hall (1962) offers the following example of a situation where different cultural assumptions about personal space are seen to collide:

A conversation I once observed between a Latin and a North American began at one end of a 40-foot hall. I watched the two conversationalists until they finally reached the other end of the hall. This maneuver had been effected by a continual series of small backward steps on the part of the North American as he unconsciously retreated, searching for a comfortable talking distance. Each time, there was an accompanying closing of the gap as his Latin friend attempted to reestablish his own accustomed conversation distance.

Many sociologists have cultivated a perspective of **cultural relativism** to counteract ethnocentrism in their professional work. Each culture has its own merits and should be seen in the context of its society. They argue that sociologists should only describe and explain the workings of a culture and should not judge it against the morality of their own culture. It is proper to assess the internal consistency of a culture or how successfully it deals with a society's problems, they claim, but it is inadmissible to moralize about the culture's goodness or badness.

A behavior that is condemned as immoral in one society may be acceptable in another society. However, in the absence of absolute standards of judgment, it is said to be arbitrary and unscientific to evaluate the moral worth of other societies. All cultures are valid when judged on their own terms. In other words, according to the cultural relativists, the only way to judge a culture is according to its own standards. To do otherwise is ethnocentric.

The idea that culture is relative to societies is reinforced in the results of cross-cultural studies. Research comparing the activities defined as immoral in different societies, past and present, has shown few rules that are universal across all societies. There is evidence that all societies oppose incest and violence within the community, although the specific types of behavior prohibited (what specific sex-partners are taboo, for example) vary markedly across cultures. Beyond this there are few moral universals. However, ideas about what is moral are present in all societies. Despite the differences among societies in what is thought to be good or bad, all have some ideas about good and bad behavior. The cultures simply differ in their detailed contents.

Culture and Social Behavior

We have seen that people's behavior is oriented to their culture and its rules. However, there is no mechanical one-to-one relationship between the culture associated with a particular situation and the behavior of a set of individuals in the situation. Therefore, we cannot predict all behavior from knowing the culture of a group.

What we are warning against is a blueprint theory of culture which supposes that it is always closely followed or that it is overwhelming and absolute in its impact on individuals' actions. We prefer to say that culture frames people's behavior, instead of rigidly determining it. By framing, we mean that people draw upon cultural meanings to define the choices available to them and to make sense of their experiences. Blake and Davis (1964) make the point in this way:

The blueprint theory of society does not fit the facts of social existence. Societies as we know them are highly active and dynamic, filled with conflict, striving, deceit, cunning. Behavior in a given situation tends to be closely related to that situation, to be strongly affected by individual interests, to be unpredictable from a knowledge of the norms alone.

Sometimes culture is a poor predictor of people's behavior simply because the rules have been poorly communicated or they are simply uninformed. It is difficult to abide by rules of which you are ignorant,

Cultures borrow things from each other. Sumo is the traditional Japanese wrestling. Pop bottles are artifacts of contemporary North American culture. The Sumo grand champion shown here is being presented with a very non-traditional trophy. Even though people's behaviour is oriented to their culture, there is no mechanical relationship between culture and behavior in particular situations.

even if you are otherwise disposed to do so. At other times there is inconsistency in the culture communicated, for instance when following the rules taught in one situation means contradicting what has been learned in other situations. Differences in beliefs about pre-marital sex in a young person's peer group versus those in his or her family is an example. Where the different rules learned are not absolutely situation-specific, then following the rules of one group can mean acting contrary to the rules of another group. It may even be the case that the ideas and rules taught within a given situation are inconsistent among themselves.

Rules also vary in the vigor with which infractions are monitored and sanctions administered. This affects the likelihood that the rules will be obeyed. In a given situation, different activities may be required, preferred, permitted, tolerated, disapproved, or prohibited. For behaviors in the middle of this continuum, predictions based on the rules may be less clear than for behaviors near the ends. Other things being equal, behavior can be more confidently predicted from strongly enforced rules.

CONCEPTS FOR DESCRIBING CULTURE

Components of Culture

We have emphasized in our definition that symbols and their meanings are essential elements of culture. These provide the basis for three types of shared ideas that warrant our attention: beliefs, norms, and values.

Beliefs. We can distinguish two broad categories of beliefs: **descriptive and normative beliefs. Descriptive beliefs** are ideas or claims about what is, was, or will be, including opinions about cause and effect relations. For example, all of the following are descriptive beliefs: politicians are dishonest; God created the universe; cigarette smoking causes cancer; Russians are superior hockey players. Descriptive beliefs may be mistaken and inaccurate, as judged by scientific rules of proof. But even factually incorrect beliefs can shape the perceptions and behavior of people who hold them. To a considerable extent our thoughts and actions are shaped by what we are convinced does, will, or did exist. An example is the beliefs of Christians in the existence and meaning of God and Jesus and the way these meanings shape and justify their actions.

Normative beliefs are beliefs about what should or ought to be. They refer to the goodness or badness of things, actions, or events; to their virtuousness or wickedness; to their propriety or impropriety. The boxed insert on the next page shows textbook definitions of different ethnic and racial groups.

We have also referred to several examples having to do with rules governing queues. Other examples are the convictions of some Mennonites that they are morally obliged to wear dark clothing in public and to use the horse and buggy as transportation. Religious doctrines generally involve normative beliefs designed to guide behavior in various situations. Many political beliefs are of the same sort. Some people have faith that a just distribution of power and wealth will result if society adopts Marxist doctrines leading to a successful class revolution, and they urge that this course be pursued. Others think the status quo should be preserved and defended at all cost. Some believe that the traditional family is the cornerstone of society and that divorce and the erosion of family ties should be resisted. Still others believe that the family can effectively take many forms, and, indeed, that it should.

Normative beliefs are illustrated in a study by Curtis and Lambert (1976). Using data from a national sample survey of adults, they inquired into the normative beliefs of Canadians regarding multiculturalism and the punishment of deviants. Respondents were asked, for example, whether they endorsed such statements as "Canada would be a better place if all people had the same national origin" (statements reflecting beliefs about multiculturalism), and "Illegal strikes should be broken up by the police" (statements reflecting beliefs about punishment of deviant acts). French Canadians seemed to attach more importance to having a culturally uniform society and to dealing harshly with acts of deviance than did English Canadians. Both of these normative beliefs, however, were modi-

fied by level of schooling, so that the more educated respondents among both French and English Canadians were more tolerant of cultural diversity and deviant behavior.

Norms. The rules regulating behavior in particular situations and applicable to specific categories of people are called **norms**. Norms may or may not correspond to our normative beliefs. People may prefer different rules in a situation (their normative beliefs), but they may nonetheless choose to honor the prevailing norms, at least for the moment.

Norms are said to be *institutionalized* when they are supported by people's normative beliefs. Sociologists, therefore, have an interest in assessing the degree of correspondence between normative beliefs and established norms. An example of a norm that is not well institutionalized is the current prohibition against capital punishment in Canada. Judging from public opinion

---

TABLE 2-1. CANADIANS' BELIEFS ABOUT CAPITAL PUNISHMENT

"Do you favor or oppose capital punishment: (a) for the killing of a prison guard or an off-duty policeman?" (b) "for the killing of an innocent person?" (c) "for murders committed by terrorists?"

	Favor	Oppose	Don't Know
For Killing Guard, Policeman			
National Sample	72%	21%	8%
For Killing by Terrorists			
National Sample	74	19	7
For Killing Innocent Persons			
National Sample	69	23	8
Men	71	23	6
Women	67	24	10
18 to 29 Years Old	64	30	5
30 to 49 Years Old	69	23	8
50 Years and Over	73	17	10
Elementary Schooling	76	13	11
Secondary Schooling	72	22	7
University	50	41	9

SOURCE: Adapted from the *Toronto Star.* "Death penalty poll shows little change." February 13, 1982, p. A11.

Textbook Images of Ethnic Groups

Pratt analyzed descriptive beliefs about various ethnic and racial groups which were conveyed in school textbooks approved for use in Ontario schools in 1968-69. Some of the textbooks from which his data were taken continue to be used in schools even today. The following table shows the relative frequency of ten terms most often used to describe four groups of people in Canadian society. As you can see, the groups were defined quite differently.

Provincial ministries of education across Canada have endeavored in recent years to "sanitize" or remove negative stereotypes from authorized textbooks. What objections, if any, do you have to such practices? Recalling the textbooks with which you are familiar, how successfully has this been accomplished? Under what circumstances would you expect textbooks to be an important source of students' beliefs about ethnic minorities?

Arabs	%	French Canadians	%	Native Indians	%	Blacks	%
great	3.9	great	4.2	savage	10.1	friendly	9.2
cruel	2.1	brave	3.9	friendly	6.1	unfriendly	5.0
feuding	2.1	courageous	3.6	massacre	4.9	savage	4.2
kind	2.1	skillful	3.3	skillful	4.0	faithful	3.4
pagan	2.1	heroic	2.7	hostile	3.8	kind	3.4
brilliant	1.6	determined	2.0	fierce	3.1	fierce	2.9
dictator	1.6	proud	1.7	great	2.3	primitive	2.6
fierce	1.6	devoted	1.6	murder	2.1	murder	2.4
friendly	1.6	famous	1.6	unfriendly	1.7	violent	2.4
resentful	1.6	daring	1.4	thief	1.6	backward	2.4

Source:

Pratt, David. "The social role of school textbooks in Canada," *in* E. Zureik and R.N. Pike (eds.), *Socialization and Values in Canadian Society, Vol. 1, Political Socialization* Toronto: McClelland and Stewart, 1975, p. 106.

polls, such as the 1981 Canadian Gallup poll whose results are summarized in Table 2-1, there is little support for the current legislation. It is also interesting to note that the size of the discrepancy varies in different parts of society. Approximately three-quarters of respondents with less than university education favored the execution of individuals convicted of murdering innocent people. The lowest level of support – one-half – was forthcoming from the university-educated respondents.

Sociologists also attempt to explain how normative beliefs may contribute in time to the modification of norms, and, conversely, how the existence of norms may lead people to adopt new normative beliefs. In the former case, for example, the use of a referendum on capital punishment would be one avenue by which people's wishes might be translated into legal norms.

As this example suggests, whether normative preferences become norms or not is broadly speaking a political process. In the latter case, human rights codes are premised on the idea that rules forbidding certain kinds of discrimination will lead people to think differently about what is appropriate and inappropriate behavior. This is also the subject matter of socialization, the process by which people learn and acquire respect for group norms (see Chapter 3).

The norms that most concern us on a day-to-day basis are situation-specific. What is prohibited behavior in one situation may be permitted, even required, in another situation. While norms of modesty generally forbid nudity, it is permitted in a number of specific situations such as bedrooms, medical examination rooms, nudist camps, and striptease joints. The general prohibition against taking human life also admits to a number of well understood exceptions, including warfare and self-defense. The significance of these distinctions is conveyed in our choice of words: murder, execution, abortion, suicide, assassination, self-defense. The word chosen conveys something about the situation involved, the people in it, and the admissibility of the act.

But not all norms are alike. For one thing, some norms take the form of written rules, as in the highway traffic act, while others are merely conveyed informally, as when a parent instructs a child how to behave in a restaurant. Some norms, such as rules of etiquette, are advisory in nature, compared to norms against theft and homicide that are more serious in their intent. Norms differ in their enforcement, too, some depending on community opinion and others on designated officers of the law. Furthermore, the origins of some norms can be traced, while the history of other norms is a mystery.

These are the kinds of distinctions that Sumner (1960), writing in 1906, sought to capture in his classification of folkways, mores, and laws. **Folkways** are rules about customary ways of behaving. Their beginnings lie in tradition, so their precise point of origin is often unknown. The violation of folkways usually results in only minor inconvenience. Since folkways deal with matters of little consequence, members of society do not have strong feelings about them and their enforcement is informal. Table etiquette is an example of folkways in our society. Eating food with the wrong fork is greeted by little more than stares and the occasional comment from nearby diners.

Mores are "must" rules, referring to "must behaviors" or "must not behaviors," which are strictly though informally enforced. The norms here are thought to touch on things held dear or sacred. Like folkways, mores are also traditional in origin. An example would be norms against showing contempt for the symbols of one's country, such as booing the national anthem. Some other examples of mores from political life were offered by the Supreme Court of Canada in its historic ruling on the Canadian Constitution in 1981. The Court observed that, "[m]any Canadians would be surprised to learn that important parts of the Constitution of Canada . . . are nowhere to be found in the law of the Constitution" (Canada, Supreme Court, 1981). Also, "Being based on custom and precedent, constitutional conventions are usually unwritten rules" (Canada, Supreme Court, 1981). Thus, the Court noted, the requirement that the Government resign if the Opposition wins a majority in a general election is a matter of convention and not of law. The sanctions supporting such political mores or conventions are broadly political rather than judicial in nature.

Laws take two forms – common and enacted. *Common law* is based on custom and precedent, reflecting the past practice of the courts. *Enacted laws* are formally codified and enacted by legislative bodies. Both types of laws are sustained by police and court actions. There are, of course, laws which people feel strongly about, such as those against treason, and others which they feel mildly or indifferently about, such as some traffic laws. The degree of feeling is generally reflected in the severity of the penalty for violations.

There are, then, three defining criteria for folkways, mores, and laws: (1) the origin of the norm (traditional versus enacted); (2) how a norm is enforced (formally or informally); (3) and the degree of importance attached to a norm by members of society (strong versus weak). When these three criteria are cross-classified, we find that there are two logical categories of norms that are empirically empty (see Table

TABLE 2-2. CLASSIFICATION OF NORMS

Type of Enforcement	Informal		Formal	
Type of Group Reaction	Strong	Weak	Strong	Weak
Type of Origin				
Traditional	Mores	Folkways	Common Law	Common Law
Enacted	—	—	Enacted Law	Enacted Law

SOURCE: Adapted from Bredemeier, H.D., and R.M. Stephenson. *The Analysis of Social Systems*. New York: Holt, Rinehart and Winston, 1962, p. 23.

2-2). These would in principle be laws that are enacted, toward which people attach either a great deal or little importance, but which are only informally enforced. Obviously, the passage of laws contemplates their formal enforcement.

Values. In every culture there are general conceptions of the desirable goals, or ends, that people should strive to attain and criteria by which actions should be evaluated. Rokeach (1974) calls these two types of **values** "terminal" and "instrumental," respectively (see the boxed insert on the following page). Values are more general in their application than either norms or normative beliefs. They constitute standards by which people evaluate goals and actions. It is for this reason that people attach a great deal of emotional importance to them.

Value analysis involves examining the basis for values within a culture, as well as the kinds of trade-offs worked between values in specific situations. We will consider the former question in the second half of the chapter. So far as the latter question is concerned, however, we should anticipate complex interactions among values because there will generally be at least several values relevant to any given situation. Canadians, for example, are said to value efficiency, meaning that they wish to economize on the use of time, money, and other resources in their activities. They also place a high value on democratic decision-making, with the result that values of democracy and efficiency periodi-

cally collide. In some situations, democratic decision-making may prove to be expensive in both time and money, while in other situations what is efficient may lose the support of the people affected. Value analysis involves identifying and explaining the kinds of trade-offs among values that cultures tolerate or require.

Pauline McGibbon and Dr. Elizabeth Bagshaw are two women who have achieved considerable status despite the restrictions of gender roles. McGibbon is former Lieutenant Governor of Ontario, and Bagshaw was a pioneer in the provision of public health services for women. (*Canapress*)

Two Kinds of Values: Instrumental and Terminal

Social psychologist Milton Rokeach has developed two classifications of values based on cross-cultural research, some of which was conducted in Canada while he taught at the University of Western Ontario. He has argued that values can take the form of terminal values, which are goals, and instrumental values, which are standards for judging the means to achieve goals. In his research, people are given a descriptive statement for each value and are asked to rank the terminal values in terms of their personal importance. They are then asked to rank the instrumental values in terms of their importance. Rokeach's two lists of values are presented here.

Source:

Adapted from Rokeach, Milton. "Some reflections about the place of values in Canadian social science," *in* T.N. Guinsburg, and G.I. Reuber (eds.). *Perspectives on the Social Sciences in Canada*. Toronto: University of Toronto Press, 1974, p. 180.

Terminal Values	Instrumental Values
A comfortable life (a prosperous life)	Ambitious (hard-working, aspiring)
An exciting life (a stimulating, active life)	Broadminded (open-minded)
A sense of accomplishment (lasting contribution)	Capable (competent, effective)
A world at peace (free of war and conflict)	Cheerful (lighthearted, joyful)
A world of beauty (beauty of nature, arts)	Clean (neat, tidy)
Equality (brotherhood, equal opportunity for all)	Courageous (standing up for your beliefs)
Family Security (taking care of loved ones)	Forgiving (willing to pardon others)
Freedom (independence, free choice)	Helpful (working for the welfare of others)
Happiness (contentedness)	Honest (sincere, truthful)
Inner Harmony (freedom from inner conflict)	Imaginative (daring, creative)
Mature Love (sexual and spiritual intimacy)	Independent (self-reliant, self-sufficient)
National Security (protection from attack)	Intellectual (intelligent, reflective)
Pleasure (enjoyable, leisurely life)	Logical (consistent, rational)
Salvation (saved, eternal life)	Loving (affectionate, tender)
Self-respect (self-esteem)	Obedient (dutiful, respectful)
Social Recognition (respect, admiration)	Polite (courteous, well-mannered)
True Friendship (close companionship)	Responsible (dependable, reliable)
Wisdom (mature understanding of life)	Self-controlled (restrained, self-disciplined)

Complexes of Culture

The concepts to which we turn next are built on the distinctions just described and are more complex in the sense that they combine the cultural elements already defined. We can therefore label them "cultural complexes."

Status. Status defines a position in society according to its rights and obligations. Status rights consist of ideas about what one may properly expect from others when one occupies a particular status. Status obligations are ideas about what others have a right to expect from you when you are in a given status. Statuses locate people in groups, organizations, and, more generally, in society at large. In groups and organizations, statuses are relative to the relationships contained in them. Other statuses, however, such as those based on age, gender, and race, are not specific to any particular group or organization. Nonetheless, they presuppose or imply interaction, as men are defined relative to women, and so on.

Of special interest to sociologists are statuses ranked by the different amounts of prestige accorded to them by members of society. Prestige rankings occur, in large part, because of beliefs about the importance of the rights and obligations defining the statuses. These beliefs have no doubt been promoted earlier, and are maintained currently, by powerful and influential groups in society. An example is professional occupations versus skilled manual workers, and the greater prestige accorded to the former by members of society. (See the occupational prestige discussion in Chapter 8.) One of the factors contributing to this prestige differential is professional associations' public promotion of the social importance of the services that their members perform, whereas there are seldom such efforts on behalf of manual workers. Professional associations do have a counterpart in unions, for some manual workers, when it comes to the related activity of pursuit of higher levels of income. But unions are less apt to blow their own horns, or their members' horns, on the issue of how indispensable their services are to society.

The most important consequence of statuses is their effect in shaping interactions among people. The shared understandings of rights and obligations among individuals in different statuses is what makes for predictable and ordered social behavior. Statuses are generally highly interrelated in the sense that their rights and obligations are defined in terms of one another. A mother, for example, cannot have that status unless and until she has a child. There are no wives without husbands, no teachers without students, no leaders without followers, no bosses without subordinates.

Statuses can be ascribed or achieved. Entry into an achieved status depends on a person's satisfactory performance of some relevant requirement. Movement into or out of an achieved status, in other words, is based on personal accomplishment or failure. What are relevant accomplishments, though, are typically prescribed by the rules of the situation. An example is passing the bar examinations and being called to the bar in order to practice law. An ascribed status, by contrast, is assigned to an individual regardless of personal merit. This assignment typically occurs at birth. Examples of ascribed statuses in our society include racial and ethnic status, gender status, and age status. Occasionally, normally ascribed statuses may be changed, as when a person undergoes a sex change operation or when a member of a racial minority "passes" as a member of the racially dominant group. But these are rare instances.

In a complex society such as Canada, each person possesses several statuses simultaneously by virtue of membership in various social categories, groups, and organizations, and the statuses defining participation in each. All of a person's statuses taken together, at any given time in his or her life, are called a status set. The existence of status sets makes for the possibility of status (or role) conflict. This is a situation in which fulfilling the obligations associated with one status (or role) interferes with the fulfillment of obligations associated with another status (or role). For example, a working mother with young children is often placed in a situation of status conflict. She assumes the status of worker and must perform her duties as, say, an accountant. She must put in long hours at her place of work, thus intruding upon her other obligations as mother and possibly as wife as well. Another example is provided by the status of foreman or forewoman. This person is caught between management and workers with competing obligations toward both. And young people often find themselves having to reconcile conflicting demands from their parents and from their peer group.

Social Institution. The concept of **social institution** refers to sets of beliefs, norms, and values that define and regulate how a society deals with the central problems common to all societies. Social institutions can therefore be thought of as cultural strategies for dealing with these problems. A social institution may subsume the activities of a wide variety of statuses and organized groups. Societies differ, of course, in the specific content of the beliefs, norms, and values defining their institutions. We can distinguish a number of institutions, including the family, politics, the economy, education, religion, science, the arts, and so on. Some of these are dealt with in Chapters 11 to 14, so we will confine ourselves here to a few brief comments about the family.

The family is a commonly recognized social institution consisting of an array of beliefs, norms, and values that govern the pattern of relationships among members of the family group. Taken together, the ideas on how these relationships are to work are labelled the family institution. In Canadian society, the rules of this institution anticipate a wide variety of family forms, including the nuclear family, common-law marriages, single-parent families, and so on. The outer limits of the family are regulated by laws concerning incest and who may or may not marry each other. Laws and practices concerning illegitimacy, inheritance, adoption, child abuse, the responsibilities of parents for the care of their children, the grounds for divorce and the division of property at the time of divorce, all address special issues in the area of kinship.

Recent changes in the laws concerning this list of issues should remind us that the shape of institutions is not engraved in stone. Legislation passed in Quebec in 1981, for example, requires that women retain their maiden names at the time of marriage and necessitates that parents decide what last name to give their children (Quebec, Civil Code, 1981).

Ideology. Sociologists define **ideologies** as emotionally charged sets of descriptive and normative beliefs and values that explain and justify how institutions of society are organized or should be organized. In Canada, we are most accustomed to ideological debate around political and economic affairs as different sides put forth their normative and policy preferences. Ideologies may, however, deal with any of the institutional areas (Mannheim, 1936; Parkin, 1972; Lambert and Curtis, 1979).

We distinguish two broad types of ideologies. Refor-

mist and radical ideologies rally the forces of change, while conservative ideologies support existing social arrangements. Reformist ideologies seek changes without challenging the basic rules and regulations, as when medicare, welfare, and unemployment insurance are established without eliminating either the unequal distribution of wealth between the owners of capital and workers, or the principle of private property that underlies our economic order. Radical ideologies call for a fundamental restructuring of society or of one of its institutions, as the Co-operative Commonwealth Federation (predecessor of today's New Democratic Party) did at the time of its founding in the 1930s. The independence movement in Quebec also seeks to restructure the Canadian state. But reformist and radical ideologies may also call for a restoration of former ways of doing things in society. An example would be a proposal to eliminate social welfare measures on the grounds that welfare programs are too costly for taxpayers and that people should take care of themselves as they allegedly once did.

Conservative ideologies are sometimes called dominant ideologies to emphasize their prevailing and ruling character. Private property and capitalism currently prevail in our society. In the context of a socialist state, however, the dominant or "conservative" ideology would be socialist. Reformist and radical ideologies in any society are called counter-ideologies to emphasize their competing, but not prevailing, character (Parkin, 1972).

According to Marchak (1975), "Ideologies are screens through which we perceive the world. . . . They are seldom taught explicitly and systematically. They are rather transmitted through example, conversation, and casual observation." The following example (Marchak, 1975) suggests how a dominant economic ideology is conveyed in an otherwise innocent exchange between parent and child:

The child asks the parent: "Why is that family poorer than us?" and receives an answer such as "Because their father is unemployed." The accumulation of such responses provides a ready index to the organization of the society in occupational terms, and with reference to age and gender roles. The child

Beliefs are a major part of culture. The Hutterites are a subculture and they believe that birth control is against the will of God. Children, who are considered gifts from God, dress like the adults. Their clothes symbolize their religious beliefs.

is informed by such responses that some occupations provide higher material rewards than others, that an occupation is essential, and that fathers, not mothers, earn family incomes. The child is not provided with an explanation for the differential between postmen and sales managers, between the employed and unemployed; between families in one income group and families in the other, but some children think to ask. There are, then, additional responses such as: "If you work hard at school, you can go to the top," or "Sales managers are more important than postmen," or "Well, if people don't work, they can't expect to get along in the world."

Counter-ideologies challenge the assumptions and beliefs of dominant ideologies. For example, they might ask (Marchak, 1975): Why is education related to occupations? What is meant by "the top," and why should people strive for it? Why is status associated with material wealth? What do sales managers do that makes them important, and to whom is their work important? Why would anyone not work when the penalties for unemployment are so severe? It is the point of counter-ideology to expose ideological inconsistencies and hypocrisies and to offer an alternative vision.

Subcultures. In a large, complex, and highly differentiated society such as our own, there is a great deal of cultural variation among the groups that make it up. Any sector of society that has a great deal of interaction within itself and whose experiences set them apart from the rest of society, will tend to develop local cultures, or what sociologists call **subcultures**. Occupational groups, such as medical doctors; ethnic populations, such as Italian-Canadians living in Toronto; age groups, such as youth or the elderly; people living in small and isolated communities in the north – each of these groups will develop sets of beliefs, norms, and values that make sense to them. Their ideas may or may not be opposed to the larger culture. For the most part, they will simply be variants of Canadian culture. Subcultures often advertise themselves to outsiders in a variety of ways, including dress, life-style, vocabulary,

The Road Hustler's Vocabulary

Sociologists are not the only group that possesses its own specialized vocabulary or jargon. So do hockey and football fans, politicians, police officers, and so on. Here is a partial list of the specialized vocabulary of the road hustler, "a confidence man whose specialty is the manipulation of card and dice games."

Amateurs (cheats) naive cheating; edge-taking by persons not into the hustling subculture

Amateurs (hustlers) rough hustlers, nonprofessionals

Bird-dog tipsters, persons providing information on parties or action people

Booster one who steals on a regular basis, a career thief

Bottoms (cards) dealing off the bottom of the deck

Clocking (money) keeping tabs on the money circulating in a game

Coolers (cold decks) prearranged decks switched in for the game deck

Cooling out (suckers) pacifying one who has been beaten for his money

Contacts man a hustling crew role, a person with access to action spots

Crack out busting out persons, quickly relieving them of their money

Crews mobs, gangs, a group of usually three or four persons hustling as a unit

Crimp (cards) marking a deck of cards by slightly bending or folding certain cards

Daub a waxy substance used for marking cards

Deadhead an unpromising target, one who provides little or no action

Double duke (cards) prearranging a deck so that two persons receive good hands

Double steer a double-cross involving a target who believes he is taking advantage of another

Fade covering a bet

False cut (cards) a simulated cut designed to maintain the present ordering of the deck

False shuffle (cards) a simulated shuffle designed to maintain the present ordering of the deck

Flats percentage dice, dice that have been sanded down on one or more sides to promote those numbers

Front man sponsor, one who establishes credibility for another

Hedge to vacillate or waver on one's involvements; to decrease one's risk taking

High roller big better

Holding out the act of keeping one or more cards out of the game for use in establishing a better hand

Hop (cards) pass, a move which restores a cut deck to its original order

Hustler one who regularly capitalizes on less than legitimate opportunities

Illegits (dice) any bogus dice

Laying the note shortchanging cashiers

Legits (dice) game dice

Little front man referring to a bonafide patron as a means of establishing credibility

Managing (a game) operating a confidence game

Mark the target, sucker

Mechanic one who manipulates cards or dice

Muscle muscle man; someone providing protection for crew members

Nut (the) expenses

Nuts (nut, the) in cards, having a "nut hand" or "the nuts" refers to having the best hand or what should be the best hand in the game

Padding a roll a technique of controlling the outcome of legitimate dice

Percentage dice dice favoring certain outcomes

Public relations (man) person promoting a hustle, a shoot-up man

Raking the game charging the players a fee or percentage for the privilege of gaming

Read paper being able to identify the face value of marked cards

Rolling (hotels, restaurants) avoiding paying for one's accommodations

Run up (cards) stacking a deck to give one player a good hand

Seconds dealing the second card from the top

Shade distractions designed to assist a mechanic or operator

Shooting up (the pot) promoting more extensive betting

Shoot-up man public relations man, one who promotes a game and game involvements

Shortcake getting less than equal share of the profits

Spreading a game starting a game

Still games regularized card games (e.g., a weekly game involving six regular participants)

Sting beating someone for his money

Stonewall Jackson a very cautious player, one who usually "waits for the nuts" before betting; an extremely knowledgeable poker player

Taking an edge gaining an advantage proscribed by "game rules"

Tops (tops and bottoms, busters, tees) dice not having all the numbers on them (i.e., some numbers are duplicated, etc.)

Weights percentage dice, dice in which lead weights have been inserted to promote certain outcomes

Source:

Prus, Robert, and C.R.D. Sharper. *Road Hustler.* Toronto: Gage, 1979, p. 169.

and so on. At the same time, these distinguishing features make subculture insiders aware of their separate, special group membership and provide additional grounds for group pride. The argot or slang of the group is a particularly obvious badge of subcultural membership. The boxed insert on this page gives examples of the slang of one such specialized subculture.

EXPLAINING CULTURE

Having labeled and defined the contents of culture, we are now prepared to consider some of the ways culture is produced and changed. The related question of how culture is transmitted to new members of society – the problems of socialization and resocialization – is dealt with in Chapter 3.

Our discussion illustrates the major themes favored by sociologists in their explanations of how culture develops. These explanations convey the kind of processes thought to be operating in the creation and change of symbolic meaning within society. We have also grouped these ideas according to the three broad perspectives from which they were drawn: symbolic interactionism, structural functionalism, and conflict.

The Symbolic Interactionist Perspective

The symbolic interactionist approach focuses on the fact that culture is the product of interaction between people in their everyday relationships. And it is here that the culture from the larger society is adapted to their daily lives. For the symbolic interactionists, the emphasis is on culture at the micro level of the relationship, rather than at the macro level of the larger society. Fluid rather than static, always open to revision, culture is situated in specific relationships and occasions (Lauer and Handel, 1977).

What is emphasized in the interactionist approach is the shared *definition of the situation*, for it is this that guides the course of interaction in the particular instance to which it applies. A definition of a situation is contained in a package of norms governing and regulating a recognizable situation, such as a classroom, a hockey game, or a bathroom. It includes norms

defining the appropriate reasons for people's participation in the situation and the goals they may properly pursue within it. It also spells out how these goals may be achieved, as well as regulating the relationships among the various participants. Because definitions are shared, they permit people to coordinate their actions in the pursuit of their goals. Seen in this way, a definition of a situation is a source of meaning for participants and observers alike, because it permits them to make sense of the situation.

Culture is seen by symbolic interactionists as the product of interpersonal negotiations. Negotiations may be formal and explicit (for example, when a contract is drafted between a union and an employer). However, most agreements are less dramatic and tangible than this, as people informally and tacitly communicate with each other about the situations in which they find themselves. Communication is often verbal, of course, but it may also consist of gestures, body language, and people's attire. One way in which this is done is through the impressions people create, sometimes intentionally and other times unintentionally, when they first encounter each other. Wearing a clerical collar, highly polished shoes, jeans, one's hair in a bun, introducing oneself as "doctor" – all have consequences for how people regard each other. Impression management and first impressions foster understandings about the meaning people attach to their relationships, their goals, and what actions are acceptable and unacceptable to them. In the words of Erving Goffman (1959),

[W]hen an individual projects a definition of the situation and thereby makes an implicit or explicit claim to be a person of a particular kind, he automatically exerts a moral demand upon the others, obliging them to value and treat him in the manner that persons of his kind have a right to expect. He also implicitly forgoes all claims to be things he does not appear to be and hence forgoes the treatment that would be appropriate for such individuals.

People have many motives governing how they present themselves and the kinds of interpretations they invite. They may or may not be conscious of these motives, and they may or may not be sensitive to the cues they convey to others. It is for this reason that counsellors advise job applicants to dress carefully for interviews with potential employers, lest they create the wrong impression. On the other hand, members of the clergy are often mindful of the stultifying effects their clerical attire has on conversation and the jokes people tell at parties.

To say that culture for symbolic interactionists is fluid and dynamic does not mean that it is unlicensed, except for the whims of the people involved. Situations physically and socially constrain what can reasonably be done in them and therefore limit the kinds of definitions that are effectively available. It is difficult to play ice hockey, for example, where there is no ice. And what we do in the classroom is surely constrained by the facts of organizational life outside the classroom. Sexual harassment policies, for instance, remind those who are forgetful that the larger community has a continuing interest in what transpires within the classroom.

A definition of the situation constrains interaction, but it is not rigid. Relationships between fellow workers or between customers and clerks sometimes turn into romantic relationships, which is to say that the relationships have been redefined. Interactionists are therefore interested in the subterranean tactics used to reconstruct relationships. Seduction, for example, refers to a class of interpersonal maneuvers, impressively labeled "realigning actions" by Goffman (1959), that bring about a redefinition of the relationship between a man and a woman. The possibility of realignment underscores the fact that actors are actively involved in exploiting and modifying culture, not merely its puppets.

The structural functionalist and conflict perspective, to which we turn next, do not necessarily contradict the symbolic interactionist approach. For one thing, much of the cultural content talked about by symbolic interactionists is not at all unique or original to a relationship. Much of it has its origins in the larger culture and is simply reworked for the more immediate requirements of a relationship. We can also easily imagine interpersonal negotiations being studied by sociologists working within the structural functionalist and conflict perspectives, even though this would not be a priority for them. It is more to the point to say that the structural functionalist and conflict viewpoints emphasize that there are important shared meanings beyond those found in small groups. In addition, these meanings are seen as less transitory and localized than the interactionist view might lead us to expect.

The Structural Functionalist Perspective

Strictly speaking, the structural functionalist perspective does not explain why some feature of culture (such as a particular norm, value, or ideology) emerges (Johnson, 1960). Rather, structural functionalism deals more with the persistence of elements of culture in a society or sub-group, a persistence explained by their positive consequences for that society or group. A norm is said to persist because it "works" in some sense. The focus of the research done within this perspective is upon elements of culture which are shared (so that they are cultural), though they may be minimally shared, as in the case of rules subscribed to by only a minority subculture of the society. For example, structural functionalists may study the persistence of codes of dress among motorcycle gangs and their consequences for the gang.

However, because a specific norm, value, or the like is functional for a society or group, it does not follow that this is the reason it was originally established. The four explanations discussed here are broadly functional in their treatment of aspects of culture as consequences of society or some part of it. It will also be apparent that these explanations, in spite of their different emphases, are complementary rather than contradictory.

By way of preface to the following interpretations, you should understand that none of them presupposes a simple one-to-one relationship, as between cause and effect. How events affect culture will depend on a variety of factors, not the least of which is the content of the culture at the time change occurs. Other factors include the structure of the society and its social and physical environment. Seen in this way, it is fairer to describe the causes of cultural change more as possibilities than as determinants. In addition, the application of these interpretations to specific societies would require that we identify their relevant peculiarities.

Culture Mirrors Society. The first explanation, and the most all-inclusive of the four, emphasizes that value systems mirror the economic, political, and social organization of the societies in which they appear. As the structure changes, so will its values. There are different versions of this thesis, but we have selected Inglehart's (1977, 1981) for purposes of illustration. In his opinion, ours is a post-industrial society, increasingly characterized by "post-materialist" concerns and values. Post-materialist values are largely intellectual, aesthetic, and social in nature. In surveys conducted in ten nations, he measured these values by respondents' support for freedom of speech and the importance of ideas in society, as well as the desire for a greater say on the job and in government, for a less impersonal society, and for more beautiful cities. Materialist values, with their emphasis on social control and economic matters, are losing ground. These values underlie the respondents' desire for a strong military establishment, the maintenance of domestic order and the fight against crime, and for economic growth, a stable economy, and price-restraint. What Inglehart (1977) calls a "silent revolution" has brought about "a shift from overwhelming emphasis on material consumption and security toward greater concern with the quality of life".

The major transformation in values described by Inglehart is the product of a number of profound social changes in the way society is organized that are occurring simultaneously. Included here are major technological innovations, such as computer-chip technology and miniaturization; changes in the occupational structure, most notably the growth of the service sector of the economy at the expense of manufacturing; the rise in real income since the Second World War; the immense expansion of higher education and the rising levels of education among the population; the wiring of the world by sophisticated mass communications into what McLuhan called a "global village;" and the appearance of a fortunate generation that has personally known neither total war nor widespread economic depression. Inglehart believes, following the psychologist Maslow (1970), that people's mental and spiritual needs become important once their more basic physical needs have been satisfied. Given these psycho-logical assumptions, he expects and finds that the same factors that produce differences between societies also engender differences within societies (Inglehart, 1977, 1981). Post-materialist values are most prevalent among groups in society, such as the young and the well educated, that have benefited most from the structural changes taking place.

Of course, history is more complex than any theory admits. Inglehart's description of modern societies sounds strangely dated now, not a decade later. Maybe he anticipated the economic and military malaise of the 1980s when he wrote of possible "counter-trends." However, "the principal evolutionary drift . . . is unlikely to be changed unless there are major alterations in the very nature of these societies" (Inglehart, 1977).

Cultural Adaptations to Technological Change. New tools increase a people's capacity to exploit their ecological setting with far-reaching consequences for their relationships with each other, and consequently for the meanings with which they invest their lives. Technology affects culture both directly and indirectly. Directly, technology creates new possibilities requiring accommodations in people's ideas, and these are communicated and shared. Indirectly, technology alters people's relationships with each other, and their altered relationships then usher in new cultural patterns. Human geographers, anthropologists, and historians have documented, for example, the profound repercussions of European weapons and utensils, obtained in trade, upon the Canadian Indian way of life. Their growing dependence on European manufacture undermined the traditional basis for native cultures.

Where new technology is obtained in trade, instead of through native invention, it is necessary to distinguish between the separate effects of the technology and the trading relationship. An example is provided by Ray, an economic geographer, who has described the introduction of new hunting technology into the Amerindian societies of colonial Canada. On the one hand, he was interested in the improved capacity of these societies to exploit their environment. Guns were clearly more efficient and deadly than arrows, and

Technological innovation affects not only our patterns of learning, but also the number and position of those who can learn. This Winnipeg student has a learning disability, but instruction through electronic means allows her to express herself in ways not possible a few years ago. (*Winnipeg Free Press*)

horses increased the hunters' dominion. On the other hand, their trading relationships with Europeans created new economic and political dependencies. But both sets of factors exerted a profound influence on the composition of native culture. A more contemporary example is Canada's well known reliance on the United States for much of its technological innovation. This means that technology and economic dependency are intertwined in their cumulative impact on Canadian culture.

Three different patterns can be discerned in the effects of technology on culture and social behavior (Ogburn and Nimkoff, 1964). The first is a dispersion or multiple effects pattern. The invention of the birth control pill, for example, might have the following effects, some of them cultural in nature: new conceptions of independence on the part of women; a sense that the arrival of children can be effectively planned

and they can be weighed against alternative investments; smaller families; new ideas about the nature of sexual morality.

The second model involves a succession of effects or derivative effects, where one effect leads to another, and so on. For example, we have probably not seen the end of the stream of effects produced by the invention of the computer. The ability to process large amounts of information in very short periods of time leads to networks of computers and information sharing. This, in time, provokes questions about the privacy of individual citizens, national sovereignty, and the need for laws to regulate access to information.

In the case of convergence, the third pattern, the effects of a number of technological innovations come together and produce a common effect. The development of birth control technology, new techniques for building high density housing with limited space per living unit, proliferation of innovations in the area of mass communication, especially satellite transmissions, jointly theaten the survival of minority language groups, such as the French in Canada.

Cultural Adaptations to Social Invention.

Technological inventions are visible and tangible, but we are apt to lose sight of the significance, for cultural change, of social inventions. Included here are new forms of social organization, new roles, new practices, and new procedures (Whyte, 1982). Consider some of these inventions that we probably take for granted: the 40-hour work week, flex-time, labor unions, the limited company, crown corporations, day-care centers, rape centers, half-way houses, franchise operations, indoor soccer, family allowances, medicare, sociology, public opinion polls, fast-food restaurants, the novel, compulsory school attendance, community colleges, multiple-choice exams, federal/provincial conferences, legal-aid clinics, lotteries, jogging, and so on. Each of these refers to a way of organizing human activity and incorporates a significant cultural component. Accordingly, sociologists are interested in explaining the appearance of these inventions, as well as identifying their effects.

Why is that person running along the darkened street? Need we fear him? Is he running away from something or after somebody? Not to worry. His attire suggests that he is a jogger, thus "explaining" this otherwise bizarre behavior. There is something new under the sun as concern for health and doing something about it has become a visible and easily recognizable phenomenon in Canada. Not only do joggers have repercussions for the economy, as manufacturers hire workers to supply the growing demand for running shoes, jogging outfits, and so on, but they also nourish our values and beliefs about physical fitness.

Think of the multiple-choice exam and the intelligence test, and what they have come to symbolize in our society. They have surely reinforced certain conceptions about the nature of knowledge and intelligence and the purposes of education. Students' success or failure has been premised on the idea that there are certifiably correct and incorrect answers to questions of knowledge, and that the purpose of their education is to find out what these pre-determined answers are. Success in the job market often depends on the belief that people can be graded, like eggs, and that some level of intelligence is necessary for employment.

Or think of the limited company – the modern corporation. As Marchak (1979) quotes the Canada Business Corporations Act, "A Corporation has the capacity, and subject to this Act, the rights, powers, and privileges of a natural person." It is a "legal fiction" that places companies on the same footing as you and I. This means that we can talk about corporations in moral terms, in much the same way we talk about individual humans. Though there may be no afterlife where companies are concerned, they can fire us, cheat us, lie to us, and pollute our environment. We can discuss whether my claims to rights infringe upon the rights of a corporation. Socialists have to contend, for instance, with the sentiment on the part of many people that the rights of corporations to own property are sacrosanct in the same way that the rights of individuals are. In other words, corporations are cultural and social inventions, and they have cultural repercussions in terms of how we think about the economy and our place in it.

As a final example of a social invention, a much older one than jogging, consider the Gregorian calendar around which we organize our lives, and which we take very much for granted. It is no exaggeration to say that the calendar is one of the chief pillars of western culture. The failure of France's Revolutionary metric calendar, introduced in 1793, to win people's loyalty over a period of 12 years, attests to the close relationship between the calendar and culture. "It is hard to overemphasize the extent to which the reformers obliterated the existing system of units of time as well as the existing time-reckoning and dating framework . . ." Zerubavel has written. "The scope of the . . . calendrical reform was almost total, since its architects strived to bring about a total symbolic transformation of the existing calendrical system" (Zerubavel, 1981). Thirty day months, ten-day weeks, decimal minutes and decimal seconds, along with non-religious labels for the days and months, were intended to establish time on a firm secular, quantitative, scientific, naturalistic, and patriotic basis. Details of the French

The French Revolutionary Calendar, 1793-1805

The French Revolution produced an interesting social invention that is by now little more than a curious historical footnote. According to Eviatar Zerubavel, a metric calendar was introduced in post-Revolutionary France in an effort to establish time on clearly scientific grounds, and to strip away all of the religious and qualitative connotations of the old system. Although metrication in weights and distances was accepted by the French population and the international community, it was never accepted as a measure of time. It offended the religious sensibilities of the French nation by seeking to undo their Christian traditions; and it effectively isolated France internationally, because few nations were prepared to concede that time should be reckoned from the founding of the French Republic. The following describes the Revolutionary or metric calendar.

1. The establishment of a new chronological dating framework. The traditional Christian Era was replaced by the Republican Era, which began on September 22, 1792, the day on which the French Republic was founded.

2. The establishment of a new annual cycle. The traditional January 1 was replaced by September 22 as New Year's Day. Not only did the year on which the Republic was founded become a standard reference point for the new chronological dating framework, the day on which it was founded became a standard reference point for the new annual cycle.

3. The uniformization of the months. Unlike the traditional Gregorian year, which consisted of 31-day, 30-day and 28- (or 29-) day months, the Republican year consisted of 12 isochronal 30-day months. The five complementary days (*Sansculottides*) were grouped together at the end of the year, as in the ancient Egyptian calendar. A sixth intercallary day was added on leap years (*sextiles*), which still fell every four years, although on the third – rather than the fourth – year of every group of four years (*Franciade*) that is, on years III, VII and XI, rather than on years IV, VIII and XII.

4. The abolition of the seven-day week and Sunday. Each 30-day month was divided into three ten-day cycles called "*décade*." Sunday was replaced by "*Décadi*," which was celebrated only every ten days, as the official rest day.

5. The decimal subdivision of the day. Days were divided into ten hours, hours into 100 decimal minutes and decimal minutes into 100 decimal seconds.

6. The introduction of an entirely new nomenclature. Aside from introducing new concepts such as *Franciade*, *Sansculottides*, *décade*, decimal minutes and decimal seconds, the reformers renamed each day and month within the new calendar. The days of the *décade* were named in accordance with their numerical order as follows: *Primidi, Duodi, Tridi, Cuartidi, Quintidi, Sextidi, Septidi, Octidi, Nonidi, Décadi*. The five *Sansculottides* were named after Virtue, Genius, Labor, Opinion and Rewards. The Catholic saints' days were abolished, and the days of the year were renamed after trees, plants, seeds, roots, flowers, fruits, farming implements, and domestic animals. The new months were named after seasonal aspects of nature in the following manner: *Vendémiaire* (vintage), *Brumaire* (mist), *Frimaire* (frost), *Nivôse* (snow), *Fluviose* (rain), *Ventose* (wind), *Germinal* (seeds), *Floréal* (blossom), *Prairial* (meadows), *Messidor* (harvest), *Thermidor* (heat), and *Fructidor* (fruits).

Source:

Zerubavel, Eviatar. "The French Republican Calendar: a case study in the sociology of time." *American Sociological Review*, 1977:42 (December 6), p. 870.

system are outlined in the boxed insert on this page. An important factor in its final abandonment by Napoleon in 1805 was the fact that its inventors underestimated the contribution of the Gregorian calendar to French culture and the hold of religious symbolism on the French people.

The Cultural Marketplace and Culture Production. Canadians should be familiar with this explanation, because much of the country's cultural policies are based on it. According to this interpretation, an important source of a society's culture is in the strength and autonomy of its **cultural infra-**

structure. This term refers to groups and organizations having a specific interest, often economic, in the creation and conservation of culture. The institutions of religion, politics, and education, of course, play an important role in creating and disseminating symbols. But beyond these institutions, we have in mind the various business enterprises, especially in the mass and specialized media, whose economic interests entail some amount of culture production. At various times, the federal and some of the provincial governments have concluded that the private sector needed encouragement or direction in meeting their cultural obligations (see, for example, Crean, 1976; Ostry, 1978). In the absence of an effective indigenous cultural infrastructure, we know that we will be served by the American infrastructure. We also know that one of the effects of this kind of dependency will be that the culture we consume will reflect American preoccupations, and not our own.

It is a useful exercise to think about what aspects of life in Canada would escape our attention were we to depend on other societies to tell us about ourselves. Many of the symbols and shared meanings that make up our culture would be borrowed from other people's experiences and would only accidentally reflect our own. On the other hand, creating an economic base for Canadian literature, from writing through publication to sales, means that our thinking about French/English relations, for example, is enriched. In a similar fashion, Canadian nationalists argued for a long time that there was a relationship between the production of Canadian doctorates and hiring them in Canadian universities, on the one hand, and the production of new knowledge about Canadian society, on the other. These observations extend no less to the production of scientific and technological knowledge, for these are dynamic ingredients of contemporary culture (see, for example, the Gray Report, 1972; Britton and Gilmour, 1978).

The Canadian infrastructure includes the following government bodies: the Canadian Radio-television and Telecommunications Commission, the Canada Council, the Social Sciences and Humanities Research Council of Canada, the Canadian Film Development Corporation; the following business enterprises: Holt, Rinehart and Winston, a Canadian subsidiary of an American publisher; McClelland and Stewart, a wholly-owned Canadian publisher; periodicals, such as *Maclean's* magazine; newspapers such as the *Globe and Mail*; and crown corporations such as the Canadian Broadcasting Corporation; and the following regulations: the Canadian content rules for television programming and for popular music on radio, the Canadian quota rule in the Canadian Football League, and preferential hiring of Canadian faculty in our universities.

The usefulness of this idea for explaining national differences in culture is shown in a study by Griswold (cited in Peterson, 1979). She wished to explain the apparent differences in literary taste between British and American novelists writing in the 19th century. Americans wrote about "isolated male protagonists combatting nature, the supernatural, or an evil society," while the British wrote about "love, marriage, and domestic bourgeois life" (Peterson, 1979). One might try to explain these differences in literary culture in terms of national character and civilization, but Griswold preferred a much more direct explanation. Prior to 1891, the United States was not a party to the prevailing international conventions respecting copyright. It was cheaper for American publishers to pirate British novels on love and marriage than to pay their own authors. This compelled American authors to turn to topics which were relatively neglected by British authors, hence the peculiar division of literary labor between the two nations. She reports that these national divisions eroded after 1891, when the United States decided to respect literary property rights.

The Conflict Perspective

All of the structural functionalist hypotheses share the idea that some factor A, perhaps technological change, leads to Z, a change in some feature of culture. Conflict hypotheses, on the other hand, are more complicated in that they posit a conflict relationship between at least two causal factors, A and B, and it is out of this relationship that Z arises. Sometimes the A and B relationship is referred to as dialectical, implying that there is a productive tension between the two.

The conflict perspective has a certain kinship to the symbolic interactionist approach. Both of them assume that interaction between A and B leads to Z. They differ in that A and B are individuals, in the case of symbolic interactionism, but groups or parts of society, in the case of conflict theory. A second difference is that the interactionists do not start from the assumption that A and B are in conflict; in fact, there is generally an assumption of a kind of cooperation between people in order to find a working consensus. Conflict theorists, alternately, start from the assumption that A and B's interests are opposed rather than mutual. It is out of the clash between their respective ambitions that culture is produced.

The conflict perspective assumes, as do the structural functionalist and symbolic interactionist perspectives, that there is a minimum level of shared culture in a society, even between parties in conflict. That is, there is some mutual understanding between conflicting parties on the character of their differing interests and the fact that their relationship is a conflictual one. Often, conflicting groups have much more than this in common, such as a common language and similar goals.

Conflict theorists, however, are more likely to emphasize the cultural differences as opposed to the similarities between groups. They also tend to focus on the relationship between the groups; on how it is defined; and on the degree, why, and with what consequences it is conflictual. As we will show, the conflict approach also emphasizes how cultural elements emerge out of conflict, and how they may even come to be shared across the groups involved. What is important to recognize in conflict is that it is nonetheless a form of sociation, and it is out of sociation or interaction that culture emerges.

We will discuss three conflict oriented explanations in this section. In all of them, cultures are created or embellished as adaptive responses to historic conflicts. Culture can be seen as an accommodation to conflict, as when groups learn to live symbolically with the ruptures that have occurred in their society and with the resulting unequal distribution of power. As ideology, culture is a weapon used by either side to buttress its position and perhaps even to alter the relationship

to its advantage, in time. In the latter case, ideology is a way of asserting the symbolic superiority of one group and the corresponding inferiority of the other group. Interpretations that explain ideology in terms of momentous historical events, such as the American Revolution, cannot be tested directly. We can study their alleged cultural residue, but the event itself can no longer be recovered and the link between it and culture verified. Nonetheless, sociologists buttress their theoretical arguments by testing them indirectly, as we shall see.

Cultural Accommodations to Historical Conflicts. This hypothesis can probably be illustrated in the history of most societies. In the Canadian case, we will draw upon the cultural accommodations that English and French Canadians have made to the battle of the Plains of Abraham and that English Canadians have made to the American War of Independence. Although the specifics would differ, the logic of what we have to say can be illustrated equally well by the cultural adaptations of the Canadian Indians to the European settlers in Canada (see Patterson, 1972).

1. The Conquest and Cultural Differences Between French and English Canadians.

Over the years a number of writers have reported striking cultural differences between English Canadians and the French-speaking people of Quebec (for example, Hughes, 1943; Taylor, 1964). English Canadians were depicted as more individualistic, materialistic, and achievement-oriented in their outlook. The Québécois were more oriented to the family and the kinship system, as well as to religious and spiritual values. They were also said to be more authoritarian in their relationships and to be more xenophobic or negative toward immigrants and foreign influences (Lambert and Curtis, 1982a, 1982b). The picture of Quebec that emerged was of a "folk society," compared to the modern, cosmopolitan society of English Canada.

We can distinguish between two broad views on the relationship between Québécois culture and society. According to the first view, the historical dominance of English Canadians in business was the natural result of their greater interest in worldly success. The Québécois were scarce in business pursuits, because of their loyalties to religious and family-oriented values. If the Roman Catholic Church was prominent in Quebec life, this reflected the wishes of the people in that province. In short, culture determined the shape of society in Quebec and in English Canada.

In more recent years, these cultural differences have been interpreted as cultural responses to more fundamental changes in the organization of Quebec society brought about by the Conquest of 1759-62 (Lambert, 1981). In this view, Quebec was effectively "decapitated" by the Conquest as much of its secular elite returned to France. One of the consequences of this decapitation was to leave the leadership of Quebec society by default in the hands of the Church. And, with the economy firmly tied into the British system of colonial trade, and with English established as the language of commerce, the Québécois were compelled to look elsewhere for national fulfillment. The emergent French-Canadian culture was one of the accommodations made by Québécois society to their new economic, political, and social circumstances. This perspective also leads us to expect that the cultural preoccupations of the Québécois will continue to change, reflecting contemporary shifts in their economic and political power.

The choice between these two points of view is a matter of some political as well as scholarly significance. If the behavioral differences between the two language groups is attributable simply to differences in cultural values, then it is tempting to conclude that people simply get what they want. If, however, cultural differences are themselves the product of who won or lost a war and the ways in which the winners have organized society, then we are more likely to raise questions about social justice and the redress of historical grievances.

2. Conflict and Cultural Differences Between English Canadians and Americans.

We distinguish between two lines of thought on the relationship between conflict and Canadian-American cultural differences. The first traces them to the quite different reactions of English Canadians and Americans to the American Revolution, while the second focuses on the ideological content of the institutions which were transplanted at particular periods in European history to North American soil.

The writing of Lipset (1963, 1965), an American sociologist, best exemplifies the first line of thought. The American Revolution was a traumatic event that left its imprint not only on the victorious Americans, but also on the defeated British Americans who, with the French, created Canada. Traces of our ancestors' historic rejection of the American Revolution are to be found even today in our institutions, culture, and perhaps even in the character of the Canadian people. Thus, according to Lipset, Canadians show greater deference to authority and are more likely to put the welfare of the community ahead of their personal interests. Americans place a greater value on achievement in their relationships with and evaluations of other people. It was these values which the losing side, the Tory United Empire Loyalists, carried to the Canadian colonies. Once established in Canada, these values have been reinforced by our British, monarchical, and religious traditions.

It was obviously impossible for Lipset to test the specific link between reactions to the American Revolution and contemporary culture. His approach, therefore, was to test the claim that the two countries differ in their values in the predicted direction. This he did using statistics on divorce, crime rates, levels of educational attainment, and government spending patterns. If Canadians put the common good ahead of self-interest, then they should be less likely to divorce; if they were more deferential to authority and more attached to the common good, they should be less likely to commit a variety of criminal offenses; if they placed less value on achievement, they should spend less money on higher education; and so on. In general, the data tended to support his picture of Canada as a more conservative nation and, by inference, his historical hypothesis. The boxed insert on the next page contains information that bears on this line of thought.

Lipset's interpretations of his findings have been criticized on a number of grounds. For example, divorce rates reflect more than people's values and their

How useful is the concept of culture in explaining differences between societies?

Critics of the concept of culture, especially the idea of cultural values, urge us to look for differences in the social structures of different societies before we attempt to explain behavioral differences between them in terms of culture. Consider the example of differences in risk-taking behavior on the part of Canadians compared to Americans (see also Gray, 1972). It is a cliché to say that Americans invest their money in risky ventures, while Canadians prefer to invest in safe blue-chip stocks or deposit their money in government-insured bank accounts. An alternative approach would be to analyze the two economies, looking for the structural features of each that encourage and discourage risk-taking behavior.

The following table is taken from an article that appeared in the *Detroit Free Press* in August, 1981. According to this article, the *Free Press* had published an article in June reporting on the much higher interest rates then available in banks in Windsor, Ontario. By August, many Americans had hurried across the border to deposit their money in Canadian banks. "Unlike the U.S.," the author wrote, "Canada does not limit interest rates financial institutions can pay on savings accounts and investment cer-

	Interest Rates	
	Windsor	Detroit
Daily interest savings account		
U.S. funds	12%	5.25 – 5.50%
Canadian funds	17 – 18.75	not available
One-year term deposit		
$1,000 (Canadian)	17.5 – 19.125	not available
One-year term deposit		
$10,000 (U.S.)	16.50	5.25 – 5.50
30-day term deposits		
$5,000 (U.S.)	17.875	5.25 – 5.50
$10,000 (U.S.)	18.125	5.25 – 5.50
$50,000 (U.S.)	18.375	5.25 – 5.50
$100,000 (U.S.)	18.5 – 18.625	17.25 – 17.75

tificates, so even small savers can benefit from the high rates now prevailing in the money markets."

According to the structural view, as opposed to the cultural view, Canadians will continue to engage in a low-risk behavior option more than Americans so long as it promises a relatively higher payoff. We need not assume different cultural values between Canadians and Americans when we see Americans responding to the same economic incentives when given the chance. This example also illustrates one of the points where the interests of economists and sociologists overlap. Sociology students studying economics might look at that discipline from the point of view of the sociologist and ask how the concepts and principles from that field might be used to explain what appear to the sociologist to be cultural phenomena.

Source:

McKinsey, Kitty. "Savers pour cash into Canada." *Detroit Free Press*, August 10, 1981, p. E1.

readiness to say "I quit." Divorce laws affect how easy it is to obtain a divorce, making it difficult to say how much of the differences between the two countries was due to values and how much to legal hurdles. To correct for this ambiguity, a number of studies have asked respondents directly about their opinions on a variety of issues. Their answers have then been used to measure value orientations. Suffice it to say that the findings from these studies are equivocal in their support of Lipset's predictions (for example, Arnold and Tigert,

1974). While finding differences in the responses of contemporary Canadians and Americans in the predicted direction would not be sufficient to demonstrate their connection with specific historical events, nonetheless the failure to find these differences must be seen as theoretically damaging.

The second hypothesis based on historical conflict is called the Hartzian thesis, named for its originator, Louis Hartz (Hartz, 1964). Its basic premise is that ideologies develop out of conflict waged by their respective proponents. Compared to the variety of contending ideologies to be found in Europe, however, the debate in North America has been exceedingly truncated. According to Hartz, immigrants to the new North American societies did not carry with them the full spectrum of ideological opinion that prevailed in the countries from which they had come. Only parts of the spectrum made the journey, with the result that these parts were free to flourish unchecked by the ideological adversaries they had known at home. The institutions founded in the new societies, therefore, bore the ideological imprint of their founders. This historical hypothesis requires that we know something about the ideological origins of our society. In the case of the United States and English Canada, the English-speaking peoples carried with them the assumptions of liberal individualism. The assumptions of conservatism and socialism were missing or under-represented among the English-speaking settlers of North America, thus permitting liberalism to develop virtually without impediment. But Quebec was another matter, because this society was founded prior to the French Revolution and represented a corporatist and authoritarian extrusion from France.

The general view presented here was later revised by Horowitz (1968) to allow for significant cultural differences between Canada and the United States. While the United States can fairly be described as a liberal society, Horowitz argued, the appearance of a "Tory touch" complicates the Canadian case. The United Empire Loyalists and our British traditions introduced distinctly non-liberal elements into English-Canadian culture. This Tory presence meant that Canadian conservatism would not be like its American cousin, and it provided the fertile ideological soil out of which an indigenous Canadian social democratic party would emerge.

Structural Contradictions and Cultural Change. Herschel Hardin, the Canadian dramatist, has described Canada as a series of three contradictions. These are French Canada against English Canada, the regions against the center, and Canada against the United States. "To get at the Canadian circum-

stance . . . is above all to see the country in terms of its contradictions–the contending forces that underlie the character of the people" (Hardin, 1974).

So long as one remains in this country, he argues, it is impossible to escape these sources of creative tension for they are "the forcing ground of our identity" (Hardin, 1974). Canadians interacting with each other around these points of division produce symbols, norms, ideology, and other elements of culture as means of coming to terms with their society and with each other. Hardin (1974) offers the following illuminating example of the impact of one of the Canadian contradictions upon a new Canadian:

One poignant case sticks in my mind, because it illustrates the leading Canadian contradiction at work on a man whose identity as a Canadian was still in the process of formation. It was during the St. Leonard controversy over whether all schools should be French-language, or whether there should be English-language instruction available as well. An ethnic spokesman caught in the crossfire protested with quiet emotion to CBC radio that his group was an innocent victim . . . because they had no ingrained hostility against French Canadians. "We're not against the French Canadians," he said. "And we're not against the English Canadians. We just want to be Canadian." It never occurred to him that having to explore this linguistic conflict and cope with it, and in intensely passionate, practical circumstances, would give him more insight into what it meant to be a Canadian than most Canadians would gather from a lifetime. Even while he was protesting, he probably had already realized there was no total escape from the contradiction other than by leaving the country. Wasn't that why he was protesting in the first place? And after going through that experience, would he ever agree that being a Canadian and an American involved more or less the same thing?

The origins of this society's culture in conflict, as sketched by Hardin, are vastly more complex than the Lipset and Hartzian theses would have us believe. The central historical conflicts were not waged centuries ago, but have persisted through the generations and into the present. Paradoxically, the forces on either side of each contradiction have strengthened their opposites while flexing their own muscles.

The "thick continuity" (Hardin's expression) of our history has created a people for those with the eyes and the patience to see. It is a commonplace for visitors from Britain or the United States to miss what is Canadian, because their sensibilities have been shaped elsewhere. Closer to home, sociology textbooks that treat Canada as a cultural extension of the United States, Hardin would argue, display this same insensitivity. Nor is it uncommon for Canadians to miss what is Canadian, because their ideology is American and borrowed. This is especially the case, he believes, when Canadians persist in seeing Canada as a free enterprise economy, either amnesiac of or blind to the fact that this country has a history rich in public enterprise.

The Dominant Ideology Thesis. This explanation emphasizes that there are dominant social classes or groups in society, a topic to be discussed more fully in Chapter 7. These classes develop ideologies that are self-justifying and hence unifying among themselves. There is great debate among sociologists about how extensively dominant ideology is disseminated in society and how important it is in maintaining the status quo. If people in the subordinate classes are not persuaded by dominant ideology, it may nonetheless intimidate them and impede their development of counter-ideologies (Abercrombie, Hill, and Turner, 1980).

If dominant ideology is to be disseminated, then it makes sense to look at the institutions assigned this task – as conflict theorists have done. Education, religion, and the mass media, in particular, have been the subject of much research and speculation in this thesis. We will limit our comments to some studies of education.

A good example of research testing the dominant ideology thesis is a study by McDonald (1978) on the establishment of the Ontario public school system by Egerton Ryerson in the 19th century. Ryerson believed that the educational system should be firmly under government control, rather than locally controlled. It should be highly regulated and uniform throughout the province, staffed by loyal and professional teachers, and open to all children. He believed that its mission was to produce the kinds of loyal citizens who would reject the ideas of republican democracy emanating from the United States. Properly indoctrinated citizens would never again participate in the kind of rebellion that had been crushed in Upper Canada in 1837. The schools should also promote harmony among the social classes. This meant persuading the working classes that "their interests were also those of the middle and upper classes, and that, as a collectivity, there was a 'common' or 'public good' towards which all must work" (McDonald, 1978).

The relationship between people's level of education and belief in dominant ideology among Canadians interviewed in 1977 was tested by Baer and Lambert (1982). Dominant ideology was signified by support for the kind of economic inequality that prevails in Canadian society and rejection of the idea that government has a responsibility for creating employment. Support for dominant ideology was greatest among the most educated respondents. Belief in dominant ideology was also greatest among people who felt that their income matched their qualifications. Doubts were most frequently expressed by the less educated and by those who felt underpaid.

The findings of the Baer and Lambert study, however, suggest that the aspirations of the founders of our educational system to indoctrinate the children from all social classes have not been fully realized. If the point of dominant ideology is social control, then its effects seem to be limited to the most educated members of society. Mann (1970) has claimed that this is all that is really necessary, for there are other ways of controlling people with less education. For one thing, the prominence given to dominant ideology in our mass media and in the educational system may simply undermine the emergence of counter-ideologies. In other words, they disorient more than they persuade. Cynicism bred by our political system, the absence of significant political options, and the control exercised by work and the fear of unemployment may lead to a sense of resignation on the part of citizens. It is less a matter of belief in the status quo, Mann argues, than it is a matter of "pragmatic acquiescence" on the part of subordinate groups in society to what appears inevitable.

TOWARD A UNIFIED PERSPECTIVE

Our treatment of the three perspectives and the explanations generated from them has implied that they are mutually exclusive. This may be a useful device for purposes of exposition, but social reality is not so simply constructed. In fact, the sensitive observer can probably detect all three processes intertwined in the creation of most cultural phenomena. We pointed out earlier that interpersonal interactions are subsumed by the two macro-perspectives, structural functionalism, and conflict. The problem is with the latter two perspectives, because they have often been defended as though they were theoretically irreconcilable.

Following Baldus (1977), we can find evidence for both processes at work in specific cases, although their mix may well differ between cases. The development of regional and provincial cultures in Canada is a case in point. On the one hand, provincially-based economies (Wilson, 1974) and cultural infrastructures operate to produce provincial or regional cultures. On the latter point, the British North America Act and its successor Canada Bill assign clear responsibilities in fields such as education to the provinces. This means that some of the factors that shape culture, as discussed above in connection with the structural functionalist perspective, have a provincial presence.

On the other hand, there are enduring rivalries and conflicts between regions, between the hinterland and metropolitan centers, and between the provinces and the federal government, as Hardin (1974) has emphasized, and these contribute to cultural variations across the country. In fact, the political scientist Cairns has argued that key instruments in the development of the "societies [and cultures] of Canadian federalism" are the governments of Canada themselves. In asserting this proposition, Cairns objects to the traditional view that sees politics and government as mere products of society; once created, they react upon society, changing it in the process. Who would deny, for example, the significance of the continuing struggle between the Ottawa and Quebec governments in producing the stuff of culture in this country?

The development and maintenance of ethnic cultures in Canada provides another example in which functionalist and conflict processes are intertwined. Once again, we can see how processes occurring within and between ethnic groups contribute to subcultures. The importance of ethnic tensions and conflicts for ethnic cultures, as between the French and the English, is well known. In addition, ethnic cultures are nourished by the institutions comprising ethnic groups. Breton (1964) has suggested the concept of "institutional completeness" to explain the persistence of ethnic communities and their cultures. He found that ethnic groups that possessed churches, periodicals, and welfare organizations, operating in their own languages, were more likely to retain the loyalty of their members. Assimilation into the dominant culture was more pronounced in institutionally incomplete ethnic groups. We can imagine a situation of maximum institutional completeness as one in which all institutions belong to the ethnic group. At this point, we might better think of such a group as a society rather than as an ethnic group. This of course is the goal to which many Québécois aspire.

SUMMARY

1. The most useful view of culture is that it is a shared set of symbols and their meanings. The effects of these shared meanings can be seen in people's actions and relationships with each other, as well as in their manufactured world.

2. Beliefs, norms, and values are the building blocks for more complex components of culture – statuses, social institutions, ideologies, and subcultures.

3. The fact that culture is defined in terms of some minimum level of sharing or consensus is common across the three basic theoretical perspectives in sociology. However, those three approaches differ on whether they emphasize the functional or conflicting origins and consequences of culture, as well as micro versus macro level interests.

4. The symbolic interactionist approach locates culture in specific relationships and situations. Culture is seen as fluid and dynamic rather than static. The principal cultural concept is the definition of the situation, and this is a product of people's negotiations with each other. Symbolic interactionists emphasize the initiative and activity of individual actors in the process.

5. According to the structural functionalist perspective, culture mirrors the society as a whole or some part of society.

6. The conflict perspective is represented by three explanations. Culture can be interpreted as an accommodation to a historic conflict, as a product of social contradictions, and as a weapon used by dominant groups to justify their privileged status and to unify themselves.

7. Each of these three perspectives is sensitive to particular themes in the creation, maintenance, and change of culture. Because the relationship between society and culture is multifaceted, it should be theoretically possible to adopt a unified approach.

8. Although some sociologists emphasize either the organization of society or culture in their explanations of social life, it should not be necessary to choose one over the other. Social process and social change within a society are best understood as products of the complex interplay between a society's structure and its culture. The task for the sociologist is to make sense of this interplay for the research question at hand.

GLOSSARY

Cultural infrastructure. Specialized groups with an interest, often economic, in the production and preservation of cultural symbols.

Cultural relativity. The idea that all cultures are equally valid and valuable and that each culture must be judged by its own standards.

Culture. Shared set of symbols and their definitions or meanings.

Definition of the situation. Beliefs and norms about an interaction setting.

Descriptive beliefs. Statements or claims about what is, was, or will be, including ideas of cause and effect.

Dominant ideologies. Ruling ideologies which explain and justify the existing ways of doing things.

Ethnocentrism. Tendency to use one's own culture as the only valid standard for evaluating other cultures, societies, and peoples.

Folkways. Traditional rules about customary ways of behaving which are informally enforced and of mild concern to society members.

Ideologies. Emotionally charged sets of descriptive and normative beliefs and values that either explain and justify the status quo or, in the case of counter ideologies, call for and justify alternative arrangements.

Laws. Norms that have been formally promulgated by a legislative body and are enforced by an executive body of government.

Material culture. Physical artifacts or products of a society embodying cultural meanings.

Mores. Traditional rules about how the individual must or must not behave which are invested with strong feelings and informally enforced.

Normative beliefs. Ideas about what should or should not be, referring especially to goodness, virtuousness, or propriety.

Norms. Formal or informal rules stating how categories of people are expected to act in particular situations, the violation of which is subject to sanction.

Social institutions. Sets of beliefs, norms, and values that define how people, groups, and organizations should resolve central and persistent societal problems.

Status. Culturally defined position in society, consisting of ideas about rights and obligations.

Subcultures. More or less distinctive beliefs, norms, symbols, values, and ideologies shared by sub-groups of a larger population.

Symbol. Anything, such as a word, gesture, or object, taken by people as a matter of convention to stand for something else.

Values. Cultural conceptions about what are desirable goals to pursue and what are appropriate standards for judging actions.

FURTHER READING

Bell, D.V.J., and L. Tepperman, *The Roots of Disunity.* Toronto: McClelland and Stewart, 1979. Describes the contours of Canada's culture and shows the differences across regions, social classes, and linguistic groups.

Christian, W., and C. Campbell. *Political Parties and Ideologies in Canada.* Toronto: McGraw-Hill Ryerson, 1974. Although organized in terms of political parties, there is extensive treatment of the ideologies of liberalism, conservatism, socialism, and nationalism in this country.

Crean, S.M. *Who's Afraid of Canadian Culture?* Don Mills, Ont.: General Publishing, 1976. A detailed description and interpretation of the personnel, groups, practices, policies, and "facts of life" affecting the arts in Canada.

Gerth, H., and C.W. Mills. *Character and Social Structure.* New York: Harcourt, Brace and World, 1953. See especially this book's discussion of social institutions and their impact on organizing society.

Hardin, H. *A Nation Unaware: The Canadian Economic Culture.* Vancouver: J.J. Douglas, 1974. This book argues that Canada has a history of public enterprise that Canadians fail to appreciate when they perceive it through the ideological categories of American business.

Lakoff, G., and M. Johnson. *Metaphors We Live By.* Chicago: University of Chicago Press, 1980. Metaphors are sources of meaning. Metaphors taken from areas of life that we understand are applied to areas that we cannot understand on their own terms. Differences in cultures can be found in their prevalent metaphors.

CHAPTER 3
SOCIALIZATION

MARLENE MACKIE

Human beings must eat to stay alive. For babies, the matter is quite straightforward. They experience abdominal discomfort; they cry; a parent responds; they suck. Adult satisfaction of this basic physiological need is more complicated. Canadians consider some things proper food (steak, hamburgers), but gag at the thought of eating equally nutritious alternatives (caterpillars, horsemeat). Food preferences (spaghetti, sauerkraut, bagels) also mark ethnic group boundaries (Anderson and Alleyne, 1979). And, of course, eating is surrounded by rules (Goffman, 1963). Even when people are ravenous, they are not supposed to attack the apple pie before the spinach. Adults who jam food into their mouths until their cheeks bulge seem disgusting, especially if they try to talk while they stuff. Plucking an interesting item from a neighbor's plate will result in raised eyebrows. So will scratching one's tonsils with a fork.

How, then, does the carefree infant become transformed into the disciplined adult? There is a one-word answer to this question – socialization. The whole story, of course, is not quite that simple.

Socialization is the complex learning process through which individuals develop selfhood and acquire the knowledge, skills, and motivations required for participation in social life. This process is the link between individual and society and may be viewed from each of these two perspectives.

From the point of view of the individual, interaction with other people is the means by which human potentialities are actualized. The newborn infant is utterly helpless. Its abilities are limited to crying, sucking, eliminating wastes, yawning, and a few other reflexes. It has no self-awareness. Though it has the potential for becoming human, it is not yet human. The physical care, emotional response, and training provided by the family transform this noisy, wet, demanding bundle of matter into a functioning member of society. It learns language, control of impulses, and skills. It develops a self. Knowledge is acquired of both the physical world and the social world. The child becomes capable of taking on social roles with some commitment. It learns whether it is female or male. It internalizes, or accepts as its own, the norms and values of, first, the family and, later, the wider society.

Effective socialization is as essential for the society as it is for the individual. Canadian society could not continue to exist unless the thousands of new members born each year eventually learned to think, believe, and behave as Canadians. Each new generation must learn the society's culture. Social order demands self-discipline and control of impulses. The continuity of our society requires that children come to embrace societal values as their own. Citizens must adhere to cultural norms because they themselves view those norms as right and proper. Cultural breakdown occurs when the socialization process no longer provides the new generation with valid reasons to be enthusiastic about becoming members of that society (Flacks, 1979). However, individuals may redefine social roles and obligations, as well as accepting them as they stand. Social change thus occurs over time (Bush and Simmons, 1981).

The heterogeneous nature of Canadian society complicates the socialization process. Although many values and norms are shared by all Canadians, differences are found by language, by region, by ethnicity, by religion, by social class, by urban-rural residence. These variations in social environment bring with them variations in the content of socialization. The perpetuation of these distinctive Canadian groups is dependent on children learning the relevant subcultural norms and values. For example, the Ukrainian-Canadian community cannot continue in any meaningful fashion unless children of this ethnic background learn to view themselves as Ukrainian-Canadians, and learn the traditions and perhaps the language of this group. Similarly, the continuation of the unique features of the Maritime region requires that Canadians who live there acquire, by means of specialized socialization, the identity of Maritimers and the special norms, values, and history of that region.

Historical events, such as the Great Depression and the Second World War, mean that successive generations of Canadians have different socialization experiences (Mannheim, 1953). For example, people who grew up during the 1930s often learned what it meant to go hungry, to give up career plans, to delay marriage. We would expect their perspective on life to contrast sharply with that of earlier and later generations (Elder, 1974).

The socialization process explains how commitment to the social order is maintained. However, it is important to note that socialization for deviance also occurs. Some folks learn to forge checks, to crack safes, and to snort cocaine.

TYPES OF SOCIALIZATION

We defined socialization as the lifelong learning process through which individuals develop selfhood and acquire the knowledge, skills, and motivations required to participate in social life. Before we go on, we should make some further definitional distinctions.

Primary socialization is the basic socialization that occurs in childhood. It involves: the development of language and individual identity, the learning of cognitive skills and self-control, the internalization of moral standards and appropriate attitudes and motivations, and some understanding of societal roles.

Death: The Ultimate Status Change

A number of years ago, Glaser and Strauss (1965) described dying as a "non-scheduled status passage." Although The New Yorker *magazine found this dry sociological terminology highly amusing, dying does represent a new social status.*

Since the fate of most people is not sudden death, socialization is required to cope with this inevitable termination of life. Individuals must come to terms with the fact of their own impending death and must relate to others as people who are dying. The amount of anticipatory socialization that can occur is slight. So how do we learn? We frequently read or hear or see mass media reports of death, but the death of strangers is an abstraction, it means very little to us. We are touched emotionally by the death of relatives or friends, but the fact that their dying occurs mostly in managed hospital settings reduces first-hand experience with death. Therefore, the actual socialization for death takes place when our own death is imminent.

Two cases of socialization for death are described below. The first concerns a group of elderly people in a retirement village (Marshall, 1975). The second describes the experiences of survivors of a coal mine disaster (Lucas, 1968). The socialization of the miners was more traumatic than that of the elderly, who had considerably more time to get used to the idea.

Marshall used participant observation and interviews to study the inhabitants of a retirement village, Glen Brae. The majority of the people there accepted the appropriateness of their own impending death. Asked if they would like to be a hundred years old,

75 percent said "no."

The remarks of one widow, aged eighty-one, show this acceptance of death: "Heavens! I've lived my life. I'd be delighted to have it end. The sooner the better. I nearly went with a heart attack. . . . I feel I've lived my life, and I don't want to be a care to anybody. That's why I'm glad to be here [in Glen Brae]."

The retirement village setting was a typical context for adult socialization generally: a formal organization with intense peer influence. Most of the residents knew that the move there was their last. Because everyone faced death, there was a feeling of common fate. This peer group socialization involved frequent discussion of death (often a taboo conversational topic in the outside world). Also, living in a community of the dying provided role models with which to anticipate dying.

Being ready to die, these elderly people were concerned with a graceful style of dying. This style involved not making trouble for anyone.

Until they were trapped underground in a Maritime coal mine disaster, on the other hand, death had been a distant prospect for the 18 survivors interviewed by Lucas. After five days of entrapment, these men began to contemplate their own death. The very real possibility of death suddenly propelled them into the role of dying. But death was a different proposition for these miners in the prime of life than for the elderly.

The prospect of premature death meant unfinished business left behind. The men were concerned about small amounts of money they owed, home projects left uncompleted, hunting trips they would never take. In comparison, the elderly had had time to put their affairs in order. Unlike the aged, who had completed their work and family roles, the miners were preoccupied with a number of social

losses which would result from their deaths. Wives would be left without husbands, children without fathers. The financial implications for their survivors also troubled these men.

Nevertheless, the elderly and the miners shared three dimensions of the dying role. First, the miners' thoughts turned to an evaluation, or final accounting, of their life achievements. As they reviewed their lives, they were pleased with their successes and disturbed by their omissions and failures. And, although Marshall does not specifically mention that the retired contemplated their accomplishments, we can be sure that they did. Second, both groups were preoccupied with a dignified manner of dying. Each miner wanted to meet death stoically and to "die like a man." Finally, both settings involved peer socialization. The opportunity to discuss their impending deaths with others sharing the same fate was of immense importance to the miners, as well as to the elderly. Because death is such a delicate subject, all had lacked the opportunity to talk about it fully before they met it face-to-face in the mine shaft or the retirement village. Fortunately, the miners were rescued, and the dying role was abandoned —for the time being.

Source:

Glaser, Barney G., and Anselm L. Strauss. *The Awareness of Dying: A Sociological Study of Attitudes Towards the Patient Dying in Hospital.* London: Weidenfeld and Nicolson, 1965; Lucas, Rex A. "Social implications of the immediacy of death." *Canadian Review of Sociology and Anthropology*, 5, 1-16, 1968; Marshall Victor W. "Socialization for impending death in a retirement village." *American Journal of Sociology*, 80: 1124-44, 1975; Mortimer, Jeylan T., and Roberta G. Simmons. "Adult Socialization." *Annual Review of Sociology*, 4: 421-54, 1978.

Adult socialization is that which occurs beyond the childhood years. Although primary socialization lays the foundation for later learning, it cannot completely prepare people for adulthood. For one thing, our age-graded society confronts individuals with new role expectations as they move through life. Moving beyond the family into the neighborhood, entering school, becoming an adolescent, choosing an occupation, marrying, bearing children, encountering middle age, retiring, and dying all involve new lessons to be learned.

Also, society changes, and people must, therefore, equip themselves to cope with new situations (for example, technological job obsolescence, war, changes in sexual mores, and energy crises).

Finally, some individuals encounter specialized situations with which they must deal. Geographical and social mobility, marital breakdown, physical handicaps, and so on all require further socialization (Brim, 1966).

Anticipatory socialization is that which occurs in advance of the actual playing of roles. This rehearsal for the future involves learning something about role requirements, both behaviors and attitudes, and visualizing oneself in the role. Children begin to practice being pupils before they ever enter school. Law students mentally try on the role of practicing lawyer. We think about being married, being parents, being widowed before we actually assume these statuses.

Resocialization occurs when a new role or a new situation requires a person to replace established patterns of behavior and thought with new patterns (Campbell, 1975). Old behavior must be unlearned, because it is incompatible in some way with new role demands. Usually, resocialization is more difficult than the original socialization; the established habits interfere with new learning. Fortunately, though, human beings retain the capacity for change across the entire life span, often assisted by organizations such as Alcoholics Anonymous and Zen (Brim and Kagan, 1980).

Resocialization is more characteristic of adult socialization than of primary socialization. However, as youngsters mature, they too are expected to discard former behavior. Block printing is fine for a first grade pupil, but a fourth grade pupil must learn to write. A two-year-old boy can cry when he is frightened, but a twelve-year boy who climbs into his mother's lap and whimpers is thought to be odd.

Resocialization necessarily confronts the individual with contradictions between old and new behavior which are sometimes confusing and sometimes painful. The fact that the nonresponsible, submissive, asexual child must become the responsible, dominant, sexually active adult (Mortimer and Simmons, 1978) illustrates one contradiction between childhood and adulthood. Also, the resocialization involved in new situations entails contradictions for adults. For example, the women's liberation movement has resulted in redefinitions of the ways men and women relate to each other. Is it chivalrous or sexist to open doors for women? Should husbands help with housework or sit back and watch their wives do it? (Campbell, 1975). More dramatic discontinuities between old and new selves are experienced by individuals who get caught up in extreme instances of resocialization, such as brainwashing, religious conversion, and "therapeutic" programs in prisons and mental hospitals.

THE LIFELONG PROCESS

We've noted that socialization is a lifelong process. Despite some anticipatory socialization during childhood, primary socialization simply cannot prepare people for roles and situations which are either unforeseeable at the moment, or which lie far ahead in the future.

Adult socialization is particularly necessary in complex, changing societies such as Canada. Here, a comparison may be made with the Hutterities, who constitute a subculture that has remained very much the same for some 450 years. Hutterites live out their lives in small rural colonies in western Canada. Everybody knows everybody else. There are few secrets, therefore nearly all adult roles are open for the Hutterite children's inspection (Mackie, 1975). Eventually, the children will inherit those very roles they see enacted before them. In cases such as these, adult socialization is less extensive than in Canadian society generally.

Although socialization continues throughout life, social science literature tells us comparatively little about the detailed processes involved in adult socialization. The main reason for this somewhat distorted focus is that primary socialization provides the ground-

Socialization is a lifelong process, and one that has been changing in recent years. Unions have traditionally been the province of males, but here men, women, and minority group workers interact to make union decisions. (*Canapress*)

work for all later learning. The major structures of personality are formed in childhood. In addition, the lessons learned during this impressionable period are the first lessons, and learning comes easily. We have already pointed out that resocialization is difficult, because old behavior must be unlearned before new behavior can be acquired. Finally, it should be noted that even when new expectations do not conflict with previous expectations, primary socialization channels and sets limits for adult socialization. For example, a person who emerges from childhood without a strong motivation to achieve is unlikely to excel in medical school.

A number of fundamental differences exist between primary socialization and adult socialization (Brim, 1966), in addition to those just considered.

1. With some exceptions, adult socialization concentrates on overt behavior, rather than on values and motives. Society assumes that adults already hold the values appropriate for a given role and that they are motivated to pursue that role. All that remains is to teach the incumbents how to behave. Universities, for example, do not attempt to convince students of the value of higher education or to motivate them to work hard at their studies. Prisons, on the other hand, are resocialization agencies, but their high rates of recidivism (of individuals relapsing into crime after imprisonment) illustrate the impracticality of wholesale attempts to alter basic values and motives.

2. While primary socialization tends to be idealistic, adult socialization tends to be realistic. Children are taught how society ideally operates and how people ideally behave. They are shielded from knowledge of how society actually operates and how people actually behave. At the same time that parents exhort children to be honest, they protect children from awareness of corruption in government and their own "fudging" of the truth. Part of growing up, then, involves the substitution of sophistication for childish naiveté.

3. The content of adult socialization is more specific than the content of primary socialization. Although there are exceptions, children learn general knowledge, skills, and behavior relevant to many roles. Adults, on the other hand, acquire information specific to particular roles. For example, children learn to read and to write. This knowledge is useful in a wide range of roles and situations. In contrast, adults learn to diaper a baby or to wire a circuit board. These sets of skills usually pertain to the parent and electronic-technician roles, and not elsewhere.

4. As a general rule, adults are socialized by formal organizations (schools, corporations), while children are socialized in informal contexts (the family and peer groups, mainly). This distinction, however, reflects a general tendency rather than a rule. The school, for example, although it is a formal organization, is an important primary socialization agency. Also, the actual socializing of adults within organizations is often done through primary relationships. For example, Mann's (1964) study of the socialization of new inmates ("fish") in an Ontario reformatory found that the prisoners were the main socializers. The administrative staff carried on a "rearguard, defensive action." Throughout life, people remain sensitive to the opinion and example of their family and friends.

5. The nature of the relationships between socializer and socializee differs in primary and adult socialization. The family is the major socializer of the child. Familial relationships are marked by high levels of both feeling and power. Because of the emotionally charged familial context and the power of the parents to mete out rewards and punishments, parents have a tremendous impact on the child. By contrast, the relationship between adult socializer and socializee is usually more emotionally neutral and more equal in terms of power. But, this does not mean that the adult socialization experience is devoid of emotion. For example, McMaster medical students are plagued by anxiety and uncertainty (Haas, Marshall, and Shaffir, 1981). Moreover, the adult socializee is often in that position voluntarily. You may choose to be an apprentice welder or a college student. The volunteer has rights that the conscript lacks in defining what will be learned and how the learning will occur. The youngest son in the Jones family, however, did not choose his fate.

NATURE VERSUS NURTURE

Since the beginning of this century, social scientists have been preoccupied with the relative contributions of biology and environment to human development. Those who have emphasized the role of biology in this nature-nurture debate argued that the individual's psychological characteristics and social behavior result from the unfolding of inherited factors, such as instincts. On the other hand, sociologists on the nurture side of the argument believed that environmental influences are all important.

Recent discoveries in biology and genetics have resulted in the problem becoming increasingly complex. Although the nature-nurture debate has not yet been resolved, scientists have now abandoned the simplistic approach of nature *versus* nurture. Both biology and environment interact to transform the infant into a functioning member of society. (See Chapter 4 for a discussion of the nature-nurture issue as it applies to gender patterns.)

Socialization provides the link between biology and culture. Biology gives human beings the capacity to learn and the ability to use language. In addition, the human infant's relatively long period of helplessness (compared with that of the lower animals) enforces dependence on adult caretakers. The resulting emotional bonds forged between parents and children are necessary for normal childhood development. This deep emotional attachment gives parents the power needed to socialize children. In other words, children are responsive to parental influence partly because they are dependent on the parents' love and approval.

EFFECTS OF SOCIAL DEPRIVATION

What happens when that parental love and approval are not forthcoming? Two specific cases impressively demonstrate the importance of socialization. Both illustrate clearly that the infant's biological potential cannot be actualized without close emotional attachments to at least one adult. The first case concerns two American children who were deliberately reared in isolation (Davis, 1940, 1947). The second case involves experiments by Harlow and his colleagues on the effects of isolation on rhesus monkeys (Harlow, 1959; Harlow and Harlow, 1962).

Children Reared in Isolation

Anna was an illegitimate child born in 1921. At the insistence of her grandfather, she was hidden away in an attic-like room until she was nearly six years old. During this period, her mother had given her enough care only to keep her alive. When Anna was discovered, her clothing and bedding were filthy. She was extremely emaciated, skeletal, and had a bloated stomach. There were no signs of intelligence; she was unable to talk, walk, feed herself, respond to people. At first, it was believed that she was blind and deaf. Four years later, she finally began to develop speech. By the time of her death a year later, she was operating at the level of the normal child of two-and-a-half. Although the possibility that Anna was born mentally deficient cannot be ruled out, Davis thinks that, "Anna might have had a normal or near-normal capacity, genetically speaking."

Isabelle was also an illegitimate child kept in seclusion. She and Anna were discovered at about the same time, at about the same age. Isabelle had lived with her deaf-mute mother in a dark room shut off from the rest of her mother's family. As a result, she had had no chance to develop speech. Instead, she made only a strange croaking noise. An inadequate diet and lack of sunshine had produced a severe case of rickets. When Isabelle was confronted with strangers, especially men, she behaved like a frightened wild animal. The child appeared to be hopelessly feeble-minded. However, her caretakers began a long, systematic training program. She went through the usual stages of learning characteristic of the years one to six, and she did this very rapidly. Within a week, she made her first attempt at vocalization. In less than a year, she could identify written words, could write, and add. By the time she was eight and a half years old, she had reached a normal level. Davis reported that she was a bright, cheerful, energetic little girl.

Isabelle had two advantages which Anna did not. She received prolonged, expert attention. She also had had the constant companionship of her deaf-mute mother. The story of these neglected children points up the primary importance of contact with reasonably intelligent, articulate people in the early years of child development.

Monkeys Reared in Isolation

Monkeys need this early contact as well. The experiments of Harlow and his associates on the effects of isolation on rhesus monkeys show that infantile social experience has crucial effects on behavior in later life.

In one of this series of studies (Harlow and Harlow, 1962), young monkeys were separated from their mothers a few hours after birth. They were caged in such a way that each little monkey could see and hear other monkeys, although it could make no direct physical contact with them. These socially deprived infants matured into emotionally disturbed adults. The monkeys sat in their cages and stared fixedly into space or clasped their heads in their arms and rocked for hours. They developed compulsive habits, such as chewing and tearing at their own bodies until they bled. They did not know how to relate to other monkeys, and were either passive and withdrawn or extremely aggressive. Harlow's work showed that there was a critical period of development during which social experience was absolutely necessary. Isolation for the first six months of life rendered animals permanently inadequate. The effects of shorter periods of isolation (60 to 90 days) were, however, reversible.

Another phase of Harlow's (1959) research involved comparing the importance of the act of nursing with the importance of bodily contact in engendering the infant monkey's attachment to its mother. Two surrogate mother monkeys were constructed. Both were wire cylinders surmounted by wooden heads. One was bare. The wire of the other was cushioned by a terry-cloth sheath. Each "mother" had the nipple of a feeding bottle protruding from its breast. Eight newborn monkeys, separated from their natural mothers, were placed in individual cages. They were given access to both types of surrogate mothers. Four monkeys were fed from the wire surrogate and four from the cloth surrogate. All the infants developed a strong attachment to the cloth mother and little or none to the wire mother, regardless of which one provided the milk. Both groups spent much more time clinging to the cloth-covered mothers than to the wire mothers. Moreover, the soft mother was sought out for security. The monkey infants were also frightened by a mechanical teddy bear, which moved toward them beating a drum. Whether the infants had nursed from a wire mother or from a cloth mother, they sought comfort from the cloth mother. These results showed the importance of bodily contact in developing the infant-mother affectional bond.

The cloth surrogate mother provided tactile comfort; however, it could not supply communication or training. Therefore, the social development of all the infant monkeys was severely and permanently impaired. Both the rhesus monkey experiments and the case histories of Anna and Isabelle show the fundamental need for childhood social experience. In addition, both show us how futile the nature-nurture controversy really is when nature and nurture are viewed as mutually exclusive alternatives.

SOCIALIZATION THEORIES

Although socialization – learning norms, attitudes, values, knowledge, skills, and self-concepts – occurs throughout life, the learning that takes place during the formative years of childhood has been of special concern to psychologists and sociologists. The family, which bears the major responsibility here, has therefore received considerable attention from these social scientists. This section considers the principal ideas involved in four theoretical approaches to childhood socialization: learning theory, Piaget's cognitive developmental approach to moral thought, Freud's psychoanalytic theory, and symbolic interactionist views on development of the self. These theoretical perspectives vary in their emphases on how learning occurs and what socialization comprises, but for the most part, they are complementary rather than opposed sets of ideas. All of them can contribute to our understanding of childhood socialization.

Learning Theory

The nature-nurture debate demonstrated that very little human behavior is directly determined by the individual's genetic makeup. For this reason, the precise mechanisms involved in learning are well worth knowing.

Three Main Types of Learning. We are concerned here with three main types of learning: classical conditioning, operant conditioning, and imitation. The last type, imitation, is probably the most important way in which children learn.

Classical conditioning was first discovered by the Russian physiologist Ivan Pavlov in his famous experiments with the salivating dog. The basic idea is quite simple (Deutsch and Krauss, 1965). Meat powder, an "unconditioned stimulus" (UCS), is placed in a dog's mouth and automatically elicits salivation, an "unconditioned response" (UCR). A neutral stimulus, such as the sound of a bell, which does not elicit salivation, is presented just before the presentation of the food. The neutral stimulus is called a "conditioned stimulus" (CS). Soon the CS by itself elicits the flow of saliva without the meat or UCS. This learned response to the bell is the "conditioned response" (CR).

The classical conditioning paradigm explains some of children's learning which is unintended by their parents. For example, a child may munch cookies while watching "Sesame Street." Before long, television becomes a signal to eat. Phobias, or irrational fears, provide another good illustration. Many social attitudes are acquired in exactly the same fashion. If, for example, a little boy has an unpleasant experience with a red-haired girl, he may (unlike Charlie Brown) go through life disliking red-haired girls.

Operant conditioning, a second type of learning, is associated with the American psychologists, E.L. Thorndike (1898, 1913) and B.F. Skinner (1953). In this case, the organism must first make a specific response. If that response is followed by a reward or a punishment, it then becomes a conditioned, or learned, response. In a typical experiment, a hungry pigeon is placed in a cage equipped with four differently colored keys. It goes through a trial and error procedure of

Conversations with a Gorilla

Are human beings the only animals capable of learning language? The answer to this controversial question depends partly on what is meant by "language." Read this account of Francine "Penny" Patterson's (1978) work and decide for yourself.

For the past six years, Penny, a developmental psychologist at Stanford University, has been engaged in teaching sign language to a gorilla named Koko. Penny decided to use the hand speech employed by the deaf, on the assumption that apes' difficulty in acquiring language might stem from inability to control lips and tongue, not from lack of intelligence. Each gesture in the sign language signifies a word or an idea.

A "molding" technique was used to teach Koko to sign. Penny took Koko's hands and shaped them into the proper configuration for a sign. At the same time, she showed the gorilla the object or activity which the sign represented. As Koko began to associate the hand movement with its meaning, Penny gradually loosened her hold on the ape's hands until the animal was making the sign by herself. At first, Koko did not take too kindly to her language lessons. Every time Penny grasped Koko's hands, the gorilla tried to bite her!

Koko's current vocabulary consists of 375 signs, which she uses regularly and appropriately. Her repertoire includes "airplane," "belly button," "lollipop," "friend," and "stethoscope." Because Penny talks to her while signing, Koko also understands hundreds of spoken words. Indeed, words like c-a-n-d-y and g-u-m have to be spelled out in her presence.

Koko's IQ on the Stanford-Binet test ranges from 85 to 95, which is slightly below average for a human child. However, the test is biased toward humans so that her actual IQ may be higher. For example, one question asks the subject to "point to the two things that are good to eat." The objects shown are a block, an apple, a shoe, a flower, and an ice-cream sundae. According to Koko's gorilla tastes, the apple and the flower are good to eat. Another question asks the child where he or she would run for shelter from the rain. The choices are a hat, a spoon, a tree, and a house. Koko, of course, chose the tree. Responses such as these must be scored as errors.

Koko's use of sign language goes far beyond indicating objects. She asks and answers questions. She tells Penny when she feels happy or sad. She shows empathy for fellow animals. Seeing a horse with a bit in its mouth, she signed, "Horse sad." When asked why the horse was sad, she signed, "Teeth."

Despite some scholars' conviction that animal intellect is tied to the here and now, Koko can make reference to past and future events. She uses the sign "later" to postpone discussion of unpleasant subjects. She deliberately lies to avoid blame. Although lying may not represent moral progress, it does involve progress of another sort: the ability to engage in "make believe," the use of symbols to describe something that never happened. For example, Penny caught the gorilla trying to poke a hole through the window screen with a chopstick. When Penny demanded to know what was going on, Koko signed "smoke" and "mouth" to indicate she had been "smoking" the chopstick.

The gorilla shows a sense of humor and insults her human companions. She gives definitions to objects; asked "What is a stove?" she points to the stove. "What do you do with it?" Koko signs, "Cook with."

Penny believes Koko is developing self-esteem. When she asked Koko, "Are you an animal or a person?" Koko instantly replied, "Fine animal gorilla."

The gorilla is toilet trained and helps clean up her room in the mobile home where she lives. However, after cleaning the floor, she usually tears up the sponge!

Source:

Summarized from Patterson, Francine. "Conversations with a gorilla." *National Geographic*, 154 (October, 1978): 438-65.

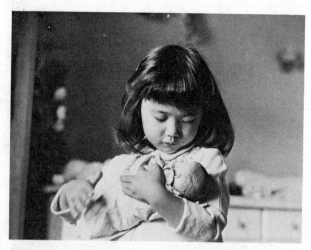

Children learn how to be masculine or feminine. Parents encourage certain behaviors, such as girls playing with dolls, and discourage others, such as boys having tea parties. Such operant conditioning is one way that children learn proper behavior for boys and girls.

pecking at the keys and, eventually, pecks the red key. The red key, when depressed, releases food. Because this particular response was rewarded, the pigeon will, after a few trials, go directly to the red key when hungry. In avoidance learning, an animal would be exposed to a noxious stimulus, such as an electric shock. In that case, it would learn to prevent punishment by pressing a certain key. In general, though, punishment is not a very reliable way of shaping future behavior. It stops unwanted behavior for the moment but, for various reasons, its effects on future behavior tend to be somewhat uncertain.

Children learn many of their socialization lessons through operant conditioning. Parents positively reinforce desired verbal response, such as "please" and "thank you." Little boys are rewarded for being brave and not crying. Little girls are rewarded for being pretty and ladylike. Parents punish unwanted behavior, such as rude talk, selfishness, or taking candy from stores without paying for it.

Although children do learn by operant conditioning, complications inevitably arise whenever results from pigeon and rat experiments are extrapolated to human beings. For one thing, experimenters consciously de-

cide what they want the animals to learn. But such human learning is accidental. In addition, human beings find a much broader range of responses rewarding or punishing than do animals. Imagine this scene. A mother and her three-year-old daughter are in the kitchen. The child is bored and wants attention. Because the mother is busy, she is ignoring the child's chatter. Eventually, the little girl repeats the word she heard her father say that morning when he cut himself shaving. The mother, shocked by the profanity, scolds the child but unwittingly reinforces the vulgar response through giving the bored child attention. Guess what the little girl learned that day?

Imitation, the third type of learning, was discovered through research on the social behavior of human beings. Bandura and Walters (1963) have shown that children can learn novel response patterns through observing another's behavior. No reinforcement or reward is required for such learning to occur. Imitative learning does not involve the gradual building up of responses required by operant conditioning.

Language appears to be learned mainly through imitation. Consider that if children had to learn speech through operant conditioning, they would be senior citizens before they mastered their native language. Each sound, syllable, word, and sentence would have to be uttered spontaneously, then systematically reinforced by the parents. Instead, children copy the language behavior of their adult models (and learn the meaning behind the language forms), just as they imitate other forms of behavior. Children are especially likely to imitate adult models who are warm, nurturant, and powerful. In families that are functioning effectively, the child's parents provide extremely influential models. Models are also provided when trial and error learning is likely to have dangerous consequences; parents *show* their children how to cross streets and how to drive automobiles.

Unintentional learning often occurs through imitation, as well as through classical and operant conditioning. Although a father may deliberately demonstrate to his son the movements involved in tying shoe laces, he does not set out to teach the boy his vocal inflections or facial expressions. Similarly, parents often tell children one thing and model quite another. For example, parents may preach that reading books is worthwhile but never read themselves. Their child is more likely to copy parental deeds than parental words.

Piaget's Cognitive Developmental Approach

The career of Swiss psychologist Jean Piaget began early. At age ten, he published an article on a rare albino sparrow in a natural history journal. Four years later, he was considered for a position as a curator in a Geneva museum. When this creative child's age was discovered, the offer was hastily withdrawn (Hetherington and Parke, 1979).

Piaget's concern with moral thought is a particularly important dimension of his general theory of how children think, reason, and remember. He observed children playing marbles and asked them to explain the game to him. He in turn talked to them about such ethical concepts as stealing, cheating, and justice. In many respects, childhood games are small-scale analogies of society. When children learn about the rules of the game, they are learning, at their level, about the norms of society. Similarly, when they learn to play game roles, they are also learning something about playing societal roles.

From his observations and discussions, Piaget concluded that two stages of moral thought exist. Children from four to eight years display the more primitive level of morality, **moral realism**. The second stage, **moral autonomy**, develops after the age of eight. Several characteristics are associated with each stage.

The moral realist judges wrongdoing in terms of the outcome of the act. Extenuating circumstances and the intentions of the wrongdoer are disregarded. For example, Piaget told his subjects stories about two boys, John and Henry, and asked them to decide which boy deserved the more severe punishment. John was summoned to the dinner table. He came immediately. As he entered the dining room, he knocked over a teacart which, unknown to him, had been left behind the door. John's collision with the teacart resulted in fifteen broken cups. The other boy, Henry, had been forbidden by his mother to eat jam. When his mother left the room, Henry climbed up to the cupboard in search of the jam and knocked a cup to the floor.

Children under seven years, in the moral realism stage, believed that John should be punished more severely. After all, John had broken fifteen cups while Henry had broken only one. However, the older children, the moral autonomists, were more concerned with the fictitious boys' reasons for acting rather than the consequences of the acts. These older children felt that Henry deserved the greater punishment, because his offense had been committed while disobeying his mother's order. John's offense, on the other hand, had been accidental.

The moral realist believes that all rules are sacred and unchangeable absolutes. Rules are handed down by adult authority, and not the slightest deviation from them should be tolerated. The moral autonomist, by contrast, views rules as somewhat arbitrary social conventions. Older children involved in a game agree that certain rules are appropriate or inappropriate to that particular game situation. When the players consent to change, new rules can be adopted.

For example, the moral realist would agree that the child able to knock the most marbles out of a circle drawn in the dirt should have the first turn. Asked why, the moral realist would answer, "That's the rule. That's the way things are done." The moral autonomist would also agree that turns are decided by this preliminary trial. However, the older child would explain the procedure this way: "Well, the first turn has to be decided somehow. There are probably other ways to do it, but we decided to do it this way, and it works fine."

Piaget believes that maturation of cognitive capacities is the primary determinant of moral thought. This cognitive development results from the interaction of genetic capacities and social experiences. According to Piaget, it is the child's interaction with peers, rather than parents, that provides crucial social experiences for the development of morality. For one thing, freewheeling games with other children show that rules are conventional products that arise out of cooperation. Parents, on the other hand, are often reluctant to debate the reasons for their rules and regulations. This

Which of these containers holds more water? Even though he has just seen the water from the short container being poured into the tall container, this child will notice only the higher water level and say that the tall, thin container holds more water.

authoritarian stance promotes the younger child's view of rules as arbitary and immutable. That briefly is Piaget's approach. Many studies have borne him out, showing that children from different cultures and social class backgrounds do go through a stage of moral realism before they reach moral autonomy.

Lawrence Kohlberg (1976) is currently studying moral development in the Piaget tradition. In his procedure, those being interviewed are asked to respond to moral dilemmas such as this:

In Europe, a woman was near death from cancer. One drug might save her, a form of radium that a druggist in the same town had recently discovered. The druggist was charging $2,000, ten times what the drug cost him to make. The sick woman's husband, Heinz, went to everyone he knew to borrow the money, but he could only get together about half of what it cost. He told the druggist that his wife was dying and asked him to sell it cheaper or let him pay later. But the druggist said, "No." The husband got desperate and broke into the man's store to steal the drug for his wife. Should the husband have done that? (Kohlberg, 1969.)

From his analysis of children's responses to these dilemmas, Kohlberg concluded that moral thought develops through six stages rather than the two hypothesized by Piaget.

Psychoanalytic Theory

Psychoanalytic theory, as formulated by the Viennese physician Sigmund Freud (1856-1939), is both a theory of personality and a system of therapy. (See Brill, 1938.) As a theorist, Freud was not an orthodox Freudian. He insisted that his psychoanalytic disciples be passive listeners and never respond emotionally to their patients. However, Freud himself gossiped, cracked jokes, offered advice, and often surprised his patients by handing them photographs of himself (*Time* Magazine, March 8, 1982).

Freud's theory views socialization as society's attempt to tame the child's inborn animal-like nature. He believed the roots of human behavior lie in the irrational, unconscious dimensions of the mind. He assumed that the adult personality is the product of the child's early experiences within the family.

Freud saw the personality as composed of three energy systems: the Id, the Ego, and the Super-ego. The **Id** is the biological basis of personality, the **Ego** is the psychological basis of personality, and the **Super-ego** is the social basis of personality (Shaw and Costanzo, 1970).

The Id is the reservoir of inborn, biological instincts. This "seething cauldron of sex and hostility" is wholly unconscious. It seeks immediate gratification; it operates according to the pleasure principle. The selfish, impulsive Id is not in contact with the reality of the external world.

Unlike the Id, the Ego develops out of the child's learning experiences with the environment. If all of the Id's desires were gratified, the Ego would never emerge. The Ego encompasses the cognitive functions of thinking, perceiving, and memory. It also contains the defense mechanisms (such as rationalization, repression, projection) which have emerged from the Ego's previous encounters with reality. Part of the Ego is conscious and part is unconscious. The Ego's primary purpose is to direct the personality toward realistic goals; it is oriented toward the reality principle. Therefore, the Ego mediates among the demands of the Id, the Super-ego, and the external world.

The Super-ego, or conscience, emerges as a result of the child's identification with her or his parents. Through reward, punishment, and example, the parents communicate society's rules to the child. When these social values and behavioral standards have been "introjected" (adopted as the child's own standards), the Super-ego censors the Id's impulses. This internal authority also guides the Ego's activities.

Freud held that every child goes through a series of personality development stages, each stage marked by sexual preoccupation with a different part of the body – the mouth, the anus, the genital area. Personality development, according to psychoanalytic theory, is essentially complete by five years of age.

Erikson's Revisions. Freud's ideas have been revised by his many disciples, especially Erik Erikson (1902-   ). Though Erikson entered Freud's Viennese circle as a 25-year-old itinerant artist, with no university degree at all, he emerged as a prominent child psychoanalyst. As well, he contributed the term "identity crisis" to our everyday language (Ewen, 1980).

Erikson's (1963, 1968) ideas about socialization differ from Freud's in four ways:

1. Erikson is convinced that the rational Ego has an important independent role in personality development. The irrational Id is played down in his thinking.
2. One function of his autonomous Ego is to preserve a sense of identity and to avoid identity confusion. While patients in Freud's time suffered from sexual inhibitions, contemporary patients are plagued with questions of who they are or what they should believe in.
3. Freud's biological theory holds that "anatomy is destiny." By contrast, Erikson's theory emphasizes

society's role in molding personality. What is really involved here is a matter of degree.
4. According to Erikson, personality development continues throughout the life cycle from infancy to old age. It does not stop at five years of age. Adolescents have the problem of establishing their identity. Young adults must establish intimacy with others in deep friendships and marriage, without sacrificing this sense of identity. Middle-aged adults are preoccupied with productivity and generativity (providing guidance for the next generation). Mature adults are concerned with ego integrity, a conviction that the life they have lived has meaning (Ewen, 1980). Growth continues through all of these developmental crises.

Other writers besides Erikson disagree with Freud's belief that personality development ends with childhood. "Life crisis," "critical transitions" (Levinson, 1978), "turning points," "passages" (Sheehy, 1974) have all recently entered popular culture, though research is needed to establish whether life transitions are biologically linked, invariant, or necessarily traumatic (Bush and Simmons, 1981). Their discussion does signal that socialization occurs over the life span.

Symbolic Interactionist Views

Symbolic interactionism, as a theoretical perspective on primary socialization, is more sociological than any of the approaches discussed so far. Like learning theory, it emphasizes the environmental influences that impinge on the child, rather than the unfolding of the child's biological capacities. (Both Piaget and Freud stressed the latter.) However, symbolic interactionism directs particular attention to the impact of the social environment. The term "interactionist" emphasizes the importance of group influences. These theorists also take issue with the Freudian position of fundamental conflict between individual and society. Symbolic interactionists view the individual and society as two sides of the same coin. One cannot exist without the other.

Interactionists and learning theorists differ on two other major assumptions. Interactionists believe that human behavior is qualitatively different from animal behavior, because humans use much more complex language. This assumption is the reason for the word "symbolic" in their title. Since symbolic interactionists feel that social scientists should focus their analysis on qualities that differentiate *Homo sapiens* from the lower animals, they adopt the related position (contradictory to behaviorists) that sociologists must study how people define and interpret reality.

Finally, symbolic interactionists emphasize the importance of the child's active involvement in role learning processes such as role taking (discussed below) and altercasting, as opposed to the more passive processes of modelling or conditioning. "Altercasting" involves casting the other person in a role we choose from him or her in order to manipulate the situation (Charon, 1979). For instance, a child may say, "Toby, you're supposed to let me use your bike, because friends are supposed to share" (Weinstein, 1969).

Although the symbolic interactionists are interested in many facets of socialization, we will concentrate here on the question of how the child acquires a self. We will consider the pertinent work of two pioneer theorists – Charles H. Cooley and George Herbert Mead.

Cooley's Looking-Glass Self. Cooley was an American sociologist who derived many of his ideas about socialization from observing and recording the behavior of his own children. He used the metaphor of the looking glass to illustrate his point that children acquire a self through adopting other people's attitudes toward them. The self is social in that it emerges out of interaction with primary group members. Its content reflects the children's interpretation of others' appraisals of what kind of person they are.

The **looking-glass self** has three elements (Cooley, 1902):

the imagination of our appearance to the other person, the imagination of his judgment of that appearance, and some sort of self-feeling, such as pride or mortification.

Notice that what is important here is the child's interpretation of other people's attitudes. This interpretation may or may not be accurate. A little boy may pick up messages from his parents that they think

he is short, fat, and clumsy, and that they think being short, fat, and clumsy is deplorable. If the assessment of his extremely authoritative parents is not countered by other sources of opinion, the boy has little choice but to define himself as short, fat, and clumsy. In all likelihood, therefore, he will feel ashamed of himself. Cooley was arguing, as we would put it today, that both self-imagery and self-esteem are social products.

Mead's Theory of the Self. In formulating his ideas about the child's acquisition of the self, Mead elaborated upon many of the insights of Cooley, his symbolic interactionist contemporary. Mead's ideas on the subject are, however, much more sophisticated than Cooley's. Mead's major work on the self is contained in *Mind, Self, and Society* (1934), a series of social philosophy lectures given at the University of Chicago, assembled after Mead's death. Although in his own lifetime Mead's impact was through ideas presented in lectures rather than through published works, he was not a charismatic teacher. In fact, he was boring. Schellenberg (1978) tells us that:

His lectures were not very dramatic occasions. He seldom looked at his students, and he spoke with little expression. Looking at the ceiling or out a window, he sat and calmly lectured on the subject of the day.

The word "self" has rather mystical connotations. In order to specify what he meant by the "self," Mead made three fundamental assumptions:

1. The newborn infant does not come equipped with a self. Although the infant is born with the physiological potential to reach this goal eventually, the self is acquired, not innate.

2. Mead defined "self" as that which is an object to oneself. At first glance, this definition does not seem to be very enlightening. However, Mead meant that the self is reflexive. To have a self is to have the ability to think about oneself and to act socially toward oneself. For most of us, the self is the most fascinating object in the world. We devote considerable time to self-contemplation. When we congratulate ourselves for an honest act or chastise ourselves for a piece of stupidity, we are acting toward ourselves.

3. The self is a communicative process, not a "thing." The self is analogous to a verb rather than a noun; it consists of the processes of thinking and acting toward oneself. The self is not a substantive entity that dwells behind the eyes or under the heart.

Genesis of the Self. Mead's complex explanation of how the child acquires a self can be summarized in a small number of central ideas.

The development of the self is dependent upon development of the capacity to use language. According to Mead, language and self develop concurrently. As a first step in developing self-awareness, the child must differentiate himself or herself as a separate "thing" from the myriad of other "things" in the environment. Through language, the child learns the names of things. This object is called a "chair," that one is called "Mommy." The child learns his or her name along with other object names: there is an object called "George." The child also learns the characteristics of objects. Fire is hot and dangerous. Chairs have four legs and are intended for sitting. Similarly, George learns what sort of object he is – a boy, little, someone who likes cookies. (See Chapter 4 for an application of this theory to gender socialization in particular.)

Both language and development of the self require "taking the role of the other." In order to communicate with another person, it is necessary to take the role of the other, that is, to adopt the other's point of view about what is being said. Suppose you greet me Monday

The family is the most important agent of socialization. The family has first and exclusive control during the early years when learning occurs rapidly. The family's social class, ethnic background, and geographical location all affect the child's socialization.

morning by asking, "How are you?" Before I can properly reply, I have to put myself in your shoes and decide whether you really want to hear all about my physical and psychological well-being or whether you are merely being polite. In the first case, I will tell you at great length how I am feeling. In the second, I will answer, "Fine, thank you."

The development of the self requires this ability to take the role of the other, which is a fundamental aspect of language use. Because the self is social, the child must be able to adopt the perspective of other people toward himself or herself. Having a self means viewing yourself through the eyes of other people.

Stages of Development of the Self. According to Mead, the ability to role play and the consequent

genesis of the self occur through the two main stages (Meltzer, 1978) described below.

1. During the *play stage,* the child begins role playing. The little girl pretends she is a mother or a teacher or a store clerk. What is important here is that the child is demonstrating the ability to adopt the mother's role (as one example), and to act back upon herself from the perspective of this role. In pretending that she is the mother scolding her imaginary child for lying, the little girl is placing herself in her own mother's shoes and reacting to her own behavior. This type of play indicates that the self is forming. However, the self at this stage is fragmentary because the child is taking the role of only one person at a time. The self lacks unity because the reflected view of

You and Your Self

The acquisition of personal identity, or a sense of self, is one of the major goals of socialization. Therefore, researchers often have occasion to measure this concept. Despite its centrality, the "self" remains elusive. One of the most frequently used measures of the self-concept is Kuhn and McPartland's (1954) Twenty Statements Test.

Before you complete this test, remember these three things.

First, the self is difficult to define. Although we know intuitively what we mean when we say we have a self, this label implies a number of related components. It can refer to the stream of consciousness, the self as experiencer of thoughts, emotions, physical sensations. As well, it implies the conviction of continuity over time. (This self who thinks, experiences, and acts

today is essentially the same self as the one who thought, experienced, and acted five and ten years ago.) Sometimes, the "self" means the director of action, the planner, and the doer. Sometimes, it means the cognitive picture of who I am, the self-concept. In addition, the sense of self encompasses an ideal self, the self that I wish I were. Related to the latter component is self-esteem, or my evaluation of myself. Finally, the material self, which includes my body and, perhaps, my possessions, seems to be involved.

The first task of researchers is to specify exactly which component of the self they wish to measure. Below, we will focus on the self-concept (Mead's "Me"), and define it as a "set of attitudes toward the self."

Second, techniques to measure the self are often vulnerable to the "social desirability effect," which is the tendency for research subjects to present a flattering view of themselves. For example, people who really regard themselves as neurotic and overweight may not care to reveal these thoughts to a researcher.

Third, measures of the self are sometimes affected by the context in which they are administered. If you complete the measure described below at university, those aspects of your self-concept related to being a student will probably be uppermost in your mind. If you complete it at home, however, family identities may supersede the student dimension of your self-concept.

The Twenty Statements Test

1. Write the numbers one to twenty on a page. The standard instructions for the test read as follows: "There are 20 numbered blanks on the page below. Please write 20 answers to the simple question "Who Am I?" in the blanks. Just give 20 different answers to the question. Answer as if you were giving the answers to yourself, not to somebody else. Write the answers in the order that they occur to you. Don't worry about logic or importance. Go along fairly quickly, for time is limited. Give yourself about ten minutes to complete the answers.

the self is a series of fragmented views, not a coherent whole.

2. A coherent self develops during the *game stage,* when the child becomes capable of taking a number of roles simultaneously. Mead used the game of baseball to explain this process. Playing baseball requires the ability to adopt several different roles at the same time. Being a catcher involves understanding the roles of pitcher, shortstop, opposing team member up to bat, and so on. The events in a particular game must be understood from all of these various perspectives. The child manages this task by forming a composite role out of all the particularized roles. Mead called this generalized standpoint from which the child viewed himself or herself the **generalized other**. He called the corresponding standpoint involved in the earlier

play stage the **significant other**. During the play stage, the child might think, "Dad says I am bad when I tell lies." During the game stage, the child now things, "*They* say lying is wrong." Behavior thus comes increasingly to be guided by an abstract moral code rather than the opinion of one individual.

Mead's ideas imply that self-development does not stop in childhood. As the person adopts new roles and encounters new situations, the self will continue to evolve (Bush and Simmons, 1981).

The "I" and the "Me." Mead's formulation of the self makes room for both a socially defined aspect of the self (which was stressed above) and a spontaneous, creative aspect of the self. The **Me** represents the self-concept, especially internalized societal atti-

---

2. Next, the researcher classifies each of the 20 answers as either "consensual" or "nonconsensual" references. By "consensual references," Kuhn and McPartland meant groups and classes whose limits and conditions of membership are matters of common knowledge (for example, student, male, wife, Baptist, youngest child). By "nonconsensual references," they meant groups, classes, attributes, or traits which require interpretation by the individual. These statements are either ones without positional reference (happy, tall) or consensual references whose meaning is obscured by ambiguous modifiers (good student, ungrateful daughter).

Go through your twenty answers and write "consensual" or "nonconsensual" beside each of them.

3. The final step is to compute your "locus score." The "locus score" is the total number of consensual references made. The TST was designed to measure Mead's "Me," the self as a social entity. The locus score is intended to provide an indicator of the social anchorage of the self, because it measures citations of social positions.

Some Comparative TST Results

You might find it interesting to compare your own TST results with some of its developers' findings. Differences do not mean that you are abnormal in any way.

1. Most people tend to exhaust all their consensual responses first, before going on to nonconsensual responses. For example, a person might describe himself as "male," "a university student," "a son," "22 years old," and then as "athletic," "skinny," and so on. However, the actual locus score may vary from none to twenty. Kuhn and McPartland argued that the self-descriptions given early are the most important ones. Therefore, they felt that the fact that the consensual responses come first provided evidence for the social nature of the self.

2. The locus score increases with age as people acquire an increasing number of social statuses. The average locus score for seven-year-olds is 5.8, and for twenty-four-year olds, 11.0.

3. Females mention their gender earlier than do males. Of those uni-

versity undergraduates mentioning gender at all, the mean rank for females was 1.7, and for males, 2.5.

4. Respondents nineteen to twenty-two years old mentioned their age in average rank order of 5.6.

5. Most TST responses fall into five general categories: social groups and classifications (such as age, gender, occupation, marital status, kinship relations, ethnicity); ideological beliefs (statements of a religious, philosophical, or moral nature); interests; ambitions; selfevaluations. The fifth category can be analyzed as an indicator of self-esteem.

Source:

Kuhn, Manford H. "Self-attitudes by age, sex and professional training." *Sociological Quarterly,* 9:39-55, 1960; Kuhn, Manford H., and Thomas S. McPartland. "An empirical investigation of self-attitude." *American Sociological Review,* 19:68-76, 1954.

tudes and expectations. The **I**, on the other hand, is the acting, unique, unfettered self.

Unlike the Freudian Id, Ego, and Super-ego, the I and the Me collaborate. The I provides individuality and initiative for behavior, while the Me provides direction for that behavior according to the dictates of society. Remember, though, that the self is a process and that the I and Me are phases of that process, not concrete entities.

Theoretical Overview

The ideas of the learning theorists, and of Piaget, Freud, and the symbolic interactionists all contribute to our understanding of childhood socialization. The learning theorists focus on the specific mechanisms involved in socialization. They tell us *how* the child learns the lessons of socialization. Piaget's work, on the other hand, analyzes the development of morality. Both Freud and Mead are also concerned with the question of how society's notions about proper behavior are internalized by the child. Their theories also address other questions. Freud emphasizes emotions, sexuality, and the unconscious. In addition, his theory provides many ideas concerning the role played by specific family members in socializing the child. Finally, Mead and Cooley emphasize the social context of child development. The linkage they isolated between emergence of self-awareness and the acquisition of language is extremely insightful. The work of these people, then, should be seen as complementary rather than competing systems of thought.

AGENTS OF SOCIALIZATION

The socialization process involves many different types of influence that impinge upon people throughout their lives. This part of our discussion will concentrate on four major socialization agents: the family, the peer group, the school, and the mass media. The agents singled out here are important because they affect almost every Canadian. In addition, they all exert a powerful influence during the impressionable childhood years.

Society has charged two of these agencies, the family and the school, with the socialization of children. Although much of the impact they have upon children is unintentional, both the family and the school also deliberately set out to equip children with the knowledge required to fit into adult society. The influence of the peer group and the media is, frequently, unintentional.

Family

A point of agreement among almost all of the childhood socialization theories that we discussed is that the family's impact upon the child transcends all the other agents of socialization. In Clausen's words (1968), "the 'widening world of childhood' spirals out from the parental home." Learning occurs rapidly during these crucial years of early childhood when the family has almost exclusive control and no relearning or contradictory lessons are involved. Moreover, learning takes place in the context of close emotional bonds. The family touches every sphere of the child's existence. The early immersion of the child within the family guarantees that the institution lays the foundation for the later and lesser influences of the other socialization agents, which are considerably more segmented. Chapter 11 offers more details about the nature and content of socialization by the family.

There is a second reason why sociologists assign primacy to the family. Various characteristics of the family orient the child to specific configurations of experiences, values, and opportunities. Growing up in the 10 percent of Canadian single-parent families is different than growing up in an "intact" family. Also, by being born into a particular family, the child automatically becomes part of a larger family – grandparents, aunts, uncles, cousins. Moreover, the family's social class position means that the child will learn one set of values, rather than another. The opportunities of a child born into an upper-middle-class family are considerably different from those of a child born into the working class. Social class, as we will see below, is the most studied demographic variation in socialization (Wright and Wright, 1976). The family's ethnic background is another important determinant of the content of socialization.

Finally, the family's geographical location is also the child's. Growing up in Toronto and growing up in rural Saskatchewan are quite different experiences.

Child as Socializer of the Parents.

The socialization that occurs within the family is a two-way process (Rheingold, 1969). The child is not just a passive recipient of parental influence. Just as the parents socialize the child, the child also socializes the parents.

Even in infancy, the child's demands and responses serve to teach the mother and father how to behave as parents. A newly married couple have, of course, many abstract ideas of what parenthood entails, which they have gleaned from observation, reading, and so on. Interaction with their first-born, however, teaches them the actual behaviors involved in the role of parents. For example, it is one thing to know that parents are responsible for their children when they are ill, and quite another to cope with a sick baby who cannot breathe properly at two in the morning.

As the child matures from infancy through adolescence to adulthood, the parents become aware of new facets of mothering and fathering. Though theorists tend to emphasize the early childhood years, it is also important to remember that the mutual parent-child influence often continues until the death of the parents.

Social Class.

Canadian society, like all other large societies, is socially stratified. (For a detailed discussion of the nature of stratification in Canada, see Chapter 8.) When sociologists talk about social stratification, they are referring to the arrangement of a "group or society into a hierarchy of positions that are unequal with regard to power, property, social evaluation, and/or psychic gratification" (Tumin, 1967). The occupations of the parents provide the best indicator of the Canadian family's social class position, and this position influences the child's socialization experiences and consequent opportunities.

Growing up in a lower-class (as opposed to a middle-class) home means less money. Satisfaction of such basic needs as housing, diet, medical and dental care, clothing, and so on is relatively less adequate. For example, poor people are more likely to grow up in overcrowded homes. The experience of overcrowding is associated with poor physical and mental health, poor child care, and poor social relations in the home (Gove, Hughes, and Galle, 1979). The amount of income at the family's disposal also determines less tangible aspects of socialization. Opportunities to read a wide variety of books, to visit museums, to travel, to attend camp, and so forth all widen the growing child's intellectual horizons, and all tend to narrow the parental purse. If the parents in a lower-class home are vulnerable to job lay-offs and unemployment, their feelings of powerlessness and insecurity will be communicated to their children. It is not surprising, therefore, that research shows adolescents from the higher social classes as having a higher level of self-esteem than adolescents from the lower social classes (Rosenberg, 1965).

Members of different social classes, by virtue of experiencing different conditions of life, come to see the world differently and develop different conceptions of social reality (Gecas, 1976; Kohn, 1977). Prince Charles' royal childhood provides an extreme example. In public, he walks behind the Queen and never refers to her as "my mother," let alone "Mummy" (Heald, 1982). Distinctive occupational backgrounds lead middle-class parents to be more likely than working-class parents to value self-direction, achievement, and deferred gratification. Blue-collar work typically requires little innovation and is highly supervised. Satisfactory performance requires conformity to external authority. In contrast, white-collar work demands individual initiative. Therefore, working-class parents value conformity in their children over self-reliance, while the opposite is true for middle-class parents (Ellis, Lee, and Petersen, 1978).

Recently, a cross-national study of child-rearing values was carried out among French- and English-speaking Canadians (as well as parents in the United States, Japan, and six European countries). Working-class parents almost everywhere were more likely than middle-class parents to be intolerant of children's insolence and temper, to restrict autonomy, to insist on good manners, and to wish to maintain male-female distinctions (Lambert, Hamers, and Frasure-Smith, 1980).

The class origins of a child remain important. They are a significant influence on the occupation that a child will eventually choose (Breton, 1972; Porter et al, 1973). Indeed, the evidence suggests that children have a high probability of achieving a class position very similar to that of their parents (Pike, 1975). Lower-class children are relatively less successful in school, leave school earlier, and have lower occupational aspirations. Middle-class parents are more likely to socialize their children to internalize the values of individualism, high motivation, and deferred gratification required for success in school (Pike, 1975).

Ethnicity.

Because Canada is not a melting pot, which culturally homogenizes its people, ethnicity exerts a major influence on many families. Although most Canadians share a common core of experiences and values, their socialization may also reflect ethnic differences in values, norms, and identity. The matter is further complicated by the fact that ethnic background and social class position are frequently related. For example, as you will see in Chapter 9, in comparison with most other ethnic groups, the British are overrepresented in the higher status occupations.

It is impossible, in the space available here, to inquire into all nuances of child socialization in nearly forty different ethnic groups. Instead, a brief discussion of English-Canadian French-Canadian similarities and differences in child training will serve to alert the reader to the fact that the term "the Canadian family" necessarily represents an abstract oversimplification (Ishwaran, 1976).

Lambert, Yackley, and Hein (1971) were interested in comparing the parent-child interaction of English-Canadian and French-Canadian parents. In order to do this, they observed the reaction of parents of six-year-olds to taped versions of a child's demands for attention, help, comfort, and displays of anger, insolence, and aggression. They found that English-Canadian mothers and French-Canadian fathers are the more active socializers in their respective families. They were more likely than their marital partners to comfort distressed children and to scold insolent children. English-Canadian parents were more punitive than their French-Canadian counterparts in their responses to children's displays of temper.

Parents of both ethnic backgrounds were harsher with boys than with girls. Both showed cross-gender favoritism. That is, mothers were more permissive with boys, and fathers with girls. Lambert et al (1971), suggest that their finding that the English-Canadian mother is the active socializer has special significance. Educational and occupational attainments are affected by the individual's need to achieve, and other studies (McClelland, 1961) have shown that the need to achieve is strengthened by mother dominance but impeded by father dominance.

French-speaking Canadian adolescents express a lower sense of control over life events than do their English-speaking counterparts for two reasons (Grabb, 1980). For one thing, the Francophones come from lower socioeconomic backgrounds, and lower SES is associated with fatalism and resignation. For another, Francophone child-rearing practices give less encouragement to children's independence and individualism.

Socialization by Siblings.

Brothers and sisters play an important role in socializing one another. An older sibling can provide a role model. The learning theorists tell us that children learn many of their socialization lessons through imitation. Also, a younger sibling gives the older child the opportunity to try some portion of the parental role on for size. Guiding and protecting a younger brother or sister helps the child internalize his or her parents' perspective. Much of the older child's influence is, of course, quite unintentional.

Sibling interaction provides practice in cooperation and competition. As Freud observed, sibling rivalry is one of the more emotional experiences encountered in growing up. Sibling comparisons have an impact on the child's developing self-image (Yussen and Santrock, 1978). All children are concerned about how smart, how big, how worthwhile they are. Children with nearby siblings arrive at some of these answers by comparing themselves with brothers or sisters. One dimension in this rivalry is sibling concern for equally

Peers are equals, and peer interaction, no matter what form it takes, constitutes a major social experience outside the home. Everyone, even the members of this punk rock band, needs the companionship and approval of peers, and the peer group remains important throughout life. (*Miller Services*)

fair treatment by parents. But, at times, brothers and sisters also provide useful allies against parents. The more adult-oriented only child benefits from the exclusive attention of the parents, but lacking siblings, may be somewhat unskilled in social relations with peers.

Peers

After the family, peers (other children approximately the same age) constitute the second most potent socialization agency. The importance of peer relations is not confined to human beings. Harlow and Harlow (1962) found that interaction with other infant monkeys compensated for most of the negative effects of the maternal deprivation undergone by the experimental groups of monkeys. The age-grading of Canadian society increases the impact of peer socialization; people in similar age categories tend to be segregated in schools, neighborhoods, and various recreational settings. Propinquity (simply being in the same place at the same time) tends to facilitate friendship.

Although children do not consciously set out to socialize one another, their need for companionship and approval results in mutual learning of a variety of information. Interaction with friends provides the first major social experiences outside the family circle. Peer relations allow children to begin to separate themselves from the family's all-encompassing influence and to develop other facets of their identity. One of the goals of socialization, remember, is the eventual ability to function independently of the family. Another point worth stressing is that peers share relatively equal power. This equality contrasts sharply with the power position of the child vis-à-vis the parents. There are some things that can be learned only from equal status peers. However, peer and family influences are not necessarily in opposition. Peers sometimes reinforce family socialization.

Peer Influence Throughout Life. From early childhood through to old age, people attach a great deal of importance to peer relationships (Brenton, 1974). Even young infants stare at each other with fascination. By the age of two, children play alongside each other. By three or four years old, this parallel play becomes shared play. Most parents know that companionship with other children is a necessity, not a luxury. They take pains to find little companions for their child and worry if their offspring does not seem to make friends. Within a few years, children are able to relate to groups of children. (Recall the emphasis both Piaget and Mead placed on games for the child's social development.) By eight or nine years, most children are concerned with having one special friend. (Many of us may remember being rejected by a best friend as one of the poignant tragedies of childhood.)

The intensity of the feelings surrounding childhood friendships provides one indicator of their importance. The amount of time spent with friends provides another. One study of American sixth grade children found that, over a weekend, these children spent more than twice as much time with their peers as with their parents (Condry, Siman, and Bronfenbrenner, 1968; cited in Yussen and Santrock, 1978).

Adolescence marks the peak of peer-group influence. The teenager's orientation to the companionship, opinions, and tastes of age-mates helps to bridge the gulf between childish dependence on the family and adulthood. Peer relations continue to matter a great deal to people in the middle adult years and on into old age. Although adults have more inner resources than children, they remain sensitive to the opinions of their friends.

Content of Peer Socialization. What do children learn from one another? Smith (1979) reminisces:

It was a pitiful wreck of a tarpaper hut, and in it I learned the difference between boys and girls, I learned that all fathers did that, I learned to swear, to play with myself, to sleep in the afternoon, I learned that some people were Catholics and some people were Protestants and some people were Jews, that people came from different places. I learned that other kids wondered, too, who they would have been if their fathers had not married their mothers, wondered if you could dig a hole right to the center of the earth, wondered if you could kill yourself by holding your breath.

Though the social scientist's answer to this question would fill volumes, it is possible to isolate at least some of the more notable types of learning. (The actual mechanisms of learning are, of course, those emphasized by the learning theorists, namely modeling and positive and negative reinforcement.)

Contact with peers provides opportunities to practice social roles and to develop interaction skills. For example, children gain experience in leader and follower roles. During Mead's game stage, they learn the meaning of all the interdependent roles involved in games, such as baseball. They learn to cooperate and to compete.

Egalitarian peer relations provide frequent opportunities for *role-making*, as opposed to *role-taking* (Gecas, 1981). While some roles are explicitly predefined in the culture and we take them, others can be created and modified to the actors' own specifications through interaction; that is, we make them. (Turner, 1962). People *take* military roles, and *make* friendship roles.

Peer interaction influences the child's self-concept. Age-mates provide a more valid source of comparison of attributes and performances than do either parents or older or younger siblings. The outcome of this self-evaluation has an impact on the child's self-image and self-esteem. The looking-glass self, then, reflects the child's interpretation of peer, as well as familial, judgments.

Peers are a source of information. Children interpret the world for one another in a manner adults cannot possibly duplicate. Adults are ignorant of many aspects of reality that matter greatly to their children, like the latest fads. Moreover, some sensitive topics are more easily discussed with peers than with adults, such as how babies are born or the etiquette of dating. Finally, that much of this peer information might be the wildest misinformation is beside the point and in no way minimizes its importance to the young people in question.

Peers influence one another's values and attitudes. The concern of parents to protect their offspring from bad influences reveals their recognition that children influence one another's values. Is religion nonsense? How important is school? Should people be judged by the clothes they wear and the amount of money they have? Piaget was well aware of the impact of peer experiences on moral development. Such ethical abstractions as rules, fair play, and honesty become meaningful in the give and take of peer interaction. Similarly, children teach each other attitudes toward such diverse subjects as eating turnips, East Indian classmates, and smoking grass.

School

Industrialized nations such as Canada assign to the school a major role in preparing children for adulthood. The knowledge and skills required to function effectively in urbanized, industrialized societies are too extensive and too complex for parents to convey to their offspring. The educational system performs two major functions for society (Parsons, 1959). The *socialization function* involves the internalization of commitment both to broad societal values and to doing the tasks that the society requires done. The *allocation function* refers to the channeling of people through programs of occupational preparation into positions in the socioeconomic structure. See Chapter 14 for details about how these functions are carried out.

Most children are eager to begin school. For the majority, enrolling in school is their first encounter with a formal institution. This significant step beyond the family circle represents "being grown up." For the first time, the child is treated not as a unique individual but as a member of a cohort. If Suzy is feeling grumpy and does not want to go out to play, her mother may abandon her plan to have a quiet house all to herself. At recess, however, regardless of her mood, Suzy will march out to the school playground with the other pupils. As a lone child at home, she gets her own way. But at school Suzy is "processed" as one of a "batch." Experiences like this prepare children for adulthood, where the demands of organizations often take priority over the individual's own wishes.

Some of the content of socialization is consciously planned; some is incidental to the school's stated goals. In addition, no two children have precisely the same school experiences. A variety of factors, such as the child's ability and temperament, the parents' attitudes toward academic success and their social class position, the teachers, and relations with the peer group, all influence what happens there. For example, to children from some ethnic minorities or from very poor environments the school may be an alien place (a resocialization context) that devalues what they have learned in their families (Gecas, 1981). Nonetheless, it is possible to offer some generalizations about the content of school socialization:

1. Formal Knowledge. The most obvious purpose of the school is to provide students with some of the information and skills required to function in society.
2. Values. Educational systems attempt to transmit to their charges some appreciation of the sentiments and goals considered important in our society (for example, motivation to achieve, individual responsibility, respect for other people's rights). In addition, the school plays a vital role in orienting the child to Canadian society as such, a function particularly important in a society such as ours, which fosters strong regional and ethnic identities and consumes American mass media.

The school also transmits values concerning ethnic groups within our society. The selection of school names serves as an interesting indicator of these values (Goldstein, 1981). Between 1880 and 1979 in Winnipeg, 79 percent of the schools were named after noteworthy Anglo-Saxons, 15 percent after persons of French origin, and only six percent after persons from other ethnic groups. Overall, this school-naming supports the preeminence of English culture. However, the decline in Anglo-Saxon names to 56 percent in the 1970s suggests a decline in popularity of Anglo-conformity.
3. Interpersonal Skills. Because elementary school represents most children's first experience in coping with the demands of a formal organization, new social skills are developed. Young pupils are confronted with impersonal rules for behavior – waiting his or her turn, being on time, cooperating – that are not rooted in parental or peer authority.
4. Self-Evaluation. Throughout childhood and adolescence, interaction at school provides reflections for the looking-glass self. The child needs to know what sort

of person he or she is, relative to others of the same age. Educational authorities judge all children according to universal criteria.

Although it is possible in general terms to comment on the school as socialization agent, Canadian schools provide young people with a wide variety of socialization experiences. For instance, Royal Military College, founded in Kingston, Ontario, in 1876, demands a 17-hour day of military discipline, ceremonial drills, and bilingual classes of their uniformed (male and female) cadets (Tausig, 1982). In 1977, a Linden, Alberta, Mennonite group that objected to the "lack of discipline, a permissive moral atmosphere and neglect of the Bible" in the public schools, formed their own "Christian" school. Religion is stressed and movies, television, and competitive sports are banned (Levy, 1979). When considering these two rather extreme examples, we should remember that school is an abstraction and children are really socialized by teachers, textbooks, and other pupils.

Teachers. When we think back to our days in elementary and junior high school, many of our thoughts revolve around particular teachers. Some are remembered as heroes or heroines and some as villains. Sometimes, we liked a particular subject, or school in general, because we had a warm, talented teacher that year. In contrast, perhaps our attitude toward school was soured by contact with an unpleasant teacher.

Teachers (and teacher-administrators) are powerful socialization agents because they are the human point of contact between pupils and the formal organization of the school (Martin and Macdonell, 1978). These people constitute young children's first exposure to adult authority outside the family. Although the teacher-student relationship is not devoid of emotion, the tie is considerably more impersonal than that of parent-child.

The teacher exercises influence on the child in several ways. He or she acts as the major vehicle for transmitting the school curriculum and associated values. The teacher interprets the wider society. As principal agents of socialization of the young, teachers play a key role in Quebec's struggle between French and English language groups (Murphy, 1981). In addition, the teacher sets up the rules of expected behavior and metes out punishment when these are broken. Finally, the teacher is a potential role model.

Textbooks. Schools also socialize through textbooks. The content of these books augments the information conveyed by teachers, and, as pupils advance through the educational system, an increasing proportion of their new knowledge is obtained through this more impersonal source.

Sociologists have been very interested in how texts affect students' attitudes towards, for example, racial groups (Pratt, 1975) and gender roles. (Pratt's research and its results are discussed in the boxed reading "Textbook Images of Ethnic Groups" in Chapter 2.) This concern for the attitudinal content of texts has its source partly in the nature of young readers. Particularly in the formative elementary school years, textbooks make up the bulk of reading material for many children. In addition, this assigned reading carries the cachet of authority because it is "official" school reading. For better or worse, therefore, texts have considerable potential for conveying social attitudes along with factual material. A related concern has been to provide children with Canadian, not American, texts. Extreme nationalism is, of course, a dangerous sentiment. However, parents are rightfully disturbed when their children are more familiar with John F. Kennedy, the Fourth of July, and the "Star Spangled Banner" than with their Canadian counterparts.

School Peers. The age-graded school system puts children into contact with a large number and variety of children their own age. Peer-group influence, noted above, is greatly accelerated once children enter school.

Some of this influence takes the form of peer reinforcement of school-related behavior, as when the children themselves adopt performance in academic work and semi-official activities such as sports as criteria for judgment of one another. In addition, school provides a context for the operation of youth subculture. Here, the socialization lessons may be irrelevant to school-sponsored values or may even contradict them.

Being accepted by one's peers is a serious matter. Research shows that children (as well as adults) sometimes judge one another by standards that seem rather odd. For example, McDavid and Harari (1966) measured grade school children's liking for particular first names, and another group of children's liking for classmates who bore these names. A high relationship was found between liking of names and liking of children. Probably the reason is that, other things being equal, people like what is familiar to them. A boy named "Peter" or "David" has a distinct peer acceptance advantage over one named "Horatio" or "Marion."

From an early age, children also respond to the physical appearances of other children. Nursery school children, whom adults judged as being physically unattractive, were not as well liked by their classmates as were more attractive children (Dion and Berscheid, 1972). Part of the reason children (as well as adults) like attractive children is that they extrapolate from appearance to assume that "beautiful is good" and "ugly is nasty." In other words, other desirable characteristics are assumed to go along with being good-looking. Conversely, unattractive children are assumed to possess undesirable traits. Peers, teachers, and other adults expect a nice-looking child to be intelligent, well behaved, and popular. Ugly children are expected to be bratty and stupid. In view of the looking-glass self notion, it is not surprising that attractive children score relatively high in self-esteem (Maruyama and Miller, 1975).

Both educational authorities and parents have been especially interested in the high school peer group and competition between its values and official school values. Considerable *homophily* characterizes this group. Homophily is the tendency to similarity in various attributes among persons who affiliate (Lazarsfeld and Merton, 1954). For example, adolescents whose friends use illegal drugs are also more likely to use drugs. The homophily stems both from a selection process where individuals choose friends who already resemble themselves and from a socialization process where individuals, irrespective of prior similarity, influence one another (Kandel, 1978). Tanner (1981) documents an association between rock music and adolescent rebellion among Edmonton, Alberta, high school students. The minority who reject school values identify with heavy rock. However, most of these students endorse school values and embrace the more conventional pop music found in the Top 40. However, when the issue is teenagers' future life goals and educational aspirations rather than their current lifestyles, parents are a more important influence than peers (Davies and Kandel, 1981).

Mass Media

The mass media – television, radio, newspapers, magazines, books, movies, records, tapes – are impersonal communication sources, and they reach large audiences. If you try to imagine what a week spent without any of these media would be like, you will gain some idea of the important part they play in the lives of most Canadians.

Child development experts have been particularly concerned about television as a socialization agent. TV has been called the "plug-in drug" (Winn, 1977). The average television set is on seven hours a day. Many children are zombie viewers, who watch anything and everything, "silent, immobile, mesmerized" (Goldsen, 1979). Canadian preschool children typically watch 20 hours a week, grade school children 22 hours (Murray and Kippax, 1979). Sleeping is the only activity that commands more of children's time. Television time is replacing hours of playtime, and, as we have seen, children learn both societal norms and social skills through their games. By the age of eighteen, children will have spent more time in front of the television than anywhere else, including school. However, the school also makes extensive use of television and other media as teaching devices. Indeed, the activities of all the socialization agencies – school, family, peer groups – are affected by the media.

The media reflect nearly every aspect of society, but these reflections are, of course, not necessarily accurate. Children see or hear world news. Their country is presented visually, along with its political leaders, diverse cultures, arts, and sports. Situation comedies picture what happens in other people's families. "Cops and robbers" shows present children with an astonishing number of violent crimes per evening. Media advertisements show children all the paraphernalia supposedly required for them to be happy, healthy, and respectable.

The ability of the media to influence children has become an extremely important issue. If children can learn to read from educational television, if they pressure parents to buy heavily advertised toys and breakfast cereals, and worse, if they learn to solve problems through violent means from watching crime shows, then the media constitute a socialization agent whose power is almost beyond imagination.

Unfortunately, tracing the direct effects of the media is a very difficult research task. When the media operate in the natural environment, their influence is one among many other factors. For example, if Peter behaves aggressively, is the cause the type of television program he watches, or his family, or his nasty temperament? On the other hand, experimental studies that attempt to control for variables besides media content become so artificial that their conclusions may not hold beyond the experimental situation.

In general, research on specific media effects does show that children are indeed influenced by their media consumption. Before we go on to describe some of this evidence, a major factor that reduces this influence must be emphasized. Children are exposed to media content in a social context. What they see and hear is monitored, at least to some extent, by parents. Similarly, their interpretation of media content is molded by the opinions of parents, teachers, and friends. Parents may forbid watching a particularly violent television series. They offer their own opinions on fighting as a way of solving differences of opinion, or the advisability of spending the contents of one's piggy bank on a heavily advertised toy. In other contexts, children are exposed to the points of view of the other socialization agents. These may or may not agree with the media's perspectives. In short, the media have an impact on children, but this impact is just one of the influences that shape a child's attitudes and behavior.

Frazer and Reid (1979) report that due to parental tutelage even young children are skeptical about television commercials and are able to differentiate commercials from programming. These researchers observed this scene. Charlie, a preschooler, is watching a Purina Cat Chow commercial featuring a number of cats dancing to the jingle, "Chow, Chow, Chow." He says, "That's dumb. Cats can't dance like that, 'cause Barney (the family cat) eats that stuff (Purina Cat Chow) and don't dance like that." His father responds, "You are very smart. You remember what we told you about TV advertising." Charlie answers, "Yea. They don't always tell the real truth, do they?"

We now turn to more specific considerations of the media as an agent of socialization.

Violence and the Media. Canada is a more violent society than we think. Public opinion polls show that substantial minorities approve of diverse forms of violence from movie portrayals of betrayed males beating up females, to use of force to keep Quebec in Confederation, to fighting in professional hockey (Smith, 1979). Most of the research on media influence upon children has been concerned with possible negative effects of exposure to violence. (For a discussion of the influence on children of the mass media's portrayal of gender roles, see Chapter 4.)

What messages, for example, do children take away from their Saturday morning cartoon sessions? Week after week, they see cartoon characters like the coyote in "Road Runner" being smashed with giant mallets, blown up with dynamite, and crushed by trains. That violence is a staple in the television diet made available to Canadian children has been well established. Waters and Malamud (1975) claim that by the time the average child is sixteen years old, that child will have witnessed more than 13 000 television killings.

Learning psychologists have shown that children imitate the behavior of adults on film. Bandura, Ross, and Ross (1963) exposed nursery school children to an adult who modeled unusual forms of physical and verbal aggression toward an inflated Bobo doll. The children themselves later displayed precisely imitative aggressive responses toward the doll. Bandura et al, report that the filmed models were as effective as live models.

Critics of the Bobo doll experiment have pointed

Youngster Dies Trying to Copy Houdini Escape

RICHMOND, B.C. (CP) – A twelve-year-old boy died while trying to recreate an escape feat performed by the famous magician Harry Houdini, says coroner Dr. Dick Talmey.

John Baartman was found Jan. 9, bound in chains, hanging from the balcony of his home in this Vancouver suburb. Police first thought the death was a suicide.

But the coroner's report released this week ruled the death accidental, saying there were no reasons for Baartman to have committed suicide. The report said the boy died of asphyxiation due to strangulation.

The boy, who was described as bright, an enthusiastic reader, and a frequent library user, was enraptured by a television movie on Houdini aired a few days before his death, the report says.

After the movie, he did library research on Houdini, apparently to try to reproduce the escape act which is believed to have involved an attempt to free himself from chains while suspended in mid-air.

Source:

The Calgary Herald, March 4, 1982.

---

out that the doll was the type of toy that invited aggression. Also, since the filmstrip used in the experiment lacked a plot, it contained no justification for the adult's violence. Therefore, its similarity to a television program has been questioned. Many other experiments, however, do support the conclusion that children are susceptible to impersonal examples presented to them through the media.

The Ontario Royal Commission on Violence in the Communications Industry (Thatcher, 1978) also found cause for concern in the way newspapers report violence. A tendency was found for newspapers to focus on the violence in isolation from the context or issues involved.

Similarly, Huggins and Straus (1978) did a content analysis of 125 classic or recommended children's books, for the period 1850 to 1970. They found that the typical children's book had two violent incidents for every fifteen pages. A third of these violent incidents involved someone being killed. These researchers found that the amount of violence remained the same over the 120-year period studied.

Two different positions exist on the effect of media violence. The observational-learning position, taking its cue from research such as Bandura et al (1963), the Bobo doll study, holds that the media do encourage children to solve their problems by violent means. Constant exposure to media content "normalizes" violence; society is violent, and that is the way things are. The opposite position is that violence in the media provides a catharsis; that is, the individual's frustra-

tions are relieved or purged through vicarious participation in media violence. Alfred Hitchcock's defense (quoted in Schellenberg, 1974) of his own television program illustrates the catharsis position:

One of television's great contributions is that it brought murder back into the home where it belongs. Seeing a murder on television can be good therapy. It can help work off one's antagonisms. If you haven't any antagonisms, the commercials will give you some.

Despite the methodological problems involved in establishing a direct causal link between media content and children's attitudes and behavior, available research tends to support the observational-learning position rather than the catharsis position. Both the Ontario Royal Commission on Violence in the Communications Industry and the United States Surgeon General's Advisory Committee report, *Television and Growing Up: The Impact of Televised Violence* (1972), expressed grave concern about violence in the media. Although other variables are involved, televised violence is one factor in the production and maintenance of violence in our society (Murray and Kippax, 1979).

Learning about Occupations. Both boys and girls learn that they must eventually choose an occupation. Canadian males have always been expected to work and to support their families; increasingly, females are discovering that adulthood involves a combination of work in the labor force and family activities. Therefore, an important aspect of the socialization

These two women have chosen occupations usually occupied by men. They're posing in their ill-fitting work clothes to demonstrate how difficult it is to find outfits to suit female linemen and mechanics. (*Winnipeg Free Press*)

process is providing children with some understanding of the world of work.

The media's beneficial socialization effects were established by DeFleur and DeFleur's (1967) study of television's role in occupational learning. (The discussion of television's contribution to occupational socialization also provides a good illustration of its unintentional influence on children; children go to television to be entertained, but while being entertained, they absorb much incidental information about their society.)

DeFleur and DeFleur attempted to measure how much a sample of 237 American children, six to thirteen years of age, knew about the work involved in and the prestige ranking of eighteen selected occupations. They also tried to disentangle the relative contributions of television, personal contact, and general culture as sources of occupational knowledge.

The children were asked to respond to cartoon-like representations of the various occupations. "Personal contact occupations" were jobs with which the ordinary child has direct contact: minister, teacher, owner of small grocery, mailman, supermarket clerk, and school janitor. "Television contact occupations" were jobs that children do not encounter personally, but which were well represented in local television programs: judge, lawyer, reporter, head waiter, butler, bellhop. Finally, "general culture occupations" are widely understood by adults in the community, but rarely seen by children, either in person or on television: bank president, electrical engineer, general accountant, skilled printer, shipping clerk, and hospital orderly.

DeFleur and DeFleur chose the three sets of occupations in order to measure the relative influence of the three sources of learning. Personal contact with an occupation proved to be the most effective source of learning. It should be noted, however, that most of these occupations are also portrayed on television. The impact of television was demonstrated by the finding that children were more knowledgeable about the "invisible" occupations shown on television, than they were about the "invisible" occupations not seen on television, that is, the general culture occupations. Moreover, children who watched television frequently were better informed than were infrequent viewers on the television contact occupations. However, the amount of viewing did not influence knowledge of the other two sets of occupations. Here, we can see how researchers attempt to isolate media influence from other types of influence.

DeFleur and DeFleur (1967) concluded that the information television provides children about occupations tends to be superficial and misleading. These stereotypes portrayed clever, unethical lawyers; temperamental, eccentric artists; burly, aggressive truck drivers; and so on.

And, as one might expect, children's knowledge about occupations was found to increase with age. A more recent Canadian study (Baxter, 1976) also found that older boys' perceptions of occupational prestige resembled adult perceptions of occupational prestige. Also, middle- and upper-class children knew more about the work roles and their relative prestige than did lower-class children.

An Overview

This section has dealt with the influence of major socialization agents: the family, the peer group, the schools, the mass media. Children are, of course, also socialized by such institutions as Sunday school and the church, by such community organizations as the YWCA and the YMCA, with their athletic and camping activities.

As children mature into adults, they encounter an increasing diversity of socialization agents that help them to learn relatively more specialized roles. For example, a considerable amount of occupational socialization occurs on the job. Young interns learn how to be effective doctors partly by attending medical school (Chappell and Colwill, 1981), and partly by practicing on hospitalized patients. Newly divorced adults are often socialized into the single role through self-help groups such as Parents without Partners. Many universities offer noncredit courses on topics such as effective parenting, coping with divorce and widowhood, and reentry into the labor market by women who have been full-time housewives for many years. On the whole, adult socialization agencies tend to be impersonal – formal organizations such as universities, technical colleges, corporations, social welfare agencies, and the like. Nonetheless, family and peers continue to be important influences throughout life.

OVERSOCIALIZATION

Throughout this chapter, we have contended that the socialization process serves both society and the individual. Societal order and continuity depend upon members learning to share values, norms, and language. Interaction and role playing rest upon these common understandings. On the other hand, socialization allows individuals to realize their potential as human beings.

Because socialization is such a powerful process, there is a danger of those who read about it ending up with what Wrong (1961) called the "oversocialized conception of man." By this term, Wrong meant that people are completely molded by the norms and values of their society. Such thoroughgoing indoctrination would, of course, destroy individuality and render nonsensical free will and responsibility for one's actions.

But this does not happen. It is quite true that people brought up in a particular society speak the same language, value much the same things, and behave in a similar fashion. Fortunately, however, they are not all identical products turned out by an omnipotent socialization factory. There are many reasons why absolute conformity just does not occur.

To begin with, each person is biologically unique. The raw material of temperament and inborn aptitudes leave considerable room for individuality. In addition, human beings possess the ability to question norms and values and to innovate. The theorists of socialization also allowed for some measure of independence. Mead acknowledged the spontaneous, creative I, as well as the socialized Me. Similarly, Freud's personality structure theory contained the impulsive, selfish Id, as well as the conventionalized Super-ego. Individuals also make roles as well as take roles, as they modify situations to suit themselves.

Furthermore, although nearly everyone is socialized within the family, the actual content of children's socialization varies from family to family. Even brothers and sisters brought up in the same home experience growing up somewhat differently. And though we can speak of societal norms and values, these are really abstractions that must be interpreted by specific agencies of socialization; the people responsible for teaching the child to fit into society have differing interpretations of these norms and values. Finally, socialization is carried out by multiple agencies, which implies that the person being socialized is exposed to diverse perspectives.

All of this means that although we can speak about Canadians in general, and in so doing distinguish them from Japanese or Brazilians, we are talking about characteristics that make Canadians similar, not identical. The existence of at least some deviant behavior within every society, including our own, testifies to the fact that no system of socialization is perfectly efficient.

SUMMARY

1. Through socialization, individuals develop selfhood and acquire the knowledge, skills, and motivations required for them to participate in social life. This symbiotic learning process is functional for both the individual and the society. From the individual's point of view, intense interaction with adult caretakers allows the infant to realize its human potentialities. Later socialization equips the person to handle societal roles. In addition, socialization insures that commitment to the social order is maintained over time.

2. Sociologists have distinguished four types of socialization. "Primary socialization" refers to the learning that occurs in childhood. It lays the foundation for all later learning. "Adult socialization" describes the socialization that takes place beyond the childhood years. "Anticipatory socialization" is the role learning that occurs in advance of the actual playing of roles. "Resocialization" occurs when a new role or situation requires that a person replace established patterns of behavior with new patterns.

3. Since the turn of the century, social scientists have been perplexed about the relative contributions of biology and environment to human development. More recently, however, evidence that both factors interact to transform the infant into a functioning member of society resulted in the abandonment of the overly simplistic nature-nurture debate.

4. There are four major theoretical approaches to childhood socialization: learning theory, the cognitive-developmental approach, psychoanalytic theory, and symbolic interactionism. Learning theory explains the precise mechanisms involved in socialization. Piaget's work focuses on the development of morality. The psychoanalytic approach analyzes the development of personality structure. The symbolic interactionists emphasize the child's acquisition of language and self.

These approaches are complementary, rather than competing, systems of thought.

5. There are four major agents of childhood socialization: the family, the school, the peer group, and the mass media. Because society has given the family and the school a mandate to socialize youngsters, both of these agencies deliberately attempt to equip them with the knowledge and values required to fit into adult society. The influence of the peer group and the media is, for the most part, unintentional.

6. Socialization is a lifelong process. Primary socialization cannot possibly equip individuals for all the roles and situations they will encounter throughout their lives. Compared to primary socialization, adult socialization tends to concentrate on overt behavior (as opposed to values and motives). It tends to be realistic, rather than idealistic; to be more specific in content; and to occur in formal organizations, rather than informal contexts. In addition, the relationship between socializer and the one socialized in the adult situation is marked by lower levels of feeling and power than in the childhood situation.

7. The "oversocialized conception of human beings" is a viewpoint that exaggerates the effectiveness of the socialization process. Socialization does not mold members of society into identical products. Fortunately, there is considerable room for spontaneity and individuality.

GLOSSARY

Adult socialization. Socialization that takes place after childhood to prepare people for adult roles, e.g., husband, mother, computer technician.

Anticipatory socialization. Role learning that occurs in advance of the actual playing of roles.

Classical conditioning. Type of learning that involves the near-simultaneous presentation of an unconditioned stimulus (UCS) and a conditioned stimulus (CS) to an organism in a drive state (the state during which needs such as hunger or thirst require satisfaction). After several trials, the previously neutral stimulus (CS) alone produces the response normally associated with the UCS.

Ego. The director of the Freudian personality. The Ego attempts to mediate among the demands of the Id, the Super-ego, and the external world. The Ego, which encompasses the cognitive functions and the defense mechanisms, is governed by the reality principle.

Generalized other. Mead's "organized community or social group which gives to the individual his unity of self." Although the equivalence of terms is not exact, "reference group" is the more modern way of referring to this notion of the organized attitudes of social groups.

I. Mead's dimension of the self which is acting, spontaneous, creative, and unpredictable. The I is seen as a component of a process, not a concrete entity.

Id. The reservoir of inborn, biological propensities in the Freudian personality structure. The selfish, impulsive Id operates according to the pleasure principle.

Imitation. Type of learning whereby a novel response is acquired through observation of another's behavior. No reward is required for such modeling to occur.

Looking-glass self. Cooley's formulation of the self as the interpreted reflection of others' attitudes. It consists of "the imagination of our appearance to the other person, the imagination of his judgment of that appearance, and some sort of self-feeling, such as pride or mortification."

Me. That dimension of Mead's notion of self that represents internalized societal attitudes and expectations. The Me is an aspect of a process, not a concrete entity.

Moral autonomy. Piaget's later stage of moral thought in which children over age eight judge wrongdoing in terms of intentions and extenuating circumstances, as well as consequences, and view rules as social conventions that can be changed.

Moral realism. Piaget's early stage of moral development in which children, four to eight years old, judge wrongdoing strictly in terms of its consequences and believe all rules are immutable absolutes.

Operant conditioning. Type of learning whereby the organism gives a number of trial-and-error responses. Those responses followed by reward (positive reinforcement) tend to be repeated on future occasions. Those responses followed by negative reinforcement, or by no reinforcement, tend to be extinguished.

Primary socialization. Socialization that occurs during childhood.

Resocialization. Replacement of established attitudes and behavior patterns.

Significant other. The particular individual whose standpoint the child adopts in responding to himself or herself during Mead's play stage.

Socialization. Complex learning process through which individuals develop selfhood and acquire the knowledge, skills, and motivations required to participate in social life.

Super-ego. The Freudian conscience, or internalization of societal values and behavioral standards.

FURTHER READING

Brim, Orville G., Jr., and Jerome Kagan (eds). *Constancy and Change in Human Development.* Cambridge, Mass.: Harvard University Press, 1980. An analysis of the extent to which childhood experiences constrain adult behavior.

Edgerton, Robert B. *The Cloak of Competence: Stigma in the Lives of the Mentally Retarded.* Berkeley: University of California Press, 1967. An anthropological study of how adult mental retardates living in the community attempt to conceal the fact of their mental retardation.

Elkin, Frederick, and Gerald Handel. *The Child and Society: The Process of Socialization.* 3rd Edition. New York: Random House, 1978. A compact overview of the subject of socialization.

Goffman, Erving. *Asylums: Essays on the Situation of Mental Patients and Other Inmates.* New York: Doubleday Anchor, 1961. How total institutions, such as mental hospitals and prisons, attempt resocialization, and how the inmates fight back.

Haas, J., V. Marshall, and W. Shaffir, "Initiation into medicine: neophyte uncertainty and the ritual ordeal of professionalization." in Katherina L.P. Lundy, and Barbara D. Warme (eds.), *Work in the Canadian Context.* Toronto: Butterworths, 1981.

Haas, Jack, and William Shaffir. *Shaping Identity in Canadian Society.* Scarborough: Prentice-Hall, 1978. A book of readings that integrates theoretical material with discussions of ethnic and occupational socialization.

Hostetler, John A. *Hutterite Society.* Baltimore: Johns Hopkins University Press, 1974. This detailed description of the Hutterites offers an interesting contrast to the socialization experiences of majority Canadians.

McHugh, Peter. "Social disintegration as a requisite of resocialization." in Gregory Stone, and Harvey A. Farberman (eds.), *Social Psychology Through Symbolic Interaction.* Waltham, Mass.: Ginn-Blaisdell, 1970. A theoretical discussion of why rehabilitation attempts fail.

CHAPTER 4
GENDER RELATIONS

MARLENE MACKIE

Female. Male. The difference that makes a difference. She can identify 25 colors, including taupe and magenta. He can identify 25 cars (Aston-Martin, Lamborgine). He defends against danger. She is afraid to go out alone after dark. She smiles more. When they are together, he does more of the talking and is more likely to interrupt her remarks (Thorne and Henley, 1975). She finds it easier to express her innermost feelings (Jourard, 1964). He thinks sexual humor is funny (Brodzinsky, Barnet, and Aiello, 1981), while she relishes jokes which satirize the status quo between the sexes.

Consider marriage. In our society, it is still the sign of the successful woman, while occupational achievement is the sign of the successful man. Witness the different connotations of bachelor and spinster. Bachelor has a romantic, carefree air, while spinster "conjures up the vision . . . of a stringy old hen with a puckered mouth" (Dahl, 1962). Therefore, it is women who show primary (though not exclusive) interest in makeup, fashionable clothing, cosmetic surgery for wrinkles and jowls, health spas, and Weight Watchers' meetings. Men, on the other hand, take responsibility for initiating contact with women (and the risk of rejection). The burden of decision-making and economic support within marriage is carried disproportionately by men. Society expects them to achieve, to compete, to be aggressive. They do not have the option to be unemployed or to fail occupationally (Safilios-Rothschild, 1974).

Education and economic experiences also differ by sex. In the twenty to twenty-four year age group, more Canadian males than females have been enrolled full-time in school in every census year since 1911 (Hunter, 1981). The number of girls studying physics and mathematics in high school is less than half the number of boys, with a corresponding absence of women in the ranks of physical scientists (Shore, 1982). Indeed, Canadian women are segregated into a relatively few, mostly low-skilled, poorly paid jobs (Armstrong and Armstrong, 1978). Women, especially unmarried women, have a more difficult time getting credit than do their male counterparts (Kryzanowski and Bertin-Boussu, 1981).

Old age is not easy for either sex. Compared to older men, older women are more likely to be poor and widowed, to be living alone, or to be institutionalized (Abu-Laban, 1980; Dulude, 1978; Matthews, 1980). Elderly men, on the other hand, generally lack the occupational prestige, income, physical strength, and sexual prowess which are considered prerequisites of masculinity in our society (Abu-Laban, 1980).

Men and women differentially experience physical and mental health. Although women are ill more often than men (Thompson and Brown, 1980), the average woman outlives the average man by seven years (Dulude, 1978). There are more females than males with the diagnosis of depression, phobia, anxiety, hysteria, and chronic schizophrenia. There are more males than females with the diagnosis of personality disorders, such as alcoholism and drug addiction, and psychophysiological disorders, such as ulcers, heart,

and respiratory illness (Al-Issa, 1980). At every age, Canadian males are more likely than Canadian females to kill themselves (Cumming and Lazer, 1981).

Women and men are socialized differently, play different roles, and have different thoughts and experiences. They live out their lives in social worlds that are separate at some points and overlapping at others. "Men and women march to different drummers;" in some respects, "they are not even in the same parade" (Bernard, 1975).

SOCIOLOGY OF GENDER RELATIONS

This chapter explores one central question: what does it mean to be female or to be male in contemporary Canadian society? Human social life always and everywhere has been built around the relationships between the sexes. Changes in these relationships thus affect the entire social structure.

The sociology of gender relations developed about 15 years ago in response to the feminist movement. Until then, with a few exceptions (Hacker, 1951; Komarovsky, 1946), the social behavior of females had been ignored by sociologists (Daniels, 1975). Sociology was a science of male society (Bernard, 1973) that emphasized those social institutions and settings in which males predominate, such as the occupational, political, and legal systems. Where women were noticed at all, as in the sociology of the family (Parsons and Bales, 1955), it was their connection with men that counted. Consequently, matters of interest to women were often neglected. For example, urban sociology overlooked the behavior of mothers and children in parks, women at beauty parlors, widows in coffee shops (Lofland, 1975). Indeed, labelling the suburbs as "bedroom communities," because the *men* leave during the day, conveys the message that what women and children do doesn't matter very much (Richardson, 1981). In addition, there was a tendency to assume that the results of studies of male behavior automatically applied to women as well (for example, that people respond to leaders generally as they respond to male leadership). On other occasions, it was assumed that what was true of men could simply be reversed for a description of women (Fuller, 1978). The traits of ambitiousness and competitiveness, for example, were often associated with masculinity and disassociated with femininity.

The sociology of gender relations attempts both to remedy the discipline's previous exclusion of the feminine perspective and to encompass the masculine side of the equation (Lipman-Blumen and Tickamyer, 1975). The gradual realization that males, too, have been trapped by traditional role definitions has led to critical analysis of the male situation (Harrison, 1978). Although the bulk of the social science literature has been written by men on topics of interest to men, consideration of the implications of cultural beliefs about maleness per se is a recent phenomenon.

Some Definitions

Before proceeding further, let us define gender and distinguish it from the closely related word, sex. According to the "Humpty Dumpty Theorem," this definition, like all definitions, is a matter of conventional usage:

> *Humpty Dumpty*: When I use a word it means just what I choose it to mean, neither more nor less.
> *Alice*: The question is whether you can make words mean so many different things.
> *Humpty Dumpty*: The question is, who is to be master, that's all (Carroll, 1896).

Sex refers to the physiological differences between males and females. In other words, the term "sex" indicates sexual anatomy and sexual behavior, that is, behavior that "produces arousal and increases the chance of orgasm" (Hyde, 1979). **Gender**, on the other hand, is what is socially recognized as femininity or masculinity (Gould and Kern-Daniels, 1977). The cultural norms of a particular society at a particular point in time identify some ways of behaving, feeling, and thinking as appropriate for females, and other ways of behaving, feeling, and thinking as appropriate for males. Below we differentiate biologically-based and culturally-based role behaviors vis-à-vis offspring (Gould and Kern-Daniels, 1977).

	Sex Role	*Gender Role*
Women	Childbearer	Mother
Men	Sperm Donor	Father

Two recent newspaper articles illustrate the sex-gender distinction. A story entitled "Cowboy captures crocheting honors" (*Calgary Herald*, January 17, 1982) describes a cattleman and former bullrider who won a blue ribbon at the county fair for his crocheted tablecloth. "I know a lot of people call it woman's work, but I can do it better than most women", says Cowboy Shorty. Maybe so, but his behavior contradicts our society's definition of masculinity.

The second story, headed "Lion tamer claims hysterectomy helps" (*Calgary Herald*, February 10, 1982), tells about an Australian woman who had the operation for career rather than medical reasons. Apparently, lions are more likely to attack females during mens-

In our society, marriage and children are still signs of the successful woman. But today women are less willing to accept the exclusive roles of housewife and mother. More and more, they are entering the labor market, if only to increase family incomes. One result is that women are no longer "stuck" at home with children as their only company. (*Miller Services*)

Signs of equal rights philosophy pop up everywhere these days. Women may now find themselves being aced out of a spot at the hairdresser's by a mere male. Robert Rocchi, 45, a printer in San Jose, Calif., likes to get a permanent during hot weather so he doesn't have to bother with his hair.

truation. For this reason, the patient was anxious to have her uterus removed. Although the woman's occupational choice also violates a gender norm (we expect lion tamers to be men), her surgery was performed because of her biological sex.

Note that the term "gender relations" is not a codeword for women. Though the women's movement stimulated remedial sociology to analyze previously ignored female behavior, it soon became evident that it is futile to attempt to study one gender in isolation from the other. Masculinity and femininity derive their meaning from the relation of one to the other. The roles most influenced by gender (e.g., husband, wife) are reciprocal roles. Moreover, the changes currently taking place in female roles inevitably affect male roles as well.

The Importance of Gender

Our argument for the importance of gender rests upon two major points. First, in Canadian society, as in all human societies, the genders are *differentiated*. A great fuss is made over the biological distinctions between female and male. Elaborate sets of meanings are built upon them. Gender's impact upon the individual begins at the moment of birth and continues until the moment of death. The parents of a newborn infant ask, "Is it a boy or a girl?" Though at this stage the infant is little more than a bundle of tissue with potentiality, members of society immediately begin to react to it in terms of its gender. It will likely be wrapped in a pink or blue blanket. It will also be given a name that usually signals its sex.

Sex-typing begins even before birth. Lewis (1972) reported that mothers-to-be responded to the activity of the fetuses in a sex-differentiated fashion. If the fetus kicked and moved a great deal, this behavior was often interpreted as a sign that the baby was male. There is a great deal of folk wisdom on this subject. For example, a child's pre-natal position supposedly indicates its sex, boys being carried high and girls low.

Parents' perception of their infants after birth continues to be sex-typed. Aberle and Naegele (1952) reported that fathers expected their daughters to be pretty, fragile, sweet, and delicate, and their sons to be athletic and aggressive. Rubin, et al (1974), interviewed 30 pairs of parents at a Boston hospital within 24 hours of the birth of their first child. Fifteen of the couples had daughters and fifteen had sons. Infant girls were described by the parents as "softer," "finer-featured," "littler," and "prettier," boys as "bigger," "stronger," "firmer," and "more alert." Although males are generally slightly longer and heavier at birth (Barfield, 1976), the hospital records showed that these particular male and female infants did not differ whatsoever in birth length, weight, or health.

Throughout life, gender permeates every social relationship and every sphere of human activity. There are girls' games and boys' games, women's work and men's work. Being a male university student is not the same as being a female university student. Being a wife, mother, divorcée, widow, or elderly woman is not the same as being a husband, father, divorced male, widower, or elderly man.

A second reason for gender's importance is that society values males more than females. The sexes are ranked. As a category, males have more prestige and power than females. Traditionally, society has not shared Maurice Chevalier's sentiment of "Vive la Différence!"

Labovitz's study (1974) illustrates the devaluation of women. He asked 335 university students to evaluate a briefly described sociology article. This same article was attributed to four different fictitious authors in order to determine the extent to which sex and ethnicity influenced student reactions. The alleged authors were Edward Blake (English-Canadian male), Edith Blake (English-Canadian female), Joseph Walking Bear (Canadian Indian), and Marcel Fournier (French Canadian). The same work was judged to be of lower quality when it was attributed to a woman than when it was attributed to a man. However, the non-Anglo-Saxon names elicited more critical evaluations than the female name, showing the parallel between gender and ethnic prejudice.

Remember the newborn infant that we spoke about a few paragraphs ago? When the parents asked the doctors which sex the baby was, in all likelihood they were hoping for a particular answer. If the baby was their first child or intended to be their only child, research shows that parents tend to prefer a boy (Markle, 1974). Which sex would you yourself prefer to be? Chances are that if you are female, you sometimes wish you were male, and if you are male, you are quite satisfied to remain that way. Why do people condone – even admire – the masculine behavior of a twelve-year-old girl and abhor the feminine behavior of a twelve-year-old boy? Even the labels for these children, "tomboy" and "sissy," communicate societal sentiments. The answer to these questions and many more just like them is clear: society values males more highly than females.

MALE-FEMALE SIMILARITIES AND DIFFERENCES

Our society emphasizes both sex and gender. Moreover, people tend to view these physiological distinctions and the cultural elaborations upon them as equally natural. Therefore, it makes sense to determine just

what these differences really are. Possible origins of such differences are explored in later sections.

Misleading Female-Male Comparisons

Because so much emotion and mystery surround male-female relations, it is not surprising that many notions about sex differences have been biased (Tresemer, 1975). We dwell on the differences between males and females and ignore their similarities. Men and women are seen as *either* this *or* that, not both. We are fascinated with the anatomical differences and overlook the fact that males and females really share much the same body blueprint. Psychological traits provide another example. We assume (correctly, as it happens) that males are more aggressive than females. However, this does not mean that *all* males are aggressive, or that *all* females are passive. Research shows that this gender difference, as well as others, can be represented as an overlapping normal curve, as in Figure 4-1. The trait appears to be distributed normally within each category, but the group means differ. Concretely,

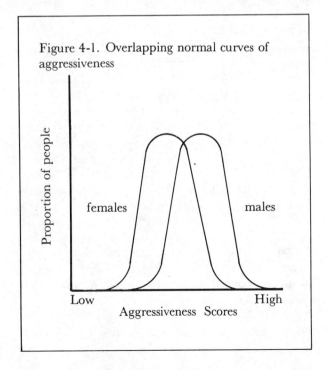

Figure 4-1. Overlapping normal curves of aggressiveness

Proportion of people

females   males

Low   High

Aggressiveness Scores

this means that both males and females vary between being highly aggressive and very unaggressive. However, the group average for males is somewhat higher. Nevertheless, a substantial number of females will be as or more aggressive than a substantial number of males (Chafetz, 1974).

The following classroom exercise makes the point that females and males are not diametrically opposite beings. Ask a number of males and females to answer "yes" to the following questions by raising their hands. How many people have blue eyes? Are 5'8" or taller? Ever consider growing a beard? Like mathematics? Know the meaning of "saute," "magenta," and "placket"? Cried at least once this month? Ever had a fist fight? Support the New Democratic Party? Like kittens? If people answer honestly (social desirability might influence some responses), you would probably find no sex difference on some questions (eye color, political party), overlapping, but gender-related responses on others (height, mathematics), and completely dichotomous responses on still others (beard, definition of words).

Physiological Differences

The biological concept of sex really has four highly interrelated aspects (Frieze, et al, 1978):

1. Genetic sex. Normal humans have 23 pairs of chromosomes. One of these pairs determines the genetic sex of the individual. With reference to this pair, males carry an X and a Y chromosome, while females carry two X chromosomes. The person's sex is determined at the moment of conception, when the egg, with an X chromosome, is united with the sperm, which carries either an X or a Y chromosome. The fertilized egg with XX are females; those with XY are males.

2. Hormonal sex. Hormones are chemical substances secreted into the bloodstream by the endocrine glands. The primary male sex hormone is testosterone, and the primary female sex hormone is estrogen. These hormones influence the development of sex glands, organs, and secondary sex characteristics.

3. Gonadal sex. The embryo's genetic sex determines whether its gonadal cells become ovaries or testes.

4. Genital sex. Males are equipped with a penis and scrotum, and females with a clitoris and vagina. Men and women differ in their reproductive functions. "Only women menstruate, gestate, and lactate. Only men produce semen" (Armstrong and Armstrong, 1978).

In addition, a number of secondary sex characteristics exist that become more pronounced with puberty (Barfield, 1976). On the average, males are taller, heavier, and have a greater percentage of total body weight in muscle and a smaller proportion of fat. Females have lighter skeletons, different shoulder/pelvis proportions, different pelvic bone shapes, and different socket shapes at the hip and shoulder. These differences contribute to women having less strength (especially in the upper body), less endurance for heavy labor, more difficulty in overarm throwing, and a better ability to float.

Psychological Differences

Only four sex differences in psychological characteristics are well established by research (Maccoby and Jacklin, 1974). Remember, though, that these abilities are both overlapping and matters of degree.

1. Verbal Ability. Included are spelling, punctuation, sentence complexity, vocabulary size, fluency, reading comprehension, creative writing, and use of language in logical reasoning (Tavris and Offir, 1977). Although boys are more likely than girls to stutter and to have reading difficulties, pre-adolescent verbal ability is otherwise equivalent. However, from the age of ten or eleven through high school, female superiority increases.

2. Mathematical Ability. Girls and boys are similar in their early acquisition of quantitative concepts and mastery of arithmetic. However, beginning at puberty, boys' mathematical skills increase faster than girls'.

3. Spatial Skills.

Males consistently excel in visual-spatial skills. These refer to the ability to visually manipulate, locate, or make judgments about the spatial relationships of items located in two- or three-dimensional space. For example, the embedded-figures test involves locating smaller figures in a larger design. Once again, there is a developmental trend, with no difference in young children and a male advantage emerging at the beginning of adolescence (Frieze et al, 1978).

4. Aggressiveness.

Males engage in more physical aggression, more verbal aggression, and more aggressive fantasies. This sex difference emerges as early as two years of age.

Conventional wisdom attributes a variety of other traits to the sexes. For example, women ("soft body, soft mind") are alleged to be less intelligent (Ellmann, 1968) or less creative. How else explain the relative absence of eminent women in history, science, art, literature? Devising a list of Canadian "great women" is a formidable task. Nevertheless, the sexes do not differ in tests of general intellectual abilities or creativity which weight fairly the particular skills at which males and females excel, such as spatial versus verbal tasks (Maccoby and Jacklin, 1974). We must also point out that for both sexes intellect is only one factor contributing to eminence. Drive and opportunity are also required.

Women are also expected to be nurturant, warm, and helpful towards children, men, and animals. Girls' doll play is often taken as evidence of spontaneous nurturance. However, it is impossible to conclude from the evidence whether women are more disposed to behave maternally than men are disposed to behave paternally. So far as dolls are concerned, they are presented to girls not boys, and much doll play is not nurturant. Dolls are hugged and tucked into bed all right, but they are also "scolded, spanked, subjected to surgical operations, and . . . even scalped" (Maccoby and Jacklin, 1974). The evidence for other supposed sex differences, such as greater emotionality, is inconclusive.

Gender and Its Source

"What," asks the nursery rhyme, "are little girls made of?" Double X chromosomes. A vagina, clitoris, and eventually, bosoms. Verbal ability. "What are little boys made of?" An X chromosome. A Y chromosome. A penis and related parts. Later, mustache, beard, or five o'clock shadow. Aggressiveness. Mathematical and spatial ability. *Not* sugar and spice. *Not* snips and snails and puppy dog tails.

However, researchers' unromantic inventory of female-male distinctions grows longer when consideration is given to fashion (long hair and pants are no longer reliable guides, but skirts are still definitive); etiquette and demeanor (who drives the car on dates, who lights cigarettes for whom?); language (which sex is more often likened to food – a dish, tomato, peach, cookie, honey, cheese cake?) (Eakins and Eakins, 1978); social roles (nurses versus soldiers, mothers versus fathers); spheres of existence (the domestic world of women versus the public world of men).

Up to this point, we have concentrated on enumerating sex differences rather than explaining them. The sections that follow will consider the causation of gender. First, though, it is important to realize that the topic of sex differences is a sensitive one for feminists (Mackie, 1977). Incidentally the term feminist applies to people of both sexes who believe in the equality of the sexes. One of the most visible male feminists, actor Alan Alda, explains "I come from a long line of women."

The recent furor over mathematical ability is a good example of this sensitivity. An article concluding that males have inherently superior mathematical ability appeared in the prestigious journal, *Science* (Benbow and Stanley, 1980). A month later, the annual meeting of the American Mathematical Society was held. At a news conference, a half dozen mathematicians of both sexes called the finding "ridiculous" and "disturbing" and said "it is virtually impossible to undo the damage" of the publicity surrounding the report. Professor Stanley observed that, "People are so eager not to believe that there is a difference in mathematical reasoning ability between boys and girls that all kinds of people are taking potshots" (*Time*, March 22, 1982).

Since there is current evidence to support both environmental and biological causation, more research is necessary to resolve the question.

Feminists' difficulty with the topic of sex differences stems, in part, from people's tendency to confuse difference with inequality and to devalue female characteristics (Favreau, 1977). Because males enjoy more power and prestige than females, our culture tends to devalue "feminine" traits, such as gentleness and expressiveness, and to glorify "masculine" traits, such as ambitiousness and competitiveness. In addition, feminists prefer explanations that emphasize socialization, not biology. If "anatomy is destiny," then the contemplation of alternatives to the gender status quo makes no sense. For example, it would be pointless for Canadian women to organize in order to seek more power in, first of all, the political parties, and second, the House of Commons, if male leadership and female powerlessness are biologically preordained. On the other hand, learned behavior patterns are arbitrary and, hence, replaceable with other behavior patterns.

While sympathy can be shown for these concerns, it is important to distinguish between wishful thinking and scientific research. Increasingly, gender specialists are coming to realize that biological, socialization, and social structural evidence all need to be carefully evaluated. These explanations will be discussed in turn.

BIOLOGICAL EXPLANATIONS OF GENDER

Are boys masculine and girls feminine because they were born that way? The question of the impact of biology upon sex differences and consequent gender elaboration has fascinated the practitioners of many academic disciplines.

Animal Research

Scientists have attempted to determine whether human sex differences are innate or learned by studying our evolutionary cousins (Tavris and Offir, 1977), the monkeys and apes. The logic here rests on the assumption that primates are like human beings, but they do not undergo the intensive learning that we do. Primate sex differences that parallel human sex differences, therefore, constitute evidence for biological causation of human sex differences.

This type of argument-by-analogy (Tavris and Offir, 1977) presents at least three problems. First, the conclusion reached depends greatly on the particular species chosen (Rosenberg, 1976). The male baboon is much more aggressive than the female baboon. Both male and female gibbons are highly aggressive (Lancaster, 1976). So far as human differences are concerned, do baboons support biological causation and gibbons social learning? Second, extrapolation from lower animal behavior to human behavior is risky "for the simple reason that humans are not non-humans" (Weisstein, 1971). As the evolutionary ladder is ascended, the effects of physiology on behavior becomes less dramatic and the role of learning more important (Frieze, et al, 1978). Third, even when the same label is used for human and animal behavior, the behaviors may not be at all comparable. Take, for instance, sex differences in aggression. The animal findings refer to measures such as threat displays, the latency of initial attack, and the outcome of fights, whereas the human studies refer to quite different measures, such as verbal aggression, teachers' ratings of assertiveness, questionnaire studies, and so on (Archer, 1976).

Do criticisms like these mean that animal studies are worthless to students of human sex differences? Not at all. But research into animal differences is best viewed as a source of hypotheses, rather than definitive answers concerning sex differences in *homo sapiens*.

The Anthropological Approach

Anthropologists have provided yet another perspective on the question: "To what extent do women's and men's psychological characteristics and social behavior have their source in physiology?" The presence or absence of **cultural universals** in the anthropological record is taken to be evidence for or against a biological explanation. If a certain type of behavior is found in many cultures, despite other sorts of variation in cultural patterns, that behavior is assumed to be biologically determined, or at least linked in some way to physiology. If, however, cultural comparisons show inconsistency, if social arrangements are sometimes this way, and sometimes that, this cross-cultural inconsistency is interpreted as evidence for social causation. Unfortunately, the method is complicated by the existence of disagreement over the meaning of cultural universal. Does it mean all known cultures, or are exceptions to be allowed? Obviously, the logic is open to the intrusion of values at this point (Rosaldo, 1980). Margaret Mead's study, *Sex and Temperament in Three Primitive Societies* (1935), illustrates the anthropological approach.

Fifty years ago, Mead set off to New Guinea to discover whether North American sex differences in temperament were innate or learned. She encountered three tribes that provided evidence. Both the men and women of the Arapesh, a mountain-dwelling tribe, displayed a gentle personality that would seem feminine in our society. Both parents participated in childbirth. Conception was believed to require repeated sexual union in order to feed and shape the child in the mother's womb. Both parents lay down to bear the child and observed the birth taboos and rituals. Mead says that, "If you comment upon a middle-aged man as goodlooking, the people answer: 'Goodlooking, Ye-e-s? But you should have seen him before he bore all those children'." Neither sex was aggressive. The ideal Arapesh male never provoked a fight, and rape was unknown. Males considered leadership to be an onerous duty.

The fierce, cannibalistic Mundugumor tribe, on the other hand, standardized the behavior of both sexes as almost pathologically masculine. Both women and men were violent and competitive. Polygyny (a man having more than one wife) provoked hostility and jealousy. Children were unwanted and weaning consisted of slapping. Sex often took the form of a rough-and-tumble athletic tryst in the bushes. The delights of these "bush encounters" were enhanced by copulating in other people's gardens, an act that spoiled their yam crops. One wonders how a society so lacking in cooperation managed to survive at all.

Among the head-hunting Tchambuli, temperament reversed Western notions of normalcy. Economic affairs were relegated to the women, while the men devoted themselves to art and ceremony. The women worked together in amiable groups and enjoyed the theatricals put on by the bickering, quarreling men. Mead described the women as "solid, preoccupied, powerful, with shaven unadorned heads" and the men as having "delicately arranged curls," "handsome pubic coverings of flying-fox skin highly ornamented with shells," "mincing steps and self-conscious mien." The women were more "urgently sexed" than the men.

Mead's analysis of these primitive New Guinean societies presents a classic argument for cultural conditioning of sex differences. However, to complicate matters, other anthropologists have arrived at the opposite conclusion. Such is the case with Goldberg's *The Inevitability of Patriarchy* (1973).

Goldberg's explanation of gender relations is built on the argument that male dominance is a cultural universal. This observation is accurate. In all known cultures, males are dominant over women of equal status and age (Frieze, et al, 1978). Although women may have a good deal of informal influence, everywhere men have some authority over women. Everywhere, males have a culturally legitimated right to female subordination. For example, even the Iroquois, who were the closest approximation that ever existed to the hypothetical form of society called a matriarchate, were not ruled by women. Women might install and depose their rulers, but Iroquois chiefs were men. These generalizations also apply to Mead's New Guinean tribes. The Arapesh wife was viewed as the daughter of her husband. Tchambuli society regarded masculine artistic and ritualistic knowledge as superior to the feminine economic knowledge (Rosaldo, 1974).

According to Goldberg (1973), biology provides the explanation for the universality of male dominance. Here is his line of reasoning. Male bodies contain more of the sex hormone, testosterone, than do female bodies. Aggressive behavior is linked to testosterone. Because of hormonal differences, males are, on the average, more aggressive than females. Therefore, patriarchy is inevitable, because the male competitive edge over women allows men always to occupy the high-status, public positions. Again, because of hormonal differences, women are better suited for motherhood and homemaking. Goldberg feels that it violates nature for women to seek public leadership. Instead, he suggests that motherhood should be more highly valued. Faced with this biological reality, societies choose to socialize the sexes so that they do not compete with one another. Females are protected from inevitable failure by being socialized into roles males either cannot play, like childbearing, or do not wish to play, such as low-status positions (Frieze, et al, 1978).

There are several difficulties contained in Goldberg's ideas. For one thing, research with humans has not demonstrated a clear link between testosterone levels and aggressiveness or competitiveness. Although male hormones and aggressiveness are related in animals, as we have seen, generalizing from animals to human beings is a risky business. Also, sex differences in aggressiveness only mean that the *average* male is more aggressive than the *average* female. *All* males are not more aggressive than *all* females. These average differences cannot explain the pervasiveness of role and status differentiation in our culture (Frieze, et al, 1978). Furthermore, in order to explain cross-cultural differences in male aggressiveness biologically, differences in testosterone levels would have to be demonstrated. In other words, we would have to establish that Mundugumor men have more testosterone surging through their systems than Arapesh men.

The anthropological record, then, does not provide us with an unequivocal answer to our question: what is the source of gender?

Psychosexual Deviations

Sex and gender taken together involve eight variables (Hyde, 1979, based in part upon Money and Ehrahardt, 1972). Earlier, we discussed four biological variables, *genetic sex*, *hormonal sex*, *gonadal sex*, and *genital sex*. Genital sex may be further differentiated into *internal accessory organs* (uterus and vagina in the female; prostate and seminal vesicles in the male) and *external genital appearance* (clitoris and vaginal opening in the female; penis and scrotum in the male). Being female or male involves three additional social psychological variables. *Assigned gender*, based on the appearance of the child's external genitals, is the gender the parents and the rest

of society believe the child to be. It is the gender in which the child is raised. **Gender identity** is the person's own conviction of being male or female, expressed in personality and behavior. Finally, *choice of sexual partner* refers to the person's sexual attraction to members of the same sex or the opposite sex or both.

In most cases, an individual is consistently male or female across the above eight variables. That is, an individual with **XX** chromosomes, has an endocrine system producing estrogen, as well as internal and external female organs. This person has been designated a female from birth, and she believes herself to be female. Finally, she is sexually attracted to males.

Occasionally, however, contradictions exist among these variables. A person whose gender identity contradicts the first six dimensions is called a **transsexual**. A person whose choice of sexual partner is at variance with the other components is called a *homosexual*. A person with contradictions among the biological variables (hormones, chromosome structure, anatomy) is called a **hermaphrodite**.

People with psychosexual abnormalities function, to a certain extent, as natural experiments that provide some insight into the question of the relative weight of biological and social causation in the development of gender. Evidence on both sides has been reported. However, the case described below reinforces the importance of gender as social assignment.

In the 1960s, the parents of perfectly normal seven-month-old twin boys took their children to a hospital to be circumcized.

The physician elected to use an electric cauterizing needle instead of a scalpel to remove the foreskin of the one who chanced to be brought to the operating room first. When this baby's foreskin didn't give on the first try, or on the second, the doctor stepped up the current. On the third try, the surge of heat from the electricity literally cooked the baby's penis. Unable to heal, the penis dried up, and in a few days sloughed off completely, like the stub of an umbilical cord (Money and Tucker, 1975).

Doctors recommended that the boy's sex be reassigned and that female external genitals be surgically constructed. The child's name, clothes, and hairstyle were feminized as the parents made every effort to rear twins – one male and one female. As the following anecdotes concerning the twins at age four-and-a-half years shows, both parents and children successfully developed "sex appropriate" attitudes and behavior. The mother, talking about the boy, reported: ". . . in the summer time, one time I caught him – he went out and took a leak in my flower garden in the front yard, you know. He was quite happy with himself. And I just didn't say anything. I just couldn't. I started laughing and I told daddy about it . . . ." The corresponding comments about the girl, went this way: ". . . I've never had a problem with her. She did once when she was little, she took off her panties and threw them over the fence. And she didn't have no panties on. But I just gave her a little swat on the rear, and I told her that nice little girls didn't do that, and she should keep her pants on . . ." (Money and Ehrhardt, 1972). For Christmas, the girl wanted dolls, a doll house, and doll carriage. The boy wanted toy garage with cars, gas pumps, and tools.

This case and others suggest that the sex by assignment outweighs biological factors in determining gender identity. For example, there were 44 cases of individuals with female chromosomes, female gonads, excessive male hormones, and ambiguous external genitals. Thirty-nine were assigned as female at birth. Thirty-seven of them developed a female identity. In contrast, all five assigned and reared as males developed male gender identity (Green, 1974). However, gender reassignment is usually unsuccessful after the age of 18 months (Money and Ehrhardt, 1972). By then, the child has the ability to understand verbal labels for gender and to view the world from a "female" or "male" perspective. Finally, we must point out that the conclusions of psychosexual abnormality research have been criticized because gender reassignment has been supplemented by appropriate surgery and hormone treatment. That is, the individual's biology has been modified to correspond to the assigned gender (Hyde, 1979).

Hormone and Gene Research

Much of the current effort to explain female language fluency and male visual-spatial ability centers on sex disparities in the brain. Although there appear to be no sex differences in brain size or structure, male and female brains seem to differ in organization (Bryden, 1979; Carter and Greenough, 1979; Goleman, 1978). The left hemisphere of the brain controls language and the right hemisphere, spatial and nonverbal functions. **Lateralization** is the term used to label the specialization in the functioning of each hemisphere. The left side is normally dominant in both sexes. However, there is some evidence that female brains are less specialized than male brains, both hemispheres being involved in the performance of verbal functions. The greater flexibility of female brains is thought by some to explain their language superiority (Barfield, 1976). Also, lateralization may be responsible for male visual-spatial superiority and consequent mathematical skill.

At the moment, the mechanisms responsible for the sex difference in lateralization, and lateralization's precise impact on spatial and verbal skills, are unclear. However, a number of hypotheses are being explored that involve connections with the sex hormones or genes (Frieze et al, 1978). The evidence so far is inconclusive.

Some researchers (Maccoby and Jacklin, 1974) believe male aggressiveness is biologically based. Males are more aggressive than females in the vast majority of societies for which evidence is available. Also, male aggressiveness shows up early in life. A high testosterone level is associated with aggressiveness in male lower animals. However, hormonal research in humans is as yet unclear.

Conclusion

Every approach to the problem of the biological foundation of female-male differences raises more questions than it answers. Biology does seem to be involved in cognitive differences and aggressiveness. As we shall see further on, biology may be indirectly involved in the male-female division of labor.

However, to search for either biological *or* environmental causation of gender patterns, to pose the question as nature *versus* nurture is a misleading and simplistic formulation of a complex question. In gender patterns, as in social behavior in general (remember the discussion in Chapter 3), both biology and environment are implicated. Biochemical and genetic factors set the stage, but culture and history provide the script for social life (Kunkel, 1977). The fact that socialization often emphasizes "natural" sex differences further complicates the situation. For example, our society provides more athletic facilities and opportunities for the physically stronger males. However, because most of the psychosocial differences between the sexes involve learning in one way or another, let us look at socialization as an explanation of gender.

SOCIALIZATION EXPLANATIONS OF GENDER

Chapter 3 defined *socialization* as the lifelong learning process through which individuals develop selfhood and acquire the knowledge, skills, and motivations required for participation in social life. *Gender socialization* involves the particular processes through which people learn to be masculine and feminine according to the expectations current in their society. As we have already seen, there exist a number of theoretical approaches to socialization: the learning, Freudian, cognitive-developmental, and symbolic interaction perspectives. Symbolic-interactionism will be emphasized here.

Each society has its **gender scripts** (Laws, 1979) for femininity and masculinity. The emotions, thoughts, and behavior of children are shaped in approximate conformity with these scripts. Gender stereotypes and occupational sex-typing tell us something about our society's script for gender socialization.

Gender Stereotypes

A **stereotype** refers to those folk beliefs about the attributes characterizing a social category on which there is substantial agreement (Mackie, 1973). The term refers to consensual beliefs about the traits people choose to describe categories of people, such as ethnic groups, old people, or university students. Stereotypes are *not* false by definition. Beyond the truism that all generalizations fail to reflect the minutiae of reality,

Institutions like the Miss Canada Pageant help to maintain gender stereotypes. The mass media presents an image of "ideal" female beauty that affects both gender socialization and occupational sex-typing. (*Canapress*)

degree of accuracy is an empirical question. Stereotypes are not "good" or "bad" or "desirable" or "undesirable." They simply *are*. The categorization involved appears to be a necessary aspect of human cognition. Our limited sensory apparatus cannot encode the multiplicity of stimuli rushing at us *de novo* or in detail. We place relevant stimuli into these categories designated important from previous personal-cultural experience and ignore the rest.

Gender stereotypes capture folk beliefs about the nature of females and males generally. Broverman, et al (1972), carried out the most thorough investigation of these stereotypes. The similarity of their findings with more recent results (Ward and Balswick, 1978) shows that despite the activities of the women's movement, gender stereotypes are remarkably stable over time. Broverman, et al, asked respondents to indicate the extent to which 122 different adjectives characterized an adult man or an adult woman. For example, if 75 percent, or more of the sample agreed that "very aggressive" was more descriptive of an average man than an average woman, then that adjective was de-

TABLE 4-1. GENDER STEREOTYPES

Competency Cluster: Masculine Pole is More Desirable

Masculine	Feminine
Very aggressive	Not at all aggressive
Very independent	Not at all independent
Not at all emotional	Very emotional
Almost always hides emotions	Does not hide emotions at all
Very objective	Very subjective
Not at all easily influenced	Very easily influenced
Very dominant	Very submissive
Likes math and science very much	Dislikes math and science very much
Not at all excitable in a minor crisis	Very excitable in a minor crisis
Very active	Very passive
Very competitive	Not at all competitive
Very logical	Very illogical
Very worldly	Very home-oriented
Very skilled in business	Not at all skilled in business
Very direct	Very sneaky
Knows the way of the world	Does not know the way of the world
Feelings not easily hurt	Feelings easily hurt
Very adventurous	Not at all adventurous
Can make decisions easily	Has difficulty making decisions
Never cries	Cries very easily
Almost always acts as a leader	Almost never acts as a leader
Very self-confident	Not at all self-confident
Not at all uncomfortable about being aggressive	Very uncomfortable about being aggressive
Very ambitious	Not at all ambitious
Easily able to separate feelings from ideas	Unable to separate feelings from ideas
Not at all dependent	Very dependent
Never conceited about appearance	Very conceited about appearance
Thinks men are always superior to women	Thinks women are always superior to men
Talks freely about sex with men	Does not talk freely about sex with men

Warmth-Expressiveness Cluster: Feminine Pole is More Desirable

Feminine	Masculine
Doesn't use harsh language at all	Uses very harsh language
Very talkative	Not at all talkative
Very tactful	Very blunt
Very gentle	Very rough
Very aware of feelings of others	Not at all aware of feelings of others
Very religious	Not at all religious
Very interested in own appearance	Not at all interested in own appearance
Very neat in habits	Very sloppy in habits
Very quiet	Very loud
Very strong need for security	Very little need for security
Enjoys art and literature	Does not enjoy art and literature at all
Easily expresses tender feelings	Does not express tender feelings at all easily

SOURCE: Broverman, et al (1972).

fined as part of the stereotype. Their findings are shown in Table 4-1.

Broverman, et al, also found that gender traits fall into a feminine *warmth-expressiveness cluster* and a masculine *competency cluster*. The latter includes characteristics such as being independent, active, competitive, ambitious. A relative absence of these traits is supposed to characterize women. In other words, relative to men, women are seen to be dependent, passive, noncompetitive, and so on. The warmth-expressiveness cluster, on the other hand, consists of attributes such as being gentle, quiet, sensitive to the feelings of others. Relative to women, men are perceived as lacking these traits.

The societal script manifest in gender stereotypes contains reference to appropriate major time and energy investments for women and men. According to this ideal division of labor, men are expected to work outside the home, marry, and support their families, while women are expected to marry, carry the major responsibility for child rearing, and rely on men for financial support and social status. Although the woman too may work outside the home, attracting a suitable mate and looking after his interests (and eventually those of her children) take priority over serious occupational commitment. The two clusters of traits reflect this division of labor.

Occupational Sex-typing

The sex-typing of occupations is a central element of the societal script for masculinity and femininity learned by children. Traditionally, women have been expected to engage in female occupations, such as secretary, librarian, nurse, elementary school teacher, while men enter male fields, such as plumbing, engineering, and law.

Even young children are aware of these norms. For example, when Barty (1971, described in Kimball, 1977) asked ten-to-thirteen-year-old Vancouver children to choose between being a doctor and being a nurse, 70 percent of the girls chose to be a nurse, while 80 percent of the boys chose to be a doctor.

Are these decade-old results outdated? Apparently not. Kalin, Stoppard, and Burt (1980) asked 156 Queen's University students to pretend they were guidance counsellors. They were presented with descriptions of 12 fictitious students in their final year of high school and asked to rate each student's suitability for study in eight occupational fields. Student gender was varied by changing first names.

Here is an example of one fictitious student:

Gloria (George) Rutherford is 19. She (he) has an IQ of 100 and maintains an average of 65 percent. Her (his) father works for a newspaper. Her (his) mother is actively involved

THE OUTCASTS   Ben Wicks

in several social events and is presently organizing a church bazaar. Gloria (George) helps to run a youth program at the church and derives much personal satisfaction out of talking with varied sorts of people. She (he) also enjoys music and works at Dominion to make enough money to invest in a high fidelity stereo. She (he) is a member of the U.N. Club at school. Gloria (George) is a good student and is a reliable individual. She (he) is on the class executive and does a commendable job. She (he) is a friendly girl (boy).

Female and male future occupations were chosen so they were all of similar social class level. The eight were social worker (F), commercial traveller (M), surveyor (M), librarian (F), engineering technician (M), nursing (F), sales manager (M), and occupational therapist (F).

Kalin, Stoppard, and Burt reported a number of interesting results. The fictitious female students were rated as more suitable for female than male occupations, while the reverse was true for the male students. The women subjects were as likely as the men to make judgments along traditional sex lines. Finally, the suitability of all the fictitious high school students, males as well as females, was rated to be higher for female than male occupations. The authors explain the last result as follows: "It is as if participants saw female occupations as easier and therefore thought that anyone could do them. If this impression is correct, participants showed a general devaluation of female occupations."

Stereotypes as Gender Socialization Content

Evidence does exist that Canadian children learn about stereotypes as part of the socialization process. Lambert's (1971) questionnaire study of the gender imagery of 7500 Canadian children, ten-to-seventeen-years-old, established that the children were aware of differential societal expectations for females and males. He reported that boys were considerably more traditional in their thinking about the genders than girls. Percival and Percival (1979) found that Maritime male university students stereotyped the sexes more than their female counterparts. Lambert's study of gender imagery also found parents' social class to be strongly related to their children's perception of gender. Greater traditionalism was found among working-class respondents. However, gender imagery was *not* related to rural-urban residence, perhaps because centralized schooling and the mass media have standardized influences for farm and city children.

French-Canadian/English-Canadian Comparisons

French-Canadian gender attitudes seem to have become increasingly egalitarian over time. Lambert (1971) found French-Canadian parents to be more traditional than English-Canadian parents. French-Canadian children, however, had less differentiated views of appropriate gender behavior than did English-Canadian children. Lambert suggests that the parental difference might be partially attributable to the higher average educational level of his English-speaking sample. This interpretation agrees with his finding of greater traditionalism in the working-class noted above.

Somewhat later studies show that although some changes were occurring, French Canadians remain quite traditional about those aspects of gender relations that concern the family. For instance, Boyd's (1975) analysis of Gallup poll results shows that French-Canadians support equality between the sexes, but only when the Gallup questions did not evoke maternal or wifely imagery. When these roles become salient, French-Canadians tend to become more traditional in their attitudes towards women.

Most recently, Hobart's (1981) study of university and technical students across Canada reports that Anglophone men now have the most traditional attitudes about marriage, followed by Francophone men, Anglophone women, and Francophone women, in order of increasing egalitarianism. Although all four categories increased in egalitarianism between 1968 and 1977 (years in which data were collected), Francophone increases for both sexes were very much greater. Egalitarian stances were adopted in formerly sensitive areas such as authority within marriage, child-rearing, household management, and women's work outside the home. According to Hobart, these data signal that recent changes have been more dramatic in French-Canadian families than among Canadian families generally. However, we suspect that the older generation of both ethnic groups remains relatively traditional in gender attitudes.

The Role of the Mass Media in Gender Socialization

Concerns about the effect on children of violence depicted in the mass media led to the studies you read about in Chapter 3. Widespread concern has also been voiced about the impact of the mass media on the development of gender attitudes and behavior. The Royal Commission on the Status of Women in Canada (1970) accused the media of perpetuating stereotyping of both sexes. Advertising was accused of presenting the "housebound-mother-wife-maid-mistress," on the one hand, and the "infallibly successful, accomplished,

virile male," on the other (Farrell, 1974). Television, magazines, newspapers, and novels have all been studied as contributors to society's gender scripts. However, only television, the dominant media influence in North American popular culture, will be discussed here.

In both children's and adult programming, males dominate the television screen (Pyke and Stewart, 1974). This "symbolic annihilation" (Tuchman, 1978) of women characterizes prime-time adventures, situation comedies, and even cartoons (which include fewer female characters presented as "anthropomorphized foxes or pussycats").

The presentation of the sexes is imbalanced in function as well as numbers. While fewer women are shown as housewives or housekeepers now than in the 1950s, the makeup of the television labor force has consistently shown little relationship to the real-life employment patterns of women (Dominick, 1979). Males are represented as occupying a disproportionately high

Not too long ago, women in the media were relegated to unimportant positions. Lately, women such as Adrienne Clarkson, Barbara Frum, and Barbara Amiel have become prominent in Canadian media. The picture shows Ms. Clarkson with her former colleagues on *The Fifth Estate*, **Bob McKeown and Eric Malling.** (*Canapress*)

percentage of the work force, a great diversity of occupations, and higher status jobs.

In 1978, briefs were presented to the Canadian Radio and Telecommunications Commission concerning the Canadian Broadcasting Corporation's portrayal of women in programming (Canadian Advisory Council of the Status of Women, 1978). While some Canadian programs were singled out as praiseworthy in their portrayal of women, the overall impression was that women are "peripheral to the cultural expression of the issues of importance to the society."

Finally, the following examples illustrate the distorted image of women in many ads shown on Canadian television (Courtney and Whipple, 1978):

- the woman who begs the male announcer not to take away her bleach
- the male announcer who convinces the hapless housewife that the peanut butter (or detergent, or deodorant, or soap . . .) she has been buying for ten years is not as good as the advertised brand.
- the woman whose self-confidence is shattered by spotty drinking glasses
- the women who scrub away in mopping contests as the male announcer looks on
- the woman who cannot read a pet-food label
- the woman who feels more like a woman because she is wearing the right bra

The key assumption is that people get their ideas about females and males, in part at least, from media presentations of gender.

The Symbolic Interactionist Perspective on Gender Socialization

Symbolic interactionists, such as Cooley and Mead, view "reality" as a matter of social definition. Socialization involves the acquisition of a self, which is also socially defined. The looking-glass self notion described in Chapter 3 holds that children learn who they are by adopting other people's attitudes towards themselves. The roles played by language and significant others in the socialization process are emphasized in this perspective. Here, we want to apply some of these themes to gender socialization (Cahill, 1980). Because gender consists of the accretion of socially-derived meanings upon the physiological female-male distinctions, symbolic interactionism seems a particularly appropriate theoretical approach to the questions that concern us.

Language and Self-Development. As a first step to self-awareness, the child differentiates herself or himself from other objects in the environment. As you learned in Chapter 3, Mead hypothesizes that the capacity to use language allows the child to learn the meaning of all these things, including himself/herself. Names form a basis, then, for the development of the self. A given name individualizes the infant and classifies it by gender. That is, baptizing a child "Barbara" simultaneously separates this infant from other infants and signifies its femaleness.

Though the child's adult socializers place it in a gender class at birth, some time must pass before the child responds to its own self in terms of gender. After 18 months, gender reassignment becomes less successful, perhaps because the child labels itself "male" or "female." By the age of three, a child can accurately and consistently answer the question, "Are you a girl or a boy?" At the same age, children show preferences for either "girl" or "boy" toys and activities (Kessler and McKenna, 1978). Thus, this self-categorization as male or female becomes a major axis of identity. However, young children do not necessarily interpret gender in the same way as adults do. For instance, they use hair length and clothing, not biology, as gender cues. This behavior is understandable in a society such as ours where the naked body is usually covered.

Socialization agents, such as the family, peers, mass media, and school, teach children what sorts of traits and behaviors go along with the female/male distinction. Parents admonish that "boys don't cry" and "girls don't sit with their legs apart." Especially in the past, children's storybooks were sex-typed. Pyke's (1975) survey of 150 Canadian children's books found few women in jobs outside the home. Women's trademark was the "perennial apron," worn "even by female squirrels." Storybook characters who had interesting adventures were most often male.

Richer's (1979) observational study of Ontario kindergarten classrooms shows how the teacher provided cues to enable children to classify "properly" the two sexes. The teacher found sex to be a practical means of organizing the children. For example, children lined up by gender to move from one activity to another – trips to the library, the gymnasium, retrieving food from their lockers, preparing to go home. Also, gender was used to motivate participation: "The girls are ready, the boys are not," or "Who can do it the fastest, the boys or the girls?" During coordination exercises, commands were given by gender: "Boys, put your fingers on your nose; girls, put your hands in your laps; boys, touch your toes." When someone slipped up here, the teacher's admonishment sometimes took this form: "Are you a girl? I thought all along you were a boy." Richer (1979) tells us that such situations left the child squirming with embarrassment. Likely, part of the reason was loss of status associated with his "demotion" from boy to girl. Be that as it may, the various socialization agents teach children both gender identity (awareness of being a member of one gender or the other) and the differential evaluation of females and males. Let us turn now to some examples of how language reinforces the ranking of the sexes.

Language and Ranking of the Sexes.

The English language (among others) denigrates women, while it asserts male superiority. Therefore, children unwittingly imbibe sexism along with language.

The "problem of the generic masculine" labels the way in which the English language fails to speak clearly and fairly of both sexes (Martyna, 1980). Here, language excludes and subsumes women through generic masculine terms which are supposed to refer to people in general: "he," "mankind," "man, the social animal," "men of good will." Or even, "Man, being a mammal, breast-feeds his young" (Martyna, 1980). The grammaticists' argument that the generic masculine implies "woman," "she," "her," – that "man" embraces "woman" – is countered by the feminists' claim that the generic masculine is both ambiguous and discriminatory. For instance, Ritchie's (1975) survey of 200 years of Canadian law concluded that the ambiguity

of the generic masculine allowed judges to include or exclude women under statutes and regulations, depending on the climate of the times or their own personal biases (Martyna, 1980).

Another way language treats the sexes differently is by regarding the female as a sex object (Eakins and Eakins, 1978). The impression is thereby conveyed that women's sexuality completely defines them, while male sexuality is only part of their identity as well rounded human beings. A male professional is assumed to be a doctor, lawyer, etc. A woman professional is assumed to be a prostitute. Research on sexual terms produced ten times as many for females as for males. Women are labelled "nympho," "hooker," "tramp," "whore," and (most devastating of all) "slut." Similar terms for men carry more positive associations and reflect, perhaps, the morality of machismo and the double standard: "Casanova," "Don Juan," "letch," "stud" (Eakins and Eakins, 1978).

There is also reverse devaluation. Here, what is admirable in one sex is disdained in the other. Probably, men fare worse in this trade-off. Labeling a woman "mannish" is less insulting than labelling a man "womanish" or "sissy." Indeed, "there are surely overtones of praise in telling a female she runs, talks, or most especially, *thinks* 'like a man.' "

Then, there are "praise him/blame her" pairs of words. He is a "chef" and expert, while she is merely a "cook." He is "master" of all he surveys, she is a "mistress" cohabiting without benefit of marriage. She "chattered," he "discussed." She "nagged," he "reminded." She "bitched," he "complained." She is "scatterbrained," he is "forgetful." She has "wrinkles," he has "character lines" (Eakins and Eakins, 1978).

Finally, occupational titles also establish males as primary, females as secondary. The majority of the titles for occupations are male (pilot, physician), and it is assumed that males occupy them. A few titles (nurse, prostitute, housekeeper, maid) belong to females. When either gender moves beyond its traditional sphere, special markers are needed – female physician, male nurse – that often cast negative connotations on the incumbent. (Then, there is the story of the children who were disappointed to discover that the "dog doctor" was only a human being [Miller and Swift, 1976].)

The point to be emphasized is that as girls and boys learn their language, they also learn something about women's place and men's place.

Parents as Significant Others.

The provocative ideas of Lynn (1959; 1969) emphasize the significance of parents in gender socialization. Lynn postulates that because of the greater availability of the mother and the relative absence of the father during early childhood, little girls easily develop their gender identity through imitation and positive reinforcement. However, little boys must shift from their initial identification with the mother to masculine identification. Because male models are scarce, they have greater difficulty than females in achieving gender identity. According to Lynn, males must learn through abstractly piecing together the intellectual problem of the definition of masculinity. Some of this learning comes from peers and from media presentations of gender stereotypes. Some results from punishment for displays of feminine behavior. Masculine behavior is rarely defined positively as something the boy *should* do. Instead, undesirable feminine behavior is indicated negatively as something he should *not* do (Hartley, 1959). Consequently, males remain anxious about gender. Females freely imitate males (in fashion, for example), but not vice versa. As adults, men are more hostile towards both the opposite sex and homosexuals than are females. Nevertheless, the boy learns to prefer the masculine role to the feminine, because being male implies countless privileges.

During childhood, the male role is the more inflexible. More pressure is placed on boys to act like boys than for girls to act like girls. Girls' problems start with adolescence:

Since girls are less likely to masturbate, run away from home, or bite and draw blood, their lives are relatively free from crisis until puberty. Before that girls do not have to conform to threatening new criteria of acceptability to anywhere near the extent that boys do (Bardwick and Douvan, 1971).

As children of both sexes reach the teenage years, they are exposed to more complex and more precisely defined norms of gender-appropriate behavior.

Peers as Significant Others.

Children's experience with age-mates is also important in learning masculine or feminine behavior. Boys and girls have different friendship patterns and different forms of play. Consequently, they acquire different sorts of social skills that have implications for their later adult behavior.

A gender difference exists in the size of children's play groups (Eder and Hallinan, 1978). Girls tend to play in small groups, especially dyads (two-person groups). Boys prefer to congregate in larger groups. Therefore, girls learn the type of interpersonal skill required by small, intimate groups, such as sensitivity to others' feelings, the ability to disclose information about themselves, and to show affection. Boys learn other sorts of skills. They learn something about group leadership and decision-making. In addition, girls protect their exclusive groups against the advances of newcomers, while boys tend to welcome new members. Likely, little girls blame themselves for the greater trouble they have in making friends.

The type of play preferred by boys versus girls (Lever, 1978) partly explains the size difference of their friendship groups. Although such differences seem to be diminishing somewhat, boys tend to play competitive games requiring teams of interdependent players with definite roles. Such games are played according to specific rules. (Hockey is a good example.) In comparison, girls prefer to converse or to play games, such as hopscotch, requiring few participants. Playing dolls or hopscotch does not demand the coordination of effort that hockey or baseball does. One result is the learning of different types of skills, and, again, they very likely carry over into adulthood.

Boys acquire the ability to coordinate their actions, to cope with impersonal rules, to work for collective as well as individual goals, to deal with competition and criticism. Girls learn to be imaginative, to converse, and to be empathetic. All these social experiences would be valuable for both genders. There is some evidence that gender differences in play have lessened over the last 30 years (Eder and Hallinan, 1978); perhaps children of both genders will eventually gain practice in both types of skills.

Conclusion. Symbolic interactionists view gender as a matter of social definition and social behavior learned during the socialization process. Other theoretical viewpoints on gender socialization are also useful. For example, Lynn's (1959; 1969) ideas really incorporate psychoanalytic and learning notions, as well as symbolic interactionism.

Many social scientists are convinced that the traditional gender stereotypes are arbitrary and even damaging scripts for socialization. Some are intrigued with the possibility of making *androgyny* rather than sex-typing the goal of socialization. The term **androgyny** combines the Greek words for male (*andro*) and female (*gyne*), and it refers to the presence of both feminine and masculine elements within individuals of both sexes (Laws, 1979). Allowing people to have both instrumental and expressive capabilities within their repertoires may help to free the human personality from the restricting prison of stereotyping (Bem, 1976). An androgynous person might characterize himself or herself as understanding, compassionate, *and* assertive, self-reliant, and ambitious. A sex-typed person, on the other hand, might use *either* the first three *or* the last three traits in self-description. Androgyny, then, refers to flexibility in gender behavior. It does not imply anything about a person's sexual orientation (Basow, 1980).

SOCIAL STRUCTURAL EXPLANATIONS OF GENDER

A structural explanation of gender means seeing what can be learned about gender by assuming that people's behavior is influenced by external social factors or patterns of social relationships, such as norms, roles, statuses, social classes, institutions. According to this perspective, gender is the result of societal, not individual characteristics. The structural functionalist and conflict perspective on gender are reviewed below.

The Structural Functionalist Explanation of Gender

Structural functionalist theorists like Parsons and Bales (1955) ask how societal arrangements, such as male-female differences, contribute to the stability and survival of the social system. The family institution is seen as functional for the society because it performs such crucial tasks as satisfaction of sexual needs, procreation, child-care, and socialization.

Role specialization of the adult family members enhances the ability of the family to perform these functions. The father-husband assumes the instrumental role, meaning that he connects the family to the wider society. In our society, this implies bringing home income from an outside job. The mother-wife, on the other hand, assumes the expressive role. She looks after the relationships within the family.

According to Parsons and Bales (1955), these structural patterns developed from a biological base. The female is the sex that bears and nurses children. Pregnancy, lactation, and human children's long period of helplessness restrict women's activities outside the home. Therefore, it is convenient for women to carry out the family's expressive functions. Men perform the instrumental tasks almost by default. Someone has to perform the instrumental role, and men's biology does not restrict their movements in the outside world.

Many feminists (Rosaldo, 1974; 1980) agree that the structural functionalists' distinction between women's domestic orientation and men's public orientation is an extremely important point. Moreover, that distinction goes a long way towards explaining female subordination. Women's dependence on men for food and physical protection makes men seem their natural superiors. Men's public activities (work in the labor market, hunting, military activities, religion, and so on) have traditionally given them privileged access to resources and symbols that enhance their power and provide disproportionate rewards. The corollary, according to Rosaldo, is that women would gain power either by entering the men's public world or by encouraging male participation in domestic life. Her solution assumes that males would lack sufficient interest in the domestic sphere to usurp women's authority there.

However, structural functionalists have been severely criticized for putting forth scientific arguments that serve to justify the traditional view that women's place is in the home. Although it is not entirely the fault of structural functionalist theorists, the "function is" translates into "the function should be" (Friedan, 1963). Just because it is functional for women to stay home does not mean that women *must* stay home. Arrangements which were convenient in preliterate societies do not necessarily make sense in contemporary societies. For one thing, women need no longer be constantly pregnant to insure survival of the species. For another, social inventions, such as day-care facilities, free women from these biological imperatives. Also, male physical strength matters much less in our society than it did in earlier societies. Anyone can "man" a computer. Moreover, newer research shows that the role segregation hypothesized by the structural functionalists is not a universal feature of family life. Aronoff and Crano (1975) examined how work was distributed among women and men in 862 societies and concluded that both sexes commonly share the instrumental function. Finally, the labels "instrumental" and "expressive" sometimes get applied on ideological rather than empirical grounds. Who says the household activities of chauffeuring, check-writing, financial management, and shopping are expressive? Who says male executives' wining and dining of clients is really instrumental? (Richardson, 1981.)

The Conflict Perspective

The analysis of the inequality of the sexes in *The Origins of the Family, Private Property, and the State* (1884), by Karl Marx's associate, Friedrich Engels, provides the starting point for a conflict theory of gender (Fox, 1982; Smith, 1977). The main idea here is that females and males are tied to the economic structure in different ways, and this difference explains why males are the more powerful gender (Nielsen, 1978).

In capitalist societies, men and women constitute two separate classes. The reason: classes are defined by their relation to the means of production, and the sexes have a unique relation to these means. The difference flows from the distinction in capitalist societies between *commodity production* (products created for exchange on the market) and the *production of use-values* (all things produced in the home). In a society based on commodity production, such as our own, house-

hold labor, including child care, is not considered real work because it lies outside the marketplace. Men have primary responsibility for commodity production, women for the production of use-values. Herein lies women's inferior status.

In a society in which money determines value, women are a group who work outside the money economy. Their work is not worth money, is therefore valueless, is therefore not even real work (Benston, 1969).

Women's unpaid work in the home, nevertheless, serves the capitalist system. To pay women for their work would mean a massive redistribution of wealth.

Women who are employed outside the home also have a different relation to the economic structure than men. For one thing, women's position in the family facilitates women's use as a "reserve army of labor" (Morton, 1972). They are called into the labor force when they are needed (during wartime for example) and sent home when the need disappears. The cultural prescription that women belong in the home assures that the women will return to the home (Glazer, 1977).

Women's primary allegiance to the family is used by the capitalist system as an excuse for deploying them in menial, underpaid jobs. A large pool of unqualified women in competition for jobs depresses wages. Women are untrained, unreliable workers because their families come first. They require less money than men because they are secondary workers anyway. Or so the argument goes.

Women's unpaid labor directly and indirectly subsidizes men's paid labor (Eichler, 1978). Women entertain husbands' business acquaintances, type, help with husbands' small businesses and farms, all without compensation. All of these services cost money when someone outside the family performs them. This sort of work allows husbands to devote their efforts to full-time paid work.

In general, the conflict perspective explains the inequality of Canadian women in these structural terms:

A glance at the Canadian social structure indicates that it is men who own and control the essential resources . . . ownership of the most important resource, the means of production, is mainly in the hands of a few men who have power over almost all women as well as other men . . . . Men also have control of the next most important resource, access to the occupational structure and control of policy making in the major areas of social life (Connelly and Christiansen-Ruffman, 1977).

Critics have attacked the notion that women constitute a special class (Reed, 1978). A few women belong to the plutocratic class, more belong to the middle class, and even more belong to the proletarian layers of society. The few rich women have little in common with the millions of poor women. Moreover, if all women compose a class – the oppressed – then all men form a counter-class – the oppressor. To some people, defining men as the main enemy of women is a serious mistake. The capitalist economic system, misguided socialization practices, vestigial traditions, or biology all offer alternative explanations.

This section completes the trilogy of theoretical perspectives on gender: the biological, social psychological (or socialization), and structural functionalist explanations. These should be regarded as complementary approaches. Focusing on all three increases our understanding of the phenomenon beyond what it would be through appreciation of any one alone. Nevertheless, the various theories of gender are as yet incomplete. One reason is the newness of the sociology of gender relations.

GENDER RELATIONS IN CANADIAN INSTITUTIONS

This section presents a brief overview of some of the ways in which female and male experiences differ in selected Canadian institutions.

The Family

Marriage and the family affect men and women differently. Indeed, Bernard (1971) argues that each family unit actually contains two families – his and hers. What evidence supports this allegation?

His and Her Priorities. Females are expected to give priority to the family and males to their occupation. Through a recent cultural innovation, women may now combine the wife-mother and career roles (Gee, 1980). However, the woman still has the cultural mandate to give priority to the family. Even when she works outside the home, she is expected to be committed to her family first, her work second (Coser and Rokoff, 1971).

This cultural mandate means that in early adulthood locating and marrying a suitable man takes precedence over investment of time and money in extensive job training. The fact that women marry earlier than men is one indication of this cultural mandate. In 1975, the average age of Canadian brides and grooms at first marriages was 22.5 and 24.9 years respectively (Kalbach and McVey, 1979). Looking ahead, the young woman's decision is not between family and work, but between family and *demanding* work. After marriage her husband and his work are what counts. If his job requires geographic mobility, she gives up her job and goes with him. Her work is disrupted by pregnancy, child-rearing, and family emergencies. But these disruptions really don't matter because her low-status work doesn't matter.

Greenglass and Devins (1982) report that although 85 percent of a sample of Canadian university undergraduate women plan to combine career and family in the future, only 10 percent anticipate working while they have pre-school children. These students' plans reflect our society's gender attitudes. Eighty percent of a national sample agreed that, "when children are young, a mother's place is in the home" (Gibbins, Ponting, and Symons, 1978). The fact that nearly 60 percent of unmarried woman between 20 and 44 are actually in the labor force (Block and Wecker, 1982) suggests that many Canadian mothers experience role conflict.

Studies of the male life-cycle (Levinson, 1978) report priority shifts over time. Men, during their twenties and thirties, during the early years of marriage and family formation, remain "largely passive spectators in the home setting." In mid-life, there tends to be a shift from this high centrality of work to a greater investment in family (Rossi, 1980). This life-cycle change happens because of some combination of age, stress, and perceived failure in work. On the other hand, the full-time housewife-mother in mid-life often becomes interested in achievement outside the home (Sheehy, 1976).

Division of Labor.

Familial priorities are closely related to familial division of labor. In the traditional marriage, husbands and wives have distinctive responsibilities labelled by the structural functionalists as instrumental and expressive roles.

Statistics Canada provides an interesting illustration of Canadian traditionalism in this area. The 1976 census for the first time gave Canadians the option of choosing whether the husband or the wife should be listed as the head of the household. Only 1.5 percent designated the wife as household head! (Davids, 1980).

Recently, sociologists have become interested in who does the work around the home. If life is to proceed smoothly, someone has to prowl supermarket aisles in search of fresh broccoli, someone has to cook dinner, someone has to scrub toilet bowls, someone has to wipe children's runny noses. That someone is usually the wife. Regardless of individual variation in talent and inclination, society consigns "a large segment of the population to the role of homemaker solely on the basis of sex" (Bem and Bem, 1971). Outside work does not let women "off the hook," they carry two jobs. A time-budget study (Meissner, et al, 1975) asked Vancouver couples to keep detailed records of how they spent their time. It showed that when a childless wife goes out to work, the husband contributes an extra 6 minutes of housework each week to the 3.2 hours he would do otherwise. In couples with young children, the husband of an employed wife contributes, on the average, an hour more of housework a week to his average of 5 hours of work in the house. In contrast, the average woman who goes out to work adds 18 hours to her weekly workload.

Our society assigns child support to the father and child care to the mother. The law requires the husband to support his children (and wife), but the wife is not similarly obliged (Eichler, 1975). As noted above, the weight of child-rearing responsibility falls on the mother's shoulders.

Marital Dissolution.

Separation and divorce affect men and women somewhat differently (Brandwein, Brown, and Fox, 1974). First, custom but not the law favors women in the area of child custody (Prentice, 1979). The mother is the custodial parent of over 85 percent of the children involved in divorce (Ambert, 1980).

The economic implications of marriages ending are often different for husband and wife. Divorce frequently spells downward economic mobility, even poverty, for the women involved (Boyd, 1977). There are a number of reasons for this situation. Women generally earn less than men. Moreover, divorced and separated women suffer from the widespread assumption that men are the chief breadwinners and women merely secondary earners. Also, women returning to the labor market after years of full-time housewifery are unlikely to be well trained. Often, the woman is supporting children and must pay for child-care while she works. Husbands often renege on child support payments. A further reason for women's economic disadvantage was the failure of the law, until recently, to recognize the financial contribution to the marriage of the wife who chose to be a full-time housewife or to work in a family business.

Divorced women are less likely to remarry than divorced men. Four-fifths of divorced men versus two-thirds of divorced women remarry (Ambert, 1980). The double standard of aging is the major factor involved here, with women's age being a greater barrier to their remarriage than dependent children. Older women have less chance of remarriage, because custom says they must marry someone at least their own age. In comparison, even much younger women are considered suitable marriage partners for divorced men.

Death still ends most marriages, and widowhood has different consequences for men and women. First of all, there are many more widows than widowers. In Canada, 82 percent of the more than one million widowed people are women (Matthews, 1980). Because men choose younger wives and women outlive men by seven years, widowers have many more opportunities for remarriage. Another difference is that widows are more likely to be poor. The reason is that they devoted their lives to their families without pay;

One Parent or Two?

The "Where Is Daddy?" controversy highlights the problem of the way parenthood is institutionalized in our society. The "motherhood mystique," which teaches that all women must experience maternity to be truly happy, tempts women into motherhood. Once women conform to this mystique, their commitment to parenthood is almost irrevocable. We can have ex-spouses (when mistakes are made in marriage) and ex-jobs (when the wrong occupational decision is taken), but rarely ex-children (Rossi, 1977). Then, mothers are expected to devote themselves full-time to their offspring in households isolated from adult company (Bernard, 1979). While society holds fathers responsible for the financial support of their family, serious childrearing is delegated to their wives.

This situation allegedly provokes several reactions from parents:

1. "Smothering, overprotective" mothers "over-invest" in their children and try to dominate their lives (Chodorow, 1978).
2. "Seductive" mothers become overly close to their sons (Flacks, 1979).
3. "Rejecting" mothers detach themselves emotionally from child-rearing. (Cross-cultural observations suggest that the greater the burden of childcare assigned to mothers, the less warmth they feel for their children [Bernard, 1979].)
4. "Escaping" mothers trade full-time motherhood for an outside job. (Incidentally, research shows that maternal employment does *not* harm children [Etaugh, 1974].)
5. "Guilty" fathers lament the confusion surrounding the father role. It seems "there's little he does or can do right" (Brenton, 1975).

6. "Resentful" fathers, unable to relate to their children, view them as economic liabilities (Brenton, 1975).

The wisdom of our traditional childrearing arrangements is now being questioned. Something is clearly wrong when 70 percent of 10 000 parents who wrote to Ann Landers about having children said they "would not do it again" (Rowe, 1977). Many experts are convinced that fathers should be responsible for half the parenting. Children would then be better off because love would not be a "scarce resource controlled and manipulated by one person" (Chodorow, 1978). Moreover, "two adults involved in the upbringing [of children] can counteract each other's more bizarre tendencies and complement each other's talents and blind spots" (Green, 1974).

in other words, they obeyed the cultural mandate mentioned on the previous page.

Work Outside the Home

Our discussion of women's cultural mandate to give the family priority and of conflict theorists' ideas about women as a reserve army of labor would lead us to expect that the labor force experiences of women and men will differ.

Labor Force Participation. Although there are more men then women who work for pay, 78 percent versus 49 percent in 1979 (Women's Bureau, Labour Canada, 1980), the participation of women in the labor force has risen dramatically since World War II. Moreover, since that time, the labor force participation of *married* women has increased five-fold. This rate of increase for married women is almost twice as fast as that for all women (Lupri and Mills, 1982). In 1979, the

female labor force consisted of 30 percent single women, 60 percent married women, and 10 percent widowed, separated, or divorced women (Women's Bureau, Labour Canada, 1980).

How is this rising labor force participation to be explained? Women's increasing education, and consequent higher earning capabilities, is one reason (Gunderson, 1976). Also, though marriage and children still reduce women's labor force participation, they are weaker deterrents now than in the past (Bruce, 1978), and women are having fewer children. The double-digit inflation over the past few years has compelled many women to enter the labor force. Finally, more clerical and service jobs have become available in the post-World War II economy, and women have been attracted to these jobs.

Sex Segregation of Work. Although the female participation rate in the Canadian labor force has risen sharply, corresponding changes have not occurred in the nature of women's work.

[Women] are still overwhelmingly slotted into specific . . . occupations characterized by low pay, low skill requirements, low productivity, and low prospects for advancement. There is women's work and there is men's work. And women continue to be disproportionately segregated into many of the least attractive jobs (Armstrong and Armstrong, 1978).

Occupational segregation by sex means that women tend to work in a relatively few traditionally female jobs, in clerical, health, teaching, and service occupations, and tend to outnumber men in these occupations (Armstrong and Armstrong, 1975). For example, since women hold about 70 percent of all clerical jobs, the office is a "female job ghetto" (Lowe, 1980). Although considerable publicity is given to female physicians, lawyers, university professors, pharmacists, each of these professions involves a tenth of one percent (or less) of all female workers (Armstrong and Armstrong, 1978).

Income. The money women derive from their work represents a key indicator of progress toward equality. The facts are unequivocal: employed women earn considerably less money than their male counterparts. From a national survey, Goyder (1981) found that Canadian women earn less than half the average income of Canadian men. If we analyze sex differences in income by marital status, we find that married women earn about 40 percent as much as married men, but that single women earn about 80 percent as much as single men, and that women in other categories earn about 60 percent as much as men in these same categories (Block and Walker, 1982). Younger, single, educated females fare better than middle-aged, married, low-educated females (Gunderson, 1976). These differences are accounted for by women's cultural mandate to give their families priority, their consequent greater involvement in part-time work and career interruptions, by discrimination, and by the lower paying jobs available to them.

Additional Characteristics of Women's Work. Women's work is more unstable than men's work. Women have higher unemployment rates than men in almost every occupation and industry and are usually the first to be laid off (Gunderson, 1976).

Women's work in the labor force *parallels* their work at home (Armstrong and Armstrong, 1978). In both contexts, they nurture others, cook and serve food, take care of the sick, sew clothes, clean rooms, wash hair. In addition, women's work typically offers *few opportunities for advancement*. Because they have less chance than men to move up a career ladder (Rosenfeld, 1979), Canadian women frequently end their working lives where they began.

Women are much less likely than men to occupy *authority* positions in work organizations. Although women's lack of qualifications is an explanatory factor, just as important are discriminatory employer policies based on the assumption that women are unfit to supervise others (Wolf and Fligstein, 1979).

Finally, fewer Canadian female workers are *unionized*; 27 percent versus 43 percent of Canadian male workers (Baker and Robeson, 1981). The main reason is that white-collar workers and part-time workers are difficult for unions to organize (Marchak, 1973).

Religion

Church organization has traditionally assigned different roles to women and to men. With few exceptions, men are the authority figures: deacons, priests, clergymen, bishops, cardinals, popes. Ceremonial ties with the deity are maintained by men. When women are permitted a role beyond member of the congregation, it is usually a service position. For example, in the Roman Catholic Church, the nuns teach and nurse, while priests celebrate mass, perform marriage ceremonies, and ordain other priests.

Iona Campagnolo, former Canadian Minister of Amateur Sport, discussing her childhood ambitions, was quoted in *Today* magazine as saying, "I always thought I'd be a missionary of some kind. Because I was a female, I never thought of becoming a minister." Although some of the large Protestant denominations, such as the United Church, have agreed after much deliberation to ordain women, the numbers involved are very small. Often, these female clergy are deflected from ministerial roles into teaching (Walum, 1977).

Women's marginal position in the churches has

serious implications for gender socialization. Ruether (1974) claims, perhaps extravagantly, that religion is "undoubtedly the single most important shaper and enforcer of the image and role of women." While children might encounter female Sunday School teachers, they again see the important roles as a male prerogative and experience only males making ceremonial contact with God. Other consequences are more indirect. As long as women remain outside the church's inner circle, the female point of view is missing on matters of considerable concern to them, such as abortion and birth control (Ambert, 1976).

The religious doctrine presented to children is also male-oriented. For instance, the male image of God, his traditional presentation as father, judge, shepherd, king, serve indirectly to buttress male supremacy on earth. If God is male, how can females be made in his image?

All of this is quite ironic in view of the fact that Canadian women tend to be more religious than Canadian men. More women are believers (Veevers and Cousineau, 1980), and they attend religious services more regularly than men (Mol, 1976).

Only a handful of studies have attempted to measure the effects of religious socialization on gender attitudes. Most focus on women. First, women who are more involved with religion are also more traditional in their gender attitudes. Second, women's religious affiliations are related to their gender attitudes. Jewish women and women without religious affiliation are relatively untraditional. Catholics and Fundamentalist Protestants are quite traditional. Mainline Protestants fall somewhere in between (McMurry, 1978). In general, it seems that religious socialization augments and reinforces other sources of gender socialization.

The School

Though most Canadian classrooms are not segregated by sex, school does not seem to be the same psychological or social environment for girls and for boys. Elementary school is a place where women teachers rule. They approve of the girl students who identify with them and scold boy students for being rambunctious. Female pupils progress through elementary (and secondary) school faster than male students (Martin and Macdonell, 1978).

During the early years of school, girls are more successful academically than boys. Girls beginning school are, on the average, two years more advanced developmentally than boys. They begin to speak, read, and count before boys do. This developmental advance is reflected in girls' academic achievement. In the early grades, girls are at least equal with boys in mathematical skill (Fink and Kosecoff, 1977). Two to three times the number of boys, as compared with girls, have reading problems. Also, boys seem to have a more difficult time adjusting to elementary school classroom demands for obedience, order, neatness. "Feminine" behavior seems more appropriate to school. Possibly, girls have already learned at home to be obedient and quiet, while boys have been reinforced for "bouncing about, questioning, being curious or aggressive" (Howe, 1974). Finally, the female authority figure in the elementary grades makes it easier for girls to identify with their teacher, and hence with general academic values (Richer, 1979).

The situation of women today very likely has something to do with the way textbooks stereotyped the sexes in the past. For instance, *The Report of the Royal Commission on the Status of Women in Canada* (1970) analyzed the gender imagery in a representative selection of Anglophone and Francophone elementary school textbooks. The versatile characters who had adventures were invariably males. In French-language textbooks, the girls "are preparing to be only mothers and housekeepers, and are portrayed as passive, self-sacrificing, and submissive." A series of readers used in Ontario featured a caricatured family. The kind, understanding father takes his children on interesting expeditions, while the mother stays home to prepare meals and to tell the children "what is best for them." The gender-typing even appeared in arithmetic books, where children were presented with problems such as: "A girl can type about 48 words per minute. She has to type 2,468 words. Can she do this in 45 minutes?" Although the elementary school curriculum is the same for girls and boys, the textbook models provide children with clearly differentiated gender imagery. From this content analysis, the Commission concluded that,

"A woman's creative and intellectual potential is either underplayed or ignored in the education of children from their earliest years." Therefore, they recommended, "That the provinces and territories adopt textbooks that portray women, as well as men, in diversified roles and occupations."

Textbooks are not the only teaching material found to contain sexist bias. A former teacher describes a social studies film called "Big People, Little People:"

It was very careful to reflect a racial mix, showing a lot of children playing adult roles with a black boy playing the mayor. But apparently the idea of female roles had never occurred to the filmmakers. Throughout the entire eight minutes, females appeared twice; the total time they were on screen was 38 seconds, and each time they were carrying mops. The committee viewing this film dissolved into hysterics. If it had been prepared deliberately as a satire on sex stereotyping, it couldn't have been done better (Nelson, 1976).

Proportionately more boys continue their education beyond high school (Hunter, 1981). Moreover, women in post-secondary education continue to enrol mostly in traditional female occupations (Robb and Spencer, 1976). Most girls want to be teachers, social workers, nurses, secretaries, not chartered accountants, engineers, architects, lawyers. Many women, by charting their destiny according to traditional gender patterns, are not developing their human potential.

The term "reversal of success" has been used to label the fact that females, the sex most comfortable in school, end up doing less well in the occupational structure. As we saw earlier, most Canadian women who work outside the home are concentrated in a small number of low-skilled, poorly-paid jobs. Research tells us that gender contributes a more formidable barrier to women's occupational achievement than does lack of resources, such as academic ability or socioeconomic background (Marini and Greenberger, 1978). Girls from poor families, from Indian or Inuit families, and from remote regions of the country, will be even more disadvantaged.

Why are women's educational ambitions so modest? Possibly, men's occupational ambitions are greater than women's, because work is a major ingredient of masculine self-esteem, and because they expect to spend a lifetime in the labor market. As they reach adolescence, males take school, the avenue to the "breadwinner" role, more seriously.

The school is only one of many agents that markets gender stereotypes and depresses women's ambitions. However, the school reflects the values of the surrounding society, and consequently, its teachers, curricula (official and hidden), textbooks, and guidance counsellors are engaged in the business of gender socialization. However, things are slowly changing. Under the auspices of the women's movement and the exigencies of the economic climate, women's lives are less determined by the family cycle. Concomitant with the recent trend toward later marriage, later initiation of child-bearing, reduced family size expectation, and the rising number of female-headed families is women's growing occupational commitment (Garrison, 1979).

WOMEN'S AND MEN'S LIBERATION MOVEMENTS

The decade of the 1960s was marked by protest against the system and demands for just treatment by Indians, blacks, the poor, university students, and, eventually, women. In 1967, the Royal Commission on the Status of Women was set up to inquire into the situation of Canadian women and "to recommend what steps might be taken by the federal government to insure for women equal opportunities with men in all aspects of Canadian society" (*Report of the Royal Commission on the Status of Women in Canada*, 1970). The feminist movement in Canada officially began with the federal government's decision to establish the Commission (Morris, 1980). Prior to this political action, women's situation was not regarded as a social problem. Three years later, the Commission tabled its report which contained 167 recommendations in the areas of the economy, education, the family, taxation, poverty, public life, immigration and citizenship, and criminal law.

Women's problems are far from being solved. To date, a number of the Commission's recommendations have not been implemented. For example, establishing 18 years as the minimum age for marriage, and amendments to the Indian Act to allow an Indian

The Changing Door-Opening Ceremony

Doors are everywhere. Car doors, house doors, university building doors, revolving doors, electric eye doors. When we confront a door, we often find ourselves involved in a ceremonial ritual.

Though, on the face of it, ceremonial rules of conduct appear to deal with minor everyday matters, etiquette acts as glue which holds together the fabric of social order. Such rules involve the routine acting-out of cultural values. In addition, they reveal the actors as considerate persons who know how to behave "properly" or, alternatively, as boors. Indeed, "the gestures which we sometimes call empty are perhaps, in fact, the fullest things of all" (Goffman, 1967).

Imagine this scene outside a 1960 classroom door. A young woman and a young man, total strangers, simultaneously reach the closed door. She steps aside slightly and waits. He positions himself, turns the knob, pulls open the door, and holds it while she enters. Once she is across the threshold, he enters behind her. The door-opening ceremony has gone smoothly, although the participants never rehearsed it.

Imagine the same scene in the 1980s. These entries in student diaries for a sociology of gender relations course indicate that the door-opening ritual no longer proceeds automatically:

I came to a door at the same time as this guy. He reached to open it for me but then I started to open it myself and he just let me do it. It was like neither of us knew what to do.

I had a 15-second encounter with a pro-libber which has left a bad taste in my mouth all day. She had a large stack of papers and I pushed open and held the door for her. I would have done this for a woman or a man. Instead of thank you I got the coldest, bitterest, most glaring stare that went right through me. I resent being seen as a Pig when I was being courteous to her as a person.

What has happened? The traditional door ceremony affirmed the nature of the social order as it was before the feminist movement. It symbolized that masculinity meant having authority, being strong, and in control and that femininity meant being dependent, frail, and passive. As this overheard conversation indicates, feminists' general challenge to the social order has had repercussions for ceremonial encounters between females and males:

Female: Well, aren't you going to open the door for me?
Male: I didn't know that girls still like boys to do that.
Female: I'm not in Women's Lib.

The present confusion about doors may eventually resolve itself into a humanitarian ritual signifying consideration for people of both sexes. A male diarist expresses this line of thought.

A male shouldn't circle *the car to open the door for a woman.*
I believe each sex should treat the other with mutual courtesy.
If a woman reaches the car first, there is nothing wrong with her opening it.

Source:

Walum, Laurel Richardson. "The changing door ceremony." *Urban Life and Culture,* Vol. 2, 1974, pp. 506-515.

---

woman who marries a non-Indian to retain her Indian status and to transmit this status to her children. Also, many new issues concern women today that were not evident in 1970. Equality in pension provisions and violence against women are two examples (Advisory Council on the Status of Women, 1979). Informal protest groups seem to have lost some of their momentum. Florence Bird, who headed the Commission, says that, "The excitement and sense of achievement generated by the response of the Royal Commission . . . have begun to fizzle" (*Chatelaine,* July 1982).

Societal arrangements are also in flux for men (David and Brannon, 1976; Dubbert, 1979; Fasteau, 1975; Komarovsky, 1976; Nichols, 1975). Because gender roles are interlocking and complementary, women's dissatisfaction has inevitably affected men. Women's critical scrutiny of the traditional ways the genders relate forced men also to become conscious of the flaws in the status quo. A few men, mostly middle-class and university educated (Snodgrass, 1974), became involved in male liberation groups in the 1970s.

Many of the social policies designed to liberate women would also liberate men (Safilios-Rothschild, 1974). If women were treated equally, both sexes would

As lifestyle and gender patterns change, the rituals of everyday married life also change. In the 1950s and 1960s, it was standard practice for the husband to leave for work each morning to earn a living for the family. The wife, for her part, stayed behind to care for the children and prepare a comfortable living environment for the "breadwinner." In the 1980s, such a standardized gender relationship does not always exist. In fact, it may be that both partners work, or that the wife is the one who leaves for work each day. (*Miller Services*)

benefit from more mature relationships. Men would no longer need to take all the responsibility for initiating contact with women, or all of the risk of rejection. True female-male friendships would become possible. Egalitarian marriage would mean the sharing of decision-making and economic responsibility. Until now, men have been morally and legally obliged to support all the dependent women and children in

their lives. They have not had the option to be unemployed, to work part-time, or occasionally to fail occupationally. Men, too, could ignore occupational sex-typing and, if they wished, enter such nurturing supportive occupations as nursing and primary school teaching, or such artistic but financially insecure occupations as ballet dancing. If women become liberated from 24-hour-a-day motherhood, men would learn more about fatherhood. Traditional masculinity has discouraged the tender, expressive, sensitive qualities. The rough, tough male has been seriously disadvantaged in establishing relationships with women, children, or other males.

Insistence that males achieve, be aggressive, and competitive, and prescriptions against emotional expression have been described as the "lethal aspects" of the male role (Jourard, 1964). The higher male suicide rates and earlier death rates may be, in part, consequences of the male role.

Women's and men's liberation groups appreciate the fact that traditional gender roles are arbitrary and damaging for both sexes. As an ideal, androgyny offers freedom to persons of both sexes. Although the difficulties inherent in altering cultural values cannot be underestimated, thought is being given to healthier definitions of masculinity and femininity.

SUMMARY

1. The sociology of gender relations examines masculinity and femininity across cultures and historical periods. This sub-discipline, which was inspired by the feminist movement, attempts to remedy sociology's previous exclusion of women.
2. Human social life is built around the relationships between the sexes. The sexes are both differentiated and ranked.
3. Biological sex has four interrelated aspects: genetic sex, hormonal sex, gonadal sex, and genital sex. Genital sex may be subdivided into internal accessory organs and external genital appearance. Social-psychological gender has three additional dimensions: assigned gender, gender identity, and choice of sexual partner. These eight variables are not necessarily congruent in the same individual.
4. There are only four well established sex diffferences in psychological traits. Females are superior in verbal ability; males in mathematical ability, visual-spatial ability, and aggressiveness. These various abilities are not absolute, but overlapping, and matters of degree.
5. According to the study of animals, the anthropolo-

gical record, psychosexual abnormalities, and hormones and genes, biology seems to be directly involved in cognitive gender differences and aggressiveness and indirectly involved in the female-male division of labor. However, both nature *and* nurture are involved.
6. Theories based on biology, socialization, and social structure are complementary explanations of gender.
7. The socialization process teaches children society's gender scripts, which include gender stereotypes and occupational gender-typing.
8. The structural approach assumes that gender results from external social factors, not individual characteristics. The structural functionalist and conflict perspectives are examples of these macrosociological theories.
9. To a great extent, women and men inhabit their own social worlds. Therefore, they have somewhat different experiences in societal institutions, such as the family, work, religion, and political institutions.
10. The women's and men's liberation movements have pressed for more egalitarian social arrangements and healthier androgynous definitions of masculinity and femininity.

GLOSSARY

Androgyny. Presence of both masculine and feminine characteristics within individuals of both sexes.
Cultural universals. Behavior patterns found in many cultures.
Gender. Societal definitions of appropriate female and male traits and behaviors.
Gender identity. The individual's conviction of being male or female, which is expressed in personality and behavior.
Gender script. The details of a society's ideas about masculinity and femininity contained, for example, in gender stereotypes and gender attitudes.
Hermaphrodite. A person with contradictions among one or more dimensions of biological sex (hormones, chromosomes, gonads, internal and external genitalia).
Lateralization. Functional specialization of left and right hemispheres of the brain.
Sex. Physiological differences between females and males.
Stereotype. Folk beliefs about the attributes characterizing a social category (e.g., the genders, ethnic groups) on which there is substantial agreement.
Transsexual. A person whose gender identity contradicts his/her biological sex.

FURTHER READING

Ambert, Anne-Marie. *Sex Structure.* 2nd ed. Don Mills, Ont.: Longman, 1976. A sociological analysis that emphasizes Canada.

Cook, C.A. (ed.). *Opportunity for Choice: A Goal for Women in Canada.* Ottawa: Information Canada, 1976. Useful statistical information and discussion on the relationship among gender and family, education, and the labor force.

Eichler, Margrit. *The Double Standard: A Feminist Critique of Feminist Social Science.* New York: St. Martin's Press, 1980. A discussion of the feminist perspective and proposals for social change.

Greenglass, Esther. *A World of Difference: Gender Roles in Perspective.* Toronto: John Wiley, 1982. A psychologist's view of gender.

Jamieson, Kathleen. *Indian Women and the Law in Canada: Citizens Minus.* Ottawa: Advisory Council on the Status of Women, 1978. Documents how the law discriminates against Indian women.

Mackie, Marlene. *Exploring Gender Relations: A Canadian Perspective.* Toronto: Butterworths, 1982. An in depth discussion of the many dimensions of gender.

Martin, M. Kay, and Barbara Voorhies. *Female of the Species.* Toronto: Methuen, 1975. An anthropological view of gender.

CHAPTER 5
AGING AND LATER LIFE

VICTOR W. MARSHALL

CAROLYN J. ROSENTHAL

In contemporary Canada, almost everyone can expect to grow old. Even in Third-World societies, for the first time, large proportions of the population can expect to live into the later years. Therefore, aging is a phenomenon of increasing interest to both lay people and sociologists.

Societies and social life are made possible only because people are born into them and pass out of them through a process of aging and dying. From the beginnings of sociology, the way in which social life has been affected by aging has interested many scholars. Karl Mannheim, a German-born sociologist, suggested a mental experiment in which we should try to imagine "what the social life of man would be like if one generation lived on forever and none followed to replace it" (1952).

Mannheim's experiment, like much science fiction

based on the idea that people might live forever, helps us to see more clearly the ways in which the organization of society has taken into account the fact that humans do not live forever but grow old and die. Wilbert Moore has described this as a paradox in which human beings are mortal, but societies are in a sense immortal (Moore, 1966). He argues that aging is both a major aspect of societal continuity and a major opportunity for social change.

Virtually every aspect of social life is affected by the growing proportion and number of older people, by the decreasing proportion and number of very young people, and by the higher average age of the population. Changes have occurred and will continue to be made in the way we allocate work and leisure at various points of the life course. Our ideas about education are less tied than they formerly were to the early years of life. Family life is changing as people find that their parents and grandparents are living to ages thought highly unlikely by Canadians at the time of Confederation. New demands are being made on the social welfare and health care systems by the shift in the age structure.

Aging has a micro and a macro side. The aging of individuals occurs in a context of aging societies. Work in this field draws on theory from all areas of sociology. There is a political economy, as well as a social psychology, of aging and virtually everything in between.

We define the sociology of aging as the scientific study of the way in which age is relevant or "makes a difference" in social life and in the organization of social life that we refer to as "social structure." Age makes a difference, and so changes in age or aging must also make a difference for both individual life and social organization. Our approach to defining the field therefore encompasses both the process of aging and the fact of age differentiation, and it includes within its scope both the experiences of aging individuals and the dynamics of social structure in relation to age.

POPULATION AGING

Before focusing on the aging of the Canadian population, it is important to recognize that population aging is a worldwide phenomenon. The United Nations uses age sixty to demarcate the older population. Currently, more than half the world's people over sixty are living in the less developed areas. The older population in the Third World is increasing at double the rate of the industrialized world. As Third-World countries industrialize and modernize, they are increasingly adopting the First World social institution of retirement. This leaves them with a growing number and proportion of older people outside the work force. The increasing old age dependency ratio (see Chapter 7) has serious repercussions in Third-World countries whose economies are very marginal and whose per capita gross national product is very low. Against this international picture, we will now turn to a consideration of population aging in Canada.

Let us begin with a basic reference point at the beginning of this century. At that time, of about 5.5 million Canadians, just 5.2 percent, were aged 65 or more. In 1981, just under 10 percent of our 23 millions were aged 65 and over. The proportion of the population over the age of 65 will be even larger in the next century. As Table 5-1 shows, around 12-14 percent of our people should be aged 65 and over, and by 2031 about 18 percent.

The Economic Council of Canada suggests that the number of people in the 65 and over category is likely to more than triple by the year 2031, reaching 7 million. Of these, a larger proportion will also be in their late seventies and eighties, because people are living not only to be old but to be very old in a much larger proportion of cases (Economic Council of Canada, 1979).

It is important to recognize that the entire complexion of our society is changing with the aging of the population. Whatever happened to the Pepsi Generation? It grew older and turned into that generation of slightly older-than-Pepsi-Generation beer drinkers featured in the television commercials.

Under reasonable population projections, the median age of the population will increase from 26.2 years in 1971 to 41.6 years in 2031 (Denton and Spencer, 1979). The median age of Canadians is now about 29.7.

Women live longer than men. Life expectancy at age 60 for males is now over 17 years; for females it is 22 years – a five-year spread. At age 70 it is 11 years for

TABLE 5-1: A PROJECTION OF THE POPULATION OF CANADA, BY SEX AND AGE, 1986 TO 2051

Sex and Age		1986	1991	1996	2001	2011	2021	2031	2041	2051
					–Thousands–					
Males:	0-19	4,137	4,389	4,639	4,701	4,683	4,986	5,135	5,270	5,498
	20-64	7,836	8,290	8,657	9,151	10,204	10,490	10,614	11,245	11,515
	65-69	395	453	466	470	608	837	925	752	963
	70-74	308	320	367	378	399	612	764	645	695
	75-79	201	226	237	271	282	366	502	552	450
	80+	178	207	238	260	314	338	474	620	596
Females:	0-19	3,928	4,160	4,393	4,450	4,430	4,715	4,856	4,984	5,200
	20-64	7,827	8,249	8,609	9,102	10,154	10,386	10,454	11,083	11,353
	65-69	487	568	564	568	744	1,045	1,122	907	1,159
	70-74	409	450	528	526	564	875	1,073	903	966
	75-79	301	357	397	466	474	624	875	938	759
	80+	345	430	530	624	806	888	1,220	1,611	1,603
Total		26,352	28,099	29,625	30,967	33,662	36,162	38,014	39,510	40,757
					–Percent of Total–					
Males:	0-19	15.7	15.6	15.7	15.2	13.9	13.8	13.5	13.3	13.5
	20-64	29.7	29.5	29.2	29.6	30.3	29.0	27.9	28.5	28.3
	65-69	1.5	1.6	1.6	1.5	1.8	2.3	2.4	1.9	2.4
	70-74	1.2	1.1	1.2	1.2	1.2	1.7	2.0	1.6	1.7
	75-79	0.8	0.8	0.8	0.9	0.8	1.0	1.3	1.4	1.1
	80+	0.7	0.7	0.8	0.8	0.9	0.9	1.2	1.6	1.5
Females:	0-19	14.9	14.8	14.8	14.3	13.2	13.0	12.8	12.6	12.8
	20-64	29.7	29.4	29.1	29.4	30.2	28.7	27.5	28.1	27.9
	65-69	1.8	2.0	1.9	1.8	2.2	2.9	3.0	2.3	2.8
	70-74	1.6	1.6	1.8	1.7	1.7	2.4	2.8	2.3	2.4
	75-79	1.1	1.3	1.3	1.5	1.4	1.7	2.3	2.4	1.9
	80+	1.3	1.5	1.8	2.0	2.4	2.5	3.2	4.1	3.9
Total		100.0	100.0	100.0	100.0	100.0	100.0	100.0	100.0	100.0

SOURCE: Denton, Frank T., and Byron G. Spencer. 1980. "Canada's population and labour force, past, present, and future.", in Victor W. Marshall (ed.), *Aging in Canada: Social Perspectives*. Toronto: Fitzhenry and Whiteside.

males and 17 years for females (*The Globe and Mail*, 19 July, 1979). In Canada there are now 130 women over the age of 65 for every 100 men. As the population grows older, it will increasingly become female in the later years due to these sex differences in mortality or longevity. By the turn of the century there will be 150 females per 100 males over the age of 65. At that time, among those aged 80 and over, it is projected that there will be about 219 women for every 100 men (Denton and Spencer, 1979, 1980). Not only is the gap in life expectancy between the sexes large, it is widening. Over about the past ten years, female life expectancy at age 60 has increased by about two years, for women, but only a quarter of a year for men.

INCOME, HEALTH, AND GENDER DIFFERENTIATION AMONG THE AGED

Just as we know there are many changes in the first years of life, we should expect there to be many changes in the last years of life. Similarly, just as the lives of young Canadians differ greatly depending on factors such as their class of origin and their gender, the same factors differentiate people in the later years. In the later years, as well, health becomes an important differentiating factor among people. In this section let us look at the ways in which all older people are not alike.

Income Differences

Probably the most critical personal dilemma facing the aging individual and, at the same time, a very important policy issue facing the society as a whole, is the provision of income security for older people. In our society, the basic sources of income for most people are tied to their participation in the labor force or to their familial connection to a labor force participant. Older people are largely excluded from the labor market by the social institution of retirement. In addition, the majority of older women have been prevented by social custom and gender discrimination in the work place from having the experience of regular, consistent labor force participation.

As recently as half a century ago, about half of the Canadian males over the age of 65 were still in the labor force. Today, most people retire before age 65.

Public transfer payments are the major source of income in retirement. Canada has a three-tiered retirement income system (Powell and Martin, 1980). The first tier consists of the federal Old Age Security program instituted in 1951 to apply to persons aged 70 and over, later lowered to age 65 (Chappell, 1980). It is non-contributory and universal. In other words, all persons aged 65 years or older who meet residence requirements receive Old Age Security payments regardless of their previous work history. Also in the first tier is the Guaranteed Income Supplement (GIS) and the Spouse's Allowance program, as well as provincial supplements. GIS benefits are paid to low income pensioners. The Spouse's Allowance is also income-tested and provides benefits to people aged 60 to 64 who are spouses of old age pensioners. Various provinces add additional income-tested support. Over half of all old age pensioners currently receive at least partial GIS benefits.

Although the first tier is designed to keep the aged population from destitution, the official policy of the Canadian government is that income security beyond the survival level is the responsibility of the individual. The second and third tiers of our retirement income system, therefore, depend on individual initiative.

The second tier consists of the Canada Pension Plan (CPP) or, in Quebec, the Quebec Pension Plan (QPP). These pension plans cover almost everyone in the labor force. They are contributory (both the employer and the employee contribute), and they solve the problem of portability that plagues the private pension system. That is, an employee who moves from one employer to another continues to be covered (Economic Council of Canada, 1979).

Contributions to the CPP have led, after disbursements, to a fund of about 19 billion dollars, which is loaned to the provinces at a modest rate of return. The CPP/QPP has thus become the principle source of debt financing for the provincial governments. Any changes in the viability of the plan will have serious repercussions for federal-provincial relations (Pesando and Rea, 1977). Some changes will be needed, because as currently funded the plan will be unable to meet obligations beyond the turn of the century.

The third tier consists of individually-made contracts, especially private pensions, life insurance, Registered Retirement Savings Plans, private annuities, and other savings schemes. In 1976, about 46 percent of employed workers were enrolled in almost 16 000 occupational pension plans which were mostly employer-sponsored. This amounts to 3.9 million workers (Economic Council of Canada, 1979). Coverage varies greatly by industrial sector. Government employees enjoy almost complete coverage, while only about 15 percent of people in retail trade (e.g. sales clerks) and almost no workers in agriculture are covered (Economic Council of Canada, 1979). Government workers or those in large, unionized industrial concerns are most likely to be covered. Class is clearly relevant here. As well, those sectors of the economy in which most women currently find employment are least likely to provide pension coverage.

Even if an employee is enrolled in a private pension plan, there is no guarantee that he or she will collect anything from it. Many currently retired persons suffer from the inadequacies of the system in earlier times (Powell and Martin, 1980). Most private pension plans have inadequate vesting provisions. Normally, employees who leave a company with less than ten years service or before the age of 45, receive only their personal contributions. Insofar as the company's contribution is viewed as deferred wages, this represents a loss to the employee. Although most Canadians change jobs frequently, and although women especially have irregular work histories, pensions are seldom "portable". Those changing jobs lose any accrued benefits.

The scope and significance of private pension plans is evident from the following: Canadian employers spend over 4 billion dollars a year for such plans, a figure amounting to about 6 percent of wages and salaries. The assets of private pension funds in Canada are growing yearly by about 6 billion dollars (Wente, 1980). Of the 16 000 pension plans in Canada, two-thirds of their assets are held by the largest 50. The funds of Bell Canada, Ontario Hydro, and CN each exceed 1 billion dollars. The assets controlled by all private pension funds in Canada are nearly one-sixth the size of Canada's Gross National Product (Wente, 1980).

The private pension industry is clearly massive in scope and in its implications on the control and direction of the Canadian economy. Nonetheless, many observers charge that it has failed almost completely to meet the income security needs of older Canadians.

Summarizing the difficulties with these plans as applied to women, Laurence E. Coward, a director of William M. Mercer Limited, says, "Better pensions for women can best be assured by improving their pay before they retire, by earlier vesting, by pensions that continue to the surviving spouse, and by pension splitting if the marriage breaks down" (*The Globe and Mail*, July 22, 1981).

Currently, however, as shown in Figure 5-1, only about 13 percent of retirement income comes from employer-sponsored pension plans, while more than 50 percent comes from public transfer programs (Powell and Martin, 1980).

Adequate understanding of the economic position of the aged also requires an appreciation of their assets. Almost 70 percent of older Canadians own their homes, a figure slightly larger than that for younger Canadians. Moreover, they are very likely to own their homes completely, unlike younger people who carry mortgages. Housing is a significant asset for the aged, but their houses are generally older, have a lower market value, and are more expensive to repair, keep up, and heat (Collins, 1978). Other assets, such as investments, do not play a large part in providing economic security for the aged.

The economic situation of older Canadians should improve in the future for a number of reasons. The CPP/QPP was initiated only in 1966 and was not fully effective until 1976. Some very old people had ceased employment prior to the full introduction of the plan. Rising labor force participation rates for women, a steady increase in the proportion of the labor force covered by private pension plans, and reform in the plans along the lines suggested above by Coward should help them somewhat to improved economic security.

Poverty in Later Life

Nevertheless, the result of these financial arrangements is that the majority of older Canadians are poor. Yet great differences in degree of economic security occur among the older population, and many of the most wealthy people in the world are old. However, in 1977 more than half of elderly Canadians received the Guaranteed Annual Income Supplement in whole or in part, bringing their annual incomes to just over $5000, still below the official government poverty line. Government transfer payments replace only 43 percent of the pre-retirement income of a single person and 68 percent of the pre-retirement income of a married couple, both of whom are pensioners (Powell and Martin, 1980). While about half of all older Canadians fall below official poverty lines, it is women, especially unmarried women and widows over 55, who are most likely to be poor. As already pointed out in Chapter 4, at least two thirds of this group survive on incomes below the official poverty line.

Not only are most older Canadians poor, but few are wealthy. Among older Canadians, 43 percent have no investment or private pension income to add to their income from public sources. Only 13 percent have more than $4000 of income from pensions or investments (Task Force, 1979).

To put the inadequacy of income security in perspective, Eichler (1982) has contrasted the situation of single parents in Ontario with the elderly. In January 1981, according to Eichler an elderly couple was guaranteed $853 per month, while a welfare family consisting of a mother, father, and three children was guaranteed only $650. Eichler sees political support for children as diminishing, while that for the elderly is growing, and she sees a danger that the young and the old might be played off against each other.

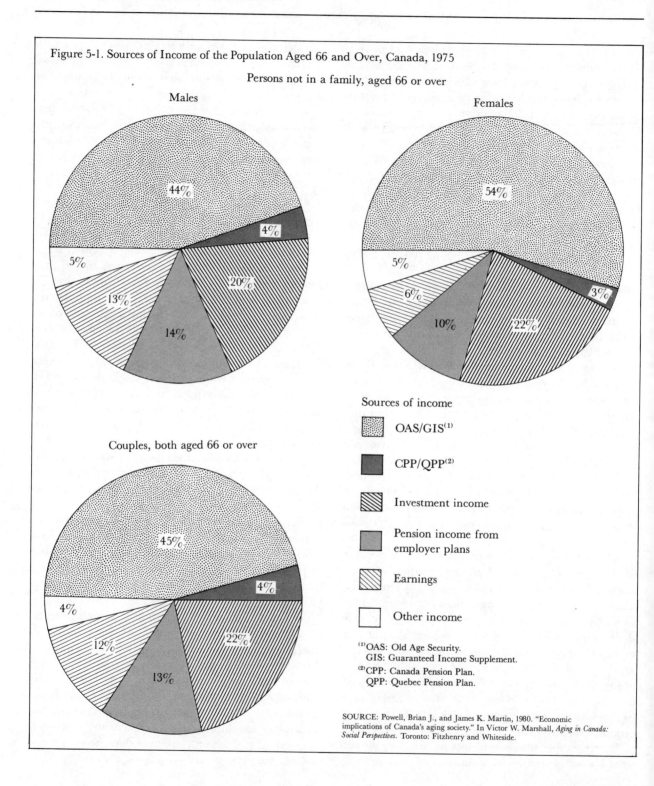

Figure 5-1. Sources of Income of the Population Aged 66 and Over, Canada, 1975

Persons not in a family, aged 66 or over

Males

Females

44%

4%

20%

14%

13%

5%

54%

3%

22%

10%

6%

5%

Couples, both aged 66 or over

45%

4%

22%

13%

12%

4%

Sources of income

OAS/GIS[1]

CPP/QPP[2]

Investment income

Pension income from
employer plans

Earnings

Other income

[1]OAS: Old Age Security.
   GIS: Guaranteed Income Supplement.
[2]CPP: Canada Pension Plan.
   QPP: Quebec Pension Plan.

SOURCE: Powell, Brian J., and James K. Martin, 1980. "Economic
implications of Canada's aging society." In Victor W. Marshall, *Aging in Canada:
Social Perspectives*. Toronto: Fitzhenry and Whiteside.

Former Governor-General Roland Michener is shown here at 81, as fit as most people half that age. The quality of health care in Canada is helping a large proportion of our population to achieve healthy, active later years.

Health

A second major differentiator among older people is health. Contrary to commonly held stereotypes, most people over the age of 65 are quite healthy. However, aging leads to an increased likelihood of a person experiencing chronic health problems, such as heart and circulatory diseases, cancer, arthritis, rheumatism, and diabetes, and to a greater severity in the effects of acute health problems. For example, an older person may take longer to recover from a simple ailment. Older people are also more likely than younger people to have multiple or compounded health problems (Bayne, 1978).

From a sociological point of view, one important way to describe how healthy people are is to ascertain whether or not they need help with everyday activities such as preparing meals. These are referred to as **activities of daily living (ADL)**. In a large study conducted by Tilquin and Associates (1980) on the South Shore of the St. Lawrence River near Montreal, community respondents were asked if they required partial or total help with the following five activities: rising and going to bed, daily personal hygiene, walking around inside the house, bathing, and shopping in summer. The proportion reporting no disability was 84 percent for those aged 65 to 69, but just 67 percent for those aged 75 and over.

The results of various Canadian community studies are remarkably similar (e.g., Cape and Henschke, 1980; Gutman, 1980). Community studies underestimate the extent of health problems among the aged, because in such studies people living at home but in very poor health are usually not interviewed. Nonetheless, some general patterns are apparent. First, most older people remain quite healthy until their late seventies or eighties. Men do not usually live that long, but if you examine the health of men and women in their seventies, you will find quite a healthy group of people.

Second, there really are important sex differences in health. This is apparent in the mortality and life expectancy data noted above and in Chapter 7. But it is also apparent in the ADL data from community studies. There is a significant upward shift in the proportion of people requiring assistance with the activities of daily living at the mid- to late seventies for men, and about the late seventies to mid-eighties for women. In this and in other areas such as economic status, it is imperative to consider older men and older women separately.

Judging from studies in the United States, perhaps 2 percent of the community-dwelling elderly are bedfast (they cannot leave their beds without assistance), and another 4 or 5 percent are homebound (they cannot leave their homes without assistance). Even if you add the institutionalized elderly to the homebound and bedfast, the view that most older people are in poor health is shown to be a myth.

This leads us to note another myth; that most older people are institutionalized. This is clearly false. Most older people live in their own homes. Less than 10 percent of Canadians aged 65 and over live in institutions such as nursing homes and homes for the aged (Schwenger and Gross, 1980; Fletcher and Stone, 1981). With increasing age beyond 65, this proportion rises to 39 percent in the 80 and over category, most of whom are women (Large, 1981). Women are more likely than men to be institutionalized on a proportional basis, and since there are more old women than men this means that a very large proportion of people in nursing homes is women.

The two major factors leading to institutionalization of the aged in Canada are health and the availability of a spouse to provide care with things like medication, bathing, preparation of meals, shopping, and housekeeping. American studies (e.g., Brody, 1978; Tobin and Kulys, 1980) have shown that upwards of 70 percent of such care is provided informally, mostly by family members such as children. (There are as yet no comparable Canadian studies.)

From a societal point of view, the fact that older people consume more health care resources than younger people is of great significance. Although they comprise less than one-tenth of the population, older people account for almost two-fifths of patient days in acute care and allied specialty hospitals (Clark and Collishaw, 1975). Ontario data (Ontario Council of Health, 1978) show that older people account for 17 percent of the services of general practitioners, 23 percent of general surgeon and internist services and even higher amounts of the services provided by some of the other specialties.

The cost of providing health care to the older population should not be viewed with alarm. Instead, we might be thankful that our society has provided conditions that will allow so many people to reach the later years. Moreover, a careful study of health care costs projected into the future (Denton and Spencer, 1980) leads to the conclusion that a quality of health care comparable to that currently provided can be realized without a major shift in the allocation of societal resources. Major changes in the cost of health care will not come from the changing age structure of the population, but rather from changes in the organization of health care delivery and in the decisions made about the level of care we wish to maintain.

For the sociologist of aging, it is as essential to take into account the health of an individual as it is for the general sociologist to take into account such factors as gender or social class. Health status is a major example of the truism, "All old people are not alike."

Gender

It should be apparent that in many respects concerns about aging and the aged are concerns about women and gender-role differentiation. Not only are most older people female, but the older female is much more likely to be economically deprived than the male who survives into the later years.

The health status of older people, as it varies by gender, has profound implications for their day-to-day experiences of physical limitation, dependency on other people, and the discomfort and pain of illness. In addition, as we will describe below in discussing family life, the all-important tasks of providing nursing care and daily assistance to the ill elderly fall mainly to women – primarily to wives and daughters.

Because gender is a major differentiator in society, the value or social status of men and women is based on different criteria. These criteria, in turn, are differentially available to men and women at different points in the life cycle. For instance, women may be highly valued for the important tasks of child-rearing which, in Canadian society, continue to be delegated primarily to them. However, by the time a woman reaches the later years, these tasks are largely replaced by grandparenting, a task which is of relatively minor social importance. Status emanating from occupation is higher for men than women for several reasons. Older men are more likely than older women to have been in the paid labor force. This situation is changing, with over half of women currently of working age in the paid labor force. However, as pointed out in Chapter 4, women continue to be located primarily in jobs of lower status and lower income than those of men. This decreases their accumulated economic worth as we discussed above, and in addition deprives them of the deference and prestige credits which are so important in a society such as ours in which social worth is closely tied to occupation. Finally, men do not retire from their major occupation until they enter the later years, whereas women retire from their major occupation – child-rearing – much earlier.

If being old is to occupy a negatively evaluated status, and if being female is similarly associated with relatively low social status in a sexist society, then being old and female places a person in what has been referred to as "double jeopardy" (Chappell and Havens, 1980). Our culture values youthful, feminine beauty (Abu-Laban, 1981; Posner, 1980). Although the low economic status and financial dependency of the older woman may be a more important cause of her low social status than her loss of youthful attractiveness, these cultural standards should not be underestimated as a factor influencing the self-esteem of older women who were strongly socialized to define their worth in these terms. Their male age-peers may also strongly adhere to these standards.

The *structural functionalist perspective*, because of its emphasis on the contribution of social statuses and role behavior to the survival and ongoing maintenance of society, tends to devalue the experiences of women in later life. In structural functionalist terms, at a highly abstract level, the major functions fulfilled by women are childbearing and child-rearing. These functions occur early in the life course, in contrast to the important economic functions attributed mainly to men, which persist longer. Alternative theoretical perspectives challenge this view. The *conflict perspective* has led to a new appreciation of the contribution of unpaid "women's work" to the wider society. Scholars within the *symbolic interactionist perspective* have directed attention to important aspects of the aging experience of both men and women that are ignored by structural functionalists and that give us a new appreciation of both the similarities and differences in the aging experience of the two genders.

MACRO-LEVEL THEORIES OF AGING

Macro-level theories of aging deal with the way in which aging individuals are tied to the society and the social status or deference accorded them. We find it useful to view these theories in relation to one very important strand of thought that can be referred to conveniently as the **modernization thesis** of aging.

The Modernization Thesis

One of the founders of the sociology of aging, Burgess, argues that as a result of "modern economic trends" the aged ". . . lost their former favored position in the extended family." In addition to a move from the extended to the nuclear family, he lists urbanization, industrialization, bureaucratization, increased leisure time, and enhanced life expectancy as factors that combine to leave the aged with little of any consequence to do in and for their society (Burgess, 1960).

This argument assumes that older people once had a more important place in society and in the family than they currently occupy. These arguments rest on a structural functionalist view of society as consisting of a number of status positions to which role expectations are attached, all of which contribute in some way to the maintenance and survival of the society.

Cowgill and Holmes (1972) developed the systematic theory of how modernization led to a decline in the status of the aged, illustrated in Figure 5-2. The theory describes four aspects of modernization: First, *modern economic technology* creates new urban occupations and leaves older occupations to become obsolete. As obsolete occupations are predominantly held by older people, their status declines relative to that of younger people in the newer, high technology occupations. Second, *urbanization* leads the young to establish new families geographically distant from their parents. This creates both residential and social segregation of the old from the young. Third, the progressively higher *educational attainment* of younger people provides them with more societally relevant knowledge than the old. Because such knowledge is itself a valued commodity, it enhances the status of the young relative to the old; in addition, the educational differences segregate the generations both intellectually and morally. Fourth, advances in *health technology* increase life expectancy. People are able to remain in the labor force for longer periods of time. This blocks upward career mobility of younger generations, leading to increased intergenerational conflict. The social institution of retirement, in this theoretical framework, may be seen as an example of such conflict and as an attempt to resolve it at a macro-social level.

The theory is, of course, much more complicated than we have described. As originally formulated (Cowgill and Holmes, 1972), it included 22 propositions. For example, one of them states that, "The status of the aged is highest when they constitute a low proportion of the population and tends to decline as their numbers and proportions increase." This rests on a notion of scarcity based on supply-and-demand thinking from economics. The refined version of the theory relies on chains of linked hypotheses that you can create by following the diagram in Figure 5-2.

Sociologists argue vehemently about the best ways to describe modernization and how to describe the status of the elderly. For a start, modernization does not progress uniformly across all four dimensions in any particular society. Nor can it be assumed that any society will progress uniformly along a single dimension from "non-modernized" to "modernized," or that modernization is an indigenous process. If social status were taken to be accurately measured by the proportion of GNP allocated to the aged for health care and pensions, then we might assume that the status of the elderly has never been higher. It is apparent, then,

that how one views the relationship between modernization and social status of the aged depends on just what is taken to be an indicator of modernization or of social status.

The social institution of retirement is seen as an indicator of decreased status of the aged, according to Cowgill and Holmes. However, Quadagno (1980) has shown that, "In England and Wales, a substantial portion of the population was retired prior to any demographic aging of the population and well before the application of modern health technology." This finding directly contradicts two of the four major postulated links between modernization and the status of the aged (see Figure 5-2).

Recent criticism (Dowd, 1980; Hendricks, 1981; Marshall, 1981a) has suggested that the modernization thesis rests on a somewhat romanticized vision of the past. Laslett (1976, 1977) has shown that, in England at least, the family and household status of the old was probably never very high and that older people were not as highly integrated into their families as is often assumed in contemporary aging research and in general studies in the sociology of the family.

The modernization theorists can be faulted for a uniform or undifferentiated view of the past. In contrast, Synge (1980) has shown great rural/urban differences in the pattern of familial care for the aged in Ontario at the beginning of this century, and Dowd (1980) has pointed to the importance of class differences in the status of the aged in the past and the present. In other words, a person's social status has always been determined by many factors in addition to age.

Despite its shortcomings, the modernization thesis, especially as expanded and articulated by Cowgill and his associates, has been valuable. By clearly enunciating the theoretical propositions implied by the theory, it has provided a major reference point for scholars in developing theory in the sociology of aging.

The Age Stratification Perspective

A second major theoretical approach also rests on the structural functionalist perspective. This is the **age stratification perspective** developed by Riley and a

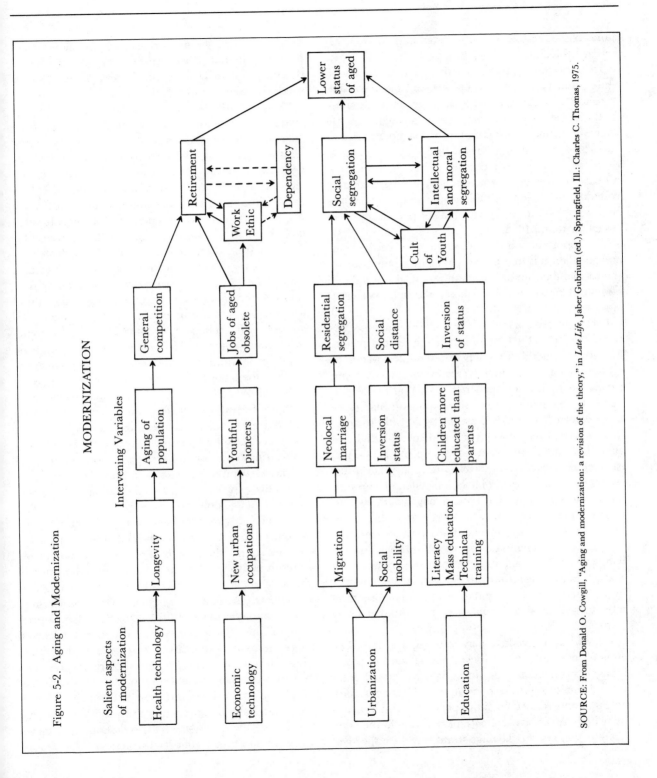

Figure 5-2. Aging and Modernization

MODERNIZATION

Salient aspects of modernization

Intervening Variables

SOURCE: From Donald O. Cowgill, "Aging and modernization: a revision of the theory," in *Late Life*, Jaber Gubrium (ed.), Springfield, Ill.: Charles C. Thomas, 1975.

number of associates (Riley, Johnson, and Foner, 1972; Foner, 1974; Riley, 1976, 1980).

To understand this perspective, it is necessary to understand two concepts: **cohort** and **age stratum**. A cohort consists of individuals, born approximately at the same time, and who move through the life course together. The definition of the boundaries of cohorts is arbitrary and based primarily on practical decisions made by a researcher rather than on theoretical considerations. For example, a researcher may compare the cohort of all people born in Canada between 1900 and 1905 with that of people born between 1950 and 1955.

The important point that distinguishes a cohort from an age stratum is that an individual or group assumes cohort membership at birth and retains it throughout life. With aging, a cohort passes through successive age strata.

Every society makes at least some distinctions between people on the basis of age or age-related events. Our society uses both a finely differentiated system of age strata based on single years of age, and a more loosely defined set of age strata based on biological, familial, and more general social phenomena. Radcliffe-Brown (1929) uses the term **age-grade** to refer to ". . . recognized divisions of the life of an individual as he [or she] passes from infancy to old age. Thus each person passes successively into one grade after another, and if he [or she] lives long enough, through the whole series – infant, young boy, youth, young married man, elder, or whatever it may be." The "whatever it may be" refers to the social and cultural basis of age differentiation. The arbitrariness underlying age grades or age strata is apparent in the recent changes in legal ages for drinking, voting, and eligibility to marry without parental consent – changes that refer to the social differentiation of adulthood from youth.

Canadian society, then, may be thought of as differentiated not only by social class and gender, but also by age stratification. Age strata have associated with them different rights, responsibilities, obligations, and access to rewards. Aging in this perspective is a process by which successive cohorts pass through the age stratification system. The age-stratification perspective in the sociology of aging brings together the notion of cohort with that of age stratum (or age-grade) in a dynamic system. The model focuses on the flow of successive cohorts through the age strata of the society.

Cohorts will vary in a number of their social characteristics, and the age stratification system is also changing over time. For example, in Canadian society, almost every successive birth cohort has entered the age stratum of old age (say, at age 65) with a higher level of income, education, and health status. Different birth cohorts have encountered the various age strata in different historical periods. The school system that the 1900 to 1910 cohort passed through was far different from that encountered by the 1950 to 1960 cohort. Some cohorts encounter adulthood during a period of economic prosperity and have an easy time entering the labor market; others reach the initial working years in a time of economic recession or depression. The cohort born 1905-1910, for example, was trying to enter the labor force at the peak of the Depression, while that born just five years later was entering the labor force during the economic recovery of World War II and afterwards. Such accidents of birth are fateful for individuals and for whole cohorts and may affect the life chances, the political attitudes, and values of the various cohorts in different ways.

Focusing on cohort differences as they unfold during passages through the age-stratified system poses an alternative explanation to one based on age. Are people of a certain age politically conservative because aging leads to conservatism or because their formative years were lived during a general societal climate of conservatism? In this view, age differences are hypothesized to result not so much from the aging or maturation of the individual as from the different experiences that individuals have as a result of their cohort membership.

For example, low fertility occurred in the Depression of the 1930s, partly because people delayed marriage and childbirth due to economic difficulties (Easterlin, 1980). This produced a relatively small birth cohort. On the other hand, during a period of economic prosperity in the later 1940s and early 1950s the large baby-boom cohort was produced. Waring (1976) uses the term *cohort flow* to describe the "movement of successive cohorts through an age-graded sequence of roles . . ." and argues that in the normal case ". . . a mutually accommodative situation obtains between the people in the cohort and the roles available to the age stratum."

When the supply of people provided by an age cohort is either too small or too large in relation to the number of available role positions, then we have a situation of *disordered cohort flow*. The societal response to this is often to change age-graded role expectations and the timing of the transitions between age strata. In response to the increasing size of cohorts entering the retirement years, and because of concern about providing economic security to this large cohort in retirement, suggestions have been made to raise the age of retirement. As another example, one reaction to the large baby-boom cohort was to expand the post-secondary educational system. This led in Canada to massive expansion of the university system during the 1970s, thereby delaying entry of many baby-boom cohort members into the labor force. As Waring (1976) points out, many nations have sought to rectify disorders of cohort flow by relying on large scale immigration or emigration. She argues, however, that attempts to maintain an orderly flow of cohorts are contained increasingly within specific societies and achieved by adjusting the age stratification system.

A major virtue of the age-stratification approach is that it emphasizes change, even if, as an outgrowth of its underpinnings in structural-functionalist theory, change is most often seen as a movement to restore societal equilibrium. It should not be assumed, however, that conflict has no place in this theoretical approach. The passing of older cohorts represents a fundamental process of social change that encompasses such basic phenomena as childhood socialization, education or training for labor-force participation, retirement, and the status passage of dying.

One example of conflict given by Foner and Kertzer (1978) concerns the timing of the transitions. Because progression through the age strata of a society is normally associated with increasing access to power and rewards (with the occasional exception of transitions at the very end of the life course, such as retirement), cohorts occupying higher age strata may seek to delay the transitions of younger cohorts, while younger cohorts may wish to accelerate their passage into a higher age stratum. Younger cohorts may wish to lower the age of legal drinking or voting. In the case of the progression into retirement, which decreases power and rewards, older workers may seek to elevate the age of retirement. However, the potential for conflict surrounding processes of cohort flow is reduced by the relative flexibility of the age stratification system in our society and by such adaptive mechanisms as skipping grades in elementary school, early or mature entry into university, and flexible retirement.

The age-stratification perspective, together with the aging and modernization thesis discussed earlier, constitute the major foci of research interest in the macrosociology of aging. It is noteworthy that both approaches exemplify the structural functionalist perspective. While both attempt to deal with fundamental processes of social change, in their different ways they view such change as orderly or smooth, and as functional for the society. Just as the modernization thesis was useful in stimulating critical scholarship from alternative theoretical premises, the age stratification approach has also generated a reaction. In Canada, this reaction has been based primarily on a conflict perspective.

The Generational Conflict Perspective

The theoretical approach of the age-stratification perspective rests on the notion of cohort. As we observed earlier, cohort is a statistical term. Tindale (1981) and Marshall (1980c) have attempted to go beyond the age-stratification approach by using the concept of **generation**. In contrast to a cohort, a generation's boundaries are not arbitrary, but depend on characteristics and social experiences shared by cohort members. A generation is a cohort, large proportions of whose members have experienced significant sociohistorical changes.

Not all single-year birth cohorts will experience profound historical and social events in the same way. A difference of a year or two, for example, may mean being too old or too young to serve in the armed forces during a major war. Generational experiences are usually thought of as cataclysmic and shaped by major changes such as depressions or wars. However, as Ryder (1965) has pointed out, "Cohorts can also be pulled apart gradually by the slow grind of evolutionary change." When a set of adjacent single-year birth cohorts is pulled away from earlier and later cohorts in this manner, the qualitative differentiation between them is recognized by the term generation (or generational cohort). While many prominent researchers have used cohort and generation interchangeably (notably Ryder, 1965; Easterlin, 1980), for some purposes in the sociology of aging it is important to remember the distinction between the two terms.

Generation, as a socially real group, is analogous to social class in that it describes differences that "make a difference" in the life chances and often in the consciousness of its members.

It is possible to talk about relationships among different generations in addition to talking about differences among them, as in the focus of age-stratification analysis. Generation members may respond to their shared fate by developing a consciousness of their kind analogous to the development of class consciousness by people similarly located in the class structure (see Chapter 8). Generational consciousness developed early in life may persist, probably with some modification, throughout life. The politically active, anti-war generation of youth and young adults formed from people born on the leading edge of the baby-boom cohort still retains its generational membership as its members pass into their mid-thirties.

The generational conflict perspective attempts to focus on generational experiences as they intersect with other bases of differentiation, especially social class and age. Class differences profoundly influence the encounter of cohort members with important historical events and should be thought of as usually causally prior to generational experiences. For example, the children of the upper class who reach prime military service age during a major war are less likely to live or to die in active military service than are the children of the lower class, despite shared cohort membership. Similar class differentiation occurs in response to fluctuations in the economy and the job market.

Tindale (1980a, 1980b, 1981) has shown how age and generational cohort differences interact with class factors to affect issues of job security among Ontario secondary school teachers. The smaller cohorts entering the school system have led to school closings and to the "redundancy" of some teachers. Younger and middle-aged teachers lack promotion opportunities within a shrinking occupational structure. Teachers with seniority are able to preserve their jobs by "bumping" teachers with less seniority from different schools in the system. Substantial tension between older and younger teachers results from this situation, and the teachers' professional associations have given serious consideration to introducing an early retirement mechanism to facilitate the career opportunities of younger teachers.

In this analysis, age is relevant because of its relationship to seniority. Middle-aged teachers are less

Identifying Generational Differences

As Karl Mannheim (1952), the leading theorist of generations, stressed, conflicting generation units may develop within any one generation, in response to the same social-historical circumstances experienced by people differentiated in other ways. Consider the different positions taken by men and by women and by people of differing social classes in your birth cohort to the cultural mandate that women give priority to the family (which is described in Chapter 4). Now, in addition, consider the stance taken by members of successively older and younger birth cohorts. Keeping in mind both gender and class differences in adherence to gender roles, can you identify cohort differences that are either incremental or qualitative? If you identify important qualitative differences, and if you can describe them in terms of differing social experiences of those cohorts taking qualitatively different positions, then you have identified a generational phenomenon. It is likely that most generational differences identified in this way would be strongly affected by social class.

"This is your conscience speaking. Don't you think it's time you retired and gave a young man a chance?"

Cartoon: Earl Engleman

likely than the young or old to perceive pressures for early retirement. They are old enough to be secure in seniority but not so old as to be subject to pressure to retire early. Generational cohort factors are relevant to the analysis, because different cohorts of teachers vary in educational attainment, job skills, and labor market experience. Some younger teachers with specialized educational qualifications resent the lack of such qualifications among older cohorts of teachers. Class is important in this analysis, because of the contradictory class location of the teaching profession. Some teachers view themselves as professionals and seek professional solutions to this problem, while other teachers opt for unionist solutions.

Analyses similar to that of Tindale might profitably be extended to the questions of the consequences of layoffs and plant shutdowns in industry. As noted earlier in this chapter Cowgill's theory of aging and modernization argued that the growing proportions of older people in the population will lead to increased intergenerational conflict over job scarcity (Cowgill, 1975). More broadly, the potential for conflict among different age groups will increase because of such demographic changes. This conflict may be affected to some degree by differences based on generational cohorts, that is, by characteristics of age groups that result from shared historical experiences. However, the potential for conflict is probably even greater because of age-group differences in the present. Just as a group of people may form a distinctive consciousness of themselves as different from others on the basis of generational experiences, they may also form such a distinctive consciousness based on age itself. This takes us to the question of subculture or minority group formation among the aged, or indeed among groups of any age.

The Aged as a Minority Group Versus the Age Irrelevance Perspective

The question of whether or not older people are qualitatively different from people of other ages has been discussed along the lines of the aged as a subculture or as a minority group. Rose (1965) argues that increasingly the aged are coming to constitute a subculture, because of their large numbers, increased vigor and health, collective concerns in fighting for adequate health care, and growing geographical segregation in areas such as small towns or in age-segregated housing. He also stresses the exclusion of older people from integration with the society through employment, but he feels that the good health and economic security of most older people would facilitate their interaction, and thereby allow them to develop a shared consciousness of themselves as older people.

Older people are discriminated against in the labor markets (Jarvis, 1972) and treated legally as a distinct category for many purposes such as pensions (Cain, 1976). The extent to which these factors lead to a shared consciousness based on age is, however, open to dispute.

The counter-arguments to the minority group thesis are many. Abu-Laban and Abu-Laban (1980) argue that minority status should be viewed as multi-dimensional and as a matter of degree, rather than as a uniform attribute of the older person. Different individuals of the same age may vary greatly in their physical characteristics, in the extent of their active participation in the society, in the esteem they are accorded by others, their power and privileges, and in their ability to resist or be exempt from the disadvantages of age.

At the macro level, the arguments against the formation of an aged minority group or subculture have been clearly articulated by Neugarten (1970). In her view, each successive cohort entering the later years is more like young and middle-aged cohorts with regard to health, educational attainment, income security, and shared social values. Therefore, the objective basis for conflict between age groups should diminish.

From the age-stratification perspective, however, Foner (1974) argues that the potential for age-based consciousness is diminished by generational consciousness. In other words, because each successive cohort entering the old age stratum brings with it its unique encounter with history, its values and interests will be different from those of previous cohorts already in the old age stratum, thereby weakening the unanimity or consensus of shared values. Foner also suggests that membership in associations that are not age-graded provides opportunities for a better understanding and greater tolerance of opposing political views. Recognition by the young that they will eventually grow older, together with tolerance by the old of the frustrations of the young, combine to reduce the potential for age-based conflict. Finally, Foner also argues that material disputes tend to cut across generational or cohort boundaries. For example, class interests might unite workers of all ages (see Kernaghan, 1982).

On the other hand, it is clear that the past decade or so has seen a tremendous increase in concerns about age. The rise of interest in aging is itself an indication of the growing importance of age, and so also is the increase in volume of political rhetoric and public policy discussion concerning pensions, health care for the aged, and related issues. An American political scientist, Cutler (1981), has in fact argued that age consciousness is itself a generational cohort phenomenon.

The Political Sociology of Aging

Other developments in the macrosociology of aging focus on the political and economic impact of population aging on the old and on the entire society. Guillemard (1977, 1980) offers yet another reason why the apparent strains toward conflict between age groups and generations have not led to much open conflict. She argues that the state actively fosters an ideology that discourages older people from recognizing their common interests and their distinctive and disadvantaged position in society. She describes the promulgation of a positive view of retirement in which retirement is seen as a time for leisure and self-expression. Failure to attain satisfaction in retirement is attributed to inadequate preparation for it by the individual. Such an individualistic ideology directs the attention of many older people away from the structural foundations of age-related poverty and leads them instead to blame themselves for their misfortune. As with many other deprived groups, an ideology is provided that contributes to their pacification by "blaming the victim" (Ryan, 1971).

Orbach (1981) has shown that recent policy initiatives directed toward the elimination of mandatory retirement in the United States and Canada (e.g. Special Senate Committee, 1979) are ideological mechanisms in the sense of pacification. He goes so far as to suggest that abolishing mandatory retirement at age 65 might mean "that the poor elderly would have to keep on working, while the well-to-do could afford to retire" (1981). In Orbach's view, the debate over mandatory retirement is a symbolic issue, and the real issue is over the continuation into retirement of lifelong class inequities.

In Canada, Bryden (1974), Chappell (1980), and Myles (1980a, 1980b) have described the persistence of an individualizing "market ideology" governing Canadian social policy toward the aged. Several sociologists (Calhoun, 1978; Estes, 1979; Marshall and Tindale, 1978-9; Matthews, 1979) have also pointed out that much of the theoretical and research activity of social gerontologists, whose emphasis has been predominantly social-psychological, serves to reinforce and legitimize this ideology.

This emphasis is reflected in undue attention in social gerontology to the adjustment of the aging individual to the society, rather than of society and its social institutions to the aging individual (Marshall and Tindale, 1978-9; Townsend, 1979, 1980).

Estes (1979) calls attention to the ways in which old age has been defined as a social problem of crisis proportions. Drawing on the symbolic interactionist approach and on conflict sociology, she argues that:

To define old age as a social problem of crisis proportions is politically useful, because such a crisis may be portrayed as not the fault of prior social inaction or economic policy, but as the result of increased longevity, retirement, declining birth rates, and so forth. In addition, the aging crisis label serves to advance the interests of those seeking expansion of government resources to deal with the crisis.

The real issue of debates over income security and pension policy, according to Myles (1980b), concerns the control over massive pools of capital. As he says, "Pension policy, then, is not primarily an issue of individual welfare, but rather an issue of power, power to control and allocate the capital generated through the savings put aside by workers for their old age."

Work in the political economy of aging reacts against the central thrust of most sociology and social psychology of aging. Canadian sociologists are making a contribution disproportionate to their numbers in the development of macrosociological approaches from the political economy perspective and, more generally, the conflict perspective.

Although the preceding material in this chapter has focused on social-structural and macro-social theoretical and practical issues, the great bulk of research interest in the sociology of aging until very recently has been social-psychological. Also, until recently most of this research has been within the structural functionalist perspective. More recently, a number of sociologists, including many Canadians, have worked within the symbolic interactionist perspective. Most of them view conflict as inherent both in the interaction among individuals and in the character of macro-social relations. Many feel the conflict and symbolic interactionist approaches provide compatible theoretical perspectives that enable the sociologist to take this broader view – considering the aging individual in an aging society (see for example: Dowd, 1980; Estes, 1979; Marshall, 1981; Marshall and Tindale, 1978, 1979).

THE FOCUS ON INDIVIDUAL ADJUSTMENT AND LIFE SATISFACTION

From the beginning, the sociology of aging has focused unduly on the adjustment of the aging individual to his or her fate in the society. This emphasis on individual adjustment reflects the overall individualistic bias of North American sociology.

Underlying this preoccupation with happiness in later life, there appears to be an assumption by social scientists that this time of life is a problem for those who pass through it, a time when people find it difficult to be happy or satisfied with life.

Three variants of structural functionalist role theory have been concerned with attempts to predict morale.

Contrary to popular opinion, most people over the age of sixty-five are healthy and not dependent on others. Happiness as aging progresses has a lot to do with peer acceptance and mate survival.

STRUCTURAL FUNCTIONALIST

These are *activity theory, disengagement theory, and continuity theory.* While these theories guided voluminous work in the earlier stages of the sociology of aging, their findings can be briefly summarized, and it is not necessary to review the theories in great detail. The factors that most strongly predict morale or life satisfaction are, in order of importance: health status, income security, and – a distant third – levels of social activity or role involvement.

Theoretical debate among these approaches focused on a structural functionalist concern with the integration of the individual in society. Individuals were considered to be tied to their society through role occupancy. **Activity theory** hypothesized that the adaptation of the individual to society was threatened by age-related declines in role occupancy. Activity theorists argued that in order to be happy in later life people should remain as active in role-relationships as possible (Palmore, 1969; Maddox, 1970; Palmore and Luikart, 1972). It should be noted that this theoretical approach is consistent both with Durkheimian structural functionalism and to a symbolic interactionist approach. As we saw in Chapter 1, Durkheim argues that few social ties lead to anomia and sometimes to suicide. According to Lemon, Bengtson, and Peterson (1972), the major argument of activity theory "is that there is a positive relationship between activity and life satisfaction and that the greater the role loss, the lower the life satisfaction." Interaction, in symbolic interactionist terms, is capable of maintaining stable self concepts or identities and, these, Lemon, Bengtson, and Peterson argue, would be the link to self-esteem and, ultimately, life satisfaction. High morale results from activity through the intermediate variable of confirming feedback from others.

Disengagement theory was explicitly formulated in structural functionalist terms (Cumming and Henry, 1961; Hochschild, 1975) and argued against the activity theory. Disengagement theory viewed the decline of activity as an inevitable and natural severing of the ties between the individual and the society which was functional to both. The society "granted permission" to the individual to disengage from active participation in social roles. This was seen as functional to society because it allowed a smooth passing of people

through the positions which make up the society, maintaining society as a *dynamic equilibrium* (see Chapter 1 for a discussion of dynamic equilibrium.)

Disengagement was also viewed as functional for the individual needing to conserve energy due to failing health. Moreover, the process of disengagement from the point of view of the individual was thought to be initiated by a heightened recognition of mortality. Reduction of activity allowed more time for the individual to prepare for death.

The debate between activity and disengagement theorists was heated and dominated the sociology of aging for many years. For the most part, disengagement theory was discredited. Major withdrawal from role relationships such as widowhood and retirement is not voluntary (Shanas and Associates, 1968). In general, as noted above, levels of activity do lead to higher life satisfaction even though this is not a strong relationship. Psychologists (e.g., Neugarten, Crotty and Tobin, 1964; Reichard, Livson and Peterson, 1962) found that psychological and sociological disengagement did not always occur simultaneously as postulated by the theory, and they stressed that there were many different styles of successful aging, depending on personality characteristics.

Translated into sociology, the idea that there are many different successful ways of aging led to the **continuity theory** (Atchley, 1977). Sociologists such as Atchley and Rosow (1973, 1974, 1976) argued with the aid of supporting data that rather than the actual level of role involvement or activity, changes in role involvement or activity were the important determinants of adaptation in later life. Some people, in other words, are life-long loners and happy to be so; others have always been happy only when busy and active with other people. Change in either direction can lead to low morale in later life.

These three approaches have produced a wealth of empirical studies. It should be noted, however, that these approaches are more similar than dissimilar to one another. Unlike other approaches to be reviewed in sections that follow, they share structural-functionalist assumptions of dynamic equilibrium and the conception of role as the major link between the individual and the society.

Related to this general approach is the assumption that middle-aged people have to be socialized to old age (Riley, Foner, Hess, and Toby, 1969). Rosow (1974) views socialization as important but inadequate in the later years because of low motivation to learn the devalued role of older persons. Symbolic interactionists, focusing on the individual as the active creator of roles, question both the existence of a role of aged person and the importance of this problem (Marshall, 1980b). They would argue that there are other more important aspects of aging that are completely ignored by these theoretical approaches. The issues discussed in the next section, for example, stand in vivid contrast to structural functionalism and its stress on the life satisfaction and adjustment area of inquiry.

IDENTITY AND IDENTITY MANAGEMENT

What is old? When is old? Is old good or bad? You are only as old as you feel – is this true? These questions point to the meaning of aging and being old to the individual. In this section, let us first examine attempts to answer these kinds of questions through survey research and then, relying on participant-observation studies, try to describe the implications of age-identification and age-definition in the lives of older people.

What Is Old?

Age is a somewhat ambiguous identity marker in our society. Physical appearance usually gives only a very rough clue to a person's age, and in any case we are not terribly clear as to how expected behavior should differ by age.

The anthropologist Fry (1976, and see discussion in Keith, 1982) asked an American adult sample to sort into piles a deck of cards depicting people in typical life situations ". . . based on their decisions regarding the appropriate age or similarity in age bracket" of the people depicted. Respondents could create as many piles as they wished to describe appropriate ages or age brackets. The average number of categories identified was five or six, depending on age, gender, marital status, education, and other variables. Some respon-dents identified as many as 15 different age categories, but others identified only two, and over 100 different terms were used to describe the categories.

Such lack of agreement as to the age categories used in our society creates some of the flexibility, but also points of tension, that we discussed in relation to age stratification theory. Our society does not in fact have a single system of age categories that encompasses all spheres of life and receives wide agreement (Waring, 1976; Hagestad, 1982).

People are not entirely sure just what it means to be old, but they have a vague feeling that it is not such a good thing. It is commonly acknowledged that ours is an ageist society in which people share negative stereotypes of the old and are likely to discriminate against them in various ways. A number of studies suggest that negative stereotypes about later life are held by young, middle-aged, and even old people (a careful, recent review is found in McTavish, 1982). However, such studies also identify some positive stereotypes about the aged.

Reviewing the research on attitudes toward old age, Kalish (1982) concludes: "Older people consistently view themselves much more optimistically than they are viewed by the non-elderly. However, when older people are asked about 'older people in general' they use very much the same stereotypes that the non-elderly use. Once again, we have evidence of the syndrome 'I'm fine, but look at those poor old people over there.'" We should expect that to the extent that stereotypes about old age are negative people will seek to exempt themselves from the status of old. This tendency for people to view themselves as young for their age, or as younger than others might view them, is frequently found in studies on this topic. Yet many people do not appear to dissociate themselves from the status of being old; nor do all older people (or younger people) view old age in highly negative terms. This suggests a more situational interpretation of the relationship between socially shared attitudes and self-identity.

Stigma and Identity Management Among the Aged

People of the same chronological age may be more

likely to see themselves as old in some kinds of situations than in others. For example, they may be more aware of being "old" when receiving a pension check in the mail, than when receiving a love letter. They may be less aware of their age when attending a symphony concert with their children, than when attending a rock concert with their grandchildren. The extent to which people think about age as a description of themselves, and even the value they place on this description, is therefore variable and situational (Matthews, 1979).

A status characteristic which is negatively evaluated but which is variable or situational in its applicability to a given individual has been called by Goffman (1963) a "weak stigma."

A number of studies describe the situational salience of the weak stigma of being old. According to Tindale (1980a), old, poor men in Hamilton, Ontario, do not

feel stigmatized when among themselves, but when dealing with outsiders they feel stigmatized and go to great lengths to attempt to manage their stigma. One method of stigma management used in encounters with strangers is information control:

The men are slow to reveal aspects of their past or personal elements in their present life except when they want to do so. The subject of family relations is the most prominent area where information is controlled . . . . When dealing with mission staff [in a hostel where they receive meals] . . . there is an implicit notion that the men are inferior and that they should improve the moral tenor of their lives. The men sometimes feign reformation, but are able to laugh behind their humble smiles, i.e., they go to church only if a meal is served in return.

In fact, Tindale says, among themselves the men maintain their own differentiation. They stigmatize as

Kuypers and Bengtson Model

Maintaining Positive Identity in Later Life: the Social Breakdown Model

Kuypers and Bengtson (1973) and Bengtson (1973) have applied Zusman's (1966) concept of social breakdown to examine identity change of the aged. They see the elderly as susceptible to stigmatizing labeling because of role loss, normative ambiguity, and a lack of confirmatory feedback from others. Such vulnerability creates a dependence on negative external portrayals as useless and obsolete. Learning to be old under such conditions of vulnerability induces people to surrender their independence and to self-identify as sick or inadequate. Each point in this cycle can become a place of formal or informal intervention to enhance the self-reliance, coping skills, and self-esteem of the individual. D'Arcy

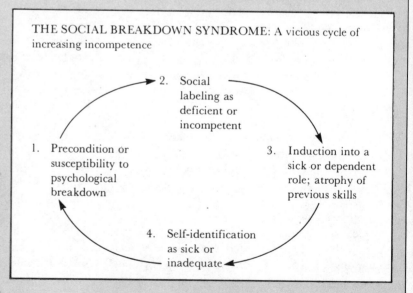

THE SOCIAL BREAKDOWN SYNDROME: A vicious cycle of increasing incompetence

1. Precondition or susceptibility to psychological breakdown

2. Social labeling as deficient or incompetent

3. Induction into a sick or dependent role; atrophy of previous skills

4. Self-identification as sick or inadequate

(1980) has presented a similar model to describe psychiatric institutionalization of the aged in Saskatchewan.

Source:
Bengtson, V.L., *The Social Psychology of Aging.* Indianapolis, Ind.: Bobbs-Merrill, 1977.

"mission stiffs" those of their peers whom they see as adopting without reservation the identity imputed to them by the public.

Similar internal differentiation for the maintenance of self-esteem is described by Hochschild (1973) as occurring among older widows living in an apartment building. When they compared themselves to people in the outside world, they saw themselves as united, but among themselves they made distinctions: ". . . she who had good health won honor. She who lost the fewest loved ones through death won honor, and she who was close to her children won honor. Those who fell short on any of these criteria were often referred to as 'poor dears.'"

Whether or not a person accepts the label "old" will determine the extent to which old people become a reference group, a source of comparison, a yardstick against which the person measures his or her own abilities, well-being, and indeed all aspects of personal identity (see Keith, 1982). Evaluations of old people and of the self are most likely interdependent in the later years and serve self-protective purposes. As Keith (1982) says, "Old people . . . think more highly of themselves than they do of old people on the whole. The old, in other words, share many stereotypes of old age, and feel good as individuals because they don't fit them."

Another adaptive strategy in the face of the weak stigma of old age is what Keith calls "community creation." While many younger people bemoan the increase in geographical age segregation exemplified by senior citizens' housing and retirement communities, Keith sees the benefits of these arrangements:

Egalitarianism insulates them from an outside status system in which they have a low position; . . . mutual aid . . . provides both material and psychic security without the high price of dependence . . . they invent responses to sex, death, conflict, or economic needs that are distinctive to their new communities . . . . As a community of age peers, old people are less dependent on their families for all social satisfactions and consequently enjoy better relations with kin.

Similarly, Marshall (1975a, 1975b) and Hochschild (1973) have shown how older people living congregatively creatively fashion ways to deal with impending death, and Rosow (1967) has found that many older people prefer congregate living because it enhances their ability to form new friendships; a finding which no doubt applies to people at many stages of the life course (e.g. students in residence, adult-only apartments).

All these ways of managing identity are also employed by the older women studied by Matthews (1979). In addition, Matthews characterizes many old people as adopting a strategic approach to organizing everyday activities so as to avoid situations that threaten their identity. This may affect such things as the timing of shopping excursions and the choice of restaurants and other public places in order to avoid contact with young people, from whom they fear disrespect.

Exchange and Dependency

One of the greatest fears of older people is that they might become dependent upon others. In Chapter 1, you were introduced to **exchange theory**. Some sociologists of aging have, formally or informally, drawn on exchange theory principles to explain identity management and social interaction patterns of the aged. In exchange theory terms, people are assumed to interact with others in order to obtain rewards, and stable social relationships will develop if both parties receive roughly equal rewards in return for roughly equal costs, or if the balance of rewards and costs is roughly equal. Dowd (1980) argues that decreased interaction with increasing age is due to a decline in the resources that can be brought to such encounters: material possessions, positions of authority, access to power resources, and strength and beauty (as socially defined). Also, as friends and family die, they cannot be drawn upon as resources, and they are lost as sources of respect (Dowd, 1980).

Exchange theory has a view of the individual as strategic and voluntaristic, and Dowd explicitly attempts to link his exchange theory approach to the symbolic interactionist perspective (Dowd, 1980). If a person is not able to offer resources or rewards to another, but needs resources that the other has, he or she may become dependent on the other. But human beings seek to maintain independence, autonomy, and control over their situations (Marshall, 1980b), and therefore they seek to avoid dependent situations or relationships.

The exchange theory perspective should be viewed as one of the most promising social-psychological approaches to understand aging. This perspective is useful in leading to understanding what might otherwise appear to be confusing, irrational behavior by individuals as, in fact, rational or strategic. Some of the older women studied by Matthews (1979) withdrew their participation in a senior center. Matthews argues that this was a calculated decision taken to avoid the costs of having to interact with the center's middle-aged staff, who viewed the women as old and therefore dependent. Withdrawal was a way for these older women to eliminate the psychological costs of dependency. Similarly, in an example cited by Matthews (1979) reluctance of older people to accept automobile rides from others was often because ". . . many disliked becoming indebted to the person who provided the ride" (Carp, 1972).

Autonomy is valued by people throughout life, but it becomes more precarious in the later years. Preserving autonomy is an ongoing, day-to-day accomplishment made even more difficult because of the ambiguous and mildly stigmatized status of old age.

LIFE COURSE TRANSITIONS

In recent years, a number of sociologists, together with demographers, historians, psychologists, and other scholars, have systematically sought to characterize aging in terms of a sequence of life course transitions (see for example George, 1980; Hagestad, 1982). This work draws on the structural functionalist approach and relates closely to work on age stratification described earlier. However, it also draws heavily on symbolic interactionism (Cain, 1964; Strauss, 1969; George, 1980). The notion of life course transition refers to "complex patterns of change and stability – or discontinuity and order" (George, 1980) that occur over the life course.

Hughes' concept of career (1971) and the derivative notion of status passage (Glaser and Strauss, 1971) are helpful in understanding life course transitions. Hughes distinguished between *objective career* (a series of social statuses and clearly defined offices) and *subjective career* ("The moving perspective in which the person sees his life as a whole and interprets the meaning of his various attributes, actions, and the things which happen to him"). Marshall (1980a) has applied the career perspective to aging ". . . to point to a person negotiating a passage from one age-linked status to another, and then to others, finally coming to the end of the passage through life at death."

Objective Careers

A number of investigators have noted that the events marking the early stages of objective careers in our society have become more compressed in time and more predictable. (Winsborough, 1978; Hogan, 1981; Hagestad, 1982). For example, the average timing of school completion fell significantly during the first half of this century, while the variability around the average age of completing school decreased. In statistical terms, the mean age decreased and the dispersion around the mean also decreased. Similar patterns showing greater standardization of life course events and an earlier timing of such events have been observed for age of entry into the labor force, age of first marriage, birth of first child, birth of last child, and marriage of last child. In a similar way, the timing of widowhood has also become more predictable but has moved to a point later in the life course (Glick, 1977; Winsborough, 1978). Some of these patterns are visible in Table 5-2.

In addition to the greater predictability already discussed, you should take note of the emergence in this century of what has come to be referred to as the "empty nest" stage of the family life course: the period of life after the departure of the youngest child which ends when the first parent dies. Rodgers and Witney (1981), who have made this comparison, also emphasize some important differences between Canadians and Americans in the structure of the family career. Canadians in the period studied delayed childbearing longer and spaced their children more closely than did their American neighbors; Canadians saw their last

Table 5-2. MEDIAN AGE AT SELECTED PERIODS OF THE FAMILY CAREER: CANADA AND UNITED STATES

Period of Birth of Mother (top) / Approximate Period of First Marriage (bottom)

Period of Family Career	80-Year Average Canada	80-Year Average U.S.	1880s / 1900s Canada	1880s / 1900s U.S.	1890s / 1910s Canada	1890s / 1910s U.S.	1900s / 1920s Canada	1900s / 1920s U.S.	1910s / 1930s Canada	1910s / 1930s U.S.	1920s / 1940s Canada	1920s / 1940s U.S.	1930s / 1950s Canada	1930s / 1950s U.S.	1940s / 1960s Canada	1940s / 1960s U.S.	1950s / 1970s Canada	1950s / 1970s U.S.
Median Age At:																		
1. First Marriage																		
Mother	22.8	20.9	24.7	21.4	23.2	21.2	22.8	21.0	23.8	21.4	23.5	20.7	21.7	20.0	20.9	20.5	21.5	21.2
Father	26.1	23.9	29.1	25.4	27.2	24.7	26.2	24.0	26.8	24.2	26.5	23.2	24.8	22.5	24.3	22.9	24.1	23.6
Difference	3.3	3.0	4.4	4.0	4.0	3.5	3.4	3.0	3.0	2.8	3.0	2.5	3.1	2.5	3.4	2.4	2.6	2.4
2. Birth of First Child	23.9*	22.4	(26.1)**	23.0	(24.5)	22.9	(24.0)	22.8	24.2 (25.1)	23.5	24.7	22.7	23.8	21.4	23.2	21.8	23.9	22.7
3. Birth of Last Child	28.1*	30.8*	(28.8)	32.9	(28.0)	32.0	(27.2)	31.0	28.5	32.0	28.2	31.5	29.2	31.2	28.8	30.1	26.3	29.6
4. Marriage of Last Child	51.1*	53.0*	(55.1)	55.4	(53.0)	54.8	(50.4)	53.0	51.1	53.2	51.0	53.2	52.0	53.6	51.6	52.7	49.1	52.3
5. Death of One Spouse	67.4*	64.7*	65.6	57.0	65.6	59.6	67.6	62.3	67.5	63.7	68.0	64.4	68.2	65.1	68.4	65.1	68.2	65.2
Difference Between Age at First Marriage and:																		
6. Birth of First Child	1.6*	1.7	(1.4)	1.6	(1.3)	1.7	(1.2)	1.8	0.4 (1.3)	2.1	1.2	2.0	2.1	1.4	2.3	1.3	2.4	1.5
7. Birth of Last Child	5.8*	10.1*	(5.1)	11.5	(4.8)	10.8	(4.4)	10.0	4.7	10.6	4.7	10.8	7.5	11.2	7.9	9.6	4.8	8.4
8. Marriage of Last Child	28.8*	32.2*	(30.4)	34.0	(29.8)	33.6	(27.6)	32.0	27.3	31.8	27.9	32.5	30.3	33.6	30.7	32.2	27.6	31.1
9. Death of One Spouse	44.6	43.9*	40.9	35.6	42.4	38.4	44.8	41.3	43.7	42.3	44.5	43.7	46.5	45.1	47.3	44.6	46.7	44.0
Difference Between:																		
10. Age at Birth, First and Last Child	4.2*	8.4*	(3.1)	9.9	(3.5)	9.1	(3.2)	8.2	4.3 (3.4)	8.5	3.5	8.8	5.4	9.8	5.6	8.3	2.4	6.9
11. Age at Birth and Marriage Last Child	23.0*	22.2*	(25.3)	22.5	(25.0)	22.8	(23.2)	22.0	22.6	21.2	22.8	21.7	22.8	22.4	22.8	22.6	22.8	22.7
12. Marriage Last Child and Death of Spouse	17.0*	11.7*	(10.5)	1.6	(12.6)	4.8	(17.2)	9.3	16.4	10.5	17.0	11.2	16.2	11.5	16.8	12.4	19.1	12.9

SOURCE of United States Data: Glick, 1977, Table 1.
*50-Year Average (1930–1970).
**Figures in parentheses are estimates.
SOURCE: Rodgers, Roy H., and Gail Witney, 1981. "The family cycle in twentieth-century Canada." *Journal of Marriage and the Family*, Vol. 43, no. 3 (August): 727–740.

These people, ranging in age from 93 to 80, haven't given up on exercise or learning. They are being instructed in the Tia-Chi-Chu'an form of Kung Fu, a system of self defense and exercise also said to be effective against symptoms of rheumatism and other ills. (*Toronto Star*)

child married earlier and survived before widowhood longer. The result is that Canadians have had, on average, longer marriages including longer empty nest periods than Americans. The difference is quite profound. About one-third of married life for Canadian couples is spent in the empty nest stage of family life, compared with about one-quarter for U.S. couples.

Family life factors such as this are consequential for intergenerational relations and for the social character of later life, because they affect the average number of children, grandchildren, siblings, and other relatives who will be available to the individual in old age. Rodgers and Witney (1981) interpret these data to suggest a pattern of long-term stability in the Canadian family cycle, but they note that recent increases in divorce and in preferences for remaining single observed in the most recent cohort may dramatically affect the family in ways of special importance to the old.

Subjective Careers

People have their own ideas about the timing of life-course transitions, and they have some sense of the appropriate timing of such events. This sense has been referred to by the term **social clock** (Neugarten, Moore, and Lowe, 1965; Neugarten and Hagestad, 1976). In relation to these social clocks, people see themselves as "on time" or "off time" – early, late, or "just right" – in getting married, forming a family, obtaining a promotion, becoming a grandparent, retiring, and so forth. Very little research has actually been done on the extent to which conceptions of life-course timing, or social clocks, are associated with sanctioning in order to keep people roughly "on time" in the life course (Hagestad, 1982), but most of us have experienced pressures (sometimes not so subtle) in this regard.

One study of cohort differences in the preferred

timing of female life events (Fallo-Mitchell and Ryff, 1982) found that young adult women preferred later ages for family career events, such as having their first child, but earlier ages for general life events, such as settling on a career choice, than did middle-aged or older women. The different cohorts attributed their own timing preferences to women of the other cohorts. Such differences in actual preferences, coupled with misperception, create grounds for potential conflict among different generations in families.

An aspect of subjective careers that has been quite neglected in the sociology of aging is the increasing awareness of finitude as age increases. That is, as people grow older, and typically when they see themselves as having about ten years to live, the fact that they are mortal becomes very important to them (Marshall, 1975b, 1980a, 1980c). This recognition is heightened by self-perceived changes in health and by the death of parents, siblings, and friends (Marshall, 1975c, 1980a; Marshall and Rosenthal, 1982). Awareness of finitude normally leads individuals to focus on their past lives in order to make sense of any past life events that lack meaning or coherence. In addition, highly aware individuals frequently focus on the meaning of death and engage in concrete preparations for it, such as the making of wills and the making of peace in their personal relationships.

Two life course transitions have been of particular interest to sociologists of aging: widowhood and retirement. Too frequently these have been viewed as the problems of the female elderly and the male elderly, respectively. It is important to bear in mind that large numbers of both men and women experience each of these transitions, though in somewhat different ways, and are affected by the transitions of their spouses and those they love.

Structural

From Working to Retirement

In an earlier section we discussed retirement as a socioeconomic institution. Our concern here is with the retirement experiences of individuals. Retirement should be seen as occurring within the context of age discrimination in employment that can either accelerate departure from the labor force or make retirement more

palatable for the worker. With increasing age, men and women in the work force frequently encounter pressure from younger employees who feel that their older co-workers are blocking advancement opportunities (Chen, 1980; Tindale, 1981). Contrary to popular belief, for almost all tasks skill at industrial work increases with age and older workers are generally as competent and often more accurate, punctual, and committed to the employer than are younger workers (Koyl, 1977).

The dictum, "Last hired, first fired" implies not only racial and gender discrimination, but also the operation of seniority rules in providing job security. Nonetheless, there is considerable evidence to suggest that older workers are more harmed by plant shutdowns and layoffs than are younger workers. A shutdown places young and old on the labor market, and the older worker is disadvantaged in that market (Sheppard, 1970; Parnes, Gagan, and King, 1981).

Most North Americans retire before reaching a formal, compulsory retirement age (Orbach, 1981). While the reasons for and implications of retirement in Canada are a major unresearched area, American data suggest that a large proportion of early retirees leave the work force for health reasons and that health impairments also significantly decrease the average number of hours worked and the rate of pay of older workers (Chirikos and Nestel, 1981).

Earlier studies noted a correlation between being retired and being in poor health, and they led to the view that retirement is a crisis that adversely affects health. However, more recent research suggests that in most instances the direction of causation is the reverse: poor health is a cause rather than a consequence of retirement, and retirement may even produce health benefits (Adams and Lefevre, 1980; Foner and Schwab, 1981).

Retirement may be a more consequential life course transition for women than for men. In many instances, women have had to struggle harder to fashion any stable career in paid employment, and they may therefore value it more (Ragan, 1977). Conversely, widowhood may be a more serious life transition for men than for women (Berardo, 1970), partly because it is "off time" in relation to social clocks. Data are scarce in these areas, but the important point is that we need to be alert to the fact that women as well as men retire, and that this transition may be experienced quite differently by men and by women.

There is no retirement from domestic labor – that form of unpaid work that is essential to the maintenance of our socio-economic order and still largely the domain of women, even if they are also in paid employment (Luxton, 1980). Whether or not the wife has also been in paid employment, the retirement of her husband might produce a profound and, at times, adverse life transition for her. Her home is no longer her castle, and she may find new difficulties with her husband around the house not quite knowing what to do with himself. Her loss of autonomy may, however, be offset by other aspects of the relationship, such as increased opportunity to express nurturance (Keating and Cole, 1980) and to enjoy leisure time with her husband (McPherson and Guppy, 1979).

Sometimes women and men retire together. For example, farm couples in Alberta were found to plan ahead together for their retirement, a gradual and mutually supportive experience in most instances (Keating and Marshall, 1980).

Not enough attention has been paid to the ways in which retirement is affected by social class and type of occupation. Retirement is, in fact, problematic primarily because of reduced income (Orbach, 1981). As with most aspects of aging, income security and good health are the critical factors influencing morale and satisfaction with life. Seeing retirement as a negative experience rests on the assumption that work is a positive experience. This assumption is clearly untrue for many individuals and may reflect the middle-class bias of many researchers. Finally, it seems apparent that retirement is both a process and an event (McPherson and Guppy, 1979) and that both must be distinguished from the state of being retired.

From Marriage to Widowhood

Until quite recently, little was known about the experience of widowhood. Most men have the bad fortune not to experience this life course transition, because most men predecease their wives. The alleged disadvantages of widowhood for women should be weighed against this alternative. Widowhood is both a process, called grieving, and a state caused by bereavement (to be bereft of a spouse). The process involves changes in identity and feelings toward the self and the deceased spouse. This process is affected by the social characteristics of the deceased and the survivor, by the nature of the death, and by the social relations that the widowed person maintains.

In general, grief is more intense in the case of a younger death and when death is relatively unexpected (Vachon, et al, 1976; Vachon, 1979; Marshall, 1980a). Many deaths of older people can be thought of as appropriately timed according to the life-course social clock. There is time for the dying person and the spouse to prepare for the death.

There is increased mortality among the recently bereaved. Because about three-fourths of the increased death rate among the bereaved is due to various types of heart disease, the term *broken heart syndrome* has been applied to this phenomenon (Parkes, Benjamin, and Fitzgerald, 1969). Although the dynamics of this syndrome are not clearly understood, they undoubtedly go beyond the stress implied in the folk dictum, "She died of a broken heart" to include the stresses of care-giving which the remaining spouse probably experienced in caring for the first to die.

Canadian research (McFarlane et al, 1980; Martin Matthews, 1982) shows that widowhood is the single most disruptive transition of the life course. Of 34 life events ranked in severity of adjustment by 375 Ontario retired women and men, widowhood was ranked first, retirement only 28th (Martin Matthews, 1982). The potential severity of the stress of bereavement may be indicated by Norris' (1980) finding that some elderly women remained committed to the role of wife for as long as ten years following the husband's death.

Women, as noted earlier, are much more likely to occupy the social status of widowhood than are men. If they do remarry, this is likely to be after a longer period of widowhood than is the case for men. Comparing a Quebec sample of widowed persons who did and did not remarry, Stryckman (1981) found that half the males had remarried within a year and a half of bereavement, while half the females remarried within four and a half years.

Much of the existing research on widowhood focuses on social support. Lopata's (1979) major conclusion about the social supports provided to older female widows is that children are the only category of kin to be active. Siblings, on the other hand, are virtually absent from the support system of widowed women according to Lopata; nor are they important in providing emotional support.

A Canadian study conducted in Guelph, Ontario, also found children to be important sources of support. But in contrast to Lopata's finding, siblings, usually a sister, were actively involved in the widow's support system. Also, two-thirds of the widows listed an extended kin member – sibling-in-law, cousin and/or niece – as part of their emotional support system. Half of these widows named a sister as one of the three people to whom they felt closest (Martin Matthews, 1982).

Matthews, applying a symbolic interactionist perspective in her research, stresses the active part that widows play in reconstructing their lives and their identities and in attributing meaning to the widowhood experience. For example, she notes that diminished social ties in widowhood may mean rejection to one widow, loneliness to another, but independence to a third (Martin Matthews, 1982). Like retirement and other life-course transitions, widowhood brings changes in identity and in social relationships. Like these other transitions it is no doubt influenced by social class, cohort, and other bases of social differentiation.

The ramifications of widowhood extend beyond the widow to other family members. If a widow is finding support from a sibling or from a child, then we should also look at the sibling or child who is providing such support. Considerations such as these lead us to a general consideration of the intergenerational family.

FAMILY AND INTERGENERATIONAL RELATIONS

One of our society's most persistent myths about the family is that the elderly are isolated from and aban-

doned by their children. This is related to a view that our family system consists of self-sufficient nuclear family units composed of parents and young, dependent children isolated from one another geographically, socially, and emotionally. When children mature and leave home, they are thought to sever ties with their parents. If this characterization were entirely accurate, the elderly would be cut off from intergenerational family life. Sociologists have therefore been very interested in investigating the family relationships of older people. Three decades of research have led sociologists to suggest that we have a *modified extended family system* consisting of many nuclear family units maintaining separate households but bound together in ongoing relationships (see Chapter 11).

The Changing Structure of the Family

Changes in mortality and fertility have made the multigenerational family more common. In the United States during the mid-1970s about one-third of the community-dwelling population over the age of 65 had great grandchildren (Shanas, 1981). Comparable data for Canada are unavailable, but we can presume our situation is similar. We may expect a substantial increase in the number of four and five generation families between now and the end of this century. People now have greatly increased opportunities to have ongoing relationships in adult life with their parents and grandparents, and with their adult children and grandchildren. At the same time, families are more and more likely to have some members who are old and frail, placing burdens of responsibility for care on other family members, especially those in the younger generation.

While families now have more generations alive than they did in the past, declines in fertility mean that there are fewer people within each generational level. Despite great cohort variability in fertility, there has been an overall trend toward fewer children. This also means that people have fewer brothers and sisters (Marshall, 1981c). Thus, we conceive of the contemporary family structure as being long and thin; it is also somewhat fragile in the sense that death or geo-

Contrary to popular opinion, most older people are neither incapacitated nor institutionalized. Although today's extended families may be smaller than they once were, the role of grandparents continues as an important facet of family structure. (*Miller Services*)

graphical mobility may have greater impact than in multigenerational families with more members.

Much research on the family life of older people has focused on their relationships with adult children. To describe this research, the following discussion is organized around certain dimensions of family solidarity (Bengtson, Olander, and Haddad, 1976; Bengtson and Marshall, 1982).

The Availability and Proximity of Kin

Most people enter the later years with a spouse. About 80 percent of men and 55 percent of women aged 65 to 69 are married; this drops to 67 percent and 31 percent respectively for Canadians aged 70 and over (Abu-Laban, 1980). In a representative community study in

Age and Friendship

We have emphasized the family and especially the parent-child relationship as an important context in which the aging individual receives social support. However, about one in five older people have no children. For them, and perhaps especially for widowed, never-married, separated, or divorced older people, friendship may be very important. The joint effects of lower fertility and higher divorce and separation rates for successive cohorts may make friendship even more important to older people in the future. Yet little is known about friendship, and, indeed, it is hard to define. Friendship may be less intense for older men than for older women, and men may be more passive and less intimate than women in later-life friendships (Abu-Laban, 1980). B. Bradford Brown has systematically reviewed the literature on friendship over the life course. The following brief excerpt suggests some important features of friendship that merit future research.

There is an ageless quality to friendship. We can make friends at virtually any age, keep them for as many years as we like, and disavow them whenever it seems necessary or convenient. Friends differ from parents, children, siblings and other kinfolk, whom we inherit at birth (ours or theirs). They aren't like a spouse, for whom we have to wait two decades and then must promise to love and live with for the rest of our life. Nor are they like neighbors and co-workers, who "come with the territory" or the job, and who, by definition, are lost as soon as we move to a new home, a new position. Unlike the other close associates of one's life, friendship is a relationship for all seasons—or for none, as we so choose.

It is perhaps this "agelessness" that has induced most researchers to ignore age as a crucial variable in friendship. To many investigators, friendship is friendship, regardless of when it occurs or how long it lasts. Yet, there are three ways in which age enters into the fabric of friendship. It is, first of all, a relational characteristic of the partners, representing the difference in age between oneself and one's friend. Although we commonly conceive of friends as age mates, there is nothing in the definition of friendship (at least as I define it in this essay) that requires them to be so. But as relational age expands, the inherent similarity between individuals diminishes. It seems likely that individuals who share the same life stage and who have lived through the same historical events would forge a different relationship than two people from separate generations.

Age can also be viewed as a temporal characteristic of the relationship. That is, friendships are formed, deepened and sustained across time. One cannot expect two individuals who have been friends for decades to relate in the same fashion as they did during the first months of their acquaintance, just as one cannot expect the "honeymoon phase" to be maintained over the entire course of marriage.

Beyond this, of course, is the individual age of each partner. As people progress across the life course, they witness changes in their abilities, experiences and developmental needs, as well as in the expectations and opportunities they have for close interpersonal attachments. Both the form and function of friendships must adjust to these developmental changes.

Each of these age-related characteristics adds to the complexity of friendship. Each, in a sense, undermines its "agelessness."

Source:

Brown, B. Bradford, "A life-span approach to friendship: age-related dimensions of an ageless relationship." In *Research in the Interweave of Social Roles: Friendship*, Toronto: JAI Press.

Hamilton, Ontario, 71 percent of men aged 70 and over but only 23 percent of women were still married. Of this older age group, 8 percent of the men and 14 percent of the women had never married (Rosenthal, 1982a). On the whole, then, while most people at age 65 have a spouse, the percentage declines as the years go by, very sharply for women.

About 80 percent of Americans over the age of 65 have at least one child (Shanas, 1981), and the Hamilton study confirms this general pattern (Marshall, Rosenthal, and Synge, 1982). About 10 percent of people over 65 have children who are themselves over the age of 65. The Hamilton study also noted a further aspect of fragility in family structure: in addition to the one-fifth of the respondents aged 70 and over who had no children, a further one-fifth had only one living child.

Siblings may be very important to older people, especially those who are childless or never married. About 80 percent of Americans aged 65 and over have at least one living sibling (Harris and Associates, 1975). We do not have comparable nation-wide Canadian data, but the Hamilton study suggests that the figures might be quite a bit lower in this country.

About three-quarters of older people have grand-children and one-third have great-grandchildren. These days, people become grandparents in middle age, often in their forties. Thus, the grandchildren of older people are often adults themselves.

Clearly, most older people have kin. However, a very small but important minority – about 5 percent or 6 percent of people over 65 – have no living spouse, children, or sibling (Riley, et al, 1968). These people find it extremely difficult to remain in the community should they suffer health losses in later life; indeed, in the United States about half of them are institutional-ized (compared with only 4.5 percent of the United States' older population as a whole). In Canada, al-though we have a higher rate of institutionalization of older people (Schwenger and Gross, 1980), it is fair to assume that here, as in the United States, people without kin are more vulnerable to being institution-alized than others their age who have kin.

Like people of all ages, married old people usually live with their spouses, and those who are widowed or never married are likely to live alone (Fletcher and Stone, 1981). In the Hamilton study, of women aged 70 and over, 23 percent lived with a spouse and a further 60 percent lived alone. Most older people prefer this living arrangement, striving for a relationship with their children that has been called "intimacy at a distance" (Rosenmayr, 1977). For people over the age of 80, living with a child is somewhat more common, partly because of age-related health problems.

Although most older people do not live with a child, they usually live near at least one of their children. About 85 percent of older people in the U.S. who have children live within an hour's trip from at least one child; these figures rise as we look at older age groups. We may assume this is related to the concern of chil-dren to keep a watchful eye on the parents' condition (Marshall, Rosenthal, and Synge, 1982) and to the health care needs of aging parents. Shanas' American and Danish data (1981) suggest that in the majority of cases community-dwelling persons aged 80 and over either lived in the same household as a child or within ten minutes of a child, with the child assuming primary responsibility as care-giver.

Interaction, Exchange, and Helping Patterns

Associational solidarity refers to the degree to which members of a family are in contact with one another, engage in shared behaviors, and interact in common activities. Contrary to popular belief, most older people experience high associational solidarity with their chil-dren. For example, in countries such as the United States, England, Denmark and Canada, about four of five older people who do have children see a child at least once a week; telephone contact is almost daily (Marshall and Bengtson, 1982; Shanas, 1981). One of the reasons for such contact is that it allows the ex-change of help.

A variety of studies point to high levels of exchange among generations of a broad range of goods and services, including assistance with home repairs, child care, grocery shopping, transportation, health care, as well as financial assistance and support (Shanas, 1981; Chappell, 1981; Marshall and Bengtson, 1982). We refer to this aspect of family life as *functional solidarity*. Contrary to popular images of older people as de-pendent, these studies suggest a more appropriate image of interdependence. Help flows across the gen-erations in both directions, with older people both giving and receiving. Certainly, the amount and type of help given and received varies by the socio-economic status of the parent and child, but, except for the extremely poor, most elderly people are more likely to give financial help to their children than they are to receive it (Moore, 1966).

The familial provision of health care is becoming increasingly prevalent as parents live into very old age and experience health losses. Care-giving responsibili-ties generally fall to persons in the second-oldest generational level in a family, who may themselves be getting on in years. Shanas (1981) argues that "for the majority of persons aged 80 and over still living in the community, a middle-aged child in the 50s and 60s or even older has assumed responsibilities [making] life in the community possible for them." The second oldest generation in families, especially women, experience added familial concerns and burdens in mid-life, leading scholars to refer to them as the "caught generation" (Marshall, Rosenthal, and Synge, 1982; Neugarten, 1979; Rosenthal, 1982a; Brody, 1981).

Consensus and Normative Solidarity

Consensus and *normative solidarity* refer to agreement among the generations on general issues (consensus) and on matters dealing with expectations (normative) for intergenerational relations. Some research (Bengtson and Kuypers, 1971; Marshall and Bengtson, 1982) suggests that both parents and children think they are in greater agreement (*subjective consensus*) than they really are (*objective consensus*). Bengtson and Kuypers, in addition, found that the parents of the college students sampled indicated subjective consensus to a greater extent than did their children; for example, they see themselves as closer in political ideology to their children than the children consider to be the case. The researchers interpret this as an example of the "developmental stake" that parents invest in the parent-child relationship. Parents devote many years to building this relationship and want it to be close and successful.

Children, too, want this kind of relationship, but they also have a stake in developing their own autonomy and independence. These differential investments of the two generations contribute to somewhat different perceptions of the characteristics of the relationship. The "developmental" in "developmental stake" refers to both changing perceptions and motivations of both child and parent as they proceed through the life course.

Affective Solidarity

Affective solidarity refers to such qualitative aspects of relationships as closeness, warmth, trust, concern, understanding, and respect. This solidarity dimension includes the feelings each partner has about the relationship and the feelings attributed to the other partner.

Research in the Netherlands (Knipscheer and Bevers, 1981) inquired of older people and their adult children whether the parent-child relationship had become better or worse compared to the past. Parents viewed the relationship as stable and thought their children would agree, but children were more likely to see changes for the better. In contrast to the discussion in the previous section, here the developmental stake principle seems to be weighted toward the younger generation taking the more positive view of the relationship. This may be a reflection of the aging parents' desire to deny growing dependency, and of the satisfaction gained by the child in contributing more to the parents' welfare as a representation of increasing equality.

In the Hamilton study (Marshall, Rosenthal, and Synge, 1982), a related aspect of affective solidarity was investigated. Adult children showed a high level of concern about health and health changes in their parents. Daughters, in keeping with traditional gender role stereotyping, showed more concern than did sons; and fathers were worried about more than were mothers. These differences, however, are variations on a theme of widespread filial concern and feelings of what has been called "filial obligation" or "filial maturity" (Blenkner, 1965; Brody, 1981). Concern was also correlated with the actual provision of health care to the parent.

The Struggle for Solidarity

Family relationships do not develop inexorably because of functional requirements of the society. Instead, they are an achievement worked out by family members in response to social and historical conditions. Among these conditions are the demographic changes affecting the family context of older people and their middle-aged children.

In the various dimensions of family solidarity that we have discussed, most families may be aptly characterized as having high solidarity. Not only does this refute myths of the abandonment of the elderly, but it occurs despite pressures on contemporary families. Economic constraints, geographical mobility, and demographic changes pose threats to family and intergenerational solidarity. Additional tensions arise out of the normal course of intergenerational life. The quest for autonomy and independence of both young and old represents one such source of tension. New members must be absorbed into families. Family relations are disrupted by death. Family solidarity on any dimension cannot simply be taken as a given that naturally characterizes family or intergenerational relations. Family members work at realizing solidarity through a variety of accommodations and negotiations, including mutual tolerance, self-deception, and role segregation (Marshall and Bengtson, 1982; Rosenthal, 1982a). Recent research on "kinkeeping" indicates that many families have one person who takes on the task of keeping the family together and that this is considered especially important in times of family crisis such as the death of a parent. The family is valued, and, because it is valued, its members work to preserve it (Rosenthal, Marshall, and Synge, 1981; Rosenthal, 1982a,b).

In summary, the ramifications of population aging at the level of the family have not demonstrated a failure of the family or the end of the family, but rather these ramifications have shown that people have transformed the family to meet new challenges.

Summary

1. The sociology of aging deals with changes experienced over the life course, with social relationships of older people, and with the implications, both micro and macro, of individual and population aging for the entire society.

2. Canada has experienced, and will continue to experience, a significant increase in the number and proportion of older people and in the average age of the population. The great majority of very old people are women.

3. It is essential to differentiate among "the aged" by health status, economic characteristics, age itself, and other social characteristics.

4. Political and social concern about population aging results in large measure from increased societal allocation of resources for health care and income security of the aged.

5. Modernization has been associated with a decline in the status of the aged. However, it cannot be assumed that old people had high status in premodern societies, nor that age is a more important criterion for assigning status than other factors.

6. Society is characterized by age differences in rights, obligations, and rewards. The age stratification system itself changes as cohorts with varying social characteristics flow through it.

7. A number of factors, including cross-cutting allegiances and differences within generations, decrease the potential for conflict based on age, while the growth of the proportion of aged people in the population and the economic implications of population aging increase the likelihood of age-group conflict.

8. Much of the sociology of aging has focused on happiness. The major predictors of happiness in later life are good health, income security, and to a lesser but important extent supportive interaction with other people.

9. It is mildly stigmatizing to be old. As a result, many people resist identifying themselves as old and adopt various interaction strategies such as controlling information and selective interaction to protect their self-esteem.

10. Old age is associated with a decrease in the resources people can exchange in interaction. This may partially explain the decreased role involvements of older people and the kinds of involvements they seek.

11. Over the past century, major life course transitions have become more predictable. Retirement is less a crisis than is usually thought, while widowhood is undoubtedly the most significant transition of later life. Also, people develop subjective views of the timing of their own transitions over the life course. Disagreements and misperceptions about the social clock are bases of tension between generational and age groups.

12. Relationships between older people and their adult children are characterized by high levels of interaction and solidarity.

13. Structural functionalist sociology has dominated the sociology of aging at both macro- and micro-levels. It provides the theoretical foundations for both modernization and age stratification theories, and for activity, disengagement, and role theories of later life adjustment.

14. Conflict theories have developed a political economy of aging that emphasizes the economics of income security for older people. Other conflict theorists have examined the ways in which age and historical generations can become bases for conflict.

15. Symbolic interactionists have rejected the equilibrium assumptions of the sociology of later life happiness and have stressed the strategic interaction of older people as they seek to maximize personal autonomy and self-esteem.

GLOSSARY

Activities of daily living (ADL). Everyday activities such as rising and going to bed, personal hygiene, and shopping.

Activity Theory. A theory which emphasizes that continuing activity through social roles is required in order to attain high life satisfaction in the later years.

Age grade/Age stratum. Socially recognized divisions that are ordered over the life course and with which are associated rights, responsibilities, obligations, and access to rewards.

Age stratification perspective. A theoretical approach that focuses on the progression of birth cohorts through the age strata of a society and, in addition, views the age stratification system as changing in response to cohort characteristics and other social phenomena.

Cohort. A group of individuals born approximately at the same time who move through the life course together.

Continuity theory. A loosely defined theoretical approach which argues that life satisfaction in the later years is enhanced by a continuation of life-long patterns of activity and role involvement, whether high or low.

Disengagement theory. A theory which argues that successful aging involves a mutual withdrawal of the aging individual and society. This is seen as functional for the society and beneficial for the individual. Such disengagement is viewed as normal and, ideally, voluntary on the part of the individual.

Exchange theory. A view of social interaction as an exchange of rewards. Individuals are assumed to seek to maximize rewards and minimize costs.

Generation. When used in other than the kinship or family sense, the term refers to a cohort, large proportions of whose members have experienced significant socio-historical experiences. Such generational experiences frequently lead to the development of shared generational consciousness.

Modernization thesis. An argument which maintains that as societies modernize, aspects of modernization such as industrialization, urbanization, increased emphasis on technology, and improved health and longevity contribute to a decline in the social status of the aged.

Social clock. Refers to socially shared expectations about the normal or appropriate timing and sequence of events over the life course. For example, people may see themselves as making slow or rapid career progress compared to general expectations, or they may see themselves as "delaying" marriage or parenthood.

FURTHER READING

Cowgill, Donald O., and Lowell D. Holmes (eds.). *Aging and Modernization.* New York: Appleton-Century-Crofts. 1972. A comprehensive statement of the "modernization thesis" of aging, with case studies of aging in diverse societies.

Marshall, Victor W. *Last Chapters: A Sociology of Aging and Dying.* Monterey, Calif.: Brookes/Cole. 1980. A broadly ranging social psychological examination, framed explicitly within the interpretive perspective, of aging and the importance of impending death for the aged.

Marshall, Victor W. (Ed.) *Aging in Canada: Social Perspectives.* Toronto: Fitzhenry and Whiteside, 1980. Twenty-six chapters representing the work of many Canadian sociologists of aging, presenting basic demographic data and empirical studies.

Matthews, Sarah H. *The Social World of Older Women.* Beverly Hills and London: Sage. 1979. An exemplary and readable examination of the lives of older women, this book draws on symbolic interactionism and exchange theory, and uses participant observation.

Myles, John S. *Political Economy of Pensions.* Boston and Toronto: Little, Brown and Company. 1983. A leading Canadian sociologist of aging provides an overview of the political economy approach.

CHAPTER 6
CRIME AND DEVIANCE

JOHN HAGAN

Deviance involves variation from a norm. In other words, to be different is to be deviant. But there is more to deviance than this. If there were not, our topic would be considerably less interesting than it is; we would simply be talking about the human diversity that surrounds us. What makes deviance a matter of great interest and importance is the reaction it provokes. Through the reactions of others, diverse human beings are singled out as both different *and* disreputable.

KINDS OF DEVIANCE

Deviance, then, is variation from a norm and the societal reaction involved. With this definition in mind, let us begin to identify several distinguishing characteristics for kinds of deviance (Hagan, 1977a).

The first of these characteristics is the *severity of the societal response*. Historically, we have responded to our most serious deviants, including first degree murderers, by making them liable to capital punishment. We may do so again (see Table 6-1). At the other end of the spectrum, some deviants, particularly those who are badly disturbed or disabled, are simply ignored. If they are slightly more disturbing, they are ostracized.

Between the two ends of this societal-response continuum, there are other types of institutional and community responses, including imprisonment, mental hospitalization, probation, fines, and out-patient treatment. The point is that these many societal responses vary in the degree to which they limit a citizen's freedom. Generally speaking, the more seriously the act of deviance is regarded, the more the freedom of the alleged deviant will be curtailed.

A second characteristic of deviance is the *perceived harmfulness* of the behavior in question. Some deviant behaviors, like forcible rape and aggravated assault, are regarded as serious because of the harm they are perceived to cause. Other forms of deviance, including some sexual predilections of consenting adults, are regarded as inconsequential because little or no perceived harm is done. Between the extremely harmful and the relatively harmless are a number of behavioral deviations from the norm that are thought to be only mildly harmful, or whose degree of harm is uncertain. Included here are activities like marijuana use. Governments have spent millions of dollars assessing the presumed harmfulness of this drug, while the public has seemed to grow steadily less interested in, and more skeptical of, government findings.

In general, however, the more harmful a form of deviant behavior is perceived to be, the more serious a form of deviance it will be regarded. The key word here is *perceived:* the point is not so much what harm these deviant acts do, but what harm they are perceived to do. As Shakespeare observed, "There is nothing either good or bad, but thinking makes it so."

A third characteristic of deviance is the *degree of agreement* there is among the public about whether an act should be considered deviant. Across nations and generations there is a high degree of consensus that some forms of behavior are indeed seriously deviant (for example, armed robbery, forcible rape, and premeditated homicide). Yet there are also many forms of behavior about which there is considerable disagreement. Included among these debated subjects, called **conflict crimes** because of conflicting opinions regarding them, are most types of drug use and many forms of sex. Finally, there are those forms of behavior about which most of us couldn't seem to care less.

Among the more intriguing subjects of our apathy are many fads and fashions. As bizarre as these styles can become, and as interesting, most of us have no strong interest in calling them deviant.

We have briefly considered three related characteristics of deviance: the severity of the societal response to the deviant activity, the perceived harmfulness of this behavior, and the degree of agreement among the public that the acts involved should be considered deviant. Taken together, these characteristics provide a measure of how serious a particular form of deviance may be regarded. In other words, the most serious forms provoke a severe societal response, are perceived as extremely harmful, and are defined as deviant with a high degree of consensus. Less serious forms of deviance result in more moderate or indeterminant forms of societal response, are perceived as less harmful, and may be the subjects of uncertainty or conflict. Finally, the least serious forms of deviance call forth only mild responses, are perceived as relatively harmless, and are subjects of widespread apathy.

Consensus Crimes

With these points in mind, we can now attach names to the kinds of deviance we have begun to identify. See Table 6-1. The first of these categories comprises the **consensus crimes** (Toby, 1974). These acts are defined by law as crimes. The criminal code of Canada specifies a large number of such criminal acts, yet only a few are widely regarded as extremely harmful, are severely punished, and are consensually identified as deviant. One such act is premeditated murder. In many nations and for many centuries, laws of a similar form have designated this type of behavior a crime. The consistency of these statutes has led some legal philosophers to call such acts *mala en se*, or "bad in themselves." A quick examination of our criminal codes, however, will convince most readers that the number of *mala en se* criminal and deviant acts is few. The lessons of history and anthropology are that most conceptions of crime and deviance are subject to change. What is called criminal in one time or place frequently is seen quite differently in another. This being so, the notion of inherent and universal evil is somewhat du-

TABLE 6-1. KINDS OF DEVIANCE

Kind of Deviance	Severity of Societal Response	Perceived Harmfulness	Degree of Agreement	Examples
Consensus Crimes	Severe	Extremely Harmful	Consensus	Premeditated Murder
Conflict Crimes	Punitive	Somewhat Harmful	Conflict	Victimless Crimes (e.g., prostitution, narcotics)
Social Deviations	Indeter-minant	Potentially Harmful	Uncertainty	Mental Illness, Juvenile Delinquency
Social Diversions	Mild	Relatively Harmless	Apathy	Fads and Fashions

bious for many people. This changeable character of crime and deviance is a salient feature of the kind of deviance we consider next.

Conflict Crimes

Our second category of deviance we will call conflict crimes. Although persons convicted of conflict crimes may receive punitive treatment from the courts, acts of this type are usually regarded as only marginally harmful and, at that, typically are subjects of conflict and debate. Legal philosophers refer to such crimes as *mala prohibita*, or "wrong by definition." It is significant that many conflict crimes were once consensus crimes, and that some of what were once conflict crimes have now achieved considerable consensus. In the former category are many of the victimless crimes, including prostitution, drug use, and many sexual acts between consenting adults. For example, during much of this century marijuana use was regarded as a serious form of narcotics abuse requiring strict legal control (Bonnie and Whitebread, 1974). Today marijuana is the subject of commission inquiries and law reform. Significantly, however, this change did not begin until marijuana use became a part of middle- and upper-class youth cultures in the 1960s. What was once a consensus crime is now a subject of conflict.

In contrast to marijuana use, rape seems to be a crime whose roots involved conflict, and whose legal definition has only recently become a focus of renewed debate. It can be argued that the historical illegality of rape is grounded in a conflict between the sexes. That

is, rape laws may have emerged out of men's efforts to protect their women, not because these women were women, but because these women were theirs. From

Consensus crimes are perceived as extremely harmful by society, and those guilty of them are controlled officially by the courts and penal institutions. Within penal institutions, however, a separate, though deviant, society is organized that has its own rules and procedures. Conflicts between "inside" rules and legal authority may lead to demonstrations such as this one in the British Columbia Penitentiary. (*Vancouver Province*)

this viewpoint, rape consists of the taking of one man's property by another. Consistent with this view is the legal fact that a husband cannot be convicted of raping his wife. Furthermore, Lorenne Clark (1976) has demonstrated that rape usually results in sentences quite similar to those handed down for robbery. For most of our Canadian experience these facts have been the subject of apparent consensus, and only recently has the conflict underlying this law become a topic of public concern.

Social Deviations

Our next category consists of **social deviations**. Many of the behaviors included in this category are not criminal, but are nonetheless subject to official control. Some are dealt with under statutes defining mental illness, others under juvenile delinquency legislation, and still others by numerous civil laws that attempt to control various forms of business and professional activities (for example, those laws dealing with securities and stock transactions). A common feature of these official measures is the vagueness with which they define their subject. In the case of business and professional activities, this vagueness may reflect an attempt to protect the powerful from public harassment; in the cases of juvenile delinquency and mental illness, however, it may be that we simply don't have clear notions of what these official categories include.

The concern in all of this is that while business and professional people may escape official control of their social deviations under such statutes, persons with fewer resources may not. Furthermore, those defined as delinquent or mentally ill may be designated as such on the basis of their perceived potential for harm, rather than on the basis of actual harm done. Finally, their assigned treatments may be of indeterminate duration, rather than for a fixed term of punishment. All of this comes from the announced desire to help rather than penalize the subjects of social deviation. But help is all too often perceived by those on the receiving end as punishment and usually constitutes some form of official control. The ineffectual history of official and unofficial responses to homosexuality is an unhappy example of the latter point.

Social Diversions

Our last deviance category is made up of **social diversions**. All of us personally or vicariously experience them. They are the variations in life-styles that help make our lives more interesting and at times exciting. Included are the fads and fashions of speech, appearance, and play. Constant among these diversions is the pursuit of pleasure, but there is, of course, extreme variation in what is regarded as pleasurable. Joggers brave subzero temperatures and exhaustion in search of the "runner's high," while surfers circle the world and endure the ravages of weather and water in their quest for "the perfect wave." As odd as many of these activities seem to most of us, however, we typically react with only a mixture of amusement and apathy to the time, energy, and resources expended by such enthusiasts. Other societies would regard our tolerance of the diverse and the bizarre as indulgent, and indeed it is. Yet that in itself does not make the behaviors involved good or bad, but simply different, diverse, and, to their participants, enjoyable.

So far we have given an extended definition of deviance, seeking to answer the question: What is it? Let us now turn our attention to the question: Where do we find it?

Using several alternative approaches (considered in detail a few pages further on) to the measurement of crime and deviance, sociologists have attempted to get some sense of reliability and validity in their knowledge of how these behaviors are socially distributed. One way of beginning this task is to compare the official statistics of crime and deviance with those gathered through one or more alternative methods. Where the findings generated by alternative methods are in agreement with the official measures, we can have some confidence in our conclusions. Where disagreement occurs, we can begin to examine possible explanations for the disparities. Often these alternative explanations can tell us a good deal, not only about the social distribution of deviance, but about the official agencies that control deviance. In the next section, we use the strategy just described to consider the distribution of crime and deviant behavior by gender and social class in Canada.

SOCIAL DISTRIBUTION OF CRIME AND DEVIANCE

Are criminal and non-criminal forms of deviant behavior randomly distributed in Canadian society? Or do these behaviors occur at different rates among identifiable social groupings in our society? Accurately identifying sources of the social distribution of crime and deviance is an important first step toward the explanation of these behaviors.

Sexual Distribution of Crime and Deviance

Criminal and non-criminal forms of deviant behavior clearly are not distributed randomly by gender. Regardless of the mode of measurement, men are significantly more likely to be alcoholic (Cahalan, 1970), addicted to illegal drugs (Terry and Pellens, 1970), and involved in the more serious forms of crime (Hindelang, 1978). This does not mean, however, that men in all ways or at all times are necessarily more deviant than women. We know that women tend to take more legally prescribed psychoactive drugs than men (Manheimer, et al, 1969) and that they report higher rates of mental illness (Gove and Tudor, 1973). But when it comes to criminal forms of deviance, men clearly exceed women. This does not mean that the relationship between gender and crime is a simple one. The disparity between the sexes fluctuates with the type of crime, time, and social setting. For example, while it has been estimated from official statistics in North America that males exceed females in crimes against the *person* on the order of more than eight to one, in recent years males exceed females on the order of four to one for crimes against property (Nettler, 1974).

The most fascinating aspect of this deviance by gender situation is the possibility that it may be changing, along with more general attitudes toward gender roles. It has been argued recently that women are increasing their involvement in all types of offenses, and more specifically that there is a rising new breed of violent, aggressive female offender (Adler, 1975).

On the other hand, it has also been suggested that the new female criminal is more a social myth than an empirical reality (Steffensmeir, 1978). Both of these arguments could have some validity. For example, it may be that the new female criminal is to be found in some areas of crime more frequently than in others. In other words, some convincing evidence suggests that certain areas of crime may be changing faster than others.

For example, a recent review (Smith and Visher, 1980) of official data and **self-report** data (based on anonymous surveys of adolescents and adults) on crime and deviance indicates that behavioral differences between the sexes are diminishing. Interestingly, this narrowing of the gap is occurring faster for minor deviant acts than for more serious crimes. Equal gender representation in the area of serious criminal behavior has clearly not yet occurred. Similarly, while the gender-deviance relationship is declining for both youths and adults, the data indicate that this trend is stronger for youths. This latter finding is particularly interesting, because it is consistent with expected effects of changing gender roles. That is, it seems likely that shifting gender role ideologies would have a greater effect upon the behavior of younger women, and this is exactly what the data indicate. These patterns of change deserve to be closely watched in the future.

Class Distribution of Crime and Deviance

The relationship between deviant behavior and class position is a matter of considerable controversy. A major reason for the controversy is a pair of seemingly conflicting assumptions. The first of these assumptions is that being a member of the lower class implies a denial of opportunities and a harshness of circumstances to which deviant behavior is a predictable response. The second assumption is that the prejudice and discrimination of official control agents and agencies result in members of the lower class more frequently becoming the targets of control. These contrasting assumptions are not necessarily mutually exclusive; the argument will be made in this and a later section that both assumptions are correct.

The official statistics of crime and delinquency make one point rather clearly: persons *prosecuted* for criminal and delinquent offenses are disproportionately members of the lower class (Braithwaite, 1981). The issue is whether this official sampling of criminals and delinquents is representative of the population from which it is drawn, or whether it is biased by, for example, selection from one class more than another. The answer to this question seems to depend in part on the type of deviance we are considering.

Self-report data have often been compared with official records to examine the class distribution of crime and deliquency. The most serious forms of crime and delinquency are seldom encountered in self-reports, however, and these comparisons therefore tend to concentrate on the less serious and most frequent types of deviant activity (Hindelang, et al, 1979). Results of the self-report studies typically show that the relationship between self-reported behaviors and class position is either weak or inconsistent (Tittle, et al, 1978; Braithwaite, 1981). For example, 47 of these studies are summarized in a review article by Braithwaite (1981), with 25 of them finding some evidence of the expected relationship, and 22 studies reporting no relationship at all. On the other hand, official statistics have traditionally shown such a relationship. The implication of these comparisons is that some class bias exists in the official reports of the most frequent forms of crime and delinquency. A recent Canadian study (Hagan, et al, 1978) reinforces this conclusion, noting that the police in particular tend to have a perception of dense, lower-class areas of the city as being the most in need of police patrol. More telephoned complaints come from these areas, for example, and the police develop a probably exaggerated idea of the relative incidence of crime and deliquency occurring there. A result is a differential allocation of police resources to patrol these areas, with higher rates of recorded crime and delinquency as a consequence, because more police are looking for, and responding to, more deviance.

Thus, self-report data reveal that such deviancy distributions to some extent may be the result of a self-fulfilling prophecy. That is, people see what they expect to see. Self-report data, therefore, have their uses, but recently more serious forms of crime have tended to be studied through surveys of victims. In the United States, these surveys have been used nationwide to examine racial involvement in common-law personal crimes (crimes against persons that have long been considered serious). These studies reveal a substantially greater involvement of blacks in the crimes of rape, robbery, and assault (Hindelang, 1978). There is also some evidence of police bias in this research, but evidence of bias is far outweighed by evidence of behavioral differences. Insofar as race and class are strongly related, this American research suggests that there is a relationship between social class and criminal behavior for serious forms of crime.

It bears repeating, however, that our conception of what constitutes a serious form of deviance is subject to change. We saw this earlier with regard to marijuana use. Within one generation, marijuana use has changed, in the assessment of many, from the alleged cause of "reefer madness" to a symbol of radical chic status. Self-report surveys reflect this change, documenting higher levels of marijuana use in the middle and upper classes than in the lower (Barter, et al, 1970; Suchman, 1968). So marijuana use patterns are changing significantly; changes in the use of hard drugs, like heroin, however, have been less substantial (Berg, 1970). Self-report and official statistics are in agreement that these hard drugs have been and continue to be used more extensively in the lower class, and their use is still generally regarded as a serious matter.

Official and alternative types of statistics have also been compared in the areas of alcohol abuse and mental illness. Official statistics in these areas, as in others, show a higher representation in the lower class. Self-report studies parallel these findings. For example, household surveys have contained the following question: "Have you or any member of your household ever had difficulty because of too much drinking?" Many of these studies report a higher incidence of such problems in the lower class than in other classes (for example, Bailey, et al, 1965; Cahalan, 1970). Similar conclusions are found in the area of mental illness. Dohrenwend and Dohrenwend (1975) report that, "The highest overall rates of psychiatric disorder have been found in the lowest social class in 28 out of 33 studies that report data according to indicators of social class."

The conclusions we can draw are as follows: serious crimes, hard-drug use, alcohol abuse, and mental illness are found more frequently in the lower class, while less serious and more frequent forms of crime, delinquency, and drug use are more evenly distributed across the social classes. It is in the latter areas that official statistics appear most dubious, because the lower class is here disproportionately selected for official attention. To some extent, doubt or confidence in a given deviance statistic depends on how such deviance was *measured*. Let us turn then from our consideration of the social distribution of deviance to a consideration of its measurement.

MEASURING CRIME AND DEVIANCE

Because many forms of deviance are *controlled* officially, they are also *counted* officially. These enumerations constitute the official statistics of deviance found in the reports of police, of criminal and civil courts, of correctional institutions, of mental health centers, and of various agencies dealing with alcohol and drug abuse. A myriad of statistics exist, therefore, and if these were as credible as they are accessible, the sociologist's task would be an easier one. Unfortunately, the same type of biases that can affect the legislation of crime and deviance (we will consider these shortly) can also affect the counting of crime and deviance. That is, organizations involved in controlling these behaviors may vary from strict impartiality, following their own interests in the types and amounts of crime and deviance they count.

Giffen (1966), for example, suggests that one latent function of processing skid road alcoholics in a "revolving door," or perpetual, fashion is that it makes the criminal justice system look both busy and efficient: the budgets of control agencies are often heavily dependent on how busy and efficient these agencies appear. Thus some statistics produced by official control agencies may tell us more about the agencies themselves than about the persons and events counted. The challenge for scholars, then, is to make sociological sense of the statistics official agencies collect.

Analysts of deviance have responded to this challenge by developing alternatives to the use of official records, such as collecting data from non-official agencies: insurance companies dealing with theft; hospitals, private physicians, and public health agencies whose records reflect much alcoholism and drug abuse; and business accounting and consulting firms that encounter much internal theft and fraud.

A second alternative is to collect and record first-person accounts generated through anonymous *self-report surveys* of adolescents and adults and personal face-to-face interviews with subjects in their natural settings. The self-report approach, as seen earlier, has been used to study crime, delinquency, alcohol and drug abuse, and the symptoms of mental illness. Personal interviews are most often used to study career deviants, those individuals who persist in deviant lifestyles.

A third approach involves surveys of the victims of crime. Done by telephone or in a door-to-door census-like fashion, *victimization surveys* provide a unique measure of deviant behavior that includes crimes committed by individuals against persons and their property.

A fourth and final approach involves actual *observations* of deviant behavior in which the observer may or may not be a participant. For obvious reasons, this approach has been used primarily in the study of the more conflict-prone forms of deviance, like homosexuality and marijuana use.

These, then, are four alternatives to reliance on official statistics, that may reflect official control and may in turn reflect official preoccupation with certain kinds of deviance.

But the question remains: Why are some forms of difference and diversity subject to official control while others are not? Scholars have been particularly concerned that part of the answer to this question involves the activities of self-interested groups and individuals. The concern is that some individuals and groups may have interests that encourage them to lobby for the official control of some types of deviant behavior. Let us therefore turn our attention next to the issue of crime and deviance legislation.

LEGISLATION OF CRIME AND DEVIANCE

Moral entrepreneurs is the term Becker (1963) uses for those individuals most active in striving for official control of deviance. These are the people whose initiative and enterprise are essential in getting the legal rules passed that are necessary to "do something" about a particular type of deviant behavior. Often these individuals seem to be undertaking a moral crusade in that they perceive some activity as an evil in need of legal reform, and they pursue this task with missionary zeal (Gusfield, 1963). Moral entrepreneurs and crusaders assume that enforcement of the wished-for legal rules will improve the lives of those who are ruled. That this is often a very dubious assumption will become clear as we consider two moral crusades that have brought legal control of two different types of deviant behavior in North America.

Narcotics and Alcohol

The moral entrepreneur most responsible for the passage of Canada's first narcotics laws was none other than Mackenzie King (Cook, 1969). King became aware of Canada's "opium problem" when he discovered that opium could be bought over the counter in Vancouver. This knowledge came to him accidentally. As Deputy Minister of Labour, he had been sent to Vancouver to supervise the payment of compensation to Chinese and Japanese businessmen who had suffered losses during the anti-Asiatic riots of 1907. Two of the claims came from opium manufacturing merchants. Shocked, King prepared a report which soon led to the Opium Act of 1908.

Along the route to becoming Prime Minister, King made a small career out of this particular moral crusade. He was selected as part of a five-man British delegation to attend the Shanghai Opium Commission in 1909. And in 1911, as a member of Laurier's cabinet,

If defiance had been enough then, we wouldn't need your money now.

Many people for many years have disagreed with the laws concerning the use of marijuana. The prevailing attitude seems to have been straight defiance. Smoke it anyway. Wherever and whenever.

The federal government's response is just as defiant. As long as it is politically questionable, the issue is avoided. Despite the scientific, moral and medical arguments put forth the government sits still.

And criminal records pile up. And people are arrested and humiliated. And people go to prison. Daily.

We at NORML CANADA have decided that we have had enough. We view the

personal use of marijuana as an activity that should not be viewed as criminal.

In order to get the government to change the laws, now, we must apply continual pressure. We have caught their attention. Our presence is continually monitored. Our latest rally at Nathan Phillips Square drew about 7,000 people and was covered by every newspaper and television station in the Toronto area. We feel we have picked up incredible momentum in a very short period of time.

In order to keep the momentum up, we have got to raise funds. We need your support. If you care about your personal liberty, join us or help us financially.

The time has never been so right.

NORML CANADA

☐ Here's my $15 annual membership fee (students $10). Count me among the concerned Canadians seeking equity in our laws and keep me informed on the issues.
☐ I'm not a joiner but here's a contribution.
☐ Please send me information about NORML Canada products (T-Shirts, etc.)
Name
Address
Code

National Organization for Reform of Marijuana Laws in Canada. Box 340, Stn. E, Toronto, Ont. M6H 4E3

Reefer madness: marijuana use was once perceived as a serious crime and was severely punished. By the end of the 1970s, simple possession had been decriminalized for one-third of the American population. How did it happen? Partly through the work of organizations such as NORML; partly because dope-smoking hippies grew up to be lawyers, doctors, and executives; partly because economic factors began to outweigh social and moral ones. How long could governments forego lost tax dollars? How long could they continue to spend millions to prosecute and imprison young offenders?

he introduced a more stringent Opium and Drug Act. By 1920, calls for still more stringent legislation were coming in the form of sensational articles in periodicals like *Maclean's* magazine. Several of these articles were authored by Mrs. Emile Murphy (1920; 1922), a juvenile court judge in Edmonton, who ultimately went on to expand her views in a book titled *The Black Candle*. The background of these efforts tells us much about the way in which moral crusades can be generated.

During the period leading up to our first narcotics legislation, Canadian doctors were probably as responsible for addiction as the Chinese opium merchants. Medications containing opiates were indiscriminately prescribed by physicians and used by patients of all classes. In fact, syrups containing opiates, particularly paregoric, were frequently used by mothers for their infants. So it was not just fear of the drug, but also hostility toward Asian immigrants, that stimulated much of the narcotics legislation. This antagonism emerged in large part from the immigration of Asian laborers to Canada. Much of the parliamentary debate that preceded the first Opium Act dealt with Oriental immigration and a proposed trade treaty with Japan that was to allow Japanese immigration.

A dramatic example of how the logically separate and distinct issues of opium and Asian immigration were tied together occurred in the 1922 narcotics debates, when the following remarks of the secretary of the Anti-Asiatic Exclusion League were read:

Here we have a disease, one of many directly traceable to the Asiatic. Do away with the Asiatic and you have more than saved the souls and bodies of thousands of young men and women who are yearly being sent to a living hell and to the grave through their presence in Canada (House of Commons Debates, 1922).

Others, like Murphy (1922), spoke of "Chinese peddlers" bringing about the "downfall of the white race."

The point is that hostile attitudes toward a minority group were an important part of the crusading and entrepreneurial efforts that resulted in Canada's first narcotics legislation.

The moral entrepreneur best known for his role in the passage of American narcotics legislation is H.J. Anslinger, the first Director of the Federal Bureau of Narcotics (Becker, 1963; Lindesmith, 1967). Anslinger used his office to arouse American public and congressional concern about what he regarded as a growing "drug menace." For example, in 1937 Anslinger published a widely circulated magazine article, "Marihuana: Assassin of Youth." As in Canada, much of this attention combined hostile attitudes toward minority groups with discussions of the drug problem (Musto, 1973). In the course of media accounts, for example, the Chinese were associated with opium (Reasons, 1974), southern blacks with cocaine (Musto, 1973), and Mexicans with marijuana (Bonnie and Whitebread, 1974). The fear was fostered that drug use by minorities posed a particularly dangerous threat to American society.

It made little difference in Canada or the United States that, as Duster (1970) reports, the upper and middle classes predominated among narcotic addicts into the second decade of this century. It was not until after the passage of America's first narcotics legislation, the Harrison Act of 1914, that this picture seemed to change. By 1920, medical journals spoke of the "overwhelming majority [of drug addicts] from the 'unrespectable parts' of society" (Duster, 1970). The technique used is called guilt by association, because by persuading the public to associate narcotics use with disenfranchised minorities, moral entrepreneurs were able to lay a foundation for a legislative prohibition against the non-medical use of drugs and for making drug use a crime. Some contemporary thoughts on drug use are contained in the boxed insert on this page.

The prohibition against alcohol offers an interesting comparison with drug legislation, because while the latter endured, the former failed. Alcohol prohibition in the United States followed from the well organized lobbying activities of the Women's Christian Temperance Union and the Anti-Saloon League. These efforts constituted a moral crusade that seemed to reflect an effort to protect an established way of life that was perceived as threatened during the early part of this century by the immigration of new Americans into the nation's cities. Joseph Gusfield (1963) argues that alcohol prohibition was a response to the fears of native, middle-class, Protestant Americans that their established positions in American life, and this style of life itself, were endangered by the urban, immigrant alco-

Cannabis Criminals

The law is an imperfect social invention. Indeed, the law produces many social embarrassments that most of us successfully ignore. One of these embarrassments is the role our laws have played in creating what Patricia Erickson (1980) calls in her recent book "cannabis criminals." Erickson has documented the details of this embarrassment in terms it may no longer be possible to ignore.

For example, did you know that by 1976 more than 100 000 Canadians had been designated "criminal" for simple possession of cannabis? Indeed, one out of every eight or nine adults charged with a crime in Canada in recent years has been pursued for their use or abuse of cannabis. While many of us assume that our attitudes, and therefore our laws, dealing with

cannabis are changing, to date changes have not occured. Instead, Erickson has demonstrated that in recent years the total criminalization for cannabis use has actually increased, with increasing numbers of persons going to prison in Canada for cannabis possession. Yet imprisonment represents only the very tip of the iceberg, and other types of dispositions have increased as well. Erickson reports that the great majority of "cannabis criminals" receive absolute or conditional discharges or fines. Many citizens may wonder why we bother, and Erickson's findings should raise this feeling from curiosity to dismay.

Adopting the sensible standard of the Le Dain Commission, Erickson examines how the costs of criminalizing cannabis offenders compare with the presumed beneficial deterrent effects of cannabis prohibition. To this end, 95 Canadians sentenced for possession of cannabis were interviewed and their responses analyzed.

The implication of Erickson's findings is a stark indictment of the logic of our cannabis laws. What she finds is that being criminalized for canna-

bis possession has negative consequences for other aspects of the individuals' lives, but no demonstrable deterrent effect in the individuals' cannabis use. Why, then, have these laws been enforced with such apparent enthusiasm?

Erickson's argument here is provocative, providing a more general and important insight into how good legislative intentions can produce bad law enforcement. The problem is that in Canada special police powers of search, the widespread availability of cannabis users, rewards to police for generating large numbers of arrests, and few restrictions on the admissibility of illegally obtained evidence in court all seem to encourage an aggressive seeking out of cannabis offenders. Unfortunately, the burden of the evidence reported in Erickson's research is that more problems have been created than solved by this type of law and its enforcement.

Source:

Erickson, Patricia. *Cannabis Criminals: The Social Effects of Punishment of Drug Users*. Toronto: ARF Books, 1980.

hol use they saw as increasing around them. As with drugs, a concerted effort was made to link alcohol with poverty, minorities, crime, and insanity.

Alcohol prohibition was only partly successful, however, and resistance to it began to emerge, particularly in the ranks of organized labor. That is, when alcohol prohibition attempted to criminalize the mass of the poor, it ran into the opposition of unions and urban political machines.

Timberlake (1963) observes that although wage earners were unable to thwart the enactment of temperance legislation, they were strong enough to insure its ultimate failure. He notes that many working men were opposed to prohibition because it smacked of paternalism and class exploitation. To them it was a hypocritical and insulting attempt to control their personal lives in order to exact greater profits for their

employers. The employers themselves had no intention of abstaining. Indeed, it is estimated that as much as 81 percent of the American Federation of Labor was "wet," a figure consistent with the claim of Samuel Gompers that the great majority of the membership opposed prohibition. In sum, it seems that alcohol prohibition failed because it attempted to define as criminal what too large and well organized a part of the poor, as well as the rich, were doing. By contrast, narcotics legislation focused more narrowly, and more successfully, on minorities of the poor, who could be defined as criminal usually without organized opposition.

Juvenile Delinquency

The work of moral entrepreneurs is often associated

with the growth of professional organizations that have their own bureaucratic interests to develop and protect. An example of this is the development of juvenile delinquency legislation and a resulting juvenile court bureaucracy staffed in large part by probation officers trained in the emerging profession of social work. The efforts that led to the separate designation of juvenile delinquency and to the development of the juvenile courts were often called "child-saving" (Platt, 1969). Parker (1976) points out that, contrary to common sense understanding:

. . . the history of child-saving in the twentieth century is not the history of improving the general conditions of child-life (because most of the battles have been won), or the history of juvenile institutions (which changed very little after the initial efforts of the founders of the House of Refuge and their imitators). It is not even the history of the juvenile court itself, because it provided, as legal institutions tend to do, a purely symbolic quality to child work. The real history of the period is a history of probation.

Probation was a new idea at the beginning of this century. Its attraction was the prospect of keeping young offenders in their homes and out of institutions. The emphasis on probation within the juvenile court movement reflected a concern for the family that pervaded the early part of this century; it was known as the Progressive Era. This was an era of extensive social, political, and legal reform work. The result was the emergence of a system of social control that was less formal and less coercive than institutionalization. The use of probation extended the range of control efforts, however, and this control was imposed largely on the families of the urban poor, often outside of court. The results of these activities can be seen in Canada and the United States.

J.J. Kelso, for instance, was a moral entrepreneur who guided the passage of Canada's first juvenile court legislation. The result of this legislation was the development of a bureaucracy, staffed in large part by probation officers (Hagan and Leon, 1977a).

Kelso began as a crusading newspaper reporter in Toronto and went on to further his own career as Ontario's first Superintendent of Neglected and Dependent Children. Possibly the most important step toward juvenile delinquency legislation in Canada came in 1893, when Kelso and others convinced the Ontario legislature to enact a comprehensive Children's Protection Act giving explicit recognition and authority to the Children's Aid Society. As a result, it became the duty of the court to notify the society prior to initiating proceedings against a boy under twelve or a girl under thirteen; an officer of the society would then investigate the charges, inquire into the child's family environment, and report back to the court. These procedures were extended the following year to federal law in an Act Respecting Arrest, Trial, and Imprisonment of Youthful Offenders. Finally, a federal Juvenile Delinquents Act was passed in 1908, incorporating and extending the earlier procedures for juveniles. Kelso was prominent in all these efforts; he promoted his work frequently and well.

It is widely believed that the juvenile court movement just described was the result of an effort to get children out of criminal courts and prisons. This effort seems to have been one of the purposes of juvenile delinquency legislation, but it was less than successful. Juveniles continued to be sent to institutions. The most dramatic consequence of the new legislation was a rapid expansion of the number of probation officers and of the number of juveniles with which they dealt. In this sense, the control of juvenile behavior was actually increased by the new legislation. And in 1924 the federal Juvenile Delinquents Act was amended to include control over adolescents "guilty of sexual immorality or any similar form of vice." In short, most of the fun of adolescence was made illegal by this act! The point is that the suspicion arises that one purpose of much of this moral reform effort was to increase the "need" for probation officers and the growth of this bureaucracy.

A diminished reliance on institutions combined with increased control, particularly through probation personnel, is apparent in other fragmentary data. The prominent reformer Frederic Almy (1902) wrote from Buffalo that, "The . . . Juvenile Court has not quite completed its first year, and no definite records have been compiled, but two results are already notable – the decrease in the number of commitments to the truant school and to reformatories, and the increase in the number of children arrested." In the same way, between 1913 and 1914 in Chicago the number of delinquents referred to court rose from 1956 to 2916, an increase of nearly 50 percent in the delinquency rate for Cook County. Haller (1970) notes that the reason for this was that 23 additional probation officers were hired in 1914. Similar points have been made by Schlossman (1977) with regard to the development of the juvenile court in Milwaukee.

A general picture begins to emerge from these reports. The Progressive Era was characterized by a widely shared view that rehabilitation should be family-centered. Advocates of such legislation, therefore, focused on the offender's home as the locus of treatment and on the probation officer as the key remedial agent. Among the most vigorous proponents were members of women's groups and persons who eventually became the "professionals" charged with responsibility for probation. Again, one suspects that a purpose of much of this moral reform effort was to increase both the need for probation officers and the growth of this bureaucracy.

To say that the legislation of deviance is influenced by individual and group interests, however, is not to say that legislation of this kind is unnecessary. Rather it emphasizes the facts that all such laws cannot be taken at face value and that individual and group interests can determine the form that various laws take. The line that separates those forms of deviance that are socially controlled, from those that are officially and criminally controlled, is a thin one.

THEORIES OF CRIME AND DEVIANCE

So much for what deviance is, where it is found, how it is measured, and how and why it is legislated against. Our chief remaining question is: How do we account for the actual phenomenon? How, that is, do we explain deviance. Accordingly, we now turn to attempted theoretical explanations of class differences in criminal and deviant behavior, as discussed above. This discussion will proceed from the three basic sociological perspectives: structural functionalist, symbolic interactionist, and conflict.

Structural Functionalism and Deviance

Structural functionalist theories regard deviant behavior as the consequence of a strain or breakdown in the social processes that produce conformity. The focus here is on institutions (such as the family and school) that socialize individuals into the conforming values of the existing society and on the ways in which this process can go wrong. An assumption of this approach is that there is wide agreement, or consensus, about what the prime values of our society are. Structural functionalist theories try to explain why some individuals, through their deviant behavior, come to challenge this consensus. In other words, why do individuals violate the conforming values that nearly all of us are assumed to hold in common?

Anomie. The roots of functionalist theory are in Durkheim's notion of **anomie** (1964, originally published 1897); this term at first meant an absence of social regulation, or normlessness. Merton (1938, 1957) revived the concept, making it refer to the consequences of a faulty relationship between goals and the legitimate means of attaining them. Merton emphasized two features of social and cultural structure: culturally defined goals (such as monetary success) and the acceptable means (such as education) to their achievement. The problem for Merton was that in our society success goals are widely shared, while the means of attaining them are not.

Merton's theory is intended to explain not only why people deviate, then, but also why some types of people deviate more than others. In particular, members of the lower class are most affected by the disparity between shared success goals and the scarcity of means to attain them. The result of this structural inconsistency is a high rate of deviant behavior.

Merton outlined a number of ways in which individuals adapt to inadequate means of attaining their goals. These methods of adapting include *innovation*, comprising various forms of economic crimes; *ritualism*, involving various forms of overconformity; *retreatism*, consisting of escapist activities such as drug abuse; and *rebellion*, involving revolutionary efforts to change the structural system of goals and means. The common feature of these separate patterns is that they all represent adaptations to failure, a failure to achieve goals through legitimate means.

Delinquent Subculture. The adaptations to failure described above occur socially as well as individually. One form of social adaptation is represented in the **delinquent subculture**. Cohen (1955) suggests that members of the lower class, and potential members of a delinquent subculture, first experience a failure to achieve when they enter school and are assessed against a "middle-class measuring rod." The result for these students is a growing sense of "status frustration." The crux of the problem is that working-class children are not prepared to satisfy middle-class expectations. The delinquent subculture therefore emerges as an alternative set of criteria, or values, that working-class adolescents can meet.

This emergence is accomplished by making subcultural values a complete repudiation of middle-class standards; the delinquent subculture expresses contempt for a middle-class life-style by making its opposite a criterion of prestige, as if to say, "we're everything you say we are and worse." The result, according to Cohen (1955), is a delinquent subculture that is "nonutilitarian, malicious, and negativistic" – an inversion of middle-class values. Yet this is only one possible type of subcultural reaction to the frustration of failure. The theorists we consider next go on to suggest three other reactions to the denial of opportunity.

Differential Opportunity. When legitimate opportunities are denied, illegitimate opportunities may be the only game in town. Cloward and Ohlin (1960) argue that to understand the different forms that criminal and delinquent behavior can take, we must consider the different types of illegitimate opportunities available to those who are seeking a way out of the working class. Different types of community settings, and the different illegitimate opportunities they offer, produce very different subcultural responses. Cloward and Ohlin suggest that three types of responses predominate: a stable criminal subculture, a conflict subculture, and a retreatist subculture.

The **stable criminal subculture** is, as its name suggests, the best organized of the three. According to Cloward and Ohlin, this subculture can emerge only when there is some coordination between persons in legitimate and illegitimate roles; for example, between politicians, police, and the underworld. One pictures the old-style political machine, with protection provided for preferred types of illegal enterprise. Only in these circumstances can stable patterns be established so that there are opportunities for advancement from lower to upper levels of the criminal underworld. The legitimate and illegitimate opportunity structures are linked in this way, the streets become safe *for* crime, and reliable criminal upward mobility routes can emerge. The relationship among opportunity structures, crime, and ethnicity is discussed in the boxed insert on the next page.

Violence and conflict, on the other hand, are disruptive of both legitimate and illegitimate enterprise. When both types of enterprise coexist, violence is restrained. In the disorganized slum, however, where these spheres of activity are not linked, violence can reign uncontrolled. Cloward and Ohlin see these types of communities as producing a **conflict subculture**. A result of this disorganization is the prevalence of street gangs and violent crime, making the streets unsafe for profitable crime.

The final type of subculture posited by Cloward and Ohlin, the **retreatist subculture**, comprises those individuals who fail in their efforts in *both* the legitimate and illegitimate opportunity structures. These "double failures," are destined for drug abuse and other forms of escape.

So far we have focused on a strain between goals and means as the source of deviant behavior in structural functionalist theory. It is this strain that theoretically produces the subcultural responses we have discussed. Before moving on, however, we should note a final form of structural functionalist theory that also takes into account those individuals who are relatively unimpressed by the goals, values, or commitments that our society emphasizes.

Control and Commitment. To have goals and means is to be committed to conformity and to be

Crime and Ethnicity: An Example of the Structural Functionalist Approach

Some of the most interesting applications of structural functionalist theories of deviance have dealt with the topic of crime and ethnicity. For example, Ianni (1972) has noted that over several generations a series of different ethnic groups has been associated with organized crime in North America. Ianni proposes the concept of *ethnic succession* to explain the changing ethnic participation in organized crime activities. Ethnic succession refers to the process by which successive ethnic groups have come to North America in search of a better life, but without the ready means to achieve it – education and job skills. They responded to this disparity through involvement in organized crime. Ianni notes that in the United States first the Irish, then the Jews, later the Italians, and most recently black Americans have been prominently involved in organized crime. As they gained access to legitimate means of attaining success, and consequently moved up the social ladder, their involvement in organized crime declined.

Ianni illustrates his argument most convincingly in a discussion of Italian involvement in organized crime. This discussion begins with an historical analysis of organized crime in Italy. Here Ianni notes that the roots of organized crime can be found in a collection of secret societies, of which the Mafia is only one. Furthermore, the word Mafia has been used in two ways: first as an adjective to describe the type of man who is known and respected because he gets things done, and second as a noun to refer to criminal organizations and societies. These meanings are often confused and may be a source of the exaggerated claims made for the existence of a single, all-powerful criminal organization. In contrast to this image of unity and omnipotence, Ianni notes that the Mafia began as a collection of local organizations in Sicily in the early nineteenth century. The emergence of the Mafia coincided with the breakdown of feudalism. In effect, the Mafia served as a middleman, paying landowners who had fled to the cities lump-sum rents for their rural estates, and then re-renting them to peasants. In other words, the Mafia filled a vacuum between the social strata in Sicily and became a source of order within the Sicilian social system. The Mafia continued to be prominent until Mussolini. Thus, the Mafia was not a single organization that could have emigrated en masse to North America.

Nonetheless, the cultural attitudes that surrounded the term "Mafia" as an adjective did begin to have an impact in North America in the 1920s, notably because of Prohibition, one result of which was to create an illegal industry well suited to a large new immigrant group whose other opportunities were minimal. Many Italians, who had traditionally produced their own wine at home, began turning their household wineries into home stills, and central organizations emerged to collect this new source of illegal profits. Later, with the coming of the Depression and the repeal of Prohibition, it became necessary for these organizations, or crime families, to enter new fields of illegitimate enterprises, particularly drugs and prostitution. By this time, however, second generation members of organized crime families were taking over, and the Italian-American involvement in organized crime was becoming more North American than Italian in character. Ianni notes that today the process of ethnic succession is working toward its logical conclusion, with declining involvement of Italians in organized crime.

Clairmont (1974) has given a parallel structural functionalist explanation of the development of a deviance service center in the Nova Scotian community of Africville. Until its displacement for industrial and harbor development in the mid-1960s, Africville was a predominantly black community located close to Halifax. This community was settled by descendants of blacks who fled from slavery in the United States during the War of 1812. Few economic opportunities were available to the residents of Africville. At the same time, the community was given the "functional autonomy" by the City of Halifax to develop in almost any way it wished: "that is, not sharing fairly in society's wealth, they . . . [were] allowed by authorities a range of behavior that would not be countenanced elsewhere" (Clairmont, 1974). A result was that during World War I a growing bootlegging trade developed, and eventually a full-scale deviance service center consisting of several vice industries emerged. Clairmont (1974) summarizes the situation in this way: "Minority group members, if oppressed and discriminated against, often find a mode of adjusting to their situation by performing less desirable and sometimes illegitimate services for the majority group." Vice industries have served this function for many generations. Lacking the legalization of all forms of vice, or the availability of economic opportunities to all who seek them, organized crime is likely to continue to serve this function for some time to come.

Source:

Ianni, Francis A. *A Family Business: Kinship and Social Control in Organized Crime.* New York: Russel Sage, 1972; Clairmont, Donald. "The development of a deviance service centre," in Jack Haas and Bill Shaffir (eds.), *Decency and Deviance.* Toronto: McClelland and Stewart, 1974.

controlled by this commitment; to have neither goals nor means, however, is to be uncommitted and thus *un*controlled. Hirschi (1969) has argued that the absence of control is really all that is required to explain much deviant behavior. There are other types of controls (besides commitment to conformity) that may also operate: *involvement*, in school and other activities; *attachments*, to friends and family; and *belief*, in various types of values and principles. Hirschi argues that deviant behavior is inversely related to the presence of these controls. Alternatively, as these controls accumulate, so too does conformity. Again, Hirschi's point is that no special strain between goals and means is necessarily required to produce deviant behavior; all that is required is the elimination of constraint.

In all the approaches we have considered, values or beliefs play some role in the causation of deviance. The presence of success goals or values without means to obtain them can produce deviant behavior, as can the absence of these goals or values in the first place. It is an emphasis on these values, and the role of the school and family in transmitting them, that ties the structural functionalist theories together.

Symbolic Interaction and Deviance

The *symbolic interactionist theories* of deviance are concerned less with values than with the role of social meanings and definitions in the production of deviant behavior. The assumption, of course, is that these meanings and definitions, these symbolic variations, make a behavioral difference. Early versions of symbolic interactionist theory focused on how these meanings and definitions were acquired by individuals *from* others; later versions of the theory have focused on the role of official control agencies in imposing these meanings and definitions *on* individuals. The significance of this difference in focus will become apparent as we consider the development of the symbolic interactionist approach.

Differential Association. One of the fathers of the North American study of crime was Edwin Sutherland (1924). Sutherland anticipated an emphasis of the symbolic interactionist perspective with his early use of the concept of **differential association**. This concept referred not only to associations among people, but also, and even more importantly, to associations among ideas. Sutherland argued that people behave criminally only when they define such behavior as acceptable. The connection postulated between people and their ideas (that is, definitions) is as follows (Sutherland, 1949):

The hypothesis of differential association is that criminal behavior is learned in association with those who define such behavior favorably and in isolation from those who define it unfavorably, and that a person in an appropriate situation engages in such criminal behavior if, and only if, the weight of the favorable definitions exceeds the weight of the unfavorable definitions.

Sutherland (1949) applied his hypothesis in a famous study of white-collar crime, arguing that individuals become white-collar criminals because they are immersed with their colleagues in a business ideology that defines illegal business practice as acceptable.

A student of Sutherland's, Donald Cressey (1971), went on to apply a form of this hypothesis to the specific crime of embezzlement. Cressey interviewed more than 100 imprisoned embezzlers and concluded that they had committed their crimes after they had rationalized, or redefined, their crime, using such lines as the following:

"Some of our most respectable citizens got their start in life by using other people's money temporarily."

"All people steal when they get in a tight spot."

"My interest was only to use this money temporarily so I was 'borrowing' it, not 'stealing.'"

"I have been trying to live an honest life, but I have had nothing but trouble so 'to hell with it.'"

Techniques of Neutralization. Symbolic interactionist theory is not exclusively concerned with lower-class deviance; it gives considerable attention to crimes of the upper and middle class as well. But when attention is turned to the underworld, the explanatory framework remains essentially the same. The key to this consistency is Sykes and Matza's (1957) observation that lower-class delinquents, like white-collar criminals, usually exhibit guilt or shame when detected violating the law. Thus the delinquent, like the white-

The Yonge St. Strip. Toronto's biggest tourist attraction during the seventies was the few blocks of its main street where sexual diversions were openly available and widely patronized. The Strip was a centre for deviant types who congregated from all over Canada.

collar criminal, is regarded as an "apologetic failure," who drifts into a deviant life-style through a subtle process of justification. "We call these justifications of deviant behavior techniques of neutralization," write Sykes and Matza, "and we believe these techniques make up a crucial component of Sutherland's definitions favorable to the violation of the law" (1957).

Sykes and Matza list five of these **neutralization techniques**: the denial of responsibility (e.g., blaming a bad upbringing), denial of injury (e.g., claiming that the victim deserved it), condemnation of the condemners (e.g., calling their condemnation discriminatory), and an appeal to higher loyalties (e.g., citing loyalty to friends or family as the cause of their behavior). Sykes and Matza's point is that crime in the underworld,

like crime in society at large, is facilitated by this type of thinking. The question remains, however: Why are underworld crimes more frequently made the subjects of official condemnation?

Dramatization of Evil. The beginning of an answer to this question appears in the early work of Franklin Tannenbaum (1938). Tannenbaum points out that some forms of juvenile delinquency are a normal part of adolescent street life – aspects of the play, adventure, and excitement that many nostalgically identify later as an important part of this period. To others, such activities are seen as a nuisance or as threatening, and they summon the police.

Tannenbaum's concern is that police intervention begins a process of change in the way in which the individuals and their activities are perceived. He suggested that there is a gradual shift from the definition of specific acts as evil to the definition of the individual as evil. Even more importantly, Tannenbaum sees the individual's first contact with the law as most consequential, and he refers to this as a "dramatization of evil" that separates the child out of his group for specialized treatment. Tannenbaum goes on to argue that this "dramatization" played a greater role in making the criminal than perhaps any other experience. The problem is that individuals thus singled out may begin to think of themselves as the type of people who do such things – that is, as delinquents. From this viewpoint, efforts to reform or deter deviant behavior create more problems than they solve. "The way out," Tannenbaum argues, "is through a refusal to dramatize the evil." He suggests instead that the less said about it the better.

Primary and Secondary Deviance. Sociologists in recent years have expanded on the version of the interactionist perspective introduced by Tannenbaum. For example, Lemert (1967) suggests the terms primary and secondary deviance to distinguish between those acts that occur before and after the societal response. Acts of **primary deviance** are those that precede a social or legal response. They may be incidental or even random aspects of an individual's general behavior. The important point is that these initial acts have little impact on the individual's self-concept. **Secondary deviance**, on the other hand, follows the societal response and involves a transformation of the individual's self-concept, "altering the psychic structure, producing specialized organization of social roles and self-regarding attitudes" (Lemert, 1967). From this point on, the individual takes on more and more of the "deviant" aspects of his or her new role. The societal response has, from this point of view, succeeded only in confirming the individual in a deviant role (Becker, 1963, 1964).

The Labeling Process. As we have developed our discussion of the interactionist perspective, it has focused more and more on the official societal reactions to deviant behavior, or on what many analysts of deviance call "the labeling process." This attention to societal labeling has focused not only on the conventional topics of crime, delinquency, and drugs, but labeling also applies to the much neglected topic of mental illness. Scheff (1966), for example, has suggested that our society uses the concept of "mental illness" in much the same way as other societies use the concepts of "witchcraft" and "spirit possession." That is, this label provides a catch-all category wherein we can place a variety of forms of **residual rule breaking** for which our society provides no other explicit labels.

Scheff (1966) observes that from childhood we all learn the stereotyped role behavior that is a part of insanity. On the basis of this knowledge, Scheff (1966) suggests that:

When societal agents and persons around the deviant react to him uniformly in terms of the traditional stereotypes of insanity, his amorphous and unstructured rule-breaking tends to crystallize in conformity to these expectations, thus becoming similar to the behavior of other deviants classified as mentally ill, and stable over time.

In other words, the labeling process of mental illness may help to create the very kind of secondary deviance it is attempting to cure.

In the end, symbolic interactionists do not insist that all, or perhaps even most, deviant behavior is caused by officially imposed labels. Official labels *are* thought, however, to create special problems for the individuals to whom they are applied, often increasing the chances that additional deviant behavior will follow. The point is that not only the actor but also the reactors participate in creating the meanings and definitions involved in the generation of deviant behavior. That the poor are more likely than the rich to get caught up in this process is acknowledged by the symbolic interactionists, and further emphasized in conflict theory, the approach we consider next.

Conflict Theory and Deviance

The most distinctive feature of the conflict theories of deviance is their focus on the role of dominant societal groups in imposing legal labels on members of subor-

Crime as Work: An Example of the Interactionist Approach

The symbolic interactionist theories of deviance place a heavy emphasis on the role of meanings and definitions in the explanation of deviant behavior. Even when these theories have been applied in the study of very different kinds of behavior, it has been emphasized that these meanings and definitions can play a quite similar role. Letkemann (1973) has illustrated this point in a unique Canadian study of career criminals. His thesis is that crime can be a form of work defined by all the elements of a profession. But to understand this contention we must see the world of crime in the same terms, that is with the same meanings and definitions, as the persons who participate in it. To do this, Letkemann conducted in-depth interviews with a sample of skilled and experienced property offenders.

One of the most striking results of these interviews is the awareness of how different the official and criminal classification of offenders can be. The problem is that legal categorizations of offenders, according to criminal code designations, often constitute distorted descriptions of offenders' career patterns. For example, while safe-cracking has been a lively and venerable criminal career in Canada, it is not a term found in the criminal code. Instead, offenders involved in this form of criminal work are often convicted of breaking and entering. This example illustrates the need to appreciate the meanings and definitions offenders attach to their own activities.

Pursuing this theme, Letkemann found that his subjects define not only their own activities, but those of their colleagues in crime, in terms of several important distinctions. The first of these distinctions is between one group referred to as "rounders,"

and a larger group referred to as "alkies," "dope fiends," and "normals." The first of these groups, the rounders, is distinguished by its commitment to an illegitimate life style, a commitment that is demonstrated in a consistent and reliable, albeit criminal, pattern of behavior. The sense here is of a concern for "honesty among thieves," in which the emphasis is on a record of consistency and integrity among peers. In sum, the rounder seems to hold and apply work standards that are not so different from those of the more orthodox professions. James Caan, the safe-cracker par excellence in the movie *Thief*, was a man's man and a rounder's rounder.

In contrast, the second group is characterized by its use of psychoactive chemicals and involvement in small-scale illegal activities, primarily theft. The alkies, dope fiends, and normals share the dedication of the rounder, but in this case their dedication is to their drug, rather than to their own illegal activities. Property crime for these offenders is a "means to an end" (drugs, alcohol), rather than an end in itself. The importance of this difference is that the dependence of the members of this group on drugs and alcohol makes them unreliable partners in criminal undertakings.

Another important distinction that Letkemann's respondents made is between "amateur" and "experienced" criminals. One identifying feature of amateur criminals is that they are primarily concerned with avoiding detection, while more experienced criminals concentrate on avoiding conviction. The point here is that experienced criminals have technical skills that make them rather easily identifiable by police. Their concern, then, is less with being detected as the culprits, than with making certain that they leave no evidence. Without evi-

dence, of course, there can be no conviction.

Skilled and experienced property offenders also distinguish among themselves according to the specializations they pursue. These offenders speak of "having a line" – that is, a generalized work preference and a related repertoire of skills. We will come back to this point in a moment; for now, let us simply note again that the defining features of a criminal occupation are seen to parallel the more conventional world of work.

A final distinction is drawn in terms of prison experience. This distinction gives new meaning to the common concern shared by labeling theorists that "prisons are schools for crime." Letkemann points out that prison experience can operate much like college or university experience: as a prerequisite to status. Furthermore, some prisons are known for the specialized contacts they allow. For example, since provincial institutions in Canada can hold an offender for no more than two years less one day, they offer little exposure to more experienced criminals. Thus, to obtain full standing as a rounder may require experience in a federal penitentiary where the more seasoned professionals are often to be found.

Letkemann goes on to describe two kinds of skills that characterize two very different criminal career paths. This description is central to his main argument that crime *is* work, often of a highly skilled form. Therefore, the argument is concerned with defining features that make it explainable, using the same principles applied to understand legitimate behavior. The first of these career paths involves surreptitious crimes; the second, overt crimes.

Surreptitious crimes include burglary, and, more specifically, safe-

cracking. These crimes emphasize mechanical skills and victim-avoidance. Persons involved in this kind of criminal work must develop a set of technical skills: working with explosives and learning how to use them to blow a safe. At the same time, they must acquire a set of techniques for gaining entry to sites where safes are used and for minimizing the chances of being observed in the course of their work. While this set of activities may be defined by law as anti-social, its more interesting feature in sociological terms is that it is so *non*social: the emphasis here is on avoiding others while engaging in criminal activity.

By contrast, overt crimes, like bank robbery, can involve a highly developed set of social, as opposed to mechanical, skills. In overt crimes, the victims are confronted and skill must be applied to handle this social event in a way that does not lead to violence. While it may often be thought that because a weapon is used an armed robbery involves no skills, the skill required is to avoid the use of a weapon. The film *Dog Day Afternoon* illustrated, at times comically, how in inexperienced hands this type of situation can escalate beyond control. As well, very basic decisions must be made. Does the getaway driver stay in the car or enter the bank? The problem is whether the waiting driver will actually wait, or panic and take off prematurely. Also, who should lead the exit from the bank? While on the one hand it might be wise for the most experienced person to lead the way, the first one out may also be the person most likely to get shot. These and other factors must be taken into account, and decisions must be made. The point is that a successful robbery is a complex accomplishment, demanding considerable social and planning skills. To the extent that these skills are conscientiously developed and applied, the criminal career will have much in common with other more conventional careers.

Symbolic interactionists remind us that criminals, like the rest of us, define their worlds and act accordingly. Often, these meanings and definitions are developed with skill and experience. The importance of this different but sophisticated world-view is well summarized by Letkemann (1973): "The model of a criminal as one who takes a craftsman's pride in his work, and who applies his skills in the most profitable way he thinks possible, is very different from the model of the criminal as one who gets kicks out of beating the system and doing evil."

Source:

Letkemann, Peter. *Crime as Work*. Englewood Cliffs, N.J.: Prentice-Hall, 1973.

dinate societal groups. The issues are how and why this happens. We will see that attention to these issues focuses as much or more on the groups imposing labels as on the individuals receiving them.

Crime as Status. For conflict theorists, crime is a status that is imposed by one group on the behavior of another. Turk (1969) suggests that, "criminality is not a biological, psychological, or even behavioral phenomenon, but a social status defined by the way in which an individual is perceived, evaluated, and treated by legal authorities." The task, then, is to identify the group(s) involved in the creation and application of this status.

Turk (1969) responds by observing that there are two types of people in society: "There are those... who constitute the dominant, decision-making category – the authorities – and those who make up the subordinate category, who are affected by but scarcely affect law – the subjects." In short, authorities make laws that in turn make criminals out of subjects. The difference is a matter of relative power. Authorities have sufficient power to make the status of some subjects' behavior criminal. For example, it is the poor who have the least power, and we can therefore expect the poor to have the highest rate of "criminalization." This process by which groups are differentially criminalized is the subject of much of the following discussion.

Legal Bureaucracy. Determining which groups in society will be more criminal than others is in large part a matter of determining which laws will be enforced. Chambliss and Seidman (1971) observe that in modern, complex, stratified societies like our own, such issues are assigned for resolution to bureaucratically structured agencies. The result is to mobilize what we can call a "primary principle of legal bureaucracy." According to this principle, laws will be enforced when enforcement increases the reward for the agencies and their officials; they will not be enforced when enforcement is likely to cause organizational strain. In other words, the primary principle of legal bureaucracy is to maximize organizational gains while minimizing organizational strains.

BEN WICKS

Of course it's unethical; it's business.

Chambliss and Seidman (1971) conclude that a consequence of this principle is to bring into operation a "rule of law," whereby "discretion at every level... will be so exercised as to bring mainly those who are politically powerless (i.e., the poor) into the purview of the law." Because the poor are least likely to have the power and resources necessary to create organizational strains, they become the most rewarding targets for organizational activities. In sum, and according to the conflict theorists, the poor constitute a disproportionate part of our crime statistics, more because of a class bias in our society and the realities of our bureaucratic legal system, than because of the behavior of the poor themselves.

A New Criminology. The type of arguments expounded in the preceding paragraphs have recently culminated in the call by a group of British researchers for a "New" or "Critical Criminology" (Taylor, et al, 1973, 1975). This group argues that the roots of our modern crime problems are intertwined with those of western capitalism. They argue further that the capitalist ideology is so strong a force that it has conditioned the very way we conceive of crime.

Suite Crime: An Example of the Conflict Approach

The conflict and critical theories are particularly important in emphasizing the role of powerful interest groups in defining what gets treated as criminal. Goff and Reasons (1978) illustrate this point in the distinction they draw between "suite" and "street" crimes. While we are all familiar with the common sense meaning of the latter, the former refers to "the illegal behavior which occurs in the business suites of the corporate, professional, and civic elites of society . . . . These types of offenses are largely carried out by persons representing an organization and are committed for individual and or collective benefits." Examples of suite crimes include misrepresentation in advertising, price fixing, fraudulent financial manipulations, illegal rebates, misappropriation of public funds, fee splitting, fraudulent damage claims, failure to maintain safety standards, and the violation of human rights. Goff and Reasons focus on anti-combines legislation to provide one example of how one type of suite crime has been defined and presumably controlled in Canada.

Canada's first anti-combines legislation was sponsored by small businessmen who, in the midst of Sir John A. Macdonald's emerging National Policy, felt their firms were at the mercy of big businesses then in the process of entering into powerful combines. Macdonald's Conservative government supported a much-amended version of this legislation, possibly to divert attention from the National Policy, and certainly to show at least symbolically that it was concerned about alleviating the economic conditions brought on by the combines. The resulting legislation was passed in 1889. The ineffectiveness of this, Canada's first combines legislation, is evidenced by the legislators' failure to establish a permanent enforcement agency at the federal level to administer the law. As well, the wording of the act left even its potential for enforcement dubious. It was not until the turn of the century that any active enforcement of anti-combines legislation began to take place.

Later governments were also slow to pursue seriously the enforcement of laws against combines. As Prime Minister, Mackenzie King displayed a reluctance to follow even the very tentative policies of American governments, showing particular antipathy for American attempts to enforce the Sherman Anti-Trust Laws. King noted that, "We have tried to avoid the error which the United States have experienced in going too far . . ." (cited in Goff and Reasons, 1978). More recent governments may have gone further than King in drafting and enforcing anti-combines legislation, but the record is not impressive.

For example, Goff and Reasons note that between 1952 and 1972, a total of 157 decisions were made against 50 corporations in Canada. These decisions were predominantly against small- and medium-sized businesses, rather than against the larger corporations, and attempts to pursue larger enterprises are actually decreasing. Nonetheless, more than half of Canada's largest corporations have been recidivists (that is, convicted more than once), with an average of 3.2 decisions registered against them.

Most interestingly, however, Goff and Reasons report that no individual has ever been jailed for illegal activities under the Combines Act. Instead, the government has usually issued Order of Prohibition penalties, rather than fining the offender or issuing other penalties, such as lowering the tariff duties on foreign products to compensate the Canadian consumer by way of increasing competition. Finally, Goff and Reasons note that since 1923, when mergers were brought under the control of the new combines legislation, only .003 percent of the total number of mergers have been charged as constituting violations of combines laws. During this same time period, the courts have found only .0005 percent of the mergers to be illegal.

Goff and Reasons note that these findings are the logical consequences of the allocation of government priorities and resources. They observe that federal authorities spend much more money to control street crimes than suite crimes. Presumably, one reason for this differential is that on a per case basis it would cost the government far more money to prosecute vigorously these complicated suite crimes than everyday street crimes. Given bureaucratic demands for productivity, this type of investment is unlikely to be made. Beyond this, conflict theory asserts that in capitalist societies the state is controlled by economic and business interests, and that we should therefore not expect the state to interfere legally in the operations of these interests. C. Wright Mills summarizes the societal implications of this interpretation: "It is better, so the image runs, to take one dime from each of ten million people at the point of a corporation than $100,000 from each of ten banks at the point of a gun. It is also safer" (cited by Goff and Reasons, 1978).

Source:

Goff, Colin, and Charles Reasons. *Corporate Crime in Canada*. Scarborough, Ont.: Prentice-Hall, 1978.

For example, the New Criminologists observe that our thinking about crime is largely in terms of "an ethic of individualism." This ethic holds individuals responsible for their acts, while it diverts our attention from the elemental structure in which these acts take place. Moreover, this individualist ethic focuses primarily on one group of individuals, the poor, making them the chief targets of criminal law and penal sanctions. By contrast, the New Criminologists argue that employers and other advantaged persons will be bound only by a civil law that seeks to regulate their competition with one another. The New Criminologists argue that the result of this type of arrangement is to create two kinds of citizenship and responsibility, the more advantaged of which tends to be "beyond incrimination" and therefore above the law (see also Hagan, et al, 1980). The boxed insert on the previous page explores the conflict theory approach to different types of crime.

THE PROCESSING OF CRIME AND DEVIANCE

One of the most important consequences of the emergence of the symbolic interactionist and conflict theories of crime and deviance has been a heightened awareness of the role official agencies play in determining what gets called criminal or deviant. This increased awareness has stimulated new kinds of research that focus on decision-making in offical agencies, including, for example, decisions made about mental hospital admissions, police arrests, plea-bargaining, and judicial sentencing. The results have often been provocative and suggestive of biases in official decision-making.

Processing Mental Illness

Doubting the accuracy with which psychiatrists distinguish the sane from the insane, Rosehan (1973) designed a unique study to test these skills in the diagnoses that lead to mental hospital admission and release. In this study, Rosehan himself and eight other individuals with histories free from mental disorders sought admission to twelve different psychiatric hospi-

tals. Each person complained of fictional symptons (hearing voices saying "empty, hollow, thud") resembling no known form of mental illness. Despite the fictitious symptoms, all of the pseudo-patients were diagnosed as schizophrenics. Immediately following admission, the pseudo-patients ceased to report symptoms and resumed what they regarded as a normal pattern of behavior. After an average period of more than two weeks, all of the pseudo-patients were released as "schizophrenics in remission." None of the individuals, in other words, was discovered *sane*. These results do not indicate, of course, that there are no differences between the sane and the insane, but they do suggest that mental hospital personnel may often overlook or mistake these differences.

It is important to note that in the above experiment the pseudo-patients were seeking admission voluntarily. Gove (1975) has observed that most people who receive psychiatric treatment do so voluntarily, and that concerned friends and relatives do not seek hospitalization frivolously for others. Indeed, there is evidence (Smith, et al, 1963) that the typical psychiatric patient performs three or more "critical acts," each of which may justify hospitalization, before commitment procedures are initiated.

Similarly, there is evidence that hospitalization is sought earlier for economically more important family members, than for those less consequential to family life (Hammer, 1963-64). Beyond this, Gove (1975) reviews a variety of studies leading to the observation that, " . . . officials do not assume illness but, in fact, proceed rather cautiously, screening out a substantial number of persons." Significantly, this results in a situation where (with the severity of personal disorder held constant) hospitalization is more readily obtained by members of the upper classes (Gove 1975). One explanation for this situation, as it relates to courts, is offered by Rock (1963): "The more important problem today is not the filing of petitions (for institutionalization) that are without cause, but rather finding a person willing to petition." Apparently, there are class differences in the willingness to assume the role of petitioner for another person. A second explanation is that some forms of treatment for mental illness may be a fate preferable to others, particularly when the other forms of response carry the stigma of criminal disrepute. This point will become clear as we turn next to the problems of alcoholism.

Processing Alcoholism

The treatment of alcoholism is perhaps the area where the connection between class background and societal response is most apparent. The descending social rank of the pesons typically receiving treatment in private sanitaria, from Alcoholics Anonymous, and from the Salvation Army will be obvious to anyone who has passed through the doors of each. The issue that underlies this situation is how members of various classes find their way into these widely varying treatment arrangements.

One way of approaching this problem is to study the admission and treatment practices of a single institution that deliberately attempts to attend to persons of varying class backgrounds. The purpose of this type of study is to determine if there are intra-organizational patterns suggestive of more general principles in the treatment of alcoholism.

Such a study was carried out by Schmidt, et al (1968), in the Toronto clinic of the Alcoholism and Drug Addiction Research Foundation. Although this study deals entirely with vountary admissions, it carried larger implications for our concern with the courts. One of the major findings of this study is that lower-class alcoholics in the Toronto clinic were more likely to receive drug related treatment from physicians, while upper-class alcoholics were more likely to receive "talking" therapies from psychiatrists. Class related treatment differences could not be explained by differences in diagnosis or age, although differences in verbal skills are suggested as an explanatory variable.

Even more interesting than these treatment differences, however, are variations by social class in the sources of referrals to the clinic. Upper-class patients are more likely to find their way to the clinic through the intermediary services of private physicians, middle-class persons by way of Alcoholics Anonymous, and lower-class persons through general hospital and welfare agency referrals. Schmidt, et al, offer the conclusion that these class patterns are attributable largely to

behaviors that result from alcohol excess tolerated in given social settings and to differences in modal drinking patterns of the class. We are particularly interested, at this point, in the role the courts play in responding to these class differences.

An understanding of the role of the courts in the societal response to alcoholism requires that we use the findings of voluntary clinic studies as a source of leads to what may be happening across agencies, and particularly in the involuntary sector. Lowe and Hodges (1972) began a progression along this route in studying the treatment of black alcoholics in the southern United States. They began their research with the operations of a single voluntary clinic, but soon left this course after finding that, " . . . any variation in amount of services given to patients within the clinic was insignificant beside the overwhelming fact that so few black alcoholics entered into service at all." This result of their research is eventually explained with the observation that black alcoholics are less likely to view admission as offering treatment, and are therefore unlikely to admit themsleves voluntarily into any program. Unfortunately, the effect is that black alcoholics find themselves the involuntary subjects of law-enforcement operations that start with the police, take fatal form in the courts, and end up in prison. Lowe and Hodges note that the courts very rarely attempt to reverse this situation with referrals to alternative treatment insitutions. This pattern is apparent for native peoples in Canada as well.

Hagan (1974b) followed up the treatment received by native and white offenders in Alberta following incarceration. On the basis of either judicial recommendation or inmate request, offenders in Alberta are considered for transfer to an open institutional setting offering a program particularly designed for alcoholic offenders. However, Hagan finds that although the target population of problem drinkers is nearly twice as large among native offenders as among whites, more whites than native offenders receive treatment in the open institutional setting. Thus, although only a minority of alcoholic offenders from either ethnic group experiences the open institution, white offenders are more than twice as likely as native offenders to find their way to this treatment setting. There are three plausible explanations for this situation. First, judges may recommend referrals of native offenders to the open institution less often. Second, native offenders may seek and accept such referrals less frequently. Third, correctional personnel may consent to the transfer of native offenders less often. It is important to note, however, that the three possibilities described are certainly not mutaully exclusive and in fact probably are mutually supportive. In other words, there may be general agreement that in its present form the open institutional setting is less beneficial for native than for white offenders.

Policing Crime and Delinquency

Winding up in a correctional institution represents the end point in a series of decisions whose pattern has been likened to that resulting from the use of a leaky seive or funnel. The point is that most persons whose cases enter the first stages of a criminal or juvenile justice system eventually are diverted or deflected from the stream that leads to institutionalization. Thus, an offense may go undetected or unsolved in the first place; or if an offender is identified, the police may decide against arrest; or if an arrest occurs, the prosecutor may decide to dismiss the case; or if the case results in conviction, the judge may decide to suspend sentence; or any number of other things may happen along the way that result in the termination of a case short of institutionalization. The issue is the extent to which these outcomes are random, legally determined, and/or socially biased.

Starting with decisions made by the police, some of the most important research has been done by Black and Reiss (1970; Reiss, 1971). Black and Reiss draw a very basic distinction between two ways in which the police are mobilized. "Reactive mobilizations" are citizen-initiated (e.g., by a telephoned complaint), while "proactive mobilizations" are police-initiated (e.g., in response to an observed incident). Eighty-seven percent of the mobilizations in the Black and Reiss research were reactive, suggesting that police work has a rather democratic character. That is, the implication is that the police usually do not seek out deviant behavior, but rather respond more often to complaints about

such behavior. As Black and Reiss note, a complainant in search of justice can make demands with which a police officer may feel she/he has little choice but to comply, and this may be a factor that affects differential rates of arrest.

However, a recent study by Ericson (1982) in a suburban Toronto jurisdiction raises some important questions about the applicability of these findings in Canada. Of 1323 encounters observed between citizens and officers in Ericson's study, 47.4 percent were characterized as proactive mobilizations, and only 52.6 percent as reactive mobilizations. "On the surface," Ericson (1982) notes, "our data reveal that patrol officers are much more assertive in producing encounters with citizens than the figures provided by Reiss, Black, and others would lead us to believe." Still, when only "major incidents" are looked at in these Canadian data, Ericson reports that more than 82 percent result from reactive mobilizations. In these incidents, complainants may still loom large in the decision-making process.

A recent study by Smith (1982), based on 742 suspect contacts with police in 24 American departments, confirms the influence of complainants but also points to the impact of suspect characteristics. This study reports that antagonistic suspects are much more likely to be taken into custody than suspects who display deference (see also Piliavin and Briar, 1964). Furthermore, black suspects are more likely to be arrested. Smith explains that part of this race effect can be accounted for by the fact that black suspects are significantly more likely to act toward the police in a hostile or antagonistic manner. Nonetheless, and apart from suspect behavior and victim demands, it remains the case that black suspects are somewhat more likely than white suspects to be arrested.

Prosecuting Crime and Delinquency

Once an individual has been arrested and charged, the media image of the court process is that of a trial by jury, with prosecution and defence attorneys assuming adversarial roles in a battle for justice. In fact, however, few criminal cases follow this adversarial pattern. The typical sequence, followed in up to 90 percent of the cases in some jurisdictions, is for the defendant to plead guilty and forfeit trial. Grossman (1969) observes, on the basis of interviews with prosecutors in York County, Ontario, that guilty pleas are an important way of avoiding the time, expense, and uncertainty of trials. The assumption is that plea bargaining is an effective way of increasing court efficiency (Blumberg, 1967). The question, therefore, is not whether plea bargaining will take place, but rather how it will occur.

David Sudnow (1965) has attempted to spell out in sociological terms the procedures involved in bargaining for reduced charges (see also Wynne and Hartnagel, 1975a,b; Hagan, 1974a). Sudnow notes first that the reduction of charges focuses on two types of offenses: "necessarily included offences" and "situationally included offenses." Necessarily included

Criminals or merely deviants? No matter which, these people's common interests and group identity may affect their relationships with society in general and the police in particular.

offenses are those that occur by legal definition in association with one another; for example "homicide" cannot occur without "intent to commit a murder." In contrast, situationally included offenses are those that occur together by convention; "public drunkenness" usually, but not necessarily, occurs in association with "creating a public disturbance." Bargaining for charge reductions works on the general premise of reducing the initial charge to a lesser necessarily or situationally included offense, as illustrated above.

Sudnow's point, however, is that the procedural rules followed in deciding what sort of a reduction is appropriate are not entirely defined by law. Rather, lawyers and prosecutors develop working conceptions of what they regard as "normal crimes": ". . . the typical manner in which offenses of given classes are committed, the social characteristics of the persons who regularly commit them, the features of the settings in which they occur, the types of victims often involved, and the like" (Sudnow, 1965). According to Sudnow, it is on the basis of these conceptions of "normal crimes" that an initial legal categorization is established; attention is then directed to determining which (necessarily or situationally included) lesser offence may constitute the appropriate reduction. As an example, Sudnow notes that in the jurisdiction he studied a burglary charge is routinely reduced to petty theft. However, "the propriety of proposing petty theft as a reduction does not derive from its . . . existence in the present case, but is warranted . . . [instead] by the relation of the present burglary to 'burglaries,' normally conceived." Finally, Sudnow notes that there must be a balance established between the sentence the defendant might have received for the original charge, and that which probably will be received for the lesser charge. This brings us to the issue of sentencing.

Judging Crime and Delinquency

Legislation outlining the sentencing responsibilities of the criminal courts in Canada entrusts to presiding judges nearly complete freedom in the determination of minimum sentences. Similarly, a wide range of discretion is allowed in the establishment of maximum penalties. The nature of the problem, however, ex-

tends beyond the absence of statutory guides to minimum and maximum sentences. Also involved is confusion regarding a basic set of principles to be used in the determination of sentences. Decore (1964) notes that even the utilization of precedents in sentencing is a matter of contradiction and doubt. A consequence is a heavy reliance on the discretion of the sentencing judge, with the implication that variation and disparity will follow. An important attempt to explain variation in criminal sentences is found in the research of Hogarth (1971).

Hogarth begins by noting that judges in the lower provincial courts in Canada have broader jurisdiction (i.e., 94 percent of all indictable cases are tried in these courts) and wider sentencing powers (e.g., to life imprisonment) than any comparable set of courts in the western world. Hogarth then provides data suggesting that Canada in the mid-1960s had one of the highest rates of imprisonment in the western world (see also Cousineau and Veevers, 1972; Matthews, 1972). However, Hogarth also presents evidence of a recent shift in this pattern, with the heavy reliance on prison sentences giving way to an increasing reliance on fines.

The most recent evidence on Canada's use of imprisonment is provided in an exceptionally careful analysis by Waller and Chan (1975). This analysis indicates that Canada's overall imprisonment rate is no higher than that of the United States and several other countries, with only the Yukon and the Northwest Territories remaining high relative to most American states. Waller and Chan are careful to emphasize the difficulties of drawing any final inferences from the data they present, and to their cautions we will add several additional comments. First, it is not surprising to find Canada's imprisonment rate per 100 000 population low relative to some other countries, particularly the United States, for Canada's serious crime rate is also relatively low. The more crucial comparisons would involve ratios of incarcerations to occurrences and convictions. Waller and Chan appropriately point out the complications in accurately computing these ratios with current official data. Second, it should be noted that where imprisonment rates are highest in Canada (i.e., in the north), native peoples are most likely to be experiencing the consequences. Finally, we can observe that while efforts to avoid incarceration through the increasing use of fines may be successful on an aggregate basis in Canada, economic and ethnic minorities unable to pay these fines remain at a continuing disadvantage. These comments should discourage any sense of complacency with our condition, a complacency that Waller and Chan clearly disavow (see also Waller, 1974).

Probably because Hogarth's research described above was based primarily in the large urban areas of Ontario, little attention was given to the social consequences of sentencing for ethnic and economic minorities, particularly native persons. Yet native persons are present in Canadian court and prison populations far beyond their representation in the general population. To understand further the influence of race and other offender characteristics on judicial sentencing, we will need to consider briefly a large body of American research.

A variety of American studies focus on the role of race, sex, age, and socio-economic status of the offender in the formation of sentencing decisions (e.g., Bullock, 1961; Green, 1961; Nagel, 1969; Wolfgang and Riedel, 1973). A review of such studies concludes that generally there is a small relationship between the extra-legal attributes of offenders and sentencing decisions (Hagan, 1974a; see also Hagan and Bumiller, 1982). However, because the authors of many of these studies have failed to take the seriousness of offense and prior records of offenders into account, it is sometimes difficult to know whether relationships reported can be taken as evidence of discrimination. For example, do blacks in the United States receive longer sentences because they are discriminated against, or because they commit more serious offenses and more frequently have prior convictions?

When these factors *are* controlled, relationships reported between extra-legal offender characteristics and sentence sometimes are reduced or eliminated (e.g., Chiricos and Waldo, 1975). However, there continues to be compelling evidence that in such areas as rape (e.g., LaFree, 1980) and white-collar crime (Hagan, et al, 1980) race and class position can make a difference in the severity of sentence received. To this extent

the symbolic interactionist and conflict theorists are clearly correct: there is more to criminal and delinquent labels than the behaviors presumed to have provoked them. There is evidence (Hagan and Albonetti, 1982) that public perceptions mirror this reality.

Interestingly, judges in Canada are frequently charged with being differentially lenient, as well as punitive, with native offenders. The charge of leniency may reflect an attempt on the part of some Canadian judges to take cultural differences into account when sentencing native offenders. However, recent evidence on this issue suggests that most judges sentence primarily on the basis of offence seriousness and prior conviction records. Thus, Hagan (1975) divided a sample of Albertan judges into two groups scoring them high and low on a a "law and order scale." He then predicted that those judges scoring high would sentence native offenders punitively, while judges scoring low would sentence leniently. Perhaps surprisingly, the results showed that "law and order" judges sentence almost exclusively on offence seriousness, while judges less concerned about such issues provided native persons only minimal leniency. More generally, this study suggests that most judges sentence most offenders mechanically without taking the time to consider their social backgrounds. This is particuarly the case, and becomes particularly problematic, with minor offenders.

We noted earlier that the police typically apprehend native offenders for minor alcohol related charges. In turn, judges typically sentence such offenders to "so many dollars or so many days." The outcome of this approach is predictable: Hagan (1974b) reports that nearly 66 percent of all native persons who go to jail are incarcerated in default of fine payments. This is nearly twice the rate for whites. One result is that in Hagan's Albertan sample native persons are represented in the prison population four times more frequently than in the general population.

One final point worth noting: there is evidence that corporate entities are playing an increasingly important role as complainants in Canadian courts, for example in cases of shoplifting. A recent study in a suburban Ontario jurisdiction (Hagan, 1982) revealed that nearly two-thirds of the victims in cases for whom an offender was charged were corporations (mostly retail stores). The corporations in this study were better able than individuals to get convictions against the accused. The implication, again, is that the courts may serve some interests better than others in our society.

Societal Strategies of Law Enforcement

The processing of crime and deviance is influenced by the general strategies employed to enforce the law. In the following paragraphs we will see that under different social conditions alternative strategies may be adopted to accomplish quite similar goals. For example, two societal strategies for maintaining legal order are the "due process" and "crime control" models of law enforcement (Packer, 1964). Societies vary in their commitment to these models, and it can be argued, *at least in symbolic terms,* that Americans give considerable deference to the due process model. This point can be made in an interesting way by comparing policies of law enforcement in the United States with those in Canada. In doing this we will note that Canada is characterized by a much more explicit commitment to a crime control model. Before we develop this comparison, it will be necessary to clarify the nature of these two models.

The **due process model** has its roots in the Enlightenment and in the notion of the English philosopher John Locke that the law can be used effectively in the defense of "natural" and "inalienable rights." Accordingly, the due process model is greatly concerned with procedural safeguards thought useful in protecting accused persons from unjust applications of criminal penalties. Where errors are to be made in law enforcement, advocates of the due process model are known for their preference that guilty persons go free before innocent persons are found guilty.

In contrast, the **crime control model** received its philosophical support from the conservative reaction to Enlightenment thought and from the arguments of the Englishman Edmund Burke that civil liberties can have meaning only in orderly societies. Thus, the crime control model places heavy emphasis on the repression of criminal conduct, holding that only by insuring order can society guarantee individuals' personal freedom. It is for this reason that advocates of crime control are less anxious than the proponents of due process to presume the innocence of accused persons and to protect such persons against sometimes dubious findings of guilt. It is not that the crime control model favors the unfair treatment of individuals, but rather that it is willing to tolerate a certain amount of mistreatment when the measures involved are seen as generally necessary, at least symbolically, for the maintenance of social order. Individual "rights" here assume a discretionary status in the hands of the authoritative figures who control them.

The distinction between the Lockean due process and the Burkean crime control models is clear, but the difference in intent is one of degree. Both have as their goal the creation and maintenance of legal order. With this in mind, one Canadian social scientist notes that the "approach which is truest to our experience and most in keeping with our capabilities is that of Edmund Burke, not John Locke. Canadians . . . are [not] creatures of the Enlightenment" (Russel, 1975). Similarly, in the following paragraphs we will see that Canada, particularly in symbolic terms, tends more than the United States toward a crime control model, and that this tendency constitutes a difference between the two countries. Some might argue that Canada's new Charter of Rights will remove this difference. However, because the roots of it (discussed below) are social and historical, we remain dubious. Time will tell. Meanwhile, the boxed insert on the following pages draws some current comparisons between the two countries.

Historically, the southern part of this continent contained resources that could be exploited with relatively less governmental involvement and control than those in the northern part (Clark, 1976). As well, the United States was conceived *ideologically* as a nation devoted to the rights and responsibilities of individuals (Lipset, 1968). One result was the formation of an ideology of individualism that, when combined with exploitable resources, allowed and encouraged more extensive variations from the norm than was the case in the northern part of the continent (Hagan and Leon, 1977b:). Quinney (1970) notes that on the American frontier local authorities were free to develop their own law enforcement policies or to ignore the problem of crime altogether. Similarly, Inciardi (1975) observes that:

the American frontier was Elizabethan in its quality, simple, childlike, and savage. . . . It was a land of riches where swift and easy fortunes were sought by the crude, the lawless, and the aggressive, and where written law lacked form and cohesion.

Put simply, the American frontier was also a criminal frontier, a model in some ways for the city life that followed. In Bell's (1953) apt phrase, "Crime is an American way of life."

As the United States developed, however, the establishment of a workable legal order also became a priority. On a formal and symbolic level, the American commitment to a due process model of law enforcement continued to be ideologically important. Countering this ideology, however, was a significant national commitment and assignment of resources to policing and punishing deviant behavior. Even though one might expect an economy of scale, because of its relatively large population, the United States actually spends more per capita on its police than does Canada, substantially more on its courts, and more as well on correctional institutions (Hagan and Leon, 1977b). As a result, the United States has produced a legal order that combines high levels of crime with a very profuse and coercive police response. Some of the historical irony of this situation is captured in Skolnick's (1975) description of the police as America's "asphalt cowboys."

In contrast, the Canadian approach was one of initially firmer, but necessarily more strategic, control (McNaught, 1975). In the east, problems of law and order were dealt with by the military, but more efficient means were required in the west. MacLeod (1976) notes that by the 1870s the American government was spending over $20 million a year just fighting the Plains Indians. At the same time, the total Canadian budget (of which defense was only a part) was just over $19 million. "It is not an exaggeration to say," according to MacLeod (1976), ". . . that the only possible Canadian west was a peaceful one."

One means of realizing this possibility was to assign the North-West Mounted Police a key role in John A. Macdonald's National Policy, giving the Mounties "power unparalleled by any other police force in a democratic country." Clark (1962) summarizes the situation this way: "In the United States, the frontier bred a spirit of liberty which often opposed efforts to maintain order. In Canada, order was maintained at the price of weakening that spirit." The point is that Canada has been able to limit its resource commitment to crime control by reemphasizing its ideological commitment to the Burkean ideal of social order first and individual rights second. In Canada, therefore, the police role has become preeminently symbolic, a reminder that social order ideologically precedes individual liberties. "Canada," notes Margaret Atwood (1972), "must be the only country in the world where a policeman is used as a national symbol."

It is interesting to speculate about the consequences that may follow from Canadian and American strategies of crime control. The consequences for the socially advantaged of both countries are much the same: both nations possess a legal order that allows the relatively safe and stable conduct of social and economic affairs. The consequences for the socially disadvantaged in each country are, however, somewhat different, or at least relatively so. Overall, crime rates are significantly higher in the United States than in Canada. Indeed, there is evidence that this gap has widened in recent years (Hagan and Leon, 1977b). Because it is the poor who are far more likely to be arrested and convicted in both countries, it is the poor who are most affected by this difference (see Hagan and Albonetti, 1982).

The American situation allows a freedom to deviate, but there is also a heightened likelihood of criminalization for those in subordinate statuses. The Canadian situation discourages deviation and at the same time decreases the proportionate likelihood of criminalization for subordinates. And, therefore, the poor are likelier to become a part of crime and deviance statistics in the United States than in Canada. This difference may reflect an important part of what is unique about the Canadian experience.

Crime Control and Due Process in Canada and the United States

The differing models of law enforcement discussed in this chapter persist in their alternative emphasis in Canada and the United States. Two examples, involving right to legal counsel and the admissibility of illegally obtained evidence, will help make our point.

1. Right to Counsel

One example of the crime control emphasis in Canadian society involves an accused person's right to counsel. The critical role of legal counsel in representing a defendant in criminal proceedings is well recognized in both Canada and the United States. The "right to effective representation," however, is an essentially American notion that has developed from an expansion of the concept of the constitutional right to be provided with counsel under the sixth and fourteenth amendments to the American Constitution. In fact, an absolute right to counsel has yet to be affirmed in Canada (Grossman, 1967).

Thus an accused person in Canada who retains counsel is entitled to counsel's assistance, but a court is not deprived of jurisdiction to try an accused person who is unrepresented by counsel. Instead, the primary concern is that the accused not be denied a "fair" trial. And on the issue of what constitutes "fairness," there are various views. For example, in 1974, in *Re Gilberg and the Queen*, the appellate division of one provincial Supreme Court advises that "counsel is not always a necessary concomitant to a fair trial."

We noted above that the right to effective representation, as an element of the constitutional right to counsel, is an evolving concept in American law. In contrast, Canadian provincial appellate courts to date have professed reluctance to address issues related to the competency of counsel at trial or have ignored the issue altogether. Even where a specific instance of a failure by trial counsel to take appropriate action is documented, appellate judges are hesitant to recognize this as justification for finding a substantial wrong or miscarriage of justice and hence for ordering a new trial.

In the 1973 case of *R. v. Draskovic*, a reason for this position is advanced: "We think it would be a very dangerous practice to review in this court the tactical procedures adopted by defense counsel, and if we thought that he should obviously have adopted some other course, then to declare the trial unfair to the accused to a degree constituting a mistrial. Many difficult decisions have to be made by a defense counsel in a trial such as this, sometimes on the spur of the moment."

It may be consistent with the crime control emphasis of the Canadian criminal justice system "to accept incompetency in the practice of criminal law if it secures the long-range goal of bringing more alleged offenders to justice" (Cohen, 1977). Yet the distinction between no counsel and ineffective counsel is one of degree, and to allow merely an appearance of representation may be misleading. In any event, we have noted that there are significant differences in "rights" to counsel in Canada and the United States. In Canada, access to counsel is more a matter of discretion than guarantee, and little

attention is directed toward the disadvantages faced by an accused subjected to incompetent representation. Mewett (1970) effectively summarizes the Canadian view of the criminal process in suggesting that with "an adequate system of legal aid" and a "desire on the part of the courts not to prejudice unfairly an accused," concern in Canada is better conceptualized in terms of "prevention of abuses" rather than "the enforcement of 'right.'" Thus, "there must be rules to safeguard the individual but those rules cannot be formulated with a disregard for the interest of the community."

2. Illegally Obtained Evidence

The "exclusionary rule" renders much illegally obtained evidence inadmissible in American courts of law. Under this rule, material or testimonial evidence may be excluded when it is obtained directly by illegal methods or, with some notable exceptions, when such evidence is indirectly secured by illegal methods.

Although there is continuing debate in the United States about the advisability of the exclusionary rule (for example, Spiotto, 1973a, 1973b), advocates for the rule typically cite two justifications: first, that application of the exclusionary rule should have the effect of deterring the police from using illegal tactics; and second, that the existence of this rule confirms the precedence given by the American Constitution to "due process" over "crime control." In short, the American position on illegally obtained evidence is an attempt, at least symbolically, to preserve and protect the constitutionally entrenched rights of individuals.

In contrast, the Canadian position and the English tradition from which it is derived are less concerned with

gravely prejudicial to the accused, the admissibility of which is tenuous and whose probative force in relation to the main issue before the court is trifling which can be said to operate unfairly." Thus, in Canada, the prime if not sole criterion of admissibility is relevance.

In summary, the Canadian attitude toward illegal evidence derives from English precedents and places concern for social order ahead of individual rights. The common Canadian response to the American rule of exclusion is that "the price paid by society for such a rule is too high" (Law Reform Commission of Canada, 1974): "the State has the right and the duty to protect and promote respect for the security of social life" (1974). To the extent that the reforms of rules regarding illegally obtained evidence are considered in Canada, they involve assigning judges increased discretion to decide the degree to which social concerns should override consideration of fairness to individuals.

Source:

Grossman, B.A. "The right to counsel in Canada." *Canadian Bar Journal*, 10:189-211, 1967; Cohen, S.A. "Controlling the trial process: the judge and the conduct of the trial." *Criminal Reports* (new series), 36:15-84, 1977; Mewett, A.W. "Law enforcement and the conflict of values." *McGill Law Journal*, 16: 1-18, 1970; Spiotto, J.E. "Search and seizure: an empirical study of the exclusionary rule and its alternatives." *Journal of Legal Studies*, 2:36-49, 1973a, and "The search and seizure problem – two approaches: the Canadian tort remedy and the U.S. exclusionary rule." *Journal of Political Science and Administration*, 1:36-59, 1973b; Law Reform Commission of Canada. *The Exclusion of Illegally Obtained Evidence*. Ottawa: Information Canada, 1974.

the rights of individuals than with relevance of the evidence. This English attitude toward evidence was expressed most candidly in the 1861 case of *R. v. Leatham*: "It matters not how you get it; if you steal it, it will be admissible in evidence." In many respects, this standard still holds. Perhaps most significantly, however, in the 1970 case of *R. v. Wray*, the Supreme Court of Canada held that a trial judge does not have the authority to exclude evidence otherwise admissible, unless that evidence would operate "unfairly" for the accused. Furthermore, in the 1975 case of *Hogan v. The Queen* it is suggested that "it is only the allowance of evidence

SUMMARY

1. Deviation consists of variation from a norm and is made socially significant through the reactions of others.

2. There are several kinds of deviance – consensus crimes, conflict crimes, social deviations, and social diversions – and these can be distinguished according to their socially determined seriousness.

3. Whether or not different kinds of deviant behavior come under official control is influenced by the activities of moral entrepreneurs and various interest groups.

4. There are a variety of means used to count deviant behavior, including data gathered by official agencies and non-official agencies, through first-person accounts, through surveys of crime victims, and through observations of deviant behavior. Comparison of these measures leads to the conclusion that serious crimes, hard-drug use, alcohol abuse, and mental illness are found more frequently in the working class, while less serious and more frequent forms of crime, delinquency, and drug use are more evenly distributed across the social classes.

5. The structural functionalist theories of deviance argue that the presence of success goals or values without the means to attain them can produce deviant behavior, as can the absence of these goals or values in the first place.

6. The symbolic interactionist theories of deviance are concerned with the role of social meanings and definitions in the production of deviant behavior.

7. The conflict theories of deviance have focused on the role of dominant societal groups in imposing legal labels on members of subordinate societal groups.

8. Consideration of the processing of various kinds of crime and deviance indicates that social as well as legal factors influence when, where, and upon whom deviant labels are imposed.

9. Two societal strategies for maintaining legal order are the due process and crime control models of law enforcement. Although the differences involved are often a matter of ideology and emphasis, at a formal and symbolic level Canada tends more toward a crime control model than does the United States.

GLOSSARY

Anomie. Term originally used by Durkheim to refer to an absence of social regulation, or normlessness. Merton revived the concept to refer to the consequences of a faulty relationship between goals and the legitimate means of attaining them.

Conflict crimes. Acts that are defined by law as criminal, are often severely punished, but are usually regarded as only marginally harmful; typically they are subjects of conflict and debate.

Conflict subculture. Illegal group activity that is prone to violence and is common in settings (e.g., "disorganized slums") where legitimate and illegitimate spheres are unintegrated.

Conflict theories of deviance. Theories that focus particularly on the role of dominant societal groups in imposing their legal controls on members of subordinate societal groups.

Consensus crimes. Acts defined by law as criminal that are widely regarded as extremely harmful, severely punished, and consensually identified as deviant.

Crime control model. Model of law enforcement that places heavy emphasis on the repression of criminal conduct, because insuring order is seen as the only way to guarantee individual freedom.

Delinquent subculture. Collective response of working-class adolescents to their failure to satisfy middle-class expectations; the result is an inversion of middle-class values.

Deviance. Variation from a norm, made socially significant through the reaction of others.

Differential association. Process by which criminal behavior is learned in conjunction with persons who define such behavior favorably and in isolation from those who define it unfavorably.

Due process model. Model of law enforcement that emphasizes procedural safeguards thought useful in protecting accused persons from unjust applications of criminal penalties.

Neutralization techniques. Linguistic expressions that, through a subtle process of justification, allow individuals to drift into deviant life-styles.

Primary deviance. Deviant behaviors that precede a societal or legal response and have little impact on the individual's self-concept.

Residual rule breaking. Category conventionally called "mental illness" that includes forms of rule breaking for which society has no specific labels.

Retreatist subculture. Group-supported forms of escapist behavior, particularly drug abuse, that result from failure in both legitimate and illegitimate spheres of activity.

Secondary deviance. Deviant behaviors that follow a societal or legal response and involve a transformation of the individual's self-concept.

Self-report survey. Paper and pencil questionnaires used with adolescents and adults to obtain first-person accounts of amounts and types of deviant behavior.

Social deviation. Noncriminal variation from social norms that is nonetheless subject to frequent official control.

Social diversion. Variations of life-style, including fads and fashions of appearance and behavior.

Stable criminal subculture. Illegal group enterprises made more persistent by the protection they receive from persons in legitimate social roles (e.g., politicians and police).

FURTHER READING

Black, Donald. *The Behavior of Law.* New York: Academic Press, 1976. One of the most widely read of recent theoretical works on the way criminal and other kinds of law actually operate in real legal settings.

Boydell, Craig L., and Ingrid Arnet Connidis. *The Canadian Criminal Justice System.* Toronto: Holt, Rinehart and Winston, 1982. An up-to-date and comprehensive collection of readings.

Chambliss, William, and Robert Seidman. *Law, Order and Power.* Reading, Mass.: Addison Wesley, 1982. A conflict perspective on criminal law and its enforcement. This book deals with all aspects of the criminal justice system and with the development of criminal law.

Durkheim, Emile. *Suicide.* John A. Spalding and George Simpson (trans.). Glencoe, Ill.: Free Press, 1964. The classic work on this form of deviant behavior. Durkheim anticipated much of what is thought modern in sociological theorizing about crime and deviance, including anomie theory and the labeling perspective.

Ericson, Richard. *Reproducing Order: A Study of Police Patrol Work.* Toronto: University of Toronto Press, 1982. This volume presents the results of the most comprehensive field study of policing done in Canada.

Griffiths, Curt T., John F. Klein, and Simon N. Verdun-Jones. *Criminal Justice in Canada.* Vancouver: Butterworths, 1980. This volume provides a concise yet comprehensive introduction to the Canadian criminal justice system, with particular attention to the police, courts, and correctional subsystems.

Hagan, John. *The Disreputable Pleasures.* Toronto: McGraw-Hill Ryerson, 1977. An integrated textbook treatment of crime and deviance with a twist: it is argued that crime and deviance can be pleasurable, albeit disreputable, pursuits.

Shearing, Clifford. *Organizational Police Deviance.* Toronto: Butterworths, 1982. This book brings together a collection of articles that broadens the subject of police misbehavior from simple corruption, which can be dismissed as a private moral failing, to pervasive patterns of official action – referred to as "structural deviance" – such as arresting, charging, harassing, and warning, which can have organizational roots.

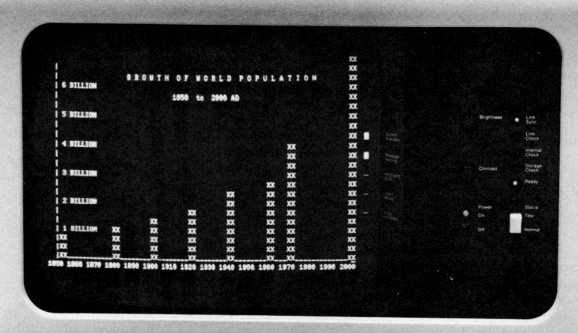

III

THE SOCIAL BASE

The fabric of life in every society is largely determined by its social base. For example, a society where people usually live to age forty is very different from one where they usually live to age eighty.

Major factors are working to shape society. The density and distribution of population, the ways in which society is stratified or divided into levels, the size and distribution of various ethnic groups, and the number and nature of formal organizations all play an important part.

Consider the fact that Canada is larger than the United States but has roughly the population of California. Or this: The world's population is expected to double in approximately 36 years – to more than 8 billion people in the early years of the next century. Chapter 7 examines the causes and consequences of the population characteristics of societies.

Every society is stratified, or ranked, in some way: leaders and followers, rich children and poor children, vice presidents and junior clerks. The ways in which societies are stratified and the degree of mobility between levels are the concerns of Chapter 8.

The interaction of various ethnic groups is important in most societies, and this is particularly true in Canada, where we are committed to maintaining the identities of different ethnic groups. Chapter 9 discusses the concepts of ethnicity and race, and their importance for understanding Canadian society.

Modern societies increasingly are arranged into large, formal organizations. Today, most of us are born and educated, work and die in formal organizations. Chapter 10 examines some of the causes and consequences of this type of social organization.

CHAPTERS

CHAPTER 7
POPULATION

ELLEN GEE

Population is a fundamental element of society. Its characteristics are important determinants of social, economic, and political structure. In turn, social organization affects the characteristics of a population.

The interrelationship between population and social factors can be seen by noting one population fact about Canadian society: compared to many non-western societies, women in Canada produce few babies. Why? The answer lies not in biology or instinct, but in the social setting in which women, and couples, find themselves. Canada is primarily an urban society, and children are more expensive and less economically useful to parents in an urban society than in a rural one. Nearly one-half of married women in Canada work outside the home, a fact that is itself related to our urban economic structure. In other words, our society provides for women an alternative that competes with the traditional child-rearing role. Also, contraception is generally accessible and acceptable in Canada. This acceptance of contraception reflects the widespread social beliefs that such behavior is not immoral, that marriage exists for reasons other than just procreation, and that we can and should control our fates as individuals.

Not only is the rate of child production subject to

social causes; it has social consequences as well. One consequence of the low production of children in Canada is that our population is becoming old. That is, proportionately we have more older people and fewer younger people than societies producing more babies per woman. An old population faces a number of potential social problems, such as housing and health care for a large number of elderly people who no longer make an economic contribution to the wider society. Because one of the social factors that helps to create an old population is a decreased emphasis on families, we may not be able to expect the family to be a major source of aid to our increasing elderly population.

Demography, a sub-field of sociology, is the scientific study of population. Demography describes and explains the characteristics of population and the processes underlying those characteristics. Nearly always, the study of both the characteristics and the processes of population encompasses an examination of social variables. Neither the society nor the population can be understood apart from the other.

There are three major characteristics of population: size, composition, and distribution. **Size** refers to the number of people in a given area. **Composition** concerns the characteristics of the people in the population, particularly with regard to age and gender. When we say, for example, that women compose approximately 51 percent of the Canadian population and that 10 percent of our population is aged 65 or over, we are talking about the composition of our population. **Distribution** refers to the geographical location of people in a population. For example, approximately 9 percent of Canadians live in Alberta; about one-quarter of the Canadian population lives in rural areas. These are facts concerning population distribution in Canada.

These population characteristics are, in turn, determined by the three demographic processes of fertility, mortality, and migration. **Fertility** refers to actual childbearing in a population. **Mortality** refers to the deaths that occur in a population. **Migration** is the movement of persons from one geographical location to another.

Perhaps most importantly, these three processes together affect change in population size. Is the population increasing or decreasing? At what pace? An examination of fertility, mortality, and migration will help us answer these questions, particularly the "why" of population change. Since "population bomb" and "population explosion" are household words, it is important to know the mechanisms underlying population change. Let us, therefore, first turn our attention to the issue of population growth.

POPULATION GROWTH

We tend to think of population change in terms of increase, but populations can also decrease. Demographers use the term **positive growth** to describe a population that is increasing, **negative growth** to refer to a population that is getting smaller.

Populations can grow quickly or slowly. A glance at Figure 7-1 shows that the world population increased relatively slowly until about 1750, and that rapid population growth is unique to the twentieth century. In 1750, the total population of the world was approximately 800 million; by 1982, it was over 4.5 billion.

Underlying the huge increase in the world's popula-

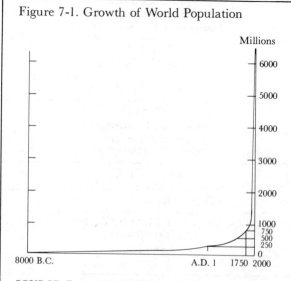

Figure 7-1. Growth of World Population

SOURCE: Durand, John. "The modern expansion of world population." *Proceedings of the American Philosophical Society*, 111:139.

tion is a changing growth rate. **Growth rate** refers to the number of people added to (or subtracted from) a population in a given time period for every 100 or 1000 people in the population. Often, growth is expressed as an annual rate per 1000 population.

The history of world population growth is one in which growth rates increase markedly over time. (See Table 7-1.) For the period from 8000 B.C. to 1750, world population grew approximately one-half person per 1000 population per year. In comparison, world population is currently growing by nearly 20 persons per 1000 population per year. This present growth rate, the highest in the history of humankind, cannot continue indefinitely. If it did, the human population would outweigh the earth it stands on in less than 1200 years from now (Coale, 1974). The present era of growth is, by necessity, a transitory phenomenon. In fact, it is expected that the annual growth rate will slow down; the United Nations' projected rate for the end of this century is 16.4.

The growth rate plays the important role of determining how fast a population will change in size. Often, demographers measure the pace of population increase in terms of doubling time. **Doubling time** is the number of years it will take for a population to double in numbers, assuming that the current growth rate remains unchanged. If the projected annual growth rate for 1980-1985 (19.5 per 1000 population) were to remain unchanged, the world's population would double in approximately 36 years. In that event, the world would contain more than 8 billion people in the early years of the next century.

Variations in Growth

So far, we have looked at population growth in terms of the world as a whole. The world's population has increased dramatically, particularly in the twentieth century, as a result of rising rates of growth. Against this background of general increase, different parts of the world have experienced different rates of growth, both in the past and in the present.

From 1600 to 1950, Europe (including the U.S.S.R.) and the areas of European settlement (e.g., the United States, Canada, Australia, and New Zealand) experienced large-scale population growth. By contrast, non-western populations grew very slowly.

The present situation is radically different. In today's world, non-western, or developing, nations are growing at a much faster pace than western populations. The annual growth rate in the developing nations is around 25 per 1000 population; in the developed world, it averages 9. In Canada, the current annual growth rate (1976-1981 average) is 11.

Projections concerning future growth suggest a continuation of the present pattern. The United Nations estimates that, at the end of this century, the growth rate in the developing regions of the world will be approximately 19. Africa, particularly, is singled out for predicted large-scale future growth, with a growth rate of just under 28 expected at the end of the century. Such a figure implies a doubling time of under 25 years. The projected growth rate (Tsui and Bogue, 1978) for the developed regions, in contrast, is 6.

Components of Growth

In order to understand the causes of growth for the world population and for the different societies that make it up, we have to look at the components of growth – the three demographic processes of fertility, mortality, and migration.

TABLE 7-1. HISTORICAL CHANGES IN RATES OF WORLD POPULATION GROWTH

Time Period	Annual Rate of Population Growth (per 1000)
8000 B.C.-A.D. 1	0.36
A.D. 1-1750	0.56
1750-1800	4.40
1800-1850	5.20
1850-1900	5.40
1900-1950	7.90
1950-1974	17.10
1980-1985[a]	19.50
1995-2000[a]	16.40

SOURCE: Coale, Ansley J. "The history of human population." *Scientific American*, 231:43; Tsui, Amy Ong, and Donald J. Bogue. "Declining world fertility: trends, causes, implications." *Population Bulletin* 33(4):38. Washington, D.C.: Population Reference Bureau.
NOTE: [a]United Nations projections

For the world, population increase is a direct result of the extent to which births (fertility) outnumber deaths (mortality). The excess of births over deaths is termed **natural increase**. (If deaths exceed births, the term "natural decrease" would be used). In addition to natural increase, a population can change in size as a result of migratory movement. **Net migration** refers to the difference between the number of immigrants (people moving into an area) and the number of emigrants (people moving away). Net migration is positive when the number of immigrants exceeds the number of emigrants and negative when emigrants outnumber immigrants.

Rate of Natural Increase.

The rate of natural increase, arrived at by subtracting what is termed the **crude death rate** from the **crude birth rate**, is usually measured as a single-year interval and is expressed as a figure per 1000 population. The formula for the computation of the rate of natural increase is:

$$RNI = CBR - CDR$$

where:

RNI = Rate of Natural Increase in a given year per 1000 population

CBR = Crude birth rate, or

$$\frac{\text{Number of births in a given year}}{\text{Mid-year population}} \times 1000$$

CDR = Crude death rate, or

$$\frac{\text{Number of deaths in a given year}}{\text{Mid-year population}} \times 1000$$

High positive values indicate that the population is growing substantially due to natural increase. Negative values indicate natural decrease. A rate of zero means that the birth rate and the death rate are identical, with no resulting change in population size due to natural increase.

Table 7-2 presents 1982 data on rates of natural increase, births, and deaths for major areas of the world and for selected countries. The highest rates of natural increase occur in Africa and Latin America. The lowest rates occur in Europe, and some European countries, West Germany, for example, are currently experiencing natural decrease. The "new" societies with a predominantly European heritage (Canada, the United

TABLE 7-2. RATES OF NATURAL INCREASE, CRUDE BIRTH RATES, AND CRUDE DEATH RATES, 1982

	Rate of Natural Increase (per 1000)	Crude Birth Rate (per 1000)	Crude Death Rate (per 1000)
World	17	29	11
Africa	29	46	17
Egypt	31	43	12
Niger	29	51	22
Ethiopia	25	50	25
Asia	19	30	11
Bangladesh	28	47	19
India	20	35	15
Japan	8	14	6
People's Republic of China	14	22	7
North America	7	16	9
Canada	8	16	7
United States	7	16	9
Latin America	23	32	8
Mexico	25	32	6
Venezuela	29	34	5
Argentina	16	25	9
Europe	4	14	10
United Kingdom	2	14	12
France	5	15	10
Spain	7	15	8
West Germany	−2	10	12
Poland	10	20	10
Oceania	13	21	9
Australia	8	15	7
USSR	8	18	10

SOURCE: *World Population Data Sheet*, 1982. Washington, D.C.: Population Reference Bureau, Inc.

States, and Australia, for example) have low rates as well, although somewhat higher than those of Europe.

Different amounts of societal variation exist in the two variables that make up the rate of natural increase: the crude birth rate and the crude death rate. Birth rates vary considerably from society to society. In 1982, the highest level was recorded in Kenya: 53 births per 1000 population. The lowest rate, 10, was registered in West Germany. In general, the level of the crude birth rate is related to the level of economic development. Developed societies experience low levels of birth rate, while Third World societies have much higher birth rates. Variations in the crude death rate, however, bear no such clear-cut relationship to the level of economic development. Many nations in the developing world have very low death rates. On the other hand, western European societies, all highly industrialized, do not experience particularly low death rates. For example, Sweden's death rate in 1981, at 11, was more than double that of Singapore.

Natural Increase and Net Migration: The Canadian Case

For most populations, natural increase plays a much more important role than net migration in affecting population growth. For the world as a whole, only natural increase is involved; for the different societies in the world, the migration component plays a greater or lesser role, depending upon a number of factors, such as political stability, economic conditions, and the like.

Canada is one society in which migration has played an important role in population growth. Canada is usually perceived as an immigrant-receiving country, and we would expect that positive net migration has played a major part in augmenting our population to its current size of just over 24 million. Let us see if the data confirm this expectation. Table 7-3 provides information concerning the roles played by natural increase and net migration in Canada's population growth from 1851, the time of the first regular census, to 1981. Immediately, it becomes clear that the factors accounting for historical development in the growth of the Canadian population are complex and vary over time.

Canada has had an uneven history in the trend of the growth rate. Growth has been substantial at some points in history and quite small at others. The early decades of the present century, particularly 1901 to 1911, and the decade of the 1950s can be singled out as times of rapid growth. On the other hand, the latter part of the nineteenth century and the decade of the 1970s are characterized by low growth rates. What accounts for this fluctuation in the trend of population growth? The answer lies in different combinations of rates of natural increase and net migration.

TABLE 7-3. NATURAL INCREASE AND NET MIGRATION IN CANADA: [a] 1851-1981

Census Year	Population (in thousands)	Average Annual Growth Rate (per 1000)	Rate of Natural Increase (per 1000)	Rate of Net Migration (per 1000)
1851	2,436	—	—	—
1861	3,230	29	22	6
1871	3,698	13	18	−4
1881	4,325	16	17	−1
1891	4,833	11	14	−3
1901	5,371	11	13	−2
1911	7,207	30	16	13
1921	8,788	20	16	4
1931	10,377	17	14	2
1941	11,507	10	11	−1
1951	14,009	17	15	1
1956	16,081	28	20	8
1961	18,238	25	20	6
1966	20,015	19	16	3
1971	21,568	15	10	4
1976	22,993	13	9	3
1981	24,187	11	8	3

SOURCES: Adapted from Beaujot, Roderic P. "Canada's Population: Growth and Dualism." *Population Bulletin*. 33(2): 6. Washington, D.C.: Population Reference Bureau, Inc. and Foot, David K. *Canada's Population Outlook*. Toronto Ont.: James Lorimer and Canadian Institute for Economic Policy,. 1982, p.4.
[a] Excludes Newfoundland prior to 1951.

Let us focus on the two periods of rapid growth first. The high growth rate in the decade of 1901 to 1911 can be largely accounted for by a large increase in the rate of positive net migration. The level of positive net migration that occurred in this decade is the highest recorded for any decade since 1851. This large excess of immigrants, relative to emigrants, reflects a change in immigration laws that took place at the time. It was the goal of the Laurier government to populate the western, rural part of the country – the prairies – with people who had a background in agricultural skills. In order to achieve that goal, immigration restrictions were liberalized, and Europeans from previously-defined "non-preferred" countries (for example, in eastern Europe) were allowed relatively easy entrance into Canada. Their movement into Canada, occurring as a wave, helped to bolster the rate of net migration. Even with this unprecedented rate of immigration, however, natural increase accounted for more than one-half of the total population growth during the decade.

In the second period of rapid growth, the decade of the 1950s, a very different picture emerges. This was not a time of unusually high positive net migration; the rate does not approach that of the decade 1901 to 1911. Even if the rate of net migration had been zero, this ten-year period would have experienced a growth rate higher than that occurring in earlier or later decades. It was a high rate of natural increase, not positive net migration, that was largely responsible for the high growth rate. As we will see later, the phenomenon known as the "baby boom," a period of high crude birth rates, occurred in the 1950s. As a result, the rate of natural increase, affected as it is by the level of the crude birth rate, was high.

The two periods characterized by low population growth rates resulted from differential combinations of natural increase and net migration. In the latter decades of the nineteenth century, negative net migration rates operated to deflate the growth rate. Why was net migration negative for the 40-year period from 1861 to 1901? How does an immigrant-receiving country like Canada end up with negative rates of net migration, especially for such a long period of time? It was not the case that immigrants ceased to enter Can-

ada. In fact, it is estimated that between one and two million people came to Canada from other countries in the period from 1861 to 1901 (Kalbach and McVey, 1979). However, greater numbers of people left Canada than entered during this time. The out-migrants, who consisted of both the Canadian-born and people who had immigrated to Canada at an earlier period in their lives, went mainly to the United States, because they were attracted to the possibilities offered by a rapidly expanding American economy.

The current period of relatively small growth is not similarly a function of negative net migration. Rather, an historical low point has been reached in the rate of natural increase, the result of our currently low birth rate.

Growth in the Canadian population, then, has resulted from the combined factors of natural increase and net migration. Of these, natural increase has played the dominant role. For most decades, the contribution of natural increase to population growth has far exceeded that of net migration. The particular role played by migration has varied over time. Migration has functioned to increase our size at some points and to lessen it at others. As a result, the pattern of migration accounts for much of the unevenness in the trend of Canadian population growth.

Malthusian Theory

One of the earliest and most influential statements regarding population growth was that of Thomas Malthus, an English clergyman and economist (for summaries of his life and work, see Bogue, 1969; Overbeek, 1974; Thompson and Lewis, 1965). Malthus wrote a series of essays expanding on his theory concerning the growth of population in relation to human welfare. Reacting against the optimism of eighteenth-century Europe, Malthus came to be viewed as a "prophet of doom," because he saw the human condition as inevitably worsening due to the working of the "principle of population."

Malthus' principle of population is that unchecked population has a tendency to grow at a rate that surpasses the ability of the means of subsistence (food) to support it. The means of subsistence, if they do

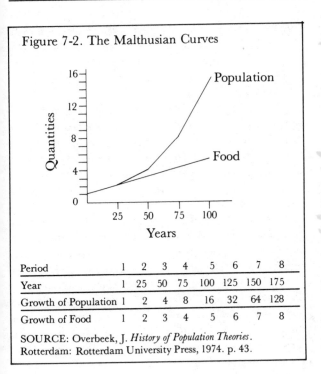

Figure 7-2. The Malthusian Curves

Period		1	2	3	4	5	6	7	8
Year		1	25	50	75	100	125	150	175
Growth of Population	1	2	4	8	16	32	64	128	
Growth of Food		1	2	3	4	5	6	7	8

SOURCE: Overbeek, J. *History of Population Theories*. Rotterdam: Rotterdam University Press, 1974. p. 43.

increase, can do so only in *arithmetic* progression (1,2,3,4,5); population increases in *geometric* progression (1,2,4,8,16). Figure 7-2 graphs the growth curves for population and for food that result from these laws of increase and shows the ever-widening gap that Malthus saw as inevitable if populations were to grow unchecked.

The tendency to reproduce at a rate exceeding the supply of food has, of course, disastrous consequences. Something has to counteract unlimited population growth. For Malthus, the checks on population are of two types: preventive and positive.

The preventive checks result from human action that operates to lower the number of births. For Malthus, the postponement of marriage was the major preventive check, because a late marrying age implies that fewer children can be born to a woman before she passes her productive years. Another type of preventive check is possible: the prevention of births within marriage by some voluntary means other than abstinence. Reflecting the times in which he lived, however, Malthus felt such action to be immoral and did not view it as a permissible preventive check.

The *positive checks*, on the other hand, result from either humans or nature operating to increase the number of deaths. War is an example of a positive check stemming from action on the part of people. Famines, plagues, and natural disasters are examples of positive checks not caused by human hands. Malthus also put forth "vice" as a positive check on population growth. For example, prostitution, a vice, is an activity that Malthus saw as having a dampening effect on the birth rate.

The operation of any of these checks prevents population from growing at its maximum rate, but Malthus did not think that the preventive checks were effective or powerful enough to do the job alone. Sooner or later, the more drastic positive checks would come into play. Therefore, the fate of humanity was inevitably governed by the laws of nature; humans were bound to over-reproduce themselves relative to the means of subsistence, and their numbers would necessarily be diminished in the end by an increased death rate.

The Malthusian position implies an acceptance of the way things are. Improvements in the living conditions of people are self-defeating, for good times lead to a lifting of the preventive checks, and the consequent population growth, following the law of geometric progression, surpasses the ability of the means of subsistence to support it.

Marx's Perspective

Although Karl Marx's writing on the subject of population was secondary to his general social and economic theory (for summaries of his views, see Bogue, 1969; Overbeek, 1974), his arguments are a direct, negative reaction to Malthusian theory, and to Malthus.

Marx objected to the Malthusian idea that there was one principle of population that applied to all types of societies. Marx argued that each "mode of production" in history was characterized by its *own* particular law of population. Feudal society, and later capitalist society for example, operated according to a law of population peculiar to each, and Marx's envisioned communist society would likewise forge a law unique to itself.

According to Marx, the "law of relative surplus population" corresponded to capitalist society. Capitalism, he believed, creates overpopulation, or a surplus of people relative to jobs, leading to high unemployment and increasing poverty. It is the nature of capitalist society to produce this end, he felt, given that in their own economic interest the bourgeoisie will continue to introduce labor-saving machinery and equipment, thus making workers obsolete. Capitalists who do not, or cannot, follow suit will be unable to meet their automated competition; their bankruptcies will lead to further unemployment among workers. However, according to Marx, capitalism not only creates unemployment, it also requires unemployment in order to insure a docile, low-paid class of laborers. As Marx saw it, the capitalist system is fraught with unemployment and underemployment, regardless of the rate of growth of the population (or labor force). Furthermore, for Marx unemployment and poverty themselves lead to a high rate of population growth as a result of the high fertility of the poor, thus compounding human misery.

Overpopulation would, according to Marx, be overcome in a communist society. He did not specify the nature of the law of population corresponding to a communist society, however. It is difficult, therefore, to know precisely how this population control would be achieved. Probably Marx believed that a new social and economic order based on communist principles could insure full employment, regardless of the rate of population growth.

Partially as a result of the lack of detail in his writing concerning population, Marx's impact on demography has been less than on most other areas within sociology discussed in this textbook. His focus upon the employment aspect of population is narrow, neglecting other dimensions of importance. In fact, it has been argued that Marx, while attempting to outline a theory of population, actually formulates a theory of employment (Overbeek, 1974). Nevertheless, his overall point that population growth and overpopulation are the product of the wider social and economic structure is indisputable. Marx understood that social factors play an influential role in population. Generally speaking, Malthus lacked this insight.

Demographic Transition Theory

A great deal of contemporary writing on population growth stems from **demographic transition theory** formulated on the basis of observed changes in population growth in western European societies (for summaries, see Coale, 1973; Stolnitz, 1964). It provides both a description and an explanation of historical change in population growth.

According to demographic transition theory, a population goes through three major stages in its transition to a modern pattern. *Stage one* is the stage of pretransition. The population is characterized by high fertility and high mortality. Birth rates are constantly high, whereas death rates fluctuate around an average high level in response to external conditions, such as the presence or absence of famines, epidemics, and so forth. Because both rates are high, the population grows slowly, if at all.

Stage two, the stage of transitional growth, consists of two phases or sub-stages. In the first sub-stage, the death rate declines, but the birth rate remains at the high level characteristic of stage one. As a result, the population grows rapidly. In the second sub-stage, the birth rate begins to decline, while the death rate continues to decrease. Because mortality decline has had a head start, the death rate remains lower than the birth rate. A high rate of population growth characterizes this sub-stage as well.

In *stage three*, the transition to low birth and death rates is complete. The rate of population growth, then, slows in comparison to stage two. The completion of transition implies *zero population growth*, or what demographers call a *stationary population*, at least in the long run. The rates of population growth in stage three and stage one are therefore similar, but they are achieved differently.

In stage three, death rates do not fluctuate; they are constantly low because the means exist to control short-term mortality crises such as epidemics. Birth rates, however, fluctuate in accordance with wider trends in society, such as economic recessions and booms. The low but fluctuating fertility level of this stage is accomplished through deliberate control of childbearing.

According to transition theory, as a population moves out of stage one into stage two and, later, into stage three, there is no turning back to an earlier stage of demographic development. Societies may differ in the pace of transition, in the time gap between death rate decline and the commencement of birth rate decline, or in the factors precipitating transition, but once begun the process is irreversible.

The theory of demographic transition (outlined in Figure 7-3) explains the course of demographic events in terms of changes in the wider social and economic environment, particularly industrialization and urbanization. The demographic characteristics of stage one result from the inability of preindustrial society to control mortality. Given an environment that continually threatens individual and group death, the predictable response is to maximize fertility. However, high fertility represents more than a reaction to high mortality. In a preindustrial society, children are economically advantageous, because they contribute to agricultural productivity at young ages and function as a source of security for aging parents. The costs of child-rearing, on the other hand, are small. The economic utility of children is buttressed by a system of social beliefs that reinforces the value of children.

Technological advance results in improvements in the production and distribution of food, in sanitation, and in medicine. A society is quick to accept these improvements, given their life-sustaining effects. As a result, death rates decline, and the first phase of transition begins.

Fertility, however, responds more slowly to modernization; declines in fertility are more difficult to bring about than declines in mortality. The high fertility of pretransitional societies is upheld by social beliefs and values that run counter to the behavioral changes reduced fertility implies.

Nevertheless, modernization eventually operates to lower fertility. Declining mortality, for example, acts as a damper on the birth rate, because one of the first groups to benefit from mortality reduction is young children. The heightened survival rate of the young serves to reduce fertility by making "insurance" births

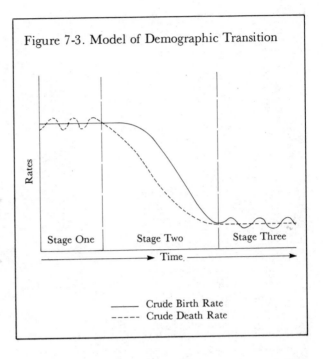

Figure 7-3. Model of Demographic Transition

less necessary. Furthermore, urbanization, one facet of modernization, lessens the productive utility of children. At the same time, the cost of child-rearing rises in an urban setting; education costs increase and big families come to be seen as liabilities.

Demographic transition theory is not without its critics (for example, Okediji, 1974). One of the major criticisms is that the theory, both as description and as explanation, has been modelled after the western experience and may not be applicable to today's Third World countries.

In fact, there is one crucial difference between demographic transition as it was experienced in the western world and the transition in today's developing countries. In the west, mortality decline was relatively slow, generally paralleling the course of economic modernization. Today's Third World countries, in contrast, have experienced very rapid declines in the death rate achieved in most cases since World War II. Also, the rapid mortality decline in the Third World has occurred, in many instances, in the absence of significant economic modernization, the result of the borrowing of western mortality-reducing technology.

Malthus and Marx: Sociological Theory in Demography

In demography, the major perspectives are Malthusian theory, Marxist theory, and the theory of demographic transition. Each concerns population growth and the determining mechanisms. They vary in terms of detail, the types of variables that are viewed as important, and the degree to which they are accepted by contemporary demographers. Demographic transition theory is the perspective that currently dominates the study of population.

Only one of the three major theoretical perspectives mentioned in Chapter 1 – the Marxist or conflict model –exists within the history of academic demographic thought. The lack of representation of the other sociological perspectives exists for at least two reasons. First, early recognition of the importance of population, and early attempts to explain population change and population processes, came from economics rather than sociology. Malthus was an economist; the early statements of demographic transition theory were formulated, in the main, by economists;

even Marx's orientation to population was largely economic, with a focus on the variable of employment. As a result, the study of population lacks a history of theoretical contribution from either structural functionalism or symbolic interactionism.

A second reason, closely related to the first one, is that demography is somewhat peripheral to mainstream sociology. While demographic variables are common within sociology, they are largely utilized as explanatory or independent variables. Demographers alone have sought to explain population variables, that is, formulated demographic variables as dependent variables. As a consequence, demography has developed theoretical perspectives that have no parallels in other branches of sociology.

FERTILITY

Natural increase (the excess of births over deaths) is a major component of population growth. For the world as a whole, it is the only component. For most societies, including Canada, it is the largest component. Because the demographic process of fertility is one of the elements of natural increase, let us now turn our attention to that process and examine it in more detail.

Demographers use the term fertility to refer to the actual childbearing of a woman or a group of women. It is distinguished from **fecundity**, which refers to the potential childbearing of a woman or group of women. Fertility is always lower than fecundity. No society has ever produced babies at a rate approaching women's

physiological capacity to do so. The production of babies at a rate lower than the biological maximum is accomplished through either, or both, of two mechanisms.

First, fertility can be consciously limited by individuals. Some action is taken with the deliberate aim of preventing the occurrence of a conception or a birth. The birth-control pill, intrauterine devices, diaphragms, foams, sterilization, condoms, and so forth are devices that prevent conception. Abstinence and coitus interruptus (withdrawal) may also be viewed in this light. Abortion, in contrast, is aimed at preventing a birth after conception has occurred.

Deliberate fertility control measures, such as those just listed, may be used at different times in the reproductive span. They may be used to postpone the beginning of family formation, to space children at desired intervals, or to prevent future births altogether. The conscious limitation of fertility, through any of these techniques and for any of these purposes, depends upon people's attitudes (is fertility control viewed as desirable, as morally acceptable?), their knowledge of effective means to control fertility, and the availability and proper use of those means.

The second fertility-limiting mechanism can be actions intended to achieve other ends. French demographer Louis Henry (1961) has introduced the term **natural fertility** to refer to the less-than-biological-maximum fertility that occurs in a population as the result of behavior not aimed specifically at modifying the number of children born but having that effect. A number of practices can be identified as having fertility-limitation effects without having fertility-limitation intentions. Prolonged lactation (breast feeding) has the effect of temporarily diminishing a woman's capacity to conceive another child. Also, some societies are characterized by a long postpartum ("following the birth") ban on sexual intercourse. Similarly, the practice of marriage postponement can effectively limit fertility, provided that the society does not have a high occurrence of illegitimacy.

These, then, are the two types of fertility control: voluntary/deliberate control, and unintentional control. To the degree that any control occurs, fertility falls short of the maximum possible.

Another factor affects fertility. Some portion of any population is involuntarily childless. People incapable, for physiological reasons, of producing children are termed "infecund." Also, some portion of any population is subfecund, people who are biologically capable of producing children but, even in the absence of any fertility-limiting measures, have difficulty doing so.

Fertility Measurement

Two types of fertility measurement exist: period and cohort. Period measures, of which the crude birth rate is one example, assess the frequency of a given event (in this case births) at one point in time, usually a year. Cohort measures, on the other hand, assess the frequency of a given event (births) occurring to a group of people (a cohort) over a longer period of time. For example, with cohort measurement, we could assess the total number of births that a cohort of women have over their reproductive span.

Period Measures. The crude birth rate is a period measure of fertility; it assesses the number of births that occur in one year in relationship to the total population. For purposes of assessing the extent to which births contribute to natural increase and, hence, to population growth, the crude birth rate is an adequate measure of fertility. For other purposes, however, more refined rates are required.

The crude birth rate is a "crude" or unrefined measure in the sense that its denominator, the total population, consists of people (like children and the aged) who do not bear children. A more refined measure limits the denominator to those directly exposed to the possibility of child-rearing, that is, women in the childbearing ages. A hypothetical example will show us the limitations in using crude measurement. Let's say there are two populations, A and B. Both have a population of 1000, and both produced 25 babies last year. The crude birth rate in both cases is 25, and we would be tempted to conclude an equivalency in fertility. However, let us suppose that population A comprised 500 people who could give birth (that is, women aged fifteen to forty-nine) and population B comprised only 350. In the event, one in 20 women had babies last year in population A, whereas in population B the ratio is one woman in 14. Looked at in this way, population B had a higher fertility level than population A, but that fact is masked when we relate the number of births to the total population.

There are several kinds of period fertility measures that are more refined than the crude birth rate. We will now look very briefly at those most commonly used.

The **general fertility rate** represents a refinement over the crude birth rate, because it restricts the denominator to women in the prime reproductive ages. In Canada in 1980, the general fertility rate was 57.9 births per 1000 women aged fifteen to forty-nine.

Age specific birth rates are a third widely used

type of period fertility measure. Age-specific birth rates for any year are obtained by dividing the number of births to mothers of a certain age by the number of women of that age in the population. These rates are useful because the rate of childbearing in any population is not uniform throughout the reproductive ages. By studying these rates, we can see the particular pattern of childbearing in a population, how it compares with other populations, and how it has changed over time.

Cohort Fertility Analysis. With period measures of fertility, the frequency of births in a given year is assessed. With cohort fertility analysis, the frequency of births occurring to a cohort of women over a longer period of time is measured. A cohort is a group of individuals who experience a "demographic event" at the same time. For example, all people born in 1960 constitute a cohort – a birth cohort; all people married in 1980 constitute a cohort – a marriage cohort.

In cohort fertility analysis, the childbearing of a birth cohort of women (or a marriage cohort of women) is traced throughout their reproductive years. It is possible, then, to assess the extent of change in the actual total number of children that different cohorts of women bear over the course of their reproductive span (completed family size) and in the timing of those births throughout that span.

We can see that cohort and period rates measure fertility from different perspectives. It is important not to place a cohort interpretation on period rates. For example, if we observe a trend of declining general fertility rates in a population, we cannot conclude automatically that the number of children born to women over the course of their reproductive years is declining. It is possible that the trend of decline in general fertility occurs because women are delaying childbearing at the present time, perhaps because of an economic recession. They could go on to have as many, or more, children as women of an earlier time. Similarly, a trend of increasing general fertility rates may reflect, not an increment in completed family size, but a trend toward childbearing at earlier ages in the reproductive span. Given that period rates are subject to these timing differences, demographers usually consider cohort measurement a more accurate representation of actual reproductive behavior in a population.

Fertility Change in Twentieth Century Canada

Over the course of this century, the level of period fertility in Canada declined. The trend, however, was not smooth. Fertility rates fell to low levels during the Depression of the 1930s, peaked for a fifteen-year period following the end of World War II, and declined during the 1960s, reaching unprecedented low levels by the end of the 1970s. The period of peak fertility is commonly termed the "baby boom;" the present low levels have been referred to as the "baby bust" (Grindstaff, 1975).

This twentieth-century trend is not unique to Canada; all western populations experienced a pattern of declining, but fluctuating, period fertility levels. Canada, nevertheless, is distinctive in the sense that our baby boom lasted longer and was higher than in other western populations. However, the boom was not equally large in all parts of Canada. For example, Quebec experienced a smaller baby boom than did other provinces.

The baby boom era is responsible for the major deviation from the trend of overall declining fertility that would be expected from demographic transition theory. What factors account for this unevenness in trend? Specifically, why did the baby boom occur?

One important variable is the timing of childbearing. Significant changes have occurred in Canada over this century in terms of when women have their children. During the baby boom era, women had their children at younger ages compared to women before and after them.

A trend toward younger age at childbearing gives rise to increasing period fertility rates. Similarly, a trend toward older age at childbearing results in decreasing fertility rates. A change in childbearing timing affects fertility level, because there are more younger women than older women in a population. If proportionately more women bear children at younger ages, more babies will be produced for the simple reason that there are more younger women. The high fertility of the baby boom period reflects a shift toward younger childbearing; the present trend of low fertility reflects a shift back to older childbearing.

The timing of childbearing in a population is itself the result of a complex of factors. One important variable is age at marriage. If women marry at young ages, the possibility exists that they will have children early in life. On the other hand, older age at marriage tends to be associated with older childbearing.

Throughout the course of the twentieth century in Canada, the average age at marriage changed significantly. For both sexes, age at marriage is younger now than in the past. For example, the mean age at first marriage for women in the twentieth century up until World War II was around twenty-five. By 1951, it had declined to approximately twenty-three years, and in 1961 it had dropped further to twenty-two years. It rose again, but by 1980 the mean age was still around twenty-three years.

The essence of the baby boom, then, was a change in the timing of events in the life span of women. Baby boom mothers married earlier than women before them and had their children in a short span after marriage. They did not go on to have significantly more children than earlier cohorts of women. Canadian census data reveal that ever-married women born between 1927 and 1931, women whose chief childbearing years occurred in the baby boom era, bore 3.3 children on average. This figure is not significantly higher than the completed family size of ever-married women of earlier cohorts. For example, ever-married women born between 1907 and 1911, women whose chief childbearing years occurred prior to the baby boom, bore 3.2 children on average. Figure 7-4 shows general fertility values in Canada from 1921 to 1979.

The heightened period fertility of the baby boom did not signify an increase in completed family size in Canada, but a change in childbearing pattern. The low fertility of the baby bust similarly reflects a change in the age patterning of childbearing to some degree. Today, women marry at relatively young ages but do not go on to have children immediately. This is a generation of postponers whose behavior reflects normative change, an economic recession, and the

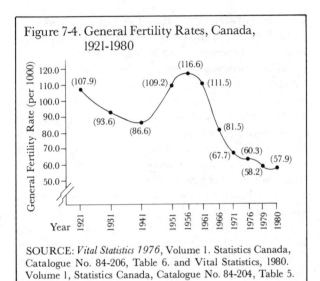

Figure 7-4. General Fertility Rates, Canada, 1921-1980

SOURCE: *Vital Statistics 1976*, Volume 1. Statistics Canada, Catalogue No. 84-206, Table 6. and Vital Statistics, 1980. Volume 1, Statistics Canada, Catalogue No. 84-204, Table 5.

availability of effective contraceptive technology. We cannot assume that their completed family size will be as low as present period fertility levels suggest, although it does seem likely that they will have smaller families than earlier generations of Canadian women, approximating two children per ever-married women on average.

Factors Affecting Fertility

Fertility level varies across societies, within societies, and over time at least in some societies, one of which is Canada. Some part of fertility variation is due to physiological variables, such as the incidence of infecundity. However, most of the variation is the result of differences in the degree that fertility is consciously limited. The degree of deliberate fertility limitation is a product of the wider social environment within which the population exists. Fertility is a social fact and, as such, a complex phenomenon. Its level is determined by a number of interacting factors. Four types of factors are particularly important: demographic, cultural, socioeconomic, and governmental. We will look at each factor separately, but it is important to remember that they are highly interrelated.

Demographic Factors. Two population-related variables play an important role in affecting fertility level: infant mortality and marriage pattern.

Infant mortality, usually measured by the infant mortality rate, refers to the incidence of death among children under the age of one in a population. For the world as a whole in 1982, the infant mortality rate was 85. In other words, nearly 9 percent of all children born in 1982 died in the first year of life. Rates varied from a high of 212 in Guinea to a low of 5.4 in Iceland. The level in Canada was 10.9.

When the level of infant mortality is high, the level of fertility is high. A high incidence of infant death creates a situation in which women produce many babies in order to insure some surviving children. Insurance births result; that is, extra babies are produced "just in case."

The marriage pattern in a population affects fertility level. Marriage pattern consists of two aspects: the average age at marriage and the proportion of people in a population that eventually marries. These two aspects tend to be related; where marriage occurs at young ages, most of the population marries. Conversely, old age at marriage and a high proportion of never-marrying people tend to occur together.

The significance of marriage pattern for fertility level lies in its effect on the exposure of women to the risk of childbearing. When virtually all women marry, and at young ages, there is greater exposure to the risk of producing children. This is so not only because more women are married for a longer period of time, but also because more are married at the time of peak fecundity, that is, at ages under thirty.

A second aspect of the effect of marriage pattern on fertility level concerns the structure of opportunities for women. If women marry at young ages, there are few alternatives for them outside the home. The focal point of their existence is their domestic role; children justify that existence.

Cultural Factors. The cultural environment that people live in also plays an important role in determining fertility behavior. Culture affects motivations in childbearing largely through the institutionalization of values guiding people about the number of children they have. These values bear directly on the acceptance (or rejection) of deliberate fertility limitation practices. Two dimensions of culture are particularly important in this regard (Okediji, 1974):

1. cultural definitions of the nature of human relations
2. cultural definitions of the human condition

Societies differ in the emphasis they place upon the importance of the individual in relation to the larger group consisting of kin and community. Where the wider group is viewed as taking precedence over the individual, children are highly valued as they increase the membership of that group. Consequently, childbearing is highly rewarded. Societies that value the larger group, and hence the production of children, are termed *familistic*. In contrast are societies like ours in which cultural values emphasize the individual over and above the wider group. The rewards for childbearing are smaller; therefore, the motivation to produce children is less.

A related aspect of the cultural view of human relations concerns definitions of appropriate gender-role behavior. If a man is a "real man" only when he fathers children, and if manliness is culturally gauged in direct proportion to the number of children he fathers, then the motivation for children is so great that their production in large numbers is virtually assured. If the cultural environment further stipulates that only male children "count," fertility will be high in order to insure that the requisite numbers of sons are born and survive. A cultural setting that assesses "maleness" according to the number of sons a man fathers is one that typically affords a low status to women. As women lack economic and political power, the only avenue open for them to enhance their status is to produce children, preferably sons. Therefore, if culture defines expected gender-role behavior according to reproductive performance, both men and women are strongly motivated to produce children and highly rewarded for so doing.

Bear in mind that all societies reward people for producing children. We can see that our society does by observing the degree of negative sentiment attached to homosexuality, voluntary childlessness, and any act or relationship that, at least symbolically, challenges parenthood. However, variations do exist in the degree to which reproduction is rewarded, resulting from differences in gender-role definitions and the extent of familism.

The second cultural factor that bears directly on fertility is the way the culture views the human condition. Cultures vary in attitude concerning the degree to which the environment can be controlled. At one end of the continuum are cultural settings characterized by what is termed fatalism (an acceptance of the way things are). Often intermeshed with religious ideology and convictions, this results in the production of as many children as is "God's will." Interference with God's will – that is, deliberate fertility control – is viewed as unnatural, immoral, or just plain impossible. More often than not, the idea of interfering does not even arise. At the other end of the continuum are environments like ours, where it is culturally defined as proper and possible that individuals exercise control over their own lives. In such an environment, deliberate fertility limitation is viewed as acceptable behavior.

Within a society, the impact of cultural factors on fertility is often assessed by examining different ethnic and religious attitudes to childbearing. In Canada, for example, women of French origin have traditionally had substantially larger families than women of British origin. In terms of religion, Catholic women have the largest families and Jewish women the smallest.

Cultural differences in family size in Canada, however, are diminishing. The fertility differential between French-Canadian women and British-Canadian women has now in fact virtually disappeared, especially for younger women.

Convergence in fertility behavior illustrates that the influence of culture on childbearing can change. It appears that the cultural environment influences the degree of initial resistance to fertility limitation practices. Once initial resistance is overcome, which typically occurs in conjunction with wider social and economic changes, a cultural group with a high fertility level can decrease its fertility very rapidly. In Canada, the province of Quebec underwent decline last, but accomplished fertility transition in the shortest period of time.

Socioeconomic Factors. We have already seen that economic development is closely associated with fertility level. All the developed countries have low levels of fertility; the developing countries experience much higher levels. We have seen that demographic transition theory regards economic modernization as a significant variable affecting fertility decline. Also, within societies there is an inverse relationship between socioeconomic status and fertility. Groups of high socioeconomic status are characterized by low fertility and vice versa. Here, we will focus on the interrelated social and economic factors that are important determinants of fertility behavior.

1. Type of economic production. In an agrarian mode of production, children are economic assets. They contribute to agricultural production at young ages and provide economic support for aged parents. At the same time, children in an agrarian setting are not expensive to rear. In other words, the economic benefits of children outweigh the costs.

In an industrial mode of production, on the other hand, children are economic liabilities. The structure and content of jobs in an urban, industrial setting exclude the participation of children. Labor force participation is dependent upon the acquisition of skills that are obtained through education. Children are no longer workers, they are students. As such, they are expensive; they do not contribute to family earnings, and their education is costly.

2. Female labor force participation. While women in all societies work, the location of their work varies in accordance with the level and type of economic production. Women in urban environments are more likely to work outside the home than women in rural settings. Also, the higher the level of economic development of the society as a whole, the greater the likelihood of female employment outside the home.

At the societal level, an inverse relationship exists between the percentage of women employed outside the home and fertility level. In other words, societies with a high rate of female labor force participation have low fertility levels and vice versa. Also, at the individual level, women who work outside the home have fewer children than women who stay home. However, it is not clear whether it is employment in the labor force that affects lowered fertility, or whether women with few children are more likely to work outside the home. It is likely that the relationship is two-way, with female labor force participation and fertility influencing each other.

One reason for the fertility-deflating influence of female labor force involvement has to do with the conflict between the worker role and the traditional female childbearing and child-rearing role. Because both are demanding roles, one strategy to accommodate the conflict is to minimize the number of children born. By constrast, when women's work occurs within the confines of the household, it is easier to coordinate that work with child-rearing tasks.

3. Mobility opportunities. The perception of opportunities for social and economic advancement affects fertility behavior. If people perceive that they have a chance to "get ahead," one way to realize that opportunity is to minimize fertility. Family resources can then be mobilized toward the goal of social and economic betterment, a goal that can more easily be attained with a small family.

The perception that opportunities exist will likely have some basis in fact. Ordinarily, people will perceive that a better life is possible even if it actually is not possible at all. The real opportunities that exist for people in a society are not equally distributed; people with higher socioeconomic status have more opportunities open to them than people of lower socioeconomic status. These differential opportunities may explain the inverse relationship between fertility and social rank.

4. Educational attainment. One very important factor determining fertility behavior is the level of educational attainment, particularly among women. High levels of educational attainment are associated with low levels of fertility. This relationship is found both across societies and within societies.

There are several factors underlying the inverse relationship between fertility and education. With increasing education, people come to define themselves and their world in a different way. Education enhances the individual's sense of self. In addition, education supports the idea that the environment can be controlled by the individual. Not only does education

create people who are willing to exercise control over their lives; it also provides the tool for that control – knowledge. Increased educational attainment breaks down traditional barriers to fertility-limitation practices, making fertility control an acceptable behavior. At the same time, the increased knowledge gained through education can be applied directly to reproduction, enhancing the likelihood of the effective use of contraception.

Governmental Factors. Governments intentionally (and sometimes unintentionally) act in ways that can affect the birth rate. Often, attempts are made to alter the birth rate in accordance with governmental aims and intentions. Sometimes, governments are successful, sometimes not.

Historically in the west, governmental attempts to influence fertility have been aimed at increasing the number of births. This pronatalist stance, mirroring a "bigger is better" mentality, is reflected in a number of strategies that have been employed regarding reproduction. The strategies implemented fall into two major categories: negative measures and positive measures. Negative measures include outlawing birth control, the criminalization of abortion, and stringent legal barriers to divorce. Canada utilized all three types of negative measures until fairly recently.

Canadian law has a restrictive history regarding birth control. Legislation concerning contraception was enacted in 1892, as part of the Criminal Code dealing with Offences Against Morality. The law did not make the use of contraception illegal. Rather, the sale, distribution, and advertisement of contraceptive products were illegal.

As such, Canadian law did not differ from that of Great Britain (Indecent Advertisements Act of 1889) and the United States (Comstock Laws of 1873). The Canadian law banning birth control remained on the books until 1969, when selling, distributing, and advertising non-abortive, contraceptive products and literature were removed from the criminal code. Therapeutic abortion was also decriminalized. Regarding divorce, Canadian law also has a restrictive history. Not until 1968 was divorce made relatively easy to obtain.

This Tokyo commuter grimly clutches his shopping bag and glares at the "back pusher" whose job it is to jam the overflow of passengers back into the subway cars. Tokyo's population approaches nine million.

Positive pronatal measures include family allowances and tax exemptions to larger families. Canada implemented a family allowance program after World War II which is still in force. In 1967, the Province of

Quebec instituted a baby bonus scheme whereby graduated allowances were paid for additional children. Also, tax benefits accrue to larger families in Canada.

Despite these governmental measures, the Canadian birth rate fell throughout the twentieth century with the exception of the baby boom era. The Canadian case, then, illustrates governmental failure to influence the birth rate. Indeed, all western societies show governmental inability to alter the course of fertility decline. If people are highly motivated to limit their fertility, they will do so, regardless of how difficult it is made for them.

The situation in today's Third World countries is radically different. There, for the most part, governments seek to limit fertility, rather than increase it as in developed countries. It would be incorrect, however, to assume that the western failure to increase fertility indicates that governmental attempts to lower fertility in the Third World are doomed. In fact, success can be expected so long as governmental attempts to lower fertility are coupled with social and economic structural change that reduces the motivation to produce children.

The strategies to limit fertility are as varied as the measures that have been employed to increase it. However, fertility-limiting measures are of two basic varieties: family planning programs and legal measures. Family planning programs take the form of an organized effort to educate people concerning the available techniques of contraception, to disseminate contraceptive products, and to propagandize the benefits of small families. Evidence suggests that family planning programs are working in many Third World countries; fertility is being reduced at a faster rate than would be expected as a result of modernization gains alone (Tsui and Bogue, 1978).

Legal measures to reduce fertility include the legalization of contraceptive devices, abortion, and sterilization, and legal restrictions concerning age at marriage. The People's Republic of China is an example where all these legal strategies have been employed in recognition of the negative consequences of too rapid population growth. Available evidence indicates that these legal strategies are facilitating fertility decline (Aird, 1978).

MORTALITY

Mortality refers to the occurrence of deaths in a population, as opposed to *morbidity*, which refers to the occurrence of illness in a population. There is some relationship between mortality level and morbidity level; that is, high mortality and high morbidity tend to occur together. The relationship is not one-to-one, however, because some illnesses are not fatal and some deaths are not due to illness.

Fertility and mortality are the two components of natural increase: fertility determines how many people will be added to a population and mortality determines how many people will be subtracted. Fertility and mortality differ in the extent to which human intervention is possible. While human beings have considerable choice about childbearing and can choose to bear no children, they have no choice about dying. Nevertheless, social and economic factors are still important in determining the mortality characteristics of a population. Also, the social consequences of mortality level and change are significant. As the model of demographic transition in Figure 7-3 shows us, mortality decline (and the subsequent gap between fertility and mortality level) is *the* factor that accounts for the rapid population growth rate that is currently being experienced in the world. Therefore, it is important to know how mortality is measured.

Mortality Measurement

At the simplest level, mortality is measured by the crude death rate. For many parts of the world, data are so limited that it is not possible to measure mortality in a more sophisticated way. The crude measurement of deaths is subject to the same limitations as is the crude measurement of births. The denominator of the crude death rate is the total population, so this type of mortality measure does not take into into account population composition differences. For example, Population A may have a higher percentage of people with high death-risk characteristics than Population B. Even if the two populations were characterized by identical levels of mortality for different types of people, Population A would have a higher crude death rate, because it has more people of the type likely to die than Population B.

Age is one significant variable affecting mortality risk. Two age groups are particularly susceptible to dying: young children, particularly children under the age of one, and old people. Therefore, if a population has a high proportion of people in these high-risk ages, its crude death rate will be proportionately inflated. This effect of age composition on the death rate explains why crude death rates in certain western populations are higher than those in some less developed countries: western populations have a much higher percentage of old people. See Chapter 5 for a discussion of this phenomenon.

Another important variable affecting the risk of dying is sex. In most populations, males die off more quickly than females. The effect of the sex differential in mortality on the crude death rate, however, is much smaller than the effect of age differences, because societies vary less in sex composition than they do in age composition.

A life table is a mathematical model that is used to estimate the average number of years that people of a given age and a given sex can expect to live, assuming that mortality rates continue at current levels. The most commonly used statistic arising from life table construction is the estimation of life expectancy at birth. Correctly interpreted, this is a particularly meaningful statistic. It tells us the average number of years that a newborn baby can expect to live. We already know that babies are a high death-risk group. If babies survive the high-risk young ages, however, their expectation of life is greater than the average for their cohort at birth. For example, if the males in a population have a life expectancy at birth of 70.2 years (as was the case in Canada in 1976), a male who has survived to the age of 20 can expect to live longer than 50.2 years. How much longer depends upon the particular age schedule of mortality existing in the male population of which he is a part. In Canada, the twenty-year-old male could expect to live 52.1 more years.

Mortality Variation

Although contemporary death rates are not as variable as birth rates, substantial differences continue to exist, globally, in life expectancy at birth. (See Table 7-4.) For the world as a whole in 1982, the average life expectancy was 60 years. The range was from 37 years in Kampuchea to 76 years in Iceland and Japan.

In past centuries, all populations existed under mortality conditions that resulted in short life expectancy. Only in the twentieth century has mortality been controlled to a degree that allows for an average world life expectancy at birth of 60 years. In the past, mortality was high for three main reasons: acute and chronic food shortage; epidemic disease; and poor public health standards (Thomlinson, 1965).

Recent increases in life expectancy have resulted from the partial control we have achieved over these traditional killers. Other factors that have contributed to overall mortality decline include the development and acceptance of germ theory, the development of immunology, and improvements in agricultural techniques. This last factor is important. Although famines took their toll on human life, probably just as significant in human history has been the continued undernourishment that weakens people to such a degree that they succumb even to mild infections.

As a population undergoes mortality reduction, the causes of death change. In a population with high mortality levels, communicable diseases are the prime cause of death. The mortality declines that have occurred are largely the result of the control of communicable diseases. With the control or eradication of such diseases, new ones emerge as the chief killers, in particular cardiovascular diseases and cancer. These new killers gain in prominence, at least in part, because the avoidance of communicable diseases allows people to live to older ages when the risks of heart disease and cancer are greater.

The three leading causes of death in Canada are general diseases of the heart, ischemic (coronary) heart disease, and cancer. This pattern is in keeping with a low mortality rate where deaths are concentrated at old ages, though some differences between the sexes can be observed. (See Table 7-5.) While the three leading causes of death for men and women are identical, men exhibit higher death rates. The fourth cause of death differs for the sexes. For men, it is accidents; for women, cerebrovascular disease. To some degree, this difference reflects the fact that women survive longer than men. As women live to older ages, they are more likely to die of diseases of old age like strokes.

TABLE 7-4. LIFE EXPECTANCY AT BIRTH, 1982

Country	Life Expectancy (in years)
World	60
Africa	49
Egypt	55
Niger	42
Ethiopia	40
Asia	58
Bangladesh	46
India	49
Japan	76
People's Republic of China	65
North America	74
Canada	74
United States	74
Latin America	63
Mexico	65
Venezuela	66
Argentina	69
Europe	72
United Kingdom	73
France	74
Spain	73
West Germany	72
Poland	71
Oceania	69
Australia	73
USSR	69

SOURCE: *World Population Data Sheet*, 1982. Washington, D.C.: Population Reference Bureau, Inc.

TABLE 7-5. DEATH RATES, CANADA, 1978

Cause of Death	Death Rate (per 100,000)
Males	
1. Diseases of the heart	288.8
2. Ischemic heart disease	259.9
3. Cancer	178.6
4. Accidents	98.0
5. Respiratory diseases	61.7
All Causes	831.9
Females	
1. Diseases of the heart	202.0
2. Ischemic heart disease	172.6
3. Cancer	138.4
4. Cerebrovascular diseases	69.3
5. Accidents	39.3
All Causes	601.8

SOURCE: *Vital Statistics, 1978*, Vol. 3. Statistics Canada Catalogue No. 84-206, Table 2.

Mortality Differentials

Almost universally, women outlive men. The gap in life expectancy favoring women is greater in developed societies than in developing societies. In the developed world, this gap has increased over time. For example, in Canada 50 years ago, female life expectancy at birth exceeded that of males by approximately two years; at the present time, the gap is about seven years.

The male-female gap in mortality in developed countries is not equal at all ages. The difference is particularly great for persons in their twenties, where the death rate for males is nearly three times as large as that for females. The major factor involved is death by accident.

In 1980, the death rate for males aged 20 to 24 due to accidents was 95.2 per 100 000; the comparable figure for females was 25.5. One reason for this large difference may be that men seem to find themselves in, or put themselves into, riskier situations. Men are more likely to work at jobs where the risk of accidental death is high; the traditional male gender role and "Give 'em hell" attitude (David and Brannon, 1976) are probable causes of this situation.

Married people have a better chance of surviving than single people. Single people, in turn, have somewhat lower death rates than the widowed and divorced. Lastly, different levels of mortality are found among various ethnic and racial groups. In Canada, one group has a particularly high mortality level and short life expectancy at birth: native Indians. Their level of infant mortality is nearly twice the Canadian average. Also, provincial averages of life expectancy at birth for both males and females are lowest for Quebec.

MIGRATION

Migration that crosses national boundaries is termed "international migration." If the movement, on the other hand, occurs within the confines of a society, the migration is said to be internal. For both varieties of migration, there are two kinds of movers: people moving into a given geographical area (in-migrants) and people moving out (out-migrants). In the case of international migration, these two types of movers are termed immigrants and emigrants.

Many arrived, like this group, with bare feet and burlap sacks. European immigrants came here early in the century, lured with promises of free land from a government eager to populate the western plains. Recent immigrants are increasingly from the Third World.

Net migration refers to the difference between the number of in-migrants and the number of out-migrants. As we have seen, net migration is one of the important components of population growth, and may be either positive (where the number of in-migrants exceeds the number of out-migrants) or negative (where the number of out-migrants is larger than the number of in-migrants). Net migration is used when referring to both international and internal migration.

International Migration in Canada

We can identify four major periods of international immigration to Canada. Initially, Canada was settled by the French. The bulk of French immigrants came to the colony of New France during the years 1608 to 1760. The total volume of French immigration was quite small, probably less than 10 000 (Beaujot, 1978).

The second period of immigration was much larger in scale, and it brought a new group to Canada, the British. Initial in-migration of the British to Canada was, in the main, via two distinct routes: from the United States when United Empire Loyalists entered Canada during the time of the American Revolution; from Great Britain when direct immigration in significant numbers occurred during the early years of the nineteenth century. The British-origin population in Canada was augmented further by an influx of Irish escaping famine in the 1840s. In the nineteenth century, other western European groups, particularly Germans, immigrated to Canada. The total volume of immigrants in this period is uncertain; for the period from 1851 to 1901, estimates range from 1.3 million to 2.3 million (Kalbach and McVey, 1979).

The third period encompasses the first three decades of the twentieth century, when an historically unprecedented number of immigrants entered Canada. Estimates range from 3.7 million to 4.6 million for the period 1901 to 1931 (Kalbach and McVey, 1979). For the first time in Canadian history, groups other than western Europeans entered Canada in significant numbers. This was the period of large scale immigration of eastern Europeans, particularly Ukrainians.

TABLE 7-6. SOURCE COUNTRIES OF IMMIGRANTS, CANADA, 1979

Country[a]	Number of Immigrants
1. Viet Nam	19,859
2. Great Britain	12,853
3. United States	9,617
4. Hong Kong	5,966
5. India	4,517
6. Laos	3,902
7. Philippines	3,873
8. Portugal	3,723
9. Jamaica	3,213
10. Guyana	2,473
All Countries	112,096

SOURCE: Employment and Immigration Canada, 1979 *Immigrations Statistics*, Table 3.
NOTE: [a] Country of last permanent residence.

The fourth period is the post-World War II years. From 1946 to 1978, 4.6 million immigrants entered Canada. During this period, immigration from non-European countries steadily increased. In the earlier part of the period, the ten leading sources of immigrants were all European countries, predominantly western European, and the United States. For example, in 1951, the ten leading countries, in order of volume, were: Britain, Germany, Italy, Netherlands, Poland, France, United States, Belgium, Yugoslavia, and Denmark. In 1979, the situation was quite different. (See Table 7-6.) Of the ten leading sources, seven were Third World countries. Nonetheless, Britain and the United States continue to be leading source countries.

Changes in the overall numbers of immigrants entering Canada reflect differences in the attractiveness of Canada to immigrants, particularly in comparison to the United States. Throughout most of our history, Canada has welcomed immigrants, viewing them as important for economic development, as long as they were of the "right" variety. Recently, there has been a change in attitude toward the volume of immigration, reflected in the establishment of a yearly quota on the total number of immigrants allowed into the country.

Changes in the ethnic origin of immigrants in Canada reflect alterations in Canadian immigration policy over time. Up until 1962, Canadian immigration policy was based on ethnic criteria to a large degree. There were "preferred" immigrants and, therefore, "nonpreferred" immigrants. Preferred immigrants were those of western European origin, people viewed as highly suitable for assimilation into Canadian society.

One of the most blatant examples of racism in Canadian immigration history was the Oriental Exclusion Act, in existence from the early 1930s to 1947. No Asians were allowed into the country, because they were viewed as a group that could never assimilate into Canadian society. In addition, Asian Canadian citizens were required by law to pay a head tax to re-enter Canada if they left for any reason, no matter how temporary the absence.

Recent changes in Canadian immigration policy have been designed to remove race and ethnicity as grounds for admission. As a result, the percentage of nonwestern Europeans and non-Europeans entering Canada has increased. See the "Immigration" section of Chapter 9 for a description of the revised system for selecting immigrants.

On the other hand, the major receiver of Canadian emigrants, both foreign-born and Canadian-born, has been the United States. As we have already seen, emigration from Canada was very high in the period from 1861 to 1901, a major concern of the authorities at the time, because the number of emigrants exceeded the number of immigrants. This situation reversed itself in the early decades of this century, due to changes in Canadian immigration policy and economic expansion. Nonetheless, emigration from Canada to the United States in greater numbers than immigration to Canada from the United States was a fact of life until relatively recently. In every year from 1950 to 1970, for example, Canada lost population in Canadian-American migration exchanges (Beaujot, 1978). Perhaps more importantly, Canada was losing trained people to the United States and not receiving comparable numbers of skilled, well-educated people from the United States. This phenomenon has been called the "brain drain." Although, on the whole, a brain drain did occur, the reverse was the case for certain occupational categories. One example is university professors. More American professors entered Canada, encouraged by short-term exemption from federal income tax payments, than Canadian professors left to go to the States.

International Migrants. Some people are more likely than others to be international migrants. One important variable is age. Younger people are more likely to desire to move into a new environment. They are also more likely to be allowed admission into a "new" country like Canada, given their potential labor force contribution.

Gender is another variable involved in international migration, but its effect has changed over time in countries like Canada. Historically, men have been more prone to international migration, although recently there has been a reversal of this traditional pattern. In 1979, for example, there were approximately 95 male immigrants for every 100 female immigrants.

A third international migration variable is marital status. Historically, single people have been more likely to migrate than married people. However, as with the gender variable, there has been a change in recent years, with married immigrants outnumbering single immigrants.

Internal Migration in Canada

Two historical aspects are particularly important when discussing internal migration in Canada. One is the fact of western expansion. In 1901, approximately 88 percent of the Canadian population resided in the Maritime Provinces (excluding Newfoundland), Ontario, and Quebec; less than 12 percent of the population lived in the western part of the country. By 1980, the western provinces (the prairies and British Columbia) had increased their share of the total population to 28 percent. The western expansion of the Canadian population has been encouraged by the Canadian authorities. The "peopling of the prairies" was one of the motivations underlying the admittance of previously "non-preferred" people into Canada in the early decades of this century.

Figure 7-5. Population Pyramids, Canada, 1881 and 1981

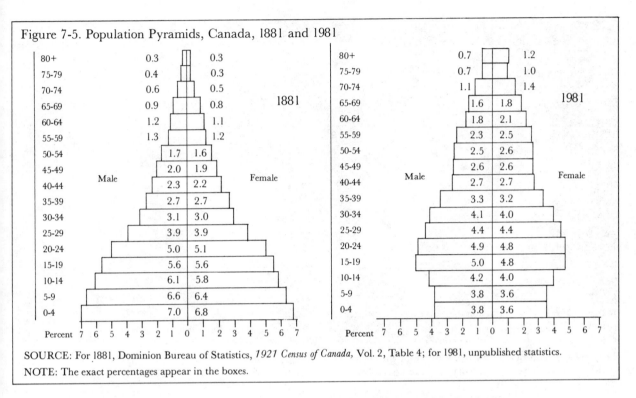

SOURCE: For 1881, Dominion Bureau of Statistics, *1921 Census of Canada*, Vol. 2, Table 4; for 1981, unpublished statistics.

NOTE: The exact percentages appear in the boxes.

The second significant aspect of internal migration in Canada is the trend to urbanization; that is, the movement of population from rural areas to urban areas. Urbanization, reflecting wider economic transformation, is a major aspect of social change within Canadian society in the twentieth century. In 1901, only 34.9 percent of the population resided in urban centers; by 1976, the percentage was 75.5. This urbanization has largely taken place along the southern rim of Canada, because few cities in Canada are any great distance from the American border.

The growth of urban Canada is only partially a function of internal migration. International migration has also played a role. When immigrants enter Canada, they are more likely to move to cities than to settle in rural areas. Up until now, the Canadian government has made no attempt to control the location of immigrants in Canada and their preference has been cities. Finally, as you will see in Chapter 15, differential fertility and mortality rates sometimes gives a relative advantage to urban populations.

CONSEQUENCES OF FERTILITY, MORTALITY, AND MIGRATION

The levels of fertility, mortality, and net migration in a population have effects upon the characteristics of that population. We have already seen that these three demographic processes operate together to determine growth rate. In addition, there are other, equally important, effects.

Age Structure

The fertility level in a population is the major determinant of **age structure**, the proportion of people in each category in a population. Age structure, or age composition, is usually represented in graphs known as population pyramids, as shown in Figure 7-5.

Demographers have identified three major types of population pyramids:

This great-grandmother enjoys a place of honor at the center of successive generations of happy and well-fed children. But Canadian fertility rates have declined since the turn of the century, reaching unprecedented low levels during the 1970s.

1. The expansive type, which has a very broad base. This type of pyramid reflects a population that has a high proportion of children, the result of high past and present fertility levels. A population with an expansive pyramid is termed a "young" population.
2. The constrictive type, which has a base that is somewhat narrower than the middle of the pyramid. This type of pyramid occurs with rapidly declining fertility levels.
3. Stationary pyramids, which have a narrower base, with approximately equal percentages of people in each age group and a tapering-off at older ages. Stationary pyramids occur when a population has had low fertility levels for a considerable length of time. A population with a stationary pyramid is referred to as an "old" population.

Fertility level is the most significant demographic variable affecting age structure, but migration can play a role as well, although it is generally a minor one. Given the age-selectivity of migration, a population that receives in-migrants will display a pyramid that has a bulge in the young working ages. Conversely, a population that loses people through out-migration will have an indentation at the age groups that are most likely to migrate out.

Figure 7-5 shows age-sex pyramids of the Canadian population in 1881 and 1981. The pyramid for 1881 is expansive, as a result of high fertility during the nineteenth century. On the other hand, the pyramid for 1981 is constrictive. The declining fertility of the 1960s and 1970s resulted in a relatively small proportion of children in 1981. The bulge in the ages from twenty to thirty-four is a direct result of the baby boom. That bulge will continue to appear in population pyramids of the Canadian population until the large cohort of the baby boom era eventually dies out. When that happens, and assuming that fertility does not increase substantially in the future, the population pyramid for Canada will be stationary.

The social and economic significance of age structure lies in what is termed the **dependency ratio** or **dependency burden**. This is the ratio of the number of persons in the economically dependent age groups to the number of people in the productive ages. Usually, the economically dependent ages are arbitrarily taken to be the ages under fifteen and the ages of sixty-five and over; that is, children and the elderly. The higher the dependency ratio, the more people in a population that must be economically supported relative to the number of supporters.

As a population undergoes fertility transition, moving from an expansive pyramid to a constrictive one, then later to a stationary one, its dependency ratio changes. First, a high dependency ratio occurs with an expansive pyramid; high fertility creates a large population in the economically dependent young ages. For example, the dependency ratio in Canada in 1881 was 74.8; that is, there were approximately 75 economically dependent persons for every 100 persons in the productive ages. Most of these economically dependent persons were children. Nearly 40 percent of the population was under fifteen; only 4 percent was sixty-five and over.

The dependency ratio lessens with a constrictive pyramid. In Canada in 1981, the dependency burden was substantially smaller than in 1881, 48.2. The dependency burden at the young ages was much smaller, because only about 23 percent of the population was under the age of fifteen in 1981. At the same time, the percentage of older people increased. In 1981, approximately 10 percent of the Canadian population was aged sixty-five and over.

Dependency burden plays an important role in economic and social development. Other things being equal, the lower the dependency ratio, the easier the economic and social modernization. A population with a lower dependency ratio will have a higher per capita output, better standard of living, greater savings, and more investment capital for development. In addition, a lower dependency burden implies that less will be spent per capita on education, especially primary education, and housing.

The societies most in need of economic and social development are, however, the same societies that have expansive pyramids and high dependency burdens. Their age structures are one stumbling block to development, because the needs of the young can be met only at the expense of production.

What will decrease the dependency ratio in Third World societies? Lowered fertility. What will lower fertility? Economic and social modernization. What will facilitate modernization? Lowered fertility and the resulting lessened dependency burden. This is the vicious circle existing in many developing countries. In order to lower fertility, they must modernize; in order to modernize, they must lower fertility.

Age structure has a seond important implication, apart from dictating dependency burden: age structure plays an important role in determining future growth of population. For example, a population that has an expansive pyramid has built into it the potential for substantial future growth. The large numbers of children will age into the childbearing years, resulting in large numbers of potential parents. Even if they have small families, the population will grow, because there are so many parents. Therefore, even if Third World countries reduce their fertility levels substantially, their populations will continue to grow; the legacy of their current age structures have what is termed "demographic momentum" built into them. A similar hypothetical situation is described in the boxed insert on the next page.

The current Canadian structure also has a demographic momentum built into it. As a result of the baby boom, a large percentage of the population is in the early childbearing ages and constitutes the bulge in our pyramid. Therefore, our crude birth rate could increase, not because we are returning to large families, but because there are many people in the childbearing ages. In fact, our crude birth rate has been undergoing a slight increase in recent years.

Sex Structure

The sex structure in a society is a direct result of the action of demographic processes, particularly mortality and migration. Sex structure is usually measured in terms of the **sex ratio**, that is, the number of males per 100 females.

Happy Birthday, Populandia!

The world's newest continent is an island called Populandia, which erupted from the Pacific last year. Blessed with balmy weather and measuring 400 by 400 miles, the unpopulated minicontinent was seen by some as a way to relieve the world's population pressures, and late in 1977 the prestigious World League of Countries (WLC) announced that starting January 1, 1978, all the babies born in the world who represented natural increase (surplus of births over deaths) would be brought up in Populandia.

In January 1978 INTERCOM reported the epochal arrival of the first baby on Populandia. Updates were published in March (when Populandia was already the 32nd largest country in the world.) June (when it gained 22nd place), and September (when it reached 14th place). INTERCOM will continue to report the latest news from Populandia, as the tiny island nation continues to grow inexorably.

Populandia has joined the giants. On January 2, 1978, for about 4/10ths of one second, Populandia had a population of 1: namely, little Beverly Ming, of the Tonga Islands, the first child to arrive on the verdant Pacific minicontinent.

But that was a year ago, right after Populandia was designated by the WLC as the repository of the world's natural increase. At 200,677 new arrivals a day, the Populandian population has mushroomed to 73, 247,105

(as of January 2, 1979) and the infant nation has stormed up through the ranks to become the 10th largest country in the world.

The toll of world population heavyweights now reads as follows: China, India, the Soviet Union, the U.S., Indonesia, Brazil, Japan, Bangladesh. Pakistan, and Populandia. And because all the nations of the world now have stable populations (the result of exporting their natural increase), Populandia can only rise.

Populandia is now growing by 199,177 new arrivals per day, instead of 200,677, an adjustment that takes into account the latest 1978 world figures for natural increase.

There are now about 457 Populandians per square mile – near the density of India – and now that the oldest citizens are beginning to toddle and move about, the island is not quite as spacious as it used to be. The vast nursery domes of tinted glass have sprouted all over the island like mushrooms, and presently, each Popu-

landian (exclusive of support staff) has about 6100 square feet of land area (an area about 78 × 78 feet) to call his or her own.

Of the approximately 122 million children born each year in the world, Populandia receives about 60 percent. Consequently, the International Year of the Child has promoted world interest in the newly created "Pied Piper" country of the Pacific. Besides regular visitors, tourists now flock to Populandia to observe the world's fertility in action and to gasp at the island's unique age structure. And on January 1, the tourists could also marvel at the tinted-glass domes, all aglow with birthday cake candles as the nurses helped little Beverly Ming and some 200,000 other Populandians celebrate their first birthday.

Source:

Intercom, 7, January, 1979:5.

In developed countries, the sex ratio at birth is typically 105. Slightly more male babies are born than female babies. After birth, however, males lose this advantage. By the older ages, women outnumber men by a substantial margin. For example, in Canada the sex ratio at ages sixty-five and over is approximately 76 (76 males per 100 females). The major factor accounting for this changing ratio is mortality. As we have already seen, the life expectancy at birth for males is shorter than that for females.

Sex ratios, particularly in the young working ages, are influenced not only by mortality but by migratory movement. In the past, receiver societies like Canada experienced an excess of males to females, and sender societies an excess of females. On the other hand, internal migration, particularly rural-to-urban migration, has tended to be female-dominated. As a result, cities tend to have sex ratios below 100, with women outnumbering men, and rural areas tend to have sex ratios over 100.

Sex ratio distortion (values of the sex ratio deviating significantly from 100) can have many effects on the wider society. One obvious effect concerns marriage chances. If there is a large excess of one sex relative to the other, the marriage opportunities for the numerically greater sex will be correspondingly lessened. Some people will have to forgo marriage because of a lack of available mates.

Other effects of sex ratio distortion vary from society to society, depending on the role of men and women in the wider social environment. For example, in a society in which productive work is concentrated in the hands of men, a sex ratio in favor of males would facilitate production, all other things being equal. There are, however, societies in which productive work is not defined as a wholly male activity. In such societies, sex ratio distortion would have different effects.

WHAT THE FUTURE HOLDS

We have already seen that in demographic terms the contemporary world can be divided into two camps, the developed societies and the developing societies. Partially as a result of the existing differences, the respective camps face different demographic prospects and issues in the near future.

Developing Societies

The developing societies are growing very rapidly – some would say too rapidly – as a result of high rates of natural increase. To lower the rate of population growth, three possibilities exist:

1. heightened mortality
2. increased emigration
3. lowered fertility

The first possibility is, of course, morally reprehensible as a course of action, one simply does not kill surplus people. The second possibility is not feasible. Where will the emigrants go? In recent years, most developed societies have increased restrictions on immigration. The third possibility – reduced fertility – is the only option available.

How is reduced fertility to be achieved? While this is a crucial question for the future of all of us, attempts to answer it have caused a deep split in both scientific and political circles. The split concerns the relative importance of demographic measures versus economic development in dealing with the problems that the Third World faces.

On one side is the "Neo-Malthusian" school of thought, arguing that family planning programs should be implemented where they do not exist and intensified where they do exist. In other words, the problem facing the Third World is defined as a demographic one of too rapid population growth as a result of too high fertility levels. On the other side is the "development first" school of thought, arguing that economic development of the Third World should be the priority. Their slogan at the 1974 United Nations World Population Meetings was, "Take care of the people, and the population will take care of itself."

As is often the case in such disagreements, neither side is totally wrong or right. The Third World faces the twin problems of rapid population growth and economic underdevelopment. Each reinforces the other, and each makes the other more difficult to solve. Both fertility reduction and economic development must therefore occur in the developing societies. One cannot occur without the other. Fertility is lowered with economic development; economic modernization is facilitated by a fertility decline that will lessen the dependency burden. Attempts to lower fertility in the absence of economic modernization are probably doomed to fail. At the same time, attempts to modernize in the face of current high rates of population growth are self-defeating. Therefore, the answer to the question posed earlier – How is reduced fertility to be achieved? – is two-fold: through intense family planning efforts *and* through economic development.

Developed Societies

The demographic situation in the developed world is entirely different from that in the Third World. Canadian fertility levels, for example, have decreased substantially over the past century. As a result, our future holds stationary growth and an "old" age structure. Stationary growth, or zero population growth, will not occur in Canada for some time yet, because of demographic momentum, the continuation of birth rates that are somewhat higher than death rates, and positive net migration. Nevertheless, stationary growth is, in the long run, inevitable.

Stationary growth is not unique to the future of the developed world. All societies will eventually reach no-growth. Similarly, all societies, before demographic transition, experienced little population growth or none. This situation was caused by high birth and death rates, rather than low birth and death rates, but the result was the same. By contrast, stationary growth in conjunction with an "old" age structure is historically unprecedented. There are no lessons to be learned from the past; the impact of our future demographic regime is somewhat uncertain and subject to speculation.

Here, in the chapter's final section, we will speculate on the future, focusing on some of the economic and social effects that are likely with an "old," no-growth population (Day, 1972). It is important to keep in mind, however, that the characteristics of developed societies in the future are only partially dependent on demography. The way in which societies respond to new demographic situations is as important as the demographic situations themselves. In other words, our future demography will have an impact on the wider social and economic environment, but it will not absolutely determine that environment.

One set of effects concerns the larger percentage of people in the older age groups. On the one hand, that larger percentage implies a greater societal need for, and a greater economic expenditure on, health care facilities. But on the other hand, there is no necessary

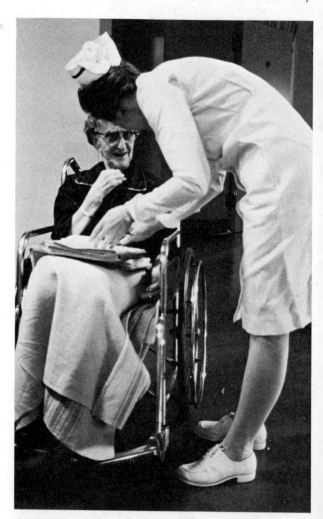

Canada had a baby boom after World War II. As the baby boomers grew up, they overflowed the classrooms. As they grow old, they will place a strain on such things as health care facilities and pension plans.

one-to-one relationship between an increasing elderly population and the need for increased health care. Much will depend upon our health habits. Societal definitions and attitudes toward age and aging may also change. Because age is at least partially defined socially, the behavior of old people could significantly change if expectations and their life conditions were transformed. Attitudinal change in the wider society may make an increasing percentage of old people less of a burden than we might suppose at first glance. In fact, an "old" age structure may lead to a lessened emphasis on age-grading as a defining principle of social organization.

An older population implies an older labor force. Consequently, opportunities for social advancement may be fewer than they are now. At least initially, this probably will be defined as a "social problem." Possible ways to deal with it include altering retirement practices and reappraising our competitive and success-oriented values. A likely demographic consequence of reduced opportunities for social advancement is a lowered rate of internal migration. If there are no better jobs drawing people to new geographical locations, these people will be less likely to move. As a result, the neighborhood and community may become, as in former times, more important aspects of peoples' lives.

Our future demographic situation may also influence the status of women in our society. Again, it is not possible to predict the demographic impact with any certainty, as much depends upon our social and cultural responses, but it does seem that developed societies like Canada face a future where a higher percentage of women will experience fewer and shorter child-care obligations, or none at all. Some lessening of child-care obligations has already occurred, and the female response has been to take on other roles, particularly the worker role. A continuation and intensification of female labor force participation therefore seems likely, and as the female gender role changes, so will the male gender role, at least in the long run. As the roles of men and women become more similar, we might expect a narrowing of the gap between them in prestige and power. This is, of course, no foregone conclusion and will depend to a large degree on changes in our value structure.

Finally, one issue often raised concerns the effect of stationary population growth on the wider economy. Does stationary population growth imply stationary economic growth? Not necessarily. Economic growth, stagnation, and decline are all possible with a stationary population. The type of economic situation that will arise depends more on the soundness of economic policies than on any specific demographic characteristics (Espenshade, 1978).

SUMMARY

1. The study of population, or demography, is intimately related to the study of society. Within demography, the important areas of study are the three demographic processes of fertility, mortality, and migration. Together, they determine population growth. Singly or in combination, they determine population composition and distribution.

2. The components of growth are natural increase and net migration.

3. Population growth in Canada reveals a history of unevenness. Natural increase has been the major component of our growth with net migration playing a variable role over time.

4. There are three major theories of population growth. Dominant at present is demographic transition theory. Based on the historical experience of the west, it provides a three-stage model of population change, with rapid growth occurring in the second state.

5. Fertility is an important element of population growth, affecting the rate of natural increase. Fertility is assessed by two types of measurement: period and cohort.

6. Fertility in Canada declined over the course of this century, with the exception of the period known as the baby boom. Variations in fertility level result from the combined action of four types of factors: demographic, cultural, socioeconomic, and governmental factors.

7. Mortality acts jointly with fertility in determining rate of natural increase.

8. As a population undergoes mortality reduction, the causes of death change.

9. Within societies, differentials in mortality exist. Women outlive men; married people have higher life expectancies than persons in other marital statuses; minority groups experience higher mortality than the national average.

10. Migration is the movement of persons from one geographical location to another. Migration is of two types: internal and international.

11. Four periods of immigration in Canada can be identified, each differing in volume and type of immigrants. Emigration from Canada, for the most part, has been to the United States.

12. Fertility level is the major determinant of age structure. The three types of age structures, graphically represented in population pyramids, are: expansive, constrictive, and stationary.

13. Age structure dictates dependency ratio or dependency burden, which plays an important role in economic development.

14. In the near future, developing and developed societies face different population issues and prospects.

GLOSSARY

Age-specific birth rate. Incidence of births in a given year per 1000 women of a given age group. The rates are calculated for five-year age groups.

Age structure. Pertaining to population, the proportion of people in each age category.

Composition. The characteristics of people in a population, particularly age and gender.

Crude rate. Frequency of an event per unit of the total population, usually 1000. Applied especially to deaths and births.

Demographic transition theory. Description and explanation of the three-stage transition or shift from high birth and death rates to low birth and death rates.

Demography. Scientific study of population.

Dependency ratio. Ratio of the economically dependent population (under fifteen, and sixty-five and over) to the productive population (fifteen to sixty-four).

Distribution. The geographical location of people.

Doubling time. Number of years it would take for a population to double its present size, given the current rate of population growth.

Fecundity. Physiological capacity for a woman or a group of women to produce children.

Fertility. Actual childbearing performance of a woman or

group of women; an important component of population change.

General fertility rate. The incidence of births in a given year per 1000 women between the ages of fifteen and forty-nine.

Growth rate. Number of people added to or subtracted from a population in a given period for every 100 or 1000 total population.

Migration. Movement of people from one geographical locale to another; can be either internal or international.

Mortality. Occurrence of deaths in a population; an important component of population change.

Natural fertility. Term used to refer to fertility that is lower than the biological maximum level, as the result of behavior not aimed deliberately at reducing childbearing.

Natural increase. Excess of births over deaths in a population during a given time period.

Negative growth. Term applied to a population that is decreasing.

Net migration. Difference between the number of in-migrants and the number of out-migrants.

Positive growth. Term applied to a population that is increasing.

Sex ratio. Number of males per 100 females in a population.

Size. The number of people, the population in a given area.

FURTHER READING

Beaujot, Roderic, and Kevin McQuillan. *Growth and Dualism: The Demographic Development of Canadian Society.* Toronto: Gage, 1982. An excellent introduction to population issues in Canada, with separate chapters on regionalism and linguistic balance.

Bouma, Gary D., and Wilma J. Bouma. *Fertility Control: Canada's Lively Social Problem.* Don Mills: Longman, 1975. A short, readable inventory of the controversial issues surrounding birth control in Canada at the present time.

Foot, David K. *Canada's Population Outlook: Demographic Futures and Economic Challenges.* Toronto: James Lorimer, in association with the Canadian Institute for Economic Policy, 1982. A recent book on Canadian demography, focusing on future demographic characteristics and their relationship to economic and policy issues.

Grindstaff, Carl F. *Population and Society: A Sociological Perspective.* West Hanover, Mass.: Christopher Publishing, 1981. A book about Canadian population that places population variables in the context of the wider society.

Kalbach, Warren E., and Wayne W. McVey. *The Demographic Bases of Canadian Society,* 2nd ed. Toronto: McGraw-Hill Ryerson, 1979. Provides descriptions of major demographic characteristics of Canadian society, with chapters on ethnicity, religion, education, labor force, family, and housing.

Overbeek, Johannes. *Population and Canadian Society.* Toronto: Butterworths, 1980. A short book on the Canadian population, describing our major demographic characteristics.

United Nations. *Determinants and Consequences of Population Trends*, Volume 1. New York: United Nations, Department of Economic and Social Affairs, 1973. A comprehensive synthesis of findings on the relationship between population trends and social and economic factors in both developing and developed societies.

Weinstein, Jay A. *Demographic Transition and Social Change.* Morristown, N.J.: General Learning, 1976. A short, easy-to-read book providing a sociological perspective on the relationship between population growth and social change.

CHAPTER 8
SOCIAL INEQUALITY

R. OGMUNDSON

Many of the readings you are asked to do at university deal with topics which are of interest to a very limited number of people. That is definitely not the case with the topics discussed here. While you are reading this chapter, it is likely that somebody somewhere is being killed because his or her opinions about social inequality happen to differ from those of someone else. On a larger scale, riots and revolutions are continually taking place, partly because those involved seriously disagree about the topics we will discuss in the following pages. If there is a Third World War, a leading cause of that war will almost certainly be ideological disputes between capitalists and communists about what brings about **social inequality** and what can be done about it.

Inequality is, apparently, a universal characteristic of social life. This inequality takes many forms: economic – some people have more money than others; social – some people are more popular than others; political – some people are more able to have their own way than others; physical – some people are taller, stronger, or better looking. The potential list of examples is almost endless.

At this point, you might well be tempted to ask:

"Why so much inequality?" Students of society have been discussing this question for thousands of years, but they have yet to agree why inequality is an apparently universal characteristic of human societies and what, if anything, can be done about it. Their disagreement stems from three sources: value judgments, interests, and scientific beliefs.

Value judgments about inequality differ. Some people feel that there is nothing seriously wrong with the inequality they see around them. Consequently, they feel that there is no serious need for change. Others disagree. They feel that inequality is thoroughly unfair. Consequently, these people favor changes. Those who oppose inequality also disagree among themselves about how far inequality should be reduced. Some would be satisfied with a moderate reduction of some types of inequality (free university education for example). Others would be satisfied only if we were all the same in as many respects as possible (for example, that we all wear the same clothes and adopt the same hair styles).

So people disagree about inequality partly because they make different value judgments about what is right and what is wrong. They also disagree because they have different **interests** to pursue. Those who are well off tend to think that things are fine just the way they are. Those who think they would benefit from a change tend to think that major changes would be a good idea. The type of change favored by an individual or group tends to correspond with the interests of that individual or group. Your sociology professors, for example, might think it is a fine idea to decrease the salaries of business executives and to increase those of factory workers. It is unlikely, however, that they would favor a reduction of their own salaries so that your student fees could be reduced!

Yet another basis of disagreement has to do with different **scientific beliefs** about the causes of social inequality. This is where the sociologist comes in. Remember that in Chapter 1 we learned that the expertise of sociologists does not qualify them to make value judgments concerning inequality which are any better than those of anyone else. Similarly, sociology professors have no more right to advance their own interests than you do. Nonetheless, the sociologist *can*

tell us what the major schools of thought on social inequality are. Furthermore, the sociologist *can* tell you what some of the facts are about inequality in Canada. What follows, then, will give you a brief overview of what sociologists have to say about social inequality.

THEORETICAL PERSPECTIVES

Theories about social inequality are similar to those about society generally. In fact, much general sociological theory began with an attempt to explain the specific phenomenon of inequality. We learned in Chapter 1 that major sociological theories can be divided into two general categories – macro and micro. In the case of social inequality, micro theories, while not irrelevant, are rarely used. We will focus, therefore, on the macro theories.

It is customary and convenient to divide macro theoretical perspectives on social inequality into two major schools, the radical and the conservative (Lenski, 1966). Briefly, the **radical perspective** is opposed to inequality; the **conservative perspective** supports it. These views go back a long way. An example of the radical view can be found in the Old Testament account from around the year 800 B.C. of the Hebrew prophets Amos, Micah, and Isaiah who denounced wealth and privilege in the society of their time. A clear example of the conservative view can be found in Hindu texts from around the year 200 B.C. in which Manu, the great lawgiver, proclaimed that social inequality was ordained by God for the good of the people. These two basic views can be traced through intellectual history from these dates to the present day (Lenski, 1966).

Contemporary radical and conservative theories are similar to those which preceded them in that they are largely **normative**. In other words, they concern themselves mainly with making value judgments about how things *should* be. They also depend heavily on making their case through the use of *deductive logic* (a form of reasoning in which particular conclusions are drawn from general principles). As noted in Chapter

1, differing views such as these survive because each illuminates some aspect of reality. However, they are limited in that they only consider part of reality and in that they do not take us much further than we were 2000 years ago.

Recently, there has been an attempt to go beyond these traditional approaches and to study inequality in a systematic, empirical fashion. This new approach tries to create a theoretical **synthesis** drawn from the best parts of the two traditional views. This approach also attempts to be analytic rather than normative. In other words, it attempts to determine what the truth *is* not what truth *should* be. This more recent approach depends as much on *inductive logic* (a form of reasoning in which general conclusions are drawn from knowledge of specific facts) as on deductive logic. It also tries to be scientific, in the naturalist sense, in its evaluation of theoretical statements about inequality.

We shall now discuss the three theoretical perspectives in turn: radical, conservative, and synthesis. After that, we will outline some of the facts concerning inequality in our society.

THE RADICAL PERSPECTIVE

The radical perspective is represented in contemporary sociology by **conflict theory**. Remember that this theory emphasizes the divergent interests to be found in any society, the conflict that necessarily takes place, and the role of coercion in maintaining social order. It views inequality as the result of the domination and exploitation of some groups by other groups. It emphasizes the injustice of inequality and suggests that something be done in an attempt to reduce it.

Marxism

According to Marxists, the key to understanding inequality lies in an understanding of material (i.e., economic) factors. This position is known as **materialism**. The basic argument in favor of this position runs something like this. We must eat in order to survive. Hence, the first activity of our species must be eco-

nomic. Only when our stomachs are full can we worry about relatively secondary matters, such as reproduction, defense, government, or art. Economic activity, therefore, is at the very base of all our other activity. Furthermore, since work takes up so much of our time and energy (both individually and collectively), it more or less determines the nature of everything else we do. Consequently, the first task of the student of human activity must be to analyze the material basis of that activity.

In order to understand economic activity, Marxists find it useful to make a number of distinctions. To begin with, the initial basis of any economic activity may be referred to as the "means of production." The means of production consist of land (i.e., natural resources of all types), labor, and capital. This distinction is not at all unique to **Marxism**. Those of you who are taking economics courses may realize that conventional economists refer to these same three elements as the "factors of production" (e.g., Samuelson, 1964). However, the Marxist approach also distinguishes two other important elements of economic activity – the "forces of production" and the "relations of production." The forces of production are the physical and social technology (e.g., tools, machines, organization) used in the productive economic activity of a given society. The relations of production are the social organization of economic activity. This organization determines who has the authority to give orders and to make decisions. In particular, it also determines how the benefits of a society's economic activity are distributed. The combination of these two elements – the technical nature of economic activity (forces of production) and the social nature of economic activity (relations of production) – is referred to by Marxists as the "mode of production."

Marxists argue that, throughout written history, the relations of production have typically been organized in such a way that a relatively few people have been able to enjoy a highly disproportionate amount of the wealth produced by the labor of the many. In the past, they say, a privileged few (e.g., emperors, kings, capitalists) have been able to live in the lap of luxury while the bulk of those who do almost all the work (e.g., slaves, serfs, workers) have been forced to live in conditions of poverty and degradation. Marxists have no difficulty making the value judgment that this inequality is outrageously unjust. Consequently, they argue that the relations of production should be changed as soon as possible. From the point of view of Marxist values and analysis, such changes are sufficiently important and desirable to justify any amount of violence and disruption that may be necessary.

According to Marxist theory, this task is initially complicated by the fact that the material substructure of society (i.e., the mode of production) is thought to determine not only the distribution of wealth, but also the political, cultural, and military affairs of a society (the "superstructure"). The wealthy few discussed earlier are able to use their money not just to enjoy themselves, but also to dominate the affairs of an entire society. They are able to control the impoverished many, because they can use their wealth to buy soldiers, policemen, professors, priests, and civil servants to perform that task for them. Hence, the dominant economic class is thought to form also a **ruling class**. (Chapter 13 contains a thorough discussion of the flow of influence from the substructures to the superstructure and back again.)

More generally, the mode of production is thought to be such a powerful force that it determines the overall nature of society for entire historical epochs. Everything – war, politics, art, music, the family – may be understood as an outgrowth of the class structure and the class struggle.

Marx argued that all of human history could best be analyzed in terms of the dominant modes of production (i.e., ancient civilizations, feudalism, and capitalism), the consequent class structure, and in turn the consequent class struggle:

The history of all hitherto existing society is the history of class struggles (Marx, 1969).

It follows from this analysis that it is not as easy as one might think initially to change the relations of production. An entire society must be completely reorganized if this goal is to be achieved. Such major changes generally require revolution, not reform. And successful revolutions are not easily arranged.

However, Marxist theory also takes the problem of change into account. Indeed, change is viewed not only as being possible, but as being inevitable. Revolutionary change is seen as inevitable because the Marxist believes that each mode of production contains within itself the seeds of its own destruction. Just as ancient civilizations gave way to feudalism, and just as feudalism gave way to capitalism, so will capitalism give way to communism. Marx (1969) put it this way:

The bourgeoisie cannot exist without constantly revolutionizing the instruments of production and thereby the relations of production, and with them the whole relations of society . . . What the bourgeoisie therefore produces, above all, are its own grave-diggers. Its fall and the victory of the proletariat are equally inevitable.

To put it another way, just as one idea (a thesis) tends to give rise to a critique (an antithesis), and thereby stimulates the emergence of yet another set of ideas (the synthesis), so do modes of production also evolve. Marx borrowed the term *dialectic* from Hegel, a German philosopher, to describe the process he believed took place. Hegel had applied the word to the evolution of ideas. When you apply the word to material matters, it is called "dialectical materialism." The Marxist approach argues that the material processes analyzed by the dialectical materialism perspective will eventually destroy the present mode of production. Consequently, the Marxist is not discouraged by the apparent difficulty in changing the relations of production in any specific historical situation. The role of the revolutionary is merely to accelerate processes already in motion.

Class Structure. In the case of countries like Canada, Marxists would feel their task is to speed up the process of transition from the present mode of production – capitalism – to the next mode of production – communism. They begin by analyzing the capitalist class structure. In addition to the bourgeoisie who possess capital and who are thus able to employ other people, and the proletariat, who work for wages, there is an intermediate class of people called the "petite bourgeoisie" who work only for themselves and generally do not employ others (i.e., artisans, independent farmers and fishermen, small businessmen). An underclass of unemployed people who do not work for wages at all is identified as the "lumpenproletariat."

It is important to note here that Marxist class position is determined by relationship to the productive process and not by relationship to the distributive process. For example, in traditional Marxist thought, a business executive earning a salary of $100 000. a year is considered a member of the proletariat, while an independent businessman making an annual profit of $10 000. is classified as a member of the petite bourgeoisie.

Finally, Marxists recognize that, in specific historical circumstances, there may also be remnants of classes from previous historical periods, such as aristocratic landowners and peasants. Notwithstanding the complications presented by the other classes, it is thought that the role of these remnants is secondary and that they will eventually pass from the scene. To quote Marx again (1969):

Society as a whole is more and more splitting up into two great hostile camps, into two great classes directly facing each other – bourgeoisie and proletariat.

The relationship between the two major classes, therefore – between the owners and workers – is felt to be the key to an understanding of capitalist society. The economic relationship between these two classes is analyzed according to the labor theory of value.

Labor Theory of Value.

In Marxist theory, the central economic relationship in capitalist society is that between capital and labor; workers exchange their labor for wages, while capitalists exchange their money for the work done. Marxists argue that the terms of this exchange are always unfair, and therefore the entire economic system is based on the **exploitation** of workers by capitalists. A crucial theory in the Marxist position on exploitation is called the **labor theory of value**. This theory argues that the value of a commodity is determined by the labor that goes into it. If this is so, it follows, according to Marxist value judgment, that workers should receive virtually all the returns for the value their labor has created. However, in a capitalist society the owners appropriate part of the benefits of production for themselves in the form of profits. Consequently, a worker's wages represent

only a fraction of the value that worker has created. For example, a worker might produce commodities worth $1000 a day but be paid only $100 a day. Indeed, Marx (1969) argued that workers would not receive even a moderate portion of the value they created, but would receive only enough to keep them alive:

Hence, the cost of production of a workman is restricted, almost entirely to the means of subsistence that he requires for his maintenance, and for the propagation of his race.

The remainder, or what is left after workers get their share, is called the "rate of surplus value," and it goes to the capitalist. Thus, concludes Marx (1969), "In the selfsame relations in which wealth is produced, poverty is produced also. . . ."

However, this very process, so central to the operation of capitalism, is thought likely to contribute ultimately to its downfall. Because underpaid workers cannot afford to buy everything they produce, capitalism is subject to periodic crises of overproduction and consequent unemployment leading to recession or depression. This spawns a pattern of ruthless competition among capitalists, which eventually reduces their number and concentrates their wealth in fewer and fewer hands. This, in turn, sets the scene for revolution.

Revolution.

Marxists predict that revolution will ultimately take place in mature capitalist societies. They expect the process to work something like this: As the economy evolves, the classes that complicate the political picture (the aristocrats, the peasants, the petite bourgeoisie) will disappear. Most of the people formerly in these classes will become members of a growing proletariat. This leaves the two major classes in a state of outright confrontation – the workers against the bourgeoisie.

As the process of business competition bankrupts more and more people (especially during the periodic economic crises), the capitalist class will become smaller and more homogeneous. As the competition turns increasingly ruthless, the rate of profit falls. In order to survive, the remaining capitalists must exploit their workers more and more efficiently and the workers will become increasingly *immiserated*. In other words, their standard of living will deteriorate both economically and psychologically.

Then, as urbanization takes place, the differences in wealth between the workers and their employers will become more and more visible. Furthermore, the workers, gathered together in huge factories and in slum neighborhoods, will be able to communicate more freely with each other. This communication will also be aided by the increasingly similar nature of their work. Gradually, an understanding of their true economic interests will emerge. As they talk among themselves, their **false consciousness** (and their concern abvout their racial, ethnic, or sexual differences) will dissolve. This false consciousness will be replaced by a **class consciousness**. The workers will come to believe that their position is neither inevitable nor just, and they will band together as an economic and political group in an effort to improve their lives.

As the time for change draws near, Marx (1969) predicted, the bourgeoisie itself will begin to fall apart. In particular, some of the brightest and best bourgeois intellectuals will join the proletariat and provide it with intellectual leadership. Sooner or later, all these various factors combine. The result is inevitable – revolution. Capitalism (the private ownership of the means of production) will be replaced by socialism (the collective ownership of the means of production).

After the upheaval of the revolution, Marxists believe there will have to be a brief dictatorship of the proletariat led by party officials and intellectuals who understand what is good for the workers. During this period, "reactionary," or bourgeois, elements will be eliminated, and the new socialist society set up. After this, however, the state will wither away because there will be no ruling class for it to serve. Within the Marxist vision, this new historical epoch based on the socialist mode of production will be unlike all the previous historical epochs. There will be no class division, no class struggle, and no further evolution of the mode of production.

Theoretical Criticisms of Marxism.
Marxist theory has been criticized from every conceivable angle. Those who would make some variation on the argument that "man does not live by bread alone" criticize the initial materialist assumptions of Marxism, insisting

that non-materialist factors are also very important to the explanation of human behavior.

Perhaps the most prominent exponent of this view has been Max Weber (1930), who argues that the very emergence of capitalism was largely due to religious beliefs. Similarly, Andreski (1968) has maintained that another non-materialist factor, the nature of military activity in a given society, is an important determinant of its degree of inequality.

Still others have maintained that Marx neglected the importance of the fact that natural resources (one of the means of production) are limited and differentially distributed, and that this influences the distribution of wealth. It could be argued, for example, that the present wealth of many Arab countries is related to the location of the world oil supply.

Still others claim that the role of technology (i.e., the forces of production) is a much more important determinant of the degree of inequality in human society than the relations of production (e.g., Lenski, 1966). Some believe that human societies require political organization in order to survive, and that it is therefore impossible for the state to wither away as Marx predicted. Indeed, it has even been argued that political organization requires inequality of authority (e.g., Wesolowski, 1969) and that inequality of authority will inevitably lead to economic and social inequality. People like Mosca (1939) and Michels (1962) have predicted that those who gain control of the state during the dictatorship of the proletariat will not voluntarily relinquish their power and privilege, but will set themselves up as a new ruling class.

There have been more specific criticisms. For example, the basic premise of the labor theory of value has been challenged. It has been argued that the value of goods depends not only on the amount of labor that goes into them, but also on the skill of the worker. For example, one student might work for 25 hours and produce an A paper, while another might work for 50 hours and produce a B paper. In particular, it has been argued that the value of a commodity depends, not on the work that has been put into it, but rather on its utility as measured by what consumers are willing to pay for it (the utility theory of value). Another specific criticism has been that of Dahrendorf (1959) who maintained that Marx misunderstood the nature

In both Marxist and capitalist societies, a few people control a large share of the wealth. They direct economic activity, hire workers, and decide wages. With control comes power, the power to determine the distribution of further wealth.

of property and ownership, and that property is merely a special case of the more general phenomenon of authority. Hence, argues Dahrendorf, the central class conflict is between those in different authority positions, not between owners and workers.

Yet another specific criticism is that of Adler-Karlsson (1970) who has argued that property consists of a collection of specific rights, not an indivisible whole, and that the relations of production can thereby be transformed by a policy of reform. Furthermore, Geiger (1969) claims that the economy dominates the political superstructure only in those relatively few specific historical circumstances in which it is allowed to develop according to its own internal dynamics. Finally, Djilas (1957), a former prominent Yugoslavian Marxist, has argued that the collectivization of the rights of property does not give power to the people, but rather to a new privileged stratum:

Ownership is nothing other than the right of profit and control. If one defines class benefits by this right, the Communist states have seen, in the final analysis, the origin of a new form of ownership or of a new ruling and exploiting class.

We do not have the space here to consider more of the theoretical criticisms of Marxism. They are innumerable. And they are aided by the facts that Marx himself never systematically outlined his ideas on class, that he was apparently inconsistent on some key points, and that contemporary Marxists take different positions on similar issues. In one way, it is often possible to show that Marx was inconsistent and/or wrong on some particular point. But in another way, it is frequently possible for a Marxist to reply that the critic misunderstands the true Marxist position.

Empirical Criticisms of Marxism. In Chapter 1, we learned that one characteristic of Marxism is its attempt to be historically specific. This makes it easier to evaluate the validity of Marxist thought. Marxists are able to point with pride to the many predictions that have come true: social groups characteristic of the feudal epoch have certainly declined; the petite bourgeoisie has declined; capitalism has been characterized by periodic economic crises; urbanization has taken place; and there have been many successful Marxist revolutions.

Conversely, critics of Marxism can identify several aspects of the modern world that have not evolved as Marx predicted: the working class has not been economically immiserated – instead, its standard of living has risen spectacularly; there is no evidence that working-class people are any more unhappy than they ever were; the working class has become more heterogeneous in skill and status levels; and Marxist revolutions have taken place mainly in underdeveloped countries – not in mature capitalist ones as Marx predicted. Furthermore, Marxist societies have not become classless societies, except in a Marxist sense. The degree of inequality is almost as great in Marxist societies as in capitalist ones. In particular, the state in Marxist societies has not withered away but has become much stronger – thus apparently supporting the opinions of people like Mosca (1939), Michels (1962), and Djilas (1965).

To many of these criticisms, Marxists often reply that the complete evolution has not yet taken place. The critic is asked to withhold final judgment. On some other matters, there is major debate. For example, there is no doubt that a major new social stratum of relatively well paid and well educated white-collar workers has appeared. Critics of Marxism consider this to be a new middle class which is replacing the petite bourgeoisie in capitalist society. Marxists reply that, since these members of the new middle class now work for wages, they have been "proletarianized" and are now part of the working class.

Similarly, there is no doubt that a significant stratum of managers and technical experts has emerged in today's large corporation. Critics of Marxism argue that the managers and/or the technostructure are now the people who make the decisions of modern business and that this has largely changed the face of capitalism (e.g., Galbraith, 1967). Most Marxists (e.g., Clement, 1975), though not all (e.g., Wright, 1978), reply that the owners are still in charge and that nothing important has changed.

Social Democracy

Marxism is not the only radical theory of inequality. It may not even be the best one. But it is clearly the most important, and so we have spent a great deal of time on it. There is one other radical theory we should consider briefly – **social democracy**.

Social democrats take positions which are, in many respects, very similar to Marxists. In particular, they share the value judgment that contemporary inequalities are unjustifiable, and they share the theoretical view that capitalist relations of production are the key to the problem of inequality in capitalist societies. However, the two views differ considerably in at least two important ways: in certain value judgments and in theory.

Theoretically, the Marxist views property as an *indivisible* bundle of rights and privileges. It follows that if the evils believed to be caused by capitalism are to be eliminated, the institution of private property must be destroyed all at once. As pointed out earlier, this almost certainly requires violent revolution. Conversely, the social democrat views property as a *divisible* collection of separate rights and privileges. It follows from this theoretical position that it is possible to eliminate these rights and privileges one by one as the need for change presents itself. From the social democratic point of view, therefore, it is theoretically possible to change the relations of production through a process of reform. So far as values are concerned, Marxists condone physical or psychological violence as a means for advancing their theories. The social democrat, on the other hand, is far more reluctant to resort to such violence (Adler-Karlsson, 1970). Consequently, the Marxist is more likely to favor revolution; the social democrat, reform.

Social democrats would argue that the wisdom of their approach is demonstrated by the fact that the available data seem to indicate that the peacefully achieved equality of social democratic societies is approximately the same as the violently achieved equality of Marxist societies.

THE CONSERVATIVE PERSPECTIVE

We have just examined at length the radical perspective on social inequality. It may be contrasted to the conservative perspective which we will discuss in this section. The conservative perspective emphasizes the mutual interests to be found in any society, the cooperation that necessarily takes place, and the role of common values in maintaining social order. It views inequality as being the inevitable result of the division of labor required to produce goods and services for the benefit of everyone. In contemporary sociology, the most prominent exposition of this perspective is **structural functionalism**. In Chapter 1, you examined structural functionalism at some length. Here, we will review the theory and discuss the structural functionalist explanation of inequality.

Structural Functionalism

Structural functionalists analyze inequality in much the same way we would analyze a piece of machinery, a computer, or a living organism. First, they try to outline the parts of the system and determine how the parts interconnect (the structure). Then they try to describe how the system behaves (the process). Finally, they look at a given social phenomenon and decide what function it appears to serve. For example, inequality obviously exists, and structural functionalists search for a reason to explain its existence.

The structural functionalist explanation of inequality runs something like this. In order to survive, a society must insure that certain needs are met. Obviously, one such need is economic – we must eat in order to survive. However, there are other needs as well. For example, there is a need for defense against enemies, for reproduction and the nurture of children, and for the care of the sick. Furthermore, political, religious, educational, and cultural needs also seem to exist. If all these needs are to be met, people must be assigned specific tasks.

Some of these tasks are dangerous (protecting the country, coal mining); others are difficult (performing a ballet, doing surgery); while others are unpleasant (cleaning latrines, castrating bulls). In all but the most primitive societies, specialized positions are created for the performance of such tasks (e.g., soldier, farmer, doctor, homemaker). Some of these positions (e.g.,

university president) are more important and/or more difficult than others (e.g., janitor). According to the structural functionalist view, people in all these positions must perform their tasks competently if a society is to prosper.

However, it is especially important that those in critical positions (e.g., general, prime minister) perform well. If this social need is to be met, people must first be motivated to undergo any training necessary for the competent performance of difficult tasks, and then be motivated to apply themselves conscientiously once they have the job for which they are qualified.

But the question arises: how are people motivated to undertake the more demanding tasks of a society? The structural functionalist reply is that motivation for the performance of difficult jobs is provided by unequal rewards. For example, they would say that your work at university is motivated, to a crucial degree, by the belief that you will some day be rewarded for it. The love of knowledge alone, they say, is unlikely to be sufficient to inspire your best performance.

According to the structural functionalist, the unequal rewards given to different social positions are a result of variations in both the social need for the service and in the supply of people available to provide that service. For example, the demand for people who can shine shoes is low, while the supply of people who can do the job is high. Consequently, rewards for shoe-shiners don't amount to much. Conversely, the demand for people who can rescue a failing company from bankruptcy (or write a hit song) is high, while the supply of people who can do the job is low. Consequently, rewards for such services are substantial.

The structural functionalist also maintains that reward levels for specific occupations differ from one society to another, because of the varying needs of different societies. Similarly, reward levels for entire social groups may also rise and fall within a given society as its needs change. For example, soldiers are likely to receive greater rewards during wars than during times of peace. These rewards need not be material, they may also be psychological in substance – prestige or popularity, for example. A priest might receive a low income but enjoy high prestige in his community. Nonetheless, inequality of rewards, of whatever kind, is thought to be necessary if performance in key positions is to be adequate. Adequate performance in these positions is necessary if a society is to survive and prosper. Hence, social inequality is necessary, inevitable, and functionally positive.

Criticisms of Structural Functionalism.

Structural functionalism, like Marxism, has been subjected to severe criticism from a number of sources. Since its most famous expositions have been cast at a very abstract level (Davis and Moore, 1945), structural functionalism has been difficult to criticize empirically in the way that Marxism can be criticized. Although it has been shown that its central propositions could be subject to empirical research (Stinchcombe, 1963), very little such research has been done. The initial results of this research tend to give moderate, though tentative and debatable, support to the structural functionalist position (e.g., Cullen and Novick, 1979).

Theoretical criticisms of structural functionalism, however, have been voluminous. It has been pointed out, for example, that human societies are not nearly so tightly organized as the systems found in machines and bodies. Hence, the implicit analogy can be misleading. Furthermore, just as the human body may have parts (e.g., the appendix) that serve no function at all or which may, in fact, be bad for the body (e.g., the ruptured appendix), so human society may also contain pehenomenon that are neither necessary nor positive (Merton, 1957).

Take slavery, for example. Conservatives used to argue that the universality of the institution of slavery indicated that slavery was necessary and inevitable. Subsequent events, however, have proven this to be incorrect. Hence, the mere existence of a phenomenon does not prove that it is necessary. Similarly, the existence of a phenomenon does not mean that it is automatically good for a society; it could be unhealthy or **dysfunctional**. Some critics (e.g., Tumin, 1953) point to the inequality of opportunity that is found in most societies as an example of such dysfunction. They argue that key positions can become filled with the lazy and stupid children of the privileged, because the bright and energetic offspring of ordinary people are not given a fair chance. Hence, through the same logic

outlined earlier, the society could suffer, because of the incompetent leadership made possible through inequality of opportunity.

Another theoretical criticism of structural functionalism has to do with the idea that two different, but "functionally equivalent," social mechanisms may be able to perform the same function in the same way that two different machines might perform the same function. For example, both a truck and a train can be used for transportation. Consequently, even if one agrees that people must receive extra motivation to perform difficult tasks, it does not inexorably follow that they can be motivated only by unequal material rewards. In theory at least, people could also be motivated on other bases: duty, honor, love, desire for power, enjoyment of work, and so forth (see Wesolowski, 1969). Besides, even if we grant that some inequality in material reward is necessary to motivate people, it does not follow that this inequality need be as great as is found in most societies. Therefore structural functional theory cannot be used as a scientific justification of extreme disparities of reward. (This is a point that structural functionalists readily concede, saying that they never argued for it in the first place.)

Finally, various criticisms of a more specific nature have been leveled at structural functionalism. It has been argued, for example, that it is no great hardship to undergo training for highly rewarded positions (e.g., to be a university student), when the alternative is to work for a living like everyone else. It has been argued in a similar way that reward levels often depend on factors other than functional importance. For example, nurses in Canada were able to demand (and get) much higher salaries after they unionized. The increase in their salaries seems attributable, not to the increased functional importance of nurses, but rather to the increased economic and political power provided by unionization.

To such criticisms, structural functionalists often reply that they have been misunderstood (Davis and Moore, 1945). In particular, they argue that their critics have confused the question of allocating rewards to positions (which we will discuss later under the heading "Inequality of Condition" (with the question of allocating individuals to positions (which we will discuss later under the heading "Inequality of Opportunity"). They say that their theory applies only to the first question and not to the second. They also point out that they took non-material rewards into account in their original theory.

Nonetheless, structural functionalists have conceded the validity of some of the points made by their critics. Notwithstanding these concessions, they point to the stubborn fact that inequality is everywhere, even in communes, *kibbutzim*, and revolutionary societies designed to eliminate such inequality. They maintain that this central phenomenon demands explanation, and that their theory is as good as anything yet developed. They invite others to do better (Moore, 1963).

One of the most powerful critiques of the standard structural functionalist position, by the Polish sociologist Wesolowski (1969), concluded with the argument that if there is a functional necessity for inequality, it has to do with the apparent social need for the unequal allocation of authority. (See also Tumin, 1953). If authority must be unequally distributed, what is to prevent those with authority from using their position to obtain unequal material and social privileges? This is a question for which no one in the radical perspective seems to have worked out a satisfactory answer.

Biosociology

Structural functionalism is the most important of the conservative theories concerning inequality in contemporary sociology. Less important – but still deserving some consideration – is the theory known as **biosociology**.

Throughout history, conservatives have tended to argue that inequality is the result of human nature. They take the position that, "Some are more equal than others." If you maintain this position, it follows that the degree of inequality cannot be changed significantly because we do not, as yet, know how to change human nature. Radicals, of course, have replied that this is all nonsense and that undesirable human behavior (incuding inequality) stems from the nature of social institutions. If you take this latter position, you can then argue that the degree of inequality can

be altered by changing social arrangements. This theoretical debate has been conducted throughout most of human history, mainly from the armchairs of the various protagonists.

Recently, however, scientists have embarked upon the empirical study of human nature and of the nature of other animal species. So far, the results have appeared to support the conservative view. Almost all animal societies, including those most closely related to humans, display clear patterns of territorial, hierarchical, and gender inequality. Human societies also display these patterns. Biosociologists argue that this provides evidence that human inequality probably has a genetic basis. Egalitarians, however, challenge the validity of the inference and argue that humans are so different from other animals that this kind of data is irrelevant. Biosociologists reply that such an opinion of ourselves is excessively conceited.

SYNTHESIS

During this discussion of the radical and conservative views of social inequality, you may have noticed that Marxism received a more generous exposition to criticism ratio than did structural functionalism. Marxism also received almost twice as much space as the conservative viewpoint. You might well argue that there has been unequal treatment of the opposing viewpoints. In this you would be correct. This unequal treatment of the two views has become standard among the contemporary generation of sociologists. The previous generation did the same thing, but in reverse: structural functionalism was emphasized, while Marxism was criticized. It is to be hoped that future generations of sociologists will transcend this fluctuation between two viewpoints that are essentially thousands of years old. If they do, it will be because the kinds of theories we discuss in the next section will have received further development.

The third major theoretical perspective on inequality might be labelled "synthesis" (or for those who may be doubtful about the achievement, "attempt at synthesis"). In Hegelian terms, the conservative view might be seen as the *thesis,* the radical view as an *antithesis,* and subsequent views as *synthesis* (Lenski,

1966). These subsequent views attempt to do just that – to produce a whole new approach made up of the best parts of the previous major views.

Weber

Perhaps the most influential attempt at synthesis was provided by Max Weber, who was under the influence of both the idealism of Hegel and the materialism of Marx. Weber agreed with Marx on many important matters, incuding the idea that a basic key to the explanation of human societies lay in economic or material considerations. He also agreed that the relationship of the propertied to the non-propertied was a central one. Weber (1969) stated, for example, that " 'Property' and 'lack of property' are . . . the basic categories of all class situations." Nevertheless, he was also of the opinion that the Marxist approach over-simplified matters and was, as a result, somewhat incomplete. In particular, Weber felt that Marx over-emphasized the role of material factors. In his own work, therefore, Weber attempted to provide a more complete overview of human society.

To begin with, Weber argued that the worker-employee relationship was not the only significant one in the economic sphere. There were at least two others: the relationship of creditors to debtors, and the relationship of producers to consumers. For Weber, the questions of high interest rates ("usury") and the "just price" of things were as likely to be important as the question of "fair wage." The practical importance of these economic relationships would probably vary from one concrete situation to another: for example, Canadian farmers might be concerned about a just price for their produce, Canadian workers about a fair wage for their work, and Canadian home buyers about high interest rates, or the "usury" of the banks (Wiley, 1967).

Furthermore, Weber argued that, aside from economic relationships, there are at least two other very important bases of inequality in human societies – the social and the political. Social hierarchies have to do with prestige and honor (status groups). Political hierarchies have to do with the distribution of power in society (parties). Weber saw these three basic hierar-chies – class (the economic), status (the social), and power (the political) – as being interrelated but somewhat independent.

Weber also argued that the key factor in the assess-ment of a person's position in the overall social hierar-chy was not whether that person happened to be an owner or an employee, but rather to what degree he or she would be able to enjoy life (life chances). This degree of enjoyment determined largely by income, but all the other economic, social, and political factors were thought to play a role as well. Those working in the Weberian tradition would argue, contrary to Marx, that the key difference between a businessman earning $100 000 a year working for someone else and a busi-nessman making $10 000 a year working for himself was the difference in income ($100 000 versus $10 000) and not the difference in their relationship to the mode of production (employee versus owner).

Weber saw bureaucratization as the master trend of our time. He foresaw the development of bigger and bigger bureaucracies which would control more and more of the lives of ordinary people. In his view, socialist or Marxist revolutions would only serve to hasten this process of bureaucratization and would do little or nothing to reduce inequality.

Sorokin

Pitirim Sorokin took a different approach to the study of inequality. This Harvard sociologist examined the data made available by our entire written history. He found that all known human societies are character-ized by inequality (Sorokin, 1927). This was true even in experimental societies like communes developed precisely for the purpose of building egalitarian communities.

Sorokin's studies indicated that even socialist and communist political parties officially dedicated to the cause of equality were always characterized by sub-stantial internal political inequality themselves. Fur-thermore, he found that there have been repeated communist revolutions throughout the history of mankind and that all failed to produce an egalitarian society that lasted for any length of time. Indeed, sincere attempts to equalize had inevitably resulted in economic catastrophes, famine, and starvation which had been curses to the very people who were supposed to benefit.

Conversely, Sorokin also found that unusually large amounts of inequality also seemed to attract what he called "levelling" forces (invasion, revolution, reform, taxation, robbery) These forces had the effect of reducing inequality to something like a normal level.

He concluded that there seemed to be both upper and lower limits to the amount of inequality characterizing human societies. If a society became too equal, it was forced to change in the direction of inequality. On the other hand, if a society became too unequal, it would somehow be forced to change in the direction of greater equality. Looking at history as a whole, Sorokin discovered a pattern of apparently trendless fluctuation in the amount of inequality.

Sorokin's findings are conservative in suggesting that inequality cannot be completely eliminated. Yet they are radical in suggesting that the amount of inequality in a given society can usually be reduced to some degree. His findings give minimal satisfaction to both conservatives and radicals, just as one would expect a genuine synthesis to do. Perhaps this helps to explain why Sorokin's work has been largely ignored.

Lenski

Contemporary American sociologist Gerhard Lenski (1966) has made the most self-conscious attempt to synthesize the traditional viewpoints. In trying to provide an empirically-based theory of inequality, Lenski, like Sorokin, studied our historical experience. His survey of the data indicated that the degree of inequality in human societies varies considerably depending upon the level of technological development (upon what Marxists call the forces of production). Within the boundaries set by technological level, he found that there seemed to be a predictable range of inequality, which had an apparent average level as well as upper and lower limits. This finding is similar to Sorokin's. (See Figure 8-1.)

Lenski attributed this apparent average level to some presumably universal or constant aspects of the human situation (for example, human nature). Likewise, he

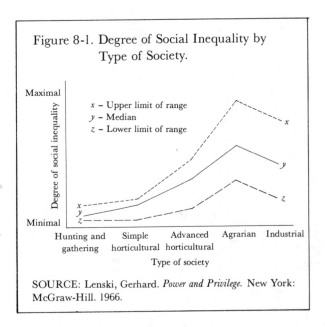

Figure 8-1. Degree of Social Inequality by Type of Society.

SOURCE: Lenski, Gerhard. *Power and Privilege.* New York: McGraw-Hill. 1966.

attributed the tendency toward variation to a number of other factors that differ from one society to another, such as environmental conditions or the degree of external threat. (See Figure 8-2).

Lenski's theory, like Sorokin's, gives little comfort to either conservatives or radicals. The fact that the degree of inequality varies substantially in contemporary societies clearly indicates that some reduction in the degree of inequality is possible in most situations. This aspect of the theory displeases conservatives. Conversely, Lenski's study indicates that many of the factors that influence the degree of inequality are, as yet, impossible to change. This aspect of the theory displeases radicals. Furthermore, as Figure 8-2 indicates, the theory is too dry and complex to be used for popular propaganda by either side. It is perhaps no coincidence, therefore, that the work of Lenski, like that of Sorokin, has been largely ignored by Canadian social scientists.

This concludes our discussion of major theoretical orientations to the problem of inequality. In the following parts of the chapter we will discuss what some of the facts regarding inequality seem to be so far as Canada and Canadians are concerned. This discussion

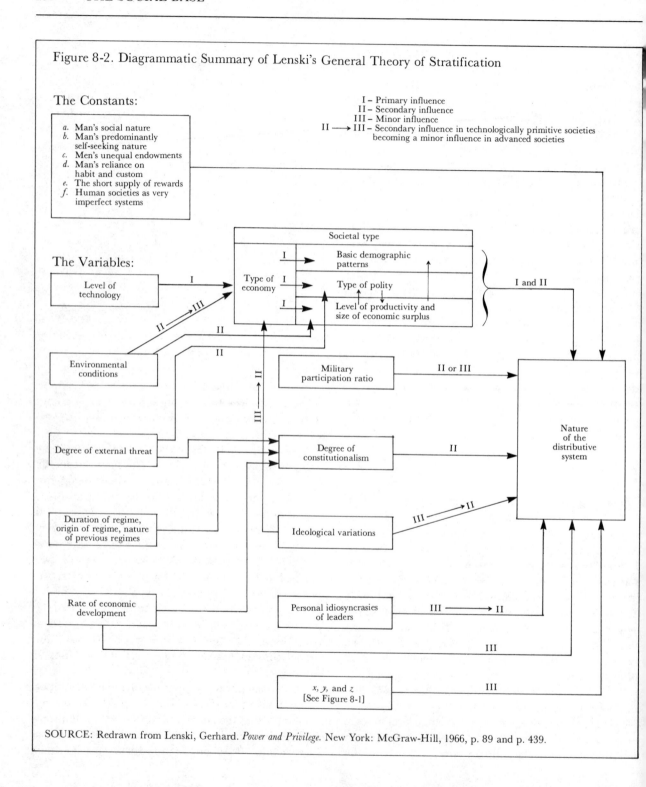

Figure 8-2. Diagrammatic Summary of Lenski's General Theory of Stratification

The Constants:

I – Primary influence
II – Secondary influence
III – Minor influence
II ⟶ III – Secondary influence in technologically primitive societies becoming a minor influence in advanced societies

a. Man's social nature
b. Man's predominantly self-seeking nature
c. Men's unequal endowments
d. Man's reliance on habit and custom
e. The short supply of rewards
f. Human societies as very imperfect systems

The Variables:

Societal type

Level of technology

Type of economy

Basic demographic patterns

Type of polity

Level of productivity and size of economic surplus

Environmental conditions

Military participation ratio

Degree of external threat

Degree of constitutionalism

Duration of regime, origin of regime, nature of previous regimes

Ideological variations

Rate of economic development

Personal idiosyncrasies of leaders

x, y, and z
[See Figure 8-1]

Nature of the distributive system

SOURCE: Redrawn from Lenski, Gerhard. *Power and Privilege.* New York: McGraw-Hill, 1966, p. 89 and p. 439.

will be divided into two major sections – **inequality of condition** and **inequality of opportunity**.

INEQUALITY OF CONDITION

Inequality of condition refers to the overall structure of rewards in a society. It involves questions like these: What is the average income? What is the range between the richest and the poorest people? What is the overall distribution of rewards? How equal or unequal is this distribution?

The Class Structure

A typical way to analyze inequality is according to class structure. In some respects, this approach is ideal because it allows the scholar to consider simultaneously almost all the factors normally associated with inequality. But it is difficult to use this approach because sociologists cannot seem to agree on what they are referring to when they use the word *class*. Every theoretician examined so far used his own criterion for class membership. Weber, for example, used "life chances," while Marx used "relationship to the means of production." Each criterion naturally gives a different picture of the class structure.

There is also disagreement about whether the word *class* should be used to refer to a category of individuals with similar characteristics, or to a cohesive social group. On this there are two schools of thought – the nominalist and the realist.

Nominalists maintain that the term *social class* best refers to an analytic reality determined by variables that do not necessarily take into account the behavior and perceptions of the people involved. For example, the category of families making $10 000 to $15 000 a year might be described as a "class" by some nominalists. This approach is used mainly by contemporary empirical social scientists.

Realists maintain that a "social class" does not exist unless the members of that class function as a cohesive group and are conscious of their mutual class membership. Most traditional theorists used some form of this definition (Wrong, 1969).

Some perspectives try to take both elements into consideration. Marxists, for example, speak of a class-in-itself (*klasse an sich*), and of a class-for-itself (*klasse für sich*), while Dahrendorf (1959) speaks of latent class groupings and manifest class groupings. Perhaps the most common usage is to refer to nominalist categories as "strata" or "socioeconomic status (SES)" categories, and to the realist groupings as "social classes."

What we find out about the Canadian class structure will naturally depend on both the definition of class (nominalist or realist) and the criterion for class membership which we use. If we use a nominalist definition of social class, there is no doubt that Canada has a class structure to which virtually everyone belongs. However, the shape and apparent nature of this class structure varies considerably depending on which criterion of class membership is adopted.

Marxist criteria indicate that we have a very small bourgeoisie or upper class, a small and declining middle-class petite bourgeoisie, and a huge working class proletariat consisting of over 85 percent of the population. If we use occupation as a criterion, we find that a middle-class, white-collar group is the dominant and growing sector of our class structure. If education is our criterion, we find that a middle-class group of high school graduates is numerically dominant in a class structure characterized by major improvement for many people during the past 40 years. In sum, Marxist criteria indicate that the class structure is dominated by a growing working class; non-Marxist criteria, like occupation and education, indicate that the class structure is dominated by a growing middle class (for data, see Ogmundson, 1981). Other criteria give somewhat different overall versions of the Canadian class structure (see, for example, Porter, 1965).

If we use a realist definition of social class there is some doubt as to whether, and to what extent, classes exist in Canada. Although pockets of apparent class consciousness have been reported here and there across the country (Rinehart and Okraku, 1974; Stevenson, 1977), less than half the Canadian population reports itself as aware of being a member of a social class (Ogmundson, 1981). If Canadians are asked simply to give themselves a class position without further guidance from an interviewer, an overwhelming majority

Regional differences affect the distribution of wealth and power. Ontario, a center for manufacturing, has traditionally enjoyed the lowest unemployment rates in the country, while underdeveloped regions have traditionally suffered the highest.

of those who respond see themselves as being "middle class." If an interviewer provides respondents with a list of class positions from which to choose, about 60 percent of the Canadian population views itself as being "upper middle" or "middle" class, while about 30 percent views itself as "working class." So it appears that, if we use a realist definition of social class, Canada either has no class structure, or has a class structure dominated by the middle class. (For further discussion, see Goyder and Pineo, 1979.)

Material Dimensions

Another useful way of examining inequality of condition is to put aside the idea of class and consider material factors alone. In this approach it is both customary and convenient to look at income distribution. The standard way to do this is to divide the national income into fifths, or quintiles, and determine how much of the national income each quintile receives. Table 8-1 indicates what happens when you treat Canadian income this way. It is interesting to note that the top 20 percent of the population consistently receives over 40 percent of the national income, while the bottom 20 percent regularly receives about 4 percent.

How should we evaluate these facts? Should we be impressed by how *equal*, or by how *unequal*, Canadian income distribution is? Initially, we might be amazed, perhaps even horrified, by how unequally and how unfairly income in Canada is distributed. But to evaluate these figures reasonably, we must put them into historical and comparative perspective. The results of such a comparison are surprising. Compared to most other countries in the world today, Canada's income distribution is unusually equal.

Perhaps this is not so remarkable when we consider that countries like Brazil, Mexico, and Puerto Rico are included. However, recent data appear to indicate that Canada's relatively egalitarian position holds even when compared to western European social democracies and to eastern European Marxist societies! This, at least, is the result if one takes the percentage of income going to the top 5 percent of households as a measure of equality of income distribution, as in

Territorial Inequality

Probably the single most important determinant of your life chances is the territory within which you are born and spend your life. International inequality is very great, indeed. A glance at the table below will show that Canadians are very fortunate, because our position is a highly affluent one.

Our present affluence, however, has been created and sustained by the sale of non-renewable resources to the rest of the world. Unfortunately, a good case can be made for the argument that we have often sold our resources far too cheaply. The experience of other countries which also enjoyed affluence through the sale of their resources indicates our present affluence is probably temporary. It is conceivable that this may directly affect your life. As one influential report stated in 1972:

> ... *before the children of today can reach middle age, most of the resources may be gone, leaving Canada with a resource-based economy and no resources (Bourgeault, 1972).*

Regional inequality within Canada is also very substantial, as shown in the table below. Ontario traditionally has the highest living standard within the country, followed by British Columbia, the Prairie Provinces, Quebec, and the Maritimes in that order. Essentially, the same basic pattern of regional inequality has been with us since at least the 1920s (Manzer, 1974).

TABLE A. GROSS NATIONAL PRODUCT PER CAPITA IN TWENTY-FOUR COUNTRIES

United States	$3575
Sweden	2549
Canada	2473
Denmark	2120
Australia	2022
France	1924
West Germany	1901
Norway	1890
Great Britain	1818
Belgium	1804
Netherlands	1554
Israel	1422
Puerto Rico	1154
Italy	1104
Hungary	1094
Poland	978
Japan	861
Chile	565
Spain	561
Mexico	455
Yugoslavia	451
Columbia	282
Brazil	267
Philippines	160

SOURCE: Tyree, et al, 1979: 416.

TABLE B. ANNUAL PERSONAL INCOME PER CAPITA IN CANADIAN PROVINCES

Province	Annual Personal Income per Capita $	(Canada=100)
Ontario	3,365	116
B.C.	3,116	107
Alberta	2,913	100
Manitoba	2,842	98
Quebec	2,626	90
Saskatchewan	2,516	87
Nova Scotia	2,304	79
New Brunswick	2,080	72
P.E.I.	1,818	63
Newfoundland	1,613	56
Canada	2,906*	100

*Excluding the personal income of Canadian non-residents.
SOURCE: *Poverty in Canada*: 51.

Table 8-2. More recently, Stack (1980) reported similar findings using the "Gini coefficient" as a measure of inequality.

It seems, then, that our national income distribution is not unusually unequal. The data indicate that a Marxist revolution would very likely accomplish little or nothing so far as further equalizing income distribution in Canada is concerned. Nevertheless, the same findings also indicate that we still have some room for improvement from the perspective of egalitarian values.

TABLE 8-1. INCOME DISTRIBUTION BY QUINTILE, CANADA

All Units
(both families and individuals)

	1951	1961	1971	1974
Highest quintile	42.8	41.1	43.3	42.4
Fourth quintile	23.3	24.5	24.9	25.0
Third quintile	18.3	18.3	17.6	17.8
Second quintile	11.2	11.9	10.6	10.8
Lowest quintile	4.4	4.2	3.6	4.0

Adapted from Gillespie, 1980.

TABLE 8-2. PERCENTAGE OF INCOME GOING TO THE TOP 5 PERCENT OF HOUSEHOLDS IN 24 COUNTRIES

Israel	13.0%
Poland	13.9
Canada	14.0
Hungary	14.0
Australia	14.3
Great Britain	15.0
Yugoslavia	15.0
Norway	15.0
U.S.A.	16.0
Denmark	16.2
Sweden	16.8
Japan	20.0
Spain	20.0
Netherlands	21.6
Puerto Rico	22.0
France	25.0
Philippines	29.0
Chile	30.4
West Germany	31.2
Mexico	32.1
Brazil	36.0
Colombia	39.4

Adapted from Tyree, et al, 1979:416.

Historically, income distribution in Canada is more equal today than it was a century or two ago. The material standard of living has also risen quite substantially during this period. From this perspective, therefore, Canadians have reason to be satisfied. However, if we narrow our historical perspective and concentrate on what has happened since the end of World War II (1945), the facts are not so clear. Indeed, this area has been the subject of one of the classic debates in Canadian sociology.

In 1974, Leo Johnson (a prominent Marxist historian now associated with the sociology department at the University of Waterloo) published a highly influential pamphlet entitled *Poverty in Wealth* which seemed to prove that income distribution in Canada was rapidly becoming more unequal and that the situation of poor people, in particular, was deteriorating in a most alarming fashion. Johnson's work, however, became subject to a powerful critique by Richard Hamilton and Maurice Pinard (1977), in which the two McGill sociologists indicated that Johnson was quite mistaken in his analysis, and that, if anything, income distribution in Canada was becoming slightly more equal.

It is impossible to go into all the details of this debate here, but it may be useful to note that part of it had to do with the units of analysis used. Johnson looked at all the individuals who filed an income tax return, including, for example, students living at home, while Hamilton and Pinard looked at the family as a whole. If you look at individuals alone, the data support Johnson. If you look at the family units, as Hamilton and Pinard say you should, the data indicate a slight trend toward greater equality.

There is as yet no apparent consensus among Canadian sociologists about which of these views is correct (Johnson, 1979a; Hamilton and Pinard, 1977; Johnson, 1979b; Cohn, 1978; Johnson, 1979a). But it is interesting to note that scholars in other disciplines hold the view that income distribution in Canada is remaining about the same or becoming slightly more equal, once factors like the changing age distribution of the population are taken into consideration (Armstrong, et al, 1977; Reuber, 1978).

Subjective Dimensions

Inequality of condition can also be studied in terms of its subjective aspects. Consideration of the subjective dimension of inequality includes topics such as class

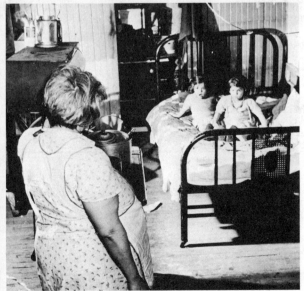

Some people have enough money to throw away. For others, the grim realities of life are an empty store on Montreal's Bonsecours St., six children to feed, a rust-encrusted basin, and colds that last all winter because there isn't any heat.

consciousness, relative deprivation, occupational prestige, the relationship of objective status to subjective status, value systems, ethnic and racial standing, and many other topics. Some of these approaches were discussed previously when we were considering some of the empirical findings concerning social class (by realist definition) in Canada. In the section that follows, we will discuss Canadian findings on occupational prestige and ethnic standing.

Occupational Prestige. One of the most commonly used measures of social inequality is occupational

The Question of Poverty

There are two basic definitions of poverty, one is an absolute definition, the other is a relative definition. An absolute definition of poverty concerns itself with whether or not people have enough money to obtain necessities such as food, clothing, shelter, and medical care. This definition corresponds with the popular understanding of the term. The measurement problem here consists of ascertaining exactly how much money is currently needed to meet "minimum" standards and to decide exactly what a "minimum" standard is. For example, should false teeth be considered a "necessity" or a "luxury"? These questions necessarily involve value judgments. Conservatives usually favor an absolute definition of poverty.

The relative definition views poverty in relation to the living standards of a given contemporary society, and not in relation to minimal physical needs, historical living standards, or living standards in other countries. In effect, this definition of poverty has to do with value judgments about how much inequality can be justified. Arguments for the reduction of poverty along these lines are really arguments for the reduction of inequality. Radicals usually favor this definition.

The measurement problem for people who take this view comes in deciding how unequal the position of a person or a family needs to be before being labeled "poor." To put it another way, the problem consists of a value judgment concerning how equal income distribution should be before a satisfactory level of equality has been achieved. The proportion of the population considered poor by this definition depends on where the "poverty line" is drawn. This, in itself, is an arbitrary decision based very much on the values and interests of the people involved. Such definitions are the usual basis for the figures on "poverty in Canada" reported in the newspapers.

For purposes of elementary exposition only, let us look at the following example. (For a technically accurate description of how a relative poverty line is drawn, see Adams, et al, 1971). Suppose the income distribution of the population is divided into deciles, or tenths. A conservative working in the private sector and forced to use this definition might draw the poverty line at the first decile. Using this line, 10 percent of the population would be considered "poor." A moderate working in a university might draw the line at the second decile; 20 percent would now be "poor." A liberal working for the welfare department might draw the line at the third decile – 30 percent would be "poor." A radical working for an independent welfare agency in need of funding might decide to draw the line at the fourth decile; no less than 40 percent of the population would now be "poor."

It is worth noting that the two definitions have some interesting arithmetic properties. If the standard of living in Canada miraculously doubled overnight, and if everyone in Canada had exactly twice as much money tomorrow, the amount of poverty in Canada would be exactly the same by a relative definition. By an absolute definition, the amount of poverty would be reduced by doubling the standard of living.

Conversely, if we were hit by a ruinous depression, and if everyone in Canada had exactly half as much money tomorrow, the amount of poverty in Canada would still be exactly the same by relative definition. In other words, since we would all be in the same boat, we wouldn't feel any more poor than we did before. By an absolute definition of poverty, the amount of poverty would be substantially increased by a depression – in the manner anticipated by common sense.

How much poverty is there in Canada? By historical and comparative standards, almost none. By an absolute definition, very little. By relative definitions, anywhere between 20 to 40 percent of the Canadian population is poor. You must decide for yourself which of these measures is most meaningful to you. (For further discussion, almost all from the radical viewpoint, see Adams, 1970; Adams, et al, 1971; "Report of the Special Senate Committee on Poverty," 1971; Canadian Council of Social Development, 1980).

prestige. Those who use it argue that this approach does more than simply provide a direct measure of a subjective dimension of inequality. They point out that it also provides an indirect measure of the material and political rewards that go with an occupational role. Furthermore, they maintain that occupation is a central determinant of the overall position of an individual or family unit in the entire social structure. Consequently, the study of occupational prestige, in their view, is a convenient way to look into the heart of a society's social inequality.

Studies of occupational prestige in Canada have indicated that white-collar workers have more prestige than blue-collar workers, and that higher educational status tends to be associated with higher occupational prestige. At the top of the scale, professionals have

TABLE 8-3. PRESTIGE RANKING OF SELECTED OCCUPATIONS

OCCUPATION	SCORE	OCCUPATION	SCORE	OCCUPATION	SCORE
U.S. Supreme Court Justice	94	people	80	a wholesale concern	66
Physician	93	Artist who paints pictures that are exhibited in galleries	78	Plumber	65
Nuclear physicist	92	Author of novels	78	Barber	63
Scientist	92	Economist	78	Machine operator in a factory	63
Government scientist	91	Musician in a symphony orchestra	78	Owner-operator of a lunch stand	63
State governor	91	Official of an international labor union	77	Playground director	63
Cabinet member in federal government	90	County agricultural agent	76	Corporal in the regular army	62
College professor	90	Electrician	76	Garage mechanic	62
U.S. Representative in Congress	90	Railroad engineer	76	Truck driver	59
Chemist	89	Owner-operator of a printing shop	75	Fisherman who owns his own boat	58
Diplomat in the U.S. Foreign Service	89	Trained machinist	75	Clerk in a store	56
Lawyer	89	Farm owner and operator	74	Milk route man	56
Architect	88	Undertaker	74	Streetcar motorman	56
County judge	88	Welfare worker for a city government	74	Lumberjack	55
Dentist	88	Newspaper columnist	73	Restaurant cook	55
Mayor of a large city	87	Policeman	72	Singer in a nightclub	54
Member of the board of directors of a large corporation	87	Reporter on a daily newspaper	71	Filling station attendant	51
Minister	87	Bookkeeper	70	Coal miner	50
Psychologist	87	Radio announcer	70	Dock worker	50
Airline pilot	86	Insurance agent	69	Night watchman	50
Civil engineer	86	Tenant farmer—one who owns livestock and machinery and manages the farm	69	Railroad section hand	50
Head of a department in a state department	86	Local official of a labor union	67	Restaurant waiter	49
Priest	86	Manager of a small store in a city	67	Taxi driver	49
Banker	85	Mail carrier	66	Bartender	48
Biologist	85	Railroad conductor	66	Farmhand	48
Sociologist	83	Traveling salesman for		Janitor	48
Captain in the regular army	82			Clothes presser in a laundry	46
Accountant for a large business	81			Soda fountain clerk	44
Public schoolteacher	81			Sharecropper—one who owns no livestock or equipment and does not manage farm	42
Building contractor	80			Garbage collector	39
Owner of a factory that employs about 100				Street sweeper	36
				Shoe shiner	34

SOURCE: Hodge, Robert W., Paul M. Seigel, and Peter H. Rossi. "Occupational prestige in the United States, 1925–1963." *American Journal of Sociology,* 70 (November 1964): 286–302. Used by permission of the University of Chicago Press.

Table as it appears in M. Spencer, *Foundations of Modern Sociology,* Prentice-Hall, 1976, p. 220.

more prestige than managers. However, both managers and professionals have substantially more prestige than clerical workers, farmers, and manual laborers. Clerical workers have slightly more prestige than farmers; farmers have slightly more prestige than manual workers. These findings are similar to those in coun-

tries like the United States, as shown in Table 8-3.

In fact, the structure of occupational prestige appears to be very similar in almost all countries and all time periods for which we have information (Treiman, 1978; Haller and Bills, 1979). As might be expected, the degree of inequality by occupational prestige in

TABLE 8-4. PRESTIGE RANKING OF RELIGIOUS, ETHNIC, AND RACIAL CATEGORIES IN ENGLISH AND FRENCH CANADA

CHART II
HIERARCHY OF ETHNIC AND RACIAL GROUPS IN ENGLISH AND FRENCH CANADA

English Canada (N = 300)		French Canada (N = 93)
English Canadians (83.1)	83	
English (82.4)	82	
British (81.2)	81	
	80	
	79	
	78	
	77	French Canadians, English Canadians
	76	Catholics (77.6)
Protestants (75.3) Scots (75.2)	75	
My own ethnic background (74.4)	74	My own ethnic background (73.7)
	73	
	72	French (72.4)
	71	English (71.0)
Catholics (70.1)	70	
Irish (69.5)	69	
	68	
	67	
	66	British (66.0)
	65	
	64	
	63	
	62	
	61	
French (60.1)	60	
	59	
Dutch (58.4)	58	
Swedes (56.6)	57	Scots (56.5)
French Canadians (56.1) Swiss (55.7)	56	
Norwegians (55.3)	55	Irish (55.2) Protestants (54.8)
	54	
	53	

Canada appears to be about the same as that found everywhere else.

Ethnic, Religious, and Racial Prestige. Another indicator of social inequality is the prestige that various categories of people experience because of an ascribed status such as race. A study of racial prestige in Canada (see Table 8-4) has indicated that Caucasians have greater prestige than non-Caucasians (Pineo, 1980). So far as religion is concerned, the same study indicates that Anglophone Canadians rank Protestants slightly higher than Catholics, and that they rank both Christian religions well above the Jewish category. Conversely, Francophone Canadians rank Catholics much higher than both Protestants and Jews. Studies of ethnic prestige indicate that the English and French categories are ranked above other ethnic categories (Pineo, 1980).

Once again, let us put these findings into historical and comparative perspective. The order of ethnic ranking in Canada appears to be similar to that in the United States. However, the degree of inequality of ethnic prestige is much greater in English Canada than in the United States (Pineo, 1980). This indicates that, in terms of egalitarian values, there is substantial room for improvement in Canada on this dimension. As substantial as our present degree of inequality of ethnic prestige may be, other evidence indicates that it

TABLE 8-4. PRESTIGE RANKING OF RELIGIOUS, ETHNIC, AND RACIAL CATEGORIES IN ENGLISH AND FRENCH CANADA (continued)

CHART II
HIERARCHY OF ETHNIC AND RACIAL GROUPS IN ENGLISH AND FRENCH CANADA

English Canada (N = 300)		French Canada (N = 93)
Danes (52.4)	52	
	51	Italians (51.3)
People of Foreign Ancestry (50.1)	50	Dutch (49.7)
Austrians (49.6) Belgians (49.1)	49	
Germans (48.7) Finns (47.6)	48	
	47	
Jews (46.1) Icelanders (45.6)	46	
	45	Belgians (45.3) Swedes (44.8)
Ukrainians (44.3)	44	Swiss (44.4)
Italians (43.1) Hungarians (42.6)	43	Jews (43.10)
Poles (42.0) Roumanians (42.1)	42	
Lithuanians (41.4) Czecho-Slovaks	41	
(41.2) Greeks (39.9)	40	Germans (40.5) Ukrainians (40.0)
	39	People of Foreign Ancestry (38.9)
	38	Hungarians (38.4) Poles (38.0)
	37	Norwegians (38.0) Austrians (37.5)
Russians (35.8)	36	
Japanese (34.7)	35	
	34	Roumanians (33.9) Greeks (33.5)
Chinese (33.1)	33	Russians (33.2) Icelanders (32.9)
	32	Canadian Indians (32.5) Czecho-
	31	Slovaks (32.4) Finns, (32.3)
	30	Danes (32.2)
	29	Lithuanians (29.1)
Canadian Indians (28.3)	28	Japanese (27.8)
	27	Coloureds (26.5)
Coloureds (26.3)	26	
Negroes (25.4)	25	Chinese (24.9) Negroes (23.5)

SOURCE: Pineo, 1979: 196-197.

is probably less than it used to be (Darroch, 1980). In other words, there has been a welcome historical trend toward the reduction of this type of inequality.

The Political Dimension

Inequality of condition can also be studied from the perspective of its political aspects. In a broad theoretical sense, power is found everywhere. Consequently, it would be possible and useful to study the typical allocation of power in all our social institutions: the school, the family, friendship cliques, the workplace, the church, and so forth. Here, however, we will concentrate on Canadian society as a whole. We will discuss

first the distribution of authority (the recognized right to make binding decisions) and then the distribution of power (ability to control the behavior of others whether such ability is considered legitimate or not).

Authority. Sociologists in Canada have tended to agree that it is useful to analyze the authority structure of our society as it appears in a number of separate realms: the economic system, the state system, and the ideological system. These systems, in turn, can be usefully analyzed according to the major institutions within them: business and labor in the economic system; the legislature, the civil service, the military, and the judiciary in the state system; and the media, the church, and education in the ideological system. It is assumed here that authority in each of these areas is hierarchically organized, and that the people at the head of these institutions (the generals, bishops, corporation directors, union leaders, deputy ministers, university presidents, cabinet ministers) form an elite that has the authority to make the major decisions for our society (Porter, 1965). Hence, whoever has power in our society must exercise it through these figures.

Perhaps the most notable finding concerning the distribution of authority in Canada is that it is largely, perhaps even mainly, located outside the country. About half the businesses, two-thirds of the unions, and about two-thirds of the media to which Canadians are exposed are externally controlled (Clement, 1975; Watkins, 1973; Ogmundson, 1980a). The military is highly integrated with that of another country (Warnock, 1970). The economic policy and foreign policy of the Canadian government is substantially limited by agreements with foreign powers (Levitt, 1970). The major churches (excepting the United Church) have their headquarters elsewhere. In other words, a substantial portion of final authority in almost every realm of Canadian life is located outside the country. The degree to which Canada is externally dominated appears to be unusually great in a comparative perspective.

Of the authority that remains in Canada, a great deal appears to be concentrated in relatively few hands. In every institutional sphere, except perhaps in education, it is possible to locate a small group of people at the heads of formal organizations who have the authority to make binding decisions for that part of our society. In the economy, just over a hundred corporations, with about a thousand corporation directors and senior executives, appear to dominate private business (see the "Corporations" section of Chapter 10 for an analysis of these holders of economic power). The labor movement is dominated by about forty organizations, headed by less than five hundred people. The media is dominated by about fifteen organizations, headed by less than three hundred people. Religion is dominated by three organizations, each in turn controlled by small numbers of people. The civil service and the legislature are also controlled by a small number of

organizations (fifteen counting all the provinces and the four major cities), which are in turn dominated by a few hundred people (Porter, 1965; Clement, 1975; Olsen, 1977).

In this sense, it is widely agreed that authority is distributed in a very unequal manner in our society. This finding does not surprise sociologists because, as you will remember, they usually agree that successful social organization requires the unequal allocation of authority. But the distribution of authority is one issue, while the distribution of power is yet another. Certain questions come to mind: Who or what has power? Who or what influences or determines the decisions which these elite groups make? On these matters sociologists have been unable to agree.

Power. There are many theories about the distribution of power in countries like Canada. Some emphasize the importance of public opinion as a determinant of elite decisions (e.g., Downs, 1957), others underline the role of pressure groups (e.g., Dahl, 1961). Still others draw attention to the role of socioeconomic strata (e.g., Alford, 1963). Some insist on the crucial importance of capitalism and the capitalist class (e.g., Miliband, 1969). Others emphasize the influence of technology and the technostructure (e.g., Galbraith, 1967). Still others argue that bureaucracies and bureaucratic elites function largely according to their own needs (e.g., Cairns, 1977).

Most of these theories tend to argue that the variable or group it emphasizes is by far the most important

"It's not what you know, it's *who* you know. And who do *I* know. You!"

one, and that the others are relatively insignificant. Some give the impression that the distribution of power is highly democratic (public opinion); others maintain that power is moderately well distributed (pressure groups); while still others argue that it is distributed in a very unequal manner (capitalists).

It is conceivable, of course, that *all* these factors influence elite decision making to some degree. Although there has been no end of traditional theorizing on these topics, there is a thoroughly insufficient amount of empirical research. In short, it cannot be honestly stated that Canadian sociologists agree on who has power in our society. Besides, even when relevant data are available, they are subject to varying interpretations. Let us look at two examples.

Earlier research clearly indicated that elite groups in Canada tended to be dominated by an atypical group of well educated males of British Protestant, upper- or upper-middle-class origins (Porter, 1965; Clement, 1975; Olsen, 1977). This pattern appeared to be particularly clear in the case of the business and media elite groups. French Canadians and people of middle-class origin were fairly often found in the church, educational, civil service, and legislative elites, but there still appears to have been a clear overrepresentation of upper-class Canadians of British origin. Females, those of working-class origins, and those who are of neither British nor French ethnic ancestry (the *third ethnics*) were hardly to be found in elite groups at all. An exception to this pattern was found in the labor elite which was more or less representative of the population in class and ethnic background, although it too had very few females.

The trend, however, is apparently toward an "opening up" of the elites to non-British, non-upper-class groups. In particular, French Canadians, Jewish Canadians, and people of middle-class origin are more and more to be found in the upper levels of our society. Furthermore, one recent study found that third ethnics are actually *over*-represented among these individuals who control $100 million or more (Kelner, 1970; Olsen, 1977; Campbell and Szablowski, 1979; Hunter, 1981).

Scholars differ in their interpretation of these data. When the early data indicated very substantial British upper-class dominance of elite groups, radicals argued that this indicated a ruling class or capitalist class dominance of elite decision making in our society (Clement, 1975). Conservatives replied that the data were not particularly meaningful, because people in these roles performed about the same regardless of their origin and background. Now that the data are changing, the two sides are switching their favored mode of interpretation. Conservatives view the opening up of the elite structure as proof that democracy works. Radicals (e.g., Olsen, 1977) now tend to argue that elite social background is of minimal significance in any case.

It is also well established that participation in the political process by Canadian citizens is unequal. The facts indicate that higher social status is associated with higher political participation (Manzer, 1974). Indeed, it appears that a fairly high proportion of Canadians at lower socioeconomic levels may not participate in the political process at all (Van Loon, 1970). At more advanced levels of activity (e.g., running for office), it is also clear that women, third ethnics, and the working class are minimally represented (Manzer, 1974). By these measures, then, there is clear political inequality associated with sex, ethnicity, and socioeconomic status. Furthermore, a great deal of data indicates that the correlation of public opinion with elite decisions, even in the state system, is often minimal. Some (e.g., Ogmundson, 1976) feel that the one point that is made reasonably clear by such facts is that public opinion is of minimal importance as a determinant of elite decision making, and the search for explanatory factors should be focused elsewhere on factors like pressure groups, social class, and the technostructure. However, this view has also been subjected to a vigorous critique (Schreiber, 1980; Ogmundson, 1980b), and no discernible consensus on the matter appears to have developed among sociologists in Canada.

Correlates of Inequality

Socioeconomic status is related to almost everything sociologists study. To begin with, of course, it is related to income and the material conditions of life. As we

TABLE 8-5. MARITAL LIFE STYLE AND SOCIAL CLASS

	HIGHBROW	UPPER MIDDLEBROW
How girl meets boy	He was an usher at her best friend's wedding	At college, in the psychology lab
The proposal	In his room during the Harvard-Princeton game	In the back seat of a Volkswagen
The wedding	In her living room, by a federal judge	College chapel (nondenominational)
The honeymoon	Mediterranean	Bahamas
Sleeping arrangements	Double bed	King-size bed or twin beds with one headboard
Sleeping attire	He: nothing. She: nothing	He: red turtleneck nightshirt. She: gown with matching peignoir
Background music	Ravi Shankar or the Beatles	Wagner
Turn-ons	Pot	Champagne and oysters
Number of children	One each by a previous marriage, or as many as God provides	2.4
Anniversary celebrations	A weekend in Dublin	He gives her a new dishwasher. She gives him a power lawn mower
If the marriage needs help	He consults her analyst. She consults his	They go (a) to a marriage counselor; (b) to the minister
Vacations	Europe in May. She takes the children to the Cape. He commutes	Europe in July. Family camping in Yosemite
Financial arrangements	Separate trust funds	Joint checking account
Who raises the children	English nanny, boarding school, and Dr. Grauber	Mommy and Daddy, Cub Scouts, and Dr. Freud

might expect, it is related also to life expectancy – as a general rule, the richer you are, the longer you can expect to live. Less obviously, it is related to fertility – poor people tend to have more children than rich people. It is related as well to child-rearing practices, courtship patterns, and the incidence of divorce. These correlates have their humorous side as shown in Table 8-5.

Socioeconomic status is also related to membership in voluntary associations – the higher your status, the greater your likely participation. Similarly, it is related to political participation – the higher your class, the greater the likelihood that you will vote and otherwise take part in the democratic process. Likewise, it ap-

pears that poor people are more likely to be obese than rich people, and that higher class people are happier than lower class people. Furthermore, socioeconomic status is related to religious behavior – lower class people tend to prefer informal religious ceremonies, while upper class people tend to prefer formal ones. Not surprisingly, then, the typical membership of the various churches is related to social class.

The list of such correlates of socioeconomic status is almost endless. As you read the various chapters of this book, you will find that almost all the behavior and attitudes discussed are related to socioeconomic status. It is interesting that many of these SES-related differences appear to be independent of income. Construc-

TABLE 8-5. MARITAL LIFE STYLE AND SOCIAL CLASS (continued)

	LOWER MIDDLEBROW	LOWBROW
How girl meets boy	In the office, by the water cooler	On the block
The proposal	After three drinks in an apartment he borrowed	In her home one night when Mom and Dad were at the movies
The wedding	City Hall	Neighborhood church
The honeymoon	Any Hilton hotel	Disneyland
Sleeping arrangements	Twin beds with matching night tables	Double bed
Sleeping attire	He: pajamas. She: pajamas	He: underwear. She: nightgown
Background music	Sound track of *Dr. Zhivago*	Jackie Gleason and the Silver Strings
Turn-ons	Manhattans and whisky sours	Beer
Number of children	3	As many as God provides
Anniversary celebrations	Corsage and dinner out	Whitman Sampler and dinner at Howard Johnson's
If the marriage needs help	He: to his successful brother. She: to her best friend	He: to the bartender. She: to her mother
Vacations	He hunts or fishes. She visits Mother with the children	They visit Brother Charlie in Des Moines
Financial arrangements	She budgets	He gets weekly allowance
Who raises the children	Mom and Dad, the Little League, and Dr. Spock	Mom, the gang, Ann Landers, and good luck

Source: William Simon and John Gagnon "How Fashionable Is Your Sex Life?," *McCall's* 94 (October 1969), pp. 58–59. Reprinted by permission of the authors and *McCall's*. From: Spencer, 1976:226–227.

tion workers, for example, will typically drink beer, while many underemployed intellectuals will insist on drinking wine. This suggests that how much money you make is one issue, while how you spend it – the life-style you adopt – is yet another. For whatever reasons, people in similar income categories often adopt different consumption habits.

INEQUALITY OF OPPORTUNITY

In the previous section we determined that rewards are distributed unequally. The obvious next set of

questions is: How do we decide who gets what? Who said he could be a big general when I am a lowly private? Couldn't I be a doctor instead of a nurse? Why can't I be rich? To answer these questions, we must talk about inequality of opportunity or, as it is also called, **social mobility**.

Marxists and social democrats make the value judgment that equality of condition is much more important than equality of opportunity. To them it is more important that the pay differential between managers and workers be reduced than that everyone have a fair chance to be manager. Therefore they tend to focus on the topics discussed in the previous section. Others take a different value position. They think it's fair that surgeons should be paid a lot more than secretaries. What concerns them most is that people should be placed in these positions on the basis of merit and not on ascribed bases like age, gender, race, language, religion, ethnicity, or social background. People who take this value position tend to devote themselves to the study of inequality of opportunity.

Views on equality of opportunity are also influenced by individual and collective interests. Those who have confidence in their ability to do well are likely to be concerned mainly with keeping the competition fair. They look forward to receiving the substantial rewards they feel will be richly deserved. Those who have less confidence in their abilities, or in the possibility of reasonably equal opportunity, are likely to be more concerned about equalizing rewards.

Distribution of Opportunity

One of the central concerns of students of opportunity has been the manner in which mobility opportunities are distributed internationally. A recent study (Tyree, et al, 1979; see also Hazelrigg and Garnier, 1976) has found that mobility opportunities vary substantially from one society to another. Some of these findings are listed in Table 8-6, and they indicate that chances for mobility in Canada are apparently among the best in the world. It is also of interest to note that mobility opportunities show no consistent relationship to whether a country is capitalist or Marxist. This particular finding indicates that a Marxist revolution would probably fail to reduce inequality of opportunity in Canada.

Socioeconomic Origins

Another central focus of those interested in inequality of opportunity has been the degree to which life chances are influenced by the socioeconomic status of an individual's parents. A study based on a national survey done in 1974 found that less than 15 percent of the variance in the occupational status of a typical Canadian male could be explained by his socioeconomic origins. When the children of farmers were removed from the analysis, it was found that only about 10

TABLE 8-6. OCCUPATIONAL MOBILITY IN TWENTY-FOUR COUNTRIES

Country	Mobility Index
Israel	−.286
Canada	−.184
Australia	−.141
U.S.A.	−.114
Great Britain	−.102
Hungary	−.068
France	−.056
Sweden	−.045
Netherlands	−.041
Denmark	−.037
Yugoslavia	.003
Norway	.008
Puerto Rico	.013
Belgium	.033
Chile	.048
Japan	.048
Mexico	.051
Spain	.062
Poland	.067
West Germany	.068
Italy	.081
Philippines	.103
Brazil	.133
Colombia	.356

Please note that a negative score indicates a higher rate of occupational mobility. In this table, Canada is second only to Israel in opportunities for occupational mobility.

SOURCE: Tyree, et al, 1979:416.

percent of the variance in the occupational status of males who were not born on farms could be explained by socioeconomic origin. As might be expected, this relationship declines even further when one looks at status transmission over three generations. When one compares the status of great-grandfathers to great-grandsons, there is no statistically significant relationship at all.

In sum, it appears that if you are a Canadian male, your socioeconomic origins will be only a minor determinant of your life chances. (On all this, see Goyder and Curtis, 1979.) Data from the United States indicate that your status inheritance will probably be even less if you are a female (Hauser, et al, 1974).

The findings also indicate that privileged parents are able to transmit their status best only when they

TABLE 8-7. Percentage of University Students of Working-Class Origin in Nine Countries

Canada	26%
Britain	25
Norway	25
Sweden	14
Denmark	10
France	8
Austria	8
Netherlands	5
West Germany	5

Adopted from Rich, 1976:16.

insure that their children obtain a high level of education. If their children are unwilling or unable to obtain schooling, the influence of high socioeconomic origin is even more limited. Finally, data from other countries indicate that the effects of initial social origin diminish even further as one moves through the life cycle. As you grow older, class origin is of less and less importance as a determinant of your position (Matras, 1980).

As always, it is useful to put these data in comparative and historical perspective. The degree of status transmission in Canada is generally similar to that found in the United States and in western European countries (Goyder and Curtis, 1979). At least one study (Rich, 1976) has indicated that opportunities for working-class children to go to university in Canada are unusually good. (See Table 8-7). There has been some suggestion that status inheritance at the higher levels of Canadian society is greater than that found in other countries (Manzer, 1974; Porter, 1965; Clement, 1975). However, Manzer's data was restricted to French-speaking Quebec, and it has been persuasively demonstrated that the methodology used by Porter (1965) and Clement (1975) artificially inflated the apparent exclusiveness of Canadian elite groups (Rich, 1976). Appropriate research methodology indicates that Canadian elite groups are probably less exclusive than those in other countries (Rich, 1976; Grayson and Grayson, 1978; Campbell and Szablowski, 1979).

The historical evidence indicates some decrease in the degree of educational inheritance in Canada since World War II (Manzer, 1974). Similar findings have been reported in the United States (Featherman and Hauser, 1978). This means that educational opportunity for the average person, compared to the privileged, is improving. At the elite level, the findings are mixed. In the case of the state elites (Olsen, 1977), the civil service elite (Campbell and Szablowski, 1979), and the Toronto elite (Kelner, 1970), it would appear the opportunities are becoming more equal. In the case of the business and media elites, it would appear that opportunities are becoming less equal (Clement, 1975). It should be noted, however, that these findings have been subject to considerable methodological criticism (Rich, 1976; Hunter, 1976; Baldwin, 1977a, 1977b).

Ascribed Status

Students of occupational mobility have also been interested in the degree to which life chances are influenced by ascribed statuses such as ethnicity, race, immigrant status, language, and gender. There is no doubt that many ascribed characteristics are associated with economic standing in Canada. (See Chapter 9 for a discussion of the socioeconomic standing of various ethnic groups.) It is widely known, for example, that women make less money than men, and that Francophones make less than Anglophones. However, there is some question as to how great the differences are, what the trend is, and how many of the differences can reasonably be attributed to discrimination stemming from the levels of social prestige among people in the various categories.

Ever since the publication of John Porter's *Vertical Mosaic* in 1965, it has been widely believed in sociological circles that ethnicity is a major determinant of individual life chances in Canada. It has also been widely believed that the role of ethnicity in Canada is unusually great (Porter, 1965; Forcese, 1980). More recent work, however, has indicated that the relationship between ethnicity and occupational status is steadily decreasing (Manzer, 1974), that ethnic background will probably have little or no influence on the life chances of young Canadians like yourselves, and that the relationship was never that strong in the first

Many ethnic groups entered Canada at a low status level, working at menial jobs. Chinese coolies, for example, provided cheap labor on the railroad. In subsequent generations, however, the relationship of ethnicity to socioeconomic class has declined. For example, Asiatic Canadians today enjoy a higher average income than British Canadians.

place (Darroch, 1980). Pineo (1976) has concluded that: ". . . no more than 2 percent of the current occupational status of the Canadian male labor force can be said to derive from ethnic origin." Darroch (1980) has shown that the role of ethnicity in Canada is not much greater than in the United States. Other research has shown that, as in Canada, the role of ethnicity as a determinant of life chances is declining in the U.S. (Duncan and Duncan, 1968; Featherman, 1971).

The outstanding exception to these findings is provided by our native peoples. The living standard of native Indians and Inuit is very low. For example, research from 1960 indicates that almost one out of every five Inuit children died in their first year of life (Manzer, 1974). This was one of the worst rates of infant mortality in the world at the time. The data also point out that the relative position of native peoples has not been improving significantly (Darroch, 1980).

This is of special normative concern because, unlike the rest of us, native peoples made no choice to take their chances and immigrate to this country. Furthermore, they have been wards of the federal government (i.e., the people of Canada) during most of the history of the country. Comparative data indicate that our treatment of native peoples has been much less enlightened than that of some other countries (Hobart and Brent, 1966). As Canadians, therefore, we must accept some responsibility for the miserable conditions they face, conditions which are far worse than those of American blacks, a group for whom we regularly express sympathy. Furthermore, the position of American blacks, unlike the position of Canadian native peoples, has been improving substantially in recent years (Featherman and Hauser, 1976a; Hogan and Featherman, 1977).

In this context, it is interesting to look at the position of immigrants in Canadian society. In most countries, it is anticipated that immigrants will come in at lower levels of society and work their way up. It is considered sufficient if they be treated fairly in this process. In Canada, however, a high proportion of immigrants, especially Anglo-Americans, are to be found in the highest levels of the occupational structure. Indeed, immigrants from many origins generally have a higher socioeconomic status than do people born in Canada (Forcese, 1980). If nothing else, this would seem to suggest a generous treatment of immigrants sharply in contrast with the treatment given to our native peoples.

The differing life chances of Anglophones and Francophones have also been the subject of considerable study. Early research clearly showed that Francophones received a considerably lower income than Anglophones, especially in Quebec. For example, in Canada in 1961 the average Francophone income was found to be about 80 percent of the average Anglophone income. Within Quebec, the corresponding figure was 64 percent (Morris and Lanphier, 1980). The early research also seemed to indicate clearly that much of this income differential could only be attributed to discrimination (Dofny, 1970; Reynauld, et al, 1967; Beattie and Spencer, 1971). To make matters worse, it appeared that the situation at the managerial-professional level had deteriorated substantially from 1931 to 1961 (Rioux, 1971). The dissemination of this knowledge helped to convert many Québécois to the separatist cause.

Here again, however, subsequent research has tended to modify the initial impression of wholesale discrimination given by earlier work. On the one hand, it has become clear that Francophones have contributed in part to their position through their mobility-related attitudes and through their failure to obtain appropriate educational qualifications (Tepperman, 1975). One study found that a full 60 percent of Anglophone/Francophone differences could be explained by education alone (Manzer, 1974). This, in turn, could be attributed largely to the previously obsolete Quebec educational system which, until the 1960s, discouraged attendance beyond elementary school (Porter, 1965).

It is also widely believed that the situation in the 1970s and 1980s was, and is, vastly better than the situation in the 1950s and 1960s when most of the earlier work was done. More recent research has indicated that Francophone/Anglophone differences are decreasing (Cuneo and Curtis, 1975; McRoberts, et al, 1976). Indeed, one subsequent study of engineers and middle-level managers have even shown patterns of discrimination in favor of Francophone Canadians (Armstrong, 1970).

Nonetheless, it is still widely believed that there is probably a significant residue of discrimination against Francophones in the Canadian labor market. Perhaps this opinion has been, or will be, rendered obsolete by contemporary social change. Only future research will tell.

Finally, there is no doubt, as you saw in Chapter 4, that there are major differences between the incomes received by males and females in the labor market. Early research clearly showed that women make much less money than men. For example, in 1961 the average annual pay for female wage-earners was about 55 percent of that for male wage-earners (Manzer, 1974). Furthermore, early research also showed that much of this difference could be attributed only to discrimination (Bossen, 1971; Robson and Lapointe, 1971; Armstrong and Armstrong, 1978).

Again, however, subsequent research has tended to modify the initial impression given by these figures (e.g., Tepperman, 1975). There is some doubt as to how much of these differences can be attributed to discrimination and how much to other factors, like women choosing to devote part of their life to homemaking. For example, one study by Sylvia Ostry (1968) began with the fact that women make about half as much money as men. By the time Ostry had finished controlling for a number of factors – hours worked, work experience, years of education, and so forth – the apparent gap had diminished from about 50 percent to about 20 percent. Ostry went on to state that even the remaining 20 percent disparity in earnings could not be entirely attributed to discrimination (Manzer, 1974).

In any event, it is widely agreed that there is still a significant amount of discrimination against women in the Canadian labor market. It may not be as great as popular reports indicate, but it is still there. And there appears to be no trend toward improvement (Carroll, 1980). Findings in the United States are similar (Featherman and Hauser, 1976b).

In a broad historical perspective, the amount of ethnic, linguistic, and gender discrimination in Canada is probably much less than it used to be. When it comes to comparison with other affluent western countries, precise data are not available in most cases. The findings on ethnicity appear to be similar to those in the United States (Darroch, 1980). The occupational situation of women is reported by McDonald (1979) to be about the same in Canada as in most other western countries. Qualitative impressions indicate that our treatment of immigrants is very likely among the most generous in the world. Conversely, our treatment of native peoples is much worse than that of some other countries (Hobart and Brent, 1966).

Other Factors

Gender is still a major determinant of life chances as measured by occupation and income. Membership in some ethnic groups (i.e., native peoples) can also play a central role in determining your opportunities in life. However, other factors, like class origin, most ethnic origins, and (probably) linguistic group, appear to play a minor role. For example, if you are a Canadian male born in an urban setting, only about 10 percent of your life chances can be explained by your socioeconomic origin and no more than 2 percent by ethnic origin. This still leaves almost 90 percent to be explained. If these factors are not crucial, then what does explain opportunities for occupational mobility in Canada? Data from other countries (e.g., Blau and Duncan, 1967) suggest that the following factors may be important:

1. Position in birth order (the first and last children have a better chance)
2. Size of family (people from smaller families have a better chance
3. Size of city (the bigger the city you grow up in the better your chances
4. Willingness to move (the greater your willingness to move, the better your chances)
5. Sex of older siblings (an older sister helps; an older brother is no help at all)

All these factors put together still only account for a small portion of opportunity for occupational mobility. It seems that sociologists are temporarily at a loss to explain more of the variance.

INEQUALITY AND SOCIAL CHANGE

What the future holds is not at all clear. At the least, it is fair to say that there is no consensus among sociologists. A few dream of the day when the classless society will somehow be created, by evolution or revolution (Marx). Some see the development of new and perhaps worse forms of inequality through a bureaucratization process occasionally assisted by Marxist revolutions (Weber). Others fatalistically take the position that a ruling class will always be with us (Mosca). Most, perhaps, accept that a certain degree of inequality will always be with us (Sorokin), because the empirical evidence to the present day shows that this will be so. But these same sociologists would argue that it is always possible to reduce inequality, or to eliminate its worst effects, through a policy of reform (the social democrats).

This last view suggests that perhaps our future is not preordained by God or by social processes but is largely in our own hands. The main purpose of sociology, some feel, lies in the development of theories which will enable our society to guide itself into a more desirable future condition. This raises the question of social policy. On this issue, some points should be made.

There is no doubt that inequalities of most kinds can be reduced to some degree. Granted, there is some question as to the exact degree to which particular forms of inequality can be reduced, but at present there seems little need to be concerned about whether we are approaching those limits. Canadians could reduce some kinds of inequality to some degree, if we had the political will to do so.

Furthermore, there is no shortage of policy ideas which are supposed to have the effect of reducing inequality. Entire books have been filled with them. (See Adams, et al, 1971.) For example, it has been suggested that educational opportunity could be somewhat equalized by reforms such as reduced tuition, increased scholarships, and subsidized housing. As well, it might be possible to reduce inequality of condition by suitable revision of our taxation system and by a reduction of regional wage differentials. Other such ideas abound; these are just a few of them.

There are, however, scientific differences of opinion about exactly which reforms are likely to be most effective. On these matters, the experts very clearly disagree. At every point along the way, there are substantial problems with our theories and even with our facts. As we have seen, we are not always sure that we even have the *facts* straight!

There are similar problems with values: How much equality do we want? How much are we willing to sacrifice in order to achieve it? Probably all of us have some personal limit. It is often argued that some equalizing programs reduce freedom and/or efficiency. We could insist, for example, that all university students wear uniforms. This would make them more equal in appearance but would certainly impinge on their freedom. Would you prefer the equality of uniforms or the freedom of personal clothing choice?

The reduction of one kind of inequality could conceivably increase other kinds of inequality – for example, centralized union negotiations might decrease regional economic equality but increase regional political inequality. Would you be willing to equalize wages across Canada at the cost of concentrating further power in Ottawa? This is the kind of value choice that must be faced.

Finally, there are problems in the differing interests of various segments of our society. Those who think they would benefit from reforms tend to support them. They adopt suitable scientific and value positions (i.e., the radical perspective) in order to validate their claim for more of society's resources. Those who think they would not benefit from such policies tend to oppose them. They, too, adopt suitable philisophical positions (i.e., the conservative perspective) in order to defend their interests. Such conflicts usually make it difficult to assess policy options in a clear-headed way.

In this context, it is worth noting that sociologists and sociology students have a material interest in whether or not attempts at equalization actually take place. We have a material interest in the expansion of some forms of aid to the underprivileged, because this provides a market for our services, consulting fees and research money for your professor, summer work and a civil service job for you. In the same way, the equalization of opportunity for university education would probably increase enrollments, make life easier for sociology students, and help to ease problems of unemployment among sociologists. So the sociologists and sociology students who argue for aid to the underprivileged may, in effect, be arguing in favor of aid for themselves. It is no coincidence that most contemporary sociologists favor the radical perspective.

A FINAL COMMENT

As you have seen, scholars who have devoted their lives to the issues covered in this chapter have been unable to agree. As a student and as a citizen you must make up your own mind about such matters. Here's some free advice. First, remember how little you know; perhaps you should read more; be sure to expose yourself to a variety of viewpoints. Second, remember that professors and authors have their limitations; do not blindly accept their lead. Third, remember that you have the right to take whatever value position you prefer, and that a sociology professor, in his or her role as professor, is no more qualified than you are to say what is right or wrong. Finally, bear in mind that your views, too, are likely to be biased by your own interests; what you think is best for the world may be, in fact, what you secretly believe is best for yourself. And just remember this: the enemy of the truth is the enemy of the people.

SUMMARY

1. Disagreements about the issue of social inequality stem from three sources: values, interests, and scientific beliefs. Values have to do with what amount of inequality is judged to be right or wrong. Interests have to do with who stands to benefit or to lose by a change. Scientific beliefs have to do with viewpoints on what causes social inequality, how much social inequality there is, and what can be done about it at what cost. Sociologists are qualified to speak only to the last point.

2. Sociological theories on inequality can be usefully divided into three types: the radical, the conservative, and attempts at scientific synthesis. Radical theories emphasize the injustice of inequality. Conservative theories emphasize the inevitability of inequality. The synthesis approach attempts to use the best ideas of both traditional approaches and to base conclusions on known facts. Examples of synthesis theories are those of Weber, Sorokin, and Lenski.

3. Canadians enjoy a very high standard of living by international standards. There is, however, substantial regional inequality in Canada.

4. By Marxist criteria, 85 percent of Canadians belong to the proletariat. By non-Marxist criteria, like occupation and education, most Canadians belong to the middle class.

5. Less than half the Canadian population reports itself as being aware of belonging to a social class. However, Canadians variously identify themselves as middle class (60 percent) or working class (30 percent) if asked to do so.

6. Income distribution in Canada is relatively equal by historical and comparative standards. There is substantial debate about whether the current trend is toward greater equality or greater inequality. There is also considerable dissensus about how much poverty we have. This depends on the definition of poverty which is adopted.

7. The structure of occupational prestige in Canada is similar to that found in the United States and other advanced countries. Different religious, ethnic, and racial groups in Canada have different levels of social prestige. The range of such differences is greater here than in the United States.

8. There is substantial inequality in the distribution of authority in Canada. A very large portion of our authority structure is controlled by foreign interests. Of the authority that remains in Canada, a great deal is controlled by upper-class individuals of British ancestry. Little is known, for certain, about the distribution of power in Canada.

9. The amount of occupational mobility in Canada appears to be unusually great by comparative standards. Class origins appear to be a relatively minor determinant of occupational opportunity in this country. This

is also true of ethnic background, immigrant status, and, possibly, language. Gender appears to be strongly related to life chances. There is evidence that native peoples are subject to considerable discrimination.

10. It is evident that Canadians could reduce some kinds of inequality to some degree if they had the political will to do so. However, sociologists do not agree on what can, or should, be done to reduce social inequality. Nonetheless, it is clear that sociologists have a material interest in seeing that some such attempts are made.

GLOSSARY

Biosociology. That branch of sociology that studies the interaction of the social order and the biological makeup of its members, especially the apparent influence of genetics on human inequality.

Class consciousness. Awareness, particularly among the working class, of common social, economic, and political conditions. May be contrasted with false consciousness, a lack of awareness of such conditions.

Conflict theory. In sociology, the theory that conflict, power, and change are permanent features of society.

Conservative perspective on social inequality. Normative theory that inequality is necessary, inevitable, and just.

Dialectical materialism. Philosophical method of Karl Marx, who regarded knowledge and ideas as reflections of changing material conditions.

Dysfunctional. Effect of social action that lessens the adaptation of a social system or that prevents the fulfillment of a social want or need.

Exploitation. Unequal social relations resulting in the acquisition of a valued commodity by the dominant individual or group. In Marxist theory, exploitation is inherent in capitalist social relations.

False consciousness. Attitude toward the social world and one's own position in it that (according to sociologists) does not accord with one's objective situation.

Inequality of condition. Situation in which various members of a society have unequal amounts of socially valued resources such as money, prestige, or power.

Inequality of opportunity. Situation in which various members of a society have unequal chances to obtain socially valued resources such as money, prestige, or power.

Interests. A basis for individual or group advancement. For example, most sociologists have an economic interest in the acceptance of the radical perspective on social inequality, while most businessmen have an economic interest in the acceptance of a conservative perspective.

Labor theory of value. Theory that the value of a commodity is determined by the labor that goes into it, in contrast to the utility theory of value, which holds that the value of a commodity is determined by what people are willing to pay for it.

Marxism. A conflict theory that emphasizes the material basis of social inequality.

Normative theory. Any theory concerned mainly with moral evaluation and the question of justice. Can be contrasted with scientific theory.

Radical perspective on social inequality. Normative theory that inequality is unnecessary and unjust.

Ruling class. Marxist terminology for a class that consists of a combination of the state and the dominant economic class. When such a combination exists, the state directly expresses the political power of that economic class (e.g., landowners in feudal society, the bourgeoisie in capitalist society, the state bureaucrats in Marxist society).

Scientific beliefs. Beliefs concerning empirical reality and how it can best be explained. Can be contrasted with normative theory and value judgments.

Social democracy. Normative theory of inequality which holds that ownership consists of a divisible bundle of rights and that satisfactory progress toward equality can be achieved through non-violent, gradual reform within the political institutions of democratic capitalist societies.

Social inequality. Situation in which various members of a society have unequal amounts of socially valued resources (e.g., money, power) and unequal opportunities to obtain them.

Social mobility. Upward or downward movement of individuals or groups into different positions in the social hierarchy.

Structural functionalism. Theoretical approach to sociological analysis based on a view of society as a complex of interdependent institutions, each of which makes some contribution to overall social stability. Functionalist theory tends to focus more on social equilibrium than on social change, and the component elements of a given society are consequently analyzed according to their specific function in system maintenance.

Synthesis. A theoretical approach to the study of social inequality that attempts to utilize insights from both the radical and conservative perspectives and that attempts to be scientific in its methodology.

Value judgment. A judgment about what is right or wrong, good or bad, desirable or undesirable. It has to do with morals and ethics. Can be contrasted with a scientific judgment about what actually exists or could exist: a value judgment has to do with how things should be, a scientific judgment with how things are.

FURTHER READING

Cuneo, Carl J. 1980. "Class, stratification, and mobility," in R. Hagedorn (ed.). *Sociology*. Toronto: Holt, Rinehart and Winston. A good neo-Marxist introduction to the study of social inequality which includes discussion of recent developments in Marxist thought.

Curtis, James E., and William G. Scott (eds.). 1979. *Social Stratification: Canada*. Scarborough: Prentice-Hall. A valuable collection of essays on social inequality in Canada.

Hunter, A. 1981. *Class Tells: On Social Inequality in Canada*. Toronto: Butterworths. An informative and recent Canadian text.

Lenski, Gerhard E. 1966. *Power and Privilege: A Theory of Social Stratification*. New York: McGraw-Hill. An ambitious attempt to develop a balanced theory about social inequality.

Porter, John. 1965. *The Vertical Mosaic*. Toronto: University of Toronto Press. An internationally recognized classic on class and power in Canada.

Sorokin, Pitirim A. 1959. *Social and Cultural Mobility*. Glencoe, Illinois: Free Press. (Originally published in 1927). A neglected classic that deserves a wider readership.

Tepperman, Lorne. 1975. *Social Mobility in Canada*. Toronto: McGraw-Hill Ryerson. The only Canadian text on this topic.

CHAPTER 9
ETHNIC AND MINORITY RELATIONS

LEO DRIEDGER

"Ethnic" comes from the Greek word *ethnos*, meaning a group bound together and identified by ties and traits of nationality, culture, and race. French Canadians, for example, promote a national and cultural ethos which originated in France. Native Indians, too, have their subcultural and racial ties and traits. The British identify with their heritage as well. Each of these three groups constitutes "ethnos."

An **ethnic group**, according to Shibutani and Kwan (1965), "consists of those who perceive of themselves as being alike by virtue of their common ancestry, real or fictitious, and who are so regarded by others." An ethnic group includes a sense of belonging, and particular ways of acting, thinking, and feeling.

Gordon's (1964) definition differs somewhat in emphasis from Shibutani and Kwan's: "An ethnic group is a group of individuals with a shared sense of peoplehood based on presumed shared sociocultural experiences and/or similar characteristics." This sense of sharing includes all dimensions of language, nationality, culture, religion, and race. This is the group's **ethnic identity**. Ethnicity is thus a very broad term, which recognizes that all people have basic historical origins, but that the form and importance of this heritage may vary from group to group. Their sense of belonging and loyalty may also vary.

When people of many different nations, cultures, religions, and races come into contact with each other, some are bound to be more numerous, or influential, or both. Thus, minority-majority relations are inevitable. In Canada, the Hutterites are a small minority because they are relatively few and because they lack political power. The Jews are also small numerically, but they have more influence than their numbers might suggest. French Canadians are a minority, except in the province of Quebec where they are the numerical and political majority. While Canadians of British origins constitute the majority in the Atlantic provinces and Ontario, they are a numerically small minority in Quebec. However, this small English minority tends economically to dominate all of Quebec (Porter, 1965). In Canada, much of the economic – as well as political power is in the hands of the British Canadians.

Wagley and Harris (1958) summarize these minority aspects into five useful characteristics:

1. minorities are subordinate segments of complex societies

2. they have special physical or cultural traits which are [usually] held in low esteem by the dominant society

3. they are self-conscious units bound together by special traits

4. membership is transmitted by descent, capable of affiliating succeeding generations

5. by choice or necessity members [usually] marry within the group

According to these general characteristics, Hutterites, native Indians, blacks, and Jews will almost always be seen as minorities in Canada. Germans, Ukrainians, Scandinavians, and Italians will also constitute minorities most of the time. The basic difference between an ethnic group and a minority group is that each of us belongs to an ethnic group or groups, while not everyone belongs to a **minority group**. Minority status, on the other hand, has to do with both the size and power of the group.

IMMIGRATION

To understand the patterns of ethnic relations in Canada, we must first analyze the demographic and ecological macrostructures. (The term "ecological" is used here in the sociologists' sense of having to do with the spacing of people and institutions, and their resulting interdependency). When did the many peoples first come to the land we now call Canada, and where have they settled? Did Canadians of various racial, ethnic, cultural, and religious origins cluster more in one region than another? If so, why? What are the implications of such varied enclaves and patterns for ethnic relations?

A Demographic History

To document the coming of Homo sapiens to Canada, we begin with the earliest native Indians and Inuit. They were followed much later by the French and British, who traded in and settled this vast territory. Later still, many other Europeans came, and, more recently, Third World immigrants. A short history will help us gain some perspective on who came when and to whom Canada belongs.

The Earliest Native Inhabitants. Anthropologists tell us that the earliest Homo sapiens came to the two American continents at least twelve thousand years ago, probably via the Bering Strait (The Indians were here, therefore, when the Europeans were still barbarians roaming the European continent). Some Indians remained food gatherers, but others turned to agriculture, and by the time the Spaniards came in the early 1500s, they found the great civilizations of the Maya, the Aztecs, and the Incas in Central and South America.

The French and the British did not find equivalent civilizations among the native Indians of what is now Canada. Indians of the central plains and northlands were food gatherers. The Hurons and Iroquois had begun farming (Trigger, 1969), however, and the natives of the west coast were engaged in large-scale fishing (Rohner and Rohner, 1970).

Canadians tend to see a very small part of the great variety of Indian groupings who live throughout the two Americas. We also often forget that the native peoples have lived in what is now Canada twenty-five times longer than any Europeans. This fact gives rise to the interesting questions raised earlier: Whose land is Canada, and what are the land rights of native peoples who have not yet signed treaties with white immigrants?

The Charter Europeans. The French in 1608 established the first European settlement in Canada at what is now Montreal. Some 150 years later the British settled permanently in this country. Those first European settlers in Canada were considered by Porter (1965) as the two **charter groups**.

In 1871, when the first census after Confederation was taken, almost all (92 percent) of the some 3.5 million people who lived in Canada were either of British (61 percent) or French (31 percent) origin. Except for a small number of Germans (6 percent), early eastern Canada was two-thirds British and one-third French. Table 9-1 lists immigrants to Canada by nationality. The 1871 census did not include the estimated one-half million or more native Indians scattered over the northern territories, because the census included only the four original provinces of the east, only a fraction of the territory which is now Canada.

The British North America Act of 1867 legalized the claims of the two original European immigrant groups for such historically established privileges as the perpetuation of their separate languages and cultures. The Royal Commission on Bilingualism and Biculturalism continued to support and encourage the charter group status of the French, even though by 1981 immigrants of other ethnic origins composed more than one-fourth of the Canadian population.

The Multi-European Entrance. Although European settlers other than French and British represented only about 7 percent of the Canadian population in 1871, more of them continued to immigrate to join the two charter groups. Table 9-2 shows that in 1901 the charter groups constituted a great majority, but by

1971 this majority had dwindled, and the 5.5 million others represented more than a quarter – 26.7 percent – of the Canadian population. While the French origin population held fairly steady at 29 percent, the proportion of British origin had dropped to 45 percent. The British and French ranked first and second, followed by the Germans, Italians, and Ukrainians.

Most of these other European groups entered Canada well after the charter groups. Many of the Germans came to Ontario as early as 150 years ago, but the majority of the others arrived in a country where the charter groups had already established the political and economic patterns. In other words, the rules were made, and the terms of admission were set down. Some of the earlier European immigrants, such as the Germans, Scandinavians, and Jews, had a relatively high status and have been upwardly mobile, but more recent immigrants, with some notable exceptions, have remained largely in the lower strata of Canadian society.

Recent Third World Immigrants. Table 9-3 shows that in 1951, shortly after the war, the leading immigrant source countries were predominantly northern European; in 1973 immigrants from Britain continued to lead, and immigrants from the United States had moved into second place, but eight of the ten leading source countries were new Third World or southern European countries. This change in immigration trends to some extent reflects the change in Canadian immigration procedure from the discriminatory system described in Chapter 7 to a point system, introduced to provide immigrants of all countries with a more equitable chance to enter Canada.

The new regulations for selection of immigrants, established in 1967 and modified from time to time, set forth nine criteria for entrance. "Independent" applicants are assessed by and awarded points according to these nine criteria; those able to score 50 or more points out of 100 are given permission to enter Canada, from any part of the world. The "nominated" applicant (intermediate between "independent" and "sponsored") is subject to the point system, but can gain extra points by means of short-term arrangements

TABLE 9-1. COUNTRY OF ORIGIN OF THE CANADIAN POPULATION [1], 1871-1981

Ethnic Group	1871[2]	1881	1901	1911	1921	1931	1941	1951	1961	1971	1981[8]
Total [3]	3,486	4,325	5,371	7,207	8,788	10,377	11,507	14,009	18,238	21,568	24,343
British Isles	2,111	2,549	3,063	3,999	4,869	5,381	5,716	6,710	7,997	9,624	10,900
English	706	881	1,261	1,871	2,545	2,741	2,968	3,630	4,195	6,246	
Irish	846	957	989	1,075	1,108	1,231	1,268	1,440	1,753	1,581	
Scottish	550	700	800	1,027	1,174	1,346	1,404	1,547	1,902	1,720	
Other	8	10	13	26	42	62	76	92	146	86	
French	1,083	1,299	1,649	2,062	2,453	2,928	3,483	4,319	5,540	6,180	6,743
Other Europeans	240	299	458	945	1,247	1,825	2,044	2,554	4,117	4,960	5,700
Austrian, n.o.s.	—	—	11	44	108	49	38	32	107	42	
Belgian	—	—	3	10	20	28	30	35	61	51	
Czech & Slovak	—	—	—	—	9	30	43	64	73	82	
Finnish [4]	—	—	3	16	21	44	42	44	59	59	
German	203	254	311	403	295	474	465	620	1,050	1,317	
Greek	—	—	—	4	6	9	12	14	56	124	
Hungarian [5]	—	—	2	12	13	41	55	60	126	132	
Italian	1	2	11	46	67	98	113	152	450	731	
Jewish	—	1	16	76	126	157	170	182	173	297	
Lithuanian	—	—	—	—	2	6	8	16	28	25	
Netherlands	30	30	34	56	118	149	213	264	430	426	
Polish	—	—	6	34	53	146	167	220	324	316	
Roumanian [6]	—	—	—	6	13	29	25	24	44	27	
Russian [7]	1	1	20	44	100	88	84	91	119	64	
Scandinavian	2	5	31	113	167	228	245	283	387	385	
Ukrainian	—	—	6	75	107	225	306	395	473	581	
Yugoslav	—	—	—	—	4	16	21	21	69	105	
Other	4	6	5	7	18	9	10	36	88	195	
Asiatic	—	4	24	43	66	85	74	73	122	286	400
Chinese	—	4	17	28	40	47	35	33	58	119	
Japanese	—	—	5	9	16	23	23	22	29	37	
Other	—	—	2	6	10	15	16	19	34	129	
Other	52	174	177	158	153	158	190	354	463	519	600
Inuit	—	—	—	—	—	—	9	10	12	18	
Native Indian	—	109	93	95	110	112	117	156	208	295	

SOURCE: Dominion Bureau of Statistics, 1961 Census of Canada, Bulletin 7:1-6, 1966, Table 1; Statistics Canada, 1971 Census of Canada, Bulletin 1.3-2, 1973, Table 1; Kubat, D., and D. Thornton, *A Statistical Profile of Canadian Society*, Toronto: McGraw-Hill Ryerson, 1974, Table f-10.
NOTE: [1] Numbers rounded to the nearest 1000.
[2] Four original provinces only.
[3] Excludes Newfoundland prior to 1951.
[4] Includes Estonia prior to 1951.
[5] Includes Lithuanian and Moravia in 1901 and 1911.
[6] Includes Bulgaria in 1901 and 1911.
[7] Includes Finnish and Polish in 1871 and 1881.
[8] 1981 Estimates.

with relatives. This new policy is designed to facilitate entry of next of kin, but it gives more non-Europeans a chance to compete for immigration as well. Thus, in the last ten years many more immigrants from non-European countries have entered Canada than previously, adding more racial, religious, and ethnic heterogeneity to our population.

Regional Ethnic Mosaic

Our discussion so far of the population patterns over time illustrates that the native Indians possessed the land first, followed by the French, the British, other European groups, and Third World immigrants. Table 9-1 shows that the various groups increased at differ-

TABLE 9-2. PERCENTAGE COMPOSITION OF THE POPULATION BY ETHNIC ORIGINS FOR PROVINCE OF RESIDENCE, CANADA, 1901 and 1971

Ethnic Origin	Total	Nfld.	PEI	NS	NB	Que.	Ont.	Man.	Sask.	Alta.	BC
1901											
British	57.0		85.1	78.1	71.1	17.6	79.3	64.4	43.9	47.8	59.6
French	30.7		13.4	9.8	24.2	80.2	7.3	6.3	2.9	6.2	2.6
Other	12.3		1.5	12.0	4.1	2.2	13.4	29.4	53.2	46.0	37.9
Total	100.0		100.0	100.0	100.0	100.0	100.0	100.0	100.0	100.0	100.0
1971											
British	44.6	93.8	82.7	77.5	57.6	10.6	59.4	41.9	42.1	46.8	57.9
French	28.7	3.0	13.7	10.2	37.0	79.0	9.6	8.8	8.1	5.8	4.4
Other	26.7	3.3	3.6	12.3	5.3	10.4	31.0	49.3	51.8	47.4	37.7
German	6.1	0.5	0.9	5.2	1.3	0.9	6.2	12.5	19.4	14.2	9.1
Dutch	2.0	0.1	1.1	1.9	0.8	0.2	2.7	3.6	2.1	3.6	3.2
Scandinavian	1.8	0.2	0.2	0.5	0.6	0.1	0.8	6.4	6.4	6.0	5.1
Polish	1.5	0.1	0.1	0.4	0.1	0.4	1.9	4.3	2.9	2.7	1.4
Russian	0.3	0.0	0.0	0.0	0.0	0.1	0.2	0.4	1.1	0.6	1.1
Ukrainian	2.7	0.0	.0.1	0.3	0.1	0.3	2.1	11.6	9.3	8.3	2.8
Italian	3.4	0.1	0.1	0.5	0.2	2.8	6.0	1.1	0.3	1.5	2.5
Jewish	1.4	0.1	0.1	0.3	0.2	1.9	1.8	2.0	0.2	0.4	0.6
Other Europe	3.9	0.2	0.2	0.8	0.4	2.0	6.1	3.8	4.1	4.1	4.5
Asiatic	1.3	0.3	0.3	0.6	0.4	0.7	1.5	1.0	0.8	1.6	3.6
Other	2.4	1.7	0.5	1.8	1.2	1.0	1.9	5.6	5.2	4.2	3.9
Total	100.0	100.0	100.0	100.0	100.0	100.0	100.0	100.0	100.0	100.0	100.0

SOURCE: Dominion Bureau of Statistics, 1921 Census of Canada, Vol. 1, 1924, Table 23; Statistics Canada, 1971 Census of Canada, Bulletin 1.3-2, 1973, Table 3.

TABLE 9-3. TEN LEADING SOURCE COUNTRIES OF IMMIGRANTS, CANADA, SELECTED YEARS

1951	1960	1968	1973
Britain	Italy	Britain	Britain
Germany	Britain	United States	United States
Italy	United States	Italy	Hong Kong
Netherlands	Germany	Germany	Portugal
Poland	Netherlands	Hong Kong	Jamaica
France	Portugal	France	India
United States	Greece	Austria	Philippines
Belgium	France	Greece	Greece
Yugoslavia	Poland	Portugal	Italy
Denmark	Austria	Yugoslavia	Trinidad

SOURCE: Manpower and Immigration, *Highlights from the Green Paper on Immigration and Population,* 1975, p. 28.

Dr. Daniel Hill is a prominent black Canadian whose work in studying cults, sects, and mind development groups has been extremely valuable in understanding these phenomena. Hill's stature and prominence have given him a strong and positive voice in Canadian ethnic and minority relations. (*Canpress*)

ent times. Table 9-2 indicates that the many groups were unevenly distributed throughout Canada. It is obvious that the various Canadian regions are very different ethnically, and we need to examine these differences.

Culturally and linguistically, Canada can be regarded as six regions: the northlands, the west, Upper Canada, Lower Canada, New Brunswick, and the Atlantic region. Today, the regions vary from multicultural and multilingual in the northwest to unicultural and monolingual in the east. High concentrations of the native people in the north, the "other" ethnic groups in the west, the French in Quebec, and the British in the east constitute an interesting mix of cultural values and social organizations.

The Northlands. The northlands include all of the Yukon, the Northwest Territories, Labrador, and roughly the upper three-fourths of the six western and central provinces (British Columbia, Alberta, Saskatchewan, Manitoba, Ontario, Quebec). As indicated so powerfully in Figure 9-1, this area constitutes about 80 percent of the Canadian land mass, though it includes a relatively small proportion of the Canadian

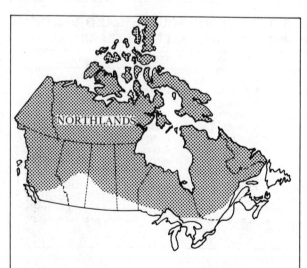

Figure 9-1. Extent of the Cultural and Linguistic Region of the Canadian Northlands.

population. Demographically, it is the area where 69 percent of the population is of native origin, and 56 percent uses its native tongue at home. Vallee and DeVries (1975) illustrate that these northern Indian peoples perpetuate multilingual and multicultural societies, where European influences are increasing but not yet dominant.

The Indian residents lived here first, and they occupy the majority of our land area. However, they constitute a very small percentage of our population, and are, economically and politically, virtually powerless. The trend, however, seems to be for Indians to come south into more urban settings, and there is strong evidence that they quickly adopt either English or (in Quebec) French; only 33 percent of Indian people in urban areas use their mother tongues (Vallee and DeVries, 1975). The northlands are multicultural and multilingual.

The West. The west, which includes the southern portions of British Columbia, Alberta, Saskatchewan, and Manitoba, was the domain of food-gathering peoples, and was settled most recently by immigrants of many European origins. The region is highly rural and agricultural; it includes a multitude of substantial British, German, Ukrainian, French, and smaller ethnic settlements. A diversity of European ethnic groups settled the region and established social instututions.

Indians comprise a significant proportion of the population on the prairies. Asiatics represent an important part of British Columbia (3.6 percent). Although many western ethnic groups seek to retain their language, the language used at home by the majority – 85 percent – is English. The west is multicultural and anglophone.

Upper Canada. Until recently, Upper Canada, now southern Ontario, was English linguistically and British culturally. It was the stronghold of the British, a charter group, whose large population promoted urban industrial growth, while it maintained a strong economic and financial base.

But lately this urban industrial area has attracted many newcomers to its labor market, especially immigrants to Toronto. These immigrants represent many cultures from northern and southern Europe, as well as the Third World. Therefore, the urban areas of Ontario are changing from being very British to highly multicultural and multilingual. These new immigrants, however, are competing for jobs, and are therefore learning English. So, although British culture is not threatened in Upper Canada, multiculturalism is on the rise.

Some 75 percent of Ontarians use English at home (Vallee and DeVries, 1975). Only about 5 percent speak French at home. Although Ontario has made some efforts to become bilingual (French and English), it appears that English is dominant, other languages subordinate. This region could best be described as Anglophone with strong multicultural trends.

Although the linguistic and cultural conditions of the west and Upper Canada may seem similar, they are very different historically. The west has been strongly multicultural and multilingual throughout its short history. But since it is less industrialized, new immigrants do not seem to be streaming into the area in large numbers. Consequently, it is not as culturally diverse as southern Ontario.

Lower Canada. In Lower Canada, now the southern portion of Quebec, 80 percent of the population speak French at home (Vallee and DeVries, 1975). Speaking English in the home seems to be declining. One reason that English has persisted in Quebec is because the economic elite tended to be English and were influential because of their industrial connections with the rest of North America. Toronto is now Canada's dominant financial and industrial base, which means that slowly business headquarters and offices are shifting to Ontario. Therefore, the power of the English business elite in Quebec will decline, and the use of French will increase.

A second reason for greater French lingual and cultural influence in Quebec is that provincial legislation favors that language. The influence of the Québécois nationalists will also result in some English interests leaving Quebec, redoubling the emphasis on French language and culture.

The more than 5 million French Canadians living in Quebec constitute the largest regional ethnic block in Canada. With their long Canadian history, their new drive for French identity, federal efforts to promote French in Canada, and provincial legislation to promote French language and culture, it is likely that southern Quebec will remain the strongest single ethnic region. Lower Canada is Francophone and multicultural.

New Brunswick. New Brunswick is Canada's only bilingual and bicultural region. About 25 percent of the residents speak French at home; about 66 percent speak English at home. Other languages are spoken in the home by fewer than 10 percent of the population. This area supports only 2 or 3 percent of Canada's population. According to Joy (1972), the French in New Brunswick will in all likelihood retain their language, because they are part of the bilingual belt adjacent to French Quebec. French-English bilingualism is therefore both a current fact and the pattern for the future. Cultures other than French and English are not represented in large numbers in New Brunswick.

The Atlantic Region. The most easterly Atlantic region (Nova Scotia, Prince Edward Island, and the island of Newfoundland) is unilingual and unicultural. Ninety-five percent of the residents in this area speak English at home (Vallee and DeVries, 1975). Their long history is largely British, and demographically they are British. Very few immigrants enter these provinces. This area supports only 6 or 7 percent of the Canadian population, and it is highly unlikely that residents of this region will push for heterogeneity. Their Indian population is very small, their black population is English speaking and small, and other ethnic groups are hardly represented.

Regionalism. This discussion of our country's cultural and linguistic composition suggests that Canada is indeed a **regional mosaic**. The differences between the multicultural and multilingual northwest and the unicultural and unilingual east are great. Indeed, New Brunswick is the only region that approaches a bilingual and bicultural condition, and it is a very small part of Canada. The recommendations of the Bilingual and Bicultural Commission (1965), with its first report advocating a bilingual and bicultural nation, have been promoted by the Federal Government of Canada. The more recent Royal Commission on Canadian Unity (1978), however, appears to stress regionalism and diversity. This latter emphasis seems to be more in line with the cultural, linguistic, demographic, and ecological realities of the nation. Canada is a mosaic of many ethnic cultures and languages. Such diversity is a source of problems, but a source, too, of opportunities for expanding our personal and national horizons, by experiencing and appreciating that rich variety which is the hallmark of Canadian society.

ETHNIC STRATIFICATION

A regional mosaic indicates the ecological distribution of ethnic groups. A vertical mosaic (Porter, 1965) indicates strata of status and prestige. Some ethnic groups are heavily represented in the upper strata of the power elite; other groups are heavily represented in the lower strata. Let us start our examination of **ethnic stratification** with a discussion of the legal status of three ethnic categories – *charter group*, *entrance group*, *treaty group* – and follow this with a discussion of the social class groupings of ethnic categories by education, income, and occupation.

Legal Ethnic Status

Charter Groups. We noted above that the British North America Act of 1867 gave the British and French, charter group status. Though the Canadian charter group status of the French is legally secure, the French have always been junior partners with the British, and they have had difficulty matching the numerical, economic, and political strength of the British. The French came to rely on regional segregation and on institutional and cultural development as a means of counteracting British dominance.

The collective dominance of the charter groups has never been seriously challenged, because of high levels of British immigration and French natural increase in population. Also, the ethnic structure of a country, in

terms of its charter and noncharter groups, is determined early and tends to be self-perpetuating. The French have held at about 30 percent of the Canadian population (although that has declined recently); the British have always been the largest ethnic group (although their proportion, too, has been dropping steadily).

At the time of Confederation the British and French in Upper and Lower Canada and the Atlantic Region (other than Newfoundland) formed a bilingual and bicultural nation, with few representatives from other countries. It is these other immigrants who are in the process of slowly changing Canada from a bicultural to a multicultural and plural society, and it is to them and their statuses that we now turn.

Entrance Groups. Many ethnic groups are not founders of the country; they enter as immigrants and are called **entrance groups**. Porter (1965) calls the position to which ethnic groups are admitted and at which they are (at least initially) allowed to function in the power structure of a society *entrance status*. For most entrance groups in Canada this position is characterized by low status occupational roles and a subjection to processes of assimilation laid down by the charter groups. This situation held and holds for immigrants generally. Less preferred immigrants, moreover, although they were allowed to enter Canada, were channeled into even lower status jobs than the norm. Because of their later entrance they were often left with marginally productive farm lands.

Some immigrants of German, Dutch, Jewish, Chinese, and Scandinavian origin entered Canada earlier than many of the others; they can be considered older entrance status groups. Many Germans, such as the ones who settled in the Berlin (now Kitchener-Waterloo) area, have been here more than 150 years; in Manitoba many have been here over a century. Many of these older immigrants have moved out of entrance status into higher educational, financial, and occupational status. The Jews, for example, placed great value on education, and have entered higher status occupations, higher on the average than those of any of the other groups, including the charter groups. Immigrants from eastern Europe, however, came in

Indians have long been at a serious disadvantage in Canadian society. Native leaders like George Erasmus (left), President of the Dene Nation, and Bob Stevenson, interim President of the NWT Metis Association, are attempting to guarantee native rights and freedoms. In the Northwest Territories, there are divisions among native groups, but most believe that a united front will be most effective in changing the status quo. (*Canpress*)

large numbers in the early twentieth century; southern Europeans came later still. Ukrainians, for example, were left with relatively less fertile rural areas to settle, and urban Italians, many of them unskilled, were left with the relatively more menial jobs. Third World immigrants who arrived during the seventies were better educated and more highly skilled than were the eastern Europeans, and often entered the higher occupational strata, but since many were different racially, culturally, and religiously, they often found competition difficult.

Treaty Status Groups. According to Frideres (1974):

Until 1755 the English followed a policy of expediency. At first they chose to ignore the Indians, but when this was no longer feasible (because of westward expansion), they chose to isolate them (through the reserve system), or to annihilate them (as in the case of the Beothuk Indians of Newfoundland).

By 1830 Indian Affairs, initially a branch of the military, became a part of the public service (Surtees, 1969). The first Indian Act was passed in 1876, and it has been revised a number of times since then. The general policy at this time was to isolate Indians on segregated reserves, thus freeing most of the land for use by Europeans.

The first treaties were made in 1850, such as the Douglas Treaty in British Columbia, and the Robinson Superior and Huron Treaties in Ontario. As Europeans increasingly moved westward, Treaties 1 to 11 were begun in southern Manitoba in 1871, a year after Manitoba became the first western province. The native Indians ceded most of their land to the Europeans, and they received in return reserved land claims, annuities of three dollars per person, and various gifts of clothing, medals, and equipment. Thus the **treaty status** groups were created.

At present there are about 100 000 Treaty Indians belonging to 550 bands, located on some 2241 reserves west of the Province of Quebec (Hawthorne, et al, 1967). Treaties with Indians have generally not been made in the five easterly provinces, most of British Columbia, large parts of the Yukon, and the Northwest Territories.

Although native peoples were the original peoples,

Treaty Indians are nevertheless wards of the federal government. Their low legal status was originally intended to restrict them to small groups, so that white Europeans could more freely occupy the land. This legal **segregation** has had the additional effect of creating many islands of inertia and poverty, with little hope of improvement. Many Indians and whites are very unhappy about this lowly legal status of Indians. Some of them question whether any of the treaties, made between literate Europeans and illiterate food gatherers, are valid. To return to our initial question: Whose land is Canada, especially the vast areas where no treaties have been signed as yet?

Socioeconomic Status

There are forms of status other than legal. The amount of income, the years of education, and the occupation in which people are engaged are all indicators of socioeconomic status. Most Canadians desire more money; those who attain it thereby gain prestige. Similarly, education is often seen as a means of obtaining well paying occupations; education is therefore also valued by many. Blishen (1967) used the combined indicators of income and education to develop a socioeconomic occupational index that ranks occupations. Pineo and Porter (1967) also ranked occupations by asking respondents to order the occupations according to prestige. Thus, various populations can be ranked by socioeconomic status, or strictly by occupational prestige. Ethnic groups can be ranked in this way as well.

Canada's Jewish population, for example, is very heavily represented in the higher prestige occupations such as the managerial and professional categories, while hardly represented in the lower, blue-collar categories. Thus a group which is not legally one of the advantaged charter groups ranks highest on the socioeconomic occupational index. The British, one of the two charter groups, rank second highest, suggesting that occupational prestige and socioeconomic status reinforce charter status to some degree; the British, in addition to being most numerous in Canada, rank high socioeconomically.

The ranking of ethnic groups by occupations also shows that the French have not fared as well socioeconomically as their charter status might suggest.

They rank in the middle, below the Jews, the British, and the Germans, but above the Ukrainians, Italians, and Indian people. Various scholars – Hughes (1943) in his study of Cantonville, Rioux (1971) in his study of Quebec society – show that even in Quebec, where the French are a large majority, the British tend to have a disproportionate socioeconomic influence. Much of the industrial capital is in the hands of non-French entrepreneurs, who dominate the higher managerial occupations. Recently, the Québécois have been working hard at gaining more control over their economic destiny. For these and many other reasons, as you saw in Chapter 8, a large French minority wishes to secede; it wishes to gain territorial, political, and economic control, so that it can perpetuate the French language and culture without fear of assimilation. Thus, and to emphasize a point made earlier, the legal charter status of the French is very much a junior partner status in Confederation (especially since it is not backed by strong socioeconomic status), and it is the effects of this junior status that the French seek to counter.

The most recent occupational data also show that immigrants, such as the Italians, are very heavily represented in the lower occupational strata, such as construction trades, manufacturing, and service. Native Indian people are especially heavily represented in the lower status occupations, and many are unemployed. Many Indians have emerged only recently from the food gathering state, and their special status under the "ward" system of the federal government has made it very difficult for them to compete socioeconomically. The middle-class curriculum in schools has not served well many Indians, and they have been reluctant to enter unfamiliar industrial occupations. Thus, Canadian Indians find themselves in the lowest socioeconomic stratum. Some writers like Cardinal (1969) have referred to them as the "niggers" of Canada, the disadvantaged targets of discrimination by Canadian whites.

Racial Differentations

If this were a chapter in an American sociology text, **race** would likely be the central theme. Eleven percent of the American population is black; America has as many blacks as Canada has people, plus some 6 million Chicanos. By comparison, Canada is predominantly Caucasian; only about 3 percent of Canadians are non-white. Canadian Indians (1.4 percent) and Chinese (.6 percent) represent the largest of the non-white groups. Some might therefore contend that race is not a significant factor in Canada, and does not need special treatment. They would be wrong.

There are at least three important reasons why race must be included as an influential factor in Canadian stratification. First, Canadian Indians, although less than 2 percent of our population, were the first inhabitants, have special legal status, and are perceived by many as belonging to another race. Second, new immigration laws now permit many more immigrants from the Third World to enter Canada than previously, and many of these are neither of European racial stock nor of Judeo-Christian religious background. Third, Canadians are greatly influenced by their neighbor to the south, and the preoccupation of Americans with racial questions also tends to affect Canadian attitudes and thinking. A brief discussion of race is therefore necessary.

Anthropologists tell us that race is an arbitrary biological grouping, and estimates of the racial component of large populations are still based on subjective opinions (Hughes and Kallen, 1974). Physical features, genetics (including blood types), and theories about racial origins have given rise to various classifications. Although there are many such classifications, "Caucasoid," "Mongoloid," and "Negroid" are the most common. Head form; face form; nose form; eye, lip, and ear form; color of hair, skin, and eyes; texture of the hair and amount of hair on the body; and stature and body build have all been used as criteria for racial classifications. Skin color (Caucasians, white; Mongoloids, yellow; Negroids, black) is the most common criterion. However, large groupings of the world's people, such as the native Indians of the Americas, the East Indians, and the Pacific Polynesians, do not fit these three categories. Many scholars, especially in the United States, also find that differences between races (such as intelligence levels) tend to disappear in controlled situations. Then why have the whites of European origin made so much of race, and of skin color especially?

Although we cannot delve deeply into the origins of racial differentiation here, it would appear that European explorers found that most of the people they encountered were of darker skin color than themselves, and were also less technologically advanced. "Technologically advanced" and "superior" tended to be equivalent in the European mind. Europeans thus developed an image of "white superiority."

Northern Europeans in particular, the dominant population in Canada, tend to be very conscious of skin color, and often classify people accordingly. Certainly, Indians in Canada, who are segregated on reserves, and who are also racially classified as Mongoloid, are accorded low status in Canada. There is already evidence that as more Third World immigrants, racially classified Negroid and Mongoloid, enter our larger cities, racial incidents tend to erupt more frequently.

Porter (1965) suggests that the idea of an ethnic mosaic, as opposed to a **melting pot** impedes the process of social mobility: "the melting pot with its radical breakdown of national ties and old forms of stratification would have endangered the conservative tradition of Canadian life, a tradition which gives ideological support to the continued high status of the British charter group." As you saw in Chapter 8, however, this situation seems to be changing; many entrance groups are gaining status educationally, occupationally, and economically, but are retaining many of their ethnic characteristics. The Jews are an excellent example of high upward mobility coupled with high maintenance of ethnic identity.

Any theory of Canadian ethnic relations must make provision for these multidimensional regional, economic, and political status structures in order to account for the factors that influence the composition of the Canadian mosaic, and also the identity of individual ethnic groups.

THEORIES OF ETHNIC CHANGE AND PERSISTENCE

What happens to the multitudes who enter Canada? How do they adjust to their new environment? Do some immigrants fare better in one region than in another? Do they simply wish to retain a separate identity, or are they determined to maintain geographic/ethnic boundaries which will keep them separate? Various theories have been developed to explain what will happen to ethnic groups in an industrial-technological society. The first two theories, assimilation and amalgamation, assume that the urban industrial forces of technology will result in vanishing ethnicity. The third and fourth theories, multivariate assimilation and modified pluralism, admit that the technological forces will change the ethnic minority, but predict that groups will retain ethnic characteristics in part, or in a changed form. The remaining two theories, ethnic conflict and pluralism, posit the maintenance of ethnic identity in both rural and urban environments. A discussion of the six theories follows.

Assimilation: Anglo-Conformity

The theory of **assimilation** has influenced North American thinking greatly since the 1920s. It is the product of an evolutionary perspective which assumes that ethnic groups are constantly becoming more like the majority culture, represented in Canada and the United States by the British. This theory tends to be deterministic; it assumes that the power of the majority will be too much for any minority group to resist, and therefore the group will assimilate into the majority.

A chief advocate of this concept was Robert Park, who contended that immigrants, when they came into contact with the new American society, either followed the course of least resistance (contact, accommodation, assimilation) or took a more circuitous route (contact, conflict, competition, accommodation, fusion) (Hughes, et al, 1950). (See Figure 9-2.) Whereas the latter route would take longer and entail considerable resistance on the part of the immigrant, the end results would be the same: assimilation and a consequent loss of distinctive ethnic identity.

There were enough minorities who did assimilate as Park predicted to keep American researchers occupied with documenting this process. For 50 years these scholars tended to ignore groups that retained a separate identity and tended to regard their separateness as a relatively insignificant and temporary factor in

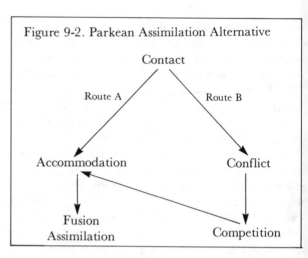

Figure 9-2. Parkean Assimilation Alternative

the total pattern of minority-majority relations. The assimilationist theory was so influential, combined with the evolutionary thinking of the day, that evidence to the contrary often made little headway.

The theory of assimilation was and is attractive, because it is dynamic. It takes into account the distinctiveness and enormous technological changes visible in North American societies. Furthermore, numerous studies show that many northern European groups, such as the Dutch, the Scandinavians, and the Germans, do lose many of their distinguishing cultural traits, such as original language use, fairly quickly. However, in the eyes of some, assimilation theory is too deterministic. That is, as a macro-theory it may explain a general process for some groups, but it does not take into account the many aspects of cultural change that may not all be moving in the same direction. Further, it does not sufficiently account for the possibility of non-assimilation by some groups. Finally, it does not address the idea that the end-type of assimilation may not be Anglo-Saxon, but something quite different.

We learn from Canadian history that many British leaders had the Anglo model in mind for the native people, the French, and everyone else. Lord Durham, for example, assumed that others would assimilate into the dominant British legal, political, economic, and cultural system (Stanley, 1960). And many seem to have hoped that somehow even the French would finally so assimilate, although via Park's more circuitous route of conflict and competition. These leaders assumed the preeminent desirability of British social institutions.

Amalgamation: Melting Pot

Amalgamation theories differ from those of assimilation by positing that immigrant groups will be synthesized into a new group. The evolutionary process is the same as that of assimilation, but the end result is a melting pot amalgam different from any of the groups involved. This concept is frequently taken by Americans to be typical of their society. They broke free of British dominance 200 years ago and created a nation ostensibly dominated by no one group. All contributed to the American dream, with its new Constitution, a multitude of cultures from many parts of the world, and a system of free enterprise. Independence and freedom were popular watchwords. It was a new nation, a new culture, a new continent, a pot to which all might contribute.

Herberg (1955) contends, however, that in America the Protestants, Catholics, and Jews have never "melted." Nor have they in Canada. The racial component, well represented in Canada by our native peoples and in America by 25 million blacks, seems not to be melting very noticeably either. To what extent other ethnic groups, such as the French, Chinese, and Italians, are melting is the subject of much research, and it is perhaps somewhat early to tell. But certainly the French in Quebec are a bulwark against amalgamation. The prophesied synthesis is slow in coming in Canada, and even in the United States where the melting pot theory is often applied, more and more scholars are having doubts about its usefulness (Kallen, 1924; Herberg, 1955; Newman, 1973).

Canada's relatively open immigration policy has provided the potential opportunity for many peoples to contribute to a melting pot. At the time of Confederation, however, the two founding peoples represented most of the population, and as we have seen their historical influence has been much stronger than any of the other groups that followed. Early British and French influences have tended to dominate early Canadian history and the lives of more recent immigrants. The two charter groups have fought hard not to amalgamate either culturally or linguistically, so that from the beginning our pot has contained ingredients that don't melt.

The synthesis of British, French, Germans, Ukrainians, Italians, Canadian Indians, and others into a recognizable national character has been a long time coming. Perhaps it is this "melting" process, more than any other, which is needed to develop a spirited Canadian nationalism. The Americans, on the other hand, have stressed amalgamation more, and have evolved a stronger feeling of nationalism than Canadians have been able to manage. Could this be why Canada is at this time seriously discussing the possibility of French separation? Perhaps too many Canadians feel that some parts of Canada are not really so much a part of them. Speculation aside, amalgamation seems not to explain the Canadian scene as well as some other theoretical perspectives. Perhaps in the future amalgamation may apply to a greater extent than it does now.

Pluralism: Ethnic Mosaic

The metaphor of the mosaic to describe the Canadian plural society is useful in answering such questions as the following: How are the tiles in the mosaic distributed? Are the tiles equal, or can some be seen as more important than others because of their size or the way in which they cluster in the total design? What would be missing if particular tiles no longer remained distinctive? The first question corresponds to the regional and spatial distribution of various ethnic groups in Canada; the second, to the status and power of the various ethnic groups within the total society; and the third, to the cultural and institutional contributions of the groups.

Cultural **pluralism** suggests that over time different ethnic groups maintain their unique identities. Cultural pluralism is often viewed as an arrangement whereby distinct groups live side by side in relative harmony. The proponent of this view was Horace Kallen, who did so for three main reasons (Newman, 1973). He argued that, first, while there are many kinds of social relationships and identities which can be chosen voluntarily, people cannot choose their ancestry. Second, each of the minority groups has something of value of contribute to a country. And third, the American constitution carried with it an assumption that all were created equal, even though there might be many distinct differences. Kallen wished to refute the reigning notions of assimilation and the melting pot.

Assimilationists and amalgamationists emphasize the overwhelming influence of social phenomena like technology and urbanization as constituting the master trend which would sweep all forms of ethnic differentiation before it. Cultural pluralism, on the other hand, tends to focus on countervailing ideological forces, such as democracy and human justice, fundamental to which are the beliefs that all people are of equal worth and all may live as they choose, providing they respect the rights of others. Whereas the preceding theories call for the disappearance of immigrant and racial groups, pluralism holds that there may be greater resistance to assimilation and amalgamation than had formerly been thought, and that the trend toward permissive differentiation already seems to be set. In

All Things in Common

Many Canadian ethnic groups – Ukrainians, Mennonites, French, Germans, and Scandinavians – seek to isolate themselves in rural block settlements, but the Hutterites have been the most successful.

All Hutterites inhabit the Canadian and the American prairies, and none remains in the countries of their origin, the Austrian Tyrol and Moravia. The Hutterites numbered about 20 000 in the 1970s, dispersed throughout some 200 colonies in Alberta, Manitoba, North and South Dakota, Montana, and Saskatchewan.

The Hutterites originated during the Protestant Reformation in the sixteenth century and are one of three surviving Anabaptist groups. (The other two are the Mennonites and the Swiss Anabaptists including the Old Order Amish). The Anabaptists were noncomformist groups who rejected infant baptism and membership in a state- or all-inclusive church. They challenged existing social, economic, and political institutions, as well as some of the reformers, including Martin Luther. Many became martyrs. As religious refugees in 1528, they began the practice of community of goods, holding all things in common. The first Bruderhof or colony was begun in Moravia, which is now

European Czechoslovakia. The first colonists were soon joined by Jacob Hutter, who became an important organizer, and from whom they were to derive their name. Hutter was burned at the stake in 1536.

Although many communal groups have emerged from time to time, the Hutterites are now by far the oldest, in existence for some 450 years. They began as a religious group, and religion is still their driving force. Curiously, they do not as a rule have a special church building for worship, but often meet in the school. They believe that all life is sacred, and that worship is only one of the many aspects of living together.

The preacher, elected by the colony, is the chief leader, in charge of the religious and organizational aspects of the community. "The Boss," the second man in authority, is in charge of the economic activities, assisted by other bosses in charge of the various agricultural operations, and so on. The women are also led by a head woman in charge of kitchen and garden operations.

Hutterites do not follow the fashion. The polka-dot kerchief, the shawls, the long dresses are the styles of the past. Hutterite women part their hair in the middle and braid it a special way. The men often button their shirts to the top; never wear ties, but typically wear suspenders. Clothes are usually dark, homemade, and conservative, although styles vary by colony. The children are dressed

Canada, we have accepted pluralist religious expressions and a diversity of political parties and ideologies. **Multiculturalism** in Canada is now also increasingly promoted, although not without some resistance.

In 1971 the government of Canada announced a policy of multiculturalism within the bilingual framework. The government sought to encourage and assist Canadian cultural groups who so desired to continue to develop their cultural heritage, while seeking also to acquire one of the two official languages and thus increasing integration into the Canadian society. Berry, Kalin, and Taylor (1977) show in their national study

that Quebec – predominantly French – and the Atlantic provinces – predominantly British – are not sold on multiculturalism, while Ontario and the west, where more of the non-charter groups reside, are more in favor of multiculturalism.

Our large French population has always made up a very substantial, very distinct tile in the mosaic. Pluralists would say, too, that the Indians of Canada's northlands represent several more, quite durable tiles in the mosaic, and that, to a lesser extent, so do Canada's blacks, Jews, Hutterites, Doukhobors, Italians, Asiatics, and many other groups, such as the

---

like miniature adults. Make-up is taboo, and a simple life is emphasized. Distinctive clothing and grooming, sacred symbols of separation and Godliness, are also effective means of ingroup boundary maintenance.

Individuals own little more than their clothes and a private chest; the rest belongs to everyone in the colony (usually 75 to 150 members). Families live in several-room apartments, and spend time together during the evenings. But, they all eat together in large dining rooms, with the adult males and females at separate tables. The children attend German school, with the teacher and his wife in charge. The children attend public school on the colony as well, in a separate schoolhouse.

Adults usually work in groups. The women cook, clean, paint, sew, and work in the gardens. Seeding, harvesting, butchering, hunting, and other activities are done in male groups.

The basic structure of the Hutterite colony is so firm that the Hutterites can freely adopt the latest technology. They place very few if any restrictions on mechanical, electrical, and any other means of production. The chicken operation may involve thousands of laying hens, in well lit,

ventilated modern barns with all the latest equipment, feeding formulae, and processing of eggs. The same is true for the hog operation and the cropping. The latest seeding equipment, super-power tractors, self-propelled combines, and trucks are in standard use. These large-scale operations make farming more economical, so that Hutterites can compete very effectively. Their simple, no-frills life style saves money, and large families provide cheap labor, so that colonies often become economic threats to the larger rural communities. They generate large profits, and pay well for new acreages required for their expansion into new colonies. Thus, some provincial governments, like Alberta, have placed restrictions on colony expansion.

The Hutterites are a very small minority, and are now confined to the prairies of North America. Hutterites are a good example of slight religious and culture change, contributing toward pluralism in Canada. But they adopt new farming techniques freely. Thus, Gordon's (1964) suggestion that some features of a minority may change more than others, certainly applies. Glazer and Moynihan's (1963) theory that no group remains unchanged, but main-

tains a core identity, is also evident among Hutterites. There is little evidence of assimilation and amalgamation. Of Germanic ancestry, and conscientious objectors to war, they have survived through difficult times. Sometimes accused of being German sympathizers, and at times labeled communists, they have been subjected to prejudice and discrimination. They have survived for centuries, however, amidst conflict and persecution, thus also constituting an object lesson in the relevance and function of social conflict.

Source:

National Film Board of Canada, *The Hutterites*. 16 mm., 1964; Hostetler, John A., and Gertrude Enders Huntington. *The Hutterites in North America.* New York: Holt, Rinehart and Winston, 1967; Hostetler, John A. *Hutterite Society.* Baltimore: Johns Hopkins University Press, 1974; Peters, Victor. *All Things Common: The Hutterian Way of Life.* New York: Harper and Row, 1965.

Ukrainians, and Germans in block settlements on the prairies. Canada's original natives, dominant charter groups, and relatively open immigration policy seem to have contributed toward a differentiated country more like Belgium or Switzerland than like either of our most influential neighbors, Britain and the United States.

Multivariate Assimilation

The central theme of Milton Gordon's (1964) *Assimilation in American Life* is **multivariate assimilation**, the theory that assimilation is not a single social process but a number of subprocesses which he classifies under the headings "cultural" and "structural." Cultural assimilation includes acceptance by the incoming group of modes of dress, language, and other cultural characteristics of the host society. Structural assimilation concerns the degree to which immigrants enter the social institutions of the society and the degree to which they are accepted into these institutions by the majority. Gordon suggests that assimilation may occur more in the economic, political, and educational institutions, while assimilation may be resisted more in the areas of religion, family, and recreation. It would seem, therefore, that the opposing processes of assimilation and pluralism may occur simultaneously, depending on the dimension of ethnic activity examined. But, as Newman (1973) points out: "Gordon contends [that] once structural assimilation is far advanced, all other types of assimilation will naturally follow."

Gordon's multivariate approach forced scholars out of their unilinear rut. But each of the seven stages or types of assimilation he established (listed in Table 9-4) tended to be oriented toward either an assimilationist or an amalgamationist target.

Gordon's major contribution is his complex multilinear, multidimensional view of the assimilation process. It has been seen as a considerable improvement on Park's assimilation cycle. Although Gordon was mainly concerned with assimilation as such, and though he did not dwell on pluralism, he did not negate plural expressions in the areas of religion, the family, and recreation. The Hutterites emphasize religion, for example, and the Jews the family.

TABLE 9-4. GORDON'S SEVEN ASSIMILATION VARIABLES

Subprocess or Condition	Types or Stages of Assimilation
Change of cultural patterns to those of host society	Cultural or behavioral assimilation
Large-scale entrance into cliques, clubs, and institutions of host society, on primary group level	Structural assimilation
Large-scale intermarriage	Marital assimilation
Development of sense of people-hood based exclusively on host society	Identificational assimilation
Absence of prejudice	Attitude receptional assimilation
Absence of discrimination	Behavior receptional assimilation
Absence of value and power conflict	Civic assimilation

SOURCE: Gordon, Milton M. *Assimilation in American Life,* New York: Oxford University Press, 1964.

Modified Pluralism

Glazer and Moynihan (1963) are able to distinguish four major events in New York history which they think structured a series of ethnic patterns in that city. The first was the shaping of the Jewish community under the impact of the Nazi persecution of Jews in Europe and the establishment of the state of Israel. The second was a parallel, if less marked, shaping of a Catholic community by the reemergence of the Catholic school controversy. The third was the migration of southern Negroes to New York following World War I and continuing through the fifties. The fourth was the influx of Puerto Ricans during the fifteen years following World War II.

Their implicit point is that the melting pot did not function in New York. They claim, further that throughout America's history the merging of the various streams of population, differentiated from one another by origin, religion, and outlook, seemed always to lie just ahead, but the looked-for co-mingling was always deferred.

Many of the European immigrants who came to Canada early in the twentieth century settled in the west. These newcomers to Canada were unskilled and very poor, and they found it difficult to assimilate. In contrast, many of today's immigrants tend to be better educated but from identifiable Third-World minorities.

Glazer and Moynihan suggest that the blacks are often discriminated against, and their assimilation is not tolerated by the majority. The Jews, with their distinct religion, do not wish to assimilate, but rather are proud of their identity. The Puerto Ricans and Irish Catholics represent combinations of these variations. Thus, over time they change, but they remain distinct ethnic groups.

Perhaps the Hutterites best represent pluralism without much change, but even here we find that in their economic farming arrangements they are quite willing to adopt the most modern methods. This would seem to suggest **modified pluralism**. Similarly, the French in Quebec are a good example of change from a dominantly rural, religious population, to an increasingly urban, industrial one. Nevertheless, this enormous shift in value orientations seems not to have affected their determination to survive as a distinct people in North America. Modified pluralism takes account of change, as do the assimilationist and amalgamation theories, but it also provides for degrees of pluralism often demonstrated in Canadian groups such as native Indians, Italians, French Canadians, Jews, Asiatics, and many others.

Glazer and Moynihan hold that all groups change, but those able to shift from traditional cultural identities to new interest foci may maintain their identities in a modified form. This view recognizes change, maintains that identification can be shifted, suggests that some groups may change more than others, and implies that the outcome may be a pluralist mixture with a non-Anglo conformity target. Indeed, Glazer and Moynihan contend that traumatic experiences, such as conflict, encourage the development of a sense of identity among minorities. And that brings us to our sixth and last theory of ethnic change and persistence: conflict.

Conflict: Dialectic of Incompatibles

The theories of assimilation and amalgamation posit an ordered society, one for the most part in a state of equilibrium, within which social change and group conflict are but temporary dislocations. By contrast, the theories of pluralism, multivariate assimilation, and modified pluralism allow for a greater measure of inherent conflict in the social system. But Georg Simmel (1950) contends that conflict is the crux of the matter, that both conflict and consensus are ever present in society. His general assumption is that all social phenomena reflect a combination of opposed tendencies.

The conflict focus, although concerned with structure and institutions, emphasizes the processes of ethnic group relations. Since conflict implies the meeting of people with dissimilar or opposite values and norms, it includes processes of competition, confrontation, and argumentation. Following Dahrendorf (1959), we will define *social conflict* as "all relations between sets of individuals that involve an incompatible difference of objectives (with regard to positions, resources, or values)."

One way to view conflict is as Marx did in *The Communist Manifesto*: "The history of all hitherto existing society is the history of class struggles." As was described in Chapter 1 and elaborated on in Chapter 8, Marx saw the relationship between the bourgeoisie and the proletariat as a class struggle between opposites, as a macro power struggle for control over the economic and political institutions of a society, and as pervasive conflict that would inevitably lead to revolution.

Marx viewed this struggle as much more serious than ethnic territorial squabbles (Bottomore and Rubel, 1963). Most ethnic groups in Canada do not aspire to such an extensive power struggle, although the FLQ movement in Quebec might be a good example of one that does. And the Parti Québécois can be seen as a milder form of conflict institution which would seek to gain sovereign control of Quebec's economic, political, and social institutions by a referendum to secede.

While conflict may take the form of revolution and secession occasionally, it is also present in lesser forms. When many subgroups and a multitude of cultures exist side by side they will maintain distinct identities, thus providing a potential for conflict of values, territorial interests, and power relationships. John Jackson (1975) studied French-English relations in the Windsor, Ontario, area and found considerable competition and conflict which he viewed as a normal outcome of the processes of power position and boundary maintenance by these groups. By the same token, Quebec's Quiet Revolution, the native peoples' quest for equal rights, the relations between adjacent ethnic prairie communities all demonstrate a constant potential for dissension. Hutterite expansion into more of the Alberta farmlands and subsequent restrictive legislation, the conflict of French and other ethnic groups over language rights and education during the Manitoba School question, Bill 22 and the conflicts of Italians and recent immigrants with the Quebec government over English education in Montreal are all examples of such ethnic countercultural conflicts (Hostetler and Huntington, 1967; Richmond, 1972).

These theories – assimilation, amalgamation, and

Louis Riel: Traitor or Hero?

Metis leader Louis Riel vividly illustrates this chapter's sociological emphases. As European immigrants invaded the native Indian lands, they disrupted a food gathering way of life. Rich farmlands for the immigrants meant eviction for the natives. Conflict was inevitable and continued until the Europeans prevailed. The Indians were herded into reserves, and to this day they remain in the lower strata of Canadian society. Many lost their former identity, and only a few are now beginning to make a new life. Prejudice and discrimination against Indians and Metis are common. People of Indian ancestry are shunted to the margins of Canadian society. Very few know what to do about it, and still fewer care.

Brilliant, eloquent, compelling, moody, sensitive, argumentative – all these words applied to Louis Riel. He was born in St. Boniface where his French father owned a flour mill, but he was educated in Montreal where he studied first for the priesthood, then, after his father died, turned to law. When the father of Marie-Julie Guernon refused Riel's request to marry his daughter, Riel packed his bags and set out for the United States . . . Chicago . . . Minnesota . . . finally back to St. Boniface, Fort Garry, and Winnipeg – places he had last seen when he was just a boy.

Now, in 1869, they were overflowing with newcomers – settlers from Ontario and the Maritimes who wanted farmland; Americans selling union with the United States; members of the Canadian Party plugging union with Canada. Sir John A. Macdonald wanted farmland. The Metis were worried and apprehensive.

The next year Macdonald bought the Metis homeland from the Hudson's Bay Company for $1.5 million and appointed William McDougall governor of the vast new territory. Riel was enraged. When McDougall tried to reach Fort Garry, he was turned back by the Metis. Riel took over Fort Garry, set up a provisional government, took several prisoners, including a man named Thomas Scott, and demanded a Bill of Rights for his people. His provisional government persisted, and Manitoba became the fifth province of Canada in 1870.

Riel's fatal error was hanging Thomas Scott. Scott had escaped and made a vain attempt to liberate Fort Garry with a handful of supporters. Scott was a troublesome, defiant Ontario Orangeman. He was tried by Metis court martial, found guilty of insubordination and executed. As news of his death spread, Ontario Orangemen demanded quick revenge. Riel was forced to flee to the United States.

Fifteen years later, in 1885, Riel was invited by the Metis in Batoche, Saskatchewan, to plead their cause with the federal government. The buffalo were now gone. Big Bear and his Cree, who had refused to sign Treaty 6 in 1876, were becoming increasingly restless. Poundmaker, one of the foremost chiefs to sign the treaty, had become bitter. In the south there was Piapot; in Alberta, Crowfoot, chief of the Blackfoot. There was rebellion in the air.

The final drama unfolded in Batoche in 1885 when Riel and his Metis fought against the Second Army sent from eastern Canada. The Metis were greatly outnumbered, short on ammunition and supplies, and the hoped-for native Indian allies did not join the final battle. It was Riel's last fight, and it was all over in a few days.

On September 18, 1885, in a crowded Regina courtroom, six English-speaking jurors pronounced Louis Riel guilty of treason. Two months later he was hanged.

Less than a hundred years later, commemorative monuments to Louis Riel stand on the legislative grounds in both Regina and Winnipeg. Hindsight leads to second thoughts. More and more the Regina execution seems unjust, and increasingly Manitobans look upon Riel as the father of their province. His grave occupies a place of honor in front of the oldest Roman Catholic basilica in the west, located in St. Boniface, which is now part of metropolitan Winnipeg. It is surrounded by the LaVerendrye monument, the French St. Boniface college, and the French Catholic archdiocese, the museum and first Grey Nuns hospital, the CBC French radio and television station, and the newly built French cultural center. Louis Riel's grave is the hub of an important Franco-Manitoba center.

The CBC film *Riel* documents the sequence of events in this western drama. Rudy Wiebe's novel *The Scorched-Wood People* (McClelland and Stewart, 1977) portrays the life and aspirations of these Metis on the South Saskatchewan River.

the rest – have been introduced to illustrate how various scholars in a variety of situations have tried to explain how immigrants in our society change, adjust, and persist in their ethnic identities. While the first three may be important ideal descriptions, few if any societies conform to any of them. And while ideal, general theories are useful, they are much too broad and sweeping to explain the many specific changes of scores of particular ethnic groups in a variety of definite regions in Canada. More precise multivariate, modified pluralist, and conflict versions are therefore needed which will account for many more of the processes of change and explain in much more detail the enormous diversity of our country.

ETHNIC IDENTITY

In our discussion of Canadian ethnicity we noted that the two charter groups, the British and the French, are by far the two largest ethnic groups in Canada.

The British have from the outset been dominant demographically, English language use is dominant outside Quebec, and British economic, political, and legal influence upon the nation is strong. The French are highly segregated in the Province of Quebec where they can maintain some of their linguistic and cultural distinctiveness by provincial government control. So much we have already determined.

The dominant industrial and political Anglo environment acts as a magnet upon ethnic minorities. Access to jobs, economic enterprise, and influence are appealing. But how do the Hutterites, the Jews, the native Indians, the French, and others retain a separate identity, when they wish neither to assimilate nor amalgamate? On the other hand, are there other racial and ethnic groups who may wish to assimilate into the Canadian society, but who are not permitted to compete equally? In this section, we will explore ethnic identity maintenance, and, in the next section, ethnic prejudice and discrimination. These are the two sides of the identity coin: voluntary and involuntary maintenance of ethnic identity.

In our discussion of ethnic identity in this section, we will look into group identification. To what extent do various ethnic groups in Canada adhere to distinctive cultures that differentiate them from the rest? Dashefsky (1976) defines group identification as:

a generalized attitude indicative of a personal attachment to the group and a positive orientation toward being a member of the group. Ethnic identification takes place when the group in question is one with whom the individual believes he has a common ancestry based on shared individual characteristics and/or shared sociocultural experiences.

Dashefsky (1976) has reviewed some of the literature on identity and identification that illustrates the many dimensions attributed to this concept:

Rosen [1965] has . . . . . . argued that an individual may identify . . . with others on three levels: First, one may identify oneself with some important person in one's life, e.g., parent or a friend (i.e., significant other). Second, one may identify oneself with a group from which one draws one's values, e.g., family or coworkers (i.e., reference group). Last, one may identify oneself with a broad category of persons, e.g., an ethnic group or occupational group (i.e., a social category). It is on the third level that ethnic identification occurs.

That, very briefly, is what constitutes identification. We turn now to the various kinds. In our discussion of ethnic identification we shall touch on six identification factors: ecological territory, ethnic institutions, ethnic culture, historical symbols, ideology, and charismatic leadership. These factors are some of the basic components of an ethnic community, and taken together they constitute what Gordon (1964) refers to as a group of individuals with a shared sense of peoplehood.

Territory

The maintenance of a separate language and culture is difficult and unlikely without a sufficiently large ethnic concentration in a given area. Minorities need territory, and they need to control this territory, within which their offspring may then perpetuate their heritage. This can best be done in a tightly knit community. Community space thus becomes an arena in which ethnic activities occur and are shared.

Joy (1972) demonstrates how, in Quebec, the French retain control of the provincial territory, where they perpetuate their language and culture through religious, educational, and political institutions. French scholars such as Rioux (1971) have shown how, historically, the French were the first Europeans to settle along the St. Lawrence River where they set up a seigneurial (manorial) system, with the long, narrow tracts of land still in evidence today. Miner (1939) describes beautifully the community life of the 1930s, in St. Denis, a typical rural French Catholic parish: everyone spoke French, attended Roman Catholic churches, and generally lived as depicted in the film, *Mon Oncle Antoine*. Gold (1975), who studied St. Pascal, the adjacent community, describes how the modern rural French parish has changed, but how territory remains very important for maintenance of rural French culture.

The Hutterites constitute a good example of a rural ethnic community, characterized by extensive boundary maintenance and controlled exposure to outsiders. Indian reserves also demonstrate ethnic territorial segregation. Chinatowns are urban examples. Most minorities cannot maintain such exclusive control over a territory; it is a goal, however, to which many minority groups seem to aspire.

Ethnic block settlements, especially in the west, are common. The Germans are heavily concentrated in the Kitchener-Waterloo area of Ontario; and the Ukrainians settled in the Aspen Belt, stretching from the Manitoba Inter-Lake region to Edmonton. Rural hinterlands often supplied migrants to the city who tended to perpetuate the urban villager way of life, as illustrated by the north end of Winnipeg, until recently the stronghold of Ukrainians, Poles, and Jews (Driedger and Church, 1974). Richmond (1972) also found extensive residential segregation in Toronto. Kalbach (1980) found historical Jewish and Italian settlement patterns in Toronto and traced how they shifted over time.

Individuals, then, can identify with a territory; it is the bounded area within which ethnic activity can take place. Territory is essential.

Ethnic Institutions

Forces of attraction are generated by the social organization of ethnic communities within their established social boundaries. Integration into one's own ethnic community, supported by the institutional completeness of the group, reinforces solidarity (Breton, 1964).

The importance of institutional completeness is that the extent to which a minority can develop its own social system, with control over its own institutions, is the extent to which the group's social actions will take place within the system. Religious, educational, and welfare institutions are therefore crucial. Driedger and Church (1974) found that in Winnipeg, for example, the French and Jews maintained the most complete set of religious, educational, and welfare institutions of all other ethnic groups. These two groups were also the most segregated, in St. Boniface and the north end respectively, where they had established their institutions. The French and the Jews identified with both territory and ethnic institutions. Residential segregation and ethic institutional completeness thus tended to reinforce each other.

Ethnic Culture

Kurt Lewin (1948) proposed that the individual needs to achieve a firm, clear sense of identification with the heritage and culture of the group in order to find a secure ground for a sense of well-being. The territory becomes a crucible, within which solid ethnic institutions can be built, and within which ethnic culture should be protected.

Ethnic cultural identity factors have been studied by numerous scholars. Driedger (1975), for example, found at least six factors that tended to influence group adherence to culture: language use, endogamy (marriage within the group); choice of friends; plus participation in religion, parochial schools, and voluntary organizations. French and Jews in Winnipeg, who were more residentially segregated and who maintained their ethnic institutions to a greater degree than some other comparable ethnic groups, also ranked high on attendance at parochial schools (79 and 74 percent respectively), endogamy (65 and 91 percent), and choice of in-group friends (49 and 63 percent). Use of the French language at home was significantly widespread (61 percent), as was French attendance in church (54 percent). Other ethnic groups, such as the

Germans, Ukrainians, Poles, Scandinavians, and British, supported their in-group cultures less actively.

Examination of territorial, institutional, and cultural identity factors suggests that they tend to reinforce each other; when individuals of a given ethnic group identify with their group along these lines, they then tend to remain relatively more ethnically distinct and proportionately less prone to assimilation. Such maintenance of distinctive ethnic features is necessary to the integrity of the Canadian ethnic mosaic.

Historical Symbols

Villagers may perpetuate their ethnic social structure and community as an end in itself, without much reference to their past and future. Among ethnic urbanites, however, a knowledge of their origins and pride in their heritage would seem to be essential for a sense of purpose and direction. Without such pride and knowledge, the desire to perpetuate tradition rapidly diminishes. The Jews expose their children to a ritualized ethnic history expressed in the form of symbols: special days, fastings, candles, food habits, and other commemorative observances. Such historical symbols can create a sense of belonging, of purpose, of continuing tradition, that are important and worth perpetuating.

A comparison of identity among seven ethnic groups in Winnipeg, indicated strong French and Jewish in-group affirmation and low in-group denial (Driedger, 1976). Jewish and French students were proud of their in-groups, felt strongly bound to them, wished to remember them, and contributed to them. The French particularly indicated low in-group denial; they did not try to hide, nor did they feel inferior about, their ethnicity; they seldom felt annoyed or restricted by their identity. The Ukrainians, Poles, and Germans felt less positively about themselves as ethnic groups, and at the same time were more inclined to deny their ethnicity. Ethnic heritage, therefore, can be a strong or weak, positive or negative influence on personal identity.

Ideology

For certain individuals, a religious or political ideology can relegate cultural and institutional values to second place. For many of the younger generation, territory, culture, and ethnic institutions seem less intrinsically valuable than for their elders. As urban ethnic youth become more sophisticated, they tend to value their ethnicity less. A political or religious ideology, however, supplies purpose and impetus; it promotes values considered more important than cultural and institutional ones.

Often, there is a very strong correlation between religion and ethnicity. Almost all French Canadians are Roman Catholic, and the parish system in rural Quebec has been studied thoroughly (Miner, 1939; Gold, 1975). Of course, Catholics have also founded many essentially ethnic urban parishes: in Quebec City, in Montreal, and in Winnipeg. Similarly, most Canadians of Polish origin are Roman Catholic, and, consequently, urban Polish parishes abound.

By the same token, Jewish religion and culture are so interdependent as to seem identical; they are so unified that the distinction between "religious" and "ethnic" tend to blur. Indeed, Zionism has been and is so strong that Jews from all over the world have migrated to Israel. Closer to home, Mennonites and Hutterites integrate and thus mutually strengthen their cultures and ideologies.

Ideology can help unite a people, but it can also divide them. The Ukrainians are a good example of divided loyalties. The Ukrainian Catholic and the Greek Orthodox faiths are and have long been opposed. This opposition has led to conflict among Ukrainians themselves, illustrating both the importance of ideology and its potentially divisive power.

Identification with religious beliefs or a political philosophy adds force and point to the question: What is the meaning of this territory, these institutions, and this ethnic culture, and why should it be perpetuated or changed?

Charismatic Leadership

The importance of charisma is demonstrated in a variety of minority movements: Martin Luther King and Malcom X among American blacks; René Lévesque among the Québécois; Harold Cardinal among Alberta Indians, to name a few. Individuals with a sense of mission often adapt an ideology to a current situation, linking it symbolically with the past, and using the media effectively to transform the present into a vision of the future.

Such charismatic leaders ordinarily use social-psychological means to gain a following. Designed to create trust, these methods forge a cohesive loyalty to both leader and in-group. The leader's commitment is passed on to the followers, resulting in new potential for change. In the beginning, the group may not be particularly oriented to territory, institutions, culture, and heritage. But slowly, as the movement ages, such structural features become more important.

Although there may be many more ethnic dimensions with which minorities identify, we have noted that territory, institutions, culture, heritage, ideology, and leaders are crucial. Different ethnic groups identify more with some of these dimensions than others, and some are more successful than others in their maintenance of a distinct community. The Hutterites have successfully survived in a rural setting, for example, and the Jews have for centuries done so effectively in the city. Any study of ethnic identity needs to explore such dimensions and foci of ethnic identification.

In many ways this discussion of ethnic identity can be capped by introducing the concept of **ethnocentrism**. Identity and ethnocentrism are closely linked. As you learned in Chapter 2, Sumner (1906) coined the term to describe the tendency of ethnic groups to view other people and groups in such a way that "one's own group is the center of everything and all others are scaled and rated with reference to it . . . . Each group nourishes its own pride and vanity, boasts itself superior, exalts its own divinities, and looks with contempt on outsiders." Although Summer seems to emphasize the negative aspects of ethnocentrism, the concept does have its positive side. Murdock (1931) thought that "positive ethnocentrism" would include a belief in the unique value of the in-group; satisfaction, solidarity, loyalty, and cooperation with it; and preferences for association with members of it. Positive ethnocentrism is akin to positive ethnic identity. Murdock also recognized negative ethnocentrism: believing in the superiority of one's own group and judging others narrowly from the group's standards; ignorance of, and lack of interest in, other groups; and potential hostility toward out-groups. Ethnic identity and ethnocentrism

can provide security and support for minority individuals and groups. However, if taken too far, these loyalties can also create problems of hostility toward out-groups, including prejudice and discrimination. It is to these negative features that we turn next.

PREJUDICE AND DISCRIMINATION

In our discussion of ethnic identity we illustrated positive features of ethnicity. There can also be many negative variations, including social distance, stereotypes, prejudice and discrimination.

Social Distance

When Simmel (1950) introduced the concept of **social distance**, he posited, among other relationships, the existence of an inversely varying association between in-group solidarity and social distance from out-groups. The closer you feel to the group, the further you feel from others. Simmel's discussion of "the stranger" shows both the nearness and farness dimensions. Consider these minority Canadians: immigrants coming as strangers to a new land; French-Canadians visiting other parts of Canada and feeling like strangers; native Indians segregated in reserves away from the urban industrial mainstream; Jewish Canadians who feel they are practicing their religion among a strange and seemingly alien majority. How can these strangers, who strongly identify with their in-group culture and tradition, retain their own social world, or "ground of identification," as Lewin (1948) would put it, and at the same time relate securely to others? We would expect minority strangers entering the environment of others to be secure only if grounded in an ethnic reference group, or if socially and psychologically motivated by the norms of such an in-group. Hence "distance" and "security" are linked concepts.

Levine, et al (1976) contend that "Simmel's utilization of the metaphor 'distance' was by no means restricted to his pages on the 'stranger,' it constitutes a pervasive and distinctive feature of his sociology as a whole." They summarize Simmel's meanings attached to distance as:

1. ecological attachment and mobility
2. emotional involvement and detachment
3. the extent to which persons share similar qualities and sentiments

Simmel himself also thought that distance could be expressed many ways. While recent work has attempted to sort out these meanings, Bogardus (1959), famous for his "social distance scale," chose to use "the degree of sympathetic understanding that functions between person and person, between person and group, and between group and group" as his measure of social distance. The Bogardus scale has been widely used, although not extensively in Canada.

As illustrated in Table 9-5, Driedger and Mezoff (1980) studied a sample of 2520 high school students to determine whom these students were willing to marry, have as close friends, etc. Students were much more willing to marry those of European origin than those of non-European origin (for the most part these latter were non-Caucasian). Willingness to marry, designated by Bogardus as measuring "nearness," seems therefore to indicate less nearness toward non-Europeans. The study also showed that as students identified more strongly with their in-group, they tended also to prefer more distance from others, possibly in order to maintain their identities. The high school students' willingness to be close friends with

TABLE 9-5. WINNIPEG HIGH SCHOOL STUDENTS' PREFERRED DEGREE OF SOCIAL DISTANCE FROM ETHNIC GROUPS

Ethnic Groups*	Bogardus' Social Distance Scale†							
	1 Willingness to Marry	2 Willingness to have as Close Friend	3 Willingness to have as Neighbor	4 Willingness to work with on Job	5 Willingness to have as Acquaintance	6 Willingness to have as Visitor only	7 Would debar from Nation	Number who Responded
	%	%	%	%	%	%	%	
European Origin								
American	75	14	5	2	2	2	2	2220
British	65	20	6	4	2	3	1	1849
Scandinavian	56	24	8	6	3	2	1	2265
Dutch	53	25	11	5	4	1‡	1	2328
Polish	51	26	9	6	4	2	2	2223
Ukrainian	50	28	9	6	4	2	2	2223
French	50	24	9	6	6	2	5	1764
German	48	25	11	7	4	3	2	2002
Italian	44	28	10	7	6	3	3	2163
Russian	41	27	11	7	6	3	5	2163
Jewish	28	34	12	7	9	4	7	1883
Non-European Origin								
Black	29	49	11	6	3	1	1	2256
Mexican	29	37	14	8	6	4	1	2262
Japanese	26	44	14	7	6	2	2	2209
Filipino	26	40	13	9	6	4	2	2147
Chinese	25	45	13	7	5	2	2	2328
West Indian	23	43	13	9	8	3	3	2131
East Indian	23	42	13	10	8	3	2	2190
Native Indian	22	41	10	10	10	3	4	2145
Inuit	19	45	13	10	8	3	2	2160

SOURCE: Driedger, Leo, and Richard Mezoff (1980).
NOTE: * In-group evaluations were deleted (e.g., the British in the sample did not evaluate their own group).
†Students were asked to indicate a single level on the scale for each other ethnic group.
‡The N's in any one cell never dropped below 20.

most non-Europeans, even though they might not wish to marry them, does seem to indicate their desire for identity maintenance. Relatively few students wished to bar these groups, or receive them only as visitors, although 11 percent preferred such a distance from the Jews. Such extreme desire for distance is in this instance most likely evidence of prejudice.

Stereotypes

A **stereotype** is an exaggerated belief associated with a category. Allport (1954) says it differs from a category in that it is a fixed idea that accompanies a category and carries additional judgments or "pictures" about a category or group. A stereotype may be either positive or negative, and is often used to justify behavior toward a specific group. Negative stereotypes of racial and ethnic groups have been and are widespread. Jews are shrewd and ambitious; Italians are heavily involved in crime; Irishmen are drunkards; native Indians are lazy and undependable; Germans are aggressive and boorish – all stereotypes, all negative. Positive stereotypes are also numerous: Asiatics stress family loyalty; Hutterites are very religious; the British are efficient.

Mackie (1974) found that her group of 590 adults, selected from organizations in Edmonton, had an overwhelming negative image of Canadian Indians as sharing neither the work nor success values of the surrounding society. The stereotype of Hutterites was mostly positive: clean-living people, religious, hard-working, thrifty, rural, law-abiding, pacifistic, sexually moral, sober; but also exclusive, opposed to higher education, old-fashioned, disliked. Mackie's sample also reported a flattering image of Ukrainians. On the other hand, Barry, et al (1977) found that in Quebec images of Ukrainians were not nearly so positive as in Edmonton, which illustrates how regional stereotypes vary. Mackie of course tried to determine how far these stereotypes conformed to fact, and to what extent they did not. She found some correlations, some exaggerations.

Prejudice

The word "prejudice" derives from the Latin praejudicium, which means precedent, a judgment based on previous decisions and experiences (Allport, 1954). Words change over time, and **prejudice** has come to mean thinking ill of others without sufficient warrant. One dictionary defines it as "a feeling favorable or unfavorable toward a person or thing, prior to, or not based on, actual experience." These definitions suggest that prejudice is unfounded judgment, and that emotions are heavily involved. While biases can be both positive and negative, we usually think of ethnic prejudice today as mostly negative, although Allport suggests that such prejudgments are prejudice only if they are not reversible in light of new facts.

Allport further suggests that prejudgment is normal and necessary, because the human mind can think only with the aid of categories or generalizations. A human being is bombarded with millions of stimuli, and it is impossible to react to them all. As a result, we tend to select only a relatively few of the many experiences available to us. In the process, the mind forms clusters for guiding daily adjustments. As we have new experiences we tend to assimilate them as much as possible to the clusters already formed. This enables us to identify related objects quickly.

These categories are also more or less emotional, depending on what the experiences of a particular individual may have been. Thus, a person may feel more negative about some experiences and some related persons than others. Some categories are more rational than others, but the process permits human beings to slip easily into ethnic prejudice. Erroneous generalizations can be made, and, indeed, some categories may reflect not merely feelings of dislike, but feelings of actual hostility.

Such tendencies toward bias are present in the media, in books, and in everyday conversation that mold our impressions. Depending on prejudicial bias, young people can be referred to as "youthful" or "immature;" people who are cautious may be reported as "discreet" or "cowardly;" someone who is bold may be considered "courageous" or "foolhardy."

While social distance from others may be the result of a desire to maintain a separate ethnic identity, it can also, as we have observed, stem from negative attitudes. Berry, et al (1977) found that those who favored multiculturalism in Canada also tended to have more positive attitudes toward others. Canadians of British and French origin, however, although they tended to have fairly positive attitudes toward each other, wished to identify less with others. Those who were more ethnocentric still, such as French Quebeckers and British Maritimers, tended to be more negative toward new immigrants and multiculturalism. Driedger and Mezoff's (1980) 11 percent who wished to have the Jews only as visitors, or to bar them from the country, certainly showed prejudicial attitudes. Indeed, in that same study a majority of the Jewish students reported that they had experienced prejudice in Winnipeg. Similarly, Cardinal (1969) claims that prejudice against Canadian Indians is common and occasionally reflected in the media.

Tienhaara (1974) found in her analysis of post-war Canadian Gallup polls that historical situations created varied responses. Polls taken in 1943, during the war, showed that a majority of Canadians thought the Japanese living in Canada should be sent back to Japan, although the respondents made distinctions between the Japanese who were Canadian citizens, and those who were not. After the war, Canadians became more tolerant, but many still favored deportation. In fact, most Japanese living on the Pacific Coast of Canada during World War II were sent inland involuntarily.

A 1955 poll taken in Canada showed that more than one-third of the respondents did not wish to have "a few families from Europe come to their neighborhood to live" for a variety of reasons: too many here now, high unemployment, etc. A national poll in 1961 showed that over one-half of the Canadians questioned thought we should continue to restrict non-whites. A poll in 1963 showed that almost two-thirds would not move if colored people came into their neighborhood, but over one-third – 38 percent – said they would or might (Tienhaara, 1974). These polls seem to indicate that, depending on historical situations and social events, there are latent or potential attitudes of prejudice among many Canadians.

Discrimination

Prejudice is an attitude; **discrimination** is action based on prejudiced attitudes. Allport (1954) argues that "discrimination comes about only when we deny to individuals or groups of people the equality of treatment which they wish." Hagan (1977) suggests that in this connection four distinctions are important: differential treatment, prejudicial treatment, denial of desire, and disadvantaging treatment. Obviously, we cannot treat everyone equally; distinctions must be made. This constitutes differential treatment. Although this may not be discrimination as such, it can be a predisposition to discrimination. Prejudicial treatment will likely lead to unfair treatment. Denial of desire involves placing restrictions on the aspirations of some members of society, such as their desire to live in any part of the city, or their desire to belong to any club, if they can afford it. (In some cities of the United States, for example, blacks cannot buy houses in strictly white neighborhoods. Jews often claim that they are denied membership in select clubs.) Disadvantageous treatment is a clear form of discrimination which may take a variety of forms.

Allport (1954) goes on to outline several forms of disadvantageous treatment. Anti-locution, or verbal expressions such as jokes and name-calling would be the mildest form. Avoidance is more severe in that prejudiced persons restrict their own movements so that they do not come into contact with undesirables. Discrimination is still more intense in that now acts of inequality, of disadvantage, extend to the ethnic or minority victim, including disadvantages in citizenship, employment, education, housing, or public accommodation. It gets worse. Physical attack, such as ejection from a community, lynchings, massacres, and genocide would be the severest form. Until recently blacks were still lynched in the United States; massacres of native Indians occurred in Canada; and the Jewish holocaust is still fresh in our memories. Religious and political persecution are constants in Northern Ireland, the Middle East, and elsewhere.

Driedger and Mezoff (1980), in their sample of 2520 high school students in Winnipeg, found that perception of discrimination varied by ethnic groups. About one-third of the students reported discrimination. Jews, Italians, and Poles perceived the greatest discrimination in the classroom and in textbooks. The Jews, especially, reported discrimination in clubs, and denial of access that was free to others. While verbal abuse was reported most often, the Jews reported vandalism, and physical attack as well. Blacks and Asians often report discrimination.

One of the things sociologists do is study the way in which society is structured for discrimination. Canadian immigration laws permit quotas and restrictions on immigrants considered undesirable. Agencies and institutions restrict the opportunities of Treaty Indians, Nontreaty Indians, and Metis. The cycle of poverty is too often nourished rather than eliminated. During World War II the Canadian government forcibly evacuated Japanese Canadians from the west coast and sent them inland because of a perceived threat to national security. The Chinese were legally restricted from voting and denied access to public places, especially in British Columbia. Laws were passed in Alberta to restrict the expansion of Hutterite colonies. While English and French languages were legally used in Manitoba, and other ethnic groups were permitted to educate their children in their own mother tongues, these rights were later changed and English alone was forced upon minorities. Racism is increasingly raising its head in urban centers such as Toronto and Montreal. Nova Scotia has discriminated against blacks. In most societies, including Canada, there are powerful attempts to control and sometimes repress minorities. Many who are able to gain control of the political and economic institutions use such power to their own advantage and often forget about the rights and aspirations of the weak. This often leads to conflict, because many minorities feel that Canada is theirs as well – it does not belong only to those who are in power.

Although studies of discrimination in Canada are few, discrimination does exist, as our native Indians, our Jews, and our non-Caucasian immigrants well know.

WHOSE LAND IS CANADA?

Whose land is Canada? The answer depends on perspective. Some came here first and lay claim to this land; others claimed it on grounds of numbers and power; still others, who have come recently, claim a right to it by virtue of a right to human freedom and dignity. What Canada will become depends on the goals that Canadias have for the future. If homogeneity is desired, then the dominant British may wield their power increasingly to select and protect Anglo-conformity. Others who desire homogeneity, like the French, may leave to form a separate nation. But can a nation be heterogeneous culturally and still move forward with purpose? Some think it can. Some fear that this will lead only to differences, discrimination, and conflict. Others believe that such pluralism is inevitable in modern industrial society. Increasingly, freedoms have been extended to include choices in religion and politics; must these also be extended to a diversity of ethnic identities? So it would seem. That is the great Canadian experiment.

Whose land is Canada? Ours.

SUMMARY

1. An ethnic group is a group of people with shared sociocultural experience and/or similar characteristics, whose members perceive themselves as alike by virtue of their common ancestry. An ethnic group that is subordinate to any other group is called a minority group.

2. Canada is a land of immigrants. The native Indians arrived first, followed much later by the Europeans. The French originally settled in what is now Quebec, followed by the British, and other north-, east-, and south-Europeans. Today, the British constitute the largest ethnic group – 43 percent – followed by the French – 28 percent.

3. Only New Brunswick approximates a bilingual and bicultural area. The rest of Canada is highly diversified ethnically and marked regionally by the various native Indian, French, British, and other European cultures. Thus, multiculturalism in a bilingual framework seems to reflect the demographic and regional facts of Canadian life.

4. Most urban industrial societies are highly stratified, and in Canada the ethnic groups are differentially located in the various strata. The British and the French, the two charter groups, have special legal language status enshrined in the Canadian Constitution. This legal advantage, together with their early arrival and large populations, make them the two most powerful groups. But the French have always been junior partners. The treaty status groups, the native Indians, were relegated to reserves by treaties that placed and kept them subordinate. The entrance groups came later.

5. With the increase of the Canadian Indian population, as well as a large influx of new immigrants, Canada has increasingly been faced with ethnic diversity. Various changes have occurred, and conflicts have arisen. Whose land is Canada? The question is on the minds of many. Official bilingualism and multiculturalism are hotly debated. No one theory seems best to explain Canadian ethnic change, though many, such as assimilation, amalgamation, pluralism, multivariate assimilation, modified pluralism, and conflict, have been suggested and studied.

6. Early in Canadian history many groups sought to maintain their ethnic identities by territorial segregation in rural communities, and some were forced into reserves and ghettos. Some believe that language is the most important means of preserving ethnic identity; others value religion most highly; still others seek to foster heritage, endogamy, and choice of in-group friends. Ethnic identity can be maintained through identification with an ecological territory, with ethnic institutions, with an ethnic culture, with historical symbols, with an ideology, or with charismatic leadership.

7. Amidst the Canadian ethnic diversity, some groups are valued more highly than others. In many cases, distances between groups simply maintain identity, but sometimes they emerge as either prejudice (a pre-judgment, usually negative and not based on actual experience, of a group of people) or discrimination (an action toward a group of people based on prejudiced attitudes).

GLOSSARY

Amalgamation. Process by which groups are blended into a melting pot where none remains distinctive.

Assimilation. Process by which a group becomes like the dominant group, and no longer remains distinctive. Also referred to in North America as "Anglo-conformity."

Charter groups. Two original European migration groups (British and French) whose legalized claims for such historically established privileges as the perpetuation of their separate languages and cultures are enshrined in the Canadian Constitution.

Discrimination. Process by which a person is deprived of equal access to privileges and opportunities available to others.

Entrance group. Ethnic group that is not a founder of the country and that enters as immigrants after the national framework has been established.

Ethnic group. Group of individuals with a shared sense of peoplehood based on presumed shared sociocultural experience and/or similar characteristics. They perceive themselves as alike by virtue of their common ancestry.

Ethnic identity. Attitude of being united in spirit, outlook, or principle with an ethnic heritage. An attachment and positive orientation toward a group with whom individuals believe they have a common ancestry and interest.

Ethnic stratification. Order in which ethnic groups form a hierarchy of dominance and socioeconomic status in a society.

Ethnocentrism. Tendency to see one's in-group as being in the center of everything and to judge other ways of life by the standards of one's own group.

Melting pot. Situation in which the amalgamation and blending of groups have left none distinctive.

Minority group. Ethnic group that is subordinate to another group.

Modified pluralism. Glazer's and Moynihan's modification of pluralism theory, describing a situation in which numerous groups maintain distinctly different cultures, ideologies, or interests; although they will be changed and modified somewhat, they will not be transformed entirely.

Multicultural. Relating to or designed for a combination of several distinct cultures.

Multivariate assimilation. Gordon's modification of assimilation theory, which maintains that assimilation is not a single social process but a number of cultural, structural, marital, identificational, attitudinal, behavioral, and civic subprocesses.

Pluralism. Social situation in which numerous ethnic, racial, religious and/or social groups maintain distinctly different cultures, ideologies, or interests.

Prejudice. A feeling (usually negative) toward a person, group, or thing prior to or not based on actual experience. Prejudging others without sufficient warrant.

Race. Arbitrary biological grouping of people on the basis of physical traits.

Regional mosaic. Distinctive ethnic patterns formed by the various regions of a country which have different combinations of linguistic and cultural groups.

Segregation. Separation or isolation of a race, class, or ethnic group by forced or voluntary residence.

Social distance. In contrast to social nearness, Simmel defines social distance as ecological, emotional, and social detachment from others.

Stereotype. Opinions and judgments of others that create an exaggerated and a typical view of a person or group.

Treaty status. Certain privileges and obligations passed on to Indian people from their ancestors who signed treaties with the Canadian government.

FURTHER READING

Cardinal, Harold. *The Unjust Society: The Tragedy of Canada's Indians.* Edmonton: Hurtig, 1969. A heartfelt call by a native Indian leader for a reversal of the Indian tragedy.

Driedger, Leo (ed.). *The Canadian Ethnic Mosaic: A Quest for Identity.* Toronto: McClelland and Stewart, 1978. An edited volume of eighteen contributions in ethnic theory, immigration, socialization, and identity.

Elliott, Jean Leonard (ed.). *Two Nations, Many Cultures: Ethnic Groups in Canada.* Scarborough, Ont.: Prentice-Hall, 1979. An edited volume of thirty contributions on the native peoples, the French, and other ethnic groups in Canada.

Henry, Frances. *Forgotten Canadians: The Blacks of Nova Scotia.* Don Mills, Ont.: Longman, 1973. Contains author interviews with blacks in thirteen Nova Scotia communities and two intensive community studies, one rural and the other urban.

Hostetler, John A., and Gertrude Enders Huntington. *The Hutterites in North America.* New York: Holt, Rinehart and Winston, 1967. An expert study of the Hutterite world view, colony life, economic, family and organizational patterns.

Hughes, David R., and Evelyn Kallen. *The Anatomy of Racism: Canadian Dimension.* Montreal: Harvest House, 1974. A discussion of the racial dimension including origin, intelligence, racism and the social dimension of stratification, discrimination, and problems of race in Canada.

Kallen, Evelyn. *Spanning the Generations: A Study in Jewish Identity.* Don Mills, Ont.: Longman, 1977. A study in Jewish identity in Toronto and the forces shaping ethnic and religious identity through the generations.

Price, John. *Indians of Canada: Cultural Dynamics.* Scarborough, Ont.: Prentice-Hall, 1979. An integrated summary of the prehistory, language, and culture of the Inuit, Algonquins, Hurons, Iroquois, and Kwakiutl.

Rioux, Marcel. *Quebec in Question.* Toronto: James, Lewis and Samuel, 1971. A sympathetic study of the French habitant and the changes initiated by the Quiet Revolution toward a free and potentially independent Quebec.

Ujimoto, Victor, and Gordon Hirabayashi. *Visible Minorities and Multiculturalism: Asians in Canada.* Toronto: Butterworths, 1980. An edited collection of twenty-five essays on Chinese, Japanese, East Indian, and other Asians in Canada.

CHAPTER 10
FORMAL ORGANIZATIONS

TERRENCE H. WHITE

In developed societies, organizations are everywhere. Governments, stores, hospitals, schools, universities, churches, restaurants, railways, airlines, funeral parlors, and massage parlors are but a few pieces in the vast organizational mosaic of Canadian society.

Ask a group of people what "organization" means, and you will receive a wide array of answers. For some, organization will be synonymous with bureaucracy. For others, organization may suggest the dull routine of work, or the community effort to raise money for a new arena, or their membership in a ski club. Organization may have more sinister connotations, evoking thoughts of organized crime and the Mafia. Ask sociologists for their views on the subject, and they are likely to respond, guardedly, "Well that depends, are you talking about voluntary associations, or formal organizations, or complex organizations, or institutions, or what?"

Such a wide range of responses is understandable, because organization is a very general term with many possible meanings. So it is necessary to narrow the focus on the term. This chapter examines the nature of organizations and their effects on our lives. Our main attention will be on formal organizations. But so we do not narrow our focus too quickly, let us begin by looking at the role of organizations in the broader social spectrum.

SOCIAL ORGANIZATION

Organizations are a universal attribute and a natural consequence of the social behavior of human beings. People are *social* in that they do not live in isolation from other people. There are, of course, always a few people who do live most of their adult lives in isolation – hermits, for example. But even they find themselves in social settings from time to time in order to get essential supplies, emergency health treatment, perhaps a bath, or whatever. Generally, no functioning human is ever totally asocial – or not for long.

The reasons for this social tendency in human beings are many. At the most basic level, the biological necessities of human procreation require social behavior if the species is to survive. Human sexual intercourse as the usual prerequisite activity to children (test tube babies notwithstanding) presupposes at least some cooperative action between two individuals. Infants resulting from such social liaisons are dependent on their parents or other adults for survival. This dependency, continuing until the child is self-sufficient, also presupposes cooperative social action. In the absence of such provisions, the species would disappear. At the most fundamental level, therefore, human social behavior is a necessity to insure human survival.

Furthermore, when people interact with others, they may find themselves developing dependencies other than those associated with mere survival. If, for example, I am a farmer and you are a blacksmith, I may find that ploughing is easier and more effective using a metal plough you have made. In return for the plough, I provide you with fresh vegetables and grain for your family. And later, if my horse needs shoeing, I bring that work to you. And so it goes.

What has happened is that in the process of our social interaction with each other, certain mutual dependencies have developed. You need the food I grow,

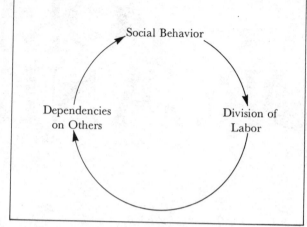

Figure 10-1. Relationships among Social Behavior Division of Labor, and Dependencies on Others.

and I need your blacksmithing skills. Unable to do everything for ourselves, we divide most of the work so that we tend to do those things at which we are good or for which we have special facilities. As a consequence, we come to rely on others for additional skills, goods, or services. That is, a basic **division of labor** results. Division of labor refers to the tendency for general tasks and roles to become increasingly specialized.

These three concepts – social behaviors, division of labor, and dependencies on others – are interrelated. (See Figure 10-1.) Human intelligence, skills, and abilities are not evenly distributed, and, as a result, social behavior eventually results in a very rudimentary division of labor. This division may be along gender and age lines, as in primitive tribes where the males are usually the hunters and the women and elderly tend to family and household duties. Or, it may be more of an occupational division, such as in our example of the farmer and the blacksmith.

The division of labor, no matter how simple or basic, leads to increasing dependencies among people which, in turn, reinforce social behavior. As industrialization or development advances in a society, the cycle of interrelationships among these three components becomes even more intense, with greater specialization in work resulting in a more complex division of labor, and so on. As a consequence, most people become bound into a web of dependency; they need others in order to survive or live in the manner to which they are accustomed. The intricacy of these developments creates an expanding need for coordination and control of the various elements in society. As this cycle of relationships develops and intensifies, the necessity for organization increases.

Durkheim and the Division of Labor

An early scholar who pointed to the link between the division of labor and the necessity for social organization was Durkheim. He was interested in the impact on societies of the increasing division of labor. In his book, *The Division of Labor in Society* (1964, originally published 1893), he focuses on the question of *social solidarity* – what is it that binds people together in larger social networks? – and what are the mechanisms that create social solidarity? He identified two types of social solidarity, mechanical and organic.

In primitive societies, Durkheim suggests that the linkages between people take the form of **mechanical solidarity**. Based on strong systems of common beliefs, the division of labor is rudimentary, with people engaged in similar tasks and having relatively high degrees of self-sufficiency. Because people are able to supply most of their own basic needs, their dependencies on others through the division of labor are not great. As a result, their social bonds are through kinship and neighborliness. Outside of the basic family unit, they get together with other people because they want to, rather than because they have to in order to survive.

But as societies evolve and become more complex, the division of labor increases, and specialization results in greater differentiation among people. No longer is everyone doing relatively similar tasks. Consequently, individual self-sufficiency decreases, and greater dependencies on others develop. Greater dependency means that people must maintain social relations in order to survive at a desired standard. This basis for social solidarity Durkheim terms **organic solidarity**.

The state of the division of labor is a critical element in Durkheim's analysis. Social behavior mediated through the division of labor, as we saw earlier, determines the development of organization. As societies evolve from mechanical to organic solidarity, specialization in the division of labor and complex interdependencies generate needs for coordination and control. In other words, they generate the need for a different type of organization.

Durkheim's focus on society as a system and his analysis of the impacts on human behavior as an aspect of societal structure are good examples of the elements in the structural functionalist approach.

Organization is a universal occurrence of human behavior and a dominant feature of our lives. We should, therefore, have a greater appreciation of what organization is and how it affects us. Before proceeding to analyze its significance, however, we should clarify its meaning.

TOWARDS A DEFINITION OF ORGANIZATION

"Organization" is a general term encompassing many interrelated elements. In order to identify the basics of organizations, let us employ an imaginary set of circumstances. You are driving in the country when you happen upon a farm where the barn is burning. Wanting to help, you join the farmer and a group of neighbors standing in front of the blaze. The necessity for action is obvious if damage to the barn is to be contained and the fire's spread to adjacent buildings averted. Fortunately, there is a waterwell in the yard, there are some buckets lying around, and there is a ladder close at hand.

Given these particulars, you can easily imagine the next step. Those at the fire start a bucket brigade, from the well to the barn and up the ladder onto the fire. Each individual performs a specific task, and probably some attempt is made to match people to appropriate tasks. The heavy chore of drawing the water from the well, for instance, is assigned to a well-muscled individual, and those afraid of height are on the ground rather than at the top of the ladder, facing the blaze.

Let us for a moment step back and analyze some of the components of this situation – the group's goals, for example. The burning barn presents a very clear challenge or goal for people on the site: to put out the fire. And as it happens, a necessary prerequisite for an organization is a goal or a series of goals, the achievement of which serves as a motivation for concerted action.

The means for achieving this goal are clear: move the water from the well onto the fire. This could be done, however, in a number of ways. The men and women could fill their own buckets and run with them to the fire. These unorganized and independent actions might be successful if the fire was small and our firefighters were all fairly strong and hardy. On the other hand, such unrelated individual actions might result in failure if the fire was large. Imagine people crowded at the well waiting to fill their buckets, people bumping into each other and spilling their water en route to the fire, and so on. Clearly, the bucket brigade organization is much more likely to realize the group's goals.

Besides the achievement of goals, our bucket brigade also encompasses some additional important concepts. First, it illustrates the use of a **technology** in goal achievement. Technology is the application of a body of knowledge through the use of tools and processes in the production of goods and/or services. In this case, the technology is based on the knowledge that water may be used to extinguish certain types of fires. The tools in this instance are simply the buckets and the ladder, while the process involves filling the buckets and passing them along a human chain to the fire. Certain additional resources are required if the technology is to function; these are the supply of water and people to fill the various roles or jobs in doing the work. Thus, in our elementary organization, the bucket brigade, the resources of water and volunteers are utilized in a division of labor employing a simple technology to achieve the goal of putting out the fire.

Back to the scene of the blaze. Good progress is being made in getting the water to the fire, but a problem has developed, one requiring coordination: the buckets, once emptied on the fire, are not being

returned to the well so that the process may be repeated. Several uninvolved children are commissioned to return the empty buckets to the well on a regular basis, thus insuring the completeness of the circuit.

An observer of the scene would be impressed not only with the need to solve problems in pursuit of the goal, but also with the communication between members of the organization as suggestions pass among them, or as they give each other encouragement or reprimands for ups and downs in performance. In addition, one person has emerged as a leader whose concern it is to coordinate the activities of the group, as well as lead in problem identification and resolution.

The reader will be relieved to learn the happy ending of this scene: the fire was speedily doused and only minor damage to the barn resulted.

To sum up, our organization, the bucket brigade, while not as complex as a metropolitan fire department or a large business, does contain the basic elements of an organization:

1. goal(s)
2. resources (e.g., water, buckets)
3. technology
4. division of labor
5. coordination
6. communication
7. leadership

An **organization**, therefore, is a collectivity in which people and resources are coordinated through a division of labor in the use of a technology to achieve a goal. Coordination, control, and problem solving are facilitated through communication and leadership.

Spontaneous Organization

Our bucket brigade has disbanded; all the stalwart men, women, and children are enjoying a well deserved rest. While it was in operation, though, the brigade constituted a good example of an organization. Furthermore, it was an example of a **spontaneous organization.**. The fire was a one-time event. The people who were at the scene of the fire linked themselves in a coordinated activity to achieve a specific goal at a particular time. The goal achieved, the organization resolved itself into individuals who went their separate ways.

Spontaneous organizations are often generated in crisis or emergency situations. Volunteers, for instance, may band together to fill sandbags and build dikes during a flood. Or, the first persons to arrive at a car accident may organize to extricate victims, provide first aid, and direct traffic. Once police and other regular service personnel arrive, this temporary organization scatters.

Spontaneous organizations may not always occur, however, even though a worthwhile goal or goals may be clear. One reason for this is that the technology to achieve the goals may not be known or readily available. Imagine, for example, a campground filled with vacationers. In the middle of the site is a large metal garbage container of the type emptied by compactor trucks. After dinner, a black bear and her two cubs stroll through the campground to the container, and the mother climbs inside and begins throwing out leftovers for her hungry cubs.

Everyone in the camp presses forward to watch the proceedings. Oblivious to the onlookers, the three bears rip open garbage bags and consume practically everything but the cans. One of the cubs climbs up and into the high-walled container to join the mother. After a while, the mother clambers out and waits for her cub to join her. But the cub can't get out. The mother's concern mounts, and she begins bellowing and tentatively charging the crowd. The longer this goes on, the more threatening her behavior becomes, and the more potentially dangerous to the many nearby children.

Adults in the crowd begin to look for some solution to the problem of getting the bear cub out of the garbage container. But no ready solutions are apparent. In this instance, participants in a possible organized action to achieve a goal are unable to proceed because no suitable technology is known to them, and the situation is compounded further by fear.

A bit later, a park warden who has been contacted by someone drives up in his truck, surveys the scene, and leaves. He quickly returns with a wooden fence-post, drives alongside the container, rolls down his window, and leaves the post against the inside wall of the container so the cub can climb out. Mother and cubs reunite and scramble into the bush, while the onlookers glance sheepishly at each other with a "Why didn't we think of that?" look.

So spontaneous organizations may fail to form because the appropriate technology either is unknown or unavailable to those at the scene. Also, of course, the goal may not always be clear, as in unfamiliar circumstances like an earthquake, or tornado, or whatever. Another possibility is that people on the scene may not be prepared to make a commitment to cooperative action for reasons of fear. This sometimes happens as people stand motionless on a dock while someone is drowning, or people ignore the pleas for help from a rape or mugging victim. No one wants to get involved. Spontaneous organization is not, therefore, an inevitability in situations calling for cooperative action. Most of the organizations with which we are familiar, however, are more enduring than the spontaneous ones we have considered so far. These are categorized as formal organizations, and we will examine them in the next section.

Formal Organization

Formalization. Earlier we referred to the circularity of the interrelationships among social behavior, division of labor, and social dependencies. We observed that as these links intensified, societies moved from what Durkheim termed mechanical to organic solidarity. Along with these developments, we suggested that people tend increasingly to be enmeshed in a dependency web where the specialized division of labor makes them more reliant on others for survival at a desired standard of living. To manage the complexity of these links, societies come to be increasingly formalized. **Formalization** is a process by which the informality of relationships in earlier social relationships is gradually replaced by varying degrees of rules, codes of conduct, laws, and other means of regulation.

Formalization is a way of guiding and regularizing human interactions; it is an attempt to avoid the chaos that would result if every human contact was completely spontaneous.

Corporations Waste Human Talent

Men and Women of the Corporation *is a topical book by Rosabeth Moss Kanter, an organizational sociologist at Yale University. Her interest was in the corporation as a workplace for men and women and she shares some of her ideas in the following interview.*

Simplified, her book says because corporations are too large, too hierarchical and not sufficiently democratic, men and women who work for them are obliged to accept "roles." This produces specific forms of behavior which are good for neither the individual nor the corporations. Kanter analyzes these roles and proposes some solutions.

You seem to be suggesting that corporations give too much importance to status and promotions. Remove those and how are you going to get people to work?

I suppose there's not much to be done about status, but in the area of promotion something can be done. Men and women can be given a chance to participate in management without necessarily being promoted.

In the present system, where people linger in ossified roles, they never get an opportunity to express themselves – hence widespread resentment. People need to express themselves, but today the opportunities are limited by job allocation.

Only specific jobs in a corporation give people motivation for success. Many men and women are motivated to be successful simply because of the type of job they have managed to acquire. These people usually end up with all the power.

Where do you see these power bases in the corporation?

The power is usually associated with jobs that involve pioneering effort, organizing or designing some product or service. Many persons achieve power because they happen to have a job that gives them high visibility, or links across to other departments, or involves travel. If you have a job in the corporation which happens to be creative or discretionary, then you will soon have power if you don't have it already.

In your book you suggest that role changes and therefore behavioral changes in a corporation can only take place by means of co-operation between people within the organization and outside public policymakers. Surely the government, itself so hierarchical, can hardly help corporations which have demonstrated flexibility, at least in pursuit of the dollar?

There is something to what you say, but you must remember that the government represents the wishes of the people and can serve two functions: one, in helping business to see that pursuit of the dollar is not the only reason for living, that quality of life on the job is important; and, two, that of a watchdog, to ensure that corporations treat people humanely.

As for corporations being flexible in pursuit of the dollar, I don't think they have been. Large corporations are extremely wasteful of human talent.

But large corporations are usually considered inherently efficient because of their "economies of scale."

Large corporations and economies of scale are a myth I don't subscribe to. Large corporations often have diseconomies of scale: they're so large and powerful, they can afford to swallow up losses.

Corporations, in my view, should be smaller, or at least work as smaller units of a co-operation of firms. If large corporations were so effective, we would hardly have the recession and inflation we're enduring these days. Yes, I have been influenced in this respect by E.S. Schumacher's book *Small is Beautiful.*

Why do you care about the difficulty people have in their corporate roles? After all, you yourself had a comfortable middle-class life.

It is because I am from the middle class that I am interested in these questions. As Marx said, "It is only the middle classes who have the time and education to confront themselves with what is going on in society."

Source:

Pearson, Alan. *The Financial Post* November 26, 1977.

Most cities, for instance, have a network of stoplights to regulate, guide, and control traffic flow in areas of congestion. We are required by the rules of the road, by law, to stop on red and to go on green. This formalization of driver behavior at controlled intersections generally provides for a relatively efficient movement of traffic. Without such formalized procedures, intersections undoubtedly would become combat zones, as converging drivers attempted to maneuver their way through the maze of uncertainty, challenges, and resulting accidents. These control procedures usually are intended to be impersonal and apply equally to all drivers, with limited exceptions for legitimate and authorized emergency vehicles such as ambulances, police cars, and fire trucks.

The intent of formalization procedures is to achieve social order and a degree of stability through the patterned conduct of individuals and social units. As a coordination mechanism, formalization is an attempt to anticipate possible variations and to reduce these to an acceptable range of desired behavior through the use of guidelines, rules, and regulations. Formalization begets formalization, and in time the resulting volume of codes necessitates that the rules be set down in written form to insure that they are consistent and enduring.

Few areas of Canadians' lives are not subject to the incursions of formalization. Governments have laws and bylaws regulating everything from traffic to trash. They certify our births and deaths, and collect taxes in between. We sign contracts, arrange mortgages and loans, and make wills for our heirs. Our clubs and associations require commitments and dues from members. Students raise their hands in class, asking teacher's permission to go to the washroom. Social contact relies on varying degrees of formalization to provide acceptable conduct and to insure stability and continuity. Formalization also may be a coordination and control technique in organizations.

In our earlier example of the bucket brigade, a spontaneous organization developed in response to the particular circumstances of the moment and disbanded when the task was completed. But others elsewhere may decide that fire protection is not something that can be left to happenstance, to the unreliable, to the serendipitous chance that people will happen to appear at the scene of a fire and successfully organize each time to battle the blaze. Instead, they elect to have in place a continuing capability to answer fire calls and to provide a ready-made organization to deal with emergencies. Volunteer fire brigade or full-time fire departments are examples of formal organizations.

Unlike the spontaneous organization – our bucket brigade – the fire department is an organization of relatively enduring character that normally outlives individual members.

You might recall from earlier chapters that a role is the behavior expected of the incumbent of a particular position. In a formal organization, the roles necessary in its division of labor are formally specified in the organization's documents, and the requirements of each role are written out in job descriptions. When the fire chief retires, the department usually does not disintegrate; instead, a new individual is recruited to fill the vacant role, and the department continues to meet its goals.

Continuity and formalized procedures are the main characteristics that distinguish a formal organization from a spontaneous organization. We now are in a position to complete our definition. A **formal organization** is a relatively enduring or continuing social collectivity in which roles and resources are coordinated through a division of labor in the use of a technology to achieve a goal or goals. Coordination, control, and problem-solving are facilitated through communication and leadership and formalized through written rules and procedures.

Spontaneous organization is encountered at different times throughout our lives, but the more profound and frequent effects upon us are from formal organizations. These will be our focus for the remainder of the chapter.

One of the first scholars to stress the importance of formalization in organizations was Weber. His perceptive analyses are reviewed in the next section.

WEBER AND BUREAUCRACY

There are many possible ways of structuring and administering an organization. From societies to

TABLE 10-1.   CHARACTERISTICS OF IDEAL TYPES OF AUTHORITY

	Rational	Traditional	Charismatic
Source of leadership	Leader has special training or expertise to occupy the position.	Leader traces origin to a traditional status, or was born into the position.	Leader has special personal qualities: e.g. magical powers, exemplary character, heroism, etc.
Name of rank and file	Members, citizens	Subjects, comrades	Followers, disciples
Grounds for obedience	Owed to a set of rules, laws, and precedents, to an office rather than the individual who fills the office.	Owed to leader out of personal loyalty because of leader's personal wisdom.	Owed out of duty to recognize a charismatic quality and act accordingly.
Form of administration	Highly trained personnel who are appointed and dismissed, whose task it is to keep written records and implement leader's policy.	Personal retainers of the leader chosen on basis of social privilege or the favoritism in which leader holds them.	Persons who are called to serve on the basis of the charismatic qualities they themselves possess.
Relationship to property	Strict legal separation between property of leaders and community.	Leader often legally possesses all property in the realm and others own only what leader gives them.	Leaders are not expected to own much but are supported through the devotion of their followers.
Form of opposition	Directed against the system.	Directed against the person of the leader.	If leader does not continue to show charismatic qualities, leader loses authority and followers leave.

SOURCE: Weber, Max. *The Theory of Social and Economic Organization.* New York: Free Press, 1964. p. 324-406. Table compiled by Kathryn M. Kopinak.

universities, one of the great problems in their survival and success is how to coordinate social behavior so that a reasonable degree of social order is maintained and attainment of desired communal goals is successful. Central to any consideration of social order are the means of control. How does a society or organization get people to cooperate? What power does it have over its members to insure conformity to established norms? Who is to wield this power?

Weber was very much intrigued by questions of social order and power. Why, he wondered, did people obey commands from persons in authority? Was it because the person issuing the command had *power* and was able to achieve his or her objectives in spite of resistance. Or, was it a question of *discipline* – that is, because people, as a condition of their membership in a group, were expected to obey.

His further analyses led him to conclude that one factor people assess before deciding whether or not to obey is the legitimacy of the authority issuing the command. From this perspective, Weber argued that there are three major bases of legitimate authority: traditional, charismatic, and legal-rational. Table 10-1 outlines these three types of authority and some of their characteristics.

Traditional Authority

Traditional authority rests "on an established belief in the sanctity of immemorial traditions and the legitimacy of the status of those exercising authority under them" (Weber, 1947). In ancient monarchies, for example, people believed in the "divine right" of their king or queen to rule. Divine right persupposes the authority of God on earth and the authority of monarch's as God's stewards. People accepted the

"Get it in writing." Reports, memos, and letters are the chief tools of management in the large organization. **Written communication ensures clarity, consistency, and objectivity, but makes not a few managers feel like paper pushers.**

legitimacy of divine right because of a belief that it was transmitted only through eligible descendents and delegated under certain conditions to members of the official court.

In past as well as present families, to choose another example, parents have traditionally exercised authority over their children by virtue of the early dependence of children on their parents for survival. Traditional authority is something we also see in a limited way in Canada with the Queen and her representatives, the Governor-General, and the various provincial Lieutenant-Governors.

Charismatic Authority

Charismatic authority, on the other hand, depends "on devotion to the specific and exceptional sanctity, heroism, or exemplary character of an individual person, and of the normative patterns of order revealed

or ordained by him" (Weber, 1947). The authority of charismatic figures derives from the belief that they are special, that they possess some exceptional ability or magic that inspires the loyalty of their followers. Such is the pervasive character of the leader of a religious cult such as the Moonies. Political charisma has been attributed to Ghandi and Nehru in India, Chairman Mao in China, Nkrumah in Ghana, John Kennedy in the United States, Pierre Trudeau in Canada, and so on. (The effect of charismatic leaders on their ethnic- and minority-group followings is discussed in Chapter 9.)

Legal-Rational Authority: Bureaucracy

We occasionally witness charismatic leadership, but by far the most frequent authority pattern we experience is Weber's third type, **legal-rational author-**

ity. It is based "on a belief in the 'legality' of patterns of normative rules and the right of those elevated to authority under such rules to issue commands" (Weber, 1947).

The underlying process of rational or legal-rational authority is formalization. As a result, the legal-rational tends to be more systematic and impersonal than either traditional or charismatic authorities. Weber argued that not only was this the case, but that organizations based on rational authority tended to have similarities, and its pure form he called **bureaucracy**. His writings on this subject were so thorough that today they are still widely used as starting points for researchers studying organizations.

Weber was curious to examine the relationships between an increasingly complex division of labor in a society and the nature of the organizations in which that labor was done. As we have already noted, his research indicated that as work and the division of labor became more complicated, there was a tendency for the organizational form in which the work was undertaken to resemble what he referred to as bureaucracy.

Weber identified certain common features of bureaucratic organizations. The first point he observed was that a bureaucracy is governed by a set of fixed and official rules and regulations. These rules outline the jurisdiction and responsibilities of each unit and usually each position in the organization. In a large hospital, for instance, the housekeeping department is charged with maintenance and upkeep of the facility, as opposed to the nursing departments charged with patient care. Within the housekeeping department, the tasks of laundry personnel are specified and are quite distinct from those of dishwashers in the kitchen area. Thus we can see that a bureaucracy has a set of comprehensive rules that govern the division of labor in the organization and clearly fix the duties and jurisdictional areas of each department and each person within it.

These governing rules lead to a second feature of bureaucratic organization, a pyramid of authority. That is, there are various levels of authority where the lower offices are supervised by the higher ones. With so many rules and regulations instructing everyone as to the expected practices and outcomes of their offices,

an extensive chain of command is necessary to monitor and oversee operations. A function of the hierarchy is to make certain that people and departments actually do what they are supposed to do and in the proper manner. A characteristic of bureaucratic authority pyramids is that each supervisor has a limited sphere of authority. His or her span of control is confined to particular subordinates, and, in turn, subordinates are expected to acknowledge and respond to the authority vested in their immediate supervisor.

A third feature of bureaucracies is that the management of the organization is based on written documents. "Get it in writing" is the key to successful bureaucratic management. These written documents, whether memos, reports, letters, or whatever, are all preserved for future reference, guidance, or clarification in the files.

A fourth feature is a function of the written rules and procedures in a bureaucracy that insure clients are treated in a consistent fashion without regard to personal considerations. This impersonality of relationships applies not only to client contacts, but also to other members of the bureaucracy.

Because the rules that govern the operation of a bureaucracy are so specific as to the duties and responsibilities of each unit and position, Weber noted a fifth feature in which there tends to be a relatively high degree of specialization in tasks. This high division of labor in a bureaucracy often means that a prerequisite for persons assuming positions in the organization is some degree of specialized training.

Finally, the presence of extensive operating rules and the impersonal nature of many of the interactions in a bureaucracy are a means of insuring that people are recruited into the organization and promoted within it on the basis of their performance, competence, knowledge, and ability. Such advancement is based on achievement criteria. That is to say, people in a bureaucracy should move ahead because they are best qualified to fill the requirements of the position as outlined in the operating rules and duties of the bureaucracy. Recruitment or advancement involving favoritism or particularism – where the basis is who you know, or because you are someone's son or daughter, or for other reasons unrelated to the demands of the job – are regarded as inconsistent with the underlying principles of bureaucracy.

These six components of bureaucracy are seen to be the minimal essentials if the organization is to operate efficiently and endure. Highly bureaucratized organizations are most likely to develop and persist in situations where the nature of the tasks essential to the organization's technology are routine and repetitive. It is also the view of many observers that as organizations grow, the necessity for control and coordination increases and, therefore, so does the tendency toward bureaucratization. We shall explore this belief more fully later.

Bureaucracies are more likely to persist when their environments are relatively stable. As we will see later, organizations seek to avoid or reduce uncertainty. A bureaucracy, with its formalized rules and authority structures, attempts to anticipate requirements and demands so that it may operate predictably and consistently. Another consequence is to ensure with the greatest probability possible that its members will perform in a predictable and consistent fashion.

Department Store Bureaucracy: An Example.

We have all experienced the standardizing qualities of bureaucracies. Most people who shop at a department store pay for their purchases with cash or the store's own credit card. These are the normal procedures, and customers who follow them are speedily processed through the cashier's line and are on their way.

But if you have ever varied from the norm and used a personal check as payment, then you have created a special circumstance. The smooth flow of customers grinds to a halt as you write your check (often having to inquire as to the date, the exact amount of the purchases, and other necessary bookkeeping details). Furthermore, accepting a check is usually outside of the specified jurisdiction of cashiers. Therefore, this variation from the norm calls into action a series of carefully orchestrated alternative procedures. The cashier rings a bell, and from somewhere the supervisor appears. The supervisor verifies the details of the check and asks, "Do you have a driver's licence, major charge card, and social insurance number?" These documents

Prisons are formal organizations, but the individuals who play the inmate roles are not usually there by choice. Therefore, prisons use force in an attempt to achieve their goal – to rehabilitate lawbreakers and return them to the society.

are carefully scrutinized and appropriate notations made on the check. Some stores may have additional procedures, such as a further clearance with a central registry and so on. Regardless of the specific details, from past experience every reader will recognize the basic scenario.

In order to avoid bad checks (and encourage use of their charge cards), stores and other businesses have highly formalized rules and procedures, and clearly specified jurisdictions of responsibilities for dealing with customer payments by check. The rules and hierarchy of authority combine to provide a consistent and reliable means of dealing with this variation from the standard expectation. One is treated the same throughout the store, regardless of the clerk or the department.

The rules were made in an attempt to anticipate variations from the norm, and if there are unanticipated difficulties, such as a man offering a live pig as payment, then these can be referred up the hierarchy to responsible authorities for a decision. But the more variations an organization regularly experiences, the more difficult it is to anticipate and cover them in the regulations. In other words, in highly changeable and uncertain circumstances, it becomes impossible to incorporate all the exceptions in the rules. If there are too many expectations, the hierarchy will eventually get plugged and bogged down in providing interpretations and directions. As we indicated earlier, a bureaucratic form of organization performs best in situations involving a routine technology in a relatively stable environment.

At about the same time Weber was studying bureaucracy, certain developments were occurring in North America that were to have a profound influence on the study and operation of organizations. We shall look at these in the next section.

THE ORGANIZATION

In the 1860s and 1870s, industrialization was well advanced in the United States and was beginning slowly to pick up momentum in Canada. With industrialization had come concentrations of workers in plants and factories and the rise of large-scale industrial organizations. In this context, a movement in North America was developing that was interested in how organizations might be made more efficient and productive.

An industrial engineer, Frederic Winslow Taylor, believed that the full potential of industrial organization was not being realized because of inefficiency and that the answer to this problem lay in more systematic management. He viewed organizations as large mechanical systems and suspected that much of their inefficiency was due to a natural tendency of workers to take it easy and not to produce at their optimal capacity.

Scientific Management

Taylor's strategy was to make every worker a specialist responsible for a single, narrowly defined task. The key, he argued, was to find the one best way to do each and every task. The means to achieve this desired state of perfection in productivity was through what he modestly called **scientific management**.

For Taylor, individual workers were simply instruments of production to be employed by management in the same way as the machines of the plant. The responsibility for finding the one best way of doing a job rests with management, because as Taylor (1947, originally published 1911) explained: ". . . the science which underlies each workman's act is so great and amounts to so much that the workman who is best suited actually to do the work is incapable (either through lack of education or through insufficient mental capacity) of understanding this science."

As the first time-and-motion specialists, proponents of scientific management sought to improve organizational productivity through more efficient procedures. To find the one best way of completing a task, they would observe workers who were thought by their supervisors to be the most capable at that job. The work patterns of these superior employees would be analyzed and broken down into their basic components, and then rearranged to make them more efficient. The worker was subsequently retrained in the job, doing it in the prescribed best way, and put on an incentive-pay-scheme so as to encourage continued use of the desired procedures.

Taylor's method became widely used because it increased productivity, and workers generally made more money than they had before. His approach was to focus on individual roles in organizations, because he believed groups tended to constrain individual productivity.

Scientific management, while successful in many organizations, was not without its critics. The methods were seen to be too employer-oriented. Unions felt that the greater efficiency derived would result in fewer jobs. On humanitarian grounds, speeding up work routines was believed to be potentially damaging to health. Highly specialized work was thought to deprive people of meaning in their work. The rapid pace caused by pursuit of income geared to exceeding a production minimum put older workers at a considerable disadvantage.

Although Taylor and the scientific management advocates were very practically oriented, they tended to have a view of organizations quite similar to Weber's. They saw the organization as an instrument for the coordination of human action in the achievement of specified objectives. All of them saw organization as a machine-like instrument, but the objective of scientific management was to fine tune the efficiency of highly specialized roles by determining the one best way for each.

The Weberian and scientific management conceptions of organizations tended to be rather narrow and limited concerned as these perceptions were mainly with an impersonal focus on internal organization structure and process. But though these conceptions came early in the development of our knowledge about organizations, they continue to have a profound influence over many practitioners today. Structure is still an important factor in the study of organizations, and we consider this dimension further in the next section.

Structure

In our definition of formal organization, we suggested that coordination, control, and problem-solving in the organization are facilitated through communication, leadership, and varying degrees of written rules and procedures. Written rules and regulations are a mechanism of formalization that Weber demonstrated to be a major component of bureaucracy. As we have seen, one function of these formalized regulations is to define the relationships among various positions composing the division of labor and to establish a hierarchy of authority. In other words, the rules describe the **organization structure**.

The relationships among various roles in a division of labor may be left to chance, as with our bucket brigade where, fortunately, enough people sufficiently coordinated their actions to get the job done. But formalization is a characteristic of formal organizations that insures a deliberate patterning of behavior so that things are *not* left to chance. Instead, the requirements in relationships for the optimal division of labor are specified in advance and serve as a model for the organization's operations.

You will recall from Chapter 2 that a position in a social network is designated as a status. President, vice-president, treasurer, and secretary are common statuses in organizations. What the occupant of a particular status is required to do is known as a role. A university department may have a vacant status, for instance, an assistant professor. They will be looking for a replacement whose likely role will be to teach some junior level courses, conduct research, and assist with minimal administrative responsibilities.

Formalization usually states how an organization's various statuses are to be arranged into some sort of a structure. The structure of an organization is the patterns of relationships between its component statuses.

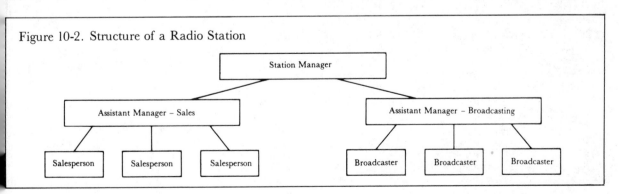

Figure 10-2. Structure of a Radio Station

Station Manager

Assistant Manager – Sales

Assistant Manager – Broadcasting

Salesperson   Salesperson   Salesperson

Broadcaster   Broadcaster   Broadcaster

The rationale for the particular structure is usually the complementary or interdependent nature of various roles for the completion of specific tasks important to the organization.

As the example in Figure 10-2 shows, a radio station may elect to group its personnel according to specialties, with the advertising and sales people in a department separate from its broadcasters. Furthermore, they may place one person in charge of each of the groups with titles such as assistant manager-sales, and assistant manager-broadcasting. At the top of the hierarchy will be a station manager. This structure not only specifies the links between various statuses based on role specializations, but also provides for a basic authority heirarchy.

The structure of an organization may be relatively simple, such as that of our radio station, or it may be very complex, with numerous statuses of various levels in a myriad of specialized departments or units, as in a multi-branch bank. Figure 10-3 describes several types of complex structures. A structure may specify an authority hierarchy such as a **centralized structure** where subordinates report directly to a supervisor (a). Or, it may be **decentralized**, where no supervisor is

The Quality of Working Life on the Shop Floor

An important aspect of the operation of any organization is the relationship between employees and management. In order to improve the labor relations, productivity, and growth opportunities for individuals in Canadian organizations, it has been argued that the quality of working life (QWL) in these settings must be upgraded. One such improvement would be the opportunity for employees to participate in organizational decision-making.

There are two fundamentally different ways in which employees may influence (participate in) decisions which affect them in their work organization. The first is indirectly, through elected representatives who meet with company officials to negotiate a collective agreement and to discuss and solve problems that pertain to that agreement as they arise over time. A variant on this form of "industrial democracy" which is common in Northern Europe but extremely rare in North America involves worker representation on the Board of Directors and on Works Councils. In this instance the worker representatives become involved in diverse and far-reaching decisions which may extend well beyond the collective agreement itself. The second way is through direct "shop floor" democracy.

QWL (as it is conceived in this booklet) focuses on the "shop floor" and involves the worker much more directly in the day-to-day decisions that affect his work or his immediate work environment. In this respect it much more closely resembles "participative management" as practised in some North American companies than "Industrial Democracy" as legislated in Germany, Sweden and a number of European countries. But even in these countries the real payoff for the worker, as well as for the organization, appears to be in shop-floor applications.

The most significant implication that QWL has for an organization is that, beyond the experimental stage, it reflects a continuing commitment to new values and the gradual development of a new philosophy of management. For QWL to be successful in the long run and to avoid becoming another fad in the long list of "miracles", both labour and management have to modify their perspectives and their roles in the organization, especially where these perspectives and roles have been militantly adversarial.

For over 50 years, North American labour relations have been characterized by union-management relations which define labour relations as something that finds expression in contract negotiations and the enforceable collective agreement that is the product of negotiations. The contract deals best with matters which are *extrinsic* to the work situation (such as compensation, leave, hours of work, etc.) and much less successfully with matters which are *intrinsic* to the work situation, those matters with which QWL is most concerned.

Reinforcing the traditional perspective of labour relations has been the dominant view on the part of labour unions that management cannot be trusted, and that consequently "if you haven't got it nailed down in a collective agreement, you haven't got anything".

Employers have not only accepted this role but reinforced it with their own attitudes toward unions and to collective agreements. For the most part employers have embraced the theory of "residual management rights", which reflects an attitude almost identical to that of the unions, as expressed above. From the employers' point of view, "If it is not in the contract it belongs to management".

The consequences of this arrangement are predictable. Unions have, to a considerable extent, denied themselves an interest in, or responsibility for, the intrinsic aspects of the quality of their members' lives at work. Management, on the other hand, has been obliged to try to achieve operational effectiveness with a workforce which has too often been encouraged by its union representatives to be as uncooperative as it can be in the workplace, short of activities which are proscribed by contract or the common law of industrial relations.

Frustration with this state of affairs has led many persons of goodwill to insist that the adversarial dimensions of industrial relations must be rejected in favour of collaborative and co-operative relationships. In the view of most union representatives, this amounts to throwing out the baby with the bathwater. They may support co-operation, but they are wary of co-option. The same may be said for many employers.

It is an underlying maxim of the market economy that employers are in business to make a profit, and that if they are to prosper and expand they must optimize that profit. The premises and motivations of North American unions are remarkably similar. Unions aim to optimize the compensation which their members receive for their labour. Since the claims of the workers for compensation are inherently a charge against the profits of the employer, it is, in their view, naive to assume that the economic pie can be cut in any way but through an adversarial process.

In the view of the writers, QWL and collective bargaining are not alternative or incompatible systems of labour relations. QWL *is not a substitute for collective bargaining*, nor a challenge to a healthy and realistic adversarial relationship at the bargaining table. As R.T. Philp of the Oil, Chemical and Atomic Workers said at a recent conference on QWL: "The collective agreement is the cornerstone of QWL." Nor is QWL a process appropriate to the division of the profits of enterprise – profits *jointly* created through the collective and collaborative efforts of management and the workers. Moreover, since in many situations QWL has demonstrated its potential for increasing profits, and consequently for improving the union's capacity to secure a good contract, neither unions nor management should object to initiatives which, at the end of the day, leave the enterprise stronger and its workers more satisfied and better paid.

While QWL neither opposes nor undermines the ordinary processes of collective bargaining, it does suggest that *unremitting* adversarial relationships provide an unsatisfactory foundation for a productive process. Continuing confrontation in labour relations increases both the direct and indirect costs of labour, threatens the quality of the product or service and reduces the reliability of the enterprise as a supplier of goods and services. QWL is not compatible with that kind of collective bargaining relationship.

QWL creates in essence a new dimension of consultation between labour and management, beyond those areas presently covered in collective bargaining. It is a process which deals effectively with matters that do not lend themselves to collective bargaining and have been too long neglected, to the detriment of both employers and workers. It provides a framework within which management and labour can work together co-operatively, in support of compatible objectives. QWL does not threaten the collective bargaining process: it complements it. The implication for labour management relations of establishing QWL relationships is not that the adversarial relationship of the collective bargaining process must be abandoned. Rather, the record suggests that an effective QWL relationship reduces the level of distrust between the two sides, and contributes to a more mature bargaining relationship.

But an effective QWL relationship is not to be achieved overnight. To be successful both parties have to have developed a fairly high degree of mutual trust, openness and respect. Where such a relationship does not exist, where both parties are locked into unending win-lose battles or where fundamental ideological differences keep them apart, the likelihood of collaborating toward common goals is severely limited. In such instances a considerable amount of time, effort and ingenuity may be required before the parties may be willing to even sit down together in a problem-solving mode.

Where union-management relations are hostile, premature attempts at introducing QWL many well lead to a worsening of relationships and make further attempts at collaboration even more difficult.

Source:

Johnston, Carl, Mark Alexander, and Jacquelin Robin. *Quality of Working Life: The Idea and its Application.* Labour Canada, 1978.

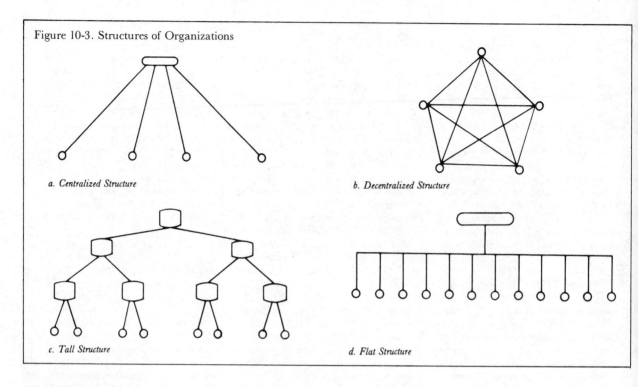

Figure 10-3. Structures of Organizations

a. Centralized Structure

b. Decentralized Structure

c. Tall Structure

d. Flat Structure

specified (b). An organization's structure may specify many levels of hierarchy and be referred to as a *tall* structure (c). Or it may be relatively *flat* with few levels in the hierarchy (d).

Simple-complex, centralized-decentralized, and flat-tall are some of the more common descriptions of organization structures. These, of course, refer to the patterns or configurations of the statuses observed.

Organization structure has remained a key variable for researchers since Weber's pioneering work, and later in this chapter we will review some of the impacts or constraints that have been found to be influential. But as this stage in our analysis, the key points are that the formal structure of an organization refers to the expected patterns of relationship among its various statuses, and that the formal structure was of primary concern for early organization researchers and theorists. A broader and more personalized view of organizations than the structural view did not begin to develop until some chance findings occurred at a large electronics manufacturing plant – the Western Electric or Hawthorne Research.

The Hawthorne Studies

Between 1924 and 1932, a series of important studies were conducted at the Hawthorne Works (plant) of the Western Electric Company (Mayo, 1946; Roethlisberger and Dickson, 1947). In the scientific management tradition, the original research was undertaken to test the relationship between the quality of the lighting under which people worked and its effects, if any, on their production. The initial results were inconclusive, the research continued, and a total of seven studies explored a range of physical conditions of work. Of the seven, four are well known: the Relay Assembly Test Room Experiment, the Second Relay Assembly Group Experiment, the Mica Splitting Test Room Experiment, and the Bank Wiring Room Observation Study (Parsons, 1974). The last study is of particular relevance to our considerations.

The work habits of the 14 men in the Bank Wiring Room were observed over time. The three soldermen, nine wiremen, and two inspectors were engaged in complicated wiring and soldering of banks of wires making up telephone exchanges. The men were paid on a piecework basis that the company intended as an incentive for groups to produce at a maximum pace. The more groups produced, the more they would be paid.

The experimenters found that in this particular group, however, the financial incentives of piecework did not urge workers to ever-increasing levels of production. Instead, the group had informally decided that wiring two exchanges a day was a reasonable output. This constituted for them a "fair day's work," and they produced steadily at that pace with little concern for the piece-rate incentive.

Not only did the group keep an eye on how much members produced, but they actively sought to bring everyone in line with group norms. If a man worked above the accepted level, he was labeled a "slave" or "speed king," and if he consistently worked below standard, he was known as a "chiseler." A person was a chiseler because he was making others in the group carry him. If sarcasm was ineffectual, other group members would give violators a sharp punch on the shoulder in what was called "binging."

These actions were seen as means for workers' groups to control changes in plant routines. It was the workers' belief that if some of them consistently produced at higher levels, then the company would expect that of everyone. Also, they had become comfortable in their relationships with other group members and were convinced that changes in rates of production caused by "rate busters" might put others out of work and lead to the break-up of groups.

Group norms on productivity in the Bank Wiring Room neutralized the effects of the company's piece-rate system. The group held its members in check and produced at a steady two units per day. Another observation was that, in spite of the rules, soldermen and wiremen rotated their jobs from time to time in order to provide some variety in their tasks and to reduce the tedium and boredom of repetitive jobs.

These finding were totally unexpected and provided researchers with new and valuable insights into the internal operations of organizations. The Hawthorne Studies diverted researchers from the machine-like view of organizations found in Weber and Taylor.

Instead, researchers discovered that individuals and groups within an organization may act in ways not predicted by formalized rules and structures. This recognition or discovery of "informal organization" represented a significant advance toward a more adequate and balanced understanding of organizations and their operations.

As we saw earlier, the formal structure of an organization refers to the expected or desired patterns of relationships and behaviors. The Bank Wiring Room Study demonstrated that there is an important additional dimension to organizational structure, the *social* dimension.

The discovery of the social dimension of organizations led to a rash of studies of so-called informal organization. Many of these confirmed the Hawthorne findings that organized work groups tend to slow production down (Mathewson, 1931; Anderson, 1944; Roy, 1952). A member of studies detailed how people in organizations cope with the working conditions created by various structural and technological arrangements. Donald Roy (1959), for example, describes his experiences as a machine operator, participant-observer doing very simple and repetitive work. (See Chapter 17 for a discussion of the advantages and limitations of participant observation as a research method.) He and his immediate group of workers spent long hours over a six-day week performing the following role:

Standing all day in one spot beside three old codgers in a dingy room looking out through barred windows at the bare walls of a brick warehouse, leg movements largely restricted to the shifting of body weight from one foot to the other, hand and arm movements confined, for the most part, to a simple repetitive sequence of place the die, punch the clicker, place the die, punch the clicker, and intellectual activity reduced to computing the hours to quitting time.

How did the machine operators cope with the tedium and meaninglessness of their jobs? Roy and his work group played little games to pass the time and made the most of social contacts. Also, they employed trivial rituals to break the routine. For example, each day one of the workers brought a couple of peaches and shared these with the others during a morning break.

This was "peach time." The same person also brought a banana in his lunch. Each day, one of his co-workers would sneak into his lunch bucket and consume the banana with much flourish and announce "banana time!"

There would be a ritual protest that his banana had been stolen, and so on. But next day, he would bring another banana, and banana time would be repeated to the delight of all the group. Peach time and banana time were followed throughout the day by "window time," "pick-up time," "fish time," and "Coke time." These little devices, not predicted by the structure or rules of the organization, helped these organizational participants to cope with their daily regimen.

The Bank Wiring Room Study and subsequent research kindled an interest in the human side of an organization and served to underscore the point that organizations were not merely structures to produce goods or services. They also contained human beings who were capable of acting and reacting. Human relations in organizations, as a result, became a major preoccupation of organization researchers. The organization became a context in which to view people at work. From this changed perspective, subsequent studies drew on a number of social/psychological theoretical resources, including those of symbolic interactionists to explore such questions as worker alienation, job satisfaction, group cohesiveness, and decision-making and change, to name but a few.

Before looking at some of these issues, it is important to stress that while this shift in emphasis from a machine-like view of organizations to a concern with what was happening to people in organizations was a major one, it did not result in a demise of scientific management or its concern for organizational efficiency and productivity. That strongly entrenched emphasis continued, and improvements in technology and advancements in automation served to keep organizations competitive. But with the addition of the human relations perspective, the study of organizations was broadened. It had become apparent that in addition to the technical system of an organization there was a social system, and a broadened sociotechnical perspective was essential to a fuller understanding of organizations (Trist and Bamforth, 1951).

Roy's study is an example of how people coped with the specific conditions of their work within an organization. It is also a good example of alienation, and this we shall explore in the next section.

Alienation

Karl Marx. In the Hawthorne Research and Roy's accounts, we were introduced to the effects that organizations have on their members. This was an aspect of industrialization and a development of large-scale work organizations that had interested Marx many years earlier. It was his view that people distinguish themselves from animals the moment they begin to produce their means of subsistence. Production of goods in order to assist one to stay alive is for him a basic social fact.

Marx believed that people can find self-fulfillment only through productive, or creative, labor. Work is a central feature of people's identities and allows them to develop to their fullest potential. As the industrialization process occurs and a capitalist system develops, however, the process of self-realization for individuals becomes frustrated and **alienation** results. That is, people begin to lose control of their destinies, because they no longer possess the major means of production. Instead, they work in organizations on someone else's machines. Expanding on this concept of alienation, Marx (quoted in Bottomore and Rubel, 1956) asks:

In what does this alienation consist? First that the work is external to the worker, that it is not a part of his nature, that consequently he does not fulfill himself in his work but denies himself, has a feeling of misery, not of well-being, does not develop freely a physical and mental energy, but is physically exhausted and mentally debased. The worker, therefore, feels himself at home only during his leisure, whereas at work he feels homeless. His work is not voluntary but imposed, forced labor. It is not the satisfaction of a need, but only a means for satisfying other needs.

For Marx, individuals experience alienation as a result of shifts in ownership patterns, changes in technology, and the rise of industrial organization. Alienation, according to Rinehart (1975), "refers to a condition in which individuals have little or no control over (a) the purposes and products of the labor process, (b) the overall organization of the workplace, and (c) the immediate work process itself." We are reminded of Roy and his co-workers looking through barred windows at a brick wall while they placed the die, punched the clicker, placed the die, and punched the clicker.

Technology. Blauner (1964) was interested in the impact that technology has on workers – how what a person does in his or her work (the technology) affects that person. In the early 1960s he looked at the secondary data analysis of workers in a number of industries in an attempt to answer the following question: Under what conditions are the alienation tendencies of work organizations the strongest, and under what conditions are they the weakest or least noticeable?

Blauner argued that technology was a key factor in an organization's distictive character. In view of this position, it is not surprising that he turned to differences in technology to see if these might explain differences in alienation levels. As a preliminary step he identified four basic technologies in the industries he studied: assembly-line, machine-tending, continuous-process, and craft.

The work processes on an assembly-line are highly particularized, so that each worker has a very small number of routine, specialized tasks to complete. Workers generally have a fixed work station, and the pace of the line determines the speed at which people work. Assembly of automobiles was Blauner's example of this technology.

In machine-tending technologies, work processes are highly routine, and worker's tasks consist of watching or tending to the needs of machines. Blauner saw textile manufacturing as representing this type of technology. In the production of textiles, large machines spin the fibers, or automated looms weave materials. The worker's role is paced by the machines, when they run out of materials the worker replaces the spools of fiber, and so on. Simple tasks are completed according to the needs of the machines.

Continuous-process is a very advanced form of technology, where a raw material such as petroleum enters one end of the operation and undergoes a number of automated conversion steps. Finished products are derived at various stages along the way. Oil refining and chemical production are examples of this technology. The complexity of the technology requires workers to be highly knowledgeable about its processes, so that the operations may be monitored and spur-of-the moment decisions made when necessary to insure continuous operation.

Craft technology is characterized by a considerable amount of hand-work. It also tends to be relatively unstandardized, because it is difficult to establish routines in a technology where the products produced vary considerably. In Blauner's sample, craft technology was represented by printers. Because of the skill involved, printers have judgmental flexibility in the organization and execution of their work.

Blauner arranged these three technologies according to the level of control, meaning, and self-expression they allowed the worker. Assembly-line work permits very small amounts of these features for individual workers, while machine-tending contains slightly more of each one. Continuous-process technology, he found, provided workers with greater control, more responsibility, and meaning in their work than in the previous two. The highest levels of control, meaning, and self-expression were found in craft technology.

Worker alienation or feelings of powerlessness, meaninglessness, self-estrangement, and social isolation, he found, were highest for assembly-line workers. These feelings diminished as technologies afforded more control, meaning, and self-expression for the workers. For his sample, therefore, alienation was lowest among printers. Blauner's findings are summarized in Table 10-2; a study by Fullan (1970) using a Canadian sample had similar results.

Whenever we have individuals, groups, or organizations interrelating there is, of course, the potential for conflict. Within organizations, labor and management may have differing objectives or views that lead to conflict, and the organization may find itself in conflict from time to time with elements in its task environment. Research on alienation also serves to remind us that factors within the organization, such as its

TABLE 10-2   BLAUNER'S FINDINGS ON TECHNOLOGY AND ALIENATION

Industry	Technology	Control Over Work	Meaning In Work	Self-Expression	Alienation
Printing	Craft	Very high	Very high	Very high	Very low
Oil Refining	Continuous Process	High	High	High	Low
Textiles	Machine Tending	Low	Low	Low	Medium
Automobile Assembly	Assembly Line	Very low	Very low	Very low	Very high

SOURCE: Blauner, Robert. *Alienation and Freedom*. Chicago: University of Chicago Press, 1964.

technology, may stimulate conflict. The perspective of conflict theory increases our sensitivity to such possibilities in organizational analysis.

Technology remains a major factor for researchers who examine the conditions in an organization that foster the development of alienation. Alienation is likely to be lowest in organizational settings where members have control, meaning, and opportunities for self-fulfillment in their roles. We saw earlier that Roy and his group of machine-tenders coped with the alienating tendencies of their roles through informal social activity. Many researchers have attempted to explore the dynamics of groups in the social structure of organizations and the impact they have on individuals and the successful attainment of organization goals. We consider these questions in the next section.

Groups in Organizations

We have been considering some of the ways in which the organization acts to influence the interaction of its members. People in organizations find themselves in a variety of circumstances. Some people work in isolation, while others work in groups of varying sizes. People working in groups may be dependent on one another to complete a joint task, or they may do their jobs independently but be in close proximity to each other. We have already seen how groups may act to influence the production standards or levels of its members.

But, of course, all groups do not influence their members to the same extent, and, in attempting to account for these differences, the concept of **cohesiveness** has proven useful.

Groups differ according to the degree its individuals perceive themselves as members, how much interest they have in belonging to the group, and how highly they regard other members of the group. Where individuals identify themselves as members of the group, where group members want the group to remain together, and where group members have a high regard for each other, there will be high cohesiveness.

Groups will vary in the degree to which these characteristics are present, and researchers have investigated what difference, if any, this makes. In other words, what variations in behavior and attitudes normally may be expected when a person belongs to a highly cohesive group as opposed to membership in a low-cohesive group.

Seashore (1954) has looked at this matter in a study of 228 groups of varying sizes comprising 5871 individuals working in a machinery factory. He sees group cohesiveness as, "an attraction of group members to the group in terms of the strength of forces on the individual member to remain in the group and to resist leaving the group." Seashore's major findings were:

1. Members of high-cohesive groups exhibit less anxiety than members of low-cohesive groups.

2. High-cohesive groups have less variation in productivity among members than do low-cohesive groups. High-cohesive groups, such as the Bank Wiring Room, establish and enforce a group standard that is usually missing in low-cohesive groups.

3. High-cohesive groups will differ more frequently and significantly from the plant norm of productivity than low-cohesive groups. High-cohesive groups will tend to have productivity levels either noticeably above or noticeably below the plant norm.

4. Whether the productivity of high-cohesive groups is above or below the plant norm is a function of the degree to which the plant is perceived by group members to provide a supportive setting for the group. If high-cohesive groups members feel secure that the group will continue to exist, they are more likely to produce above the plant norm than high-cohesive groups where the organizational setting is not as supportive.

5. Similarities in members' ages and educational levels are not related to the degree of cohesiveness in a group. Instead, group cohesiveness is positively related to opportunities for interaction by members, and this is most likely to occur in smaller groups of relatively stable composition.

Seashore's findings on group cohesiveness are entirely consistent with our expectations based on some of the studies we have reviewed previously. Roy's (1959) cohesive group, for instance, provided a relief from the alienating tendencies of their work through such social diversions as "peach time" and "banana time." In relation to individual attitudes, White showed that the opportunities individuals have for belonging to cohesive groups and other social networks were more important factors than organization size. And, of course, we recall the impacts of group standards on productivity as shown in the Bank Wiring Room Study.

Cohesiveness, alienation, and its positive counterpart, job satisfaction, are examples of the types of research interests that have been pursued since the Hawthorne Studies. The organization is a setting in which human behavior and the social system can be viewed and improved understanding sought. One final example, and an important one, that we will consider in the following section concerns opportunities for

organization members at the lower levels to be involved in decision-making.

Decision-Making

Decision-making is a central component in the operation of organizations. Decisions involving the purposes of an organization and the means for their pursuit are a constant matter of concern for organization members. These policy matters are often long-term, but at almost every instant of an organization's activity there are problems to be solved and decisions of the moment to be made. As we saw earlier, organizations are structured with an authority hierarchy that usually is charged with assuming the dominant role in decision-making. As a matter of fact, in many organizations this decision-making role becomes a jealously guarded exclusive right of management.

We should also bear in mind that the technology with which a person works may afford very little opportunity for flexibility and decision-making. This was the case in Blauner's study with the assembly-line and textile workers in contrast to those in continuous-process and craft technologies. There have been many research efforts since the Hawthorne Studies to examine the possibly good effects that a more broadly based decision-making structure and process have on participants. But before considering these, we should return to the Hawthorne Studies to look briefly at the Relay Assembly Test Room Experiment.

Relay Assembly Test Room Experiment. The Relay Assembly Test Room Experiment took place at the Hawthorne Works of the Western Electric Company from 1927 to 1932. It involved the study of a small group of women (several members of the group changed at one point) making relay assemblies for telephones. In the tradition of scientific management and industrial psychology, the researchers were interested to see if changes in conditions affecting worker fatigue would result in increased productivity and morale. The assembly of a telephone relay was completed by a single worker and required about a minute's time. As a result of the large number of relays produced by a worker each day, it was relatively easy to

Employee-Owned Firm Shows Profit

It has been suggested that if employees of an organization owned a piece of the business, their interest in its operations would be very much enhanced. There are growing numbers of applications of this principle in Canada.

Byers Transport Ltd., the employee-owned trucking company, continued to show strong growth in business and profits during 1976.

The Edmonton-based company also continues to be in the spotlight as a working example of industrial democracy.

The long-established trucking company had been acquired from its founders by Pacific Western Airlines to complement the airline's northern service.

The provincial government, when it became the owner of PWA, decided to get out of the trucking industry and in the spring of 1975, with the help of long-term financing by the Alberta Opportunity Company, sold Byers to its employees.

The company employees, who made the highest bid for the then money-losing operation, turned Byers into a profitable operation after one full year of operation.

The combination of care and increased productivity is continuing to pay off, says R.A. (Sandy) Slator, Byers president. "Through the end of November, profits were up 15 per cent over last year and the freight volume increased 20 per cent."

"We will make or surpass all our forecasts," Mr. Slator said during an interview in the Byers headquarters, at 7420 125A Avenue.

Mr. Slator and other Byers employee-shareholders get a lot of practice at being interviewed. The employee-owned business has captured the attention of newspapers, business publications and academic institutes.

Richard Long, a post-graduate student at Cornell University, Ithaca, New York, has spent more than six weeks around the trucking company headquarters and plans to use the company as the main subject of a Ph.D. thesis.

The company is one of the best and most successful examples of an employee-owned company in North America, Mr. Long said.

Initially, 125 of the firm's 175 employees purchased stock in the firm, Mr. Slator said. "We now have 103 shareholders and the staff has increased to about 200."

Those employees who sold their stock did so in almost all cases because they were leaving the company and only employees can hold stock in Byers.

"We are going to have to make more effort to sell shares, given up by retiring employees, to new employees," Mr. Slator admitted. There has been a tendency for employees, already holding stock, to purchase additional shares when they become available.

The employee-shareholders in Byers elect a board of 10 directors of whom two are selected from the drivers, dockworkers and clerical staff, one is selected from the foreman-supervisory-junior management level, one from middle management; three from senior management, one from the North and two from outside the company.

The directors are elected to one-year terms. Mr. Slator said 18 people were nominated for the last election and nine of those elected had served on the board before.

The current directors are: Harvey Norstrom, a pick-up and delivery driver within the city; Mrs. Karen Guttinger, accounts payable supervisor; Floyd Shannon, a purchasing supervisor; John Bubel, controller; John Bell, systems operations manager; Mr. Slator, president; Bill Jenkins, Yellowknife terminal manager; Glyn Edwards, an Edmonton lawyer, and R.T. Eyton, president of Pacific Western Airlines.

There is one vacancy on the board as the result of the resignation of a driver who left the firm recently.

The employee-shareholders have been rewarded with a dividend equal to 20 per cent of the current value of the stock at the end of the first year's operation.

It is still four months from the company's year-end, but the board is expected to declare an interim dividend at its next meeting, Mr. Slator said.

The profits do not appear to be coming at the expense of wages. The company's drivers and dockworkers are members of the Teamsters Union and receive rates competitive with other companies.

Byers, which added successful runs to Grande Cache and Hinton in the last year, plans further expansion for 1977, Mr. Slator said.

The biggest limitation on any company's ability to expand is the availability of good management people, he said. Byers has a program aimed at educating its staff so that it can promote from within.

"We have a full training program for all employees which pays the cost of any course they choose on its successful completion."

Source:

Campbell, Tom. *Edmonton Journal,* January 3, 1977.

observe the effects on productivity of any changes introduced.

The normal work-week before the start of the experiment consisted of 48 hours and included Saturday mornings. The only break provided during the day was a brief lunch period. The changes introduced in the Relay Assembly Test Room Experiment centered largely on rest pauses and the length of the work-day and work-week. One of the first changes was the introduction of two five-minute rest breaks during the day; after five weeks, this was changed to two ten-minute rest breaks; then after four weeks, six five-minute breaks, and so on. As these minor changes were introduced, and effects on behavior and attitudes of the workers were noted.

During the majority of the changes introduced, the workers' attitudes and morale remained good, their productivity increased, and their absenteeism decreased (Parsons, 1974). Most observers have tended to attribute the positive outcomes of the Relay Assembly Test Room Experiment to the cohesive work group. Prior to the experiment, the women were members of a large department of 100 members. This meant that there were not the opportunities to form cohesive groups that were available in the test of the smaller Bank Room.

Much later, analysts re-examined the data of these experiments and argued that although the cohesive nature of the work group was an important factor, equally important was the fact that the women in the experiment had an opportunity to participate in decisions about matters that affected them, an opportunity that they had not had before. As Blumberg (1968) has observed:

I believe that a major, although of course not the exclusive, explanation for the remarkable increases in productivity and morale lay in the crucial role which the test room workers played in determining the conditions under which they worked. The operatives, from the very beginning of the experiment, were drawn into the decision-making process and achieved a large measure of direct and active control over their tasks and working conditions. In other words, a small but genuine dose of workers' participation was introduced into the test room. . . .

It is important to note that their participation in decision-making was not contrived or irrelevant to their work; instead it was as Blumberg has described, "genuine." In addition to cohesiveness, the lesson to be learned from the Relay Assembly Test Room Experiment is put most succinctly by Kahn (1975): "Real participation has real effects. When people take a significant and influential part in decisions that they value, the quality of decisions is likely to be improved and their implementation is almost certain to be improved."

There have been many organization studies that examined the amount of control individuals have in their work, and as in Blauner's (1964) study on technology and alienation, there has been a remarkable consistency in reporting positive association with job satisfaction. Where control and relevant participation in decision-making are present in organizations, individuals more likely have higher job satisfaction and lower alienation. There are fewer studies on these effects on productivity, but those that have been undertaken are less clear-cut. That is, control and participatory decision-making may or may not have direct positive relationships with individual performance levels.

We have briefly reviewed the sorts of things researchers concerned with human relations in organizations have looked at since the Hawthorne Studies. The organization has been the setting in which human behavior has been examined and the dimensions of the social system explored. In some instances, such as the studies on technology and alienation, the linkages between the social and the technological systems have been considered. But in general, people, either as individuals or in groups within organizations, have been the main units of analysis. This was clearly the case in the references to group cohesiveness and participatory decision-making. We will return to consider the current applications of these insights later in the chapter when we discuss organization design.

Just as the Hawthorne Studies shifted the focus of organization research 30 or so years ago, so also did a more recent view of organizations, the "open system." We shall explore this and its current impacts in the next section.

OPEN SYSTEMS AND TASK ENVIRONMENTS

Most of the materials we have reviewed so far have tended to reflect a very simple view of organizations as **closed systems**. According to this concept, organizations are relatively self-contained units where particular structural arrangements and individual behavior patterns may be accounted for by factors internal to the organization. Max Weber, as we saw, saw organizations or bureaucracies as mechanisms for control of participants, and his overriding interest was with internal mechanisms and operations. Similarly, the human relations studies we considered were interested in organizations only insofar as they provided a context within which to assess attitudes and to view groups and individual behavior. These essentially closed system approaches, as has just been suggested, conceive of organizations as autonomous social entities; the analytical approach is largely one of short-range observation and deduction, because of a belief that "all consequences of action are contained within the system and all causes of actions stem from within it" (Thompson, 1967).

But there has been a gradual tendency to regard this closed-system view of organizations as too narrow, because organizations are also part of a larger social system (Barnard, 1938; Selznick, 1949; Clark, 1956; Parsons, 1960). Organizations do not operate in a vacuum. They are located in a multi-faceted environment. They are affected by governments and their legislation, by customers and suppliers, by competitors, and by numerous other external bodies and groups. An organization may attempt to insulate its internal operations as much as possible, but an organization's total environment will ultimately affect even these. Figure 10-4 depicts, in simplified form, an organization as an **open system**, where the organization is dependent for its viability in part on external inputs and outputs.

A fish processing plant, for instance, buys raw fish from fishermen, packaging materials, fuel, and so on from suppliers and hires its workers from the community. These are inputs from the outside that are necessary for the organization's operation. The organi-

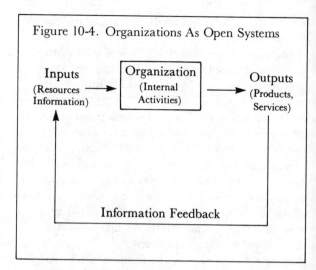

Figure 10-4. Organizations As Open Systems

zation's internal procedures combine these resources in such a way that the fish are cleaned, filleted, and packaged (they are transformed into a finished package). But, once again, without sales of the products to outside customers, the organization cannot survive. Information about the success of their products, the availability of various input resources, and so on provide feedback for the organization that is important in determining its future moves. The words of John Donne, "No man is an island, entire of itself," apply equally well to organizations.

Task Environment

When we regard an organization as an open system, we take a more realistic but more complex view of it, because in order to comprehend its operations we not only need to understand its internal workings, but we need as well to identify those elements in its environment that significantly influence it. We must determine not only how an organization reacts to its environment, but also how it acts to influence and control its environment.

Furthermore, if we become concerned with an organization's environment, we are confronted with the problem of exactly defining the boundaries of that environment. Is an organization's environment everything external to it? Technically, this is the case, but

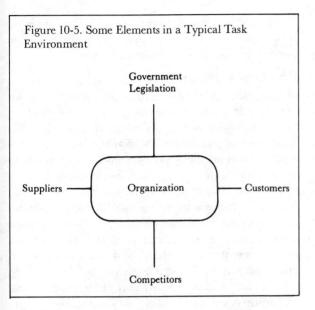

Figure 10-5. Some Elements in a Typical Task Environment

Government Legislation

Suppliers —— Organization —— Customers

Competitors

A Brooklyn College professor is suing his college on the grounds that he was fired because he is an alcoholic, and the government is arguing that it is illegal for colleges to prefer sober professors to alcoholics because alcoholics are considered handicapped persons under the 1973 Rehabilitation Act.

In most task environments, supplies and customers are equally important, and related to these are an organization's competitors. But to determine accurately the components of a task environment, we should also consider four significant sub-areas: the political, the sociocultural, the physical, and the economic.

Political Environment. We have already discussed, to some extent, the political component of an organization's task environment. Government legislation, we noted, affects in some way or other virtually all of an organization's activity. After the November, 1976, election of the Parti Québécois in Quebec, for example, many organizations in that province have had to accelerate the switch to conducting their affairs in French. Others have elected not to comply with the government's language requirements and have relocated elsewhere in Canada.

This movement out of Quebec as well as the flight of small oil servicing firms from Alberta to the U.S. after the shutdown in oil exploration caused by the National Energy Policy are examples of organizations exercising the options available to them. They are shopping around for the best deal – searching, that is, for more appropriate task environments.

Organizations, of course, may and usually do lobby to influence developments or changes in government legislation so they will not have to relocate. **Lobbying** consists of activities by various interest groups wishing to state their cases to politicians in the hope of influencing the course of legislation. We tend to think of lobbying as an American phenomenon, but it is well established in Canada and could probably be considered almost a growth industry. Lobbying occurs for example, when fishermen argue for a 200-mile offshore limit, textile and shoe manufacturers request protective tariffs against cheaper imports, police chiefs argue for the return of capital punishment, farmers bargain for milk or wheat subsidies or improved grain transporta-

practically speaking there will be elements in the environment that are more important to one organization than to others. A manufacturer of air conditioners, for instance, is likely to be more concerned with customers living in very warm regions than with people in colder areas. Dill (1958) has suggested that in analyzing organizational environments it is useful to think of a **task environment**, or those elements in an organization's environment that "are relevant or potentially relevant to goal setting and goal attainment."

Figure 10-5 depicts a typical manufacturing organization's task environment. In Canadian society, organizations are influenced by a wide range of government legislation whether at the federal, provincial, or municipal level. Legislation governs hours of work, pollution and noise limits, safety, union activity, health standards for products or services, taxation, competition practices, exports, imports, building codes, and so on. A comprehensive list would be so long that it would save considerable space to list those areas of an organization's existence *not* affected by government legislation.

O'Toole (1981) provides a chilling example of how legislation and court interpretations in the extreme can pull internal organizational operations away from a reasonable standard of common sense:

tion policies, doctors state their case for higher medicare fees, and autoworkers demand a limit on sales of foreign cars.

The increasing importance that business organizations attach to the political sector of their task environments is mirrored in business publications containing a steady stream of articles on the subject. The following titles are typical examples: "Business Urged to Increase Role in Society"; "How to Deal with the Invisible Partner: Government"; "Business Tells Its Story: After Years of Silence, Companies Are Finally Speaking to the Public."

The Business Council on National Issues (BCNI) is a powerful group of chief executive officers from Canada's largest corporations who formed to represent business interests more articulately and actively to the federal government. BCNI was formed, says one executive, because: "The system of business representation through the traditional channels – the Canadian Chamber of Commerce, Canadian Manufacturers Association, and other business groups – has simply broken down" (*The Financial Post*, April 30, 1977). Chapter 13, *Polity*, discusses the role of government in more depth.

Organizations also interact with governments through contributions to political parties at election times. And in some task environments, the political norms require that organizations make "gifts" or "bribes" to government officials in order to oil the gears of government bureaucracies. The word chosen depends on your point of view.

Canadians tend to regard such practices as characteristic of other societies, but in an article on preferred gift-giving patterns in various societies one American publication advised businessmen on appropriate protocol when in Canada: "*Canada*. Gifts to government employees are delicate now thanks to a crackdown on them. White lilies are for funerals. French and California wines are greatly appreciated, and Eskimo and Indian crafts – stone sculpture, wood carvings – are highly prized" (*Business Week*, December 6, 1976).

The political component of task environments is very important for organizations, and certainly in Canada such relationships are characterized by varying degrees of interaction. Also, government legislation should not be viewed narrowly as setting constraints for organizations because in many instances legislation presents important opportunities as well.

Physical Environment. The physical component of an organization's task environment is often a major consideration. The weather in Canada is frequently a factor in organizational planning. It may affect the location of organizations, for example. Fruit or vegetable growers are likely to be somewhat restricted as to where they locate their orchards or vineyards, because of the need for warm summers, water, and moderate winters. Engineers in northern Alberta have found that conveyor belts transporting tar sands function more smoothly in spring and summer than at wintertime temperatures of −40 Celsius when huge frozen lumps damage and plug the equipment.

Geography and topography may affect organizations. Ski resorts are more likely to be located in the mountains. Some organizations may wish to be near lake regions in order to emphasize the opportunities for recreation activities when recruiting employees. The availability of raw materials, such as water, minerals, wood, energy sources, and so on will be a major determinant of organizational locations.

The most visible and negative feature of the interrelationship between organizations and their physical environments is pollution. There have been many highly publicized examples of this in Canada. Water has been polluted by cities, by factories, mines, mills, and so forth, as sewage, chemicals, and other contaminants run into lakes and rivers. Few of Canada's lakes and rivers are not affected in some way, and as a result fishing and recreation activities often are curtailed, if not halted. In many areas our skies are filled with smoke and dust, and pollution increasingly manifests itself in the form of radiation, noise, cancers, and so on.

Economic Environment. The economic recession of the late 70s and early 80s has had a significant negative impact on organizations. A growing number are in serious trouble. Soaring interest rates, high labor costs, declining consumer demand, competition from cheaper and sometimes more attractive imports, increasing tax and royalty burdens, aging plants and

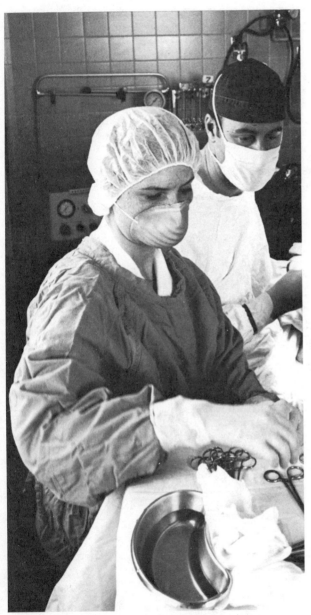

Hospitals are an example of structured organizations in which the responsibilities of each type of employee are specified by regulations and, in many cases, legislation, as well as collective agreements. Nurses, for example, are responsible for certain kinds of patient care, including in the operating room. They may not, however, perform many medical procedures and do not clean or cook for patients.

technologies have all combined to create enormous pressures on organizations – big and small alike.

Plant shutdowns, massive layoffs and unemployment, bankruptcies, and work-sharing schemes are all symptoms of this critical period. As a result, the economic sub-area today has become a dominant element in task environments for most organizations in Canada and the industrialized world.

The bulk of organizational theory and research has been generated during the economic boom years since World War II. Continuous growth, therefore, is an underlying assumption of these theories and models. Not surprisingly, managers have generally been ill-equipped to deal with the consequences of a prolonged economic downturn. Such difficult circumstances provide unique opportunities for researchers to gain new insights into the operations of organizations under a broader range of environmental conditions.

Sociocultural Environment. The sociocultural features of an organization's task environment are increasingly important. We have already mentioned the significance of matters related to language for organizations in Quebec. Lucas (1971) and Perry (1971) have given excellent accounts of the relationship between organizations and their host communities. In those communities where there is a diversity of industry, with a number of companies, no single one is likely to dominate the affairs of a community. But what of those where there is but a single dominant industry? It was on these communities that Lucas focused in his study.

In order to be classed as a single industry town, 75 percent of the population had to work in one organization. Lucas found that there were 636 such communities in Canada with a combined population of over 900 000 persons. Most of them had mining, lumbering or pulp mills, or railways as their sole industries. He found that this heavy reliance on a single industry was a precarious existence for many communities, a fact reflected in the attitudes and behavior of the citizens. They tended to be somewhat resigned and fatalistic about their situations. They feel there is little they can do; the company controls not only their working lives, but also their community. Lucas (1971) comments:

Corporate Chiefs Tread Fine Line

The cleavage between federalists and separatists in Quebec politics provides an excellent opportunity to observe business organizations in interaction with an important element in their task environments. The following account illustrates the dynamics, strategies, and risks for some organizations at the time of the province's 1980 referendum on sovereignty-association.

Annual meeting time in Montreal. Sadly, with the head office departures of recent years, the season isn't what it used to be.

Not everybody has moved to Toronto, however, and Montreal's office towers are still populated by a fair number of Canada's leading corporate chieftains who emerge annually to ventilate their thoughts on Quebec's political and economic life.

If any theme can be extracted from this year's crop of shareholder outings it's that the business community is unabashedly – even passionately – federalist. Its message is clear: Canada must remain united. And while it's seldom stated explicitly, the federalist message implies another: The Parti Québécois must be defeated.

Paul Desmarais, chief executive of Power Corp. of Canada Limited: "Quebec federalists bear the brunt of the fight and the separatists would just love us to give it up – just love it. I don't think Canadians outside the province really want us to give it up. And I hope they will realize how crucial, how important their support is."

Budget Betrays Business

Other executives – notably Alex Hamilton, president of Domtar Inc., and Jean de Grandpré, chairman of Bell Canada – voiced anti-PQ sentiments at their annual meetings a few weeks ago.

And early this month Pierre Côté, president of the Conseil du Patronat, whose membership includes more than 100 of the largest corporations in the province, blasted the PQ for undermining business confidence through manipulation and betrayal.

The business attacks on the PQ came just as the government appeared to be enjoying some improvement in its relations with the business community. At a recent provincial conference of business, labor and government leaders, the executives attending felt they had received a sympathetic hearing from PQ ministers and Premier René Lévesque, who appeared supportive of many business positions.

But when the provincial budget failed to deal with a major business concern – high taxation of better-paid Quebec residents – many businessmen felt betrayed and began entertaining the suspicion that they were being deceived and manipulated.

By aggressively moving to the attack, however, the business community runs the risk that the attack will backfire and be used by the government to gain popular support. In any popularity contest between business and the PQ, the government holds an upper hand and could easily emerge the winner by renewing its portrayal of big business as the centre of the anglophone power structure that is keeping Quebeckers under foot.

"If business wants to play politics we can play politics," Natural Resources Minister Yves Bérubé said in an interview with the Times shortly after Domtar's Hamilton criticized language restrictions.

"Until I heard about Mr. Hamilton's comments, I thought he was a good guy, a reasonable man," said Bérubé. "But now I'm not so sure."

As the referendum on sovereignty-association approaches, the participation of business in the debate is likely to lead to even more strained business-PQ relations. While the PQ could capitalize on a strongly belligerent business opposition, it would be to the government's greater advantage to have a relatively neutral and benign business community to deal with during the debate.

A delicate balance will have to be struck by business. For the time being, however, the best that can be said about business-PQ relations is that they are in a state of flux.

Wait and See Attitude

"Apparently the government has adopted a more positive attitude toward business," says Roger Hamel, president of the Quebec Chamber of Commerce. "There appears to have been an improvement, but let's wait and see."

Hamel, who is Quebec corporate vice-president for Imperial Oil Ltd., tends to take a more positive view of Quebec's prospects than many of his associates. "We have a socialist and separatist government and it's creating a lot of tensions," says Hamel. "But governments come and go and economic cycles come and go. I feel my mandate is to draw attention to many of the positive aspects of Quebec."

In the eyes of most French-speaking Canadians, says Hamel, the rules of the game have been changed for the better.

It is impossible to tell at this point, but it may be that there is a difference of opinion between French and English businessmen in Quebec over language legislation.

Hamel, whose flawless unaccented grasp of English could put even the most articulate Toronto executive to

of service at Simpsons Ltd. department store in downtown Montreal is an example of "monumental change."

In his view, no government, whether it's the PQ or a succeeding Liberal government, will abandon the legislation. The only possible area that might be changed involves English-language education in the schools.

Under current rules, a person moving into Quebec does not have absolute right to send his children to English-language schools. It is this rule that has drawn strongest criticism from executives such as Mulroney, who called the provisions "silly, vexatious and self-defeating."

This aspect of language policy is only adding further damage to Montreal's status as a head office city, businessmen say, because executives from outside Quebec refuse to move here. Higher taxation imposed by the PQ on Quebec residents who earn more than $30,000 is viewed as another deterrent.

In the eyes of the PQ government, however, Montreal's corporate leaders are just "playing politics" by continually harping on the language and taxation issues.

Says Bérubé: "How many people in a company like Domtar earn more than $30,000? It's a minuscule percentage. The lower cost of housing in Montreal alone makes up for the difference. Anyway, it would cost next to nothing for a company to pay an executive a little more money to make up for the difference in tax rates."

On the language issue, Bérubé notes than an executive moving into Quebec from another province can obtain education exemptions for his children for three-year periods.

shame, sees the adoption of French as the working language in the province as a major step forward for Quebec's French-speaking population.

With the adoption of French, many well-trained young people are now entering business with a greater sense of pride and self-confidence.

Language of Service

On a more basic level, Hamel adds, the fact that French is now a language

Source:

Corcoran, Terence. *Financial Times of Canada.* May 14, 1979.

They know that their future depends upon impersonal forces outside their community such as head office decisions, government policies, and international trading agreements. They do not presume to be their own gods. Their interest in local government is as casual as such interest always has been.

Lucas further reports that people in single-industry communities have a sense of temporariness, a general insecurity about what happens if the company goes broke or leaves town. What will they do then? Will the town collapse? Will they have to move on? This Canadian malaise is evident in newspaper headlines: "When Wood Demand Falls, Terrace Shudders," "Collingwood Economy Goes on the Line as Many Shipyard Workers Face Layoffs," "Sudbury Waiting for More Bad News."

Perry (1971), in his book *Galt, U.S.A.*, shows how the nature of the ownership of organizations may affect a community. He studied what was then Galt (now Cambridge), Ontario, a place where more than 60 percent of the manufacturing industry was American-owned. He describes the impacts that this substantial ownership had on the cultural patterns of the community, on the entrepreneurial spirit of citizens, and other matters related to what he calls "the subculture of the subsidiaries."

Just as Lucas (1971) had found in single-industry communities, Perry observed that dominance of the Galt economy by American firms tended to create a sense of powerlessness among many community members. He describes a labor relations problem between Canadian members of an "international" (American-controlled) union and the Canadian managers of an American-owned subsidiary company. The position of the manager of the subsidiary company he calls "messenger-boy management."

Messenger-boy management, which has no real wage-setting power but goes through the motions of bargaining, actually has an adverse effect on labor relations. In a sense, the subsidiary manager is never so naked as when he sits down across from the union men from his own shop. They respect power, and they scorn pretense. The messenger-boy manager carries offers back and fourth between the ultimate authority and the union. This takes time, and he stalls (Perry, 1971).

We saw above that customers or clients are an important part of most task environments. As consumers of products or services they provide necessary revenue to support the economic viability of the organization. But customers or clients may have other impacts, sociocultural impacts, on organizations. For example, notions of social responsibility and good corporate citizenship have become more clearly articulated by increasing numbers of consumer and citizen advocacy groups. These interest groups may succeed in shifting public opinion so that organizations have to be more responsive or to take on tasks not formally theirs.

In the late 1960s in Canada, a definite movement developed, the underlying assumption of which stated briefly was that industrial development is good, but not at all costs. In response, organizations increasingly came to be responsible for their actions and could no longer assume that grateful communities would continue to absorb all the consequences of development. Increasingly, for example, organizations must take responsibility for the pollution they create.

Many people began to question the profit motive. They asked questions about "exorbitant profit levels." Concerned companies responded by sponsoring advertising in support of the profit motive. Schools are feeling this shift as business, unions, and other interest groups argue that their perspectives should be incorporated into school curricula.

Interest or pressure groups are a noticeable outcome of the social unrest of the sixties. Canadians have not been great litigators, but the 1970s saw some collective or class actions against organizations, as in the cases of the Firenza Owners and the Rusty Ford Owners.

Another part of the social responsibility movement was the notion that members of organizations should not be simply passive recipients of the services and cultural activities of their communities and societies. Instead it was increasingly expected that these members should provide leadership and resources in the development of these services. As a result, organizations in Canada are becoming more active in support of the arts and culture and in community affairs generally.

Figure 10-6 depicts some of the important task-environment elements divided into the four main areas: political, sociocultural, physical, and economic. The examples given are by no means complete, and their

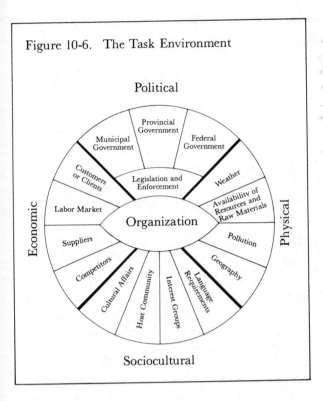

Figure 10-6.   The Task Environment

Political

Provincial Government

Municipal Government

Federal Government

Customers or Clients

Legislation and Enforcement

Weather

Economic

Labor Market

Organization

Availability of Resources and Raw Materials

Physical

Suppliers

Pollution

Competitors

Geography

Cultural Affairs

Host Community

Interest Groups

Language Requirements

Sociocultural

relevance for any specific organization will vary. Also, it is important to realize that although we have dealt with each of the four task-environment subdivisions separately, what happens in one area may have consequences in another. That is, there is interaction among the four areas. If, for instance, public opinion (sociocultural) becomes persuasive about a particular state of pollution (physical), then politicians (political) may be moved to provide pressure, or legislation, or even funds to force or encourage organizations to take desired action on the matter. And finally, it is worth emphasizing that organizations and environments are in a state of dynamic tension where an organization's role may be either proactive or reactive, or both.

Complexity and Change in Task Environments

Earlier we identified and discussed four major subdivisions within task environments. Dill (1958) characterized task environments further as being *homogeneous* or *heterogeneous*, and *stable* or *rapidly shifting*. Homogeneous-heterogeneous refers to the relative complexity in the task environment. Does the organization produce a single product for a single customer. This would be a highly homogeneous task environment. Less homogeneous would be the production of a single product for multiple customers. The production of multiple products for multiple customers would create a highly heterogeneous task environment.

The stable-rapidly shifting characterization refers to the amount of change in the task environment. A single product for the same customer every time would be a very stable task environment, when compared with a single product for a different customer each time.

Researchers have considered the effects of various task environments on organizations. Lawrence and Lorsch (1967), for example, were interested in a combination of these two characteristics. They concluded that the shifting-heterogeneous task environment contained the greatest degree of uncertainty, and the stable-homogeneous, the least. They wanted to determine those organizational characteristics required to deal effectively with different levels of uncertainty. "Such a question," said Lawrence and Lorsch (1967), "is quite different from the central theme of most organizational studies, which have tended to focus on the question of what is the one best way to organize, irrespective of the external environmental conditions facing the business."

These researchers selected three industries to represent various points along a continuum of task environment uncertainty. The plastics industry was the most uncertain, the standardized container industry the least uncertain, and the packaged food industry was roughly in the middle. Their findings are summarized in Table 10-3.

Lawrence and Lorsch found that, as a result of the changing complexity of task environments, organizations in the plastics industry created many specialized roles to deal with various dimensions of their environments. This role differentiation led to problems of integration; control and coordination of the more diverse roles required continual mechanisms of conflict and problem resolution. As a result, the uncertainty

---

TABLE 10-3   UNCERTAINTY IN THE TASK ENVIRONMENT AND CONSEQUENT STRUCTURES AND PROCEDURES

	Plastics Industry	Packaged Foods Industry	Standardized Containers Industry
Environmental Uncertainty	High	Medium	Low
Role Differentiation	High	Considerable	Low
Decentralized Decision making	High	Considerable	Low
Conflict Resolution	Heavy management involvement across levels	Some management involvement across levels	Heavy reliance on bureaucratic hierarchy

SOURCE: Lawrence, Paul R., and Jay W. Lorsch. *Organization and Environment: Managing Differentiation and Integration.* Cambridge, Mass.: Harvard University Press, 1967.

---

generated by the task environment necessitated structures and processes (1967) where "the lower and middle echelons of management had to be involved in reaching joint departmental decisions; these managers were centrally involved in the resolution of conflict. In resolving conflict all the managers relied heavily on open confrontation."

Conflict resolution in a changing environment needs to be based on familiarity with the current situation and to be relatively speedy to insure appropriate solutions. When the ship is sinking, fast action is required. You cannot wait for a response to the captain's request for action from the general manager at head office, who in turn contacts the vice-president operations, who must clear his directives with the president. A steep hierarchy is not conducive to fast response time – something that is required in uncertain environments like the plastics industry.

By contrast, the Lawrence and Lorsch study found that the low uncertainty in the task environment of the standardized container industry meant that events could be anticipated in advance in much the same way as we earlier described for bureaucracies. As a result, specialized roles for dealing with the environment were not required, and the formal hierarchy of the organization was suited to the resolution of problems. Middle-managers did have some influence, but the real power rested with those at the top.

The packaged food industry was structured and acted in a manner closer to the plastics industry than to standardized container operations. Because they experienced a fair degree of uncertainty, organizations in packaged foods had different roles for their environmental contacts and decentralized decision-making. But, "the major difference between them was that the plastics organization appeared to be devoting more of its managerial manpower to devices that facilitated the resolution of conflict," according to Lawrence and Lorsch (1967).

The comparative results of Lawrence and Lorsch's research are summarized in Table 10-3. This is an important study, because it clearly shows that successful organizations adopt structures and procedures appropriate to the conditions of their task environments.

These two researchers also provided some insights into the dynamics of management required under situations of varying uncertainty. However, more explicit statement of the suitability of particular management styles to varying environmental contingencies is contained in an earlier study by Burns and Stalker (1961). They sampled 20 firms in the British electronics industry. In their interviews with managers they observed two idealized and polarized styles of management, the mechanistic and the organic.

Mechanistic management is typically bureaucratic in style. Everyone's duties and responsibilities are precisely defined. Communication is filtered upwards through a formalized hierarchy of authority, and in this way control is maintained by those at the top.

By contrast, the **organic management** style is much less formalized. Reliance on the formalized hierarchy is less evident. Instead, decisions are based on knowledgeable suggestions, whether they come from the top or the bottom of the hierarchy. As a result, communication patterns are much more open and tend to be lateral as well as horizontal. Commands give way to consultation, and status differentials are of minor import. Duties and responsibilities are not clearly defined and are subject to change as conditions warrant.

You may have guessed under what conditions each management style was most prevalent. Burns and Stalker (1961) observed that the organic style was usual among electronics firms in particularly uncertain or unstable task enviroments where new problems seeking new solutions are the norm. The mechanistic style typified managers in electronics firms in relatively stable, unchanging task environments.

In our review of the open system's model of organizations we noted the importance of task environments to organizations and their operations. Not only that but we saw how organizations adapt to the particular demands of their environments by altering their structures and processes. We also argued that organizations are not merely reactive but that they adopt proactive strategies where they attempt to influence or change parts of their task environments.

In addition, we noted that government legislation provides not only constraints on organization behavior, but opportunities as well. In the next section we shall explore this more fully when considering incorporation processes and the corporations that result.

CORPORATIONS

Canadian federal and provincial governments have large volumes of legislation that relate to organizations within their jurisdictions. This legislation may regulate labor practices, pollution controls, product standards, and a host of other organizational subjects. There is, however, a segment of these statutes that is particularly relevant to organizations as such, and it is concerned with corporations. These laws in particular provide both constraints on organizations and some unique opportunities. It is little wonder then that the dominant business mode in Canada is the corporation.

The simplest way to conduct business, however, is as a **sole proprietor**. A person purchases the necessary local business operating permits and sets up shop. A little corner store or small typing service will likely be sole proprietorships. These owners use their own resources to establish and develop their businesses. They reap the profits of their efforts, but if they get into financial difficulty, legally they are in a position of *unlimited liability*. This means that not only may the assets of the business have to be sold to satisfy creditors, but "the owner's personal assets such as house, furniture, car, and stocks, may be seized, if necessary, to pay the outstanding debts of his business. Thus a person's life-savings could be wiped out by a business failure" (Amirault and Archer, 1976).

Sometimes persons may wish to collaborate in a business venture and establish a **partnership**. The partnership operates in much the same way as a sole proprietorship, but there are additional people and sources of money on which to base the venture. Unlimited liability is generally also a feature of partnerships, and one has to be very careful about selecting partners, because all are responsible for partnership debts. If, for instance, one partner cannot meet his or her fair share of the debts, the other partners must assume it. The sole proprietorship and partnership are easy and convenient to start, but the unlimited liability situation is a risk that could be very costly for participants.

A **corporation**, on the other hand, is a legal entity that interested persons may create if certain criteria are met. The founders incorporate their joint venture with a provincial or the federal government. Operating capital is provided by the sale of stocks, and the affairs of the corporation and the rights of shareholders are overseen by a board of directors. The major advantage of the corporation is that it affords the shareholders *limited liability*, in that they stand to lose only to the extent of their investment in the corporation. Other personal effects are not liable to claims by creditors. There are other advantages for this legal entity, the

The walkers in Miles for Millions are among the hundreds of thousands of Canadians who volunteer time to work toward a common goal. Voluntary organizations may be quite informal, but many use a hierarchal structure, and the boards of some well-known ones interlock with major business boards.

corporation, such as separation of ownership and management, possibly lower income taxes, enduring existence, and so on (Amirault and Archer, 1976; Smyth and Soberman, 1976).

These advantages have made the corporation the dominant organizational form in developed societies, and most of the organizations we have studied throughout this chapter are corporations. Two questions that have been of considerable interest to organizational

researchers in Canada concern the sources of power and control in Canadian corporations and the patterns of existence for these corporations.

In his major work, *The Vertical Mosaic*, Porter (1965) examines the locus of power in various sectors of Canadian society. Of particular interest to us is his study of what he refers to as "economic power." That is, who controls big business? He was concerned with how the large corporations were administered and how they formed links with other corporations. Because many of Canada's biggest corporations are largely- or wholly-owned subsidiaries of large U.S. or British corporations, the power probably rests with the board of directors of the parent companies.

In Chapter 8 you learned that economic authority in Canada is concentrated in relatively few hands. That information comes from Porter who discovered that among the largest corporations there is a very frequent tendency for directors of one corporation to sit on the boards of others. This situation of a common director or directors on two or more corporation boards creates an interlock between these boards and their corporations. There are striking patterns of interlocking directorships, and key individuals in these networks hold large numbers of such posts. This is particularly true of bank directors.

The central figures identified in this interlocking directorship matrix constitute Porter's economic elite. In assessing their backgrounds he found that in many respects they are a very homogeneous group. They attended similar private schools and universities; intermarry; belong to similar clubs, organizations, and churches; and maintain close ties in their social and political activities.

Clement (1975) provides a more up-to-date analysis and finds similar trends, although the economic elite tends to be even more exclusive than in the past and shows little evidence of penetration by persons of lower social origins. Even more recently, Clement (1977) has extended his view of the corporate elite because: "It is no longer possible to provide an adequate understanding of the power structure of Canadian corporations without expanding the horizons of study outside into the United States and, to a limited extent, beyond."

The work of Porter and Clement provides valuable data and insights for readers on the nature of power in large corporations and the extent to which it is controlled by a relatively small elite group.

White (1978) examined a range of variously sized corporations with different patterns of ownership (Canadian versus foreign, private versus public) to determine the locus of control within them. He found that the size of the corporation was not as important a factor as ownership in explaining the activity of corporate boards

of directors. For example, boards of independent or parent corporations were more active in control than those of subsidiaries. This is not to suggest that subisidiary corporations are not closely monitored, but that the mechanisms are somewhat different:

Control of subsidiaries by parents is considerable, but it usually tends to be exercised through management links rather than by the subsidiary's directorate. In subsidiary corporations in our sample there is at least one senior manager in the parent who is responsible for subsidiary operations. The chain of command from the parent to the subsidiary is through this responsible authority in the parent to his subordinate who heads the subsidiary. This link is the control coupling for the parent, a bypass around the subsidiary's board which in most instances is little more than a legally-prescribed structural adornment (White, 1978).

A second important factor, related to board of director control or lack thereof, was the composition of the board. If the board was made up of some directors who were outsiders, not employees of the corporation, then the board was more active than if it consisted solely of inside directors.

Corporations and foreign ownership remain dominant factors in Canadian life, and organization researchers have only begun systematically to explore their impacts.

SUMMARY

1. The need for organization is consistent with the social nature of humans. Basic divisions of labor result in increasing interdependencies, and, in order to maintain some degree of social order, preliminary forms of organization are generated.

2. The establishment of an organization centers on goal attainment. Its establishment may be spontaneous, left to chance or circumstance, or it may be established and maintained in a more formalized manner.

3. Early theorists and researchers regarded organizations as closed systems and were mainly concerned with their formal structures and processes. The technical system tended to be a primary focus. Only with the accidental discoveries of the Hawthorne Studies did a more balanced view include the social system as well.

4. In the scientific management perspective of organizations, individual workers are regarded as instruments of production to be employed by management in the same way as machines. Efficiency is achieved by finding the one best way to do each and every task.

5. Technological or organizational arrangements that fail to give people reasonable control over important aspects of their work, and that deprive them of social contacts and meaning in their tasks, are likely to result in worker alienation.

6. Every organization interacts with other organizations. Those elements outside itself that affect its operations or directions constitute the organizations's environment.

7. Corporations are legal creations that allow people to establish organizations while minimizing their personal liabilities. Most organizations in business and industry are corporations.

GLOSSARY

Alienation. Individuals' feelings that, as workers, they are small, meaningless parts of an insensitive production system over which they have little control

Bureaucracy. A formal organization based on the application of legal-rational principles.

Centralized structure. Structure of an organization in which authority and decision-making are concentrated in a few people at senior levels.

Charismatic authority. Authority that is based on the belief that the individual leader is special and possesses some exceptional ability or magic, which inspires loyalty in the followers.

Closed system. Theoretical perspective of organizations as relatively self-contained units where particular structural arrangements and individual behavior patterns may be accounted for by factors internal to the organization.

Cohesiveness. Conditions whereby individuals identify themselves as members of the group, members want the group to remain together, and group members have a high regard for each other.

Corporation. Legal entity created for purposes of conducting business, which has an existence separate from that of its members while providing them with limited liability.

Decentralized structure. Structure of an organization in which authority and decision-making are widely distributed among people at various levels.

Division of labor. Process whereby general tasks and roles become increasingly specialized.

Formal organization. Relatively enduring or continuing social collectivity in which roles and resources are coordinated through a division of labor in the use of a technology to achieve a goal or goals. Coordination, control, and problem-solving are facilitated through communication, leadership, and varying degrees of written rules and procedures.

Formalization. Process by which the informality of relationships is gradually replaced by varying degrees of rules, codes and conduct, laws, and other means of regulation.

Legal-rational authority. Authority based on belief in the legality of formally specified rules and relationships.

Lobbying. Activities by special interest groups aimed at influencing government legislation.

Mechanical solidarity. Feeling of people in primitive societies that they are held together by kinship, neighborliness, and friendliness.

Mechanistic management. Management style in which duties and responsibilities are precisely defined, communication is filtered upward through a formalized hierarchy of authority, and control is maintained at the top.

Open system. Theoretical perspective of organizations where particular structural arrangements and individual behavior patterns may be accounted for by a combination of factors internal to the organization and its external environment.

Organic management. Management style in which decisions are based on knowledgeable suggestions, communication patterns tend to be lateral as well as horizontal, duties and responsibilities are not rigidly defined, and status differentials are of minor importance.

Organic solidarity. Dependencies among people in developed societies created as a result of a more specific division of labor.

Organization. A collectivity in which people and resources are coordinated through a division of labour in the use of a technology to achieve a goal. Coordination, control, and problem-solving are facilitated through communication and leadership.

Organization structure. Patterns of relationships among organization statuses.

Partnership. Joint business venture where normally all partners experience unlimited liability equally.

Scientific management. Taylor's term for achieving perfection in productivity by finding the one best way to do each and every task.

Sole proprietorship. Simplest manner in which to establish a business where the sole owner experiences unlimited liability.

Spontaneous organization. Temporary coordination of individuals and resources that disbands when its task or mission has been completed.

Task environment. Those elements in an organization's environment that are relevant or potentially relevant to setting goals and attaining goals.

Technology. Application of a body of knowledge through the use of tools and processes in the production of goods and/or services.

Traditional authority. Authority that is based on followers' belief that their king or queen has a "divine right" to rule that is transferred down through eligible descendants.

FURTHER READING

Coleman, James S. *Power and the Structure of Society.* New York: W.W. Norton, 1974. Traces the development of corporations as unique legal creations for the transaction of business affairs.

Kiesler, Sara B. *Interpersonal Processes in Groups and Organizations*; MacKenzie, Kenneth D. *Organizational Structures*; Pfeffer, Jeffrey. *Organizational Design*; Tuggle Francis D. *Organizational Processes*: Arlington Heights, Ill.: AHM Publishing Corporation, 1978. A series of books that examines contemporary directions in the study of organizations.

March, James C., and Herbert A. Simon. *Organizations.* New York: John Wiley, 1958. A good description of the many facets of organization structure and operation.

Ouchi, William. *Theory Z.* Reading, Mass.: Addison-Wesley, 1981. A description of the adaptations Japanese organizations have made of conventional organization designs for their particular needs and culture.

Perrow, Charles. *Complex Organizations: A Critical Essay.* Glenview, Ill.: Scott, Foresman and Company, 1972. A critical view of major theoretical perspectives on organizations.

Thompson, James D. *Organizations in Action.* New York: McGraw-Hill, 1967. Discussion of approaches to the study of organizations and development of a framework for their analysis.

Zald, Mayer N. (ed.). *Power in Organizations.* Nashville: Vanderbilt University Press, 1970. A collection of articles exploring the nature of power structures and relationships in a variety of organizational settings.

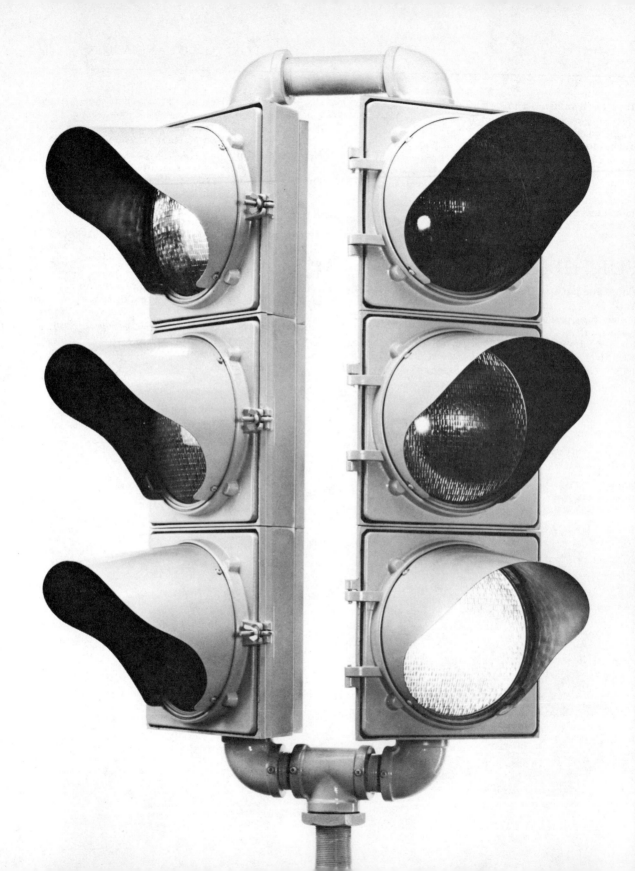

IV
SOCIAL INSTITUTIONS

Institutions are defined as relatively stable sets of norms, values, and beliefs developed to resolve the recurring problems faced by all societies. Institutions are a central part of social structure and are major factors defining society.

Family, religion, polity, and education are the social institutions considered in this section of the book. They are found in every society. The emphasis here is on Canadian institutions, but each chapter also deals with these institutions as they appear in other societies and discusses how the various sociological perspectives have been used to analyze them.

Marriage and the family is the concern of Chapter 11. How we are socialized into family roles and ethnic differences among Canadian families are discussed. Other topics included in this chapter are getting married, staying married, divorce, and family violence.

Every society defines which religious beliefs are proper, the correct way to honor god(s), and the ac-ceptable procedures involved in becoming a priest or minister. Chapter 12, *Religion*, defines what religion is, and why it is important to the individual and society. How do we explain the universality of and the differences in religion, and what is its future in Canada? This chapter explores such questions.

How do people govern themselves and maintain order in society? Chapter 13, *Polity*, examines the political process, including the role of the individual, pressure groups, political parties, and the state. Explanations of these processes, along with a look at the future of Canadian polity, are discussed.

Every society has some systematic way of educating its members. In our society this is accomplished largely in schools. What is the purpose of these schools? What differences do they make? How are they organized? Is there equal opportunity for all to be educated? How is the educational system changing in Canada? These are some of the issues explored in Chapter 14.

CHAPTERS

CHAPTER 11
THE FAMILY

EMILY M. NETT

There is no one Canadian family. With its distinctive geography and history, Canada is much too heterogeneous to have one or ten or twenty distinctive family types. As the geographical setting, and as the social class, religious, ethnic, occupational, and other groupings vary, so too do our families.

Who would dispute this contention by Frederick Elkin (1964) that variety is the essence of Canadian family life? From personal encounters with families in everyday life, and from the many fascinating reports on the diversity of specific groups in Canada, we know that "multiformity" is a fact. Merely listing the names of a few groups in which the family has been studied by sociologists and anthropologists in recent years acquaints us with the patchwork quality of the "Canadian family" quilt: Chinese, Doukhobors, Dutch, urban working class (predominantly of British origins), English Protestant, farm families, French, Hungarians, Hutterites, Indians, Inuit, Italians, Japanese, Jews, Lebanese Muslims, Sikhs, suburban middle class, and Ukrainians (Larson, 1976).

On the other hand, Elkin puts forth the equally valid notion of the family as an old and venerable institution in human society generally and Canadian society specifically. As an institution it is an organized aspect of Canadians' social existence, established and perpetuated by various norms or rules. Those rules, affect most Canadians, particularly as codified in family law: everyone wanting to marry must be certified, no woman can marry more than one man at a time, and all parents are legally and financially responsible for their dependent children.

Other rules, frequently unspoken and often informal, appear to affect the overwhelming majority of Canadian families. For example, there is the rule of residence known as *neolocality*, the cultural norm that newlyweds should move into their own residence rather than that of the husband's parents (*patrilocality*) or the wife's (*matrilocality*). It is one of those commonly understood rules learned by boys and girls who grow up hearing mother-in-law jokes, listening to stories about the dire consequences for marital happiness of outside interference from meddling kin, and heeding the advice to newlyweds on the importance of privacy to good marital adjustment. This rule is enforced only by custom, but it resulted in the last census in approximately 80 percent of all dwelling places in Canada being **nuclear family households** (a residence consisting of one family only), and only 2 percent being **extended family households** (a residence shared by two or more related nuclear families).

Are there contradictions in saying some Canadian families are different from others, that the Canadian family is not the same as some in other countries, and yet that Canadian families duplicate all human families? If there is a paradox in these statements, it is more apparent than real; that is, definition and perspective go a long way to resolve it. As we hope to demonstrate in this chapter, it is indeed true that the Canadian family is like all other families, like some other families, and like no other family.

DEFINING FAMILY

What do we mean by *a* family or *the* family? Canadians tend to have a somewhat specialized notion of a family. When we think of a family, we think of a wife, her husband, and their dependent children. Why? Because the married couple and their offspring are the relatives our family rules indicate should share a home.

Many problems arise in using that popular picture, or stereotype, as a definition of family. First, it is like a family snapshot, a picture of a domestic unit frozen at a certain point in its ever-changing cycle; second, it

obscures differences between family households and other family groups; and third, it confuses the people with the institution.

Family Household and Family Groups

Actually, a **family** is that group of people considered to be related to each other by blood or marriage. Notice, however, that the definition does not merely say "related," but "considered to be related." This is important because adopted children can be included, as well as common-law spouses, for example. Conversely, certain "blood" relatives can be excluded depending on how descent is traced from the ancestors. Of course, no one lives with all the persons to whom she or he is considered to be related. When you marry you usually no longer live with your parents, but they remain part of your family. A family is, therefore, more than those who live together at any given time; it extends to a wider social group of related persons (the *kin network*).

The kin who share a household, usually a smaller group than those considered to be related, is called the *domestic family* or the *family household*. Of course, not all households or dwellingplaces include families. Often, unrelated persons live together, or a person lives alone. In Canada in 1976 about 5 percent of all households were constituted by two or more unrelated persons, and their number was more than double what it was 25 years earlier in 1951. In the same period of time one-person households more than tripled, and the percentage more than doubled, from 7.4 percent in 1951 to 16.8 percent in 1976. The great majority of households, however, are family households as Figure 11-1 shows.

The domestic family in Canada is, therefore, numerically normative as well as culturally normative. In other words, most people live the way society says they should, in nuclear family households. The nuclear family is defined by the census as follows:

. . . a husband and wife (with or without never-married children, regardless of age) or a parent with one or more children who have never married, living in the same dwelling.

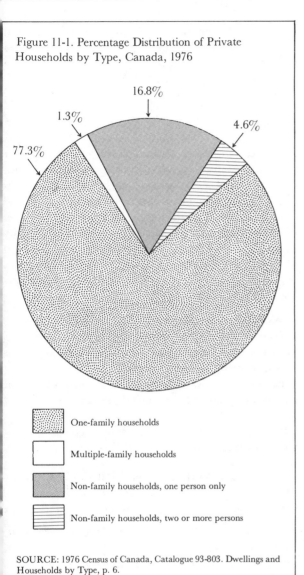

Figure 11-1. Percentage Distribution of Private Households by Type, Canada, 1976

16.8%

1.3%

4.6%

77.3%

☐ One-family households

☐ Multiple-family households

☐ Non-family households, one person only

☐ Non-family households, two or more persons

SOURCE: 1976 Census of Canada, Catalogue 93-803. Dwellings and Households by Type, p. 6.

A family may consist also of a man or woman living with a guardianship child or ward under 21 years for whom no pay was received.

It should be noted that contrary to the popular belief that a one-parent family is a totally different form, it too is a nuclear family. A husband and wife (legally married or common-law) also constitute a nuclear family. In fact, in 1976 only slightly more than one out of five Canadian nuclear family households contained the stereotypical four persons. So, whereas more than two-thirds of Canadians live in nuclear families, at any given time, about one-third of all nuclear families have no children in them, and one-tenth have but one parent.

As mentioned above, one problem with defining a family as two parents and their offspring who live together is that families are then perceived as static rather than as the growing and developing entities they really are. Think about the families you knew in 1981 and then imagine how they must have looked when the previous decennial census was taken (1971) and how they will look when the next one is taken (1991).

Any given domestic family changes very much in composition from one census decade to the next. Children are born, grow up, and leave home; parents separate, divorce, or die; other people, related and unrelated, come and go. Nuclear families also combine or share a dwelling place for varying periods of time. For example, should one of the adult children in a nuclear family marry (or adopt a child) and continue living in the parental dwelling, the household is then classified as a *two-family household* in census terms, or, in anthropological terms, an *extended family household* (extended over generations). It could also be extended laterally, as when brothers marry and their wives and children share a house or apartment, or when a woman shares her bed and board with two men. In some societies these forms are institutionalized as the *joint family* and the *polyandrous family*, and are therefore preferred, but in Canada they are relatively rare events. The trend has been for the proportion of dwellings shared with relatives to decline each decade since 1931 (from 6.7 percent in 1951 to 2.0 percent in 1971 to 1.3 percent in 1976). Availability of housing has probably been the major factor in the decline. Therefore, a housing shortage could result in more families doubling up once again.

The great majority of Canadians live in some kind of nuclear household, but they belong to a much larger family, or kin network. In fact, our kin-family relationships have been termed a *modified extended fam-*

ily system, because they consist of several nuclear families and individuals bound together by interaction, emotions, and obligations. When persons leave their domestic *family of orientation* (the one into which they were born or adopted) and establish their own residence or get married (their *family of procreation*), they do not generally cut themselves off emotionally or behaviorally from parents and siblings. Instead, they maintain those ties and add new ones with their spouse's kin.

Most Canadians will determine who are their kin by tracing relatives through both their mother's and father's sides of the family (*bilateral descent*). They would have to include at least their **primary relatives** (mother, father, sister, brother, daughter, son, husband or wife) and their *secondary relatives* (paternal and maternal grandparents, uncles and aunts, and the same for the spouse, or in-laws).

A bilateral descent system is not the only kind, however, since in many societies and in some Canadian subcultures the rule is *unilineal descent.* The Lebanese Muslims of Alberta, for example, traditionally include in their notion of family only those persons related to them through the male line. This system is known as *patriliny.* Another and contrasting type of descent system, *matriliny,* includes only relations through the female line. Because both these systems exclude all persons related by marriage, a woman marrying into a patrilineal system has the unusual (not to her, but to most of us) experience of not being considered a part of the "family," even though she lives in the same household with her husband and children! She belongs to her father's and brother's family, and she returns to their household if and when her husband divorces her. In Canada, where the laws and their enforcement assume bilateral descent, Lebanese Muslims sometimes experience conflict at the time of divorce. Following Canadian traditions, the courts are more likely to grant custody of children to the mother; according to traditional norms, Lebanese children belong with and belong to the father and his family.

Children in Canada are customarily given the family name of their father, and this practice frequently causes confusion about the kind of descent system we have. This custom is called *patronymy,* and it may be a vestige of **patriarchy**, or institutionalized male dominance in domestic affairs. In fact, it is more than custom, because although there is no law that requires the wife to take her husband's family name, legitimate children must take their father's name.

The Family Institution

As you've probably noticed, it is difficult to discuss *a* family, or a group of related people, without becoming involved in a discussion of *the* family as an institution. The family institution (as opposed to actual mothers, fathers, aunts, uncles, and so forth) is the set of socially constructed, socially shared, and socially transmitted cultural norms that establish the pattern of relationships among members of the family group. It includes the standards and guidelines for the following family behaviors:

1. getting married (family formation)
2. establishing a home (residence)
3. exchanging goods and services among related persons (roles, descent, and inheritance rules)
4. deciding with whom to have sex and under what conditions (marital, premarital, extramarital sexual norms)
5. caring for children and teaching them proper behavior (socialization)

Our set of rules defining the family institution actually refer to a **conjugal family** system. Goode (1970) sees the principles involved as constituting an ideology:

The ideology of the conjugal family proclaims the right of the individual to choose his or her own spouse, place to live, and even which kin obligations to accept, as against the acceptance of others' decisions. It asserts the worth of the individual as against the inherited elements of wealth or ethnic group. The individual is to be evaluated, not his lineage. A strong theme of "democracy" runs through this ideology. It encourages love, which in every major civilization has been given a prominent place in fantasy, poetry, art, and legend, as a wonderful, perhaps even exalted experience, even when its reality was guarded against. Finally, it asserts that if one's family life is unpleasant, one has the right to change it.

The assertions of the conjugal family system are thus

contrary to those of the traditional family, emphasizing happiness and adjustment of family members rather than passing down traditions from one generation to the next.

As the name implies, in a conjugal family institution the unity in family relationships stems from the marriage linkage rather than parent-child ties (as in lineage systems). Therefore, the institution includes such normative features as marriage prior to the birth of children, participant choice of marriage mates, neolocality of residence, bilateral descent, and inheritance disregarding age or gender of children. The importance of the marriage relationship is embedded in our language usage. For example, when a marriage is voluntarily dissolved we say the family has been "broken up." Strictly speaking this is not true, because the nucleus of custodial parent and child still constitutes a domestic family and the non-resident parent continues to be part of the child's kin network, or wider family. Marital break-up in our system is equated with family instability. This does not occur in a lineage system where generational solidarity is the important feature.

The family as an institution is an abstraction; no one has ever observed directly a normative system. The Canadian family is a product of all the more or less formal rules and regulations that provide the general social scripts upon which individual Canadian families of varying backgrounds can elaborate their particular performances. The family institution can be discovered both by examining the behavior of large and representative numbers of families and by studying the official codes of the society.

This abstraction of the Canadian family, takes on substance as we survey statistics, employ public opinion polls, and delve into the family law and family policies of the government. Families as perpetuators of ethnic traditions or regional folkways, or as responses to social class conditions, however, must still be observed in their everyday behavior, interviewed in depth, and surveyed with questionnaires. But first things first. Before sketching in the outlines of the Canadian family and all its varieties, let us briefly turn our attention to the origins of the human family and the importance of the family in human society.

THE BIOLOGICAL BASES OF THE FAMILY

In both human and nonhuman primate societies, **biosocial units** can be found. The biosocial unit is not a family, but it is the basis of the family group. It is a reproductive unit consisting of the three sets of relations: between adult females, adult males, and the issue of their sexual union. One relation is that of the mating or heterosexual pair. Another is that of the female and her offspring. A third is that of the offspring and an adult male (not necessarily the progenitor, or biological father).

The biosocial unit is important among all primates because:

1. the newborn are extremely dependent and require a relatively long period of learning to integrate into the group in which they must live in order to survive

2. there is no mating season, but rather a monthly cycle of fertility in primate females

3. physical survival depends on the interdependency of highly social animals of different ages, genders, and physical conditions associating together in small bands or troops

These characteristics are shared by monkeys, apes, and early humans. An excellent illustration is found in Washburn and De Vore's (1961) study of baboon behavior and social structure. Chapter 3, *Socialization*, discusses these characteristics in more depth.

The different kinds of biosocial units found among nonhuman primates appear to be quite specific to the kind of species. Gorillas have strong bonds between the dominant male and his females, whereas chimpanzees bond along lines of the female and her offspring of both genders, until the young males reach puberty and until the young females give birth, at which point the bond dissolves. Other species of anthropoids have other kinds of biosocial units. In the process of human evolution the biosocial units have become only a nucleus in more extended family groupings, and variations can be found within our species in the relative importance of any one of the three basic relations. Human families may be organized along female-offspring bonds, male-offspring bonds, female-male bonds, or all three.

Biosocial Units in the Baboon Troop

The infant is nursed by the very protective female, who enjoys a privileged place at the center of the band by the dominant males, until it is weaned and enters a playgroup where it learns all the social skills needed for complete integration into the troop.

Adult baboons form consort pairs at the edge of the troop's activities where they briefly mate. The bond, or relation, of the longest duration, approximately two years, is the nursing female-infant bond. The sexual relation is the most temporary, lasting a few minutes in some cases or several hours if the couple groom each other. Neither interferes with the other, however, since both are internally regu-

lated. That is, a lactating female is not sexually receptive or attractive, and a female is both attractive (swelling and reddening of the buttocks, in addition to odor) and receptive only when in oestrus.

Dominant males keep close to nursing females while the troop is on the move through the grasses, and it is the males who supervise the rough and tumble activities of the juvenile play groups.

Source:

Summarized from Washburn, S.L., And Irven DeVore. "The Social Behavior of Baboons and Early Man," in S.L. Washburn (ed.), *Social Life of Early Man.* Chicago: Aldine, 1961. pp. 96-100.

Biological Changes

The biological changes in the hominids were many, and we assume they occurred as family forms were evolving. Some of the important changes for family development were: bipedalism and hand dexterity; increased brain size and complexity; stereoscopic vision; a very fine coordination between the eye, hand, and brain; appearance of the lumbar curve and accompanying rebalancing of the skeleton with the subsequent narrowing of the pelvis; lessening of the sense of smell; loss of hair; loss of the estrus cycle; and a diet change from essential vegetarianism to the inclusion of more concentrated proteins.

The human female's posture was upright, and her birth passage was smaller than that of her hominid ancestors; the human infant was less mature *(neoteny)* and more helpless than the pongid (ape) infant. The estrus cycle, in which mating occurs only in the few hours of the month when the female is likeliest to conceive, changed to a menstrual cycle in which human females are receptive to sexual intercourse even when pregnant and nursing. Diet changes created a greater reliance on animal protein, which had to be hunted or

fished for, thus providing the basis for a *commensal unit* (literally "table mates," a unit in which food is shared), in addition to the nursing and mating units.

Social Changes

Consider the tremendous effect on social life of those biological transformations, which probably represent adaptations to the new edge-of-the forest environment to which hominids had moved when they left the trees.

Consider, more particularly, the potential threat to the survival of our species that neoteny and menstruation represent. Because the sexual and maternal activities of the mother were no longer separated by internal mechanisms, a nursing female could theoretically abandon or at least neglect her newborn in pursuit of a protracted sexual liaison. Mother's milk could be assured for the infant only with a relatively stable or permanent sexual relationship between adult female and male, and only if the mates or their surrogates assumed responsibility for the newborn could it survive.

On the other hand, sharing food among the group made biosocial units more cohesive than previously.

From what is known of the few existing foraging tribes today, it is safe to say that the bulk of our ancestors' diet, the vegetarian part, was probably provided by women, children, and the few aged, gathering roots, herbs, berries, fruits, and occasionally even small animals. Less than half the food supply was contributed by adult male hunters, and that sometimes sporadically and undependably. Women were also the sole source of food for infants. (The relatively low protein content of human milk, requiring women to be frequent nursers, may have been what limited mobility of females and their participation in hunting.) These biosocial changes, along with the discovery of fire about two million years ago, may have been the occasion of division of labor by gender, so important in early human existence (Ambert, 1976; Tavris and Offir, 1977).

Furthermore, it is almost unthinkable that such developments could have unfolded without the concurrent invention of symbolic communication, what we call language. Our hominid ancestors, remember, were less and less internally regulated in their behavior. The external regulations regarding copulation and child-care are social norms, norms imply rules, and rules are impossible without language. (You saw in Chapter 2 that symbols and their meanings provide the basis for shared ideas, including norms.) If human infants were to learn the norms, therefore, close emotional attachments with particular communicative adults were necessary during the infant's developmental years. Our female and male ancestors came to be interdependent in a way that their ancestors were not, and this evolving state of affairs became symbolically communicable. Two powerful symbols in particular have come down to us through the millennia, gathering force en route, the bed and the hearth. The symbol for economic and emotional interdependencies is the hearth, the place where food was brought to be cooked and shared; the symbol for sexual attachment is the shared bed. Only humans, among the primates, share the pleasures of hearth and bed – even the nomads among us.

The home is more than a place, or collection of shared comings and goings, just as the family is more than a collection of persons. The hearth represents the warmth or affection that develops between the individuals in a family unit. In addition, the blood and marriage lines in a family represent for every person bridges to a past and a future, as well as a social map of the present. Homes make it possible for men and women and their children to love and cooperate; the family institution enables them to transcend the imperatives of food and sex, and create normative worlds of elaborate design.

Why the Family?

. . . We now understand why it is so wrong to try to explain the family on the purely natural grounds of procreation, motherly instinct, and psychological feelings between man and woman and between father and children. None of these would be sufficient to give rise to a family, and for a reason simple enough: for the whole of mankind, the absolute requirement for the creation of a family is the previous existence of two other families, one ready to provide a man, the other a woman, who will through their marriage start a third one, and so on indefinitely. To put it in other words: what makes man really different from the animal is that, in mankind, a family could not exist if there were no society; i.e., a plurality of families ready to acknowledge that there are other links than consanguineous ones, and that the natural process of filiation can only be carried on through the social process of affinity.

Source:

Lévi-Strauss, Claude. "The Family," in Harry L. Shapiro (ed.), *Man, Culture, and Society.* New York: Oxford University Press, 1960. p. 277.

Filial piety (respect and care of parents) and romantic love (one-and-only mate), two important notions associated with family systems in different times and places, are far removed from the biosocial imperative, but they indicate the range and power of our human emotions and intellect. Family systems, in all their diversity and change, are sociocultural adaptations which human beings, within the limitations of biology, make to their physical and social environments. Such systems distinguish humans from other animals who live in biosocial units but who neither entertain the idea, nor contemplate their own experience, of the reality of family.

THE FAMILY AND SOCIETY

Comte said that the family is the basic social unit. His statement has been repeated in many forms. Exactly what did he mean?

First, the family possesses a moral character that makes it different from other social units; humans in families have changed themselves from more or less self-sufficient animals whose survival, if not social behavior, was regulated largely by instinct, into cooperative, altruistic, and moral creatures. They could do this mainly because the symbol-making capacity results in abstract thinking. Conceptualizing units of people as belonging together because they are related by blood or marriage, and as separate from others because they are not so related, is a distinctly human characteristic. If there were no rules about who can mate with whom, there would be none of the social combinations that arise from the differentiation and coordination of family units. There would be only hordes or bands similar to those found among non-human primates today. Second, the family is the basic social unit because family units make possible, besides moral behavior, new social units based on conscious cooperation.

The Incest Taboo

In the first sense, the family is the basic societal institution because it does precisely what no other social arrangement can do and what biology no longer does for human beings: it regulates sexual behavior and, therefore, reproduction.

The most fundamental mechanism involved in regulating sexual behavior is the incest taboo learned by very young children in the home. The incest taboo is the (frequently) unspoken rule that prohibits persons from having heterosexual relations with at least their intimate kin in all societies and certain other relatives in most others. In Canada, the Criminal Code prohibits sexual relations between father and daughter, mother and son, and brother and sister. The various provincial marriage acts specify the prohibited degrees of consanguinity (relationship by blood) and affinity (relationship by marriage) between two people wanting to get married.

The prohibited degrees of relatedness in most acts have little to do with the genetic consequences of procreation between relatives. Often a woman may not marry her stepfather (even after her mother's death), nor may a man marry his half-brother's daughter. In the Manitoba Marriage Act, for example, the prohibited degrees of relatedness appear to have been classified as first, second, and third. Cousins, being related in the fourth degree, are free to marry.

The effect of the incest taboo, then, is to insure that mating establishes new biosocial units and, at the same time, social bonds between the families of the mates. It has other organizational consequences, such as preventing confusion in roles (making certain you do not become "your own grandpa!"), and preventing sexual rivalry from entering into interpersonal relations, thus making it easier to perform household tasks without emotional disruption. The incest taboo epitomizes the stable order possible only if sex and reproduction are regulated by the family.

Marriage

The relationship between the heterosexual couple who are societally approved as mates is called **marriage**. Marriage is the other side of the incest taboo, that is, societal approval of who can mate with whom in contrast with who must not. Marriage is found in all human society. From the viewpoint of the society, marriage is social permission for reproduction, even if not all marriages actually produce offspring, and even if some children are conceived and born before the marriage ceremony. Stephens (1963) defines it thus:

a socially legitimate sexual union, begun with a public announcement and undertaken with some idea of permanence . . . and with a more or less explicit marriage contract, which spells out reciprocal rights and obligations between spouses, and between the spouses and their future children.

Marriage assures that all children born into a society will have parents or other adult kin of both sexes to care for their needs as they develop into human beings and to teach them what they must know to fit into their society. These are the other functions of the family – placement and socialization of children. Therefore, the three *universal functions* (or four, depending on how you look at it) of the family as a human institution are: regulating sex and reproduction, legitimating children, and nurturing them so that it is possible for them to learn the norms and values of the culture, and inculcating those norms and values.

In societies that have not reached the stage of differentiation represented by civilization (i.e., city living, which surplus subsistence makes possible), the family as a household and kin group is also responsible for providing for other personal and social needs, such as religion, specialized education, health care, and the production of goods and services. That is, these institutions are embedded in the family, rather than differentiated and represented by specialized groups and organizations designed for these purposes. The traditional Inuit are a good example of *institutional embeddedness* in the nuclear family household, where the husband-father is religious leader as well as upholder of the law.

Strictly speaking it is inaccurate to say, as some do, that contemporary families have "lost" functions. It is more accurate to say that in urban, industrial society some of the tasks performed by families in other kinds of societies are shared between family groups and specialized agencies such as schools, churches, hospitals, offices, and factories.

EVOLVING FAMILY FORMS

Family patterns are adaptations to the physical and cultural environment. Long-term changes in the variety of family forms and the conditions under which they occur are inferred from archaeological and ethnographic materials. In general, the relationship between technological development and family patterning has been well documented. Some forms, such as nuclear households, appear to be associated with both the simplest and most complex societies, such as the several-thousand-year-old traditional Inuit and the nation states of contemporary Western civilization. Extended households, on the other hand, appear to be more frequently found in agricultural societies. Hunter-gatherers, too, reflect the current state of technology in their family patterning. Although a rather strict division of labor based on gender is characteristic of hunters and gatherers, the economic interdependency between the genders in these types of society also makes for somewhat egalitarian relationships between wife and husband. For example, recent studies of the !Kung people, as the boxed insert on the next page shows, indicate that settlement in agricultural villages of the once basically nomadic group has resulted in the loss of status, autonomy, and influence for women.

Historical studies show that our current family system has evolved in a most uneven way. Some of its features are of great antiquity, and others, in the lifespan of humanity, are as recent as yesterday. Moreover, these features of the present conjugal system are the result of belief systems as dissimilar as Judeo-Christian religions on the one hand, and various secular streams on the other, in addition to politico-economic trends including much more than technology.

For instance, monogamous marriage, nuclear households, an open mate-selection system, and egalitarian relations in the family are by no means twentieth-century phenomena. Monogamy as a tradition goes back as far as the ancient Hebrews. Nuclear family households appear to have replaced the extended stem family in Europe as early as the sixteenth century, when the development of trade and commerce drew the rural population to the cities for wage development. Romantic love, as the ideal basis for marriage, on the other hand, appeared as recently as the beginning of the last century. Mate selection in both New France and New England during the seventeenth century was already a matter of participant choice, but romantic love was not the ideal basis.

Loss of Equality for !Kung Women

The !Kung* have lived as hunters and gatherers in the Kalahari Desert of South Africa for at least eleven thousand years, but recently they have begun to settle in agrarian villages near those of the Bantus. Settlement began about fifteen years ago, and all but about 5 percent of the 30,000 !Kung now live by farming and keeping herds of domestic animals.

One aspect of this change has been the loss of equality for these newly-agrarian women. The remaining !Kung hunter-gatherer women enjoy a higher status because of the role they play in contributing to the band's food supply. Since they gather at least half the group's food, these women, of necessity, are as mobile as the men, who make up the other half by hunting. Women and men leave the camp equally often to obtain food. Those who do not seek food on a given day, women and men, remain in the camp and share in taking care of the children.

The women in the new !Kung farming settlements, however, have

far less mobility than the men and contribute less to the food supply. The men leave the village to clear fields, raise crops, and care for the cattle of their Bantu neighbors; the women remain in the village where they prepare food and take care of the shelters.

Since the men work for the Bantus, they learn the Bantu language. Thus when the Bantus deal with the !Kung, they deal exclusively with the men. This practice, together with the men's emulation of the male-dominated Bantu society, contributes to increasingly subservient roles for !Kung women.

*The exclamation point refers to an alveolar-palatal click. The tongue tip is pressed against the roof of the mouth and drawn sharply away, producing a hollow, popping sound.

Source:

Kolata, Gina Bari. "!Kung hunter-gatherers: feminism, diet, and birth control." *Science*, 185, 1974.

By the same token, the idea of equality between marital partners may have had its conception in the French Revolution, but only with social changes in this century has the concept gained wide popular approval and become feasible for couples. Legal rights resulting from the two militant phases of the women's movement in North America (suffrage and liberation), a sexual revolution which began to undermine the double sexual standard, and perhaps more importantly the swell, from a trickle into a flood, of women entering the labor force and limiting the size of their families have effaced all but the lingering vestiges of patriarchy from the marriage relationship.

Numerous explanations have been formulated for the emergence of new family forms and interaction patterns. Let us briefly examine a few of these explanations and relate them to the three major perspectives employed in this textbook.

Historical Factors and Theoretical Perspectives

Systematic study of the family began in Europe, with the writings of early sociologists, anthropologists, and economists. Names that immediately come to mind are the most influential social thinkers of the last century and the early part of this one. Some of these names you have encountered in Chapter 1 and elsewhere in this textbook. They are Comte, Marx, Engels, Morgan, Le Play, Durkheim, and Weber. With their scientific attention focused on the macrocosm, or society as a whole, they viewed the family as one important part that fitted into an overall pattern.

Structural Functionalism. For some of these thinkers the puzzle was: how do the functions the family performs integrate with those of the institutions of religion, politics, and economics? The **structural functionalist** approach gave rise to speculations about the origins of the family in human society and the family's universal functions, which we touched upon earlier in this chapter.

The basic structural functionalist assumption is that expected behavior, or norms in the family, can in large measure be explained or predicted by knowing what the other institutions in society are. This assumption has also been useful in investigating family changes, although not all structural functionalists have been interested in change. Parsons, for example, was more interested in the way family patterns are maintained than in the way they are transformed. Some who have stressed change are Farber (1964), Goode (1970), and Scanzoni (1972). Farber associates the main features of the emerging family system with the loss of family and community control over mate selection, sex codes, and divorce. Goode, among others, finds the changes in our family system linked to the Industrial Revolution and its ideological and institutional consequences. Although Scanzoni criticizes the structural functionalism of Parsons and considers himself an exchange theorist, he attributes the changes in families to conflicts between the sexes as interest groups in the wider society. More specifically, he believes that the extension of the ideology of individualism and the diminishing importance in modern (urban, industrial) society of ascribed roles opens up the possibility of all roles being achieved. In any of these macro-explanations, people do not appear; rather, social structures and ideological structures determine family behavior.

Symbolic Interactionism. Weber's interest in relationships and the social meanings to social actors of their behavior represents a turning point in the study of social groups. Shortly after the turn of the century the conceptual framework that came to be known as **symbolic interactionism** entered into the work of American sociologists interested in families. C.H. Cooley observed his infant daughter learning language and, mirroring the actions of her parents, evaluating herself in their terms. Thus he provided a family case study of the "looking glass self" similar to G.H. Mead's idea of role playing and "taking the role of the other." (The work of these theorists was described in detail in Chapter 3.) Burgess (1931) first applied the symbolic interactionist perspective to the family when he defined the family as a unity of interacting personalities. According to Burgess (1931):

. . . this meant a living, changing, growing thing. The actual unity of family life has its existence not in any legal conception, nor in any formal contract, but in the interaction of its members. . . . The family lives so long as interaction is taking place and dies when it ceases.

This perspective restricted the definition of family to the group of people who customarily live together. It stressed the more or less shared meanings communicated and reinterpreted during the process of interaction among family members. It gave rise to a set of concerns different from those of the earlier European investigators. Questions were asked about attraction of young people to each other, adjustment in marriage, and effective parenting. Berger and Kelner (1971) may be most representative of this approach. Like Aldous (1974) they view change as the result of the conflicts caused by ambiguities that develop between the two persons playing the roles of wife and husband. Partners who may or may not have shared meanings about roles at the outset of marriage either establish an effective way of communicating or do not. When communication fails to bridge the gap opened by the different experiences of their daily lives, or does not help to meet the expectations of the many roles they choose or have thrust upon them, marital adjustment suffers. By talking through their roles, by negotiating with each other, couples can create new shared understanding and establish the basis for gaining the self-esteem they both seek in marriage. As conflicts are resolved, a new family unity is achieved and often new roles are created. To a considerable extent people determine the pattern of their own family life.

Conflict Theory. In Canada, the third sociological perspective, **conflict theory**, was adapted as a model for understanding the family. Feminist concern that the oppression of women was a peculiar result of the corporate structure of contemporary society resulted in Marxist theory being applied to the domestic family

(Smith, 1973). In this sense, conflict theory as an approach to family study has been a distinctively British-Canadian approach. And in fact, Americans have been behind Canadians in applying the conflict approach to the study of the family.

The Marxist perspective is somewhat similar to structural functionalism in that the unitary aspect of the social world is stressed. In other words, the family is viewed as integrally tied to the social structure. The difference, however, is that from the Marxist point of view there is no question of separating the family system from other aspects of social relations. In fact, the very notion of distinguishing the family from the economic institutions of society is frowned upon, because the separation is believed to be a consequence of the corporate society that fosters a situation wherein all work except housework is "rationalized." In this chapter we will use the Marxist conflict approach in the discussion of housework and the problems entailed in making marriage an equal partnership between women and men.

The conflict model has pointed up the class interests served by the sexual division of labor in both the home and the labor force. Women's role in the labor force is determined by what they do at home; as well, the needs of the economy and the nature of jobs available to women affect the roles they play at home. Because women are usually paid so little and rely on skills appropriate to low-paid work outside the home, they generally find themselves financially dependent on marriage. From this perspective, it is the rise of capitalism that explains the historical changes in working-class family households and the exploitation of women, their dependency, and the subsequent mutual resentment of husbands and wives (Fox, 1980). As long as the capitalist corporate class dominates, family life, in all but that class, can only become more disorganized and more difficult for all persons in the family. It is the internal dynamics of capitalism that create change.

Clearly, all three sociological approaches can add new dimensions to our understanding of families in Canada. Present family arrangements are comprehensible in the context of the institutional structure and functioning of all human families, the interaction of family members based on the creation and usage of symbols, and the division of labor between the genders that is carried over from the current societal mode of production.

CONJUGAL FAMILIES TODAY

What are the salient characteristics of contemporary Canadian families? Five of them, listed below, represent a modification of the work done by Adams (1975). The first three will be discussed in greater detail in this section, the last two in separate sections.

1. A central service performed by Canadian families, both in their formation and continuation, is to provide affection and meaning for members of the mass society.

2. Providing income for domestic families is now the task of all adult members, some of whom tend to serve as a reservoir of unpaid labor and a reserve army of low-paid workers who can move in and out of the labor force as needed.

3. Whereas primary socialization is as much a function of the family as ever, such tasks as educating children for occupations and citizenship and providing recreational opportunities and health services have increasingly come to be shared with other agencies.

4. Because of the historical and geographical reality that Canadian society represents, a wide range of subcultural variety exists within the overall family patterns. The political and cultural dominance of the French in Quebec and parts of the Atlantic Region and the English in Ontario and western Canada has left its mark. The dominance of the middle and upper classes in government, schools universities, and mass media, however, has created pressure for uniformity. This dominance has meant that the ideals and expectations of families of native groups and later immigrants tend to be submerged. But these ideals and expectations, as well as rural-urban differences, must be acknowledged.

5. The family in Canadian society includes inconsistent aspects and fragmentary changes as well as subcultural variation. It is far from disclosing a logical coherent pattern.

Since World War II, an increasing proportion of Canadian women have taken jobs outside the home. One consequence has been that the roles of mother and father have changed somewhat, with fathers taking a more active part in the care and teaching of children.

Affection

Affection as the binding part of conjugal families is so much taken for granted that we may find it difficult to imagine what traditional, or **legalistic families** were like (Burgess, 1971).

Consider, for example, Tevye and Golda, the husband and wife in *Fiddler on the Roof*, who discovered that they loved each other after twenty-five years of living and working together – even though their marriage had been arranged. Contrast their situation to the predicament of the couple separated in 1979 by the Canadian government, which asserted that the two persons were guilty of marrying *without* love. Moksudor Rahman was deported by Canadian immigration authorities who said his marriage to Hafiza Rahman was not out of love but arranged to give him an edge in gaining landed immigrant status.

European colonists in North America discontinued the practice of arranged marriage, and individuals have been free to choose their spouses since the settlement in New France and New England in the early part of the seventeenth century. But because of the harsh realities of pioneer life, which required everyone to have a spouse, because of the short supply of women, and because of the high death rate and frequently short marriage span, the choice was usually based on considerations other than emotional ones. Financial matters were as always very important, as was the prospect's ability to perform the tasks traditionally assigned to each gender. The point here is that participant choice need have nothing to do with romance.

As life in the settlements became more stable, romance entered into the now longer courting relationships. At least by the time of Confederation, couples were expected to be in love, as well as to have the role requisites, that is, the male to be an adequate provider and the female a good homemaker. By the late 1930s, however, urban dating had replaced the family- and community-centered courting pattern, and young people looked for definite individual traits, as opposed to role requisites, in their prospective mates. During a more extended period of heterosexual association under informal conditions, they searched for their one-and-only, believing that marriage would invariably result in everlasting happiness.

Perhaps contemporary Canadians are more sophisticated about both love and marriage than were their grandparents. After all, an estimated 10 percent of university students live in heterosexual arrangements

Women of Three Rivers: 1651–63

For women in Three Rivers, as throughout New France, all roads led to matrimony. The scarcity of women, the economic difficulties of existence, and the constant danger had one important result: all girls became wives and all widows remarried. Consequently, the study of these women becomes a study of the legal and social effects of marriage.

Most Canadian girls married between the ages of twelve and sixteen, thirteen being the most common age. Marguerite Crevier married Jacques Fournier at the age of twelve; at the time of her second marriage she was sixteen. Her sister Marie married Nicolas Gatineau when she was thirteen. Marie Vien married Jean Lanqueteau at the age of thirteen, and was widowed at fifteen.

Widows at Three Rivers in the 1650s were, alas, numerous. But permanent widowhood was almost as unusual in the colony as spinsterhood. It was the rule to marry well within the year. Some widows remarried within three months and others even sooner.

Source:

Summarized from Foulche-Delbosc, Isabel. "Women of Three Rivers: 1651–63," in Susan Mann Trofemenkoff and Alison Prentice (eds.), *Essays in Canadian Women's History: The Neglected Majority*. Toronto: McClelland and Stewart, 1977, pp. 14-26.

prior to marriage. Even so, love is sentimentalized. Love, rather than tradition or roles, is most likely to be viewed as the social glue that cements members of the family. Affection, or the feeling of belonging, rather than societally agreed upon duties, is what keeps families together. Most couples do not even know that Canadian law clearly defines the responsibilities of wife and husband, and that whether or not their marriage has been a legal one (certified and solemnized), they are required to perform the roles incorporated in the statutes of their province covering marriage and family (Saunders, 1975). It is generally only in times of crisis that two people discover the ways in which the political state is involved in their marriage.

To some extent this reliance in everyday family life on the positive force of affection, to the exclusion of roles and tradition, is related to a decline in the influence of the more formal source and supports for the other Canadian social institutions – the churches and the courts. Both have vested interests in traditions being perpetuated, and lately both have experienced much pressure to be more responsive to the new conditions of social life. To give the impression that the law and religion are inconsequential in contemporary marriage and family life would, however, be very misleading. Religious marriage ceremonies are still common, and most Canadians do have their marriages certified by registering them with the province in which they reside.

This relatively new requirement for marriage – love – is more than an emotion, or positive feelings flowing between two or more persons. Love is also patterned behavior. When we are "in love," or when we are acting in loving ways, we follow the scripts that society provides. We learn to love according to what is considered appropriate in our society. This means we are taught whom we can love, how we should feel about the objects of our love, and how we should behave when we are with them. Most of our beliefs and attitudes about love form complexes, or sets of related expectations.

We expect that marriage should begin in love; we expect that, ideally, the couple will love only each other sexually, and only after the wedding; we expect them to remain lovingly together until death parts them. This is more true in Catholic French Canada where divorce is discouraged. It is true to a lesser extent among Anglicans and Protestant denominations, where secular ideas have gained a foothold, including the ideas that premarital sex between loving, responsible persons may be all right, and an unloving marriage can destroy both family unity and the personal integrity of family members.

The law, as opposed to the church, has been somewhat more responsive in the matter of divorce. Providing grounds that bear more directly on the quality of the marriage relationship (marital breakdown, or not living together for three years) rather than emphasizing violation of moral stricture (sexual exclusiveness) is

one step in the direction of recognizing the importance of the spouses' total commitment to each other, including their positive feelings and respect.

Kinship Relations. With **kinship** relations, as with marriage, the key word in Canadian families is affection. In an urban society where achievement, self-reliance, conjugalism, and financial independence are emphasized one expects to find a lessening emphasis on kinship networks. Nevertheless, such networks continue to function and to be important to individuals, even in modified form. That is, compared to kin arrangements in agrarian societies, urban kin networks are more likely to be "voluntary, selective, and relatively free from normative pressures or a sense of compelling obligation to be part of it" (Ramu 1976).

The few studies of kin relations in Canada indicate a high degree of kinship solidarity among Canadians, with personal preference being an important factor in contacts between relatives. It is on the basis of liking, rather than degree of kin and a specified obligation, that most decide whether to associate with the husband's or the wife's parents, or both. Adult children maintain contacts with their parents and in-laws by means of frequent mutual visiting and telephoning when they reside in the same city or community. Telephoning and writing, as well as periodic visits, are somewhat determined by the closeness of the kin tie and the sentiment attached to it. Money and services, such as babysitting, house building and repair, etc., flow between adult married children and their parents on the basis of the affection established over the years that parents were rearing the children, rather than because of a compulsion to do so, or legal requirements (Irving, 1972). A recent study in Edmonton has discovered that home ownership for some young couples is only possible with kin support (Kennedy and Stokes, 1980).

Family solidarity becomes even more important as persons grow old. There is a myth abroad that the elderly in North America are shoved into institutions needlessly and neglected by their families. Nothing could be further from the truth. As Chapter 5 pointed out, the fact is that in North America today three out of four older persons belong to kin networks of four generations. As for living arrangements, most of them live with their spouses. After widowhood, they live alone but near an adult child, until unable to care for themselves, usually when very old or sick. Surprisingly, a much higher proportion of persons over 80 years of age live with an adult child than are institutionalized. Add to that those who live as close as 10 minutes away from one of their children, it is possible to account for at least half of all persons 80 years and over.

Recent studies indicate that families are primary sources of services for the elderly. This is especially true in regard to care-giving for the ill and incapacitated (Snider, 1981; Marshall, Rosenthall and Synge, 1981). Families also provide meaning and continuity in the lives of older persons, including those who live alone or in institutions.

Labor and Income

From the settlement period in New France until Confederation, the basic economic unit was the family, independently providing for most of its needs. All family members – men, women, and children – contributed directly and obviously to the support and maintenance of this unit, and there was no distinction made between "working women" and those who stayed at home. As one historian puts it, "The value of women as economic partners in the struggle for existence was a matter of general agreement" (Griffiths, 1976).

In 1871 roughly 82 percent of the Canadian population was rural. By 1971 the figure had dwindled to 24 percent, with less than 7 percent being rural farm population. In fact, by 1900 family production was rapidly being replaced by factory production. The effects on **gender roles** and behavior were remarkable. Chapter 4, *Gender Relations*, and Chapter 7, *Population*, have explored some of the issues mentioned here. Chapter 15, *Urbanization and Urbanism* takes a closer look at this rural to urban shift.

The first role to change was that of father and husband. Farmers are employed near their residences, in frequent association with their wives and children. Their urban counterparts, however, work in factories and offices, on construction jobs, and operating trucks,

buses, and airplanes. They are employed for eight or more hours a day at considerable distance from where they live. Many are absent for days or weeks at a time if their jobs involve travel.

As the rural-urban shift took place husbands became providers, wage-earners, for their families and, as part of an industrial unit, produced goods and services for the market. During the early stages of industrialization, women's work continued to be in the domestic unit, providing labor in the form of maintaining the home and caring for small children. But the role of children, like that of their fathers, also changed. Urban children became less involved in work at home, because it was more important that they either contribute to family incomes or, with the later introduction of child labor laws and compulsory education, prepare themselves for employment by attending school. As a result, children required more care, became more costly, and remained financially dependent longer.

Prior to the turn of the century, working-class wives in cities like Montreal and Toronto often contributed to family incomes, even if they were not employed in factories and offices. They took in washing, sewed, and did piece work at home. Since that time, as more youth have remained out of the labor force, more wives have been entering. This shows up to some degree in trends in labor force participation by gender. Shortly after the turn of the century, approximately 90 percent of the male population over fourteen years of age was in the labor force, and 16 percent of females of the same age.

The participation rate for males has declined, until by 1979 it was only 78 percent, while, as you saw in Chapter 4, the rate for females has increased steadily to a high of almost 50 percent. Participation rates also show that married women are increasingly entering the labor force at the same time that married men are just about holding their own, a trend that really took off during World War II.

These changes in labor force participation have had tremendous consequences for the family and the economy. As a legacy of the recent past, the association of home with women and work with men has become so close that many have come to think of it as natural and inevitable. At least the myth has been persistent that women and children have always been dependent on males for survival, and men on women for maintenance and child care. The fact is, however, that the family as a consumer of goods and services produced outside the home, in organizations managed and directed mostly by males, is a very recent phenomenon associated with industrialization and urbanization. Prior to that, women organized and engaged in most of the activities involved in providing food, clothing, and other necessities for rural family life. A minority of domestic families now conform to the stereotype of the breadwinning father, the homemaking mother, and their dependent children.

The opposing trends in male and female *labor force participation* by no means indicate a coming reversal in the roles of husband as provider and wife as homemaker. The decline in male participation can be explained both by early retirement and by the longer period devoted to education by young men, and not by wives assuming the main-provider role in two-parent families or by husbands relinquishing it during the early years of their fatherhood.

Clearly, however, the Canadian family is still in transition. The roles played by husbands and wives appear to be extremely responsive to changes in the economy. The influx of Canadian wives into the labor market is not the result of the women's liberation movement as many inaccurately believe. The most likely spur was World War II. By 1951, 30 percent of all women in the labor force was married, and by 1961 this figure had risen to 50 percent. From the advent of the women's liberation movement in the middle 1960s, until 1971, the increase was only 7 percentage points.

In fact, married women work outside the home because of job expansion in the economy and the financial needs of many Canadian families. The low income of husbands is the most powerful determinant of wife employment. The average earnings of a wife whose husband provides a lower-middle-class life-style can raise the family's standard of living to the class above.

Still, the majority of Canadian wives (57 percent) was not in the labor force in 1976. They were nonetheless, working. Wives work at home; referring to a married women as either a "housewife" or a "working wife" is linguistic malpractice. Housework, performed mainly by women, is indeed work, as anyone can attest who has spent any time doing it. Valuable as its contribution to the family and society is, however, it is not paid work. Luxton (1980) has shown, in her book *More Than A Labor of Love*, how wives cater to their husband's needs because the wage labor of working-class husbands is so important to family subsistence. In the process of making certain he performs his job for the company, the wife's work at home becomes invisible and unacknowledged.

Wives may be either full-time homemakers or they may be in the labor force, but even the latter are also homemakers. The main burden of keeping house, preparing meals, doing the laundry, and attending to all the chores associated with family maintenance usually falls to the wife, whether or not she is in the labor force. In fact, the employed wife does almost as much work at home as the full-time homemaker, and she gets no more help from her husband than the wife who is home all day. For example, although one out of four husbands of employed women spends time cleaning house (along with cooking, the most time-consuming regular chore), he spends on the average four hours a week at it. Compare this with an estimated eight out of ten employed wives who spend nine hours a week cleaning house (Meissner, 1975).

Urban wives are not merely consumers as the myth has it; they are co-producers of income with their husbands, and they are simultaneously producers of valuable services in the home. For the vast majority of Canadians, the family is the basic economic unit for which income is both earned and spent. In spite of increased labor force participation by married women, the division of labor in the family is such that the husband obtains the greatest share of income for the family through his employment in a labor market that discriminates against women's equal participation. The wife performs financially uncompensated work in the home, and as a result the husband is able to make a greater financial contribution to the family income (Armstrong and Armstrong, 1978).

Attitudes favorable to greater equality of social and

occupational opportunity for women are now characteristic of the majority of Canadian adults (Nett, 1979).
Espousal of the egalitarian ideal most often occurs
among young persons, women, and in response to a
generally worded question, although few Canadian
adults think the wife's role should be that of housewife
and mother only.

The two aspects of marriage associated with gender
roles – who makes the decisions and who performs
which tasks – appear to be interrelated as well as affected by the employment of the wife outside the
home. Generally, joint decision-making appears to be
rarer than allocation of decision areas along rather
traditional gender lines. Although Canadian families
have been considerably democratized, in practice many
couples maintain special domains of competence over
which each spouse has authority by gender. Women
are expected to make decisions about meals, the
purchase of children's clothing, home decorating, grocery shopping, and house cleaning. Husbands have
responsibility for home repairs and car upkeep. Perhaps
more sharing occurs in the areas of family recreation,
finances, and child care than in activities associated
with keeping the family home and properties in

running condition. On the whole, couples think there
should be more sharing but they appear to be unable
or unmotivated to achieve it.

The effect of the wife's outside employment on the
marital relationship has generally been viewed as important in her gaining more influence in decision-
making, or having as much power in the marriage.
Not only is she contributing to the family's wealth, but
she gains a degree of independence which the full-time
homemaker lacks. Women who know that they have
an alternative to marriage, because they have the
work skills and employment experience to earn a living,
are less likely to be satisfied with a subordinate role in
marriage. In marital negotiations, employment can be
a bargaining chip. A deterrent to wives' participation
in the labor force is the presence of young children, as
Table 11-1 shows.

Socialization

Socialization is the process whereby the individual
learns to control biological drives, is taught the norms
and values of society, and acquires an identity or
self-concept. As you saw in Chapter 3, children are
born without the habits, beliefs, attitudes, and ways of
behaving that come to constitute their personalities.
They also lack the knowledge of the patterned ways of
behaving required by their culture. Throughout the
vast sweep of human experience, and in a number of
today's human societies, socialization has consisted
chiefly of learning directly from parents and kin. In
tribal and peasant societies the world over, impulse
control, skills, proper attitudes, and a sense of one's
own history and value are the unconscious result of
the close association of parents and children in the
everyday round of work and play. In more complex or
differentiated societies like urban Canada, children
are perceived as a very special category of persons
whose development has been exhaustively charted and
whose care has been minutely prescribed. Furthermore, in urban societies the task of teaching skills and
values is viewed as being more rationally carried out
by formal organizations such as schools.

During the settlement of Canada, the various churches played important roles in educating the young,

**TABLE 11-1. LABOR FORCE
PARTICIPATION OF EVER-MARRIED
WOMEN[1] AGED 25 TO 34, BY AGE OF
YOUNGEST CHILD, CANADA, 1971**

Age of Youngest Child	Percent of Women in Labor Force
No child	79.4
Less than 1	25.4
1-1.99	29.8
2-2.99	32.5
3-3.99	35.4
4-4.99	38.2
5-5.99	40.4
6-6.99	45.8
7-7.99	49.8
8-8.99	53.2
9-9.99	56.0

SOURCE: Unpublished statistics provided in Cook, Gail C. A. (ed.).
Opportunity for Choice: A Goal for women in Canada. Statistics Canada in
association with the C.D. Howe Research Institute, 1976, p. 30.
NOTE: [1]Ever-married women are those who have at some time been
married, but are not necessarily married at the time of the survey.

Twenty-year-old former cheerleader Debbie Pratt is following in her father's footsteps. She was one of three women who broke a sex barrier in West Virginia in 1975 when they hired on as underground coal miners. Traditionally jobs like truck driver, construction worker, airline pilot, bus driver, police officer, postal carrier, and coal miner were thought too dirty or too demanding for women. But women are increasingly seeking out these jobs, because they are bored in offices, they like the outdoors, or they like the bigger salaries.

but up until the early part of the eighteenth century most children were taught to read and write by their parents and acquired the elements of their religious beliefs at home. As late as the nineteenth century, most people still believed that education was the primary concern of the church and home. In 1900, just over half of the Canadian population between the ages of five and nineteen years of age was attending school. By 1971, the proportion had jumped to almost 80 percent. Until Confederation, only the children of affluent families attended high school, and this was doubly true for girls who primarily had access only to private schools. Very few rural children went to high school. Chapter 14, *Education*, looks at these trends in detail.

In one sense, impulse control, cultural transmission, and identity are inextricably intertwined. In another sense, modern societies, as compared with traditional ones, tend to assign to the family more responsibility for aspects of personality development, such as impulse control and identity, and less to teaching the culture. Each newborn child is to some extent a guarantee of the culture's survival, but the transmission of cultural norms is another matter. It is a question of degree how much of this transmission is the task of the family and how much is handed over to the schools.

The process of replicating in the next generation the family's pattern of norms and values is known as *orderly replacement of the culture.* In slow-changing or technologically simple societies it is possible for families to perform this task almost unaided. On the other hand, in mass society the focus is on the uniqueness both of each individual produced in the family and of each generation. Recognizing that rapid social change

A Loving Father

My father was an infinitely gentle man. When I see him – as I do often, now that the death of that sad invalid has liberated my true, my real father – it is always in the posture of tender protection. What was it Hamlet said of the dead king? "So loving to my mother That he might not beteem the winds of heaven Visit her face too roughly." My father was like that. If he could have carried us through the world on his shoulders, he would have done so. One of the few conflicts of his life, I think (he was a man simple and straight, not vexed by division), was the pull between the desire to give us everything and the need to keep us safe.

"Papa, I want a cap gun!"

"What for darling? You should hurt yourself?"

Scornful, impatient, I stamped my Buster Brown shoes (oxfords, for the sake of my arches). "You can't get hurt with a cap gun. Everybody else has one!"

So I got my pistol, and the little red roll of paper caps to carry. When the moment came – wait until Sammy Horton sees *this*! – I handed Papa the weapon and he fired . . .

No single world will conjure up the quality of my father's generosity. It was not permissiveness: a feeling for what one did and did not do was strong in our household. It was not indulgence in any ordinary sense. I think of it, rather, as a special sensitivity to need. When, as a child, I waked crying because the dark got in my nose, he was beside me in an instant. Then he would light the lamp and sit at the foot of the bed, singing softly:

*Lule, lule, lulinke
Shlof nu shlof meyn meydele,
Sleep now, sleep my little girl,
Ah, ah, lulinke,
Lule, lule, lulinke. . . .*

Source:

Maynard, Fredelle Bruser. *Raisins and Almonds: The Rich Memoir of a Childhood on the Canadian Prairies.* Don Mills, Ont.: Paperjacks, 1978, pp. 159–161.

---

requires new modes of adaptation, mass societies stress the importance of the family in instilling in children the notion of who they are and of their own worth as persons. Rather than being the primary goal of the family, transmission of cultural values is merely a means to the development of a conscience, or the effective internalization of those values. Redefinition of the culture by each generation is the result.

In Canada, the extremes of families replacing the culture in orderly fashion or redefining it for each new generation are found only in certain small segments of the society. The experience of most persons in the family is one of making strong identifications with other family members during their early years. As they grow older they acquire skills, attitudes, and values from extra-familial agencies like day care,

nursery school, public or parochial schools, churches, hospitals, recreational clubs and organizations, and many others with which they increasingly come in contact.

Besides these theoretical implications, there is the question of whether or not socialization in the family is on the decline. Two issues are involved in this question. One is the existence of fewer children to be socialized. The second is whether the influence of parents on children is lessening, relative to outside influence.

Declining Birth Rates. If the number of children in the family is used as the indicator of socialization, there is no question about the decline in function. Fertility rates for Canadian women in the hundred years between 1871 and 1971 dropped by more than half. Married women born in 1874 gave birth on the average to 4.5 children throughout their entire childbearing years. The average number of children born to women in their childbearing years in 1971 was 2.28 for those of British ancestry and 2.53 for French. As you saw in Chapter 7, at the present time Canada is experiencing its lowest birth rate ever. It would appear that the young women entering their childbearing years since the early part of the 1970s will, in increasing numbers, have small families or remain voluntarily childless.

Perhaps one of the most important features of this reduction in births is the shortening of the time span during which women complete childbearing. Most women today have their families in a span of less than ten years, whereas twenty years ago it was double that. At present, about two-thirds of all births are to women in their early and middle twenties. Also, the occurrence of large families, those of five children and more, is dwindling yearly.

Childfree marriage is much talked about, but as yet there is no real way to determine the extent to which Canadian couples are choosing this alternative. Until recently there was little societal support for such marriages, because parenthood included a set of legitimations stemming from religious and community beliefs in the moral superiority of the fertile couple. More recently, marriage without children has become tolerated if not actually approved. It is a fact that the average number of children in families with parents under twenty-five years of age declined between 1961 and 1971, and the birthrate for teenaged women declined significantly in these same years. But only time will tell if these couples are delaying having children or have decided they want none. It is worth noting, however, that the longer women delay having children, the less likely they are to have any. Only 5 percent of Canadian women under twenty-two years of age at the time of marriage remain childless, compared to about 15 percent of those over twenty-two.

Canadians' then, *are* having fewer children to socialize in the family. But, are parents less influential in the important task of child-rearing? Let us now consider this question.

Parental Influence on Child-Rearing. How much do parents influence their children? There is little reason to believe that parents are playing less important roles in determining the social positions of their children or in shaping their children's perception of society. Parental influence can be seen in children's early identification with their parents' politics, in the unusually high proportions of university graduates from ethnic groups that traditionally value learning and education, and in the continuing similarities of gender-role orientations between generations. Families have also been found to be important in the mobility aspirations of their youngsters, as well as in determining whether their children are familistic or individualistic. Social class is a strong determinant in children's values and behavior (Gecas, 1979). To say that families continue to exercise the most control over the development of children growing up in them is not to downplay the effects of other socializing agencies such as schools, churches, neighborhood and playground peer groups, and television. Remember, however, that the family is primary in several ways: as you saw in Chapter 3, the family has the child first almost exclusively in the early formative years; it also has the capacity for creating the closest and most enduring psychological bond the child will have.

Questions arise as to which parent in a two-parent household is more influential in the lives of children. There are good logical arguments to substantiate either one, but until further evidence is forthcoming we must assume both parents are equally important in the tasks of socialization. The roles in the family, however, have changed over time. The role of father in socialization of children has always been important in Canadian society, but during the early years of industrialization the father's role in looking after and teaching children became somewhat minimized. Lately, the employment of mothers appears to be changing this situation. Such employment has been responsible in part for blurring the distinction between the mother's and the father's roles in child care and socialization. One survey shows that one-third of all children whose mothers work for pay were being supervised by one other family member in the home. (Canada Department of Labour, 1970). That member was not a grandmother, not an older sister, but the father of the child. This undoubtedly reflects the "helping" aspect of the father's role in child care in the two-parent household.

At present, girls and boys generally do not distinguish to a great extent between the authoritarian and emotional roles played by their parents. They describe their mothers as well as their fathers as sources of punishment, and they perceive their male parent as well as their female parent as offering love, advice, and encouragement (Nett, 1979). There are subcultural variations, but even in groups in which the father is the traditional authoritarian, the role is much modified by the age and gender of the children and the personality of the father. As an idea, the stricter role of the father appears to be undergoing considerable modification in French Canada, where it has been upheld until recently. Parental roles seem more flexible than marriage roles in the nuclear family.

VARIATIONS UNDER PRESSURE FOR UNIFORMITY

Region, history, and culture create diversity in family life. However, as Ishwaran (1971) has observed: "a different, but related, set of factors – processes of urbanization and industrialization, based on modern technology – produces pressure for uniformity. Consequently, what one actually finds is a whole range of variations continuously under pressure for uniformity." Granted, but whatever the pressure toward urbanization, in 1971 20 percent of Canadians did not live in urban areas. What influence does their rural experience, farm and non-farm, have on diversity or uniformity in Canadian family life?

Part of the regional factor in family life is the incidence of poverty in various areas of Canada (see Table 11-2). Some regions, notably the prairie provinces, have average poverty rates for families, whereas others such as British Columbia and Ontario have the lowest rates, while the Atlantic Region and Quebec

TABLE 11-2   INCIDENCE OF LOW INCOME FOR ECONOMIC FAMILIES, BY REGION

Region	Percent of families below low income cut-offs[1]
Atlantic Provinces	14.1
Quebec	12.1
Ontario	9.7
Prairie Provinces	11.4
British Columbia	11.0

SOURCE: Wargon, Sylvia T. *Children in Families*. Statistics Canada Catalogue 98-810, p. 99.
NOTE[1]: Families with income below the "low income cut-offs" are families "in poverty." The term "low income cut offs" replaces the earlier phrase "poverty lines" in the data compiled by the Survey of Consumer Finance (CIED, 1979).

have the highest percentage of families with low incomes.

Ethnicity, or distinctive cultural and social heritages of native and immigrant groups, is another way the family varies in Canada. Multi-culturalism is not merely a numerical fact, but such a highly touted feature of the society that it constitutes an ideology. In 1971, almost three out of four Canadian families had heads whose origins were either British (45 percent) or French (27 percent). The remaining 28 percent were fragmented into fourteen ethnic categories; one of which, "all others," included in turn twelve additional groups. The dualism resulting from original North American settlements in New France and New England has been important. At the same time, the influence of the British extends far beyond their numerical superiority. It seems reasonable, though, that there should be at least as many patterns of family life in Canada as there are ethnic groups.

It is fascinating and perhaps novel that within Canada can be found much of the diversity known to exist in human families throughout the world's history, although the impact of this diversity on the general outlines of the Canadian family is minor (Ishwaran, 1971; Larson, 1976; Wakil, 1975). Let us briefly examine here the range of variety in three areas: mate selection (family formation), marriage interaction, and socialization of children.

Mate Selection

Mate selection can be left up to the man and woman involved (participant choice), or it can be taken entirely out of the couple's hands (arranged, by family or community elders), or it can be a combination of the two. In North America arranged marriages were the rule for the original inhabitants (i.e., Inuit and Indian), but among the European settlers in the New World the common practice became for individuals to contract their own marriages. Marriage was often a matter of necessity and convenience for individuals who made their own choices in role terms; the man would seek a wife as helpmate and mother for his children, and the women would look for a protector and a father for her children. The tradition that developed was self-selection. As social conditions became more settled, the pattern changed only slightly in order to accommodate a concept of romantic love and desired personality factors as important factors in the choice.

Arranged marriage, then, has never been a Canadian tradition, although it was the ideal way for forming families for some Canadian groups. The Kwakiutl Indians of British Columbia are an example. In one village studied in 1970, 60 percent of those above the age of thirty-five had had their marriages arranged; under the age of thirty-five, no one had. Netsilik Inuit marriages were traditionally arranged at the time of the child's birth; today this practice is rare.

But even if the family does not attempt to control completely who marries whom, it does try to restrict the choices of the young persons. Perhaps the Hutterites are the best example in Canada. The first marriage rule, religious and subgroup **endogamy**, and the second one, colony **exogamy**, account in large part for the difference between marriage in this group and among English and French urban residents. According to the first rule, individuals should not marry non-Hutterites; they should marry within the Hutterite religious group (*Leut*). Within the *Leut*, however, a woman from one colony is expected to marry a man from another colony, as in the following description of a Hutterite wedding (Hostetler and Huntington, 1967):

The couple had known each other for at least five years, but had only visited one another about five or six times. The bride had never been to the groom's colony. . . . The young man asked his parents if he could be married; then he asked the first preacher who, in turn, asked the council (the governing body of the colony). He was given consent of his colony and a letter to the preacher of the girl's colony. . . . Her parents gave their consent and then asked their daughter if she accepted the young man.

In general, a high degree of control over mate selection is associated with ethnic groups in which organized religion or religious beliefs play an important part in the family life. Jews are another group in Canada to whom religious endogamy is important and for whom preservation of the in-group, even in urban settings, is crucial (Latowsky, 1971).

The one thing parents fear more than anything else is the marriage of their children to non-Jews. To forestall this, parents tend to favor residence in a predominantly Jewish neighborhood or, for the more liberal [sic] oriented, an area that has "at least a sprinkling of Jews," to increase the probability of their children meeting and marrying fellow Jews. One mother living in a predominantly non-Jewish area became concerned when her teen-age daughter began interdating exclusively and reports that the family has since moved back into the ghetto . . . so that she [her daughter] can at least meet some Jewish boys.

This kind of unobtrusive and subtle direction can be observed for other strongly religious groups.

For most Canadians, however, the choice is more open to the preferences of the young persons themselves. At the extreme, couples even have the option of marrying first and informing parents after the fact. Indeed, secrecy is often the rule with those who are cohabiting instead of legally marrying. More women than men fail to inform their parents about their premarital heterosexual cohabiting arrangements, but even a significant number of males are reluctant to do so. With more young persons living away from home, however, in university residences or in their own apartments in anonymous areas of urban centers, this alteration in dating patterns becomes increasingly possible.

In no segment of Canadian society is there random choice, or an absence of social criteria that enter into the question of who marries whom. Upper-middle-class suburban parents, for example, who subscribe to the romantic view that their children's marriages ought to be founded on love, sympathy, compatibility, and personality, manage nonetheless to launch their offspring into marriages that are not notably different from those that might have been arranged in a caste system based on race, creed, color, and money. Whereas such parents no longer closely supervise and advise their young people, they have indeed influenced them to observe the informal norms of endogamy.

Marriage Interaction

Increasing numbers of Canadian women and men view marriage as an equal partnership. This does not mean that the view is the majority one, or that there are no other socially shared notions of what the best arrangements between spouses should be. Nor does it

Couples think there should be more sharing, but they are far from achieving it. One task men like to help out with is cooking. (*Miller Services*)

follow that couples who believe in equality are therefore necessarily able to achieve it.

Throughout a good deal of written history, societies have believed that a husband has title to his wife, exactly as he did to a purchased slave. The present marriage contract, the terms of which are typically unknown to the contracting parties (an ignorance applicable to no other legal contract), derives from English Common Law under which the husband and wife were merged into *one* legal identity, that of the husband. Under this common law doctrine, called *coverture*, a married woman was a legal nonperson. She gave up control of her property to her husband, and she could not make a contract in her own name. If she earned money, it went to him; if they separated, the children were his; if she committed a criminal act in his presence, he was held responsible.

A woman therefore was considered to be property and as such could legally control none of her own. Most of the legal barriers to wives owning property were removed by the passage of the Married Women's Property Acts in England in the nineteenth century. They affected Canadian women as well, and in this century the provinces enacted additional laws which have further changed the status of married women. But a hundred years later, the basic legal obligations between husbands and wives are still determined by English Common Law.

The marriage contract is a statement of property rights, and in many ways the law assumes the central concept of the wife as a chattel to her husband. She is expected to live where the husband decides, or he can charge her with desertion. He is legally responsible for debts she incurs in order to provide herself and their children with the essentials, and it is therefore difficult to establish credit in her name. She cannot charge her husband with rape if he forces her to have sexual relations with him. The courts consider it a "reversal of normal roles" for a wife to be the major wage-earner. Thus the law is one of the restraints "upon a man wishing to share equal happiness with his wife," which W. Thompson deplored in his 1827 "Appeal to One-Half of the Human Race."

Despite anachronisms in some features of the marriage law, however, no group in Canada literally upholds the idea of wife-as-property, or the extremes of the patriarchial ideal. True, several religious groups do hold to the notion of the husband-father as the patriarch within the nuclear-family unit. Calvinist Dutch farm families, for example, cling to their official ideology of the father as the "pastor" of the family and "lord" of the home. Yet in two-thirds of these families both parents were found to mete out punishment to the children. Similarly, the Hutterites invest the husband with full authority, which is also moderated in actuality. In working-class urban families, too, the idealized authoritarian role of the father is a far cry from reality.

In contrast to the wife-as-property concept, a less traditional but increasingly frequent pattern in Canadian society is that of the wife-as-complement. In it the wife can expect more than the satisfaction of minimal needs. She expects companionship during leisure time, communication, and understanding; she expects to be her husband's friend and not his chattel. The Jewish upper-middle-class urban family appears to be a good example here. Because of the wife's traditional role in keeping Jewish values alive in the home, her contemporary role includes assisting her husband's career by entertaining and involving herself in community activities. The wife-as-complement is unlikely to be in the labor force herself, and although she can disagree with her husband and prevail, her husband, as the provider, possesses more resources and retains more authority.

A variation of the wife-as-complement is the wife-as-junior-partner, the status more likely to be ascribed to wives in the labor force. Because most wives enter the labor force to supply their families with extra money, and because their jobs are therefore not as critical to family survival as are their husbands', they have a subordinate position in decision-making. One indication of this quasi-egalitarian status, touched on earlier, is that they add their labor-force job to their homemaking duties. Urban working-class wives are perhaps most typical, although farm wives, in Saskatchewan for example, may also be junior partners to their husbands. In such a situation, the wife and husband are jointly involved in making a success of the family farm enterprise, with the eventual help of

their adult children and spouses residing close by. The women are expected to help the men in the fields and in other farm jobs, but the line is seldom crossed the other way. Farm men and ranchers do not cook or do housework unless their wives are incapacitated.

The wife-as-equal is probably rare. As yet no descriptions of this status situation have been published for Canada. The most likely conditions under which this equality would be achieved include an urban residence (or separate residences), a marriage in which both partners are young and well educated, and in which both have careers as professionals or high level managers. The marriage would probably be childfree, and the partners at least middle class but probably higher.

The spousal arrangement in the average Canadian family of British or French origin, then, is somewhere between wife-as-complement and wife-as-junior partner. Furthermore, there is probably very little difference between the French and British when sample groups are controlled for rural-urban residence and social class.

Socialization of Children

A tension exists between the two extremes of the child-socialization dimension discussed earlier, orderly replacement and continuous redefinition of the culture. How involved are families of various categories in passing on to the next generation the beliefs and behavior systems of their group? Orderly replacement is more likely to be the goal of socialization in rural and religiously based families, or in those whose ethnic group maintains viable subcultural oganizations. Some indicators of success at orderly replacement are the survival of language and unique traditions, the persistence of positive attitudes toward traditional life-styles, and the ability to isolate the young from nonfamily influence or provide them with extra-familial reinforcements of values taught in the home.

Perhaps French-Canadian families have been the most effective in the endeavor to maintain a cultural identity, insofar as the French have suffered the least loss of language in a nation where English speakers are the majority. The French, along with Jews and

Ukrainians, have also subscribed more heartily than have some subgroups to the importance of the mother's role in the early years of child care. Jewish women, as representative of urban groups, and Ukrainian women, more rural, have been reluctant to enter the labor force while there are children in the home. On the other hand, women of Japanese origin, perhaps because of a more secular orientation, appear less affected by the presence of children in their decision to take outside employment.

Farm families also seem to be effective in instilling in children the desire to continue in their parents' way of life. Even though employment opportunities are usually greater in the cities, the home farm or ranch in southwestern Saskatchewan also exerts a strong pull. Hutterites of German origin constitute a similar case; their communal farm life is reproduced with only slight variation in the next generation.

By the same token, emphasis on the sanctity of family life has helped mold a familistic, or collective, orientation among French Canadians, which has tended to be seen as somewhat inimical to success in the business world. It is not certain, however, that family and business are incompatible. Family reputation and loyalty, for example, appear to be main motivations for educational striving among many recently arrived minority groups in Canada, including Greeks and Italians, as well as Chinese and other non-Europeans. The family in these groups is seen as mediating between the individual and the other institutions in the new society.

FAMILY INCONSISTENCIES AND PROBLEMS

No family system is entirely coherent or logical. Although the tendency is for the various rules and behaviors to complement each other and to make sense in the overall pattern which constitutes the family as an institution in society, some aspects of the family will always appear to be out of place. There are many reasons for this. For one, humans are never completely rational and consistent in their beliefs and actions.

Furthermore, the moral order is constantly in the process of being collectively revised as social conditions change. And perhaps most importantly, the family is a type of control mechanism. Groups with more resources are better able to make the rules, abide by and enforce them, and mold their own lives to them or change them to suit their life-style. Powerless and marginal persons or groups (like working-class families) have more difficulty living up to family ideals and standards.

Striking incongruities in our family system can be observed in the issues of inequality between the genders, inadequate child-care provisions, divorce law and procedures, and family violence. Let us look briefly at the first two issues and in greater detail at the latter two. Finally, we will discuss how they are related among themselves and to social class distinctions in Canada.

Spousal Inequalities

There is a basic inconsistency in the Canadian view of the family. On the one hand, the family is seen as the single remaining sanctuary in mass society where persons can find meaning and participate fully as individuals. On the other hand, the person whose task is to minister to the needs of the family members and maintain the household is isolated, marginal, and devalued. As you saw in Chapter 4, Canadians recognize the importance of the home and the necessity for someone to keep it going, yet they give no tangible reward for the labor of the wife. The occupational hazards of the full-time homemaker are evident in the case of the wife who is divorced after years of contributing to the family's well-being, but who finds that these services have not been recognized in the divorce settlement as the equivalent of her husband's contribution. Widows are in the same position. Of women older than seventy years of age 70 percent have only government pensions and allowances to live on, whereas this is the case for only 40 percent of men. Never having been in the labor force and not eligible for their own or their husband's pension payments, widows are among the poorest persons in Canada.

The images of Greta Garbo and John Gilbert bespeak romance and surrender. Romance is an important prelude to most Canadian marriages, but after it fades, the marriage partners must decide what they rightfully can demand of and expect from each other.

Child Care

It is inconsistent, moreover, or at least extremely awkward, that with the increasing number of families that depend on income from both parents, society has not solved the problem of no one being at home to look after the children. Almost one out of five married women with children under the age of six years works outside of the home full-time, and the figure for women with children over six years is one in four (see Table 11-3). Because nuclear-family households with children seldom have more than one or two adults present,

during the past ten years an increasing number of groups and individuals have begun to perceive day care as one of the necessary support services to promote and strengthen family well-being. But though day-care centers in Canada increased from about 700 in 1971 to almost 2000 by 1977, providing for over 81 000 children, only a very small percentage of all children of employed mothers are presently cared for outside their own home or someone else's. Table 11-3 shows the common belief to be incorrect that maternal employment outside the home has resulted in children being shunted in great numbers into day-care centers.

TABLE 11-3.   CHILDREN REGISTERED IN DAY CARE

Age in Children	Total Children in Day Care	Total Children with Mothers in Labor Force[1]	Percentage of Children in Day Care
Under 3	15,237	291,000	5.23
3 to 5	58,626	365,000	16.06
6 and over	7,788	2,108,000	.36

SOURCE: *Status of Day Care in Canada*, 1977. National Day-Care Information Centre. Social Service Programs Branch. Ministry of National Health and Welfare.
NOTE: These figures, as of March 1977, were estimated by the Women's Bureau, Labour Canada.

Individual couples are left to themselves to solve the dilemma of how to provide both financial well-being and supervision for their youngsters. Some couples decide to remain childless. In some families, the wife is employed part-time, and the husband helps at home. Others have the wife taking time out from the labor force when the children are very small and returning to employment when they reach school age. Still others rely on unsupervised family day care, the main form all across the country. Should their solutions misfire, parents must shoulder the blame for failing their children. Whether such societal solutions will emerge in this country as Kamerman (1980) reports have been institutionalized by most European countries is unknown. It is clear, however, that child-care provisions that support the family and make it stronger are most inadequate in Canada. Facilities are available, but parents often worry about their quality. Those who suffer directly are the children whose needs are left unmet. Indirectly, society pays for such inattention in its rates of suicide, mental illness, crime, alcohol and other drug abuse.

Divorce

Divorce presents several more inconsistencies. Before discussing them, let us consider some facts.

Divorce rates in Canada have soared between 1961, when they were 1.67 per 1000 married women, and 1979 when they reached 10.5 per 1000 married women. As Figure 11-2 shows, the upward trend began the year following the liberalization of the Divorce Act in 1968. It has continued to increase ever since, although at a smaller change in rate.

It is difficult to explain what causes divorce rates to rise as they have. Certainly, a change in the grounds for divorce made it easier for persons who were unhappy to divorce. Fewer people can divorce if adultery is the only legal grounds, as it was prior to 1968. More acceptable and more nearly accurate grounds for divorce, such as mental and physical cruelty and marriage breakdown, make it more accessible. In addition to relaxation of divorce laws, Ambert (1980) cites many other societal factors. Among them are reduced religious influence, a secularized view of marriage, increased independence of individuals from families, the emancipation of women, a lack of psychological emancipation of men, increased longevity of both spouses, and a surfeit of choices available to individuals. Such changes create a climate in which divorce has become more socially acceptable and more feasible as an alternative to an unhappy marriage.

When one seeks the people most likely to divorce, however, a different set of causes or motives emerges. Marriages at greatest risk are those in which are found youthful spouses and premarital pregnancies, brief acquaintances, unhappiness in the marriages of the spouses' parents, dissimilarity of backgrounds, family disapproval, alcoholism, mental problems (especially for husbands), total career immersion, problems of communication, sexual problems, adultery, the effect of children, and the emotional immaturity of the couple.

In 1979 the median duration of all marriages at the time of divorce was ten years, meaning that half of all divorces were finalized before the couples had been married ten years. On the average, divorce occurred even earlier if the couple had been married when the woman was still a teenager.

Remarriage has become a part of the love-and-marriage scene in Canada. Most divorced persons remarry fairly soon after the divorce (although, as you'll recall from Chapter 4, a higher percentage of

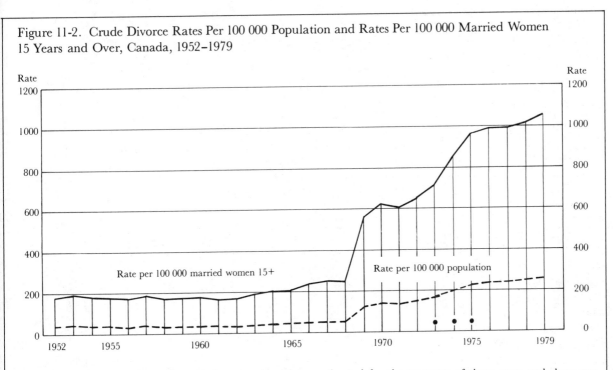

Figure 11-2. Crude Divorce Rates Per 100 000 Population and Rates Per 100 000 Married Women 15 Years and Over, Canada, 1952–1979

• Corresponding populations of married women have been estimated for the purposes of these rates and these are subject to revision when official estimates are available.

SOURCE: Vital Statistics Vol. II. Marriages and Divorces 1979. Statistics Canada, Catalogue 84-205.

men than women remarry). By 1979, 14 percent of all brides had been previously married and divorced. The change from marriage for life to an increasingly frequent pattern of marriage, divorce, and remarriage is the switch from lifetime monogamy to **serial monogamy**. The pattern is also sometimes referred to as serial polygamy.

Comparing the 1978 and 1979 Canadian crude divorce rates with recent rates in 25 other countries, only three others are higher, while 14 are considerably lower. The higher ones are the United States, the Soviet Union, and Australia. Four countries have rates similar to Canada's: Denmark, Hungary, Sweden, and the United Kingdom. That Canadian statistics present a more traditional pattern than do those of the United States is probably due to Canadian couples being

slightly older at the time of the first marriage and experiencing fewer divorces and consequently fewer remarriages (remarriages tend to be less stable). These differences, in turn, probably stem from the religious and ethnic compositions of the two countries, particularly the large French-Catholic element in Canada.

Even with a relatively high divorce rate, in the United States most marriages continue to be lifelong commitments. A statistic of one out of three marriages ending in divorce means that two out of three, or 67 percent, will be terminated by the death of one of the spouses. Couples who are entering a first marriage for both the bride and the groom have an even lesser risk of divorce, because 84 percent of such marriages last until the death of one of them.

Public opinion regarding whether there should be

Figure 11-3.   Number of Lone-Parent Families, by Marital Status of Head, Canada, 1951-1976

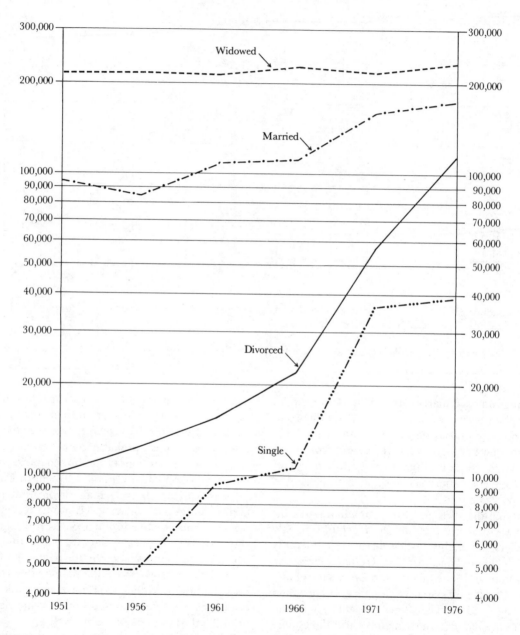

SOURCE: Wargon, Sylvia T. *Children in Canadian Families*. Statistics Canada, Catalogue 98-810, p. 68.

concern about the frequency of divorce today does not seem to have crystallized. There is a segment of the population that views a divorce rate of ten per 1000 marriages in existence with alarm. On the other hand, Ambert probably has put her finger on the attitude of the great majority when she says:

It is now widely accepted in specialist's circles, and even among laypersons, that an unhappy marriage can be more detrimental than divorce, both to adults and to children. . . . It is also being recognized that divorce can be viewed as a beginning rather than an ending; the beginning of a new life, often a much better life.

It seems unlikely at this point that the public will favor a tightening of divorce laws in order to reduce the incidence. In fact, many are aware of incongruities in the reformed law.

It is inconsistent to require that the couple enter marriage in love, and then insist that the loss of love is insufficient reason to terminate that marriage. The present divorce process involves adversary procedures that pit the spouses against each other. An extensive body of opinion in law, medicine, and the social and behavioral sciences asserts that legal procedures wherein one spouse must be found guilty or at fault and the other blameless are inappropriate to contemporary marriage. Although reform of federal divorce law in 1968 improved the situation, even the grounds of separation for three years is not the same as a couple's mutual agreement that it is in their best interests and those of the children for their marriage to be dissolved. In the words of the Law Reform Commission of Canada (1975):

. . . the present procedures in divorce seems unduly formal, sometimes involved, and always expensive. It is not conducive to a therapeutic or conciliatory approach and often frustrates the possibility of preserving the marriage or resolving collateral issues on a reasonable basis acceptable to both spouses. . . . What appears to be necessary is . . . to eliminate the fault concepts. . . .

Canadian advocates of further divorce reform are not recommending the no-fault divorces obtainable in the United States since 1975 in some states, but instead a type of divorce conciliation.

One-Parent Families

As well as making an issue of rising divorce rates, the popular press often focuses attention on the alleged increase in one-parent families. Numerically, solo-parent domestic families have increased, but so have two-parent families. It is correct, however, that the rate of increase for one-parent families is somewhat greater.

As a percentage of all families in existence, the trend for solo-parent families has not changed much since 70 years ago when figures were first made available by the census. It has fluctuated only very slightly around one out of ten families. The smallest percentage of one-parent families was reported in 1956. The relative stability in the percentage figure is due to remarriage and the inherent dynamic in the domestic family cycle. The low point in 1956 undoubtedly represents the time when death rates had declined to a point where marriages were more likely to last until children were grown and divorce was still difficult to obtain.

Figure 11-3 shows the slight increase in the total number of lone-parent families in recent years, and the changes in the marital status of parents heading such families. Thus, in an earlier time the parent was more likely to be widowed or separated (married); now the divorced and never-married (single) occur more frequently than formerly. Figure 11-3 does not show that overall there has been a drop in the number of children residing in one-parent households. The decline is the result of smaller numbers of children per family.

The differential effects on children of voluntary (divorce and separation) versus involuntary (death) marital dissolution is not known. In any event, one-parent families in Canada today appear to be societally tolerated arrangements in which more persons than previously can expect to live at least temporarily, as a child or an adult, sometimes by choice and sometimes not. They may be statistically deviant, but not culturally. They can be found in all societies and in all historical periods, even in those that forbid divorce or stigmatize the family. The stigma may be more harmful to children than the condition.

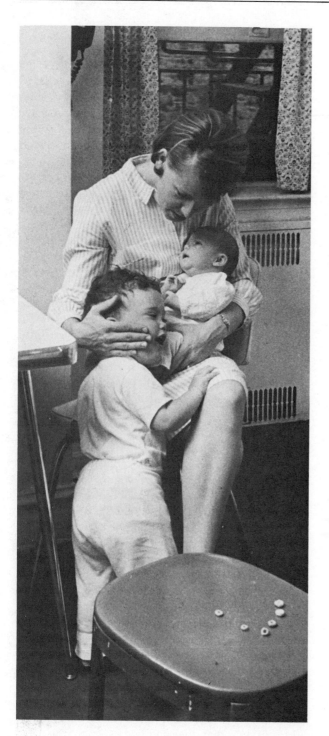

A high proportion of solo-parent families are headed by women whose incomes, on the average, are low. Many live in substandard or subsidized housing. Some share households with other families like theirs or with relatives. (Miller Services)

Concern about the numbers of solo-parent families in our society undoubtedly arises because of three related facts: a high proportion of the heads of such households are women, the average income is much below that of two-parent households, and female heads have been getting younger in recent years. It is too soon to know whether the slight increase noted by Wargon (1979) in younger female heads of families sharing living accommodations with other families and persons is a trend or not.

Family Violence

It is inconsistent that Canadians consider love to be important in marriage and in the parent-child relationship, and at the same time tolerate a high incidence of violence.

Wife Battery. According to Lewis (1982) "family violence" is one of several euphemisms for wife battering, because it is women who are beaten in the vast majority of cases (72 percent). According to the best estimates, one in ten Canadian women experiences violence, physical or psychological, to which she does not consent, expressed toward her by a husband or a live-in lover (MacLeod, 1980). Husband battering also exists, but occurs much less frequently, is generally an act of desperation or retaliation, is not long-term, and seldom results in injuries. Family violence frequently leads to death, as indicated by the figure of 20 percent of Canadian homicides being the result of one spouse killing the other. Almost all these cases are wives murdered by their husbands.

Spousal violence also leads to divorce if the grounds for divorce are any indication. One-third of all divorces in 1979 were granted on the grounds of physical or mental cruelty. The number of cases (20 000), plus the fact that a large proportion of petitioners are women, belie the notion that women are passive about or helpless in their situation. Probably included here are those women who have the resources required to leave a violent husband (which few women have), namely an education or job training, supportive friends or family, and perhaps legal assistance. Wife abuse, incidentally, is not confined to any one group, social class, or geographic region. Middle and upper-class wives may have almost as much difficulty leaving a violent husband as poorer women, because the wife-beater's wife seldom has access to money, even if she herself is employed. Hers is the husband who controls the purse-strings, and, in fact, tries to maintain complete control over her.

As Lewis (1982) points out, most women do not leave marriages capriciously. They have been socialized to keep trying to please their husbands, and their kin who know about the violence of the situation may advise them to make more adjustments in their marriage, especially if the husband is a "good provider." Above all, there is little support for the battered wife from formal agencies or their representatives, such as police, doctors, lawyers, or welfare workers. The idea that the family is a private matter, plus the notion that if a woman is mistreated it must be her own fault, create almost insurmountable barriers for women trying to get help (MacLeod, 1980; Lewis, 1982).

Family violence appears to be part of a larger cycle of violence. That is, there is childhood experience of violence in the histories of spouse abusers, murderers, and child abusers. The facts, however, are more complicated than the popular assumption that growing up in a violent home is what causes an adult to be involved in violence in the family of procreation. In regard to wife abuse, gender differences are found. A relatively small number of battered women come from violent childhood homes; in fact, women who observe violence as children are less likely to be battered. On the other hand, what little is known about their husbands is that a high proportion have been beaten as children. It appears that boys learn violence at home; girls fail to learn how to prevent or avoid it in their later conjugal relationships.

Child Abuse. The extent of child abuse can be estimated, and these estimates depend very much on the definition used. One estimate is that at least 59 500 Canadian children were physically abused by 35 000 parents in 1979, the International Year of The Child (for a description of estimation procedures, see Manitoba Proceedings, 1977). An unknown number of children are neglected or harmed psychologically by their parents. Two other kinds of familial child abuse are sexual abuse and victimization as the result of child-stealing by a parent after divorce. Based on U.S. estimates, in Canada there are annually over 500 cases of father-daughter incest. According to Herman and Hirschman (1977) incest "appears to follow the general pattern of sexual abuse of children in which 92 percent of the victims are females, and 97 percent of the offenders are male." Child-stealing, estimated to involve one child in each 22 divorces (Agopian and Anderson, 1981), does not distinguish its victims by gender. Fathers are more likely to be offenders, probably because custody is less often granted to them by the courts.

Violence toward children in families is not easy to explain. For one, so little is known about incidence and variation from one culture to another, within different historical periods, and by various sectors in society. There can be no doubt of terrible treatment of children in some past times and of laws granting parents enormous power over their children, including death. Child abuse is by no means a recent phenomenon. Attention is drawn to it now because it is inconsistent with our ideals of family life.

A second reason violence toward children cannot be easily explained is because of the many facets or what Gil (1977) has termed "levels of causation." As with divorce, both societal and personal factors can be found. Our attitudes toward children as belonging to their parents (especially to their fathers, who believe they have extensive rights over them), our widespread beliefs that force is a legitimate means for attaining ends, the great amounts of stress and frustration induced in individuals by work situations (for all occupations), and financial needs in our society are only a few of these social factors. The triggering contexts our family-work patterns provide can lead to abuse even with normal parents. Unresolved rage resulting from job frustrations, anger due to unemployment or an ex-spouse's failure to provide support, or from any of a number of pent-up emotions, may lead to loss of control directed toward the most helpless and vulnerable persons there. Added to these conditions, however, is the fact that these very same family contexts are favorable to the development in children of intense intra-psychic conflicts and various forms of psychopathology. Even though it is people in families who commit violence against children, and they are ultimately responsible for what they do, it is societal structures that provide the explanation of how it can happen.

Family Inconsistencies with Other Institutions.

In other parts of this chapter and in the section above on family violence, we have alluded to financial realities as problematic for many families. It is not merely a problem that many domestic families are poor, however. It is indeed frustrating and limiting not to have sufficient resources, whether wages or welfare, in order to keep body and soul together. More to the point, socio-economics are important because they are so pervasive. They determine the ways people and families must organize themselves in order to perform the basic family functions (regulating sex and reproduction and the nurturing and socializing of the young), and at the same time at least minimally maintain the members of the family household. The same is true of the gender structure of our society, which is inextricably bound up with economic institutions and also pervades familial relationships. Social class is not merely a cultural fact for Canadians; it is an existential one. It provides the opportunities for or sets the limits to families achieving the cultural ideals. Wealth (or its lack) and the way families acquire it and use it probably condition family life in Canada today more than any other single factor. Male dominance, as suggested by the earlier discussions of working-class sexual antagonisms and of wife abuse

and incest, is closely linked to ideas of property. Even the plight of one-parent families and the day-care situation is tied up with patterned discrimination against women. Our economic institutions, therefore, provide much of the grist for the inconsistency mill of the family system today.

Basic differences exist between the organization of middle-class and of working-class families, not to mention those in the upper classes. Households are central to the matter, because they are the important economic groups in our society. Middle-class families live more or less in conformity to the conjugal ideal. In terms of households, this means that financially each one is relatively independent of other kin, mainly because income sources are dependable and adequate. Income is provided primarily by the husband's employment, although financial aid from parents and parents-in-law who can afford it is expected in the early years of marriage. While the children are small, one wage earner is frequently sufficient; child-care outside the home is often not even an issue.

Working-class households are maintained in an entirely different manner. It is by means of women-centered networks of malleable domestic units of various kinds (two-parent, one-parent, extended, one-person, etc.) that such families are kept going (Rapp, 1982). By means of these networks, all individuals are provided every manner of service and emotional support needed. The member families care for children of a working sister, telephone and take meals to an elderly uncle living alone nearby, repair a brother-in-law's broken steps, take in for a night a sister-in-law whose husband has beaten her, and put up during a season a young nephew from another city who is working at a temporary job. The women comprising the networks utilize various sources of income, including their men's wages, their own supplements, and welfare and old age security checks. They distribute money *across* households where it is needed and with remarkable economy in order to keep the adults working on their underpaid and unreliable jobs and to keep children fed, clothed, and looked after. It is truly remarkable that many of us, who grew up in families that made these kinds of adaptations to poverty or financial marginality and subsequently escaped, have forgotten how different such situations are from middle-class families. These adaptations are not organized as lineal investments in resources (among grandparents, their adult children, and grandchildren) as in the middle class, but as lateral distributions (among siblings and their spouses and children, etc.). The binding principle of such networks is not spousal companionship, but maternal concern that extends beyond one's own children and household to other kin. As Rapp has concluded:

To achieve a normative family is something many categories of Americans are prevented from doing because of the ways that their households plug into tenuous resource bases. And when normative families are achieved, it is at substantial and differential costs to both men and women.

With policy makers under pressure at present to reduce public funding for programs for the elderly as well as children, there is some danger in sociologists' having discovered the existence of networks of families that fend for themselves even under difficult circumstances. Will the provincial and federal governments exploit these families even further? Family support of the elderly, like day care for children, hardly affects middle-class couples whose parents plan for retirement, invest in private pensions, own paid-up mortgages on their houses, insurance policies and other property. To the women in working-class networks it means added burdens of all kinds, and to the men it spells more opportunities to fail as providers. To the children it means generational tensions, as well as the gender ones they already experience at home.

It is inconsistent to promote an ideology of individualism and conjugalism in family relationships at the same time as the political, economic, and gender structures promote defensive dependency and kinkeeping.

SUMMARY

1. The family, as a social arrangement that normatively ties together the group of people considered to be related to each other by blood or marriage, is the most basic of our institutions. The three functions performed by families in all societies are: controlling sex and regulating reproduction, placing infants and children in the society, and socializing these offspring.

2. Additionally, the family can perform certain other tasks for its members: maintenance, protection, and gratification of personal needs. Family relationships are primary and are characterized, at least ideally, by deep and intense communication, involvement of the total person, and intimacy.

3. Families throughout the world vary considerably in their structure and functioning. There are myriad rules regarding mating, marriage forms, and authority relations; residence of family members; descent and inheritance; and exchange between kin.

4. In the western part of the world generally, and in North America specifically, the family has been undergoing a series of transformations that began even before the Industrial Revolution. Recent changes appear to have accelerated in Canada and the United States, and with modernization they are rapidly spreading to other parts of the world.

5. The Canadian family can be characterized as serially monogamous; highly endogamous in respect to race, religion, and ethnicity; residentially neolocal and nuclear; bilateral in descent; and democratic in authority pattern. Mate selection is by choice of the participants, and kin relations are maintained voluntarily. This family system, the conjugal family, represents the beliefs and behavior patterns of the politically dominant middle-class Anglo group, and is shared with the same groups in the United States, Great Britain, and many northern European nations.

6. In Canadian society, which takes pride in its pluralism, there are also geographical, racial, ethnic, and religious variations in the patterns of family life. Strong pressures toward uniformity, however, are evidenced in the tendency for convergence between French and English, and rural and urban patterns.

7. There are many incongruities in our family system, including marital inequalities, inadequate child-care, outmoded divorce laws and procedures, and various forms of violence taking place within families. Basic differences exist in the organization of middle-class and working-class families, stemming from the tenuous resource base of the latter and perpetuated by institutionalized gender differences in property concepts, wages, and financial independence.

8. Although there is much discussion of the decline in family stability and the rise of alternatives to family arrangements, there is also every indication that the family as an institution will persist. It had its origins in our humanity and will end when the species does. The particular present form, however, the conjugal family system, is another matter. There is little doubt that this system is highly dependent upon the supports that can be extended to it by other societal groups and institutions, some of which have not yet emerged in the mass society. It is also certain that the present form continues to evolve. The family's future depends much on the past.

GLOSSARY

Biosocial unit. Reproductive group consisting of relations between the mates, the female and offspring, and the male and offspring. It is the basis for family groups.

Conflict perspective on the family. Approach to understanding and explaining all social arrangements, including the family, as determined by capitalism as a mode of production in the society which creates antagonism between groups or categories.

Conjugal family. One name for the contemporary family institution which has as its center monogamous marriage and includes bilateral descent and neolocal nuclear households tied together in a wider network of kin, all supported by an ideology of affection, individualism and choice, and privacy.

Endogamy. Formal and informal rules that require marriage within one's group or community.

Exogamy. Formal and informal rules that require marriage outside one's group or community.

Extended family household. Household comprised of a nuclear family plus other relatives. It may consist of three generations, or collaterals like siblings, or polygamous marriages, or all of these ways of extension.

Family. *A* family refers to any group of people considered to be related to each other by blood (genetically) or marriage. Such persons are one's "kin." *The* family refers to the social arrangements which tie together members of the family group, normatively establishing the relationships between the persons filling various positions, and defining boundaries, rights, and duties.

Family household. The related persons who reside together or share a household.

Gender roles. Culturally defined positions and activities that are considered gender-appropriate within the family (or society).

Kinship. System in which are spelled out the persons who are considered to be related either by birth or marriage or both, and the expected rights and obligations between them.

Legalistic family. Traditional family system in western society in which roles were clearly defined and family members were tied together by obligations or duties which were legitimated by religious codes. "Legal" refers not to government statutes, but to the moral standards, or social norms, as regulatory.

Marriage. Socially approved and relatively permanent heterosexual relationship, in which are designated, more or less explicitly, reciprocal rights and obligations between spouses and between them and their children.

Nuclear-family household. Household in which resides the family group of a wife and her husband and their unmarried children, or alternately, a single parent and dependent children, or a heterosexual couple.

Patriarchy. Family arrangement in which only the males (father, husband, sons) have legitimate power or authority vested in their positions.

Primary relatives. Those kin who are one degree removed from a person genealogically. They include your mother and father, brothers and sisters, daughters and sons, and spouse. Secondary and tertiary relatives are more distantly related.

Serial monogamy. Societally accepted pattern of more than one spouse in a person's lifetime, as long as that person is married to only one spouse at a time; that is, it requires divorce and remarriage. Sometimes referred to as "serial polygamy."

Socialization. Process whereby individuals learn to control their biological drives, are taught the norms and values of society, and acquire an identity or self-concept.

Structural functionalist perspective on the family. Theoretical framework which provides a basis for organizing and explaining facts about the family by assuming that the family institution, with its universal functions, is more or less integrated with other social arrangements and changes as they are modified.

Symbolic interactionist perspective on the family. Theoretical framework which organizes and explains facts about the family by viewing family groups as two or more persons communicating with each other in order to arrive at shared meanings of their experiences.

FURTHER READING

Armstrong, Pat, and Hugh Armstrong. *The Double Ghetto: Canadian Women and Their Segregated Work.* Toronto: McClelland and Stewart, 1978. One of the best documented theoretical discussions of the relationships between the two segments of labor, the home and the rationalized work place, by gender.

Irving, Howard. *The Family Myth: A Study of Relationships Between Married Couples and Their Parents.* Toronto: Copp-Clark, 1972. A study of Toronto social agency families which demonstrates that the interaction of married couples and their parents is not part of a problem, but actually a potential strength upon which the couple and the social worker can build.

Johnson, Laura C., and Janice Dineen. *The Kin Trade: The Day Care Crisis in Canada.* Toronto: McGraw-Hill Ryerson, Limited, 1981. An examination of private day care in Canada and an assessment of it in terms of the goal of a quality day care place for ever child who needs one.

Luxton, Meg. *More Than a Labour of Love: Three Generations of Women's Work in the Home.* Toronto: Women's Press, 1980. A case study of life in working-class families at three points in time in a northern community, depicting women's domestic work in relationship to husbands and children.

MacLeod, Linda. *Wife Battering in Canada: The Vicious Circle.* Hull, Quebec: Canadian Government Publishing Centre, 1980. Based on materials obtained from interviews with women in shelters across Canada, a picture is drawn of the conditions in which family violence occurs and is institutionalized.

Ramu, G.N. (ed.). *Courtship, Marriage, and Family in Canada.* Toronto: Macmillan, 1979. Essays by seven contributors identity and synthesize concepts and research findings for such issues as ethnic perspectives, socialization for gender roles, divorce and remarriage, and non-traditional family and marriage in the Canadian family.

CHAPTER 12
SOCIOLOGY AND RELIGION
REGINALD W. BIBBY

Religion has been present in virtually every society since the beginning of time. To be sure, its influence has varied with culture and century. In different places and in different eras, religion has known both its dark and golden ages. Moreover, changes such as the rise of rationalism and the advent of modern science and technology have led many observers to predict its demise. Yet religion lives on into the present, embraced by at least a minority in all cultures. Consequently, social scientists have given considerable attention to religion.

Sociology, as discussed in chapters 1 and 17, uses the scientific method of investigation to study social life. In doing so, it seeks to understand reality by relying on what we perceive through our senses, on perceptions that are empirical and can be verified. Sociologists can thus discover patterns of behavior and develop theories to explain these patterns. Religion, on the other hand, has traditionally asserted that the world we know through the senses is just part of a greater reality which – because of the clear limitations of perception – can be known only through faith. Historian Arnold Toynbee (quoted in Cogley, 1968) noted:

> The world is not limited to that part of it which is accessible to the human senses and which can therefore be studied scientifically. . . . The key to a full understanding of this part [may] lie in that other part of the world which is not accessible in this way.

Science and religion, therefore, represent two different approaches to knowledge. In their pure form they are compatible. Science deals with the perceivable. Religion with the non-perceivable. Science, and sociology, then, are unable to make statements about the faith claims of religion – for example, that there is a God or that God is the source of events or ideas. These are supernatural claims that cannot be resolved by science. Conversely, as Durkheim (1965) pointed out, religion "can affirm nothing that [science] denies, deny nothing that it affirms." Conflict between the two arises only when they invade each other's territory, such as when people believing in a literal Biblical account of creation want equal time in the science classroom with the proponents of evolution.

Sociology's focus is on religion's social component. People hold beliefs, worship together, possess attitudes, relate to others, vary in terms of their mental health, and display a wide variety of life-styles and social characteristics. While sociology cannot pass judgment on the truth of religious claims, it can explore questions relating to the social aspects of those claims – who believes what, the relationship between individual commitment and group support, the personal and societal factors that influence the inclination to be religious, and the impact that religious commitment has on one's attitudes and behavior. As Weber (1964) put it: "The essence of religion is not even our concern, as we make it our task to study the conditions and effects of a particular type of social behaviour."

What is important for our purposes is not whether religious beliefs are true, but rather that they are presumed to be true, and therefore have potential consequences for individual and social life.

THEORETICAL TRADITIONS

Much of the work done in the sociology of religion has been influenced by the approaches taken by three individuals: Karl Marx, Emile Durkheim, and Max Weber.

Marx and Conflict

Marx (1970) asserted that "Man makes religion; religion does not make man" and argued that man has "found only his own reflection in the fantastic reality of heaven, where he sought a supernatural being." This human creation, Marx felt, compensated the deprived and represented "the self-consciousness and self-esteem of a man who has either not yet gained himself or has lost himself again."

Central to Marx's thought on religion is the belief that religion serves to hold in check the explosive tensions of a society. Aligned with the interests of the dominant few, religion soothes the exploited majority like an anesthetic – "the opium of the people" (1970) – blinding them to the inequalities at hand and bottling up their creative energies. Consequently, its use by the masses is encouraged as a subtle tool in the process of economic exploitation.

Marx, therefore, saw religion as an inadequate salve for a sick society. When the sickness is remedied, there will be no need for the salve.

Marx accordingly viewed his criticism of religion as an attempt to show people the chain that was binding them, in order that they could remove it. To criticize religion was to enable an individual to think, act, and fashion his or her reality as one who has lost illusions and regained reason.

Yet so intertwined are society and religion that attacks on religion are often attacks on society. Marx pointed out, for example, that the attacks on feudalism were above all attacks on the church, because revolutionary social and political doctrines were simultaneously theological heresies (Marx, 1964).

Durkheim and Collectivity

Durkheim was an inheritor of nineteenth century positivism, which held that the scientific study of society – in contrast to a preoccupation with religious or philosophical speculation – would produce an understanding of social life that would rival the achievements of the natural sciences. The son of a Jewish rabbi and raised in a Catholic educational tradition, Durkheim ended up an atheist and anticleric. His work is covered in detail in Chapter 1.

In *The Elementary Forms of the Religious Life*, Durkheim (1965) argued that religion has a social origin. Through living in community, people come to share common sentiments with the result that a **collective conscience**

"So much for . . . Christianity"

The social principles of Christianity justified the slavery of Antiquity, glorified the serfdom of the Middle Ages and equally know, when necessary, how to defend the oppression of the proletariat, although they make a pitiful face over it.

The social principles of Christianity preach the necessity of a ruling and oppressed class, and all they have for the latter is the pious wish the former will be charitable.

The social principles of Christianity transfer . . . all infamies to heaven and thus justify the further existence of those infamies on earth.

The social principles of Christianity declare all vile acts of the oppressors against the oppressed to be either the just punishment of original sin and other sins or trials that the Lord in his infinite wisdom imposes on those redeemed.

So much for the social principles of Christianity.

Source:

Marx, Karl, and Friedrich Engels. *On Religion.* New York: Schocken Books 1964, p. 83.

---

is formed. It is experienced by each member, yet is far greater than merely the sum of the individual consciences. When individuals have the religious feeling of standing before a higher power, they are in fact in the presence of a greater reality. This reality is not a supernatural being, however, but rather the collective conscience of society. So it is that as humans experience society they conceptualize the idea of "God;" yet, in actuality, God is no more than a symbol for society.

This alleged experience of the supernatural is accompanied by a dual classification of all things into **profane or sacred**. In Christianity, for example, sacred objects have included the cross, the Bible, and holy water. Religious beliefs articulate the nature of the sacred and its symbols, while religious rites are developed as rules of conduct prescribing how men and women should act in the presence of the sacred.

Since all societies feel the need to uphold and reaffirm their collective sentiments, societal members come together as a church. According to Durkheim: "The idea of religion is inseparable from that of the church," because it is "an eminently collective thing" (1965). Even when religion seems to be entirely within the individual conscience, society is still the source that nourishes it. Besides meeting needs at the individual level, claims Durkheim, religion creates and reinforces social solidarity. Collective life is thus seen as both the source and the product of religion.

Accordingly, Durkheim defines religion as "a unified system of beliefs and practices relative to sacred things . . . which unite into one single moral community called a church, all those who adhere to them" (1965).

For Durkheim, religious thought and scientific thought are closely related. Religion, like science, tries to take the realities of nature, man, and society and translate them into intelligible language. Yet while both pursue the same end, scientific thought is a more perfect form than religious thought.

In 1922, Durkheim observed that the times were characterized by "moral mediocrity." He readily acknowledged the decline of traditional Christianity. Unlike Comte, however, Durkheim did not predict the end of religion. Although the forms of expression might change, the social impetus that gives rise to religion will remain, and with it religion. Likewise, Durkheim contended that there will always be a place for religious explanations. Science is fragmentary and incomplete, he wrote, advancing too slowly for impatient people. Religion will therefore continue to have an important role in explanations.

Weber and Ideas

Weber was trained in law and economics. As we saw in Chapter 1, his interest in the origin and nature of modern capitalism led him into extensive debate with Marx and stimulated much of his work in the sociology of religion. Weber did not concern himself with the question of whether or not religion is ultimately true or false. Rather, he recognized that it has a social dimension which can be studied according to its nature and relationship to the rest of life. Apart from its supernatural emphasis, Weber maintained that religion is largely oriented toward *this* world. As a result, he argued that religious behavior and thought must not be set apart from the range of everyday conduct. The term **Protestant ethic** is commonly associated with Weber, stressing as it does the importance of work performed well.

In *The Protestant Ethics and the Spirit of Capitalism* (1958) for example, Weber examined the possibility that the moral tone characterizing capitalism in the western world can be traced back to the influence of the Protestant Reformation. He stated in his introduction, "The following study may thus perhaps in a modest way form a contribution to the understanding of the manner in which ideas become effective forces in history."

Similar to early University of Chicago symbolic interactionists, such as W.I. Thomas and George Herbert Mead, Weber maintained that ideas, regardless of whether they are objectively true or false, represent one's definition of reality. Consequently, they have the potential to influence behavior. In Thomas' famous phrase, "If we define things as real, they are real in their consequences."

Accordingly, Weber emphasized the need for interpreting action through understanding the motives of the actor (*Verstehen*). Such an awareness is to be sought, he said, through placing oneself in the roles of those being studied.

Weber took religion seriously as a factor that can influence the rest of life. He noted that ideas, regardless of their truth or falsity, may have important consequences on behavior. This is not to say that Weber saw religious ideas as completely independent causal factors. Rather, he recognized that religious ideas are involved in highly complex processes of interaction with many other factors in producing behavior. In analyzing behavior, however, Weber did insist that religious ideas must be considered among such factors.

According to Parsons (in Weber, 1963), Weber early became aware that he needed to study other societies as well in order to take culture into account in examining the influence of religion. After *The Protestant Ethic* in 1905, therefore, Weber embarked on a number of comparative studies of religion which unfortunately

were left incomplete at his death. In *Sociology of Religion* (1963), which was compiled and translated after his death, he noted that god-conceptions are strongly related to the economic, social, and political conditions under which people live. The birth of the gods of light and warmth, rain and earth has been closely related to practical economic needs; heavenly gods ruling the celestial order have been related to the more abstract problems of death and fate. In political conquest the gods of the conquered are fused with the gods of the conqueror, reappearing with revised characteristics. Furthermore, the growth of *monotheism* (belief in one god) is related to goals of political unification.

Beyond the social sources of the gods, Weber dealt with such major themes as religious organization and the relationship between religion and social class. He discussed the function of priests, prophets, and *routinization* (the important process whereby a personal following is transformed into a permanent congregation). Weber further noted that different groups within society vary in their inclination to be religious: the peasants are religious when they are threatened; the nobility find religion beneath their honor; the bureaucrats view religion with personal contempt, while regarding it as a manipulative tool; the solid middle class see it in ethical terms and, to varying degrees, accept it; the artisans freely adopt religion; and the working class supplant it with other ideologies.

Freed from concern with the truth of falsity of religion, Weber's work represents a major step forward from the positivistic approach to religion.

RELIGION: ITS NATURE

In defining religion for social scientific study, we might begin by noting that humans develop systems of meaning to interpret the world. Following Stark and Glock (1968), some systems commonly referred to as "religions" have a supernatural referent, while others do not; the latter could be viewed as human-centered or **humanist perspectives**. The former differ from the latter on one critical point: religion has a concern for life's meaning, while humanist perspectives have a concern for making life meaningful. Humanist Bertrand Russell states this difference well: "I do not think that life in general has any purpose. It just happened. But individual human beings have purposes" (quoted in Cogley 1968).

In short, religious perspectives imply the possibility that our existence has a meaning preceding that which we as humans decide to give to it. In contrast, humanist perspectives play down the search for the meaning of existence in favor of a new concern for making existence meaningful. If life has meaning beyond that which we assign to it, that meaning lies with some supernatural or trans-empirical reality; the dismissal of a trans-empirical referent indicates a change in the questions being asked.

Religion, then, for our purposes, can be defined as a system with a supernatural referent which is used to address life's meaning. Humanist perspectives, on the other hand, are empirically-based systems used to make life meaningful. This chapter focuses upon the former.

Personal Religiosity

Individuals obviously vary in their levels of religious commitment or religiosity, and a major issue in the scientific study of religion is how to define and measure **personal religiosity**. The hurdle is a most important one, for until we can first specify what constitutes religiousness, we cannot proceed to examine the characteristics of the religious – namely, the sources and the consequences of the commitment of religious people.

Most of the early empirical work in the field used one of three basic indicators to determine religiosity: affiliation, membership, or church attendance. One early analysis, Lenski's (1961), for example, featured differences in areas like economic and educational attainment by Protestant, Catholic, and Jewish categories. It should be apparent, however, that knowing someone is a Protestant tells us very little about the person's actual commitment to the Christian faith. Categories such as Mennonite or Hutterite have similar limitations as commitment indicators. In these two cases, religiosity versus ethnic affiliation has to be demonstrated. In the same way, church members may be active or inactive, committed or uncommitted. And

church attendance, while indicative of religious group participation, has the disadvantage of excluding people who could – by our definition – be very devout yet not active in religious organizations.

In recent years, therefore, social scientists have been inclined to view religious commitment as many-faceted or multi-dimensional. Glock and Stark's proposed dimensions may offer the best scheme for analyzing religiosity without introducing a church involvement or Christian theological bias. Briefly, they contend that while the religions of the world vary greatly in the details of their expression, considerable consensus exists among them as to the more general ways in which religiosity is manifested. Glock and Stark cite four such manifestations: belief, practice, experience, and knowledge, referring to them as the core **dimensions of religiosity**. Put succinctly, within these dimensions the religiously committed are expected to hold certain beliefs (concerning the supernatural and life after death, for example), engage in specific practices (like prayer and worship), experience the supernatural, and possess a basic knowledge of the content of their faith.

Two major national surveys (Bibby 1975, 1981) offer interesting data on personal religiosity in this country. As Table 12-1 indicates, Canadians exhibit relatively high levels of belief, practice, experience, and knowledge. Indeed, only 4 percent maintain that they do not believe in God, just 13 percent dismiss altogether the possibility of life after death, and only 23 percent claim they never pray. On the surface, late twentieth-century Canadians would therefore seem to be a highly religious people. However, important questions can be raised concerning the depth of this apparent religiosity. When, following the lead of Glock and Stark, we observe the extent to which the people of this country manifest commitment on all four dimensions, only one in five Canadians gives preliminary evidence of being committed to a traditional version of Christianity.

Collective Religiosity

Some might argue that it is possible to be religious without having anything to do with religious organizations such as churches or synagogues. But most social

TABLE 12-1.   RELIGIOUS COMMITMENT, ALONG FOUR DIMENSIONS, CANADA

Dimension			Percentage
BELIEF			
God		"I know God exists, and I have no doubts about it"	46
		"While I have doubts, I feel that I do believe in God"	20
		"I don't believe in a personal God, but I do believe in a higher power of some kind"	16
		"I don't believe in God"	4
		Other[1]	14
Jesus		"Jesus is the Divine Son of God, and I have no doubts about it"	46
		"While I have some doubts, I basically feel that Jesus is Divine"	22
		"I think Jesus was only a man, although an extraordinary one"	16
		Other[2]	16
Life After Death		"There is life after death, with rewards for some people and punishment for others"	19
		"There must be something . . . but I have no idea what it may be like"	40
		"I am unsure whether or not there is life after death"	16
		"Reincarnation expresses my view"	7
		"I don't believe there is life after death"	13
		Other[3]	5
PRACTICE			
Private Prayer		"Regularly, once a day or more"	28
		"Regularly, many times a week"	9
		"Sometimes"/"Only on special occasions"	40
		"Never or hardly ever"	23
EXPERIENCE			
God		"Yes, I'm sure I have"	20
		"Yes, I think I have"	23
		"No"	57
KNOWLEDGE			
Who Denied Jesus	"Peter"		54
	"Judas"		19
	"I don't know"		20
	Other wrong answers		7

SOURCE: Data derived from Bibby, Reginald W., "Project Can80," 1982.
NOTE: [1]"I find myself believing in God some of the time, but not at other times;" "I don't know whether there is a God, and I don't believe there is any way to find out;" and a write-in option.
[2]"I feel that Jesus was a great man and very holy, but I don't feel him to be the Son of God;" "Frankly, I'm not entirely sure there really was such a person as Jesus;" and a write-in option.
[3]"There is life after death, but no punishment;" and a write-in option.

scientists would argue the contrary, that personal religiosity is highly dependent upon **collective religiosity** – group support of some kind. Such dependence is not unique to religion, but rather it stems from a basic fact of life: the ideas we come to have are largely the product of our interaction with other people. However creative we might like to think we are, the fact of the matter is that most of the notions we have about life and ourselves can fairly easily be traced back to the people with whom we have been in communication – family, friends, teachers, authors. The point is that we come to hold few ideas, religious or otherwise, in isolation from others.

Moreover, if we are to retain ideas, we need the continuing endorsement of those ideas by other people – not necessarily a lot of people, but at least a few who think as we do. For example, we could not believe for long that in our society physical beauty begins at forty unless such a minority view was supported by others. To make such a claim would be to invite considerable ridicule, producing a strong temptation on our part to undertake a quick about-face. On the other hand, if

In many nations, church and state are separate. Communism has no place for religion, but politics and religion can be quite similar. Archbishop Jozef Glemp, leader of the Roman Catholic Church in Poland, has made many public statements with political overtones. He and his church are greatly concerned with the condition of Polish society, the union Solidarity, and the activities of the Polish government in suppressing dissent. In Poland, the church has become a forum for and symbol of social justice. (*Canapress*)

we can find others who believe as we do, our viewpoint takes on heightened credibility for us, precisely because we are no longer arguing such a position in isolation. As the group grows, so does our confidence in our minority view. And, who knows, if the group becomes sufficiently powerful – financed generously by not a few well-wishers over forty – it might succeed in convincing the rest of society that physical beauty does indeed begin at forty.

The point is not that we as individuals are incapable of creativity, but rather that the ideas we possess have for the most part been socially imparted and are socially sustained. In this light Durkheim (1965) contends:

. . . it is the church of which he is a member which teaches the individual what these personal gods are, what their function is, and how he should enter into relations with them . . . the idea of religion is inseparable from that of the church.

In complex societies where religious orientations compete with non-religious ones, the existence of social groupings that can transmit and sustain religious ideas is essential to the maintenance of those ideas. And over the centuries, religion has not lacked for such supportive groups.

Church-Sect Typology. Those who have examined religious groups in predominantly Christian settings have historically found themselves dealing with two major kinds of organizations. On the one hand there have been numerically dominant groupings – be they the Roman Catholic Church in medieval Europe, the Church of England, or the so-called mainline denominations in Canada and the United States (Episcopalian, Anglican, Methodist, Presbyterian, and the United Church of Canada). On the other hand, smaller groups that have broken from the dominant bodies have also been common. These smaller groups have ranged from the Waldensians of the twelfth century, through the "protestants" four centuries later, to the Baptist and Pentecostal splinter groups found in virtually every major North American city today. Therefore, not surprisingly, sociologists studying religious groups have given considerable attention to a conceptual scheme featuring these two major organizational forms. The framework, known as **church-sect typology**, represents an attempt to describe the central characteristics of the two types, as well as account for the origin and development of the sect.

In perhaps its earliest formulation, Weber differentiated between church and sect primarily on the basis of each group's theology (works versus faith) and relationship to society (accommodation versus separation). Weber noted the irony in the sect's development: while initially a spin-off from an established church, the sect gradually evolves into a church itself (Gerth and Mills, 1958). The sect movement is at first characterized by spontaneity and enthusiasm which, in time, gives way to institutionalization and routinization. Thus the sect was seen in dynamic terms by Weber,

Television news cameras film Hindu holyman Babaji as he chants sutras by the Jumma River. All religions have a supernatural referent. Hindus, for example, aspire to the state of nirvana.

moving toward the end of the church-sect continuum. Niebuhr (1929) used the dynamic relationship between church and sect as an explanation for the appearance and ultimate absorption of new religious groups in Europe and the United States.

Church-sect typology has been extensively employed in the sociology of religion. It has been the central framework in a number of key studies, both American (for example, Niebuhr, 1929; Pope, 1942; Demerath, 1965), and Canadian (for example, Clark, 1948; Mann, 1962). The terms "church" and "sect," "church-like" and "sect-like" have, moreover, been household words in the discipline.

Over the years, modifications in this typology have been numerous as analysts have sought to deal adequately with diverse forms of religious organization. Becker (1950) and Yinger (1946) have sought to expand the simple church-sect dichotomy. Yinger, for example, using the three criteria of membership, accommodation to society, and extent of bureaucratization, put forth six major types of organizations: the *universal church, ecclesia, denomination, established sect, sect, and cult*. Examples of each of these six types would include respectively: the Roman Catholic Church in thirteenth century Europe, a state church such as the Church of England, the United Church of Canada, the Quakers, the Jehovah's Witnesses, and Scientology. A refinement in the predominantly Roman Catholic and Protestant Canadian setting has been offered by Millett (1969). He has maintained that immigrants to Canada with a church-like background have exhibited sect-like behavior in the face of economic struggles and isolation. He suggests that such religious groups can be seen as minority churches which, with accommodation and assimilation, eventually evolve into indigenous churches.

In recent years, however, church-sect typology has been discarded by a large number of sociologists because of its apparent limitations as an analytical tool.

Organizational Approaches.

The result of this increasing dissatisfaction with church-sect typology has been a growing tendency to study religious groups in the same manner that sociologists examine other groups – by using an organizational approach. The obvious advantage to this approach is that sociologists of religion can draw upon the extensive organizational literature available and have access to well developed concepts and analytic frameworks.

From an organizational point of view, a given congregation might be examined in the following terms:

1. the nature and the sources of its members
2. its formal and informal goals
3. the norms and roles established to accomplish the group's purpose
4. the controls used to insure that norms are followed and roles are played
5. the success the group experiences in pursuing its goals

Studies of this kind include Harrison's (1959) pioneering examination of the American Baptist Convention, and Westhues' continuing analyses (1973, 1978) of the Roman Catholic Church in which he views that organization as a type of nation-state. Although such case-study types of research are still relatively few, they can provide considerable insight into the nature of religious groups.

Looking, for example, at Protestant churches, one notices that members are typically the offspring of previous members, and geographical mobility is the prime factor in the determination of group sizes. Bibby and Brinkerhoff (1973, 1982), in following 20 theolo-

gically conservative groups in Calgary over 15 years, found that some 70 percent of new members had come from other conservative churches, while approximately 20 percent were the children of members. Only about 10 percent of the new members had come from outside the conservative groups, and even here they commonly had been fairly active in other, more theologically liberal churches, such as the United Church.

Because new members come primarily from an existing pool, churches are in considerable competition with each other. One area of competition is leadership, and smaller, lower status congregations are usually at a severe disadvantage to larger and more prestigious groups. One researcher found in an analysis of eight American denominations that ministers have standards comparable to those of secular executives when it comes to interchurch movement (Mitchell, 1966). Comfort and success loom large, with the result that "attractive" churches in all denominations search further for their ministers and hold them longer than those deemed less attractive. A study of over 500 southern Baptist ministers similarly revealed that the dominant pattern of ministerial movement is from smaller to larger congregations (Wimberley, 1971).

Such competition does not stop with ministers and other church workers. Physical attributes and range of services are also significant, with the result that churches tend to build structures as lavish as their resources will permit. They likewise expand their services and personnel – as do secular businesses – in keeping with their economic means. And in the pursuit of members – who have been observed to pick their churches as carefully as they pick their golf clubs – congregations run the risk of compromising their product in order to attract the consumer. As Demerath and Hammond (1969) have pointed out, "Competition among churches is often resolved not in favor of the most religious but precisely in favor of the least."

The conscious and unconscious goals of Protestant churches vary by congregation and members. As with those of other social groupings, these goals commonly appear to be in conflict. Metz (1967) has drawn attention to the reality of "formal goals" derived from religious doctrine (for example, spiritual growth) versus "survival goals" derived from the need simply to keep the congregation alive (for example, numerical growth). Glock, et al (1967) have suggested that churches have difficulty reconciling the pastoral or "comfort" function with that of the prophetical or "challenge" function. One particular clergyman quipped that he couldn't decide whether his church buildings were locker rooms or hospitals!

Still other observers (Herberg, 1960; Hoge, 1976) have noted that North American Protestantism has historically known tension between an emphasis on individual versus social redemption. Driedger (1974), for example, in a study involving 130 Winnipeg Protestant clergymen, found theologically conservative ministers to be far less inclined to favor social change than their theologically liberal counterparts.

Despite this apparent divergence in what people expect their religious groups to be doing, there is good reason to believe that churches survive and, to varying degrees, thrive precisely because different goals are realized. A rather extreme but informative example has been offered by Bibby and Mauss (1974) in an examination of the skid road mission. The mission operators, skid roaders, and suburban supporters all appear to have very different informal goals. The operators need employment, the skid roaders need food and lodging, and the suburbanites need an outlet for their talents. Yet the mission nonetheless functions in such a way as to allow these varied goals to be attained. And thus, somewhat ironically, the skid road mission survives, even though it largely fails to accomplish what it is officially claiming to do, namely, rehabilitate homeless derelicts.

To the extent that groups do achieve their official or formal goals, it is essential that they establish norms for thought and action, and roles for members to play. These norms and roles are in turn facilitated by communication, which coordinates the interaction, and by the use of social controls in the form of rewards and punishments.

Brannon (1971) has argued that many Protestant groups, reliant as they are upon volunteers, have considerable difficulty executing goals in this norms-roles-communication-social control pattern of efficient organizations. Congregations compete for volunteer members and are dependent upon them for attendance, financial support, and general participation. While they can establish norms concerning belief and behavior, as well as assign organizational roles for members to perform, churches have few and weak methods of social control in such a buyer's market. In short, says Brannon, churches are, "painfully vulnerable" organizations. The clergy receive no exemption from such organizational fragility. On the contrary, they are commonly highly dependent on these volunteer parishioners, which has important implications for what the clergy can do and how they can do it.

The overall result is that congregations may often be primarily "paper organizations." Yet the informal structure of churches bears watching. One study of small churches found that individuals without formal leadership have considerable influence: long-standing members were observed to have a voice beyond their formal roles; people who gave the most money had to be consulted on key decisions; relatives of official leaders had unofficial input (Chalfant, et al, 1981). Another study of churches large and small has documented the presence of inner circles – or groups that tend to control the affairs of local congregations (Houghland and Wood, 1979). While the researchers concluded that such groups often arise because of the absence of strong ministerial leadership, it seems equally plausible that inner circles also function to restrict such leadership.

The Canadian Situation. Affiliation with religious groups has been widespread in Canada since the founding of this country. Close ties have been apparent between the British and the Church of England, Methodism, and Presbyterianism; between the French and the Roman Catholic Church; between other ethnic groups and the churches of their homelands. Such general affiliation continues to be very common in Canada. As of the latest available census figures, less than 5 percent of Canadians indicated that they had no religious preference (see Table 12-2). Although group preferences clearly differ in various parts of the country, on a national basis Protestants and Roman Catholics each compose approximately 46 percent of

TABLE 12–2. RELIGIOUS PREFERENCE, CANADA, 1971

Denomination	Canada	Nfld	PEI	NS	NB	Que	Ont	Man	Sask	Alta	BC	Yukon	NWT
	%	%	%	%	%	%	%	%	%	%	%	%	%
Anglican	12	28	6	17	11	3	16	12	9	11	18	25	36
Baptist	3	–	6	13	14	1	4	2	2	3	3	5	1
Greek Orthodox	2	–	–	–	–	1	2	3	3	3	1	1	1
Jehovah's Witnesses	1	–	–	1	–	–	1	1	1	1	2	3	2
Jewish	1	–	–	–	–	2	2	2	–	–	–	–	–
Lutheran	3	–	–	2	–	–	3	7	10	8	5	5	2
Mennonite	1	–	–	–	–	–	–	6	3	1	1	–	–
Pentecostal	1	5	1	1	3	–	1	1	1	1	2	1	2
Presbyterian	4	1	12	5	2	1	7	3	2	4	5	4	1
Roman Catholic	46	37	46	36	52	87	33	25	28	24	19	25	41
Salvation Army	1	8	–	1	–	–	1	–	–	–	–	–	–
Ukrainian Catholic	1	–	–	–	–	1	1	6	4	3	–	1	–
United Church	17	20	25	21	14	3	22	26	30	28	25	17	9
Other	3	1	3	1	2	–	3	2	3	6	6	4	2
No Religion	4	–	1	2	2	1	4	4	4	7	13	9	3
TOTALS	100	100	100	100	100	100	100	100	100	100	100	100	100

SOURCE: Computed from *Yearbook of American and Canadian Churches: 1975*, New York: Abingdon Press.
NOTE: All figures are rounded percentages.

the population. The remaining 8 percent consist of Jews (1), other religions (3), and people with no religious preference (4).

Beyond mere affiliation, more Canadians – over 50 percent – claim to belong to churches than to any other voluntary group. According to various polls, approximately one in three say they attend services weekly, and roughly the same proportion of people with school-age children expose those children to church schools.

At the same time, however, there has been a considerable decline in church attendance in recent years, as indicated by the Gallup Poll findings presented in Table 12-3. Since approximately the end of World War II, Protestant attendance has dropped off from 60 to around 30 percent, leveling off at that point in the last few years. As for Roman Catholics, the decline appears to have started around 1960, continuing downward from roughly 85 to 50 percent in the early 1980s.

This attendance drop is further documented in the *Project Canada* national surveys. While one in three Canadians claim they currently are weekly service

TABLE 12-3. CHURCH ATTENDANCE FOR ROMAN CATHOLICS AND PROTESTANTS, CANADA, SELECTED YEARS

"Did you happen to attend church (or synagogue) in the last seven days?"

	1946	1956	1965	1975	1981
	%	%	%	%	%
Roman Catholics	83	87	83	61	51
Protestants	60	43	32	25	29
Total	67	61	55	41	37

SOURCE: Canadian Institute of Public Opinion.

attenders, two in three maintain they were attending weekly when they were growing up (Bibby, 1979a). Given the dependence of personal religiosity on collective religiosity, this attendance decrease seems destined to manifest itself in a reduced level of personal religious commitment. What we may well be witnessing at present is something of a "belief lag." Many people have rejected the churches, yet retain ideas that date back to childhood participation. Without similar exposure, however, it is doubtful that their children will know a comparable belief level.

To be sure, the majority of people who claim religious group affiliation will probably continue to use those organizations for certain rites of passage, notably marriages and funerals. However, the proportion of people who are actively involved in religious groups has clearly dropped fairly dramatically. This situation, of course, may change. Indeed, some observers contend that it is changing, that there is a renewed interest in religion. But an accurate assessment of trends needs to be based not on impression or intuition, but rather on a comprehension of the societal and individual factors that influence religious commitment and the lack of it. Let us now turn to this question of the sources of commitment.

RELIGION: ITS SOURCES

Much important early work in the scientific study of religion focused on primitive or simple cultures in which religion was highly pervasive. It is not surprising that in this context observers sought to understand the sources of individual commitment – since little variation was apparent – rather than the origin of religion itself.

However, individual differences in religion's importance in modern societies has called for explanations that can explain why some people and not others are religious. To date these explanations have tended to be either individually or structurally focused.

Individual-Centered Explanations

At least four dominant "person-centered" explanations of religious commitment have emerged. In essence, these explanations are probably as old as the major religions themselves.

Reflection. The need to comprehend reality is widespread among humans. Geertz (1968) notes:

It does appear to be a fact that at least some men – in all probability, most men – are unable . . . just to look at the stranger features of the world's landscape in dumb astonishment or bland apathy without trying to develop . . . some

notions as to how such features might be reconciled with the more ordinary deliverances of experience.

In the course of reflecting on the meaning of existence, people have commonly concluded that life has a supernatural dimension. As Weber (1963) puts it, religion is the product of an "inner compulsion to understand the world as a meaningful cosmos and take up a position toward it." For some, religion appears to be the result of considering, with the Psalmist (8:3-4), one's place in the universe:

When I consider thy heavens, the work of thy fingers, the moon and the stars, which thou has ordained; What is man, that thou art mindful of him?

Canadians who say they often think about questions pertaining to origin, purpose, happiness, suffering, and death are generally somewhat more likely than others to exhibit religious commitment (Bibby, 1980). Yet the tendency is very slight. Fewer than one in three of the people in Canada who often raise these so-called ultimate questions give evidence of being religiously committed. At the same time, some of the committed do not give evidence of raising the questions. Indeed, some 10 percent of Canadians who exhibit traditional Christian commitment say that they never have thought about life's origin and purpose. For this latter group, learning would appear to be supplanting a conscious quest for meaning.

Socialization. A second person-centered explanation of religious commitment sees religiousness as primarily the result of learning. If people are exposed to a social environment which is positive toward religion – an entire society, a community, a reference group (that is, family, peers), many would be expected to "be religious." As Freud (1962) put it, many would seem to learn religion just as they learn the multiplication table.

Particularly important to religious socialization – as with socialization generally – are primary family and friendship groupings along with organizations such as churches and synagogues. This latter organizational involvement has in turn been attributed commonly to two types of factors: *association* and *accommodation*.

Where the crazy fish swims . . .

In one of the most astounding exhibitions of religious fanaticism in recent history, some 900 followers of the Reverend Jim Jones' People's Temple commune in Guyana committed mass suicide in November, 1978. Their commitment, along with that of other sect and cult members, has commonly been explained in terms of deprivation.

Canapress

Today's cults are seeking the simple ways of life, an escape from social turbulence. Dr. Robert Lifton, a Yale University psychiatrist and authority on brainwashing, says: "There's some kind of historical phenomenon here. When people are facing dislocations of rapid social change and the present looks frightening, there is often a cry for a return to absolute simplicity in the rules of living. People seek to return to a past of perfect harmony that never was. When they find their fundamentalist principles threatened by the outside world believers have many times chosen suicide as a way of immortalizing their purpose."

Certainly mass suicide, though mercifully rare, is not an unheard-of-phenomenon. A few years after the death of Christ, 960 Jews killed themselves in the besieged fortress of

Masada rather than yield to Roman soldiers, while in 1944, when the Americans took the Japanese island of Saipan, hundreds of men, women and children leaped off a cliff into the ocean rather than surrender. As Dr. Edwin Shneidman, a leading suicide expert at the University of California, says: "In the altruistic suicide the pressure of the group can be so powerful that suicide may not be the individual choice but it is nonetheless demanded. If you're in the Marine Corps and the sergeant says it's time to go, you can't just say, 'Gee, Sarge, I prefer not to.'"

But in the case of a cult there is

another factor involved – the leader – and Manhattan psychiatrist Richard Rabkin draws a disturbing analogy about him. Says Rabkin: "A school of fish has no real leader. If one fish strays he comes back into the school. But if you brain-damage that fish and he goes on ahead, the others will follow him. He becomes the leader not because of anything he has, like charisma, but because of what he's lacking."

Source:

Maclean's, December 4, 1978, p. 36.

The human inclination for association has frequently taken the form of religious group involvement. In Canada and the United States, churches and synagogues have played an important role in the social life of both native-born and immigrant people in communities both large and small. Participation has undoubtedly had a variety of functions, including a person's search for identity, social status, and group solidarity. Not surprisingly, participation has been observed to follow class and ethnic lines. Hiller (1976), for example, comments that Canadian immigrant churches have played a vital role in providing an ethnic anchor in an alien society.

Accommodation to social pressures, notably of a

TABLE 12-4. RELIGIOUS SOCIALIZATION AND COMMITMENT, SELECTED CATEGORY FINDINGS

	Weekly Atten- dance	See Selves As "Very Religious"	Christian Commit- ment
	%	%	%
IN CHILDHOOD			
Father's Commitment			
"Very Religious"	45	43	29
"Not Very Religious"	20	5	12
Mother's Commitment			
"Very Religious"	41	36	26
"Not Very Religious"	18	4	8
Childhood Attendance			
Weekly	35	19	20
Less than Weekly	20	12	10
IN ADULTHOOD			
Partner's Commitment			
High ("Very Religious")	79	82	46
Low ("Not Very Religious")	10	3	8
Religious Friends			
Yes	83	35	49
No	25	15	14
School-Age Children			
Yes	32	17	17
No	29	18	17
Service Attendance			
Weekly	—	44	37
Less than Weekly	—	5	8

SOURCE: Data derived from Bibby, Reginald W. "Project Canada," 1976.

primary group variety, seems to be another source of religious participation. For example, one marital partner may become more religiously committed in response to the hopes and expectations of the other, friends in response to friends (Gerlach and Hine, 1968), and parents in response to school-age children (Nash and Berger, 1962; Nash, 1968). In tightly knit religious communities, accommodation, like association, would seem to be an obvious contributor to religious involvement.

The *Project Canada* analyses have unveiled a noteworthy relationship between the commitment of respondents and their parents (Bibby, 1980). Close to one in two Canadians with fathers or mothers perceived as very religious are themselves weekly attenders, as compared to one in five of the respondents with not very religious parents. The parallel figures in the case of religious self-image and traditional Christian commitment are approximately 40 versus 5 percent for the former and 30 versus 10 percent for the latter (see Table 12-4).

On the other hand, the relationship between childhood religious service attendance and adult commitment is weaker. Weekly attendance as children does not necessarily lead to a similar level of participation in adulthood. Only 35 percent of Canadians who attended weekly as children are still doing so as adults. Conversely, 20 percent who were not weekly attenders as young people are involved on that level now. Childhood attendance is also tenuously related to both religious self-image and traditional Christian commitment.

The religious socialization of children appears to be important in the generation of commitment, but with the family rather than church exerting the greater influence. Such findings are consistent with those of Hunsberger (1980), whose analyses of students at Wilfrid Laurier University and The University of Manitoba led him to conclude that emphasis on religion in childhood is positively associated with later religiosity.

Table 12-4 also confirms that the commitment level of one's spouse is strongly related to personal commitment, while association with religious friends also has a noteworthy effect. The presence of school-age children is not, in and of itself, tied to commitment for Canadian parents generally. As would be expected, given the previously discussed dependence of personal religiosity on organized religion, a strong relationship exists between church attendance and both religious self-image and Christian commitment. The relationship, however, is far from perfect. Less than one-half of the weekly attenders (44 percent) see themselves as very religious, while only about one-third (37 percent) exhibit traditional Christian commitment.

In adulthood, then, the commitment level of one's spouse and friends, along with church attendance, appear to be the factors most strongly associated with personal commitment.

Deprivation. A third person-centered explanation that has long been popular with both scholar and layman is that the religious are drawn primarily from society's deprived or disadvantaged. Such people turn to religion as a means of compensating for their deprivation. The idea has received considerable Judaic-Christian support (e.g., "Blessed are the poor in spirit . . . Blessed are the meek") and has characterized the thinking of such influential social scientists as Marx and Freud. Glock and Stark (1965) contended that five types of deprivation are predominant in the rise and development of religious and secular movements: economic, social, organismic (physical or mental), psychic, and ethical. The first three are self-explanatory; psychic deprivation refers to the lack of a meaningful system of values, and ethical deprivation to having one's values conflict with society.

Yet if deprivation is measured using so-called objective indicators such as income, health, and social relationships, it is neither consistently nor strongly related to religious commitment in either the United States (see Roof and Hoge, 1980) or Canada (Hobart, 1974; Bibby, 1980). This is not to say that deprivation is never a significant factor for some individuals and some religious groups. But it is to say that, generally speaking, the committed in North America are not any more or less disadvantaged than other people.

Emotional Predisposition. A person's emotional posture toward religion would seem to be another determinant of commitment. Judaic-Christian writers noted centuries ago that receptivity was a key component of interaction between God and man. Conversely, social scientists have observed, along with religious leaders and laity, that many people show scant interest in religion for what appear to be essentially emotional reasons. Mauss (1969), for example, points out that a number of religious defectors claim that churchgoers are hypocrites, that God deserted them in time of need, that churches are interested only in money, and so on. Although such reasons may be plausible, they commonly appear to camouflage other factors that have contributed to an emotionally expressed negativism toward religion. Mauss recalls Allport's (1950) observations concerning people who

drift away from religion because of guilt and shame. McCann (1967) is also cited as seeing the "seed for future agnosticism" sown in unhappy, unsatisfying, or rigid family environments.

The point here, then, is that religious commitment seems to require an emotional posture which, if not positive, is at least not negative.

In the *Project Canada* survey, Canadians were asked to indicate any of the following factors that may have contributed to a reduction in their religious activity:

1. the absence of God in time of need
2. the restrictions religion places on life
3. religion was forced on me as a child
4. increasing awareness of hypocrisy

For analytical purposes, if any of these factors was cited as being "very important" in decreased participation, then the respondents were regarded as having a strongly negative emotional posture toward religion. If none was seen as "very important" but one or more of the factors were said to be "somewhat important," they were viewed as somewhat negative. The citing of no factors resulted in a "neutral" designation.

A neutral emotional predisposition was found to be associated to some degree with attendance, religious self-image, and traditional Christian commitment. Yet it is important to keep in mind here that being non-negative toward religion most certainly cannot be equated with religious commitment. Well over 50 percent of Canadians who are neutral do not attend weekly, do not regard themselves as particularly religious, and do not exhibit traditional Christian characteristics.

Structural-Centered Explanations

So far we have examined what we might call "kinds of people" explanations of religious commitment. What these explanations have in common is their emphasis on the individual; he or she is said to turn to religion out of reflection, socialization, or deprivation, assisted by an emotional outlook that is not antagonistic toward religion. An adequate understanding of commitment, however, must also take into account the societal context in which people find themselves, and its influence upon religious inclination. Individual religiosity is not formulated in a vacuum; it is highly dependent upon the larger social environment in which individuals and their reference groups are located. Clark (1948), for example, has argued that in Canada's past the tendency of sect-like religious groups to emerge was tied directly to the existence of unstable conditions produced by factors such as immigration and economic depression. With industrialization and increased prosperity and stability, sects tended to evolve by a process of **denominationalism**.

The climate provided by modern industrial societies for religion is a subject of considerable controversy. On the one hand, there are those who claim that religion is experiencing a decline, in pervasiveness and influence, that parallels the rise of industrialization. Such a **secularization argument** dates back at least to Comte, Marx, Freud, and Durkheim. On the other hand, there are a number of observers who claim that religion – traditional or otherwise – is making a comeback; it is persisting in part because people have experienced dissatisfaction with modern industrial living and its emphases on rationalism and materialism.

The actual influence of modern cultures on the tendency of people to be religious or otherwise is not at all clear. Considerable cross-cultural research is necessary to clarify the picture. The specifics of this secularization-persistence controversy, as well as some of the research findings available to date, will be dealt with in more detail when we examine the future of religion at the end of this chapter.

At this point, however, we want to explore how some of the correlates of industrialization – such as urbanization, higher education, work-force participation, and exposure to mass media – are related to religious commitment in Canada.

Following the secularization argument, in a highly industrialized society the culture as a whole will exhibit a pervasive secularity, so that such correlates should not differentiate strongly the committed from the noncommitted. Indeed, in time rural dwellers should come to resemble their urban counterparts in being nonreligious; the same should be true of high school dropouts and college graduates, the retired and those under the age of thirty. The reason for this lack

TABLE 12-5. INDUSTRIALIZATION CORRELATES AND COMMITMENT, SELECTED CATEGORY FINDINGS

	Weekly Attendance	See Selves As "Very Religious"	Christian Commitment
	%	%	%
Community Size			
Farm and Rural Non-Farm	42	27	24
Metropolis (over 400,000)	25	14	14
Education			
High School or Less	31	20	17
University Degree or More	28	12	11
Work Force Participation			
Not Employed Outside the Home	38	27	25
Employed Outside the Home	27	12	14
Media Exposure (Television)			
Watch less than 15 hours[1]	34	20	22
Watch more than 30 hours	23	9	8

SOURCE: Data derived from Bibby, Reginald W. "Project Canada," 1976.
NOTE: [1] Weekly.

of differentiation is that the culture is so secularized that no sector of the population remains untouched. But at this point in Canadian history, when the nation is being posited as highly but hardly completely secularized, we would expect some portions of the population to be less secularized than others – specifically those less influenced by industrialism.

The *Project Canada* findings support such an argument. As community size, education, work force participation, and media exposure increase, commitment tends to decrease slightly (see Table 12-5). These data suggest a highly secularized society, but one where industrialization correlates still have a slight negative impact on religiosity. Interestingly, there is a tendency for the industrialization-secularization pattern to be reflected in the regions of the country: the Atlantic Region and Quebec have the highest levels of commitment, followed by the Prairie Provinces, Ontario, and British Columbia.

An Assessment

Religion finds itself competing in modern societies that have a "this world" outlook. Emphases upon science, technology, and human progress are accompanied by the expectation that a person's attention, capabilities, and energies will be directed toward the successful living out of everyday life. This **industrial world view** is perpetuated quite unconsciously by virtually every major institution and assimilated with equal lack of awareness by the average person.

To the extent that people in an industrializing, secular country like Canada are religiously committed, the key sources of their committment do not lie with institutions such as the media, education, or the work world; nor with reflections on the fact of disenchantment; nor with the desire for compensation in response to deprivation. Rather, the people in this country who are religiously committed tend to be those so socialized. Religion, like so many other things, is transmitted through relationships, primarily learned from and supported by family and close friends, with the assistance of the churches.

But with the industrialization of Canada, two important developments have occurred that seriously affect this kind of transmission of religion. First, the influence of family-friendship-church has been reduced by the advent of other decisive socializing agents, not the least of which have been other peer groups, mass media, and the modern educational system. These agents are typically concerned with everyday life and thus, however inadvertently, function to instill the industrial world view with its empiricism-materialism emphases. Consequently, while religious socialization is the key contributor to religious commitment, for these reasons its impact is relatively light.

Second, besides the decreasing effectiveness of religious socialization, with the decline in personal religious commitment, socialization of a religious nature is simply not as common as it once was. Some 15 percent of the men in the 1975 *Project Canada* national survey viewed themselves as very religious, while 25

percent so designated their fathers. The women likewise indicated a similar decline in commitment, from 45 percent for their mothers to 19 percent for themselves.

In short, religious socialization is the key determinant of commitment. But socialization efforts – when they are made – are commonly neutralized by a strongly secular culture. The result is a decrease in the number of people who are even attempting to religiously socialize their children. Therefore, from one generation to another there is a decline in religious commitment and in attempts to socialize offspring.

RELIGION: ITS CONSEQUENCES

From the standpoint of social scientist and layperson alike, one of the most significant questions about religion is that of consequences. Given its continuing presence in the modern world, does religion have an impact upon individuals that extends to their relations with other people, or is it largely irrelevant? Further, if such an influence exists, what is its nature? Does religion tend to contribute to individual and societal well-being, or is it inclined to produce anxiety and guilt, social indifference, and bigotry? Still further, if religion has an impact, positive or negative, to what extent is this impact unique to religion, and to what extent is it common to other institutions?

To some of the early observers of society such as Comte, Marx, and Freud, the expected demise of religion made the answers to these questions fairly obvious: the death of religion would mean the death of its influence. The persistence of religion in highly industrialized societies, however, has given the question of its consequences renewed social scientific relevance.

Religions do indeed claim to have consequences for individuals and hence for societies. Christians, for example, are likely to tell us that mature followers of the faith should find it influencing them personally and their relations with others. Specifically, Christianity claims that the committed will experience joy, satisfaction, peace, and hope. In addition, the tradition asserts that committed and mature Christians will be characterized by love in their relations with other

"Do you have love in your heart?"

Christian commitment has historically been associated with humanitarian ideals and practice. Yet, like other religions, it also has on occasion known socially undesirable consequences. Following is one such bizarre manifestation of commitment, taken not from the middle ages in Europe, but from the middle 1970s in the state of Washington.

YAKIMA, Wash. (AP) In three years of life, David Weilbacher knew brutality, pain and humility – forced upon him by the people who made up his world. But those three years never gave David enough time to understand or fight back.

The blond and dimpled child was too young to know why the people he trusted to provide security would beat him repeatedly with sticks and tell him he did not have love in his heart.

He could not comprehend what "the devil" was, much less understand why they felt it had to be driven from his body.

The five people who made up David's world are in the Yakima county jail, across town from where the three-year-old is buried.

They can't see the small stone grave marker, which says "David Weilbacker." The name is misspelled – an ironic finality for the people to whom David, in his last months of life, was not David at all.

David's mother, Debra Marie Weilbacher, was 19 when she and her son moved to the yellow house, used as a church by those who lived there, in a neighborhood of crumbling streets and poverty on Yakima's southeast side.

Debra's four-year marriage to David's father had ended, and she looked to members of the religious household to help her overcome the emptiness. Edward Leon Cunningham, 51, told her God was his master, and he was God's messenger.

Also living in the house were Cunningham's wife, Velma, their daughter Carolyn, 27, and Lorraine Edwards, a former schoolmaster of Debra's. All are awaiting sentencing on manslaughter and assault convictions in David's death . . .

Cunningham began to point out things about David to the family . . . wetting his pants, smearing his waste on the bathroom wall. The child smelled wicked, too, for some unknown reason. Once he put glass chips in his shoes and wore them.

David acted like he would rather be an adult than a child, although he had a laugh, a foolish laugh, that seemed to be neither young nor old. In the end, it was clear, particularly to Cunningham, that David was possessed by the Devil.

The spankings began in April, the family says. Cunningham had pointed to something in the bible which he belived was the answer. "Withhold not correction from the child; for if thou beatest him with a rod he shall not die. Thou shalt deliver his soul from hell."

Twice a day for four months, the paddles – lath sticks 18 inches long, sanded and rounded – were passed around to each family member. each took his turn swatting David a few times or many times, on his legs, his rear, his back, his arms – almost everywhere except the genitals and the kidney area.

"Do you have love in your heart," Cunningham would say to David.

"Yes," David would say.

"Then show it," Cunningham would say.

David would hug and kiss Cunningham, who didn't think the three-year-old was being honest. So he would pass the stick to the next family member to use on David.

On the morning of July 22, Debra remembers picking David off the floor after an extra-long spanking. A tiny splotch of blood appeared on his lips, and the family saw little David raise his fists and growl. Then he stopped breathing.

They put David in a sealed room in the back of the house and waited for God to resurrect him.

On Sept. 1, Sgt. Robert Langdale went to the house, acting on a tip from Mrs. Cunningham, who began to suspect her husband after the Anti-Christ prophesy didn't come true. Langdale went to the back bedroom, to the door where deodorant had been sprayed to stop the smell. He burst through the door into the fly and maggot-infested room and got the shock of his life.

With his gas mask on, Langdale looked under the sheet on a cot and saw something that was bloated, eaten black, three feet-long and three years old.

A pathologist later would say there was no way he could tell how David died. But he had a guess, and he guessed David was beaten to death.

"That's the way it goes," Carolyn .Cunningham said after the convictions were announced.

Source:

Associated Press, November 24, 1976.

people and that this love will be exhibited in such qualities as concern for others, acceptance, benevolence, forgiveness, self-control, honesty, and respect. In living out such a love norm, Christians are expected to follow ethical guidelines such as the Ten Commandments, the Sermon on the Mount, and the teachings of the Apostle Paul. At the same time, religious groups certainly differ on specific norms. Logically, if an issue such as abortion is perceived as "religiously relevant," one would expect that the attitudes of the committed would be influenced; if not, their attitudes would simply vary according to other factors such as age and education.

Social scientists exploring the causal effects of Christianity, then, give their attention to two main areas: personal characteristics and relations with others. However, they do not limit the possible outcomes of their research to those predicted by religion. Rather, they also freely explore commitment's possible latent or unintended consequences. One religious counselor tells of dealing with a distraught young woman who exclaimed, "My troubles began the day I became a Christian!" (Southard, 1961). The sociologist keeps an open mind to such a possibility. Similarly, the ideal of Christian love does not stop the researcher from probing the incidence of Christian hostility.

Individual Consequences

It is interesting that Marx and Freud essentially conceded that religion contributed to positive personal characteristics such as happiness, satisfaction, and hope. Their adverse criticism rested in their belief that such qualities were based upon illusion rather than reality. However, their concessions were largely speculative rather than empirical.

Actual research on consequences of individual commitment is surprisingly limited and further suffers – along with consequence studies generally – from serious methodological flaws. *Time-order* is often vague, so that one does not know whether religion is the cause, the effect, or simply correlated to something like happiness; the *strength of relationships* is not always specified; and *controls* for other explanatory factors are commonly

inadequate (Bouma, 1970; Wuthnow, 1973; Bibby, 1979c). A very recent effort to update Lenski's previously mentioned religious factor, for example, fails to demonstrate time-order in maintaining that religious activities lead to greater involvement with family, neighbors, and organizations (McIntosh and Alston, 1982).

Even apart from methodological shortcomings, the research findings on religion and what we might generally refer to as "mental health" are contradictory. Rokeach (1965), summing up a number of his studies, wrote:

We have found that people with formal religious affiliation are more anxious (than others). Believers, compared with non-believers, complain more often of working under great tension, sleeping fitfully, and similar symptoms.

Yet researchers have consistently found a negative relationship between religious commitment and *anomia* (Lee and Clyde, 1974) – a characteristic of valuelessness and rootlessness that Srole (1956) sees as related to anxiety. Further, as early as the work of Beynon (1938), Boisen (1939), and Holt (1940) involvement in groups such as sects and cults was seen as providing revised self-images and hope in the face of economic and social deprivation – a theme echoed by Frazier (1964) for American blacks, Whyte (1966) for Canadian rural-urban immigrants, and Hill (1971) for West Indian immigrants to Britain. Lindenthal, et al (1970) found in a New Haven, Connecticut, study of some 1000 adults that a positive correlation existed between church affiliation and mental health, a finding corroborated by Stark (1971) using a California sample.

Bibby's (1979c) analysis of the consequences of personal religiosity in Canada suggests that Canadians who exhibit religious commitment are slightly more inclined than others to claim a high level of happiness, to find life exciting, to express a high level of satisfaction with family, friends, and leisure activities, and to view death with hope rather than with mystery or even fear. However, when controls are introduced, and the impact of variables like age, education, and community size is taken into account, the apparent modest influence of commitment is found to dissolve. This occurs on a national level as well as among Roman Catholic, United Church, Anglican, and conservative Protestant members.

In short, religious factors appear to have no more influence upon personal characteristics than secular characteristics. Religion is at best only one path to a positive mental state. Moreover, it frequently is not as important as such variables as age, education, or employment, even among active church members.

Interpersonal Consequences

One of the first empirical attempts to examine the relationship between religious commitment and compassion was carried out by Kirkpatrick in 1949. Using a sample of Minnesota students and other adults, Kirkpatrick found that religiously committed people were actually somewhat less humanitarian in their outlook than others.

Some twenty years later, two important studies gave support to Kirkpatrick's findings. Stark and Glock (1968), in their classic examination of American religiosity, contended that traditional Christian commitment ("orthodoxy") was negatively associated with social concern ("ethicalism"). They did note, however, that this was true for Protestants but not for Catholics, where the relationship was slightly positive. In an attempt to explain this difference, they suggested that Protestants are more inclined than Catholics to see social problems as being solved through God's changing of individuals. Catholics – and more theologically liberal Protestant groups – assume the limitations of man and therefore attempt "to offer moral guidance for the conduct of man-to-man relationships" (Stark and Glock, 1968).

Rokeach (1969), drawing on a representative American sample of some 1400 adults, similarly observed that religious commitment on a national level was negatively related to social compassion. In the case of Roman Catholics, however, he found that no relationship (positive or negative) existed. Rokeach concluded: ". . . the results seem compatible with the hypothesis that religious values serve more as standards for condemning others . . . than as standards to judge oneself by or to guide one's own conduct."

These findings, however, do not go unchallenged.

Research conducted on some specific religious groups–on Mennonite students by Rushby and Thrush (1973) – and in certain localities – in a southwestern American city by Nelson and Dynes (1976) – has found a positive relationship between commitment and compassion.

Considerable research has also been carried out exploring another facet of interpersonal relations – prejudice. Gorsuch and Aleshire (1974) reviewed all the published empirical studies on the topic through the mid-1970s and concluded that the key to understanding conflicting findings is in the way religious commitment is measured. If church membership is used as the measurement, members are more prejudiced than those who have never joined a church. If beliefs are used, the theologically conservative are more prejudiced than others. And, if church attendance is the measure of commitment, then the marginal church member shows more prejudice than either the nonactive or the most active members. Gorsuch and Aleshire (1974) conclude:

The results of the present review are clear: the average church member is more prejudiced than the average nonmember because the casual, nontheologically motivated member is prejudiced. The highly committed religious person is – along with the nonreligious person – one of the least prejudiced members of our society.

These researchers point out, however, that the precise role of organized religion in the influencing of prejudice is unclear. Sophisticated studies that measure the impact of churches on individuals over time simply have not yet been done.

The *Project Canada* analysis has disclosed that the religiously committed in Canada do not differ significantly from others with respect to their interpersonal relationship attitudes (Bibby, 1979c). They hold a similar view of people, claim a comparable level of compassion, and appear to be no more or less tolerant of deviants, minority groups, and people of other religious faiths than other Canadians. Further, no noteworthy differences are apparent in the interpersonal attitudes held by Protestants and Roman Catholics, in contrast to the findings of Rokeach (1969) and Stark and Glock (1968).

At this point it is important for us to pause and ask

TABLE 12-6. COMMITMENT AND MORAL ATTITUDES (Percentage Opposed)

	Pre-Marital Sex[1]	Extra-Marital Sex[1]	Homo-sexu-ality[1]	Abortion: Rape[2]	Abortion: Child Unwanted[3]	Porn-ography[4]	Marijuana[5]
	%	%	%	%	%	%	%
Service Attendance							
Weekly	38	76	83	29	81	55	87
Less Than Weekly	7	43	54	8	42	28	66
Religious Self-Image							
"Deeply Committed"	33	71	81	27	75	51	86
"Not Religious"	5	37	50	4	30	21	64
Other	7	46	53	9	47	30	65
Christian Orientation							
Yes	38	72	84	35	85	55	92
No	11	49	58	10	46	32	68

SOURCE: Data derived from Bibby, Reginald W. "Project Can 80," 1982.
NOTE: All the above responses represent opposition to the following possibilities.
[1]The responses on premarital, extramarital, and homosexual relations are "Always wrong."
[2]The legal availability of abortion when "she became pregnant as a result of rape."
[3]The legal availability of abortion when "she is married and does not want to have any more children."
[4]The legal limitation of the distribution of pornographic materials to persons of all ages.
[5]The legalization of the use of marijuana.

ourselves, should we really expect religion to be making a unique contribution in such areas as happiness and compassion at this stage in Canadian history? In highly specialized industrialized societies, religion becomes only one component of interpersonal norms. Valued relational characteristics such as compassion, integrity, and diligence are emphasized by virtually everyone – the family, the school, youth groups, voluntary associations, mass media. Norms specific to work and play, on the other hand, are largely created and disseminated within the business and social contexts in which they are used. The predictable result, in Berger's (1961) words, is that the religious would be expected to "hold the same values as everybody else, but with more emphatic solemnity." The paths to interpersonal norms – as with valued personal characteristics – are many, with religion being at best one path for what seems to be a decreasing number of people.

At the same time, there is one area where the Christian religion still appears to speak with a fairly loud if not necessarily unique voice – the area of personal morality, notably sexuality. Here, Christian churches with varying degrees of explicitness tend to function as opponents of moral innovation. Examples include opposition to the changing of sexual standards, to the increased availability of legal abortion, to the legalization of pornographic material, and to the legalization of prohibited drugs.

Table 12-6 reports findings that support this argument. Religiously committed Canadians are more inclined than others to hold negative attitudes toward nonmarital sexuality, homosexuality, abortion, pornography, and the use of marijuana. A national study of Canadian Mennonites has also found commitment to have consequences for the moral rather than the social sphere (Driedger, Currie, and Linden, 1982).

Yet the *Project Canada* analysis has found that even here the influence of religion both nationally and by religious groups, while important, is generally no more significant than the year of one's birth (Bibby, 1979c). What this means is that the era in which a person was born is just as important a determinant of opposition to moral innovation as religious commitment, with opposition to change increasing with age.

Religious commitment in Canada, then, appears to have a measure of distinctive influence not so much in

Birth, marriage, and death – these three crucial events are the central to religion. An essential function of religion is to help people deal with death. The experience of bereavement is often enought to bring religious drop-outs back into the fold.

the areas of personal characteristics or interpersonal relations – where secular alternatives abound – but rather in the sphere of moral innovation.

Societal Consequences

Religion's influence can be examined not only in terms of individuals and social interaction but also with reference to society as a whole. From at least the time of Marx and Durkheim observers have argued that religion contributes to solidarity. Marx was particularly critical of the way in which he felt religion was fused to the interests of the powerful, to the point where political and theological heresies were synonymous. Similarly, Durkheim saw the supernatural as both reflecting the nature of a society and functioning to unite it.

To be sure, however, religion can sometimes also be disruptive. Efforts on the part of Protestant leaders to bring about social change (Crysdale, 1961; Allen, 1971) have challenged the Canadian status quo. From one vantage point, Roman Catholicism in Quebec can be seen as contributing to considerable ethnic and regional cohesion. From another point of view, such a solidifying function can be seen as disruptive to Canadian unity. The divisive role of religion can further be seen in the Protestant-Catholic strife in Northern Ireland, the Islamic resurgence in Iran, and the Roman Catholic clergy's call for political and economic change in Latin America (see, for example, Westhues, 1973). Disruption is also evident in the activities of specific religious groups, including Canadian Doukhobors and youth-oriented cults. Conflict occasionally takes place over the dissenting views of Christian Scientists and Jehovah's Witnesses on the subject of blood transfusions, and over the pacifist stance of Quakers and Mennonites.

Nevertheless, Berger's (1961) observation of some twenty years ago still seems generally valid: while an adequate sociological theory of religion must be able to account for the possibility of dysfunctions, Durkheim's assertion that religion integrates societies aptly describes religion in America. Religion, at least that mainline segment of organized Christianity that embraces the largest number of affiliates, appears largely to endorse culture, rather than to challenge it; to reinforce North American society as we know it, rather than to call for its reformation. As Hiller (1976) has put it: "There are times, then, when religion can be a vital force in social change. . . . But as a general principle, we can say that in Canada organized religion has generally been a conservative force supporting the solidarity of the society. . . ." Historically the Protestant churches have reflected the British position of legitimizing authority through supporting government, offering prayers, for example, for its success in securing order and justice (Fallding, 1978).

The primary reason for such a conservative situation has already been illustrated in the area of personal consequences of commitment. Our culture seems to inform religion more commonly than the reverse. The result, in the words of one Canadian theologian is that religion has difficulty saying something to the culture

Opposition to Moral Change

Opposition to moral innovation can be seen in the following wireservice stories.

TORONTO (CP) Salvation Army women went to war today on alcoholism, gambling and lotteries, permissiveness in society, pornography, abortion and Sunday opening of stores.

Recommendations were contained in a manifesto issued at the second national congress of women attended by 3,000 delegates from across Canada. . . .

Dealing with alcoholism, the congress recommended the drinking age be raised and there be strict control on liquor advertising. It also suggested that the number of liquor outlets be restricted.

Claiming a "distress at the rate at which lotteries are multiplying in Canada," the congress said it deplored the fact that the federal and provincial governments have "permitted this unfortunate means of raising money" with its "disastrous results, particularly among lower-income groups in society."

Rejecting the highly vocal and "completely unsupportable pleas" for abortion on demand, delegates fully endorsed its policy that "abortion be granted only on adequate medical grounds after a therapeutic abortion committee has considered all the implications." (April 24, 1976).

* * *

NEW YORK (AP) The church had spoken gently and compassionately. But the ensuing actions hit hard among Presbyterian homosexuals.

"It hurt," says Chris Glasser, a ministerial candidate and homosexual. "It was a contradiction between words and deeds."

The odd sequence came in the final minutes of the United Presbyterian governing assembly in San Diego, Calif., last week.

"I'd believed what they had said, but it was just a lot of words," says Sandra Brawders, a Princeton Theological Seminary student who had declared her homosexuality to the assembly. "That's why it hurt so much."

The assembly had decided to prohibit active, declared homosexuals from ordination although it had called for love and care toward homosexual members. Assembly delegates also decided in its closing session to exclude the homosexual group from church recognition. (June 3, 1978).

* * *

VANCOUVER (CP) Modern Bible translations were the chief concern this summer at the fourth annual Fundamental Bible Conference of North America meeting in Cambridge, Mass.

"The main conflict and issue facing all believers is still the question of Bible versions," Mark Buch, pastor of The People's Fellowship Tabernacle, Vancouver, B.C., recently reported.

Mr. Buch, who submitted a postconference report, was a speaker at the event. Another Canadian, Perry Rockwood of the People's Gospel Hour radio broadcast, Halifax, N.S., also participated. . . .

Mr. Buch said the conference also warned "against the social gospel, long championed by modernists and lately given new impetus by the new evangelicals. "Though popular with man, we find no scriptural warrant for calling the church or individuals to programs of social betterment or reformation. Furthermore, we attest that our hope is not to get along with everyone; it is not the improvement of the world nor do we find in the scriptures any grounds for believing the church will bring in the kingdom of God."

The National Association for Evangelicals was cited "for its inconsistencies and compromise with apostasy" and the National Council of Churches and World Council of Churches dubbed "Satan inspired" in the forefront of one world church and government plans, Mr. Buch said.

The meeting also repudiated feminist and women's liberation groups, both secular and religious, saying women are being encouraged "to disobey the Bible by demanding equality instead of being in submission to Christ and to their husbands in the church and home." (Oct. 16, 1976).

Source:

Canadian Press; Associated Press.

---

that the culture is not already saying to itself (Hordern, 1966). Rather than standing apart from culture, religion is commonly colored by culture – its product rather than its source.

This pattern can be seen in the association between religion and social class. Since at least the time of Weber, social scientists have drawn attention to the relationship between class characteristics and religious ideas and practices. Niebuhr emphasized that the church-sect cycle was largely a response to economic deprivation and ensuing social mobility. The religiously neglected poor, he said, fashion a new type of Christianity that meets their own distinctive needs, proceed to climb the economic ladder through the influence of religious discipline, and then, "in the midst of a freshly acquired cultural respectability, neglect the new poor succeeding them" (Niebuhr, 1929). He offered examples including the Quakers, Methodists, and the Salvation Army. Observing religion in Alberta in the first half of this century, Mann (1962) noted that prairie people were inclined toward an informal and emotional expression of religion, in contrast to the structured and less personal style of eastern Canadians. New groups consequently arose in response to this void.

In like manner, congregations through to the present day have commonly displayed considerable class homogeneity. However alarming this may be to those who hold that churches should know the presence of people from all classes, it nevertheless is not surprising. As we saw in Chapter 2, *Culture*, to the extent that people in our society interact, they understandably gravitate toward those who share a common life-style. We socialize with similar people, we date and marry those who are like us. We assume the central importance of common interests. Accordingly, when people meet to share their faith, including ideas and worship forms, they are most comfortable with people of a similar class (and not uncommonly ethnic) background.

Yet one of the results of such a pattern is that supernatural imagery (God, Jesus, heaven, hell) along with worship forms (hymns, prayers, sermons) come to be shaped along distinctive class lines. The "Lord Jesus" and "mansion over the hilltop" of the lower middle class are relatively foreign to the "Christ our Savior" and "life eternal" of the upper middle class. In Berger's (1961) words: "Their ethics and aesthetics, not to speak of their politics, faithfully mirror [their] class prejudices and tastes."

Religion commonly mirrors culture. To the extent that it does so, it gives supernatural endorsement to culture, and indeed functions as social cement. Only when certain segments of society develop ideas in opposition to the dominant societal norms and attribute them to a supernatural source is religion potentially divisive. There is good reason to believe that the dominant religious groups exercise considerable social control over the legitimation of such deviant ideas (for example, the gay religious community's assertion "God loves gay people too").

To be sure, there are not a few observers who decry the inability of religion to rise above culture. Theologian Paul Tillich (1966) has written that religion "cannot allow itself to become a special area within culture, or to take a position beside culture." In describing the social roots of denominationalism, Niebuhr (1929) called such division "an unacknowledged hypocrisy, a reflection of the inability of churches to transcend the social conditions." Herberg (1960) stated that religion in America seems to possess little capacity for rising above national consciousness. "The God of judgment," he said, "has died." Berger (1961) has claimed that American religion is not unlike a nation-serving imperial cult, a state religion unconsciously affirmed.

Nevertheless, religion's inclination to mirror culture, rather than to stand apart from it, seems to be the inevitable result of humans, however unintentionally, creating religion in their own image. To the extent that this is true, religion can only be expected to lean toward personal and societal endorsement rather than toward personal and societal judgment.

RELIGION: ITS FUTURE

Since social scientists first turned their attention to religion, they have been divided on the question of its future.

Comte asserted that the world was experiencing an ever increasing level of rationalism, with religious ideas progressively giving way to metaphysical and then scientific modes of thought. Marx and Freud also saw religion as being replaced by reason, a movement that would usher in a superior quality of life.

Durkheim, on the other hand, was among those who saw religion persisting. Religious explanations, he said, may be forced to retreat, reformulate, and relinquish ground in the face of the steady advance of science. Yet religion will survive, because of both its social sources and functions (for an important discussion of the applicability of Durkheim's predictions to the current new religious movements, see Frances Westley, 1978).

This secularization-persistence debate has not diminished in recent years.

A little bit of hell . . .

The potential of religion to contribute to conflict has been dramatically illustrated in contemporary Northern Ireland.

In Fermanagh, one of the six counties of Northern Ireland, a Catholic butcher was found shot dead, impaled on meat hooks in his own refrigerator. He had been castrated, his testicles crammed into his mouth.

In Belfast, the capital of Northern Ireland, a businessman was called to the city morgue to identify his secretary's body after she and her Catholic lover had been murdered by Protestants. She had been ripped open, a crucifix jammed into the wound.

In County Tyrone two brothers and a sister were blown apart by a boobytrap bomb. The girl was eight months pregnant, but this was not known until some time later, when her unborn baby was discovered several hundred feet away among the debris and wreckage of the explosion.

On Friday, May 17, 1974, three cars were hijacked in Belfast, packed with explosives and driven south to Dublin in the Irish Republic. They were left on Parnell Street, Talbot Street, and South Leinster Street. (After office hours these streets are thronged with commuters hurrying to railway stations for their trains.) I happened to be walking across the playing fields of Trinity College and was some 300 yards away when, at 5.30 p.m., the car on South Leinster Street exploded. Even at a distance the shock waves were staggering. An acrid brown cloud of smoke drifted over the area. Racing to South Leinster Street I was confronted by a sight I am not likely to forget. A young woman who had been alongside the car when it blew up was killed instantly, smashed against a wall and cremated in a sheet of flame. Across the street another woman lay dead. In nearby Leinster Lane an old man weltered in a huge pool of frothing blood, both his legs blown off. He flopped about like a seal as the blood spread terribly.

The car in Talbot Street exploded at five-twenty-seven. Seven people were killed. The body of a man was taken from the window of a department store: faceless, its limbs enmeshed with those of a dead woman. Limbs and flesh were scattered about the street. There were bursts and splashes of blood everywhere. Scores of injured lay sprawled grotesquely in the street, shrieking for help. Twelve cars were wrecked.

The bomb in Parnell Street exploded at 5.30 p.m. Five people died instantly. A baby was blasted into the cellar of a pub. A man's leg was blown away. So was half his skull, which lay bloody on the pavement, like a bowl of bone. One woman walked to a hospital and collapsed, a fragment of the exploded car lodged in her back. Time literally stood still; the force of the blast had stopped all the clocks in the area at exactly five-thirty.

That same evening a car-bomb exploded in Monaghan Town in the Irish Republic at 7 p.m. It had been placed in Church Square, the town's main shopping centre. Five people were killed, and 16 were injured. The final tally for the day was 30 dead and several hundred maimed and injured. All were civilians.

This is the reality of contemporary Ireland, the complexities of religion, race, history and politics reduced to the simplicity and immediacy of terror. There are no longer any clean hands in Northern Ireland, where rival paramilitary groups, Catholic and Protestant, each infatuated and imprisoned by its own mythology, have been locked in mortal combat for . . . long years.

Source:

de Santana, Hubert. *Maclean's.* May 3, 1976, p. 36.

The Holy Roman Rollers

The charismatic renewal movement among Roman Catholics has been seen by some as evidence of a response to the limits of the modern industrial world. Others, however, view it as probably a short-term "irregularity" in the secularization trend.

Against a background of strumming guitars and a rattling tambourine, the People of Joy kiss and embrace. Only a week before, they filled the 200 seats in St. Gerard's Parish Hall in Calgary. Tonight, there's standing room only until a couple of dozen more chairs are pulled from storage. By 8.15 p.m. everyone is belting out glory hallelujah: "With sanctified hearts and hands that are raised, come join a song of praise to our God." Arms outstretched, bodies swaying, the crowd radiates contentment.

Punctuating their prayers with cries of "praise" and "glory," they rise – one after another – to testify to prophecies fulfilled, to pray for healing, to recount visions. One woman faints. A man speaks in tongues. A father announces: "Christ has a new soldier in his army": an eight-pound boy to be named Christian. By 9.30 p.m., the more energetic are step dancing in the aisles, while musicians lead the rest in a rousing rendition of "the Holy Ghost will set your feet a-dancing." It's a celebration straight out of Elmer Gantry of the Holy Rollers. But the People of Joy are mostly Roman Catholic adherents of the Catholic pentecostal movement that is growing – they claim – at the rate of one new Canadian group every day.

At the heart of Catholic pentecostalism, more frequently called the Charismatic Renewal movement, is the concept of an extraordinarily personal God. "He is going to take away the things we rely on," one convert assured the People of Joy as he recounted a dream about losing his job. Sure enough, he was subsequently fired, but "The Lord was beside me," and he was so joyful "I couldn't wait to get home and tell my wife." Another man, without a decent mattress to sleep on, woke one morning to find a mattress in his garbage. He had chores to do, so "I told the Lord to leave it there awhile." By the time he returned, there were three complete beds in the refuse. "Hallelujah," the crowd shouts.

As a group, the Catholic pentecostalites are fluent and articulate, riding a high that's irresistibly infectious. "And every one of them came out of darkness," says Father Denis Phaneuf of Saskatoon, one of the seven-member committee set up to guide the movement in Western Canada. According to Charismatic Renewal's voluminous writings, the movement sprang up simultaneously at three American universities in the late Sixties, then spread to Canada about 1969. Numbers, adherents agree, are "irrelevant" because the movement is growing so rapidly. But Quebec, with 1,000 known prayer groups, is the acknowledged Canadian leader. . . . The West claims 10,000 converts.

Like Protestant pentecostals, Charismatic Renewal leans heavily on a literal intepretation of the Bible, although Catholics steer clear of strict fundamentalism. . . . They accept Biblical references to being baptized in the Holy Spirit, to the laying on of hands by fellow worshippers, to the gift of tongues, and to the powers of prophecy and healing. In charismatic prayer groups, miracles still happen, God speaks to people personally in dreams and/or visions, and He heals the sick (usually the spiritually ill but occasional physical ailments as well).

Speaking or singing in tongues – messages transmitted via an unknown language – is a regular event for the "born again" – people who have welcomed Jesus into their hearts.

Officially, the Roman Catholic church views the movement as further evidence of the Holy Spirit at work. Pope Paul VI has personally given Charismatic Renewal his blessing. Canadian bishops have likewise issued a generally favorable declaration, although their message warns of excessive emotionalism and the dangers of a fixation on tongues, prophecy or healing.

Priests and nuns are prominent in prayer groups, but Charismatic Renewal is primarily a lay movement that cuts through age and religious barriers. The People of Joy range from babies in diapers to the geriatric set. Some 60% are Roman Catholic, the rest run the gamut of other religions. Father Phaneuf's own conversion came without his having heard of the Charismatic Renewal movement. During a prayer group, "I heard the voice of the Lord saying, 'My son, you are born again.' And from that day, I wanted to pray day and night."

Just why the Roman Catholic church should now be ripe for renewal is a question "everyone struggles with," Father Phaneuf says. "There are greater forces of darkness and cultural disintegration now than mankind has ever before experienced." Thus the birth of a movement adherents believe is bigger than any the church has ever experienced.

Source:

Maclean's. November 15, 1976.

The Secularization Argument

According to the proponents of the **secularization argument**, traditional religion has experienced a decline parallel to modern industrialization. The increase in specialized activities has led to a reduction in the number of areas of life over which religion has authority, including meaning. Such a trend can be seen in the loss of influence of the church in Europe since the medieval period, or in a similar loss of territorial authority experienced by the Roman Catholic Church in Quebec since approximately 1960.

Secularization further involves the adopting of an empirical-material outlook, the industrial world view, whereby the individual's focus and commitment are given to reality as known through the senses. Social change correlates, such as urbanization, urban growth, higher education, technological development, work force participation, an emphasis upon consumption, and the advent of mass media, are seen as factors contributing to this secularization of consciousness.

The Persistence Argument

Other observers, however, have questioned this posited decline of religion as it has been traditionally known. They argue instead for the viability of religion. There are various forms of this **persistence argument**. In the manner of Durkheim, Davis (1949) has contended that because of the functions that religion performs, its future is not in question. Although there is a limit to the extent to which a society can operate guided by illusion, says Davis, there is also a limit to which a society can be guided by sheer rationality. He therefore argues that while religion will certainly experience change, including the birth of new sects, it is unlikely to be replaced by science and technology.

In a similar fashion, Bell (1977) has argued that a return to the sacred is imminent. Following three centuries of rational and material emphases, the limits of modernism and alternatives to religion are beginning to be experienced. "We are now groping for a new vocabulary whose keyword seems to be limits," says Bell. New religions will consequently arise in response to the core questions of existence – death, tragedy, obligation, love.

Another well known argument for the persistence of religion in industrial societies is offered by Parsons (1964). Christianity, according to Parsons, continues to flourish in the modern western world, "most conspicuously in the United States." Parsons further asserts that specialization need not be equated with a loss of significance for religion. On the contrary, religious values have now pervaded society and religion is presently being sustained with unprecedented efficiency, precisely because religious organizations can concentrate on religion. He further sees "the individualistic principle inherent in Christianity" as contributing to religious autonomy, a situation in which the individual is responsible for deciding what to believe and with whom to associate in the social expression and reinforcement of commitment. Far from being in a state of demise, then, Christianity for Parsons is characterized by institutionalization and **privatization**.

Still another proponent of the persistence of religion is Greeley (especially, 1972), who calls the secularization argument a myth. Greeley criticizes the common forms of the argument and concludes that contemporary religion does indeed face pressures and is certainly unimportant for some. But he contends that such pressures and variations in commitment are not unique to our time, and expresses confidence in religion's future.

On the one hand, then, there are a number of social scientists who see industrialization and its specialization, and empirical-material features as having a negative effect, largely irreversible, upon religious commitment. On the other hand, there are observers who question such a relationship – Davis and Bell its permanence, and Parsons and Greeley its existence. The manner in which industrialization actually influences religious commitment is therefore still very much in question.

The Preliminary Evidence

The debate over modern industrialization's relationship to religion, however, is clearly one that needs to be resolved not around the seminar table but rather by examining what is happening in the world – literally. Adequate data must of necessity be cross-cultural, if industrialization's effect upon religion is to be understood apart from specific societal idiosyncrasies.

International Poll Data. In a significant summary of international Gallup Poll data, Sigelman (1977) reports that religious commitment measured by belief in God, life after death, and self-reported commitment tends to be highest in developing Third World countries and lowest in highly industrialized western European countries (see Table 12-7). Consistent with the industrialization-secularization hypothesis, the commitment level of an increasingly industrialized Canada lies between these two extremes.

Though such international findings do not exclude the possibility of a return to religion, as envisioned by Bell, at this point in history the data appear to support the secularization thesis. A clear-cut, contrasting return to religion pattern is not presently visible.

There is one important societal exception to this general relationship between industrialization and religion – the United States. In that country commitment levels remain high. Yet following such writers as Herberg (1960), Berger (1961), and Luckmann (1967), the United States may not be exempt from industrialization's effects. While outwardly still alive and well, American religion also gives considerable evidence of being secularized not only from without

but also from within. These observers argue that religious organizations are being increasingly infiltrated by American culture, with the result that secularization does not stop at the church steps.

But this process works both ways. Religion has historically been strongly embedded in American ideology and continues to play a significant role in powerful nationalistic tendencies or what Bellah (1967) and others have referred to as **American civil religion**. As Herberg (1960) has put it:

Americans, by and large, do have their "common religion" and that "religion" is the system familiarly known as the American Way of Life . . . . By every realistic criterion the American Way of Life is the operative faith of the American people.

As a result, says Herberg, "To be a Protestant, a Catholic, or a Jew are today the alternative ways of being an American." More recently, Mauss and Rokeach (1977) have argued:

Any comparisons between the United States and other countries in religious matters must take into account the unique part that religion has played in the history of the United States . . . . In America, a declaration of belief in some kind of deity is little more than an affirmation of the national heritage. [This is why] belief in deity can easily coexist, as it always has in America, with continuing increases in educational levels and in scientific advancements.

However, even in the U.S., mainline denominations have known considerable membership losses since the 1960s. Some observers have pointed out that prior to that time institutional religion in America prospered because the values expounded by Protestants, Catholics, and Jews were consistent with conservative political and family values (Nelsen and Potvin, 1980). But with the post-1960s shift in values, religion no longer is experiencing its previous level of establishment. Instead, an increasing level of disestablishment is most pronounced among the affluent young.

Accordingly, the affluent, educated, culture-affirming mainline denominations have been hit the hardest thus far. But the trend will eventually spread to the more conservative denominations as well (Hoge and Roozen, 1979).

TABLE 12-7. BELIEF IN GOD AND LIFE AFTER DEATH, AND IMPORTANCE OF RELIGIOUS BELIEFS FOR SELECTED COUNTRIES AND AREAS

	God	Life After Death	Beliefs: "Very Important"
	%	%	%
Britain	76	43	23
Canada	89	54	36
France	72	39	22
India	98	72	81
Italy	88	46	36
Japan	38	18	12
Scandinavia	65	35	17
United States	94	69	56
West Germany	72	33	17
Africa	96	69	73
Far East	87	62	71
Latin America	95	54	62
North America	94	67	54
Western Europe	78	44	27

SOURCE: Compiled from Sigelman, Lee. "Multi-nation surveys of religious beliefs." *Journal for the Scientific Study of Religion*, 16, 1977:290.

Most religions have sacred objects that are used in their rituals. The shofar is a ram's horn with no reed or manmade means of reproducing sound. The ancient Hebrews used it as a trumpet in battle; today it is used at Rosh Hashanah and Yom Kippur.

In sum, relative to other countries religion in the United States continues to flourish, yet nevertheless gives evidence of experiencing the secularizing tendencies of modern industrialization.

The Canadian Situation. We have already observed that to varying degrees Canadians assert belief in God, claim to pray to or experience God, believe in the divinity of Jesus, and maintain that there is life after death. Yet while the people of this country do not exclude the supernatural, they nevertheless do not give evidence of adhering to a well defined **religious meaning system**. Indeed, as we noted earlier, perhaps only one in five Canadians give even preliminary evidence of being committed to a traditional type of Christianity. A majority, almost 75 percent, have a

fragmented, unfocused religious orientation. The remaining 25 percent exhibit "other religion" or "no religion" tendencies (Bibby 1982).

Significantly, despite the extensive publicity given the so-called new religions, only about 1 percent of Canadians claim to be strongly interested in activities and groups such as TM, Hare Krishna, the Moonies, Eckankar, and Scientology. Only approximately one-half of those expressing strong interest are actually participating in any groups. The possibility that interest and involvement are transitory is suggested by the finding that almost another 3 percent of Canadians say that they had once been strongly interested in one or more of the new religions. A recent related study of new religion participation in Montreal found that, although participation is high, adherents typically establish peripheral ties with groups and then drop out (Bird and Reimer, 1982).

Such findings suggest that, contrary to popular belief, the new religions are not functioning as alternatives to traditional religion for large numbers of people.

The majority of Canadians, rather than searching for old or new religious answers, appear to give only passing attention to so-called ultimate questions (that is, life's purpose, suffering, and death). This seems to be in part because people are preoccupied with life itself, and in part because they have resolved these questions. Because Canadians commonly possess fragmented Judaic-Christian ideas instead of a system of belief, they are inclined to respond to ultimate questions with empirically-based explanations. Life is seen as having no meaning beyond that which we assign it; suffering is viewed as an inevitable part of existence; death is looked on as a mystery that defies knowledge.

Such a secular outlook is reflected in additional national survey findings. Some 80 percent feel that science will gain greater influence by the end of the century, and over 50 percent say the same of education. Yet less than 10 percent indicate such optimism about the future of Protestantism, Catholicism, or Judaism, and 20 percent feel that atheism will gain in influence. Further indicative of the increasing prevalence of the industrial world view is the finding that Canadians who describe themseles as "once active but no longer active in religious groups" cite not only organizational, but also belief factors as reasons for their disaffiliation. Along with skepticism about both the goals (53 percent) and integrity (56 percent) of religious groups are the responses: "decreasing interest in ultimate questions" (41), "increasing disbelief" (40), and "conflict between religion and science" (35) (Bibby, 1979a).

To what extent does such a secular outlook represent a change from the past? No one really knows. Detailed comparative information on personal religious commitment in years gone by is simply unavailable.

Nevertheless, the question of change can be addressed by recalling two of our previous findings pertaining to organized religion and the correlates of industrialization. We have already seen that organized religion in Canada has been experiencing a dramatic numerical drop. Churches are losing many of their active members and failing to replenish them through immigration, birth, and **proselytism**. Given the crucial role of the religious group in the formation and sustenance of religious beliefs, such a marked decline in religious group participation can be expected to reflect itself in a diminished level of commitment to Judaic-Christian ideas. Religious privatization may give hope to the pro-religious, but if it is groupless, it is an untenable dream.

We have also seen that industrial correlate variables, such as community size, education, work-force participation, and media exposure, continue to have a slight but consistently negative impact on religious commitment. Further, such a decline in religiosity has increased with the passage of time. Industrialization, therefore, appears to be contributing to the decline of traditional religion in Canada.

Given the state of organized religion in this country and the apparent negative effects of these industrialization correlates, it seems reasonable to conclude that religious commitment in Canada is being adversely influenced by modern industrialization. Barring a change in such causal relationships such lessening of commitment will undoubtedly continue. This is not to say that religion will disappear altogether, or that there will not be some short-term irregularities in the decline trend. But the pervasiveness of commitment to traditional religion in Canada may well be a thing of the past.

SUMMARY

1. Sociology uses the scientific method to study religion, in contrast to religion, which explores reality beyond that which can be known empirically.

2. The sociology of religion has been strongly influenced by the theoretical contributions of Marx, who stressed the compensatory role of religion in the face of economic deprivation; Durkheim who emphasized both the social origin of religion and its important social cohesive function; and Weber, who gave considerable attention to the relationship between ideas and behavior.

3. Religion can be defined as a system of meaning with a supernatural referent used to interpret the world. Humanist meaning perspectives make no such use of the supernatural realm, attempting instead to make life meaningful.

4. Personal religious commitment has increasingly come to be seen as having many facets or dimensions, with four being commonly noted: belief, practice, experience, and knowledge.

5. Collective religiosity instills and sustains personal commitment. The theologically-centered church-sect typology has been increasingly abandoned in favor of organizational analyses that examine religious collectivities in the same manner as other groups. In Canada, organized religion has experienced a considerable decline in participation during recent years, which has critical implications for commitment at the individual level.

6. The variation in levels of individual commitment characterizing complex societies has led to explanations with individual and structural emphases. Reflection, socialization, deprivation, and emotional predisposition have been prominent among the former explanations, while the dominant structural assertion has been the secularization argument.

7. The key source of religious commitment in an industrializing Canada is socialization. Although it is located in a highly secular milieu, religion's socialization efforts are decreasing both in incidence and impact.

8. Religion appears to be at best one of many paths leading to valued characteristics such as personal happiness and compassion.

9. Although religion sometimes has a disruptive impact, it more commonly seems to contribute to social solidarity, frequently mirroring the characteristics of groups and societies.

10. Historically, observers of religion have been divided on its future, asserting both secularization and persistence hypotheses. Internationally, the secularization argument appears to have substantial support.

GLOSSARY

American civil religion. Tendency for nationalistic tendencies in the United States to have many characteristics similar to religions; established Judaic-Christianity is drawn upon selectively.

Church-sect typology. Framework, dating back to Weber, that examines religious organizations in terms of ideal-type church and sect characteristics.

Collective conscience. Durkheim's term, referring to the awareness of the group being more than the sum of its individual members; norms, for example, appear to exist on a level beyond the consciences of the individual group members.

Collective religiosity. Religious commitment as manifested in and through religious groups; key to the creation and sustenance of personal religiosity.

Denominationalism. Tendency for a wide variety of Protestant religious groups to come into being, seemingly reflecting variations not only in theology but also – and perhaps primarily – in social characteristics.

Dimensions of religiosity. Various facets of religious commitment; Stark and Glock, for example, identify four: belief, experience, practice, and knowledge.

Humanist perspectives. Systems of meaning used to interpret the world that do not have a supernatural referent (e.g., communism, scientism).

Industrial world view. Outlook associated with industrialization, characterized by empiricism (the limiting of reality to that which can be known through the senses) and materialism (the commitment of one's life to the pursuit of empirical reality).

Persistence argument. Assertion that religion will continue to have a significant place in the modern world, either because it never has actually declined, or because people can absorb only so much rationality and materialism.

Personal religiosity. Religious commitment at the level of the individual.

Privatization. Parsons' term for the alleged tendency of people to work out their own religious beliefs and associations in an individualistic, autonomous manner.

Profane and the sacred. Two categories by which Durkheim claimed all things are classified; the sacred represents those things viewed as warranting profound respect, the profane encompasses everything else.

Proselytism. Effort to convert people from outside of one's religious group or faith; also called evangelism.

Protestant ethic. Term associated with Weber, referring to the Protestant Reformation emphases of Calvin, Luther, and others upon the importance of work performed well as an indication of living one's life "to the glory of God;" key characteristics include diligence, frugality, rational use of time.

Religion. System with a trans-empirical referent which is used to address life's meaning.

Religious meaning system. Systems of meaning used to interpret the world which have a supernatural referent (e.g., Christianity, Hinduism, astrology).

Secularization argument. Theory that religion as it has been traditionally known is declining continuously and irreversibly.

FURTHER READING

Clark, S.D., *Church and Sect in Canada.* Toronto: University of Toronto Press, 1948. A Canadian classic that examines the social factors contributing to the rise of different types of religious groups in this country.

Crysdale, Stewart, and Les Wheatcroft (eds.). *Religion in Canadian Society.* Toronto: Macmillan, 1976. One of the few works available dealing with the social-scientific study of religion in Canada with articles by leading scholars in sociology, anthropology, and history.

Glock, Charles Y. (ed.). *Religion in Sociological Perspectives.* Belmont, Calif.: Wadsworth, 1973. Provides a succinct summary of some of the most significant empirical studies in religion conducted by "the Berkeley school."

Needleman, Jacob, and George Baker (eds.). *Understanding the New Religions.* New York: Seabury Press, 1978. Twenty-nine essays exploring the nature and sources of new religions in the United States; interdisciplinary, drawing upon top scholars in a number of fields.

Neibuhr, H. Richard. *The Social Sources of Denominationalism.* New York: Henry Holt and Company, 1929. A classic attempt to probe the role social factors (e.g., economics, nationality, race, region) had in creating denominationalism in Europe and America.

Westhues, Kenneth (ed.). *The Canadian Journal of Sociology* 3, Spring, 1978. A valuable collection of articles by leading academics comparing organized religion in Canada and the United States. Groups include mainline and conservative Protestants, Roman Catholics, Jews, Mennonites, and Mormons.

CHAPTER 13
POLITY

KATHRYN M. KOPINAK

In 1980, 118 590 immigrants to Canada took out citizenship (Secretary of State, 1980). They completed the process of becoming a member of the Canadian polity by making this commitment,

I swear (or affirm) that I will be faithful and bear true allegiance to Her Majesty Queen Elizabeth the Second, Queen of Canada, Her Heirs and Successors, according to law and that I will faithfully observe the laws of Canada and fulfil my duties as a Canadian citizen.

Although many of us take our status as citizens for granted, people joining us from other parts of the world are often eager to become legal members of the Canadian polity because it will afford them political freedoms and the protection of private rights that may not have been available in their countries of origin. The comparison that their situation evokes brings into focus the unique character of the Canadian **polity**, that political unit which is territorially defined as Canada, including our particular social, cultural, and economic life.

While we may find the contemporary political scene in Canada exciting, humorous, or otherwise, it is nevertheless important to understand that our polity has developed in response to particular historical events, and has not always existed in its present form. For example, women could not exercise the most basic right of citizenship, the franchise, until 1918. Native people could not vote in federal elections until 1965. With the patriation of the constitution in 1982, our political character continues to change and develop. Changes such as these make us aware that political life is a continuous social process, as well as a set of institutions.

This chapter examines the Canadian polity using the three sociological perspectives set out in Chapter 1. It will describe the internal structure of the Canadian polity, analyze how it functions, and discuss the ways in which different groups of people participate in the institutions that constitute this structure. In order to understand the role of these institutions, a brief historical look at their origins will introduce the more specific case of Canada.

THE HISTORICAL DEVELOPMENT OF THE MODERN POLITY

Citizenship has evolved over the last two hundred and fifty years in the western world. Civil rights, such as those in our Charter of Rights, first developed in Britain during the eighteenth century. Political rights, such as the right to vote and hold office, were extended in the nineteenth century. Social rights, like the right to a minimum standard of living to share fully in the social heritage of the polity are still being contested in the twentieth century (Marshal, 1964). With these changes, the polity has become a much more complex and specialized structure than it had been in the feudal era. Moreover, curious contradictions have occurred because of the different rates at which the three types of rights developed. Although most people in the western world might be equal before the law, because of the more complete development of political rights, the social inequalities based on characteristics like class, gender, and ethnicity have prevented all of them from the full exercise of these political rights. This is a uniquely modern inconsistency, in which status may not always be proportionate to power. For example, every Canadian citizen has or will have the legal right to run for federal office, but for those who do not have the appropriate education and party connections, the opportunity to exercise this right is lost.

The modern polity, based on the British model, developed over several centuries in response to particular events in the history of modern capitalism. The civil rights component of citizenship referred to above was in fact promoted by capitalists who proved more progressive on this issue than their feudal predecessors. These rights allowed the individual to operate as an independent unit in the competitive market economy and simultaneously absolved the capitalist of any social responsibility for the individual's welfare. In the pre-capitalist period the aristocracy had taken some responsibility for the well-being of the serfs and was bound to take care of them in bad times. But in the new system, capitalists accumulated for themselves any surplus that was produced and took no responsibility for the worker.

As early as the twelfth century in Britain, judicial institutions began to be established to define and defend the civil rights of the individual. Parliament then became much more developed and continued to define the political powers of the national government as a separate institution. Later, mass media began to arise, in the form of newspapers, partly as a response to the rights of freedom of speech, freedom of religion, and so on.

As civil rights were extended in Britain, some individuals could increasingly move into occupations in which they might prosper and, if they husbanded their resources, move up the class scale. Once they had reached a certain level of prosperity, they might also enjoy the political rights that went along with this class position. In addition, successive Reform Acts extended the franchise to those who owned less and less property and continued to reduce the qualifications for becoming a candidate. Finally, in 1918, the vote and the right to run for office became available to all British men, regardless of wealth or property. Until 1920, Canadians had to own a certain amount of property in order to vote.

To further the enjoyment of these new political rights, other institutions developed in the polity. Political parties and interest groups arose to give new voters real access to the political process, as well as to articulate their interests at the national and provincial levels. The old aristocracy was also eager to capture these new votes through parties and interest groups, lest new organizations be formed that did not favor them.

This brief historical review demonstrates how the development of the modern polity has brought under public regulations many of those activities formerly considered private prerogatives. This continues today,

Figure 13-1. The Polity

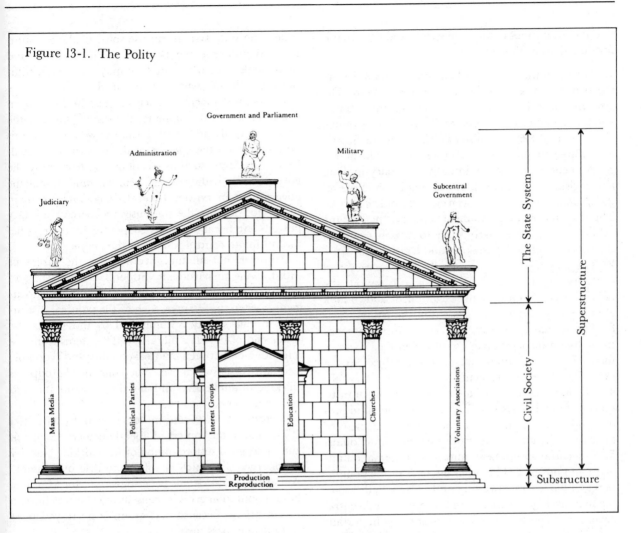

with more laws passed and more police attention to injustices that occur in the most intimate realms; like the beating of wives by husbands and the abuse of children by parents. With the development of citizenship in the last two and a half centuries, the group of institutions regulating public life have become what is defined as the **state system**. That which is still considered private, or what is left after the state developed as a separate system, is **civil society**. Civil society includes that area of social life in which we conduct our everyday, domestic affairs. Thus, it is in the sphere of civil society that we make arrangements for housing, choose who will we eat with, and so on.

As indicated above, some political institutions link civil society to the state system. And because economic forces are seen as fundamental to much of political life, such forces are analytically considered as separate from civil society and as an independent level of social structure. Economic activity constitutes society's base. Civil society and the state system are two levels of the **superstructure**, resting upon this **substructure**, or base. These three components of the polity – the substructure, civil society, and the state system – with their constituent parts, are represented in Figure 13-1.

The State System. Miliband (1973) has summarized the institutions in the state system and their manifest functions in this way:

1. The government and parliamentary assemblies are the two most visible bodies in the state system. The government includes the Prime Minister, the cabinet, and some administrative bodies like the Privy Council Office and the Prime Minister's Office that are directly answerable to the Prime Minister. The role of the government is to take the initiative in policy-making and legislation. Parliamentary assemblies include all those candidates who have been elected from all parties. Those members of parliament who are not in the cabinet or the ruling party share to a lesser extent in the processes of policy-making and legislation.

2. The administration includes the bureaucracy and civil servants. Its official function is to carry out the policies decided upon by the government and to look after the day-to-day management of the polity.

3. The military, security, and police forces are entrusted with the legitimate use of violence or coercive force. These institutions are officially subject to the executive of the government.

4. The judiciary is one of the more independent institutions of the state system. Its official function is to protect and defend individuals from the infringement of their rights by other state institutions and individuals.

5. Subcentral government units move information upward and downward between the mass of the population and the federal government. In Canada, these are the provincial governments. In this country, subcentral governments possess jurisdiction over many important areas, such as education, culture, and recreation. They are more powerful than subcentral governments in many other parts of the world.

This, then, is the state system that officially wields power and that has become separated from civil society over a long period of time.

Civil Society. Miliband also indicates several other parts of the polity that have political roles to play, but that are part of civil society rather than the state system. These include political parties, pressure groups, churches, and mass media, as well as other institutions. These latter institutions link civil society to the state. The state system can use some of these institutions to influence the behavior of individuals, and individuals in their private lives may use these institutions to influence what happens in the state.

In liberal democracies such as those in the western world, civil society dominates the state. Although the state is the only body with formal power, it holds this power through the consent of the governed. Formalized procedures (such as elections) exist whereby the governed can withdraw their consent and unseat the government in power. Liberal democracies remain stable not because the state uses its coercive military power, but becaue people cooperate in their belief that ultimate control rests with the people.

However, not all the governed use the threat of withdrawing their consent with equal effectiveness to control the government in power. As we will document later in the chapter, each of the political institutions in civil society is dominated by those from the upper end of the class hierarchy. This stems from the contradiction between political equality and economic inequality discussed above. When one social group has this kind of intellectual and moral leadership, it is said to be hegemonic.

Hegemony is a concept developed by Gramsci (1971), and in the context of liberal democracies means "the ideological subordination of the working class by the bourgeoisie, which enables it to rule by consent" (Anderson, 1977). It has been suggested, for example, that a population gives its consent to government by a certain group, because that group is portrayed positively in the mass media.

In societies undergoing social change, hegemony can also be used to mean "an historic phase in which a given group moves beyond a position of corporate existence and defense of its economic position and aspires to a position of leadership in the political and social arena" (Hoarse and Smith, 1971). An example of a group that became hegemonic in this way is Poland's union Solidarity. During the 1970s, Communist party leaders put several plans into effect that they hoped would bring a modicum of economic security to a people starved for the most basic consumer goods. When these economic plans failed, and the entire world economy moved toward recession, the

Polish people refused to accept economic failure. They formed the union Solidarity and began to struggle with their government for more political and social freedoms, as well as economic reforms. They became hegemonic to the extent that they were able to wrest the consent of the Polish people away from a party leadership sympathetic to the Soviet Union and to mobilize the people in order to gain more liberties, like a temporary freeze on food prices, some Saturday holidays, radio broadcasts of church services, and so on.

Solidarity was not able to maintain this hegemony, because the military institution within the Polish state system took complete control, declaring martial law. In fact, most totalitarian polities do not usually maintain themselves through hegemony in civil society. Characteristically, the state expands to engulf civil society so that the division between the two becomes blurred (Anderson, 1977). In this type of polity, the military and security portion of the state successfully coerces people into cooperating with the state. Other institutions in the state system also assume an enlarged role.

The distinction that has been drawn between the state system and civil society, and the concomittant importance of hegemony in both stable and changing societies, makes it clear that the sociological study of political life must include more than government and politicans. To study that which is political means to study those individuals and institutions that wield power.

Weber defined **power** as the ability of an individual or group to control, influence, or manipulate others' behavior, whether they wish to cooperate or not. From our discussion it is clear that power is wielded not only by the institutions in the state system, but also by the political institutions in civil society. It is therefore important to understand that the state system is not synonymous with the political system, and that power may be wielded in both public and private life. Later we will see that what happens in the base of society influences the form that politics takes at all levels.

This introduction has its roots in the conflict approach to the study of politics, because the conflict theory is the dominant paradigm in Canadian political sociology. The next section of this chapter will explain this and the other two approaches.

THREE PERSPECTIVES

In this section, we will use the three basic sociological perspectives – conflict, structural functionalism and symbolic interaction – to shed light on political life in Canada. Each approach emphasizes a different aspect of political life, although symbolic interaction can be used by both conflict theorists and structural functionalists to enrich their analyses. The structural functionalist and the conflict perspectives are more likely to constitute opposing viewpoints on the same issue and to have differing policy implications.

Conflict Theory

Conflict theory maintains that the operation of the state system and the political institutions in civil society reflect the way people are related to each other in the productive process. From the conflict perspective, then, those who own, have authority over or control natural resources, factories, technical processes, and the like, are also predicted to be more powerful in the government and other institutions of the state system than those who are wage laborers and have little control or authority in the labor process. This perspective also predicts that those who are predominant in the productive process will be hegemonic in the political institutions of civil society, such as the mass media, interest groups, and so on.

In this ruling position, the dominant class can propagate a set of ideas, an ideology, that justifies or legitimates its dominance and attempts to prevent social change that is not to its advantage. This ideology is dispersed through institutions like the mass media, the schools, and in some cases the church. Influence can be seen as going primarily from the base to the superstructure. But once a social system is established, influence also flows from important institutions within the superstructure (like government) to the base in order to maintain social relations the way they are – to maintain, in other words, the status quo.

An in-depth discussion of the conflict perspective can be found in Chapter 8. Each of the later subsections of this chapter will demonstrate how people's relation to each other in the labor process is reflected in political life and how those in political institutions can in turn effect the productive process.

Structural Functionalism

Unlike conflict theorists, who see the modes of production and reproduction as the prime movers in political affairs, structural functionalists consider values, norms, attitudes, and other cerebral processes as the basic determinants of political life. As one of the best known spokesmen for *structural functionalism*, Talcott Parsons (1960) sees the state as the institution specializing in "society's goal achievement." This means that it is the job of the state to arrive at the collective commitments, obligations, and conscious goals of the society as a whole without favoring any particular group within society.

Parsons points out that political acts in the United States are judged by how well they provide for economic adaptation and mastery of the physical conditions of life. Other important goals are progress and improvement. Porter (1965) believes that the Canadian political system lacks such clearly articulated goals. While Americans express particular social values in phrases such as "life, liberty, and the pursuit of happiness," our watchwords are phrased in more geographic terms, as in "from sea to sea." If there is a major Canadian goal, Porter believes it is an integrative one, expressed in such wishes as the desire to maintain national unity.

Despite this emphasis on collective goals, structural functionalists do not deny the existence of conflict or inequality. On the contrary, they see it as important that the existing balance between competing groups be maintained so that society will remain stable. In modern industrial societies, structural functionalists believe that economic, social, and political inequality is necessary for the realization of collective goals by the state. Therefore, they support rule by a political elite. Prolonged political participation on the part of the mass of people is considered an unstabilizing force for society as a whole. This view of the world sees it as necessary that differential rewards be provided for those with the most political skill, so that leadership will be maintained by those with the most expertise.

Symbolic Interaction

Symbolic interaction theory does not embrace entire systems but analyzes interaction between smaller numbers of people. This, however, does not make it inapplicable to the study of political life. Although they have approached the problem from different directions, both conflict theorists and structural functionalists have hypothesized and found that a very small proportion of people in the modern polity actually wield power and can be considered political activists. Much of the work of the symbolic interactionist perspective, on the other hand, can be used to understand the small number of political actors who, through the use of the mass media, define the political situation for us (Hall, 1973).

Symbolic interactionists do not view political life as in any way abnormal or outside the rules that govern other behavior. As a result, they can apply the same techniques they use in analyzing everyday life to the study of political life. Although they do not view politics as unusual, they do consider politics as something that happens outside of institutions, as an order that is negotiated and constantly in a state of flux (Effrat, 1973). They are particularly interested, therefore, in the give and take that goes on in parliamentary debate and in the symbolic manipulation that occurs in the pageantry surrounding leadership.

While structural functionalists might use symbolic interaction to show how collective goals come to be generated, conflict theorists could use it to show how political systems devise ideologies that legitimate their activities. The point is that the symbolic interaction perspective can help us understand the use of symbols and images in the public forum. (See the boxed insert on this page.) The use of symbols in this area is extremely important in defining the situation and in bringing people together in groups or pulling them apart. For example, when English-speaking Canadians in favor of national unity call the Lévesque government "separatist," they emphasize its potential to fragment the country. When the Lévesque government refers to itself as *indépendantiste*, it is attempting to show the justice of its claims by identifying itself with other regimes that have overthrown tyranny.

Put Out More Flags

This article, which appeared in a British publication, shows how national symbols can be used to unite or divide a polity.

IF YOU HAPPEN to live in an industrial area there is one thing to be said for the slump; it's a lot quieter at night. As more and more factories, foundries, and mills close or go onto short time, the great clangings, bangings, and hisses that used to emanate from them and resound through the surrounding terraced streets until all hours exist now only in the memory.

Walking through one such district the other night the only sound I could hear was a low chattering. I asked a passerby what it was. "Sewing machines," he replied. "But I thought the textile trade was worse off than most," I said. "Certainly, every dress shop and gents' outfitters I pass seems to be having a closing down sale." "Too true," he answered, "but that place is making flags for the Royal wedding in July."

A few inquiries quickly showed that this was no isolated case. Right across the country the flag makers are working at full belt. From large firms with contracts to decorate The Mall and Constitution Hill, down to back street workshops turning out tiny tatters of red, white, and blue for tiny tots to wave at village fetes, the trade has not had it so good since the British Empire was wound up in the fifties and sixties.

Then they shared with the fireworks manufacturers in the great bonanza of orders that poured in from Tanzania and Togoland, Ceylon and the Seychelles. The present boom will inevitably be shorter but it promises to be nearly as sweet.

Oddly enough flags, like fireworks, seem to have originated in China. There are records showing that the founder of the Chou dynasty (1122BC) had a white flag carried in front of him wherever he went. Further, a low relief sculpture on the tomb of one Wou Leang T'sue of the Han dynasty, who died around 200BC, depicts cavalrymen with small flags on their lances. From China the use of flags seems to have travelled to India and the Middle East. Mohammed's followers carried black banners and it is generally assumed that the Crusaders who went to fight for the Holy Land copied the idea from the Saracens. This would seem to explain why the motif on most early European flags was a cross in one form or another.

From the Middle Ages on, the significance of flags grew and their making and meaning developed into a vast complex of lore and laws inextricably bound up with chivalry and heraldry. Firm rules governed their design, display, and even their size. Henry VIII laid it down that a king was entitled to eight yards, a duke seven, an earl six, and a baron five. The flag of a knight bachelor was a pennon which had swallow tails. To mark a deed of valour on the battlefield the king could, if he chose, cut off the swallow tails, converting it into a square banner and promoting its owner into a Knight Banneret or, as we have it nowadays, a baronet. A similar association between flag and rank lies behind the term ensign. It was originally applied to a British junior officer whose duty it was to carry the ensign or flag. It is obsolete here now, but the American navy still uses it.

Civilians can sometimes be as fascinated by flags as soldiers and sailors. They are called Vexillologists, a term coined from the Latin vesillum, a military standard, by Mr Whitney Smith, formerly professor of political economy at Boston University and believed to be the only full-time professional vexillologist in the world.

There are Flag Institutes in America, Britain, and many other countries, including Czechoslovakia, and Mr Smith keeps them in touch with one another through a quarterly magazine, the Flag Bulletin, which he edits from the Flag Research Centre in Massachussetts. He explains this world-wide interest by pointing out that more than half the independent nations have designed and adopted their national flags since the last war. Not only that, but they keep changing them. Syria changed its flag four times in 13 years, while Zanzibar had as many in only 18 months.

For most civilians, however, interest in flags tends to wane between periods of national crisis or celebration. Flags seem only to get into the news when some drunken holidaymaker unwittingly insults the symbol of his host country, when planning authorities object to some overenthusiastic display of them, or when controversies break out in conservative newspapers about when, where, and how they should be displayed on public buildings. And I would be surprised if a whole new controversy is not even now brewing up about the expense in the present hard times of those now being feverishly sewn together in readiness for July 29. As so often happens a device intended to unite people ends up dividing them.

Source:

Harry Whewell, *The Manchester Guardian*, April 12, 1981.

THE SUBSTRUCTURE

Figure 13-1 represents the classic Marxist metaphor of the polity as an edifice or building. The foundation or bottom floor, which consists of the dominant **modes of production** and reproduction, is the base. In the Canadian polity, the base includes the capitalist mode of production, both industrial forces of production and the relations of production between owners and wage-laborers and the reproduction of the species and of labor-power, both of which have been the jobs of women. Just as the top floors of any building rest on, or are supported by, the foundation, so also the modes of production and reproduction have a determining influence on civil society and the state system. We will see how this occurs in the following two sections.

Production

The question in which we are interested when we ask about the role of production in the polity is: How does a person's position in the relations of production influence the kind of political activities in which he or she will become involved? We noted in the last section that although individuals may be equal before the law, they may wield differing amounts of power because of their links to the productive process. This is the topic on which we would like to expand in this section.

Before considering how a person's links with the productive process can influence his or her political position, however, we must have a clear picture of all the possible types of political activity. Van Loon and Whittington (1981) have prepared a hierarchy of electoral participation (see Figure 13-2). This hierarchy is cumulative, meaning that those who engaged in the activities at the top of the list will probably have also engaged in those listed below. For example, people who have been political candidates will likely have already worked in other candidates' campaigns, been a member of a party, tried to convince others how to vote, and so on.

Of course, a hierarchy of electoral participation does not tell the whole story. There are several other ways people can participate in politics. Writing a letter to the editor of a newspaper, phoning a call-in radio

Figure 13-2. A Hierarchy of Electoral Participation

Gladiatorial Level
5%
- Holding a public office
- Being a political candidate
- Holding an office within a party
- Soliciting party funds
- Attending a strategy meeting or planning a campaign

Transitional Level
40%
- Contributing money to a political party
- Being an active party member
- Contributing time to a campaign
- Attending a meeting or rally

Spectator Level
- Contacting a public official or politician
- Attempting to convince people how to vote
- Initiating a political discussion
- Being interested in politics
- Exposing oneself to political stimuli
- Voting

show, participating in an intestest group such as a labor union or businessman's association, or boycotting expensive food in the supermarket all may influence the political process much more directly than working through the electoral system. Research done by political scientists to date, however, tends to concentrate on the electoral level, and much of our information is about people's activities in this sphere.

The types of electoral politics in which most people are involved cluster at or near the bottom of the hierarchy. Van Loon and Whittington (1981) report that only 5 percent of the Canadian population participate at the "gladiatorial" level, including soliciting party funds, planning party strategy, and standing as a candidate for election. About 40 percent participate at what they have called the "transitional" level, contributing time or money to a party or being an active party member. Most Canadians tend to be political spectators. According to a 1974 survey, fewer than 5 percent of Canadians have never voted, and 80 to 90 percent follow election campaigns in the media and by informal talk with friends. (Van Loon and Whittington, 1981).

As you may have already guessed, those at the top of the class ladder are also those most likely to participate at the gladiatorial level in the hierarchy of electoral participation. The higher a person's income the more likely he or she is to engage in politics at the gladiatorial level. Those elected to office come overwhelmingly from the professional ranks, and university educated people are more likely to become directly involved in approaching government officials.

There may be several reasons why those who are less privileged are less active at the electoral level. At this point, we can present some alternatives and suggest that this is a good problem for future research. If upper-middle-class people are the stars of the political theater, working-class people may be de facto excluded by the particular manners and language in which the performance is scripted. Working-class people may have less leisure time to spend on things like electoral politics, or they may conclude that their political goals will be more readily reached outside the electoral sphere. Rinehart (1978), for example, has argued that the strikes that reached an all-time Canadian high in 1974 and 1975 are the most obvious expressions of working-class discontent. He has suggested also that, because of their subordinate position in society, the immediate problem for workers is not in what we have called the ideological realm of politics, but in the pragmatic. Workers are concerned with their continued existence and act on these interests at the shop-floor level.

The overwhelming evidence from contemporary research on the class background of those who hold positions in the state system is that the upper end of the class hierarchy is not only over-represented, but it forms an elite closed to those who originate in other parts of the social structure. Clement (1975) examined the class background of those prominent in all institutions in the state system and determined how often members of the economic elite tended to take positions in the state elite for short periods of time. Amost four out of ten of the economic elite either had held some position in the state system or had a close relative who had. In recent years, overlap between the corporate and political sectors has increased rather than decreased. The boundaries of this elite, through which outsiders may not pass, are marked by private schools and private clubs.

Olsen (1977) also found that the political, judicial, and bureaucratic sectors of the state are made up primarily of middle-class Canadian males of British and French ancestry. While political sociologists all agree that the upper end of the class hierarchy is over-represented in the state system, one of the questions currently being debated is whether this elite should be seen as a foreign one, or whether a substantial component of the state elite is indigenous to this country. Regardless of the origin of this group, the findings indicate that there is something in Canada that can be considered a ruling class.

It is because of this imbalance in the way people from different social classes are represented in the political structure that our polity and polities like it are called liberal democracies. In a **liberal democracy**, everyone has the legal opportunity to participate in politics, and the structure is constitutionally democratic. But in fact only a limited few do participate at the highest level. A still more accurate term for this type of system might be "bourgeois democracy," since those who do the most participating are from the middle class or higher.

Once in power, members of the elite identify the interests of the country with their own interests, and have been found to implement policies that enable their class to profit. In the *Manifesto of the Communist Party*, Marx and Engels (1975) contended that, "The executive of the modern state is but a committee for managing the common affairs of the whole bourgeoisie." Although most political sociologists now consider this to be an oversimplification, the political situation in Canada does provide many examples of the overlap and alliance between the privileged and those who govern. Many of the founding fathers of Confederation were eminent financiers, railwaymen, or land speculators, and it has been suggested that one of the motives for the new union was to protect the economic interests of this group (Naylor, 1972). John A. Macdonald, for example, was president of the Manufacturer's Life Assurance Company. George-Etienne Cartier was a

"... would the minister not agree?"

The Employment Development Fund is one of the mechanisms by which the Ontario government attempts to create a favourable economic climate for investment by industry and to keep unemployment rates low. The question has been raised, however, as to whether industry has not taken unfair advantage of governments' willingness to subsidize them, and played individual governments off against each other, locating in the jurisdiction of the one that proves to be the highest bidder.

For example, on May 24, 1979, the Ontario government announced that it would provide TRW Canada Limited, which manufactures parts for automobile steering systems, with a grant of $420,000 through its Employment Development Fund to expand its plants in St. Catharines and Tillsonburg. At this time, Mr. Bradley, MPP for St. Catharines, replied that helping healthy companies is not a credit to you ... They've expanded already." When given an opportunity to pose a question at Queen's Park a few days later, Bradley had this to say:

In view of the fact that I attended a sod-breaking ceremony in St. Catharines on April 6, four days before the announcement of the Employment Development Fund in the provincial budget on April 10, and in view of the fact it was known in business circles months before the budget was brought down that TRW was to establish a plant outside of St. Catharines, would the minister not agree the expansion is taking place as a result of favourable markets being taken advantage of by a capable management and a competent work force? Would the minister not agree that ... the $420,000 really represents a windfall to TRW?

This was one of several grants given to what were considered well-established industries in Ontario in the spring of 1979. Political journalist Hugh Winsor was the first critic to call this bribery. He elaborates:

Of course, there is nothing illegal in giving away taxpayers' money in this fashion. Indeed, there is some suggestion that Mr. Grossman is doing a good job of it, if you are convinced that that is the only way companies are going to be persuaded to do what it is in their interest to do anyway. There is an important question of policy involved here and Ontario is in a genuine dilemma because it is competing with other jurisdictions that have also been drawn into the auction.

Those who support the government funding of private industry would say that the question of policy is whether governments should allow companies to go to other jurisdictions, while those against this practice would say that the question of policy is whether the government should take money from the have-nots, through taxation, and give it to the haves.

A survey conducted by the London Free Press in 1981 to follow up on the results of the granting of these monies, found that instead of creating new jobs, it had been invested in capital expenditures, like equipment, which later sat idle because of the downturn in the economy. The results of the newspaper's survey showed that "Of five Southwestern Ontario companies which shared more than $1 million in direct grants from the Ontario Employment Development Fund, none was able to report the government aid had increased employment."

Source:

Legislature of Ontario Debates. No. 52. Third Session, Thirty-first Parliament, pp. 2121–22; Legislature of Ontario Debates. No. 58. Third Session, Thirty-first Parliament, p. 2375; Hugh Winsor, "Sweet deals questioned," *Globe and Mail*, May 29, 1979; Gordon Sanderson "Ontario's job creation program a dismal flop," *London Free Press*, March 7, 1981.

director of the Grand Trunk Railway. Alexander Tilloch Galt was an executive in the British American Land Company.

Concerning the differential access of social classes to political power, an interesting comparison can be drawn between the conflict theories just presented and the structural functional viewpoint of Robert Presthus (1973). In a study that looked at governmental, bureaucratic, and interest group elites in an attempt to find which groups had the most influence on the political process, Presthus arrived at findings strikingly similar to those presented above. In his sample of the political elite, he found that 71 percent of members of parliament, 68 percent of directors of interest groups, and 97 percent of bureaucrats were from the upper middle class or higher. Also, the background of these people showed that interpersonal networks had been important in their recruitment into the elite, and that those with less privileged backgrounds did not have opportunities for the same mobility.

But Presthus (1973) interprets the political results of this phenomenon differently. His interpretation agrees that in fact the system of elite accommodation reinforces the status quo in Canada and protects the strong against the weak. Unlike Clement (1975), however, Presthus sees the restriction of access to political resources as necessary to the survival of the Canadian political system. Without elite rule fragmentation of the political system would result, because most Canadians come from different ethnic groups and religions and have varying regional loyalties, while elites are socialized into a more homogeneous class culture and therefore find communication and compromise easier. Olsen (1977), on the other hand, does not see accommodation at the elite level as necessarily leading to stability, but calls it a "rather fragile structure of alliances," which, he implies, could change quite drastically if there is dissent from those lacking the same access to the political process as the elites.

Reproduction

Just as Marxists have proposed that people's political activities are related to their positions in the production of commodities, socialist feminists have recently suggested that political behavior also depends on how a person is involved in reproduction. In our society, the bearing of children has important implications in the division of labor. Those who bear children are also socially defined as most appropriate for the roles of child-rearer and homemaker. Traditionally, motherhood has limited women's roles to the private sphere of civil society, whereas fatherhood has not implied such a restriction. On the contrary, it has propelled men into the work force to "bring home the bacon." Chapter 11, *The Family*, discusses these divisions, roles, and definitions in depth.

Women, then, are de facto excluded from much political activity in the public sphere, because their time is taken up in child-rearing. This is not the only reason, however, for their concentration in civil society. Once a culture includes child-rearing and homemaking in the job description for biological motherhood, women are kept in the private sphere of the home performing a task that has been called the **reproduc-**

Socialist feminists suggest that political behavior depends on an individual's involvement in reproduction. Women, who bear the children, tend not to participate. Men, who bring home the bacon, do. But many women have become politicized around the abortion issue.

tion of labor-power. As Smith (1977) has pointed out, the reproduction of labor-power involves taking care of the physical and emotional needs of husbands, so that the latter may return to the work force each day refreshed. It also includes raising children who will be suited to particular types of occupations and social positions. The school, as we will see in Chapter 14, collaborates in this task, so that young people are prepared to step into their parents' class position.

Without the work that women perform in the reproduction of the species and the reproduction of labor-power, capitalism could not continue. To put this another way, the productive work men do in capitalist societies would be impossible without the reproductive work women do. This is not to deny that women are working outside the home at an increasing rate. Almost 40 percent of the Canadian work force is made up of women. Even when women work outside the home, however, they still have primary responsibility for reproduction. Look at any women's magazine published in the last five years and you will find numerous articles discussing how women can best balance a job with home responsibilities. The women's liberation movement has also had some success in broadening the roles of men to include the enjoyment of child-rearing and homemaking. But balancing their work and home responsibilities has not become such a big issue for men.

Men are often exposed to contemporary issues in the workplace, where they participate with other men in political discussion and debate. Women's work is more often carried out alone in the home. Not only does work bring men into the public realm more often than women, but men are more likely to discuss public issues in work related organizations such as labor unions, professional organizations, and even fraternal clubs.

The social networks into which women are integrated, on the other hand, are often those made up of family members, or those organizations concerned with family care and safety in their immediate communities (like the Home and School Association). Lynn and Flora (1973) found that the role of mother (not the number of children) decreased political participation for American women, because they spent most of their time with other mothers who lived near them. Almost all their interaction took place in child-centered neighborhoods impervious to political messages. Morris, et al (1969) found that Canadian women not in the labor force were more likely to describe themselves as nervous and not very confident in their dealings with civil servants than were women in the labor force.

Simply getting a job outside the home is no solution to the problem of women's low political participation, however, since outside employment adds more responsibilities to an already busy schedule. Morris, et al (1969) also found that among employed persons in Canada with a similar educational background, 8 to 10 percent more men than women could be classified as having a "high" knowledge of government jurisdiction. When the researchers compared these same men with women comparably educated who were not employed outside the home, women's rates of political knowledge fell still further behind men's.

Her analysis of voting studies has led McCormack (1975) to suggest that there are, in fact, two political cultures based on gender. Because of the traditional specialization of women in the jobs of child-rearer and homemaker, women have not acquired the vision, skills, or vocabulary for ideological politics. They have developed a different way of understanding politics based on their experience of the world.

McCormack suggests that while men are likely to make political decisions on the basis of expedience, women are more likely to use moral values in their political evaluations. While men are more likely to take the political position that the rest of their social class takes, women are more likely to identify with those who have status and authority, seeking continuity rather than change. This may be because women know well that they do not control the reins of power and fear that any change might be for the worse. Their conservatism might be explained by their dependence. At any rate, McCormack points out that both political cultures are flawed but could come together in a healthy polity, a third political culture based on the absence of the polarization of the sexual division of labor.

We can better understand the politics of the women's liberation movement by looking at the concentration of women's activities in civil society. One of the principles of the early women's movement was the notion that the personal should be political. Women were tired of men who advocated equality and liberation on the international front but did not bring these principles closer to home. In politicizing the personal side of life, the women's movement made a number of demands on society, which were at first received as totally apolitical.

The issues women promoted depended primarily on how they saw power being used to limit their autonomy. These limitations were necessarily in the personal realm because of prescribed gender roles. Young, unmarried women engaged in courtship became politicized around issues of sexuality and the control of their bodies. Married women examined the give and take in their married relationships and often found them uneven. Issues have emerged in the last 15 years that political parties have had to consider in order to maintain women's support: publicly funded child-care, English language courses for immigrant women, more equitable property settlements between divorcing spouses, removal of abortion from the criminal code, the designation of rape as assault, and so on. If such demands are won, then women's role in reproduction would no longer limit them socially or politically, but would help extend their role in the polity.

Women in Electoral Politics

It does not require a great amount of sophisticated research to determine that women are almost absent from the Canadian state system and play minor roles in political institutions in civil society. All we need do is watch the proceedings of the House of Commons on television to get a notion of the masculine character of electoral politics. While less than 5 percent of all MPs elected in Canada in 1980 were women, the fact that there is international variation in this statistic shows that the proportion of women in federally elected office need not necessarily remain so low. Comparing 12 countries in 1977, Vallance (1979) found that the percentages of women in parliament ranged from a low of 1.7 in France to a high of 23.5 in Finland.

Why are women not more prevalent in federally elected offices? Although there are no significant differences between the voting rates for men and women, men participate in almost all other political activities more than women do. Women are present in political parties, but they are active mainly at the less powerful levels – stuffing envelopes and canvassing at election time. With the rise of feminism, however, more women have become interested in electoral politics, and their rate of candidacy has increased.

The few women who do hold public office are more likely to do so at the municipal level than the provincial, and at the provincial rather than the federal. Vickers (1978) calls this the **pyramidal pattern**: the higher the political position and the greater the power it controls, the smaller the percentage of women occupying such positions. There is also a pyramidal structure within the municipal arena, with the highest number of women running for school board, the next highest for alderperson, and the fewest running for mayor or reeve. Most women who run campaigns and win elections do so at the municipal level. Vickers

Agnes Macphail was the first woman ever elected to the House of Commons and served as an MP for a longer period than any other woman (1921–1940). A pragmatic politician, Ms. Macphail at one time stated, "The way to get things out of a government is to back them to the wall, put your hands to their throat, and you will get all they have."

concludes that this level is relatively more open to participation by women in Canada because it is a less desirable arena for participation to men. It also makes sense that women would be more willing to be candidates here, because winning would not involve moving away from their families to the provincial or federal capital. Furthermore, they might have more expertise at the municipal level, because they are involved, through their care of the family, in the management of their immediate community.

Brodie (1977) conducted preliminary research on the 44 women provincial legislators elected between 1950 and 1975, and her data give some indication as to how women may be successful at this level. For example, women legislators were more frequently elected in the west than in the east. Like male legislators, women tend to come from relatively privileged class backgrounds, but they are not so concentrated as men in the business and legal professions. In terms of political experience, most of the women legislators had held office at the municipal level and had used this office as a stepping stone to and training ground for provincial office. Most interesting is the fact that 77 percent of the women provincial legislators in Canada from 1950 to 1975 were recruited in urban ridings by the party in power. A candidate is more likely to win if her party is strong, but this may also indicate that only well established parties are willing to recruit women candidates in elections.

The fate of successful female provincial candidates is also an interesting story. With the rise of feminism, parties have seen it as advantageous to make women legislators highly visible by promoting them quickly to cabinet positions. Brodie, however, indicates that this is little more than tokenism, because only three of the 44 women legislators secured cabinet posts which were crucial to the provincial government, such as education and public works. The other 11 women promoted to a provincial cabinet served as window-dressing ministers without portfolio, or were given "housekeeping" duties such as social services, consumer affairs, and housing.

Women have been dismally absent from the House of Commons. While the increased political activity on the part of women has made a difference in the proportion of women elected municipally, it is questionable whether there has been any impact federally. It may appear that more women are becoming involved federally – many more are running for office – but in order to show that this too is not mere tokenism, one must examine the data carefully.

At the provincial and federal levels political parties serve as recruiting structures that screen out candidates they consider inappropriate for one reason or another. If a candidate is to win at the provincial or federal level, she must have a strong party organization supporting her. Kohn's (1980) study of women in the Canadian national legislature shows that political parties have been too prejudiced to nominate women candidates to run in ridings where the party had a good chance of winning. Vickers found that between 1945 and 1976, only 33.4 percent of all female candidates ran for the Liberal or Progressive Conservative parties, the two with the strongest party organizations and the most resources. The New Democratic Party ran more women candidates than either of the other two parties, but these were most frequently in ridings where that party did not have a reasonable chance of winning. Except in British Columbia, the NDP has fielded the lowest number of female candidates in ridings where that party has had a reasonable chance of winning.

Even when women are elected at the federal level, this lack of party support is reflected in their relative lack of strength in office. Examining all women elected to the House, Kohn (1980) found that a very high proportion of them had their careers terminated by being defeated. He concluded that "a large number seemed to represent swing districts, where the national party fortunes might well make or break the incumbents."

This section has concentrated on illustrating the structural barriers that prevent women exercising the full rights of citizenship. We have seen how their role in reproduction excludes them from the ideological public arena and how political parties act as barriers through which they have not yet been allowed to pass freely. Reinforcing these structural barriers is the factor of political socialization; that is, women are taught to believe that politics is not an appropriate activity for them and that the attributes which make a good politician (like aggressiveness, expediency, competitiveness) are by nature masculine.

With the rise of feminism, however, the socialization of women into passive political roles has become less predominant. Some research has been conducted on the reversal of this ideological process. Kopinak (1978), for example, found that education increases women's political efficacy (belief that the political system is responsive to them) more than any other factor. And that while getting a better job and a higher income make men feel that they are more suited for politics, these factors have little effect on women's political behavior or attitudes. The route to greater political participation of women, then, is twofold:

1. removal of the structural barriers that impede women's participation
2. resocialization of women to reinforce the appropriateness and legitimacy of their presence in public life

THE SUPERSTRUCTURE

As Figure 13-1 indicated, civil society is that part of the polity that joins the base, the substructure, of society to the state system. Although it contains some institutions that play political roles, it is significant because it is that part of the polity in which people conduct their everyday lives, in the domestic and private spheres.

Civil Society

One of the ways in which civil society joins different parts of the polity together is through the production and reproduction of basic values, beliefs, and attitudes that allow us to define common politial goals, as well as the boundaries between groups that disagree. These norms, values, and beliefs in which political life is embedded and from which it takes its meaning are called **political culture**. Political culture includes the spirit and morale that help bind a people together, the values and sets of beliefs that shape collectivities into coherent groupings giving them common meanings and purposes, and the ideologies that create and heal cleavages. Political culture is the glue that holds a polity together, or allows communication to take place so that collective goals can be defined. Because of their emphasis on subjective phenomena, theories such as symbolic interaction are most readily (although not exclusively) applied to the study of political culture.

In a survey conducted just after the 1974 federal election (Clarke, et al, 1979), most Canadians were positive about the Canadian polity but negative about the political actors in it. Most of the respondents felt that Canada was a democratic political system and that

the people were genuinely represented. They thought that Canadians themselves, however, were dull, passive, unexciting, and politically apathetic and that politicians were "terrible," "crooked," "doing a bad job," "out for themselves," and "wasting the money we pay in taxes." When asked how they would best describe politics in Canada, they complained that the important issues were not being dealt with by government. These issues included (in order of importance) inflation, rising prices, pensions, unemployment, and taxes. Only one-half to one-third of the respondents felt a sense of efficacy. Only 52 percent believed that the government cared what they thought, 44 percent felt they had a say in what the government did, 33 percent disagreed that government and politics were so complicated that they could not understand what was going on.

Johnston and Ornstein's (1979) analysis of national data collected in 1977 revealed that when we look at people in different social classes, it is clear that there is not one homogeneous political culture throughout the country. As one moves down the class ladder, people tend to agree more that politics and government are so complicated they can't understand what's going on, to disagree with the use of strike-breakers, to think the government should put more effort into assisting the unemployed and compensating injured workers. As one moves up the class ladder, there is less support for social welfare measures like improving health and medical care, building public housing, aiding the poor, protecting the rights of native people, and eliminating gender discrimination.

A further way in which political culture in Canada has been observed to join people into groups is on the basis of ethnicity. Since the election of the Parti Québécois in Quebec in 1976, for example, political sociologists have been especially interested in the existence and configurations of French- and English-Canadian political cultures in order to predict future political scenarios for the country.

The Québécois political culture remains distinctly different from that in the rest of Canada, and the future relationship between this one province and its neighbors remains uncertain. The Parti Québécois lost the referendum on sovereignty-association in 1980, failing to receive a mandate from the Quebec people to proceed with plans to be more politically separate from the rest of Canada while maintaining economic ties. The Quebec government did manage, however, to take a stand against the other provinces in the constitutional debates that preceeded the patriation of the Constitution in 1982. This is a longstanding cleavage in Canadian political culture that will continue to test the creativity of Canadian politicians for some time to come.

Political Parties and Voting. Why do people vote the way they do? Maybe people vote the same way that their parents did; maybe they identify with a particular party early in life and refer to it in adulthood when they need to understand politics; perhaps they vote on the basis of their attraction to the leader or the local candidate; or maybe they vote on the basis of current issues. This question of why people vote the way they do is of interest not only to political scientists, but also to the party faithful who at each election organize campaigns based on their understanding of voting behavior aimed at "pulling out the vote." Despite all these attempts to find out why people vote the way they do, some detractors have suggested that since the Liberal Party has won 11 out of 15 elections in Canada since 1926, voting does not really make much difference because there is little change anyway.

Clarke, et al (1979) have attempted to resolve this question by studying survey data collected from national samples after the federal election campaigns of 1974, 1968, and 1965. Although there is no one explanation to account for the way everyone votes, these political scientists discerned four important groups of Canadian voters that should be closely watched to predict the outcome of an election.

Two of these categories are defined on the basis of the kind of loyalty a person feels to a particular political party. The first type, constituting the majority of Canadian voters, are those who have a *flexible* allegiance to a particular party, either because they support different parties in federal and provincial politics, or because they have voted for different parties in the past. In contrast to this group is the second type, those who have a more *durable* allegiance to a political party, those who are more likely to support the same party

This cartoon, which appeared during the 1980 federal election campaign, portrays the voters' rejection of the choices presented to them. (*The Globe and Mail, Toronto*)

both federally and provincially and not to have changed the party they supported in the past.

Voters who have a durable party allegiance are therefore likely to stay with the same party. This means that the best predictor of the way they will vote is the way they have voted. While for those with a flexible party allegiance, it is still important to know how they voted in the past, the image of the leader, recent party performance, the issues arising in the campaign, and the way they are dealt with can be deciding factors. Those flexible voters who are very interested in the election are much more likely to vote on the basis of issues, while those not very interested are likely to vote on the basis of their attraction to the party leader.

The Liberal Party formed a minority government after the 1972 election, but won a landslide victory in 1974, giving it a large majority of the seats in the House. Many commentators have accounted for this by suggesting that many who voted for the Progressive Conservatives and the New Democratic Party in 1972 switched their votes to the Liberals in 1974. While Clarke, et al (1979) found that there was a great deal of switching in the 1974 election, this switching was in all directions, cancelling out its impact on the outcome of the election. For example, nearly as many voters moved from the Liberals to the NDP as from the NDP to the Liberals. Half again as many voters were found to have switched from the Liberals to the Conservatives as switched from the Conservatives to the Liberals. In fact, more voters left the Liberals than joined them from other parties. How, then, did they win their 1974 majority?

To answer this question, we must look at the other two groups of voters (Clarke, et al, 1979). The electorate is not limited to people who may or may not change the party for which they are voting. There will always be **new voters** who were ineligible to cast ballots in the previous election. There are also **transient voters** who have been eligible, but who for one reason or another have not cast their votes in one or more previous elections. In 1974, these new voters and transient voters cast their ballots overwhelmingly for the Liberals, tipping the scales in their favor despite the fact that more voters in the other two categories had switched their votes away from the Liberals than had switched their votes to the Liberals.

The outcome of Canadian elections, then, can best be understood in terms of the behavior of four groups of voters: durable partisans, flexible partisans, transients, and new voters. Some relationships have been observed between voting and other variables such as region. For example, those from Quebec are more likely to vote Liberal than those from western Canada. These relationships, however, are not necessarily permanent, and realignments can take place because the majority of the Canadian electorate falls into the flexible partisan category. Thus, "presently observed regional differences in support of various parties may be subject to substantial change in any given election" (Clarke, et al, 1979). Although political scientists and politicians have spent enormous amounts of time and money trying to find the right formula to predict election outcomes, no one can know exactly what will happen before the campaign begins and the four categories of voters confront the issues and the leaders.

Because of the large proportion of flexible voters who actually do make their voting decisions during an election campaign, Clarke et al (1979) conclude that Canadians do make political choices. The Liberal Party has been the one most often in power in modern Canada, because it has been able to turn many short-term factors to its advantage. Other parties have the same potential as the Liberals for capturing the votes of those who do make careful political choices. Therefore, change is possible within Canadian electoral politics.

Mass Media. The potential for the mass media to be instruments both for the powerful to control society and for the powerless to right injustice has given the media a Jekyll and Hyde character and linked them in a love-hate relationship with political activists at all points in the ideological spectrum.

In Orwell's prophetic novel *1984*, the media are used to spread patriotic propaganda that fires the population with zeal in support of international conflict. In movies like *Network* and *The China Syndrome*, the media liberate information vital to the prevention of catastrophe and encourage people to shout from the rooftops that they're mad as hell and aren't going to take it any more. Leaving aside the question of whether art imitates life, or life imitates art, we can, of course, find real-world referents for both these functions of the media.

The Canadian Broadcasting Corporation, created in the 1930s, and the National Film Board, conceived and organized during World War II, were both vehicles for using national culture as a form of defense. The 1940 CBC Annual Report stated:

Even in time of peace, national radio has played an increasingly important role in welding together the diverse elements of our population; in wartime it serves also to interpret policy, by bringing the country's leaders in constant contact with listeners, and to sustain morale by means of programs that adequately interpret the will of the whole Canadian people to prosecute the war to a vigorous conclusion by every means in its power.

This strategic action is an example of the state system, or more specifically the military institution within it, using an institution in civil society to mobilize the population in a particular way. Once the war was over, the mandate of the publicly owned media in Canada became to create a cultural milieu in which a national identity could emerge. In the media, as in all other political institutions, however, not all parts of the public have been equally represented. This has extremely important implications when we look at the media, because those who are most involved have the opportunity to define the public interest and have their view accepted as the Canadian one.

One of the characteristics of the media in Canada is the concentration of ownership in the hands of a few people. Newspapers, as well as radio and television stations, are owned by a very few. Clement (1975), in his analysis of the concentraiton of media ownership in Canada, notes that there is an overlap between media elites and economic elites. Over seven-tenths of the total media elite are from upper-class origins. Because elites move from the corporate sector to the media, it is difficult to imagine that the view of the world presented in the media does not represent those elites. Instead, those who are most influential in deciding media content continue to represent the ruling class. Clement reconfirmed Porter's (1965) finding that personnel are recruited to important positions in the media institutions primarily through kinship, rather than upward mobility.

The Royal Commission on Newspapers in Canada (Kent, 1981) found that because so few companies own so many newspapers, Canadians' right to free expression is threatened. The commission recommended the passage of new laws placing limits on the number of newspapers a chain could own, enshrining the independence of editors of newspapers owned by chains, and giving tax incentives to high quality papers. It also proposed that committees made up of representatives of newspaper owners, staff, and the community be set up to advise chain-owned newspapers and monitor annual reports from the newspapers.

Endres (1977) shows how the media and other institutions that create and transmit culture are also important in the accumulation of capital. As well as invest-ing money in artists who can develop a distinctively Canadian culture, for example, the Secretary of State invests in large buildings capable of housing theater companies. These enrich the construction industry and provide amusement for tourists and the indigenous bourgeoisie. Similarly, the Special Senate Committee on Mass Media (1970) found that the owners of the Canadian press were more concerned with profits than providing high quality newspapers. Working-class people, by contrast, rarely attend theaters, ballets, operas or other forms of "high culture." The cultural form in which they participate is popular culture, and much of it comes to them daily through television.

Television maintains the status quo in at least two ways: by encouraging a consumer ethic through advertising and by ideological manipulation. Advertising creates desires for things that are beyond our basic needs and teaches us to make fine distinctions between a multitude of products that do approximately the same thing.

Endres (1977) says that, "In Canada, ideological manipulation of the cultural needs of the working class is carried out so well by the American-owned electronic media that there is no need for the state to play a role." While a great deal of research still needs to be done to understand exactly how this "ideological manipulation" takes place, Vidmar and Rokeach (1974) have studied the reactions of Canadian and American viewers to the now-defunct TV program *All in the Family*. Their findings indicate that relatively more prejudiced people tended to watch the show more frequently than others, to identify more with Archie than Mike, and to perceive Archie as making better sense than Mike and as winning their arguments. Such viewers also thought that Archie "told it like it was" with his use of racial and ethnic slurs. The authors conclude that this program tended to reinforce prejudice and racism, rather than combat it, and they also note that impressionable white children have picked up, and are using, many of the old racial slurs Archie resurrected. Such is the strong and pervasive influence of the media.

The media are assumed to have such an important influence on public opinion that there are specific laws in Canada about how they can be used during

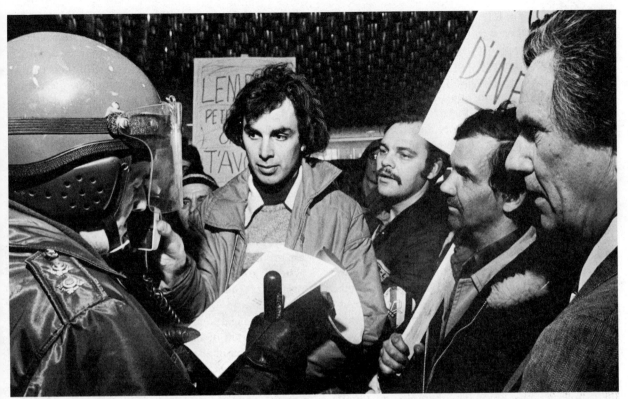

The riot squad reads an eviction order to striking employees of *La Presse* and *Montréal Matin*. The police are bound to maintain order and protect property, but strikers often see them as agents of employers, accomplices in the accumulation of capital.

political campaigns. During the 1974 federal election campaign, the media gave the most attention to party leaders, with the effect that personalities were magnified and local issues downplayed. The public, for their part, were exposed to campaign messages most often through television, with those exposed through newspapers being a somewhat smaller group. Of all the media, radio exposed the fewest number of people to political messages during the campaign.

Whether or not the amount of money and time spent on media advertising makes any difference is still an open question, however, because it was found that those who saw, heard, or read nothing about the campaign in any of the media were just as likely to change the way they voted as those who followed the campaigns very closely in the media (Clarke, et al, 1979). As with Archie Bunker, people may select the

media passages most like the views they already hold and use these messages to reinforce their opinions rather than change them. Either way, the status quo remains intact.

The investigative newspaper reporting that brought to light the Watergate scandal and finally unseated a President of the United States in 1974 reminded us most forcefully that people *can* use the media to change the state system, to change the status quo.

McCormack (1978) has given several examples of how the media have been involved in the process of social change in Canada. One example involves the CBC and the NFB, which not only have fulfilled the defense and national unity functions noted above, but have also acted as training grounds for the development of writers, actors, directors, and musicians in this country. With these professionals has come the awareness of the impact of foreign media in Canada and the necessity for further nurture of a Canadian culture through the protection of Canadian media. Out of this awareness has come recent legislation that supports a more competitive Canadian periodical press by discouraging advertising in non-Canadian magazines. Because of this legislation, there is no longer a Canadian edition of *Time* magazine, and the number of Canadian magazines originating in this country has increased.

McCormack also cites another example of the use of media by people who wish to change the form of society: the growth of "underground" media as organs of the 1960s counter-culture. These newspapers and magazines, sometimes short-lived but usually full of vitality, rejected the idea of journalist as purveyor of "facts" in an unbiased way. Their journalists were activists whose goal was to mobilize people as well as to inform them. To accomplish this they addressed themselves to minorities and the underprivileged, rather than to the public at large, and used their publications as networks holding together entire social movements.

No one but the Prime Minister can demand free media time to deliver important political messages. In 1970, however, the Front de Liberation du Québec used the media to broadcast its manifesto when it kidnapped Pierre Laporte and James Cross. This action met with some success. A poll taken at the time showed that while almost no Quebeckers supported FLQ kidnapping and bombing tactics, many agreed in principle with the manifesto (Rioux, 1971). The use of the media engaged the entire Canadian population in FLQ politics and forced Canadians to take sides on and think through issues to which they might never otherwise have been exposed.

These examples are important because they demonstrate the possibility that the media can be used by people to send influence upward to the ruling part of society. But we must be clear that this is not the usual way media are used. Because of the predominantly one-way flow of communication in television, radio, and newspapers, it is difficult for those who do not already have some input into decisions that affect the media to "talk back." This does not mean, however, that we should stop trying to do so. Those who now

make media decisions do so because they can draw on the resources of the upper class. Therefore, some affirmative action is necessary to allow those from less privileged backgrounds to participate in their culture as it is manufactured and transmitted in the media. This includes state support of the media and the arts and the granting of greater support to artists and performers.

Interest Groups. An **interest group** consists of individuals who have a particular economic interest or social cause to promote. These groups, or the lobbyists they hire, attempt to persuade those in the state system to act in ways favorable to them. The Canadian Manufacturer's Association, for example, is an interest group that lobbies the various parts of the state system (government and bureaucracy) so that laws profiting it (like tariffs on foreign goods) will be passed and remain in effect. Interest groups exist at the federal, provincial, and municipal levels of government. An association of taxi drivers may donate money to the campaigns of all municipal candidates, for instance, hoping that whoever is elected will be favorable to their later requests for fare increases. Not all interest groups act solely on behalf of their members. Some may organize around altruistic motives, such as the Elizabeth Fry Society that lobbies in the interest of women convicted of criminal offenses (Van Loon and Whittington, 1981).

Like parties, interest groups link civil society to the state system. Drawing on Durkheim's notions of social integration, Presthus (1973) says that interest groups are structural mechanisms linking individuals in the private sphere with those in authority who can protect and/or promote their interest at a public level. Political elites, for their part, receive useful advice that serves as a guide for policy-making.

Interest groups differ from parties in that they never assume formal authority and responsibility for running the government (Presthus, 1973). Neither do they pretend to represent the majority of people. Instead, interest groups try to convince bureaucrats and legislators of the appropriateness of their cause through direct contacts and briefings, by advising those in power on courses of action, and by getting their own membership to act in support of their policies by letter-writing, boycotts, and so on.

Interest groups and political parties are organizationally separate in this country, with only the labor unions making formal alliances with any one party, the NDP. While political parties are responsive to the population mainly at election time, interest groups must be ready to try to influence the government whenever an issue relevant to them arises. It has been suggested that political parties furnish decision-makers, but interest groups influence political decisions (Van Loon and Whittington, 1981). Members of parliament are involved to differing degrees in decision-making, creating a situation in which powerful interest groups may have more influence over some decisions than some backbenchers.

More Canadians belong to interest groups than to political parties, yet this does not mean that interest groups reflect a broad spectrum of society. Presthus' (1973) research indicated that leaders of interest groups are drawn from the same elite as leaders of government and the economy: "The web between the so-called private and public elite," he tells us, "is virtually seamless." In his sample of 1150 interest group leaders, MPs, and high-level bureaucrats, Presthus found a high degree of homogeneity in the class background and career preparation of the three groups. The great majority were from the upper middle and upper classes.

Those whose economic and educational backgrounds are most dissimilar to the elite find it most difficult to operate successfully as interest groups. This may be because one of the most effective ways of pressuring the government is through personal contacts with acquaintances in the bureaucracy. These types of relationships are cultivated more easily if the leaders of interest groups share the manners, tastes, and outlook that come from having a common class background. Presthus (1973) found that legislators and bureaucrats did not give their attention equally to all the interest groups that sought them out, but that "those who work with their brains enjoy advantages over those who work with their hands."

Although labor interest groups have the largest membership, they are the least effective and find it most difficult to influence government policy. This may be one of the reasons they are the only interest group with any long-term affiliation with the NDP. Those having the most efficacious access to the cabinet were found to be professional, business, educational, welfare, and labor groups, in that order.

Influence flows both to and from the state system through interest groups. Many Canadian governments have taken a **corporatist** stance, meaning that they have felt overburdened by the task of governing and have delegated some of their functions to private groups. In turn, these groups advise the government on the policies most relevant to them (Presthus, 1973). Although interest groups may influence the state by having their point of view incorporated into legislation before it even reaches the House, their close contact with bureaucrats and legislators also tends to weaken that influence. That is, a group finds it difficult to be critical of policies about which that group has already been consulted. Interest groups may act as a check on the excessive use of power by government, but they also disseminate information and get their members to cooperate in the administration of government policies.

In fact, interest groups may be so useful to the state system that it may initiate them where none already exist. When bureaucrats have difficulty getting legislators to accept their point of view, they have on occasion encouraged the growth of interest groups through funding and sharing information. As a result, those in power find it more difficult to ignore the combined bureaucratic/interest group point of view.

Interest groups also perform an important administrative function through the self-regulation of their members. The government would have to expand its bureaucracy substantially if it had to supervise the training and certification of physicians, lawyers, dentists, etc. In return for their freedom to police themselves, interest groups find it necessary to make their relationship with government a cooperative one most of the time. That physicians can opt-out of health insurance programs and leaders of unions can be imprisoned for advising their membership not to return to work indicates that the cooperative nature of the relationship between interest groups and government is not absolute, although it has been the norm throughout most of Canadian political history.

FREEDOM FOR GAY MEN & WOMEN TO SHOW AFFECTION IN PUBLIC !!!

Any group wanting social change must work within civil society to effect change in the state system. The gay rights movement, for example, often uses organized marches and ensuing media attention as a vehicle to carry their demands up to elected representatives.

The class background of interest group leaders and the relative failure of those interest groups representing the less privileged sectors of society make it clear that this political institution in civil society reinforces and helps to maintain inequality. The groups that compete for power, and all that it can bring, by no means have equal opportunities for success. The anti-democratic nature of our polity is lamented by Presthus (1973) who suggests that what is needed is more effective political socialization through formal educational institutions to foster the "realization among young people that higher learning has other objectives than occupational success."

Presthus is assuming that if more Canadians were highly educated, they would understand the degree of inequality that exists and would also know how to correct it. Until such a transformation takes place, however, we are left with a situation of elite hegemony in political affairs. As Kautsky (Milibrand, 1973) said some time ago, "The capitalist class rules but it does not govern . . . it contents itself with ruling the government."

The State System

Individuals in civil society are concerned with meeting their own privately defined goals. But decisions at the level of the state system apply to society as a whole. Even if a particular state system is legitimized by the principle that the best government is the least government, that individuals should be left alone to fight their own battles without state interference, the principle still applies to the whole of society because the state system promotes it.

The state system can play this universal role because it is the only part of the polity with authority to legislate, command, or dominate, as it sees fit. Although there may be individuals and groups in civil society who are leaders because of their hegemony in political institutions, only those who hold positions in the state system can legitimately wield power in a legal way (for example, by declaring the War Measures Act).

The elaboration of the concept of **authority** was one of the major contributions Max Weber made to political sociology. As you saw in the section "Weber and Bureaucracy" in Chapter 10, Weber described three different ideal types of authority to which people might voluntarily submit: traditional, charismatic, and legal-rational. The last of these types is the most characteristic of Canadian polity.

The institutions that make up the state system were listed in the introductory part of the chapter with their manifest or formal functions. In the following sections, we will examine each state institution and describe its interrelationship in the Canadian polity.

Before that, however, we should say a few words about how the state operates vis-a-vis the other parts of the polity shown in Figure 13-1. In the section on the base or substructure, we said that the modes of production and reproduction had a determining influence on the rest of the polity. As we discovered in the sections on civil society, however, this determination is not a simple phenomenon. Once established, the superstructure assumes an influence of its own, or in Althusser's (1971) words, has a "relative autonomy" and exercises a "reciprocal action" on the base. He suggests that the joint function of civil society and the state system is to reproduce the relations of production and reproduction.

You will recall that the relations of production are located in the base of society and consist of the way people are socially oriented to the productive process: whether they are owners, wage-laborers, or members of some other class fraction. To reproduce the relations of production, therefore, means to keep people in their positions as owners, wage-laborers, and so on. The state system can, because of its authority, reproduce these relations of production through direct decree. The state can, for example, pass laws that freeze wages. In civil society, the political institutions also attempt to influence the relations of production: interest groups such as the Canadian Manufacturers' Association try to maintain or improve their class position, the media present a particular image of Canadian society, and so on.

Social theorists are only beginning to discuss the mode of reproduction and the reproduction of the social relations of reproduction. With the present development of biological science, we have only one mode of biological reproduction. In recent years, however, there has been technological innovation on the forces of reproduction within this mode; birth control techniques allow women to decide how many children they will bear and when they will bear them. This technological innovation has had important repercussions in the superstructure, where women have entered public life as the proportion of their lives spent in biological reproduction has dropped. The state, for its part, has influenced the mode of reproduction by allowing the dissemination of birth control information and materials and by decriminalizing abortion. Right to Life organizations can be seen as an interest group in civil society that is attempting to exert political influence to reverse this change in the mode of reproduction.

Any group within the polity wishing to change the form of the polity must work through the political institutions in civil society, as well as trying to change the state itself. The political institutions of civil society can be used to carry new definitions of reality upward and the government's policies downward.

Government and Parliament. The government is constituted by the regime in power. In Canada, this includes the Prime Minister and the cabinet, who hold formal executive power. The Prime Minister is clearly the most powerful individual in the government, having the power to appoint the cabinet and control it once it is in operation. The Prime Minister and the cabinet are the most important people in the legislative and policy processes. There are two other parts of the government which are not elected. The Privy Council Office (PCO) can be assigned special responsibilities by the Prime Minister. In the past these have included the administration of federal-provincial relations and the study of American ownership of industry in Canada. The Prime Minister's Office (PMO) administers a great deal of the Prime Minister's affairs and is a connecting link between the Prime Minister and the public.

Parliament is formally made up of the Crown (which since 1947 has delegated all its effective powers to the Governor General), the House of Commons, and the Senate. While the Prime Minister and the cabinet within the House of Commons have the greatest power over legislation and policy-making, other MPs may also share in this process, depending on their numbers relative to the governing party. When a party has a strong majority, it need pay little attention either to its own backbenchers or the opposition members. The smaller the proportion of seats the governing party has, the more it is likely to share power with those outside the cabinet on both sides of the House.

At election time political parties make it appear that there are large differences among them. But Miliband (1973) argues that all political parties in liberal democracies are strikingly similar in their agreement on the existing economic and social system of private property and class relations. Miliband does not think that political parties are in favor of radically different social systems, rather they simply quibble about the best way to manage the existing economic system with its built-in inequalities. Most often they quibble about how much they should intervene to keep the economy running smoothly.

Parliamentary rules contribute to cooperation among political parties. Once dissenting parties agree to field candidates for political office, they have agreed to play by a set of rules that limits the kinds of changes they can bring into being. In Canada, those MPs whose parties are defeated in an election, and whose task it therefore becomes to attack the party in power during the question period, are called Her Majesty's *Loyal Opposition*. They also serve with members from all other parties on committees in which a certain amount of cooperation is necessary. One of the government's purposes in involving the opposition in the planning stages is, of course, to make it less likely that the opposition will obstruct legislation in the House. Add this initial and continuing involvement to the trading of support for issues that goes on in parliamentary systems, and it is no wonder that the partisan affiliation of members becomes more and more difficult to determine.

There is empirical evidence that the Canadian people see the major political parties as committed to the existing economic structure. Using Meisel's national survey of the 1965 federal election, Ogmundson (1975) re-analyzed some of the data with particular attention

TABLE 13-1. CLASS IMAGES OF CANADIAN POLITICAL PARTIES, 1965

NDP	Créditistes	Social Credit	Conservatives	Liberals
2.7	3.2	3.4	4.4	4.4

to a question that asked respondents to rate parties on a scale from 1 "for the working class" to 7 "for the middle class." He then averaged the scores that all respondents gave to each of the parties. The midpoint of this scale is 4. Ogmundson found that respondents placed both the Liberals and Conservatives in the same place, a little to the right of center. The mean scores for all parties are indicated in Table 13-1.

Canadian voters, therefore, see little difference in the class positions of the only two parties ever to form a government in this country. On the contrary, both of them are viewed as more "for the middle class" than any other Canadian political party, although they are certainly not perceived as being far right.

Sub-central Governments. Sub-central governments are small-scale replicas of the more general state system of which they are a part. Often, they are incomplete and do not contain all of the state institutions. For example, not all Canadian provinces have provincial police forces; when they do not, the federally organized RCMP fulfills the function for them. The relationships between class and power that hold in the federal government are often replicated at this level. The Alberta government, for example, is ruled by the Conservatives who represent the petit bourgeois interest of those in the natural resource industry. Newfoundland is another case in point. Ontario, although also represented by a Conservative government for over 40 years, is intimately linked with the industrial bourgeoisie of that province.

Administration. The administration, or bureaucracy, in the Canadian state system is made up of full-time civil servants appointed because of their specialized skills. The importance of an administrative branch of the state is especially clear for modern nations. There

During the seventies, power shifted from the judicial and parliamentary branches of the state system to the bureaucratic and executive branches. Federal and provincial bureaucracies expanded, and structures such as the Privy Council gained new importance.

must be a body responsible for minding the day-to-day business of the nation while the House is not sitting and between elections. Moreover, elected representatives cannot be expected always to possess the technical expertise necessary to make important decisions alone. Ideally, civil servants collect information at the direction of elected representatives, present it to them in an unbiased fashion, allow the legislators to make decisions, and then execute the government's policy to the best of their ability.

Civil servants, however, are not automatons functioning in a structureless environment. Like other social actors, they are individuals with particular world views, and they work in social organizations that have efficiency and self-maintenance as high priority goals. Given these facts, it is important to know just how powerful the bureaucratic administration is relative to the government and the other institutions within the state system.

Whether or not a civil service can be neutral depends on how it is appointed. Some nations, Britain for example, emphasize merit in their appointments, while others use administration appointments to repay political favors and maintain party loyalty – **patronage**. It is reasonable to expect that people who get jobs because they were faithful to a particular party will support that party in their work. Party loyalty, then, can be a source of administrative power.

Whether or not civil servants can be unbiased in serving a government that did not appoint them depends on the degree of difference between the government that appointed them and the one they now serve. We noted above that most Canadians do not perceive a great deal of difference between the Liberals and Conservatives on important issues. It therefore seems reasonable to assume that only the most partisan bureaucrats would find it difficult to serve one or the other of these parties equally well. The occasions in Canadian history in which the neutrality of the administration has become an issue have been the times when the change in government has been between parties that have more obviously different goals. For example, Sterling Lyon made a great show of dismissing NDP-appointed civil servants when he led the Progressive Conservatives to power in Manitoba in 1977.

In China, this phenomenon has been called the "red and expert dilemma." The question is: Should administrators be appointed on the basis of their commitment to party philosophy, or their possession of specialized skills regardless of their political position? But surely, the question does not have to be either/or. The answer must be a compromise, for in the field of government, where administrators are creating new social structures that attempt to alter the form of society, experts must believe government changes are possible before they can use their expertise to implement these changes.

Administrative power over the government also varies with the particular issue under consideration. Presthus (1973) found that although the cabinet was the major focus for most interest groups, there were many issues over which an interest group could get more control if it lobbied the bureaucracy. Professional, educational, and business groups concerned with the licensing of their members went first to the civil service. Welfare and social-recreational groups that wanted to influence intra-organizational policy were also most effective when they lobbied the bureaucracy, rather than the government or any other branch of the state.

Most researchers agree that administrative influence over government is likely to be conservative. Olsen (1977) found that the top levels of the federal and provincial bureaucracies contained more people from classes below the upper middle class than did the political-judicial elite, which in turn is drawn from lower in the class system than the corporate elite. Olsen argued, however, that such people have to adopt the perspective of the ruling class in order to "make it" in the civil service. Thus, although their class origins may be different from the rest of the ruling elite, the functions administrators fulfill are the same as the functions of those who originated in classes above them.

Military and Security Forces. The military, paramilitary, security, and police forces are the only groups within the polity that can legitimately use physical force. The use of such force is specified in legislation, and the government is the institution to which the military and security forces are directly accountable. As Miliband (1973) says, "The formal constitutional position of the administrative and coercive elements is to serve the state by serving the government of the day."

Historically, the coercive institutions of the state system in Canada have been well developed. Their function is to defend the polity from its enemies and maintain social order. The military and security forces

tend to see themselves as ideologically unbiased, yet their interpretation of what is in the national interest and what particular form the social order should take is noteworthy in that it is highly conservative. (See the section on "The State" in Chapter 16 for a discussion of patterns in the Canadian state's responses to perceived threat.)

Canadian military and security forces have a long history of involvement in the suppression of legitimate dissent: the Winnipeg General Strike of 1919 (see the boxed reading "Bloody Saturday" in Chapter 16), the Regina riot of 1935, the Vancouver Post Office demonstration of 1938, and the implementation of the War Measures Act in 1970. Police forces have also been used in several industrial disputes, to facilitate, as O'Connor (1973) and others would say, the accumulation of capital. During strikes, for example, police often interpret their maintenance of the social order to mean intervening on behalf of the employer, protecting only the capitalist's interests. The police serve the state, which theoretically represents all the people, yet police never intervene of behalf of the picketers to keep factories closed during strikes. These different interpretations by employers and employees play up the contradiction between the equality of individuals before the law and their simultaneous inequality in the economic system.

It is clear what kinds of formal authority the police in Canada have, but their just exercise of this authority has been questioned. As Hogarth (1979) notes, alleged abuse of authority has also occurred recently in Australia, New Zealand, the United Kingdom, and the United States, indicating, perhaps, symptomatic strains in liberal democracies rather than a peculiar fault in our own country. Nevertheless, there are some ways in which Canada's police-and-the-law situation is unique.

Lipset (1965) has argued that Canadians have more respect for authority than Americans. The police in Canada are a national symbol. Souvenir Mountie dolls are sold in dime stores across the land, and the Mountie image is stamped on Canadian coins. Perhaps because of the esteem in which military and security forces are held, Canadians appear slow in checking abuse of the law by police and have suggested instead that if police break the law (by opening mail, for example), then the law should be changed. Our very language indicates an unwillingness to see security forces in an unfavorable light. One of the many inquiries into police abuse of the law conducted in 1978 was called an inquiry into police "wrongdoing." If anyone else had committed the acts under investigation, they would surely have been called crimes.

Hogarth (1979) suggests that our acquiescence in the abuse of the law by police is part of a shift away from individual rights in favor of state power. He finds it interesting that when police break the law for their own gain (taking a bribe) they are sternly brought to justice. But illegality carried out in the interests of "national security" we are loath to condemn. Hogarth (1979) dates the beginning of this shift (away from individual rights and toward state power) to the declaration of the War Measures Act in 1970.

Indeed, the nature of police crimes so far uncovered indicates a confusion of state security with security of the party in power, of social order with the particular form Canadian order has taken in the past. Because of this confusion, political groups have been denied free competition through the action of security forces. In 1970, the offices of the Praxis Institute (a publicly and privately funded organization which worked on issues such as day care, tenants' rights, working mother's problems, and the poor people's movement) were burglarized and files stolen. These files later turned up in the hands of the RCMP. Richard Henshel (1977, 1978) is one of many critics suggesting that it was from these files that a blacklist was drawn up containing the names of Praxis members and 21 civil servants who supposedly constituted an extra-parliamentary opposition. Retired security service director John Starnes testified at the hearings of the McDonald Commission that in 1973 the RCMP broke into an office of the Parti Québécois, took computer tapes containing party membership lists, copied them, and returned them before dawn. Included also in the inventory: breaking and entering at l'Agence de Presse Libre, stealing files, and later burning them. This agency had distributed news of the sort carried by the underground media of the sixties. In other words, l'Agence was a behind-the-scenes force in the change-oriented counterculture

media. No crimes were ever uncovered by the security forces through these illegal activities, no convictions resulted, no acts of terrorism were prevented.

Statements by former solicitors-general concerning these charges have been to the effect that the security forces in this country are not in fact accountable to the government. Henshel has called them "a police force out of control," and one former solicitor-general has termed them a "state within a state."

Whether or not security forces illegally influenced political affairs in this country on their own initiative or with the approval of the government in power is still to be fully disclosed. Either way, it will be an important point in understanding the Canadian polity, for if security forces have done these things autonomously, then there is reason to believe that as state institutions they might be considered more central to the political process than the government. If they have done these things at the behest of the regime in power, then we must speak not only of the abuse of the law by the security forces, but also of the abuse of law and privilege by the particular parties in power.

Judiciary. The administration and the military constitutionally serve the government under the Constitution, but the Canadian judiciary is legally defined as independent of both the cabinet and the legislature. The judiciary in most modern polities can act as a conservative force against rapid change by the government of the day through its power to review legislation. This does not happen automatically in Canada, as it does, for example, in the United States, but the judiciary can review laws and interpret them when those laws are crucial in deciding a particular case before the courts.

The Canadian judiciary has gained increasing visibility and importance because of its important role in interpreting the Charter of Rights in our Constitution. Much of the wording of the Charter is deliberately vague and unclear, in order to gain agreement from the provincial premiers on its inclusion in the Constitution. It is the courts, however, that will finally define its content by hearing test cases and setting precedents.

Whether or not the judiciary in Canada is above

conflicting class interests is an open question. Olsen (1980) shows that judges have the same social class background as the ruling class, but he did not test whether this has any effect on their rulings. He also presents copious evidence that political partisanship biases the selection of judges. The Prime Ministers of Canada have traditionally appointed to the bench people who are known to be affiliated with the Prime Minister's party and who have often been electoral candidates and served as federal or provincial members. This brings into question the ability of the judiciary to make fair judgments in cases with political implications, especially in provinces where one party has held power for an extended period of time (as in Ontario) and has therefore appointed almost the entire judiciary in that province. The patronage nature of judicial appointments also brings into question the fairness in cases having to do with third parties (the Federal NDP and Social Credit parties) that have never formed a government and have therefore never been able to appoint sympathetic judges.

One of Olsen's (1980) most interesting contributions is the demonstration that different levels of the court system serve different segments of the class hierarchy. Of the 437 cases reported in the *Canada Supreme Court Reports* from 1971 to 1975, he found that 62 percent, almost two-thirds, were concerned with regulating business relationships or relationships between professionals and their clients. He estimates the proportion of the Supreme Court's workload "dealing directly with the lower half of the class structure" would probably be no more than 15 to 20 percent.

Those at the bottom of the class hierarchy tend to use the lower courts, where traffic, automobile, and alcohol offenses, as well as petty crimes such as shoplifting, prostitution, theft and assault, are heard. If different classes appear before different levels of the judicial system, this may constitute differential and unequal treatment, regardless of whether or not there is bias on the part of individual judges. Those who use the higher courts are almost without exception those who can pay.

The complexity of the judicial system in Canada mystifies all but the most educated. The jurisdictions of provincial and federal courts sometimes overlap and this makes access by all but the most tutored difficult. Both these factors contribute to the fact that people from the lower end of the class hierarchy are much less likely to use the courts, even if they believe they are in the right and have a strong case.

The inconsistency of different court decisions (although not individual judges) also makes it difficult for those without legal skills to understand how the courts can best serve them. An example of such inconsistency occurred in 1976 when the Canadian Labour Congress declared October 14 a day of protest, during which all Canadians were encouraged to stop work to protest wage and price controls. The Ontario Labour Relations Board ruled that workers did not have the legal right to take part in the work stoppage. The British Columbia Labour Relations Board rejected an application to prohibit unions from participating, and went on to define the day of protest not as a strike, but as a political protest in which citizens had a right to take part. Labour relations boards are regulatory boards that function as quasi-courts. The Canada (federal) Labour Code defines "strike" in the same broad way as the Ontario Code. If there had been a test, therefore, the federal government could conceivably have agreed with the Ontario ruling. In the case of this one event, the most we can say is that the judiciary was divided in its support for the right of the trade union movement to this form of political expression.

In Canada, the weakness of much of our labor law is a deterrent to unionization of the two-thirds of Canadian workers who are not unionized. There are federal and provincial laws that make it illegal for an employer to fire or discipline an employee for joining or helping to organize a union, but such laws are enforced so laxly that they might as well not be on the books. Labor relations boards are also too slow in processing applications for certification of unions as legal bargaining units, giving ample time for the employees' commitment to be weakened through management harassment by the time the vote is taken (Finn, 1977).

The situation whereby the courts most frequently come into contact with unions is the strike. In an examination of the judicial treatment of picketing from 1948 to 1963, Mackay (1963) observes that because of the specification of the law, and the way it has been interpreted by judges, the trade unions and their members have been found liable for civil and criminal injury throughout this period. This leads him and others to conclude that any form of remotely effective picketing has become illegal. The picket as a weapon in strikes, then, has been prevented by legislation and also by the judiciary's interpretation of the law. This has important implications for the political expression of the working class when we remember that working-class people do not participate very often in electoral politics. Instead, they take a pragmatic approach that makes conflict in the workplace their most important political tool.

Frequently, when governments have legislated legally striking workers in the public sector back to work, union leaders have sometimes encouraged workers to stay out in order to win the strike. The courts, for their part, have convicted labor leaders for providing such counsel and have given them jail sentences. While the courts may be complying with the letter of the law (and this is not perfectly clear) by convicting labor leaders, it is questionable whether these acts show the courts to be impartial umpires between government and labor.

Although the rule of law is supposed to represent a consensus of all the people, its application is sometimes felt to oppress large segments of the population. The internment of the Japanese during World War II was perfectly legal but was seen as a great injustice by them. Similarly, the declaration of the War Measures Act in 1970 reinforced the feeling of many Quebeckers that they are a colonized people. The question of whether the judiciary delivers different amounts of justice to those in different social classes and ethnic groups is an important one. The equality of all people before the law was a crucial advance in the transition from feudal to modern times, and we should not consider the erosion of such rights lightly. If there is a system of class justice rather than universal justice, then it would mean that the judiciary is not, in fact, an independent state institution, but one that serves the interests of some more than others.

AN APPRAISAL

The first point that emerges from our discussion of the institutions in the Canadian state system is that they are not related to each other in the expected patterns. In the decade between 1969 and 1979, power shifted from the judicial and parliamentary systems to the bureaucratic and executive ones. Both the federal and provincial bureaucracies have grown, and some structures have gained renewed importance within them, such as the Prime Minister's Office, the Privy Council Office, and the Treasury Board. These structures are not responsible to the legislature as a whole, but only to the executive in the form of the Prime Minister and the most trusted cabinet ministers. Thus, we do not have the simple supremacy of administration over government. Rather, we have the use of the administration by the executive with little legislative consultation. Policy-making has also become more removed from the parliamentary system and is now often handled in first ministers' conferences. Although all the first ministers are elected, the proceedings of these conferences are not responsible or accountable to any particular body, and there are no rules for voting, or for implementing decisions. Much of their deliberation takes place behind closed doors. The resultant policy is at least two or three steps removed from the democratic process, if it can be said to be procedurally democratic at all.

Hogarth (1979) characterizes this as the emergence in Canada of political executives with powers similar to those in the American system, but with few of the checks and balances. He explains this change by suggesting that the concept of "office" has been eroded, so that public servants operate ahistorically; that is, outside any tradition by which they judge their conduct and without a vision of a future ideal state. Instead, they are "caught up in the immediacy of the power struggles that are played out in their offices, and guided only by expediency, the game becomes more important than the result."

Hogarth's notion of the erosion of the concept of office is also interesting because it is central to the rational type of authority supposedly operating in the

Canadian polity. In Weber's ideal type legal-rational authority, the notion of office is integral, rather than the individual who fills the office. Members of a system based on legal-rational authority do not owe their loyalty to individuals, but to an impersonal order made up of offices and defined by law.

SUMMARY

1. Polity refers to a form of government or administration, or to a politically organized unit.

2. The polity can be compared to a building. The foundation or bottom floor is the substructure or base, consisting of the dominant modes of production and reproduction. The second floor of the building is civil society. The top floor is the state system. Civil society and the state system together constitute the superstructure.

3. The relations of production are located in the substructure of society and consist of the way people are socially oriented to the productive process: whether they are owners (the bourgeoisie) or wage laborers (the working class). Canada has a capitalist mode of production.

4. Conflict theorists maintain that social change originates in the mode of production and works its way up to the superstructure of the polity. Structural functionalists consider values, norms, attitudes, and other cerebral processes as the basic determinants of political life. The symbolic interactionist perspective can be used to understand the small number of political actors who, through the use of the mass media, define the political situation for us.

5. Electoral participation usually progresses through three levels: spectator, transitional, gladiatorial. Most Canadians tend to be political spectators.

6. In a liberal democracy, everyone has the legal opportunity to participate in politics, but only a limited few participate at the highest levels. Those who participate most are from the middle class or higher.

7. Political behavior depends on, among other things, how a person is involved in reproduction. Within the superstructure of the polity, women have entered public life as the proportion of their lives spent in biological and social reproduction has dropped.

8. Civil society is that part of the polity in which people conduct their everyday lives. The mass media, political parties, interest groups, education, churches, and voluntary associations are political institutions within civil society.

9. The norms, values, and beliefs in which political life is embedded and from which it takes its meaning are called political culture. Political culture is constituted at the level of civil society.

10. The state system is the only part of the polity with authority to legislate, command, or dominate as it sees fit. The state system consists of the judiciary, the administration, government and parliament, the military, and subcentral government. During the 1970s, power shifted from the judicial and parliamentary systems to the bureaucratic and executive ones.

11. There are three ideal types of authority: traditional, charismatic, and legal-rational.

GLOSSARY

Authority. Power that is legitimized and institutionalized in a society or other social system, and to which people consent. Authority may take one of three forms: traditional, charismatic, or legal-rational.

Civil society. That sphere of social life in which people conduct their everyday affairs and fulfill individual needs. Civil society can be thought of as connectng the state system with the economic substructure, while being separate from both of these areas of social life.

Corporatism. Notion that government is overburdened and should delegate some of its tasks to private groups, which in turn would advise the government on policies most relevant to them.

Forces of production. That which workers work on, including land and minerals, tools and all instruments of labor, and the techniques they have devised in their work.

Hegemony. Intellectual and moral leadership or direction by a high status group through its predominance in the political institutions of civil society. Also the phenomenon of a particular group being able to win social, political, and economic struggles in a society.

Interest group. Group organized to secure certain objectives that the members value or regard as beneficial to themselves.

Liberal democracy. Polity in which all members have the legal right to participate in political affairs, but in which only a small number, usually those at the top of the class hierarchy, actually do participate.

Mode of production. Way of producing (for example, the capitalist mode of production) that combines the forces and relations of production. Each mode of production represents a combination of a fundamental class relation, labor process, and form of extraction of surplus labor.

New voters. Voters who were ineligible to cast their votes in the previous election because they were too young or not citizens.

Patronage. Political party's awarding of benefits or favors to those who have shown loyalty to it in the past.

Political culture. Values, beliefs, and attitudes which are the basis of political behavior. The political culture of a people contains the memory of historical events important in the group's development and the symbols which crystallize the subjective meaning that their polity has for them.

Polity. Form of government or administration; a politically organized unit.

Power. Ability of an individual or group to control, influence, or manipulate others' behavior whether those others wish to cooperate or not.

Pyramidal pattern. Pattern of political participation whereby members of a group participate more often in the less powerful positions in the state system than they participate in those which have the greatest control.

Reproduction of labor-power. Regeneration of the individual so that he or she is able to continue working every day. This regeneration includes physical upkeep (food, clothing, rest), as well as the regeneration of the emotional well-being and the social skills that are necessary to perform a particular kind of labor.

State system. That segment of the polity which has the authority to rule and control. Depending on the type of polity in which the state is found, it may include one or more institutions.

Substructure. Base, or infrastructure, of society, including both the mode of economic production and the mode of biological reproduction.

Superstructure. The state system which contains political and legal institutions, and civil society (which includes some political institutions which have an ideological function).

Transient voters. Those who were eligible to vote, but who for one reason or another have not cast their vote in one or more previous elections.

FURTHER READING

Mann, Edward, and John Alan Lee. *RCMP vs. The People: Inside Canada's Security Service.* Don Mills: General Publishing, 1979. A study in investigative sociology that demonstrates how illegal acts by members of the security service emerge from the organizational structure of the RCMP rather than the errors of individuals.

Marchak, Patricia. *Ideological Perspective in Canada.* Toronto: McGraw-Hill Ryerson, 1975. This book is about two versions of the Canadian reality. One of these describes Canada as a liberal democracy governed by representatives elected by a majority of adult citizens. The second describes Canada as a society ruled by a hereditary oligarchy and multi-national imperialist corporation.

Milner, Henry. *Politics in the New Quebec.* Toronto: McClelland and Stewart, 1978. A class analysis of politics in Quebec. This book is the best source available for English-speaking undergraduates on Quebec independence.

Olsen, Dennis. *The State Elite.* Toronto: McClelland and Stewart, 1980. This book examines in more detail the state and state elite in Canada.

Rowbotham, Sheila. *Woman's Consciousness, Man's World.* Harmondsworth: Penguin, 1975. A discussion of the development of the new feminist consciousness and a description of the social changes from which it originates. This book is also important in explaining the role of women in the capitalist state and the part they play in the production of commodities.

CHAPTER 14
EDUCATION

JOS. L. LENNARDS

Education is an institution that affects us all. By law you are compelled to attend school for at least ten years, but the great majority of young people in Canada spend more than this required minimum in school. From kindergarten to high school graduation, the average young Canadian presently spends about 17 000 hours in school. In addition to this, a substantial segment of the young population pursues further full-time education at the post-secondary level. Going to school is such a regular part of growing up that it seems difficult to imagine how the socialization process could proceed without it. As we saw in Chapter 3, education is an important agent in the socialization process. For the greater part of human history, however young people were prepared to assume adult responsibilities without the benefits of a system of universal schooling.

Universal public education is a modern invention, dating from the nineteenth century. One of the main promoters in Canada of a state-supported system of mass schooling was Egerton Ryerson. As superintendent of education in Upper Canada from 1844 to 1876, Ryerson played a major role in formulating and implementing a series of legislative acts which, by 1871, had resulted in the establishment of a provincially controlled system of free and compulsory schooling for all young people. The main features of the Ontario system of education were subsequently adopted by the Atlantic and western provinces.

To gain some perspectives on the historical uniqueness of our educational situation, it might be useful to contrast it with earlier practices. Education in the early nineteenth century consisted of a patchwork of formal and informal arrangements. Children of "common" people learned much of what they needed to know either at home or in apprenticeship training at the work place. Formal training at an elementary level was offered: for a fee in private schools, organized by individuals or churches; in the local, government-aided common schools; and, at no cost to the poor, in large schools run by charitable organizations. The majority of children received some schooling, but attendance was seasonal and brief. Still Ontario data indicate that this mixture of formal and informal, of publicly supported and privately financed instruction produced basic literacy for the greater part of the population (Graff, 1975).

The introduction of a state-supported system of compulsory schooling in 1871 constituted a sharp break with previous practices. It meant, first of all, that education had achieved a new social significance. Schools were turned into government-supported organizations, because they were perceived to perform important public functions. Because of this, voluntary participation was no longer acceptable, and students were compelled to attend. Education had become too important to be left to the discretion of parents. Henceforth, the family would have to delegate part of its responsibility for the socialization process to the schools.

This shift in the role of the school, from an agency serving private purposes to an instrument for the attainment of public ends, was accompanied by changes in the organization of education. The educational system was transformed into a bureaucracy, with regulatory power centralized at the top. Authority over such important areas as teacher certification, curricula, and school texts was transferred to the state. Diversity was replaced by uniformity; schools were required to operate within common guidelines formulated and enforced by a central, state administration.

In this chapter, we will focus mainly on the first aspect of education – its social significance. Why has education become an important social institution? What role exactly does it fulfill in our society? What determines the ebb and flow of support for education? How effectively does it discharge its public responsibilities? Has educational expansion delivered on its promises? Have the benefits been equally distributed? What are some of the main factors producing unequal educational outcomes? These are the topics to be discussed in this chapter. They are more than just theoretical issues, part of the ongoing debate between structural functionalist and conflict theorists. They are also of immediate importance to you. What is happening to the educational system is also happening to you.

Before we proceed, however, let us clarify what we mean by education. In this chapter the word carries a specific meaning. It is not interchangeable with either socialization or learning. Although education involves both, not all socialization or learning takes the form of education. Here, **education** means the deliberate, organized transmission of values, knowledge, and skills. It implies the notion of a set of actors – teachers and students – meeting at a designated time, in order to pursue systematically a defined learning objective in a setting deemed appropriate for the purpose at hand. Schools are therefore educational organizations, but educational activities also take place outside of school in such forms as apprenticeship training, English language courses for immigrants, lecture series, and religious instruction in Sunday school.

Because of their central importance we will concentrate here on schools and universities only. The passage to adulthood for young people in our society is channeled through these organizations.

THE FUNCTIONS OF EDUCATION

The most widely recognized aim of the educational system is to facilitate the transition from participation in the primary relationships of the family to involvement in the affairs of the larger society. What are the social positions considered to be so essential that prep-

Growing Up In School

One of the crucial stages in a young person's transition toward adulthood is adolescence. The psychological task at this stage is the development of a firm identity, a sense of what you are and what you want to become. It involves a search for purpose in life. "Where am I going?" and "What do I want to commit myself to?" The resolution of this identity crisis is the general developmental task of adolescence.

Prolonged education has made the school into the central social setting within which adolescents confront the problem of identity formation. But do schools provide students with an appropriate maturational environment? Are they good places in which to grow up and discover your identity? Is it a good thing that the task of preparing young people for adult life has been delegated to such a great extent to the educational system? A number of scholars have argued that the school setting provides an incomplete basis for the attainment of many important maturational objectives (Coleman, et al, 1974).

Schools are oriented to developing self-centered skills that expand a person's instrumental resources, especially in the economic area. But schools do less well in developing other sets of skills that are crucial to the process of identity formation. They provide, for instance, little opportunity for developing a sense of self-direction and responsibility. Students occupy a subordinate position in the school system. The student role does not allow for much initiative and self-management. Students are given assignments rather than responsibilities. The ends to which their activities are directed are determined by the school, and their job in carrying out their duties requires little decision-making and little discretionary judgment. Because little responsibility for managing one's affairs is given, little training for self-direction takes place. Responsibility cannot be taught where freedom of choice is absent.

The student role has a second characteristic that reduces the ability of the school to generate a sense of self-involvement and, hence, responsibility. In school, knowledge is taught, rather than acquired through experience. Schools are information-rich, but action-poor. The realities of the outside world are presented in an abstract fashion. Students are made aware of the choices they face, but they are given little opportunity to learn from experience what the choice of a particular cause of action entails. Schools teach cognitive understanding without providing students with an experience-based access to this understanding. Separated from the world of experienced reality, students find it difficult to establish the personal relevance of what they are learning.

Schools provide an incomplete environment for the socialization of the young. They do not offer a sufficiently wide range of maturity promoting experiences. Schools are not the right places in which to face the most pressing of adolescents' concerns: the formation of a secure identity. The task of moving toward adulthood needs to be recognized in such a way that young people are no longer shielded from responsibility and meaningful experience. Several proposals have been advanced in this regard, such as:

1. The introduction of a voucher system for youth. Vouchers, equivalent in value to the average cost of perhaps three years of college education, would be given to young people at age sixteen to be used at their discretion for schooling or other forms of skill training. The advantage of such a system would be that it places the resources required for further schooling directly into the hands of young people, who will now be given a chance to take responsibility for managing their own education. Under these conditions, a much higher degree of self-involvement can be expected.

2. Alternation of school and work. One way of providing youth with opportunities for obtaining experience is to encourage movement between school and workplace. Students could spend part of their time in a work setting related to the educational studies they are pursuing. This would help them establish the personal relevance of what they are learning and, at the same time, present them with a realistic opportunity for testing the strength of their interest and commitment to their chosen line of study.

Source:

Reference is to Coleman, James S., et al. *Youth: Transition to Adulthood*. Chicago: University of Chicago Press, 1974.

---

aration for them has been brought under the province of the educational system? Participating in society involves membership in four key areas: the economy, the social stratification system, the polity, and the culture of the society. The educational system fulfills a specific function with regard to each of these areas.

The Economy

In any society, the socialization process is bound to be tied to the economy. Preparation for adulthood always involves training in the practical skills required to become a productive member of society. In the past, except for the most specialized occupations, much of this training took place on the job. Today, the school has come to occupy a central role in the occupational training process at all levels of the occupational hierarchy.

Apprenticeship programs and other forms of on-the-job training still exist, but their contribution to the total occupational training process has been greatly reduced. The basic vocational training for the overwhelming majority of jobs in our society takes place within the educational system. Training and apprenticeship programs build on the foundation laid by the school. Education has become the major agency of occupational socialization. **Occupational socialization** refers to the students' preparation for entering the job market. The economy depends for its operation on an adequate supply of efficient and motivated workers. One of the tasks of the educational system is to maintain this flow.

Social Stratification

As we saw in Chapter 8, social inequality or social stratification is a pervasive aspect of social life. You are born into a particular class (*class of origin*), and, as adults, you occupy a position in the social stratification hierarchy (*class of destination*). These two can be, but are not necessarily, the same.

Inequality is a potential source of conflict in all societies, and it makes the smooth assimilation of people into the social structure problematic. As long as occupations carry unequal amounts of benefits in income and prestige, it can be fairly assumed that people will try to "better themselves"; that is, they will tend to avoid the less rewarded positions in favor of the more attractive ones. Social stratification, then, introduces an element of status competition. To deal with this problem, societies have developed strategies for regulating the process of status acquisition.

Two basic strategies can be distinguished, each based on a different type of eligibility criterion. The crucial distinction here is between ascriptive and achievement criteria.

The allocation of persons to positions on the basis of ascriptive criteria leads to a system of closed competi-tion in which the range of positions for which new cohorts can compete is determined at birth. That is, the class of destination is determined by the class of origin. When achievement criteria are recognized as the basis for status allocation, the competition is not closed, but open. Future position is not a function of initial placement, but of an individual's effort and ability. Under the closed system your final position is identical with your starting position, but in the open system social position at birth is only a temporary status that does not restrict how far you are allowed to move. Instead of ending up where you started, you arrive at the position you have earned.

In their pure forms, these two strategies for status allocation hardly exist. Completely open and completely closed competition represent two extremes. Still, this typology gives us a useful tool of analysis, because most societies gravitate toward one side or the other. According to their central tendency, then, societies can be characterized as either open or closed. Like other advanced industrial societies, Canada subscribes to the principle of open competition for status allocation. This has important ramifications for the role of education.

In a *closed society* education fulfils a mainly passive role. Its function is not to change students' class positions, but to confirm them after the fact by teaching students the skills and values appropriate to their class of origin. In a closed society the purpose of university education, for example, is "to put the icing on the cake." Gentlemen attend in order to become "cultivated." Education is largely a consequence, rather than a determinant, of social class position, and it serves to stabilize social class positions across generations (see Figure 14-1).

In an *open society* education operates under a different mandate. Its task is to play an active, interventionist role in the allocative process. Rather than simply being a transmitter of the stratification system, education becomes an independent "assignment office for social chances" (Schelsky, 1961). Instead of accepting class of origin as a determinant of future status, the school functions as society's testing agency, screening claims to future status on the basis of standards presumed to be relevant and objective. Its task is to

Figure 14-1. Closed Society: Education as an Institution of Social Inheritance

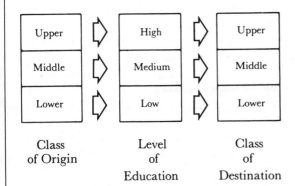

Educational selection: according to class background

Allocation: according to educational level

Class of Origin		Level of Education		Class of Destination
Upper	⇨	High	⇨	Upper
Middle	⇨	Medium	⇨	Middle
Lower	⇨	Low	⇨	Lower

Figure 14-2. Open Society: Education as an Institution of Social Mobility

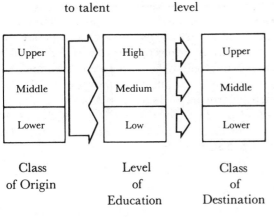

Educational selection: according to talent

Allocation: according to educational level

Class of Origin		Level of Education		Class of Destination
Upper		High	⇨	Upper
Middle		Medium	⇨	Middle
Lower		Low	⇨	Lower

provide everyone with an equal chance to compete and to assess a student's class of destination on the basis of talent and ability. In an open society, the school functions as the arena where the status passage from class of origin to class of destination is publicly negotiated (see Figure 14-2).

As a social selection agency, the task of the school is to identify, allocate, and certify talent. The educational system in our society is supposed to operate as an independent review board giving people a fair hearing before making its decision on what their social stratification credentials are. Consequently, schools are places where students are tested, where their academic achievement is evaluated and compared to that of their peers, and where, based on a comparative assessment of their performances, they are channeled in appropriate directions. Students emerge from this process with a diploma, certificate, or degree that qualifies them for entrance to a particular level of the social stratification hierarchy.

It is not enough, however, to have a system for assessing status claims. What happens when someone is not happy with the assessment? A way to insure that people respond favorably to status allocation is also necessary. Given the existence of social stratification, a favorable reaction of the members of a society to their class of destination cannot be taken for granted. Allocative decisions may give rise to serious discontent, especially among those facing limited prospects. The process of status induction, therefore, also includes a second, subjective, component. People need to be taught two things concurrently: what their place is and acceptance of that decision. As the major social selection agency, the school is not only involved in the screening process, but also functions as an instrument of status socialization. The task of the educational system is twofold: to select fairly, and to generate compliance with the outcome of the selection process.

How is compliance generated? What exactly does status socialization entail?

First, **status socialization** implies regulation of ambition. This means that students' aspirations need to be brought into line with the school's estimation of their abilities. Bright students are to be encouraged to have high aspirations, while poor, but ambitious, students need to be "cooled-out" (Clark, 1960). The main problem associated with the processing of ambition is that students' aspiration levels are strongly influenced by their social class. The educational system is expected to neutralize the impact of this powerful factor by either raising or lowering class-based ambition levels, depending on its independent assessment of talent. Therefore, schools do not only evaluate performance, they also offer guidance counseling.

Second, status socialization implies legitimation. Allocation means that people have different levels of access to privileged positions. In order for people to accept the allocation process, particularly those people who receive fewer benefits, they must not only learn to be realistic about their mobility prospects, but they must also come to believe in the appropriateness of the principles governing the allocation process. As Marx pointed out, systems of social inequality generate their own ideologies of justification. Once this happens, the existing system of privileges becomes more firmly entrenched, since notions of justice can now be harnessed in its defense. Inequality is no longer a fact of existence with which one has to come to terms pragmatically, it is transformed into a normative state of affairs. Social stratification becomes a social reality that rightfully exists and commands our approval.

In our society, the justification for social stratification is provided by a meritocratic ideology. In a **meritocracy**, social inequality is warranted as long as privileges are distributed on the basis of established merit, and as long as all people have an equal chance to prove themselves. The educational system serves as a major agency for implementing meritocratic ideology. Schools try to convince students of the importance of their selective criteria, so that educational achievement comes to be seen as the standard by which social merit is to be assessed. Schools also attempt to create confidence in the fairness and accuracy of their assessment procedures, so that educational success or failure is accepted by students as a true manifestation of their ability.

The school, then, is expected to function both as an agency promoting social mobility according to talent and as an agency promoting acceptance of social stratification. The same processes that make the school a place of opportunity also transform it into an instrument of social control for the stratification system. The provision of equality of opportunity implies the notion of status training. Social selection and status socialization are complementary activities. They define, from different angles, the social stratification mandate of the school in the open society.

The Political Order

Learning to participate in social life includes, as a third component, preparation for membership in the political order. Your initial encounter with authority takes place in the family, and you receive your first political training at home. Learning to be a child involves learning to be a subordinate and to follow directives, learning to anticipate that violations of the rules will call forth negative sanctions, and learning to accept parental authority as being oriented toward your own good. But, because authority in the family is personal and takes on a variety of forms from one unit to another, your early socialization does not prepare you adequately for the formally organized and uniform authority structure of the larger society. As residents of a particular municipality, province, and country, you must also learn to deal with the demands of public authority.

In Canadian society, public authority is organized along democratic lines. Democratic government is based on the consent of the governed and represents an attempt to make authority accountable to the people. Accountability requires, as its counterpart, responsiveness. As citizens, we are called upon to become politically involved, to speak up for our interests, and to monitor the performance of our elected representatives. The task of preparing us for this type of active participation in the affairs of society has been given to the educational system. Part of the school's effort, therefore, is directed toward democratic **citizenship training**: Courses in history and civics are included in the school curriculum for this reason.

Culture

All the functions of education identified so far have one element in common: all aim at preparing students for life in a socially differentiated society in which each person will occupy a particular niche in the division of labor. But participating in society implies one additional dimension: learning to be members of the same community. One of the central aims of the educational system, from its very inception, has been to create a common cultural identity, as discussed in Chapter 2. The common school was meant to serve as an agency of social integration, bringing people from different classes, ethnic background, and religions together, and connecting the local community to the larger society. In its cultural function the educational system attempts to foster a sense of collective identity and purpose. We learn in school that we are a people bound together by common traditions. We are taught about the components of our common cultural heritage and what distinctive qualities and achievements we collectively value. Finally, schools do not only inform, they also appeal to our sentiments. They attempt to capture our commitment and loyalty, so that what we have in common becomes a source of self-identification and pride.

Human Enlightenment

In the preceding discussion we have highlighted the role of the school as a preparatory agency easing our entrance into the existing social order. The importance of the educational system as an instrument for role socialization should not be underestimated, but it would be one-sided to define its teaching mandate solely in these terms. The task of the educational system is not just to serve the demands of society and to mold our personalities accordingly. One important function of education is personality development as a value in its own right. Official curriculum guidelines frequently include statements to the effect that education should lead to "the full development of each child's potential" and that it should develop "the moral and aesthetic sensitivity necessary for a complete and responsible life" (Ministry of Education, Ontario, 1975).

Universities are not far behind in expressing their commitment to liberal education as a nonutilitarian search for self-enrichment. From the Greeks, who believed that the educated person should live "the exam-

ined life," we have inherited the notion of education as worthy to be pursued for its own sake. In this perspective, the function of the school is to enhance the capabilities of the individual, particularly the ability to reason, and to lay the basis for self-realization and autonomy.

A final function of education also derives from our cultural commitment to knowledge as an end in itself. The school is expected to do more than to preserve and pass on the collective wisdom of the past. The educational system also functions as a source of innovation. At the higher levels in particular, centers of learning are involved in both the transmission and creation of knowledge. They are places where new scientific ideas are born and developed, where new interpretations of our cultural tradition are undertaken, and where our existing stock of knowledge is subjected to critical examination and modification in light of changing circumstances.

The Basic Reference Points

These, then, are the major functions of education:

1. to be the major agency of occupational socialization
2. to identify, allocate, and certify talent; and to function as an instrument of status socialization
3. to train students for democratic citizenship
4. to create a common cultural identity
5. to develop the student's personality and human potential; and to function as a source of innovation

Having identified the major functions of education, we now have a framework for analyzing the interaction between education and the larger society in more detail.

Before proceeding with this analysis we should point out that these are not the only interconnections that can be made between education and other areas of social life. Schools also have latent functions that produce side effects which in an unintentional and/or unrecognized way sustain certain social phenomena. A latent function of high schools and post-secondary institutions, for example, is to provide a dating and marriage market. Schools also fulfil a custodial function, providing the day care that enables mothers to join the labor market. At the same time, schools prevent youngsters from entering the work force, thereby alleviating unemployment and the social dissatisfaction it creates.

In the following analysis, we will focus mainly on the five manifest functions enumerated above. They represent the publicly recognized contributions of education, and they furnish the key justification for its institutional support. The list provides us, therefore, with a set of basic reference points for analyzing the institution of education in its societal context.

One good starting point for a macrosociological analysis of education is to ask how much weight is attached to each of the manifest functions. Not all of them receive equal emphasis, and systems of education differ depending on the dominant priority scheme. What, in our society, are the functions that receive high and low priority? What are the areas of performance on which public concern is mainly focused? If the school is criticized for not doing a good job, what type of complaints receive widespread public attention, and what type of criticism fails to arouse much general interest? The answers to these questions provide us with important clues to the nature of the power field within which the educational system is located.

The list of manifest functions serves a second useful analytical purpose. It allows us to identify more precisely the nature of the contradictions and controversies that accompany the operation of education in our society. Tensions and debates can be reduced to three causes.

First, while a particular function is generally considered to be important, there might exist disagreement about how to define it more specifically. In fact, the greater the importance attached to a particular function, the more likely it is that such differences of opinion will occur. A good example in Canada is the historical conflict about the cultural role of the school. What does creating a common cultural identity entail? Whose culture should the school promote? Should the goal be assimilation or cultural pluralism, the melting pot or the mosaic?

Second, tension results from the fact that a particular

Passage from childhood to adulthood leads through the school. Do our schools teach young people to think, to reason, to make decisions and to act responsibly? Or to record facts and then regurgitate them on cue? Or simply to conform?

function might involve contradictory demands. For example, we have seen that our society subscribes to the principle of open status competition. As a result, the educational system is expected, on the one hand, to extend and equalize educational opportunities and, on the other hand, to sort out the more able from the less able students. In other words, the school is supposed to create and raise the aspirations of students and, at the same time, to block the educational opportunities of the less talented pupils, thereby limiting their stratification prospects. How realistic is it to expect that these two tasks can be accomplished simultaneously? Can the one be achieved only at the expense of the other?

Third, in addition to these two internal types of contradictions, there also exist external contradictions among the various functions. One controversy concerns the conflicting demands of human enlightenment versus role training. The pendulum of educational reform seems to swing back and forth between these poles. At the elementary and secondary levels of the educational system, it is expressed as a conflict between a child-centered type of education and a concern for the basics. An increased emphasis on the former inevitably produces, in reaction, a demand for a renewed emphasis on "the three Rs" (readin', ritin', 'n' rithmetic). At the university level, a similar, seemingly perpetual tug-of-war is conducted between those who support a more humanistic and general type of education and those who are in favor of a more specialized and professionally oriented curriculum.

Another, much less widely debated, contradiction exists between the political and the cultural socialization functions of the school. In its cultural role, the school is engaged in nation building. It tries to increase people's identification with their society and to instill feelings of solidarity and national pride. But political citizenship in a democracy requires an attitude not of blind loyalty, but of critical involvement, of conditional approval. Actually, we often see that democratic citizenship training is sacrificed for or confused with nation building and that patriotism and docility, rather than informed consent, is the desired result.

EXPANSION

The Canadian educational system has undergone several profound and fundamental changes in recent decades. In this section we will describe these changes and then relate them to the underlying shift in perspective on the functional significance of education.

From Elite Preparatory to Mass Terminal

In 1951, only 46 percent of Canada's fourteen to seventeen year olds was enrolled on a full-time basis in the senior high school level of education (grades nine and up). Ten years later the figure had increased to 72 percent; in 1971 it had reached 98 percent (Statistics Canada, 1978). Beginning in the 1960s, the Canadian educational system moved decisively and rapidly into a new phase: from an **elite preparatory** system it has been transformed into a **mass terminal** system (Trow, 1961). The third phase of development, mass preparatory, where most students continue through post-secondary education is beginning to emerge in the United States.

Until the 1950s, the function of the high school in Canada was, basically, to prepare a relatively small group of students for advanced studies. The demands of the universities largely determined the curriculum and the philosophy of secondary education, especially at the senior level. But during the sixties, there was a rapid expansion in the number of students who continued to matriculation – from 49.8 percent in 1961 to 80 percent in 1971 (Statistics Canada, 1973). This rapid expansion changed the educational system in a fundamental way.

Mass terminal education produced a new set of organizational demands. The secondary school system had to accommodate itself to a much wider range of educational interests. No longer could it orient itself toward just the needs of the university. And the post-secondary sector, having lost control over the direction and nature of secondary education, had to deal with a more heterogeneous and much larger student population. Here, we will concentrate on the quantitative

TABLE 14-1. TRENDS IN FULL-TIME ENROLLMENT, BY LEVEL, CANADA 1951-1979

	1951	1961	1971	1977	1979
Elementary-Secondary					
Kindergarten-Grade 8	2,230,300	3,514,900	4,096,100	3,788,000	3,505,100
Grade 9 and up	394,500	894,900	1,726,500	1,704,900	1,701,300
Subtotal	2,624,800	4,409,800	5,822,600	5,492,900	5,206,400
Post-Secondary					
Non-University	27,200	53,400	173,800	227,000	251,400
University	63,500	128,600	323,000	367,500	371,400
Subtotal	90,700	182,000	496,800	603,500	622,800
TOTAL	2,715,500	4,591,800	6,319,400	6,096,400	5,829,200
Post-Secondary enrolment as percentage of 18-24 age group	6.0	10.6	18.5	19.6	19.1

SOURCE: Adapted from Statistics Canada, *Historical Compendium of Education Statistics from Confederation to 1975.* Ottawa, 1978, pp. 16-17; Statistics Canada, *Education in Canada, 1980,* Ottawa, 1981, pp. 56 and 63.

dimension of this transformation and on its external, social causes and consequences.

Table 14-1 shows the startling speed with which the Canadian educational system moved into its new phase. Between 1951 and 1971, the total student population more than doubled – it increased by a factor of 2.33. This increase was partly a product of the post-war baby boom. The eligible student population, those in the five to twenty-four age group, grew in the same period by a factor of 1.83. But the greatest share of the growth resulted from increased participation levels. The most rapid increase in student enrollment occurred at the senior-secondary (grade nine and up) and the post-secondary levels, where attendance is a matter of choice. Between 1951 and 1971 the senior-secondary sector grew by a factor of 4.38, the post-secondary, non-university sector by a factor of 6.39, and the university sector by a factor of 5.09.

Part-time university enrollment expanded at an even faster rate. Between 1962 and 1971 the number of part-time students grew from 43 990 to 185 387, a factor of 4.21 (Statistics Canada, 1978). Full-time university enrollment during the same period increased by a factor of 2.29 (Statistics Canada, 1978).

To teach this vastly expanded student population a great number of additional instructors were recruited. Between 1950 and 1971 the number of full-time teachers in elementary and secondary schools almost tripled (1:2.93) from 89 682 to 263 126. At the university level, the full-time faculty body grew from 5339 to 27 557, a factor of 5.16 (Statistics Canada, 1978). Because graduate programs at Canadian universities had just started to expand, many of the university instructors recruited during this period were of foreign origin and/or had received their graduate training abroad, particularly in the United States. So large was the recruitment effort that, in spite of the rapid growth in student population, the teacher-pupil ratio actually declined. In the elementary-secondary sector it dropped from 1:25.5 in 1961 to 1:21.4 in 1971; at the university, it decreased from 1:14.7 to 1:8.4 during the same ten-year period.

In 1971, Canada had 68 universities, 16 of which were affiliated with another Canadian university. Only 44 of these institutions had been in existence ten years earlier. Many of the new universities had roots in the religiously affiliated sector. At the post-secondary, non-university level a whole new set of institutions was created to bridge the gap between high school and university. In most provinces, the only fields of study available at the post-secondary level outside the university had been nursing and teacher training. The 1960s saw the emergence of a new and comprehensive, alternative branch of post-secondary education: the community college. In 1960 only 29 institutions of this kind existed; by the end of the decade their number had increased to 133.

The community college sector constitutes the most rapidly growing part of post-secondary education. The name and function of these colleges differ according to province. In the west, they are sometimes called Junior Colleges; in Ontario, Colleges of Applied Arts and Technology (CAAT); in Quebec, Collèges d'enseignement général et professionnel (CEGEP). In British Columbia, Alberta, and Quebec, the colleges offered both vocational training and two years of university level studies, from which a student could transfer to a university. In the other provinces, the colleges formed a separate stream; their specific objective was to provide a comprehensive career alternative to university education. Teacher training was largely transferred to the university, while nursing programs were incorporated into the community colleges.

The simultaneous and rapid expansion of the secondary and post-secondary sectors had a tremendous impact on expenditures. In 1950, only 2.4 percent of the Gross National Product (the total amount of goods and services produced in Canada) was allocated to educational spending. By 1961 it had risen to 4.9 percent, and in 1971 it had reached 8.8. Since then the percentage has hovered somewhat below this level. No other advanced industrial society, including the United States, has made such a high financial commitment to education.

The greatest proportion of the increase in expenditures occurred at the post-secondary level. University expenditures, for example, increased at an annual rate of 15 percent between 1950 and 1971 (Statistics Canada, 1978). The burden of these expenditures was increasingly borne by the government. In 1950, tuition fees accounted for 26 percent of university income, and private financing accounted for an additional 15 percent, so that only three-fifths of the total expenditures came from public sources. In 1961, the combined share of tuition and private support had dropped to 30 percent; in 1971 to 18 percent (Statistics Canada, 1978). More than four-fifths of all university revenues are now derived from governmental sources.

The Impetus to Expansion

In 1975 a group of foreign experts (OECD, 1976), commissioned to review recent educational policy in Canada, characterized the development we have just noted in this way:

Until the late 1940s, Canada could be counted as one of the less developed (educationally) of the great democracies. Today, it is numbered clearly among the educational leaders. . . . It is hardly an exaggeration to talk about a second great Canadian pioneering achievement.

What was behind this sudden leap of education into a position of institutional prominence? Obviously, a profound change in the functional importance attached to education must have taken place. What was the nature of this change?

The impetus for the enormous expansion of the Canadian educational system came from two sources. One was the growing belief in the central significance of higher education as a source of national strength. The other was the desire to create a more just society.

Productivity. The recognition that higher education could be a source of national strength dates from the 1940s. Prior to World War II, universities were seen as regional institutions important chiefly to the province in which they were located. The war effort created a great demand for scientific research and highly trained personnel, and with this came the realization of how much the nation's survival and development depended on the university sector. In the immediate post-war period, the federal government for the first time started to give direct financial support to the universities to assist them in meeting the expenses created by the influx of veterans who, supported by government grants, enrolled in large numbers.

When the veteran program and the accompanying

subsidies were about to expire, a Royal Commission was appointed to study the federal role in the arts, letters, and sciences (Royal Commission, 1951). Headed by Vincent Massey, the commission took special note of the state of higher education, documented the precarious financial situation the universities and especially the humanities faced, and recommended that the federal government embark on a program of annual grants to the universities to help them meet operating costs. The recommendation was accepted, and, beginning in 1951, the federal government became involved in the financial support of the post-secondary sector on a regular basis. The *Massey Report* based its recommendations on the fact that universities were national institutions vital to the preservation and growth of Canada's cultural identity. This cultural argument carried some weight, but the real push for expansion came from a different direction.

In the wake of economic fluctuation during the 1950s, the Canadian government set stable economic growth and the reduction of unemployment as two of its national priorities. It realized that the weakness of the Canadian economy had a structural source, and that the goal of sustained economic development could only be attained by shifting the economic base of Canadian society from resources to industry. The society to be taken as a model of how to achieve industrial strength was the United States. According to the economic theories in vogue in the United States, economic growth in an advanced industrial society depended foremost on *human capital*.

The core postulate of the **human capital theory** was that knowledge had replaced muscle and physical capital as the principal factor of production. It was the fusion of science with industry that made possible the great increases in productivity on which economic prosperity depended. Advanced industrial societies were "knowledge societies," and organized technological rationality was the key to their economic success. If knowledge was the strategic resource of an advanced industrial society, then the educational system was its key institution, for it could produce the scientific ideas on which innovation depended and the skilled manpower required to operate the system. In an "expert society" (Clark, 1962), education as a means for mobilizing human capital had become a crucial type of investment.

If education was a key component of economic growth, then the level of schooling of the Canadian labor force in comparison to that of the United States was a matter of concern. In 1961, among the male labor force in the twenty-five to thirty-four age group, 14.7 percent of American workers had university degrees compared to 6 percent of Canadians; 57.2 percent of the same group in the United States had completed four years of high school, compared to only 28.2 percent in Canada.

Even more striking was the fact that the differences in educational attainment were highest for the youngest age group. For the fifty-five to sixty-four age category, the gap between the educational levels of the Canadian and American male labor force was not so wide (Porter, 1967). The conclusion was obvious. If Canada were to catch up with its industrial neighbor, then the educational gap between the two countries needed to be closed. This required a drastic expansion and reform of the existing educational system. For too long Canada had relied on immigration to supply highly skilled personnel. From now on, our own educational system had to be equipped to undertake the crucial task of meeting industrial society's ever increasing demand for expertise. This was the opinion expressed in the sixties by the influential Economic Council of Canada in its first and second annual reviews (1964, 1965) and by sociologist John Porter in his pioneering study, *The Vertical Mosaic* (1965).

Social Justice. The second major force behind educational expansion was the desire to create a more just society. As S.D. Clark (1976) noted, the post-war period was a time of social ferment. Barriers to social and geographical mobility were breaking down, and new groups were trying to enter the mainstream of social life. A revolution of rising expectations was taking place, especially among the middle class. The steady increase in the proportion of students opting for university education, for example, dates from the early fifties and was well under way before the government became involved financially. Everyone, it seemed, wanted a bigger share of the pie. To accommodate

Recent changes in economic and social structures suggest that in the future education will continue from the cradle to the grave. These youngsters in Peking are learning from the poster that, "When your classes are finished, you run to your home. But Mama will not be there, for she has gone to school."

these pressures, an active policy of promoting opportunities through improved access to educational institutions was adopted by Canadian governments during the sixties. Social justice demanded that all people, regardless of gender, region, or social class, would be given an equal opportunity to develop their talents.

The appeal of this policy rested on more than just social grounds. It also served important economic functions. Both social justice and efficiency demanded talent mobilization, and education could satisfy these two objectives simultaneously. It was this identity between social and economic objectives that provided such a powerful justification for educational expansion.

In addition to being economically attractive, the policy of relying primarily on the educational sector to bring about a more just society had important political advantages as well. It provided a way of meeting

rising social aspirations without having to undertake more radical reforms.

The policy of equality through education was based on a narrow definition of what constitutes social justice. The concern was with opening up opportunities for individual advancement: equal chances to become unequal. The system of social inequality as such, the shape of income distribution, was not under attack. What was offered was fairness of selection procedures (equality of opportunity), not fairness of results (equality of condition).

Mobility Strategies

In pursuing this goal of equal opportunity for all, Canadian education underwent a distinct shift in social orientation. The nature of this change can best be

The rod was not spared, and these children do not look spoiled. But neither do they look too happy. The Ontario Public Health Department took this photograph to illustrate inadequate lighting conditions in turn-of-the-century classrooms.

described in terms of the typology developed by American sociologist Ralph Turner (1961). The basic assumption behind Turner's typology is that because schools are important social selection agencies, their organization will be determined by the prevailing ideas about how social mobility ought to proceed. Turner distinguishes two modes of upward mobility: a sponsored mobility and a contest mobility. Turner (1961) characterized **sponsored mobility** this way:

Elite recuits are chosen by the established elite or their agents, and elite status is given on the basis of some criterion of supposed merit and cannot be taken by any amount of effort or strategy. Upward mobility is like entry into a private club, where each candidate must be sponsored by one or more of its members. Ultimately, the members grant or deny upward mobility on the basis of whether they judge the candidate to have the qualities they wish to see in fellow members.

In contrast to this is Turner's (1961) **contest mobility**:

. . . a system in which elite status is the prize of an open contest and is taken by the aspirants' own efforts. While the "contest" is governed by some rules of fair play, the contest-ants have wide latitude in the strategies they may employ. Since the "prize" of successful upward mobility is not in the hands of the established elite to give out, the latter are not in a position to determine who shall obtain it and who not.

This difference in mobility is related to the nature of the stratification system, particularly the elite structure, of a particular society. Sponsored mobility will be found in societies where one particular group has been able to establish cultural control, so that only the attributes it values will form the basis for elite selection. Contest mobility emerges in societies where no status group has been able to establish a monopoly over elite credentials. Historically, England and continental Europe belong in the former category; the United States, in the latter. This has been reflected in the organization of their respective educational systems.

Contest Mobility. In the United States, the educational system is organized to encourage students to stay in the competition as long as possible and to teach them whatever skills are useful in attaining high rewards. Within the American educational system, **contest mobility** is characterized by:

1. lack of early selection and allocation of students to different streams; all students attend the same comprehensive high school
2. relative ease of transfer between types of programs and institutions
3. relative openness of the curriculum

Because no elite has monopolized elite credentials, the school system has no legitimate criteria for excluding certain subjects as inappropriate. American schools and universities offer a curriculum that ranges from traditional arts and science subjects to home economics, and financial support is offered to both scholars and football players. Any skill that is in demand is considered legitimate and worthy of inclusion in the curriculum. The educational system is structured in such a way that selection is postponed as long as is practicable to permit a fair race. Junior colleges offer second chances to those students who were not successful in their first attempt to qualify for university entrance. The onus is on the educational system to prove ineptitude for elite positions, and not on the student to prove special worth. The problem of creating an open contest is met by creating diversified curricula in a unitary structure, where transfer chances are optimized.

Sponsored Mobility. The purpose of education in a **sponsored mobility** system is to identify and select those with elite potential as early as possible in order to insure control over their training. This purpose is articulated into:

1. early selection and segregation of students into different streams
2. prescribed curricula aimed at the cultivation of qualities deemed necessary by the established elite
3. restriction of transfer possibilities from non-elite to elite training institutions

If a student does not make it into the university stream at an early age, his chances of ever getting there are slim. The desire to control the content of the selection process leads to the creation of prescribed curricula in a binary or tripartite structure precluding transfer.

Historically in Canada education has followed mainly a sponsored mobility tradition, although in the western provinces the American model has been influential.

The prevailing belief was that higher education was the privilege of a carefully screened intellectual elite, rather than the right of as many people as possible. With the post-war emphasis on educational accessibility, however, this has changed, and in recent decades the Canadian educational system as a whole has moved in the direction of contest mobility, particularly at the secondary level. Abolishing departmental exams, looser university entrance requirements, breaking down the rigid structure of the curriculum by introducing a credit system, abolishing Latin (the traditional symbol of elite status) as a required subject – all these curriculum changes were clearly motivated by a desire to loosen control over elite credentials and to encourage students to stay in the race as long as possible.

But these sentiments were not as evident in post-secondary educational policy. We noted earlier that in the majority of provinces community colleges were established as a separate system, not to be systematically associated with the university sector. Even though the idea of mass education was generally accepted at the secondary level, support for such a policy at the post-secondary level was much more guarded. Here the remnants of sponsored mobility thinking can still be observed.

The Case of Quebec. Among all the provinces, it was in Quebec that the economic and social ideas we have just outlined had their greatest educational impact. The Liberal government of Jean Lesage, which came to power in 1960, committed itself to a policy of *rattrapage*, of catching up with social and economic development elsewhere. Education became one of the main targets of this modernization drive.

Before the 1960s, the provincial government had had little control over the education system. Public education was divided into two sectors: one Catholic and largely French, and the other Protestant and largely English. In addition to this public Catholic-French sector, there was also an extensive network of private educational institutions operated by the Catholic Church. Each sector was autonomous in matters related to organization, curriculum, examinations, and teacher certification. Power resided in a Catholic Committee and a Protestant Committee. Together these committees formed the Council of Public Instruction. It is indicative of the lack of coordination between these two sectors that between 1908 and 1960 the Council never once met as a body.

The English-Protestant school system had evolved much like its counterparts in other provinces and offered a wide selection of courses, ranging from vocational and commercial courses to university preparation through an interlocking network of public elementary and secondary schools. The Catholic system was organized in quite a different manner. Free, public education was available at the elementary level, but secondary and higher education was provided by private institutions controlled by the Catholic Church. Francophone students could obtain secondary education leading to university study, for a fee, at the classical colleges, sponsored and supported by various religious orders. These colleges, all affiliated with the arts faculties of one of the three private French universities (Laval, Montreal, Sherbrooke), offered an eight-year program comprising both high school and undergraduate liberal arts education. Upon graduation, students received a B.A. from the parent university.

The quality of education offered at the classical colleges and these three universities was high, but it had a limited intellectual range. Both types of institutions were oriented toward the humanities and the traditional professions (law, medicine) and placed low priority on scientific and technological subjects. Francophone students who wanted to enter a faculty of science could do so only after completing 15 years of schooling, while an English-Protestant student could start science studies upon matriculation from grade eleven.

French-Catholic education in Quebec prior to the 1960s provided the purest example in Canada of a sponsored mobility system. The elite and the masses were separated at an early age. Because cultural control was in the hands of one group, elite training restricted itself to the cultivation of the qualities favored by the Catholic Church.

In the early sixties, all this changed. The so-called Quiet Revolution initiated by the Lesage government represented a shift in ideological orientation away from the past to the present. Modernization was to be embraced rather than feared, and government power would be the major instrument through which the desirable changes would be introduced. The Lesage government recognized from the outset that a reform of the educational system was crucial and appointed a Royal Commission of Inquiry on Education, the Parent Commission, to undertake a complete examination of all aspects of the educational system.

One of the Parent Commission's first recommendations was that a Ministry of Education be created. This recommendation was implemented in 1964. The effect of the new Ministry of Education was to secularize the control structure and to reduce sharply the role of the Catholic and Protestant committees. Henceforth, the committees would have power to regulate only in moral and religious matters. In all other areas, full authority for education rested in the hands of the government.

This done, the government was able to act on the other recommendations made in the five volumes of the *Parent Commission Report*. The Francophone educational system was upgraded by the introduction of free, public secondary schools. Secondary education in Quebec now lasts for five years and is patterned on the contest-mobility model of the comprehensive high school – *l'école polyvalente*. Secondary schools now serve all categories of students, separate programs were abolished in favor of a credit system with various levels, and the curriculum now includes all subject areas.

At the post-secondary level in Quebec, the new CEGEPs offer both a two-year university program and advanced technical training of two or three years duration. Unlike other provinces, this college education is free and is not organized on a binary basis. All students at the post-secondary level, both those who are headed for the university and those who are headed for the labor market, receive their education in the same institution. In its commitment to accessibility, comprehensiveness, and ease of transfer, then, Quebec has moved farther than any other province in the direction of contest mobility.

Can We Be Excellent and Equal Too?

A reservation frequently expressed in conservative circles is that equalizing educational opportunities inevitably entails lowering academic standards. High quality, so the argument goes, can only be maintained in an elitist system. *More* necessarily means *worse.* Inequality is the price we have to pay for excellence. The progress of bright students will be endangered when they are mixed with students of average ability.

Are excellence of academic standards and equality of access irreconcilable objectives? One answer to this question can be found in the studies conducted by the International Association for the Evaluation of Academic Achievement. These studies contain information about the performance of students in at least twelve different countries on internationally devised math and science tests (Husen, 1967; Comber and Keeves, 1973). The secondary school system in the countries selected range from very selective (Germany, France) to comprehensive (United States).

Which system provides more equality of educational opportunities? Upper-class students are over-represented and lower-class students are under-represented in all countries, but the rate of under-representation of lower-class students is significantly higher in the selective school system. The more selective the school system, the greater the social bias.

Is the lack of equality in selective systems compensated for by their excellence in academic achievement? The legitimation of elitism rests on its supposed superior results. How do the graduates of the academic programs in the selective and comprehensive systems compare on math or science test scores? The average math and science score among United States high school graduates taking these subjects is far below, for instance, that of their West German counterparts. But this should come as no surprise. The West Germans taking these subjects represent a small group of academic survivors, 4 to 5 percent of the relevant age group, while in the United States about 18 percent of the age group were taking math or science in the graduating class. If you compare the top 4 percent with the top 18 percent, the results are predictable. So the two systems cannot be compared on the basis of the average score for the whole student population. The question has to be refined.

Is it possible within a comprehensive system to produce an elite comparable in size and quality to the one produced by the selective system? Let us compare the average math or science score of the top 4 percent of the students in the United States with the average score of the top 4 percent of students in other countries. In such a comparison, the United States' top 4 percent average score is about the same as that of most selective European countries. In the whole study, none of the comprehensive systems ranks among the five countries at the bottom. So more does *not* mean worse. But neither is there evidence that less means better. The selective systems do not all rank at the top. They do not produce an elite superior to the elite cultivated in the comprehensive system.

What can we conclude from this? The price to be paid by selective systems in lack of equality cannot be justified. On the grounds of both justice and efficiency of performance, comprehensive systems seem to be preferable to selective systems. They are more egalitarian, produce as good and as big a crop of top students, and, as far as the majority of the student population is concerned, bring more people along further.

Source:

References are to Husen, Torsten (ed.). *International Study of Achievement in Mathematics: A Comparison of Twelve Countries*, 2 vol. Stockholm: Almqvist and Wiksell, 1967; Comber, C., and John P. Keeves. *Science Education in Nineteen Countries: An Empirical Study.* New York: John Wiley and Sons, 1973).

DISILLUSIONMENT

The 1970s witnessed a great change in public support for education. All governments began to curtail their educational spending. Today, educational policy issues have to do with declining school enrollments, school closures, and teacher and faculty layoffs. Clearly, the boom period in education is over. Education has entered an era of institutional retrenchment.

It was to be expected. Education grows and contracts in response to the demographic factors outlined in Chapter 7. The post-war baby boom had finally worked its way through the schools, and by about 1977 the size of the student population at the primary and junior high school levels had decreased sharply. This demographic decline will continue through the 1980s. Since the 1960s, the number of births in Canada has been falling and the repercussions of this will continue to be felt through all levels of the educational system.

But demographic factors alone cannot explain the reduced support for education. As Table 14-1 indicates, the participation rate in post-secondary education has slowed down also and had even started to decline by 1979. Somewhere along the line the belief in the value of education was badly shaken and a certain disillusionment set in. Many felt that the policy of educational expansion had failed to deliver the promised economic and social benefits.

The Economic Failure

Students now realize that post-secondary education does not automatically give them access to a well paid job. The educational requirements in the job market have been steadily rising, and the purchasing power of a degree has declined accordingly. Twenty-five years ago a B.A. put you into the competition for a high status position; in today's inflated educational market an advanced degree is required to obtain the same competitive advantage. Both Canadian and American studies (Harvey, 1974; Freeman, 1976) have convincingly demonstrated that the personal rate of return on education has been falling in recent years.

However disappointing these facts might be, they do not by themselves justify the conclusion that post-secondary education has failed to deliver the goods. Rather, it can be argued that the expectations of the mobility benefits to be derived from post-secondary education have not kept up with changing circumstances. Only in an elitist system can students expect that an attractive position will be available to them upon graduation. In a contest-mobility system, such a guarantee does not exist. Contest-mobility systems do not try to protect the social value of a degree by restricting the number of competitors. But the social expectations appropriate to the previous elitist system still survive and create disappointment when students

discover that their education does not give them the social stratification advantages that tradition has led them to expect. A more realistic way of assessing the value of post-secondary education as a mobility strategy is to determine to what extent it confers an advantage in comparison to other forms of education.

As far as protection against unemployment is concerned, the answer is clear – unemployment tends to be lower among those with more education. In June 1978, Canada's unemployment rate stood at 8.0 percent, but at 14.3 percent for the 15 to 24 age group. A study conducted at this time on the work experience of 1976 post-secondary graduates two years after graduation found an overall unemployment rate of 7.8 percent. This is below the Canadian average and almost half as low as the unemployment rate for the relevant age group. The average unemployment rate for community college graduates was lower (6.7 percent) than that for university graduates (8.2 percent), but the average full-time salary of the latter group was about $3 000 higher, or $15 200 versus $12 300 (Clark and Zsigmond, 1981). The absolute purchasing power of post-secondary education may have declined, but as long as it still confers a relative competitive advantage in the job market, the argument in favor of educational expansion is not necessarily invalidated.

The expansionist policy *is* challenged, however, when it can be demonstrated that the price of upward mobility has been rising because of an artificial inflation of educational currency. This seems to be the case. In a book cleverly entitled *Education and Jobs: The Great Training Robbery,* Berg (1970) presents evidence that the escalation of educational credentials is not justified by the growing complexity of jobs. Educational requirements have risen in excess of skill levels.

The relationship between education and the economy, then, seems to be more complex than the human capital theory suggests. The educational level of the labor force in an advanced industrial society is high, but not necessarily because expertise has become a functional necessity for an increasing number of jobs. While it cannot be denied that some jobs are highly specialized and require extensive educational preparation, it is also clear that other occupations have educa-

TABLE 14-2. FULL-TIME POST SECONDARY ENROLLMENT AS A PERCENTAGE OF THE RELEVANT AGE GROUP, BY LEVEL AND GENDER, CANADA, SELECTED YEARS

	18-21 Age Group Non-University		18-21 Age Group Undergraduate		22-24 Age Group Graduate		18-24 Age Group Total Post-Secondary	
	M	F	M	F	M	F	M	F
1960-1961	2.9	7.1	16.2	5.4	1.6	0.3	11.9	7.4
1970-1971	7.6	7.5	25.8	15.5	4.9	3.5	21.9	14.3
1979-1980	12.7	13.8	18.6	16.1	3.9	2.2	20.0	18.2

SOURCE: Adapted from Statistics Canada, *Education in Canada, 1973*. Ottawa, 1973. Table 35, pp. 150-151; Statistics Canada, *Education in Canada, 1980*. Ottawa, 1981, Table 6, p. 63

tional entrance requirements that cannot be justified on strictly technical grounds. Contrary to the human capital argument, rising educational requirements are not just a reflection of the increasing complexity of the occupational structure. To a large extent, education functions as a purely formal credential, as a screening device unrelated to the knowledge requirements of the job.

The Social Failure

If educational expansion has not produced the expected economic benefits, what about the other reasons for its support? Has the belief in the importance of education as a promoter of social justice been justified? Here, too, disappointment has set in. In spite of the attempt to make education more accessible, the basic inequalities of gender and social class have not been overcome. Expansion has resulted in increased participation rates for all groups, but reduction of inequality has to do with relative gains. The crucial question is whether group disparities in educational achievement have been significantly narrowed.

Gender Disparities. Gender has been a traditional basis of inequality. To what extent has expansion succeeded in making education more equally accessible to both males and females? These are the main research findings:

First, gender inequalities have been reduced at the secondary level, in that girls are now as likely as boys to finish high school. Also, equal proportions of boys and girls are enrolled in academic programs leading to university studies. As Synge (1977) has pointed out, however, within academic program boys are more likely to take science and mathematics, while girls tend to concentrate on arts and social sciences.

Second, this relative equality at the secondary level is only partly matched at the post-secondary level. As the last column of Table 14-2 indicates, there is still a difference between the proportions of the respective gender/age group enrolled full-time in post-secondary education, although the disparities have narrowed. In general, the lower the level of education, the greater the equality between the genders. The greatest overall gains for females have been made at the undergraduate level. In 1979, at the B.A. level, 49.1 percent of the degree recipients were female; but at the M.A. level female students received only 36.0 percent of the degrees, and at the doctoral level 20.5 percent (Statistics Canada, 1981). At the master's and doctoral level, males still heavily outnumber females.

Third, although females have increased their proportional representation at the undergraduate level, the increase is distributed unequally among different types of programs. The average female undergraduate enrolment rate in 1979 was 45.4 percent, but it was only 34.0 in medicine, and 36.4 in law, as compared to 61.5 in fine arts and 67.7 in education (Statistics Canada, 1981).

These research findings indicate that some progress

has been made toward bridging gender disparities, but females still have a long way to go toward educational equality.

Class Disparities. Of all the barriers to equality none has received more political attention than class of origin (see Chapter 8). No other topic has been investigated more fully than the relationship between education and social stratification, but in trying to assess the extent to which expansion has improved the educational opportunities for lower-class students, it is difficult to arrive at exact conclusions. Social class has been measured in so many different ways that it is not always possible to relate research findings directly to each other and to develop comparisons over time. But we can identify a general pattern, even though we are unable to be precise (OECD, 1975; for Canada: Breton, 1972; Porter, et al, 1973; Anisef, et al, 1980).

First, in spite of all efforts, students from the lower classes are less likely to be enrolled in academic programs on the secondary level, even when they possess the academic ability for university study. In 1971 in Ontario, for instance, almost all (96 percent) of the bright students from the upper class in grade twelve were enrolled in the academic program; only 77 percent of the bright students from the lower class were in the program of study that matched their talent (Porter, et al, 1973). Canada-wide data collected in 1965 showed a similar pattern (Harvey and Lennards, 1973). There is a correlate to this finding. Low-ability students from the upper class are enrolled disproportionately in academic programs.

The school system seems to have great difficulty in "warming up" the aspirations of bright lower-class students and "cooling out" the aspirations of not so bright upper-class students: 72 percent of upper-class students whose scores on a mental ability test placed them among the bottom third were in the academic program, as compared to 38 percent of lower-class students of similarly low ability. Low ability at the upper end of the scale has a much less inhibiting effect on educational plans than at the lower end.

Second, lower-class students are less likely to continue their education after high school at the post-secondary level. This holds true regardless of talent.

The proportion of bright students in grade twelve expecting to go to work after graduation was found to be twice as high in the lower class that it was for other students (Porter, et al, 1973).

Third, lower-class students who decide to continue their education at the post-secondary level are more likely than upper- or middle-class students to enroll in a community college (Porter, et al, 1973).

Fourth, in addition to class inequalities in access to higher education, there are also class inequalities within higher education. Among the different faculties, law and medicine have the highest enrollment ratio of upper-class students, while education has the lowest. Upper-class students are also more likely to continue their education at the graduate level (Harvey and Lennards, 1973).

Fifth, both Canadian and international data indicate that educational expansion has not succeeded in reducing existing social class differentials in university attendance. Proportionately, lower-class students have not improved their representation; as a group they are still as heavily under-represented as before. The major beneficiary of the expansion of the university has been the middle class (for Canada, Pike, 1978; for U.S.A., Carnoy and Levin, 1976).

One general conclusion emerges clearly from this: while expansion has led to a democratization of educational opportunities for individuals from previously disadvantaged sectors, it has been less successful in reducing existing group inequalities. The number of lower-class and female students receiving higher education has increased, but so has the size of the male and upper- and middle-class student population. In relative terms, no major victories have been won. It can even be argued that the policy has had detrimental effects in certain areas. In a number of ways, expansion has reinforced, rather than weakened, the existing structure of inequalities.

Decreasing Equality. The massive increase in the supply of university graduates has resulted in an inflation of educational credentials. To the extent that this upgrading of educational requirements is artificial and bears no relationship to the actual job skills required, education has turned into a new form of job discrimination. Qualified people are denied access to jobs on the basis of irrelevant criteria. Career lines previously open to persons without extensive training are now closed, and job ceilings based on education have reduced the possibility of working your way up through the ranks.

The price of educational expansion has been lost job opportunities. This price is paid largely by those whose educational investment has not kept up with the rate of inflation. The social composition of this group will be obvious from the preceding discussion.

The escalation of educational job requirements has produced a second unfortunate effect: it has canceled the relative gains to be achieved by attaining additional years of schooling. This has made entry into the mainstream of society more difficult for groups that start from a low position as latecomers to the social mobility process. Native people are an example of a group that labors under this special handicap. Educational expansion only improves mobility prospects as long as it confers a competitive advantage. In the past, when educational entrance requirements for access to middle-level jobs were not high, it was possible to improve your opportunities considerably by spending a few more years in school. But the educational entrance fee to middle positions has risen sharply. To achieve the same relative improvement, a much greater educational investment is required. In fact, as long as the inflation of educational credentials continues unchecked, disadvantaged groups will have to run harder simply not to fall further behind.

Under these conditions, how fair is it to expect that these groups have an equally good chance, through education, to catch up with the main pack? The problems faced by latecomers in the race are different. To the extent that we refuse to admit this and rely on education as the major avenue of social advancement, we put these groups at a considerable disadvantage and, at the same time, rationalize their failure as deserved. ("Other groups have done it in the past. Why can't they?")

We have just identified two ways in which educational expansion has made matters worse for groups with the least educational attainment. There is a related question: Who has profited most from it? The benefits of increased educational opportunities have accrued to the groups that were well placed in the race at the start. As a result of educational inflation, the competition for good jobs has now moved up to a higher level and requires more years of education. The cultural and motivational advantages possessed by middle- and upper-class students enable them to meet these demands and to maintain or even increase their relative position. Our discussion of inequalities within higher education is of particular relevance in this regard.

The high hopes that spurred the rapid development of the Canadian educational system have been shaken. Educational expansion has brought about an escalation of educational prerequisites. As a result of this development, the economic and social underpinnings of the expansionist educational policy have been removed. Opening up access to higher education is of little social benefit when, in response to a greater supply of university graduates, educational requirements for employment are raised by a similar amount. The economic base of educational policy is also undermined, because the artificial upgrading process does not guarantee a high return on educational investment, on either the societal or the personal level. Neither justice nor efficiency are automatically assured by the expansion of the educational system.

The present disillusionment with the policy of educational expansion provides us with a good sociological opportunity for assessing the nature of the support base for education. Increased opportunities for schooling can be defended on a number of grounds. Studies of the effects on attitude of higher education have demonstrated, for instance, that university education makes an important contribution to the goal of democratic citizenship training. Support for civil rights, degree of tolerance, willingness to participate in political activities, level of political awareness – all of these qualities, relevant to the operation of a democratic society, increase with education (Harvey and Lennards, 1973). As the Massey Royal Commission pointed out (1951), education is also vital to the cultural life of a society. Universities are important instruments of nation building, and, on the individual level, they are sources of personal self-enrichment. These possible rationales for educational expansion have not been invalidated by recent developments, but they seem unable to arrest the decline of public confidence in the benefits to be derived from schooling. Public support for education appears to expand or decline largely in accordance with its perceived economic relevance and, tied to this, its perceived mobility value.

Why has the policy of educational expansion failed to deliver the expected economic and social goods? In the next two sections we will review the attempts undertaken by sociologists to answer this question. First, we will present some theoretical explanations of the role of education that challenge the guiding rationale of educational expansion. Second, we will review the empirical research efforts to locate the sources of inequality.

THE THEORETICAL PERSPECTIVES

Until recently, the dominant framework for analyzing the role of education in modern society had been provided by the human capital theory. As Collins (1971, 1979) has noted, human capital theory, translated into sociological terms, is a version of the structural functionalist theory of social stratification (discussed in Chapter 8). When discussing education, a combination of these theories creates the idea of technological fuctionalism.

Technological Functionalism

The basic premises of **technological functionalism** are:

1. the skill requirements of occupations in our society are constantly increasing
2. talented people need to be recruited to fill the more highly skilled jobs
3. the educational system is the place where the selection and training of talent occur
4. rising skill requirements for occupations therefore require an expansion of the educational system

Educational requirements reflect the functional needs of the occupational structure. Employers assess the skill level required for particular jobs and set the educational entrance requirements accordingly. The relationship between education and the labor market is technically determined.

But in this chapter we have presented data that cast serious doubts on the accuracy of this view of the role of education in modern society. The function of education cannot be explained in these purely instrumental terms. We saw earlier that educational requirements for employment often bear little relationship to the knowledge demands of the job. The disappointing results of the policy of educational expansion might, therefore, be related to the weakness of its theoretical base. Indeed, the functional view of the relationship between education and the labor market has been challenged from two quarters, both of which approach education from a **conflict perspective** and both of which stress the non-technical relevance of educational certification.

The Weberian Challenge

Like Marx, Weber saw society as a constellation of conflicting interest groups (Bendix, 1962; Zeitlin, 1973); but, unlike Marx, Weber believed that the struggle for social advantages takes place on more than one front. In addition to economic power there is status power. Status power depends on one's position in the cultural order. It is acquired by monopolizing the possession of particular cultural attributes and using them as a basis for establishing social superiority. Status power is obtained by the formation of status groups. Those who advance the same claims start associating with each other and act out their claim to deference by creating a distinctive way of life (taste, manners, opinions, leisure activities, and so on). This serves to differentiate them from others and becomes a mark of social distance and exclusiveness (Gerth and Mills, 1958).

To the extent that a status group's claim to cultural superiority is accepted by other groups, its demands are treated with deference and its power is legitimized. Thus, status power based on deference is an important social resource, and status groups need to be recognized, according to Weber, along with social class as basic units of organization of the social stratification system.

Drawing on these Weberian ideas about the importance of status groups, Collins has advanced a conflict interpretation of the role of education in our society (Collins, 1971, 1979). The link between educational certification and jobs has little or nothing to do with technical competence; it rests on the desire to impress others. Advanced education functions as a status attribute, a mark of social distinction that enables its possessors to convince others of the importance of their work.

Impression-management plays a central role in the occupational world. For many jobs the degrees of competence required is difficult to assess. The expertise of engineers can be evaluated readily; they make tangible products and, as long as their bridges do not collapse, their competence is accepted. The work speaks for itself and claims for income can be staked out on this basis. But what about the work of teachers, civil servants, bank managers, doctors? Here the product is not clearly visible, and the criteria for adequate performance are not at all obvious. For example, what exactly does a bank manager contribute, and what is required to be a good one? The product does not speak for itself, and such occupations face a credibility problem. They are confronted with the task of creating trust in the importance and competence of their services. It is here that education comes in.

According to Collins, educational certification operates as such a trust generating device in our society. Educational credentials are widely recognized and generally accepted symbols of competence. By making them a condition for entrance, occupations and organizations secure for themselves the needed confidence and awe from the public. If it is that difficult to enter, the job must be important and demanding; because the practitioners form a selective group, their competence can be taken for granted. Exclusiveness breeds prestige. It makes you look better. Prestige so obtained can, in turn, be converted into claims for higher income. A basic strategy of occupational groups in search of advancement has been to raise the educational requirements and then to command a salary commensurate with "the increased importance and difficulty of the job." Collins maintains that the upgrading of educational requirements is largely artificial. Educa-

tional credentials are social weapons used by occupations and organizations in the struggle for social advantages.

The explanation of the link between education and jobs constitutes only one of Collins' theoretical concerns. A second major objective is to demonstrate how a theory of status group competition explains why, as we noted earlier, educational requirements have been steadily rising. An increased supply of educated persons reduces the prestige value of education. What was previously a mark of distinction (a B.A. or B.Sc., for example) becomes merely a mark of average respectability. In response to this devaluation of education, educational entrance requirements will be raised in order to restore the lost prestige value: a Master's degree may now be required for a job that used to call for a Bachelor's degree. This, in turn, will trigger a further round of educational inflation. Unless we take the drastic step of making formal educational requirements for employment illegal, Collins sees no end to this spiral (Collins, 1979).

The Marxist Challenge

The second challenge to the functional interpretation of the role of schooling in modern society comes from Marxism. In *Schooling in Capitalist America* (1976), Bowles and Gintis present a radical critique of the notion that education promotes social justice. They view schools not as instruments of social and economic progress serving the needs of a technological and meritocratic society, but as agencies of social control and repression serving the interests of the economic elite. As such, the main task of the school is to produce workers who will accept their positions within the capitalist system.

The key to the analysis of the education system, claim Bowles and Gintis, is the structure and functioning of the capitalist economy. Under capitalism the social relations of production are characterized by alienation and domination. Workers are treated as commodities exchanging their labor for wages in the hierarchically organized division of labor. Schools prepare individuals for the world of alienated and stratified work relationships. They reproduce labor power.

Like Collins, Bowles and Gintis reject the premise that the relationship between education and the labor market has a strictly technical base. Education is important primarily for non-knowledge-related reasons. It fosters the type of workers' consciousness required by the nature of the capitalist work situation. Workers must be psychologically prepared to accept their positions in the productive system. This psychological preparation is accomplished by the creation of a correspondence between the social relations of production and the social relations of education, a correspondence between workplace and classroom.

Schools are organized like factories, and the educational process is analogous to commodity production. Students have little control over the content of their work, and they are spurred on by grades and other external rewards. Schools, in other words, teach students to accept meaningless, alienating work for the sake of future rewards (the paycheck). The authority relations between teacher and students replicate the hierarchical division of labor. Students are permitted limited freedom and autonomy and are taught to be docile and passive. "Students are rewarded for exhibiting discipline, subordinacy, intellectually as opposed to emotionally oriented behavior, and hard work independent from intrinsic task motivation" (Bowles and Gintis, 1976).

The way in which schools reproduce the values and personality characteristics necessary in a capitalist society varies according to the level of the occupational structure to which their graduates are headed. The social organization of instruction for future manual workers is not the same as that for future managerial personnel, because their work situations differ.

Lower-level workers perform tasks requiring little discretion and responsibility, and their work is closely supervised. Consequently, discipline among vocational students tends to be strict and emphasis is placed on punctuality and unquestioned rule-following. Higher-level workers must be flexible and innovative and must work autonomously without direct supervision. Their efficiency depends on the extent to which they have an internalized work ethic.

This flexibility is reflected in the social atmosphere of the college-oriented program. The emphasis is on "soft socialization" rather than on behavioral control. Students are permitted more choice in their activities, and the interaction between teacher and students is more relaxed. Instead of demanding blind obedience, the program encourages students to be cooperative, to be involved, and to choose voluntarily what is good for them. This is merely another version of social control – internal, rather than external compliance. It does not change the objective of schooling. The function of education is to teach the appropriate type of labor discipline. The social organization of the schools is shaped by the demands of the capitalist production process.

Because the capitalist order is based on inequality, it is unrealistic, warn Bowles and Gintis, to expect that education can produce a more egalitarian society. Schools try to convince people that selection is meritocratic, but they are essential props for the reproduction and legitimation of existing inequalities. Educational expansion has not been more successful in promoting justice, because the policy has been based on the wrong assumptions about the relationship between schooling and society. Schools are dependent institutions serving the interests of the capitalist elite. As long as capitalism persists, schools will never be instruments of social liberation.

Shortly, we will turn to an assessment of the theories discussed in this section. But, first, let us continue this exposition of how structural functionalist and conflict theorists differ in their approach to another important topic.

THE SOURCES OF INEQUALITY

The difficulty encountered by the school in extending equal opportunities to all has spawned a vast research literature. Empirical location of the social determinant of educational success has been a major preoccupation of the sociology of education. This literature is informative in two ways: it identifies fairly precisely the nature of the obstacles experienced by lower-class

In 1901, most of the nation's work was mechanical, and manual training classes prepared boys for jobs in a factory. In the electronic seventies, Japanese primary school kids punched answers into a computer and checked a monitor to see if they were correct.

students; and it illustrates how each of the two major theoretical perspectives – structural functionalist and conflict – studies the problem of inequality in a different way.

Defining the Problem

The major contribution of empirical research has been to demonstrate that social class functions not only as a barrier to **equality of access** to education, but also as a barrier to performance in education. Scholarships, the regional spread of post-secondary educational institutions, the equalization of teachers' salaries and of school resources in general – all these things remove the external barriers to equal participation in education. But equality of access is not enough. The strategy of equalizing educational resources, while politically convenient in its assumption that the problem can be solved by administrative changes, is based on too narrow a view of the nature of the handicaps experienced by students from underprivileged groups. It assumes, that, once you have equal access there are no further differences between the social classes in their ability to profit equally from the opportunities available to them. This is not accurate. It is not enough to provide equal entrance to the race so long as not all social classes are equally able to participate in the competition.

Consequently, the task of the educational system is to equalize starting positions by providing **equality of nurture**; attention and resources must be distributed according to students' need. This definition of the role of the school has important policy implications. The burden of proof for providing equality of educational opportunity now shifts from the student to the educational system. Instead of just making learning opportunities available to those who, by their social class background, are well equipped to take advantage of them, the school is called upon to play an active, interventionist role and to compensate for milieu disadvantages. It is up to students to prove themselves, but it is also up to the school to insure that all students participate in the race under equal conditions.

Home Environment

Sociologists have located the social determinants of unequal school performance both in the home and in the school environment. What are some of the salient intellectual and motivational factors that have been singled out as blocking the potential of lower-class students? Let us turn to the home environment first.

Achievement Motivation. Researchers have consistently found that school performance is related to aspirations for educational success. Lower-class children do worse in school, it is argued, because they do not receive enough home encouragement. Their parents visit school less frequently and tend to have lower ambitions for them. This conclusion that lower-class children and their parents have less of a desire to succeed needs to be critically examined, because it results partly from the way ambition has been measured.

Often, ambition levels are inferred by asking parents and students about their specific educational aspirations. Aspirations for university education, for instance, are viewed as an index of a strong desire to succeed. Such a measurement is based on the assumption that the goal of higher education is equidistant for individuals from all social classes. But the desire to attend university may or may not signify a high level of ambition. As a measure of the actual distance to be traveled, it indicates a very high degree of ambition for lower-class students and only a moderate degree for upper-class students. To avoid the problem that occurs when striving for a specific goal is taken as an index for level of ambition, Breton (1972), in his study of Canadian high school students, measured ambition in terms of a general desire to succeed. His findings reveal that lower-class boys and girls tended to be more ambitious than is generally assumed: 44 percent of lower-class boys expressed a high ambition to succeed, as compared with 42 percent of middle-class and 36 percent of upper-class boys; the percentages for girls were, respectively, 38, 28, and 24.

Language Use. Starting with the work of Bernstein (1973, 1974, 1976), sociologists have tried to relate social class differences in educational achievement to social-class differences in language use. According to Bernstein, lower- and middle-class persons use different language codes identified, respectively, as a restricted and an elaborated code. The **restricted language code** is characterized by its use of implicit, context-bound meaning, while the **elaborated code** meanings are explicit and universal.

An example can best illustrate the difference. Five-year-old, middle-class and lower-class children were asked to tell a story in response to four pictures: some boys playing football, the ball going through a window, a man making a threatening gesture, a woman looking out of the window, and the boys moving away. A middle-class child told the following story:

Three boys are playing football and one boy kicks the ball and it goes through the window the ball breaks the window and the boys are looking at it and a man comes out and shouts at them because they had broken the window so they run away and then that lady looks out of her window and she tells the boys off (Bernstein, 1970).

Based on the same pictures, a lower-class child told this story:

They're playing football and he kicks it and it goes through there it breaks the window and they're looking at it and he comes out and he shouts at them because they'd broken it so they run away and then she looks out and she tells them off (Bernstein, 1970).

The first story can be understood without reference to the pictures, the second one cannot. Children in middle-class families are encouraged in their speech and writing to elaborate their meanings, to be explicit and specific, so that their language is understandable to all, including outsiders. Lower-class language is more particular: it is the language of insiders, and it is accessible only to those who have knowledge of the context out of which it generated.

What is the educational significance of these language codes? How do these different ways of communicating affect school performance? One interpretation given to Bernstein's work is that the different language codes reflect differences in cognitive skills. The restricted code is an inferior form of speech. Students who have been taught to communicate in this mode do not perform well in school, because they suffer from a cognitive deficit. They have been raised in an unstimulating, "culturally deprived" environment that has stunted their verbal and, hence, analytical ability. Whether it is accurate to portray Bernstein's analysis as a deficit theory will be considered shortly. For now, let us move out of the home and into the school.

School Environment

Several characteristics of the school environment are sources of inequality of nurture for lower-class children.

Influence Structure. Inequalities in educational performance derive from inequalities in the normative support available to students in their immediate school environment. One major source of influence is teacher expectations. The best known study of teacher expectations and their possible self-fulfilling effect is that of Rosenthal and Jacobson (1968). In this study, students in an elementary school were given a general achievement test at the end of the 1964 academic year. Teacher expectations were created by claiming that the test had been developed to identify intellectual late bloomers, who could be expected to show unusually large achievement gains during the coming academic year. In the fall, a few children in each classroom were identified to the teachers as "late bloomers." These students had been randomly selected, so that no factual basis existed for the expectations induced in the teachers. When, in the spring, all students were retested, the data showed some evidence that the children who had been identified as late bloomers did indeed make more intellectual gains than the others. Rosenthal and Jacobson concluded that the favorable expectations they had created caused these gains to occur. Teacher expectations have a self-fulfilling effect on students.

The Rosenthal and Jacobson (1968) study has been criticized for its methodological weakness, and attempts to replicate it have not produced consistent findings. Studies using a naturalistic, rather than an experimental approach have yielded less ambiguous results (Brophy and Good, 1974). Instead of manipulating or creating teacher expectations, these naturalistic studies take as their point of departure the teachers' own expectations of students, as they actually exist. Teacher expectations have proven not to be automatically self-fulfilling, however, and not enough is known about how the process actually operates at the classroom level.

With regard to lower-class students, there is some evidence that some teachers make judgments about a student's academic potential on the basis of such factors as neatness of dress, general deportment, and home background (Silberman, 1970). A certain number of teachers probably form stereotyped opinions about what can be expected from certain categories of students, but there is little systematic information on how widespread stereotyping is and who is most adversely affected by it. For this information, sociologists will have to undertake more detailed analyses of classroom behavior.

A second source of influence on academic achievement is the student body. Several researchers have established that aspirations are affected by the social-class composition of the student population. Lower-class boys in predominantly middle-class schools have been found to possess higher aspirations than lower-class boys in working-class schools (Wilson, 1959). Because schools recruit their students from the areas in which they are located, residential segregation is a built-in source of inequality in our school system. In the United States, busing has been introduced as a means of equalizing peer group support for aspirations.

Selection Procedures. To the extent that schools rely on IQ tests to assess a student's academic ability, lower-class students are put at a disadvantage. Intelligence consists of two components: an innate, genetically determined potential; and a learned, environmental element that determines how far that potential will be fulfilled. The more favorable the nurture, the more a person's natural ability will flourish. No test can measure innate potential; we can only establish nurtured ability. IQ tests, therefore, favor those who have received good intellectual nurture and systematically underestimate the reservoir of talent existing among lower-class students.

In addition, IQ tests are often culture-bound. Lower-class children score less well, simply because they have

Vandalism is a continuing problem in today's schools. Is such mindless violence a result of failure in society generally, in the home environment, or in education in particular? Would education be more relevant and successful if it responded to the needs of the students, or is it the students' responsibility to respond to the current structures of education?

not had exposure to the type of situations emphasized in the tests. A final consideration to keep in mind is that test-taking is a performance. It is a challenge of a particular kind. Only students possessed of a truly competitive spirit will be able to generate the motivation required for answering questions that have little intrinsic relevance. Lower-class students generally are less well prepared to perform in this fashion. When they are given special training in taking IQ tests, however, their scores improve dramatically (Boocock, 1972).

The Missing Dimension: Cultural Transmission. We have identified the range of variables generally included in a structural functional analysis. Before introducing the contribution of conflict sociologists, we might pause for a moment and consider what this selection of variables implies about the way the relationship between schooling and inequality is conceived. School performance is seen as a product of ability and motivation. Because of deficiences in both home and school environments, these educational

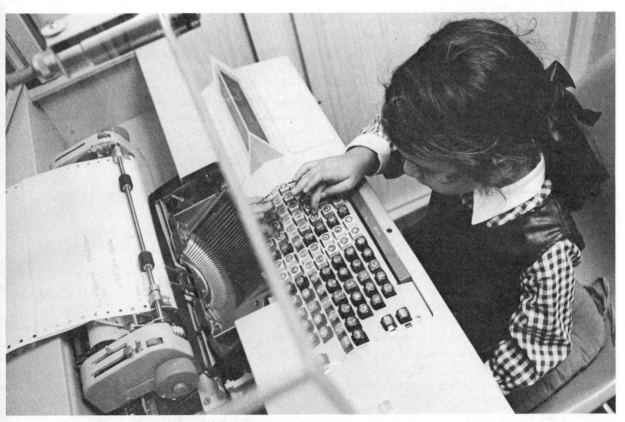

Electronics have dramatically changed every part of our lives: how we think, how we learn, how we work, and how we play. Computers are an extension of the human brain, and logically play an important role in educating people for a highly technological society.

resources are not equally nurtured among lower-class students and students from families of higher status. The kinds of remedial action undertaken to equalize nurturing conditions are twofold.

To remedy the deficiencies of the home environment, preschool compensatory programs are introduced to help bridge the distance between the culturally deprived child and the school. Even though the roots of unequal performance lie in the interaction between home and school environments, policy intervention is directed primarily at the former. Preschool enrichment programs such as Head Start try to cultivate in the students the characteristics required for adaptation to the school. The problem is defined largely as one of

cultural deprivation in the home, rather than of cultural unreceptiveness in the school. As Bernstein (1970) rightfully claims, the concept of compensatory education "serves to direct attention away from the internal organization and the educational content of the school and focus our attention onto families and children." The cultural standards of the school are not questioned, rather the inability to live up to them is seen as evidence of a deficiency in the home environment. In this context the reception given to Bernstein's analysis of language codes becomes understandable.

The restricted code, because it deviates from the accepted norm, comes to be seen as an index of linguistic deprivation, rather than of linguistic difference. The unequal school performance of lower-class children is seen in that light. There is, however, a much simpler and more accurate explanation of the relationship between restricted code use and school failure. Lower-class children are handicapped in school, not because they lack verbal and cognitive ability, but because their normal mode of communication is not accepted as an appropriate form of discourse. Forced to suddenly switch to an unfamiliar language code, these children perform poorly. This is then interpreted as lack of general ability. It is this inability of the school to adjust its cultural standards that creates the problem for the lower-class child.

With regard to the school, we see a similar blindness to its cultural aspect. Where it is recognized that attributes of the school environment might also provide unequal conditions for nurture, corrective policies have been aimed primarily at improving the organization and technique of instruction (increasing per student expenditure, abolishment of rigid procedures and IQ tests, attractive teaching material). In other words, the school sources of inequality are taken to be related to the way the educational service is delivered, not to its content. What is being taught, the curriculum, the very nature of the school as a system of cultural transmission, is not seen as a possible cause of inequality.

From a social stratification point of view, this neglect of the role of the school as an agency of cultural transmission appears to contain a serious oversight. Schools are not neutral institutions. They teach certain values, they select certain subjects for inclusion in the curriculum, they call upon particular skills, and, in so doing, they give cultural recognition and social stratification advantages to certain groups over others.

Bourdieu (1974) has coined the term "cultural capital" to refer to the curriculum role of the school in maintaining social inequality. According to him, schools are institutions that present upper-class culture as an objective measurement of merit. Because of this orientation, upper-class parents are able to provide their children with the type of cultural resources required for educational success. Privileges are still passed on from one generation to another, only the form of inheritance has changed. What counts now is not economic, but cultural capital.

The necessity to study the school as a medium of cultural transmission has been forcefully brought to attention in recent years by conflict sociologists. According to Bernstein (1971), schools are institutions that define what counts as knowledge (curriculum), how knowledge is to be transmitted (pedagogy), and what counts as a valid realization of it (assessment procedures). What determines the selection in each of these areas? Who loses and who gains as a result of the particular selection? Raising these questions increases our awareness of the way the school is involved in the social stratification process.

THEORIES: A COMPARISON

We have presented the relationship between education and society from both a technological functional and a conflict perspective. By way of summary, let us identify systematically the major points of difference between these two approaches. Under the conflict perspective we include both the Weberian (Collins) analysis and the Marxist (Bowles and Gintis) analysis. Let us start with the four major points of difference:

1. Societal determinants of education. Technological functionalists see education as an instrument for the attainment of societal needs. Both the size of the educational system and the curriculum are determined by the technological requirements of talent production in an expert society. But conflict theorists see education as an instrument of domination; not functional needs, but group interests determine the nature and shape of education.

2. Stratification role of education. For technological functionalists, education functions as an instrument of social mobility in the meritocratic society. Educational selection takes place according to objective, universalistic criteria. The conflict perspective sees education as an instrument of social class reproduction. Schools provide status socialization. They teach students to accept their future class position and legitimize the process by which they arrive at their destination. Because the criteria of educational selection favor the cultural capital of the privileged groups, schools also perpetuate the inheritance of social advantages.

A Fable – The Animal School

Once upon a time, the animals decided they must do something heroic to meet the problems of a new world. So they organized a school.

They adopted an activity curriculum consisting of running, climbing, swimming, and flying. To make it easier to administer the curriculum, all the animals took all the subjects.

The duck was excellent in swimming, in fact, better than his instructor. But, he only made passing grades in flying and was very poor in running. Because he was slow in running, he had to drop swimming and stay after school to practice running. This was kept up until his web feet were badly worn, and he was only average in swimming. But average was quite ac-

ceptable in school, so nobody worried about that – except the duck.

The rabbit started at the top of his class in running, but had a nervous breakdown because of so much make-up work in swimming. The squirrel was excellent in climbing, but he developed frustrations in flying class because his teacher made him start from the ground up instead of from the tree-top down. He developed charlie horses from overexertion and then got C in the climbing and D in running.

The eagle was a problem child and was severely disciplined. In climbing classes he beat all the others to the top of the tree, but insisted on using his own way to get there.

At the end of the year an abnormal eel who could swim exceedingly well, and could also run, climb and fly a little, had the highest marks and was class valedictorian.

The prairie dogs stayed out of school and fought the tax levy, because the administration would not add digging and burrowing to the curriculum. They apprenticed their child to a badger and later joined the ground hogs and gophers to start an independent school.

Source:

Reavis, George H. *Phi Delta Kappa.*

3. Relevance of education as a credential. Educational requirements reflect the technological needs of the labor market, according to technological functionalists. Education is used as a screening device for assessing technical competence. Both versions of the conflict perspective agree that education is used as a non-technical attribute. Collins claims that education is a resource in the competition for social status. In order to maintain the prestige on which their privilege rests, elite occupations will increase educational requirements in response to an increased supply of more highly educated persons. For Bowles and Gintis, education is relevant because it produces appropriately socialized workers. It is an instrument of social control. Educational requirements shift in response to changes in the nature of the production process. Monopoly capitalism, with its attendant bureaucratization, has produced a need for dependable workers with an internalized labor discipline. Hence, the increased demand for graduates from the higher levels of the educational system.

4. Sources of unequal academic achievement. The technological functionalists are well aware of the discrepancy between the ideal and the real meritocratic society and are concerned about increasing equality of educational opportunity. They believe that the obstacles of equality are in principle removable and that the determinants of inequality in school performance are located either in the home environment or in the delivery system of the school. But conflict theorists claim that inequality of educational opportunity is inevitable. Discrimination is embedded in the cultural operation of the school system. Education is not a neutral institution standing outside the social stratification system; it is a constituent part of it. Schools decide the basis on which social stratification entitlements are to be granted. Only certain skills and values are taught in the schools and receive cultural recognition. Inevitably, therefore, certain groups and individuals will be favored over others.

The conflict perspective on education emerged in the 1970s in opposition to the conventional wisdom about education embodied in the technological functional view. Because of the polemical thrust of the argument, little attempt has been made to explore possible areas of agreements. For example, functionalists would have no trouble accepting that the school functions as an instrument of both mobility and social control. Social selection according to talent and status socialization into the meritocratic ideology are complementary rather than alternative ways of defining the social stratification function of education in our society.

Similarly, with regard to the relevance of education as a credential, Collins (1971) admits that "at appropriate points" the technical skill argument will have to be considered. Although status competition provides the principal dynamic behind the rise in educational requirements, changes in the technical requirements of jobs have also contributed to the process (Collins, 1971). The exact role of both of these factors needs to be investigated further.

Despite disagreements on many substantive issues, technological functionalism and the Marxist version of conflict theory have similar views on the relationship between education and society. Both see schools merely as reflections of the demands of the wider society. What happens in schools is substantially determined by the technological requirements of society, or by the economic needs of the capitalist elite. We may call this the **empty box view of education**. Schools as organizations do not seem to possess a life of their own; they are merely passive transmitters of outside influences.

But there is a danger of oversimplification inherent in such an approach. As an example of this danger, let us take Bowles and Gintis' (1976) analysis of the correspondence between the social relations of classroom and marketplace. The authors postulate that the correspondence between classroom and marketplace is not accidental. Schools are bureaucratically organized and teach passivity and docility, they claim, because such behavior is functional from the point of view of the capitalist elite. But this ignores alternative explanations.

A system of mass public education faces unique problems of organizational control generated from within. Unlike other organizations, public schools have no say in the selection of clients. They are not allowed to follow selective admission procedures; they must accept every student in their area, regardless of motivation or ability. Unlike other organizations, schools cannot get rid of their failures. Students are legally obliged to attend until age sixteen. Faced with a captive student population, what steps can schools take to create positive commitment? Here again, the

options are limited. For many students, learning is boring and generates little intrinsic interest. The universal incentive which the school can offer is an external one: grades. Grades are promises of future rewards; they are pieces of investment in your career. But grades work only as an incentive to those who are ambitious and are doing well. To a failing or low-achieving student school has little pay-off to offer. Disciplinary practices in the school can be seen as an attempt to deal with the constraints imposed by the need to motivate and control a captive clientele. Emphasis on strict rule following will be found in the lower streams of all schools, regardless of the nature of the economic order, because the discipline problem will be most severe where the school has few tangible benefits to offer.

Similarly, classroom management will present fewer problems among students who can see that their education is going to pay off. Soft socialization practices can replace emphasis on rule following among college-oriented students. All of this may be functional as socialization for the workplace, but it is fallacious to infer that workplace requirements had a direct causal impact on school organization. Such an inference ignores the fact that these are organizational tendencies to be found in all types of society, once mass public education is introduced.

Not only does school organization produce pressures of its own, teachers and students have also some control over the way they respond to pressures. Both technological functionalist and conflict explanations of schooling too readily assume that life in school is a mechanistic response to outside demands. But teachers do not always behave in the way the system wants, and students do not always follow what teachers say. Teachers have a high degree of classroom autonomy. As you know from your own experience, within the same educational institution you can find considerable variation in teaching style and emphasis. Teacher autonomy is one of the reasons why it has proven so difficult to change the educational system. Similarly, students have their own way of dealing with the demands of the school system. They develop many responses, ranging from challenging the authority of the teacher (Hargreaves, 1967) to attempts to control the workload, so that they can "make it" (Becker, Geer, Hughes, 1960).

Life in school represents a negotiated, rather than an unilaterally imposed, social order. Teacher and students are neither free to conduct the education process as they see fit, nor are they completely constrained by the system. What happens in individual classrooms is a product of societal pressures, organizational conditions, and the type of coping strategies teachers and students manage to develop in response. A full analysis of the educational system needs to do justice to all these factors.

THE FUTURE OF EDUCATION

The story is told of an old man who returned to his birthplace after a long absence. Many things had changed, but there was one place where he felt immediately at home: his old school. This is not surprising; the basic social pattern of education has changed little since the beginning of this century. Schooling was then, and to a large degree still is, an age-specific enterprise pursued in the early stages of a person's life before entering the world of work. It takes place in isolation from the rest of the community within the walls of a building or group of buildings. Schooling is based on group instruction. Students are differentiated according to their age into grade levels and within each grade they take classes. Advancement proceeds from one grade level to the next. It is a teacher-directed process. Classes are run by teachers who are the experts in charge of the educational process. Familiar as this social framework might be, it is unlikely to survive your lifetime.

One major trend already under way is the change from education as an age-specific process to education as a lifelong endeavor. In the future, education will extend from cradle to grave. The growth of the two-wage family and the other related changes discussed in Chapter 11 are already creating strong pressures for the provision of day-care centers for the very young. In time, these facilities will be made available on the same basis as public schooling – as a right for all.

Regulations will be tightened, the amateur will be displaced by the certified expert, and day care will be turned into early childhood education.

At the other end, education will not be completed once we enter the world of work. Given the rate of scientific and technological change, the stock of knowledge and skill we have acquired between the ages of five and twenty-four will not suffice for a lifetime. We will need to return to education for professional upgrading and new career training. But lifelong learning will not be motivated by instrumental considerations only. Education will also be pursued for intrinsic reasons: as a means or self-enrichment and self-realization. The cultural motive of self-fulfilment is also gaining strength in our society, and it is fed by, among other things, the increase in the number of highly educated persons. Education tends to create its own demand.

The opening up of new markets for education will be accompanied by a weakening of the monopoly held by the school system, particularly at the post-primary level. Financial and technical considerations will bring this about. Education is a labor-intensive rather than a capital-intensive enterprise. That is, we use people to produce educational outcomes rather than machines. Salaries of the teaching staff constitute the largest cost item of the educational budget. Expansion of education will be costly, unless we can find alternatives to the traditional, labor-intensive teaching methods. The development of the microcomputer and the video disc make such a change in instructional technology possible. For many subjects, high quality and attractive educational material will become available at reasonable cost. This will lead to the creation of a decentralized (you can plug in at home or at work), geographically dispersed network of learning opportunities of which schools are only one part. In order to provide for a common socialization experience, children will still be required to attend school, but they also will study at home; instruction and promotion will be more individualized. The teacher role will change from that of a dispenser of knowledge to that of a manager and facilitator of a student-centered learning process.

These are some of the directions education is likely

to take in the future. The speed and exact scope of these changes is difficult to predict. They will not be universally welcomed; some groups whose interests will be affected, will no doubt oppose them. For a sociologist, all this will guarantee that education will continue to be an area worthy of investigation.

SUMMARY

1. State-supported, universal schooling is a modern invention, dating from the nineteenth century.

2. The functions of education are: occupational socialization, social selection and status socialization, democratic citizenship training, creation of a common cultural identity, development of personality and human potential, and innovation.

3. Education is likely to be surrounded by controversy. First, not all of the functions of education receive equal public support. Evidence has been presented to show that the economic and the social-stratification function have received the strongest emphasis. Second, some of the functions of education contain internal and external contradictions, and disagreement about the specification of objectives is not uncommon.

4. The impetus for the massive expansion of the educational system in Canada since the 1950s has come from two sources: a concern for economic productivity, and a concern for social justice. Human capital theory provided the economic rationale for educational expansion. Social justice without major revision of the educational system provided the social rationale.

5. In terms of its social orientation, the Canadian educational system has shifted from sponsored mobility to contest mobility. The Quebec educational system is an example of this trend.

6. One of the main effects of educational expansion has been an escalation of educational requirements. This has undermined both its economic and social rationale. Although some absolute gains have been made in the area of social justice, in relative terms existing gender and class inequalities have not been resolved.

7. The sociological counterpart to human capital theory is technological functionalism, a perspective that sees the school as a neutral instrument for satisfying the technological needs of society. There are two alternative, conflict interpretations of the role of education: Collins has presented a Weberian, and Bowles and Gintis a Marxist, inspired theory of education. Both stress the role of the school as an instrument of domination.

8. Two strategies for improving educational opportunities can be distinguished: equality of access and equality of nurture. Both imply different responsibilities for the school system.

9. Two home based and three school related sources of unequal nurture have been identified. They are, respectively, achievement motivation and language use; and the influence structure of the school, selection procedures, and cultural transmission. Structural/technological functionalists and conflict theorists differ in the emphasis placed on these factors.

10. The functional and conflict perspectives have been compared along four dimensions: societal determinants of education, the stratification role of education, the relevance of education as a credential, and sources of unequal academic achievement. Some of the differences are more apparent than real and represent differences in emphasis. Others are more substantive. Both perspectives have been criticized for ignoring the study of school life as a variable in its own right.

11. Education in the future will be lifelong, and schooling will be part of a larger network of educational facilities. Instructional technology will make available more individualized and decentralized forms of learning.

GLOSSARY

Citizenship training. Preparation for political participation in the affairs of a democratic society.
Conflict perspective. Sociological perspective which sees education as an instrument of domination.
Contest mobility. Open competition for elite status.
Education. Deliberate, organized transmission of values, knowledge, and skills.
Elaborated language code. Way of communication that makes meanings explicit and universal.

Elite preparatory. Stage of educational development in a society in which the majority of students do not finish high school, and the function of the high school is restricted to preparing a select group of students for university education.

Empty box view of education. View that schools are passive transmitters of outside influences, with no life of their own.

Equality of access. Removal of external barriers to educational participation.

Equality of nurture. Removal of barriers to educational performance.

Human capital theory. Economic theory that the skill level of the labor force is the prime determinant of economic growth.

Mass terminal. Stage of educational development in a society in which secondary education has become universal, but post-secondary education is pursued by a minority only.

Meritocracy. Society in which merit constitutes the basis for social stratification and in which all people have an equal chance to display their talents and to be evaluated fairly.

Occupational socialization. Preparation for entering the job market.

Restricted language code. Way of communication that leaves meanings implicit.

Sponsored mobility. Competition for elite status on the basis of criteria set by the existing elite.

Status socialization. Process of teaching people to accept their position in the social stratification system. It includes two components: "ambition regulation" and "legitimation."

Technological functionalism. A perspective which sees rising educational requirements as a reflection of the increased complexity of the occupational structure.

FURTHER READING

Husén, Torsten. *The School in Question: A Comparative Study of the School and Its Future in Western Societies.* Oxford: Oxford University Press, 1979. A wide ranging international assessment of the central problems confronting secondary education.

Illich, Ivan. *Deschooling Society.* New York: Harper and Row, 1972. A fundamental attack on institutionalized schooling. Controversial and stimulating.

Karabel, Jerome, and A.H. Halsey (eds.). *Power and Ideology in Education.* Oxford: Oxford University Press, 1977. An excellent selection of readings on the macrosociology of education, incorporating all the major theoretical perspectives. The introductory chapter by the two editors is particularly worthwhile.

Murphy, Raymond. *Sociological Theories of Education.* Toronto: McGraw-Hill Ryerson, 1979. Less innovative than the Karabel and Halsey reader, but solid in its discussion of the mainstream literature, and unique in its thorough assessment of the Canadian contributions to the field.

Prentice, Alison. *The School Promoters: Education and Social Class in Mid-Nineteenth Century Upper Canada.* Toronto: McClelland and Stewart, 1977. Examines the most important formative period in the history of Anglophone Canadian education and analyzes the ideas and actions of Egerton Ryerson from a conflict perspective.

V
SOCIAL CHANGE

For thousands and thousands of years, human beings, or their ancestors, walked, or rode horses, or sailed ships. In 1926 the rocket was invented, in 1934 the jet engine. In 1969 we walked on the moon. The world is changing, and the rate of change itself is accelerating.

It took more than a million years for the world's human population to reach about a quarter billion, at the year A.D. 1. It took an additional 1650 years for the population to double, to about one-half billion. But it took only about 200 years for it to double again, to one billion in 1850. Less than 100 years later, in 1930, it was two billion. It doubled again in 36 years, reaching four billion in 1976. By the year 2000 it will double again to eight billion. What will your world be like in a decade or two?

For a very long time the role a person played in youth was not much different from that played in later life: a farmer was a farmer; a parent was a parent. Today roles change constantly. For example, sociologists estimate that ten years from today, half the jobs now available to high school graduates will have faded out of existence. They will have been replaced by jobs that do not exist today.

Social change is an essential ingredient of our society. Most of the earlier chapters include some discussion of social change in particular areas, such as the family and education.

The chapters in this section of the book deal with very important aspects of this process of change. Chapter 15, *Urbanization and Urbanism*, discusses one of the major social changes of modern times, the population shift from rural to urban concentration. This chapter examines the extent, the causes, and the consequences of urbanization, emphasizing urban life in Canada.

Chapter 16, *Social Movements*, is a more general and theoretical treatment of social change, giving special attention to groups promoting or resisting change. The focus is the role of such social movements in Canada.

Whether through organized groups or individual effort, whether conscious or unconscious, rational or intuitive, sane or crazy, social change is one constant on which we can depend.

CHAPTERS

CHAPTER 15
URBANIZATION AND URBANISM

A. R. GILLIS

Some urban sociologists wonder whether their area should be seen as separate sub-field of sociology. Most would argue, however, that the area is indeed unique, with a distinct subject, a special way of looking at social life, and a discrete body of knowledge. Like other sub-fields, urban sociology includes both structural functionalist and conflict viewpoints, as well as historical and contemporary approaches. Symbolic interactionism has not been popular with urban sociologists (which probably means that urban sociology is not popular with symbolic interactionists). Also, students of cities typically include the physical environment as an important variable in their research. This not only distinguishes urban sociology from other areas, but it is the basis for a link with applied fields such as social policy, planning, and architecture. This side of urban sociology pleases utilitarians and bothers purists. In any case, a concern with the physical as well as the social environment often distinguishes those of us who study cities from other sociologists.

It is hard to define "city" in a way that will please

you've really got far.

What is an Urban Area?

Current definitions of "urban" vary widely from one country to another. In Greece, for example, municipalities and communities containing fewer than 10,000 people are not classified as urban; in neighboring Albania any towns with 400 or more are. In Canada, the minimum population necessary for a locality to be classified as urban (a Census Urban Area or CUA) is 1000, while in the United States the figure is 2500.

These different definitions of "urban" make international comparisons difficult. Statistics Canada tells us that approximately 75 percent of the Canadian population lives in urban areas, and the United States census reports roughly the same figure for that country. But it is important to realize that the level of urbanization in the United States is, from the Canadian standpoint, understated. In fact, the proportion of the American population living in towns of 1000 or more is greater than 75 percent.

Here is another definitional problem: classifying a village containing 1000 people (or for that matter 2500 people) as an urban area has little intuitive appeal. For most of us, "urban" brings to mind places like Tokyo, New York, Montreal, or Toronto, rather than Gimli, Manitoba, or Gibson's Landing, B.C., both of which are classified as urban areas in Canada. In view of this incongruity, Statistics Canada (then the Dominion Bureau of Statistics) developed in 1931 the concept of Census Metropolitan Area (CMA) in the hope of offering a more satisfactory description of the number of Canadians who were living under urban conditions, if not in urban areas.

A CMA was defined as a principal city with at least 50,000 inhabitants; an urbanized core with a density of at least 1000 population per square mile; or an area outside the central city but with a labor force of which at least 70 percent were engaged in nonagricultural activities or with a total population of at least 100,000.

The United Nations uses the following classification scheme:

Big City   — a locality with 500,000 or more inhabitants.

City   — a locality with 100,000 or more inhabitants.

Rural Locality —a locality with fewer than 20,000 inhabitants.

Thus, Canada's definition of a CMA is roughly equivalent to the United Nations' classification of "city" and the definition of "city" presented at the beginning of this chapter.

So how urban are Canadians? Well, the fact that the country is 75 percent urban does not mean that each of us is three quarters urban and one quarter rural in orientation. A sociologist would say that this sort of reasoning is an example of an *ecological fallacy.* The characteristics of an aggregation are not necessarily displayed in the same proportions in each of the members that make it up. Urban sociologists, who examine collectivities such as cities or neighbourhoods and draw conclusions about the individuals who live in them must be particularly careful of these problems of aggregation and disaggregation.

Three out of four Canadians live in urban areas, and one does not. Furthermore, in 1981 one of two lived in a "Big City" (a metro area of 500,000 or more), and three of ten were in metropolitan areas of one million or more (Montreal, Toronto, or Vancouver). This suggests that Canada is an urban society. And it is. However, as Rex Lucas (1971) pointed out, ". . . many people in Canada live nowhere. "In addition to the six million who live in rural areas, many more live in small, one-industry towns of 30,000 or less. When we call Canada an urban society, then, we should keep in mind that a substantial proportion of the population still lives in rural areas and small towns.

Source:

Kalbach, Warren E., and Wayne W. McVey. *The Demographic Bases of Canadian Society*, 2nd ed. Toronto: McGraw-Hill Ryerson, 1979, p. 140; *Demographic Handbook for Africa*, Addis Ababa: United Nations Economic Commission for Africa, 1968, p. 38.

everyone. Architects, planners, and civil engineers, for example, are mainly interested in planning, design, and physical factors, and the way they view and define "city" reflects this. Since social scientists are concerned with social life, their view of the city and what they regard as its distinct features lead them to a somewhat different definition.

Sociologists see the **city** as a large concentration of people who work in a wide range of interdependent occupations which, for the most part, do not involve the primary production of food. It is important to note that this definition does not ignore the physical characteristics of the city. "Large concentration of people" implies that the number and density of people in cities is noteworthy as an urban characteristic. In fact, many urban sociologists suspect that population density and other environmental factors have a major impact on social life in cities.

The sociological view of cities is useful because it points to variables that allow us to explain where, when, and why the first cities were built, how cities grow and spread, and how and why people who live in cities differ from people who don't. These are important questions for sociologists, especially in view of the recent and continuing rural-to-urban shift of the world's population.

THE ORIGIN OF CITIES

Until recently, social scientists thought that the first permanent settlement with enough people in it to be called a city was built about 5000 years ago in the Middle East. However, recent archaeological evidence suggests that the first walled city may have been built 8000 to 10 000 years ago. (In fact, one of the first cities may have been Jericho, a city far more famous for its destruction than its construction.) In any case, since Homo sapiens has existed for at least 250 000 years, it is clear that the natural history of humanity has been almost exclusively in wilderness and rural environments.

That humans have spent so little of their time on earth living in cities suggests to some scholars that pastoral living is our natural or preferred way of life. This may be true, but for the most part our ancestors' life in the wilderness was probably less indicative of preference than necessity. Until about 8000 B.C. people were simply unable to sustain urban populations.

Agricultural Surplus

According to our definition, a city is a large number of people who inhabit a relatively concentrated area. To feed these people, a great amount of food must either be produced in and around the area or be brought into it from further away. Moving great amounts of food long distances requires relatively sophisticated technology, and growing a great amount of food in a concentrated area requires high-yield agriculture. Neither of these requirements is easy for people with primitive skills. To make matters worse, a large proportion of the urban population is not engaged in the production of food, so the rural residents who are growing food must not only supply themselves, but others as well.

Even if early humans had been inclined to live in cities, then, they would not have been released from primary food production to become urbanites. As people advanced technologically – developing the plow, domesticating draft animals, discovering high-yield grains, and inventing more efficient systems of transportation – larger **agricultural surpluses** could be taken from a wider range of environments. However, these and other important innovations emerged only relatively recently in the natural history of humans.

In view of all this, it is not surprising that the first cities were built in the rich alluvial valleys of the Tigris, Nile, and Indus rivers, and, somewhat later on, in similar environments in Central America. These sites allowed people with simple technology to grow a surplus of food in a relatively concentrated area and to feed a relatively large number of people who were not themselves contributing to the production of food.

Limiting Factors

Sociologists point to several factors that may have caused people to produce a surplus of food and construct cities. Two major types of factors can be distinguished: limiting factors and motivating factors. **Limiting factors** include the natural environment and the technical ability of people to alter it. Limiting factors determined where cities could not be built. **Motivating factors** include cultural values and social structure as forces that may have encouraged people to build the first cities.

The Natural Environment. According to Bronowski (1973), the first cities resulted indirectly from the emergence of a new relationship between people and a specific part of their physical environment: wheat. Wheat for making bread resulted from the accidental cross-fertilization of several kinds of wild grasses. The seeds of the new plant had a low chaff content that separated easily from the kernel. This impaired their dispersal by the wind, and might

Images of the City

The word "city" brings various images to the minds of various people. And specific cities, because of their traits, physical symbols, and nicknames, elicit different images – New York, world status; Washington, politics; Chicago, virility; and San Francisco, elegance.

Traits tend to be emphasized or exaggerated by nicknames. Nicknames are particularly popular in the United States. In Canada, we have the "Cradle of Confederation" (Charlottetown), the "Forest City" (London), the "Stampede City" (Calgary), and the "Gateway to the North" (Edmonton). Montreal competes with both San Francisco and Paris, Ontario, as "The Paris of North America." Most nicknames are positive and often reflect boosterism, but as with other stereotypes, this need not always be

the case; one of Toronto's nicknames is "Hogtown."

Some cities also have physical symbols, which may or may not be functional. The Golden Gate Bridge symbolizes San Francisco, while also allowing access to Sausalito; but the St. Louis Arch has no function but to symbolize St. Louis as "The Gateway to the West." A unique natural silhouette, like Montreal's Mount Royal, can also symbolize a city, as can a constructed silhouette, like the New York skyline.

The most distinctive city monument in Canada is probably the CN Tower in Toronto. The tower serves as a communications center, and is gradually gaining world-wide recognition as *the* symbol for the city. However, it is not at all clear what meaning we should attach to this monument. Suggestions range from an exclamation point, through more Freudian phallic interpretations.

Specific cities vary in the nature of

their overall ambience or image. In comparing popular images of New York, Paris, London, Milgram (1970) found that New York was distinguished primarily on the basis of architecture and "the pace of life." In contrast, London elicited images of its citizens and social quality, while Paris brought to mind *both* physical and social characteristics equally. Like the image of "city" itself, then, both physical and social characteristics seem to be important in describing the character of specific cities, with some more physical and others more social (Lynch, 1960).

Source:

Selected references to Milgram, Stanley. "The experience of living in cities." *Science*, 167: 1461-168, 1970; Lynch, Kevin, *The Image of the City*. Cambridge, Mass.: M.I.T. Press, 1960.

have caused the extinction of the new hybrid. The chaff contains cellulose and cannot be used for energy by humans, but the kernel is an efficient source of energy. So the hybrid was a good food source for humans, who saw the value of the new plant and replaced the wind as its principal means of dispersal. Thus, people and wheat became involved in a mutually beneficial relationship. Human involvement allowed the plant to thrive, and the plant's high yield reduced the amount of work required to produce food for human survival.

This relationship was the basis for the development of agriculture and provided an important and desirable alternative to the hunting, gathering, and herding economies that had previously characterized human societies.

The discovery and domestication of wheat (and of corn in Central America) allowed both plant and people to settle in mutually advantageous locations (such as the Mesopotamian Basin). This settlement and the ease of storing wheat greatly helped people to create a surplus of food. A family head could support a larger family and would need to devote less time and energy to producing food for survival.

Furthermore, this would also allow some family heads to be released entirely from food-producing activities, while other family heads continued to work full-capacity to feed themselves, their families, and all those not engaged in food production. The presence of ideal growing conditions and a high-yield grain, therefore, set the stage for agriculture, the production of a surplus, the division of labor, and the emergence of cities.

Technology. Ideas and technology helped humans to construct favorable environments for the production of an agricultural surplus and to build the physical artifacts that contain urban populations. Natural environments, in contrast, often forced people to be nomads. When game or edible plants disappeared from one region because of overhunting, overgrazing, or a change in the season, people had to move on to where game and edible plants were more abundant. People who lived in these conditions were hardly in a position to settle down and construct cities. It was agricultural technology that gave people more control over their natural environment and allowed them to settle.

The application of ideas has frequently changed the natural environment, making it a more productive and less punishing place to live. People have discovered and even developed a wide variety of high-yield crops (like wheat) and learned how to care for them by improving natural environments with various devices ranging from fertilizer to irrigation. Technology has vastly improved the capacity of people to extract surplus food from the physical environment and greatly extended the range of environments that will tolerate large numbers of people and cities.

City walls and private and public buildings represent alterations of a natural environment to suit certain human needs. Walls protect people from external threats, and buildings provide protection from extremes in climate. Concentrating large numbers of people in cities does, however, pose challenges concerning shelter, transportation, sewage disposal, and so forth. These challenges cannot be met with the methods used in rural areas, where the scale is small and the population is dispersed. Thus, a city can be seen as a technical device that alters or controls the effects of the natural environment by substituting for it a *built environment*.

So far, then, we can see that humans applied technology to the natural environment in two ways important for the origin of cities. First, technology altered environments to exploit or increase agricultural potential for the production of surplus food. Second, technology allowed people to replace natural environments with built environments. This not only protected people from natural threats, but also solved many of the problems associated with large numbers of people living in close quarters. Technology made people less vulnerable to the limitations and variability of their natural environment.

The natural environment and technology combine to allow the possibility of surplus food and the construction of cities. An agreeable natural environment means that simple technology may suffice for the survival of persons or plants. But complex technology means that a disagreeable natural environment may be improved. The absence of a minimal combination of natural environment and technology, however, means that a city cannot be built. We can conclude from this that certain environmental conditions, whether natural or altered, are necessary for the origin of cities.

The first cities emerged in natural settings hospitable to plants and people. Necessarily so, because of the low level of technical development 10 000 years ago. The plow, after all, was not even invented until the fourth century B.C. (Palen, 1975). Later, as people extended their knowledge and skills concerning environmental improvement, cities were constructed on a wider range of sites.

Motivating Factors

Although an agreeable environment, whether natural or improved, is necessary for the origin of cities, it is not sufficient. Just because people can stockpile a food surplus does not guarantee that they will do so. For example, Tuan (1974) notes that some areas of New Guinea provide their inhabitants with more food than they can eat. Yet they have not stockpiled a surplus that would allow a division of labor between food producers and others. As a result, urbanization has not occurred. This example points out that the part played by the environment in the origin of cities is that of limiter, not motivator.

The New Guinea natives have had little or no experience with cities; so it is therefore hard to argue that their failure to stockpile food and to urbanize reflects a preference for rural living. Instead, sociologists argue that certain structural or cultural factors (or both) are necessary before a population can urbanize. These characteristics are absent in the New Guinea population. Before cities can exist, people must be divided at the very least into food producers and nonproducers. Sociologists have several explanations for the development of this division of labor.

Cultural Values. Social scientists who favor a structural functionalist model of society (for example, Davis, 1955f) stress that general and widespread economic benefits accrue from large-scale operations and a division of labor. They therefore argue that the first

cities arose because the original inhabitants recognized these economic benefits and wanted to realize them.

On the other hand, the origin of the first cities may have had less to do with economics than with religion. According to Adams (1960) and Childe (1950), the first public buildings were temples that often doubled as granaries. Priests may have been the first nonagricultural workers, forming the nucleus of urban society. They gave spiritual sustenance, supported and spread cultural values, and supervised the collection and storage of the agricultural surplus as tribute.

This argument is generally consistent with a functionalist view of the relationship between culture and social structure, where social organization is seen as a manifestation of cultural values. These views focus on cooperation, consensus, and the importance of cultural values as the motivation for developing cities. But it is also possible – and according to many sociologists, more likely – that conflict and dissensus were the social forces that produced the initial division of producers and nonproducers of food, which resulted in the first cities.

Social Structure. From a conflict perspective, the division of labor into food producers and nonproducers resulted from the victimization of the former by the latter. In other words, nonproducers took food from farmers who were then forced to extract still more nourishment from the environment in order to survive. From this viewpoint, the creation of surplus food accompanied or followed, rather than preceded, the division of labor and the first cities.

The nonproducers, then, were a ruling elite ensconced behind the walls of cities. They created an agricultural surplus by forcing farmers to produce more food to avoid starvation, or at least to increase their rural standard of living. This situation also encouraged the invention of more labor-saving agricultural technology (Polanyi, 1957; Sjoberg, 1960).

Sociologists vary in their opinion of how much force had to be used to get farmers to give their food to the ruling elite. Outright pillaging, institutionalized taxation, and exchange for protection and other services involve different degrees of open coercion. Exchanges of this kind involve less force than fraud (and then

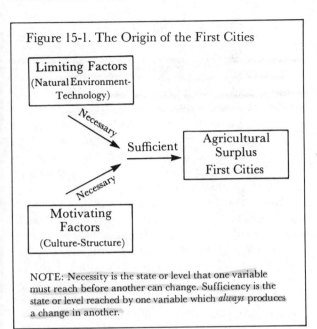

Figure 15-1. The Origin of the First Cities

Limiting Factors
(Natural Environment-
Technology)

Necessary

Sufficient

Agricultural
Surplus
First Cities

Necessary

Motivating
Factors
(Culture-Structure)

NOTE: Necessity is the state or level that one variable must reach before another can change. Sufficiency is the state or level reached by one variable which *always* produces a change in another.

only if the exchange can be deemed unfair by some absolute standard). It is at this point that the conflict argument shades off into a consensus view of the relationship between cities and their **hinterland** (the surrounding area from which a city draws its food and other raw materials).

In any event, culture, structure, or both in combination (Mumford, 1961) can be seen as necessary motivating effects on the development of the first cities. Like the natural environment and technology, however, culture and/or structure are not by themselves sufficient to account for the first cities. Unless a surplus is possible (and the natural environment and technology may or may not permit this) the motivation to produce surplus food will be fruitless and disappear (along with many of the people). So, both limiting and motivating factors are necessary but not sufficient individual variables to cause the first cities. It is not until these factors are considered together (See Figure 15-1) that there is satisfactory explanation for the origin of the first city, in Mesopotamia, about 10 000 years ago. For more general discussions of this approach, see Schnore (1958), Duncan (1959), Duncan and Schnore (1959), and Tilly (1974).

URBANIZATION

Urbanization refers to an increase in the proportion of a population living in areas defined as urban. Increases have most often occurred through people migrating from rural to urban areas and, as you saw in Chapter 7, to other countries. But it is important to realize that urbanization can also occur through differential fertility and mortality rates that sometimes give a relative advantage to urban populations, although fertility and mortality differentials have been more important in affecting **deurbanization** (a decrease in the proportion of population inhabiting urban areas). Historically, higher rates of fertility typical in rural areas have on occasion combined with higher rates of urban mortality (especially during plagues) to create a deurbanizing effect on a population (Tilly, 1976).

Urbanization: The Ancient Period

Ancient cities were small by today's standards and contained only a tiny proportion of the world's population. Athens, the great city of classical Greece, peaked with a population of 120 000 to 180 000. Both limiting and motivating factors kept the population of Athens low; poor soil and simple agricultural technology combined with a cultural preference for small cities to limit growth (Davis, 1955; Palen, 1981).

The other great city of the ancient period was Rome. A more generous natural environment, technical advances (especially in the areas of agriculture, and the transportation of people, produce, and water), a more complex division of labor, and a cultural interest in expansion all joined to push Rome far beyond the size of Athens. Estimates of the size of ancient Rome, whose population peaked just before the birth of Christ, range between 250 000 and 1.6 million (Palen, 1981).

Deurbanization: The Middle Ages

Rome was the largest and most powerful city the world had ever seen, but when the Roman Empire fell (around the fifth century A.D.), neither the city nor its population could be maintained. When the Vandals cut the city off from its grain-producing areas in Africa,

Rome was crippled, and its population ultimately dwindled to less than 25 000 (Palen, 1981).

The demise of the Roman Empire, like the decline of Greece before it, involved the disorganization of an extensive social network, with a city at its center. All roads had indeed led to Rome; they carried raw materials, food, and laborers to the city, and armies from it to collect taxes, maintain order in the provinces, and extend the empire's frontiers. The fall of Rome heralded a period of deurbanization and the return of Europe to rural life. The vast network developed by Rome withered, and outlying localities were forced once again into isolation and self-sufficiency. During urban growth, people flowed into the city on all the roads that led to Rome. In decline, the same roads took those people away. People returned to the land and to local rather than imperial domination. According to Pirenne (1939), Europe entered the Dark Ages, 600 years of economic and cultural stagnation. Whether this should be viewed as "stagnation" is moot. The Dark Ages have also been called the Middle Ages, a time of great social and cultural stability and, perhaps, individual happiness (Huizinga, 1924).

Cities and Culture

The rise of Athens and Rome were accompanied by dramatic developments in the arts, science, and other dimensions of culture. After the fall of Rome, Europe did not again begin to urbanize until the eleventh century, when once again innovations in abstract and material culture began (Huizinga, 1924; Pirenne, 1939).

We saw earlier that cultural factors affected the origin of cities. The reverse is also true: cities affect culture and civilization. Athens and Rome are exemplary in this respect, having developed and disseminated the classical traditions and the bases for Western civilization.

One way to understand the cultural contributions of Athens, Rome, and other great cities is by viewing the city as a mechanism for controlling time (Innis, 1951). Because they did not have to grow food to feed themselves, and because of the efficiency of a more complex social organization, citizens of cities like Athens and Rome may have had more leisure time than did their rural counterparts (Herskowitz, 1952). Inadequate leisure time can be seen as a limiting factor that prevents innovation and experimentation. Pushing back the amount of time spent on agricultural work freed people to do other things.

In addition, cities attracted and sustained creative people from a wide range of rural regions and different sociocultural systems. (The same factors that caused individuals to break away from local ties and migrate to cities may also have inclined them to be innovative in other ways.) The concentration and social interaction of creative people with different cultural backgrounds would have been fertile ground for the growth of new ideas and cultural change. In fact, this is a good description of a university as well as a city.

The motivating factor for many cultural advances may have been the need of the urban elite to keep records concerning the taxation of the hinterland and the administration of the empire. Primitive accounting may have led to the development of writing, mathematics, and related fields. Also, advances in the sciences may have resulted from pressure to improve agricultural technology (Childe, 1950).

Athens and Rome illustrate that the causal arrow between urbanization and the development of culture can go both ways. In other words, cities are not only the products of the ideas and values of people; they are also the agents of innovation and cultural change.

Reurbanization: The Renaissance

In the eleventh century Europeans began to return to the cities. These were small by today's standards. According to Max Weber (1958), each city had the following features:

1. a fortification
2. a market
3. a court of its own and at least partially autonomous law
4. a related form of association (guilds, professional associations)
5. at least partial political and administrative autonomy

Weber thought that cities like this were characteristic of Europe and had an important effect on the European economy.

By the fourteenth century the economy of Europe was becoming a city-centered, trade-oriented version of capitalism. The feudal self-sufficiency of the medieval period was in decline. Cities provided farm workers with a place to live, greater freedom, and a better occupational deal than did the feudal manor. As a result, serfs increasingly fled the farm to the cities. The urbanization of Europe contributed to the destruction of the feudal economy and the concentration of capital in cities (Marx, 1965, originally published 1889). In this sense, then, the city affected the structure, as well as the culture, of western societies.

The development of cities in Europe during the Renaissance was associated with important changes in culture (such as the Protestant Reformation), as well as in the economy (such as the rise of modern capitalism). The major effects on cities during this period were the forces of urbanization discussed above and the countervailing force of deurbanization caused by the bubonic plague. In a three-year period the Black Death killed about one-quarter of the population of Europe. By 1400 one-third of Europe's total population was dead from the plague. The mortality rate was highest in the cities, and more than half of the urban residents died (Zinssen, 1965; Langer, 1973; McNeill, 1976). This pattern reflected the inadequate garbage and sewage disposal in most cities, as well as the greater ease with which communicable diseases spread in high-density settings.

In the short run, then, the bubonic plague had a deurbanizing effect on the European population. But in the long run the Black Death dealt the final blow to feudalism and actually accelerated urbanization. The death of so many peasants totally depleted the already weakened supply of rural farm workers. Those who survived left for the cities, where the plague had created a severe labor shortage. By the fifteenth century, the forces of urbanization had countered the forces of deurbanization, and European cities began growing again.

Plagues continued into the seventeenth century, but never again affected the size or distribution of the population the way they had in the latter part of the fourteenth century. (The descendents of the survivors of the fourteenth century plague were probably more resistant to the Black Death.) But the mortality rate from all causes continued to be higher in cities than in the countryside until the end of the nineteenth century. This mortality rate, combined with the typically lower rate of urban fertility, meant that heavy migration to the cities was required for urbanization to continue.

The Modern Era

The urbanization of Europe proceeded slowly until late in the eighteenth century, when the population grew quickly, partly because of a sudden drop in mortality rates. This decline probably resulted from Jenner's invention of the smallpox vaccine in 1792 and a general improvement in health attributable to a significant increase in the amount and availability of food. This was made possible through several important advances in agricultural and transportation technology (McKeown, 1976). Extra food not only allowed a larger population to be better nourished, but released more people from agricultural occupations and rural areas. Many migrated to the cities, and for the first time in history close to 10 percent of the human population inhabited urban localities.

Apart from the natural environment, the most important factor limiting the expansion of cities is technology. Over the centuries people have used a wide range of techniques to extract larger and larger surpluses from an increasingly wide range of natural environments. Because of this, technologically advanced societies have been able to take laborers from agricultural occupations and reallocate them to other tasks in urban centers. The most important technical advance in this respect was the Industrial Revolution.

The Industrial Revolution replaced animate sources of energy (humans, horses, oxen) with inanimate sources of energy (mainly fossil fuels like coal, oil, or gas, but also electricity). This involved the substitution of machines for tools as energy converters. For example, the horse collar and harness are tools that direct horse-power into pulling. But the tractor is a machine

How many farmers would it take . . .?

Between fifty and ninety farmers were required to produce sufficient food to sustain themselves and *one* person in the first cities. This tiny surplus kept the population of the earliest cities small. As technology improved, the number of farmers required to sustain an urbanite decreased. By the beginning of the nineteenth century the number of farms required to sustain an urban family had been reduced to nine, and the second-largest city in the world was London with a population of 900,000. (The largest was Edo [Tokyo] at 1 million.) The Industrial Revolution has further decreased the number of farmers required to sustain an urbanite and increased the potential size of cities.

Today, in the United States, for example, one farmer can sustain him-

self or herself and approximately forty-five other people. Fewer than 5 percent of the employed population are engaged in agricultural occupations, and the largest metropolitan area in the country is New York, with more than 16 million people.

Source:

Davis, Kingsley. "The origin and growth of urbanization in the world." *American Journal of Sociology*, 60:430, March, 1955; Rozman, G. "Edo's importance in the changing Tokugawa society." *Journal of Japanese Studies*, 1(1):91-112, 1975; Palen, John. *The Urban World*. New York: McGraw-Hill, 1975; Gist, Noel P. and Sylvia F. Fava. *Urban Society*, 6th ed. New York: Thomas Y. Crowell, 1974.

that transforms inanimate energy into pulling power.

The Industrial Revolution, centered in nineteenth-century England, had at least three major effects on the city. First, the application of its principles to agriculture greatly increased the efficiency of farm workers and the size of the surplus they could produce. This probably released many workers from agriculture and created a pool of laborers available for work elsewhere (McQuillan, 1980). Second, the application of its principles to transportation (rail, ship, auto, and ultimately air) greatly extended the territory upon which an urban area could draw. This effectively increased the amount of food and raw materials that could be brought into the city in a short time. (Territorial extension of this kind had special implications for Canada, because it allowed England to draw even more than previously upon the colony as a supplier of wheat.) Third, the application of these principles to factories resulted in a new type of city – the manufacturing city. Ironically, in view of the nature of the revolution (men and animals replaced by machines), there was also a growth in demand for laborers as

factory workers on the line. So the Industrial Revolution was also a social revolution. People and capital, which had been dispersed throughout rural areas, became concentrated in factories which were themselves concentrated in cities.

These effects combined to expand greatly the potential for the proliferation and growth of cities. Instead agricultural productivity meant that there was more food to send to cities. More efficient transportation technology meant that greater amounts of food would be sent faster and further than before, and the urban promise of consumer goods and employment attracted millions of rural migrants.

It is interesting that although technology allows people to extract larger surpluses of food from deserts, barren land, and the floor of the sea, some environments still deny surplus food to people. For example, we have not yet learned to control the central African tsetse fly, which carries sleeping sickness. Indigenous wildlife seems immune to the disease, but these animals are valuable neither as sources of food nor as draft animals. High-yield domestic beef, dairy, and draft animals, however, are susceptible to sleeping sickness. As a result, we are still unable to convert vast expanses of prime grazing land into a food surplus because of our present technical inability to control the tsetse fly.

Although technical advances cannot overcome all environmental limitations, human technology has enabled people to live in urban areas like Yellowknife in northern Canada where surplus food cannot be produced. Instead, a surplus is produced far to the south and transported to the city. Only modern technology allows the rapid transportation of massive amounts of material such long distances.

Urban Futures

The last two centuries have seen a flood of people moving from rural to urban areas around the world. Urbanization has been most intense in industrialized countries, for the reasons outlined above. For example, the United Kingdom was one of the first countries to industrialize, and was also one of the first countries to experience a massive movement of people to the cities. As a result, England is now one of the most urbanized countries in the world, with about 70 percent of its population living in large cities, and 80 percent in urban areas.

The rate of urbanization of the world's population is shown in Table 15-1. Both columns show that between 1800 and 1950 the urban population of the world was doubling every 50 years. After 1950, however, the urban population was tripling every 50 years.

The projected population of the urban areas of the world for the year 2000 is 61 percent, with 42 percent living in cities with populations greater than 100 000. Like all projections this one assumes that current trends will continue. However, there are signs that the rate of urbanization in some industrialized countries, including Canada, is starting to decline and may even reverse (Bourne, 1978).

Modern industrial countries are already heavily urbanized. Between 70 and 80 percent of the inhabitants of industrialized countries now live in urban areas. It is unclear whether a much greater proportion of these populations will be able to do so. Even now some

TABLE 15-1. PERCENTAGE OF WORLD URBAN POPULATION, ACTUAL AND PROJECTED, 1800-2000

	Urban (over 20 000)	Large Cities (over 100 000)
	%	%
1800	2	2
1850	4	2
1900	9	6
1950	21	13
1975	42	26
2000	61	42

SOURCE: Davis, Kingsley, "The origin and growth of urbanization in the world." *American Journal of Sociology*, 60:430, March, 1955; Davis, Kingsley. *World Urbanization*, 1950-70, vol. II (1972), pp. 126-127.
NOTE: Percentages are rounded.

cities in industrialized countries have spread so much that their boundaries are beginning to merge. The result of this process is called a **megalopolis** (or conurbation). North American examples of this phenomenon includes the urban belt extending from Massachusetts to Virginia along the east coast of the United States, and the "Golden Horseshoe" stretching from Toronto to Niagara around the west shore of Lake Ontario.

Also, it is unclear whether nonindustrialized countries will industrialize, as western countries have. Our industrial and urban growth depends on the consumption of fossil fuels, particularly oil and gas (see Figure 15-2). It now seems that this consumption cannot continue indefinitely. Supplies are finite. In fact, if urban industrialized countries do not soon develop more energy-efficient machines and make greater use of other energy sources (like hydro, solar, or atomic power), deurbanization and deindustrialization will begin. The natural environment limits the degree to which we can urbanize, and we have developed the technology to extend urban limits greatly by converting fossil fuel to energy. In fact, oil, gas, and coal are a crucial part of the natural environment and may act as limiters themselves – by disappearing.

In view of this, it is hard to predict future levels of world urbanization. Projections suggest a highly urbanized world. However, as we just noted, projections are

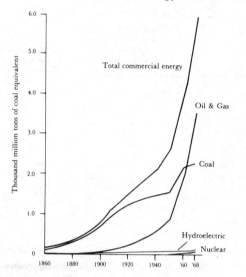

Figure 15-2. World Use of Energy Sources

Total commercial energy

Oil & Gas

Coal

Hydroelectric

Nuclear

SOURCE: Gist, Noel P., and Sylvia F. Fava: *Urban Society*, 6th ed. New York: Thomas Y. Crowell, 1974, p. 30.

NOTE: World use of coal, oil, and gas has boomed in a single century. The substitution of inanimate sources of energy for the work energy of men and animals is one of the hallmarks of industrialization. Used to propel machines, these new sources of energy have enormously increased productivity. (*Population Bulletin*, April 1971, p. 10. Based on data from Political and Economic Planning, *World Population and Resources*, London: George Allen and Unwin, 1964; and United Nations, *World Energy Supplies*, 1958 (#1), 1960 (#3), and 1970 (#13)).

based on existing trends, such as the consumption of fossil fuels, which may not continue. Deurbanization is a possibility. It happened when Rome fell, and it could happen again.

Urban Networks in Canada

Urbanization began in what is now Canada some time after French colonization in the seventeenth century. By the mid-1600s, the outposts of Quebec, Montreal, and Trois Rivières each contained fewer than 1000 people, but by 1765 Quebec City and Montreal had grown into towns of more than 5000. It is noteworthy that at this time New France was about 25 percent urban, and less than 10 percent of the population of

the 13 American colonies lived in urban areas. This reflects the fact that New France was more of a commercial center based on the fur trade, than an agricultural colony, like its southern neighbors.

By 1825, Fort York (Toronto) was a garrison of about 2000 people, while both Quebec and Montreal had passed 20 000. By the mid-1800s, Montreal was a city of more than 50 000, and both Quebec and Toronto had populations of over 30 000. In the Maritimes, Saint John and Halifax competed for regional dominance. Each contained more than 20 000 people. About 7 percent of the populations of the Maritimes, Lower Canada (Quebec), and Upper Canada (Ontario) lived in cities of 20 000 or more in 1850, compared with a world figure of 5 percent (Stone, 1967). In 1867, then, Canada was an urbanized country by world standards.

Stone (1967) notes that "Canadian urban development probably had its 'take-off' toward high levels of urbanization in the 10-15 years following Confederation in 1867." In this respect, Canada followed the pattern of urban growth in northwest Europe and the United States. In the twentieth century, the urbanization of Canada continued, lagging slightly behind that of the colonial powers of the western industrial world, but far ahead of most other colonies and former colonies.

Canada's pattern of urbanization, like that of the United States, moved from east to west. Several things caused this. These include limiting factors: the physical environment, transportation technology, and the harsh climate of the north and our continuing difficulty in coping with it. Motivating factors were also important. These included increasing population-resource pressure in eastern Canada, and the attraction of the continent's natural resources (initially furs, later wheat and fossil fuels). Let us now examine both factors in detail.

Limiting Factors. The first Europeans landed on the east coast of North America. The wooded environment was hard to penetrate, given the level of European technology. But native technology, in the form of the canoe, allowed rapid movement along rivers and lakes. So during the exploration of the con-

Figure 15-3. Population Distribution by Census Divisions, Canada, 1976

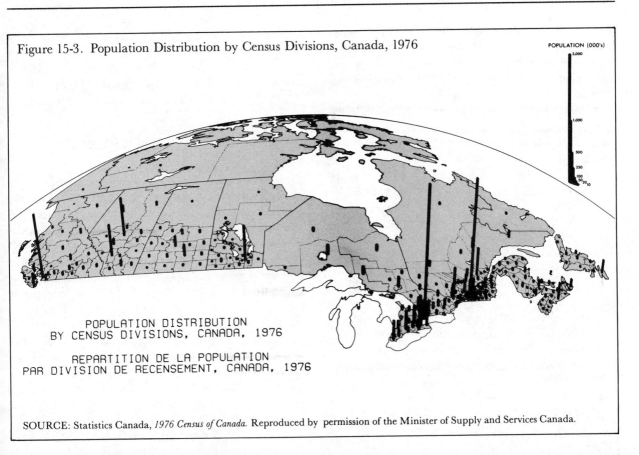

POPULATION (000's)

POPULATION DISTRIBUTION
BY CENSUS DIVISIONS, CANADA, 1976

REPARTITION DE LA POPULATION
PAR DIVISION DE RECENSEMENT, CANADA, 1976

SOURCE: Statistics Canada, *1976 Census of Canada.* Reproduced by permission of the Minister of Supply and Services Canada.

tinent, water was the principle means of transportation.

As the Europeans pushed their frontier westward and tamed the wilderness, towns and cities sprang up behind them as forts and service centers. Most of these began as ports on the east coast. Cities like St. John's, Halifax, St. John, and Charlottetown were built near natural harbors that gave ships protection from the sea. Quebec, Montreal, and Trois Rivières were situated on the St. Lawrence River in key natural locations favoring defense and transportation needs. Montreal, for example, was built at the point where the St. Lawrence narrows. Here people and goods were transferred from ocean-going ships to vessels that could proceed westward on the St. Lawrence and Ottawa rivers, while furs and other raw materials travelled eastward on the St. Lawrence.

Generally, the largest cities in Canada and the United States were eastern ports for ocean-going ships.

In the United States, places like Boston, New York, and Philadelphia were and still are among the largest and most influential cities in the country. In Canada, however, the St. Lawrence allowed the penetration of ocean-going vessels farther west. As a result, the east coast of Canada was partially by-passed and developed differently from that of the United States. For a general discussion of the importance of the St. Lawrence in Canada's development, see Creighton (1956), Lower (1939).

The westward movement of settlers in Canada was hampered to the north by climate, muskeg, and black flies, and to the south by the political boundary with the United States. Settlement, therefore, was largely confined to a westward expansion along this border. Because of these and other limiting factors, most Canadian cities are located on waterways and relatively near the United States border. In the last 20 to 30 years, however, developments in transportation have increased our technical ability to cope with the Canadian environment. This, and the lure of oil and other raw materials in the north, has produced increased movement away from the American border.

Because Canada was colonized from east to west, Canadian cities differ greatly in age; a city like Quebec contains a wider range of old and new buildings than does a city like Calgary. This, and the tendency for newer cities to be built on grids, with numbered rather than named streets, and a car rather than a pedestrian orientation, gives a very different character to eastern and western cities. Eastern cities seem more picturesque, established, and European. In contrast, the cities of Manitoba, Saskatchewan, and Alberta seem more modern, efficient, and American.

The westward thrust of Canadian urbanization can be seen in Figure 15-3. Halifax, St. John, and Kingston were the fourth, fifth, and sixth largest cities in 1851. But within a century all three were surpassed by the western cities. The most recently constructed cities, Edmonton and Calgary, are now the fastest growing in the country. This reflects the importance of wheat, cattle, and especially oil in Canada's northwest. (See Clark, 1968; Kerr, 1968; Bourne, 1975; Hiller, 1976 for discussions of the development of the Canadian urban system.)

Motivating Factors. By 1867 most of the arable land in the eastern provinces was occupied (Stone, 1967), so migration flowed west. The scarcity of eastern land and the lure of assorted natural resources probably provided most of the motivation for the drive to the west.

The discovery and settlement of Canada by Europeans was part of a widespread pattern of colonialism, particularly on the part of Britain and France. Like other colonies, Canada specialized as a supplier of staples and raw materials to the European countries. Because of this, European colonial powers were able to divert the energy they would otherwise have spent on primary production (the production of food and other raw materials) to manufacturing and other urban industrial activities (Innis, 1927, 1940).

With the decline of the British Empire and the ascendancy of the United States, Canada became less attached to England and more closely tied to the United States. Today, Canada supplies raw materials to the metropolitan areas of the United States in exchange for manufactured goods and services.

Models of Development and Dependency

Development. Social scientists note that the nature of the relationships between countries is often the same as that between a **metropolis** and its hinterland. Metropolitan countries, regions, or cities send manufactured items, ideas, and technology to underdeveloped rural areas in exchange for labor and raw materials. Again, the effects of such relationships on the hinterland are a source of continuing debate among social scientists. Sociologists who emphasize culture, consensus, and structural functionalist models stress the benefits of the relationship to both parties and the system as a whole. They point to the great advances in medical care and general standard of living that association with the United States has brought to underdeveloped countries. Just as Athens and Rome developed and disseminated advances in arts, science, and technology to their hinterlands, so too the United States is seen by structural functionalists as doing the same for its hinterland, including Canada and less developed areas of the world.

Dependency. Conflict theorists are less persuaded of these mutual benefits and focus more on the political-economic nature of the relationship between metropolitan areas and their hinterlands. They argue that the benefits to the hinterland from this association go largely to a small, local, *indigenous elite* and to the *comprador elite*, the representatives of the metropolis who live in the hinterland and manage the economy. Furthermore, the relationship pressures the economy of the hinterland to become heavily specialized in the production of raw materials needed by the metropolis. Narrow economic diversification, particularly in the manufacturing sector, increases the strength of the relationship between metropolis and hinterland. This

Since about 1950, the world's urban population has been tripling every 50 years. In Canada, many of these new urbanites live in highrise apartment buildings like these in Vancouver's inner-city West End.

increases the dependency of the hinterland on the metropolis for goods and services that might have been produced locally. Conflict theorists see such economic dependency as leading to political powerlessness, retarded or even reversed industrial development, and the erosion of indigenous culture and its replacement with a mass culture that either justifies or obscures the whole arrangement. As well, the needs of the metropolis, not the interests of the hinterland, prevail. If the resources of the hinterland are nonrenewable (such as oil), the area risks not only underdevelopment, but also abandonment by the metropolis when the resources become depleted or obsolete (for detailed discussions see Innis, 1930, 1940; Frank, 1969; Wallerstein, 1974; Bell and Tepperman, 1979).

In Canada, the **dependency theory** is most often applied by Toronto-based nationalists to the relationship between this country and the United States (for example, J. Laxer, 1973; Warnock, 1974). However, it is important to note that on the international level, "Canada is in the 'semi-periphery' of the world economy" (Beaujot and McQuillan, 1982). Some parts of the country, notably southern Ontario and west Montreal, are considerably less peripheral than others. So the relationship between the urban industrial region of Canada and the rest of the nation can be viewed from the metropolis-hinterland perspective, too (Davis, 1971). For example, some historians believe that the Maritimes would have been better off if they had not become a satellite of Upper Canada and lost their potential for local industrialization, urbanization, economic and political independence, and cultural integrity (Acheson, 1977). Central Canadians protected their own manufacturing interests by imposing tariffs on competing items imported from the United States. So Maritimers had to pay more for manufactured goods than they would have paid if they had remained independent (see also Marsden and Harvey, 1979). A similar stance has been adopted by Quebec separatists, and in recent years by the increasingly wealthy and isolationist western Canadians.

From this viewpoint, the development and dissemination of Canadian nationalism reflects the struggle of central Canada with the United States for dominion over the Canadian hinterland (Berger, 1969, 1970). Like continentalist perspectives that overlook differences between Canada and the United States, nationalist arguments may trivialize or ignore regional differences and disparities within Canada. In fact, S.D. Clark (1966) has suggested that anti-Americanism in Canada has often been used to divert attention from regional disparity within the country by focusing discontent on an external threat. Unlike the continentalist argument, however, the nationalist argument implies that U.S. ties foster regionalism and that the people of the hinterland would be better off if they were less dependent on the United States.

This may or may not be accurate. Dependency theory argues that metropolitan areas benefit more than their hinterlands from the association, and such benefits wind up disproportionately either in the cities of central Canada or in the metropolitan regions of the United States. In either case, then, without industrial decentralization the Canadian hinterland will be relatively deprived.

At present, links among Canadian and American urban centers are stronger than those among more loosely coupled regions within Canada (Lithwick and Paquet, 1968; Caves and Reuber, 1969; Bourne, 1975). This suggests that insofar as the Canadian hinterland is dominated by metropolitan areas, these areas are located disproportionately in the United States.

Dependency theory can be applied on a world level to assess relationships among countries, on a national level to describe the relationship among regions within countries, or, as it was originally developed, on a regional level to characterize the relationship between the city and the hinterlands.

A Tale of Two Cities. The drift from the British to the American economic sphere had important effects on the urban structure of Canada. Although the rise of the west may yet change things, "Canada's metropolitan development has been a tale of two cities: Montreal and Toronto" (Laxer, 1975). Partly because of its location on the St. Lawrence, Montreal was the dominant metropolis during the early, British-ruled years. But, as our ties to the United States grew, Toronto's links to New York through the Great Lakes,

the Erie canal, and the railway system gave the Ontario capital an edge over Montreal as an exporter. This, and the richness of southern Ontario farmland, broke the commercial dominance of Montreal in the middle of the nineteenth century, and the ascendency of Toronto began (Spelt, 1955). Montreal's banks, with their London connections, continued to have a strong national influence well into the twentieth century. But after the Depression, the construction of American auto plants in southern Ontario greatly added to the power of Toronto. By the end of the Second World War, Montreal's banks and head offices began moving westward to Toronto (Spelt, 1973). This trend continued, and in 1976 metropolitan Toronto's population had finally surpassed Montreal's. Between 1976 and 1981 Toronto's metropolitan population grew another 7 per cent, reaching nearly 3 million. At the same time, Montreal's metropolitan population grew only .9 percent, to just over 2.8 million. However, the most impressive growth rates were registered by Alberta's oil-rich cities, reflecting the westward shift of the Canadian population (see Table 15-2). As in the past, the future of urban Canada may indeed be "a tale of two cities." But if current trends continue, they may be Calgary and Edmonton, not Montreal and Toronto.

Urban Ecology

Social scientists have a number of explanations for the ways in which individual cities grow. The most influential of these was developed by Ernest W. Burgess (1925) at the University of Chicago. His general orientation is known as **human ecology**, a term developed by Burgess and two of his colleagues, Robert E. Park and Roderick D. McKenzie. It refers to the application of ideas from plant and animal ecology to the study of the relationship between humans and their physical habitat (Park, Burgess, McKenzie, 1925; McKenzie, 1968).

The Concentric Zone Model. Burgess constructed a model of **concentric zones** and applied to it the following concepts from the ecology of nature: segregation, competition, invasion, succession, and natural areas.

TABLE 15-2. POPULATION FOR CENSUS METROPOLITAN AREAS, RANKED BY 1981 POPULATION SHOWING PERCENTAGE CHANGE, 1976 AND 1981

Rank	CMA	1976[1]	1981	Percentage Change
1	Toronto, Ont.	2,803,101	2,998,947	7.0
2	Montreal, Que.	2,802,547[2]	2,828,349	0.9
3	Vancouver, B.C.	1,166,348	1,268,183	8.7
4	Ottawa-Hull, Ont./Que.	693,288	717,978	3.6
5	Edmonton, Alta.	556,270[2]	657,057	18.1
6	Calgary, Alta.	471,397[2]	592,743	25.7
7	Winnipeg, Man.	578,217	584,842	1.2
8	Quebec, Que.	543,158	576,075	6.3
9	Hamilton, Ont.	529,371	542,095	2.4
10	St. Catharines-Niagara, Ont.	301,921	304,353	0.8
11	Kitchener, Ont.	272,158	287,801	5.8
12	London, Ont.	270,383	283,668	4.9
13	Halifax, N.S.	267,991	277,727	3.6
14	Windsor, Ont.	247,582	246,110	−0.6
15	Victoria, B.C.	218,250	233,481	7.0
16	Regina, Sask.	151,191	164,313	8.7
17	St. John's, Nfld.	145,400[2]	154,820	6.5
18	Oshawa, Ont.	135,196	154,217	14.1
19	Saskatoon, Sask.	133,793[2]	154,210	15.3
20	Sudbury, Ont.	157,030	149,923	−4.5
21	Chicoutimi-Jonquière, Que.	128,643	135,172	5.1
22	Thunder Bay, Ont.	119,253	121,379	1.8
23	Saint John, N.B.	112,974	114,048	1.0
24	Trois-Rivières, Que.	106,031[3]	111,453	5.1

[1] Based on 1981 area
[2] Adjusted figures due to boundary changes
[3] Defined as CMA for 1981 Census

SOURCE: *Statistics Canada Daily*. Tuesday, March 30, 1982, p. 3.

Segregation refers to a tendency for certain activity patterns (such as commercial or residential activities) or certain groups of people (such as income or ethnic groups) to cluster and try to segregate themselves by excluding other activities or groups from "their" territory. To the extent that they are successful they form a *natural area* (a relatively homogeneous neighborhood with respect to the specific activity or group).

Competition occurs when one activity or group attempts to invade the territory of another. To the extent that such an *invasion* is successful and the incumbent activity or group is driven out, *succession* has occurred.

Burgess used the city of Chicago as the basis for his model of concentric zones. To be appreciated, the model must be seen as dynamic rather than static. The concentric zones are not very good descriptions of the actual form of a city. (Few cities actually look like a bulls-eye, and when applied to Chicago itself almost half the model falls into Lake Michigan as shown in Figure 15-4.) Instead, the concentric zones describe different patterns of urban activities and their tendency to concentrate, segregate, and create natural areas. The competition between activities for scarce space, and the territorial invasion and succession of activities and people represent the growth patterns of urban areas.

Burgess' zones radiate from the center of the city:

I. The central business district (CBD), which in Chicago is known as the Loop

II. the zone of transition

Figure 15-4. Burgess' Concentric Zone Model Applied to Chicago

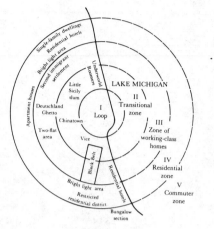

SOURCE: Redrawn from Burgess, Ernest W. "The growth of the city: an introduction to a research project," in George A. Theodorson (ed.), *Studies in Human Ecology*. Evanston, Ill.: Row, Peterson, 1961, p. 41.

III. the zone of working-people's houses
IV. the middle-class residential zone
V. the commuter zone

These five zones form the basis of the Burgess Model, although two additional zones have sometimes been included (Wilson and Schulz, 1978)
VI. peripheral agricultural areas
VII. the hinterland

Zone I is the central business district, the commercial as well as the geographic center of the city. Retail shopping areas, entertainment centers (night clubs, restaurants, theaters, hotels, and the like), and office buildings abound in the inner core of the CBD. The edge of this zone includes wholesale businesses, markets, and warehouses.

Because of its centrality, the land in Zone I is the most valuable in the city. In fact, this land is so expensive that only commercial enterprises usually have the combination of motivation and money necessary to buy it. In the competition for scarce space near the center of the city, then, commercial activities typically win over residential activities.

Zone II – the zone of transition – is where the action is. As the name suggests, this region is the battle zone, the arena for the competition between residential and commercial activities, with the latter usually destined to drive out the former. That is, the commercial activities in the CBD expand into a sector that formerly contained houses and related residential activities (child-rearing, house-related work, leisure activities, sleeping, and the like). An important effect of the invasion is the deterioration and devaluation of the areas as a residential environment. As residences devalue, they become a source of cheap rental housing. Speculators hold them for the potential commercial value of the land on which they are situated. In the interest of minimizing the costs of holding such property, they spend little or no money to maintain the buildings. At the same time, owners attempt to maximize the number of renters these buildings contain. The result is the crowded, deteriorated housing which we call slums.

It is likely, but not certain, that the invasion of commercial activities will result in succession, segregation, and a natural commercial area. Slums can endure when the expected commercial expansion fails to occur.

The cheap housing in Zone II permits people with low incomes to live in the city: the poor and unemployed, immigrants with little money, the physically and mentally handicapped, and others who survive through illegal commercial activities (mugging, theft, and the sale of illicit commodities and services such as drugs and prostitution). Because of this, the transitional zone has been seen as "disorganized."

As waves of immigrants arrive in the city, they often locate in the cheap housing of the transitional zone. Arrival of members of new ethnic groups amounts to the invasion of an area. This prompts locals to move out in order to maintain the integrity of their own ethnic group. As the members of ethnic groups become able to afford better housing, the pull of purely residential zones combines with the push from invading groups to bring them out of Zone II. In this way, just as commercial activities invade, compete with, and succeed residential activities, so too do some ethnic groups invade the territories of others and succeed the original inhabitants of the neighborhood.

Zone III contains inexpensive houses often inhabited by the upwardly mobile children of immigrants in the transitional zone. (In Chicago there are typically semi-detached houses.) The upwardly mobile children of the residents of Zone III, in turn, would try to move further out to the suburbs, into the commuter zone.

Zone IV is the zone of better residences, where the middle class lives; Zone V is the commuter zone, where people with cars live in middle, upper-middle, and upper-class suburbs. Most of the residences in zones IV and V are single, detached houses.

Like all ideal types, the concentric zone model reflects reality in some times and places better than it does in others. But this model does allow some important general insights into the processes and form of urban growth.

For example, Burgess is accurate in his observation that activities and groups tend to concentrate within specific areas of cities. In fact, recent studies show that over the last few decades socioeconomic and ethnic residential segregation has increased in the cities of both the United States and Canada, especially in the larger ones (Marston and Darroch, 1971; Richmond, 1972; Balakrishnan, 1976, 1979). Also, Burgess was generally correct in noting that the socioeconomic status of urbanites increases directly with the distance of their residences from the city center. That is, in the United States, higher status people have been more inclined to live farther from the center of cities than have people in lower socioeconomic strata.

Although these observations seem accurate for many North American cities, it must be emphasized that Canada and the United States are industrial societies whose cities are relatively new. In other countries where the development of cities preceeded industrialization, or where industrialization has not occurred, these patterns are not always found. For example, in pre-industrial cities, slums are more likely to be on the outskirts of the city. The residences of the wealthy are located downtown. The general tendency for commercial and residential activities to be segregated, with commerce at the center of the city, seems also to be a modern industrial phenomenon. In pre-industrial cities many shopkeepers live in the same building in which they conduct commercial activities (Sjoberg, 1960).

The concentric zone model should be applied with care. Both cultural constraints and the physical environment have occasionally produced incongruities between the Burgess model and urban realities. For example, cultural constraints in the form of zoning laws have often kept commercial activities from pushing into residential areas. Also, in a number of North American cities, there have recently been successful attempts to reclaim for residential purposes deteriorated sections of both commercial and transitional areas. (This is known as gentrification.) Toronto's Cabbagetown is exemplary in this respect. So, commerce need not always invade and succeed residential areas.

In other instances, the physical environment may prevent the operation of the forces Burgess observed in Chicago. Vancouver, for example, bounded on one side by mountains and on the other by the sea, appears to have developed an outer ring containing both commercial and residential sections. These are connected and contain residents who neither work nor live "in town" (Hardwick, 1971).

Although the concentric zone model was developed in Chicago in the 1920s, it continues to be relevant. The patterns of segregation, competition, invasion, and succession Burgess described can still be observed in many North American cities. However, application of the model is restricted. It does not fit pre-industrial cities or smaller cities and towns. Furthermore, topographic factors and cultural values can produce important deviations from the Burgess model, even in large industrial cities. The concentric zone model should be seen as an ideal type; it generally illustrates the operation of certain ecological principles in large cities in industrial societies, in particular the United States. Seen this way, the model has value.

The Sector Model. Social scientists have produced other models of city growth in an attempt to improve on the concentric rings. Hoyt (1939) proposed a **sector model** of urban expansion. It emphasizes transportation arteries rather than concentric rings. Like Burgess, Hoyt believed that activities and groups are segregated into natural areas, and that cities expand outward.

Suburbanization

Suburbanization refers to an increase in the proportion of urban residents who live on the periphery of central cities. Suburbanization in the United States took off with the baby boom in the period following World War II. By 1970, about one-third of the urban population lived in incorporated or unincorporated areas on the edge of cities. The suburbanization of the United States has largely resulted from migration from the cities.

In addition to this absolute growth in the suburban population, many of the largest central cities have been declining in population since the 1960s. This decline, of course, helps to account for the dramatic increase in the proportion of urbanites living in suburban areas. Crime, racial violence, air pollution, and other urban problems have been important push or motivating factors for millions who have migrated to the suburbs in the United States.

Although Canadian cities are relatively free from the problems that plague the inner cities of the United States, great numbers of Canadians have also been moving to the suburbs in recent years. In fact, by 1976 over half (50.8 percent) the population of Canada's metropolitan areas lived in the suburbs. (For details on the suburbanization of the Canadian population see Kalbach and McVey, 1979.)

It is important to realize that the suburban population of a given metro area cannot always be calculated by subtracting the city population from the metro population. For example, in 1981 the population of metropolitan Calgary was 599 743. So was the population of the city itself. This does not mean that Calgary has no outer fringe. It simply means that the political jurisdiction of the city extends well beyond the edge of the city as a physical entity. In cases like this you will often see a sign in the middle of nowhere welcoming you to a particular city, which may or may not be visible in the distance. This most often happens with newer cities in the west.

In contrast to the Calgary situation, there is metropolitan Toronto with a 1981 population of 2.99 million. The population of the city was 599 217. This suggests that the Toronto metro area resembles a doughnut and is about 80 percent suburbs. However, what it also reflects is the borough system of the metropolitan government. Old suburbs such as Etobicoke and York have not been annexed by Toronto, even though after years of urban expansion they are no longer on the fringe of the metro area. They are self-governing boroughs.

Types of suburbs can be distinguished on the basis of their developmental histories. For example, some suburbs began as villages and may have grown into small autonomous towns before being annexed or engulfed by the expanding city. Other suburbs gradually emerged on the periphery of cities, while still others were created by developers as "instant communities" on previously unoccupied land. (Like modern cemeteries, the latter are typically given names promising meadows, trees, streams, and other symbols of rural nostalgia. But names such as Meadowvale, Parkdale, and Mount Pleasant are more likely to represent wishful thinking than an accurate description of past, present, or even future topography.

These three types of suburb differ in their patterns of social life as well as in their developmental histories. The sudden creation of the instant suburb usually results in a relatively homogeneous area with respect to age, life cycle, income, and, of course, length of residence in the area. On the other hand, the annexed village contains both long-time residents of the village and newcomers from the city; these residents differ not only in the length of time they have lived in the suburb, but also in age, life cycle, income, education, and other important variables. This results in the presence of different, and often competing, interest groups in the area (Fischer, 1976). (For an interesting description of community divisions and conflict arising from such heterogeneity in engulfed suburbs, see Westhues and Sinclair, 1974.)

Source:

References are to Kalbach, W.E., and Wayne G. McVey. *The Demographic Bases of Canadian Society*, 2nd ed. Toronto: McGraw-Hill, 1979; Fischer, Claude S. *The Urban Experience*. New York: Harcourt, Brace, Jovanovich, 1976; Westhues, Kenneth, and Peter R. Sinclair. *Village in Crisis*. Toronto: Holt, Rinehart and Winston, 1974.

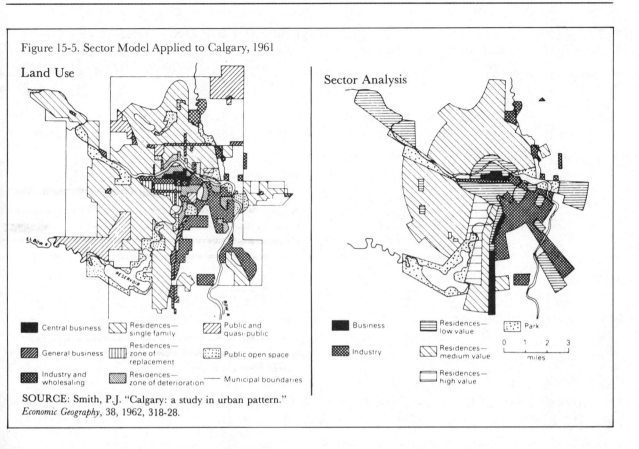

Figure 15-5. Sector Model Applied to Calgary, 1961

Land Use

Sector Analysis

■ Central business	◪ Residences— single family	▨ Public and quasi-public
▨ General business	⦀ Residences— zone of replacement	⬚ Public open space
▨ Industry and wholesaling	◪ Residences— zone of deterioration	— Municipal boundaries

■ Business	▤ Residences— low value	⬚ Park
▨ Industry	◪ Residences— medium value	
	▭ Residences— high value	

0 1 2 3
miles

SOURCE: Smith, P.J. "Calgary: a study in urban pattern." *Economic Geography*, 38, 1962, 318-28.

But Hoyt argued that the commercial and residential areas and different ethnic and income groups expanded from the center of cities in wedge-shaped sections, along natural boundaries and transporation arteries.

The sector model accounts for the existence of high-rent residential areas near the center of cities (such as Forest Hill in Toronto and Westmount in Montreal) and accentuates the importance of traffic arteries. In this way the sector model, as illustrated in Figure 15-5, is an improvement over the concentric zone model, which was developed at a time when traffic arteries, especially highways, had less impact than they have today.

The Multiple Nuclei Model. Like Burgess and Hoyt, Harris and Ullman (1945) believed that activities and groups were segregated within areas of cities. But Harris and Ullman rejected the idea that these natural areas radiated from the center of the city in either concentric rings or sectors. Instead, as Figure 14-6 shows, they saw the city as a series of centers, or *nuclei*, that attract similar activity patterns or social groups, and repel others. For example, the University of Western Ontario in northwest London and the University of Alberta in south-central Edmonton are the nuclei for several smaller colleges and schools, a number of research institutes, a university hospital (related to the medical school), a variety of student-related service centers (such as bookstores, recreational facilities, and, of course, taverns), as well as both faculty and student housing. Other nuclei emerge around mutually supporting (or symbiotic) commercial activities (such as law firms, insurance companies, and real estate offices), industrial activities, and residences.

The **multiple nuclei model** is the most recently developed of the three models of urban expansion. Perhaps this is the reason it seems most applicable to those cities that have developed with the automobile

Figure 15-6. Multiple Nuclei Model of a City

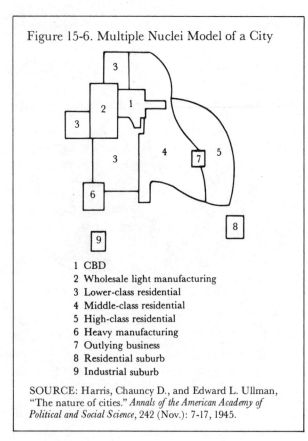

1 CBD
2 Wholesale light manufacturing
3 Lower-class residential
4 Middle-class residential
5 High-class residential
6 Heavy manufacturing
7 Outlying business
8 Residential suburb
9 Industrial suburb

SOURCE: Harris, Chauncy D., and Edward L. Ullman, "The nature of cities." *Annals of the American Academy of Political and Social Science*, 242 (Nov.): 7-17, 1945.

as a major means of transportation. The car has allowed a much greater degree of decentralization of facilities and city sectors.

The concentric zone model, the sector model, and the multiple nuclei model are three ideal types. Each stresses different aspects of city growth. They are alike in portraying competition, segregation, and natural areas as characteristic of urban areas, and all three were developed from observations of relatively new cities in an advanced capitalist society. The models differ in the extent to which they emphasize the invasion and succession of economic activities in residential areas, and the relation of the different areas to each other. No single model perfectly fits any specific city. However, all three models emphasize factors that to varying degrees affect the expansion of all cities, at least in the United States.

Canadian and U.S. Cities. It is always tempting for sociologists to generalize from the observations they have made. After all, general rather than specific statements are a goal of social science. But sociologists who study cities must be careful. Most of the published observations we read were made in the U.S., not Canada. The similarities between the two societies are certainly great, probably much greater than the differences. But there are differences. And some of these affect the nature of Canadian and U.S. cities.

Canadian and U.S. cities differ in several important ways. First, the former are higher in density and are more compact than their U.S. counterparts. Cities in the United States are troubled by urban sprawl to a much greater degree than those in Canada. Probably because of their tax breaks on mortgage interest, a higher proportion of people in the U.S. live in their own single, detached houses (Goldberg and Mercer, 1980).

Second, like their U.S. counterparts, Canadian cities have lost population from their core areas in recent years. However, the growth of Canadian suburbs has involved neither the widespread departure of inner-city taxpayers nor the outright abandonment of residential housing. As a result, the centers of Canadian urban areas have stayed economically, physically, and socially viable. In fact, the core areas typically contain the most desirable (and expensive) housing. In contrast, the core areas of many U.S. cities contain a visible underclass who cannot leave because they are unemployed, or poorly paid. The rate of violent crime is six times greater in the U.S. than in Canada, and much of the criminal activity occurs in these areas. For their part, Canadian cities are relatively safe and are perceived as such by their residents (Bourne, 1975). The socio-economic and criminal activity differences between the suburbs and cities are much greater in the U.S. than in Canada.

Third, Canadians use public transit much more often than do their southern neighbors. The lower rate of crime and the compact form of Canadian cities probaby have a lot to do with this. However, the U.S. society may also be more auto-oriented than ours. There are more cars and, accordingly, more highways. The federally funded freeways that cover U.S. cities are another distinctive feature of that country's urban areas (Goldberg and Mercer, 1980). Whether this orientation to autos reflects a cultural difference, or whether it is another manifestation of the higher standard of living in the U.S. is unclear.

These differences indicate that all the models of city growth developed in the U.S. probably fit their cities better than ours. This is not to say that the models are irrelevant for Canadian cities. It simply means that they should be applied with care, and perhaps modified for the Canadian context. Even within Canada, cities differ dramatically in form, so a particular model will fit some better than others. Montreal, for example, is a compact city of apartments and renters (Linteau and Robert, 1977). In contrast, Toronto is far more American, a sprawling city of single, detached houses, homeowners, and highways.

URBANISM

Besides trying to explain the origin, growth, and proliferation of cities at the *macro* level of analysis (large units of analysis such as the society, or community), sociologists have given a great deal of attention to the *micro* level (the effects of urban environments on social life and individual well-being). These studies of individuals and small groups involve more social-psychological than purely sociological orientations. However, the same variables (environment, technology, structure, and culture) employed at the macro level can be used as limiting and motivating factors in explaining things at the micro level.

Urbanism refers to the attitudes, beliefs, and behaviors or life-styles of people who live in cities. Many sociologists think that there is a great difference in the life-styles of residents of urban and rural environments. Furthermore, the changes required of people who move from one to the other can produce a variety of social psychological problems. Some social scientists believe that it is urbanism itself, rather than the change from a rural life-style to city living, that causes psychological disorders among urban dwellers and social disorganization. In any case, sociologists have been inclined to argue that there are important differences in rural and urban life-styles.

Gemeinschaft and Gesellschaft

In 1887, the German sociologist Ferdinand Tönnies produced one of the first analyses of rural-urban differences. He argued that rural social organization involves small populations; close, personal relationships between people, most of whom share common values and a respect for tradition; a collective orientation or sense of identity; informal social control; and strong kinship ties to extended families. Tönnies referred to such systems as **Gemeinschaft** ("community") organizations.

On the other hand, urban systems contain many people with different values and more individualistic attitudes. Interpersonal relationships tend to be temporary, impersonal, and specifically focused. Nuclear, rather than extended family orientations predominate, and social control is formal, with laws, courts, and police. Tönnies called this type of organization **Gesellschaft** ("association") in its orientation.

In rural areas and small towns, people are likely to know one another in a variety of contexts and statuses. For example, your dentist may also be a client or customer of yours, belong to the same clubs or friendship groups as you do, live in the same neighborhood, and be married to your cousin. When you go to the dentist, your relationship is more than just that of dentist and patient. You have a number of common interests, and lots to talk about (if you can talk with a hand in your mouth). In contrast, in large cities a visit to your dentist is likely to be the only time you see each other in a six-month period. You are not likely to know each other in other contexts, and apart from the weather, have little in common. Marvin Harris (1981) argues that because of this you will get better service in the rural setting, where people are more likely to care. A botched extraction or filling may deprive a dentist of a golfing partner and friend as well as a patient.

Tönnies' work was the basis for a number of similar rural-urban analyses. Durkheim's "mechanical" and "organic solidarity" (see Chapter 10), Miner's "folk-urban continuum," and Parsons' pre-industrial and industrial "pattern variables" parallel Tönnies' views of the differences between rural and urban life. However, the most important intellectual offspring of Tönnies' work is probably Lous Wirth's article, "Urbanism as a Way of Life," written in 1938.

Urbanism as a Way of Life

Wirth drew heavily on the earlier ideas of Georg Simmel (published in 1950), as well as those of Tönnies in developing his argument. Simmel argued that urban environments involve a continuous and intense bombardment of stimuli. The sounds, sights, and smells of the city, along with the press of large numbers of people, form a combined assault on the nervous systems of its residents. According to Simmel, urbanites cope with such high levels of stimulation by developing techniques to filter the onslaught of information and noise. People in cities, therefore, learn to ignore irrelevant information as they engage in their routine work and leisure activities. Urbanites can sleep with the sounds of traffic in the background, ignore intimate conversations occurring between other people within listening distance, and treat most of those with whom they interact with a minimum of interpersonal involvement.

As we noted before, cities contain large numbers of people in specialized and interrelated roles. According to Simmel, coordination and planning are necessary to bring the right people together in a particular place at a specific time. For example, the removal of your tonsils usually requires the coordinated efforts of at least one physician, an anesthetist, several nurses, and many other technicians and workers to prepare the equipment and the room for the event. All these people, in addition to you and your tonsils, must meet at a specific location at a specific time. Without this coordination, the operation could not be performed. Such coordination of specialists and locations produces pressure on urbanites to be punctual. Because of this, the residents of urban areas are more often in a hurry than are their country cousins. So life in the city is sometimes seen as a rat race.

If city folks invest emotion and time in every person they meet, take notice of every sound they hear, and pay attention to every new or different sight they encounter, they will always be behind schedule. Both individuals and social systems would break down. In order to cope, people in cities move and think quickly. They learn to act on little information and avoid becoming bogged down with details.

In Simmel's view, the more relaxed, personal, and spontaneous way of living in rural societies simply does not allow the individual to deal effectively with the demands of the city. People in rural and urban areas think differently and engage in different lifestyles, and those who migrate from rural to urban areas must learn to live like urbanites, and do as the Romans do. (For an updated elaboration of Simmel's argument see Milgram, 1970.)

Wirth (1938) extended Simmel's argument and focused more on the social than on the psychological side of urban life. Wirth believed that urbanism was a type of social organization found in the city. He thought that the elements of the urban environment that have the greatest impact on social life are the size, density, and social heterogeneity of the urban population, and he based his model on these three variables. Wirth argued that these factors reduce community integration, encourage self-interest, and produce superficial, impersonal and segmented social relationships. This leads to psychological withdrawal, anomie (normlessness), and low morale. Wirth's picture of life in the city, then, is largely negative.

The views of Simmel and Wirth are examples of *environmental determinism*, the idea that the physical environment can affect or determine people's attitudes, behaviors, or conditions. The urban environment is seen to cause people to be different from their rural counterparts. This is not, however, the only way sociologists explain rural-urban differences in life-style. Other sociologists believe that differences between people in one environment and another reflect cultural or structural factors and *selection*. Both the Wirth and the selection models are shown in vector form in Figure 15-7.

Selection

Herbert Gans (1962a, 1962b, 1967) argues that Wirth overstated the impact of the urban environment on social life. Gans believes that any relationships that size, density, and social heterogeneity of populations have to urbanism are more likely to reflect **selection** than causation. He also suggests that large heterogeneous cities are made up of small homogeneous neighborhoods. Gans called these neighborhoods urban villages and argued that the people who live in them

City Size and Social Life

Just as groups are more than the sum of their parts, "Big cities are not just bigger versions of smaller ones, but different things" (Simmons and Simmons, 1974:32).

The size of urban populations is directly related to a variety of socially relevant factors, some good and some not so good. Large cities can supply specialized goods and services that smaller cities and towns cannot. For example, if only one out of every five hundred people is interested in paying for a massage, and two hundred clients are required to sustain a massage parlor, cities of fewer than one hundred thousand people (the "threshold" population for massage parlors) will in most cases be unable to support such a service. People in smaller communities, then, must travel to larger cities for this service. Fisher (1976) points out that the same principle holds for the formation of special interest groups. That is, individuals with relatively unusual interests, such as spouse-swapping, body-building, or Zen Buddhism, are more likely to find people with similar interests in large rather than small cities. As a result, voluntary associations catering to these activities are rarely found in small communities, and larger cities are more likely to attract and contain visible clusters of people with atypical or even deviant preferences.

The optimum size of cities has for centuries been debated by philosophers, planners, and social scientists. Estimates range from Plato's 5040 to Le Corbusier's 3 million. Unfortunately, the ideal size for one factor is not necessarily the most appropriate for another. For example, a city of 1 million is more likely to have a higher crime rate than a city of 100,000, but a city of 1 million is also likely to contain a university, a museum, a symphony, or a zoo. Whether these facilities are worth a higher crime rate involves a judgment of value.

In Canada the cities that contain the most satisfied citizens seem to be cities of medium size. For example, Victoria, St. Catharines, Ottawa-Hull, London, and Saskatoon are the five most popular places to live, at least from the viewpoints of the residents. However, it is important to recognize that the differences in level of satisfaction between the most and least popular cities is small. Further, even the people in the least popular urban area (Saint John) are reasonably pleased with their city. In view of this, and remembering the importance of self selection, there is no guarantee that if the citizens of that New Brunswick city, especially the young ones, were all moved to Victoria they would prefer living there, since Victoria contains a high proportion of older people. Most people, for whatever reasons, have chosen to live in larger cities and not moved and "voted with their feet" for the smaller ones.

According to the *Financial Post*, this is the ranking of Canadian cities by satisfaction of residents:

1. Victoria
2. St. Catharines
3. Ottawa-Hull
4. London
5. Saskatoon
6. Kitchener
7. Charlottetown
8. Quebec
9. Toronto
10. Halifax
11. Vancouver
12. St. John's
13. Chicoutimi
14. Calgary
15. Thunder Bay
16. Winnipeg
17. Edmonton
18. Sudbury
19. Hamilton
20. Montreal
21. Windsor
22. Regina
23. Saint John

Source:

Simmons, James, and Robert Simmons. *Urban Canada*, 2nd ed. Toronto: Copp Clark, 1974, p. 32; Fischer, Claude S. *The Urban Experience*. New York: Harcourt, Brace, Jovanovich, 1976; Webb, Stephen D. "Crime and the division of labour." *American Journal of Sociology*, 18:643-56, 1976; Gibbs, Jack, and Maynard Ericson. "Crime rates of American cities in an ecological context." *American Journal of Sociology*, 82(3):605-20, 1976; Wilson, James Q. "The police and the delinquent in two cities," *in* Stanton Wheeler (ed.), *Controlling Delinquents*. New York: John Wiley, 1968. *Financial Post*, August 4, 1979, p. 8.

are protected from any impact that size, density, and heterogeneity may have.

Selection theorists allow that situations or behaviors and places may be related, but they do not see physical environment as a cause. For example, the area of a city with the highest number of deaths is probably the area containing the largest number of hospitals. But it is unlikely that the hospitals are killing people. Instead, many of those who are about to die are taken to hospitals. So people with certain traits can move to a specific area, while others stay where they are or move elsewhere. This is selection.

Earlier we saw that some areas of the city, like the transitional zone, contain cheap, high-density housing and socially heterogeneous populations. The people who live there are not wealthy, and many are plagued

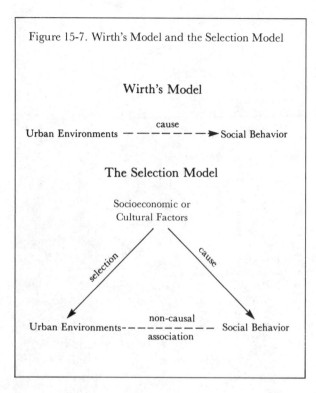

Figure 15-7. Wirth's Model and the Selection Model

Wirth's Model

Urban Environments — — — — — cause — — — → Social Behavior

The Selection Model

Socioeconomic or
Cultural Factors

selection   *cause*

Urban Environments — — — — — — — — Social Behavior

non-causal
association

For example, the urban industrial social structure is highly specialized and contains a great number of occupations that require large amounts of training or experience. This specialization is much less pronounced in rural, less industrialized social systems. Rural workers must often engage in a wide variety of tasks, rather than in a few highly specialized ones. Farmers and fishermen, for example, must have a wide range of skills that extend far beyond pure farming or fishing. Both must know carpentry, machine repair and maintenance, first aid, and so forth. In contrast, a worker in an urban automobile plant requires specific skills to build one part of a car. When other workers combine their special skills, cars take shape on an assembly line. In this way, then, urban industrial societies try to maximize efficiency with systems of interrelated, specialized jobs.

Rural and urban economic structures affect the way people behave in their work. These structures, rather than the physical environment, may affect other aspects of social and psychological life. For example, discomfort and psychological disorders may result from spending long hours at a specialized task on an assembly line. Psychological strain and other maladies, then, could be more common in urban than rural environments, but due to specialized occupational pressures, rather than the demands of the urban environment.

Furthermore, the different requirements that rural occupational structures make on individuals probably provide an important basis for the selection of people into the two environments. Persons with interests and/or abilities in a wide range of occupational activities will be in greater demand in rural than in urban areas. In fact, people with diversified skills often find so little demand for their abilities in cities that they are unemployed or paid very low wages in menial occupations. According to S.D. Clark, such people constitute the "new urban poor" (Clark, 1978).

These, then, are the major questions social scientists have about the effects of the urban environment on people. Some, like Simmel, Wirth, and Milgram, argue that elements of the urban environment actually shape and determine human attitudes and behaviors. Others, like Gans, argue that social and cultural factors, rather than the environment, affect people's lives.

with a variety of poverty-related troubles. In contrast, the suburbs are typically homogeneous, low in density, and contain middle-or upper-income populations. Density and heterogeneity, then, are related to an array of problems. But in this example, income determines both residence (through selection) and suffering as well. To conclude that density or heterogeneity is causing these problems, is a spurious interpretation. From a selection standpoint, then, the physical environment is merely a place where action occurs. It is not important as an independent variable.

The selection argument can also be used to explain rural-urban differences in behavior. According to Simmel (1950) and Wirth (1938), cities cause people to behave in particular ways, and therefore people in rural and urban areas are different. A selection argument denies the causal impact of the environment. Instead, demographic, cultural, and socioeconomic variables cause people to behave in specific ways and to either stay in rural areas or migrate to cities.

Population Density and Social Pathology

In 1962 John Calhoun found that when rats are subjected to high population density for long periods of time they change their behaviors. They engage in aberrant activities: rape, aggression, asexuality, careless mothering, infanticide, and cannibalism, among others. Calhoun attributed these behaviors, which he considered symptoms of social pathology, to excessive population density.

It seems obvious that extremely high population densities *can* cause all sorts of unpleasant experiences for rats and humans. The relevant question then concerns the *level* of population density it takes to produce symptoms of crowding in people, and what people *do* about it.

Most research on humans has produced conflicting results, but the general absence of extreme social pathology in areas of the world with relatively high densities (like Hong Kong and Calcutta) suggests that even higher densities are probably required before people begin to behave like Calhoun's rats (Gillis, 1979a).

Unlike rats, people develop techniques enabling them to overcome many unpleasant aspects of their physical environments. They have come up with a variety of ways of "cocooning" or protecting themselves from stimulus overload (Altman, 1975). For example, watching television may be a way of psychologically withdrawing from potentially unpleasant surroundings such as those with high population densities (Gillis, 1979b).

Population density probably does affect people, but the types and levels of density in the Calhoun experiment have little relevance for understanding what the effects are on people or why they occur. In any case, Canadians need not worry too much about becoming cannibals, at least not because of excessively high population density.

Source:

Calhoun, John B. "Population density and social pathology." *Scientific American*, 206:139-48, 1962; Gillis, A.R., "Household density and human crowding: unravelling a non-linear relationship." *Journal of Population*, 2(2):104-17, 1979a; Altman, Irwin. *The Environment and Social Behavior.* Monterey, Calif.: Brooks/Cole, 1975; Gillis, A.R. "Coping with crowding: television, patterns of activity, and adaptation to high density environments." *The Sociological Quarterly*, 20:267-77, 1979b; Newman, Oscar. *Defensible Space.* New York: Macmillan, 1972.

Environmental Opportunities and Constraints

Michelson (1976) has developed a viewpoint that falls between the environmental determinist and social selection perspectives. He suggests that persons with particular life-styles are attracted to specific environments and repelled by others. This is because particular places discourage or inhibit certain kinds of behaviors, and people who engage in these behaviors will avoid these environments. In housing, for example, there is usually a lack of fit between workshop activities and highrise apartments. Few highrise buildings provide either adequate soundproofing or the space these workshop activities require. As a result, people committed to the pursuit of this hobby will be pressured to select more appropriate residences.

Similarly, the suburban housing environment is often seen as the most conducive of home-centered and child-oriented styles of life. For this reason couples with young children usually prefer living in single, detached houses in the suburbs than in other types of housing in the city. According to S.D. Clark (1966), it is more the desire for an affordable, single, detached house than the suburban environment that seems to attract young married people to the suburbs. On the other hand, people with fewer or older children are often less child-oriented and are more likely to enjoy the facilities of a downtown environment as a place to live. (For discussions of the relationship between life cycle and housing environment, see Clark, 1966; and Michelson, 1976, 1977.) In this view there are relationships between specific behavior patterns, general styles of life, and the urban environment. The physical environment is neither irrelevant, as the selection argument suggests, nor a determinant, as Simmel and Wirth described it.

Michelson's (1976) view of the relationship between environment and behavior on the micro level is the same as the one we took earlier in looking at the origin of cities. That is, the physical environment can act as a limiter, and prevent people from doing things. This is the case for building cities as well as for workshop activities in the home. The physical environment does not so much motivate human behavior, as Wirth (1938) suggested, as it limits or allows activity to occur. Again, some environments are necessary (if not sufficient) for the occurrence of certain behaviors. Warm climates or flat topography limit the possibility of alpine skiing, and highrise apartments discourage or inhibit boat-building as a hobby. Because of this, statistical associations can be found between environments and behavior.

Cities and Social Networks

Although social scientists have several explanations for rural-urban differences in attitudes, behaviors, and conditions, it is unclear exactly what differences actually exist between rural and urban life-styles. For example, the social isolation, psychological withdrawal, and anomie that Wirth (1938) attributed to urbanites is also found in rural populations (Leighton, 1959). It is not at all clear that such disorders are more prevalent among urban than among rural populations (Webb and Collette, 1977, 1979; Crothers, 1979). This probably means that, like life in the city, life for many people in rural areas is no bed of roses. The strain of the assembly line may be more than matched by the physical and mental strain of farming, fishing, and the like. The belief that life is somehow better in the countryside probably reflects romantic nostalgia for a rural past, an increasing ignorance of many of the harsher respects of country life, and a tendency to take for granted many urban conveniences, such as high pay, access to specialized medical care, dental care, and education.

If characterizations of rural life have been too favorable, most descriptions of urban life have been too unfavorable (White and White, 1962). Urban life seems less atomized or anomic than Wirth and the Chicago school believed. Jacobs (1961), Wellman (1979), Reiss (1959), and others argue that city folks have friends, too, and are involved in important social networks that are analogues to communities. Just because these

networks are not physically indentifiable, like small towns and villages, does not preclude their existence. Instead, such social networks may flourish in urban areas as "communities without propinquity" (Webber, 1963; Gillis and Whitehead, 1970). Even extended families with frequent and intense interaction are maintained in cities, although residences may be physically distant (Young and Willmot, 1957; Pineo, 1971). People in cities may indeed be less likely to be friends with the next door neighbors. But the reason for such unneighborly behavior may have less to do with the size, density, and social heterogeneity of the urban population than it has to do with the fact that city people frequently change residence. This results in friends and relations being widely dispersed, and also gives people less time to get to know their neighbors. In small rural communities intimate contacts are more likely to live nearby because they move less often. In any case, people in cities seem to draw their friends more from their place of work or their voluntary associations (recreational clubs) than from their neighborhoods.

City dwellers are not as friendly or helpful to strangers as are rural residents either (Fischer, 1981; Franck, 1980). This, and the fact that urbanites are not very friendly with their neighbors, could lead one to think of the city as socially cold. But it is not. City folks merely draw a sharper distinction between friends and strangers and have a larger proportion of friends who do not live close to them. These represent important differences in the form of rural and urban friendship ties, rather than differences in their number or strength.

Differences in individual and group life in rural and urban areas may have been more dramatic when Wirth published "Urbanism as a Way of Life" in 1938. At that time, many of the residents of Chicago had been raised in rural areas, and the urbanism Wirth described may have been their way of adapting to what, for them, was an unfamiliar environment. Most North Americans are now considerably more familiar with urban environments, both from firsthand and second-hand experience. The mass media, especially television, bring urban values, beliefs, and behaviors to rural regions. Just as many urbanites are now fans of "country" music, many rural residents may adopt urban life-styles without actually spending much time in cities. As a result, rural and urban styles of life many have converged over the last few decades.

Finally, there is evidence that North American cities have changed in theoretically important ways since Wirth's time. More and more people are moving to smaller, socially homogeneous suburbs, and the centers of cities are declining in population size and density. Reductions in size, density, and heterogeneity of urban (and suburban) environments may have all but eliminated the social and psychological impact of these variables (Guterman, 1969). However, for some city dwellers, density and heterogeneity may still cause malaise. For example, people who have little money and few housing alternatives often have to live in areas where density and heterogeneity are high. When this happens they are more likely to suffer from psychological strain. So the combination of Wirth's factors and an inability to escape may produce the effects he observed in Chicago on a more widespread basis (Gillis, 1983).

Urban Deviance

Sociologists and criminologists generally agree that the rate of crime is higher in urban than in rural areas, and that the larger the city, the higher its crime rate is likely to be (Webb, 1972; Fischer, 1976; Gibbs and Ericson, 1976). Several explanations are feasible.

One viewpoint, drawn from the arguments of Simmel and Wirth, centers on the freedom and anonymity found on city streets. Urbanites seem more tolerant of non-conformity (Stephan and McMullin, 1982), and are less likely to get involved in the problems of strangers. Furthermore, bystander indiference not only allows deviants to get away with their behaviors, such indifference may even provoke deviance. Many of the strange sights and activities seen in the city may be expressions of individualism and attempts to gain recognition, to be a "somebody" (Rainwater, 1966). Because this is hard to do with an audience of blasé urbanites, some efforts go beyond the bizarre to damaging property and shocking or injuring passersby.

A nude pedestrian and nobody pays attention. According to some social scientists, urbanites learn to avoid stimulus overload by ignoring many of the things that go on around them.

This view suggests that both creativity and expressive crime can come from the same source. In fact, creativity and deviance can be hard to distinguish. The graffitti covering New York subway cars can be seen as an artistic and stylized form of vandalism. Street musicians often break local laws when they perform, and the shocking affectations of punk rockers and skin-heads may be the precursors of tomorrow's fashions. Even the Hell's Angels can be seen as a sometimes dangerous manifestation of this "hey look at me!" phenomenon. They are somewhere between a loose-knit band of demented thugs and modern knights, cultural symbols representing romance and freedom (Thompson, 1968).

If anonymity increases with the size of localities, then, the expression argument not only accounts for differences between rural and urban areas, but also for differences between small and large cities. Furthermore, once areas become known as centers of expressive deviance, they may attract colorful characters and repel more conservative people. On a broad scale, California can be seen as a mecca for both bizzare and creative people. On a more specific level, San Francisco and New York probably attract non-conformists for this reason, and on an even more confined level, areas of cities do the same. Greenwich Village in New York has attracted strange people for years. In the 1960s the Haight-Ashbury area of San Francisco drew "hippies" from all over the continent. So did Yorkville in Toronto; now the deviant service center in Toronto is the Yonge Street strip. Selection, then, may also account for some of the deviance we see in rural and urban areas. The adventurous go where the action is. In so doing they deprive their home area of their eccentricities which are added to what Baudelaire calls "le chaos des vivantes cités" – the chaos of the living cities.

Although Thrasher (1927) argued that deviance can be expressive and even fun, most of his colleagues in the Chicago school believed that deviance was the result of the breakdown of social order. In 1972 Oscar Newman produced an interesting variant of this argument. He suggested that some types of urban architecture prevent surveillance and control in neighborhoods, and even within apartment buildings. High walls, underground parking areas, long corridors, and hidden spaces such as stairwells discourage or physically prevent residents from feeling responsible for what happens in these places. Criminals can lurk behind walls or in stairwells and loiter in hallways where they are neither bothered by the police nor the residents. Because of these design factors associated with high-density housing, some areas of the city have higher rates of crime than others (Gillis, 1974).

Newman's view of the action of physical environment is similar to Michelson's and Bronowski's, discussed earlier. That is, the physical environment, in this case urban architecture, can prevent or allow action, rather than motivate it. Law-abiding people are not driven to thoughts of mayhem by the sight of a stairwell. But someone with mugging or rape on his mind may be deterred by the absence of a secluded space.

Although Newman's view accounts for differences in crime rates among buildings, neighborhoods, and areas of the city, other explanations also fit the data. One of these is drawn from the symbolic interactionist tradition.

Areas of the city with high-density housing by definition contain a lot of people. Because of this, the police pay more attention to them as likely trouble spots. In contrast, it makes little organizational sense to deploy many police in low density areas. There are neither many potential victims nor offenders in these locations. Consequently, some areas are overpatrolled while others are underpatrolled. Because of this, incidents in high-density areas are more likely to be detected and processed as criminal offences than in low-density areas. (This occurs independently of the socioeconomic status of the populations involved). On the basis of "seek, and ye shall find," rather than actual differences in rates of criminal behavior, some areas have higher rates of crime than have others (Hagan, et al, 1978; Stinchcombe, 1963).

A similar argument can be used to explain differences in rural and urban crime rates. In rural or smaller urban areas, the police are more informal and less likely to process minor offences as crimes. In larger cities with modern, more bureaucratic police forces, minor offenes are more likely to be processed as crimes (Wilson, 1968).

It is interesting to see that both the under and over control viewpoints give logical explanations of these differences in crime rates. In fact, recent studies show that both views may be empirically accurate, depending on the nature of the offence (Gillis and Hagan, 1982). This, and the observation of Lohdi and Tilly (1973) that the size of cities is directly related to some types of crime but not others, suggests that the relationship between city size, crime, and social control is complex. It will get more attention from criminologists and urban sociologists in the future.

NEW URBAN SOCIOLOGY

Dependency theory and a Marxian conflict orientation are the bases of **new urban sociology** (Zukin, 1980). For adherents, urbanization is not just the proportion of a given population that lives in areas defined as urban. Instead, urbanization refers more to the localization of labor, the concentration of capital, and the integration of hinterlands into the capitalist world system (see, for example, Castells, 1976, 1977; Harvey, 1975, 1976). Urbanism refers to "the culture of industrial capitalism" (Zukin, 1980).

The relationship between industrialization and urbanization is strong. Some non-industrialized countries do contain cities, but few industrialized countries are not highly urbanized. The new urban sociologists

---

Planning and Progress

When social change is agreeable, we call it "progress;" when it is intentional we call it "planning." Urban or town planning involves attempts to improve life by intentionally changing the structure or management of urban environments; it is a concrete expression of social policy.

Sociologists and other social scientists contribute to planning on both conceptual and methodological levels. Sociological concepts and research motivate, guide, and justify changes in both the design and management of urban areas. For the most part, however, it is probably in the critical evaluation of planning efforts that sociology makes its most important (if not its most appreciated) contribution to the field (Gans, 1970; Smith, 1979).

Whether a specific plan or design is progress is not always easy to determine. What is useful or beautiful to some people may not appeal to others. Planners, architects, and developers may consider a project successful for a variety of aesthetic, technical, and economic reasons. But they are rarely affected by the projects they produce, and have little in common with the people who are. Planners, architects, and developers are usually highly educated, middle class, cosmopolitan, and male. As such, they are not representative of the population.

Because differences in social class, life-style, and gender affect the way people "fit" with the urban environment (Gillis, 1977; Michelson, 1976; 1977), declaring a project successful (or a change as progress) on the basis of the professional's reports may be premature. User evaluation studies should be conducted.

For example, many attempts to clear slums and relocate residents in modern, efficient, and socially integrated public housing projects have been apparent successes. That is, planners, architects, and other professionals have assumed that slum dwellers would prefer newer housing to older buildings and disorganized neighborhoods. While this may be true, professionals often overlook the presence of important informal organizations flourishing in physically deteriorating neighborhoods (Whyte, 1943; Jacobs, 1961; Gans, 1962b). Furthermore, they often overestimate the likelihood of such organizations emerging in new, socially integrated housing developments. To residents who value local community over modern housing, then, such developments may be worse to live in than the slums they left behind.

From the viewpoint of nonresidents, clearing slums is aesthetically pleasing. And placing former residents in integrated housing projects may be seen as socially valuable. Contrast their reactions with those of the residents and it becomes clear that some people will define a change as progress, while others will not. It is noteworthy that when such differences of opinion develop, those who are most directly affected by a change do not necessarily win. Instead, professional policymakers and planners are more likely to prevail, especially if the opposition is not socially powerful. Clairmont and Magill (1974) showed this clearly in their detailed account of the destruction of Africville, a black community in the north end of Halifax.

Sociologists and other social scientists contribute to both people and planning by conducting evaluative research on the effects of planned change. Although the results of such studies often place policymakers, planners, and their products in a bad light, and although they may not provide solutions to the problems they uncover, evaluative research of this type is important. It provides a voice for people who might otherwise be unheard. It also alerts misguided meliorists to inadequacies in their plans. Without this information, mistakes would continue to be made and more progressive solutions (should they exist) could remain undiscovered.

Source:
Gans, Herbert J. "Social planning: a new role for sociology," in Robert Gutman and David Popenoe (eds.). *Neighborhood, City, and Metropolis.* New York: Random House, 1970.

recognize this relationship and argue that patterns of urbanization not only reflect industrialization, but also the forces of capitalism. From their viewpoint, urban sociology has traditionally focused on at least irrelevant and at most intervening variables, rather than the ultimate political-economic causes. Structural functionalists are seen in this way as missing the point, because such views do not take account of the industrial capitalist context in which they make their observations.

For example, James Lorimer (1978) argues that the proliferation of high-rises in Canadian cities occurred because this type of housing gave developers the biggest payoff. Lower density housing is cheaper on a per-unit basis, and is also more popular with planners. The majority of consumers still hope to live in low-density housing and see it as an integral part of family life. Research in Calgary and Edmonton has shown that living in high-rises is related to psychological strain in women with children at home, and that the higher they live the worse it is (Gillis, 1977).

According to new urban sociology, the combination of industrial technology and the pursuit of profit, rather than construction costs, the preferences of planners, or consumer demand, has determined the physical character of Canadian cities. Furthermore, because demand has outstripped supply, urban residents are now faced with either paying a much higher proportion of their incomes to own a house in the city, or leaving for the suburbs. The dream of house ownership has pulled many to the suburbs, while others abandon the dream and try to make their life-style conform to high-density housing downtown.

New urban sociologists also suggest that the traditional viewpoints serve the state by defining urban social movements as "deviance" or disorganization. The urban environment is blamed for producing violence and misery. This deflects attention from the fact that these behaviors represent attempts by exploited people to challenge an oppressive elite.

For example, in their study of the effects of urbanization on collective violence, Lodhi and Tilly (1973) found that collective disorders (such as riots) vary independently of other types of crime. This is not surprising, because unlike other crimes many "contentious gatherings" seem to be politically motivated (Lupsha, 1976; Tilly, 1976). New urban sociologists contend that classifying these activities together as urban violence, disorganization, or deviance not only obscures important differences in their origins, but justifies their repression by the state (Castells, 1977).

In some respects new urban sociology is neither new nor urban, in part because it is based on previously developed Marxian conflict theory and the dependency model. Also, a concern with the physical environment has characterized urban sociology in general, yet new urban sociology either ignores physical factors altogether or reduces their importance from a leading to a supporting role. In spite of this, though, new urban sociology contributes to the sub-field; it integrates the area into more mainstream sociology and points out new directions for students of cities to follow. However, followers should not go too far. For example, the specific emphasis on capitalism and industrialization is of no benefit to sociologists who focus on the origin and growth of cities in non-industrial, non-capitalist settings. In view of our earlier discussion, the motivation for constructing the first cities may indeed have been the exploitation of one group by another. But this extends far beyond capitalism. The new urban sociologists' fixation with advanced capitalism seems unnecessarily narrow.

Just as the early urban sociologists treated some urban social groups as maladjusted, so some of the new urban sociologists view these groups as heroic resisters or embryonic revolutionaries – rebels in an urban paradise, an anti-capitalist conscience. To put it mildly, "this may be a mistaken appraisal" (Zurkin, 1980). Lodhi and Tilly's (1972) study suggests that not all those who engage in urban violence can be seen as politically motivated. Similarly, just as traditional scholars may have overstated the impact of the physical environment, new urban sociologists may be too inclined to disregard it. Defining urban areas solely in terms of labor, capital, and social structure facilitates and extends Marxian views of social life. But for students of cities, the definition is less satisfactory. "Cities are, above all, places whose analysis requires a sense of spatial and physical structure. . . ." (Tilly, 1981). For these reasons, new urban sociology is un-

Territoriality, Community, and Ideology

Peace! You never know what peace is until you walk on the shores or in the fields or along the winding road of Abegweit on a summer twilight when the dew is falling and the old, old stars are peeping out and the sea keeps its mighty tryst with the little land it loves. You find your soul then . . . you realize that youth is not a vanished thing but something that dwells forever in the heart. And you look around on the dimming landscape of haunted hill and long white sand-beach and murmuring ocean, on homestead lights and old fields tilled by dead and gone generations who loved them . . . you will say, "why . . . I have come home!"

Many ethologists, who study the behavior of non-human animals, are convinced that people have an innate willingness to defend their home area and the people in it. They call this "territoriality." Whether it is innate or learned, a form of territoriality seems to exist in humans. The closer to home they are, the more likely they are to protect the person and property of other people (Gillis and Hagan, 1983).

Sociologists disagree about the importance of the physical environment as a determinant of community. Some, such as Reiss (1959), have placed great emphasis on a territorial factor; while others, such as Martindale (1964), have ignored the importance of territory and focused exclusively on the ideas of social interaction, shared values, and group consciousness. Because a specific territory may contain several distinct, and even competing, groups, most sociologists seem now to regard territory as a nonessential component of urban or rural communities. However, Westhues and Sinclair (1974) note that, "While the physical setting is not the only important factor that leads to community formation, it is a basic and important one. Physical boundaries may create an isolated group, hence limiting the social interaction which is necessary for community formation." Westhues and Sinclair also point out that the physical environment can help symbolize *community* for its members:

When there are real physical boundaries, like mountains or rivers, that delimit a particular geographic area, the people in that area are more likely to develop a sense of social cohesion. When the village limits encompass distinctive scenery, that scenery can come to symbolize in an important way the distinctiveness of the social life that goes on there.

Applying these principles on a broader scale helps us to understand how the residents of a place like Prince Edward Island are able to maintain a well defined collective identity in spite of its small size (about 125 000 people) and the strong political and economic pressures to merge with one or more of the other Atlantic provinces. The nine miles of water in the Northumberland Strait symbolically, as well as physically, separate the province and its residents from the mainland. Further, the outstanding beaches and unusual soil color of P.E.I. have been used as symbols for the uniqueness of Islanders and their style of life. (Listen to Nancy White's song "Red is the Soil.")

Whether people in specific communities have a distinctive life-style, and if it is distinct, whether it is bet-ter than life elsewhere, is difficult to determine. However, as Westhues and Sinclair point out, the accuracy of this notion may be far less important than its effects. They call (1974) such beliefs community ideology: "A set of beliefs distinctive to the community which serves to justify its existence, to give residents a sense of pride in living there, and to unify the residents as a result of that pride." Community ideology is based on historical and geographical individuality and may be an important component of community survival, particularly in the case of small towns (or provinces) whose young people face economic enticement to migrate to larger centres.

Community ideology helps small localities to resist total depletion through migration by offering intangible rewards to people who stay. "The basic item in community ideology is simply that living in the village is better than living elsewhere . . ." (Westhues and Sinclair, 1974).

Source:

References are to Gillis, A.R., and J. Hagan. "Bystander apathy and the territorial imperative. *Sociological Inquiry* (forthcoming), 1983; Reiss, Albert J., Jr. "The sociological study of communities." *Rural Sociology*, 24: 118-30, 1959; Martindale, D.A. "The formation and destruction of communities," in G.K. Zollschaun and W. Hirsch (eds). *Explorations in Social Change*. London: Routledge and Kegan Paul, 1964; Westhues, Kenneth, and Peter R. Sinclair. *Village in Crisis*. Toronto: Holt, Rinehart and Winston, 1974. The quote at the beginning of this insert is from "Prince Edward Island," by Lucy Maud Montgomery, *The Spirit of Canada*, 1939, quoted in Bolger, Francis W.P., Wayne Barrett, Anne Mackay. *Spirit of Place: Lucy Maud Montgomery and Prince Edward Island*. Toronto: Oxford University Press, 1982.

likely to supplant the more traditional perspectives. But by substituting the interests of profit-seeking capitalists for the arbitration of the market as a determinant of urban form, new urban sociology brings a challenge and a new vitality to the sub-field.

The author wishes to thank Larry Bourne, Gordon Laxer, Kevin McQuillan, Ian R. Robertson, and Charles Tilly for their comments and suggestions.

SUMMARY

1. Sociologists define a city as a large concentration of people engaged in a wide range of interdependent occupations that, for the most part, do not involve the primary production of food.

2. The shift of the human population of the world from rural to urban areas has been associated with technical, organizational, and cultural developments that have allowed the development of large agricultural surpluses. The Industrial Revolution seems to have had the largest effect on urbanization.

3. The urbanization of Canada followed temporarily the patterns in industrial Europe and the United States and generally proceeded from east to west.

4. At present about three-quarters of the Canadian population live in urban areas. In recent years, the most obvious change in the Canadian urban population has been within cities; many have stopped growing or are even declining in population, while their suburbs have grown dramatically.

5. One of the most important explanations of the relationship between metropolitan areas and their hinterlands is the dependency model. This perspective has also been used to explain the relationship between countries and between regions within countries. It is one of the bases for new urban sociology.

6. Several perspectives have been developed that incorporate ecological principles to explain the growth of an individual city. The concentric zone, sector, and multiple nuclei models are three of these. All have some applicability within the large cities in industrial North America, but more in the U.S. than in Canada.

7. Social scientists have developed various explanations for the existence of a distinct urban way of life (urbanism). The most important of these theories is

Wirth's. He focused on the size, density, and social heterogeneity of urban populations and argued that these factors cause segmental social relationships, social isolation, and psychological withdrawal. But recent evidence suggests that the current impact of these variables may not be as great as it was in the past.

GLOSSARY

Agricultural surplus. Quantity of food greater than that required to meet the needs of its producers.

City. Large concentration of people engaged in a wide range of interdependent occupations that, for the most part, do not involve the primary production of food.

Community. Identifiable self-conscious group with shared common interests. Communities may or may not have a territorial base, and they vary in their level of self-sufficiency.

Competition. Action of two or more groups or activities that attempt to occupy the same area.

Concentric zone model. Model of the city in which economic and residential activity patterns and social groups are segregated in concentric zones, with economic activities located at the center of the city, and residential activities located toward the periphery.

Dependency theory. Theory that the economies of hinterland areas become so specialized in primary industries (such as farming, fishing, or the extraction of raw materials) that trade with metropolitan areas for manufactured goods and services is necessary for the hinterland population to maintain a given standard of living. This places the hinterland in a politically disadvantageous position.

Deurbanization. A decrease in the proportion of population inhabiting urban areas.

Gemeinschaft. Tönnies' term for relatively small organizations characterized by a commitment to tradition, informal social control, intimate interpersonal contact, a collective orientation, and group consciousness.

Gesellschaft. Tönnies' term for relatively large organizations characterized by formal social control, impersonal contact, an orientation to individualism, and little commitment to tradition.

Hinterland. Rural or non-industrialized region from which a city or metropolitan area extracts labor, food, and other raw materials.

Human ecology. Application of ecological principles such as competition, invasion, and succession to the scientific study of human behavior.

Limiting factors. Variables that can prevent or inhibit change in other variables.

Megalopolis. Greek term for the most powerful of several cities in a given country or region. The term is now used to describe an unbroken urban region created when the borders of two or more metropolitan areas expand into each other; also known as conurbation.

Metropolis. Relatively large urban area containing a city and its surrounding suburbs. The term has also been used to refer to an industrial region or society that transforms raw materials extracted from its hinterland.

Motivating factors. Variables that can produce or encourage changes in other variables.

Multiple nuclei model. Model of a city as several specialized areas located along and connected by major traffic arteries such as highways. Unlike the concentric zone and the sector models, the multiple nuclei model does not suggest that zones radiate from the center of the city.

New urban sociology. This perspective, based on Marxian conflict theory and the dependency model, emphasizes the impact of industrial capitalism on the form of urban areas and the lives of the people they contain.

Sector model. Model of a city as a series of wedge-shaped sectors radiating from the center of the city, each containing different activities or land use and separated by major traffic arteries or natural boundaries.

Segregation. Tendency of specific activities or groups to cluster and exclude other activities or groups from occupying the same region or neighborhood.

Selection. Viewpoint that relationships between the physical environment and behavior reflect the migration or movement of people with particular characteristics to particular places.

Suburbanization. Increase in the proportion of a given population living on the outer limits of a metropolitan area.

Urbanism. Set of attitudes, beliefs, and behaviors that are thought to be characteristic of city dwellers.

Urbanization. Increase in the proportion of a given population inhabiting areas designated as urban.

FURTHER READING

Bronowski, Jacob. *The Ascent of Man.* London: British Broadcasting Corporation, 1976. Chapter 2, "The Harvest of the Seasons;" Chapter 3 "The Grain in the Stone;" and Chapter 8 "The Drive for Power" are particularly relevant to the study of cities.

Clairmont, Donald, and Dennis Magill. *Africville: The Life and Death of Canadian Black Community.* Toronto: McClelland and Stewart, 1974. A detailed account of the destruction of Africville, a settlement of blacks in the north end of Halifax, the motivations behind this "urban renewal," and the effects of relocation on community members.

Clark, S.D. *The Suburban Society.* Toronto: University of Toronto Press, 1966. This monograph discusses the forces affecting the suburbanization of Toronto.

Clark, S.D. *The New Urban Poor.* Toronto: McGraw-Hill Ryerson, 1978. An analysis of the rural roots of the emerging urban poor in Canada.

Gist, Noel P., and Sylvia Fava. *Urban Society*, 6th ed. New York: T.Y. Crowell, 1974. A comprehensive coverage of nearly all aspects of urban sociology.

McGahan, Peter. *Urban Sociology in Canada.* Toronto: Butterworths, 1982. An examination of most of the models and theories developed by urban sociologists, with special attention given to Canada.

Michelson, William. *Man and His Urban Environment: A Sociological Approach*, 2nd ed. Reading, Mass.: Addison-Wesley, 1976. Reviews the literature concerning the relationship between urban environments on the one hand and people's preferences and behaviors on the other; and presents the author's perspective on environmental opportunities/constraints.

Palen, John J. *The Urban World*, 2nd ed. New York: McGraw-Hill, 1981. Like Gist and Fava, this is another excellent general text in urban sociology.

Simmons, James, and Robert Simmons. *Urban Canada*, 2nd ed. Toronto: Copp Clark, 1974. A description of the Canadian urban system and its development.

Westhues, Kenneth, and Peter R. Sinclair. *Village in Crisis.* Toronto: Holt, Rinehart and Winston, 1974. An interesting study of community life, and change in a small Ontario town (Elora) on the fringe of larger urban centers.

CHAPTER 16
SOCIAL MOVEMENTS AND SOCIAL CHANGE

J. PAUL GRAYSON

L.M. GRAYSON

"I never had no use for Reds . . . nor for Red talk but a man gets to look at things different when they hit him where he lives." His voice rose suddenly in anger. "Lookit!" he cried, "look at the bunch of you boys here . . . no jobs, no place to go, no future, runnin' around the country like a pack of dogs. Give me another coupla years of this kind of thing, an' goddamit, I'll be headin' a parade myself." (Baird, Waste Heritage)

Few participants in social movements are fanatics. Like the speaker in the above passage, many feel a sense of real injustice. Many are angry. Many are impatient. A few feel frustrated and despondent. All have this in common: they want change or they want to stop change.

Some get what they want. It may be a job. It may be a revolution. It may be, as far as they are concerned, an assured place in the hereafter. Most, however, do not achieve their goal. Instead, after a flurry of activity, they are back where they started.

Whether or not they are successful, there is a cost to be paid for such activity. For some participants the price is small: a few hours here and there, at a demonstration or on a street corner distributing pamphlets. Others pay more: days, months, even years of organizing, speech-making, and marching. If the struggle is violent, some pay with their lives. Such, for example, is the case in contemporary Central America and South Africa.

The potential costs are not always a deterrent. For centuries people have accepted them. In pre-Christian Rome, a slave revolt nearly crippled society. In the Middle Ages, Europeans spilled Moorish blood in their attempts to deliver the Holy Land from the heathen. The Moors, for their part, repaid in kind. More recently, the Polish people, through the trade union Solidarity, demonstrated their willingness to die in order to bring about fundamental political, economic, and social changes. Although the scale of violence is far smaller, Canadian unionists, too, have witnessed bloodletting (during the Winnipeg General Strike of 1919, for example). For them and for many others, the struggle to introduce or to resist change has been long and dangerous.

In Canada, there is considerable information available on social movements, although the treatment of various movements and regions has been uneven. Until recently, for example, the Maritimes have not been analyzed as extensively as, say, the west. The available literature reveals what may be a significant characteristic of studies of Canadian social movements. It was noted in Chapter 1 that, with few exceptions, the major analyses have not been undertaken by sociologists, but by political economists and historians.

The reason for this is not entirely clear. Until the 1960s there were relatively few sociologists in Canadian universities. The study of various phenomena that sociologists might define as their preserve was therefore undertaken by those in other disciplines. But even today, most analyses of past and contemporary movements are not undertaken by sociologists. Perhaps sociologists in Canada are simply less interested in social movements than in ethnic studies or other areas of inquiry. Then again, it may be that contemporary funding agencies view social movements as a low priority for research. Finally, perhaps the Canadian situation is not atypical – the study of social movements may have fallen to nonsociologists in other countries as well.

PERSPECTIVES ON SOCIETY

The way in which we analyze social movements will largely depend upon the more general ideas we have about the way society works. (The most important of these general ideas have been outlined in the early sections of this book.) For this discussion of social movements, let us review briefly the three traditional sociological perspectives on society, especially those aspects that are most important for the study of social movements.

Three Traditional Views

Until very recently the dominant North American view of society was structural functionalism. The most important assumptions of this view are:

1. the society is a system composed of interrelated subsystems
2. that within the total system, there is a tendency for a change in one subsystem (for example, the economy) to lead to accommodating changes in other subsystems (the family)
3. that the subsystems are able to interact because of a value consensus
4. that within the total system there is strain toward maintaining a moving equilibrium

Many other assumptions could be added to the list, but these are the most important for the study of social movements.

The second important view is symbolic interaction. While this approach, like the structural functionalist, has a number of variants, it too has certain underlying assumptions:

1. that human behavior is a consequence of the ways in which, in particular social settings, participants define what their behavior should be (in terms of their sense of identity, their understandings of what is generally expected in such situations, and so forth)
2. that identity and understandings are themselves products of previous social encounters
3. that the totality of individuals interacting with one another on the basis of these understandings is what constitutes society

The third major view of society is Marxist. In contrast to structural functionalism, with its notion that harmony is and should be the general principle underlying social activity, **Marxism** stresses the pervasiveness of conflict. Marxists assume that in modern capitalist societies like Canada:

1. there is a fundamental objective cleavage, primarily between the interests of labor and those of capital
2. capital maintains the upper hand through physical repression and, more importantly, through the acceptance by all classes of ideologies that are consistent with the interest of capital
3. despite this dominance (because objective and opposing interests can only be concealed and never eradicated) the potential for social change and the emergence of social movements is ever present

Breakdown and Solidarity

In the introduction to its study of violence in a number of European countries, one team of sociologists and social historians makes some observations that are important to the study of social movements. They argue that theories of violence can be divided into those stressing breakdown and those emphasizing solidarity. The **breakdown theories** (Tilly, et al, 1975) maintain that collective violence is a byproduct of social change. Furthermore, these theories argue that processes of change such as urbanization and industrialization tend to undermine or diminish existing controls over antisocial behavior at the very time when the processes of change are themselves causing uncertainty and strain among individuals. The theories emphasizing solidarity (1975) argue that violence develops out of the struggle of competition for power among clearly defined groups.

Although these comments are directed specifically to the phenomenon of violence, they apply equally to the study of social movements. Theories falling into the breakdown category include structural functionalism and symbolic interaction, while Marxism is the main inclusion in the solidarity category. In many analyses of actual social movements, researchers borrow concepts from both general perspectives.

Breakdown in Canada. An example of the break-down position based on structural functionalist assumptions is provided by a study of the rise of the Social Credit in Quebec (Pinard, 1971). The general position underlying this work is that the Social Credit Party, which forced itself into the public eye by winning 25.9 percent of the Quebec popular vote in the federal election of 1962, can be analyzed by utilizing the notions of **structural conduciveness** and **structural strain**. In general, conduciveness can be viewed as the social arrangements that support or deter the rise of a movement. In Quebec, a two-party system, in which the Liberals had for some time won most of the federal seats, provided the conditions under which it was possible for the Social Credit to achieve considerable electoral success. Because some voters considered the Liberal performance inadequate and viewed the Conservatives as a weak alternative, they supported the Social Credit.

However, as Pinard (1971) indicates: "structural conduciveness is not a sufficient condition for the rise of a new ... movement. ... Another condition is necessary: strains must also be present." The strains referred to are the various phenomena that in sum represent the inadequate functioning of society, or, to use the more dramatic term, its breakdown. The disadvantaged economic position of many workers and farmers was a source of strain in Quebec in the early sixties. Stated simply, within the breakdown perspective the success of the Social Credit can be attributed to the following: features of the two-party system (an example of structural conduciveness); and the inability of a society to provide some of its members with an acceptable standard of living (an example of structural strain). In combination, these and other factors characterize a form of breakdown.

A more distinctively Canadian example of the break-down approach that manifests some of the ideas related to symbolic interaction and structural functionalism is offered in a number of works by S.D. Clark (1948; 1959; 1968; 1975). In all his analyses of social movements, Clark concentrates on the particular features of Canadian society that have generated movements of religious, political, and social protest. One of Clark's major concerns is the disruptive effect of frontier circumstances on institutions that were appropriate to older, settled parts of the country, or to Europe.

In seventeenth-century Quebec, eighteenth-century Nova Scotia, nineteenth-century Upper Canada, and twentieth-century Saskatchewan and Alberta, the patterns are similar. Individuals in frontier circumstances are confronted with new problems, for which existing institutions offer few solutions. There is thus created a good deal of uncertainty and strain.

If suitable leaders are available to mobilize the population, social movements emerge to provide people with ideas for new forms of behavior that are more appropriate to frontier circumstances. In backwoods Upper Canada, for example, itinerant preachers provided the population with a form of worship that was simple and appropriate to their life circumstances. They generated a much needed community sentiment that existing churches, being upper class and urban oriented, were unable to foster. The consequence was the success of religious fundamentalism in Upper Canada in the early and middle years of the last century (Clark, 1948).

Solidarity in Canada. One of the earliest analyses in which a **solidarity theory** can be detected is in an examination by L. A. Wood (1975, originally published 1924) of Canadian farmers' movements from their beginnings to the 1920s. For Wood, the impetus to collective action was rooted in the farmers' material circumstances, which generated a form of solidarity:

A naive ... class consciousness had begun to grow up in the farming communities in pioneer days. The evolution of this class consciousness was due in the main to the similarity of each pioneer's fight for supremacy; to the common economic problems that were presented to each in turn, and to the status of isolation from town life which was the pioneer's lot.

Despite the presence of agrarian pioneer class consciousness, it was not until much later that a broader class consciousness developed among farmers.

Class consciousness among farmers grew with the accumulation of capital in large centers, the growing diversification of manufacturing, the agrarian demand for new goods, and improvements in transportation. The farmer, Wood (1975) points out:

suddenly awoke to find himself caught in an industrial network of which he had heretofore known nothing, and was driven to relate the problems of agriculture, already thronging

[sic] for solution to all the other variegated phases of production.

Once they had made the connections among these various factors, farmers from coast to coast then combined to struggle for their common benefit through political means. Their solidarity in these matters derived from their common agrarian experiences and their ability therefore to discuss common grievances.

A more recent examination of a solidarity-based social movement is Resnick's (1977) analysis of English-Canadian nationalism. Although nationalism is by no means a new phenomenon, Resnick locates its post-World War II manifestations in the changing class structure of Canadian society. More important for our discussion is his typification of specific movements that emerged in the late sixties. Groups such as the Committee for an Independent Canada and the leftist Waffle group arose in Resnick's view primarily as vehicles of expression for the interests of a "new petite bourgeoisie" comprised of some professionals, large numbers of civil servants, teachers, and so on. In the past few years, this class has grown rapidly. With waning American influence, the members of the new petite bourgeoisie more and more view an economic and politically independent Canada as a precondition for the continuing viability of their class.

Similar sentiments, Resnick feels, are shared by increasing numbers of workers. Their main interest is in the deindustrialization that has resulted from Canada's dependence on the American economy. A comparable analysis was carried out over a decade ago of the newly emerging separatist movement in Quebec (Guindon, 1975, originally published 1964).

For purposes of the current discussion, it should be stressed that Resnick and Guindon have in common the idea that movements have come into existence as a consequence of conflict between, or among, different contenders in a power struggle and not from a breakdown of social bonds. Both analyses, therefore, are solidarity-based.

An Assessment

Overall, it can be argued that the solidarity perspective has more validity than the breakdown perspective.

The fundamental weakness of the breakdown perspective is simply that many of its assumptions are ill-founded. (This does not apply to the concrete analyses of all its practitioners.) For example, as Tilly, et al (1975) demonstrate, phenomena such as crime rates, which are usually viewed as manifestations of breakdown, have little relationship to other forms of breakdown such as rates of violence and suicide. At what point, then, can we actually say that breakdown has occurred?

A second key assumption of the breakdown perspective is that the most alienated and marginal of individuals are those most prone to the lure of social movements. A number of sources suggest that this assumption is erroneous. In fact, quite the reverse has been found (Oberschall, 1973). On numerous occasions it is evident that participants in social movements are typically integrated into the various sectors of society. Indeed, this integration is one of the mechanisms most conducive to collective mobilization.

This said, we must concede difficulties with the solidarity perspective. Some of its adherents tend to ignore, or inadequately deal with, certain social phenomena that do not appear at first to be centered on power struggles. We frequently think of power struggles occurring over material things. But struggles also take place in the realm of ideology (Laclau, 1977; Poulantzas, 1978).Many religious movements could be cited in support of this point. Moreover, religious and other ideologies frequently veil particular material interests expressed in social movements. In the early days of capitalism, for example, there is good reason to believe that large numbers of the faithful may have switched from Catholicism to Protestantism because the economic behavior permitted by the latter was more in keeping with their material well-being (Tawney, 1954, originally published 1926). At the same time, ideologies can be thought to have a dynamic of their own. One of the tasks that challenges the researcher is to identify which of the two possibilities fits any concrete situation.

Furthermore, individuals working in the solidarity tradition frequently fail to state what they mean by "social movement." In Canada, for example, the term has been used to describe various phenomena ranging from sporadic collective protests to the full-fledged organizational behavior of contemporary unions. In many cases the only common theme uniting the various usages is opposition to what can be referred to as the "Canadian establishment."

These shortcomings notwithstanding, it can be argued that the major social movements in Canada have in many ways been manifestations of power struggles. But there are a significant number that cannot be seen to best advantage as contenders in power struggles if the use of the term is restricted to what we usually call the political arena. It must be recognized that power struggles also occur in the ideological realm.

WHAT IS A SOCIAL MOVEMENT?

There is considerable fuzziness surrounding definitions of social movements. Part of the problem stems from the unwarranted assumption that everyone knows what a social movement is in the first place. Confusion also characterizes discussions of the difference between social movements and political parties. In Canada, this distinction is often a difficult one to make, because many social movements have tried to operate through existing political structures. This holds true, in particular, for most parties on the Canadian left, like the Co-operative Commonwealth Federation/New Democratic Party (CCF/NDP). Whether or not movements change in a fundamental sense once they enter the formal political process and cease to be social movements is an important question.

Although Wood (1975) does not state a precise definition of social movements in his work on farmers' movements, he does identify some salient features. Such features include:

- a change of attitude among participants
- an ideal towards which members aim
- a desire by members for energetic and inspirational leadership
- intellectual guidance to achieve the ideal
- complete loyalty on the part of members
- a willingness to minimize the significance of the individual and maximize the importance of achieving the ideal

All of this is true. But Wood is identifying a movement according to what it implies for its participants. He does not tell us the potential consequences of the movement on the structure of society.

A more recent definition of social movements is offered in a discussion of the fortunes of the CCF. During the Depression, the CCF offered solutions for obvious social ills. Consequently, it has served as a focus of the debate concerning the difference between social movements and political parties. According to Young (1969), "The 'pure' party seeks electoral victory, the movement seeks some major social change or reform." Young (1969) elaborates:

A movement is "a group venture extending beyond a local community or single event and involving a systematic effort to inaugurate changes in thought, behaviour, and social relationships." A movement seeks fundamental change and may or may not use political means to achieve it; a party seeks power for its leaders through electoral success. Its leaders may or may not then use this power to achieve goals similar in nature to those sought by a movement; and it is customary for party leaders to use their power in such a way as to ensure their continuance in office, even if this means ignoring or perverting their goals.

Young maintains that by entering the political arena a social movement need not necessarily shed its social movement characteristics. History reveals, however, that many do.

The minimal definition that we will use in this chapter is simple and to the point. **Social movements** will be defined as forms of behavior in which a large number of people try to bring about or resist social change (Clark, Grayson, and Grayson, 1975). Clearly, parts of this definition are similar to the other definitions. But this one is different in an important way; it contains the notion that social movements frequently attempt to stop social change as well as to implement it. Just a few years ago there were a number of groups, such as Canadians for One Canada, who tried without success to prevent changes to the Constitution. A workable definition of social movements must contain not only the idea of promoting change, but also that of preventing change.

We have said this is a minimal definition because

we do not want to confuse social movements with attempts by numerous other social bodies to introduce or prevent social change. The state is one such body. As you saw in Chapter 13, in Canada the repressive apparatus of the state – the police, army, judiciary – has been used against unionists in many strikes (Abella, 1974; Bercuson, 1978). In the Winnipeg General Strike of 1919, for example, then Prime Minister Robert Borden feared that the situation in Winnipeg would fan the flames of discontent elsewhere (Torrance, 1977). In Borden's view, repression was therefore justified. Some strikers were arrested; others were shot.

In other situations, the state has attempted to foster the illusion of promoting change. One such initiative involved an effort in 1975 to insure that women were not excluded from top federal bureaucratic positions. By early 1979, however, it was revealed that despite the rhetoric of change, the number of women in these positions had in fact declined, although the salary differential between males and females had narrowed slightly.

Structural Crystallization and Change Potential

If the concept of social movement is to have validity, it must be distinguished from other bodies that attempt to initiate or prevent change. One such distinction is the state of flux of the movement itself (Clark, Grayson, and Grayson, 1975). In other words, one of the characteristics of social movements is that they are less **structurally crystallized** than institutions like the state. In social movements, the roles of the participants are often ambiguous, the level of commitment is variable, the chain of command is hazy, goals are frequently unspecified. At the same time, movements are more structurally crystallized than groups like crowds, which might also be concerned with change.

Differentiating a social movement from an institution solely on the degree of crystallization poses some difficulties. A revolutionary movement, for example, might be placed in the same category as the gay liberation movement and in a different category from a structurally crystallized communist party in a capitalist society. In its potential for changing the exist-

"... what is really wrong with the BNA Act"

Canadians for One Canada was a clear example of a movement that wished, in 1979, to block social change. The movement felt that proposed constitutional re-arrangements were unnecessary, divisive, and wrong. Those who supported such a position were exhorted to make their views known through letters and petitions.

It's time to take some positive steps before Canada is split apart.

If you agree that the Trudeau constitutional changes are divisive and wrong for Canada, what can you do about it?

Beyond joining and supporting Canadians for One Canada, here are some positive actions you can take.

WRITE YOUR MEMBER OF PARLIA-MENT to say that you're against the unseemly haste to change the very nature of Canada by 1 July 1979 ... without you and other Canadians having a chance to have a "say" in the process. ...

CALL HOTLINE RADIO SHOWS – whenever a politician, regardless of party, is on ... or anyone speaking on Canada. Ask questions on "official" bilingualism and national unity. Ask who really wants Trudeau's constitutional changes. Ask what is really wrong with the BNA Act that has served Canada well for 112 years. Keep calling. You'll get through. ...

In short, take positive action. Join Canadians for One Canada. Speak out and write to all who can help stop Trudeau's proposed changes to our Constitution. Act soon, before it's too late.

Source:

Canadians for One Canada, No. 1, 1979:4.

---

ing social structure, however, the revolutionary group might well have more in common with the communist party than with the gay liberation movement.

Perhaps what is required, then, is to recognize the relatively uncrystallized nature of social movements, while at the same time examining all social groups according to their degree of structural crystallization and their potential for promoting or resisting social change. Figure 16-1 outlines the possibilities in this approach. The horizontal axis refers to the degree of structural crystallization characteristic of a social body. In other words, the degree to which roles, authority structure, goals, and so on are clearly defined. Taking the whole society as the reference point, the vertical axis expresses the **change potential** of that body. Various institutions and movements can then be placed in the appropriate quadrants.

This procedure enables us to distinguish among **institutions** and social movements in terms of their potential to promote or prevent social change. Those movements with considerable potential, "high power movements," are located in quadrant 1. Quadrant 2 contains those with little potential to cause or resist change, the "low power movements." In a similar manner, quadrant 3 contains "low power institutions;" quadrant 4, "high power institutions."

This classification scheme must be used with caution. For one thing, the potential of a group to promote or resist social change varies considerably from society to society. The Communist Party in Canada, for example, is ineffectual in its potential to promote change. In France and Italy, it could well form a government. For another thing, the placing of bodies in the quadrants can be only approximate. It cannot be carried out on a finely graded scale. Moreover, it is easy to err when assessing the change of contemporary movements and institutions. In the twenties and thirties, for example, there was good reason to believe that agrarian parties like the United Farmers of Alberta, the Social Credit, and the left-leaning CCF would result in significant change. It is now clear that such movements were not successful in bringing about fundamental changes to the Canadian capitalist system.

Despite these caveats, the general scheme presented in Figure 16-1 has at least two advantages for the examination of social movements. First, it helps in assessing the change potential and degree of structural crystallization among various bodies in *one* society (see Figure 16-2). In Canada, for example, as the economy deteriorates and the number of layoffs accelerates, a loose nationalist movement based on what has sometimes been called the new petite bourgeoisie and the working class has the potential to induce greater change than an equally uncrystallized gay liberation movement. At the same time the role of the state is crucial. Without doubt the state will resist any changes that imply a major departure from the status quo. Moreover, the state's ability or power to resist change will be greater than a nationalist movement's ability to introduce it. This prognosis is supported by findings suggesting powerful links between the Canadian and American economic elites whose interests are in opposition to those of the nationalist movement (Clement, 1977). As a result, the state is located higher in relation to the vertical power axis in Figure 16-2 than is the nationalist movement.

Under the same conditions the highly crystallized churches in Canada, despite some radicals among the clergy, are likely to have little potential to introduce change. At the same time, the churches are unlikely to resist actively the efforts of others, unless they define these activities as "ungodly."

The second advantage of the general scheme of Figure 16-1 is that it can help to assess the change potential and degree of structural crystallization among similar groups in different societies (see Figure 16-3). Once again, the communist parties provide an institutional example. The potential of the French or Italian Communist Party for change is far greater than that of the Party in Canada. When movements, rather than institutions, are examined, it can be hypothesized that

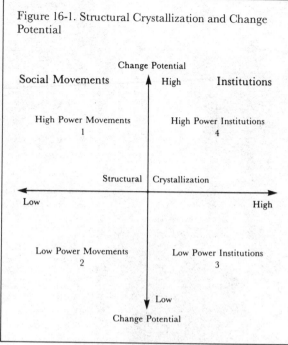

Figure 16-1. Structural Crystallization and Change Potential

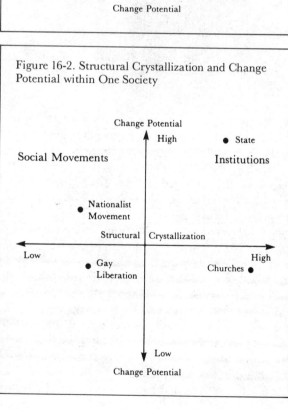

Figure 16-2. Structural Crystallization and Change Potential within One Society

Bloody Saturday

The six week long Winnipeg General Strike ended on Wednesday, June 25, 1919. The previous Saturday a silent parade of war veterans in support of the strike was met by mounted charges of the North-West Mounted Police. In the end two people were killed and thirty more were in hospitals.

Whether the police used their authority without discretion, or whether some person in the crowd precipitated the crisis, does not seem clear. But in an event of this kind, with the atmosphere electrically charged as it was, little was necessary to ignite the spark and set aflame the passions of the excited crowd. . . .

The representatives of the Canadian government from the beginning seem to have aggravated the trouble rather than have pacified it. When they arrived in Winnipeg they found two parties lined up if not in battle array, certainly in battle humor. Instead of declining to deal with either party and summoning moderates from the two sides, the cabinet ministers seem to have thrown their entire influence and strength with the extremists opposing the strikers. Under such circumstances it is not surprising that they made little headway. . . .

The riot of Saturday is a worrying and deplorable incident which cannot have but evil results whatever may be the ultimate outcome of the whole distressing disturbance, and makes more difficult all efforts looking toward permanent labor peace.

The incident will injure the labor faction most, which up to this time has shown much self-control and patience under very great provocation.

Source:

Calgary *Albertan*, June 23, 1919.

the women's movement, for example, may have similar impacts on all three societies over a number of years, because of the comparable strength of the movements and the comparable degree of receptivity within the three societies.

MOVEMENTS AND CLASSES

In analyzing any social movement, it is not enough to classify it according to the degree of structural crystallization and its potential to introduce social change. Other aspects of a movement warrant consideration. Primary among these are the movement's class interest base, its class base, its focus, and its action orientation (see Figure 16-4).

Class Interest Base

The **class interest base** refers to the social classes or class fractions (divisions within classes) whose interests are promoted by the activities of the movement. In Canadian society, following the practice established by Panitch (1977), Poulantzas (1978), and Resnick (1977), it is possible to distinguish, first, a class that owns the means of production. This class, as noted in Chapter 8, is referred to as the bourgeoisie. A second group, a proletariat, or working class, consists of those who exchange their labor for wages. The organizations that employ this working class are owned and controlled by the bourgeoisie. The petite bourgeoisie consists primarily of small businessmen and farmers who employ little or no labor, yet own their farms or machinery. In recent years an additional class, the **new petite bourgeoisie**, has been identified. In this group are included civil servants, some professionals, teachers, technocrats, and so on – people who do not own their means of production but who politically and ideologically often align themselves with the bourgeoisie. Obviously, the size of these classes and their relations to one another can vary from period to period and from society to society. In contemporary Canadian society, the largest classes are the proletariat, or working class, and the new petite bourgeoisie. The most powerful, though, is the bourgeoisie.

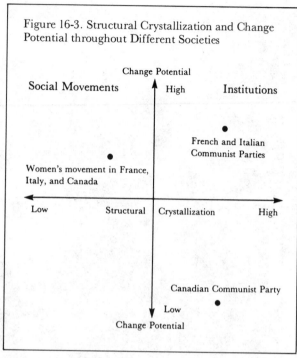

Figure 16-3. Structural Crystallization and Change Potential throughout Different Societies

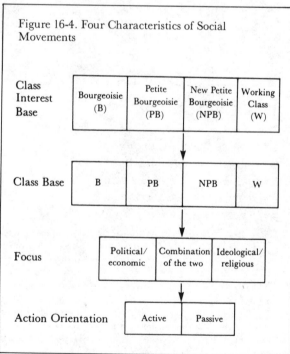

Figure 16-4. Four Characteristics of Social Movements

Many, but not all, social movements can be seen as serving the interests of one or more of the classes identified above. With good reason, we tend to assume that socialist movements will support the interests of the working class. We might also assume – perhaps erroneously – that movements like twentieth-century fascism in Germany and Italy were primarily consistent with the interests of the bourgeoisie. In fact, a number of scholars has suggested this link. In many instances, however, in what Laclau (1977) terms "popular-democractic struggles," social movements may serve the interests of a number of classes simultaneously. Such a state of affairs may be manifested in many of the anti-imperialist movements seen in Third-World societies. In the case of each movement, it is therefore imperative to attempt to identify its class interest base.

Class Base

Separate from class interest base, the **class base** of a movement can be defined according to the class position of movement participants. The class base can, but need not, be distinct from the class interest base of a social movement. German fascism, for example, arose when the political power of the bourgeoisie was far less than its economic power. At the same time, no other class was strong enough to govern. The German Nazi Party created the political conditions for the bourgeoisie to live up to its economic potential, but the members of the Party came mainly from the petite bourgeoisie and some elements of the working class. Despite its class base, therefore, the Nazi Party can be seen to some extent as serving the interests of the bourgeoisie (Laclau, 1977).

Focus

As Figure 16-4 indicates, a social movement, independent of its class interest base and class base, can **focus** its activities in different realms. Movements that focus on the political/economic arena attempt to introduce change in things like government, economic enterprises, and so on. The Maritime rights movement, which in the 1920s attempted to halt the economic and political decline of New Brunswick, Nova Scotia,

and Prince Edward Island, can be seen as a political/economic-focused movement. So can some union movements that focus their activities on purely economic matters, like higher wages. At the other extreme, we can think of ideological and religious movements that attempt to introduce change in the realm of ideas (the Hare Krishna and anti-nuclear movements, for example).

Usually, however, movements focus their activities on both political/economic and ideological concerns. The youth movement of the 1960s, for example, sought to change both the relations of the people to the state and the distribution of goods in society. These matters, in one sense, fall within the realm of the political/economic. At the same time, many participants in the youth movement were interested in the adoption of new life-styles and in the definition of new social priorities. While there is some overlap, we can think of the latter interest as belonging to the realm of ideology (Westhues, 1975). In the scheme employed here, movements are defined in terms of their emphasis on certain elements in either the political/economic or in the ideological realm.

Action Orientation

The last consideration in Figure 16-4 is the **action orientation** of the movement. There are two possibilities. First, the primary objective of the movement can be to promote or to prevent changes in the world. In this case its orientation is active. Second, the primary objective can be to change movement participants. In this case its orientation is passive. Revolutionary movements are good examples of the former. Certain religious sects that practice withdrawal from the world are examples of the latter. With the possible exception of the Rebellion of 1837, Canadians have not seen examples of revolutionary movements. Movements like Hare Krishna, whose participants attempt to withdraw from many social conventions, are far more common.

Again, as with earlier categories some overlap is inevitable. The women's movement, for example, focuses its primary efforts on promoting changes in the world, but it also tries to raise the consciousness and change the behavior of its members.

HINTERLAND MOVEMENTS

An examination of the origins of social movements in Canada and in other modern capitalist societies reveals that many develop from the inherent tensions among the classes outlined in Figure 16-4. In Canada, the United States, and elsewhere, a number of movements resulting from such tensions have taken on apparent regional characteristics. Indeed, one of the defining characteristics of many significant Canadian social movements is that they have involved the struggle of class fractions located in the hinterland.

The terms *hinterland* and *metropolis* may be defined in many ways. In his analysis of Canadian society, Davis (1971) identifies certain features of each that warrant mention here:

Hinterland means, in the first instance, relatively under-developed or colonial areas which export for the most part semi-processed extractive materials – including people who migrate from the country to the city for better educational and work opportunities. . . . Metropolis signifies the centers of economic and political control located in the larger cities.

A system of unequal exchange exists between such regions. Quite simply, more is taken out of the hinterland than is put in. This is the **metropolitan-hinterland relationship** discussed in Chapter 15.

The Maritimes and the West

In analyzing the emergence of turn-of-the-century Maritime marketing cooperative movements, Sacouman (1979) makes implicit use of the metropolis-hinterland distinction. He argues that such cooperative movements are best seen as attempts on the part of identifiable working-class and petit-bourgeois class fractions – such as Nova Scotian coal miners and inshore fishermen – to improve their position in an externally controlled system of exchange. One of the forms taken by these movements was the introduction of retail cooperatives, so that exorbitant profits could be kept out of the hands of the middlemen. By and large, however, such movements did very little to improve the place of disadvantaged class fractions in a mode of production that

worked increasingly to the benefit of an externally located bourgeoisie.

In somewhat similar fashion, Overton (1979) examined the Newfoundland neo-nationalist movement of the 1970s. He found (1979) that an increasing number of the new petite bourgeoisie, supplemented by certain elements of the petite bourgeoisie (notably small business), were beginning to question whether Newfoundland should continue in Confederation:

Local business interests are more and more seen to be at odds with national priorities and policy. Actions in the national interest are often seen to favour Ontario capitalists. . . . The interest in greater political and economic independence among the entrepreneurs of the new middle class and their associated professional groups is grounded in the need for improved conditions of trade and capital accumulation.

One consequence of this neo-nationalist movement was a "Buy Newfoundland" campaign intended to keep business profits inside the province.

In terms of the change-potential grid discussed earlier, the cooperative movements can be classified as low power movements. On the basis of available evidence, so can the Newfoundland neo-nationalist movement. Furthermore, the broad class base of the Maritime rights movement notwithstanding (Forbes, 1975), it would not be going too far to suggest that the Atlantic provinces have not yet produced a high power movement. A partial explanation for this, at least so far as the working and petite bourgeoisie classes are concerned, is suggested by Brym (1979):

Third parties representative of the interests of petty primary producers or of workers (or of both) have tended not to emerge because these classes are relatively powerless. And their powerlessness is . . . largely explicable in terms of the character of underdevelopment in the region.

In the case of both the cooperative and the Newfoundland neo-nationalist movements, the class interest base has corresponded to the class base. The focus of activities has largely been on the political/economic realm, although the Newfoundland movement also places a considerable emphasis on ideology – on the need to preserve declining folkways. In terms of their action orien-

Forty Thousand Strong

The Fishermen's Protective Union, founded in 1908, has been described as "the most imaginative and innovative political movement that Newfoundland ever produced." Led by the energetic William Coaker, the FPU promoted a high degree of solidarity among its members. The following selection from a poem titled "Forty Thousand Strong" illustrates the spirit and cohesiveness of the movement.

WE ARE COMING Mr. Coaker from the East, West, North and South,
You have called us and we're coming to put our foes to rout,
By Merchants and by Governments too long we've been misruled,
We're determined now in future and no longer we'll be fooled,
We'll be brothers all and freemen and we'll rightify each wrong,
We are coming Mr. Coaker and we're forty thousand strong.

We are coming Mr. Coaker and though sharp shall be the fight,
Yet we trust in you our Leader, and our God will do the right,
All our beacon fires are lighted and we see them brightly burn;
With our motto, "No Surrender" all our enemies we will spurn,
Led by you we'll never falter, God shall help our cause along
We are coming Mr. Coaker and we're forty thousand strong.

Source:

The Fishermen's Advocate, St. John's, September 20, 1913.

tation, both are active; both have attempted to change external social conditions rather than themselves.

Some of the factors leading to the emergence of social movements in the Maritime provinces can also be found on the Canadian prairies. The most important factor is the relationship that prairie agriculture has had to the "golden triangle" (Toronto-Ottawa-Montreal) where political, financial, and industrial interests are centered. Although the debate concerning the motivations of the Fathers of Confederation continues, there is no doubt that, by the turn of the century, businessmen regarded the prairies as one of the foundations of Canadian prosperity. The prairies served as a market for eastern manufactured goods which were protected by tariffs from foreign competition. The prairies also provided wheat for an increasingly lucrative world market. But because the means of transportation (the CPR), the financial institutions, and industrial enterprises – all of which were essential to the activities of the farmer – were controlled by eastern capitalists, the terms of the exchange of manufactured goods for wheat did not favor the prairie farmer. In fact, the nature of eastern exploitation was sufficiently clear to the prairie farmers that the turn of the century brought movements aimed at the improvement of their lot.

As in the Maritimes, prairie farmers formed marketing cooperatives in an attempt to eliminate rapacious middlemen; in 1906, they formed the Grain Growers' Grain Company; in 1911, the Saskatchewan Cooperative Elevator Company; in 1923-24, the Saskatchewan Wheat Pool (McCrorie, 1971). Despite ideological overtones, these movements clearly focused on the economic realm. Their active orientation to change was based on a class referred to as "independent commodity producers," or petite bourgeoisie (Macpherson, 1955). The class interest base likewise comprised independent commodity producers. The power potential of these movements, however, was low.

This was not true of the political ventures of prairie producers, which in many instances qualify as high power movements. Farmers formed the base of several third party movements that had the potential, if not radically to change the position of the farmers in the national system of production and exchange, at least

"... if Mr. Aberhart says it is so"

For many Albertans in the 1930s, William Aberhart, a well-known religious leader and teacher, symbolized hope in the midst of Depression. His oratorical skills, reputation, and charisma went a long way in convincing the people that Social Credit was the answer to their economic difficulties. The following report of the response of the people of Camrose to Aberhart illustrates the trust he had inspired.

Mr. Aberhart has the absolute confidence of Social Credit of Alberta. As one dear old lady said: "I don't claim

to understand the fine points of the system, but if Mr. Aberhart says it is so, then I am sure everything will be all right." It is a pleasure to feel the temper of the audiences. There are many, many thousands who will back him to the last ditch. . . .

His heart burns for the welfare of the common man. It would be refreshing to have a churchman at the head of our government. Who is better fitted to carry out the teachings of Jesus Christ than a believer and doer of Christianity?

Source:

Alberta Social Credit Chronicle, August 17, 1934.

---

to alter that position. Through the federal Progressive Movement of 1921, and the subsequent election of various farmers' parties to political office at the provincial level, certain reforms were introduced. Perhaps the most important provincial manifestion of farmers' political concerns was the emergence of the Social Credit party in Alberta and the CCF in Saskatchewan. Both developed in the early years of the Depression.

Both parties have served as the focus of a continuing debate among Canadian scholars. It was formerly believed that these movements represented different ends of the political spectrum – the Social Credit was right wing; the CCF was socialist (Lipset, 1950). More recently, however, scholars have stressed the common class base of these two movements and have concluded, generally, that both the Social Credit and the CCF should be viewed as populist responses (of independent commodity producers) to the domination by eastern financial and industrial interests (Naylor, 1972; Sinclair, 1975; Conway, 1978).

Despite the credibility of these examinations, they perhaps give too little attention to differences that distinguish social movements at the ideological level.

As Laclau (1977) points out in his analysis of populism, just because apparently similar ideologies are accepted by comparable classes in different locations, it does not mean that the importance of individual elements of the ideologies is the same in each case. To the degree that social movements must be distinguished according to both their class base and ideology, this is an important concern. Ideology aside, however, prairie movements have been manifestations of class conflicts that have taken on some regional characteristics.

It is also clear that the metropolis-hinterland class divisions that gave rise to former movements – the recent wealth of Alberta notwithstanding – continue to characterize the Canadian situation. Recent western separatist stirrings reinforce this point. Moreover, the circumstances that have facilitated the development of movements in western Canada are not entirely unique. A comparison of western separatism in Canada and Australia, for example, indicates a number of parallels, including the presence of concrete economic grievances felt by those directly engaged in commodity production (Pratt, 1981).

The Quebec Hinterland

Despite the fact that the city of Montreal forms one corner of the golden triangle, many analysts examining Quebec's social movements have emphasized the province's hinterland status. From this perspective, movements like the early Parti Québécois can be viewed as attempts on the part of certain hinterland class fractions – like the Quebec new petite bourgeoisie – to improve their position within the national system of exchange. Other analysts have viewed numerous Quebec movements – the Nationalist League, formed at the turn of the century (Levitt, 1975); the Union Nationale, a product of the Depression (Quinn, 1963); the Parti Québécois (Desbarats, 1976; Saywell, 1977) – primarily as nationalist movements concerned with the preservation of Quebec's cultural and linguistic integrity.

A more recent analysis, however, has effectively synthesized both these perspectives. According to Bélanger and Saint-Pierre (1978), most movements in Quebec are best seen as forms of conflict between classes that assume what we would call ethnic, cultural, or nationalistic proportions. Bélanger and Saint-Pierre (1978) argue that:

By crossing the boundaries of social class, cultural and linguistic domination introduces a particular dimension in class relations. Its concrete definition can be found in discriminatory cultural and linguistic practices, but its effects vary according to the position occupied in class relations.

Bélanger and Saint-Pierre further suggest that the class-interest base of the PQ, which must now be treated as an institution rather than a movement, comprises a number of elements. Primary among these are factions of the Quebec petite bourgeoisie opposed to the Anglo-American control of the economy. Added to this group are factions of the new petite bourgeoisie, like the intellectuals whose major concern is with the preservation of culture and language. The interests of the working class are secondary to those of the petite and new petite bourgeoisie.

Even though existing studies (Pinard and Hamilton, 1978) have not used the idea of class in a way that

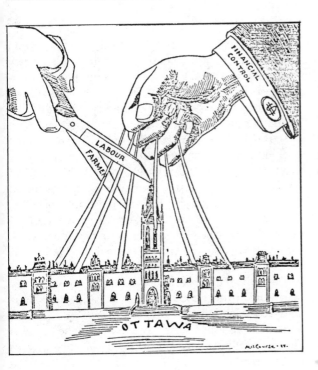

In 1935, William Aberhart promised Alberta's disillusioned farmfolk up to $25 a month for every man, woman and child if they would elect him the first Social Credit premier of Alberta. His new party swept to victory like a prairie fire.

enables us to assess accurately the class base of the PQ, it is nonetheless clear that the party has gained a great deal of support from the new petite bourgeoisie. It is equally clear that the focus of PQ activities is both political/economic and ideological. Although the party does not suggest a change in the relations of classes to the means of production, it does advocate measures that would improve the position of certain class fractions in a "national" system of exchange. In fact, one way to accomplish this is to take Quebec out of Confederation altogether. Such a move would promote the ideological goal of mintaining language and culture. It would also give the petite and new petite bourgeoisie greater political power. In view of the potential impact of these eventualities on Canadian society, the PQ must be termed high power. At this stage in its development, however, it makes more sense to treat the PQ as an institution rather than a movement. This distinction is reflected in the fact that the PQ has experienced increased internal dissension from members who feel the Party has sacrificed its fundamental goals in order to maintain political power.

The Ontario Hinterland

If we consider Canadian society as a whole, the golden triangle – Toronto-Ottawa-Montreal – must be viewed as the metropolitan center. Most of Canada's economic elite currently live in this triangle, and a large section of the Canadian economy is controlled from there (Clement, 1978). Several movements that have emerged in Ontario, outside the golden triangle, have taken on characteristics of hinterland movements. Certainly this is true of the farmers' movements that emerged in the nineteenth century and the early years of the twentieth.

Chief among these were the Grange Movement, the Patrons of Industry, and the United Farmers of Ontario. Although all emphasized particular problems faced by farmers, there were a number of common concerns, among them the problems associated with the farmer's unequal position in the system of exchange vis-a-vis urban industrialists and merchants, monopoly control of the economy, and, particularly after 1900, rural depopulation. In trying to deal with general problems, however, each adopted somewhat different

tactics. The Grange, for example, which entered Canada from the United States in 1872, abstained from political action, but "from the outset, it fulfilled a very high purpose through the educative and cultural influences which it brought to bear on the agricultural communities" (Wood, 1975, originally published 1924).

The Patrons of Industry took a different tack. Like the Grange, the Patrons had their roots in the troubled circumstances of farmers south of the border; unlike the Grange, they did not shy away from political involvement. In fact, they elected seventeen members to Queen's Park in the provincial election of 1894. The Patrons could not maintain the momentum of this victory, but the United Farmers of Ontario in 1919, led by E.C. Drury, actually formed a government. Despite a creditable legislative record, the farmers were not to repeat this victory in subsequent years. For one thing, rural depopulation was biting into their class base. For another, the movement was fraught with internal disputes. As a consequence, the interests of farm producers were relegated to secondary status in Ontario.

METROPOLITAN MOVEMENTS

Within the golden triangle, the major movements of the closing years of the nineteenth century grew out of tensions between the urban industrial bourgeoisie and the working class. Hence the trade union movements. Unionism was not the only working-class movement, however. As S.D. Clark (1948) points out, a number of religious movements, like the Salvation Army, also found fertile soil among the workers. If unionism was in the class interests of workers, as defined in this chapter, movements like the Salvation Army were not. If anything, the Salvation Army enhanced the class interests of the bourgeoisie. Through its emphasis on individual solutions to the problems of poverty and on the efficacy of hard work, it helped fashion a conscientious and placid work force for the emerging factories. In contrast to the unions, whose focus was political/economic, the Salvation Army concentrated on the religious.

A Union Man Testifies

The union movement in the nineteenth century was very weak and consequently had little success in bringing about social change. Membership was small, and the resistance of employers was high. Frequently, employers refused to hire workers who were known to have engaged in union activities. One method used to keep potential activists out of the factories was the insistence that new employees have permits signed by their previous boss. This practice was revealed in the hearings held by the Royal Commission on the Relations of Labour and Capital, 1889.

In reply to specific questions regarding the suitability of union men for employment, the witness explained the difficulties that organized labor encountered.

A. We were black-listed some years ago; I am not certain of the date, but I think it was in September, 1882. At that time each shop was paying a different price, and the boys were all complaining that some other employer was getting his cigars made cheaper, and they were arguing that something must be done in the matter. We appointed a committee to wait on each employer, and when they went to arbitrate with them in the morning the men found the doors locked and their tools out in the hall. The masters might call it a strike, but it was a lockout. Our intention was not to strike at all.

Q. You have spoken about a black-list?

A. Yes; I will give you information about that.

Q. Is that the reason you are not working in London now?

A. Yes; some time after that, I think a week or so, the bosses caused a paragraph to be inserted in the London papers, stating that those people who had been working for them were a lot of robbers, and so forth, and I believe they pledged themselves under a bond – I do not know the amount exactly – not to employ those men for a term of three years.

Source:

Hearings of the Royal Commission on the Relations of Labour and Capital, 1889, p. 136.

And compared to the unions, the action orientation of the Salvation Army falls more toward the passive. The potential for such religious movements to deter fundamental social change might be viewed as high. For exactly the opposite reason – the ability to introduce change – union movements could in some instances be characterized in the same fashion. In the case of either union movements or religious movements, however, the potential was not often realized.

Movements like the unions and the Salvation Army were not confined to the golden triangle. They could be found wherever tension existed among the various classes. There is no doubt, though, that the intensity of tensions could and did vary from time to time and from place to place. Proof of this assertion is provided by the Winnipeg General Strike of 1919 and the brief success of the One Big Union movement in western Canada (Bercuson, 1978).

While trade union activity continues, the unions are now better characterized as institutions than as movements. Exceptions may include some of the Canadian "breakaway" unions currently attempting to reduce dependence on large American union federations (White, 1975).

Given the institutional nature of contemporary unions, with few exceptions, it is doubtful that they will achieve major changes in the structure of Canadian capitalist society. Most have accepted the general principles of the system. At best they are concerned with insuring that union members receive a reasonable share of the economic pie. It is also true that the bourgeoisie have in most instances come to accept the existence of unions. Strikes notwithstanding, many analysts claim that unions contribute to effective control of the work force.

To conclude this section on metropolitan and hinterland movements, we should emphasize that geographical distance from the metropolitan center corresponds to imbalances in the national system of exchange, even for members of the same class. For example, a constant complaint of prairie farmers is that, compared to Ontario residents, they are required to pay relatively

It's Hard Not To Think of the Gay

The gay liberation movement does not have a clear class interest base, nor does it have a metropolitan-hinterland dimension. Nonetheless, the movement has challenged certain widely held assumptions regarding sexuality and has pressed for specific changes in legislation, employment, and social attitudes. Like many other movements, this one has had to deal with both factionalism and the loss of momentum that oftentimes accompanies institutionalization.

No one knew and no one cared at the time, but something was indeed happening to public life in Canada that rainy August day in 1971. About 100 homosexual men and women were in Ottawa to march on Parliament . . . to demand their rights. In 1969 Parliament had established, as Pierre Trudeau put it, that the state had no place in the bedrooms of the nation; homosexuals were therefore free to do as they wished, as consenting adults in private. But they wanted more than that: equality in jobs, living accommodation, government, the armed forces, and society in general. . . .

The official public start of the gay movement in Canada was the founding in 1969 of the University of Toronto Homophile Association and this summer gays will celebrate the tenth anniversary of that event with a national conference of gay organizations in Ottawa under the umbrella of the Canadian Lesbian and Gay Rights Coalition. But the movement became firmly institutionalized with the foundation . . . of the Community Homophile Association of Toronto (CHAT). In the early days the movement was devoted to counselling – usually to assuring individual gays that they weren't the only people in the world who felt lonely and persecuted. Later, splinter groups formed, and the gays divided into radical and conservative wings.

Source:

Saturday Night, March 1979, p. 3.

high prices for manufactured goods, to the advantage of eastern-based industrialists. In addition, the metropolitan concentration of capital means fewer employment possibilities and consequent higher unemployment for hinterland residents. This situation, in turn, means lower wages even for members of the work force who are employed. In short, the metropolis-hinterland relationship increases those tensions arising from class divisions in society. When Quebec is considered, these factors are further complicated by the linguisitic and the cultural. Movements arising in various parts of the country have in many cases reflected these differences.

THE SUCCESS OR FAILURE OF MOVEMENTS

The metropolis-hinterland distinction, useful in examining some social movements, is less useful in examining others. In addition, although the class base of a movement can usually be identified, it is often difficult to connect the class base to a distinct class-interest base. These statements are true for the multifaceted youth movement that emerged in the sixties.

Judging from university sit-ins, no part of the country seems to have been unaffected by young people's concern with "repressive bureaucracy." And, despite the essentially petite and new petite bourgeoisie origins of the participants in the movement, it is difficult, when considering both its political and countercultural aspects, to link it to a particular class-interest base. The same can be said of the gay liberation movement. Most of its activities are confined to large cities, but it manifests no metropolis-hinterland dimension. Despite a petite and new petite bourgeoisie leadership, it is difficult to identify a class-interest base for this movement.

Another difficulty in examining social movements, in addition to those posed by class-interest base and class base, is the fact that social movements do not just appear out of nowhere. There are factors that facilitate or deter their emergence. Some of these can be found in the larger society in which the movement must operate. Those we can call *external factors*, and we will examine three of them: conjunctural conditions,

sympathy and counter movements, and the role of the state. Other factors that will contribute to the success or failure of a movement derive from the movement itself. These we can call *internal factors*, and we will examine four of them: organizational base, ideology, factionalism, and leadership.

EXTERNAL FACTORS
Conjunctural Conditions

Whether or not a movement will succeed depends, to a degree, on the nature of, and relations among, classes in society at any given moment. Collectively, we call these **conjunctural conditions**. A movement may possess characteristics that usually guarantee success, but if conjunctural conditions are not right, it is doomed. The Canadian Nazi movement, for example, which enlisted several thousand members prior to the outbreak of World War II, had able leaders, a coherent ideology, and ample funds (Betcherman, 1975). Yet it failed. The reason can be found in the relations among classes in Canada. We mentioned earlier that Nazism was successful in Germany because the political power of the bourgeoisie was far less than its economic power. At the same time, no other class was sufficiently strong to govern. It was into this void that the Nazis stepped. In Canada, bourgeois dominance was clearly established. There was no such power vacuum. Consequently, there was little chance of success.

Sympathy and Counter Movements

Closely related to the nature and relations of classes in society are the presence or absence of what have been called **sympathy** and **counter movements** (Clark, Grayson, and Grayson, 1975). The sympathy movement is one that supports the general objectives of the original movement. It may or may not have the same class-interest base and the same class base as the main movement. For example, movements in Canada advocating abortion on demand have received considerable support from the more amorphous women's movement. Counter movements, on the other hand, are those that spring into existence in an attempt to offset the activities of a movement with which they disagree. The ProLife movement sprang up to oppose the abortion movement. The Pro-Canada Committee arose in Quebec after the 1976 Parti Québécois victory to thwart the PQ in its attempts to achieve sovereignty association. Usually, counter movements have a different class-interest base and class base than the original movement.

The State

Of even more consequence to a social movement than the activities of sympathy and counter movements is the position of the state. Through its repressive and ideological apparatuses as discussed in Chapter 13, the state is perhaps the institution that can have the most effect on the success or failure of social movements. Numerous religious movements are simply ignored, for example, because their activities pose no threat to "peace, order, and good government." In other cases, the state has been known to support movements. During the 1960s, for example, in an attempt to harness some of the energy of the youth movement, the federal government sponsored the Company of Young Canadians. Its goal was to carry out good works among the dispossessed of Canadian society. Eventually, the fervor of the sixties waned, the budgets of federal departments were trimmed, and the Company of Young Canadians was dropped.

In other cases, the state simply opposes social movements. It opposed a number of radical political movements in the 1930s. In Ontario, at least, groups like the communists were declared illegal under Section 98 of the Criminal Code, and Tim Buck, leader of the Canadian Communist Party, was sent to Kingston Penitentiary for his "criminal" activities. Clearly, in Canada, even if the power potential of a movement is low, the state is most likely to oppose it if it perceives it as a threat to the ruling class.

In a number of instances, as you saw in Chapter 13, the Canadian state, through the military and police, has engaged in mass violence to insure the defeat of forces regarded as a threat to the principle of "peace, order and good government." In examinations of the Red River uprising of 1869-70, the North-West rebel-

lion of 1885, the Quebec City riots of 1918, the Winnipeg General Strike of 1919, and the Regina riot of 1935, Torrance (1977) identified patterns in the response of the state to what it regarded as threatening circumstances. As some of these occurrences involved social movements, they are worth mentioning.

The first pattern is that in all five cases the state was concerned with the incendiary potential of events. In the North-West rebellion, for instance, Torrance (1977) notes:

The spectre haunting the government was the prospect of the Metis defiance setting off a chain reaction that would bring under arms the large Indian population scattered across the Northwest.

A second pattern is the tendency of the state to regard leaders as criminals and followers as having been misled. Torrance (1977) points out:

The main body of the violent have been seen as well-intentioned dupes who must be subjected to the politics of influence in order to wean them away from the sway of their malevolent leaders. The leaders have been branded as deviant members of society, interested only in manipulating others for their own illegitimate purposes.

Torrance identifies a third characteristic response of the state as a reluctance to deal with grievances leading to collective protest. It is not difficult to see why. To deal with grievances would be to recognize their validity. The fourth pattern she notes is that in all five cases the government attempted to use diplomacy as well as repression in dealing with its adversaries. This was certainly true in the Red River uprising led by Louis Riel in 1869-70. As Stanley (1960) notes: "Sir John Macdonald . . . while pursuing a policy of conciliation and concession [with the Metis] was quietly making preparations for the sending of an expedition . . . in the spring." Part of the explanation for this dual approach may be found in the concern of the state to maintain public opinion on its side.

It is clear that many of the responses dealt with by Torrance were evident once again in the state's reaction to the October Crisis of 1970. Given the historical record, it is likely that the state will violently intervene in future situations where it regards the collective

Through its police and its military, the state can attempt to crush any social movement it perceives as a threat to social order. The state has intervened on several occasions in Canadian history, and this has often led to violent confrontations.

political demands of groups as threatening to certain interests. Obviously, the state can be very influential in helping or hindering the growth of any social movement.

INTERNAL FACTORS

Organizational Base

One of the primary factors that can impede a social movement is the absence of an **organizational base** upon which the movement can build. The organizational base can be viewed as pre-existing social bodies on which social movements are able to base their activities. These social bodies can be communal, like the family, tribe, or clan, where interactions involve the individual's total being. Or they can be associational, like voluntary associations or trade unions, where individuals are treated in accordance with one of their many facets. In many cases, as with the Catholic Church, these social bodies can cross class divisions. In others, like the unions, they parallel them.

Frequently, these organizational bases can serve as communication centers in which individuals can air grievances and obtain information on issues of concern to them. For example, the study groups of the Calgary Prophetic Bible Institute served as the organizational base for the Social Credit movement in Alberta. In so doing, these study groups provided a contact point for Social Credit adherents and a forum for discussion and the exchange of information. In other instances, organizational bases provide candidates for leadership of the new movement. They may even provide an ideological matrix that enables movement participants to place their concerns in a broader social framework. Whatever their nature, organizational bases make an important contribution to the success of a social movement.

The mere existence of an organizational base, however, is not enough to assure the success of the movement. A good example of a movement that failed, despite an impressive organizational base, is offered by Forbes (1975) in his discussion of the Maritime rights movement of the 1920s. Alarmed by their decreasing fortunes in the national scheme, a considerable number of Maritimers of all classes reasoned that:

Co-operation was essential if the three Atlantic provinces were to counteract the eclipse of their influence which resulted from the rise of the West and the growing metropolitan dominance of Central Canada (1975).

Part of the solution for regional ills would be provided by a union of the Maritime Provinces which would permit not only a more efficient use of available resources, but would also facilitate more effective lobbying in Ottawa.

Because Maritime decline adversely affected the fortunes of all classes, it is not surprising that the call for Maritime union was endorsed by a cross-section of groups and organizations, such as the Maritime division of the Canadian Manufacturers' Association, retail merchants' organizations, the United Farmers, federations of labor, and toward the end of the decade by the Maritime Fishermen's Union. Despite this impressive organizational base, the movement failed. As Forbes points out, none of their "aspirations was capable of realization with the continued decline of the economic and political status of the Maritimes in the Dominion" (1975). Clearly, the presence of an organizational base is not enough in itself to guarantee success of a social movement.

Ideology

The inexorable economic pull of central Canada helped doom the Maritime rights movement to failure. In other cases, the absence of a clearly articulated **ideology** has had an equally disastrous effect. Many people consider ideology to be a system of beliefs regarding the ways in which society works or should work. Others add that belief systems legitimize the dominance of certain classes over others. In addition, ideology is seen as a backdrop against which individuals interpret their everday experiences. Frequently, social movements provide their adherents with a system of beliefs that runs counter to what is socially acceptable. Ideologies of social movements often provide a view of reality that may suggest to the participants the means whereby they can change their circumstances. Not all ideologies, however, comprise beliefs that accurately reflect the real possibilities available to those desirous of change.

One movement that failed to develop an appropriate ideology was the federal Progressives. To everyone's surprise, in 1921, Canadian farmers elected 65 Progressives to the House of Commons (Morton, 1950). It was difficult, however, to sustain this momentum, partly because movement supporters could not agree on a common ideology. The so-called Alberta wing of the movement advocated what was called "group government," while the Manitoba wing never really viewed the Progessives as anything but an extension of the federal Liberal Party. There was, then, a lack of consensus regarding strategy, tactics, and goals. Coupled with other problems, this absence of a shared ideology was fatal to the movement.

In contrast to the Progressives, the Waffle movement, which grew in the womb of the New Democratic Party in the late 1960s, developed a fairly clear ideology. It was evident to Wafflers that various social injustices found in Canada could be alleviated only by a joint policy of nationalism and socialism, and only after the stranglehold of American corporations on the Canadian economy had been broken. Despite its relatively

"We aim to replace the present capitalist system"

The ideology of the Co-operative Commonwealth Federation formed the basis of the Regina Manifesto of July 1933. In this Manifesto the CCF clearly expressed its system of beliefs regarding the way in which society should work.

We aim to replace the present capitalist system, with its inherent injustice and inhumanity, by a social order from which the domination and exploitation of one class by another will be eliminated, in which economic planning will supercede unregulated private enterprise and competition, and in which genuine democratic self-government, based upon economic equality will be possible. The present order is marked by glaring inequalities of wealth and opportunity, by chaotic waste and instability; and in an age of plenty it condemns the great mass of the people to poverty and insecurity. Power has become more and more concentrated into the hands of a small irresponsible minority of financiers and industrialists and to their predatory interest the majority are habitually sacrificed. When private profit is the main stimulus to economic effort, our society oscillates between periods of feverish prosperity in which the main benefits go to speculators and profiteers, and of catastrophic depression, in which the common man's normal state of insecurity and hardship is accentuated. We believe that these evils can be removed only in a planned and socialized economy in which our natural resources and the principal means of production and distribution are owned, controlled and operated by the people.

clear ideology, however, in the end the Waffle movement fell to pieces. By itself, then, ideology is not enough to guarantee success either.

Factionalism

Frequently, the inability of movement participants to develop a coherent and accepted ideology becomes manifest in the organizational structure of the movement. In other cases, the ideological divisions are extensions of pre-existing organizational fissures. In either case, the movement is confronted with **factionalism**, a condition in which different groups composing the movement's general membership develop different ideologies, leaders, or bases.

Most movements, in one form or another, experience factionalism. Those that deal with it effectively can continue with their activities. Those that do not either disintegrate or become ineffectual, their strength sapped by internal disputes. The social gospel movement provides a good example of factionalism.

Concerned at the turn of the century with the abuses of a growing urban industrial society, many Protestants advocated a return to the true spirit of Christianity as a remedy for social ailments (Allen, 1971). Among these advocates it was possible to identify a conservative, a progressive, and a radical wing. The conservatives, while they attacked the evils of such things as alcohol and poverty, still placed a heavy emphasis on individual salvation. In contrast, the radicals emphasized the redemption of society as a logically prior step to the reform of individuals. In true Canadian fashion, the progressives had one foot in either camp.

More important, the conservatives had a disproportionate number of supporters from established Protestant churches, like the Anglican. The radicals drew a disproportionate number of their followers from less orthodox churches, like the Methodist. The different groups had different spokesmen. The more familiar of these, like J.S. Woodsworth, were associated with the radical wing. After the demise of the social gospel movement, many radicals went into other movements, like the CCF – Woodsworth was one of the founding members – which in a number of ways continued the type of criticism initiated by the social gospellers.

Even though the different wings of the social gospel movement had in many instances been able to cooperate, there is no question that the movement's overall effectiveness was limited by factionalism. This is nowhere clearer than in the Winnipeg General Strike of 1919: the radicals supported the strikers, while the conservatives were sympathetic to employers. A more recent example of how factionalism can limit the effectiveness of a movement is provided by the breakup of the Pro-Canada Committee, which was designed to fight the Parti Québécois proposal for sovereignty association for Quebec.

Leadership

The leadership of a social movement is often crucial to its success. The tasks of leaders are difficult. They must provide the movement with direction. They must also be able to help blend the participants and any factions into a fairly unified body. (In short, they must embody what Weber called *charismatic authority*; see Chapter 10.) Such abilities are rare.

Lenin possessed both of these abilities. While he had long been the leader of the Bolsheviks, his absence from Russia in the early days of the Russian Revolution in 1917 contributed to a situation in which the Bolsheviks were prepared to support a form of bourgeois democracy under the leadership of Kerensky. The position of Trotsky, however, leader of the rival Mensheviks, was that the revolutionary impetus should carry the Revolution past bourgeois democracy and into socialism. But the Bolsheviks, influential in the newly formed soviets and unions, refused to listen. Only when Lenin returned to Russia and began to urge a tactic similar to Trotsky's did the Bolsheviks begin to act in a way that would eventually lead them to power.

It would be difficult to argue that the decisions of the leaders of Canadian movements have been as portentous as those made by Lenin in 1917. On the other hand, the organizational and personal characteristics of many leaders have had serious implications for the movements they led. It is clear, for example, that the current Parti Québécois in many ways bears the imprint of its founder, René Lévesque. A former journalist, television personality, and Liberal cabinet minister, he enjoys considerable popularity among the press and general public (Desbarats, 1976). His role in the nationalization of Quebec's hydroelectric institutions, under the government of Jean Lesage, demonstrated qualities of tough-minded and efficient administration. We cannot conclude that without Lévesque there would have been no successful separatist movement in Quebec – the PQ, after all, was only one separatist movement among many – but there is no doubt that the eventual direction taken by the several movements that joined the PQ had a great deal to do with the priorities and vision of René Lévesque, its leader.

SUMMARY

1. Analyses of social movements can be distinguished in terms of their fundamental assumptions. Those characterized as breakdown theories assume that social movements result from a breakdown of social bonds or consensus. Those referred to as solidarity theories assume that movements arise as a consequence of struggles for power in society. The former theories underlie structural functionalist and symbolic interactionist views of society. The latter derive more from the Marxist view.

2. Social movements can, in general, be defined as attempts on the part of large groups of people to introduce or prevent social change.

3. Other social bodies also attempt to introduce or prevent change. To appreciate the distinctive features of particular social movements, it is therefore necessary to look at all social bodies in terms of their degree of structural crystallization and potential to resist or introduce change.

4. Social movements can be distinguished by their class-interest base, class base, focus, and action orientation.

5. Large numbers of Canadian social movements have taken on the characteristics of struggles between the metropolis and its various hinterlands.

6. Some social movements are unconnected to the metropolis-hinterland dynamic. Others are difficult to assign to a class-interest base.

7. Social movements do not appear randomly on the historical stage. A number of factors are responsible for their emergence, and for their success or failure. Some are external to the movement – conjunctural factors, etc. – others are internal, like the presence or absence of a clear ideology.

8. Social movements appear to be a permanent feature of society. In Canada, as elsewhere, groups of people have always struggled to either introduce or prevent social change.

GLOSSARY

Action orientation. Characteristic of a social movement: either active, to resist or promote changes in the world; or passive, to change movement participants.

Breakdown theories. Theories holding that social movements result from a breakdown of social bonds and/or a lack of consensus.

Change potential. Potential of a social movement to promote or resist social change.

Class base. Class origins of participants in a social movement; class base may or may not be distinct from class-interest base.

Class-interest base. Social classes or class fractions whose interests are promoted by a movement.

Conjunctural conditions. The nature of relations between classes at a given movement in time.

Factionalism. Condition of a social movement in which different groups within the membership develop conflicting ideologies, leaders, and/or bases.

Focus. Realm into which a social movement directs its activities – political/economic or ideological.

Ideology. A system of beliefs regarding the ways in which society works or should work.

Institution. Sets of beliefs, norms, and values that define how people, groups, and organizations should resolve central problems, and the individuals, organizations, and groups whose organized activity deals with the problems.

Marxism. View of society that sees conflict as the underlying social principle.

Metropolitan-hinterland relationship. Relationship characterized by an unequal system of exchange among various areas of the country.

New petite bourgeoisie. Class that does not own its means of production but ideologically and politically aligns itself most often with the bourgeoisie. This class includes civil servants, teachers, and professionals.

Organizational base. Pre-existing social bodies on which social movements can base their activities.

Social movement. Behavior in which a large number of people try to bring about or resist social change.

Solidarity theories. Theories holding that social movements result from a struggle for power in society.

Structural conduciveness. Social arrangements that support or deter the development of a movement.

Structural crystallization. Degree to which the role of participants, the level of commitment, the chain of command, and the goals of a movement, etc., have been clearly defined.

Structural strain. Phenomena that represent the inadequate functioning of society.

Sympathy and counter movements. Movements that support (sympathy) or oppose (counter) an emerging social movement.

FURTHER READING

Allen, Richard. *The Social Passion.* Toronto: University of Toronto Press, 1971. The standard reference for information on the social gospel movement at the turn of the century. The section on factionalism is especially good.

Betcherman, Lita-Rose. *The Swastika and the Maple Leaf.* Toronto: Fitzhenry and Whiteside, 1975. An interesting account of the rise and fall of the Canadian Nazi movement. The regional strengths and variations of the movement are clearly demonstrated.

Brym, R., and R.J. Sacouman (eds.). *Underdevelopment and Social Movements in Atlantic Canada.* Toronto: New Hogtown Press, 1979. Written from a Marxist perspective, the articles in this book are among the best available on Maritime social movments.

Clark, S.D. *Church and Sect in Canada.* Toronto: University of Toronto Press, 1948. The religious movements analyzed in this book span almost two centuries. The work is, perhaps, Clark's most significant contribution to sociology in Canada.

Clark, Sam, J. Paul Grayson, and L.M. Grayson (eds.). *Prophecy and Protest: Social Movements in Twentieth-Century Canada.* Toronto: Gage Educational Publishing, 1975. A number of articles, written from varying perspectives, on social movements in Canada. It is the only general text available on this topic.

Lipset, S.M. *Agrarian Socialism.* Berkeley: University of California Press, 1950. A classic interpretation of the rise of the Cooperative Commonwealth Federation (CCF) in Saskatchewan during the 1930s.

Morton, W.L. *The Progressive Party in Canada.* Toronto: University of Toronto Press, 1950. Morton gives the classic interpretation of the roots of Canadian Progressivism, particularly in the west. The significance of factionalism in hastening the demise of the movement is well documented.

Pinard, Maurice. *The Rise of a Third Party.* Englewood Cliffs, N.J.: Prentice-Hall, 1971. Pinard attempts to apply structural functionalist theory to the study of the Social Credit Party in Quebec.

Pratt, Larry and Garth Stevenson (eds.). *Western Separatism: The Myths, Realities, and Dangers.* Edmonton: Hurtig Publishers, 1981.

Resnick, Philip. *The Land of Cain.* Vancouver: New Star Books, 1977. Written from a Marxist perspective, the book provides a good analysis of the class basis of post-World War II Canadian nationalism.

Young, Walter. *The Anatomy of a Party.* Toronto: University of Toronto Press, 1969. In analyzing the federal CCF, the author attempts to isolate the factors leading to the transition of the movement into an institution.

VI
RESEARCH METHODS

Throughout this book you have read about surveys, participant observation, interviews, rates, averages, standard deviations, correlations, and significant findings. This final section is concerned with what these terms mean.

Chapter 17, *Social Research*, describes how sociologists conduct their research. The approach here is to see the reader as a consumer of information. Divorce rates, crime rates, life expectancy, percentage employed, average income – such statistics are the stuff of life, the content of the daily news. The impact of oil pipelines on the environment, the effect of television violence on children, the legalization of marijuana – our response to such issues determines our future. When presented with research findings, we need to ask several questions. How was this research done? Is it good research? What do all these averages, rates, and percentage mean? Are the findings rational? Are they relevant? Are they true?

The intention in Chapter 17 is to help you to evaluate for yourself the vast amounts of information concerning society that are reported in the news media – and in this book.

CHAPTER
17
SOCIAL RESEARCH

CHAPTER 17
SOCIAL RESEARCH

ROBERT HAGEDORN

R. ALAN HEDLEY

Sociologists writing a chapter or book on social research methods realize full well that few students approach the subject with wide-eyed enthusiasm. However, these same sociologists are not dissuaded from their venture, because they know that a sound knowledge of how research should be carried out leads to more valid results and more appropriate interpretations of these results.

In the last ten years or so, several authors have adopted the stance that science can be fun and have attempted to attract students (and their professors) with such titles as *The Sociologist as Detective* (Sanders, 1974), *Social Statistics Without Tears* (Johnson, 1977), and *Fist-Fights in the Kitchen* (Lewis, 1975).

The point is that an understanding of the process of social research is necessary if you plan to become a professional researcher, and extremely useful even if you do not. You are constantly being called upon to evaluate the results of research. Reading your daily newspaper, purchasing a car, writing or evaluating reports in your work, even buying a bottle of aspirin – all these things require you to arrive at some interpretation or conclusion. A knowledgeable appreciation of how these facts came about or were arrived at – that is, of the research process – is essential to a sound interpretation of what they mean.

It is the purpose of this chapter to provide you with enough information so that you may begin to evaluate critically not only the results of scientific research found in the library, but also the mass of information with which you are bombarded daily. Social research is not undertaken only by academics. Whenever questions are posed, observations made, and conclusions drawn, research is done. In our daily lives, we are constantly involved in the research process. The rest of this chapter describes the various stages of the formal research process and some of the obstacles we must avoid in order to arrive at clear answers to the questions we address.

PLANNING AND DOING RESEARCH

Robert Burns observed that the best laid schemes of mice and men often go astray. His observation applies with particular force to social research: we should plan and design our research as carefully as possible, but when it comes to carrying it out, we should realize that *inevitably* there will be problems – some we may have expected and some not. There is no such thing as an absolutely perfect piece of research that answers once and for all the particular questions posed. Competing alternative explanations will always be possible for two reasons. First, snags, difficulties, and obstacles are inherent in the research process. Second, even if it were possible to anticipate and thus avoid these snags, it is impossible to design one piece of research with findings that simultaneously are unambiguous, have general applicability, and pertain directly to the real world.

If is extremely important to realize these inherent limitations at the outset, and we will address them throughout the chapter. Because of them, every single research result may be accepted only tentatively. We can never know with absolute certainty. However, if we are careful in designing and conducting research, and if the same result is repeated upon several occasions, we can have confidence in that result.

The research process by its very nature involves

Figure 17–1. The Stages of Social Research

1. Select the problem.
2. Review previous research on the problem.
3. State the hypothesis (predict what you will find).
4. Construct indicators for all variables in the hypotheses (operational definitions).
5. Set up the research design.
6. Select appropriate sample or population.
7. Decide upon data collection method(s).
8. Collect the data.
9. Analyze the data.
10. Interpret the data (write the research report).

---

uncertainty. We can't get around this, but we can suggest ways to reduce the uncertainty and thus increase our confidence in the results (see Figure 17-1). Think of the research process as an obstacle course and a series of decision points. Researchers have learned a great deal about these obstacles and the kinds of decisions possible. Furthermore, they can estimate the kinds of difficulties you will confront or the uncertainty you will face should you not make or not be able to make the appropriate decision. This is the kind of information you will need when you come to assess the overall results of research, whether it involves social problems or what kind of breakfast cereal you are going to eat.

THE RESEARCH PROBLEM

You are reading a newspaper article on juvenile delinquency. You observe that most delinquents reported have addresses in the predominantly poor areas of your city. You might conclude on the basis of this casual observation that there is something about being poor that causes delinquency. However, you want to test this proposition systematically before you are convinced. If you pursue this hunch – for at this stage that is all it is – you will then be engaged in genuine social research. What do you do? How do you go about it?

First, you should become familiar with previous research on delinquency. Are there any studies on delinquency? Have other researchers noted the relationship between social class and delinquency? Is it a

The Scientist and the Citizen

Whether or not you do research, the results of research will affect you.

It has been a common refrain in recent years that the Canadian public has a very limited knowledge of science and technology, despite the fact that developments in these areas have brought and will continue to bring about countless changes in the fabric of daily life. Many of today's developments hold tremendous potential both to improve the quality of human life and to put it at serious risk, but Canadians are largely unaware of their implications.

Treatment of science-related issues by the media has led many people to believe that scientists are the only people who can understand the subject matter of science and that it would be best to leave science to the scientists. But the applications of the products of science are too important to leave the subject to scientists alone.

Many important decisions to be made by our politicans in the near future deal with the products of science. The CANDU reactor, the dangers of asbestos, mercury and arsenic, communications satellites and a tar sands development are all examples of science-related matters

that will have a profound effect on the lives of Canadians. Yet the legislators who are making the decisions have a very limited knowledge of science. Of the 264 Members of Parliament, 61 are businessmen, 60 are lawyers, while 7 are engineers and technologists and 5 are university teachers and researchers by profession. A survey carried out during lobbying efforts by the CAUT and the CFBS during December 1976 and April 1977 indicated that the level of comprehension of science-related issues and scientific research was lowest among those M.P.'s surveyed who were businessmen prior to their election. Lawyers were rated second to last in their comprehension of the situation.

One overriding theme that emerged from the lobbying efforts was the need to generate public interest in science in order to influence government decisions. Without public input into science-related decisions, the horrors resulting from the effects of past applications will continue. Incidents such as the dumping of poisonous wastes into the Love Canal in the United States, an action which led to the contamination of entire neighbourhoods more than 20 years later, will become an all too familiar story. But effective public response to such decisions cannot take place until people

have made informed choices about them, based on reputable sources of information. The source of that information should be those who know whereof they speak – the scientists. . . .

While important steps have already been taken, much remains to be done to accomplish the long-term goals of those engaged in "bringing science to the people." Popularization of science will rely to a great extent on the cooperation of Canada's scientists, and it will be their responsibility to ensure the accuracy of statements made in the media concerning developments in their areas of research. It will also be necessary to encourage journalists and students of journalism to consider science writing as a specialty and to encourage a concern for accurate science writing. The final responsibility, however, rests with the members of the general public to become knowledgeable and involved in matters which could ultimately have a profound effect on their daily lives.

Source:

From Simpson, Catherine. "Science in the public eye." *Canadian Association of University Teachers Bulletin*, 26:3, May 1979, p. 15. Catherine Simpson was Project Assistant with the Task Force on Public Awareness of Science and Technology in Canada.

---

well established relationship repeated in many studies? Depending upon the answers to these questions, you may or may not decide to proceed with your own research. In all serious research undertakings, however, a review of the research literature relevant to the problem is a necessary first step. Because science is a cumulative process, you first want to know how your own research compares to other studies of the same thing.

Next, it is necessary for you to write down the relationship you expect to find among the variables in which you are interested. A **variable** is a factor that can differ or vary from one situation to another or from one individual or group to another. Delinquency is a variable in that some people are more or less delinquent than others, while some may not be delinquent at all. Similarly, social class is a variable. People may be upper, middle, or lower class. In your statement of relationship, you may propose that the lower the social class, the greater the likelihood of delinquency.

This is an **hypothesis**, a prediction of what you expect to find in your research.

The variable that you are attempting to explain – delinquency – is the **dependent variable**; i.e., the variation in this factor is dependent upon or caused by some other factor – in this case, social class. The causal factor – social class – is called the **independent variable**. In other words, you are saying that depending upon what social class an adolescent is from, there will be a greater or lesser chance of delinquency. If people are upper class, the chances of delinquency are slight; if they are lower class, the chances are relatively great. This is your hypothesis.

After you state your hypothesis, it is then necessary to find out if the relationship hypothesized actually exists. This involves measurement, but how do you measure social class and delinquency? How do you differentiate between upper and middle class? How do you know whether a person is delinquent? At this stage, it is necessary to construct measuring instruments of your variables.

Remember your original observation in the newspaper. How did you first measure social class and delinquency? Because you know your city well, and consequently where the rich kids and the poor kids live, your measure or indicator of social class in this case was residential area. Your indicator of delinquency was the arrests of juveniles reported in the paper. **Indicators** are measures of variables in the same way that a thermometer is a measure of temperature. For any one variable, there are, potentially, a variety of indicators to measure it.

For example, would the cases of delinquency reported in the paper for any particular day (one indicator) be identical to the arrests actually recorded by the police for the previous day (another indicator)? Probably not. The police list would no doubt be longer, while the newspaper list would contain a biased representation – biased certainly from the point of view of startling or newsworthy cases, and biased probably by class. Apprehended children of prominent citizens might not be listed, because of their parents' influence or position. In any event, it is extremely likely that the two lists (your two indicators) would be different.

The construction or selection of appropriate indicators of variables is crucial to the research process. The indicators you choose can influence your results dramatically and cause you to draw wrong conclusions. For example, does arrest necessarily imply guilt? No, you decide, but conviction does. But if you choose to use official conviction records, instead of lists of arrests, as your indicator of delinquency, other problems arise. In some cases, for instance, delinquents are handled informally by the courts, and no official record is maintained. Furthermore, conviction records would give you a list of only those found guilty. What about those who committed indictable offenses but were neither arrested nor convicted?

By now you will appreciate that achieving correspondence between variables and indicators is a difficult process. The process is called the *operationalization* of variables, and the measures or indicators adopted together constitute your **operational definitions**. Depending upon what operational definition you use for delinquency, your results will differ, and it is important to realize that this difference will be produced by the measurement process itself – not by changes in the actual incidence of delinquency. This is why in the overall evaluation of research results it is necessary to judge the appropriateness of what is actually being used to measure what.

Edmund Vaz (1965), a sociologist interested in delinquency, has devised an interesting operational definition of this variable, a checklist of nineteen activities that are violations of the law for juveniles (see Figure 17-3). Adolescents are asked to respond to this checklist by indicating how often, if ever, they have engaged in each activity. Although there are difficulties with Vaz's operational definition (will people tell the truth about their illegal behavior?), nevertheless it does avoid the problem of recording only those who have been caught for their offenses. You will also note that if one researcher used official records to measure delinquency, while another used self-reported behavior, the discrepancy produced could be due the different operational definitions and not the incidence of actual delinquency.

Vaz's measure of social class involves two indicators: the occupation of the father and his highest level of education attained. (Because juveniles assume the social

Figure 17-2. Operational Definition of Delinquency Checklist

How often have you done each of these things?

Offences	Never	Once or Twice	Several Times	Quite Often	Very Often
1. Driven a car without a driver's license					
2. Taken little things that did not belong to you					
3. Skipped school without a legitimate excuse					
4. Driven beyond the speed limit					
5. Participated in drag races along the highway with your friends					
6. Engaged in a fist fight with another boy					
7. Been feeling "high" from drinking beer, wine, or liquor					
8. Gambled for money at cards, dice, or some other game					
9. Remained out all night without parents' permission					
10. Taken a car without owner's knowledge					
11. Been placed on school probation or expelled from school					
12. Destroyed or damaged public or private property of any kind					
13. Taken little things of value between $2 and $50 which did not belong to you					
14. Tried to be intimate with a member of the opposite sex					
15. Broken into or tried to break and enter a building with the intention of stealing					
16. Sold, used, or tried to use drugs of some kind					
17. Bought or tried to buy beer, wine, or liquor from a store or adult					
18. Taken money of any amount from someone or place which did not belong to you					
19. Taken a glass of beer, wine, or liquor at a party or elsewhere with your friends					

SOURCE: Adapted from Vaz, E.W. "Middle-class adolescents: self-reported delinquency and youth culture activities." *Canadian Review of Sociology and Anthropology*, 2, 1965, 52-70.

class of their parents, it becomes necessary to measure class by this means.) The two indicators are then combined to form an index or overall operational definition of social class. Figure 17-3 outlines the progress of our research problem to this point.

The hypothesized relationship between social class and delinquency may be tested in a variety of ways. Unfortunately, we may obtain a variety of answers, depending upon what operational definitions are used. In fact, as you saw in Chapter 6, just such a discrep-

ancy is obtained in the strength of the relationship between social class and delinquency, depending upon whether official records or self-reported behavior is used to measure delinquency. Obviously, if we encounter these kinds of difficulties in systematic, rigorous research, we should certainly be wary of accepting casual observations at face value.

In the next section, we will deal with some of the problems involved in the very crucial process of measurement.

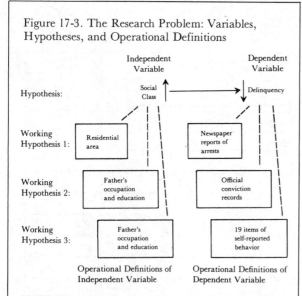

Figure 17-3. The Research Problem: Variables, Hypotheses, and Operational Definitions

NOTE: The predicted relationship – hypothesis – between social class and delinquency is presented in the top part of the diagram. The arrows refer to the direction and type of the expected relation. Social class, the independent variable, influences or causes differential rates of delinquency, the dependent variable. The higher the social class (arrow pointing up), the lower the delinquency rate (arrow pointing down). The boxes represent the indicators of the independent and dependent variables.

PROBLEMS IN MEASUREMENT

So far in this chapter we have indicated some of the difficulties involved in the measurement of variables and the testing of hypotheses. We will now address this issue directly, because measurement is the weakest part of the research process. As any chain is only as strong as its weakest link, so too are research results only as good as the measurements used to produce them.

Achieving valid results is a major goal of all research. **Validity** is the result of having measured what you intended to measure. This sounds simple enough, but it is one of the most elusive goals in research, because we can never be certain that we are indeed measuring what we want. Earlier, for example, we considered the process of constructing operational definitions for variables. We can never know with absolute certainty whether we have achieved valid measurement of variables, but there are indirect ways of estimating validity and at the same time increasing our confidence in research findings. It is to these strategies we now turn.

Reliability

Reliability is the stability of results over time using the same measuring instrument, or the equivalence of results at one time, when more than one investigator uses the same instrument. The argument for reliability is that if we can achieve a consistent result over time or with several investigators, we are measuring what we want, and therefore we probably have valid operational definitions. However, the argument is weak, because it is possible to measure a variable reliably but invalidly.

Early research on the measurement of intelligence is a good case in point. Although researchers could consistently produce the same result with their IQ tests (reliability), it was later discovered, as you saw in Chapter 14, that the tests contained a cultural and class bias, and were thus not measuring exactly what was intended (invalidity). White, native English speaking, middle- and upper-class individuals averaged higher on IQ tests than did nonwhite, non-native English speaking, or lower-class individuals, not because the former were more intelligent, but because use of written English (paper and pencil tests) is a more central, and therefore more familiar, feature of their lives.

Consequently, although reliable measures still constitute an important aspect of social research, a reliable measurement is not necessarily a valid measurement. We can, however, be more confident in a consistent result than in one that fluctuates randomly.

Replication

Replication, the systematically repeated measurement of a given relationship, is one of the bywords of science, and it suggests that any single finding by itself is or should be unconvincing. Only with repeated corroboration and confirmation should researchers express confidence in the validity of their findings.

In his classic study, *Suicide* (1964b, originally published 1897), cited in Chapter 1, Emile Durkheim employed two types of replication. His hypothesis was that the more integrated individuals are into their society, the less likely they are to kill themselves. He argued that being married is an indicator of social integration, a bond that links individuals to the larger society. Therefore, married people should have a lower suicide rate than single people.

First, Durkheim tested his hypothesis in all the provinces of his native France for which he could obtain relevant data (official statistics) on the marital status of suicide victims. Each province therefore constituted a separate, independent test of his hypothesis, and its repeated confirmation lent considerably more credence to the hypothesis than it would have if it were upheld only once. Second, Durkheim reasoned that individuals are linked to society through all the various social institutions that constitute it. The family is but one social institution; religion and work are others. He constructed separate operational definitions for each of these institutions in an attempt to test the applicability of his general hypothesis that individual social integration is related inversely to suicide. With the confirmation of his hypothesis for each of the several operational definitions he employed, he became more confident that he was indeed measuring what he intended.

By now, many of you will appreciate that there are two common themes in the measurement strategies presented above: variation and repetition. The key to validity is varied and repeated measurement. The use of several indicators measured by a variety of methods upon several occasions should produce a common core of findings.

RESEARCH DESIGN

If your professor claimed that the lecture method of instruction was superior to all others in producing greater overall student achievement, how would you go about testing this claim or establishing its truth? After a research problem has been selected, previous studies examined, hypotheses formulated, and operational definitions constructed, it becomes necessary to plan systematically how the research will be undertaken. This is called research design and it is the next stage of social research.

We must draw up a deliberate plan or design prior to the actual research in order to eliminate competing alternative explanations for the results we obtain. If the lecture method is employed and class achievement is extremely high, can we say that achievement results directly from the method used? Depending upon how the research is designed, we can be more or less confident in answering yes or no. Research design forces us to anticipate systematically the difficulties we will confront, the decisions we will have to make, and the explanations possible for the results we will achieve.

Classical Experimental Design

In science, the ideal type of research design has for many years been the **classical experimental design**. It allows researchers to obtain relatively clear, unequivocal results, that are largely attributable to the design's features:

1. Two equivalent groups are selected. Equivalence is judged in terms of the dependent variable – in the example used, student achievement. If the two groups are not similar in achievement before the experiment, any difference found could be due to the initial difference between the groups, not the result of the independent variable – the lecture method. Equivalence may be obtained either by randomly assigning individuals to one or the other group on a probabilistic basis, or by matching individuals with respect to the dependent variable and then assigning, again randomly, one member of each matched pair to one group and the other member to the other group.

2. One group, called the **experimental group**, is subjected to the independent variable, in this case, the lecture method of instruction. The other group, the **control group**, is treated identically to the experimental group, except it is not subjected to the independent variable. It could receive its instruction via the discussion method, for example.

". . . they rushed tumultuously to the cathedral."

I constructed four miniature houses of worship – a Mohammedan mosque, a Hindu temple, a Jewish synagogue, a Christian cathedral – and placed them in a row. I then marked 15 ants with red paint and turned them loose. They made several trips to and fro, glancing in at the places of worship, but not entering.

I then turned loose 15 more painted blue; they acted just as the red ones had done. I now gilded 15 and turned them loose. No change in the result; the 45 traveled back and forth in a hurry persistently and continuously visiting each fane, but never entering. This satisfied me that these ants were without religious prejudices – just what I wished; for under no other conditions would my next and greater experiment be valuable. I now placed a small square of white paper within the door of each fane; and upon the mosque paper I put a pinch of putty, upon the temple paper a dab of tar, upon the synagogue paper a trifle of turpentine, and upon the cathedral paper a small cube of sugar.

First I liberated the red ants. They examined and rejected the putty, the tar and the turpentine, and then took to the sugar with zeal and apparent sincere conviction. I next liberated the blue ants, and they did exactly as the red ones had done. The gilded ants followed. The preceding results were precisely repeated. This seemed to prove that ants destitute of religious prejudice will always prefer Christianity to any other creed.

However, to make sure, I removed the ants and put putty in the cathedral and sugar in the mosque. I now liberated the ants in a body, and they rushed tumultuously to the cathedral. I was very much touched and gratified, and went back in the room to write down the event; but when I came back the ants had all apostatized and had gone over to the Mohammedan communion.

I saw that I had been too hasty in my conclusions, and naturally felt rebuked and humbled. With diminished confidence I went on with the test to the finish. I placed the sugar first in one house of worship, then in another, till I had tried them all.

With this result; whatever Church I put the sugar in, that was the one the ants straightway joined. This was true beyond a shadow of doubt, that in religious matters the ant is the opposite of man, for man cares for but one thing; to find the only true Church; whereas the ant hunts for the one with the sugar in it.

Source:

Mark Twain. "On Experimental Design." Source unknown. Reprinted from Cummings, L.L. and W.E. Scott, Jr. (eds.). *Readings in Organizational Behavior and Human Performance*. Homewood, Ill.: Irwin and Dorsey, 1969.

3. Both the experimental and control groups are measured on the dependent variable twice. The first measurement (Time 1) occurs *before* the introduction of the independent variable to the experimental group. The second measurement (Time 2) takes place *after* the experimental group has received the effects of the independent variable. In this case, one section of an introductory sociology class could be given a test at the beginning of the course to determine its current level of sociological knowledge. It would then receive its instruction by lecture. Another equivalent introductory section would be administered the identical test, but it would then receive instruction via the discussion method. Both sections would be given the same or an equivalent test at the conclusion of the course.

4. The difference between Time 1 and Time 2 for each group is computed (Time 2 minus Time 1). Then any difference in outcome between the experimental and control groups can be attributed directly to the effect of the independent variable. Provided that the groups are equivalent at the outset, and that they are treated identically in every respect except for the introduction of the independent variable to the experimental group, any difference in result between the two groups can only be due to the independent variable. All of these features of the classical experimental design are presented in diagram form in Figure 17-4.

For decades, the classical experimental design has been the norm against which social scientists have judged the adequacy of their research designs. However, it is not perfect. Two problems can arise in generalizing from experimental results. One is that people in an experiment may be *sensitized* and therefore respond differently than people not in the experiment. For example, people who see a violent movie in an experimental situation may be **sensitized** to the fact that

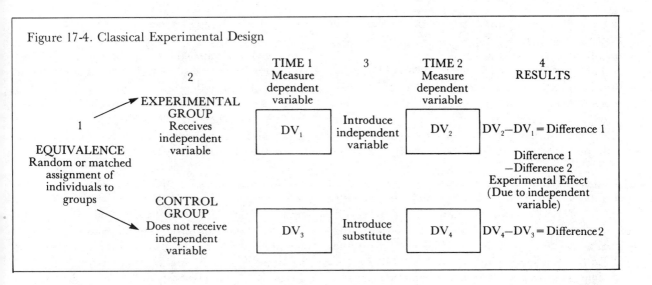

Figure 17-4. Classical Experimental Design

In the figure:

1 EQUIVALENCE Random or matched assignment of individuals to groups

2 EXPERIMENTAL GROUP Receives independent variable

CONTROL GROUP Does not receive independent variable

TIME 1 Measure dependent variable: DV_1

3 Introduce independent variable

TIME 2 Measure dependent variable: DV_2

4 RESULTS: $DV_2 - DV_1 = $ Difference 1

Difference 1 $-$ Difference 2 Experimental Effect (Due to independent variable)

DV_3 Introduce substitute DV_4 $DV_4 - DV_3 = $ Difference 2

they are in an experiment and respond differently from similar people who see the same movie on a Friday night.

The second problem is that in the social sciences experimental subjects are volunteers and usually students. This is not a representative sample of the general population and, consequently, the results of the experiment may be quite biased.

Furthermore, in many research situations it is simply impossible to design research ideally with equivalent experimental and control groups. In these cases, it is necessary to use deviations from the classical design while recognizing the limitations inherent in them.

Perhaps the most used design in sociological research is the **cross-sectional design**. Two or more groups with varying degrees of an independent variable are measured at one time to determine how they compare with respect to a dependent variable. For example, much research has been undertaken on the effects of university education (independent variable) on the values of students (dependent variable). Common in these studies is a comparison of representative groups of students from each year of university. To the extent that year groups vary in the predicted direction (regarding, for example, values such as conservatism), it is concluded that university education is primarily responsible.

In order for this conclusion to be the appropriate one, however, it must be assumed that each year group was equivalent at the beginning of its university education. The assumption cannot be validated with this type of design, and thus competing explanations must be considered as possible alternatives. For example, changes in student values could be due to the aging process of the students and not to university education. Is our hypothesis necessarily wrong? No. The point is that circumstances frequently force us to go with a less than ideal design. This does not mean, however, that we can learn nothing, nor that what we learn is wrong. Provided that we are careful in designing our study, and realize fully the alternative explanations possible, we can still do good research and make modest contributions to scientific knowledge in spite of deviations from the classical experimental design.

It is also important to recognize that in sociology we are often faced with *after* situations for which it is difficult or impossible to set up control groups. Independent variables, such as the changing of school boundaries, the closing of a plant, or the occurrence of a tornado, happen without sociologists' advance knowledge. We may wish to study their effects on individuals, but it is impossible to know what these people were like or how they felt before these events. Also, we have no way of knowing whether the groups we are comparing were equivalent prior to the occurrence of these independent variables.

Furthermore, we cannot say to the graduating class of a local high school that this half will go to university (experimental group) and this half will not (control group). Instead, the graduates themselves determine the groups. Sociologists, quite rightly, exert little control over people's lives, but this lack of control does make their job more difficult. Some researchers have taken to the laboratories in an attempt to recreate social reality on a small scale. Their findings are, however, often criticized as artificial and negligibly applicable.

To sum up: most researchers keep the classical experimental design in mind when planning their studies. Even though it is often impossible to apply these ideal designs, knowledge of the particular discrepancies between the researchers' own designs and these ideals allow the researchers to anticipate difficulties.

SAMPLING

At the same time the research design is being planned, thought must be given to the appropriate sample or population of groups, individuals, or behaviors upon which to test the hypothesis. A **population** (or universe) is that body of individuals (or other social units) in which you are interested and to which you will generalize your findings. A **sample** is a smaller representation of this whole, the group that is actually studied. Providing that the sample has been carefully selected, according to well defined sampling procedures, reliable and valid inferences can be drawn about the larger population.

Taking a sample is not something we do independently of the research we are undertaking. It is an integral part of the research process, and how we do it can greatly influence the kinds of results we achieve. For example, 30 or 40 years ago many hypotheses concerning general social behavior were tested on samples of university students. The researchers were university professors, and their students were convenient guinea pigs. University students, however, are not typically representative of society, and consequently the findings could not properly be generalized to the larger population. University students are on the average younger, more educated, of a higher social class, and more homogeneous in their values than the larger society of which they are a part. Any or all these characteristics could systematically affect the results, and therefore they would be specific to this particular group and not appropriate to society in general.

Consider the popular advertising ploy, "Four out of five doctors surveyed recommend. . . ." At first glance, this appears to suggest that 80 percent of all doctors solidly support Brand X. However, in order to interpret this statement accurately, we must ascertain the sampling process involved. Were the doctors surveyed a representative sample of the Canadian Medical Association? Were they employees of the company selling Brand X? Quite obviously, a "yes" to either of these questions would evoke different levels of confidence in Brand X. Consequently, as with the other stages of research we have discussed, it is necessary to know how individuals or groups were selected in order to assess the findings properly.

Why We Sample

You might think that taking a sample is not as good as making a complete enumeration of the entire population. In many cases, however, it is better, and here is why:

1. Destruction of the universe. This ominous phrase is intended simply to suggest that absolute certainty can be too dearly bought. For example, suppose your doctor asks, "What is your blood type?" Would you prefer the doctor to take a sample of your blood or to test the entire population – that is, to take *all* of your blood? This is not a unique example. In some cases, it is necessary to take a sample rather than a complete enumeration, because to do otherwise would destroy the entire universe.

Consider the claim by the local light bulb company that its product burns an average of X hours. What is the factual basis of this claim? Sampling is necessary. If the company tested its entire population of products, it would have no light bulbs to sell. That is, it would have destroyed the entire universe. We have heard that a foolproof method of distinguishing real pearls from fakes is to immerse all specimens of both categories in vinegar. But those that dissolve will be the genuine pearls – a costly way to achieve certainty.

2. Cost. In most research, cost considerations are extremely important. Obviously, if we can obtain essentially the same information at a lower cost, we will do so. Sampling allows just such savings, and, provided that it is done according to accepted procedures, the data obtained are no less accurate than those from a complete enumeration.

3. Accessibility to all elements within the universe. In very large populations, such as Canadian society, it is difficult, costly, and time consuming simply to locate all the people. Criminals actively avoid being located, many indigents have no fixed address, and occupationally mobile people are constantly relocating. An estimated 1.93 percent of the Canadian population was not counted during the 1971 Census, and Kalbach and McVey (1979) argue that this group is different in particular, significant ways from those people who were counted:

The census tended to miss more persons in British Columbia (2.89 percent) than elsewhere, more divorced persons (5.47 percent) than those of other marital statuses, those who rented (2.82 percent) rather than those who owned their own homes, and those who lived in mobile homes (12.03 percent), etc. In other words, the more socially and economically mobile persons, i.e., young adult males, recent immigrants, and those not related to the head of their households, are more difficult to locate in a census operation.

Because of these differences, the census itself is not a completely accurate representation of the Canadian people, even though the attempt was made to count everyone. Thus, we see that a sample can actually be a more accurate representation of a population than attempts at a complete enumeration, because more time and money *per unit* can be spent in locating relatively inaccessible cases. Consequently, inferences drawn from a sample to a population can be more valid than those drawn from an enumeration, again provided that proper sampling procedure is observed.

Types of Samples

First and foremost, a sample should be *representative* of the particular population or universe from which it is drawn. There are many dimensions along which a sample may be representative, but the researcher, whenever possible, should attempt to represent those characteristics that pertain directly to the problem being studied. In the social class/delinquency problem discussed earlier, the sample should mirror the distribution of social class within the target population (for example, Canadian secondary students). Because the actual incidence of delinquency is not known and is not easily discernible, it would be impractical to attempt to fill the sample with the same proportion of delinquents and non-delinquents as are found in the universe. But because gender is related to delinquency (the rate is higher for boys than for girls, although as noted in Chapter 6, the gap is narrowing), some attempt should be made to match the gender distribution of the sample to this population. Otherwise, the results could be misleading, and may be misinterpreted.

To the extent that the population is relatively *homogeneous*, that is, to the extent to which each element of the universe is similar with respect to the problem being studied, sampling is much easier, and any sample is likely to be representative. For example, whether your doctor samples your blood from your finger or your toe is unlikely to make a difference. If the population is *heterogeneous*, however, great care must be taken in selecting a sample that reflects this heterogeneity. For this reason, samples of heterogeneous populations should generally be larger than those drawn from homogeneous universes.

There are two main categories of samples. **Random samples** (also known as *probability samples*) are designed to be representative, and the degree to which they are can be estimated very accurately. **Nonrandom samples** (sometimes known as *nonprobability samples*) are also drawn to be representative, but the extent of representativeness cannot be determined. Nonrandom samples are, however, easier and less costly to take. The defining characteristic of a simple random sample is that each element within the universe has an equal chance (probability) of being selected into the sample.

There are many varieties of random samples, but this feature is central to all of them. Because of it, random samples are likely to be representative of the populations from which they are drawn.

Random Samples. An essential aspect of random samples is that the population must be explicitly defined or identified. In order for each element to have an equal probability of selection, all elements must be listed. Suppose that you wished to take a random sample of your class, or your university, or your town. It would first be necessary to make a list of all the people that comprise these populations. In many cases, lists already exist (class lists, student directories, registrar records, voting lists, city directories, telephone books, tax records). But you must insure that these lists correspond to your target population, that is, to the population on which you want to make generalizations. Voting lists contain only adults, telephone books contain only those people with listed telephones, and so probably exclude the very poor, the highly mobile, and those who desire privacy.

Once a list of the particular population is in hand, a random sample is relatively easy to draw. Literally, you may draw names out of a hat, or, if the list is very long, number the people (elements) on the list, and then consult a table of random numbers to determine which elements are selected. Tables of random numbers are generated by a computer in such a way that no pattern exists within the numbers; they are randomly listed. Table 17-1 provides an example of a random sample drawn in this fashion from a numbered population of 80 elements.

Somewhat easier to select than a random sample is a **systematic sample**. In this case, the first element is selected at random, and then every fourth, twelfth, or fifteenth name thereafter, depending upon what numerical proportion of your population you wish your sample to be. Care must be exercised in taking systematic samples, however, in that lists generated for some other purpose may be biased. For example, if you wished to make a survey of a newly constructed housing tract, and used a list of addresses provided by the city, you could conceivably have in your sample only those people who lived on corner lots. Enough housing studies

---

TABLE 17-1. A SIMPLE RANDOM SAMPLE OF 20 ELEMENTS; SELECTED FROM A TABLE OF RANDOM NUMBERS OUT OF A POPULATION OF 80

34	14	17	68	26	75
45	39	(17)	26	(95)	
02	06	77	(85)	67	
05	(86)	66	11	(97)	
03	(87)	14	16	73	

NOTE: Circled numbers are deleted from the sample because either they have already been included in the sample, or they do not represent numbers in the population.

---

have been conducted over the years to show that people living on corner lots are significantly different from other residents (for example, corner lots are usually more expensive than other lots). Consequently, your systematic sample would not be representative of all people living in the surburb.

Another popular random sample is the **stratified random sample**. This type of sample takes into consideration the characteristics that may be relevant to the study and represents them in the sample in proportion to their representation in the population. Returning to the social class/delinquency problem, you could take with relative ease a random sample stratified by gender of all secondary school students in your city. Essentially, this involves taking two simple random samples or two systematic random samples – one of all boys and the other of all girls. The stratified random sample does not leave to chance the appearance of relevant variables in the sample. Thus, if these variables are known before the study, a stratified random sample is to be preferred over simple or systematic random ones.

It is possible to stratify on more than one variable at a time. For example, if the list of secondary school students also contained addresses, and if it were possible to approximate social class with neighborhood, then six simple random samples could be drawn – upper-, middle-, and lower-class boys, and upper-, middle-, and lower-class girls. This example should suggest that the more variables chosen upon which to stratify (and the more categories within these variables), the more difficult and tedious the sampling becomes. Thus, stratified random samples are seldom stratified on more than two or three variables, even though many more might be directly relevant to the problem at hand.

A more complex type of random sample is termed **multistage**. Generally used with very large populations, it consists of descending stages of random samples toward a level where the use of lists of individuals is practical. Continuing with the social class/delinquency problem, you might want to study this relationship among all secondary school students in Canada. Even if you could secure lists for every high school in the country, however, the chore of taking a simple, systematic, or stratified sample at this stage would be immense. Instead, it would be much more feasible to take a random sample of school districts, perhaps stratified by province. From this sample, it would then be possible to draw a random sample of schools. And finally, at the third stage, you could then take a stratified random sample of students by gender from your sample of schools. In this fashion, a multistage random sample eliminates the tedium and near impossibility of the task and avoids the problem of sampling a population for which no lists exist. This example illustrates that the type of sample drawn is very much related to the kind of problem you have and the population on which you want to generalize.

Nonrandom Samples.

The major argument for all random samples is that they are representative of the populations from which they were drawn. While this is extremely important to any researcher, there are other factors to consider. Sometimes a case can be made for nonrandom sampling.

Nonrandom samples are usually considerably cheaper than random ones. In a random sample, it is necessary to locate specifically selected respondents who might not always be immediately accessible. Because of this feature, costs increase. People randomly selected who are not at home must be recontacted at a later date. In a nonrandom sample, by contrast, particular individuals are not chosen. If someone does not answer the door, the next-door neighbor may be substituted. Respondents randomly chosen might not all live in the same geographical area. Consequently, greater expense is involved in reaching these individuals than in nonrandom samples that are usually geographically clustered in order to cut costs. Thus, while random samples may be more representative than nonrandom ones, they are also more costly.

Another argument for nonrandom sampling is the difficulty encountered in obtaining a random sample. Suppose that you were interested in determining those factors responsible for the apathy regarding student affairs on your campus. In order to get a representative cross-section, you decide to take a random sample stratified by year level. Questionnaires are mailed out, and you obtain a mere 30 percent return, perhaps because of the apathy you are trying to study. How representative is your sample now, particularly in relation to the problem being studied? The point is that there are often serious and sizable discrepancies between the sampling *plan* and its actual *execution*. The greater these discrepancies, the less preferred is the random over the nonrandom sample.

In some cases, it is simply impossible to take a random sample, and if knowledge is to be gained, a nonrandom sample must be used. For example, in a well known study comparing the job satisfaction of people from various countries, Inkeles (1960) used Soviet refugees to form his Russian sample. For a variety of reasons, refugees cannot be considered representative of the Russian labor force. However, if Soviets are to be included in the comparison, no other options exist. Similarly, if a researcher is interested in various aspects of crime and deviance, it is impossible to take a random sample of criminals and deviants. The population is not known, and a nonrandom sample is therefore the only alternative.

The most common type of nonrandom sample is a **quota sample**. A quota sample is the nonrandom equivalent of a stratified random sample. The researcher determines which characteristics of the population are important to the study (for example, gender, age, education, occupation, residential area) and then selects a sample with the same proportions of these characteristics as are found in the population. However, because the population is not explicitly defined (that is, listed), each individual does not have an equal chance of being selected, and therefore the sample is not random. In fact, it may be biased in several important ways. Interviewers, in order to fill their quotas, will tend to select those individuals who are most immediately available, and these people could be significantly different from others who are less accessible. Quota sampling has, however, been found to be relatively inexpensive and relatively representative. It is used considerably in market research and public opinion polls.

One important final note on sampling should be made. We are often engaged in sampling without being aware of it. For instance, the time (of the day, week, month, or year) that we choose to do our research can bear on the results. Time for most people is extremely patterned. Most work during the day, engage in more leisure activities during the weekend, get paid at certain times during the month, and are apt to take holidays at regular times of the year. Because we are so time-bound, this should be taken into consideration in the overall research plan and some attempt made to reduce its impact.

Also, the context in which we conduct our research can affect the results. For example, most people are consistently different at work than at home. Researchers have also found that individuals respond differently when alone than when in groups, and the constitution of various groups themselves often affects response.

DATA COLLECTION

Once you decide what problem you are interested in, the basic research design you plan to use, and the sample or population you plan to study, you then gather the data needed to solve your problem. Actually, these decisions are not made sequentially, so you will already have thought of how to gather the data. It is a fact of life that your decision usually will be affected by considerations of money and time, and will likely be a compromise between the best way to collect data and what time and money will allow.

There are two ways of gathering data: asking people for the information you want, or observing their behavior or the products (**physical trace evidence**) of their behavior. To illustrate these ways: if you are interested in the drinking patterns of a community, you could ask a sample of the residents how much and how often they drink; or you could attempt to learn their actual drinking behavior by observing them in bars, homes, and liquor stores; or you could gather physical trace evidence by counting bottles in their garbage cans.

Let us consider the first or our data gathering methods – asking for it. There are two ways of asking people for information: by questionnaires and by interviews. The questions can be either highly structured with fixed response categories or they may be open-ended, allowing more flexibility of response.

Questionnaires

A questionnaire is a series of questions to be answered by the *respondent*. It may be handed out at work or school, or mailed directly to a person's home. If you sample the general population of an area, the respondents are spread out over a fairly large geographical area, so because of time and money a mail questionnaire may be your only choice. The questionnaire will include a letter informing the person of the purpose of the questionnaire, how she or he was chosen, reasons encouraging the person to respond, and, usually, assurance of anonymity. A stamped, addressed, return envelope will be included, and follow-up letters may also be sent out to increase the rate of response.

The importance of constructing a good questionnaire cannot be overemphasized. Following is the preferred procedure for making a structured questionnaire. You first formulate the questions (indicators) that you believe measure the variables of interest. Once you have constructed the items composing the measures of your concepts, and the response categories, you pretest them. Ideally, this involves sampling a group similar to the group you intend to survey. You then analyze the results of the pretest to see if they make sense, and interview the pretest subjects to see if the questions mean the same thing to them as they do to you. You can also partly determine if any of the items, as well as the whole set of items, is biasing the results. That is, are the questions worded in such a way that they are forcing or indicating to the respondents how they

Questionnaire Sources

Frequently it is not necessary to construct your own questionnaire. Rather, you can use items or questionnaires developed by others. Many of these have been carefully pretested and their degree of reliability has been established. Some major sources for finding such questionnaires and scales are: *Measures of Social Psychological Attitudes*, by John Robinson and Phillip Shaver, 1973; *Measures of Political Attitudes*, by John Robinson et al., 1968; and *Measures of Occupational Attitudes and Occupational Characteristics*, by John Robinson et al., 1969. All of these are from the Survey Research Center, Institute for Social Research, University of Michigan. Three other general sources for obtaining various scales and questionnaire items are: *Scales for the Measurement of Attitudes*, by M.E. Shaw and J.M. Wright, McGraw-Hill, New York, 1967; *Handbook of Organizational Measurement*, by James Price, D.C. Heath, Lexington, Mass., 1972; and *Handbook of Research Design and Social Measurement*, 2nd ed., by Delbert C. Miller, David McKay, New York, 1970. Should you be interested in using a questionnaire to collect data, these are good places to look for questions that may suit your problem.

should answer? For example, you ask the question, "How old are you?" Suppose a person answers, "Twenty." And you ask, "Are you really twenty right now?" and the reply is, "No, I'm nineteen right now, but I'm closer to twenty than nineteen." Consequently, you rephrase your question and ask, "How old are you, to your nearest birthday?"

Interviews

The procedures used for constructing questionnaires are essentially the same as those used for constructing interview schedules. Since interviewing involves human interaction, however, the potential for problems is greater than with questionnaires, mainly because personal characteristics of researchers and respondents must be considered. Research using face-to-face interviews must be designed so that the results of the study are not the consequence of the interviewer's character-

istics. Age, gender, race, dress, general appearance and behavior, a raised eyebrow, a vocal inflection – all can influence the respondents' answers. The chances of this occurring are so great that many books have been written about the interviewing process and techniques for minimizing such influence.

The interview itself may vary from a brief, structured session to a lengthy, complicated, unstructured one lasting a few hours. The structured interview uses a schedule which is essentially a questionnaire that is read to the respondents in a specified order. A schedule that specifies only some questions is called semi-structured; a schedule that simply indicates the general area to be explored is called unstructured.

There are advantages and disadvantages to structured as opposed to unstructured interviews. The structured interview is easy to score, reduces interviewer bias, is more easily replicated, and is more reliable than an unstructured interview. On the other hand, the major advantage of the unstructured interview over the structured one is that the interviewer can explore the respondents' answers. This type of interview is, however, dependent upon the skill of the researcher in winning the respondent's confidence and in asking the appropriate questions. It presents serious problems of interpretation; it is also low in reliability and difficult to replicate. Consequently, the tendency is to use structured interviews. However, if the problem being researched is very sensitive (for example, human sexual behavior), or if little is known about the topic being researched, an unstructured interview may be the best technique to use.

The advantages of interviews over questionnaires are:

1. interviews generally can be longer
2. the populations are less restricted, because the respondents need not be able to read or write, but merely to understand the language of the interviewer
3. the response rate is usually higher
4. the identity of the respondents is known, which is very useful in determining differences between respondents and nonrespondents

Major disadvantages of the interview compared to questionnaires are:

1. expense; this problem is becoming so severe that large interview surveys are mainly being undertaken now only by large public and private research institutes (e.g., Gallup and Roper), and telephone interviewing is becoming increasingly popular as a means to avoid some of the expense involved in individual interviews

2. interviewer effects, that is, the degree to which the results are affected by characteristics of the interviewer

Observation

Both questionnaires and interviews measure opinions, attitudes, and perceived behavior. But they do not measure actual behavior, and actual behavior may be crucial for certain problems. Because of this drawback – nonmeasurement of actual behavior – and because of the problems associated with questionnaires and interviews, some studies employ various types of observation. "Observation" is the term applied to methods of gathering data without direct questioning. There are basically two different types of observational techniques. One is highly structured and is called nonparticipant observation or just observation. The second type is participant observation.

Nonparticipant Observation.
Like other structured techniques, nonparticipant observation is based on developing explicit categories in order to increase reliability and replicability, and to reduce observer bias. This is much easier said than done. It is extremely difficult to obtain accurate and objective observations. If, for example, we were to observe aggression among children in a particular playground, and if we did not carefully arrive at a common definition of "aggression," our observations would be quite different. Some of us might see very little aggression; others would witness a great deal, depending upon our subjective understanding of the term. If a child picks up a toy and looks as if she is going to throw it at another child, some would record this as an aggressive act; others would not. So in order to insure that we observe the same things in the same way, careful operational definitions of our categories are required.

An example of the problems involved in constructing good operational definitions is provided in an observational study of military leadership (Davis, et al, 1954). The researchers were interested in "ways of giving orders," seen as varying on a democratic-authoritarian continuum. Originally, they assumed they would simply record whether or not an order was democratic or authoritarian. They soon discovered, however, that in many instances they could not even be sure whether an order had been given. For example, a sergeant in a car pool says, "Is there a wrench?" and a private stops what he is doing and brings the sergeant a wrench. Was an order given? They solved the problem by writing down anything that a noncommissioned officer said that could in any way be interpreted as an order, and then three people classified the notations into "orders" and "nonorders." Where two out of three coders agreed that the statement was an order, it was included in the analysis.

Participant Observation.
Systematic nonparticipant observation, using two or more observers to study the same interaction with predefined categories, has not been widely used in sociological research, probably because of the time and expense involved. **Participant observation**, on the other hand, has been widely used and has resulted in some of the classics of sociological research.

Participant observers are part of the social setting in which they observe events. There is wide variation in the degree of participation by the observer. In an extreme form, the observer is a member of the group being observed, and the group is unaware of the observer's role.

A less intense form of participant observation occurs when the researcher stays with a particular small group or lives in a community. In this case, the researcher usually participates in some of the group's activities while observing them. The members of the group or community are aware that they are being observed. This technique was used by Whyte (1943) in his classic study of a street corner gang in an Italian slum in the Boston area. Whyte lived in "Cornerville" for three and a half years and participated in most of the group's activities. They knew he was engaged in research but, presumably, they did not care.

Participant observer Ned Polsky, who had himself played pool since he was thirteen, spent many hours participating and observing the behavior of American poolroom hustlers. Here, in Montreal, Polsky observes an opponent's shot in the Canadian game of snooker.

The third type of participant observation involves the least participation of the researcher in the activities of the group. In this type of observation, the researcher takes on the role of the objective, neutral observer. The group members know they are being observed, and the observer does not usually participate in the group's activities while observing the group. A person observing a classroom, for example, might spend several hours a day for several weeks recording the various behaviors of the class members; a sociologist might observe a work group over a similarly long period of time. There are two basic differences between this type of participant observation and nonparticipant observation. First, the observers do not have preconceived categories for scoring their observations, and, second, they tend to spend a much longer time in the field.

There are several advantages to participant observation:

1. The observations take place in a natural setting. An observational study of workers at their place of work, as opposed to an experimental study of students in a laboratory doing the same kind of work, is more natural and for this reason may be more easily generalized. That is, the findings are more likely to be true of workers in general than only of the experimental subjects.

2. By observing over a long period of time, the researcher gathers a great deal of information on many variables. Also, the dynamics of changes that occur in the situation can be explored. Other methods are rarely this adaptable.

3. The observer can record the context, including the emotional reactions of the subjects, in which the behavior occurs.

4. First-hand experience enables the observer to acquire some sense of the subjective meanings that events have for the subjects.

5. Lastly, an observer who has established good relations (rapport) with the people being observed may be able to ask sensitive questions that would otherwise not be allowed.

There are, however, at least five major problems associated with participant observation:

1. There is a lack of reliability, stemming from the selective perception of the lone observer. (In this type of research there is nearly always just one observer.) The observer will have a particular theoretical orientation, interest, and training – all of which are likely to affect the perception, recording, memory, and interpretation of the events observed.

2. Observers who are not complete participants may sensitize their subjects by their presence. **Sensitization** concerns the alteration of subject behavior because of the presence of the observer. If, when they are being observed, the behavior of children in a classroom is different from their normal behavior, the observer is not getting a true picture of children's classroom behavior.

3. If an observer is a member of the group, the observer's role in the group greatly restricts the observations that can be made. You read in Chapter 10 about one such participant observer. In his role as a machine operator, Donald Roy could not observe other work groups, his foreman, or other superiors. He was restricted to one room in one building with one group (Roy, 1959).

4. It is difficult to participate in any continuing group without becoming involved in it. If involvement occurs, loss of objectivity results, and the possibility of bias

increases. Also, even if the other members of the group are not sensitized by the observer, the behavior of the group itself changes as a result of the observer's participation.

5. Most observers must wait for occurrences of the behavior in which they are interested (e.g., children's playground aggression), and it is possible that this behavior may not occur during their time of observation.

Furthermore, with the exception of complete participant observation, all these data gathering methods – questionnaires, interviews, and observation – have one disadvantage in common: the people being researched know they are being studied, and there is the possibility that they therefore will behave differently than they otherwise would. This in turn means the results may be biased.

Unobtrusive Data Gathering. This disadvantage, awareness on the subjects' part that they are being studied, is not inevitable; there are unobtrusive data gathering methods. Any type of research procedure conducted in such a way that the subjects do not know they are being studied is called unobtrusive. Such measures are rarely reactive, that is, they do not sensitize subjects, or, to put it another way, subjects do not react to being studied. One type of widely discussed unobtrusive measure is the use of physical trace evidence (Webb, et al, 1981), which can be classified as either erosion or accretion. *Erosion measurements* include any type of data occurring from human behavior that results in the wearing away of some physical object. Examples of erosion indicators are the wearing away of tiles at an art or museum exhibit (popularity), or the wear on library books (use), or the wear on children's shoes (activity). *Accretion measurements* include any type of data resulting from human behavior that leaves some physical trace. Examples of accretion indicators could include garbage, archaeological evidence such as pottery and tools, and graffiti. Although seldom used as a major basis of social research, unobtrusive measures can be extremely important for ascertaining the degree to which the other techniques may have sensitized subjects, as well as being used as direct and indirect measures in their own right.

Content Analysis

The last data collection technique we will discuss is based upon secondary analysis and is called **content analysis**. Content analysis is "any technique for making inferences by objectively and systematically identifying specified characteristics of messages" (Holsti, 1969) – examining the speeches of political candidates, for example, or searching newspaper ads for sexist bias. Content analysis is, then, a systematic procedure for examining the content of recorded information. It renders objective the usually casual and superficial judgments we make of communication content.

There are special problems with content analysis. First is the problem of coding the data or determining the categories. For example, if you want to study changes in gender role presentation in women's magazines, what categories do you count, what characteristics of women's roles do you look at, and how can you construct exhaustive and reliable categories? You might count the number of fictional heroines who are single as opposed to the number married, the number who work, the types of jobs, and the number with and without children. It should be pointed out, however, that even determining who is a heroine is sometimes difficult.

The second special problem is selecting a sample. In the above example, which magazines do you look at, and, secondly, what time periods do you choose? Virtually any content analysis of mass media involves both a sample of the media (specific books, television shows, or newspapers) and a sample of time. For instance, you might look at a random sample of two women's magazines for a ten-year period. The following example of a content analysis concerned with collective violence will make these problems clear.

As part of a general study of collective conflict and violence, Jackson, et al (1977) did a content analysis of violence in Ontario. Their first problem was what source to choose. After seriously considering all the alternatives, they chose the daily newspapers as being the most appropriate. Their next problem was to decide which paper or papers to use. Given the laborious nature of content analysis and the limitations of time and money, they chose one, *The Globe and Mail*, as

the best for their purposes. The next problem was selecting a time period. Again, after much deliberation, they chose the period from January 1, 1965, to December 31, 1975. It is important to choose a time period that is not too short and that might thus be affected by a short-term deviation (a major historical event). But at the same time it must be short enough to keep it within manageable limits. From *The Globe and Mail*, for the ten-year time period, a random sample of 209 issues was drawn. Even in this time period, the researchers had to scan approximately 15 000 pages of newsprint.

The next task was to operationalize "collective violence." Violence was defined in terms of property damage and injuries; violence was "collective" if it involved fifty or more participants. Figure 17-5 is one of the results of their study, showing collective violence in Ontario.

If this example illustrates well the difficulties in doing content analysis, it also demonstrates the advantages of such research:

1. the data are accessible and inexpensive
2. the data cover a long time period; this makes content analysis very useful for studying trends
3. these data are also seen as unobtrusive, that is, they are not reactive
4. content analysis can be used to study the larger society or macrosociological problems

Content analysis also has several main disadvantages. First, almost all the material used is screened or processed, and the researcher does not know what selection processes have occurred. It is obvious that a government-censored newspaper is not a very good source of unbiased data. But to some extent all material used in content analysis has been selected by someone for some purpose, and therefore an objective picture may not be possible. Second, content analysis is a very laborious and time-consuming process; this may be one of the reasons it is not used more frequently.

The third disadvantage is that it is very difficult to avoid a great deal of judgment and subjectivity in the coding process and in making inferences. This, of course, introduces bias. The amount of bias can be reduced, but for many types of content analysis it

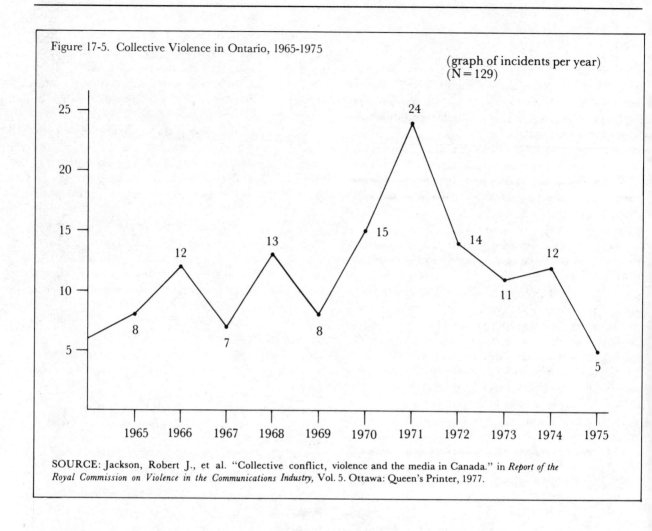

Figure 17-5. Collective Violence in Ontario, 1965-1975

(graph of incidents per year)
(N = 129)

SOURCE: Jackson, Robert J., et al. "Collective conflict, violence and the media in Canada." in *Report of the Royal Commission on Violence in the Communications Industry,* Vol. 5. Ottawa: Queen's Printer, 1977.

probably cannot be eliminated. The fourth and final disadvantage is that, historically, content analysis has been mostly used for descriptive and comparative purposes and not for the study of relationships or causal analysis, although there seems to be no inherent reason why it cannot be used for these studies.

Which Is Best?

This brings to an end our discussion of the main ways in which social scientists collect their data, and the advantages and disadvantages of each method. It is important to remember that there is no reason to consider any particular method as better than or in competition with the others. Social reality should look the same no matter what technique is used to observe it. Sample surveys using questionnaire or interview schedules are the most common method employed by sociologists to collect data. This reliance on one method implies the disadvantages previously discussed. The best approach is probably to use as many different techniques as you can. Then, if the same reality is observed with a variety of methods, relatively more confidence can be placed in the validity of the findings.

The computer has made it possible to analyze staggering amounts of research information quickly and efficiently. The many pieces of information are coded and entered into a computer. The computer then transforms these raw data into relevant statistics.

DATA ANALYSIS

Analysis of data is a complicated and difficult process. Our concern is not that you learn how to analyze data. Rather, we want to stress the interpretation of the major statistics used in sociological analysis. We hope to make you more competent as consumers of social research. To accomplish this, we will briefly discuss, first, the processing of data and, second, the statistics used to decribe those data. Because most data in sociology are still gathered by questionnaires or interview-surveys, we will restrict our description to this form of data collection.

Processing the Data

If you do an honors thesis based on a questionnaire containing 30 items and given to 200 students, you would end up with 6000 pieces of information – a relatively small number. Even so, it is impossible to analyze the data by flipping through the pages of the questionnaires. Most questionnaire results are analyzed by computers. The first step in this process is to code the data. This involves making up a code book in which each variable is assigned a column number(s). A *column number* refers to one of the 80 columns on a computer card. For example, gender may be recorded in column 3 with row 1 equalling male, row 2 equalling female, and row 3 equalling all other responses including nonresponses. When this has been done, the next step usually is to go through each questionnaire and transfer the data to a code sheet. The code sheet contains nothing but the numbers that represent the respondents' answers to the questionnaire.

Coding, then, is reducing the information to a standardized form and always involves a loss of data. For example, in coding census occupations, thousands of occupations must be lumped together. Sociologists, for example, are pooled with several other occupations including penologists and social ecologists. Demographers are coded with statisticians and actuaries. This basic coding is irreversible; you cannot, after the fact, combine demographers with sociologists (Pineo, et al, 1977). In the coding process you therefore have to be concerned with validity and reliability. A code is valid if it puts like phenomena in the same category or assigns the same values to similar phenomena. A code is reliable if different coders obtain identical or similar results when coding the same data. Both of these should be checked carefully.

After the data are transferred to code sheets, the common procedure is to have them keyed into a computer, which can then analyze them. An increasingly popular technique is to use questionnaire answer sheets, like the answer sheet students use for taking objective tests. These can be read by machine and entered directly into a computer. If you decide to do the analysis by hand using a calculator, however, you will still find it more convenient to put the data on code sheets and work from them.

Quantitative Data Analysis

The enormous amount of information usually gathered in survey research is incomprehensible in raw form. The data are useful only when reduced to some relevant statistic. **Statistics** has two basic definitions. First, statistics mean numbers, that is, the actual data gathered. When someone says, "Statistics show the Tories will win," they are using statistics in this sense. Average age at marriage, average income, percent Liberal, and so on are examples of statistics defined as numbers. Second, statistics refer to the theories and techniques that have been developed to manipulate data. Percentages, rates, averages, and measures of relation are statistics in this sense. In either sense, statistics concern the manipulation of numbers.

One of the first statistics you might use to make sense out of your data are percentages, rates, or ratios. For most problems there is little sense in comparing, for example, the provinces of Ontario and Manitoba on the total number of births, deaths, suicides, or crimes. Obviously, Ontario is going to have more of all of these because of its larger population. Even if Ontario had a low crime rate and Manitoba a high one, Ontario would have more crimes. If we want to compare these two or any two units that differ greatly in size, we must control for this factor. This can be done by computing percentages, ratios, or rates.

Instead of computing births, deaths, suicides, and crimes, we compute birth rates, death rates, suicide rates, and crime rates. For example, the crude birth rate, as you saw in Chapter 7, is the number of births divided by the population of a given community and multiplied by 1000. This mathematical operation eliminates population size as a factor and thus makes possible meaningful comparisons between groups of different sizes. Percentages provide the same kind of control. The point is that it is not meaningful to compare groups without knowing their sizes. For example, 50 people in group A are alcoholics and 100 people in group B are alcoholics, but there are 100 people in group A and 400 in group B. Then 50 percent of group A are alcoholics compared to 25 percent for group B. For a research example of the use of percentages, see Table 17-2.

Such statistics are usually easy to compute, are necessary for comparing groups of different sizes, and are easy to interpret. Nevertheless, there are certain questions that can be asked to help interpret these statistics:

1. What is (are) the operational definition(s) of the variables?
2. What is the sample or population?

TABLE 17-2. MARITAL SATISFACTION/ HAPPINESS FOR WIVES AND HUSBANDS BY WIFE'S WORK STATUS AND PRESENCE OF CHILDREN.

Those "very satisfied" or "very happy" with marriage

	Wives		Husbands	
	Percent	(N)	Percent	(N)
Total sample	49	(397)	41	(387)
Wife's employment status:				
Not working for pay	48	(237)	38	(242)
Working full-time[1]	53	(97)	50	(109)

[1]Working 30 hours or more per week.

SOURCE: Adapted from Lupri, Eugen, and J. Frideres. "The quality of marriage and the passage of time: marital satisfaction over the family life cycle." *Canadian Journal of Sociology*, 6(3), 1981, 291.

3. What can the specific statistic be compared with?
4. What is the reverse conclusion?

The following example deals with each of these four questions.

On page six of the morning paper appeared the following headline: "30% Failures in Forces' Fitness Test" (*Victoria Colonist*, May 15, 1979). The size of the headline alone suggested that the armed forces were falling apart.

1. What is the operational definition or measure of fitness? In this case, fitness meant that a male under 30 had to be able to run 1.5 miles, 2,400 meters, in less than 14 minutes.
2. What is the sample or population? In this case it was 67 000 military personnel. There was no statement as to what the population was, how this sample of 67 000 was drawn, or what proportion of the population it represented. This lack of information made it very difficult to interpret what the 30 percent failure rate meant. If all 67 000 were combat troops who presumably should be in good physical condition, 30 percent failure would seem to be more serious than if the group comprised deskbound officers and enlisted men. Also, since the fitness test was defined in terms of males, one might presume that none of the 67 000 were females. But this is only a presumption.

3. What can we compare this 30 percent failure with? No data were given as to the failure rate for the general population, but a major was quoted as saying, "I would suggest the fitness level is slightly above that of the general population but not a great deal better." No evidence was given to support that statement. The article did point out that five years ago 50 percent failed. If the tests were comparable, this would suggest considerable improvement in fitness of military personnel. So is the military falling apart or upgrading itself?
4. What is the reverse conclusion? If the headline had said, "70% Pass Forces' Fitness Test" would you have interpreted the statement differently? The meaning behind the headline is often elusive. The next time you read that one in four marriages ends in divorce, remember that three out of four do not.

Measures of Central Tendency

Frequently, it is necessary to use summary statistics that describe group characteristics. One of the most common of these are measures of **averages**. An average is an important measure because it reduces the data to one meaningful value that is readily understood and easily communicated. We often refer to averages – the average person, average weight, average height, average income, average grade point – and the typical person on the street.

Briefly, there are three types of averages – the mode, median, and mean. The **mode** is the most frequently occurring score or category in a distribution. The **median** is the category or point above and below which half the total frequency lies, or it is the middle category that divides the frequency in half. The **mean** is what we usually think of when we use the word average. It is the value obtained by adding all values in the distribution and dividing by the number in the distribution. Another way of thinking of the mean is that it is the amount of something that everyone would have if each person had the same. In a group of five people, if two have one dollar, one has three dollars, one five dollars and one forty dollars, the mode is one dollar, the most common category. The median is four have one dollar and one has forty-six dollars, persons having more than three and two less than three. The mean is ten dollars: add up the five scores and divide by the total number, fifty divided by five equals ten.

In describing the central tendency or typical value of the group, the researcher must select the average that best reflects this typical value. The mode is very unstable. In our example, if one member who had a dollar finds four more, the mode is now five. Should that member be lucky enough to find thirty-nine dollars, the mode would be forty. So one score can drastically change the mode.

The mean is by far the most widely used measure, because it is used to compute many other statistics, and because it is more stable across samples. Its major disadvantage is that it is unduly affected by extreme scores. This should be clear from the example, where the mean of ten is not very descriptive of the typical value of the group, because of the one person with forty dollars and the two with only one dollar each. If the distribution had been two with five, one with ten, and two with fifteen, a mean of ten would be a more accurate description of the average amount of money in this group.

The median is not as useful as the mean for computing other statistics and can itself be difficult to compute. However, if the data are not quantifiable, or if there are extreme scores, the median will most likely be the most accurate description. Consequently, if you have reason to believe that there are extreme scores or values, usually true of income data, be wary of the mean, and tend to prefer the median.

It is probably obvious at this point that you can have very different looking distributions, but that the mean can be the same. This fact implies that to interpret an average, to know how accurately it describes the population, you need to know what the distribution is like. More specifically, you need to know how far group members depart from the mean. Another way of saying this is that you need to know how the scores are dispersed, or spread, around the mean. In the previous example of five people, where each has ten dollars, there is no dispersion, and the mean tells you exactly what each member has. In the case where

three dollars; it divides the frequency in half, two however, there is great dispersion around the mean, and it is therefore an inaccurate description of the typical value of the group. It simply does not contain much meaningful information. Averages can be misleading and uninformative, therefore, and that is why an accompanying dispersion measure can be helpful.

In order to inform the reader of the accuracy of the average, a measure of **dispersion** is usually given. Almost all the dispersion measures you will encounter are based on deviations from average scores, either the median or the mean. The statistic you will most frequently encounter is called the **standard deviation**, **SD**. The larger the SD, the greater the spread of values around the mean or the less the group members are alike. In our example, the SD for the first distribution is zero and for the second distribution eighteen. (Eighteen is obtained by subtracting each score from the mean, squaring these figures, and summing the squares, then dividing the sum of the squares by the number of people, and taking the square root.) A measure of dispersion, then, helps you determine the degree to which an average is an accurate description of the typical values of the group. If you ever go swimming in a strange lake and are told the average depth is twenty feet, find out the standard deviation *before* you dive in.

Measures of Association

The measures we have been discussing are used to describe a single variable, such as income, births, or crime. However, sociologists are seldom interested in collecting facts for the sake of facts. Usually they want to know how these facts are related to each other. If they calculate a crime rate, it is to see if it is related to some other variable, like gender or income. It is relationships that sociologists try to explain. This, in turn, means that they must determine the degree to which the variables they are interested in are related.

There are many ways to measure **association** and each one may be interpreted in ways different from the others. However, some general comments will aid you in interpreting these measures. The measures most often used in sociology are *gamma, tau, rho, lambda,* and *r* (Pearson Correlation Coefficient). Most measures of association, and all of the ones just mentioned, have values between zero and one. Values close to zero indicate a low relationship, those near one indicate a high relationship. In other words, the higher the value the greater the relationship between any two variables.

The direction of the relationship is also included in these statistics. Direction can be **positive (direct)** or **negative (inverse)**. A positive relation occurs when one variable increases as the other variable increases, or when one decreases as the other decreases. The two variables move or change in the same direction. For example, many students attend university because of a belief in a positive relationship between education and income. That is, as education increases, income increases. A perfect positive relationship equals +1.00. On the other hand, a negative relation occurs when one variable increases as the other decreases. For example, as age increases, athletic prowess decreases. A perfect negative relationship equal −1.00.

As we stated previously, there is no one simple interpretation for the various statistics. However, for the most commonly used measure, r^2, the simplest interpretation is in terms of r^2, which is the variance explained. If our $r = .70$, $r^2 = .49$, which is the proportion of the variance explained by one variable on the other. In our example, 49 percent of the variance in income is explained by education. This also means that 51 percent of the variance in income is not accounted for by education. With other measures, it is necessary to rely on the magnitude of the relationship in order to interpret it; the closer to 1 the particular measure is, the greater the relationship between them.

In order to make easier a decision about the correct interpretation of these measures (percentages, rates, and measures of association), sociologists frequently report a "P value." Generally, at the bottom of a table you will see $P = .05$ (or some other value), or a statement like, "correlation significant at 0.05 level." This statistic is telling you that the correlation is not due to chance. Put another way, if the study were done over again, you would find approximately the same correlation.

In the social sciences, if a relation could occur at the .05 level, or .01, or .001, it is considered statistically significant. To say that the finding is statistically significant is only to say that the finding is very unlikely to be due to chance. To say that this is not a chance finding, however, is not to say what it is. And it should not be confused with being theoretically or practically significant. However, it does mean that whatever was found is likely what is there, that is, if you do the study again, you will likely find the same thing.

We hope that this brief review of data analysis will give you a feel for how data are processed and analyzed. Furthermore, we hope that the discussion of the major statistics used in the analysis of data will enable you to read with heightened understanding the tables and charts in this book and to some extent interpret the statistics for yourself.

THE VALUE OF RESEARCH METHODS

Knowledge and understanding of what is involved in the research process enables consumers of research findings to assess independently the results and to arrive at their own conclusions. Depending upon how the research was undertaken, what kind of design was used, the sample taken, and the data collection methods employed, the results may be more or less valid. The informed consumer can evaluate results in light of these considerations.

As a fruitful exercise in critical evaluation, you can use what is contained in this chapter to assess the research reported in other chapters of this book. Questions such as, "How do you know?" and "Can any other factors explain this result?" and "Under what conditions does this assertion hold?" should constantly come to mind. To the extent that you develop this critical appreciation of research, you will not be obliged to accept the claims of others on faith. Even if you never undertake a single piece of research in your lifetime, it is essential to have knowledge of what is involved in social research.

SUMMARY

1. Hunches, personal problems, observations, conversations, and theory are all sources of research problems.

Whatever the source, the steps in researching a problem are: familiarization with previous research and writing on the problem; stating the relationship you expect to find between your independent and dependent variables; constructing operational definitions of the variables.

2. The basic problem in measurement is achieving validity – measuring what you intend to measure. Reliability checks and replication are ways of solving the problem of validity. The key to validity is varied and repeated measurement.

3. The purpose of a research design is to eliminate alternative explanations for the results. The ideal, although not perfect, design is the classical experimental design. A well used deviation from the classical design is the cross-sectional design.

4. In sociology, most research involves a sample rather than the total population. The major concern in sampling is attempting to make the sample representative of the population. To achieve a representative sample, random sampling procedures are usually employed. Types of random samples are: simple random, systematic, stratified random, and multistage. Sometimes it is impossible or too costly to use random sampling procedures. In these cases, nonrandom samples such as quota samples are used.

5. All data collection is based on asking or observing, and can be structured or unstructured. The most commonly used techniques in sociology are structured questionnaires, structured interviews, and participant observation. A particularly useful method for already recorded information is content analysis. All these techniques have advantages and disadvantages that determine their usefulness for a particular research problem.

6. After quantitative data have been collected, they are submitted to analysis. This frequently involves coding the data and keypunching them on cards or tapes for analysis by computers. Various statistics are used to describe the data and to tell how important findings and relationships are. The emphasis in this section is on how to interpret the major statistics used in sociological research.

GLOSSARY

Association. Statistical relation between two or more variables. The most common measures of association are *gamma, tau, rho, lambda,* and *r.*

Average. A measure that reduces data to one meaningful value.

Classical experimental design. Research design that involves the comparison of two equivalent groups at two points in time to determine the effects of an independent upon a dependent variable.

Coding. Process of transferring answers in a questionnaire into usable data.

Content analysis. Any systematic procedure for examining the content of recorded information; usually applied to the mass media.

Control group. The comparison group that is denied the effects of the independent variable in the classical experimental design.

Cross-sectional design. Research design in which two or more groups with varying degrees of an independent variable are measured at one point in time to determine how they compare with respect to a dependent variable.

Dependent variable. The variable that research attempts to explain according to how it is affected by some other variable(s).

Dispersion. Statistics that describe the spread in the scores of a distribution.

Experimental group. The comparison group that is subjected to the independent variable in the classical experimental design.

Hypothesis. Prediction of what you expect to find as a result of research; a statement of relation between two or more variables.

Independent variable. Causal or explanatory variable.

Indicator. Empirical measure of a variable.

Mean. Sum of all of the scores divided by the number of scores; the score each case would have if the variable were distributed equally.

Median. Score that divides a distribution into two equal parts.

Mode. Score that occurs most fequently in a distribution.

Multistage random sample. Combination of random samples through several stages.

Negative (inverse) relation. Relation in which two or more variables change in opposite directions; as one increases the other decreases.

Nonrandom sample. Easier and less costly to take than a random sample, but the degree of representativeness cannot be calculated.

Operational definition. Precise set of instructions enabling a researcher to measure indicators that correspond to variables; operational definitions enable different researchers to get the same results when measuring the same phenomena.

Participant observation. Situation in which the researchers, in varying degrees, take an active part in the situation they are directly observing.

Physical trace evidence. Observational data based on accretion or erosion.

Population. Largest number of individuals or units of interest to the researcher.

Positive (direct) relation. Relation in which two or more variables change in the same direction; as one increases the other increases, or as one decreases the other decreases.

Quota sample. Sample with the same proportion of certain characteristics as found in the population; the nonrandom equivalent of a stratified random sample.

Random sample. Sample in which each element within the population has an equal chance of appearing; also called *probability sample.*

Reliability. Consistency of results over time or with several investigators.

Replication. Systematic repeated measurement of a given relationship.

Sample. Small representation of a population.

Sensitization. Process by which subjects become aware that they are being studied.

Standard deviation (SD). Measure of dispersion based on deviations from the mean.

Statistics. Actual numbers; and the theories and techniques used to manipulate data.

Stratified random sample. Series of random samples designed to represent some population characteristic.

Systematic sample. Sample in which the first element from a population is selected at random followed by every succeeding *nth* element.

Validity. Property of measurement whereby what is measured is what was intended to be measured.

Variable. Factor that can differ or vary from one situation to another, or from one individual or group to another; a concept that has more than one value.

FURTHER READING

Hammond, Philip E. (ed.). *Sociologists At Work.* New York: Basic Books, 1964. A collection of essays by sociologists on how they conducted their own research projects and the problems they encountered.

Johnson, Allan G. *Social Statistics Without Tears.* New York: McGraw-Hill, 1977. A painless introduction to social statistics.

Kaplan, Abraham. *The Conduct of Inquiry.* San Francisco: Chandler, 1964. Explores how we know something is true and how we explain the social world in a clear way.

Labovitz, S., and R. Hagedorn. *Introduction to Social Research.* 3rd ed. New York: McGraw-Hill, 1981. A highly readable, small book that treats in slightly more detail the issues raised in this chapter.

Smith, H.W. *Strategies of Social Research.* 2nd ed. Englewood Cliffs, N.J.: Prentice-Hall, 1981. Chapter 5 is a very complete description of structured observational techniques.

REFERENCES

Abella, Irving. (ed.). 1974. *On Strike*. Toronto: Lorimer.

Abercrombie, Nicholas, Stephen Hill, and Bryan S. Turner. 1980. *The Dominant Ideology Thesis*. London: George Allen & Unwin.

Aberle, D., and K. Naegele. 1952. "Middle-class fathers' occupational role and attitudes toward children." *American Journal of Orthopsychiatry*, 22:366-378.

Abu-Laban, Sharon McIrvin. 1980. "Social supports in older age: the need for new research directions." *Essence*, 4:195-210.

Abu-Laban, Sharon, and Baha Abu Laban. 1980. "Women and the aged as minority groups: a critique," pp. 63-79 in Victor W. Marshall (ed.), *Aging in Canada: Social Perspectives*. Don Mills: Fitzhenry and Whiteside.

Acheson, T. W. 1977. "The maritimes and Empire Canada," in D. J. Bercuson (ed.), *Canada and The Burden of Unity*. Toronto: Macmillan.

Adams, Bert N. 1975. *The Family: A Sociological Interpretation*. 2nd. ed. Chicago: Rand McNally.

Adams, I. 1970. *The Poverty Wall*. Toronto: McClelland and Stewart.

Adams, I., et al. 1971. *The Real Poverty Report*. Edmonton: Hurtig.

Adams, O. B., and L. A. Lefevre. 1980. *Retirement and Mortality: An Examination of Mortality in a Group of Retired Canadians*. Ottawa: Statistics Canada, Health Division (Cat. no. 83-521E, Occasional).

Adams, Robert M. 1960. "The origin of cities." *Scientific American*, 203(September):153-172.

Adler-Karlsson, G. 1970. *Reclaiming the Canadian Economy*. Toronto: Anansi.

Agopian, Michael W., and Gretchen L. Anderson. 1981. "Characteristics of parental child stealing." *Journal of Family Issues*, 2(4):471-484.

Aird, John S. 1978. "Fertility decline and birth control in The People's Republic of China." *Population and Development Review*, 4:225-253.

Alder, Freda. 1975. *Sisters in Crime*. New York: McGraw-Hill.

Aldous, Joan. 1974. "The making of family roles and family change." *Family Coordinator*, 23:231-235.

Alford, Robert R. 1963. *Party and Society: The Anglo-American Democracies*. Chicago: Rand McNally.

Al-Issa, Ihsan. 1980. *The Psychopathology of Women*. Englewood Cliffs, N.J.: Prentice-Hall.

Allen, Richard. 1971. *The Social Passion: Religion and Social Reform in Canada, 1914-1928*. Toronto: University of Toronto Press.

Allport, Gordon W. 1950. *The Individual and His Religion*. New York: Macmillan.

Allport, Gordon W. 1954. *The Nature of Prejudice*. New York: Doubleday.

Althusser, Louis. 1971. "Ideology and ideological state apparatuses," in Louis Althusser, *Lenin and Philosophy and Other Essays*. New York: Monthly Review.

Altman, Irwin. 1975. *The Environment and Social Behavior*. Monterey, Calif.: Cole.

Ambert, Anne-Marie. 1976. *Sex Structure*. 2nd ed. Don Mills, Ontario: Longman Canada.

Ambert, Anne-Marie. 1980. *Divorce in Canada*. Toronto: Academic Press.

Amirault, Ernest, and Maurice Archer. 1976. *Canadian Business Law*. Toronto: Methuen.

Anderson, C. A. 1944. "Sociological elements in economic restrictionism." *American Sociological Review*, 9(August): 345-358.

Anderson, Grace M., and J. M. Alleyne. 1979. "Ethnicity, food preferences and habits of consumption as factors in social interaction." *Canadian Ethnic Studies*, 11:83-87.

Anderson, Perry. 1977. "The antinomies of Antonio Gramsci." *New Left Review*, 100(January):5-78.

Andreski, S. 1968. *Military Organization and Society*. Berkeley: University of California Press.

Anisef, P., J. G. Paasche, and A. H. Turritin. 1980. *Is the Die Cast?* Toronto: Ministry of Education / Ministry of Colleges and Universities.

Archer, John. 1976. "Biological explanations of psychological sex differences," in Barbara Lloyd, and John Archer (eds.), *Exploring Sex Differences*. New York: Academic Press.

Armstrong, D. 1970. *Education and Economic Achievement*. Ottawa: Information Canada.

Armstrong, D., et al. 1977. "The measurement of income distribution in Canada: some problems and some tentative data." *Canadian Public Policy*, 3:479-488.

Armstrong, Hugh, and Pat Armstrong. 1975. "The segregated participation of women in the Canadian labour force, 1941-71." *Canadian Review of Sociology and Anthropology*, 12(Part 1):370-384.

Armstrong, Pat, and Hugh Armstrong. 1978. *The Double Ghetto: Canadian Women and Their Segregated Work*. Toronto: McClelland and Stewart.

Arnold, S. J., and D. J. Tigert. 1974. "Canadians and

Americans: a comparative analysis." *International Journal of Comparative Sociology*, 15(March-June):68-83.

Aronoff, Joel, and William D. Crano. 1975. "A re-examination of the cross-cultural principles of task segregation and sex role differentiation in the family." *American Sociological Review*, 40:12-20.

Atwood, Margaret. 1972. *Survival: A Thematic Guide to Canadian Literature.* Toronto: Anansi.

Baer, Douglas E., and Ronald D. Lambert. 1982. "Education and support for dominant ideology." *Canadian Review of Sociology and Anthropology*, 19(2):173-195.

Bailey, M. B., P. W. Haberman, and H. Alksne. 1965. "The epidemiology of alcoholism in urban residential areas." *Quarterly Journal of Studies on Alcohol*, 26:19-40.

Baird, Irene. 1937. *Waste Heritage.* Philadelphia: John Lippincott.

Baker, Maureen, and Mary-Anne Robeson. 1981. "Trade union reactions to women workers and their concerns." *Canadian Journal of Sociology*, 6:19-31.

Balakrishnan, T. R. 1976. "Ethnic residential segregation in the metropolitan areas of Canada." *Canadian Journal of Sociology*, 1(1):481-498.

Balakrishnan, T. R. 1982. "Changing patterns of residential segregation in the metropolitan areas of Canada." *Canadian Review of Sociology and Anthropology*, 19(1):92-110.

Baldus, Bernd. 1977. "Social control in capitalist societies: an examination of the 'problem of order' in liberal democracies." *Canadian Journal of Sociology*, 2(3):247-262.

Baldwin, E. 1977a. "The mass media and the corporate elite." *Canadian Journal of Sociology*, 2(1):1-27.

Baldwin, E. 1977b. "On methodological and theoretical 'muddles' in Clement's media study." *Canadian Journal of Sociology*, 2(2):215-222.

Bandura, A., Dorothea Ross, and Sheila A. Ross. 1963. "Imitation of film-mediated aggressive models." *Journal of Abnormal and Social Psychology*, 66:3-11.

Bandura, A., and R. H. Walters. 1963. *Social Learning and Personality Development.* New York. Holt, Rinehart and Winston.

Bardwick, Judith M., and Elizabeth Douvan. 1971. "Ambivalence: the socialization of woman," in Vivian Gornick, and Barbara K. Moran (eds.), *Woman in Sexist Society.* New York: Signet Books.

Barfield, Ashton. 1976. "Biological influences on sex differences in behavior," in Michael S. Teitelbaum (ed.), *Sex Differences: Social and Biological Perspectives.* Garden City, N.Y.: Anchor Books.

Barnard, Chester. 1938. *The Functions of the Executive.* Cambridge, Mass.: Harvard University Press.

Barter, James T., George Mizner, and Paul Werme. 1970. "Patterns of drug use among college students: an epidemiological and demographic survey of student attitudes and practices." Unpublished. Department of Psychiatry, University of Colorado Medical School.

Barty, M. 1971. "Fear of success." Unpublished manuscript.

Basow, Susan A. 1980. *Sex-Role Stereotypes: Traditions and Alternatives.* Monterey, Calif.: Brooks/Cole.

Baxter, E. H. 1976. "Children's and adolescents' perceptions of occupational prestige." *Canadian Review of Sociology and Anthropology*, 13:229-238.

Bayne, J. R. D. 1978. "Health and care needs of an aging population." Paper prepared for the National Symposium on Aging in Ottawa.

Beattie, C., and B. Spencer. 1971. "Career attainment in Canadian bureaucracies." *American Journal of Sociology*, 77:472-490.

Beaujot, Roderic P. 1978. "Canada's population: growth and dualism." *Population Bulletin*, 33(2):36.

Beaujot, Roderic, and Kevin McQuillan. 1982. *Growth and Dualism: the Demographic Development of Canadian Society.* Toronto: Gage.

Becker, Howard. 1963. *Outsiders: Studies in the Sociology of Deviance.* New York: Free Press.

Becker, Howard. 1964. *The Other Side: Perspectives on Deviance.* New York: Free Press.

Becker, Howard, Blanche Geer, and Everett Hughes. 1960. *Making the Grade.* New York: Wiley.

Becker, Howard, and Leopold Von Wiese. 1950. *Systematic Sociology.* Gary, Ind.: Norman Paul Press.

Bélanger, Paul, and Céline Sainte-Pierre. 1978. "Dépendence économique, subordination politique et oppression nationale: le Québec 1960-1977." *Sociologie et Sociétés*, 10:2.

Bell, D. 1953. "Crime as an American way of life." *The Antioch Review*, 13:131-154.

Bell, Daniel. 1977. "The return of the sacred: the argument on the future of religion." *British Journal of Sociology*, 28:419-449.

Bell, D., and Lorne Tepperman. 1979. *The Roots of Disunity.* Toronto: McClelland and Stewart.

Bellah, Robert. 1967. "Civil religion in America." *Daedalus*, 96:1-21.

Belson, W. A. 1969. "The extent of stealing by London boys and some of its origins." Survey Research Centre, London School of Economics.

Bem, Sandra L. 1976. "Probing the promise of androgyny," in Alexandra G. Kaplan, and Joan P. Bean (eds.), *Beyond Sex-role Stereotypes: Readings Toward a Psychology of Androgyny.* Boston: Little, Brown.

Bem, Sandra, and Daryl J. Bem. 1971. "Training the woman to know her place: the power of a nonsonscious ideology," in Michele Hoffnung Garskof (ed.), *Roles Women Play: Readings Toward Women's Liberation.* Belmont, Calif.: Brook/Cole Publishing.

Benbow, Camilla Persson, and Julian C. Stanley. 1980. "Sex differences in mathematical ability: fact or artifact?" *Science* 210(December 12):1262-1264.

Bendix, Reinhard. 1962. *Max Weber: An Intellectual Portrait.* New York: Doubleday.

Bengtson, Vern L. 1973. *The Social Psychology of Aging.* Indianapolis and New York: Bobbs-Merril.

Bengtson, Vern L., and J. A. Kuypers. 1971. "Generational differences and the developmental stake." *Aging and Human Development,* 2(no. 4):249-260.

Bengtson, Vern L., and Victor W. Marshall. 1982. "The three faces of generations." Paper presented at the conference of the International Sociological Association, Mexico City (August).

Bengtson, Vern L., Edward B. Olander, and A. A. Haddad. 1976. "The 'generation gap' and aging family members: toward a conceptual model," in Jaber F. Gubrium (ed.), *Time, Roles, and Self in Old Age.* New York: Human Sciences Press.

Benston, Margaret. 1969. "The political economy of women's liberation." *Monthly Review* 21:13-27.

Berardo, Felix M. 1970. "Survivorship and social isolation: the case of the aged widower." *The Family Coordinator,* 1 (Jan):11-25.

Bercuson, David. 1978. *Fools and Wisemen: The Rise and Fall of the One Big Union.* Toronto: McGraw-Hill Ryerson.

Berg, D. F. 1970. "The non-medical use of dangerous drugs in the United States: a comprehensive view." *International Journal of Addictions,* 5(4):777-834.

Berg, Ivar. 1970. *Education and Jobs: The Great Training Robbery.* New York: Beacon Press.

Berger, Carl. 1969. *Imperialism and Nationalism 1884-1914: A Conflict in Canadian Thought.* Toronto: Copp Clark.

Berger, Carl. 1970. *The Sense of Power: Studies in the Ideas of Canadian Imperialism, 1867-1914.* Toronto: University of Toronto Press.

Berger, Peter. 1961. *The Noise of Solemn Assemblies.* New York: Doubleday.

Berger, Peter, and Hansfried Kellner. 1971. "Marriage and the construction of reality," in Hans Peter Drietzel (ed.), *Recent Sociology No. 2: Patterns of Communicative Behavior.* New York: Macmillan.

Bernard, Jessie. 1971. "The paradox of the happy marriage," in Vivian Gornick and Barbara K. Moran (eds.), *Woman in Sexist Society.* New York: Mentor Books.

Bernard, Jessie. 1973. "My four revolutions: an autobiographical history of the ASA." *American Journal of Sociology* 78:773-791.

Bernard, Jessie. 1975. *Women, Wives, Mothers: Values and Options.* Chicago: Aldine.

Bernstein, Basil. 1970. "Education cannot compensate for society." *New Society,* 26(February):345.

Bernstein, Basil. 1971. "On the classification and training of educational knowledge," in M. Young (ed.), *Knowledge and Control: New Directions for the Sociology of Education.* 3 vols. London: Routledge & Kegan Paul.

Bernstein, Basil. 1973, 1974, 1976. *Class, Codes and Control.* London: Collier-Macmillan.

Berry, John W., Rudolf Kalin, and Donald M. Taylor. 1977. *Multiculturalism and Ethnic Attitudes in Canada.* Ottawa: Supply and Services.

Betcherman, Lita-Rose. 1975. *The Swastika and the Maple Leaf.* Don Mills: Fitzhenry and Whiteside.

Beynon, Erdmann D. 1938. "The voodoo cult among Negro migrants to Detroit." *American Journal of Sociology,* 43(May): 894-907.

Bibby, Reginald W. 1976. "Project Canada: a study of deviance, diversity, and devotion in Canada." *Codebook.* Lethbridge: The University of Lethbridge.

Bibby, Reginald W. 1979a. "The state of collective religiosity in Canada." *Canadian Review of Sociology and Anthropology,* 16:105-116.

Bibby, Reginald W. 1979b. "Religion and modernity: the Canadian case." *Journal for the Scientific Study of Religion,* 18:1-17.

Bibby, Reginald W. 1979c. "Consequences of religious commitment: the Canadian case." Paper presented at the Annual Meeting of The Society for the Scientific Study of Religion, October, San Antonio, Texas.

Bibby, Reginald W. 1980. "Sources of religious commitment: the Canadian case." Presented at the Annual Meeting of The Society for the Scientific Study of Religion, October, Cincinnati, Ohio.

Bibby, Reginald W. 1982. "Project Can80: a second look at deviance, diversity, and devotion in Canada." *Codebook.* Lethbridge: The University of Lethbridge.

Bibby, Reginald W., and Merlin B. Brinkerhoff. 1973. "The circulation of the saints: a study of people who join conservative churches." *Journal for the Scientific Study of Religion,* 12:273-283.

Bibby, Reginald W., and Merlin B. Brinkerhoff. 1982. "Circulation of the saints revisited: a longitudinal look at conservative church growth." Presented at the Annual Meeting of The Society for the Scientific Study of Religion, October, Providence, Rhode Island.

Bibby, Reginald W., and Armand Mauss. 1974. "Skidders and their servants: variable goals and functions of the skid road rescue mission." *Journal for the Scientific Study of Religion,* 13:421-436.

Bird, Frederick, and Bill Reimer. 1982. "Participation rates in new religious movements and para-religious movements." *Journal for the Scientific Study of Religion,* 21:1-14.

Black, Donald J. and Albert J. Reiss, Jr. 1970. "Police Control of Juveniles." *American Sociological Review,* 35(February):63-77.

Blake, J., and K. Davis. 1964. "Norms, values, and sanctions," in R. E. L. Faris (ed.), *Handbook of Modern Sociology.* Chicago: Rand McNally.

Blau, Peter M., and O. D. Duncan. 1967. *The American Occupational Structure.* New York: Wiley.

Blau, Peter M. and Richard A. Schoenherr. 1971. *The Structure of Organizations.* New York: Basic Books.

Blauner, Robert. 1964. *Alienation and Freedom.* Chicago, Ill.: University of Chicago Press.

Blenkner, M. 1965. "Social work and family relationships in later life with some thoughts on filial maturity," in E. Shanas and G. Streib (eds.), *Social Structure and the Family: Generational Relations.* Englewood Cliffs, N.J.: Prentice-Hall.

Blishen, Bernard R. 1967. "A socio-economic index for occupations in Canada." *Canadian Review of Sociology and Anthropology*, 4:41-53.

Block, W. E. and M. A. Walker (eds.). 1982. *Discrimination, Affirmative Action, and Equal Opportunity.* Vancouver: The Fraser Institute.

Blumberg, Abraham S. 1967. *Criminal Justice.* Chicago: Quadrangle Books.

Blumberg, Paul 1968. *Industrial Democracy.* London: Constable.

Blumer, Herbert. 1962. "Society as symbolic interaction," in Arnold Rose (ed.), *Human Behavior and Social Processes: An Interactionist Approach.* Boston: Houghton Mifflin.

Bogardus, Emory S. 1959. *Social Distance.* Los Angeles: Antioch.

Bogue, Donald J. 1969. *Principles of Demography.* New York: Wiley.

Boguslaw, R. and G. R. Vickers. 1977. *Prologue To Sociology.* Santa Monica: Goodyear.

Boisen, B. 1939. "Economic distress and religious experience." *Psychiatry*, May.

Bonnie, Richard J. and Charles H. Whitebread. 1974. *The Marihuana Conviction.* Charlottesville: University Press of Virginia.

Boocock, Sarane. 1972. *An Introduction to the Sociology of Learning.* Boston: Houghton Mifflin.

Bossen, M. 1971. "Manpower Utilization in Canadian Chartered Banks." *Studies of the Royal Commission on the Status of Women in Canada*, No. 4. Ottawa: Queen's Printer.

Bottomore, T. B. 1964. *Karl Marx, Selected Writings in Sociology and Social Philosophy.* New York: McGraw-Hill.

Bottomore, T. B., and M. Rubel (eds.). 1956. *Selected Writings in Sociology and Social Philosophy.* New York: McGraw-Hill.

Bottomore, T. B., and Maximilian Rubel. 1963. *Karl Marx.* Middlesex, England: Pelican Books.

Bouma, Gary D. 1970. "Assessing the impact of religion: a critical review." *Sociological Analysis*, 31:172-179.

Bourdieu, P. 1974. "The school as a conservative force: scholastic and cultural inequalities," in J. Eggleston (ed.), *Contemporary Research in the Sociology of Education.* London: Methuen.

Bourne, L. S. 1975. *Urban Systems: Strategies for Regulation.* London: Oxford University Press.

Bourne, L. S. 1978. *Emergent Realities of Urbanization in Canada: Some Parameters and Implications of Declining Growth.* Research Paper No. 96. Centre for Urban and Community Studies, University of Toronto.

Bowles, Samuel, and Herbert Gintis. 1976. *Schooling in Capitalist America: Educational Reform and the Contradictions of Economic Life.* New York: Basic Books.

Boyd, Monica. 1975. "English-Canadian and French-Canadian attitudes toward women: results of the Canadian Gallup Polls." *Journal of Comparative Family Studies*, VI: 153-169.

Boyd, Monica. 1977. "The forgotten minority: the socio-economic status of divorced and separated women," in Patricia Marchak (ed.), *The Working Sexes.* Vancouver: University of British Columbia.

Braithwaite, J. 1981. "The myth of social class and criminality reconsidered." *American Sociological Review*, 46(1):36-57.

Brandwein, Ruth A., Carol A. Brown, and Elizabeth M. Fox. 1974. "Women and children last: the social situation of divorced mothers and their families." *Journal of Marriage and the Family*, 36:498-514.

Brannon, Robert. 1971. "Organizational vulnerability in modern religious organizations." *Journal for the Scientific Study of Religion*, 10:27-32.

Brenton, Myron. 1974. *Friendship.* New York: Stein and Day.

Brenton, Myron. 1975. "The paradox of the contemporary American father: every day is Mother's Day," in John W. Petras (ed.), *Sex: Male, Gender: Masculine.* Port Washington, N.Y.: Alfred.

Breton, Raymond. 1964. "Institutional completeness of ethnic communities and personal relations to immigrants." *American Journal of Sociology*, 70:193-205.

Breton, Raymond. 1970. "Academic stratification in secondary schools and the educational plans of students." *Canadian Review of Sociology and Anthropology*, 7:17-34.

Breton, Raymond. 1972. *Social and Academic Factors in the Career Decisions of Canadian Youth.* Ottawa: Information Canada.

Brim, Orville G., Jr. 1966. "Socialization through the life cycle," in Orville G. Brim, Jr., and Stanton Wheeler, *Socialization After Childhood: Two Essays.* New York: Wiley.

Brim, Orville G., Jr., and Jerome Kagan. 1980. "Constancy and change: a view of the issues," in Orville G. Brim, Jr., and Jerome Kagan (eds.), *Constancy and Change in Human Development.* Cambridge, Mass.: Harvard University Press.

Britton, John N. H., and James M. Gilmour. 1978. *The Weakest Link: A Technological Perspective on Canadian Industrial Underdevelopment.* Background study 43. Ottawa: Science Council of Canada.

Brodie, M. Janine. 1977. "The recruitment of Canadian women provincial legislators, 1950-1975," *Atlantis*, (Spring): 6-17.

Brody, Elaine. 1978. "The aging of the family," *Annals, American Academy of Political and Social Science*, 438:13-27.

Brody, Elaine M. 1981. "'Women in the middle' and family help to older people." *The Gerontologist*, 21(no. 5):471-480.

Brodzinsky, David M., Karen Barnet, and John R. Aiello.

1981. "Sex of subject and gender identity as factors in humor appreciation." *Sex Roles*, 7:561-573.

Bronowski, J. 1973. *The Ascent of Man.* London: British Broadcasting Corp.

Brophy, J. E., and T. L. Good. 1974. *Teacher-Student Relationship.* New York: Holt, Rinehart and Winston.

Broverman, Inge K., Susan Raymond Vogel, Donald M. Broverman, Frank E. Clarkson, and Paul S. Rosenkrantz. 1972. "Sex-role stereotypes: a current appraisal." *Journal of Social Issues*, 28:59-78.

Brown, B. Bradford. 1981. "A life-span approach to friendship: age-related dimensions of an ageless relationship." *Research in the Interweave of Social Roles: Friendship*, Vol. 2:23-50.

Bruce, Christopher J. 1978. "The effect of young children on female labor force participation rates: an exploratory study." *The Canadian Journal of Sociology*, 3:431-439.

Bryden, K. 1974. *Old Age Pensions and Policy-Making in Canada.* Montreal and London: McGill-Queens University Press.

Bryden, M. P. 1979. "Evidence for sex-related differences in cerebral organization," in M. A. Wittig, and A. C. Petersen (eds.), *Sex-Related Differences in Cognitive Functioning: Developmental Issues.* New York: Academic Press.

Brym, R. 1979. "Political conservatism in Atlantic Canada," in R. Brym and R. J. Sacouman (eds.), *Underdevelopment and Social Movements in Atlantic Canada.* Toronto: New Hogtown Press.

Brym, R., and R. J. Sacouman (eds.). 1979. *Underdevelopment and Social Movements in Atlantic Canada.* Toronto: New Hogtown Press.

Bullock, Henry A. 1961. "Significance of the racial factor in the length of prison sentences." *Journal of Criminal Law, Criminology, and Police Science*, 52:411-417.

Burgess, E. W. 1925. "The growth of the city," in Robert E. Park, Ernest W. Burgess, and Roderick D. McKenzie, *The City.* Chicago: University of Chicago Press.

Burgess, Ernest, W. 1931. "The family as a unity of interacting personalities." *The Family*, 7:3-9.

Burgess, Ernest W. 1960 "Aging in western culture," in Ernest W. Burgess (ed.), *Aging in Western Societies.* Chicago and London: University of Chicago Press.

Burgess, Ernest W., Harvey J. Locke, and Mary Margaret Thomas. 1971. *The Family*, 4th ed. New York: Van Nostrand Reinhold.

Burns, Tom, and G. M. Stalker. 1961. *The Management of Innovation.* London: Tavistock Institute.

Bush, Diane Mitsch, and Roberta G. Simmons. 1981. "Socialization processes over the life course," in Morris Rosenberg, and Ralph H. Turner (eds.), *Social Psychology: Sociological Perspectives.* New York: Basic Books.

Cahalan, Don. 1970. *Problem Drinkers.* San Francisco: Jossey-Bass.

Cahill, Spencer E. 1980. "Directions for an interactionist study of gender development." *Symbolic Interaction*, 3:123-138.

Cain, Leonard D., Jr. 1964. "Life course and social structure," in Robert E. L. Faris (ed.), *Handbook of Modern Sociology.* Chicago: Rand McNally & Company.

Cain, Leonard D., Jr. 1976. "Aging and the law," in Robert Binstock, and Ethel Shanas (eds.), *Handbook of Aging and the Social Sciences.* New York: Van Nostrand Reinhold.

Cairns, A. 1977. "The governments and societies of Canadian federalism." *Canadian Journal of Political Science*, 10: 695-726.

Calhoun, Richard B. 1978. *In Search of the New Old: Redefining Old Age in America, 1945-1970.* New York and Oxford: Elsevier.

Campbell, C., and G. Szablowski. 1979. *The Superbureaucrats.* Toronto: Macmillan.

Campbell, Ernest Q. 1975. *Socialization: Culture and Personality.* Dubuque, Iowa: Wm. C. Brown.

Canada, Supreme Court. 1981. *The Supreme Court Decisions on the Canadian Constitution.* Toronto: James Lorimer.

Canadian Advisory Council on the Status of Women. 1978. *The Status of Women and the CBC: A Brief by the Canadian Advisory Council on the Status of Women to the Canadian Radio-Television and Telecommunications Commission.* Ottawa: Queen's Printer.

Canadian Advisory Council on the Status of Women. 1979. *Ten Years Later: An Assessment of the Federal Government's Implementation of the Recommendations Made by the Royal Commission on the Status of Women.* Ottawa: Queen's Printer.

Canadian Council on Social Development. 1980. "The Extent of Poverty in Canada," in J. Harp and J. Hofley (eds.), *Structured Inequality in Canada.* Scarborough, Ont.: Prentice-Hall.

Cape, Ronald D. T., and Philip J. Henschke. 1980. "Perspective of health in old age." *Journal of the American Geriatrics Society*, 28(no. 7):295-299.

Caplow, Theodore. 1971. *Elementary Sociology.* Englewood Cliffs, N.J.: Prentice-Hall.

Cardinal, Harold. 1969. *The Unjust Society: The Tragedy of Canada's Indians.* Edmonton: M. G. Hurtig.

Carnoy, Martin, and Henry M. Levin. 1976. *The Limits of Educational Reform.* New York: David McKay.

Carp, Frances M. 1972. "Retired people as automobile passengers." *The Gerontologist*, 12(1):66-72.

Carroll, Lewis. 1896. *Through the Looking-Glass.* New York: Random House (1946 edition).

Carroll, M. 1980. "The gap between male and female income in Canada." *Canadian Journal of Sociology*, 5(Fall): 359-362.

Carter, C. S., and W. T. Greenough. 1979. "Sending the right sex messages." *Psychology Today*, 13(September):112.

Castells, Manuel. 1976. "Theory and ideology in urban sociology," in C. G. Pickvance (ed.), *Urban Sociology: Critical Essays.* London: Tavistock.

Castells, Manuel. 1977. *The Urban Question.* London: Edward Arnold.

Caves, R. E., and G. L. Reuber. 1969. *Canadian Economic*

Policy and the Impact of International Monetary Flows. Toronto: University of Toronto Press.

Chafetz, Janet Saltzman. 1974. *Masculine/Feminine or Human?* Itasca, Illinois: Peacock.

Chalfant, Paul H., Robert E. Beckley, and C. E. Palmer. 1981. *Religion in Contemporary Society.* Palo Alto, Calif.: Mayfield Publishing Company.

Chambliss, William, and Robert Seidman. 1971. *Law, Order, and Power.* Reading, Mass.: Addison-Wesley.

Chappell, Neena L. 1980. "Social policy and the elderly," in Victor W. Marshall (ed.), *Aging in Canada: Social Perspectives.* Don Mills: Fitzhenry and Whiteside.

Chappell, Neena L. 1981. "Informal support networks among the elderly." Paper presented to meetings of the Society for the Study of Social Problems, Toronto (August).

Chappell, Neena L., and Betty Havens. 1980. "Old and female: testing the double jeopardy hypothesis." *The Sociological Quarterly,* 21(Spring):157-171.

Charon, Joel M. 1979. *Symbolic Interactionism.* Englewood Cliffs, N.J.: Prentice-Hall.

Chen, Mervin Y. T. 1980. "Age and closeness of supervision," in Victor W. Marshall (ed.), *Aging in Canada: Social Perspectives.* Don Mills, Ontario: Fitzhenry and Whiteside.

Childe, J. Gordon. 1950. "The urban revolution." *Town Planning Review,* 21:4-7.

Chiricos, Theodore, and Gordon Waldo. 1970. "Punishment and crime: an examination of some empirical evidence." *Social Problems,* 18(Fall):200-217.

Chirikos, Thomas N., and Gilbert Nestel. 1981. "Impairment and labor market outcomes: a cross-sectional and longitudinal analysis," in Herbert S. Parnes (ed.), *Work and Retirement.* Cambridge, Mass.: M.I.T. Press.

Clairmont, Don, and Dennis Magill. 1974. *Africville: The Life and Death of a Canadian Black Community.* Toronto: McClelland and Stewart.

Clark, Burton R. 1956. *Adult Education in Transition.* Berkeley, Calif.: University of California Press.

Clark, Burton R. 1960. "The 'cooling-out' function in higher education." *American Journal of Sociology,* 65(May):569-576.

Clark, Burton R. 1962. *Educating the Expert Society.* San Francisco: Chandler.

Clark, Sam, J. Paul Grayson, and L. M. Grayson (eds.). 1975. *Prophecy and Protest: Social Movements in Twentieth-Century Canada.* Toronto: Gage.

Clark, J., and N. Collishaw. 1975. "Canada's older population." Staff Paper. Ottawa: Long Range Health Planning, National Health and Welfare.

Clark, Lorenne. 1976. "The offense of rape and the concept of harm." Unpublished manuscript. University of Toronto.

Clark, S. D. 1948. *Church and Sect in Canada.* Toronto: University of Toronto Press.

Clark, S. D. 1959. *Movements of Political Protest in Canada.* Toronto: University of Toronto Press.

Clark, S. D. 1962. *The Developing Canadian Community.*

Toronto: University of Toronto Press.

Clark, S. D. 1966. *The Suburban Society.* Toronto: University of Toronto Press.

Clark, S. D. 1968. *The Developing Canadian Community,* 2nd ed. Toronto: University of Toronto Press.

Clark, S. D. 1975. "The post Second World War Canadian society." *Canadian Review of Sociology and Anthropology,* 12:1.

Clark, S. D. 1976. *Canadian Society in Historical Perspective.* Toronto: McGraw-Hill Ryerson.

Clar, S. D. 1978. *The New Urban Poor.* Toronto: McGraw-Hill Ryerson.

Clark, W., and Z. Zsigmond. 1981. *Job Market Reality for Post-Secondary Graduates.* Ottawa: Statistics Canada.

Clarke, Harold D., L. LeDuc, J. Jenson, J. H. Pammett. 1979. *Political Choice In Canada.* Toronto: McGraw-Hill Ryerson.

Clausen, John A. 1968. "Perspectives on childhood socialization," in John A. Clausen (ed.), *Socialization and Society.* Boston: Little, Brown.

Clement, Wallace. 1978. "A political economy of regionalism in Canada," in Daniel Glenday, et al. (eds.), *Modernization and the Canadian State.* Toronto: Macmillan.

Clement, Wallace. 1975. *The Canadian Corporate Elite.* Toronto: McClelland and Stewart.

Clement, Wallace. 1977. *Continental Corporate Power.* Toronto: McClelland and Stewart.

Cloward, Richard, and Lloyd Ohlin. 1960. *Delinquency and Opportunity: A Theory of Delinquent Gangs.* New York: Free Press.

Coale, Ansley. 1973. "The demographic transition reconsidered." *International Population Conference.* Liege, Belgium: International Union for the Scientific Study of Population.

Coale, Ansley. 1974. "History of human population." *Scientific American* 231:251.

Coale, Ansley, and Edgar M. Hoover. 1958. *Population Growth and Economic Development in Low Income Countries.* Princeton, N.J.: Princeton University Press.

Cogley, John. 1968. *Religion in a Secular Age.* New York: The New American Library.

Cohen, Albert. 1955. *Delinquent Boys.* New York: Free Press.

Cohn, W. 1978. "On inequality in Canada." *Canadian Review of Sociology and Anthropology,* 15:399-401.

Coleman, James S., et al. 1974. *Youth: Transition to Adulthood.* Chicago: University of Chicago Press.

Collins, K. 1978. *Women and Pensions.* Ottawa: The Canadian Council of Social Development.

Collins, Randall. 1971. "Functional and conflict theories of educational stratification." *American Sociological Review,* 36 (December):1002-1019.

Collins, Randall. 1979. *The Credential Society: An Historical Sociology of Education and Stratification.* New York: Academic Press.

Comber C., and John P. Keeves. 1973. *Science Education in Nineteen Countries: An Empirical Study.* New York: Wiley.

Connelly, Patricia. 1977. "The economic context of women's labour force participation in Canada," in Patricia Marchak (ed.), *The Working Sexes*. Vancouver: University of British Columbia.

Connelly, Patricia, and Linda Christiansen-Ruffman. 1977. "Women's problems: private troubles or public issues?" *Canadian Journal of Sociology*, 2:167-178.

Conway, J. F. 1978. "Populism in the United States, Russia and Canada: explaining the roots of Canada's third parties." *Canadian Journal of Political Science*, 11:1.

Cook, Shirley. 1969. "Canadian narcotics legislation, 1908-23: a conflict model interpretation." *Canadian Review of Sociology and Anthropology*, 6(1):36-46.

Cooley, Charles H. 1902. *Human Nature and the Social Order*. New York: Scribner's.

Coser, Rose Laub, and Gerald Rokoff. 1971. "Women in the occupational world: social disruption and conflict." *Social Problems*, 18:535-554.

Courtney, Alice E., and Thomas W. Whipple. 1978. *Canadian Perspectives on Sex Stereotyping in Advertising*. Ottawa: Advisory Council on the Status of Women.

Cousineau, Douglas and J. E. Veevers. 1972. "Incarceration as a response to crime: the utilization of canadian prisons." *Canadian Journal of Criminology and Corrections*, 14(January):10-31.

Cowgill, Donald O. 1975. "Aging and modernization: a revision of the theory," in Jaber F. Gubrium (ed.), *Late Life*. Springfield, Ill.: Charles C. Thomas.

Cowgill, Donald O., and Lowell D. Holmes. 1972. *Aging and Modernization*. New York: Appleton-Century-Crofts.

Crean, S. M. 1976. *Who's Afraid of Canadian Culture?* Don Mills, Ont.: General Publishing.

Creighton, Donald. 1956. *The Commercial Empire of the St. Lawrence*. Toronto: Macmillan.

Cressey, Donald. 1971. *Other People's Money: A Study of the Social Psychology of Embezzlement*. Glencoe, Ill.: Free Press.

Crothers, Charles. 1979. "On the myth of rural tranquillity: comment on Webb and Collette." *American Journal of Sociology*, 84(6):1441-1445.

Crysdale, Stewart. 1961. *The Industrial Struggle and Protestant Ethics in Canada*. Toronto: Ryerson Press.

Cumming, Elaine, and William H. Henry. 1961. *Growing Old: The Process of Disengagement*. New York: Basic Books.

Cumming, Elaine, and Charles Lazer. 1981. "Kinship structure and suicide: a theoretical link." *The Canadian Review of Sociology and Anthropology*, 18:271-282.

Cuneo, C. 1980. "Class, stratification, and mobility," in R. Hagedorn (ed.), *Sociology*. Toronto: Holt, Rinehart and Winston.

Cuneo, C. and J. Curtis. 1975. "Social ascription in the educational and occupational status attainment of urban Canadians." *Canadian Review of Sociology and Anthropology*, 12:6-24.

Curtis, James E., and Ronald D. Lambert. 1976. "Educa-
tional status and reactions to social and political heterogeneity." *Canadian Review of Sociology and Anthropology* 13(2):189-203.

Cutler, Neal E. 1981. "Political characteristics of elderly cohorts in the twenty-first century," in Sara B. Kiesler, James N. Morgan, Valarie Kincade Oppenheimer (eds.), *Aging: Social Change*. New York: Academic Press.

Dahl, R. 1961. *Who Governs?* New Haven: Yale University Press.

Dahl, Roald. 1962. *Kiss Kiss*. Harmondsworth, England: Penguin Books.

Dahrendorf, Rolf. 1959. *Class and Class Conflict in Industrial Society*. Palo Alto, Calif: Stanford University Press.

Daniels, Arlene Kaplan. 1975. "Feminist perspectives in sociological research," in Marcia Millman, and Rosabeth Moss Kanter (eds.), *Another Voice: Feminist Perspectives on Social Life and Social Science*. Garden City, N.Y.: Doubleday Anchor.

D'Arcy, Carl. 1980. "The manufacture and obsolescence of madness: age, social policy, and psychiatric morbidity in a prairie province," in Victor W. Marshall (ed.), *Aging in Canada: Social Perspectives*. Don Mills, Ont.: Fitzhenry and Whiteside.

Darroch, A. Gordon. 1980. "Another look at ethnicity, stratification, and social mobility in Canada," in J. Goldstein, and R. Bienvenue (eds.), *Ethnicity and Ethnic Relations in Canada*. Toronto: Butterworths.

Dashefsky, Arnold. 1976. *Ethnic Identity in Society*. Chicago: Rand McNally.

David, Deborah S., and Robert Brannon. 1976. *The Forty-Nine Percent Majority: The Male Sex Role*. Reading, Mass.: Addison-Wesley.

Davids, Leo. 1980. "Family change in Canada, 1971-1976." *Journal of Marriage and the Family*, 42:177-181.

Davies, Mark, and Denise B. Kandel. 1981. "Parental and peer influences on adolescents' educational plans: some further evidence." *American Journal of Sociology*, 87:363-387.

Davis, A. K. 1971. "Canadian society and history as hinterland versus metropolis," in R. J. Ossenberg (ed.), *Canadian Society: Pluralism, Change and Conflict*. Scarborough, Ont.: Prentice-Hall.

Davis, F. James and Robert Hagedorn. 1954. "Testing the reliability of systematic field observations." *American Sociological Review*, 19(3):345-348.

Davis, Kingsley. 1940. "Extreme social isolation of a child." *American Journal of Sociology*, 45:554-564.

Davis, Kingsley. 1947. "Final note on a case of extreme isolation." *American Journal of Sociology*, 54:432-437.

Davis, Kingsley. 1949. *Human Society*. New York: Macmillan.

Davis, Kingsley. 1955. "The origin and growth of urbanization in the world." *American Journal of Sociology*, 60:429-437.

Davis, K. and W. Moore. 1945. "Some principles of stratifiction." *American Sociological Review*, 10:242-247.

Day, Lincoln H. 1972. "The social consequences of a zero population growth rate in the United States," in Charles F.

Westoff and Robert Parke, Jr. (eds.), *United States Commission on Population and the American Future: Demographic and Social Aspects of Population Growth*. Washington, D.C.: Government Printing Office.

Decore, John V. 1964. "Criminal sentencing: the role of the Canadian courts of appeal and the concept of uniformity." *The Criminal Law Quarterly*, 6(February):324-380.

DeFleur, Melvin L., and Lois B. DeFleur. 1967. "The relative contribution of television as a learning source for children's occupational knowledge." *American Sociological Review*, 32:777-789.

Demerath, N. J., III. 1965. *Social Class in American Protestantism*. Chicago: Rand McNally.

Demerath, N. J., III, and Phillip E. Hammond. 1969. *Religion in Social Context*. New York: Random House.

Denton, Frank T., and Byron G. Spencer. 1975. "Health-care costs when the population changes." *Canadian Journal of Economics*, 8(1):34-48.

Denton, Frank T., and Byron G. Spencer. 1979. "Some economic and demographic implications of future population change." *Journal of Canadian Studies*, 14(1):81-93.

Denton, Frank T., and Byron G. Spencer. 1980. "Canada's population and labour force: past, present, and future," in Victor W. Marshall (ed.), *Aging in Canada: Social Perspectives*. Don Mills: Fitzhenry and Whiteside.

Desbarats, Peter. 1976. *René*. Toronto: McClelland and Stewart.

Deutsch, Morton, and Robert M. Krauss. 1965. *Theories in Social Psychology*. New York: Basic Books.

Dill, William R. 1958. "Environment as an influence on managerial autonomy." *Administrative Science Quarterly*, 2(March):409-443.

Dion, K., and E. Berscheid. 1972. "Physical attractiveness and social perception of peers in preschool children." Unpublished research report.

Djilas, Milovan. 1957. *The New Class*. New York: Praeger.

Dofny, J. 1970. *Les Ingénieurs Canadiens-Français et Canadiens-Anglais à Montréal*. Ottawa: Ontario.

Dohrenwend, Bruce P., and Barbara S. Dohrenwend. 1975. "Sociocultural and social-psychological factors in the genesis of mental disorders." *Journal of Health and Social Behavior*, 16(4):365-392.

Dominick, Joseph R. 1979. "The portrayal of women in prime time, 1953-1977." *Sex Roles*, 5:405-411.

Dowd, James J. 1980. *Stratification Among the Aged*. Monterey, Calif.: Brooks/Cole.

Downs, A. 1957. *An Economic Theory of Democracy*. New York: Harper.

Driedger, Leo. 1974. "Doctrinal belief: a major factor in the differential perception of social issues." *The Sociological Quarterly*, Winter: 66-80.

Driedger, Leo. 1975. "In search of cultural identity factors: a comparison of ethnic students." *Canadian Review of Sociology and Anthropology*, 12:150-162.

Driedger, Leo. 1976. "Ethnic self identity: a comparison of ingroup evaluations." *Sociometry*, 39:131-141.

Driedger, Leo. 1980. "Ethnic and minority relations," in R. Hagedorn (ed.), *Sociology*. Toronto: Holt, Rinehart and Winston.

Driedger, Leo, and Glen Church. 1974. "Residential segregation and institutional completeness: a comparison of ethnic minorities." *Canadian Review of Sociology and Anthropology*, 11:30-52.

Driedger, Leo, Raymond Currie, and Rick Linden. 1982. "Traditional and rational views of God and the world." *Review of Religious Research* (forthcoming).

Driedger, Leo, and Richard Mezoff. 1980. "Ethnic prejudice and discrimination in Winnipeg high schools." *Canadian Journal of Sociology*, 6:1-17.

Dubbert, Joe L. 1979. *A Man's Place: Masculinity in Transition*. Englewood Cliffs, N.J.: Prentice-Hall.

Dulude, Louise. 1978. *Women and Aging: A Report on the Rest of Our Lives*. Ottawa: Canadian Advisory Council on the Status of Women.

Duncan, Beverly, and Otis Dudley Duncan. 1968. "Minorities and the process of stratification." *American Sociological Review*, 33(3):356-364.

Duncan, Otis Dudley. 1959. "Human ecology and population studies," in Philip M. Hauser and Otis Dudley Duncan (eds.), *The Study of Population*. Chicago: University of Chicago Press.

Duncan, Otis Dudley, and Leo F. Schnore. 1959. "Cultural, behavioral, and ecological perspectives in the study of social organization." *American Journal of Sociology*, 65:132-146.

Durkheim, Emile. 1938. *The Rules of the Sociological Method*. Sarah A. Solovay and John H. Mueller (trans.), George E. G. Catlin (ed.) Glencoe, Ill.: Free Press.

Durkheim, Emile. 1964a:1893. *The Division of Labor in Society*. George Simpson (trans.). Glencoe, Ill.: Free Press.

Durkheim, Emile. 1964b:1897. *Suicide*. John A. Spaulding and George Simpson (trans.). Glencoe, Ill.: Free Press.

Durkheim, Emile. 1964a:1893. *The Division of Labor in Society*. George Simpson (trans.). Glencoe, Ill.: Free Press.

Durkheim, Emile. 1964b:1897. *Suicide*. John A. Spaulding and George Simpson (trans.). Glencoe, Ill.: Free Press.

Durkheim, Emile. 1965:1912. *The Elementary Forms of the Religious Life*. New York: Free Press.

Duster, Troy. 1970. *The Legislation of Morality: Law, Drugs, and Moral Judgment*. New York: Free Press.

Eakins, Barbara Westbrook, and R. Gene Eakins. 1978. *Sex Differences in Human Communication*. Boston: Houghton Mifflin.

Easterlin, Richard. 1980. *Birth and Fortune: The Impact of Numbers on Personal Welfare*. New York: Basic Books.

Economic Council of Canada. 1964. *First Annual Review*. Ottawa: Queen's Printer.

Economic Council of Canada. 1965. *Second Annual Review*. Ottawa: Queen's Printer.

Economic Council of Canada. 1979. *One in Three.* Ottawa: Economic Council of Canada.

Eder, Donna, and Maureen T. Hallinan. 1978. "Sex differences in children's friendships." *American Sociological Review,* 43:237-250.

Edgerton, Robert B. 1967. *The Cloak of Competence: Stigma in the Lives of the Mentally Retarded.* Berkeley: University of California Press.

Effrat, Andrew. 1973. "Power to the paradigms," in Andrew Effrat, *Perspectives In Political Sociology.* Indianapolis: Bobbs-Merrill.

Eichler, Margrit. 1975. "The equalitarian family in Canada?" in S. Parvez Wakil (ed.), *Marriage, Family and Society: Canadian Perspectives.* Toronto: Butterworths.

Eichler, Margrit. 1978. "Women's unpaid labour." *Atlantis,* 3(Part II):52-62.

Eichler, Margrit. 1982. *Families in Can. Today; Recent Changes and Their Policy Consequences.* Toronto: Gage, (forthcoming.)

Elder, G. H. 1974. *Children of the Great Depression.* Chicago: University of Chicago Press.

Elkin, Frederick. 1964. *The Family in Canada.* Ottawa: The Vanier Institute.

Elkin, Frederick, and Gerald Handel. 1978. *The Child and Society: The Process of Socialization.* 3rd ed. New York: Random House.

Ellis, Godfrey J., Gary R. Lee, and Larry R. Petersen. 1978. "Supervision and conformity: a cross-cultural analysis of parental socialization values." *American Journal of Sociology,* 84:386-403.

Ellmann, Mary. 1968. *Thinking about Women.* New York: Harcourt Brace Jovanovich.

Endres, Robin. 1977. "Art and accumulation: the Canadian state and the business of art," in L. Panitch, *The Canadian State.* Toronto: University of Toronto Press.

Engels, Friedrich. 1942:1884. *The Origin of the Family, Private Property, and the State.* New York: International Publishers.

Ericson, Richard. 1982. *Reproducing Order: A Study of Police Patrol Work.* Toronto: University of Toronto Press.

Erikson, E. H. 1959. "Identity and the life cycle." *Psychological Issues,* 1.

Erikson, Erik. 1963. *Childhood and Society.* 2nd ed. New York: Norton.

Erikson, Erik. 1968. *Identity: Youth and Crisis.* New York: Norton.

Espenshade, Thomas J. 1978. "Zero population growth and the economies of developed nations." *Population and Development Review,* 4:645-680.

Estes, Carroll L. 1979. *The Aging Enterprise.* San Francisco: Jossey-Bass Publishers.

Ewen, Robert B. 1980. *An Introduction to Theories of Personality.* New York: Academic Press.

Fallding, Harold. 1978. "Mainline Protestantism in Canada and the United States: an overview." *Canadian Journal of Sociology,* 2:141-160.

Fallo-Mitchell, Linda, and Carol D. Ryff. 1982. "Preferred timing of female life events: cohort differences." *Research on Aging 4,* 2(June):249-267.

Farber, Bernard. 1964. *Family: Organization and Interaction.* San Francisco: Chandler.

Farrell, Warren. 1974. *The Liberated Man.* New York: Random House.

Fasteau, Marc F. 1975. *The Male Machine.* New York: Delta.

Favreau, Olga Eizner. 1977. "Sex bias in psychological research." *Canadian Psychological Review,* 18:56-65.

Featherman, David. 1971. "The socio-economic achievement of white religio-ethnic subgroups: social and psychological explanations." *American Sociological Review,* 36(2):207-222.

Featherman, D., and R. Hauser. 1976a. "Changes in the socioeconomic stratification of the races, 1962-1973." *American Journal of Sociology,* 82:621-651.

Featherman, D., and R. Hauser. 1976b. "Sexual inequalities and socioeconomic achievement in the U.S., 1962-73." *American Sociological Review,* 41:462-483.

Featherman, D., and R. Hauser. 1978. *Opportunity and Change.* New York: Academic Press.

Feuer, Lewis S. (ed.). 1959. *Marx and Engels: Basic Writings on Politics and Philosophy.* New York: Doubleday/Anchor.

Fink, Arlene, and Jacqueline Kosecoff. 1977. "Girls' and boys' changing attitudes toward school." *Psychology of Women Quarterly,* 2:44-49.

Finn, Ed. 1977. "Deterrents to unionization." *Labour Gazette* (Aug.) 341-346.

Fischer, Claude S. 1976. *The Urban Experience.* New York: Harcourt Brace Jovanovich.

Flacks, Richard. 1979. "Growing up confused," in Peter I. Rose (ed.), *Socialization and the Life Cycle.* New York: St. Martin's Press.

Fletcher, Susan, and Leroy O. Stone. 1981. *Living Arrangements of Canada's Older Women: Their Implications for Access to Support Services.* Ottawa: Statistics Canada.

Foner, Anne. 1974. "Age stratification and age conflict in political life." *American Sociological Review,* 39 (April): 187-196.

Foner, Anne, and David Kertzer. 1978. "Transitions over the life course: lessons from age-set societies." *American Journal of Sociology,* 83(5):1081-1104.

Foner, Anne, and Karen Schwab. 1981. *Aging and Retirement.* Monterey, Calif.: Brooks/Cole.

Forbes, E. R. 1975. "The origins of the Maritime Rights movement." *Acadiensis,* 5:1.

Forcese, Dennis. 1975. *The Canadian Class Structure.* Toronto: McGraw-Hill Ryerson.

Forcese, D. 1980. *The Canadian Class Structure.* 2nd ed. Toronto: McGraw-Hill Ryerson.

Fox, Bonnie (ed.). 1980. *Hidden in the Household.* Toronto: The Women's Press.

Fox, B. (ed.). 1982. *Hidden in the Household: Women's Domestic Labour Under Capitalism.* Toronto: Women's Press.

Franck, K. A. 1980. "Friends and strangers: the social experience of living in urban and non-urban settings." *The Journal of Social Issues*, 36(3):52-71.

Frank, André Gunder. 1969. *Capitalism and Underdevelopment in Latin America.* New York: Monthly Review Press.

Frazer, Charles F., and Leonard N. Reid. 1979. "Children's interaction with commercials." *Symbolic Interaction*, 2:79-96.

Frazier, E. Franklin. 1964. *The Negro Church in America.* New York: Schocken Books.

Freeman, Richard B. 1976. *The Overeducated American.* New York: Academic Press.

Freud, Sigmund. 1962: 1928. *The Future of an Illusion.* New York: Doubleday.

Frideres, James S. 1974. *Canada's Indians: Contemporary Conflicts.* Scarborough, Ont.: Prentice-Hall.

Friedan, Betty. 1963. *The Feminine Mystique.* Harmondsworth, England: Penguin.

Frieze, Irene H., Jacquelynne E. Parsons, Paula B. Johnson, Diane N. Ruble, and Gail L. Zellman. 1978. *Women and Sex Roles: A Social Psychological Perspective.* New York: W. W. Norton.

Fry, Christine L. 1976. "The ages of adulthood: a question of numbers." *Journal of Gerontology*, 31(2):170-177.

Fullan, Michael. 1970. "Industrial technology and worker integration in the organization." *American Sociological Review*, 35(December):1028-1039.

Fuller, Mary. 1978. "Sex-role stereotyping and social sicence," in Jane Chetwynd, and Oonagh Hartnett (eds.), *The Sex Role System: Psychological and Sociological Perspectives.* London: Routledge and Kegan Paul.

Galbraith, J. K. 1967. *The New Industrial State.* Boston: Houghton Mifflin.

Gans, Herbert. 1962a. "Urbanism and suburbanism as ways of life," in Arnold M. Rose (ed.), *Human Behavior and Social Processes.* Boston: Houghton Mifflin.

Gans, Herbert. 1962b. *The Urban Villagers.* New York: Free Press.

Gans, Herbert. 1967. *The Levittowners: Way of Life and Politics in a New Suburban Community.* New York: Pantheon.

Gans, Herbert. 1970. "Social planning: a new role for sociology," in Robert Gutman and David Popenoe (eds.), *Neighborhood, City and Metropolis.* New York: Random House.

Gans, Herbert. 1972. "The positive functions of poverty." *American Journal of Sociology*, 78:275-289.

Garrison, Howard H. 1979. "Gender differences in the career aspirations of recent cohorts of high school seniors." *Social Problems*, 27:170-185.

Gecas, Viktor. 1976. "The socialization and child care roles," in F. Ivan Nye (ed.), *Role Structure and Analysis of the Family.* Beverly Hills, Calif.: Sage.

Gecas, Viktor. 1981. "Contexts of socialization," in Morris Rosenberg, and Ralph H. Turner (eds.), *Social Psychology: Sociological Perspectives.* New York: Basic Books.

Gee, Ellen M. Thomas. 1980. "Female marriage patterns in Canada: changes and differentials." *Journal of Comparative Family Studies*, 11:457-473.

Geertz, Clifford. 1968. "Religion as a cultural system," in Donald Cutler (ed.), *The Religious Situation.* Boston: Beacon.

George, Linda K. 1980. *Role Transitions in Later Life.* Monterey, Calif.: Brooks/Cole.

Gerlach, Luther P., and Virginia H. Hine. 1968. "Five factors crucial to the growth and spread of a modern religious movement." *Journal for the Scientific Study of Religion*, 7:23-40.

Gerth H., and C. Wright Mills. 1958. *From Max Weber: Essays in Sociology.* New York: Oxford University Press.

Gibbins, Roger, J. Rick Ponting, and Gladys L. Symons. 1978. "Attitudes and ideology: correlates of liberal attitudes towards the role of women." *Journal of Comparative Family Studies*, 9:19-40.

Gibbs, Jack, and Maynard Ericson. 1976. "Crime rates of American cities in an ecological context." *American Journal of Sociology*, 82(3):605-620.

Giffen, P. J. 1966. "The revolving door: a functional interpretation." *Canadian Review of Sociology and Anthropology*, 3(3):154-166.

Gil, David. 1977. "Child abuse: levels of manifestation, causal dimensions, and primary prevention." *Victomology*, 2(2):186-195.

Gillie, Oliver. 1979. "The great I.Q. fraud." *Atlas*, Feb.: 26-28.

Gillis, A. R. 1974. "Population density and social pathology: the case of building type, social allowance, and juvenile delinquency." *Social Forces*, 53(2):306-314.

Gillis, A. R. 1977. "High-rise housing and psychological strain." *Journal of Health and Social Behavior*, 18(4):418-431.

Gillis, A. R. 1979a. "Household density and human crowding: unravelling a non-linear relationship." *Journal of Population*, 2(2):104-117.

Gillis, A. R. 1979b. "Coping with crowding: television, patterns of activity, and adaptation to high density environments." *The Sociological Quarterly*, 20:267-277.

Gillis, A. R. 1983. "Strangers next door: an analysis of density, diversity and scale in public housing projects." *Canadian Journal of Sociology* (forthcoming).

Gillis, A. R., and J. Hagan. 1982a. "Bystander apathy and the territorial imperative." *Sociological Inquiry* (forthcoming).

Gillis, A. R., and J. Hagan. 1982b. "Density, delinquency and design: formal and informal control and the built environment." *Criminology*, 19(4):514-529.

Gillis, A. R., and Paul C. Whitehead. 1970. "The Halifax Jews: a community within a community," in Jean Leonard Elliott (ed.), *Minority Canadians: Immigrant Groups.* Scarborough, Ont.: Prentice-Hall.

Glaser, Barney G., and Anselm L. Strauss. 1971. *Status Passage.* Chicago: Aldine, Atherton.

Glazer, Nathan, and Daniel P. Moynihan. 1963. *Beyond the Melting Pot.* Cambridge, Mass.: M.I.T. Press.

Glazer, Nona. 1977. "Introduction to part two," in Nona Glazer and Helen Youngelson Waehrer (eds.), *Woman in a Man-Made World*. 2nd ed. Chicago: Rand McNally.

Glick, P. 1977. "Updating the family life cycle." *Journal of Marriage and the Family*, 39:5-13.

Glock, Charles, Benjamin Ringer, and Earl Babbie. 1967. *To Comfort and to Challenge*. Berkeley, Calif.: University of California Press.

Glock, Charles, and Rodney Stark. 1965. *Religion and Society in Tension*. Chicago: Rand McNally.

Goffman, Erving. 1959. *The Presentation of Self in Everyday Life*. Garden City, N.J.: Doubleday Anchor.

Goffman, Erving. 1963. *Behavior in Public Places*. New York: Free Press.

Goffman, Erving. 1963. *Stigma*. Englewood Cliffs, N.J.: Prentice-Hall.

Gold, Gerald L. 1975. *St. Pascal*. Montreal: Holt, Rinehart and Winston.

Goldberg, M. A., and J. Mercer. 1980. "Canadian and U.S. cities: basic differences, possible explanations, and their meaning for public policy." *Papers of the Regional Science Association*, 45:159-183.

Goldberg, Steven. 1973. *The Inevitability of Patriarchy*. New York: William Morrow.

Goldsen, Rose K. 1979. Review of Marie Winn, *The Plug-in Drug: Television, Children and the Family*, in *American Journal of Sociology*, 84:1054-1056.

Goldstein, Jay. 1981. "Has the popularity of Anglo-conformity waned?: a study of school naming events in Winnipeg, 1881-1979." *Canadian Ethnic Studies*, 13:52-60.

Goleman, Daniel. 1978. "Special abilities of the sexes: do they begin in the brain?" *Psychology Today*, (November): 48-49, 51, 54-56, 58-59, 120.

Goode, W. J. 1970. *World Revolution and Family Patterns*. New York: Free Press.

Gordon, Milton M. 1964. *Assimilation in American Life*. New York: Oxford University Press.

Gorsuch, Richard, and Daniel Aleshire. 1974. "Christian faith and ethnic prejudice: a review and interpretation of research." *Journal for the Scientific Study of Religion*, 13:281-307.

Gould, Meredith, and Rochelle Kern-Daniels. 1977. "Toward a sociological theory of gender and sex." *The American Sociologist*, 12:182-189.

Gove, Walter. 1975. "Labelling and mental illness: a critique," in Walter Gove (ed.), *The Labeling of Deviance: Evaluating a Perspective*. New York: Halsted Press.

Gove, Walter R., Michael Hughes, and Omer R. Galle. 1979. "Overcrowding in the home: an empirical investigation of its possible consequences." *American Sociological Review*, 44:59-80.

Gove, Walter, and Jeanette Tudor. 1973. "Adult sex roles and mental illness." *American Journal of Sociology*, 78(January): 812-835.

Goyder, John C. 1981. "Income differences between the sexes: findings from a national Canadian survey." *The Canadian Review of Sociology and Anthropology*, 18:321-342.

Goyder, John C., and James E. Curtis. 1979. "Occupational mobility in Canada over four generations," in J. Curtis, and W. Scott (eds.), *Social Stratification: Canada*. 2nd ed. Scarborough, Ont.: Prentice-Hall.

Goyder, J., and P. Pineo. 1979. "Social class self-identification," in J. Curtis, and W. Scott (eds.), *Social Stratification: Canada*. 2nd ed. Scarborough, Ont.: Prentice-Hall.

Grabb, Edward G. 1980. "Differences in sense of control among French- and English-Canadian adolescents." *The Canadian Review of Sociology and Anthropology*, 17:169-175.

Graff, Harvey J. 1975. "Towards a meaning of literacy: literacy and social structure in Hamilton, Ontario, 1861," in Michael B. Katz and Paul H. Mattingly (eds.), *Education and Social Change: Themes from Ontario's Past*. New York: New York University Press.

Gramsci, Antonio. 1971. *Selections from the Prison Notebooks of Antonio Gramsci*. Translated and edited by Quintin Hoare and Geoffrey N. Smith. New York: International.

Gray Report. 1972. *Foreign Direct Investment in Canada*. Ottawa: Government of Canada.

Grayson, J. P., and L. M. Grayson. 1978. "The Canadian literary elite: a socio-historical perspective." *Canadian Journal of Sociology*, 3(3):291-308.

Greeley, Andrew. 1972. *The Denominational Society*. Glenview, Ill.: Scott, Foresman.

Green, Richard. 1974. *Sexual Identity Conflict in Children and Adults*. Baltimore, Md.: Penguin.

Greenglass, Esther R., and Reva Devins. 1982. "Factors related to marriage and career plans in unmarried women." *Sex Roles*, 8:57-71.

Griffiths, N. E. S. 1976. *Penelope's Web*. Toronto: Oxford University Press.

Grindstaff, Carl F. 1975. "The baby bust: changes in fertility patterns in Canada." *Canadian Studies in Population*, 2:15-22.

Grossman, Brian A. 1969. *The Prosecutor*. Toronto: University of Toronto Press.

Guillemard, Anne-Marie. 1977. "The call to activity amongst the old: rehabilitation or regimentation," in Blossom T. Wigdor (ed.), *Canadian Gerontological Collection I*. Winnipeg: Canadian Association on Gerontology.

Guillemard, Anne-Marie. 1980. *La vieillesse et l'Etat*. Paris: Presses Universitaires de France.

Guindon, Hubert. 1975: 1964. "Social unrest, social class and Quebec's bureaucratic revolution," in Sam Clark, et al. (eds.), *Prophecy and Protest: Social Movements in Twentieth-Century Canada*. Toronto: Gage.

Gunderson, Morley. 1976. "Work patterns," in Gail C. A. Cook (ed.), *Opportunity for Choice: A Goal for Women in Canada*. Ottawa: Information Canada.

Gusfield, Joseph. 1963. *Symbolic Crusade*. Urbana, Ill.: University of Illinois Press.

Guterman, S. S. 1969. "In defence of Wirth." *American Journal of Sociology*, 74(5):492-499.

Gutman, Gloria M. 1980. "The elderly at home and in retirement housing: a comparative study of health problems, functional difficulties, and support service needs," in Victor W. Marshall (ed.), *Aging in Canada: Social Perspectives*. Don Mills: Fitzhenry and Whiteside.

Haas, Jack, and William Shaffir. 1978. *Shaping Identity in Canadian Society*. Scarborough: Prentice-Hall.

Hacker, Helen Mayer. 1951. "Women as a minority group." *Social Forces*, 30:60-69.

Hagan, John. 1974a. "Extra-legal attributes and criminal sentencing: an assessment of a sociological viewpoint." *Law & Society Review*, 8(3):357-383.

Hagan, John. 1974b. "Criminal justice and native people: a study of incarceration in a Canadian province." *Canadian Review of Sociology and Anthropology Special Issue*, (August): 220-236.

Hagan, John. 1975. "Law, order, and sentencing: a study of attitude in action." *Sociometry*, 38:374-384.

Hagan, John. 1977. "Finding discrimination: a question of meaning." *Ethnicity*, 4:167-176.

Hagan, John. 1982. "The corporate advantage: the involvement of organizational and individual victims in a criminal justice system." *Social Forces* (forthcoming).

Hagan, John, and Celesta Albonetti. 1982. "Race, class and the perception of criminal injustice in America." *American Journal of Sociology* (forthcoming).

Hagan, John, and Kristen Bumiller. 1982. "Making sense of sentencing: a review and critique of sentencing research." In Al Blumstein (ed.), *Research on Sentencing* (forthcoming).

Hagan, John, A. R. Gillis, and Janet Chan. 1978. "Explaining official delinquency: a spatial study of class, conflict, and control." *Sociology Quarterly*, (Summer):386-398.

Hagan, John, and Jeffrey Leon. 1977a. "Rediscovering delinquency: social history, political ideology, and the sociology of law." *American Sociological Review*, 42(4):587-598.

Hagan, John, and Jeffrey Leon. 1977b. "Philosophy and sociology of crime control: Canadian-American comparisons." *Sociology Inquiry*, 47(3-4):181-208.

Hagan, John, Ilene Nagel, and Celesta Albonetti. 1980. "The differential sentencing of white-collar offenders in ten federal district courts." *American Sociological Review*, 45:802-820.

Hagestad, Gunhild O. 1982. "Life-phase analysis," in David J. Mangen, and Warren A. Peterson (eds.), *Research Instruments in Social Gerontology, Vol. 1, Clinical and Social Psychology*. Minneapolis: University of Minneapolis Press.

Hall, E. T. 1962. "Our silent language." *Americas*, 14(February):6.

Haller, A. and D. Bills. 1979. "Occupational prestige hierarchies: theory and evidence." *Contemporary Sociology*, 8:721-734.

Haller, Mark. 1970. "Urban crime and criminal justice: the Chicago case." *Journal of American History*, 57:619.

Hamilton, Richard, and Maurice Pinard. 1977. "Poverty in Canada: illusion and reality." *Canadian Review of Sociology and Anthropology*, 14(2):247-252.

Hammer, Muriel. 1963-64. "Influence of small social networks on factors of mental hospital admission." *Human Organization*, 22(Winter):243-251.

Hardin, Herschel. 1974. *A Nation Unaware: The Canadian Economic Culture*. Vancouver: J. J. Douglas.

Hardwick, W. G. 1971. "Vancouver: the emergence of a 'core-ring' urban pattern," in R. L. Gentilcore (ed.), *Geographical Approaches to Canadian Problems*. Scarborough, Ont.: Prentice-Hall.

Hargreaves, D. H. 1967. *Social Relations in a Secondary School*. London: Routledge & Kegan Paul.

Harlow, Harry F. 1959. "Love in infant monkeys." *Scientific American*, 200(June):68-74.

Harlow, Harry F., and Margaret Harlow. 1962. "Social deprivation in monkeys." *Scientific American*, 207(November): 136-146.

Harris, Chauncy D., and Edward L. Ullman. 1945. "The nature of cities." *Annals of The American Academy of Political and Social Science*, 242(November):7-17.

Harris, Louis, and Associates. 1975. *The Myth and Reality of Aging in America*. A study for the National Council on the Aging, Inc. Washington, D.C.: The National Council on the Aging.

Harris, Marvin. 1981. *America Now: Why Nothing Works*. New York: Simon and Schuster.

Harrison, James B. 1978. "Men's roles and men's lives." *Signs*, 4:324-336.

Harrison, Paul. 1959. *Authority and Power in the Free Church Tradition: A Social Case Study of the American Baptist Convention*. Princeton, N.J.: Princeton University Press.

Hartley, Ruth E. 1959. "Sex-role pressures in the socialization of the male child." *Psychological Reports*, 5:457-468.

Hartz, Louis. 1964. *The Founding of New Societies*. New York: Harcourt, Brace and World.

Harvey, David. 1975. "The political economy of urbanization in advanced capitalist societies: the case of the United States," in Gary Geppert and Harold M. Rose (eds.), *The Social Economy of Cities*. Beverly Hills, Calif.: Sage.

Harvey, David. 1976. "Labor, capital, and class struggle around the built environment in advanced capitalist societies." *Politics and Society*, 9:265-295.

Harvey, Edward. 1974. *Educational Systems and the Labour Market*. Toronto: Longman.

Harvey, Edward, and Jos. Lennards. 1973. *Key Issues in Higher Education*. Toronto: Ontario Institute for Studies in Education.

Hauser, R., et al. 1974. "Race and sex in the structure of occupational mobility in the United States, 1962." *Working Paper 74-76*. Madison: Center for Demography and Ecology, University of Wisconsin.

Hawthorne, H. B., et al. 1967. *A Survey of Contemporary*

Indians of Canada, Vols. 1 and 2. Ottawa: Indian Affairs.

Hazelrigg, L., and M. Garnier. 1976. "Occupational mobility in industrialized societies: a comparable analysis of differential access to occupational rank in seventeen countries." *American Sociological Review*, 41:498-511.

Heald, Tim. 1982. "A job well done." *Today Magazine*, 6(February):7-11.

Hendricks, Jon. 1981. "The elderly in society: beyond modernization." Paper presented at joint meetings, GSA and CAG, Toronto.

Henry, Louis. 1961. "Some data on natural fertility." *Eugenics Quarterly*, 8:81-91.

Henshel, Richard L. 1977. "Controlling the police power." *Canadian Forum*, (Nov.):11-13.

Henshel, Richard L. 1978. "Forgetting about police crime." *Canadian Forum*, (Mar.):10-11.

Heberg, Will. 1955. *Protestant, Catholic, Jew.* New York: Doubleday.

Herberg, Will. 1960. *Protestant, Catholic, Jew*, rev. ed. New York: Doubleday.

Herman, Judith, and Lisa Hirschman. 1977. "Father-daughter incest." *Signs*, 2(4):735-756.

Herskowitz, Melville. 1952. "Population size, economic surplus, and social leisure," in Melville Herskowitz (ed.), *Economic Anthropology.* New York: Alfred A. Knopf.

Hetherington, E. Mavis, and Ross D. Parke. 1979. *Child Psychology: A Contemporary Viewpoint.* 2nd ed. New York: McGraw-Hill.

Hill, Clifford. 1971. "From church to sect: West Indian religious sect development in Britain." *Journal for the Scientific Study of Religion*, 10:114-123.

Hiller, Harry H. 1976. *Canadian Society: A Sociological Analysis.* Scarborough, Ont.: Prentice-Hall.

Hiller, Harry H. 1976. "The sociology of religion in the Canadian context," in G. N. Ramu, and Stuart D. Johnson (eds.), *Introduction to Canadian Society.* Toronto: Macmillan.

Hindelang, Michael J. 1978. "Race and involvement in common law personal crimes." *American Sociological Review*, 43(1):93-109.

Hindelang, Michael J. 1979. "Sex differences in criminal activity." *Social Problems*, 27(2):143-156.

Hirschi, Travis. 1969. *Causes of Delinquency.* Berkeley, Calif.: University of California Press.

Hoare, Quintin, and Geoffrey N. Smith, (eds. and trans.). 1971. *Selections From the Prison Notebooks of Antonio Gramsci.* New York: International Publishers.

Hobart, Charles. 1974. "Church involvement and the comfort thesis in Alberta." *Journal for Scientific Study of Religion*, 13:463-470.

Hobart, Charles. 1981. "Sources of egalitarianism in young unmarried Canadians." *The Canadian Journal of Sociology*, 6:261-282.

Hobart, C., and C. Brent. 1966. "Eskimo education Danish and Canadian, a comparison." *Canadian Review of Sociology and Anthropology*, 3:47-66.

Hochschild, Arlie Russell. 1973. *The Unexpected Community.* Englewood Cliffs, N.J.: Prentice-Hall.

Hochschild, Arlie Russell. 1975. "Disengagement theory: a critique and proposal." *American Sociological Review*, 40(5):553-569.

Hogan, Dennis P. 1981. *Transitions and Social Change: The Early Lives of American Men.* New York: Academic Press.

Hogan, D., and D. Featherman. 1977. "Racial stratification and socioeconomic change in the American North and South." *American Journal of Sociology*, 83:100-126.

Hogarth, John. 1971. *Sentencing as a Human Process.* Toronto: University of Toronto Press.

Hogarth, John. 1979. "The individual and state security." *Social Sciences in Canada*, 1(1):10-11.

Hoge, Dean. 1976. *Division in the Protestant House.* Philadelphia: Westminster Press.

Hoge, Dean R., and David A. Roozen (eds.). 1979. "Some sociological conclusions about church trends." *Understanding Church Growth and Decline.* New York: Pilgrim Press.

Holsti, Ole R. 1969. *Content Analysis for the Social Sciences and Humanities.* Reading, Mass.: Addison-Wesley.

Holt, John B. 1940. "Holiness religion: cultural shock and social reorganization." *American Sociological Review*, 5(October):740-747.

Homans, George C. 1961. *Social Behavior: Its Elementary Forms.* New York: Harcourt, Brace, and World.

Hordern, William. 1966. *New Directions in Theology*, Vol. 1: *Introduction.* Philadelphia: Westminster Press.

Horowitz, Gad. 1968. "Conservatism, liberalism, and socialism in Canada: an interpretation," in Gad Horowitz, *Canadian Labour in Politics.* Toronto: University of Toronto Press.

Horton, Paul B., and Chester L. Hunt. 1972. *Sociology.* 3rd ed. New York: McGraw-Hill.

Hostetler, John A., and Gertrude Enders Huntington. 1967. *The Hutterites in North America.* New York: Holt, Rinehart and Winston.

Houghland, James G., and James R. Wood. 1979. "Inner circles in local churches." *Sociological Analysis*, 40:226-239.

Howe, Florence. 1974. "Sexual stereotypes and the public schools," in Ruth B. Kundsin (ed.), *Women and Success: The Anatomy of Achievement.* New York: William Morrow.

Hoyt, Homer. 1939. *The Structure and Growth of Residential Neighbourhoods in American Cities.* Washington, D.C.: Federal Housing Authority.

Huggins, Martha D., and Murray A. Straus. 1978. "Violence and the social structure as reflected in children's books from 1850 to 1970," in Mary Alice Beyer Gammon (ed.), *Violence in Canada.* Toronto: Methuen.

Hughes, David R., and Evelyn Kallen. 1974. *The Anatomy of Racism: Canadian Dimensions.* Montreal: Harvest House.

Hughes, Everett C. 1943. *French Canada in Transition.* Chicago: University of Chicago Press.

Hughes, Everett C. 1971. *The Sociological Eye: Selected Papers.* Chicago: Aldine, Atherton.

Hughes, E. C., et al. (eds.). 1950. *Race and Culture, Volume 1, The Collected Papers of Robert Ezra Park.* Glencoe, Ill.: Free Press.

Huizinga, Johan. 1924. *The Waning of the Middle Ages.* New York: St. Martin's.

Hunsberger, Bruce. 1980. "A reexamination of the antecedents of apostasy." *Review of Religious Research*, 21:158-170.

Hunter, A. A. 1976. "Class and status in Canada." in G. N. Ramu, and S. D. Johnson (eds.), *Introduction to Canadian Society.* Toronto: Macmillan.

Hunter, Alfred A. 1981. *Class Tells: On Social Inequality in Canada.* Toronto: Butterworths.

Husen, Torsten (ed.). 1967. *International Study of Achievement in Mathematics: A Comparison of Twelve Countries*, 2 vols. Stockholm: Almqvist and Wiksell.

Hyde, Janet. 1979. *Understanding Human Sexuality.* New York: McGraw-Hill.

Inciardi, J. A. 1975. *Careers in Crime.* Chicago: Rand McMally.

Inglehart, Ronald. 1977. *The Silent Revolution: Changing Values and Political Styles Among Western Publics.* Princeton, N.J.: Princeton University Press.

Inglehart, Ronald. 1981. "Post-materialism in an environment of insecurity." *American Political Science Review*, 74:4 (December):880-900.

Inkeles, A. 1960. "Industrial man: the relation of status to experience, perception, and value." *American Journal of Sociology*, 66:1-31.

Innis, Harold A. 1930. *The Fur Trade in Canada: An Introduction to Canadian Economic History.* New Haven, Conn.: Yale University Press; 1927, Toronto: Oxford University Press.

Innis, Harold A. 1940. *The Cod Fisheries: The History of an International Economy.* New Haven, Conn.: Yale University Press.

Irving, Howard I. 1972. *The Family Myth.* Toronto: Copp Clark.

Ishwaran, K. 1971. "The Canadian family: variations and uniformities," in James E. Gallagher, and Ronald D. Lambert (eds.), *Social Processes and Institutions: The Canadian Case.* Toronto: Holt, Rinehart and Winston.

Ishwaran, K. (ed.). 1976. *The Canadian Family*, rev. ed. Toronto: Holt, Rinehart and Winston.

Jackson, John D. 1975. *Community and Conflict: A Study of French-English Relations in Ontario.* Montreal: Holt, Rinehart and Winston.

Jackson, Robert J., et al. 1977. "Collective conflict, violence, and the media in Canada," in *Report of the Royal Commission on Violence in the Communication Industry.* Vol. 5. Ottawa: Queen's Printer.

Jacobs, Jane. 1961. *The Death and Life of Great American Cities.* New York: Random House.

Jarvis, George K. 1972. "Canadian old people as a deviant minority," in C. Boydell, C. R. Grindstaff, and P. E. Whitehead (eds.), *Deviant Behaviour and Societal Reactions.* Toronto: Holt, Rinehart and Winston.

Johnson, A. G. 1977. *Social Statistics Without Tears.* New York: McGraw-Hill.

Johnson, Harry M. 1960. *Sociology: A Systematic Introduction.* New York: Harcourt, Brace and World.

Johnson, Leo A. 1972. "The development of class in Canada in the twentieth century," in G. Teeple (ed.), *Capitalism and the National Question in Canada.* Toronto: University of Toronto Press.

Johnson, Leo A. 1974. *Poverty in Wealth.* Toronto: New Hogtown Press.

Johnson, Leo A. 1979a. "Income disparity and the structure of earnings in Canada, 1946-74," in J. Curtis, and W. Scott (eds.), *Social Stratification: Canada.* 2nd ed. Scarborough, Ont.: Prentice-Hall.

Johnson, Leo A. 1979b. "Class, status, and power," in J. Fry (ed.), *Economy, Class, and Social Reality.* Toronto: Butterworths.

Johnston, William, and Michael D. Ornstein. 1979. "Social class and political ideology." Paper presented at the meetings of the American Sociological Association, Boston.

Jourard, Sidney M. 1964. *The Transparent Self.* New York: Van Nostrand Reinhold.

Joy, Richard J. 1972. *Languages in Conflict.* Toronto: McClelland and Stewart.

Kahn, Robert L. 1975. "In search of the Hawthorne effect," in E. L. Cass, and F. G. Zimmer (eds.), *Man and Work in Society.* Toronto: Van Nostrand Reinhold.

Kalbach, Warren E. 1980. "Historical and generational perspectives of ethnic residential segregation in Toronto, Canada: 1851-1971." Research Paper No. 118. Toronto: Center for Urban and Community Studies, University of Toronto.

Kalbach, Warren E., and Wayne W. McVey. 1979. *The Demographic Bases of Canadian Society.* 2nd ed. Toronto: McGraw-Hill Ryerson.

Kalin, Rudolf, Janet M. Stoppard, and Barbara Burt. 1980. "Sex-role ideology and sex bias in judgments of occupational suitability," in Cannie Stark-Adamec (ed.), *Sex Roles: Origins, Influences, and Implications for Women.* Montreal: Eden Press.

Kalish, Richard A. 1982. *Late Adulthood: Perspectives on Human Development.* 2nd ed. Monterey, Calif.: Brooks/Cole.

Kallen, Horace M. 1924. *Culture and Democracy in the United States.* New York: Liveright.

Kamerman, Sheila B. 1980. *Parenting in an Unresponsive Society: Managing Work and Family Life.* New York/London: The Free Press.

Kandel, Denise B. 1978. "Homophily, selection, and socialization in adolescent friendships." *American Journal of Sociology*, 84:427-436.

Keating, Norah C., and Priscilla Cole. 1980. "What do I

do with him 24 hours a day? Changes in the housewife role after retirement." *The Gerontologist*, 20(1):84-89.

Keating, Norah, and Judith Marshall. 1980. "The process of retirement: the rural self-employed." *The Gerontologist*, 20(4):437-443.

Keith, Jennie. 1982. *Old People as People*. Toronto: Little Brown and Company.

Kelner, M. 1970. "Ethnic penetration into Toronto's elite structure." *Canadian Review of Sociology and Anthropology*, 7:128-137.

Kennedy, Leslie W., and Dennis W. Stokes. 1980. *Extended Family Support and the High Cost of Housing*. Edmonton Area Series Report No. 15. Edmonton, Alberta: Population Research Laboratory.

Kent, Tom. 1981. *Royal Commission on Newspapers*. Ottawa: Supply and Services Canada.

Kernaghan, Kenneth. 1982. "Politics, public administration and Canada's aging population." *Canadian Public Policy*, 7(1):69-74.

Kerr, Donald. 1968. "Metropolitan dominance in Canada," in W. E. Mann (ed.), *Canada: A Sociological Profile*. Toronto: Copp Clark.

Kessler, Suzanne J., and Wendy McKenna. 1978. *Gender: An Ethnomethodological Approach*. New York: John Wiley and Sons.

Kimball, Meredith M. 1977. "Women and success: a basic conflict?" in Marylee Stephenson (ed.), *Women in Canada*. Revised edition. Don Mills: General Publishing.

Kirkpatrick, Clifford. 1949. "Religion and humanitarianism: a study of institutional implications." *Psychological Monographs*, 63(9).

Knipscheer, K., and Anton Bevers. 1981. "Older parents and their middle-aged children: symmetry or asymmetry in their relationship." Paper presented at the International Congress of Gerontology, Hamburg, Germany, July 11-17.

Kohlberg, Lawrence, 1969. "Stage and sequence: the cognitive-developmental approach to socialization," in David A. Goslin (ed.), *Handbook of Socialization Theory and Research*. Chicago: Rand McNally.

Kohlberg, Lawrence. 1976. "Moral stages and moralization: the cognitive-developmental approach," in T. Lickona, *Moral Development and Behavior*. New York: Holt, Rinehart and Winston.

Kohn, Melvin L. 1977. *Class and Conformity*. 2nd ed. Homewood, Ill.: Dorsey.

Kohn, Walter S. G. 1980. *Women In National Legislatures*. New York: Praeger.

Komarovsky, Mirra. 1946. "Cultural contradictions and sex roles." *American Journal of Sociology*, 52:184-189.

Komarovsky, Mirra. 1976. *Dilemmas of Masculinity*. New York: W. W. Norton.

Kopinak, Kathryn M. 1978. "Sex differences in Ontario political culture." Ph.D. Dissertation, York University.

Koyl, L. F. 1977. "The aging Canadian," in Blossom T.

Wigdor (ed.), *Canadian Gerontological Collection 1*. Winnipeg: Canadian Association on Gerontology.

Kryzanowski, Lawrence, and Elizabeth Bertin-Boussu. 1981. "Equal access to credit: lenders' attitudes toward an applicant's sex and marital status." *International Journal of Women's Studies*, 4:213-232.

Kunkel, John H. 1977. "Sociobiology vs. biosociology." *The American Sociologist*, 12:69-73.

Kuypers, Joseph A., and Vern L. Bengtson. 1973. "Competence and social breakdown: a social-psychological view of aging." *Human Development*, 16(2):37-49.

Labovitz, Sanford. 1974. "Some evidence of Canadian ethnic, racial, and sexual antagonism." *The Canadian Review of Sociology and Anthropology*, 11:247-254.

Laclau, Ernesto. 1977. *Politics and Ideology in Marxist Theory*. London: N.L.B.

LaFree, Gary. 1980. "The effect of sexual stratification by race on official reactions to rape." *American Sociological Review*, 45:842-854.

Lambert, Ronald D. 1971. *Sex Role Imagery in Children: Social Origins of Mind*. Study #6, The Royal Commission on the Status of Women in Canada. Ottawa: Information Canada.

Lambert, Ronald D. 1981. *The Sociology of Contemporary Quebec Nationalism: An Annotated Bibliography and Review*. New York: Garland Publishing.

Lambert, Ronald D., and James B. Curtis. 1979. "Education, economic dissatisfaction, and nonconfidence in Canadian social institutions." *Canadian Review of Sociology and Anthropology*, 16(1):47-59.

Lambert, Ronald D., and James B. Curtis. 1982a. "Opposition to multiculturalism among Québécois and English-Canadians." *Canadian Review of Sociology and Anthropology*, 19 (forthcoming).

Lambert, Ronald D., and James B. Curtis. 1982b. "The French- and English-Canadian language communities and multicultural attitudes." *Canadian Ethnic Studies*, 7:3.

Lambert, Wallace E., Josiane F. Hamers, and Nancy Frasure-Smith. 1980. *Child-Rearing Values: A Cross-National Study*. New York: Praeger.

Lambert, W. E., A. Yackley, and R. N. Hein. 1971. "Child training values of English-Canadian and French-Canadian parents." *Canadian Journal of Behavioural Science*, 3:217-236.

Lancaster, Jane Beckman. 1976. "Sex roles in primate societies," in Michael S. Teitelbaum (ed.), *Sex Differences: Social and Biological Perspectives*. Garden City, N.Y.: Doubleday Anchor.

Langer, William. 1973. "The black death," in *Scientific American* (ed.), *Cities: Their Origin, Growth and Human Impact*. San Francisco: W. H. Freeman.

Large, Mary-Jane. 1981. "Services for the elderly." *Ontario Medical Review*, (January):38-41.

Larson, Lyle (ed.). 1976. *The Canadian Family in Comparative Perspective*. Scarborough, Ont.: Prentice-Hall.

Laslett, Peter. 1976. "Societal development and aging," in Robert Binstock, and Ethel Shanas (eds.), *Handbook of Aging and the Social Sciences.* New York: Van Nostrand Reinhold.

Laslett, Peter. 1977. "The history of aging and the aged," in Peter Laslett, *Family Life and Illicit Love in Earlier Generations.* Cambridge: University Press.

Latowsky, Evelyn. 1971. "Family life styles and Jewish culture," in K. Ishwaran (ed.), *The Canadian Family.* Toronto: Holt, Rinehart and Winston.

Lauer, Robert H., and Warren B. Handel. 1977. *Social Psychology: The Theory and Application of Symbolic Interactionism.* Boston: Houghton Mifflin.

Law Reform Commission of Canada. 1975. *Working Paper 13: Divorce.* Ottawa: Information Canada.

Lawrence, Paul R., and Jay W. Lorsch. 1967. *Organization and Environment: Managing Differentiation and Integration.* Cambridge, Mass.: Harvard University Press.

Laws, Judith Long. 1979. *The Second X: Sex Role and Social Role.* New York: Elsevier.

Laxer, Gordon. 1975. "American and British influences on metropolitan development in Canada 1878-1913." Paper presented to the Annual Meeting of the Canadian Sociology and Anthropology Association.

Laxer, Robert (ed.). 1973. *Canada Ltd.: The Political Economy of Dependency.* Toronto: McClelland and Stewart.

Lazarsfeld, P. F., and R. K. Merton. 1954. "Friendship as a social process," in M. Berger, T. Abel, and C H. Page (eds.), *Freedom and Control in Modern Society.* Princeton, N.J.: Van Nostrand.

Lee, Gary, and Robert Clyde. 1974. "Religion, socioeconomic status, and anomie." *Journal for the Scientific Study of Religion,* 13:35-47.

Leighton, Alexander. 1959. *My Name is Legion.* New York: Basic Books.

Lemert, Edwin. 1967. *Human Deviance, Social Problems, and Social Control.* Englewood Cliffs, N.J.: Prentice-Hall.

Lemon, B. W., V. L. Bengtson, and J. A. Peterson. 1972. "An exploration of the activity theory of aging: activity types and life satisfaction among in-movers to a retirement community." *Journal of Gerontology,* 27:511-523.

Lenski, Gerhard. 1961. *The Religious Factor.* New York: Doubleday.

Lenski, G. 1966. *Power and Privilege.* New York: McGraw-Hill.

Lever, Janet. 1978. "Sex differences in the complexity of children's play." *American Sociological Review,* 43:471-483.

Levine, Donald N., Ellwood B. Carter, and Eleanor Miller Gorman. 1976. "Simmel's influence on American sociology." *American Journal of Sociology,* 81:813-845.

LeVine, R. A., and D. T. Campbell. 1972. *Ethnocentrism: Theories of Conflict, Ethnic Attitudes, Group Behavior.* New York: Wiley.

Levinson, Daniel J., et al. 1978. *The Seasons of a Man's Life.* New York: Ballantine.

Levitt, Joseph. 1975:1969. "The birth of the nationalist league," in Sam Clark, et al. (eds.), *Prophecy and Protest: Social Movements in Twentieth-Century Canada.* Toronto: Gage.

Levitt, K. 1970. *Silent Surrender.* Toronto: Macmillan.

Levy, Joanne. 1979. "In search of isolation: the Holdeman Mennonites of Linden, Alberta and their school." *Canadian Ethnic Studies,* II:115-130.

Lewin, Kurt. 1948. *Resolving Social Conflicts.* New York: Harper.

Lewis, Debra J. 1982. *A Brief on Wife Battering With Proposals on Federal Action.* Ottawa: Canadian Advisory Council on the Status of Women.

Lewis G. H. (ed.). 1975. *Fist-Fights in the Kitchen: Manners and Methods in Social Research.* Pacific Palisades, Calif.: Goodyear.

Lewis, Michael. 1972. "Culture and gender roles: there's no unisex in the nursery." *Psychology Today,* 5(May):54-57.

Lindenthal, Jacob, Jerome Myers, Max Pepper, and Maxine Stern. 1970. "Mental status and religious behavior." *Journal for the Scientific Study of Religion,* 9:143-149.

Lindesmith, Alfred R. 1967. *The Addict and the Law.* New York: Vintage Books.

Linteau, P., and J. Robert. 1977. "Land ownership and society in Montreal: an hypothesis," in Gilbert A. Stelter, and Alan F. J. Artibise (eds.), *The Canadian City: Essays in Urban History.* Toronto: McClelland and Stewart.

Lipman-Blumen, Jean, and Ann R. Tickamyer. 1975. "Sex roles in transition: a ten-year perspective." *Annual Review of Sociology,* 1:297-337.

Lipset, Seymour Martin. 1950. *Agrarian Socialism.* Berkeley, Calif.: University of California Press.

Lipset, Seymour Martin. 1963. *The First New Nation: The United States in Historical and Comparative Perspective.* New York: Basic Books.

Lipset, Seymour Martin. 1965. "Revolution and counter-revolution: Canada and the United States," in Thomas Ford (ed.), *The Revolutionary Theme in Contemporary America.* Lexington, Ky.: University of Kentucky Press.

Lipset, Seymour Martin. 1968. *Revolution and Counterrevolution: Change and Persistence in Social Structure.* New York: Basic Books.

Lithwick, N. H. G., and G. Paquet. 1968. "Urban growth and regional contagion," in N.H. Lithwick and G. Paquet (eds.), *Urban Studies: A Canadian Perspective.* Toronto: Methuen.

Lofland, Lyn H. 1975. "The 'thereness' of women: a selective review of urban sociology," in Marcia Millman, and Rosabeth Moss Kanter (eds.), *Another Voice.* Garden City, N.Y.: Doubleday Anchor.

Lohdi, A. Q., and Charles Tilly. 1973. "Urbanization, crime and collective violence in 19th century France." *American Journal of Sociology,* 79(2):296-318.

Lopata, Helena Z. 1979. *Women as Widows: Support Systems.* New York: Elsevier.

Lorimer, James. 1978. *The Developers.* Toronto: James Lorimer and Company.

Lowe, George D., and H. Eugene Hodges. 1972. "Race and treatment of alcoholism in a southern state." *Social Problems*, (Fall):240-252.

Lowe, Graham S. 1980. "Women, work and office: the feminization of clerical occupations in Canada, 1901-1931." *Canadian Journal of Sociology*, 5:361-381.

Lower, A. R. M. 1939. "Geographical determinants in Canadian history," in Ralf Flenley (ed.), *Essays in Canadian History*. Toronto: Macmillan.

Lucas, Rex A. 1971. *Minetown, Milltown, Railtown: Life in Canadian Communities of Single Industry.* Toronto: University of Toronto Press.

Luckmann, Thomas. 1967. *The Invisible Religion.* New York: Macmillan.

Lupri, Eugen, and Donald L. Mills. 1982. "The changing roles of Canadian women in family and work: an overview," in Eugen Lupri (ed.), *The Changing Roles of Women in Family and Society: A Cross-cultural Comparison.* Leiden, Neth.: E. J. Brill (forthcoming).

Lupsha, P. A. 1976. "On theories of urban violence," in P. Meadows and E. Mizruchi (eds.), *Urbanism, Urbanization and Change.* 2nd ed. Reading: Addison-Wesley.

Luxton, Meg. 1980. *More Than a Labour of Love: Three Generations of Women's Work in the Home.* Toronto: The Women's Press.

Lynch, Kevin. 1960. *The Image of the City.* Cambridge, Mass.: M.I.T. Press.

Lynn, David B. 1959. "A note on sex differences in the development of masculine and feminine identification." *Psychological Review*, 66:126-135.

Lynn, David B. 1969. *Parental and Sex-role Identification: A Theoretical Formulation.* Berkeley: McCutchan.

Lynn, Naomi, and Cornelia B. Flora. 1973. "Motherhood and political participation: the changing sense of self." *Journal of Political and Military Sociology*, 1:91-103.

MacCoby, Eleanor Emmons, and Carol Nagy Jacklin. 1974. *The Psychology of Sex Differences.* Stanford, Calif.: Stanford University Press.

Mackay, R. S. 1963. "Peaceful picketing and the criminal code." *Current Law And Social Problems.* Toronto: University of Toronto Press.

Mackie, Marlene. 1973. "Arriving at 'truth' by definition: the case of stereotype inaccuracy." *Social Problems*, 20:431-447.

Mackie, Marlene. 1974. "Ethnic stereotypes and prejudice: Alberta Indians, Hutterites and Ukrainians." *Canadian Ethnic Studies*, 6:39-52.

Mackie, Marlene. 1975. "Defection from Hutterite colonies," in Robert M. Pike, and Elia Zureik (eds.), *Socialization and Values in Canadian Society*, Vol. 2. Toronto: McClelland and Stewart.

Mackie, Marlene. 1977. "On congenial truths: a perspective on women's studies." *Canadian Review of Sociology and Anthropology*, 14:117-128.

Mackie, Marlene. 1982. *Exploring Gender Relations: A Canadian Perspective.* Toronto: Butterworths.

MacLeod, Linda. 1980. *Wife Battering in Canada: The Vicious Circle.* Hull, Que.: Canadian Government Publishing Centre.

MacLeod, R. C. 1976. *The North-West Mounted Police and Law Enforcement, 1873-1905.* Toronto: University of Toronto Press.

Macpherson, C. B. 1955. *Democracy in Alberta.* Toronto: University of Toronto Press.

Maddox, George L. 1970. "Themes and issues in sociological theories of human aging." *Human Development*, 13:17-27.

Mann, Michael. 1970. "The social cohesion of liberal democracy." *American Sociological Review*, 35(3):423-439.

Mann, W. E. 1962. *Sect, Cult, and Church in Alberta.* Toronto: University of Toronto Press.

Mann, W. E. 1964. "Socialization in a medium-security reformatory." *Canadian Review of Sociology and Anthropology*, 1:138-155.

Mannheim, Karl. 1936. *Ideology and Utopia.* New York: Harcourt, Brace, and World.

Mannheim, Karl. 1952. "The problem of generations," in P. Kectskemeti (ed.) *Karl Mannheim: Essays in the Sociology of Knowledge.* London: Routledge and Kegan Paul.

Manheimer, Dean I., Glen D. Millinger, and Mitchell B. Balter. 1969. "Use of marijuana among the urban cross-section of adults." Unpublished manuscript.

Manitoba Proceedings. 1977. *Manitoba Child Abuse Symposium.* Winnipeg: Manitoba Department of Health and Social Development.

Manzer, R. 1974. *Canada: A Socio-Political Report.* Toronto: McGraw-Hill Ryerson.

Marchak, M. Patricia. 1973. "Women workers and white collar unions." *Canadian Review of Sociology and Anthropology*, 10:134-147.

Marchak, Patricia. 1975. *Ideological Perspectives on Canada.* Toronto: McGraw-Hill Ryerson.

Marini, Margaret Mooney, and Ellen Greenberger. 1978. "Sex differences in occupational aspirations and expectations." *Sociology of Work and Occupations*, 5:147-175.

Markle, Gerald E. 1974. "Sex ratio at birth: values, variance, and some determinants." *Demography*, 11:131-142.

Marsden, Lorna R., and Edward B. Harvey. 1979. *Fragile Federation: Social Change in Canada.* Toronto: McGraw-Hill Ryerson.

Marshal, T. H. 1964. *Class, Citizenship, and Social Development.* New York: Doubleday.

Marshall, V. W. 1975a. "Socialization for impending death in a retirement village," *American Journal of Sociology*, 80(5): 1124-1144.

Marshall, V. W. 1975b. "Organizational features of terminal status passage in residential facilities for the aged." *Urban Life*, 4:349-358.

Marshall, V. W. 1980a. *Last Chapters: A Sociology of Aging and Dying.* Monterey, Calif.: Brooks/Cole.

Marshall, V. W. 1980b. "No exit: an interpretive perspective on aging," in Victor W. Marshall (ed.), *Aging in Canada: Social Perspectives*. Toronto: Fitzhenry and Whiteside.

Marshall, V. W. 1980c. "Aging in an aging society: cohort differences, conflicts and challenges." *Multiculturalism* 4(1): 6-13.

Marshall, V. W. 1981a. "State of the art lecture: the sociology of aging," in John Crawford (ed.), *Canadian Gerontological Collection III*. Winnipeg: Canadian Association on Gerontology.

Marshall, V. W. 1981c. "The changing family relationships of older people." QSEP Research Report No. 5, Program for Quantitative Studies in Economics and Population, McMaster University.

Marshall, V. W., and Vern L. Bengtson. 1982. *"Generations: conflict and cooperation,"* in Ursula Lehr (ed.), New York: Springer (forthcoming).

Marshall, V. W., Carolyn J. Rosenthal, and Jane Synge. 1981. *"The family as a health service organization for the elderly."* Paper presented at the Annual Meeting of the Society for the Study of Social Problems. Toronto, August.

Marshall, V. W., Carolyn J. Rosenthal, and Jane Synge. 1982. "Concerns about parental health," in Elizabeth W. Markson (ed.), *Women and Aging*. Lexington, Mass.: Lexington Books.

Marshall, V. W., and Joseph A. Tindale. 1978-9. "Notes for a radical gerontology." *International Journal of Aging and Human Development*, 9(2): 163-175.

Marston, W. G., and A. G. Darroch. 1971. "The social class of ethnic residential segregation: the Canadian case." *American Journal of Sociology*, 77(3):491-510.

Martin, Wilfred B. W., and Allan J. Macdonell. 1978. *Canadian Education: A Sociological Analysis*. Scarborough, Ont.: Prentice-Hall.

Martindale, D. A. 1964. "The formation and destruction of communities," in G. K. Zollschaun and W. Hirsch (eds.), *Explorations in Social Change*. London: Routledge and Kegan Paul.

Martyna, Wendy. 1980. "Beyond the 'he/man' approach: the case for nonsexist language." *Signs*, 5:482-493.

Maruyama, G., and N. Miller. 1975. *Physical Attractiveness and Classroom Acceptance*. Social Science Research Institute. Los Angeles: University of Southern California. Report 75-2.

Marx, Karl. 1965: 1867-1895. *Capital: A Critical Analysis of Capitalist Production*, Vol. 1. New York: International Publishers.

Marx, Karl. 1969. "On class," in C. Heller (ed.), *Structured Social Inequality*. New York: Macmillan.

Marx, Karl. 1970: 1843. *Critique of Hegel's 'Philosophy of Right'*, Annette Jolin and Joseph O'Malley (trans.). Cambridge, Mass.: Harvard University Press.

Marx, Karl, and Frederick Engels. 1975. *Manifesto of the Communist Party*. Moscow: Progress.

Maslow, Abraham A. 1970. *Motivation and Personality*. 2nd ed. New York: Harper and Row.

Mathewson, S. B. 1931. *Restriction of Output Among Unorganized Workers*. New York: Viking Press.

Matras, J. 1980. "Comparative social mobility." *Annual Review of Sociology*, 6:401-431.

Matthews, Anne Martin. 1980. "Women and widowhood," in Victor W. Marshall (ed.), *Aging in Canada: Social Perspectives*. Don Mills: Fitzhenry and Whiteside.

Matthews, Anne Martin. 1982. "Canadian research on women as widows: a comparative analysis of the state of the art." *Resources for Feminist Research* (forthcoming).

Matthews, Sarah H. 1979. *The Social World of Old Women: Management of Self-Identity*. Beverly Hills and London: Sage.

Matthews, Victor. 1972. "Socio-legal statistics in Alberta: a review of their availability and significance." Edmonton: Human Resources Research Council.

Mauss, Armand. 1969. "Dimensions of religious defection." *Review of Religious Research*, 10:128-135.

Mauss, Armand, and Milton Rokeach. 1977. "Pollsters as prophets." *The Humanist*, May-June, 48-51.

Mayo, Elton. 1946. *The Social Problems of an Industrial Civilization*. Cambridge, Mass.: Harvard University Press.

McCann, Richard. 1967. "Developmental factors in the growth of a mature faith," in Richard D. Knudten (ed.), *The Sociology of Religion*. New York: Appleton-Century-Crofts.

McClelland, D. C. 1961. *The Achieving Society*. New York: Van Nostrand.

McCormack, Thelma. 1975. "Toward a nonsexist perspective on social and political change," in M. Millman and R. Moss Kanter, *Another Voice*. New York: Anchor.

McCrorie, J. 1971. "Change and paradox in agrarian social movements: the case of Saskatchewan," in R. J. Ossenberg (ed.), *Canadian Society*. Toronto: Prentice-Hall.

McDavid, John W., and Herbert Harari. 1966. "Stereotyping of names and popularity in grade-school children." *Child Development*, 37:453-460.

McDonald, L. 1979. "Wages of work: a widening gap between women and men," in J. Curtis, and W. Scott (eds.), *Social Stratification: Canada*. 2nd ed. Scarborough, Ont.: Prentice-Hall.

McDonald, N. 1978. "Edgerton Ryerson and the school as an agent of political socialization," in N. McDonald, and A. Chaiton (eds.), *Edgerton Ryerson and His Times*. Toronto: Macmillan.

McFarlane, A. H., G. R. Norman, D. L. Streiner, R. Roy, and D. J. Scott. 1980. "A longitudinal study of the influence of the psychosocial environment on health status: a preliminary report." *Journal of Health and Social Behaviour*, 21:124-133.

McIntosh, William Alex, and Jon P. Alston. 1982. "Lenski revisited: the linkage role of religion in primary and secondary groups." *American Journal of Sociology*, 87:852-882.

McKenzie, Roderick D. 1968. *On Human Ecology*. Chicago: University of Chicago Press.

McKeown, Thomas. 1976. *The Modern Rise of Population*.

New York: Academic Press.

McMurry, Martha. 1978. "Religion and women's sex role traditionalism." *Sociological Focus*, 11:81-95.

McNaught, K. 1975. "Political trials and the Canadian political tradition," in M. L. Friedland (ed.), *Courts and Trials: A Multi-Disciplinary Approach*. Toronto: University of Toronto Press.

McNeill, William H. 1976. *Plagues and Peoples*. Garden City, N.Y.: Doubleday.

McPherson, Barry, and Neil Guppy. 1979. "Pre-retirement life-style and the degree of planning for retirement." *Journal of Gerontology*, 34(2):254-263.

McQuillan, K. 1980. "Economic factors and internal migration: the case of nineteenth-century England." *Social Science History*, 4(4):479-499.

McRoberts, Hugh A., et al. 1976. "Différences dans la mobilité professionnelle des francophones et des anglophones." *Sociologie et Sociétés*, 8(2):61-79.

McTavish, Donald G. 1982. "Perceptions of old people," in David J. Mangen, and Warren A. Peterson (eds.), *Research Instruments in Social Gerontology, Volume 1, Clinical and Social Psychology*. Minneapolis: University of Minnesota Press.

Mead, G. H. 1934. *Mind, Self, and Society*. Chicago: University of Chicago Press.

Mead, Margaret. 1935. *Sex and Temperament in Three Primitive Societies*. New York: Mentor Books (reprint of original edition by William Morrow and Company).

Meissner, Martin, Elizabeth W. Humphreys, Scott M. Meis, William J. Scheu. 1975. "No exit for wives: sexual division of labour and the cumulation of household demands." *The Canadian Review of Sociology and Anthropology*, 12(Part 1): 424-439.

Meltzer, Bernard N. 1978. "Mead's social psychology," Charles W. Morris (ed.), in Jerome G. Manis, and Bernard N. Meltzer (eds.), *Symbolic Interaction: A Reader in Social Psychology*. 3rd ed. Boston: Allyn and Bacon.

Merton, Robert. 1938. "Social structure and anomie." *American Sociological Review*, 3(October):672-682.

Merton, Robert. 1957. *Social Theory and Social Structure*. Glencoe, Ill.: Free Press.

Metz, Donald. 1967. *New Congregations: Security and Mission in Conflict*. Philadelphia: Westminster Press.

Michels, R. 1962. *Political Parties*. New York: Collier.

Michelson, William. 1976. *Man and His Urban Environment*. 2nd ed. Reading, Mass.: Addison-Wesley.

Miliband, Ralph. 1969. *The State in Capitalist Society*. London: Weidenfeld and Nicolson.

Miliband, Ralph. 1973. *The State in Capitalist Society*. London: Quartet Books.

Miller, Casey, and Kate Swift. 1977. *Words and Women*. Garden City, N.Y.: Doubleday Anchor.

Miller, Delbert C. 1970. *Handbook of Research Design and Social Measurement*. New York: David McKay.

Millett, David. 1969. "A typology of religious organizations suggested by the Canadian census." *Sociology Analysis*, 30:108-119.

Millet, Kate. 1970. *Sexual Politics*. New York: Doubleday.

Miner, Horace. 1939. *St. Denis: A French-Canadian Parish*. Chicago: University of Chicago Press.

Ministry of Education, Ontario. 1975. *Education in the Primary and Junior Divisions*. Toronto: Queen's Printer.

Mitchell, Robert. 1966. "Polity, church attractiveness, and ministers' careers." *Journal for the Scientific Study of Religion*, 5:241-258.

Money, John, and A. A. Ehrhardt. 1972. *Man and Woman, Boy and Girl: The Differentiation and Dimorphism of Gender Identity from Conception to Maturity*. Baltimore, Md.: Johns Hopkins University Press.

Money, John, and Patricia Tucker. 1975. *Sexual Signatures: On Being a Man or a Woman*. Boston: Little, Brown.

Mol, Hans. 1976. "Major correlates of churchgoing in Canada," in Stewart Crysdale, and Les Wheatcroft (eds.), *Religion in Canadian Society*. Toronto: Macmillan.

Moore, W. 1963. "But some are more equal than others." *American Sociological Review*, 28:13.

Moore, Wilbert. 1966. "Aging and the social system," in John C McKinney, and Frank T. de Vyver (eds.), *Aging and Social Policy*. New York: Appleton-Century-Crofts.

Morris, Cerise. 1980. "'Determination and thoroughness': the movement for a Royal Commission on the Status of Women in Canada." *Atlantis*, 5:1-21.

Morris, R. and C. M. Lanphier. 1980. "French-English relations as a social problem: present inequalities." in J. Goldstein, and R. Bienvenue (eds.), *Ethnicity and Ethnic Relations in Canada*. Toronto: Butterworths.

Morris, Ray, et al. 1969. *Attitudes Toward Federal Government Information*. Downsview: Institute for Behavioral Research, York University.

Mortimer, Jeylan T., and Roberta G. Simmons. 1978. "Adult socialization." *Annual Review of Sociology*, 4:421-454.

Morton, Peggy. 1972. "Women's work is never done," in *Women Unite! An Anthology of the Canadian Women's Movement*. Toronto: Canadian Women's Educational Press.

Morton, W. L. 1950. *The Progressive Party in Canada*. Toronto: University of Toronto Press.

Mosca, G. 1939. *The Ruling Class*. New York: McGraw-Hill.

Mumford, Lewis. 1961. *The City in History: Its Origin, Its Transformations, and Its Prospects*. New York: Harcourt, Brace, and World.

Murdock, G. P. 1931. "Ethnocentrism," in E. R. A. Seligman (ed.), *Encyclopedia of the Social Sciences*, Vol. 5. New York: Macmillan.

Murphy, Emily F. 1920. "The grave drug menace." *Maclean's Magazine*, 33(3):1.

Murphy, Emily F. 1922. *The Black Candle*. Toronto: Thomas Allen.

Murphy, Raymond. 1981. "Teachers and the evolving structural context of economic and political attitudes in

Quebec society." *The Canadian Review of Sociology and Anthropology*, 18:157-182.

Murray, John P., and Susan Kippax. 1979. "From the early window to the late night show: international trends in the study of television's impact on children and adults." *Advances in Experimental Social Psychology*, 12:253-320.

Musto, David F. 1973. *The American Disease: Origins of Narcotic Control.* New Haven, Conn.: Yale University Press.

Myles, John F. 1980a. "Institutionalizing the elderly: a critical assessment of the sociology of total institutions." in Victor W. Marshall (ed.), *Aging in Canada: Social Perspectives.* Don Mills: Fitzhenry and Whiteside.

Myles, John F. 1980b. "The aged, the state, and the structure of inequality," in John Harp, and John Hofley (eds.), *Structured Inequality in Canada.* Toronto: Prentice-Hall.

Nagel, Stuart. 1969. *The Legal Process from a Behavioral Perspective.* Homewood, Ill.: The Dorsey Press.

Nash, Dennison. 1968. "A little child shall lead them." *Journal for the Scientific Study of Religion*, 7:238-240.

Nash, Dennison, and Peter L. Berger. 1962. "The child, the family, and the 'religious revival' in suburbia." *Journal for the Scientific Study of Religion*, 2:85-93.

Naylor, R. T. 1972. "The ideological foundation of social democracy and social credit," in G. Teeple (ed.), *Capitalism and the National Question in Canada.* Toronto: University of Toronto Press.

Naylor, R. T. 1972. "The rise and fall of the third commercial empire of the St. Lawrence," in Gary Teeple (ed.), *Capitalism and the National Question in Canada.* Toronto: University of Toronto Press.

Nelsen, Hart M., and Raymond H. Potvin. 1980. "Toward disestablishment: new patterns of social class, denomination, and religiosity among youth?" *Review of Religious Research*, 22:137-154.

Nelson, Fiona. 1976. "Sex stereotyping in Canadian schools," in Gwen Matheson (ed.), *Women in the Canadian Mosaic.* Toronto: Peter Martin.

Nelson, L. D., and Russell Dynes. 1976. "The impact of devotionalism and attendance on ordinary and emergency helping behavior." *Journal for the Scientific Study of Religion*, 15:47-59.

Nett, Emily M. 1979. "Socialization for sex roles," in G. N. Ramu (ed.), *Courtship, Marriage and Family in Canada.* Toronto: Macmillan.

Nett, Emily M. 1981. "Canadian families in social-historical perspective." *Canadian Journal of Sociology*, 6(3):239-259.

Nettler, Gwynn. 1974. *Explaining Crime.* New York: McGraw-Hill.

Neugarten, Bernice L. 1970. "The old and the young in modern societies." *American Behavioural Scientist*, 14(1):13-24.

Neugarten, Bernice L., W. Crotty, and S. Tobin. 1964. "Personality types in an aged population," in B. L. Neugarten (ed.), *Personality in Middle and Late Life: Empirical Studies.* New York: Atherton.

Neugarten, Bernice L., and Gunhild O. Hagestad. 1976. "Age and the life course," in Ethel Shanas, and Robert Binstock (eds.), *Handbook of Aging and the Social Sciences.* New York: Van Nostrand Reinhold.

Neugarten, Bernice L., J. Moore, and J. Lowe. 1965. "Age norms, age constraints, and adult socialization." *American Journal of Sociology*, 70(6):710-717.

Newman, Oscar. 1972. *Defensible Space.* New York: Macmillan.

Newman, William M. 1973. *American Pluralism.* New York: Harper and Row.

Ng, M. 1977. "Social class and Canadian politics: replication and extension." Unpublished Master's thesis. University of Manitoba Sociology Department.

Nichols, Jack. 1975. *Men's Liberation.* New York: Penguin.

Niebuhr, H. Richard. 1929. *The Social Sources of Denominationalism.* New York: Holt and Company.

Nielsen, Joyce McCarl. 1978. *Sex in Society: Perspectives on Stratification.* Belmont, Calif.: Wadsworth.

Norris, J. E. 1980. "The social adjustment of single and widowed older women." *Essence: Issues in the Study of Aging, Dying and Death*, 4(3):135-144.

Oberschall, Anthony. 1973. *Social Conflict and Social Movements.* Englewood Cliffs, N. J.: Prentice-Hall.

O'Connor, James. 1973. *The Fiscal Crisis of the State.* New York: St. Martin's.

OECD. 1975. *Education, Inequality, and Life Chances*, 2 vols. Paris: Organization for Economic Cooperation and Development.

OECD. 1976. *Reviews of National Policies for Education: Canada.* Paris: Organization for Economic Cooperation and Development.

Ogburn, William F., and Meyer F. Nimkoff. 1964. "The social effects of innovation," in W. F. Ogburn and M. F. Nimkoff, *Sociology*, 4th ed. Boston: Houghton Mifflin.

Ogmundson, Rick. 1975. "Party class images and the class vote in Canada." *American Sociological Review*, 40:505-512.

Ogmundson R. 1976. "Mass-elite linkages and class issues in Canada." *Canadian Review of Sociology and Anthropology*, 13(1):1-12.

Ogmundson, R. 1980a. "Towards study of the endangered species known as the Anglophone Canadian." *Canadian Journal of Sociology*, 5:1-12.

Ogmundson, R. 1980b. "Liberal ideology and the study of voting behaviour." *Canadian Review of Sociology and Anthropology*, 17:45-54.

Ogmundson, R. 1981. "Social inequality," in R. Hagedorn (ed.), *Essentials of Sociology.* Toronto: Holt, Rinehart and Winston.

Okediji, Francis O. 1974. "Changes in individual reproductive behavior and cultural values." *Lecture Series on Population.* Bucharest, Rumania: International Union for the Scientific Study of Population.

Olsen, Dennis. 1977. "The state elites," in Leo Panitch

(ed.), *The Canadian State: Political Economy and Political Power.* Toronto: University of Toronto Press.

Olsen, Dennis. 1980. *The State Elite.* Toronto: McClelland and Stewart.

Ontario Council of Health. 1978. *Health Care for the Aged.* Toronto: The Ontario Council of Health.

Orbach, Harold L. 1981. "Mandatory retirement and the development of adequate retirement provisions for older persons," in George Gasek (ed.), *Canadian Gerontological Collection II.* Winnipeg: Canadian Association on Gerontology.

Ostry, Bernard. 1978. *The Cultural Connection.* Toronto: McClelland and Stewart.

Ostry, S. 1968. *The Female Worker in Canada.* Ottawa: Queen's Printer.

O'Toole, James. 1981. *Making America Work.* New York: Continuum Publishing.

Overbeek, Johannes. 1974. *History of Population Theories.* Rotterdam: Rotterdam University Press.

Overton, James. 1979. "Towards a critical analysis of neo-nationalism in Newfoundland," in R. Brym and R. J. Sacouman (eds.), *Underdevelopment and Social Movements in Atlantic Canada.* Toronto: New Hogtown Press.

Packer, H. 1964. "Two models of the criminal process." *University of Pennsylvania Law Review,* 113:1-68.

Palen, John. 1981. *The Urban World.* 2nd ed. New York: McGraw-Hill.

Palmore, Erdman. 1969. "Sociological aspects of aging," in Ewald W. Busse, and Eric Pfeiffer (eds.), *Behavior and Adaptation in Late Life.* Boston: Little, Brown.

Palmore, Erdman, and Clark Luikart. 1972. "Health and social factors related to life satisfaction." *Journal of Health and Social Behaviour,* 13(March):68-80.

Panitch, Leo. (ed.). 1977. *The Canadian State: Political Economy and Political Power.* Toronto: University of Toronto Press.

Park, Robert E., Ernest W. Burgess, and Roderick D. McKenzie. 1925. *The City.* Chicago: University of Chicago Press.

Parker, Graham. 1976. "The juvenile court movement." *University of Toronto Law Journal,* 26:140.

Parkes, C. M., B. Benjamin, and R. G. Fitzgerald. 1969. "Broken heart: A statistical study of increased mortality among widowers." *British Medical Journal,* 1:740.

Parkin, Frank. 1972. *Class Inequality and Political Order.* London: Paladin.

Parnes, Herbert S., Mary G. Gagen, and Randall H. King. 1981. "Job loss among long-service workers," in Herbert S. Parnes (ed.), *Work and Retirement.* Cambridge, Mass.: M.I.T. Press.

Parsons, H. M. 1974. "What happened at Hawthorne?" *Science,* 8(March):922-932.

Parsons, Talcott. 1959. "The school as a social system." *Harvard Educational Review,* 29:297-318.

Parsons, Talcott. 1960. *Structure and Process in Modern Societies.* New York: Free Press.

Parsons, Talcott. 1964. "Christianity and modern industrial society," in Louis Schneider (ed.), *Religion, Culture, and Society.* New York: Wiley.

Parsons, Talcott and Robert F. Bales (eds.). 1955. *Family Socialization and Interaction Process.* Glencoe, Ill.: Free Press.

Patterson, E. Palmer, II. 1972. *The Canadian Indian: A History Since 1500.* Toronto: Collier-Macmillan Canada.

Percival, Elizabeth, and Terrance Percival. 1979. "Is a woman a person? Sex differences in stereotyping." *Atlantis,* 4:71-77.

Perry, Robert L. 1971. *Galt, U.S.A.* Toronto: Maclean-Hunter.

Peterson, Richard A. 1979. "Revitalizing the culture concept," in *Annual Review of Sociology,* Vol. 5. Palo Alto, Calif.: Annual Reviews.

Piaget, Jean. 1928. *Judgment and Reasoning in the Child.* New York: Harcourt.

Piaget, Jean. 1932. *The Moral Judgment of the Child.* New York: Harcourt.

Pike, Robert M. 1975. "Introduction and overview," in Robert M. Pike, and Elia Zureik (eds.), *Socialization and Values in Canadian Society.* Vol. 2. Toronto: McClelland and Stewart.

Pike, Robert M. 1978. "Equality of eductional opportunity: dilemmas and policy options." *Interchange,* 9(2):30-39.

Pike, Robert M., and Elia Zureik (eds.). *Socialization and Values in Canadian Society.* Vol. 2. Toronto: McClelland and Stewart.

Piliavin, Irving, and Scott Briar. 1964. "Police encounters with juveniles." *American Journal of Sociology,* 70(Sept.):206-214.

Pinard, Maurice. 1971. *The Rise of a Third Party.* Englewood Cliffs, N. J.: Prentice-Hall.

Pinard, Maurice, and Richard Hamilton. 1978. "The Parti Québécois comes to power." *Canadian Journal of Political Science,* 11:4.

Pineo, Peter C. 1971. "The extended family in a working-class area of Hamilton," in Bernard Blishen, et al. (eds.), *Canadian Society.* Toronto: Macmillan.

Pineo, Peter. 1976. "Social mobility in Canada: the current picture." *Sociological Focus,* 9(2):120.

Pineo, Peter. 1980. "The social standing of ethnic and racial groupings," in J. Goldstein, and R. Bienvenue (eds.), *Ethnicity and Ethnic Relations in Canada.* Toronto: Butterworths.

Pineo, Peter C., and John Porter. 1967. "Occupational prestige in Canada." *Canadian Review of Sociology and Anthropology,* 4:24-40.

Pineo, Peter C., et al. 1977. "The 1971 census and the socioeconomic classification of occupations." *Canadian Review of Sociology and Anthropology,* 1:91-102.

Pirenne, Henri. 1939. *Medieval Cities.* Princeton, N.J.: Princeton University Press.

Platt, Anthony M. 1969. *The Child Savers.* Chicago: University of Chicago Press.

Polanyi, Karl. 1957. In C. M. Arensberg and H. W. Pearson (eds.), *Trade and Markets in the Early Empires*. Glencoe, Ill.: Free Press.

Pope, Liston. 1942. *Millhands and Preachers*. New Haven, Conn.: Yale University Press.

Porter, John. 1965. *The Vertical Mosaic: An Analysis of Social Class and Power in Canada*. Toronto: University of Toronto Press.

Porter, John. 1967. *Canadian Social Structure: A Statistical Profile*. Toronto: McClelland and Stewart.

Porter, Marion, John Porter, and Bernard Blishen. 1973. *Does Money Matter?* Toronto: Institute for Behavioural Research, York University.

Posner, Judith. 1980. "Old and female: the double whammy," in Victor W. Marshall (ed.), *Aging in Canada: Social Perspectives*. Don Mills: Fitzhenry and Whiteside.

Poulantzas, Nicos. 1978. *Classes in Contemporary Capitalism*. London: Verso.

Powell, Brian J., and James K. Martin. 1980. "Economic implications of Canada's aging society," in Victor W. Marshall (ed.), *Aging in Canada: Social Perspectives*. Don Mills: Fitzhenry and Whiteside.

Pratt, David. 1975. "The social role of school textbooks in Canada," in Elia Zureik, and Robert M. Pike (eds.), *Socialization and Values in Canadian Society*, Vol. 1. Toronto: McClelland and Stewart.

Pratt, Larry, and Garth Stevenson (eds.). 1981. *Western Separatism: The Myths, Realities and Dangers*. Edmonton: Hurtig Publishers.

Prentice, Beverly. 1979. "Divorce, kids, and custody: a quantitative study of three legal factors." Paper presented to the annual meeting of the Canadian Sociology and Anthropology Association, Saskatoon, Saskatchewan.

Presthus, Robert. 1973. *Elite Accommodation in Canadian Politics*. Toronto: MacMillan.

Price, James L. 1972. *Handbook of Organizational Measurement*. Lexington, Mass.: D. C. Heath.

Pyke, S. W. 1975. "Children's literature: conceptions of sex roles," in Robert M. Pike, and Elia Zureik (eds.), *Socialization and Values in Canadian Society*, Vol. 2. Toronto: McClelland and Stewart.

Pyke, S. W., and J. C. Stewart. 1974. "This column is about women: women and television." *The Ontario Psychologist*, 6:66-69.

Quadagno, Jill S. 1980. "The modernization controversy: a socio-historical analysis of retirement in nineteenth century England." Paper presented at Meetings of the American Sociological Association, New York, N.Y. (August).

Quebec Civil Code. 1981. "Rules respecting the solemnization of civil marriage." *Gazette officielle du Québec*, 113(15, part 2):1263-1266.

Quinn, H. 1963. *The Union Nationale*. Toronto: University of Toronto Press.

Quinney R. 1970. *The Social Reality of Crime*. Boston: Little, Brown.

Radcliffe-Brown, A. R. 1929. "Age organisation – terminology." Letter to the editor, *Man*, 29:21.

Rainwater, Lee. 1966. "Work and identity in the lower class," in Sam Bass Warner Jr. (ed.), *Planning for a Nation of Cities*. Cambridge: M.I.T. Press.

Ramu, G. N. 1976. "Courtship, marriage and family in Canada," in G. N. Ramu, and Stuart D. Johnson (eds.), *Introduction to Canadian Society: Sociological Analysis*. Toronto: Macmillan.

Rapp, Rayna. 1982. "Family and class in contemporary America," in Barrie Thorne, and Marilyn Yalom (eds.), *Rethinking the Family: Some Feminist Questions*. New York and London: Longman, Inc.

Ray, Arthur J. 1974. *Indians in the Fur Trade: Their Role as Hunters, Trappers and Middlemen in the Lands Southwest of Hudson Bay 1660-1870*. Toronto: University of Toronto Press.

Reasons, Charles. 1974. "The politics of drugs: an inquiry in the sociology of social problems." *Sociological Quarterly*, 15(3):381-404.

Reed, Evelyn. 1978. "Women: caste, class or oppressed sex?" in Alison M. Jaggar, and Paula Rothenberg Struhl (eds.), *Feminist Frameworks: Alternative Theoretical Accounts of the Relations between Women and Men*. New York: McGraw-Hill.

Reichard, S., F. Livson, and P. G. Peterson. 1962. *Aging and Personality*. New York: John Wiley and Sons.

Reiss, Albert J. 1971. *The Police and the Public*. New Haven, Conn.: Yale University Press.

Reiss, Albert J., Jr. 1959. "The sociological study of communities." *Rural Sociology*, 24:118-130.

Resnick, Philip. 1977. *The Land of Cain*. Vancouver: New Star Books.

Reuber, G. 1978. "The impact of government policies on the distribution of income in Canada: a review." *Canadian Public Policy*, 4:505-529.

Reynauld, A., et al. 1967. "La répartition des revenus selon les groupes ethniques au Canada." *Report to the Royal Commission on Bilingualism and Biculturalism*. Ottawa: Queen's Printer.

Rheingold, Harriet L. 1969. "The social and socializing infant," in David A. Goslin (ed.), *Handbook of Socialization Theory and Research*. Chicago: Rand McNally.

Rich, H. 1976. "The vertical mosaic revisited." *Journal of Canadian Studies*, 14-31.

Richardson, Laurel Walum. 1981. *The Dynamics of Sex and Gender*. 2nd ed. Boston: Houghton Mifflin.

Richer, Stephen. 1979. "Sex-role, socialization and early schooling." *Canadian Review of Sociology and Anthropology*, 16:195-205.

Richmond, Anthony H. 1972. *Ethnic Residential Segregation in Metropolitan Toronto*. Toronto: Survey Research Center, York University.

Riley, Matilda White. 1976. "Age strata in social systems," in Robert Binstock, and Ethel Shanas (eds.), *Handbook of Aging and the Social Sciences*. New York: Van Nostrand Reinhold.

Riley, Matilda White. 1980. "Age and aging: from theory

generation to theory testing," in Hubert M. Blalock, Jr. (ed.), *Sociological Theory and Research: A Critical Approach*. New York: The Free Press.

Riley, M. W., and A. Foner. 1968. *Aging and Society: Volume One – An Inventory of Research Findings*. New York: Russell Sage Foundation.

Riley, Matilda White, Anne Foner, Beth Hess, and Marcia Toby. 1969. "Socialization for the middle and later years," in David Goslin (ed.), *Handbook of Socialization Theory and Research*. Chicago: Rand McNally.

Riley, Matilda White, Marylin Johnson, and Anne Foner. 1972. *Aging and Society, Vol. 2: A Sociology of Age Stratification*. New York: Russell Sage Foundation.

Rinehart, James W. 1975. *The Tyranny of Work*. Toronto: Longman Canada.

Rinehart, James W. 1978. "Contradictions of work-related attitudes and behavior: An interpretation." *Canadian Review of Sociology and Anthropology*, 15(1):1-15.

Rinehart, J., and I. O. Okraku. 1974. "A study of class consciousness." *Canadian Review of Sociology and Anthropology*, 11(3):200.

Rioux, Marcel. 1971. *Quebec in Question*. Toronto: James, Lewis and Samuel.

Rioux, Marcel. 1973. "The development of ideologies in Quebec," in G. A. Gold, and M. A. Tremblay (eds.), *Communities and Cultures in French Canada*. Toronto: Holt, Rinehart and Winston.

Ritchie, Marguerite. 1975. "Alice through the statutes." *McGill Law Journal*, 21:702.

Robb, A. Leslie, and Byron G. Spencer. 1976. "Education: enrolment and attainment," in Gail C. A. Cook (ed.), *Opportunity for Choice*. Ottawa: Information Canada.

Robertson, Ian. 1977. *Sociology*. New York: Worth Publishers.

Robinson, John, and Philip Shaver. 1973. *Measures of Social Psychological Attitudes*. Ann Arbor, Mich.: University of Michigan.

Robinson, John, et al. 1968. *Measures of Political Attitudes*. Ann Arbor, Mich.: University of Michigan.

Robinson, John, et al. 1969. *Measures of Occupational Attitudes and Occupational Characteristics*. Ann Arbor, Mich.: University of Michigan.

Robson, R., and M. Lapointe. 1971. *A Comparison of Men's and Women's Salaries and Employment Fringe Benefits in the Academic Profession*. Ottawa: Queen's Printer.

Rock, Ronald, Marcus Jacobson, and Richard Janopaul. 1968. *Hospital Admission and Discharge of the Mentally Ill*. Chicago: University of Chicago Press.

Rodgers, Roy H. and Gail Witney. 1981. "The family cycle in twentieth century Canada." *Journal of Marriage and the Family*, 43(3):727-740.

Roethlisberger, F. J., and W. J. Dickson. 1947. *Management and the Worker*. Cambridge, Mass.: Harvard University Press.

Rohner, Ronald P., and Evelyn C. Rohner. 1970. *The Kwakiutl: Indians of British Columbia*. New York: Holt, Rinehart and Winston.

Rokeach, Milton. 1965. "Paradoxes of religious belief." *Information Service*, National Council of Churches, February 13, 1-2.

Rokeach, Milton. 1969. "Religious values and social compassion." *Review of Religious Research*, 11:3-23.

Rokeach, Milton. 1974. "Some reflections about the place of values in Canadian social science," in T. N. Guinsburg and G. L. Reuber (eds.), *Perspectives on the Social Sciences in Canada*. Toronto: University of Toronto Press.

Roof, Wade Clark, and Dean R. Hoge. 1980. "Church involvement in America: social factors affecting membership and participation." *Review of Religious Research*, 21:405-426.

Rosaldo, Michelle Zimbalist. 1974. "Woman, culture, and society: a theoretical overview," in Michelle Zimbalist Rosaldo, and Louise Lamphere (eds.), *Woman, Culture, and Society*. Stanford, Calif.: Stanford University Press.

Rosaldo, Michelle Zimbalist. 1980. "The use and abuse of anthropology: reflections on feminism and cross-cultural understanding." *Signs*, 5:389-417.

Rose, Arnold, L. 1965. "The subculture of the aging: a framework in social gerontology," in Arnold M. Rose, and Warren A. Peterson (eds.), *Older People and Their Social World*. Philadelphia: F. A. Davis.

Rosen, B. C. 1965. *Adolescence and Religion*. Cambridge, Mass.: Schenkman.

Rosenberg, Miriam. 1976. "The biologic basis for sex role stereotypes," in Alexandra G. Kaplan, and Joan P. Bean (eds.), *Beyond Sex-role Stereotypes: Readings Toward a Psychology of Androgyny*. Boston: Little, Brown.

Rosenburg, M. 1965. *Society and the Adolescent Self-Image*. Princeton, N.J.: Princeton University Press.

Rosenfeld, Rachel A. 1979. "Women's occupational careers: individual and structural explanations." *Sociology of Work and Occupations*, 6:283-311.

Rosenhan, D. L. 1973. "On being sane in insane places." *Science*, 179(19):250-258.

Rosenmayr, Leopold. 1977. "The family – a source of hope for the elderly," in Ethel Shanas, and Marvin B. Sussman (eds.), *Family, Bureaucracy and the Elderly*. Durham, N.C.: Duke University Press.

Rosenthal, Carolyn J. 1982a. "Generational relations and succession: A study of authority and responsibility in families." Doctoral dissertation, Dept. of Sociology, McMaster University.

Rosenthal, Carolyn J. 1982b. "Family responsibilities and concerns: a perspective on the lives of middle-aged women." *Resources for Feminist Research* (forthcoming).

Rosenthal, R., and L. Jacobson. 1968. *Pygmalion in the Classroom*. New York: Holt, Rinehart and Winston.

Rosow, Irving. 1967. *Social Integration of the Aged*. New York: Free Press.

Rosow, Irving. 1973. "The social context of the aging self." *Gerontologist*, 13(Spring):82.

Rosow, Irving. 1974. *Socialization to Old Age*. Berkeley and Los Angeles: University of California Press.

Rosow, Irving. 1976. "Status and role change through the life span," in Robert H. Binstock, and Ethel Shanas (eds.), *Handbook of Aging and the Social Sciences*. New York: Van Nostrand Reinhold.

Rossi, Alice S. 1977. "Transition to parenthood," in Arlene S. Skolnick, and Jerome K. Skolnick (eds.), *Family in Transition*. Toronto: Little, Brown.

Roy, Donald. 1952. "Efficiency and 'the fix': informal intergroup relations in a piece-work machine shop." *American Journal of Sociology*, 57:427-442.

Roy, Donald. 1959. "Banana time-job satisfaction and informal interaction." *Human Organization*, 158-169.

Royal Commission of Inquiry on Education (Parent Commission Report), Vol. 1. 1963. Quebec: Government of Quebec.

Royal Commission on National Development in the Arts, Letters, and Sciences (Massey Report). 1951. Ottawa: Queen's Printer.

Royal Commission on the Status of Women in Canada. 1970. *Report*. Ottawa: Information Canada.

Ruether, Rosemary R. (ed.). 1974. *Religion and Sexism: Images of Woman in the Jewish and Christian Traditions*. New York: Simon and Schuster.

Rushby, William, and John Thrush. 1973. "Mennonites and social compassion." *Review of Religious Research*, 15:16-28.

Russel, P. H. 1975. "The political role of the Supreme Court of Canada in its first century." *Canadian Bar Review*, 53:576-593.

Ryan, William. 1971. *Blaming the Victim*. New York: Pantheon Books.

Ryder, Norman B. 1965. "The cohort as a concept in the study of social change." *American Sociological Review*, 30(6): 834-861.

Sacouman, R. J. 1979. "The differing origins, organization and impact of Maritime and prairie co-operative movements to 1940," in R. Brym and R. J. Sacouman (eds.), *Underdevelopment and Social Movements in Atlantic Canada*. Toronto: New Hogtown Press.

Safilios-Rothschild, Constantina. 1974. *Women and Social Policy*. Englewood Cliffs, N.J.: Prentice-Hall.

Samuelson, P. 1964. *Economics*, 6th ed. New York: McGraw-Hill.

Sanders, W. B. (ed.). 1974. *The Sociologist as Detective*. New York: Praeger.

Saunders, Ivan. 1975. "Canadian law and marriage," in S. Parvez Wakil (ed.), *Marriage, Family and Society: Canadian Perspectives*. Toronto: Butterworth.

Saywell, John. 1977. *The Rise of the Parti Québécois*. Toronto: University of Toronto Press.

Scanzoni, John. 1972. *Sexual Bargaining: Power Politics in the American Marriage*. Englewood Cliffs, N.J.: Prentice-Hall.

Scheff, Thomas. 1966. *Being Mentally Ill: A Sociological Theory*. Chicago: Aldine.

Schellenberg, James A. 1974. *An Introduction to Social Psychology*, 2nd ed. New York: Random House.

Schellenberg, James A. 1978. *Masters of Social Psychology: Freud, Mead, Lewin, and Skinner*. New York: Oxford University Press.

Schelsky, H. 1961. "Family and school in modern society," in A. H. Halsey, et al. (eds.), *Education, Economy, and Society*. Glencoe, Ill.: Free Press.

Schlossman, Steven. 1977. *Love and the American Delinquent*. Chicago: University of Chicago Press.

Schmidt, Wolfgang, Reginald Smart, and Maria Moss. 1968. *Social Class and the Treatment of Alcoholism*. Toronto: The University of Toronto: Addiction Research Foundation, Monograph No. 7.

Schnore, Leo F. 1958. "Social morphology and human ecology." *American Journal of Sociology*, 63:620-634.

Schreiber, E. 1980. "Class awareness and class voting in Canada." *Canadian Review of Sociology and Anthropology*, 17:37-44.

Schwenger, Cope W., and M. John Gross. 1980. "Institutional care and institutionalization of the elderly in Canada," in Victor W. Marshall (ed.), *Aging in Canada: Social Perspectives*. Don Mills: Fitzhenry and Whiteside.

Seashore, Stanley E. 1954. *Group Cohesiveness in the Industrial Work Group*. Ann Arbor, Mich.: Survey Research Center, University of Michigan.

Selznick, Philip. 1949. *TVA and the Grass Roots*. Berkeley, Calif.: University of California Press.

Shanas, Ethel. 1979. "Social myth as hypothesis: the case of the family relations of old people." *The Gerontologist*, 19(1):3-9.

Shanas, Ethel. 1981. "Old parents: middle-aged children." Paper presented at the meetings of the International Association of Gerontology, Hamburg, Germany, July 11-17.

Shanas, E., P. Townsend, D. Wedderburn, H. Eriis, P. Milhoj, and J. Stehouwer. 1968. *Old People in Three Industrial Societies*. New York: Atherton Press.

Shaw, Marvin E., and Philip R. Costanzo. 1970. *Theories of Social Psychology*. New York: McGraw-Hill.

Shaw, M. E., and J. M. Wright. 1967. *Scales For the Measurement of Attitudes*. New York: McGraw-Hill.

Sheehy, Gail. 1974. *Passages: Predictable Crises in Adult Life*. New York: Dutton.

Sheehy, Gail. 1976. *Passages*. Toronto: Clarke, Irwin.

Sheppard, Harold L. 1970. *Toward an Industrial Gerontology*. Cambridge, Mass.: Schenkman.

Shibutani, Tamotsu, and Kian M. Kwan. 1965. *Ethnic Stratification: A Comparative Approach*. New York: Macmillan.

Shore, Valerie. 1982. "Women steered away from science says council." *University Affairs*, (April)23:4.

Sigelman, Lee. 1977. "Multi-nation surveys of religious beliefs." *Journal for the Scientific Study of Religion*, 16:289-294.

Silberman, Charles. 1970. *Crisis in the Classroom*. New York: Random House.

Simmel, Georg. 1950. "The metropolis and mental life," in Robert Gutman and David Popenoe (eds.), *Neighborhood,*

City, and Metropolis. New York: Random House.

Simmel, Georg. 1950. *The Sociology of Georg Simmel*, Kurt Wolff (ed.). Glencoe, Ill.: Free Press.

Simmons, James, and Robert Simmons. 1974. *Urban Canada.* 2nd ed. Toronto: Copp Clark.

Sinclair, Peter. 1975: 1973. "The Saskatchewan CCF: ascent to power and the decline of socialism," in Sam Clark, et al (eds.), *Prophecy and Protest: Social Movements in Twentieth-Century Canada.* Toronto: Gage.

Sjoberg, Gideon. 1960. *The Preindustrial City.* Glencoe, Ill.: Free Press.

Skinner, B. F. 1953. *Science and Human Behavior.* New York: Macmillan.

Skolnick, Jerome. 1975. *Justice Without Trial: Law Enforcement in a Democratic Society.* New York: Wiley.

Smith, Dorothy. 1973. "Women, the family and corporate capitalism," in Marylee Stephenson (ed.), *Women in Canada.* Don Mills, Ont.: General Publishing.

Smith, Dorothy E. 1977. *Feminism & Marxism.* Vancouver: New Star Books.

Smith, Dorothy E. 1977. "Women, the family and corporate capitalism," in M. Stephenson (ed.), *Women In Canada* Don Mills: General Publishing.

Smith, Douglas. 1982. "Extra-legal determinants of arrest: some new evidence on some old questions." *Social Problems* (forthcoming).

Smith, Douglas, and Christy Visher. 1980. "Sex and involvement in deviance/crime: a quantitative review of the empirical literature." *American Sociological Review*, 45(4):691-701.

Smith, Kathleen, Muriel Pumphrey, and Julian Hall. 1963. "The 'last straw': the decisive incident resulting in the request for hospitalization in 100 schizophrenic patients." *American Journal of Psychiatry*, 120(September):228-232.

Smith, M. 1979. *The City and Social Theory.* New York: St. Martin's.

Smith, Robert Paul. 1979. "Kids, clubs, and special places," in Peter I. Rose (ed.), *Socialization and the Life Cycle.* New York: St. Martin's Press.

Smyth, J. E., and D. A. Soberman. 1976. *The Law and Business administration.* Toronto: Prentice-Hall.

Snider, Earle E. 1981. "The role of kin in meeting health care needs of the elderly." *The Canadian Journal of Sociology*, 6(3):325-336.

Snodgrass, Jon. 1975. "The women's liberation movement and the men." Paper presented to the Pacific Sociological Association Meetings, Victoria, B.C.

Sorokin, P. 1927. *Social and Cultural Mobility.* New York: Free Press.

Southard, Samuel. 1961. *Pastoral Evangelism.* New York: Abingdon Press.

Special Senate Committee on Retirement Age Policies. 1979. *Retirement Without Tears.* Ottawa: Ministry of Supply and Services.

Spelt, Jacob. 1955. *Urban Development in South-Central Ontario.* Toronto: Collier-Macmillan.

Spelt, Jacob. 1973. *Toronto.* Toronto: Collier-Macmillan.

Stack, S. 1980. "The political economy of income inequality: a comparative analysis." *Canadian Journal of Political Science*, 13:273-286.

Stanley, George F. G. 1960. *The Birth of Western Canada: A History of the Riel Rebellions.* Toronto: University of Toronto Press.

Stark, Rodney. 1971. "Psychopathology and religious commitment." *Review of Religious Research*, 12:165-176.

Stark, Rodney, and Charles Glock. 1968. *American Piety.* Berkeley, Calif.: University of California Press.

Statistics Canada. 1973. *Education in Canada 1973: A Statistical Review for the Period 1960-61 – 1970-71.* Ottawa: Supply and Services.

Statistics Canada. 1978. *Historical Compendium of Education Statistics From Confederation to 1975.* Ottawa: Supply and Services.

Statistics Canada. 1981. *Education in Canada 1980.* Ottawa: Supply and Services.

Steffensmeier, Darrell J. 1978. "Sex differences in patterns of adult crime, 1965-77: a review and assessment." *Social Forces*, 58(4):1080-1108.

Stephen, G. E., and D. R. McMullin. 1982. "Tolerance of sexual nonconformity: city size as a situational and early learning determinant." *American Sociological Review*, 47:411-415.

Stephens, William. 1963. *The Family in Cross-Cultural Perspective.* New York: Holt, Rinehart and Winston.

Stevenson, P. 1977. "Class and left-wing radicalism." *Canadian Review of Sociology and Anthropology*, 14:269-284.

Stinchcombe, Arthur L. 1963. "Institutions of privacy in the determination of police administrative practice." *American Journal of Sociology*, 69:150-160.

Stolnitz, George J. 1964. "The demographic transition: from high to low birth rates and death rates," in Ronald Freedman (ed.), *Population: The Vital Revolution.* New York: Anchor.

Stone, Leroy O. 1967. *Urban Development in Canada.* Ottawa: Dominion Bureau of Statistics.

Strauss, Anselm. 1969. *Mirrors and Masks.* Mill Valley, Calif.: Sociology Press.

Stryckman, Judith. 1981. "The decision to remarry: the choice and its outcomes." Paper presented at the joint scientific meeting of the Gerontological Society of America and the Canadian Association on Gerontology, Toronto, November 8-12.

Suchman, Edward A. 1968. "The hang-loose ethic and the spirit of drug use." *Journal of Health and Social Behavior*, 9(2):146-155.

Sudnow, David. 1965. "Normal crimes: sociological features of the penal code in a public defender office." *Social Problems*, (Winter):255-276.

Sumner, W. G. 1906. *Folkways.* New York: Ginn.

Surtees, R. J. 1969. "The development of an Indian reserve policy in Canada." *Ontario History*, 61:87-98.

Sutherland, Edwin. 1924. *Criminology*. Philadelphia: Lippincott.

Sutherland, Edwin. 1949. *White Collar Crime*. New York: Dryden.

Sykes, Gresham, and David Matza. 1957. "Techniques of neutralization: a theory of delinquency." *American Sociological Review*, 22:664-670.

Synge, Jane. 1977. "The sex factor in social selection processes in Canadian education," in Richard Carlton, Louise A. Colley, and Neil MacKinnon (eds.), *Education, Change and Society*. Toronto: Gage.

Synge, Jane. 1980. "Work and family support patterns of the aged in the early twentieth century," in Victor W. Marshall (ed.), *Aging in Canada: Social Perspectives*. Don Mills: Fitzhenry and Whiteside.

Tannenbaum, Frank. 1938. *Crime and the Community*. Boston: Ginn.

Tanner, Julian. 1981. "Pop music and peer groups: a study of Canadian high school students' responses to pop music." *The Canadian Review of Sociology and Anthropology*, 18:1-13.

Tausig, Christine. 1982. "At Royal Military College: days filled with challenge." *University Affairs*, (January):3-5.

Tavris, Carol, and Carole Offir. 1977. *The Longest War: Sex Differences in Perspective*. New York: Harcourt Brace Jovanovich.

Tawney, R. H. 1954: 1926. *Religion and the Rise of Capitalism*. Toronto: Mentor Books.

Taylor, Frederic W. 1947: 1911. *Scientific Management*. New York: Harper and Row.

Taylor, Ian, Paul Walton, and Jock Young. 1973. *The New Criminology: For a Social Theory of Deviance*. London: Routledge & Kegan Paul.

Taylor, Ian, Paul Walton, and Jock Young. 1975. *Critical Criminology*. London: Routledge & Kegan Paul.

Taylor, N. W. 1964. "The French-Canadian industrial entrepreneur and his social environment," in M. Rioux and Y. Martin (eds.), *French-Canadian Society*, Vol. 1. Toronto: McClelland and Stewart.

Tepperman, Lorne. 1975. *Social Mobility in Canada*. Toronto: McGraw-Hill Ryerson.

Terry, Charles, and Mildred Pellens. 1970. *The Opium Problem*. Montclair, N.J.: Patterson Smith.

Thatcher, T. C. 1978. "Report of the Royal Commission on violence in the communications industry," in Mary Alice Beyer Gammon (ed.), *Violence in Canada*. Toronto: Methuen.

Thomas, W. I. 1928. *The Child In America*. New York: Alfred A. Knopf.

Thomlinson, Ralph. 1965. *Population Dynamics: Causes and Consequences of World Demographic Change*. New York: Random House.

Thompson, Hunter. 1968. *Hell's Angels*. New York: Ballantine Books.

Thompson, James D. 1967. *Organizations in Action*. New York: McGraw-Hill.

Thompson, Mary K., and Julia S. Brown. 1980. "Feminine roles and variations in women's illness behaviors." *Pacific Sociological Review*, 23:405-422.

Thompson, Warren, and David Lewis. 1965. *Population Problems*. 5th ed. New York: McGraw-Hill.

Thompson, William. 1970: 1825. Appeal of One Half The Human Race. Women Against The Pretentions of the Other Half Men to Retain Them in Political, and Thence in Civil and Domestic, Slavery. In Reply to a Paragraph of Mr. Mil's Celebrated "Article on Government." New York: Burt Franklin.

Thorndike, E. L. 1898. *Animal Intelligence*. New York: Macmillan.

Thorndike, E. L. 1913. *The Psychology of Learning*. New York: Columbia University.

Thorne, Barrie, and Nancy Henley. 1975. "Difference and dominance: an overview of language, gender, and society," in Barrie Thorne, and Nancy Henley (eds.), *Language and Sex: Difference and Dominance*. Rowley, Mass.: Newburg House Publishers.

Thrasher, Frederic. 1927. *The Gang*. Chicago: University of Chicago Press.

Tienhaara, Nancy. 1974. *Canadian Views on Immigration and Population: An Analysis of Post-War Gallup Polls*. Ottawa: Manpower and Immigration.

Tillich, Paul. 1966. *On the Boundary*. New York: Scribner's.

Tilly, Charles. 1974. "Ecological triangle," in Charles Tilly (ed.), *An Urban World*. Boston: Little, Brown.

Tilly, Charles. 1976a. *"Sociology, history and the origins of the European proletariat."* Working Paper No. 148. Center for Research on Social Organization, Ann Arbor, Michigan: University of Michigan.

Tilly, Charles. 1976b. "A travers le chaos des vivantes cites," in P. Meadows, and E. Mizurchi (eds.), *Urbanism, Urbanization and Change*. 2nd ed. Reading: Addison-Wesley.

Tilly, Charles. 1981. "The urban historian's dilemma: faceless cities or cities without hinterlands?" CRSO Working Paper No. 248. Ann Arbor: Center for Research on Social Organization, University of Michigan.

Tilly, Charles, Louise Tilly, and Richard Tilly. 1975. *The Rebellious Century: 1830-1930*. Cambridge, Mass.: Harvard University Press.

Tilquin, D., C. Sicotte, T. Paquin, F. Tousignant, C. Gagnon, and P. Lambert. 1980. "The physical, emotional, and social condition of an aged population in Quebec," in Victor W. Marshall (ed.), *Aging in Canada: Social Perspectives*. Don Mills: Fitzhenry and Whiteside.

Timberlake, James H. 1963. *Prohibition and the Progressive Movement: 1900-1920*. Cambridge, Mass.: Harvard University Press.

Tindale, Joseph A. 1980a. "Identity maintenance processes of old poor men," in Victor W. Marshall (ed.), *Aging In*

Canada: Social Perspectives. Don Mills: Fitzhenry and White-side.

Tindale, Joseph A. 1980b. "Generational conflict: class and cohort relations among Ontario public secondary school teachers." Doctoral dissertation, Department of Sociology, York University, Toronto.

Tindale, Joseph A. 1981. "Social class, social closure, and the role of the state in generational analyses." Paper presented at the joint scientific meeting of the Gerontological Society of America and the Canadian Association on Gerontology, Toronto, November, 8-12.

Tittle, Charles, Wayne Villemez, and Douglas Smith. 1978. "The myth of social class and criminality: an empirical assesment of the empirical evidence." *American Sociological Review*, 43(5):643-656.

Tobin, Sheldon S., and Regina Kulys. 1980. "The family and services," in Carl Eisdorfer (ed.), *Annual Review of Gerontology and Geriatrics*, Vol. 1, New York: Springer.

Toby, Jackson. 1974. "The socialization and control of deviant motivation," in Daniel Glazer (ed.), *Handbook of Criminology.* Chicago: Rand McNally.

Tönnies, Ferdinand. 1957: 1887. *Community and Society (Gemeinschaft und Gesellschaft).* New York: Harper Torchbooks.

Torrance, Judy. 1977. "The response of Canadian governments to violence." *Canadian Journal of Political Science*, 10:3.

Townsend, Peter. 1979. *Poverty in the United Kingdom.* Berkeley and Los Angeles: University of California Press.

Treiman, D. 1978. *Occupational Prestige in Comparative Perspective.* New York: Academic Press.

Tresemer, Davis. 1975. "Assumptions made about gender roles," in Marcia Millman, and Rosabeth Moss Kanter (eds.), *Another Voice: Feminist Perspectives on Social Life and Social Sciences.* Garden City, N.Y.: Doubleday Anchor.

Trigger, Bruce G. 1969. *The Huron: Farmers of the North.* New York: Holt, Rinehart and Winston.

Trist, E. L., and K. W. Bamforth. 1951. "Some social and psychological consequences of the Longwall method of coal getting." *Human Relations*, 4:3-38.

Trow, Martin. 1961. "The second transformation of American secondary education." *International Journal of Comparative Sociology*, 2:144-165.

Tsui, Amy Ong, and Donald J. Bogue. 1978. "Declining world fertility: trends, causes, implications." *Population Bulletin*, 33(4). Washington, D.C.: Population Reference Bureau, Inc.

Tuan, Yi-Fu. 1974. *Topophilia: A Study of Environmental Perception Attitudes and Values.* Englewood Cliffs, N.J.: Prentice-Hall.

Tuchman, Gaye. 1978. "Introduction: the symbolic annihilation of women by the mass media," in Gaye Tuchman, Arlene Kaplan Daniels, and James Benet (eds.), *Hearth and Home: Images of Women in the Mass Media.* New York: Oxford University Press.

Tumin, M. 1953. "Some principles of stratification: a critical analysis." *American Sociological Review*, 18:387-394.

Tumin, M. 1967. *Social Stratification: The Form and Functions of Inequality.* Englewood Cliffs, N.J.: Prentice-Hall.

Turk, Austin T. 1969. *Criminality and the Legal Order.* Chicago: Rand McNally.

Turner, Ralph H. 1961. "Modes of social ascent through education: sponsored and contest mobility," in A. H. Halsey, Jean Floud, and C. Arnold Anderson (eds.), *Education, Economy, and Society.* Glencoe, Ill.: Free Press.

Turner, Ralph H. 1962. "Role-taking: process versus conformity," in Arnold M. Rose (ed.), *Human Behavior and Social Processes: An Interactionist Approach.* Boston: Houghton Mifflin.

Tyree, A., et al. 1979. "Gaps and glissandos: inequality, economic development, and social mobility." *American Sociological Review*, 44:410-424.

U.S. Department of Health, Education, and Welfare. 1972. *Television and Growing Up: The Impact of Televised Violence.* Report to the Surgeon General from the Scientific Advisory Committee on Television and Social Behavior. Washington, D.C.

Vachon, M. L. S. 1979. "Identity change over the first two years of bereavement: social relationships and social supports." Doctoral dissertation, Department of Sociology, York University, Toronto.

Vachon, M. L. S., A. Formo, K. Freedman, W. A. L. Lyall, J. Rogergs, and S. J. J. Freeman. 1976. "Stress reactions to bereavement." *Essence*, 1(1):23-33.

Vallance, Elizabeth. 1979. *Women In The House.* London: Athlone Press.

Vallee, Frank G., and John DeVries. 1975. *Data Book for the Conference on the Individual Language and Society.* Ottawa: Canada Council.

Van Loon R. 1970. "Political participation in Canada: The 1965 election." *Canadian Journal of Political Science*, 3:376-399.

Van Loon, Richard, and Michael S. Whittington. 1981. *The Canadian Political System.* 2nd ed. Toronto: McGraw-Hill Ryerson.

Vaz, E. W. 1965. "Middle-class adolescents: self-reported delinquency and youth culture activities." *Canadian Review of Sociology and Anthropology*, 2:52-70.

Veevers, J. E., and D. F. Cousineau. 1980. "The heathen Canadians: demographic correlates of nonbelief." *Pacific Sociological Review*, 23:199-216.

Vickers, Jill M. 1978. "Where are the women in Canadian politics?" *Atlantis*, Spring 40-51.

Vidmar, Neil, and Milton Rokeach. 1974. "Archie Bunker's bigotry: a study of selective perception and exposure." *Journal of Communications*, 24(1):36-47.

Wagley, Charles, and Marvin Harris. 1958. *Minorities in the New World.* New York: Columbia University Press.

Wakil, S. Parvez (ed.). 1975. *Marriage, Family and Society: Canadian Perspectives.* Toronto: Butterworths.

Waller, Irvin. 1974. *Men Released from Prison.* Toronto: University of Toronto Press.

Waller, Irvin, and Janet Chan. 1975. "Prison use: a Canadian and international comparison." *Criminal Law Quarterly*, 47-71.

Wallerstein, Immanuel. 1974. *The Modern World System.* New York: Academic Press.

Walum, Laurel Richardson. 1974. "The changing door ceremony." *Urban Life and Culture*, 2:506-515.

Walum, Laurel Richardson. 1981. *The Dynamics of Sex and Gender.* 2nd ed. Boston: Houghton Mifflin.

Ward, Dawn, and Jack Balswick. 1978. "Strong men and virtuous women: a content analysis of sex roles stereotypes." *Pacific Sociological Review*, 21:45-53.

Wargon, Sylvia T. 1979. *Canadian Households and Families: Recent Demographic Trends.* Ottawa: Statistics Canada.

Waring, Joan. 1976. "Social replenishment and social change," in Anne Foner (ed.), *Age in Society.* Beverley Hills, Calif.: Sage.

Warnock, J. 1970. *Portner to Behemoth.* Toronto: New Press.

Warnock, John W. 1974. "Metropolis/hinterland: the lost theme in Canadian letters." *Canadian Dimension*, 10(2):42-46.

Washburn, Sherwood L., and Irvin De Vore. 1961. "The social behavior of baboons and early man," in S. L. Washburn (ed.), *Social Life in Early Man.* Chicago: Aldine.

Waters, H. F. and P. Malamud. 1975. "Drop that gun, Captain Video." *Newsweek*, 85(March)10:81-82.

Watkins, M. 1973. "The trade union movement in Canada," in R. Laxer (ed.), *Canada Ltd.* Toronto: McClelland and Stewart.

Webb, Eugene J., et al. 1981. *Nonreactive Measures in the Social Sciences.* Boston: Houghton Mifflin.

Webb, Stephen D., and John Collette. 1977. "Rural-urban differences in the use of stress-alleviative drugs." *American Journal of Sociology*, 83:700-707.

Webb, Stephen D., and John Collette. 1979. "Rural-urban stress: new data and new conclusions." *American Journal of Sociology*, 84(6):446-452.

Webber, Melvin. 1963. "Order in diversity: community without propinquity," in L. Wingo, Jr. (ed.), *Cities and Space: The Future Use of Urban Land.* Baltimore, Md.: Johns Hopkins Press.

Weber, M. 1930. *The Protestant Ethic and the Spirit of Capitalism.* London: George Allen and Unwin.

Weber, Max. 1947. *The Theory of Social and Economic Organization.* (Translated by A. M. Henderson and Talcott Parsons). New York: Free Press.

Weber, Max. 1958. *The City.* D. Martindale and G. Neuwirth (trans.). New York: Free Press.

Weber, Max. 1958. *The Protestant Ethic and the Spirit of Capitalism.* New York: Scribner's.

Weber, Max. 1963. *Sociology of Religion.* Boston: Beacon Press.

Weber, Max. 1964. *The Theory of Social and Economic Organization*, A. M. Henderson and Talcott Parsons, (trans.). New York: Free Press.

Weber, Max. 1964. *The Theory of Social and Economic Organization.* New York: Free Press.

Weber, M. 1969. "Class, status, party," in C. Heller (ed.), *Structured Social Inequality.* New York: Macmillan.

Weinstein, Eugene A. 1969. "The development of interpersonal competence," in David A. Goslin (ed.), *Handbook of Socialization Theory and Research.* Chicago: Rand McNally.

Weisstein, Naomi. 1971. "Psychology constructs the female, or the fantasy life of the male psychologist," in Michele Hoffnung Garskof (ed.), *Roles Women Play: Readings toward Women's Liberation.* Belmont, Calif.: Brooks/Coles.

Wellman, Barry. 1979. "The community question: the intimate networks of East Yorkers." *American Journal of Sociology*, 84(5):201-231.

Wente, Margaret. 1980. "The new power of the pension funds." *Canadian Business*, 53(3):33, 40-41, 88, 90, 92, 95, 99.

Wesolowski, W. 1969. "Some notes on the functional theory of stratification," in C. Heller (ed.), *Structured Social Inequality.* New York: Macmillan.

Westhues, Kenneth. 1973. "The established church as an agent of change." *Sociological Analysis*, 34:106-123.

Westhues, Kenneth. 1975. "Inter-generational conflict in the sixties," in Sam Clark, et al. (eds.), *Prophecy and Protest: Social Movements in Twentieth-Century Canada.* Toronto: Gage.

Westhues, Kenneth. 1978. "Stars and stripes, the maple leaf, and the papal coat of arms." *Canadian Journal of Sociology*, 3:245-261.

Westhues, Kenneth, and Peter R. Sinclair. 1974. *Village in crisis.* Toronto: Holt, Rinehart and Winston.

Westley, Frances. 1978. "'The Cult of Man': Durkheim's predictions and new religious movements." *Sociological Analysis*, 2:135-145.

White, Morton, and Lucia White. 1962. *The Intellectual Versus the City.* Cambridge, Mass.: Harvard University Press and Militi Press.

White, Terrence H. 1975. "Canadian labour and international unions in the seventies," in Sam Clark, et al. (eds.), *Prophecy and Protest: Social Movements in Twentieth-Century Canada.* Toronto: Gage.

White, Terrence H. 1978. *Power or Pawns: Boards of Directors in Canadian Corporations.* Toronto: C.C.H.

Whyte, Donald. 1966. "Religion and the rural church," in M. A. Tremblay and W. J. Anderson (eds.), *Rural Canada in Transition.* Ottawa: Agricultural Economics Research Council of Canada, 79-92.

Whyte, William F. 1943. *Street-Corner Society: The Social Structure of an Italian Slum.* Chicago: University of Chicago Press.

Whyte, William Foote. 1982. "Social inventions for solving human problems." *American Sociological Review*, 47(1):1-13.

Wiley, N. 1967. "America's unique class politics: the interplay of the labor, credit, and commodity markets." *American Sociological Review*, 32:529-541.

Wilson, Alan B. 1959. "Residential segregation of social classes and aspirations of high school boys." *American Sociological Review*, 24:836-845.

Wilson, James Q. 1968. "The police and the delinquent in two cities," in Stanton Wheeler (ed.), *Controlling Delinquents*. New York: John Wiley.

Wilson, John. 1974. "The Canadian political cultures: towards a redefinition of the nature of the Canadian political system." *Canadian Journal of Political Science*, 7(3):438-483.

Wilson, Robert A., and David A. Schulz. 1978. *Urban Sociology*. Englewood Cliffs, N.J.: Prentice-Hall.

Wimberley, Ronald C. 1971. "Mobility in ministerial career patterns: exploration." *Journal for the Scientific Study of Religion*, 10:249-253.

Winn, Marie. 1977. *The Plug-in Drug: Television, Children and the Family*. New York: Viking.

Winsborough, Halliman H. 1978. "Statistical histories of the life cycle of birth cohorts," in Karl Taeuber, L. Bumpass, and J. Sweet (eds.), *Social Demography*. Don Mills: Academic Press.

Wirth, Louis. 1938. "Urbanism as a way of life." *American Journal of Sociology*, 44:3-24.

Wolf, Wendy C., and Neil D. Fligstein. 1979. "Sex and authority in the workplace: the causes of sexual inequality." *American Sociological Review*, 44:235-252.

Wolfgang, Marvin, and Marc Riedel. 1973. "Race, judicial discretion and the death penalty." *The Annals of the American Academy of Political and Social Science*, 407(May):119-133.

Women's Bureau, Labour Canada. 1980. *Women in the Labour Force, 1978-1979, Part I: Participation*. Ottawa: Minister of Supply and Services Canada.

Wood, L. A. 1975: 1924. *A History of Farmers' Movements in Canada*. Toronto: University of Toronto Press.

Wright, Erik Olin. 1978. *Class, Crisis and the State*. London: New Left Books.

Wright, James D., and Sonia R. Wright. 1976. "Social class and parental values for children: a partial replication and extension of the Kohn thesis." *American Sociological Review*, 41:527-537.

Wrong, D. 1969. "Social inequality without stratification," in C. Heller (ed.), *Structured Social Inequality*. New York: Macmillan.

Wrong, D. H. 1961. "The oversocialized conception of man in modern sociology." *American Sociological Review*, 26(April): 183-193.

Wuthnow, Robert. 1973. "Religious commitment and conservatism: in search of an elusive relationship," in Charles Glock (ed.), *Religion in Sociological Perspective*. Belmont, Calif.: Wadsworth.

Wynne, Derek, and Tim Hartnagel. 1975a. "Plea negotiation in Canada." *Canadian Journal of Criminology*, 17(1):45-56.

Wynne, Derek, and Tim Hartnagel. 1975b. "Race and plea negotiation: an analysis of some Canadian data." *Canadian Journal of Sociology*, 1(2):147-155.

Yinger, Milton. 1946. *Religion in the Struggle for Power*. Durham, N.C.: Duke University Press.

Young, M., and P. Willmot. 1957. *Family and Kinship in East London*. London: Routledge & Kegan Paul.

Young, Walter. 1969. *Anatomy of a Party*. Toronto: University of Toronto Press.

Yussen, Steven R., and John W. Santrock. 1978. *Child Development*. Dubuque, Iowa: Wm. C. Brown.

Zeitlin, Irving M. 1973. *Rethinking Sociology*. Englewood Cliffs, N.J.: Prentice-Hall.

Zerubavel, Eviatar. 1981. *Hidden Rhythms: Schedules and Calendars in Social Life*. Chicago: University of Chicago Press.

Zinssen, Hans. 1965. *Rats, Lice and History*. New York: Bantam.

Zukin, Sharon. 1980. "A decade of the new urban sociology." *Theory and Society*, 9:539-574.

Zusman, J. 1966. "Some explanations of the changing appearance of psychotic patients: antecedents of the social-breakdown concept." *Milbank Memorial Fund Quarterly*, 64(Jan.):1-2.

CREDITS

The publishers thank the following sources of reprint material used in this book. We have attempted to trace the ownership of copyright for all materials used, and will gladly receive information enabling us to rectify any errors in references or credits.

CHAPTER 1

Photograph, page xiv, by Clive Webster. Photograph, page 2, courtesy of Miller Services Ltd. Photograph, page 5, courtesy of the Bettman Archive. Photograph, page 8, courtesy of the Bettman Archive. Photograph, page 9, courtesy of Miller Services Ltd. Photograph, page 14, courtesy of Harvard University. Photograph, page 15, courtesy of Miller Services Ltd. Photograph, page 17, courtesy of The Granger Collection. Photograph, page 19, courtesy of University of Toronto. Photograph, page 20, courtesy of Miller Services Ltd. Photograph, page 22, courtesy of Miller Services Ltd.

CHAPTER 2

Photograph, page 26, by Clive Webster. Photograph, page 28, courtesy of National Film Board. Insert, page 31, reprinted from Oxford University Press. Photograph, page 34, courtesy of Coca-Cola Limited. Insert, page 36, reprinted by permission of The Canadian Publishers, McClelland and Stewart Ltd. Photograph, page 36, courtesy of Canapress Photo Service. Photograph, page 38, courtesy of Canapress Photo Service. Insert, page 39, reprinted from University of Toronto Press. Photograph, page 42, courtesy of National Film Board. Insert, page 43, reprinted by permission of D.C. Heath and Company. Photograph, page 47, courtesy of Canapress Photo Service. Insert, page 49, reprinted from *American Sociological Review.* Insert, page 53, reprinted from *Detroit Free Press.*

CHAPTER 3

Photograph, page 58, courtesy of Miller Services Ltd. Insert, page 61, reprinted by permission of Canadian Association of Sociology and Anthropology. Photograph, page 63, courtesy of Canapress Photo Service. Photograph, page 67, courtesy of Canada-Wide Feature Service. Photograph, page 68, courtesy of National Film Board. Photograph, page 70, courtesy of National Film Board. Photograph, page 73, courtesy of National Film Board. Insert, pages 74-75, reprinted by permission of Department of Sociology, Southern Illinois University. Photograph, page 79, courtesy of Miller Services Ltd. Insert, page 85, reprinted from *The Calgary Herald.* Photograph, page 86, courtesy of Canapress Picture Service.

CHAPTER 4

Photograph, page 90, courtesy of Canapress Picture Service. Photograph, page 93, courtesy of Miller Services Ltd. Photograph, page 102, courtesy of Canapress Photo Service. Cartoon, page 106, courtesy of Ben Wicks. Photograph, page 106, courtesy of Canapress Photo Service. Insert, page 118, reprinted from *Urban Life and Culture.* Both photographs, page 119, courtesy of Miller Services Ltd.

CHAPTER 5

Photograph, page 129, reprinted by permission of *The Spectator,* Hamilton, Ontario. Photograph, page 129, courtesy of Canapress Photo Service. Cartoon, page 137, reprinted from *Industry Week.* Photograph, page 139, courtesy of Miller Services Ltd. Insert, page 142, reprinted from Bobbs-Merrill. Photograph, page 146, courtesy of Canapress Photo Service. Photograph, page 150, courtesy of Miller Services Ltd. Insert, page 151, reprinted from JAI Press.

CHAPTER 6

Photograph, page 156, courtesy of Canapress Photo Service. Photograph, page 159, courtesy of Canapress Photo Service. Photograph, page 164, from a poster, courtesy of National Organization for Reform of Marijuana Laws in Canada. Insert, page 166, reprinted from ARF Books. Insert, page 170, reprinted by permission of Russell Sage Foundation. Photograph, page 172, courtesy of *Toronto Star.* Insert, pages 174-75, reprinted by permission of Prentice-Hall, Inc. Photograph, page 175, courtesy of Canada-Wide Feature Service. Cartoon, page 176, courtesy of Ben Wicks. Insert, page 177, reprinted by permission of Prentice-Hall, Inc. Photograph, page 185, by Ken Elliott.

CHAPTER 7

Photograph, page 190, by Clive Webster. Photograph, page 192, courtesy of Miller Services Ltd. Photographs, page 202: left, courtesy of the Bettman Archive; right, courtesy of Miller Services Ltd. Photograph, page 209, courtesy of Wide-World Photo. Photograph, page 212, courtesy of Public Archives, National Photography Collection. Photograph, page 216, courtesy of Public Archives, National Photography Collection. Photograph, page 218, courtesy of United Nations. Photograph, page 220, courtesy of National Film Board.

CHAPTER 8

Photograph, page 231, courtesy of Miller Services Ltd. Photographs, page 240: top, reprinted from *The Montreal Star*; bottom, courtesy of Miller Services Ltd. Photographs, page 243: top, courtesy of Miller Services Ltd.; bottom, courtesy of Canada-Wide Feature Service. Photograph, page 254, courtesy of Ontario Ministry of Industry and Tourism.

CHAPTER 9

Photograph, page 260, courtesy of *Toronto Star*. Photograph, page 265, courtesy of Canapress Photo Service. Photograph, page 269, courtesy of Canapress Photo Service. Photograph, page 274, courtesy of National Film Board. Photograph, page 277, courtesy of Foote Collection, Manitoba Archives. Photograph, page 279, courtesy of Archives of Ontario.

CHAPTER 10

Photograph, page 290, courtesy of Miller Services Ltd. Photograph, page 296, courtesy of Miller Services Ltd. Insert, page 296, reprinted by permission of *The Financial Post* and Alan Pearson. Photograph, page 299, courtesy of Miller Services Ltd. Photograph, page 301, courtesy of Miller Services Ltd. Photograph, page 304, courtesy of Public Archives, National Photography Collection. Insert, page 312, reprinted from the *Edmonton Journal*. Photograph, page 317, courtesy of National Film Board. Insert, pages 318-19, reprinted by permission of *Financial Times of Canada* and Terence Corcoran, associate editor. Photograph, page 319, courtesy of Miller Services Ltd. Photograph, page 324, courtesy of National Film board.

CHAPTER 11

Photograph, page 328, by Clive Webster. Photograph, page 330, courtesy of National Film Board. Photograph, page 336, courtesy of Miller Services Ltd. Insert, page 336, reprinted from Aldine Publishing Company. Photograph, page 337, Courtesy of National Film Board. Insert, page 337, reprinted from Oxford University Press. Photograph, page 340, courtesy of Miller Services Ltd. Insert, page 340, reprinted by permission of American Association for the Advancement of Science. Photograph, page 343, courtesy of Miller Services Ltd. Insert, page 344, reprinted by permission of The Canadian Publishers, McClelland and Stewart Ltd. Photograph, page 349, courtesy of Canadian Press Photo. Photograph, page 350, courtesy of Miller Services Ltd. Insert, page 350, reprinted by permission of Doubleday and Company, Inc. Photograph, page 354, courtesy of Miller Services Ltd. Photograph, page 357, courtesy of Miller Services Ltd. Photograph, page 362, courtesy of Miller Services Ltd.

CHAPTER 12

Photograph, page 368, courtesy of Miller Services Ltd. Insert, page 371, reprinted from Schocken Books. Photograph, page 375, courtesy of Canapress Photo Service. Photograph, page 376, courtesy of Canada-Wide Photo. Photograph, page 381, courtesy of Canapress Photo Service. Insert, page 381, reprinted from *Maclean's*. Insert, page 386, courtesy of Associated Press. Photograph, page 390, courtesy of Miller Services Ltd. Insert, page 391, courtesy of Associated Press. Photograph, page 393, courtesy of Associated Press. Insert, page 393, reprinted from *Maclean's*. Insert, page 394, reprinted from *Maclean's*. Photograph, page 397, courtesy Canada-Wide Photo.

CHAPTER 13

Insert, page 407, reprinted from *The Manchester Guardian*. Photograph, page 411, courtesy of Miller Services Ltd. Photograph, page 413, courtesy of Ontario Archives. Cartoon, page 416, reprinted by permission of *The Globe and Mail*, Toronto. Photograph, page 419, courtesy of Canada-Wide Photo. Photograph, page 422, courtesy of Miller Services Ltd. Photograph, page 425, courtesy of Miller Services Ltd.

CHAPTER 14

Photograph, page 432, courtesy of *Toronto Star*. Insert, page 435, reprinted from University of Chicago Press. Both photographs, page 440, courtesy of National Film Board. Photograph, page 445, courtesy of Magnum Photo. Photograph, page 446, courtesy of Ontario Archives. Photograph, page 449, courtesy of Miller Services Ltd. Photographs, page 457: top, courtesy of Ontario Archives; bottom, courtesy of Canadian Press Photo. Insert, page 463, reprinted by permission of Phi Delta Kappa Society.

CHAPTER 15

Photograph, page 468, by Clive Webster. Photograph, page 470, courtesy of National Film Board. Insert, page 472, reprinted from McGraw-Hill Ryerson. Photograph, page 474, courtesy of Ministry of Industry and Tourism. Photograph, page 480, courtesy of United Nations. Table 15-1, page 481, reprinted from University of Chicago Press. Figure 15-3, page 483, reprinted by permission of Ministry of Supply and Services. Photograph, page 485, courtesy of Miller Services Ltd. Photograph, page 490, courtesy of Miller Services Ltd. Insert, page 490, reprinted by permission of McGraw-Hill Ryerson Ltd. Figure 15-5, page 491, reprinted by permission of Clark University. Photograph, page 499, courtesy of Associated Press.

CHAPTER 16

Photograph, page 506, courtesy of Canapress Photo Service. Photograph, page 513, courtesy of Miller Services Ltd. Insert, page 513, reprinted from *Canadians for One Canada*. Photograph, page 515, courtesy of Manitoba Archives. Insert, page 515, reprinted from *The Calgary Albertan*. Insert, page 519, reprinted from *The Fishermen's Advocate*. Insert, page 520, reprinted by permission of Alberta Social Credit Party. Photograph, page 520, courtesy of Canadian Broadcasting Corporation. Cartoons, page 521, reprinted from the *Winnipeg Free Press*. Photograph, page 524, courtesy of Canadian Press Photo. Insert and photograph, page 524, reprinted by permission of *Saturday Night Magazine*. Photograph, page 527, by Ken Elliott. Insert, page 529, reprinted by permission of the New Democratic Party.

CHAPTER 17

Photograph, page 532, courtesy of Miller Services Ltd. Photograph, page 534, courtesy of Control Data Canada Limited. Insert, page 537, reprinted by permission of Canadian University Teachers Association. Figure 17-2, page 539, reprinted by permission of The Canadian Association of Sociology and Anthropology. Photograph, page 551, courtesy of Canada-Wide Feature Service. Photograph, page 555, courtesy of Miller Services Ltd.

INDEX

NAME INDEX

SUBJECT INDEX